The True Adventures of
JOHN STEINBECK,

WRITER

Steinbeck in London, December 1962. *(Erich Auerbach Collection, FRPS.)*

The True Adventures of
JOHN STEINBECK,
(WRITER)

A BIOGRAPHY BY
Jackson J. Benson

NEW YORK
THE VIKING PRESS

Previously unpublished photos, writings, and letters of John Steinbeck
Copyright © 1984 by Elaine Steinbeck
Letter of Katherine Beswick Copyright © 1984 by the Estate of Katherine Beswick
Letter of Carol Brown Copyright © 1984 by William Brown
Letter of Robert Capa Copyright © 1984 by the Estate of Robert Capa
Letters of Pascal Covici are used by permission of Pascal Covici, Jr.

LIBRARY OF CONGRESS CATALOGING IN PUBLICATION DATA
Benson, Jackson J.
The true adventures of John Steinbeck, writer.
Includes index.
1. Steinbeck, John, 1902–1968—Biography.
2. Novelists, American—20th century—Biography.
I. Title.
PS3537.T3234Z616   1984   813'.52   [B]   82-17534
ISBN 0-670-16685-5

Portions of this book appeared originally in: *American Literature*, "John Steinbeck and
Farm Labor Unionization: The Background of *In Dubious Battle*," by Jackson J. Benson
and Anne Loftis, 52:2, pp. 194–223, copyright © 1980 by Duke University Press.
Reprinted by permission. All rights reserved; *Modern Literature*, "John Steinbeck and the
Man from Weedpatch," copyright © 1976 by Temple University; *Novel: A Forum on
Fiction*, "John Steinbeck the Novelist as Scientist," Spring, 1977.

Grateful acknowledgment is made to AMS Press, Inc., for permission to reprint excerpts
from Petrarch's *Sonnets and Songs*, translated by Anna Maria Armi.

Additional acknowledgments appear in the "Prefatory Notes" section beginning on page xi.

Printed in the United States of America
Set in Janson
Designed by Victoria Hartman

For the woman in my life,
Sue Ellen

And for the women in his life who made this book
possible:
Beth, Carol, Elizabeth, Shirley, and Elaine

Q: How do you look upon yourself as an author?
A: I have never looked upon myself as an author.... I don't think I have ever considered myself an author. I've considered myself a writer because that's what I do. I don't know what an author does.

—John Steinbeck, interviewed in Sweden
after receiving the Nobel Prize for Literature, 1962

Preface

This is the story of a man who was a writer. He cared about language, and he cared about people. He didn't want to be famous or popular—he just wanted to write books. But he became both. From among the many serious writers of our time, he became for a great many people, here and throughout the world, the one writer who counted, the one who touched them. He made words sing, and he made people laugh and cry. He also made them think—about loneliness, self-deception, and injustice. And in all that he wrote, he testified to his belief that everything that lives is holy.

He created men and women we cannot forget—Tom Joad and Ma, Cal and Cathy, Jody and Billy Buck, Lennie and George, Danny and Pilon, and Doc and Mack. They live with us, and for some of us, they are a part of what we are. This man wrote a lot of good books, and that, after all, is what a writer should do.

Though everyone knew his books, few really knew the man. John Steinbeck was shy and very private. On those rare occasions when he allowed himself to be interviewed, he steadfastly refused to answer personal questions. He felt that attention should be focused on his work, rather than on his life, and that if too much notice was given to him, he would be unable to do his work. He wrote largely out of his own experience, but unlike most of his contemporaries, he wrote very little about himself.

Thus, until the publication of his letters in 1975, relatively little was known about him beyond the public facts, and even these were sometimes in error. Various myths sprang up about him, some of which, such as the alleged trip to Oklahoma to research the Okies, he took delight in encouraging. During his life he was frequently confused with Hemingway in the public's mind, and was sometimes complimented for having written *God's Little Acre*. At various times he was accused of being a communist, a fascist, a puritan, and one of the most immoral men that ever published a book in the United States. He was none of those things.

My first job in writing this book has been to get the facts straight. But beyond that, my most important task has been to try to bring a man alive, a very complicated man who led a very vivid and eventful life. Since being a writer is not an occupation but a state of being, I have talked about how he came to write what he did, where he got his material, and how he went about trying to get it on paper. Steinbeck was a man and writer who had a deep attachment for his environment, and so I have tried to bring a sense of those environments in which he lived and worked into the book. And since his most famous writings had a particular social-historical context, I felt it was important to investigate that context and his relations to it in some detail.

In my thirteen years researching and writing this book I have had the cooperation and help of Steinbeck's family and many close friends, and for their help and many kindnesses I am extremely grateful.

I have tried to be as objective as possible in treating both the life and the works, although I confess that I have sympathy for both.

Prefatory Note

LETTERS

For the most part, letters quoted have been documented in the text of the book itself. If the name of the recipient of a letter from John Steinbeck is not given in the introduction to the letter or excerpt, it is usually given in abbreviation in parentheses following the quotation, as is the date of the letter. Occasionally, because of the brevity of the quotation and so as not to interrupt the flow of the text, a letter excerpt will be documented in the notes. If a specific date is not given in the introduction, at the end of the quotation, or in the notes, the letter had no date and cannot be assigned one from its contents.

Since most of Steinbeck's letters, until the last part of his life, were originally undated, and since most dates that appear on them were placed there by others, the reader should consider all such dates to be approximate. Most characteristically, Steinbeck would scrawl a day of the week at the top of his correspondence. Some dates have been assigned by the recipient according to postmark, according to date received, or according to an estimate of the day sent; others have been placed on letters by secretaries, dealers, and librarians. Needless to say, these dates are often wrong, sometimes off by as much as a decade. However, I have used a date assigned to a letter if it seemed reasonable in respect to other evidence; when the date is clearly wrong, I have assigned a date myself—usually a month and a year, but sometimes a season and a year.

The quotations from letters have been taken, in almost every case, either from the original or from a carbon or photocopy of the original. The exceptions—letters to which I had no access in the original—have been taken from the published selected letters, *A Life in Letters*. However, I have made no attempt to correlate my quotations throughout the book with *A Life in Letters* because nearly half the letters used in my text do not appear in that volume and because many of the letters in that collection were edited. Rarely have I made any changes in the text of the letters—a half dozen or so corrections of obtrusive spelling errors and two or three insertions of punctuation for clarity—and where I have omitted sentences or passages from my quotations, I have indicated the omission by the use of ellipses.

All the letters written by John Steinbeck have been reproduced by permission of Mrs. John Steinbeck. The letters by Pascal Covici are published by permission of Pascal Covici, Jr., and the letter by the former Carol Steinbeck by permission of William Brown.

I would like to thank the following institutions and individuals for physical access to and permission to use the letters owned by them. Where a correspondence is referred to in my text or notes by abbreviation, that abbreviation follows the name of the recipient in the list that follows:

Permission by the Stanford University Libraries (M263 The John Steinbeck Collection, Department of Special Collections) for letters by Steinbeck to Elizabeth Otis (JS/EO), Carlton A. Sheffield (JS/CS), Webster F. Street (JS/WS), Katherine Beswick (JS/KB), Carl Wilhelmson (JS/CW), Max Wagner (JS/MW), Robert Cathcart, and Amasa ("Ted") Miller (JS/TM). Also for letters by Katherine Beswick to Steinbeck (KB/JS). [Original access to letters by Steinbeck to Otis, Sheffield, Street, Wagner, Cathcart, and Miller provided by the recipients.]

Permission by the Humanities Research Center, University of Texas, Austin, for letters by Steinbeck to Pascal Covici (JS/PC) and Robert O. Ballou. Also for letters by Pascal Covici to John Steinbeck (PC/JS).

Permission by the Bancroft Library, University of California, Berkeley, for letters by Steinbeck to Gwyndolyn Steinbeck (JS/GS), George Albee (JS/GA), Ritchie and Natalia Lovejoy, Joseph Henry Jackson, Ben Abramson (JS/BA), and A. Grove Day. Also for a letter by the former Carol Steinbeck to George Albee. [Original access to Day letters provided by recipient.]

Permission by the University of Virginia Library, John Steinbeck Collection (#6239, etc.), Clifton Waller Barrett Library, for letters by Steinbeck to Louis Paul, Eugene Solow, and Wilbur Needham.

Permission by the Houghton Library, Harvard University, for letters by Steinbeck to Lawrence Clark Powell.

Permission by Mrs. Mary Alice Johns for letters by Steinbeck to Tom Collins (JS/TC); Mrs. Margaret Judah for letters by Steinbeck to her (JS/MG); Mrs. Lynn Loesser for letters by Steinbeck to her and her husband, Frank Loesser; Joseph Bryan III for letters by Steinbeck to him; Robert Wallsten for letters by Steinbeck to him; Mrs. John Steinbeck for letters by her husband to her; Dr. Denton Sayer Cox for a letter by Steinbeck to him; Thomas Guinzburg for a letter by Steinbeck to him; and Nathaniel Benchley for a letter by Steinbeck to Peter Benchley.

Access to the following letters was provided by Mrs. John Steinbeck or by publication in *A Life in Letters:* John Steinbeck to Bo Beskow (JS/BB), Annie Laurie Williams (JS/ALW), Elia Kazan (JS/EK), and Eugène Vinaver.

MANUSCRIPTS

Except for quotations from the journals, which are acknowledged below, credits for access to various unpublished Steinbeck materials are provided in the notes at the end of the book. I have also noted if, at present and as far as can be known, a manuscript is no longer in existence (lost) or in the hands of a dealer or collector (in private hands). All quotations from unpublished manuscripts, journals, papers, and memoranda by John Steinbeck have been reproduced by permission of Mrs. John Steinbeck, who has sole right to their publication.

I would like to thank the following institutions for physical access to and permission to use the journals owned by them:

Permission by the Stanford University Libraries for the journal that accompanied the composition of *To a God Unknown.*

Permission of the Humanities Research Center, University of Texas, Austin, for the journal that accompanied the composition of *The Grapes of Wrath.*

Permission of the Pierpont Morgan Library for the journal that accompanied the composition of *Travels with Charley in Search of America.*

Permission of the Steinbeck Research Center, San Jose State University Library, San Jose, California, for the journal that accompanied the composition of the stories later published in *The Long Valley* and of *Of Mice and Men.* (The author is responsible for the authenticity and assumes liability for all quotations from these materials. No portion of this unpublished material may be used or reproduced in any manner whatsoever without the written permission of the Steinbeck estate and the Steinbeck Research Center, San Jose State University Library.)

Contents

Illustrations follow pages 62, 250, 492,
844, 958, 1022

The True Adventures of
JOHN STEINBECK,
WRITER

Prologue

Most serious writers, in their heart of hearts, have some concern for artistic immortality. But John Steinbeck didn't really care about it much one way or the other. His perspective was too broad, and his sense of self-importance too small. What he cared about was writing itself. He didn't write for fame, although occasionally he enjoyed being famous; he didn't write for money, although there were times when he needed money; he wrote because he loved to write, because he was addicted to it.

If you understand his writing habit, then a good many things about his career become understandable. He loved the words, the shape, the sound, the history of meaning; he delighted in the magical properties of language; he even got satisfaction from the touch of pencil and paper. Behind nearly everything that he wrote there is a man enjoying himself, surprised and delighted that words work the way they do. In *Cannery Row* he articulated that joy:

> The word is a symbol and a delight which sucks up men and scenes, trees, plants, factories, and Pekinese. Then the Thing becomes the Word and back to Thing again, but warped and woven into a fantastic pattern. The Word sucks up Cannery Row, digests it and spews it out, and the Row has taken the shimmer of the green world and the sky-reflecting seas.

If you also understand that Steinbeck had a comparatively meager sense of self-importance, his career becomes even more understandable. He could be corny, know he was being corny, and still enjoy it without worrying about the consequences. He could write something like "Fishing in Paris" and not even consider the possibility that this might affect his readers' reactions to his more serious work. He carried a certain amount of innocence with him throughout his lifetime both as to his own work and to others' reaction to it. What an unpleasant sort of business for those who demand that a writer shape his own career like a sculptor carving his own image as a monument to himself.

The Aunt Sally that haunted Steinbeck was Henry James. Our neo-Jamesean expectations have been that every writer "progress" from simplicity to complexity, that every novel by a writer be a further refinement of the familiar, that every thread of the fabric of a writer's life be tied to his art, and that every public statement be a quotable pronouncement.

But Steinbeck almost never followed our expectations for him. Like Mark Twain before him, Steinbeck wrote about what interested him. And like Mark Twain's wife, who tried very hard to civilize her husband, the critics were after Steinbeck during much of his career, shaking their heads, clucking their tongues, trying to convert him to a decent sense of artistic responsibility.

But Steinbeck just could not stand respectability; he always took off for new territory, sometimes tripping over his own feet, but always going his own way. It may be that the most important single thing in his personal history as it affected his writing was that as a young man he was employed in hard physical labor close to the earth for extended periods of time. By contrast, in the rarefied atmosphere of Jamesean sensibility, one would be hard put to imagine bare hands touching bare ground. With all of the virtues the mountain man may display in the wilderness of his own affections, he appears but a buffoon in the drawing room of our academic formulations. And except for a few moments in his career when it appeared that he was a Marxist, Steinbeck demonstrated considerable talent for offending literary gentlemen. That he rubbed so many of the right people the wrong way may be reason enough to love him.

For no matter how long a list of faults one might construct in response to Steinbeck's fiction, there is something so engaging at the heart of his best work that it is impossible to dismiss that work completely. He was not a terribly profound writer, although sometimes more profound than he was taken to be. There is little in his work that is extraordinarily subtle or complex. And although he devised a number of story-telling techniques of his own, he was not a great innovator of fictional forms. No, whatever it is that makes its impression on us is less obvious than such things as these.

I would suggest that his work attracts our special attention and affection because he was a lover of life, rather than a hater of life. And closely allied to his love for living is another attitude that gains our attention and favor: he never uses his work, overtly or covertly, to declare his superiority.

The sense that Steinbeck is a writer in tune with the rhythms of life is partly due to the fact that he was not a writer obsessed with himself. He sent his feelings outward. There is life in this very act of reaching out, and life in the very fallibility of the act. In an age that often appears to be dominated by writing which is essentially the autobiographical exploration of the writer's own morbid psyche, Steinbeck was exceptionally unautobiographical in his work. There is more than a little truth in the neurotic theory of art—that great art is often the product of an artist driven and inspired by severe anxiety and insecurity—and the fact that Steinbeck was, with all his problems, an unusually healthy man helps to explain both what is missing from his work and that special quality that makes it distinctive. His greatness, if one is willing to call it that, comes not from his wound, but from his wholeness.

His humanity was exposed in his writing in those qualities which are quite opposite to the postures of superiority or weary knowledgeability and disillusionment which have become so common to modern prose: in a sense of fun, a probing curiosity, and a capacity for wonder. As we read through his work, we feel that his is a point of view that is open to experience and interested in nearly everything. We may even detect the speaker reacting to objects or situations which we find unremarkable; while the reaction may not always be profound or even new, it almost invariably strikes us as genuine. This genuineness brings a vitality and intensity to Steinbeck's fiction that illuminates it beyond whatever radiance may be generated by theme or subject.

A sense of fun, a probing curiosity, and a capacity for wonder—all of these are qualities that we associate with childhood, and there was a good deal of the child in Steinbeck throughout his life. He was a big man who took great delight in small things. He never got too old to take things for granted or to accept the unacceptable. The child in Steinbeck, as the child in Twain, was very often the writer's best part.

The childish sense of wonder was also present in his feeling that the act of writing was a sort of miraculous thing, and I think he thought it was sort of a miracle that he could spend his life doing it. At the end he tended to think of himself as a failure, and in this he was his own harshest critic, never satisfied with what he had done.

A writer out of loneliness is trying to communicate like a distant star sending signals. He isn't telling or teaching or ordering. Rather he seeks to establish a relationship of meaning, of feeling, of observing. We are lonesome animals. We spend all life trying to be less lonesome. One of our ancient methods is to tell a story begging the listener to say—and to feel—

"Yes, that's the way it is, or at least that's the way I feel it. You're not as alone as you thought."

It is so hard to be clear. Only a fool is willfully obscure. . . .

To finish is sadness to a writer—a little death. He puts the last word down and it is done. But it isn't really done. The story goes on and leaves the writer behind, for no story is ever done.

Because he succeeded more often than not in getting us to say, "Yes, that's the way it is," his story will not soon end. This book is about what it feels like to be a writer, that heaven and hell, the fun and the torture.

PART ONE

The Long Valley

CHAPTER I

J ust as his father would get on his horse and ride off to be alone, John Steinbeck had to get away from his house, from his family. Perhaps it was this impulse to get away that brought him so close to nature so young. The emotions stirred by childhood communion with nature, the excitement of secret experiences and private discoveries, stayed with Steinbeck throughout his life. In *East of Eden* he recalls such feelings:

> Under the live oaks, shaded and dusky, the maidenhair flourished and gave a good smell, and under the mossy banks of the water courses whole clumps of five-fingered ferns and goldybacks hung down. Then there were harebells, tiny lanterns, cream white and almost sinful looking, and these were so rare and magical that a child, finding one, felt singled out and special all day long.

Even as a young child, his friend Max Wagner recalls, Steinbeck had places of his own, places tucked in among the wooded, brushy banks of nearby drainage ditches, places where he could sit and dream and watch the movements of the birds and small animals. Looking back, he said, "I can remember my childhood names for grasses and secret flowers. I remember where a toad may live and what time the birds awaken in the summer—and what trees and seasons smelled like." Here he was part of what he saw and heard and smelled in the early morning of a long day in late spring in the fields around Salinas, California, the hills near the Hamilton ranch, or among the rocks that circled the tidepools below the Steinbeck summer home at Pacific Grove.

His parents and the peculiar nature of his surroundings also led him in this direction. On the one side, Steinbeck's father had a special regard for nature and man's place in it. Perhaps this regard was in part the Old Country heritage passed on to him by his own father, but for whatever reason, Steinbeck's father felt the constant need to be plugged into the soil, to feel its vibrations. Even the smallest things in nature were important. Man must conserve, for man was part of the pattern, the chain of life. On the other side, Steinbeck's mother had the sense that all things about us are enchanted, if we had but the eyes to see. There was the potential for magic everywhere and in every experience, and just as there were good and bad people, there were good and bad places—and special places.

To these influences must be added the majesty and power of the landscape of the central California coast—its redwoods and rugged mountains, its river valleys and rolling hills, and its remarkable shoreline of rocky cliffs and windblown cypresses and pines, bays, estuaries, and beaches. All of this, at the turn of the century, alive with mountain lion, deer, wild boar, wildfowl, fish, and sea animals. Vast expanses, sometimes beautiful, sometimes awe-inspiring, often desolate and oppressive, with very few roads, very few houses, and very few people.

Of all this varied terrain, the young Steinbeck seemed to develop a particular affinity for the seashore. Just as he always had a garden, always had a dog, he lived whenever he could near the sea—during the first half of his life by the Pacific and for the last half, by the Atlantic. In *Travels with Charley,* he describes his journey from ocean to ocean. As he approaches the West Coast, he finds himself drawn toward the sea, toward the Pacific, his "home ocean":

> I . . . grew up on its shore, collected marine animals along the coast. I knew its moods, its color, its nature. It was very far inland that I caught the first smell of the Pacific. . . . I believe I smelled the sea rocks and the kelp and the excitement of churning sea water, the sharpness of iodine and the under odor of washed and ground calcareous shells. Such a far-off and remembered odor comes subtly so that one does not consciously smell it, but rather an electric excitement is released—a kind of boisterous joy.

From the time he was born to the time he left to go to college, he spent part of nearly every summer at the beach. From late spring to early fall, there were weeks or long weekends at the ocean, as the families who knew each other in Salinas grouped together again in Pacific Grove, often making the journey together by train. The children were taught to swim when they were very young. They took hikes along the water and into the nearby hills around Asilomar. They were out in the morning and home at twilight. All day they built forts, collected shells, and when the tide was out, discovered the animals in the pools among the rocks.

Part of every summer was also spent with Uncle Tom Hamilton at the ranch near King City, where, by contrast with the summer fog at Pacific Grove, the sun beat down every day on the dry, rounded hills and sharp gullies. There were some chores to do among the animals and in the garden, but mostly there was time to blaze trails across the rock outcroppings and through the brush and dry grass. The Hamilton ranch was, in part, the model for the Tifflin ranch in *The Red Pony*, and like Jody, John found a special place where he could be alone with his thoughts and where the sound of water might bring renewal: "Jody traveled often to the brush-line behind the house. A rusty iron pipe ran a thin stream of spring water into an old green tub. Where the water spilled over and sank into the ground there was a patch of perpetually green grass. . . . This place had grown to be a center-point for Jody." When he had been punished, the water soothed him; when he had been mean, the meanness left him; and when he sat in the grass listening, "the barriers set up in his mind by the stern day went down to ruin," and he could sit and dream dreams of adventure and triumph.

II

In those years, at the turn of the century, Salinas was a small town of twenty-five hundred people, a town that had grown up at a crossroads near the end of a narrow valley pinched longways into California's coastal mountains. Salinas's main street was the road that ran south and then west to the Pacific Ocean and to the old Spanish town and first state capital, Monterey. Salinas originally served the cattle ranches that had developed along the river valley and on the eroded, brown hills nearby, and although there were as many farms as ranches by the time of Steinbeck's childhood, a large number of saloons at the center of town were a proud reminder of a Western past. Houses clustered on each side of what is now South Main Street, the less wealthy on one side and the more affluent on the other. The Steinbeck home, on the right side of town, was a two-story, Midwestern-Victorian frame house, painted white, with a white picket fence.

Salinas was surrounded by fields, which intruded here and there among the houses at the edge of town and which gave a boy quick release from the watchful eye of mother or an older sister. It was a town where the kids rode horses, if they had them, or bicycles down paths in vacant lots grown rank with wild oats and mustard and out to the nearby farmland. The town had been built on flat, marshy land, and although by this time much of the swamp had been filled in, there was still a lot of marshland left. Looking back, Steinbeck could remember lying in his bed at night and listening to the constant croaking of the frogs in the damp darkness outside the rusty screen of his bedroom window.

In such a town the social order was usually very simple. In addition to the "founders," those two or three of the early settlers who had made fortunes, those who achieved money and responsibility became the upper class—the banker, the lawyer, the doctor, the large store and factory owners and operators, with the more affluent farmers and ranchers as auxiliary members. The Steinbecks were never very wealthy, but the father's employment, if considered alone, would have placed the family along the lower edge of Salinas society. However, they assumed a prominence in the town somewhat beyond a merely marginal position, largely on the basis of their character and activity: the father had great integrity and was generally well liked; the mother, well-educated for her time and personable, was extremely socially active.

Superficially, the family of John Steinbeck's birth was very much like families across the country at that time—families with a slightly higher than middle income, with a good number of children, a large comfortable house, and no marked eccentricities to mar their respectability. Viewed from a distance, the family appears to match the caricature of middle-class life—the stern father, a bit formal perhaps, but tenderhearted; the lively, strong-minded mother with social ambitions, a manager who holds the family together; the older girls, trying to arrange a social life with parents who want them home from dates too early; and the little brother, precocious and mischievous, who is babied by the parents and a chore to his teenage sisters.

On closer view, however, there were a number of things about this family that were out of the ordinary. For one thing, it had, at least on the Steinbeck side, an extremely romantic past, a history that John always intended to write about at length, but never did. I suspect that his knowledge of it, combined with an imagination already stimulated by literature, set up expectations for adventure that high school and college could not possibly fulfill. No wonder, after a year of college, he suddenly left a note for his startled roommate announcing that he was going to China.

The journey, or as I suppose I should say, THE JOURNEY, to California was made by both Steinbeck's paternal and maternal grandparents.

While much of Steinbeck's fiction deals with the family—relations between husband and wife, parents and children—much of it also deals with the transplanted family, with those who move into California from the "East" and who confront a nature awesome in its beauty, power, and potential for wealth and disaster. Steinbeck reverses, in a sense, the Henry James theme of the American who confronts the sophistication of European society by bringing the American to the ultimate frontier, to a place almost incomprehensible to sensibilities formed in tamer surroundings. The Joseph Waynes, the Adam Trasks, the Joads hardly know whether they have found paradise or hell.

Steinbeck's paternal grandparents began their journey to California from the Holy Land, moving from one Promised Land to another. John Adolph Grosssteinbeck, Steinbeck's paternal grandfather, was from an area near Düsseldorf, Germany. During the early 1850s, John Adolph and his brother, both cabinetmakers, accompanied their sister and her husband, a Lutheran missionary, to Jerusalem on horseback.

A few years earlier, great-grandfather Dickson had decided to take his family—his wife, two sons, and three daughters (one of whom, Almira, became Steinbeck's grandmother)—to the Holy Land from Leominster, Massachusetts, in order to work to convert the Jews to Christianity. The younger son, who had gone to the Holy Land before Dickson arrived with the rest of the family, had recently died of tuberculosis, and the two Grosssteinbeck brothers became acquainted with the Dicksons by making the coffin. The two brothers courted the two eldest Dickson girls, were successful, and the four rode by horseback to the Mount of Olives, where they were married.

Great-grandfather Dickson's plan to convert the Jews was simple, but based more on religious zeal than on a practical knowledge of either the Jews or the Holy Land. He would acquire some land, and through the application of scientific farming methods, make the desert bloom. This example would teach the Jews how to raise their standard of living, and in the euphoria of their new-found wealth, they would be converted to an appreciation of the New Testament.

There were many problems with this Protestant agricultural crusade, of course, chief among them that the Jews were a persecuted minority in what at that time was a province of the Turkish empire, and association with Christians could only make their situation worse. A second major problem was that although great-grandfather Dickson went ahead with his farm plan, there was no labor force except slaves. Yankee Dickson could not abide that, and thus he and his family worked themselves almost to death carving out a farm in the desert by themselves. They were attacked by a tribe of Bedouin, and during the attack, John Adolph's brother was killed and Dickson's wife raped.

Everything they had worked so hard for, beyond the fields themselves, was destroyed and all their possessions stolen. The only thing they could do was return to the United States. On the way to the Holy Land, the Dicksons had been shipwrecked; on the way back, the youngest daughter was attacked by the sailors aboard the ship and died as a result of the mauling.

John Adolph, who now called himself more simply "Steinbeck," and his bride, Almira, settled in New England where he worked as a woodcarver. Shortly before the Civil War, they moved to Florida, and a short time after the war broke out, John Adolph was drafted into the Southern army. At the same time his brother-in-law, the only surviving Dickson son, went into the Northern army. Steinbeck's father, John Ernst, was born in Florida during the war, one of six boys.

John Adolph had no allegiance to the Southern cause whatsoever, and at the first opportunity, shed his uniform and escaped to the North. From the North, he and the Dickson family made appeals to the Confederate government, and through the kindness of a Southern general, Almira Steinbeck and her children were allowed to go to New England. Nearly a decade later, John Adolph made his way west to California, where he bought ten acres of land near Hollister (about thirty miles northeast of Salinas). Almira followed later with the children, crossing the continent by train, and the family first went into dairy farming, then raised fruit, and finally established a flour mill.

Steinbeck's father, John Ernst Steinbeck (his son had the same name, although "senior" and "junior" were not used), grew up to become an accountant and manager. He began working for the Southern Pacific Milling Company in King City, was transferred to Paso Robles, and then moved to Salinas to manage the Sperry Flour Mill. This was a moderately important position in Salinas, but in 1910 Sperry stopped milling flour in California. Steinbeck was offered a job with a milling company in the northern part of California, but turned it down. By this time the Steinbecks had found their place in the community.

Although Steinbeck had lost his job, he still had a substantial bank account, and, with the great economic caution that was traditional in his family, he searched for a way to go into business for himself. He felt a feed store offered the most security. He had had some experience buying and selling grain, and, after all, in a community like Salinas, people would always need grain and feed. He hadn't reckoned on the automobile.

For someone who connected so strongly the happiness of his family with his own economic success, the failure of the store—on top of having lost his job earlier—became a nearly devastating experience. In a sense, this was the family's own Great Depression, and even though the losses were eventually made up, the Steinbecks never again could quite think of themselves as "well off." Mrs. Steinbeck had acquired much the same fear of debt from her parents, and the store failure reinforced the economic caution of both. This meant, as the younger Steinbeck mentions in his portrait of his mother, that even though his parents had the money, "neighbors had new gadgets as much as two years before we did."

One of the friends that Mr. Steinbeck had made in Salinas was Charles Z. Pioda, who, as manager of the Spreckels Sugar plant, the largest factory in and around Salinas at that time, was one of the most influential men in the area. Pioda and the senior Steinbeck were both Masons, and their wives were in the Order of the Eastern Star. When the feed store went under, Pioda got his friend a job in the sugar refinery office as a bookkeeper, and for a few months, Mr. Steinbeck took the little narrow-gauge train from Salinas to the Spreckels plant, some two or three miles south of town.

Near his office at the refinery, he had a garden plot, and that was all that was necessary to make him happy in his new job. But the job was not really large enough for his abilities, and when the incumbent Treasurer of Monterey County died, Pioda and other prominent friends arranged for Mr. Steinbeck to be appointed to fill the remainder of the term. As treasurer, the senior Steinbeck did not make a large salary, but he had found a position that he was well fitted for, as well as one that had some measure of prominence and responsibility. Its only drawback was that he had to run for office periodically—Steinbeck's father was a reserved and nonpolitical type.

In the years before his father died in 1936, John would occasionally go to his father's office and "mind the store" while his father was away on county business. While sitting at his father's desk, he would work at his fiction, filling the pages of his father's discarded ledgers with his neat, but almost illegibly small handwriting. All the early manuscripts are in these ledgers (although while Steinbeck was at Lake Tahoe in the later 1920s, he used letter paper, and running out of that, used the margins and blank spaces in old magazines), and he apparently preferred them because they made his writing portable. He was known to have taken his ledger, pen, and ink bottle into the woods—to get away from the people that always seemed to gather when he had work to do—and having found a suitable rock, he would sit down and write for three or four hours. Then he would count his words, enter the total on the back cover, and stroll back to the house to join family and friends for lunch.

Mr. Steinbeck was a large yet gentle man. He was, by contrast with his wife, rather quiet and somewhat withdrawn, and he was sensitive. In the words of one of his daughters, "He suffered for people in their trouble." But he had harsh blue eyes, and people who did not know him were sometimes afraid of him. He was an accountant—organized, punctual, tidy, with beautiful handwriting. Yet, he was an outdoor man, too, perhaps a man who really belonged on the farm.

He loved to garden and taught all his children to love it (his son had to have a garden everywhere he went, even in New York City). Steinbeck senior raised chickens in back of the house in Salinas, kept a cow over at the flour mill, and occasionally butchered a hog for the family. He also kept a horse and spent what spare time he could riding about the countryside. So, although John Steinbeck grew up in town, it was almost as if he had been raised on a farm. Not only was it important to the father that his children be close to the soil, but it was important that they know about animals. When he was four, John was given his own Shetland pony, Jill, and like Jody in *The Red Pony*, he was expected to care for her.

There was much frustration in the relationship of young Steinbeck and his father, as well as much love. When very young, John was a happy-go-lucky kid, and his father was strict and expected a great deal from his children, particularly his boy. While it was true that as the only boy John was the most spoiled of the children in some ways, he was also the most often in trouble, never quite measuring up to the standards of self-discipline and hard work that his father tried to impose.

There were no spankings in the Steinbeck household, but there were tongue-lashings. And while Mrs. Steinbeck was mistress of the withering look, Mr. Steinbeck was master of the slow burn and the silent treatment. The deep frustration of both Jody in *The Red Pony* and Cal in *East of Eden*—that is, the feeling that there is no pleasing one's father and a deep sense of guilt and unworthiness in the face of one's father's expectations—had some basis in Steinbeck's own youth.

Steinbeck's father appears to have been the prototype for the many strong, silent Westerners in his son's fiction, men who repress their feelings and who are made stern by the effort to carve out a life under difficult circumstances. Steinbeck liked his father and even, later, felt a bit sorry for him, but also felt that he probably never really knew him very well:

> I remember his restlessness. It sometimes filled the house to a howling although he did not speak often. He was a singularly silent man—first I suppose because he had few words and second because he had no one to say them to. He was strong rather than profound. . . . I often wonder about him. In my struggle to be a writer, it was he who supported and backed me and explained me—not my mother. She wanted me desperately to be something decent like a banker. She would have liked me to be a successful writer like Tarkington but this she didn't believe I could do. But my father wanted me to be myself. Isn't that odd. He admired anyone who laid down his line and followed it undeflected to the end. I think this was because he abandoned his star in little duties and let his head go under in the swirl of family money and responsibility. To be anything pure requires an arrogance he did not have, and a selfishness he could not bring himself to assume. He was a man intensely disappointed in himself. And I think he liked the complete ruthlessness of my design to be a writer in spite of mother and hell.

III

Steinbeck's mother is also reflected in his fiction. Her youth as a school teacher is used as a basis for Molly Morgan's background in *The Pastures of Heaven*; some of her characteristics in middle age appear in the dominating, proper women of Steinbeck's short stories; and many of her best qualities—her cheerful strength, her sociability, her capable management—are given to Ma Joad in *The Grapes of Wrath*. She is pictured more directly in *East of Eden*, with her parents and other members of the Hamilton family.

The westward journey of this side of Steinbeck's family began in Bally Kelly, in Northern Ireland, where Samuel Hamilton, the writer's maternal grandfather, was born. When he was seventeen he came to the United States, and a year later married Elizabeth Fagen (who was born in the United States, but whose family was also from Northern Ireland) in New York City. About 1850, a year after he was married, Samuel Hamilton went to California on a sailing ship around the Horn, and a short time later his wife joined him, going by way of the Isthmus of Panama.

Samuel had a sister already living in San Jose, and he and his wife settled in that area. One child had died in New York, and another, Lizzie, came to California with her mother; six others, including Steinbeck's mother, Olive, were born in San Jose. After living in San Jose for nearly twenty years, the Hamiltons moved to nearby Soquel, and then, in 1871, to Salinas. In 1872, Samuel Hamilton signed the Salinas city charter, and a year or two later, the Hamiltons homesteaded a ranch near King City, about sixty miles south of Salinas, near the southern end of the valley. Further sections of one hundred sixty acres were filed for each of the children until something like sixteen hundred acres of land was gathered into the ranch. But the land was poor and dry. Fortunately, Samuel Hamilton not only had faith, but a good deal of skill. He was able to keep going by blacksmithing for the neighborhood, not only repairing farm machinery, but improving on it by his own invention.

Olive Hamilton was one of nine children, the youngest of five daughters. At the age of fifteen she left the ranch to go to secondary school in Salinas to prepare for a teaching career, which, as Steinbeck suggests in *East of Eden*, was an honor, a bit like having a priest in the family in Ireland. At the age of seventeen she took her county board examinations, and the following year she was teaching in a one-room schoolhouse fifteen miles south of Monterey, traveling to work on horseback every day.

Later, she taught in another one-room school near King City, and it was there that she met her future husband. In these teaching assignments she taught everything—reading, math, science, history, geography, art, and music—and to all ages. Some of her pupils, fourteen and fifteen years old, towered over her, and it took as much courage as energy and knowledge for her to do her job. Her son said of her, "Olive had not her father's brilliance, but she did have a sense of fun, together with her mother's strong and undeviating will. What light and beauty could be forced down the throats of her reluctant pupils, she forced."

Steinbeck's mother had no intention of becoming a rancher's wife, and yearned instead for town—its comforts, its stability, and its social life. At the time she met John Ernst Steinbeck, he had built and then become manager of the flour mill in King City. When he sued for Olive's hand, she accepted. Eventually, John became the manager of the mill in Salinas; Olive had the family, the house, and the position she had desired in the largest town in the long valley.

Olive Hamilton Steinbeck was a formidable woman, with remarkable energy and determination. She was, as her mother before her, forceful and practical-minded, yet, as her son notes, her actions were often based on feelings rather than ideas: "External realities of a frustrating nature she obliterated by refusing to believe in them, and when one resisted her disbelief she raged at it." Unlike her mother, Olive was a creature of society rather than of religion. She was outgoing, knowledgeable, firm, sometimes fun-loving, often opinionated, and always busy.

She was the kind of woman, as some of her neighbors have suggested, who is thought of as wearing the pants in the family, but this was a matter of visibility, rather than actual authority, which was, in fact, divided rather evenly between husband and wife. She was also thought of as snobbish, but a better term might be "proper." When a new neighbor was introduced to her at a social gathering, the neighbor might graciously invite her to "drop in" any time for a cup of coffee, blissfully unaware of the fact that Olive Steinbeck never just "dropped in" on anyone.

What people remember most about her was that she was the kind of person who could take charge and get things done. She belonged to a number of clubs and, as one of her children put it, "spent a good deal of time on strangers," arranging meetings, programs, banquets, and fund-raising drives. Although she might delegate some of the work, she was impatient with those who didn't have the same devotion and stamina that she had, and she would more than likely end up taking over most of the work herself.

Her schedule was so heavy that I suspect her children wondered if she really belonged to them or not. Two of John's closest childhood friends, Glenn Graves and Max Wagner, have mentioned that he spent a good deal of time at their houses when he was young, Glenn recalling that after Steinbeck's older sisters had gone to college, his mother "practically raised" John. Later, when he was in his early teens, John spent a lot of time in Mrs. Wagner's kitchen, where he heard the story that became "How Edith McGillcuddy Met Robert Louis Stevenson." In fact, John began rather early in life the practice of hanging around adults, some of whom didn't really appreciate having him constantly underfoot.

People with courage, will, and ambition—people who get things done—are usually thought of as deliberate, and if not logical, at least down-to-earth. But with all her practical will and determination, Mrs. Steinbeck was also very emotional and imaginative. A mystic and a romantic, her sensitivity to art was not a cultural façade, but a genuine part of her response to life.

Steinbeck has given the credit to his father for supporting him in his desire to become a writer, but he also should have given credit to his mother for getting him started. It was she who planted the seed with her bedtime stories of enchanted forests, she who encouraged her son to use his imagination, to discover a world made up of both the seen and the unseen, and to perceive the nature of things intuitively and poetically, and not only by the common sense that alone was valued in the masculine society of a "frontier" town.

Furthermore, she created a climate in the Steinbeck home which makes the emergence of Steinbeck the writer understandable, a milieu in which stories were told, books read, songs sung, verse and prose read aloud, and classical recordings played. It was a home in which there was an abundance of books and magazines to be thumbed through and sampled. In a time and place that considered magazines a waste of money, the Steinbecks always subscribed to several, including *Youth's Companion, National Geographic, Century Magazine,* and, later, *The Saturday Evening Post* and *Collier's.* The Steinbeck children always received gift books for birthdays, and there was a family collection of books in a large mahogany bookcase with glass doors. In addition, Mrs. Steinbeck encouraged the use of the library, which was nearby, and the children went there frequently.

Although Mrs. Steinbeck no longer taught after she was married, she was known by all to have been a teacher. In the Steinbeck home it was expected that all the children would get decent grades and—somewhat unusual for that time—that they would all go on to college. What happened to them if they got into trouble at school? "We didn't," remembers John's older sister Elizabeth. "We weren't allowed to—all the teachers were friends of our parents."

CHAPTER II

Even as a child there was a good deal of perversity in John. In a society in which masculinity was defined as independence, he felt he was surrounded by female authority. When his mother was off doing something cultural, as she often was, there was at least one older sister around that had to be reckoned with. He recalled later in life that his mother was "loving and firm with her family, three girls and me, trained us in housework, dish washing, clothes washing, and manners. When angered she had a terrible eye which could blanch the skin off a bad child as easily as if he were a boiled almond." As a youngster, John was brash, stubborn, and lazy, and his misbehavior was sometimes so persistent that he left his parents shaking their heads in exasperation. "I don't know about John," Mrs. Steinbeck sighed on one occasion. "He'll either be a genius or amount to nothing." Nor was he a favorite with the neighbors. One of them described him as "rotten-spoiled . . . an overgrown kid with a big belly."

One of his jobs was delivering the morning *Salinas Index*, but long after his papers should have been delivered, he was often discovered sprawled on somebody's front lawn, daydreaming or fast asleep. What energy he did expend seemed always to be used in outwitting authority. He took up smoking in his early teens and developed elaborate schemes to escape detection. He had a cache of tobacco and papers in the basement, another outside the school grounds, and a third under a loose floorboard in the church, which he used as a hiding place during Boy Scout meetings. When his father discovered what he was doing, he promised him a gold watch if he would forbear smoking until he was twenty-one. This offer only led to an acceleration of ingenuity.

One friend recalls that from very early, John "had the reputation for a loner; he was quiet; while all the kids would hang out in the vacant lot across the street from the Steinbeck house, he would never join in."

Yet, another, closer perhaps, said, "We had a little gang around the neighborhood, and he was kind of the leader." The gang changed a bit over the years. When John was young, it was Glenn Graves, John Murphy, Johnny Burgess, and sometimes Bill Welt. Later, at the end of grade school, it tended to be Glenn, John Murphy, and Max Wagner. If John was not always the leader, he was very often the strategist, his fertile imagination stimulated by a stream of ideas that came to him from adventure books read to him by his parents and older sisters.

Beyond the usual tales from such writers as Robert Louis Stevenson, Alexander Dumas, and Sir Walter Scott, there were readings from *Pilgrim's Progress, Paradise Lost,* and the Bible. But the strongest influence of all on this young boy's imagination appears to have been fairy tales, myths, and legends. His sister Esther remembers reading the Greek myths to him as a child, and John himself read Hans Christian Andersen and Malory.

There was a curious split in the foundations of his imagination produced by his early experiences with literature: on the one hand, there was a deep attachment to Romance, to the fantastic, magical, and adventurous; on the other, there was a deeply ingrained feeling for the harsh judgments of fundamentalist religion. The imagery and implications of *Pilgrim's Progress* were very real to him, and the image of a stern grandfather (a memory he could not have possibly had) reading solemnly and with all finality from the Bible came back periodically to haunt him.

This split was reflected in Steinbeck's perception of his mother's theology, which he declared was "a curious mixture of Irish fairies and an Old Testament Jehovah." It was reflected also in the split that he felt was his inheritance from the personalities of his parents. He thought of himself divided between the Irish that he had received from his mother and the Prussian he had inherited from his father (his father was really German, but Steinbeck made a point of calling him "Prussian"). Steinbeck's first wife, Carol, reacting to that self-perception, felt that she should discourage the Irish in her husband's writing—which she associated with sentimentality and rhetorical embellishment—and encourage the Prussian, the realistic and disciplined.

The *Morte d'Arthur* was the initial stimulus for Steinbeck's becoming a reader. It provoked his first interest in language, and it generated a lifelong interest in Malory:

One day, an aunt gave me a book and fatuously ignored my resentment. I stared at the black print with hatred, and then gradually the pages opened and let me in. The magic happened. The Bible and Shakespeare and *Pilgrim's Progress* belonged to everyone. But this was mine—secretly mine. It was a cut version of the Caxton "Morte d'Arthur" of Thomas Malory. I loved the old spelling of the words—and the words no longer used. Perhaps a passionate love for the English language opened to me from this one book. I was delighted to find our paradoxes—that "cleave" means both to stick together and to cut apart. . . . For a long time, I had a secret language.

John and his younger sister, Mary, would read the Arthur tales together and then recreate them in play, going into the fields with lath swords, cardboard helmets, and the pony, Jill, to search for the Grail. Mary and John had established a special relationship. While she was assigned the role of squire, she more often acted the part of Sancho Panza. When her brother was young, she got most of his jobs for him. She tried to steer him away from trouble, and when trouble came, she tried to moderate the consequences.

During their teenager years, Mary was his friend when he had almost no real friends, and for a long time, he would confide in her and no one else. She joined him in conspiracy against the world. Out of the "secret language" they had together there evolved a spiritual link that seemed at times to touch on the supernatural. For a time, Mary grew away from her special relationship with her brother by joining the real world, becoming a sorority girl, and then marrying a wealthy young businessman—embracing the respectability that her brother scorned. John, refusing to give in, struggled to preserve in his mind and then in his work the secret world they had created together.

II

John went through a primary school, which in Salinas was called the Baby School, and then on through grammar school to the eighth grade. At the fifth grade, he skipped a year (with several others in his class), which made him a year younger than most of his classmates all through high school. This was probably a major factor in putting him out of touch with his peers, for not only was he younger, but he matured, socially and physically, late for his age. He was big and awkward, going first through a "string bean" stage and then ending up with wide shoulders and barrel chest, and still some baby fat around his face and waist. Later, after six or seven years of hard labor in his late teens and early twenties, his body would get tough, but in high school, he didn't exert himself very much. He was the kind of boy who was always well-dressed, although not very neatly, and who stood around the school yard or near the front steps before school with his hands jammed in his pockets and his stomach out a bit. He was uncomfortable. A member of his class in high school recalls: "He was withdrawn. When he talked to you alone, he was fine—but in a group, no. He was an introvert when others were around."

As a junior in high school in the spring of 1917, John contracted pleural pneumonia and came very close to dying. He was taken home from Pacific Grove on the train, barely able to breathe. His father met them at the station, looked at his son, and declared to the family, "John is going to live." Dr. Murphy had to break through the rib cage in order to drain off the pus, and for weeks John's fate seemed in doubt. Once the worst was over, the doctor advised that it would help John's recovery if they moved him to a warmer climate, so Olive Steinbeck took him to a ranch near Jolon at the southern end of the Salinas Valley.

When he had recovered from the pneumonia, as John remembers,

it came time for me to learn to walk again. I had been nine weeks in bed, and the muscles had gone lax and the laziness of recovery had set in. When I was helped up, every nerve cried, and the wound in my side . . . pained horribly. I fell back in bed, crying, "I can't do it! I can't get up!"

Olive fixed me with her terrible eye. "Get up!" she said. "Your father has worked all day and sat up all night. He has gone into debt for you. Now get up!"

And I got up.

Two or three days later, he became terribly upset when his mother wouldn't let him go off into the hills and hike. "You're trying to make a baby out of me!" he complained.

Not many of his classmates remember him in high school. He stayed with the boys and stood in the background. He seldom raised his hand and volunteered to recite, seldom took part in the horseplay that erupted when the teacher left the room. He did just enough schoolwork to get the above-average grades that would satisfy his parents. Nevertheless, there were two teachers who saw in him something exceptional. One was his freshman composition teacher, Miss Cupp, who thought of him as her prize student. She praised him and encouraged him, reading his compositions to the class and holding them up as models. Although discomfiting, the experience apparently helped to give him confidence, for shortly afterward he made up his mind to become a writer and started writing stories on his own.

The other teacher, Miss Hawkins, was encountered later in math and economics classes. She was young and attractive, and he fell in love with her, worshiping her from afar. He also admired her because she was a maverick who went her own way, earning the hostility of several of the other teachers. Sensing his admiration, she used it in order to encourage him to chart his own course and persist with his ambition. Steinbeck was not much of a math student, but he felt he learned more from Miss Hawkins than from any of his other teachers.

The things that Steinbeck read in his English literature classes were typical for that time, and some of the works that were assigned were less advanced than the literature he had been reading on his own. In later years he commented on his early reading by saying that he remembered certain books "that were realer than experience—*Crime and Punishment* was like that and *Madame Bovary* and parts of *Paradise Lost* and things of George Eliot and *The Return of the Native.* I read all of these when I was very young and I remember them not at all as books but as things that happened to me."

Beyond several plays by Shakespeare, the emphasis in school was primarily on Romantic and Victorian prose and poetry, and included such works as Sir Walter Scott's *The Lady of the Lake* and Henry Wadsworth Longfellow's *Hiawatha* and *Evangeline.* Besides four years of English literature and composition, he took three years of math, two years of science, two years of history, and four years of language (two of Latin and two of Spanish). There was also a course in typing his first year, a year on the staff of the yearbook as a sophomore, and a year of "Government and Economics" as a senior. All in all it was a standard "college prep" course.

The "cadets," which John served in, was the predecessor of the high school R.O.T.C. program and was put into the schools in response to World War I. On certain days of the week during the school session, the boys wore their uniforms to school and drilled with Springfield rifles. Every few weeks, on a Saturday morning, they were taken to a range for target practice, and their shoulders would be sore for the remainder of the weekend. But the cadets had another function in addition to preparing for battle. There was an acute farm labor shortage during these war years, and the cadets program was a convenient way to organize the boys for work in the fields. All of Steinbeck's farm work experience during his time in high school came as a result of being drafted into the fields through the cadets.

When the farmers needed help, they would call, and the cadets would be brought out in buses. Some of the work was picking fruit, but most of it was in the bean fields. There was a very wet season in 1918, and the farmers needed more help than usual. Arrangements were made so that the boys reported to the high school at three-thirty in the morning, and they were taken to the fields to hoe beans for two or three hours before school started. At harvest time, the school was shut down for two weeks, and the boys were taken to the bean fields, where they pulled the vines out by hand and laid them in rows. For their work Steinbeck and the others were paid thirty-five cents an hour.

In judging Steinbeck's activity in high school, a good many journalists and biographers have depended on the Salinas High School yearbook, *El Gabilan*, published at the time of Steinbeck's graduation. In the yearbook, one gets the impression of a very active, socially successful student. There are pictures of him on the basketball and track teams, and he is listed as the senior class president, as a leading member of the cast of the school play, as an officer in the school cadets, and as an associate editor of the yearbook. But all of this is misleading.

Salinas High School had at that time only twenty-four graduating seniors. Nearly everyone was involved in some activity, and about half the class appears to have been involved in nearly everything that went on. While the election of John Steinbeck as senior class president for the second semester suggests that he was a very popular, socially active boy, just the opposite was true. Members of the class cannot remember him as president and in retrospect can't think how, considering his shyness and lack of popularity, he could have been elected. He did not have any really close friends in high school. The old gang had broken up—Max Wagner was two years behind Steinbeck and Glenn Graves one year. The closest he got to any kind of friendship with someone in his own class was with Bill Black, probably the most popular boy in the class and a successful athlete. Although he was a friend, Steinbeck was jealous of his success.

Steinbeck was a failure as an athlete. Because the school was so small, just about anybody who wanted to compete could, and he did make the track and basketball teams. But despite a willingness, he was heavy, slow, and not well-coordinated. He was also a bust in drama. Although his role, "Justin Rawson," is listed in the school playbill at the top of the cast list for *Mrs. Bumpstead-Leigh*, his part was a minor one. Later, as a justification for turning down speaking engagements, Steinbeck pointed to his acting experience as a disaster, noting that he muffed the one line—an exaggeration, the part wasn't that small—he was supposed to deliver. Nor was his position with the school cadets very exalted. As "Right Guide," one of four for Company 200, he barely made the officer roster. He had no enthusiasm whatsoever for marching around in an ill-fitting uniform and even less for getting up at three in the morning to work in the bean fields.

His one successful participation in high school affairs appears to have been his associate editorship of the yearbook, to which he contributed a number of signed and unsigned articles. They are well-written, and the wit that shows through in some of them seems to be a step above the usual yearbook humor:

> The English room, which is just down the hall from the office, is the sanctuary of Shakespeare, the temple of Milton and Byron, and the terror of Freshmen. English is a kind of high brow idea of the American language. A hard job is made of nothing at all and nothing at all is made of a hard job. It is in this room and this room alone that the English language is spoken.

While he may have had no really close friends in high school, he got along fairly well with the boys, particularly on a one-to-one basis. It was the girls who thought of him as a dud—he didn't belong in their social world at all. He didn't date or go to the school dances, and never attended (or wasn't invited to) any of the many private parties that were given during his senior year. One reason for his failure with girls might have been a painful experience during his first year in high school. His mother coerced him into going to a dancing class; he didn't want to go, but did. When he got to the dancing class, he was wearing a pair of large, clumsy boots, and when the girls saw what he had on, they laughed at him. The experience became for him one of those nightmare moments of adolescence that come back to haunt us at odd times the rest of our lives.

Twenty years later in a journal that he kept intermittently during and after the time he wrote *The Grapes of Wrath*, Steinbeck jotted down some of his memories of high school:

> I remember how grey and doleful Monday morning was. I could lie and look at it from my bed, through the rusting screen of the upstairs window. It had a quality of grey terror of its own and the

washing machines clanking in the basement and Mary playing the dull scales on the piano. What was to come next I knew, the dark corridors of the school and the desks in the ill-lighted rooms shining fiercely [in] the grey light from the windows, and the teachers, weekend over, facing us with more horror than that with which we faced them. Then the . . . [blank] . . . subjects in which no one was interested. And then one young teacher who aroused us all to ecstasies over economics when really we were merely aroused to sexual maturity by her light pretty figure and her own new-come maturity. M. [probably Max Wagner] told me he kissed her on a horse and promptly fell off the horse. M. knew about such things while I (dope that I was) thought that I loved sociology when I loved the teacher. This was not unique for me. . . . I wonder what became of that teacher. She was so pretty. But the long jawed dark ones who were not pretty got no spark from us and taught us very little. At that time, knowing little about the precocity of personality, I should have said Bill Black would have passed us all because I could not see that his very excellences were the rheostat of his mediocrity. Were I to look again and try to judge a future, I should pick a tortured child, frantic with uncertainties and unhappy in his limitations. Ed [Ricketts] riding a milk street car from illicit fornication to stoke a furnace from then to study, cursing a day and night that had no time for sleep. . . . And even after all these years I remember the envy at his [Bill Black's] ease.

Bill Black recalls Steinbeck as a nice sort of guy: "I may have been his closest friend in high school—or as much as anybody." He remembers being invited up to Steinbeck's room and hearing him read aloud manuscripts of "wonderful stories" that John had written.

III

When does a writer's apprenticeship really begin? One of John's childhood friends remembers gathering with the neighborhood children in the Steinbeck basement and listening to John tell ghost stories. Others remember that when he was a little older, he brought his friends together in the attic or the basement, arranged them in a circle, and read stories and poems to them. From the time he was very young, his sister Esther recalls, "John always had to write things." He wrote verses for place cards used at parties and dinners; he wrote verses to commemorate special events—when his dog Jiggs was run over by a fire engine, he wrote a poem for the tombstone. Since he was usually without a job and seldom had any money, he wrote poems to give as gifts, such as this one for his mother's birthday:

Ah! any gift that I could bring
would be a meagre, paltry thing,
Before the gift of God, which he,
Created on this day for me.

Sometime around his freshman year in high school, he decided to be a writer. He really wasn't quite sure how to act on that decision, except to retire to his room and write. For the next few years, he spent much of his time at home in his upstairs bedroom, sitting at his desk, staring out the window, daydreaming, and writing. Although he went to school, played some part in the life of the family, and saw some of his friends occasionally, he became, as much as practicable, a recluse. Occasionally, he had to break away, and he took long walks into the countryside or, at night, through town.

While he still played with verse, most of his writing now was devoted to short stories. Many years later, he outlined his procedure:

I used to sit in that little room upstairs . . . and write little stories and little pieces and send them out to magazines under a false name and I never knew what happened to them because I never put a return address on them. But I would watch the magazines for a certain length of time to see whether they had printed them. They never did because they couldn't get in touch with me. . . . I wonder what I was thinking of? I was scared to death, to get a rejection slip, but more, I suppose to get an acceptance.

Though he sent his stories off anonymously, he still wanted approval. He selected Bill Black and read some of his stories to him. He wanted Black to know that even if he couldn't play basketball very well, he could do something better than anyone else around. He also picked out a neighbor, Lucile Gordon Hughes, who had been editor of the high school paper, was interested in writing, and knew that John liked to write. She was also the sister-in-law of Irene Hughes, perhaps the most popular girl in John's class. Irene was first-semester senior class president, editor of the yearbook, and the lead in the school play. She was the center of everything that John was outside of in terms of parties and social events. Whether John was trying to impress Irene Hughes indirectly, or just needed someone outside the family who had some vague connection with writing to listen to his work, Mrs. Hughes was still an odd choice. She really didn't like him and tried to make that clear.

He was either too dense to get the message, or so desperate to find what he thought was a qualified listener that he didn't care. At any rate, for several long periods during his junior and senior years in high school, about twice a week he would cross the street to where Mrs. Hughes was living with her parents and her husband. John would arrive at about five o'clock, the worst possible time of day for Mrs. Hughes, since she had things to do in preparation for dinner. She didn't like him interfering with her work, but he would follow her around and read his latest manuscript to her.

She was polite enough to listen when she could, but had no hesitancy, under the circumstances, about being blunt in her criticism. The most memorable characteristic of his writing at that time was its strained vocabulary. Mrs. Hughes thought that he must be using a thesaurus, for invariably he chose the largest words one could find to express anything he was trying to express. She told him frankly, time and time again, "You use too many long words. You're showing off. No one could understand what you're talking about." He seemed to feel complimented by this, rather than hurt. He always stayed too long, and Mrs. Hughes had to ask him, as politely as her irritation would allow, to leave.

Mrs. Hughes remembers looking up and seeing him sitting near the window of his bedroom. Occasionally she would see him bending over at his writing, but more often she would see him staring into space. Once when a load of lumber was delivered to the Steinbeck house, John just sat at his window while his father struggled, all by himself, to unload it. Mrs. Hughes's husband saw the whole thing and got so angry that he wanted to drag the boy downstairs by the scruff of the neck.

John Steinbeck sitting by his window became almost a local landmark. One contemporary remembers being among a group of high school kids driving by the house: "Hey, John! Hey, John! Johnny! Steinnie! Hey, John—you got any ideas yet, John?" The girls laughed, and the boys waved, and the roadster putted on down the street and around the corner.

IV

Steinbeck was not a particularly attractive youngster. In his reclusiveness and shyness, he developed a protective arrogance that alienated many of those around him. He tried to gain affection and acceptance, but often failed. Only a few outside his family showed much warmth toward him, most notably Max Wagner's mother and his teacher, Miss

Hawkins, and both women were, in their own ways, also outsiders. His rebellion took on a somewhat different form from that of most young people: despite conflicts with his parents, he maintained his affection for them and, instead, developed a resentment for the community as a whole. As he left high school and went to college, Salinas came to symbolize for him the accumulated total of all the small embarrassments and rejections that he felt he had suffered at the hands of others during the years of growing up. For many years he nourished a hatred for his home town, adding up its faults as he perceived them—its narrow-mindedness, its prejudices, its clannishness, and the hypocrisy of its respectability. And for many years, the people of Salinas returned his hostility.

It was in response to this pattern of social failure and separation that he developed a rich inner life—he once said in a letter that half of his life while growing up was composed of dreams and fantasies. Fabricated from materials supplied by the attitudes and values of his parents, the foundation of this inner life was a special relationship he developed with nature and with language. The essence of the relationship was what could be called a belief in magic. Over and over again in looking back on his childhood, Steinbeck uses such words as "secret," "special," and "magical": he has secret places in nature to which he can retreat, the Santa Lucias are "curious secret mountains," the discovery of a rare flower is "magical" and evokes a "special" feeling, and in reading Malory, the "magic" happens. Such language points to the ability that Steinbeck had—and kept for all his life—to take delight in small things and to be open to the possibility of the wonderful.

His use of the word "magic" calls up the intensity, the excitement, the sense of discovery of childhood. He carried this mode of feeling with him out of childhood, sustaining it first by reading and then by writing. As a youngster, like so many readers, he found that printed words had a generative power. He found that they stimulated his imagination, gave substance to his dreams, and provided satisfactions that life itself all too often lacked. And like many readers, he wanted to generate that same wizardry himself.

Through adolescence he developed an ever-growing passion for language—he became entranced, literally, with the feel, the sound, and the look of words, which was accompanied by an equally intense absorption in the transformational possibilities of literature. By his mid-teens, his inner life, his plot to capture the future, was based on his hope for an apprenticeship in incantation. The Arthurian legends, Greek myths, and tales of Hans Christian Andersen were not just his earliest experiences with literature; they provided the motivation, basic form, and direction for the initial creation of the persona of John Steinbeck the writer.

These early stimulants to imagination provided for him a special status, a special "set of glasses" that only he could wear. As a young child he found the power to entertain or to frighten the neighborhood children with the stories he could tell or read. Later he could insulate himself against the shocks and rejections of adolescence, not just by escaping into a dream world, but also by assuming a perspective by which he alone could make judgments. He could view the world—and did—with a superior, bemused detachment, for he was the maker of magic. If he was solitary, it was because he was the chosen knight on a solitary quest in an enchanted land. He was not really part of "their" world, where he could be hurt, but rather, they were part of his world and subject to his judgment.

He believed in fairy tales, but in the way that very romantic boys and young men believe in them—as a hope for something special, as a metaphor for that which is creative and aspiring within them, and as a kind of blarney and bluster by which they communicate with other "initiates" and, when they are of age, flatter young ladies. When he was twenty-two, he wrote to his friend Carl Wilhelmson, whom he considered a kindred spirit:

> Do you think that I do not know of the blue magic? I was instructed in it from the start. My earliest memories are of my mother's telling me how men could become bright shining creatures with great white wings and all through the chanting of simple incantations. The spell took rather long to work however and I went to other wonderful things which could be done. . . . These charms must be worked very carefully. You must get the vowel sounds exactly right and then there are waggles of the head and forward motions of the index finger. . . . I have tried the charm for romantic love but always I have failed on the vowel sound or moved my head out of turn, and the thing failed. I think I will stop that one for a while and learn the chant which will bring me success first and then happiness. [4/24]

This is the kind of young talk, of course, that embarrasses the older man—Steinbeck burned such letters whenever he could get hold of them. In the same letter, Steinbeck mentions that he has written six short stories, one of which he calls a "fairy tale" (it "packs a sting not to be noticed at first") and goes on wryly to compare himself to "the needle in Hans Christian Andersen which imagined itself a scarf pin because it had a nob of sealing wax on its end, 'I know what I am.'"

Many readers have been shocked when, after reading several of Steinbeck's better-known works, they have picked up his first novel, *Cup of Gold*, expecting more of the same and found instead a lush, lyric fantasy, loaded with metaphor. Actually, the novel, which Steinbeck worked on from the time he was twenty-two until he was twenty-six, is a rather good compilation of his thoughts, attitudes, and tastes up to that point. The pirate Henry Morgan's search in the novel—which could be called a search for magic—is really a metaphor for Steinbeck's own search. Indeed, Steinbeck himself thought of the novel in autobiographical terms, as indicated in a letter to a Stanford friend and fellow aspiring writer, Grove Day: "The book was an immature experiment written for the purpose of getting all the wise cracks (known by sophomores as epigrams) and all the autobiographical material (which hounds us until we get it said) out of my system" [12/5/29].

In *Cup of Gold* young Henry Morgan determines at fifteen to chart his own course in the world. He wants to leave home to pursue a vague dream of fulfillment, which, in the course of time, becomes a quest for something very close to the Grail of the Arthurian legends. Henry's mother, who speaks with Steinbeck's mother's Irish lilt and who has her disposition and "second sight," opposes his journey, preferring instead that he remain and follow a more conventional life close to home. Henry's father, however, reluctantly agrees that his son's quest is necessary. To himself, he muses, "Why do men like me want sons?" He decides:

> It must be because they hope in their poor beaten souls that these new men, who are their blood, will do the things they were not strong enough nor wise enough nor brave enough to do. It is rather like another chance with life; like a new bag of coins at a table of luck after your fortune is gone. Perhaps the boy is doing what I might have done had I been brave enough years past. Yes, the valley has smothered me, I think, and I am glad this boy of mine finds it in his power to vault the mountains and stride about the world.

Although Steinbeck did try to sail to the Far East in his youth and did manage in his early twenties to sail to New York to seek his fortune, leaving the valley was for him primarily an act of will, an inward voyage of heart and imagination. It was not, however, a voyage without its hardships and privations. For nearly twenty years he followed his star with little encouragement, and his material resources, meagre at best, often ran very low. He endured battles with disappointment and self-doubt, shipwreck after shipwreck of publisher bankruptcy, and rejection after rejection at the gates of nearly every major periodical in the country. And like his hero Henry Morgan, when he reached his cup of gold, he began to doubt that it was what he had wanted after all. The great irony of this first novel was that it forecast the course of his life so accurately, his conversion from "piracy" to "respectability"—even the conferring on him of the equivalent of knighthood by the Nobel Committee and the King of Sweden.

His search for magic, however, never abated, and in looking back, what he claimed to have written throughout his life were "fairy tales" that had the truth in them. As late in his apprenticeship as 1932, in a preface to his first attempt to write a play, he thought that he might call his play "The Wizard," and noted, "My theme old as the shriveling world and as live—magic." And in the final scene of his last work of fiction, *The Winter of Our Discontent* (1961), the central character, Ethan Hawley, is saved from death by the magic of the family talisman.

CHAPTER III

Steinbeck carried a number of interests over from high school to college. His ancient history and Latin led him to take several courses in classical literature, as well as a course in elementary Greek, and these, in turn, formed the basis for a lifelong interest in Greek and Roman texts, which he pursued by extensive reading, primarily in translation. (Although he never would have admitted it, there was a good deal of the scholar in his makeup—when he could study things on his own terms.) His success in high school writing led him to an English major in college, with an emphasis on creative writing and journalism, as well as to some writing for the university literary magazine. His high school cadet experience led to several years of pleasurable horseback riding in the R.O.T.C. cavalry at Stanford, where the trainees were allowed to ride the horses during off hours just about any time they wanted.

And his year of typing in high school led to a lifetime of poorly typed manuscripts (on those few occasions when he tried to type them himself) and letters. Once at Stanford he offered to help a classmate and stayed up all night typing a paper the student would have otherwise submitted in handwriting. "You can't turn that paper in that way," Steinbeck had protested, and, with characteristic impulsiveness, added, "Let me type it for you so that you can get a decent grade." Early the next morning a bleary-eyed Steinbeck gathered the pages of the typescript and handed them to his friend, who was very grateful until he got an "F" on the paper because of the typographical errors and poor spelling.

John attended Stanford University, off and on, for six years, from the fall of 1919 to the spring of 1925. Measured by ordinary standards, his career at Stanford was not a success. When he left the university for the last time, he had completed the equivalent of less than three years of full-time attendance. His record was pockmarked with incompletes, withdrawals, cinch notices (warnings of possible failure), and long leaves of absence. Toward the end, he sometimes registered for classes, sometimes didn't—often informally auditing whatever courses appealed to him and on occasion forgetting that he had already taken or audited a course until the quarter was half over.

Eventually, he learned to use what was available to him at the university for his own ends, and since the academically elite university is one of the most intimidating institutions conceived by man, Steinbeck deserves some credit for working out his own education on his own terms. He gradually gave up the idea of getting a degree and developed a system whereby he went to school half the year and worked the other half. The various jobs he held during his university years not only provided the money to go to school (his parents put his sisters through college but let him fend pretty much for himself), but also provided a variety of experiences that he was later to draw on for his writing. During the two quarters of the year when he was at Stanford, he took the courses he thought would best help his writing. All in all it was a balanced and sane curriculum, but it took him about three years to develop it.

When he arrived in October 1919 to register for his first quarter, he was not prepared to cope with the challenges of university life. He was seventeen, immature, and bull-headed, and he thought he knew a good deal more than he actually did. He was very shy and yet, at the same time, a terrible show-off in some ways. He had rebelled at home and now he was free to carry out his rebellions at whatever pitch he wished. Furthermore, his academic preparation was mediocre—he had coasted through high school without much effort. Now he faced stiff competition from outstanding students in an institution that took pride in its high academic standards.

Had he been motivated, he might have succeeded, but he was not. He came to Stanford without enthusiasm, mechanically carrying out his parents' expectations for him. He looked forward to the life of a writer, and he couldn't see how another four years of schooling could help him become the Jack London he dreamed of becoming. If it had been up to him, he would have thrown himself into life, taken a ship to the Far East, or become a newspaper reporter in New York.

Of course Steinbeck's parents knew by this time that their son was determined to become a writer, but they had no idea how lasting his affection for writing might be. They weren't opposed to his plan, but they were realistic about it. They knew that even if their son applied himself diligently—a characteristic that he was not known for—his chances of becoming an important, well-known writer were very slim.

They were very concerned that all their children, son and daughters, have the opportunity to become successful and secure. If, after college, John stilll wanted to write, well, he could go ahead and try. Mrs. Steinbeck hoped that in the meantime he would change his mind and become a community leader—a banker, a lawyer, or even a minister. But nothing could have been further from her son's own plans and sympathies. He did go to Stanford to please his parents, but his heart wasn't in it.

In the years following World War I, Leland Stanford Junior University was, nevertheless, a pleasant place to suffer through one's education. Built in the middle of a wheat field, surrounded by the 8,940 acres of Senator Leland Stanford's Palo Alto ranch, the campus had a rural flavor and an informality which set it apart from the traditional private universities of the East. A large quadrangle, the campus opened in all directions—to the inside, with its arches, colonnades, courts, and gardens, and to the outside, with groves of trees, playing fields, and the sun-browned hills that stretched out into the western horizon.

As a freshman, John Steinbeck shared a room with George Mors on the first floor of the men's dormitory, Encina Hall, a four-story heavy sandstone building that overlooked the dining hall and the men's gym and playing fields beyond. Inside Encina, long, dim hallways, gray with brown wood, were lined with heavy wooden doors that opened into moderately large rooms, each with a window or two, a washbasin, two desks, two beds, and a closet. The window was good for looking and leaning out of during long afternoons; the top of a trunk was a good table for cards; and a closet a good place to stash forbidden material. The halls were good for snapping towels on the way back from the showers, or for water fights or kickball until the noise attracted the resident. In the late afternoon groups would gather, moving from room to room. "Let's go eat" was the call, and they would troop down the stairs and across to the eating clubs and dining hall. And in the evening, "Anybody going into town?"

Stanford's motto was "The Winds of Freedom Blow," and Steinbeck embraced the motto passionately. He learned to drink—he'd been but an amateur at home—and to play poker. Though Steinbeck celebrated his freedom, he was not always very cheerful, but, by turns, cocky, depressed, exuberant, and withdrawn. At times he declared he didn't care. Stanford couldn't teach him anything useful he didn't already know. Drinking bouts, horseplay, and late hours led to missed classes and late papers. He would go to the library to get away from the distractions of the dorm, but after a half hour he couldn't stand it any more, and he'd get up and get out. He walked the campus and the hills and rode the cadet horses out into the countryside.

Two decades later, when he was trying to write *The Grapes of Wrath*, Steinbeck, filled with the misery of attempting to get his work done in the face of constant interruption, wrote, "It's just like slipping behind at Stanford. Panic sets in. Can't organize." He was to have recurring nightmares about these first quarters at Stanford for the rest of his life. Bill Black, who was also at the university, stopped by occasionally to see his high school buddy, and saw drinking and card-playing, but not much studying. Black's main impression from his visits was how worried George Mors was about his roommate.

Mors and Steinbeck were opposites in many ways and made an odd pair. One was immature and at loose ends, a free spirit who would become an artist; the other was a self-controlled, clean-cut, precise young man who would become an army engineer. Mors was the son of a struggling middle-class family from nearby Los Gatos, and in contrast with Steinbeck, he was serious about his schooling. But the two got along well, perhaps because Mors could mind his own business when he needed to and because he, too, enjoyed a good joke. The difference was that Mors knew when to stop, whereas Steinbeck's passions led him almost always to excess. Without Mors's steadying influence, Steinbeck probably would not have lasted as long as he did in his first tenure at the university.

Steinbeck could not have been the easiest roommate to get along with. His shyness kept him from making friends, and the high ratio of boys to girls on campus made it nearly impossible for him, as a freshman, to get a date. In class, he kept to himself and tried to avoid being called on by sitting well back in the classroom and mumbling when asked to recite. He tried out for the freshman football team and failed. He was expected to go home every weekend, and while he had some homesickness and was glad to get away from the campus, he resented having to go. Friday evenings, Bernard Freire would pick up Steinbeck at Mountain View, a small town south of Palo Alto. Freire collected the beet samples from the Spreckels ranches, and, at the request of Charles Pioda, gave Steinbeck a ride in his truck on his way back to the factory. They would stop about halfway home at Gilroy, and Freire would feed Steinbeck at a truck stop and pay for it out of his own pocket. Steinbeck, unhappy and absorbed in himself, rarely had anything to say, not even "thank you."

Steinbeck did not spend every weekend at home, however. Whenever he could, he made the excuse that he had to stay at school and study in the library. Then, as Mors recalls, he would head for San Francisco. It was during these weekend sojourns that he tried to find out as much as possible about what he might have missed growing up under his parents' supervision in a small town. Years later he wrote, "I was going to Stanford. I was very broke and couldn't indulge in as much sweet-scented sin as I wished, but what I did manage to chisel in on was in San Francisco. Who needed Paris or the silken sewers of Rome when there were Bush Street apartments and the Pleasure Domes of Van Ness Avenue?"

By the time he was halfway through his second quarter, Steinbeck had two cinch notices, and a letter was sent to his parents. He completed only seven of fifteen units his first quarter, and then was stricken with a serious case of the flu during winter quarter and an acute appendicitis attack during spring quarter, so that he ended the year having completed only three classes. Following his appendicitis operation in May, he stayed at home in Salinas and waited for Mors to finish the term. Steinbeck's father had been able to line up jobs for the two of them with a surveying crew that was working in the Big Sur area south of Monterey, a job they thought would be easy. But the western slopes of the Santa Lucias are extremely rugged, and they found themselves hauling their rods and chains up steep canyons and through thick, unyielding brush, trying to avoid poison oak and rattlesnakes. The food was terrible—so bad that they began to dread the approach of mealtimes and, as Mors recalls, began to hate the foreman, who had special meals prepared by the cook, his wife. After several weeks, they could take no more, and so Steinbeck's father got them jobs with the maintenance crew at the Spreckels factory.

Mors lived with the Steinbecks for the rest of the summer. On weekends he went with them to the beach house in Pacific Grove, and the two boys slept in cots on the sleeping porch. One Sunday when it was too cold to go swimming, John told George that he knew how they could have some fun. He grabbed a couple of gunnysacks and led his roommate to a wooded area near Asilomar, which abutted a row of expensive homes. He picked up two sticks from beneath a pine tree, gave one to George along with one of the gunnysacks, and instructed him to follow his lead. John got down on his hands and knees and crawled forward cautiously for a few yards, looking here and there as he advanced. Then, with a sudden leap, he lifted his stick overhead and whacked it down on a pinecone. As if recovering a trophy, he held it up briefly for George to see and thrust it into his sack.

John continued this dramatization of a snipe hunt for fifteen or twenty minutes, and George, who hadn't the slightest idea what his friend was doing, followed, trying his best to emulate John's enthusiasm. To each of George's questions, John answered, "Just wait—you'll see." Finally, John told him not to look up, but that the people in the houses were peering at them from their front windows. He got up and led George to a place where they could hide and still watch the houses. In a few minutes, one after another, curious men came outside to walk around under the trees in an effort to find out what the boys had been up to. John enjoyed himself immensely as he watched the puzzled homeowners searching and conferring.

Mors remembers this scene as more typical of Steinbeck than anything else he witnessed when the two were together. It was an outrageous pantomime by a gleeful prankster bent on provoking the protective zeal of the respectable property owner. As such, the scene presents a kind of archetypal cartoon of the Steinbeck character. There was something of the boy whacking pinecones in much that Steinbeck would write over the years—dramatizations designed to irritate the respectable and confound the narrow-minded.

Steinbeck's work experiences as a teenager and young man had considerable impact on his writing, especially as his experiences enlarged his view of life and made him, over a period of several years, less self-centered. Most of his work up through the time he left Stanford at age twenty-three was for Spreckels Sugar and was obtained as a result of his father's friendship with the plant manager. During the summer before his senior year and right after graduating from high school, Steinbeck worked in the main plant itself, helping the carpenter-shop foreman, who found that his helper was usually more trouble than he was worth. He had to give John hell for slacking off on the job, for wandering off into corners and scribbling on paper. During that second summer, John was fooling around in the machine shop and got iron filings in his eyes, and they had to be bandaged for two weeks, while Mary became a seeing-eye sister.

It was as a carpenter's helper that he returned to Spreckels in the summer of 1920, after resigning his position as "civil engineer." In the years that followed, he performed two other kinds of jobs for Spreckels at various times: during the summer (and on one occasion during the spring) he worked on the Spreckels ranches; in the later summer and fall during the sugar beet harvest, he worked in the plant as a bench chemist. Spreckels owned or leased ranches from below King City in the south to Santa Clara in the north. Each ranch had a bunkhouse or two, a cook house, and a superintendent's house. The main business of the ranches was to raise sugar beets, but they also raised hay and alfalfa, had milk cows, and ran some cattle, although the land was more likely to be leased out part of the year to others for grazing. Each ranch had a small semipermanent crew for maintenance and feed operations. They were helped with these chores by the bindlestiffs and hobos who worked their way north every year up the line of Spreckels ranches. They'd get a meal at the southernmost ranch, find out what the work situation was in the valley, and then travel north to where there was work, living on one or more of the company ranches as long as they were needed. Lennie and George in *Of Mice and Men* are such bindlestiffs (although they drift in from the northern part of the state), who find work at the Spreckels ranch number 2, just south of Soledad on the west side of the Salinas River, joining the maintenance crew at haying time. Depending on the time of year, the bindlestiffs would move on from the ranches to Monterey to try to get work in the canneries. It was these men who became the models for Mack and the boys in *Cannery Row.*

Handling the beet crop was another matter. After the rainy season of March and April, the fields were plowed with steam-driven plows, which ran on cables for 1500 or 1800 feet, and seed was dropped in furrows far enough apart for a wagon to pass between them at harvest time. Once a crop was planted, Spreckels hired a tremendous number of men to maintain the fields throughout the entire ranch system. The crop had to be thinned, and then, during the summer growing season, the beets were irrigated by ditches, which had to be dug and then kept free of weeds. At harvest time, the fields would be flooded and the beets plowed out. Crews would top the beets by hand and stand them on their butt ends in rows.

Most of this work was handled by crews of foreign nationals, either Japanese, Mexicans, or Filipinos. One of two Steinbeck stories published in Stanford literary magazines during his time at the university is about an Anglo girl who gets involved with a Filipino crew boss. His description of the crew and its pattern of living has the ring of having come from actual observation:

A coal fire roared in the bunkhouse of the foreign camp. The Filipinos sat on the floor with their feet under them. From the outside the howling wind came through the cracks in the house and made the burlap hangings move restlessly. Burlap tacked loosely on the walls, a littered floor of dust colored wood, a few boxes to sit on, and the fat-bellied stove, that was the lounging room of the bunkhouse. Three of the pock-marked, brown men played cards on the floor under a coal oil lamp. They threw down their cards without a word. No one was talking in the room. Ten or twelve more of the squatty figures were dumped about the room, half smiling because there would be no work in the beet fields the next day. Pedro, the boss, sat on a box near the stove, great head on chest, his palms pressing on his temples while the fingers worked busily in his tangled black hair.

This scene came out of his experience during the years 1921 and 1922, when there was a long gap in his Stanford education. After an abortive attempt to return to school in the fall of 1920, Steinbeck had gone to the San Francisco area for several weeks and then ended up on a Spreckels ranch near Chualar, about ten miles south of Salinas. He was signed on as a straw boss, not to direct work gangs like the one pictured above, which already had a boss-contractor, but to supervise pick-up crews made up of casual workers. He was good at this work, born with the knack of getting along well with such laborers, and he picked up enough scraps of Spanish and Tagalog to communicate with them. He could make a fine insult. When one of the workers gave Steinbeck some trouble, John told him, *"Pon un condo sobre la cabeza"* or "Pull a condom over your head." He said later that he heard that phrase repeated for years.

The sugar beets mature in the late summer and fall and should be harvested before the first freeze. Since the harvested beets do not store very well, the idea is to harvest and process the beets continuously, field by field. Samples were brought in from all the Spreckels ranches regularly to be tested, and, on the basis of those tests, each ranch was scheduled for harvesting. After working in the fields from early spring, Steinbeck switched to working with the processing crew at the plant. He lived at home during these periods, and every morning and evening rode the narrow-gauge railroad to and from Spreckels. The processing season ran from late August to the middle of December, and the usual schedule was for each worker to work days half the season and nights the other half. The shifts ran twelve hours, changing at seven a.m. and seven p.m. Steinbeck worked as a bench chemist and earned 32½ cents an hour.

Working as a "chemist" or "running a bench" of fifteen or twenty people didn't require any technical training; the job was essentially a matter of running perfunctory tests on the beet distillate.

Steinbeck conducted the tests over and over again during his long shift throughout his first season, but in the fall of 1922 he was promoted to running a bench, or supervising, which gave him more time, especially on the night shift, to squeeze in some writing. It had become more and more habitual with him since his second year of high school to take time for his writing wherever and whenever he could. Actually, he could have stayed in the fields working with the beet harvest until the late fall if he had wanted to. But working in the plant was easier, and he could write during the slack periods—no one would bother him as long as he got his work done.

Running a bench, Steinbeck supervised a crew, as he had in the field, and had custody of all the apparatus and chemicals. One of the chemicals used in testing was alcohol, and early in the fall of 1922, he discovered that great quantities of it were missing from inventory. Since this was during Prohibition, the conclusion was obvious. To test his suspicions, he loaded the alcohol with phenophthalein—an acid indicator used in the tests, but also a powerful laxative—and before the shift was over, the culprits were easily identified. Later in the fall, he had either mellowed or adopted a double standard. He appeared at the Stanford–University of California "Big Game" wearing a large, heavy overcoat, and when the subject of drink came up, he opened his coat; there, pinned neatly to the lining, were row upon row of laboratory vials filled with grain alcohol.

Many of the hardest and dirtiest jobs at the sugar mill were done by Mexican laborers. Some have the impression that Steinbeck got much of his information about the Mexican-Americans and *paisanos* second- and third-hand, but he knew them well from childhood on. His friend Max Wagner had lived in Mexico until he was twelve, and together they were friendly with a number of Mexican families in Salinas, especially the Sanchez brothers, with whom Steinbeck ran around in his late teens. From his association with the Mexican nationals who worked at Spreckels, he picked up several of the characters and stories that he used later in *Tortilla Flat*: the ex-corporal of Mexican cavalry whose wife is stolen by a captain; the old Mexican who hangs himself for the love of a fourteen-year-old girl; and Sweets Ramirez, who is paid for her favors with a sweeping machine without a motor. This storing of material, not only stories but also metaphors and even phrases, was typical of Steinbeck, and since he did not keep systematic notes, he apparently kept such things in his head for use ten or fifteen years later.

Such diligence was both a blessing and a curse. Once he developed a fondness for a phrase or an anecdote, he not only remembered it but was determined to use it somehow. The stories of the ex-corporal and the old man are forced into *Tortilla Flat*, and don't really fit either in subject matter or tone. Such stubborn insistence was demonstrated also by his fondness for leprechauns. His writing and conversation during his college years were burdened by Irish whimsey. His determination to act the Romantic Irish rogue and to argue incessantly for the existence and importance of the "little people" had the opposite effect from the one he intended: rather than charming, it became absolutely nauseating. Another example occurs in *East of Eden*. Steinbeck had been saving up an anecdote about his mother in a flying machine for thirty years, and by God, he was going to use it. He never really learned the lesson that most good writers have to learn and that is to leave things out of a narrative that don't fit, even if you are terribly fond of them.

In the fall of 1920 Steinbeck returned to Stanford to try again. He came back under a lot of pressure—he was on academic probation and had several "incompletes" to make up from the previous year. Perhaps the pressure was too great and he felt defeated before he even got started. He avoided the reckoning as long as possible:

> Once in college I went flibberty geblut [*sic*] and got to going to the library and reading what I wanted instead of what was required. I got behind and then I got so far behind that I could not possibly catch up.

In the face of almost certain disaster, Steinbeck showed a certain bravado. One of the extracurricular rituals every year at Stanford was the "Tie-Up," a game of capture between freshmen and sophomore males, which took place on a large playing field. One of the few surviving photographs of Steinbeck at Stanford shows him and George Mors standing together in front of the crowd, stripped to the waist—the only ones so "clad"—and greased like Roman wrestlers. Steinbeck is staring at the photographer with a challenging smile on his face.

It was during this time that Steinbeck became a hasher at one of the sorority houses. Hashers served lunch and dinner, cleared the tables, and then washed the dishes, in return for which they received their meals and to some extent were considered "one of the family"—that is, the women didn't pay much attention to them, considering them more as brothers than as possible suitors. Three or four years later, Steinbeck said that the experience destroyed his romantic awe of women—witnessing them without makeup, eating with their hands, and belching at the table. But this wasn't true. He had a deeply ingrained double standard throughout his life which categorized some women to be conquered and others to be placed on a pedestal. Despite all his bragging in his younger years, he remained relatively naive about women throughout a good part of his life—and it caused him no end of trouble.

About halfway through the quarter he realized he couldn't make it academically. He had been kidding himself and now he had run out of time. George Mors woke up on a Sunday morning to find a note that read: "Gone to China. See you again sometime." The note also asked Mors to release his animals (Steinbeck had accumulated a canary, a chipmunk, and a turtle, as well as some goldfish in a bowl) and to send the rest of his things home to his sister in Salinas. Apparently Mary was the only one he wanted any communication with, under the circumstances, and he had no intention of facing his parents.

Steinbeck did go to San Francisco, his friends learned later, and tried to ship out to China, but didn't have any papers or sea experience and couldn't get a berth. His romantic dream of sailing aboard a freighter, Jack London fashion, had to wait. He moved in with a friend for a couple of weeks, but couldn't find work. His position was embarrassing: he had committed himself to a dramatic course of action and had been unable to carry it out. He was undecided what to do—he felt he couldn't go home and yet he was broke. Apparently—the chronology is not clear here—he hitchhiked south, stopping overnight at one point at George Mors's mother's grocery store and lying to her about where he was going and why. Then he went on down below Salinas and got a job, this time on his own, at one of the Spreckels ranches. For some reason, perhaps because he was laid off from his job, he went back to Oakland that Christmas, and again staying with a friend, worked in Capwell's Department Store selling men's furnishings during the holiday season.

The friend in this instance was Robert Bennett, and he has provided us with an amusing view of Steinbeck at eighteen in a pamphlet published in 1939 called *The Wrath of John Steinbeck*. Bennett draws a picture of an *adolescent formidable*, who acts the iconoclast in his strong-minded pronouncements on "girl-struck" boys (declaring his intellectual independence), and socialism (displaying his practical knowledge of the working man).

Although comic in tone, the pamphlet does provide some serious insights into the early manifestations of long-held Steinbeck beliefs.

Steinbeck's comments to Bennett on socialism have particular interest, in that throughout much of his life he shared a number of ideas with the socialists, was accused of being a socialist or communist on various occasions during the thirties, and yet never endorsed or advocated socialism as a system. Here he gives the impression of being too proud of his intellectual independence to become involved in such a political movement:

> I have been working on a ranch down the country and, incidentally, arguing Socialism with the laborers. Do you know Bob, nothing can kill Socialism in the minds of thinking people quicker than the arguments of the grubbers. It is so plainly a matter of getting something for nothing with a little revenge thrown in that the idea is sickening. Your arguments were logical and broad. Too broad perhaps for there can never be successful Socialism so long as such narrowness and greed as I have seen, exist.

What bothered Steinbeck most about our society was that in a land of plenty—a plenty so visible in California—large numbers of people could still go hungry. At a relatively early age, he had broken out of the mold of middle-class sensibility, had lived among those who actually did lack food and the means to obtain it, and had developed a strong sense of social justice, giving vent to the same indignation he was to express so forcefully in *The Grapes of Wrath* nearly two decades later. The central incident described by Bennett in his essay shows this indignation in action.

A few days before Christmas, after they had worked all week at Capwell's, Bennett took Steinbeck home with him for the weekend. Sunday morning they allowed themselves, reluctantly, to be talked into going to church. Bennett, his mother, and Steinbeck walked several blocks to the nearby Methodist Church, where they sat through a sermon on "spiritual hunger." As the long-winded preacher piously derided real bread in favor of that which would feed the soul, young Steinbeck began mumbling retorts under his breath, a rumbling made up of such comments as, "a lot of crap . . . if the soul is immortal, why worry about it . . . it's the body that . . ." Finally, when the minister intoned, "Ho, every one that thirsteth, come ye to the waters; and he that hath no money, come ye, buy and eat! Wherefore do you spend money for that which is not bread, and labor for that which satisfieth not? Ho, hearken diligently unto me, eat and let your soul delight itself in fatness," Steinbeck could not contain himself any longer. He burst out loud with, "Yes, you all look satisfied here, while outside the world begs for a crust of bread or a chance to earn it. Feed the body and the soul will take care of itself!"

It wasn't very polite—Bennett's mother "looked as though she wanted to crawl into her pocketbook"—but Steinbeck felt it needed saying and he had courage enough to say it. Robert Bennett may have been the only one who really heard what Steinbeck had to say on that day, but more would later.

CHAPTER IV

There was no doubt that Steinbeck had the necessary fire to make a writer—enough stubbornness, individuality, and ambition to get him through the lean years. What he lacked at the age of twenty-one, after a more than two-year absence from school, were the technical skills of fiction writing and enough general knowledge to give his work intellectual depth and maturity. Pressured by his parents' expectations for him and motivated, at last, by a realization that he needed more schooling to do what he wanted to do, he applied for readmission and returned to Stanford.

From November 1920 until January 1923, he had worked as a salesman, ranch hand and straw boss, bench chemist, and, during the winter and spring of 1921–22, as a laborer with a dredging crew, cutting a slough from Salinas to Castroville. (He and another boy, Budd Peaslee, were hired by the county surveyor to carry chain, wading waist-deep through swamp, in order to put in the marker stakes for a canal route designed to drain the swamps on the outskirts of town.) He had learned a lot about people and about himself during this period.

Although he occasionally lived with his parents during these years, he became more and more independent of them, traveling about on his own and often living by himself. He cut himself off from friends of high school and college days—his companions, when he had any, were the laborers with whom he worked. He had his first full-scale sexual experiences with a woman who was not a prostitute, and, so he claimed later, his first minor brush with the law. "Vagrancy" was a charge that hung over the head of any unemployed laborer on the road away from friends or family.

While moving from job to job, trying to find himself, he never deviated from his ultimate goal of becoming a writer, never seemed to doubt his ultimate success. He appeared, also, to be always gathering material. He wasn't able to keep a systematic notebook for his ideas, but he did write down ideas on miscellaneous scraps of paper, which he stuffed into his pocket, later emptying them into a dresser drawer. He was liable to stop and scrawl a note or two at almost any time, even while making love to a girl in the back seat of a car.

Sometime during this period he was on the road near San Francisco and stopped to join a hobo camp. These hobos were mostly young men, many out-of-work World War I veterans, on their way north to Oregon to look for jobs in the lumber camps and mills. Steinbeck mentioned his name and said he was trying to become a writer. He asked the man next to him if he had ever tried to write a novel. "No," the man replied. "Well," said Steinbeck, "it's the hardest thing in the world." He was looking for stories, he said, and if anyone had a good story, he'd pay him for it. Several of the men told funny stories or jokes, but Steinbeck said that wasn't what he was looking for. He wanted a "humanistic" story. "Do you know what I mean by a 'humanistic story'?" he asked.

One young man, whose name was Frank Kilkenny, said, "Yes. I know what you're looking for." And he proceeded to tell a story about himself, when he was fourteen and living in Oregon. His father had died and his mother had taken a job as a housekeeper on the Coast. He set out from the farm on which he had been working to join his mother, and as there were few roads in that part of the country in those days, he traveled cross-country. As he got near the Coast, he found himself confronted by a canebrake that seemed to stretch for miles. As he tried to cross through the field, he found he couldn't see beyond the cane that surrounded him and he began to lose his direction. The sun was frequently hidden by clouds or fog, and he found himself rushing in this direction and that in an attempt just to escape from the cane. After four days of frantic activity with no food or water, he escaped from the huge field, made his way to a nearby farm house, and collapsed. The farmer, a Finn, carried him into the house and into the bedroom and laid him on a bed.

The farmer and his wife tried to feed the boy, but he was in such bad shape that he was barely conscious and could not keep anything in his stomach. He drifted in and out of consciousness, and the farmer was clearly worried that he was dying. As he lay on the bed, he could hear the Finn and his wife arguing, but he couldn't make out what they were saying. After a time, the woman, who had been sitting on a rocker in the other room nursing a baby, came into the bedroom. She pulled the boy's head onto her lap and gave him her breast, and he fed for a few minutes and went to sleep.

Kilkenny turned to Steinbeck, who had been taking notes all this time, and asked, "Is that the kind of story you're looking for?" "Yes," he said, "I can use that," and he paid Kilkenny two dollars.

Steinbeck returned to Stanford more mature in some ways, but he still maintained his defensive posture of superiority in respect to both the university and most of its students. If anything, his period of independence had strengthened that feeling, rather than dissipated it. He returned, however, with confidence and a clearer sense of direction: this time he would do it his way. He'd get the grades necessary to stay in school, but he was going to take only those courses that would help him do what he wanted to do; he had no intention of fulfilling graduation requirements. While his parents and his teachers knew what he was up to, the university never officially sanctioned his plan, and he became the bane of the registrar's life. From the time Steinbeck reentered, to the time he left for good in June of 1925, the registrar tried, by persuasion and threat, to get him to finish his lower-division requirements, but to no avail. Steinbeck followed what interested him.

What interested him could be nearly anything—from elementary Greek, to a course in the medical school on the dissection of cadavers. According to one of Steinbeck's friends at the time, Frank Fenton, Steinbeck successfully argued for this latter course with his English department advisor on the basis that he "wanted to know more about people." The medical school would not admit him on the necessary special-study basis, but the incident does point up Steinbeck's early concern with people as physical organisms. (The incident also suggests that with all his early romanticism, he still developed a naturalistic philosophy of man, on his own, many years prior to the influence of the marine biologist, Ed Ricketts.) More usually, however, what interested him were classes in writing, literature, history, and classics, and he worked hard enough to get mostly B's and more A's than C's.

At registration that January, Steinbeck ran into Carlton "Dook" Sheffield, a friend from earlier Stanford days. Steinbeck complained that he had been put in with a roommate who had pasted pictures of naked women on all the walls of their room. "Personally," he told Sheffield, "I like naked women, but I don't really care to be surrounded by pictures of them." So they arranged to switch roommates, Steinbeck moving into Sheffield's room in the basement of Encina Hall. Sheffield had come to Stanford from Long Beach, where he had been working in a shipyard until he decided there must be a better way to make a living. He was of medium height and build, soft-spoken, but with a wry wit that apparently had attracted Steinbeck's attention when they had taken French together as freshmen. The two of them had gotten together on a regular basis for boxing sessions on Saturday mornings. The gloves were Sheffield's, but Steinbeck, bigger and more aggressive, showed no gratitude. The sessions usually consisted, as Sheffield tells it, "of his hitting me and my falling down and getting up and being hit again."

The two had several things in common. They were both English majors, both wanted to be writers, and both were nonconformists with a sense of humor. A case in point was the decor of their room. They piled a trunk on top of a moving crate and covered the whole thing with red cloth. Then they hung a canopy over the two-level platform, putting a blond doll at the top of what they began to think of as an "altar" and a figure of a "sacrificial knight" below. They discovered by accident that when they lit a can of Sterno, it created an eerie effect, taking all the color out of the room. They would invite friends down to the room for a drink, and when the friends came, they were startled on opening the door to see, according to Sheffield, "a salami on the floor with this ghastly light that turned everything a greenish gray, a horrible gray, and there we were on our knees, worshipping the Goddess of Chastity." For survivors, drinks were provided from the end of a piece of laboratory tubing that ran under the door of the closet back into a corner, where a wine keg sat on a cradle.

Steinbeck was able now to indulge in such college highjinks without letting this part of his life undermine his ability to function. He had shed some of his shyness and began to carve a place for himself in the campus community. The two usual keys to acceptance and status for a college man in those days, of course, were belonging to a fraternity (or eating club at Stanford) or participating in athletics. The role that Steinbeck chose for himself was made up of equal parts of literary genius, iconoclast, and roisterer. Part of this pose was a great scorn for things typically collegiate, yet at least a small part of this scorn was no doubt the envy of the outsider. Some clue to his mixed emotions in these matters can be found in his early effort to make the football team, and failing that, his signing up for polo (as part of the R.O.T.C. program) each quarter during his second tenure at Stanford. He was a skillful rider, but no one seems to know how successful a polo player he was; in fact, none of his acquaintances recalls ever seeing him play. Any number of people, however, recall seeing him dressed in his polo outfit, striding about campus. His riding breeches became his panache.

Several of those close to Steinbeck, including Dook Sheffield, belonged to one or another of the eating clubs and at various times tried to recruit him as a member, but Steinbeck could not hide his disdain for such things and probably would have been blackballed even if he had allowed himself to be proposed. When one of his friends, Dean Storey, joined a fraternity in his senior year out of sheer loneliness (Steinbeck by this time was living off campus), Steinbeck made it clear that he thought Storey had become too collegiate for words. He threatened to gather some of his tough acquaintances from local pool halls and bring them to the fraternity house as Storey's guests for dinner.

Steinbeck's sister Mary, who by now was also at Stanford, had turned into a very attractive girl, and relations between brother and sister were sometimes strained as Mary became a part of the social scene that her brother despised. One afternoon Webster Street met Steinbeck dressed in his polo outfit on the way to his sister's sorority, where he was to help with the decorating for a dance to be held that evening. The two young men worked all afternoon, moving furniture and climbing stepladders, and when they were through, they stood around for several minutes admiring their handiwork and waiting for an invitation to the dance. Mary, mindful of her brother's possible behavior, offered nothing but thanks and goodbye.

And indeed, her brother was a poor risk, for his greatest glory seemed to come from saying or doing the most outrageous things he could think of. One such attack on campus snobbery was a classic, at least according to Steinbeck's telling of it in a letter to Dook Sheffield (who had since graduated and returned to southern California). The formal junior prom was the campus social event of the year, and Steinbeck, for whom such affairs were usually anathema, made a plan to attend in style. During one of his periodic sorties into the nightlife of San Francisco he had made the acquaintance of two beautiful Chinese girls, twin sisters, and he made arrangements that he and a friend, Montgomery Winn, should take them to the prom. Mary, knowing nothing about the girls, offered to let them come to her sorority house to freshen up after their trip from San Francisco, and before going to the dance. Having picked up the girls in the city and brought them to Palo Alto on the train, the two young men could not find a taxi anywhere near the station, so Steinbeck ran into town in an effort to beg, borrow, or steal some kind of transportation to campus. He came back with a very old, broken-down, panel truck that he later claimed was a Chinese laundry wagon.

It is hard to realize today just how much prejudice there used to be among the genteel against old rattletrap cars, but it is sufficient to say that as the jalopy pulled into the driveway of the sorority, among the luxury cars of wealthy alumni, it became an immediate social disaster for Mary Steinbeck. It is also hard to realize just how much prejudice there was, in California particularly, against Orientals in the 1920s. As the girls emerged smiling from the rusting hulk of a delivery truck, beautifully turned out in their formal Oriental dresses, one can only suppose that outrage turned into a sort of numbness.

And there were poetic gestures of other kinds as well. Stanford was not a church school, properly speaking, but the Leland Stanfords had been religious people who had given their fortune to establish a university in memory of their only child. It was their aim that the university provide a wholesome environment, one in which the highest moral values would be affirmed, and that the Memorial Church at the center of the campus become a spiritual beacon, casting its light on all gathered at the university. While drinking was far from unknown on campus (there were a number of bootleggers in the nearby hills), it had been forced into hiding by decrees (enacted in response to a series of incidents involving drunken mobs of students) banning drink from campus residences and punishing drunkenness by suspension. Only Steinbeck would have such a burning need to defy authority as to bring a gallon of red wine with him to the Inner Quad, and to stay all night watching the stars, leaning against a palm tree in front of Memorial Church. It is also said that he got up early one morning and altered the carillon so that the bells rang out "How Dry I Am" on the hour. So delighted was he with what he had done that he went around telling everyone about it and ended up, once again, in trouble with the dean's office.

Although Steinbeck had been an "outsider" for some time, it wasn't until his second try at Stanford that he really began to cultivate the role with relish. He was old enough now so that he was able to make some progress with girls at the university—his body had toughened and he had an air of experience—although he usually stayed away from sorority types and concentrated on those whose needs were more physical than social. He did not very often "date" girls—that was too collegiate—but instead usually took out girls who were also outsiders in some way, and who lived off campus. They walked and talked, drank and argued, and had sex.

Having sex, and having it in a rather direct way, without the complicated college courtship ritual, was part of his role as an independent.

His sexual adventures soothed an ego bruised by earlier rejections and gave him material by which he could, in the telling, impress his friends with his casual *savoir faire*. The many stories in this vein that survive probably tell more about Steinbeck's personality than they tell about his activities, since the stories came from him in the first place.

Each of the stories, for one thing, appears designed to be at least mildly shocking. For example, he told Dean Storey the day after the event that he had taken two girls, both graduate students in English and both considered cold and unapproachable, out by Frenchman's Dam and had intercourse with one of them. He hadn't made any preparations, so he took the girls home and fixed his partner up with a douche of vinegar and whiskey. (Steinbeck was always pleased with his scientific ingenuity in such matters.) Storey couldn't figure out how he could have managed to have intercourse with one girl while the other was present, so he asked Steinbeck how he worked it. "Oh," he said, "she just looked the other way." The story also points up some distinctly unpleasant aspects of the Steinbeck character at this point in his life—a crudeness of sensibility, and, perhaps more important, a selfish masculine smugness that may have had some acceptance in a boys-will-be-boys college atmosphere of fifty years ago but is hardly tolerable today.

These stories of sexual prowess also seem invariably to contain some element of the grotesque in them—a one-legged maid, a douche made out of toothpaste, a "Turn of the Screw" intercourse while rolling down a hill, and intercourse with an irascible, rather masculine woman professor. This predilection to shock, often with grotesque material, sometimes humorous and sometimes simply unsavory, is a trait that manifests itself again and again in Steinbeck's personality. It is a trait that later surfaces in Steinbeck's fiction as a major mode of expression, a mode that continues past the mid-point of his career, appearing during those years in which, most critics agree, his creative powers were at their strongest. This predilection may be in large part the basis for the posture taken by the storyteller who savors the amoral exploits of the *paisanos* of *Tortilla Flat* or of the bums in *Cannery Row* and who enjoys the affront to respectability provided by his description of Casy's irreverent thrashing about in the bushes, after his sermon, with lusty and inspired girls from his congregation.

The strength of this impulse in Steinbeck's writing would seem confirmed by the almost gratuitous grotesquerie of such scenes as the one that describes Connie and Rose of Sharon having intercourse on the truck coming into California while on another part of the truck Ma lies near her dying mother. A biological view of man? Perhaps. But there is a crude Western sensibility at work here that is unpleasant to most readers, even those too sophisticated to be shocked by such things. The more one becomes familiar with the Steinbeck personality, the more one realizes how directly the eccentricities of his fiction reflect that personality. There is a certain amount of fiction written, both popular and literary, that seems almost neutral, that appears constructed or anonymous, in the sense that any skillful writer could have written it. By contrast, nearly everything Steinbeck wrote appears to be clearly the product of a strong, unique individual. While his writing is seldom autobiographical, it is often very personal.

II

The in-group of the out-crowd at Stanford during this period was composed of those loosely tied to the literary magazine and the English Club. Donald Stevens recalls asking Professor McClellan after a literature class, "What is this English Club? Is it worth joining?" McClellan replied, "Stay away. A fellow named Steinbeck comes every meeting and insists on reading his stuff to everyone." The club was an informal group of students and faculty devoted to extending the reading and discussion of literature beyond the classroom, and, since a large number of students in the club were also enrolled in creative-writing classes, to the reading and discussion of student writing. In connection with the club, the English faculty gave prizes for the most distinguished writing in the various literary forms each year. In his final year, Steinbeck won the prize for best essay, and his friend Carl Wilhelmson won the short-story award.

The club became a kind of base for Steinbeck's social and creative life at Stanford. Most of the people he came to know well at school were interested in writing, and he met many of them, including several of the girls he took out, for the first time at the English Club. The group was composed of students a bit older and more sophisticated than the average run of undergraduates. Several, such as Webster Street and Carl Wilhelmson, were World War I veterans; several were graduate students; and a few, such as John Breck, were well beyond college age. Over a period of two or three quarters, Steinbeck became a dominant personality in the club, partly because he was extremely opinionated and the gathering gave him a forum in which to speak his mind, partly because several of the English faculty associated with the club came to recognize his talent and this recognition gave him standing, and partly because his single-minded devotion to writing made him the most productive member of the group—he always had something to read aloud. Webster Street recalls that one among many stories he read at these gatherings was about God sending the angel Michael down to earth "to see what the hell the matter was down there. But Michael got involved and had to be rescued."

He did not confine his readings to the club, however; he seemed almost compelled to read his work to anyone willing to listen—to his fellow writers, to girls of his acquaintance, and occasionally to friends gathered for a party. At Encina, he almost invariably read his stuff to Sheffield (regardless of what other things his roommate had in mind to do) and then went out to stalk the halls, at all times of the day or night, looking for other victims—Frank Fenton, Dean Storey, Vernon Givan, and a half dozen others unwilling to throw him out and too patient to cut him off. This practice, which began in high school, he carried on throughout his life. While there is no doubt that he made changes after reading his stories to others, he didn't seem to read them primarily for the purpose of revision. On the contrary, he seldom invited or welcomed suggestions. And by contrast with his aggressiveness in seeking out an audience, he seemed embarrassed by the reading itself, fumbling with the pages, rushing through the sentences, and often slurring or mumbling words in his haste and self-consciousness. When he was through, he would thwart any comment of praise or criticism by starting to talk of something else, meanwhile getting up to pace the room to get rid of bottled-up emotion. Many years later, a recently married Elaine Steinbeck found herself listening to chapters from a novel in progress. Thinking that her husband wanted her opinion, she started to give it, when he quickly and impatiently interrupted her: "No, no"—he shook his head emphatically—"I don't want a critique."

One of the professors most involved with the English Club was Margery Bailey, who rented a large house on campus (in which she had several men students as roomers, including Webster Street) and on Sunday afternoons put on "salons" for selected students in English, usually the most promising of those in the English Club. She served tea and read aloud from various works, usually novels. Street remembers that she went through several books during the months he and Steinbeck attended her gatherings, but the one that sticks in his mind is Rebecca West's *The Judge*. "She would read just about anything with great feeling and understanding," he recalls, "and her diction was just about perfect."

In a way, Steinbeck became a protégé of Margery Bailey's, although their relationship was a strange one. Bailey was a Yale Ph.D. and a strong-minded, dogmatic, fierce dragon of a woman. Even in Steinbeck's time, when she was young and not long out of graduate school, she had already acquired a reputation, and she eventually become one of the most legendary figures on the Stanford campus. While she was famous for her forceful and inspired teaching, she was even more famous for her intolerance, arbitrariness, and eyebrow-singeing wrath. She and Steinbeck agreed on one thing—she despised collegiate manners and customs.

Two such opinionated people shouldn't be able to get along, and they didn't. But Bailey's specialty was intimidation—and Steinbeck wouldn't be intimidated. He stayed with her through several classes, and even though she seemed to dislike him thoroughly—she couldn't abide his masculine arrogance—he won her grudging admiration for his work. He was so little intimidated that he even dared to needle her. One very warm evening at Bailey's house, Steinbeck was dressed in a T-shirt, and there was a large scar visible on his shoulder. Bailey asked him how he got it, and he said, "A Mexican woman with whom I was copulating bit me." Bailey went into a rage and wouldn't talk to him for several weeks afterward. But in the quarter before Steinbeck left Stanford he took an advanced composition class from her, and she singled his work out, reading each one of his essays to the class. A strange bracketing—Miss Cupp reading his compositions aloud to the freshman English class at Salinas High School and Margery Bailey reading his compositions aloud to his last writing class in college.

Asked years after about Steinbeck, Bailey expressed some admiration for his mature work. But later, when Steinbeck was one of the two or three best-known writers in the world, he wrote her a long, rather sentimental letter on the occasion of her retirement. She never replied; he should have known better.

III

Steinbeck was one of the very few important writers of his generation to receive a significant amount of training in a college creative-writing program. Although Stanford did not offer a formal degree in creative writing, it did offer a series of courses in the writing of poetry, drama, and fiction within the English curriculum, and there were also courses available in advanced composition and in journalism. Steinbeck took all of these except play writing—the professor, David Gray, decided he was unqualified, since he was technically still a lower-division student.

One of the first of these courses was Verse Writing and Prosody, taught by William Herbert Carruth. On the first day of class Carruth asked his students to write a statement of their qualifications to take the class, one of those questions that students never know how to answer, since if they had any real qualifications, they probably wouldn't be taking the class. Steinbeck temporized, in part, as follows:

> Professor Carruth:
> As to your question about my training in versewriting. Certain events such as love, or a national calamity, or May, bring pressure to bear on the individual, and if the pressure is strong enough, something in the form of verse is bound to be squeezed out. National calamities and loves have been few in my life, and I do not always succumb to May. From this you can see that my poetic activity has been limited to
> > a. one war
> > b. two girls
> > c. three years

And it goes on, getting worse sentence by sentence. Fortunately, Carruth was a kindly man with a sense of humor; otherwise Steinbeck would have had to skip verse writing as well as play writing.

Dook Sheffield and Steinbeck took the class together during spring quarter, when the weather was beautiful. A poem was due every class period, and it was a tough deadline to meet. Sometimes Carruth would suggest a topic or a particular rhythm to work with, but usually they were on their own to create as they could. After the poems were in hand, as Sheffield remembers, the class would meet out "on the grass and John and I would try to see under the girls' skirts and so on," while Carruth gave a critique of each student's poem.

Steinbeck's approach to verse writing was often lacking in seriousness. Sheffield remembers one verse of Steinbeck's submitted to the class, which began:

> And so we manned the brigantine, with Chinks and yellow
> Malays—
> They couldn't speak the language of the Irish and the Dutch.
> Had to feed 'em rice and things, they wouldn't eat with falays,
> Take 'em as a people, they don't amount to much.

There was an asterisk after "falays" which led to a footnote: "This is a corruption of a Malay coastal hybrid term meaning 'knives and forks.'" For all his good nature, this was simply too much for Carruth.

Steinbeck wrote verse for much of his life, but most of it was comic parody and light verse for his own and his friends' amusement. One poem which has gained a kind of fame in Steinbeck circles was a very bawdy mock-heroic epic "Ballad of Quid Pro Quo," composed while he was working at Tahoe a year after college and distributed by mail to his friends. Another written while in college (but not for class) was "Ode to the Virgin," which ended:

> Poor Mary, whom the insidious spirit met
> And furnished all effect without a cause.

As Dean Storey recalls, "He used to love to turn out stuff like this, especially if he thought he could jolt or shock somebody." At least two serious poems survive from Steinbeck's work for Carruth, and there is a series of love poems written to his second wife, Gwyn, which has also survived.

Unlike Hemingway and Faulkner, Steinbeck never considered the possibility of working hard at poetry, perhaps because he recognized early his own lack of talent, but more probably he wasn't serious-minded enough. His mind moved through corridors of humor and satire, animated, at this age, by the pleasure of amusing or upsetting the people around him. These qualities tie him by temperament to Twain and were to bring him, throughout much of his career, into some of the same difficulties as a writer that Twain experienced: lapses of taste, lack of firm control of materials, and a tendency to over-value the trivial and overemphasize the obvious. Despite his lofty aims, his temperament drove him again and again toward that which amused him.

It is difficult to tell just how much prose Steinbeck wrote during these years, but circumstances suggest that it was quite a bit. He was writing both on his own and for assignments while at school, and when he was away from school working, he apparently continued to work on his fiction regularly. Among the few courses he had completed as a freshman were two quarters of English composition, but not satisfied with his previous work, he repeated these courses, Narration and Exposition, on his return to Stanford. He followed this with two quarters of advanced composition and an upper-division course in essay writing, and he took two more prose-writing courses within the journalism program: Feature Article, getting an A, and News Writing, getting a D. The difference in grades seems to suggest something about Steinbeck's talents, and the lower grade seems to foreshadow his difficulties as a news reporter in New York two years later. He also took Short-Story Writing for one quarter and repeated it as an auditor.

His short-story teacher, Edith Ronald Mirrielees, had the most profound effect upon him of all his Stanford professors. By personality and appearance she was almost the opposite of Margery Bailey, slender, frail, and gentle, whereas Bailey was heavyset, heavy-featured, and heavy-handed. She had been born in a small town in Illinois, and after having taught in the country schools of Montana for six years, she came to Stanford as a student in the early days of the institution, stayed to do some graduate work, and then was hired as an instructor. She published a number of short stories, including several that appeared in such major periodicals as *Atlantic Monthly,* and after Steinbeck's time, published a short-story-writing text and two short-story anthologies. She frequently taught during the summers at the prestigious Bread Loaf School of English and the Bread Loaf Writers' Conference.

In the words of Dean Storey, who had her as a teacher for two quarters, Miss Mirrielees was "one of these odd, prissy, little old-fashioned women who you couldn't imagine John getting along with, and yet he had the greatest admiration for her, and he would take whatever she told him about what he wrote." The main reason he got along with her was that she knew what she was talking about, and he needed what she knew. She was the kind of teacher perfect for creative writing in that she could put on the pressure and be extremely critical and demanding, while at the same time be encouraging where encouragement was justified.

Steinbeck wrote Carl Wilhelmson that she was "very kind, she hates to hurt feelings. She says that she thinks my stuff ought to be published but she doesn't know where. Don't get the idea that I am swimming against an incoming tide of approbation. I'm not. For every bit of favorable criticism, I get four knocks in the head" [5/24]. Steinbeck became her star pupil—perhaps her all-time star pupil—and yet he never got more than a B from her. At first this irritated him, and he complained that he knew the reason she walked so stiffly—she kept all her A's stuck up her rear—but he spent so much time with him that he at last accepted her grading as a form of encouragement to do better.

Her attitude toward teaching writing was that you can't really teach someone to be a writer, you can only help someone who has the talent to help himself become a better writer than he is. In her book on writing, the first version of which she was preparing while Steinbeck was still one of her students, Mirrielees stated her general philosophy in these words:

Writing can never be other than a lonely business. Only by repeated, unaided struggles to shape his yet unwritten material to his own purpose does a beginner grow into a writer. There are a few helps towards general improvement which it is feasible to offer, there are many specific helps in the work of revision, but help in the initial shaping of a story there is none. That is the writer's own affair.

Webster Street, who took Mirrielees's short-story-writing class during the same period that Steinbeck was working with her, recalls that she had three basic tenets. The first was to ask yourself, after having written a story, whether or not you had accomplished what you set out to do. The second was to ask, Is it convincing to the reader? And the third, perhaps the most important, was to ask, Is it true? Street adds, "It was the fabric she was thinking of as the sense of 'truth.' It may not be true in a universal sense, but it may be true in relation to the fabric of the story." In her teaching, there was great emphasis on a common-sense approach, on clear logic, and on the questions of what is believable and why.

On a more specific basis, her approach was just what Steinbeck needed. The main faults of his early fiction were wordiness, overornamentation (usually with metaphor), and a tendency to get lost along the way while trying to impress the reader. Mirrielees was known to be particularly strict in response to all of these. She led Steinbeck to be more concerned about just what it was he wanted to say, and she drove him to the revision that he was often reluctant to do. In a letter to Robert Cathcart, Steinbeck reported that "she does one thing for you. She makes you get over what you want to say. Her only really vicious criticism is directed toward turgidity, and that is a good thing" [3/1/29]. In her book, Mirrielees places great emphasis on revision and has this to say about wordiness and writing to impress the reader:

The "lean, terse style" is one towards which most beginners can profitably struggle. . . . For most stories and most writers, deliberate ornamentation needs much scrutiny before it is allowed a place in finished work. Phrases pushing up like mushrooms above the level of the narrative have a habit of turning out to be toadstools on later inspection. "Take out whatever you particularly like" is hard counsel, but oftener than not it is wise counsel as well.

Steinbeck did not take to such advice immediately; that is, he was not able to put it into practice to the extent that he should have. But he did

accept it as part of his critical consciousness—the more important alter-
ation in the long run. His experiences with Mirrielees began an internal
critical battle that lasted for close to a decade. He did not become a successful writer, measured in sales or in critical response, until the mid-
thirties, when he published such works as *Tortilla Flat, In Dubious
Battle,* and *Of Mice and Men*—and it is with the writing of these works
that, significantly, he finally achieved his own lean, natural-sounding
style. Until that time, he had struggled—with a critical consciousness
largely provided, I suspect, by Mirrielees—year by year, work by
work, to sharpen his writing and impose ever more severely the self-
discipline required to achieve that kind of style. In fact, one can actually trace this effort and its results from the early *Cup of Gold,* which
had its origins in college, through *To a God Unknown,* and *The Pastures of Heaven,* to the more disciplined prose of the first part of *The
Red Pony,* and then to the mastery displayed in the novels of the mid-
thirties.

Steinbeck's published college writing consisted of one poem and two
stories. The stories, "Fingers of Cloud: A Satire on College Protervity"
and "Adventures in Arcademy [*sic*]: A Journey into the Ridiculous,"
appeared in the February and June issues of the *Stanford Spectator.*
Although they display some of the typical vices of college literary-
magazine writing, they also exhibit in incipient form many of the traits,
good and bad, that would appear in his later work.

"Adventures in Arcademy" is an "I-am-above-it-all" satire-allegory
of life at Stanford, remarkably similar to E. M. Forster's "The Other
Side of the Hedge." In "Arcademy" a narrator takes a journey across
an *Alice in Wonderland* landscape filled with strange and mysteriously
suggestive sights and odd people involved in nonsensical activities. The
fabric is of paradox and non sequitur, which constantly hint at a wisdom hidden in the folds of the allegory. But the allegory is so obscure
that not even Steinbeck's contemporaries were able to translate very
much of it. In general, it appears to be attacking the conformity and hypocrisy of college life, the self-absorption of a doctrinaire faculty, and
the moralistic posture of the administration. We see President Ray
Lyman Wilbur, whose constant preachment against drinking and driving is mocked: "From far off a Voice was heard, wailing: 'Gasoline and
alcohol will not mix.' . . . There was much of the grandeur in the last,
which goaded the workers to greater efforts with their bottles." And we
see the dean of women as the "gray goose of some authority" scolding
the coeds and warning them about compromising themselves morally

in terms of minor things, while she remains blind to the far more serious activities which the girls are indulging in right under her nose.

For the most part, this early story predicts those traits we have come to think of as Steinbeck vices rather than virtues: there is the moralizing about other people's moralizing that we see later most obviously in works such as *Tortilla Flat, The Grapes of Wrath,* and *Cannery Row.* Connected with this trait is a pretentious, formalized diction, which crops up particularly when his characters make moral or philosophical pronouncements. This kind of language is most noticeable in the language of Doc in *In Dubious Battle* or of Lee in *East of Eden,* but on a broader scale, the tendency to switch suddenly to formal diction and stilted syntax in the middle of a passage that is generally colloquial becomes, in fact, one of the major idiosyncrasies of Steinbeck's prose. There is also in this story the evident effort to make things mysteriously significant.

"Fingers of Cloud," the other story, is a much better piece of work. It is about a retarded girl, apparently in her late teens, who leaves home, wanders aimlessly about the countryside, and during a heavy rainstorm finds refuge in the bunkhouse of a Filipino work gang. She marries the Filipino boss, Pedro, and leads a pampered life, except on those occasions when he beats her. The beatings and her Filipino husband's blackness, his sweaty back, and the three horse heads placed in the fire barrel by the superstitious work gang begin to irritate her, so at the end of the story she wanders away, just as at the beginning of the story she had left her home, impulsively, without any particular objective in mind.

The story does display some weaknesses characteristic of Steinbeck's writing during this period. It is rather supercharged with figurative language:

> The sky was splitting. A cruel, crooked line of light brought Gertie to a sitting position. Then there was a crash as of two giant freight cars hurtling together and the pop-pop of fragments falling on the roof of a tin warehouse. Suddenly the black air broke to pieces, the hills sounded and resounded, the moving air moaned, drew back and charged, buffeting and tearing at the ground.

And there is some unsureness and inconsistency of diction and tone. The rather stark image "The street sickened, became weed filled, and died" (which describes rather well in passive terms Gertie's movement out of town) contrasts jarringly with the preciousness of "a little hill which pretended to be a mountain" at the end of the same paragraph.

But the touch is relatively firm, the dialogue, even in its Filipino Pidgin English, is natural-sounding, and the description is lively. There are some passages that are artful enough to suggest a future mastery— the description of the bunkhouse and men that I quoted in a previous chapter, a scene in which a bootlegger stops by to sell the workers whiskey, and two small scenes of confrontation between Gertie and her husband near the end of the story. The subject matter is also indicative of things to come. There is the mixture of romance-fantasy, approaching at times the poetic, with the realistic, which in places runs beyond the mundane into the ugly. There is also the fascination with the grotesque—Gertie, for example, is not only retarded (reminding us, of course, of Steinbeck's rather frequent use of such characters in his later fiction), but an albino as well. And there is just the touch of a suggestion that Gertie, aimless, self-gratifyingly sensual, and uneducated, may be part of a rather harsh allegory, a satire of the thoroughly Wasp college girl in a confrontation with the real world. Whether Steinbeck had this in mind or not, as an albino, her sexual relations with the "black" Filipino provide an extreme contrast certainly designed to shock the college reader of the mid-1920s as much as possible.

Entry and front porch, Steinbeck family home, 132 Central, Salinas. (© 1983 Richard L. Allman.)

John Ernst Steinbeck, Sr.,
at the time of his marriage.
*(John Steinbeck Library,
Salinas, Steinbeck Archives.)*

Olive Steinbeck at the time
of her marriage.
*(John Steinbeck Library,
Salinas, Steinbeck Archives.)*

Elizabeth Hamilton,
John's maternal grandmother.
*(John Steinbeck Library,
Salinas, Steinbeck Archives.)*

Samuel Hamilton, John Steinbeck's
maternal grandfather.
*(John Steinbeck Library,
Salinas, Steinbeck Archives.)*

The Salinas Valley, looking toward the Santa Lucia Mountains.
(© 1983 Richard L. Allman.)

Beach outing: John between his father and mother, holding up hat; Elizabeth standing behind John; Esther, second to right of Elizabeth. *(Courtesy Mrs. E. G. Ainsworth, John Steinbeck Library, Salinas, Steinbeck Archives.)*

Mary and John on Jill, the "red pony." *(Courtesy Valley Guild, John Steinbeck Library, Salinas, Steinbeck Archives.)*

Main Street, Salinas, at the time of Steinbeck's early childhood. (*Courtesy California State Library.*)

John and Mary, with mother on porch, circa 1913.
*(Courtesy Mrs. E. G. Ainsworth, John Steinbeck Library,
Salinas, Steinbeck Archives.)*

Yearbook photo of Salinas High School track team: John, far right, back row.
(John Steinbeck Library, Salinas, Steinbeck Archives.)

Lunch break while
varmint shooting down
by the river:
Glenn Graves, left.
Photo by John with
delayed shutter.
(Courtesy Glenn Graves.)

John and father in front of Salinas home, circa 1918. *(Courtesy Mrs. E. G. Ainsworth,
John Steinbeck Library, Salinas, Steinbeck Archives.)*

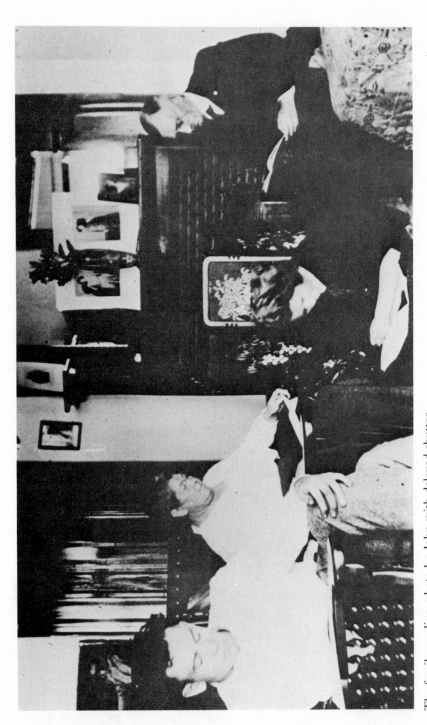

The family reading: photo by John with delayed shutter.
(*Courtesy Valley Guild, John Steinbeck Library, Salinas, Steinbeck Archives.*)

CHAPTER V

J ohn and his sister Mary enrolled for the summer quarter of 1923 at Hopkins Marine Station, conveniently located near the Steinbeck summer cottage in Pacific Grove. Hopkins, part of Stanford, was acting during the summer as an extended campus of the university, offering not only the life sciences (its normal function was as a graduate facility for the study of marine biology), but some humanities courses as well. Steinbeck signed up for a full load, taking general zoology and two English courses (Margery Bailey taught one of them).

Despite the fact that he had just successfully completed two quarters at Stanford with good grades, he probably enrolled during the summer at the urging of his sister as part of his penance for previous academic sins. He may also have been attracted by this statement in the Hopkins Marine Station *Bulletin* for 1923: "The particular advantage of work at the station is the possibility of observing and studying a large number of live animals while these are still fulfilling their role in the general scheme of marine and terrestrial life." There is no doubt, however, that this was a rather special general zoology class and that it had a lasting effect on a student who was already primed, by previous experience and inheritance, with a deep interest in nature and natural processes.

The course was taught by C. V. Taylor, a student of Charles Kofoid at the University of California, Berkeley. We can guess at the philosophical direction of this course, as elementary as it may have been, from the climate of thought in the Zoology Department at Berkeley, which at this time was strongly influenced by William Emerson Ritter. Ritter's doctrine was of the organismal nature of life. It was based upon his belief that "in all parts of nature and in nature itself as one gigantic whole, wholes are so related to their parts that not only does the existence of the whole depend upon the orderly cooperation and interdependence of its parts, but the whole exercises a measure of determinative control over its parts."

Richard Astro, who in his book on the Steinbeck–Edward Ricketts relationship explores these matters in some detail, points out that it was Ritter's conclusion that it is the duty of the true naturalist to take as his life's work the task of understanding the organismal basis of living nature. Since " 'one's ability to construct his own nature from portions of nature in general is a basic fact of his reality,' man can grasp the essential principle of the organismal unity of life and, at the same time, know himself more fully."

Nearly all of Steinbeck's published fiction was to reflect to some degree or another "the essential principle of organismal unity of life." It would be one of the main things that marked his work as different from that of his contemporaries, and it would become one of the main sources of confusion concerning his work, as humanistically guided critics attempted to judge ecological parables. Throughout his career, Steinbeck would wonder—in letters and conversation—why writers of fiction seemed unable to deal with man, not as individuals isolated, but as part of the human and general ecology. The answer was, of course, that very few writers, even the so-called naturalists, could accept in their hearts the idea that man was basically a biological entity.

Edmund Wilson would strike the theme for a generation of critics when he perceived what Steinbeck was doing, but was unable to understand what it meant. Instead of a difference in philosophy, Steinbeck's biological view of man is described by Wilson as a weakness in his conception of character, as an unconscious shortcoming in his skill as a writer:

> Mr. Steinbeck almost always in his fiction is dealing either with the lower animals or with human beings so rudimentary that they are almost on the animal level. . . . Mr. Steinbeck does not have the effect, as Lawrence or Kipling does, of romantically raising the animals to the stature of human beings [apparently to Wilson a more palatable "distortion"], but rather of assimilating the human beings to animals. . . . This animalizing tendency of Mr. Steinbeck's is, I believe, at the bottom of his relative unsuccess at representing human beings.

The implicit conflict between Wilson and Steinbeck suggested in these comments involves much more than a question of Steinbeck's skill as a creator of fictional characters: it really has to do with the question, "What is man?" Steinbeck's answer was complicated, in that he had more than one answer and his answers could be seen as contradicting each other to some extent, and his views changed slightly as his life changed. But his sense of man as part of nature remained constant. From time to time, his sense of man's place in nature received both instruction (as from his father, from his class at Hopkins, and from his relationship later in life with the marine biologist Ed Ricketts) and reinforcement (as from his immersions in nature as a child, his outdoor work as a teenager and young man, and his years following college spent, often completely alone, at Lake Tahoe). He was conditioned throughout much of his early life to see nature and to regard it seriously.

Yet, Steinbeck was also conditioned to accept the traditional view of man, as expressed by Wilson, which dominated the literature that inspired him to become a writer. This produced an inner conflict that has had its larger, outward counterpart in contemporary culture.

Whether religious or humanistic, our anthropocentric view of the universe has allowed us to concern ourselves only with man's spiritual or moral fate, while our industrialization has raped our environment almost beyond remedy. We worry that too many material goods may spoil man, not that too many material goods may spoil nature. That man may have a biological fate dependent on the physical ecology seems to have never, until recently, occurred to most of us. That man's morality may have more to do with the biological consequences of his actions, as seen within the whole of nature, than with his immediate welfare or eventual spiritual destiny is an idea that would have seemed outrageous to most of us only a few years ago. The irony of our situation is that the origins of religion can be found in the effort by man to deal with the mysteries of nature, and now that nature is no longer nearly so mysterious as it was in pre-history, we still tend to deal with it (including the facts of our own nature—birth, illness, decay, and death) on the same basis.

Language, from myth and ritual, to literature and history, to bureaucratic paperwork, starts by purporting to describe reality and ends up becoming reality. Caught between the realities of nature and language, Steinbeck oscillated between them, never totally satisfying their conflicting claims, yet dramatizing in his life and work the existence and importance of the conflict. Nearly every basic relationship of man to the earth and its creatures is explored at one time or another in his fiction, from the religious to the economic and from the primitive to the American Western. The conflicts underlying this exploration made the literature imperfect as art, but gave it, at the same time, a prophetic significance. How is one to account for a young man who, on the one hand, wants to learn about human beings by examining dead bodies in a medical-school class and, on the other, claims to see leprechauns?

II

The summer of 1923 allowed Steinbeck to return to the seashore of his childhood for an extended period of time. He delighted in the house at the beach that he and Mary would have, apart from the family, to themselves. He was an inveterate fixer-upper who had fun finding new ways of solving old problems—sticky drawers, balky drains, and broken-down, beach-house furniture. At Hopkins, the classes were small and the instruction relaxed, and he and Mary were in the same classes, making study easier.

In zoology, there were long hours in the lab, but also field trips and collecting expeditions. One, echoed many years later in the great frog hunt and escape of *Cannery Row*, grew out of the need to collect toads for class dissection. John, who claimed to know all about such things, led a party made up of Mary, her fiancé, and several other students—armed with flashlights and gunnysacks—to the outskirts of Pacific Grove, where they discovered a tribe of toads and dazzled them into submission.

Returning to the house, they deposited their catch in the drawers of an old dresser for the night, where the toads thumped and bumped, making sleep nearly impossible. In the morning John and the others hauled the dresser to the station and carried it into class in triumph. As they set it down, the drawers slid open, and several dozen toads—far more than needed—immediately escaped, creating havoc throughout the lab. What had begun as an effort by John to impress everyone with his biological expertise had ended in disaster—but on second thought, he decided that it really couldn't have turned out more enjoyably if he had planned it that way.

Not long after the summer began, John and his sister were joined by Dook Sheffield, who had been invited to stop for a visit on his way home to Long Beach. Sheffield had just been graduated from Stanford, and it was a time for celebration—many trips to the bootlegger's—as well as, for the Steinbecks, study. Wine parties, picnics, long walks, afternoons of fishing, and late-night bull sessions followed one another as the days of summer stretched into weeks and the summer quarter at Hopkins came to an end.

In early September Steinbeck returned to Salinas, where he lived with his parents and took up again the lonely job of chemist at the sugar mill. At about this time he began the practice, which he carried on throughout his life, of using letters as a way of warming up for his writing. Dook was now in southern California, and Steinbeck used him as his sounding board. During his long shift at the plant, much of the slack time late at night and early in the morning was taken up with writing long, often playful, experimental letters, which included bits of stories, sketches, and verse. None of these early letters to Sheffield have survived (Steinbeck burned them), but he did write to Sheffield's sister, Marion, in much the same manner. Here he comments playfully about his return to the sugar factory:

> Night work claims me. My tremendous powers are now directed at the manufacture of sugar. Just on the face of it, one might conjecture that a disposition so exposed might take on saccharine qualities, and such is in reality the case. I was becoming so sweet that the tips of my fingers got sticky thus interfering with my work and I assure you that it took tons (literally tons) of citric acid to bring myself back to normal.... I am in jail now until December and nightly my caroling voice can be heard for miles surging in the joy of living. That is it could be heard if the machinery didn't make so much noise.

Then in a more serious vein he notes:

> I read a delightful epigram the other day, author unknown. *"La vie est un jour de mi-carême, quelques-uns masquent, moi, je ris."* [Life is like a day of carnival; some wear masks—myself, I laugh.] That is all very fine but it can't be done. You may think that you thumb your nose at life but in the end they take your mask off and the smile is rigid and underneath the true mouth is gnarled in pain.... My favorite and progeny is "Love is a mutual flattery." I believe that implicitly and yet I know that very few people do, and in the case of love all that matters is what you think anyway. [9/21/23]

He finishes the letter with a parody of Dook's efforts at free verse. Such letters were not only a way for him to exercise his imagination, but probably also kept him sane and functioning.

There was almost no one in Salinas that he cared to see any more, except on occasion Glenn Graves. No one shared his enthusiasms or his outlook, and he was just barely civil to old acquaintances if he happened to meet them on the street or in the hardware store. Now that he was beginning to find himself outside the place where he had grown up, he brooded a bit about the wrongs and snubs of an earlier time and the years spent as an outsider in high school and developed a deep resentment of Salinas. He had assumed a small amount of eccentric glamour at Stanford, but at home he was just John Steinbeck, odd man out.

Following the pattern he was to pursue his last three years of college, Steinbeck left his job in December and returned to Stanford for the winter and spring quarters of 1924. Dook was gone, and there would be no more roommates. This year he roomed alone on the fifth floor of Encina. Byron Madison Taylor, who had the room across the hall, remembers him as almost a recluse, a man "somewhat beaten down, with no great self-confidence, but nevertheless a man under the great inner tension of an enormous drive." Bull sessions, in one room or another, were common, the topics usually women, politics, and athletics. Taylor recalls that during these discussions Steinbeck did display what we would call today a social awareness: to illustrate his arguments, "he spoke often of the plight of the farm workers around Salinas, his hometown." And he knew what he was talking about, since by this time he had lived and worked with them.

The term "recluse," however, is a little misleading—Steinbeck was actually developing a wider circle of acquaintance than he had ever had before. Nearly everyone in Encina, at least on the fifth floor, seems to have known him. Frank Fenton, later an English professor and acting president of San Francisco State, became, in the absence of Sheffield, the primary target for Steinbeck's readings. Carl Stroland, a reformed "street tough" who went on to become a professor; Dean Storey, who became an M.D. and worked for Stanford; and Vernon Givan, who became a civil engineer in the Palto Alto area—all came to know Steinbeck fairly well. He also developed somewhat closer and longer-lasting ties with several members of the English Club—Carl Wilhelmson, John Breck, Grove Day, and Katherine Beswick.

These and another dozen acquaintances one could name illustrate a further paradox of the Steinbeck personality—he was a near-recluse who knew a lot of people. The main thing that seems to have set him apart was not his reclusiveness so much as his "enormous drive," his single-mindedness. He made a strong impression on those near him because he rejected the traditional goal of becoming "well-rounded." Few other students were so certain of where they wanted to go and how they were going to get there as he. Charles McNichols, president of the

English Club at that time, recalls that his impression of Steinbeck was that he had "no other interests or talents that I could make out. He was a writer, but he was that and nothing else."

When the school year ended, Dook Sheffield joined Steinbeck at his home in Salinas for what was to be a frustrating summer. Because he knew the foreman, Steinbeck was able to get Dook and himself jobs at the Spreckels factory in Manteca (in the Central Valley, southeast of San Francisco). This was a "small run" sugar mill used to start and finish the season. John wrote to Carl Wilhelmson from Manteca in July of 1924:

I think rebellion man's highest state. All that we regard most highly in art, literature, government, philosophy, or even those changes which are the result of anatomic evolution had their beginnings in rebellion in an individual. Here you will say that rebellion for its own sake is not good, but even that I deny, for many things are and have been found in rebellion for its own sake.

In the *Enemy of the People*, the Doctor says in his last speech that the strongest man in the world is he who is most alone. That line has come to mean more and more to me. . . .

Duke and I came up here to try to make some money, because we plan to go to Mexico City in a small car about the first of October, and for that certain resources are necessary. Whether we get there is doubtful. . . .

We are very comfortable here. We live in the Spreckels Club House [a satiric reference to a Spreckels Sugar Company bunkhouse for laborers], which resembles a very select hotel and only holds about sixteen. The food is very good, and we have only to kick at the long hours and the lack of any day of rest during the week. However, there is more money to be made in this kind of work.

I will have to do this letter by installment for I get sleepy very quickly, and then there is a sort of torpor which comes from spending twelve hours of every day in a roar of machinery. . . .

The other night Duke and I went into Stockton and went into some very large gambling joints run by Chinamen. It was interesting, particularly the hangers-on who were there, apparently lived there to touch the winners. Gambling people have a queer suspicion that it is bad luck to refuse to give these people something.

It would be a mistake to think of this statement regarding rebellion as anything but personal—he was never a political radical, and political action of any kind was the last thing in the world that he would have had on his mind at this point in his life. But his identification with the position of Dr. Stockman in the Ibsen play suggests that he, too, saw himself as the lonely idealist, a man cast out from and opposed by the respectable majority—a man ahead of his time, radical in his adherence to principle and in his vision.

As the letter suggests, the job was sweaty, noisy, and nasty. The temperature in Manteca in the summer is commonly ninety to a hundred or more degrees. Add to that the heat from the cookers in the plant and you have twelve hours of hell, day after day without a break. Finally, they could take it no longer, and in a burst of frustration—the only time in his life he did such a thing—Steinbeck deliberately picked a fight with a fellow worker and got himself fired. But instead of heading for Long Beach right away, Steinbeck and Sheffield made the mistake of going up to the big city for a day or two of recreation. When they woke up, somewhere in San Francisco, their heads hurt and they found that nearly all their money was gone. They had just enough to pay for gas to get them to Long Beach in Dook's mother's car.

Dook and John had developed a number of routines over the years that they had known each other. One involved drawing some unknowing person into a heated argument by proposing something totally preposterous, and then working him in such a way that, although he began by defending common sense, he would end up advocating the outrageous without realizing it. When the two of them were together, they had lovely arguments about such things as whether tomorrow was Sunday or would be Sunday and the finite qualities of infinity.

Sometime during the summer, perhaps stopping off at the Steinbeck beach house on their way down to Long Beach, they visited a "little old ladies' philosophic society" in Pacific Grove. Steinbeck introduced the two of them as students of religion, and began talking to the group about the monad theory of the individual as a center of spiritual force. Each of the two young men threw in whatever double-talk came to mind, spinning an exotic metaphysical web that held their audience entranced. The women asked questions of their visitors, and the visitors asked questions in return. When the visitors got up to leave, the members of the society implored them to return, for they had cleared up so many philosophical points for them. "John," according to Sheffield, "did things like that so earnestly."

They were determined to get to Mexico, and when they got to Long Beach they searched for a way to make some money. An ad in the paper caught their attention: it offered good profits to those willing to sell a certain brand of radio that supposedly sold itself. They talked Sheffield's mother into staking them to the necessary capital, and, using her car and her gasoline, they drove through the neighborhoods, assaulting one door after another. There may have been something of the confidence man in Steinbeck, but a salesman he was not. Neither Sheffield nor Steinbeck knew a single thing about radios. The Echophone Radio, "three tubes, fully guaranteed, includes Everready AB battery," had a "Talking Tape" antenna, which the salesman was supposed to drape around the room on the ceiling molding, and a wire ground to be attached to a water pipe. When the two young men came into a prospective customer's home, John would carry in the apparatus, but refused to do any of the talking. Dook would begin his spiel, while the two of them would climb up on the furniture in order to hang the Talking Tape around the living room. By the time John had found a water pipe or radiator for the ground, the customer would be surrounded by a maze of wires. John would try to fade into a wall somewhere, as Dook went into his demonstration: as the radio warmed up and went on, a series of loud squeals and crackles would assault the ears of the confused customer, who had long since decided not to spend a hundred dollars on this monstrosity. Dook remembers:

> Every time we went to a place and got turned down we would be so discouraged that we would say, "That is enough for today" and we would go swimming, or go park in downtown Long Beach and watch the girls go by. Eventually we sold one to my aunt for a hundred dollars, and we got our commission of five dollars. Then we wore out two sets of batteries listening to her radio.

In the meantime, John had made friends with the young woman who lived in the apartment above the Sheffields', and through her mother, two young men got the contract for sending out the Christmas Seals to the City of Long Beach. They spend two weeks stuffing and addressing envelopes, and each earned seventy-five dollars. This was enough for John to get home on, so the day after he was paid, he went downtown and took the bus.

Late in 1924, Steinbeck returned to Salinas and to what had become his fall routine. Every evening he walked to the terminal, dressed in his overcoat and carrying his lunch pail, to catch the commuter train for his shift at Spreckels. Every morning in the cold fog, just as it was getting light, he got aboard the train to ride back home and go to bed just as everyone else was starting the day. The night shift was a godsend. Not only was he left to himself at the plant, but he was able to avoid the complications of family life at home.

The following January, he went back to Stanford for the last time. Rather than returning to Encina, he found a room off campus, first in a house on Emerson Street and then in another on Webster Street (the address appealed to him). He finally ended up living in part of a tackroom, attached to a stable, behind a house on Palo Alto Avenue. It had been used as a combination toolshed-woodshed, and Steinbeck must have talked the owners into renting, for no one would have had the courage to offer it for rent. It was damp, since it stood near the bank of Francisquito Creek, and only half of it, a little more than six feet by six feet, had been cleared for living space. There was no stove, gas, water, or electricity; urgent bathroom problems had to be taken to the main house; and it was infested with pill bugs and spiders. He put his battered Corona typewriter on a wooden box and bought an old army cot, which he put near the wood stacked at one end of the shed. He made do with water from a garden spigot and a little outdoor fire pit. He called the place "The Sphincter" and paid five dollars a month rent.

Inside he had a pile of old gallon jugs, which he had collected for wine making. Since part of the reason for living in the shack was to get away from people and get more work done, the wine making might have been a mistake. Visitors started coming so often and the demand was so great, that neither John nor the wine was able to work for very long. Dean Storey remembers that "we usually let it get about half ripe and then some night we would be down there and someone would get enthusiastic and we would drink the whole jug and wind up the next day with the most god-awful hangover you ever saw." There was a certain romance attached to living in his shed; it demonstrated his poverty and dedication. The wine parties, sometimes with "mixed company," added further color to a slightly unsavory reputation.

One of the things that made day-to-day life bearable at his tackroom living quarters was that a friend had her home only a block or so away, and Steinbeck spent a good deal of his time there. Her name was Elizabeth Smith, although she was known on campus as John Breck, one of several masculine pseudonyms she used as a newspaper columnist and short-story writer. The fact that she had placed several stories in national magazines had immediately impressed Steinbeck, who had met her at English Club meetings (some of which had been held at her house the year before).

Breck was an attractive blonde, divorced, in her late thirties, who lived with her two teenage daughters. She was an independent, sharp-tongued, and sardonic woman with some bitterness as a result of trying to gain recognition in a man's world. But she developed a soft spot for Steinbeck, who seems to have had a talent for cultivating the sponsorship of older women. For her part, Breck was interested in a series of young men, paying for their college expenses and bringing them into the family. The Breck household was, to say the least, a peculiar one—part soap opera and part situation comedy. If situation comedy, then Breck would have been the liberated but blithely impractical divorcée, mother of Polly, her unconventional but tough-minded teenage daughter. Steinbeck would have been the sardonic, wisecracking neighbor, always hanging around as if he owned the place, treating everything in the house as if it were his. Add to this a stimulating mixture of visitors: Margery Bailey, who came periodically to cry on Breck's shoulder over her always tragic love affairs; various Stanford professors, including two relatives of hers; a series of tradesmen, who never got paid for their services; most of Steinbeck's friends, including Toby Street, Carl Wilhelmson, and Dook Sheffield (and on a couple of occasions, Steinbeck's mother and sister—God knows what they thought); and a number of Stanford students interested in music, who were invited by Polly to practice in the Breck living room—drums, piano, saxophone, a whole group.

If the household is seen as soap opera, we must spotlight, first, John Breck, born Elizabeth Anderson (a.k.a., in later years, Elizabeth Smith, E. C. A. Smith, John Barton, and John Breck), who was the favored daughter of a rich, midwestern industrialist. The father, who had been divorced by his first wife on the grounds of impotency, married a second time, determined to assert his masculinity and clear his good name. He had six children, the oldest of whom was Elizabeth, who became the primary, living proof of his potency. She was a spoiled child, who graduated to her present life through a series of gothic houses, some bizarre shooting incidents, and a strange marriage, determined, with the help of some inherited money and child-support payments (money which was seldom applied to the children), to become a successful writer.

Move the spotlight now to Elizabeth's oldest daughter, Polly Smith. Pert, sarcastic, and independent, she was always in long pants at a time when it was disgraceful for a girl in her late teens to be wearing pants in downtown Palo Alto. She was arrested by the police chief for smoking in public and put on probation. She and an engineering professor at

Stanford bought an airplane that was sold by the government as unsafe to fly, and Polly, without any flying lessons, flew it by herself all around the area. During football games at the university, she would drop red and white parachutes in the neighborhood of the stadium. One day one of the parachutes, weighted by a rock, failed to open and landed very near a lady hanging up a wash on her backyard clothesline. Polly was arrested again, and still again when she offered five-minute rides in the plane for $2.50.

As far as Polly was concerned, Steinbeck was obnoxious and his continual presence around the house embarrassing. His presence was difficult to explain; at almost any time he would barge in the front door, and regardless of who was there or what was going on, he'd take over. He'd stalk across the living room to a paneled wall and then slide down against it until he was sitting on the floor with his feet stretched out in front of him. He had at this point in his life affected the wearing of his grandmother's fringed biddy shawl, which, as he sat on the floor, he would adjust on his massive shoulders. Then he would begin a low, mumbled commentary. If Polly's musician friends were there, he'd mumble things like, "Why do you waste your time on these ninnies?" or "Do you call that terrible noise music?" After a time, visitors always began to wonder, Who is that guy? And Polly would say, "That's not my friend; he's a friend of my mother's."

Breck had built a writing studio behind her house, and it was there that Steinbeck actually spent most of his time. It became almost a clubhouse for Steinbeck and his friends. He or Toby Street might wander in to play a game of chess with each other or with Breck, and there was always a lot to talk about. In addition to writing itself, one subject that Breck had an interest in, which also interested her visitors, was man's relations with his environment, both philosophically and as a matter of biological interdependence. Much of her writing dealt with the drama of man in a confrontation with the wilderness, and earlier in her career she had seen the gradual pollution of the Detroit River (on which she lived at that time) and had written a long article detailing the damage and warning of the consequences. But she got nothing but rejection notices, on one of which the editor said, "Your writing is excellent, but don't you think you could leave us on a higher note?" She wrote back, "No, you asses, I can't."

Beyond literary discussion, her sponsorship, and his use of her household facilities, it is hard to say just what Steinbeck's relation with Breck actually involved. Breck once told Ted Miller, another member of the English Club, who later acted informally as Steinbeck's agent in New York, that when Steinbeck walked into the room, it gave a woman goosepimples, but that when Miller walked in, nothing happened at all. Miller also remembers overhearing Steinbeck read one story to Breck entitled "What I've Learned from Girls," in which he purported to catalogue his experiences "over the years" with women. Some of this bragging and flirting may have been reflected in his major writing project of the period; trying to extend a short story, "A Lady in Infra-Red," into a novel. It may have been a joke between them that Steinbeck used Breck's real first name, Elizabeth (which she disliked), as the name for the object of his hero's passion.

Steinbeck might withdraw from all society for two or three days of constant writing, but more often his writing was confined to the mornings. His mornings always began with a hot pot of coffee, thanks to Breck, who had her daughter Polly make the delivery on the way to school. Then he worked on first drafts in longhand, with a fine-tip fountain pen that created a very small script on the lines of old ledgers from his father's office. Second drafts and revisions were sometimes typed, as were final copies (his typing was painfully slow and poorly done—at the insistence of her mother, Polly retyped the handwritten revision of "A Lady in Infra-Red"). Despite his many activities during this period, his writing seemed to be going very well. He wrote Carl Wilhelmson in the late spring of 1924:

> Do you wonder why I keep writing and writing when I know of nothing to be gained by it? I will tell you—when this clawed creature is tearing in my chest, the scribbling of words appears to propitiate it momentarily. That is a sacrifice to the great Cat-God life. I am sorry that you are so lonely, Carl. . . .
>
> I have done several stories (you are kind enough to seem interested). The tale of the mechanic who had his arm pulled off, and who cursed God for it, is done, and I should like to have you see it. Then there is a story of Henry Morgan, and a light piece, whose content is not lightness, of a tired shop girl who talked to a Greek nymph in the fountain of the Hill Street park in Los Angeles. I have written the Jael-Sisera story, and there are several others. Some of them are fairly good, though I can get very few outside myself to believe that.

All the stories specifically mentioned in the letter, except for the one about the mechanic, have survived. What is striking is their variety and vitality, as if Steinbeck was experimenting and having a great deal of fun doing so. In another letter, written a few weeks earlier to Wilhelmson, he lists some of the same stories (plus a story set in a Salinas whorehouse and a "pleasant little story of an old nun") and says that "about the only thing that can be said for them is that they do not resemble anything which has ever been written." While this boast is not quite true, it does indicate the effort he was making to achieve a distinctive voice.

There are at least two characteristics of these stories that have some importance for his later work. First, the experimentation is not so much concerned with style and structure (although there is some) as it is with creating unusual situations peopled with unusual characters. This effort would seem to forecast his later success in producing memorable characterizations as viewed within out-of-the-way perspectives—such as Danny and the Pirate as seen within the perspective of the ne'er-do-well *paisanos* in *Tortilla Flat* or Lennie and George as seen within the perspective of the hopeless lot of the bindlestiffs in *Of Mice and Men*. Second, these stories reflect the dichotomy so pervasive in his work between the romantic and the realistic. Here it appears almost as if these two modes are grappling with each other for supremacy, trying to force the writer to come to some kind of decision.

His first decision in this regard might be said to have been the "wrong" one, in that he chose to develop and expand the story of the English pirate Henry Morgan, taking the better part of the next four years to transform "A Lady in Infra-Red" into the manuscript for his first published book, *Cup of Gold*. Although both the novel and the story it grew out of could be roughly categorized as historical romance, in that they both deal with derring-do adventures, unrequited love, exotic locales, and historical figures and events (employed with a great deal of poetic license), on closer inspection neither really fits into the spirit of this category very well.

Cup of Gold, to which I will refer in more detail later, is a retelling of the Grail search and is too impressionistic and allegorical to be called historical romance. The short story, which is only vaguely related (in the version we have) to the novel, uses the conventions of romance while at the same time making fun of them. Henry Morgan is depicted both as a rapacious animal ("buffalo" and "bull") with tiny, sparkling eyes, and as a buffoon, who is made a fool of by a woman with the mind of a child and tricked by the people he has conquered. While this is a good story, it is clearly a story without a market—too ironic and too realistic in some of its details for the women's magazines of that time and too romantic and exotic in its materials for the publishers of literary fiction.

Much the same "in-between" quality is manifested in the other two surviving stories. The "light piece, whose content is not lightness, of a tired shop girl who talked to a Greek nymph in the fountain of the Hill Street park in Los Angeles," is called "The Nymph and Isobel." Once again, a woman is being pursued by a man with evil intent and our sympathies are drawn to the victim. In this story, Steinbeck also very cleverly draws forth the ironic contrast between the real and the poetic, between the tawdry, desperate, lower-class existence of the human girl and the idyllic, pastoral life of a mythical water sprite. Differences in language, imagery, and attitude are all brought to bear in emphasizing the dramatic split between the "civilized" (in the worst sense) and the natural, the real lives we lead and the fictions we have invented to make life more beautiful.

The third item that Steinbeck mentions is a retelling of a Bible story from the fourth chapter of Judges, which he calls "The Nail." The most impressive aspect of the story is the skill by which the author maintains a biblical tone throughout with very little sense of awkwardness or artificiality. Further, although it may have made the story unpublishable, the reversal of the biblical "message" is very subtly accomplished: instead of focusing on how the Lord has once again freed the people of Israel from oppression, the story suggests that the Canaanites' way of life was richer and far more beautiful than what, in Steinbeck's story, is seen as the sterile, deadly fanaticism of the Jews.

Although none of these stories was salable, all of them are of publishable quality—they are unusual, skillfully executed, and do mark the young writer as having talent. Taken along with a couple of other stories written at about the same time—"The Days of Long Marsh" and "East Third Street" (the latter may have been written the following year in New York)—they would seem to be far more advanced than anything written by Hemingway, Faulkner, or Fitzgerald at the same age. Then why did it take Steinbeck so much longer to publish anything of real consequence and to gain any degree of critical recognition?

For one thing, the Californian, who was slightly younger (and who missed the war that the other three writers had joined at the end) was isolated on the West Coast—he had no famous tutors, prominent literary friends, or entrée into publishing circles. He was very bashful about even submitting his manuscripts for publication, let alone work-ing to promote himself with the right people. For another, he seems to have been nearly unconscious of the current literary tide. While Hemingway, for example, was reading and being influenced by Ger-trude Stein, Ezra Pound, and James Joyce, Steinbeck was reading whatever happened to attract his interest, including writers then cur-rent who are now nearly forgotten, such as Brian Oswald Donn-Byrne. It was his reading of Byrne's *Brother Saul* that had inspired his story of Jewish-Roman conflict based on the Bible, "The Nail."

In a letter to Max Wagner's mother in the fall of 1924, he revealed a taste for rather eccentric reading:

> You asked me what I had been reading. Here is the last list which we brought from the library, The Book of the Dead from existing papyri, Les Femmes Savantes of Molière, which I had never read in French before and a low detective tale labeled L'Homme du Dent d'Or by a man of whom I never heard, and who in the French fashion manages to get his murder accomplished in a bed-room; La Barraca of Ibañez, which is shorter and I think more ef-fective than his others; some short stories by Katherine Fullerton Gerould, and she certainly is the master of her kind of short stories. I have just finished the autobiography of Casanova and The Judge by Rebecca West which is a wonderful piece of writing. If you haven't read it you must for it is one of the best things I have read in many a day. In a maniacal period this summer I went through Pushkin and Turgenev.

Allowing for a small amount of bragging in regard to his expertise with foreign languages and the quantity of reading, his list reflects some of the same qualities expressed by the fiction he was writing—a deter-mined individualism and a taste for variety, expressed here as a broad-ranging curiosity. He saw himself not just as a young man in rebellion, but as a writer set upon finding his own voice, his own way, despite the many forces surrounding him which were set upon making him con-form. He had written to Marion Sheffield the previous fall:

> Who so arbitrarily caught in folds of silken sunlight, and look at the grief-steeped moon and cry,
> "I am the world, and the world is forty-seven cents."
> That is beautiful but doubly untrue. I must live, it is true, but no power can decree how I must live. And I do not intend to live on a broad dark moor, peoples [sic] with numbers, decked with diseases,

stifled with toads, singing, "I will look at the moon in a little." There are four prophets of orthodoxy, each more orthodox than the other and every one a philistine. There is no choice. I must follow one of these prophets.

He then writes a little allegory, describing each of the prophets in turn: the first chants of peace, the second whispers of whirling arms and insane wisdom, the third speaks of sackcloth and ashes, and the fourth lies, speaking of "little buildings of blocks, and everyone knows that blocks are reserved for the Gods." Then he continues:

These prophets are good Jewish prophets, brought up in the accepted manner. They are rationalists mostly. One sneers, "Where would literature be today if the race were gifted with external reproduction." Another breaks in, "What would be the use of literature in that case." Another shrieks, "Literature must suffer" and the fourth, "I sleep." And thus, not willing to trust even the most orthodox of prophets with my lovely life, I take the advice of the second to-day, tomorrow I will follow in the footsteps of the fourth, the next day the first will be my very own prophet and in the end the third will lead. [9/21/23]

One could dismiss this sort of thing as the rantings of a post-adolescent mind, as the blarney of a very romantic young man showing off, playing with images and words. To do so, however, may be a mistake, for the voice of this letter may be, after all, the voice of the essential Steinbeck, the Steinbeck of prophecy, vision, and magic in *Cup of Gold;* of Druidism, biblical legend, and vegetation myth in *To a God Unknown;* of curses, ghosts, and fairy lore in *The Pastures of Heaven;* of the Garden of Eden, magic circles, and totemism in *The Long Valley.* If the Steinbeck of magic, myth, and folklore tends to be gradually displaced during the course of his career in favor of a realistic, socially conscious, and scientifically minded Steinbeck, perhaps, just perhaps, this was a loss, rather than a gain as most critics have assumed. Perhaps the "prophets of orthodoxy" won. Ted Miller, Stanford friend and his first literary agent, has said that in his opinion *Cup of Gold* was Steinbeck's best novel, for Steinbeck's greatest talent lay in his ability to depict vividly his fantasies.

PART TWO

Apprenticeship

I n the meantime, he had fallen in love. Her name was Margaret Gemmell, and she was a bit spoiled, a bit conceited, and a bit snobbish. Whether he ever got to know her well, as she was, is doubtful. He wanted someone to adore, someone to put on a pedestal. Even in his thinking about women there was a romantic-realistic split: he created Margaret in his mind as he wanted her to be, and then was struck deaf, dumb, and blind by his creation. Therefore, it is not quite accurate to say that she led him around by the nose, with half-negligent ease and a certain amount of amusement.

For her, it began as a kind of challenge. She had friends who were interested in writing, and they had told her of Steinbeck. He had returned to school once again (for the winter and spring quarters of 1925) and was known to be coming to an early evening get-together of some people from the English Club. "Steinbeck's going to be there," her friends told her, "and if you want to see what this genius looks like, here's your chance." She found him shy, and he drank, she thought, to cover up his shyness. "The entire evening he talked to me about his leprechauns," she recalls, "and it just sounded like a blurb to me, and I was never so disappointed." This might have ended it except that they had a class together—Edward Maslin Hulme's History of European Thought. Hulme was one of the stars on campus, and Steinbeck looked forward to his witty, sardonic lectures, never missing a class. (According to Frank Fenton, the story "St. Katy the Virgin" [1936] began as a bawdy poem inspired by a Hulme lecture on canonization during the Middle Ages.) Steinbeck began walking out at the end of class with Margaret and talking to her. For some time, nothing happened between them—but apparently he was brooding about her and making plans. When he finally did ask her out, it was to go to dinner in San Francisco, a grandiose scheme that would have been quite ambitious even for the wealthier young men at Stanford.

They took the train into the city and a taxi from the Southern Pacific station to a little French restaurant near North Beach. They were shown into a small booth in the rear, and after they were seated, the curtains were pulled. On the wall, dominating the scene, was a large picture of Parisian dancers, slightly risqué, as if to suggest that dining in this restaurant could be a romantic adventure. Before even looking at the menu, Steinbeck put his arms on the table, leaned toward her, and asked, "Are you afraid of me?"

The dialogue for the scene may well have been long rehearsed. Dumbfounded, she could not pick up her line, and after a moment could only answer honestly, "No, I'm not."

He took her on several such dates to San Francisco, dates that in each case must have been planned and saved for over a long period of time. Once he took her to see Jane Cowl playing in *Romeo and Juliet* and then to an expensive restaurant afterward. They found they enjoyed riding the ferry to Oakland and back and would sometimes go back and forth two or three times. On the ferry or sitting in the coach car on the return to Palo Alto, there would often be long lulls in the conversation, and she would wonder what this "genius" might be thinking about. Always analytical toward their relationship, she thought it odd, perhaps even received some satisfaction from finding that the young man who so many thought might become a great writer someday was so often at a loss for words.

When he did talk, his conversation often lapsed into rather self-conscious disquisition. He spoke of spending hours watching the track team work out. The runners, their movement liquid yet powerful, reminded him of greyhound dogs. At times, rather formally, he would tell her how pretty she was. Then he would lecture her on what she should do: you have a great advantage, he'd tell her; no one would suspect that you are so intellectual, and you can get away with so much. But I'm afraid, he would say, if you're not careful, you'll wind up like every other pretty girl—caught up in marriage and children, thwarted and unfulfilled. You have to have a career.

On occasion he would take her to Searsville Lake near the Stanford campus, and after he parked the car, would sit there tongue-tied, never making a move. On a busy street, he could be personal and clever, but when they were alone he would freeze completely. Both he and Margaret used the library often as a place to study. A couple of times, as she was coming out of the library with friends, they would say, "Look, there's Steinbeck under that big oak tree and all he does is watch you walk down the path." She remembers wondering why he didn't just come up to her and ask to walk with her. But he couldn't: "If it was set, and he'd called me, and planned something, then I think he gulped and went through with it."

In June of 1925, he left Stanford, but Margaret's attraction for him continued for more than a year afterward—he returned on several occasions to see her and to take her out. However, Stanford's attractions for him diminished rapidly. He carried an affection for Edith Mirrielees, for a few good friends he met as roommates or in the writing program, and a burden of regret and a sense once again of having been an outsider and a failure. His relationship to Stanford became somewhat similar to his relationship with Salinas. In later years he might bring up the name of his university as a defense against Ivy Leaguers he encountered at New York cocktail parties, but for the most part, he didn't much care for Stanford, and Stanford didn't much care to be identified with him.

He left college at loose ends, without any specific path toward success in mind, only the knowledge that his apprenticeship would have to continue. He had written Carl Wilhelmson in the early spring:

> God knows where I will be after this summer. I think that I have had all of the college I deserve and so I must face the economic situation or run away from it after next quarter.
>
> There is an opening in the Andes Mountains, and there is an opening in advertising in Chicago, and I can get a job doing legwork on the *Examiner* in S.F. Divergent, no?

Thwarted in his previous attempts to go to China and Mexico, he apparently began later in the spring to think more and more of trying to make his way as a writer in New York. In the meantime, he would have to get a job of some kind in California in order to raise the money for the trip. An opportunity came to him before school ended from Webster Street.

Webster "Toby" Street was a wild man—a boisterous companion, heavy drinker, and good storyteller. He had been wounded in World War I, losing an eye and two fingers, and had come to Stanford as a "Federal Student," with plans of becoming a lawyer. He was also interested in writing and took several creative-writing courses at the university—the germ of Steinbeck's novel *To a God Unknown* came from a play Street had written for one of those classes. Steinbeck had met him two years earlier at the get-togethers at Margery Bailey's house.

During that time they had become good friends, Steinbeck serving as best man at Street's wedding. In fact, before the wedding, the mother of Street's fiancée, Mrs. Price, came by Steinbeck's shack to check out her future son-in-law. Having heard that Steinbeck was of a good, well-to-do, church-going family, she wanted to get his candid opinion of Webster Street. As Steinbeck recalled the incident, Mrs. Price, a very proper matron, sat on his cot right above a scantily dressed girl who had been secreted under the bed at Mrs. Price's approach. The girl lay in the dust, trying desperately to control the impulse to sneeze, while Steinbeck went on for twenty minutes confirming his own virtue and extolling that of his friend.

Mrs. Price owned the lodge and resort on Fallen Leaf Lake in the High Sierra just south of Lake Tahoe. Street and his bride were scheduled to live at the resort for the summer, and he was to perform various odd jobs around the place to earn their keep. He got Steinbeck a job helping him with the maintenance work and driving the mail stage every day into Tallac on Lake Tahoe. This move to join a friend for what seemed at the time just another summer job was more fateful for Steinbeck than he realized, for he was to spend the better part of four years in the area. If the first part of his apprenticeship was tied to Stanford and Spreckels, the second was characterized by his association with Lake Tahoe.

Situated in the middle of a rugged mountain range, the Tahoe area in the mid-1920s was relatively unpopulated; the deep colors of the lake, sea-like in its great expanse, were only occasionally broken by the wakes of fishermen's boats. The shoreline was dotted here and there with fishing camps, tents or lean-tos, and less often with resort hotels or clusters of housekeeping cabins, sometimes with a dance pavilion built out over the water. There were also private estates with imposing summer homes and private wharves and beaches. This was the time of the Tahoe Tavern on the northwest shore and Camp Richardson at the south end, of the Drum and Pope estates, of the Baldwins and the Brighams. The summer was a time of dusty heat and the smell of pines and the slam of screen doors, of the snorting of horses on the trail and the slap of water against the long shoreline. Everybody knew everyone else, and the trout were bigger than you could believe. In winter the edge of the lake would freeze and the snow was deep, drifting over the pointed roofs of the smaller cabins. Mail and supplies were delivered to isolated and frozen outposts along the shore by a steamer that circled the lake once a week.

To get to Fallen Leaf Lake, you took a rutted, dusty road first east and then south from Tallac at the southern end of Tahoe. The road wound here and there through stands of second-growth pine and across alpinelike meadows and then along the southeastern shoreline of Fallen Leaf Lake. The resort was around the tip of the long lake on the southwestern shore, with Mount Tallac rising 9,735 feet in the near-distant background. The resort itself consisted of a two-story lodge, two kitchen–dining halls (one for the help), housekeeping cabins, tent platforms, and a boathouse. The founder, William Whitman Price, was a Stanford professor and naturalist who had visited the area regularly to do studies of animal and plant life for the Smithsonian and who, in 1896, opened a boys' summer camp in a canyon above Fallen Leaf. As parents of the boys became enthusiastic about the area and wanted to join their children, Price decided to move to the shore of the lake and open a resort campground. Mrs. Price, Toby's mother-in-law, took over the management in the early 1920s after the death of her husband, and continued to run the place in the spirit in which it had been founded, as a kind of summer camp for families. Girls from Stanford and Berkeley were hired every summer to help the Chinese cooks in the kitchens and to serve the family-style meals. It was to this paradise of mountain beauty and plentiful coeds that Steinbeck came in the early summer of 1925.

His primary duty was to drive a large, sixteen-cylinder Pierce-Arrow to Tallac (a small store and post office) on the big lake every day to pick up and deliver guests and their baggage and to gather freight, supplies, and mail for the resort. Always fascinated by machines of any kind, and at this point in his life enamored of cars, John took great delight in driving the Pierce-Arrow. Toby remembers that the engine was so smooth that when you started it up, you could barely hear it run. In addition to driving the mail stage, John joined Toby in doing carpentry work, repairing railings and replacing porch floors on the cabins and building an office for the resort. They also tried to do something about the electrical system, a water-powered generator that put out a weak and usually faltering direct current—as the water in the creek got lower during the summer, the lights blinked and got dimmer. Mrs. Price asked them to go up to where the creek ran through a series of basins before it hit the turbine and dam them to hold the water so that the following summer the water flow could be regulated.

They had to move huge granite boulders and in some cases change the shape of the basin itself, and Toby was surprised to find that

John, somewhere, had learned all about blasting and how to handle dynamite, even how to set off a charge under water with a fuse. (He probably learned these things while working on the dredging of the Salinas-Castroville slough several years before.) The two of them carried, rolled, and pried large rocks into place, drove steel into the ground and into the crevices in the large granite boulders of the basin lip, and mixed and poured concrete to tie everything together.

One would think that after this kind of activity, Steinbeck would be too tired to do anything else, but he did spend some time in the evenings chasing coeds. He played no favorites. Mrs. Price was a very matronly sort, and she took care of her girls as if she were running a sorority. If they wanted to leave the resort to go over to the big lake, they had to get a pass from her, and she made sure that none of them was out after nine o'clock. The Pierce-Arrow was parked in a garage near the lodge, and every evening at nine, Mrs. Price would go into the darkened garage and rout everyone out of the back seat.

On their days off Toby and John sometimes went fishing. Ignoring the local lakes and streams, they usually hiked five or six miles to the headwaters of the South Fork of the American River. They used spinners, and if the trout were biting, they'd catch a tubful and bring them back for the employees' kitchen. But Toby was now a married man, and John more often spent his days off the way he spent most of his evenings, alone in his tent, reading or writing. Robert Sears remembers John's silhouette cast by lantern light against the canvas wall of his tent, as he sat, evening after evening, at his little writing table.

Sears and another boy, Joe Stearns, both just out of high school, had been hired by Mrs. Price to bus tables during the day and play in the small combo at night. Both boys had heard of Steinbeck (another instance of his notoriety before he was famous), and since they both aspired to be writers, they worshiped him as a hero and found him even more glamorous for his eccentricities.

After getting to know John and telling him of their interest in becoming writers, the boys began to visit his camp once or twice a week:

John talked to us very seriously about what he was doing. Telling us all about how you write short stories, taking us very seriously, you know, and pontificating to the nth degree. And he read two or three of his unpublished stories to us and told us how wonderful they were. . . . But he was really in his manner an extremely modest man who talked, nevertheless, with a great deal of conviction about what he was doing. . . . I mean the fiction really came through, and I think that was one of the things that impressed us very much.

Here was a man who was a real man—I mean, my God, you know, five by five, tremendous physique and tough and had all the macho characteristics, boasting about his conquests in all the whorehouses he knew and so on. And yet, at the same time, he had this great sensitivity and was not afraid to express his emotions openly in stories, and comment on them. It was really quite an experience.

As Toby and John worked on the dams into the fall, Toby gave up going back to Stanford for the autumn quarter. Finally it got too cold to work very effectively (John told Toby that they shouldn't try to handle dynamite if there was any danger of freezing), and during the first week of November the two of them packed up (Toby's wife had already returned to Palo Alto) and began a memorable trip back to the Bay Area. They cranked over John's old Model-T, which had been sitting neglected in the hot sun all summer, and chugged along, the car bucking and missing, until they got to the long incline at Emerald Bay. There the car stalled completely, and they had to take turns pushing it all the way up that hill and every other hill until they got to Truckee. Route 40 from Truckee to Sacramento is nearly all down hill, and they were doing fine until they heard a terrible "Clack! Clack! Clack!" from underneath the car just as they were getting close to Sacramento. When they got out, they discovered that all the wooden spokes on the wheels, dried out from a summer in the sun, had come loose and were beginning to fall off. John stopped for repairs, but Toby abandoned ship, taking the bus home.

A week later Dook Sheffield met Steinbeck as he got off the bus in Los Angeles. Dook had taken a job teaching English at Occidental College, and John stayed with him a few days at Eagle Rock until the ship he had booked passage on was due to leave for New York. On a bright cloudless day late in November, Dook took John down to the docks at Wilmington, where he got aboard the Luckenbach freighter *Katrina*. They waved and shouted at each other as the ship moved slowly from the dock. The drama of departure was short-lived, however, as the boat moved across the harbor only to stop again for several hours. Still standing at the railing, Steinbeck found himself next to a man strangely dressed for a warm southern California day in an overcoat. The man, as Steinbeck was to discover later, was Mahlon Blaine, an artist and illustrator who had made a small reputation for himself in New York.

Without speaking for some time, they leaned over the rail together, looking at Long Beach, on a ship where nearly everyone spoke a foreign language:

John: "Isn't 'Iowa by the Sea' beautiful?"

Mahlon: "My God, you speak English!"

II

Steinbeck's trip to New York aboard the *Katrina* is notable primarily for the fact that he was able to see the Caribbean first-hand, and Panama City, which were the settings for the adventures of Henry Morgan in "A Lady in Infra-Red," which, over the next few years, would be extended into *Cup of Gold.* He was also able to have his own adventure in Havana, where he escorted a very attractive lady around the city in an open carriage and purchased numerous drinks of fruit soaked with rum in order to pass the time pleasantly and to ward off tropical fever. When he arrived in New York, he had only three dollars in his pocket, and the world suddenly turned from sunshine to darkness:

> From a porthole then, I saw the city, and it horrified me. There was something monstrous about it—the tall buildings looming to the sky and the lights shining through the falling snow. I crept ashore—frightened and cold and with a touch of panic in my stomach.

His panic accurately forecast a wild and strange stay in New York, a Hogarthian mixture of ribaldry and nightmare. He started by looking up his sister Beth in Brooklyn and borrowing thirty dollars from his brother-in-law, who worked for the James Stewart Construction Company, and who was able to get Steinbeck a job as a laborer on the construction of Madison Square Garden, wheeling 100-pound barrows of concrete along scaffolding. One hundred pounds is a heavy load to push and balance, even for a big man, and Steinbeck found that the punishing work hour after hour nearly killed him. He was but one in a long line of barrow-pushers, most of whom were thin, sinewy blacks. Tough and experienced, they talked and sang while Steinbeck puffed and struggled, barely making it up each time and wondering if he had enough strength to make just one more trip. "Just one more trip" rang in his head hour after weary hour as he bulled his way onto the planks and set his shoulders to balance the load—one small slip and the barrow would be gone. The promoters of the construction project were in a hurry to get the job done, and the days stretched to ten and fifteen hours. If the day was too long for you, there were a hundred men waiting to take your place. There were no Sundays. One day melted into the next:

> My knowledge of the city was blurred—aching, lights and the rear of the subway, climbing three flights to a room with dirty green walls, falling into bed half-washed, beef stew, coffee and sinkers in a coffeepot, a sidewalk that pitched a little as I walked, then the line of barrows again.

It was cold and dark in the cavernous interior of the Garden. Construction lights, naked bulbs strung out along the scaffold, sent long beams down through the planks and gave the shadowy line of men just enough light to know where they were, but not enough to show them where they were going. Big salamanders of glowing red coals were set here and there on the ground in the center of the cavern for the men to warm their loads of mortar to keep them from freezing. Long after the cold and work had cut off all feeling in his hands and feet, Steinbeck would stop to warm himself, just for the moment of rest. One day five or six weeks after he began work—he couldn't remember afterward how long it had been and probably didn't even know at the time—a worker stumbled on the scaffold high up near the ceiling. He fell to the ground near where Steinbeck was standing. Steinbeck looked down and saw that the man "was red when he hit and then the blood drew away like a curtain and he was blue and white under the working lights." That night he got his time and never returned.

Almost as if on cue, Steinbeck's rich and successful uncle, Joe Hamilton, came into town. Hamilton owned an advertising agency in Chicago and had connections everywhere. Like a business tycoon in a 1920s Hollywood movie, he set up headquarters in a swank suite at the Commodore Hotel and, to the amazement of his work-dazed nephew, ordered food and drink from room service whenever the impulse struck him. He punctuated his conversation every now and then by lifting the phone and firing off a telegram. Uncle Joe did have pull and was able to get Steinbeck a job on the New York *American.* One might think that this sudden ascension out of hell would have created in Steinbeck a sense of thanksgiving which would have led him to express his gratitude by making a prodigious effort to succeed in his new job. But there was something terribly perverse in him that caused him to take his good fortune as a matter of course and to mess up his opportunity. Perhaps he just couldn't stand being rescued.

Nevertheless, his life, for a time, changed radically for the better. He had been living in a room in Brooklyn. Now he took a room on Gramercy Park in Manhattan. Shortly after moving he wrote to Margaret at Stanford:

> Isn't this a nice address? George Bellows painted here, in this very house. The little park has a high iron fence and locked gates, and I have a key. Half a block over is Third Avenue with an elevated and all the pawn shops in the world, and two blocks in the other direction is Fifth Avenue and fur shops.
>
> I lived in Brooklyn for a while in a house as old as trees. And there was a ghost, an old lady ghost, most charming old creature and she smiled at me. . . . People are dashing no place like mad things so they can return to do nothing. The L crashes by, the streets are black with soot. . . . I think my leprechauns are dead. It is so long since they have come mumbling about the door. All dead—there was no room for them. They could not be worked nor sold nor eaten.

In the pressure cooker of the big city, his muses had indeed abandoned him and would not return for some time.

His new room was up six flights of stairs in the old Parkwood Hotel and cost him seven dollars a week. Mahlon Blaine, the artist he had met aboard the *Katrina*, lived on the first floor. The rooms were dingy and small and infested with cockroaches and bedbugs. Blaine used to come up, pull the grease-stained pictures from the wall where the bedbugs would hide, and then kill them one after another with his thumbnail. (A version of this scene was used by Steinbeck years later in *Tortilla Flat*.) This and his habit of taking out his glass eye and making it reappear in odd and anatomically confusing places endeared him very quickly to Steinbeck, and the two of them, plus Stanford friend Ted Miller, began to hang out together. They trooped around the streets of New York, exploring whatever took their fancy—uptown, downtown, or Coney Island. At Luna Park there was a band concert on the weekends, and they discovered that an hour before the concert started, the man who played the cymbals would come and, all alone and with studied intensity, practice his part. They made it a habit to come every weekend and sit with deep concentration and watch him practice; when the concert began, they left.

They often ate out together, frequenting the Astor—a cheap little cafeteria just around the corner from the Parkwood. A favorite, when they could afford it, was Ticino's, on the second floor of a building in Greenwich Village, which offered a fine steak for thirty-five cents and had a good red house wine. On one occasion, after Steinbeck had run into Bill Black, who was also in New York to make his way in the world, the two of them, along with four or five others from Stanford, had a boisterous all-night reunion at the Italian restaurant. Black remembers walking Steinbeck back in the morning, through the streets north of the Village, up the long flights of stairs, to John's really terrible room. Nearly every weekend there was a party in Blaine's larger apartment downstairs, a party sanctified, in the midst of Prohibition, with sacramental wine.

In the meantime, John had fallen in love once again. He wrote Dook Sheffield that it was a typical New York romance—they had seen each other through the windows of their rooms, which faced each other from adjoining buildings. Two strangers, lonely in the big city, found happiness together as their destinies merged for a time. But she was a beautiful showgirl and he was a starving writer, and she wanted a more secure future. When he refused to subvert his art to go into advertising and make a lot of money, she left him to run off with a banker, marrying and settling down to domesticity and children in Peoria, Illinois.

The amazing thing about this fairy tale was that it—or most of it— was true. Mary Ardath was a statuesque beauty who worked at the *Greenwich Village Follies* as a showgirl for a hundred dollars a week— four times what Steinbeck was making as a reporter. After meeting Steinbeck, Mary seemed to cling to him like a safe harbor. Ted Miller recalls seeing her, on several occasions, standing over John and rubbing his neck and shoulder muscles as he sat relaxing in a chair, talking to his friends. Every night he waited for her outside the stage door, and nearly every night she would take him to dinner and try to talk him into getting a better job. She finally gave up on him after several weeks of trying and did marry a banker. But that is not the real ending of the story: after having settled down and had her children, she couldn't stand it and came looking for John in California—with children in tow.

His friends reacted to his loss of Mary with various expressions of disbelief, for not only was she beautiful, she had been his meal ticket for weeks. Mahlon Blaine, however, took it personally. As John recalled several years later, "I remember Blaine's words when he knew I had broken with her. 'God damn you! You have let go of the most perfect pair of legs in the world.' He simply had thought that he would have a free model for the rest of his life."

John may have met Mary as he claimed, although it would not have been unlike him to make such a thing up, particularly since he had just begun to return to his writing and was working on a series of "New York romances." Or, he might have met her as one of a group of chorus girls that lived in and near his building. He became friendly with them, and eventually he appears to have acted as a sort of older brother to the group:

> They have been very good friends and sources of unlimited information. Four of them fed me for two weeks, and for my part, I have rubbed backs to cure hysteria, preached Nietzsche to a wounded would-be suicide, and entertained a mother while her daughter went wrong pleasantly and not in the least hurtfully. They tell me oceans of troubles (99% pure imagination) knowing they will be laughed at. But you would be surprised at how many of them are self-educated and informed. Of the educated, nearly all are spiritualists or Christian Scientists of varying enthusiasm. This latter class is acting a part created for it by the confessional magazines. . . . Really I have been lucky to get under their guard. I find them very interesting, like rather clever and very pretty children. I have stores of tragi-comedy for years of dearth.

Indeed, the detail of the Christian Scientists among the girls suggests that he did store these impressions in order to use them nearly twenty years later when he was writing of Dora and her girls in *Cannery Row.*

I have quoted above from two letters to Margaret, and I should mention that Steinbeck maintained a continuing sentimental attachment for her while he was in New York, even during his affair with Mary. Before leaving for the East, he had stopped by to see her and had told her that there were no other courses to take at Stanford that were worth his time and that he was leaving shortly for New York. He asked if he might write to her while he was away. She said yes, certainly, thinking that although she cared little about him personally, she would very much like to have some letters written by him. Distance helped him put her on a pedestal, and there was something, too, of the longing for home in his letters:

> Margaret Gemmel, [sic] be friends with me. I do want a tie to the half-round hills. I'll give you anything I have to give. Nothing much but words, which have a market value of three fourths of a cent now. There is every human reason why you should ignore this.

His letters are addressed to "Margaret, with the swinging step" and contain a good deal of self-pity and Irish whimsey. Just as he had built a story around his relationship with Mary, he was creating another fiction with Margaret: the struggling young artist, homesick and alone in the big city, who places himself at the mercy of that cold and distant beauty who had rejected him at home.

In the meantime, as a cub reporter on the *American*, he was given small, unimportant events to cover, and he did so half-heartedly. On one assignment he was to go out and observe "Courtesy Day"—a day proclaimed by the mayor in response to a breakdown in courteous relations in the city. John went to a poor Jewish neighborhood, where he found little kids with sticky hands pawing at strangers, and he reported that he didn't think that this was an appropriate response for that particular day.

Years later he recalled that "they gave me stories to cover in Queens and Brooklyn and I would get lost and spend hours trying to find my way back." He also found himself getting emotionally involved with the people he was supposed to write about and then trying to kill the story to protect the people. With all of his difficulties, his uncle's continuing influence with the editors apparently saved him, for instead of being fired, he was reassigned to cover the federal courts in the old Park Row Post Office. But reporting the courts was a job for an experienced hand, not a cub. It required a knowledge of the system, the cultivation of inside sources, and a nose for that telltale detail that covered a possible scandal. The old-timers did what they could to keep him going and point him in the right direction. "They pretended that I knew what I was doing, and they did their best to teach me in a roundabout way." They even covered for him when he didn't show up for work, but all their kindness wasn't enough, in the end, to save him: two days after Mary left him a "Dear John" note, he was fired. After getting his notice from the paper, he returned to Gramercy Park in high spirits and told Blaine and Miller that he had reached a plateau of accomplishment—he had been fired by a Hearst newspaper. At last, he declared, he had some credentials as a writer.

At first he was optimistic. He was sure, now that he knew the city better, that he could land some kind of writing job, and he tried each of the New York newspapers, but without any luck. He looked for other kinds of writing jobs, then tried to make enough money to live on by free-lancing feature stories to the newspapers, but with very little success. With large staffs of their own, the papers were reluctant to purchase anything from the outside. He did develop one story as a freelancer that he was proud of, and he sent a copy to Dook. He had found Kid McCoy, the former prizefighter, working at the unlikely job of putting up the quotations on the board in one of the large brokerage houses. During his last weeks as a reporter—probably at the expense of his newspaper job—he had been working at his fiction again, and he continued to work on his short stories even during this period of uncertainty. Ted Miller recalls stopping by his room day after day and nearly always finding him at his writing table.

One of the stories that had been giving him a lot of trouble was an allegory, which was developed as a character study of a man and his wife. The man was a feckless character, and the woman was quite disturbed by his failure to be serious about life (a conflict which recurs again and again in Steinbeck's fiction). Because of his failure to provide, she was forced to become the mainstay of the family, while all the time nagging him about his impractical dreaming. Ostensibly, the story dealt with the familiar subject of the Irish wife sustaining the ne'er-do-well Irish husband; allegorically, it suggested the oppositions between imagination and reality, creativity and pragmatism, which were later developed in such characterizations as that of Steinbeck's Irish grandparents, Samuel and Liza Hamilton, in *East of Eden,* and in the conflict of Junius Maltby and Mrs. Munroe in *The Pastures of Heaven.*

Another story of the same period was based on the familiar barroom joke of the trained flea or ant: a woman watches a cockroach for some time, turning it on its back, observing it struggle, and then nudging it back on its feet and blocking its attempts to escape. While watching it in fascination, she theorizes about its family and its hopes—providing the insect with an almost human identity—and then she crushes it beneath the heel of her shoe. Here, in his search for material, Steinbeck had to look no further than the baseboards of his own room.

During the spring of 1926, Steinbeck began to get a little desperate. He fell behind in his room rent and from time to time went hungry. Occasionally he went to his sister's apartment to get a solid meal, but she recalls that he "may have been hungry, but he was very proud, and he would rather walk than admit he needed carfare." Toby Street received a letter from Steinbeck on used copy paper and sent in a homemade envelope. He sent him back postage stamps, hoping to encourage him to write more often. Ted Miller, who of the three young men on Gramercy Park was the only one who seemed ever to have any money, picked up the tab whenever he could get John out to a restaurant.

John had been sending out some of his stories to various magazines, hoping for a sale and enough money to keep going. Then, Blaine suggested that he send a batch of his stories to a book publisher to see if he could get a short-story collection published. John sent several of the stories he had on hand to Robert M. McBride & Company, a publisher which at that time had some reputation for taking chances with unknown writers, and a little more than a week later, he received a note asking him to come to the publisher's office for a discussion of the manuscript. When he got there, he was taken in hand by one of the junior editors, Guy Holt, who told him that he liked the stories very much. If Steinbeck would write a half dozen more stories of the same quality, Holt was sure that he could get approval for publication.

In response to this encouragement and at the same time just about at the end of his rope, Steinbeck went to work with feverish application. He holed up in his room, working day and night and living on little more than a few cans of sardines and a box of crackers. Possibly because most of the new stories he had on hand were set in New York, that connection became a major unifying device for the projected volume. In a letter to Margaret, Steinbeck bragged that some "small tales of this blundering old idiot of a city" had resulted from his being "lucky enough to get under her makeup." He took his story "A Lady in Infra-Red" and rather awkwardly attached an introduction that tried to convince the reader that the narrator had picked up the story from a "Sixth Avenue cobbler"— "I heard it in New York, well, because everything worthwhile comes to New York sometime or other"—then valiantly plunged into his story of piracy in the Caribbean.

Other surviving stories that might have been written for the collection include an untitled Christmas story, "East Third Street," and "The White Sister of Fourteenth Street." None of these new stories are as good as several stories he had written previously. By and large they tend to be slick and sentimental—perhaps resulting from haste. Furthermore, the story of urban life does not appear to have been particularly suited to his talents.

"The White Sister of Fourteenth Street," for example, is a Runyonesque story told by a street-wise narrator about Elsie Grough, "one of those trif [sic] little pieces you see waiting in front of subway entrances." Elsie is the sort of gum-chewing, empty-headed but attractive girl who gets her ideas from movie magazines that we see emerge later in the characterization of Candy's wife in Of Mice and Men. Elsie spends most of her evenings at a dance palace called Harmony Gardens, and one night spies a man who reminds her of her favorite screen star, an

Italian. Angelo becomes her "Wop-papa," and together they become a "pair"—"Fourteenth Street watched and envied them" as every night they took in a movie and went to a dance.

One evening, however, Angelo takes her instead to a dingy little theater to watch an Italian opera. Elsie doesn't understand what's going on, but decides to keep quiet for fear of offending Angelo, who is so deeply immersed in the opera that he forgets Elsie's existence. As they come out of the theater, Angelo has been so moved that, like the rest of the audience except Elsie, he is in tears. Determined to impress him with her knowledge and experience, Elsie asks him the name of the opera, *La Monaca Bianca*, in English—*The White Sister*. Ready for his answer, she casually mentions that she had seen it before, "years ago with Lillian Gish. . . . It was a swell movie." When she looks up from making up her face in her compact, Angelo has disappeared from her side.

The story is told somewhat self-consciously—the figurative language is too heavy and the 1920s New York slang is overdone. Nevertheless, it is a pretty good attempt at light comedy, the sort of thing that if it had been cut a bit, might have found a market as a "short, short" in the Hearst Sunday supplement. Though it is not a quality piece, like the other two stories it is nothing to be ashamed of, especially for a young man who needed money in order to eat. It seems probable that Guy Holt may have given him some advice to "pep up" his stories a bit and make them a little more appealing to the general reader. And since Steinbeck a year later insisted that a much better story of his appear under a pen name, one has the feeling that he was deliberately "prostituting his art" in preparing this collection for publication. A half dozen years later he was again desperate for money and made another attempt to write for popular taste, this time a detective novel, and failed on that occasion also.

After several weeks of frantic composition, he returned to McBride & Company with his completed stories, but found that Holt had left to work for another publisher. Instead, he was ushered in to see a new young editor, well-dressed, self-important, and very literary, who impatiently listened to Steinbeck's explanation of Holt's commitment. With the air of a man really too busy to be bothered with such things, the editor refused even to look at the completed manuscript. Holt's ideas were his own, and McBride was in the process now of upgrading its list. It had no plans to publish a story collection at that time. The man was just the kind of man that Steinbeck could not abide, and the pressure over the last weeks had been enormous. He went berserk. He shouted and raged and threatened to tear the editor limb from limb and started to do so. He was half-carried out of the office, down the stairs, and ejected onto the sidewalk, his manuscript pages slipping from his grasp and floating out in a trail behind him.

In the back of his mind Steinbeck had kept the thought that he had an ace in the hole, that when things got bad enough, he could go back to laboring. Now seemed like the time.

But by that time short feeding had taken hold. I could hardly lift a pick. I had trouble climbing the six flights back to my room. My friend loaned me a dollar and I bought two loaves of rye bread and a bag of dried herrings and never left my room for a week. I was afraid to go out on the street—actually afraid of traffic—the noise. Afraid of the landlord and afraid of people. Afraid even of acquaintances.

In this state of dejection and terror, his only course of relief was to go home. Ted Miller, who had some legal business with the Port Authority, wrote a letter to the Port Captain and got John a job as a "workaway" on another Luckenbach ship, this time headed for San Francisco. Working for the steward, he was brought back to his hashing days at Stanford: he helped serve the meals and clean up. Letters to both Sheffield in California and Miller in New York told of his shipboard activities. He quickly bounced back to good health and high spirits, and within days of leaving port he had won the goodwill of the crew by fighting and decking the ship's bully. He gained even more popularity by writing funny-bawdy verses for them, and love letters to send back to their wives and girl friends.

He arrived in San Francisco in the early summer of 1926. He went home for a few days to Salinas, then to Palo Alto for two weeks to visit Sheffield, who was still working on his M.A. in English. He called up Margaret and sent her into a state of shock—she hadn't expected to see him again, but agreed to see him that evening. What had been, perhaps, just an exercise in fantasy and nostalgia for him had apparently become, in the last hard weeks before leaving New York, a serious romantic possibility. She had come to represent for him "the half-round hills" of California, the warmth of home. Margaret, for her part, began to feel some guilt for leading him on, but didn't know how to handle the situation. When he took her out that evening, she firmly played the part of a good friend and reacted with deliberate vagueness to any other possibilities. John got the message. The next day, he left for Fallen Leaf Lake to join Toby Street for the remainder of the summer.

CHAPTER VII

Among the people Steinbeck had met during his two summers in the Tahoe area was Mrs. Alice Brigham, the wealthy widow of a prominent San Francisco surgeon, who had a large summer home on the south shore of Lake Tahoe on a tract of land that ran from the lake all the way up the slopes of Mount Tallac. Since she was friendly with Mrs. Price, it was probably through Mrs. Price's recommendation that Steinbeck was offered the job of caretaker at the Brigham estate.

In addition to Mrs. Brigham, the family included her two married daughters and their husbands—the Ebrights and the Kemps—and seven grandchildren, ranging in age from five to nineteen. The two sons-in-law, one an officer in the Navy and the other a mining engineer, were seldom at Tahoe, so Steinbeck was hired on in the early fall of 1926 as a sort of "man about the place," to watch over things, chauffeur Mrs. Brigham, run errands, and help get the place ready for winter. When the family was in residence, it employed six or seven servants: a cook, two Filipino house boys, and several Indians to maintain the lawn and grounds and to do the laundry. But Steinbeck's position was more than that of a hired man; probably because of his connection with Stanford and with Mrs. Price, he became something on the order of an associate member of the family. He ate with them and often joined them for outings of one kind or another. Although they thought of him as a "little crazy," the Brighams, young and old, became very fond of him.

The Brigham summer home consisted of a large rectangular living room, with bedrooms in each of the corners of the house, and a full bath between each pair of bedrooms. A porch ran around three sides of the house, but not at the back, where, in the living room, there was a huge stone fireplace with an impressive hearth of black river pebbles, which ran several feet into the room. A considerable portion of Dr. Brigham's library was housed on the shelves on either side of the room, and Steinbeck had the use of this library when the family was gone. That winter, he searched through the books for a dictionary, but was unable, to his amazement, to find one. He wrote to Toby Street: "If you can find a small but complete dictionary lying about anywhere send it to me. I have none, and apparently the Brighams are so perfect in their mother tongue that they do not need one." But the library did contain many rare books and expensive editions, and Steinbeck borrowed a copy of Herodotus, which he sampled during the lonely days after the family was gone.

Besides the house, the Brigham property had several other buildings including kitchens and dining rooms for the family and help, servants' quarters, a small dairy, an ice house, and a caretaker's cottage. The cottage, like the main house, had been built of wood, with bark nailed to the outside to give it a rustic appearance. Steinbeck had two of three small rooms in the cottage for his use: one room had a cot and a little wood stove; the second had a table, which Steinbeck used for writing, and a crude wardrobe; and the third, a sort of attached lean-to, was used by the family for storage and as a woodshed. The buildings fit very well into the trees. A well-kept lawn ran from in front of the house down toward the edge of the bluff overlooking the lake, the wharf, and the family boats.

The Ebright part of the family liked to stay into the fall as long as possible, until the mining-engineer son-in-law was convinced that to stay any longer might result in their being snowbound. When the weather began to look very threatening, everything was loaded into the Packard, and Steinbeck drove them to Tahoe City, where they would catch the narrow-gauge railroad into Truckee to connect with the Southern Pacific.

For his part, Steinbeck drove back around the lake, to face a loneliness far darker than even his first weeks in New York City. Driving past the boarded-up summer homes, the deserted resorts, the empty piers stretching out over the gray, whitecapped water, he would realize there is nothing so bleak and sad as a summer place at the beginning of winter. Back at the Brighams', he would be by himself in his little cabin, surrounded by unused buildings, as the first heavy storm of the season howled through the tall trees. Along the southern crescent of the large lake, there was no more than a handful of people, each at least two or three miles from his nearest neighbor—and when the heavy snow came, it might as well have been a hundred miles. The clouds seemed to drop to the tops of the trees, and soon it became impossible to tell the difference between the white ground, the falling snow, and the clouds. It's as if all the doors in the whole world have softly closed tight. A person has a right to feel some panic.

That winter Steinbeck wrote to Toby:

Do you know, one of the things that made me come here, was, as you guessed, that I am frightfully afraid of being alone. The fear of the dark is only part of it. I wanted to break that fear in the middle, because I am afraid much of my existence is going to be more or less alone, and I might as well go into training for it. It comes on me at night mostly, in little waves of panic, that constrict something in my stomach. But don't you think it is good to fight these things? Last night, some quite large animal came and sniffed under the door. I presume it was a coyote, though I do not know. The moon had not come up, and when I ran outside there was nothing to be seen. But the main thing was that I was frightened, even though I knew it could be nothing but a coyote. Don't tell any one I am afraid. I do not like to be suspected of being afraid.

For the man snowbound in a primitive cabin, the worst moment of the day has nothing to do with fear, only cold. That moment comes at daylight when it is necessary to get out of a warm bed in the semidarkness, cross the freezing room in underwear and bare feet, and light the stove. Steinbeck worked hard on a system to avoid this horror. He set a cup full of kerosene on the very edge of the wood hole and tied a string to it for the twelve or fifteen feet to his bed. He practiced throwing a lighted match from his cot to the hole in the stove top. He would wake up in the morning, pull the string, strike a match on the bed frame, throw the match—sometimes several—and the inside of the stove would harrumph into flame—sometimes.

To fight off the unknown terrors, Steinbeck somehow obtained a pistol, which, because of his melodramatic frame of mind, he did not always use very wisely—as we shall see. To establish some communication with the outside world, he wrote numerous letters, to Toby Street, Dook Sheffield, several girls of his acquaintance, and his parents. His parents, naturally, were somewhat concerned about their son's sojourn in the frozen wilderness. Nearly every week they sent him a large package containing a dozen carefully wrapped eggs and other foodstuffs. They were apparently more concerned that he might starve to death than perish from the cold. In the letter to Toby in which he admits his fear of being alone, he asks him to stop by and reassure his parents of his relative safety and comfort:

If, on going through Salinas, you have the time, you might look in on my folks and tell them there is little possibility of my either starving or freezing. Be as honest as you can, but picture me in a land flowing with ham and eggs, and one wherein woolen under-drawers grow on the fir trees. Tell them that I am living on the inside of a fiery furnace, or something.

The mail was his lifeline, and waiting for and then getting the mail became an obsession. Delivery was made by the steamer *Nevada*, which in decent weather circled the lake, stopping at the Camp Richardson pier about two miles from Steinbeck's cabin. The arrival of the boat, about twice a week, was the major, the only, social event of the area. Caretakers miles around, and a few sourdoughs who stuck out the winter for the laboring jobs in the early spring, gathered at the pier. The steamer's whistle echoed back and forth over the lake, giving everyone considerable notice of its docking, and the men came, bundled in their heavy Pendletons and parkas, breath steaming through their beards, to wait for the boat. They came by ski or by sled; having nei-ther of these, Steinbeck made himself a pair of snowshoes out of sap-lings and rawhide. If you needed supplies, you could send a list back with the steamer to the Tahoe Mercantile Company in Tahoe City, and the steamer would bring them on the next trip.

Steinbeck was always worried that somehow he might miss the steamer. Although he had never failed to hear the whistle, he could en-vision wind conditions or distractions whereby in his cabin he might miss it. There was an old "bell house" on the lake that, years before, had sat at the end of a pier. Visitors to the Brighams' who came by boat would disembark and ring the bell to announce their arrival. That pier was now gone, but by rowing to the shed, which still stood well out from shore, Steinbeck was able to attach a fishing line to it, which he ran across the water and then up over the bluff and across the snow to his cabin. At the end of the line, he rigged a little bell. He instructed the *Nevada*'s captain to pull on the line on his way by the Brighams'— which he did. The local game warden, apparently at a loss for some-thing to do during the long winter, saw the fishing line running out into the water and accused Steinbeck of fishing out of season.

The local game warden was quite a character. Steinbeck described him and their first meeting in a letter to an old girl friend, Kate Beswick—a little story that might be called "An Evening's Entertainment in the Sierra Nevada":

Now it is several days later and late at night. Shumacher and Otto are sleeping in the woodshed. Shumacher's snores are like quiet screaming. But first I should tell you something about Shumaker and then about today. He is a game warden of Germanic extraction. Last summer in Truckee he killed a highwayman with a pistol though the other man was shooting at him. Consequently he is viewed with apprehension and alarm and admiration by the countryside. I had had him pointed out to me, but I had never gone close to him, and naturally I shared the alarm if not the admiration.

Today was a perfect day until two o'clock this afternoon. I got up before daylight and went out on the lake and by sunrise I had a thirty two inch trout, the largest I have caught this winter. I named him Ajax and put him in the spring house until dinner time. Today I had set aside for spading. Now there is nothing pleasanter than spading when the ground is soft and damp. You turn a spade full and then carefully knock all the lumps to pieces and you go on for hours without thinking about anything. And as though this delightful practice were not enough, I was also catching angle worms. This allayed the beast in me and took care of the hunting instinct. Consequently the morning was fine and I was enjoying myself when the clouds came up and it began to rain. I cursed and came in the house.

About three o'clock I looked out of the window and there was a procession coming out of the woods. First came Shumacher with an enormous pack on his back about the size and general plan of a summer cottage. After him strolled he whom I afterwards came to know as Otto. Otto was a dog about six feet long but without much more than three inches of clearance. He wasn't a dachshund. God knows what he is.

Omar, my airdale, greeted the cavalcade with every show of enthusiasm. He has licked every dog in the country and so he greets every stranger happily. I must say that Schumacher gave me the figits [sic] what with Ajax lying in the spring house. Omar's hospitality had by this time overwhelmed him and he set about vanquishing Otto. It was while he was joyfully eating off Otto's right hind leg that I threw a bucket of water on him without taking it out of the bucket. Shumacher had regarded the battle philosophically. When it was over he remarked, "Vell, I gez Otto don't can fight so goot." Then he turned on me, "You been breaking the law lately?" he asked. I was full of caution. "Well, no, not lately. They ain't been biting good since the last storm." I affect the patois up here because good English will get a man talked about quicker than anything else. "Why do you ask?" I inquired. "Vell, I ain'dt had a goot trout for tree wiks." But I was not to be taken in. Too often are the simple tricked by the dignity of the law. "If you could stand a pork sausage or two," I ventured, "why, I have some good fat ones and fresh."

He assented and stayed to supper. We had eight pork sausages apiece. And after dinner he began unpacking his knapsack. First came a dark colored demijohn of whiskey and second (you could never guess) a small mandolin. It was remarkably good corn whisky and we drank half a gallon. I am still sober for a wonder, perhaps because I wanted to stay sober. During the evening we had music. I played my new book of the New World Symphony to him and he learned to pick out the Largo on his tinny strings. Then he sang some low German love songs for me, and, if I understood some of the words correctly, they were lower than anything we have in English.

Finally Schumacher who had been taking two drinks to my one, slumped gently to the floor and I put him to bed in the woodshed with Otto lying at his side. It doesn't sound like much to tell it but really it was all kinds of fun, or else I have been so long alone that very little amuses me.

Sitting alone in his cabin with very few demands on his time from his job, Steinbeck at first found it difficult to do any serious writing. He had wanted to be alone and then found that he was too much alone. Lost in a sea of freedom to write, he passed the time writing letters and reading, and he began to adopt the eccentric housekeeping and eating habits of a bachelor: he would cut up a slab of bacon, fry it until it was crisp, and then eat the whole thing, with his hands, out of the pan. In the sourdough tradition, beans became his specialty, boiled in a large iron pot with a bacon rind from early in the morning until late at night. You could spoon beans right out of the pot for a week, two or three meals a day.

Besides keeping an eye on things, there were two chores that Steinbeck was supposed to complete before the family returned in the early summer. One was putting in the ice. At the coldest part of the winter, Steinbeck was required to go out to the frozen pond in a meadow on the Brigham property and with a hand saw cut blocks out of the twelve-inch-thick ice. When he had cut four or five chunks, he would load them onto a sled and then drag the sled two hundred yards from the pond to the icehouse. Enough ice had to be cut, hauled, stacked, and finally covered with sawdust to provide for the family during the summer and well into the fall. The second chore was to cut and split enough firewood to supply the fireplace in the main house for the same length of time. This job was something he was supposed to start in the fall and then work on through the winter, but the wood-cutting didn't appeal to him at all, and he kept putting it off and putting it off.

In late February or early March of 1927, Steinbeck met Lloyd Shebley, who became his closest friend during his remaining time in the Tahoe area. Shebley was a pleasant, husky, good-looking young man of about Steinbeck's age who had quit college to go to work for the Fish and Game Department. His family had been with the department for two generations, and his grandfather had helped start it. That winter Shebley had been transferred temporarily to the Tallac Hatchery, to open and operate it until late July. He got off the steamer at Camp Richardson, and Steinbeck was there, as always, to get his mail. A horse-drawn sled was going their way, so they both hopped aboard, Steinbeck standing in the back, reading his mail. When they got to the hatchery, John offered to help Lloyd with his luggage, since the Brigham place was nearby. They unloaded Lloyd's stuff and started across the snow for the hatchery, but one strand of barbed wire blocked their path.

Suddenly Steinbeck drew his revolver and shot several times at the wire in an effort to sever it, but to no avail. Shebley, who didn't even know that Steinbeck had a gun on him, was understandably quite startled and began to wonder what kind of a fellow he had gotten mixed up with. He found out later that Steinbeck carried the gun around with him whenever he made a trip of any distance from his cabin. Shebley finally kicked the wire down.

Despite such a strange beginning, the two became good friends in relatively short order. Shebley, who had no interest in writing and little in literature, was taken aback by his friend's need to arrange nearly everything on the basis of whether he could get his daily writing in or not. By this time, Steinbeck had overcome his initial lethargy and had begun his final assault on the manuscript for his first novel, *Cup of Gold,* an effort he was to continue daily for more than a year. As far as his new friend was concerned, Steinbeck was a slave to his typewriter.

John stayed overnight at the Tallac Hatchery a few times, and Lloyd stopped by frequently in the evenings for coffee. John told him of his adventures and misfortunes in New York City and showed him a copy of *Sorcerer's Apprentice,* a best-selling book with illustrations by Mahlon Blaine, which Blaine had mailed to him. On occasion, he and

Lloyd would sit around with a bottle of bootleg gin (while there was little else in the area, there was a bootlegger), and Lloyd would go through the dictionary John had obtained, picking out strange words and challenging Steinbeck on the meaning. He was seldom able to stump him.

Shebley's job was to put out gates on Taylor Creek in order to trap the trout as they came upstream to spawn. He would then gather the eggs and fertilize them, thereby producing a 90 to 95 percent hatch rate. But that spring there was a log jam on Taylor Creek, which interfered with the process. Shebley sent a message to Bert West, superintendent of the Tahoe district, asking permission to hire Steinbeck temporarily to help him free the logs. They didn't have chain saws in those days, so they used muscle and a little bit of dynamite, and they faced the constant danger of getting soaking wet in freezing water. (They did go into the freezing water once voluntarily. Steinbeck had heard from local Indians that a quick dip in icy water was good for the health. So when they were passing a shallow cove, John—who must have been a very convincing fellow—talked Lloyd into jumping in with him, while snow was still on the ground and ice crystals floated at the edge of the lake.) Steinbeck spent two weeks working on the logs with Shebley, going back to his cabin at the Brighams' each night. For some reason, the fact that Steinbeck had two jobs enraged Shebley's boss, Bert West, when he found out about it, and he would have fired him, except that Shebley led him to believe there was no one else immediately available. What West didn't know was that his two employees were using State property—ten-gallon milk cans normally used for planting fish—in order to make fig wine. But the wine was its own punishment.

When only a few weeks remained before the family would return for the summer, Steinbeck had to do something about cutting the wood for the fireplace. He hired a man to do most of the heavy work, one of several he would hire that spring and the following one to cut and split wood. Actually, the job required a hand more experienced at lumbering than Steinbeck. The big trees had to be cut down, a tricky proposition for a novice working alone, and then cut into four-foot rounds by using a drag saw. Each round was three or four feet in diameter and was split by boring a hole into the center of the open grain, tamping black powder into the hole with a fuse, and then lighting the powder to blow the round apart. After that, the job was finished with a splitting bar and wedge.

Steinbeck went out of his way to get to know the bindlestiffs that he hired, as well as the other laborers who drifted around the area, working sometimes as caretakers, sometimes as loggers, construction workers, mill hands, or ranch hands. He wanted to hear their stories and find out where they'd been and what they'd done. One fellow who helped him cut the wood was a man named Matt Dolan, who had been in Alaska. When he saw Steinbeck writing, he asked him what he was doing, and Steinbeck said, "I'm writing a book." Dolan told him, "Well, I can tell you how to make a lot of money writing a book. I know a fellow who done it on the Klondike." Since Dolan had been in the Yukon, the gold fields, and Cripple Creek, he'd tell Steinbeck everything—what he had for breakfast, what he had for dinner, what he had for supper—and then Steinbeck could write a book, just like this other fellow had. All it would cost Steinbeck was twenty-five cents.

When the Ebright family came for their vacation in late May, Steinbeck was given several weeks of vacation of his own. He drove home to Salinas, visited long enough with his parents to assure them he was all right, and then headed for the beach house in Pacific Grove. He spent most of his time there alone (his parents came over for the weekends), soaking up the ocean atmosphere and relaxing. He also made a trip or two to Palo Alto and San Francisco to look up old friends. During one of these trips he stayed with Toby Street and his wife, Frances, and it was on this occasion that he talked at some length with Toby about a play Toby had been working on called "The Green Lady." This discussion was the beginning of Steinbeck's involvement in the material that would eventually become the basis for *To a God Unknown*, his third book by publication, but composed both before and after his second, *The Pastures of Heaven*.

Toby's play had developed out of a short story he had written earlier, "Somethin' o' Susie's," which takes place on a ranch in Mendocino County, then a relatively wild and heavily forested area in Northern California. The central character in the story is the rancher Andy Wane, who finds that his favorite child, his daughter Susie, has been changed by her three years away at college. In an effort to keep her from growing away from him entirely, he forbids her to return to school, but she determines, with the support of her mother, to go back anyway, and at the end, her father sadly accepts her decision. He sees this as his loss, but he also seems to feel that his daughter will lose that close connection with the land that he values so highly in his own experience and that he has tried to encourage his daughter to value as well.

From this rather mild character sketch of a father at odds with his daughter, Street had been struggling to create what he had outlined as a very strange and unconventional three-act play. The earlier story shows Andy as having a close, but indefinite and undefined connection with nature. He has taught his daughter the "priceless secrets of his hills" until she, on her own, responds to nature with a "passion for knowing." But college has diverted this passion toward books, books that talk about things that Andy doesn't understand. In the play, Andy's closeness to the land becomes an attachment similar to that of a man for a woman, a love secretive, perverse, even sexual. His wife, who guesses at his secret, tells her daughter, "When he don't come home of a night—when he stays out there—with her—and I know he's layin' down with— But never mind; you wouldn't understand what I mean by that." To further complicate matters, Andy gets his perverse love for the land mixed up with his strong attachment for his daughter, suggesting that he harbors incestuous feelings for her, which he disguises from himself and others as parental concern and protectiveness.

Parallel with the story, the play shows Andy refusing to let his daughter return to college and Susie's determination to leave anyway. However, in the play, Andy's refusal is connected to his unwillingness to sell off part of his beloved forest to the lumber companies in order to raise money for his daughter's education, so that his desires to keep his daughter and to keep his forest are brought together. The first act of the play ends with Andy's range on fire, threatening to destroy his trees, and with Susie's threat to leave for college, regardless of her father's wishes. Street had written three drafts of the play, but had been unable to get beyond the first act. Too many conflicts were leading in too many different directions, and he was disturbed by the theme of incest, which had emerged unplanned.

After talking over the play and its problems with Steinbeck, Street jotted down some notes for revision, but he was unable to solve the problems to his own satisfaction and gave up on it. Since Steinbeck had expressed interest in the material, he gave the manuscript to him to do with as he wished. Steinbeck's first thought was to write a novel based on Street's material, listing Street as coauthor. This he did, the following year, so that the first draft of *To a God Unknown* was called "The Green Lady" and listed John Steinbeck and Webster Street as authors. At this point, the overall design of the projected novel (the draft was never finished) followed Street's play and his notes for finishing the play rather closely. However, during these months of 1927 Steinbeck was still busy working on the final manuscript of *Cup of Gold,* so that he could do little more than think about the project. According to several references in letters of the time, he apparently did spend a number of hours trying to work out the novel in his mind during the fall and winter of 1927–28. It was almost as if this project attracted him more than the novel he was trying to finish—certainly by this time he was beginning to weary in his struggle with Henry Morgan.

Street's play apparently held a great fascination for him, and it is easy to see why. He had already been involved at length with one lady, the "Lady in Infra-Red," as a symbol of aspiration, and the yearning, both sexual and idealized, in the "Green Lady" was similar, although much closer to his pantheistic view of the world. The material of the play also, no doubt, appealed to his impulses toward the mysticism of nature and toward the grotesque. There were a lot of things in this story that would prove shocking to middle-class sensibilities. But despite the weird nature of the play's action, Street's characters—Andy Wane, his wife, and his children—have a genuine rural flavor, and there are many good realistic details in the play. So the importance of this material with respect to Steinbeck's career is not just that it provided the basis for his next novel, but that it brought him for the first time to his primary subject: the interaction between members of a farm family in a rural California setting.

Steinbeck drove back to the Tahoe area in the middle of June and worked for the Brigham family for the remainder of the summer. At this time, Steinbeck renewed acquaintance with Bob Cathcart, who was working three or four miles away, helping to tear down the old Tallac Hotel for the owner, Anita Baldwin. Cathcart was a Stanford student, and, like Toby Street, was pursuing his interest in writing and drama while working toward a law degree. He was also a member of the English Club, although he joined after Steinbeck's time. Cathcart started dropping over to see Steinbeck at his cabin, and Steinbeck would read him passages from his novel in progress. Cathcart remembers that he was very diffident, ostensibly, about his manuscript, indicating that he realized that it wasn't very good and asking, modestly, for Cathcart's reactions. But Cathcart detected something in his manner that suggested he secretly felt his work was damn good and he didn't really care, one way or another, what Cathcart's thoughts about the novel might be.

Shebley, too, had been very much aware of his friend's work on the "Henry Morgan story." During the previous spring, when they were together quite a bit, Steinbeck would pass him a few sheets of the manuscript to look at now and then, and every once in a while, he would read parts aloud. Steinbeck had stacks of writing piled here and there around his cabin. Shebley's reaction to what he read and heard was that Steinbeck seemed to be trying to make the novel as complex as possible.

During the spring he had apparently taken to reading and writing outdoors, for all summer long members of the Brigham family found teacups and glasses that he had absentmindedly left here and there in the woods around the estate—a habit which added to his reputation of being a bit eccentric. That summer he took on an added task. Since the Ebrights liked to stay on into the fall, they asked Steinbeck to tutor their two sons, Charles and Harold, who were nine and seven years old. As a teacher, Steinbeck's main concern was to get along with the boys with as little trouble as possible. He was very easy on them and made their doses of English and arithmetic as palatable as he could.

And he could be very charming with children. While he was friendly with the boys, he made a special effort to become friends with one of Mrs. Brigham's granddaughters, Catherine Kemp, who was often made miserable by the teasing of her two brothers and her two male cousins. He had a rapport with youngsters like Catherine, since he felt in looking back at his own childhood that he, too, had been left out and alone. In *Journal of a Novel* from the perspective of middle age, he wrote, "I can remember this sorrow at not being a part of things from very early in my childhood. Maybe from my very first birthday party." He had made friends with books and created a world of mystery and adventure, inhabited with gnomes, and fairies, and leprechauns, and ghosts—usually very benign ghosts. One has the feeling that Steinbeck, like his character Tularecito in *The Pastures of Heaven*, thought at times, even as an adult, that if he only dug deeply enough, he could discover his own people. Perhaps in certain children he did discover his own people.

He often read aloud to Catherine, from books such as *Tom Sawyer* and *Huckleberry Finn*. She remembers that

> we used to sit by a gopher hole with a gun and wait for the gophers to come out. The lawn was beautiful around the house, my grandmother's house. He was a very, very interesting, warm man who kept to himself, except for our friendship. We were very good friends and used to share things. I was attracted to him because I thought he was crazy, and then I decided that I must be crazy too when we became such good friends.

She and Steinbeck and occasionally a brother would go hiking together. Often the family went on picnics up behind Cascade Lake (which the Brighams owned), sometimes even as far as Desolation Valley, and Steinbeck would go along. He and Catherine and others would go on long walks. He had sharp eyes and a keen interest in everything there was to see in the mountains: the trees, plants, rock formations, and animal traces.

The dog would go, too. By this time, as we saw in his letter about the game warden, Steinbeck had acquired an Airedale as another weapon against loneliness (later he would have two). He was a find, a good dog who loved children and had a lively personality. The next winter Steinbeck wrote to Catherine and in mock concern announced that his dog had learned to swear. Where he had learned such a thing he could not imagine.

One day Catherine and a brother happened to be near where a cow was beginning to give birth to a calf. This was something that they felt they could not deal with alone, and so Catherine said, "I'll go get my friend, and he'll know what to do." She remembers racing up to his cabin and saying that he had to come right away because there were all sorts of things going on in the corral. And of course, he came right away, and they all sat on the fence that was around the corral and watched the calf being born. As they watched, he carefully explained to them what was happening.

This incident appears to have been the basis for the paragraph in the *Sea of Cortez*, written in 1940, in which the author discusses the genteel view of such natural processes as reproduction. He wrote:

A man we know once long ago worked for a wealthy family in a country place. One morning one of the cows had a calf. The children of the house went down with him to watch her. It was a good normal birth, a perfect presentation, and the cow needed no help. The children asked questions and he answered them. And when the emerged head cleared through the sac, the little black muzzle appeared, and the first breath was drawn, the children were fascinated and awed. And this was the time for their mother to come screaming down on the vulgarity of letting the children see the birth. This "vulgarity" had given them a sense of wonder at the structure of life, while the mother's propriety and gentility supplanted that feeling with dirtiness. If the reader of this book is "genteel," then this is a very vulgar book, because the animals in a tide pool have two major preoccupations: first, survival, and second, reproduction.

But Catherine did not remember the hysteria of the mother (perhaps predictable and therefore ignored) as much as the kindness and patience of the caretaker and the sense of wonder he conveyed in response to nature. The next summer, before he left the employment of the Brighams, he gave Catherine his old Corona portable that had been with him through Stanford and on which he had finished one novel and had begun another. It had been nearly worn out by his hammering, but he spent several happy days tinkering with it in order to make it work as well as possible. She was twelve, and she had a typewriter that she could carry with her in its own black leather case.

For the most part his relations with the family were pleasant, and aside from some feelings of loneliness, the summer had been a good one. He was able to relax and at the same time get a good deal of his own work done, although he was never satisfied with the pace of his writing. He wrote to Carl Wilhelmson:

Just now I find great difficulty even in getting physical work done. It is too pleasant to lie on the beach and go in the water occasionally, and these people make practically no demands on me. My time is my own. I am merely a kind of surety of safety and a super watchman. They have five servants so I have little to do, and they go out of their way to prove to me that they do not consider me a servant. I have my meals with them and am included in everything they plan. Sometimes this is not to my liking, but it cushions my crazily sensitive pride.

During the summer and fall of 1927, his writing had gone very well. He had imposed a sharp discipline on himself, making sure that he wrote every day, and he recorded the number of words he wrote at the end of each session in order to develop a habit of steady progress. He had received some encouragement the previous March when he published his first short story professionally in *The Smokers Companion*. The new magazine, subtitled "A National Monthly for Hearth and Home," was edited by Gerald Fitzgerald, a friend of Mahlon Blaine's. Steinbeck, not particularly impressed with the magazine or its title, insisted on using a pseudonym, "John Stern." He made no great effort to advertise his first success among his relatives and friends.

The story is labeled by the editor "A Charming Fantasy," and it is. "The Gifts of Iban," as the fantasy was called, is one of the best-written of Steinbeck's early stories. It is a sad love story, lightly treated, set in an enchanted forest where the trees have scarlet trunks and the people are fairies who live in little houses carved of ivory. Iban, maker of songs, offers silver and gold to his beloved, Cantha, in order to win her love. Cantha's pragmatic mother, however, would have her marry Glump, King of the Gnomes, who is very rich, but very ugly. By contrast with Glump's real riches, Iban's turn out to be nothing more than the golden shafts of sunlight that filter through the trees and the silvering of the undersides of the forest leaves by moonlight. Cantha's discovery that Iban's gifts are more poetic than substantial causes her eventually to turn away from him, leaving him heartbroken.

To write such a story for adults and to keep it from becoming cloying and precious requires more skill than one might expect. Steinbeck succeeds partly by force of imaginative detail and partly by maintaining an ironic distance from his material—what fools these fairies be. Unlike the carefree creatures we read about as children, these fairies are consumed (except for Iban) by concern for middle-class human values of status and respectability. The date of publication and the mood of the story (suggesting, possibly, Steinbeck's rejection by Margaret) indicate that it was probably written in the late spring or summer of 1926.

The themes of the story—the isolation and defeat of the poet by society; the ideal (personified in the beautiful, unobtainable woman) which inevitably slips through the fingers of the quester; the destructiveness of material wealth and human pride—are much the same themes of his novel, which he finally completed in late January of 1928. *Cup of Gold* is not so much a historical novel as it is another fantasy-allegory. The brutish Morgan of "A Lady in Infra-Red" becomes in the novel a more complex, if not a more noble, character. The fact that Steinbeck, as we noted earlier, saw the novel as "autobiographical" indicates that although he probably did not identify himself with his hero directly, he did feel that his character indirectly reflected his own situation and progress.

From our perspective, the fact that there should be any identification at all is strange. Critic Joseph Fontenrose has acutely perceived the popular *Captain Blood* by Rafael Sabatini (1922) as a major source of inspiration for Steinbeck's telling of the Morgan story, yet there is an important difference between the ways the two pirates affect the reader. Captain Blood is likable, and if not always likable, at least admirable. Morgan, as Steinbeck depicts him, is neither. This is the main reason why the novel, if one wishes to ignore its symbol and allegory, cannot be read as a good adventure story. Throughout, Morgan is mean, ungenerous, self-centered, and distant. If he is such a thoroughly unpleasant person, what does this say about Steinbeck's view of himself?

Whatever connections Steinbeck may have seen, those available to us seem rather remote and generalized. Possibly the novel tells the story of Steinbeck's own growing up, moving from the grandiose dreams of youth to the disillusionment of experience. Perhaps in Morgan's self-centeredness and violence there is a rough parallel to Steinbeck's own excesses and rebellions. But it is Morgan's condition, which throughout the novel becomes more and more solitary, that would seem to best match Steinbeck's view of himself in his mid-twenties. That there appears, from the outside, to have been no real reason for his feelings— during these years he nearly always had at least one friend nearby— would seem irrelevant. He had them nevertheless. He felt very, very alone.

Like Morgan he was shut off from society while pursuing a dream of accomplishment that he felt, with some justification, no one else understood. That he chose to isolate himself in the mountains was, once again, irrelevant to his feelings. If he had not stubbornly pursued his dreams, he might not have lost Mary and Margaret, he might not be so poor all the time, he might be living among friends. Always acting the outlaw in the face of convention, he was not entirely different, perhaps, from the pirate of his novel.

If Morgan's boyhood dreams are lofty, Steinbeck's literary goals, as demonstrated in his first novel, appear to be equally so—in many ways it was his most ambitious novel. He wanted to make it sing in the great tradition of English literature; he wanted to give it epic scope, to convert the Morgan of history to a universal figure of Faustian proportions whose story would illustrate the greatest literary theme of all: the folly of human vanity. Whatever inspiration may have been provided by *Captain Blood*, Hawthorne's fiction, or James Branch Cabell's *Jurgen*, Steinbeck's novel does not really come out of the novel tradition so much as it does out of myth and poetry. The style is distinctly literary (as versus the modern, colloquial style of his more famous novels) and owes much, as has been pointed out by the critic Peter Lisca, to Renaissance drama. It is a style heavily infused with figurative language, archaisms, and lush descriptions. Such a style, combined with recurring symbolism and constant allusion to mythic themes, creates a texture that is so ornate as to make the novel dreamlike and abstract.

The author's ambitiousness is also apparent in his choice of lofty models and sources. His treatment of the Morgan story, as such critics as Lisca and Fontenrose have pointed out, makes use of the myth of the Grail Quest, the Faust legend, the myth of the conquest of Troy, and the myth of the dying-and-rising god. Fontenrose goes even further by diagnosing the use of more than a half dozen other themes or motifs from legend and folklore, including material in the novel that relates to the Argonauts, the myths of Odysseus, Orpheus, and Pan; the Druid mysteries; sailor and ghost lore; and the legend of El Dorado. The list is impressive, but also suggestive of a kind of desperation, as if Steinbeck had stored up ammunition and was determined to attract the notice of the literary world or bust in one gigantic display of fireworks. Unfortunately, so many suggestions, symbols, and parallels present a great many possibilities that are never developed. Like Morgan, an excess of ambition led him to attempt and expect too much.

Taken alone, however, the novel is not a bad one, but taken with Steinbeck's later works, it probably deserves its fate as the least read and least appreciated of all his novels. After reading *The Grapes of Wrath* and *Cannery Row*, the reader may feel that this book does not even seem to have been written by the same person. Yet after one has read the early short stories that precede it, its subjects and techniques appear to be an almost inevitable part of the sequence of his work. And there are signs, however dim, of things to come. Steinbeck's treatment of Morgan, for example, is rather typical of his distant and often unsympathetic presentation of certain central characters in later novels: Joseph in *To a God Unknown*, Mac in *In Dubious Battle*, Juan Chicoy in *The Wayward Bus*, and Adam Trask in *East of Eden*, in particular, seem less human beings with whom we can identify or sympathize than specimens chosen for scientific interest that we can hold up and examine.

There are also indications in this first novel of the biological determinism that plays such a large part in later novels. And as in the early stories, we find refutations of middle-class propriety, particularly, in this novel, as noted by Peter Lisca, of the repressions by proper society of healthy sexuality. The point is made in *Cup of Gold* that prostitutes may be fine people who honorably provide a valuable service; and this unconventional idea recurs in later works, most notably with the story of the Lopez sisters in *Pastures of Heaven* and the treatment of Dora and her girls in *Cannery Row*.

Finally, the *Cup of Gold* character Merlin becomes the prototype of that important and pervasive character in Steinbeck's works, the "wise man." This figure may have had its first appearance in Iban (if "The

Gifts of Iban" was written before the final draft of the novel was started). Like Iban, Merlin is a poet, a maker of songs, and is separated from society by his devotion to art and his ability to see through the human passion for wealth and power. At the beginning of the novel he looks into young Morgan's face and is able to predict both his success and his ultimate frustration. The old Welshman's name suggests that he is a descendant of the Arthurian character and therefore a poet in the old sense, as priest and magician as well.

Critic Warren French is right in his assertion that Steinbeck's essential sympathy is with Merlin, and he sees the novel's theme as an endorsement of the "artistic calling": "Despite the superficial pirate story, *Cup of Gold* really contrasts, therefore, the man [Morgan] who pursues the grail of power and finds he must compromise with society or be destroyed and the man [Merlin] who pursues the grail of art and transcends society." The contrast is there, but so little space is given to Merlin that it is hard to think of him as anything more than a subsidiary aspect of Steinbeck's depiction of a man driven toward a dream impossible to realize. Furthermore, power and riches mean little in themselves to Morgan as he reaches out for his ideal, and while his means are brutal and venal, his ideal—combining the cup, the city, and the ideal woman into one transcendent grail objective—is not without aesthetic and poetic aspects.

But the important point in regard to Merlin is that he comes out of Steinbeck's childhood, out of the work, *Morte d'Arthur*, which initiated him into a love of literature and which, probably more than any other factor, influenced him to become a writer. And from that seed evolves a whole series of Merlin-like characters who, although not always exactly like the character we encounter in *Cup of Gold*, seem to represent for Steinbeck an aesthetic-philosophical priesthood, a pipeline to the absolute through poetic vision. The Merlin character is usually not important so much for what he does in any given work, as for what he is. He presents an example and a perspective. Although he may be, and usually is, a minor character, his role is extremely important, since Steinbeck's fiction is almost always concerned with the drama of seeing, rather than the drama of acting.

CHAPTER VIII

Steinbeck was prone to exaggeration and liked to make up fictions about himself. He sought to give his life drama. At Stanford and during the years that followed, he enjoyed playing various roles that would attract attention. As is sometimes the case with writers, he occasionally got the fictions he read, the fictions he wrote, and the fictions he "lived" mixed up. Later in life, he said on several occasions that in looking back he could no longer distinguish those things he had made up about himself from those things that had actually happened. And he wished any future biographer luck in trying to unscramble one from the other. One such fiction might be called the "when I was a boy, I had to walk five miles through the snow in order to get to school" sort of exaggeration. Like Thoreau at Walden Pond, Steinbeck liked to think of his winters at Lake Tahoe as having been spent completely alone.

In the spring of 1928, he reported to a Stanford friend,

> I have been eight months here with no one about me. And I have been getting out the seven deadliest and furbishing them. Have come to the conclusion that only lust and gluttony are worth a darn. The others greed and so forth are dull and unpleasant enough to be virtues. But lust and gluttony are old favorites of mine and I intend to work them to the limit. I wish I were a Catholic. It would be nice to tabulate my delinquences before a priest.

And in a letter to Grove Day in November of 1929, he declared, "I went into the mountains and stayed two years. I was snowed in eight months of the year and saw no one except my two Airedales." This became a standard line, and he no doubt came to believe it. He may have had the number of dogs right, but the rest of the statement misses by three months each year and several people. Lloyd Shebley was nearby at the Tallac Hatchery from about the first of March both years; two or three times a week he talked to the steamer captain and anybody else who happened to be around when the *Nevada* docked; and both winters he had visitors.

In his letters at that time, he mentions "visitors," plural, but the only one he identifies is Carl Wilhelmson. Wilhelmson had been invited by Steinbeck to stay with him at the Brigham place during the darkest months of the two winters he worked as caretaker, and Wilhelmson did come both years, but did not stay very long on either occasion. Wilhelmson was the only one of Steinbeck's closest friends who was still unmarried, and Steinbeck thought of him as a kindred spirit, someone who was also devoting his life to writing. In addition, Wilhelmson was a nonconformist, and his life, independent and adventuresome, stirred Steinbeck's admiration. He was a young man who had seen a great deal.

Born in Finland, Wilhelmson had run away from home in his early teens to go to sea aboard a windjammer. After a couple of years as a sailor, he jumped ship in Chile, was put into jail, and then was hired as a policeman by the very authorities who had arrested him. Later he signed on to a British sailing ship, which took him to Vancouver, and he worked his way south through the Northwest, on lumber mills and farms, until he got to the San Francisco Bay area. There, he was drafted into the Army to serve in World War I, and was sent to Texas. He was only in the Army a few months when he contracted a lung disease and was given a medical discharge. He went back to the Bay area and was able to enroll at Stanford as a "special student." He had only a grade-school education, but had been further educated by experience and by omnivorous reading.

Steinbeck met him at English Club meetings in the spring of 1923, and thereafter, as the letters from Steinbeck to Wilhelmson that I have quoted indicate, they became very close. What attracted Steinbeck to him, aside from his adventurous life, was his seriousness about his writing. Of all the many college friends of Steinbeck's who were interested in becoming writers, Wilhelmson was the most dedicated and probably the most talented. He would eventually publish a novel called *Midsummernight*, about the midsummernight festival in Finland, and a children's book, *Speed of the Reindeer*, also about Finland. He wrote a third book manuscript, "Blind Bargain," about a lost weekend of gambling (he was himself addicted to gambling), but it never found a publisher. He worked very hard on the manuscript, and according to those who have read it, it was extremely well done. But the times, the early 1930s, were bad. The failure to get this book published finished his writing career.

One has to wonder, looking at their early lives, what made the difference between a Steinbeck and a Wilhelmson. Why was one eventually a successful writer and the other not? A major factor in Steinbeck's favor may well have been his persistence, which at times was almost superhuman. To work as hard and as long as Wilhelmson did on "Blind Bargain," knowing that it is a good manuscript and still not be able to find a publisher, can break a writer's spirit.

On the other hand, Steinbeck, who had his own problems, kept on going, regardless. He had great difficulty finding publishers, and he had to find a new publisher for every book, since each would publish his book and then go bankrupt. His books were hardly ever advertised and were often omitted from publishing lists and announcements. They were seldom reviewed, sold poorly (not even earning Steinbeck's advance payment), and were remaindered shortly after they were issued.

After three books, Steinbeck seemed to have made no progress at all—no one seemed to know who he was, and *Tortilla Flat* was being batted around from publisher to publisher as if the author had never written a word before. Nevertheless, with incredible internal stamina, he simply went on to yet another novel. Although he was often discouraged and depressed, he took his failures in stride—the financial disasters of his publishers and the wayward path of *Tortilla Flat* even become family jokes.

Eventually, with persistence, his luck turned. *Tortilla Flat* finally found a publisher, and its fresh perspective and colorful material made it a small success. His fame grew rapidly with each book that followed—*In Dubious Battle, Of Mice and Men,* and *The Grapes of Wrath*—in large part, of course, because the more he wrote about things he knew, the more dynamic and convincing his work became. But also, unlike Wilhelmson, he was lucky in his subject, the dispossessed farm laborer, a figure who was emblematic for many readers of all that had gone wrong with society during the Great Depression.

But Steinbeck's letters throughout his early ordeal suggest that he probably would have gone on writing even if he had not had any popular success. And he would have preferred, given a choice, only a moderate success—recognition from a few and enough money to get by. On numerous occasions, before he gained any success, he fretted over the possibility of having too much and the damage that might bring both to his psyche and to his ability to write honestly. He became very proud of his ability to get along with very little money and thought of it as a badge of honor, as essential to his artistic independence.

But what was it in Steinbeck that wouldn't let him stop writing no matter what happened? Perhaps it was the Victorian energy, the high standards of personal success, which, regardless of a conscious rejection, stayed with him as an inheritance from his parents. Perhaps, at the same time, his rebellion drove him to his work—his heavy drinking, his iconoclasm, and his compulsive writing all being of one piece, a kind of rage to establish his own identity. Whatever the deep-seated causes may have been, the result was an unreasoning, vague, emotional conviction that all joy and love were somehow inevitably tied up with his writing, and that whatever was beautiful or sublime or worthwhile in life could only be obtained, not as the product of his work—fame and fortune—but through the process of writing itself.

After Stanford, Carl got a job teaching English in Japan. Steinbeck regretted his leaving the country (although he left for New York himself shortly thereafter), since he enjoyed his company and the long midnight conversations in which they let their imaginations roam free, and there was something supportive and encouraging to Steinbeck in having a friend nearby who applied himself so assiduously to his writing. He also found it very funny to think of Carl, so gentle and so serious, teaching English to Japanese in his heavy Finnish accent, and when discussing this with friends, he would roar with delight at the thought of a whole generation of Japanese who spoke an English so tinged with Finnish that no one could understand them.

Carl had come to Tahoe for a visit during Steinbeck's first winter there, 1926–27, but it turned out to be a disaster. Two people could not share a cabin that small without getting on each other's nerves, and Carl left after only a brief stay. That summer, however, Steinbeck proposed that Carl come once again; this time each would have separate sleeping quarters:

> I will arrange for you to sleep in the kitchen or the dining room [attached to the big house] so that there will not be the crowdedness of last year. . . . Separate work rooms would obviate the nervousness and ill temper we evidenced last year. . . . Please make an effort to convince yourself that this would be a good plan. It would make my winter more pleasant and more useful (because of the added incentive to work) and it might make you feel far better than you have been.

Carl did come and stayed for several weeks, but once again their relations turned sour and his visit did not turn out as Steinbeck had hoped. In a letter to Dook at the end of February 1928, he reported Carl's departure:

Carl went away a few days ago. His last words were: "I know I'm a hypochondriac but I can't help it. I must go someplace else." I think he was sorry to go. A great part of his reason consisted in the fear that his nervousness inceived [sic] a like nervousness in me, and that I was thereby kept from working. That was partly true. Also, he had a cold which would not leave him, and he was worried about it most of the time. So you see, I am alone again, and, though I am very lonely, there is some relief on me. Perhaps I can get to work now.

In the same long, rambling letter, he reports his feelings upon completing the *Cup of Gold* manuscript, his activities, and plans for the future.

My failure to work for the last three weeks is not far to find. I finished my novel and let it stand for a while, then read it over. And it was no good. The disappointment of that was bound to have some devastating, though probably momentary effect. You see, I thought it was going to be good. Even to the last page, I thought it was going to be good. And it is not. . . .

I have a new novel preparing [*To a God Unknown*], but preparing very slowly. I am not quick about such things. They must roll about in my mind for an age before they can be written. I think it will take me two years to write a full-length novel, counting the periods when I walk the streets and try to comb up courage enough to blow out my brains. . . .

I have been cutting wood violently to keep from being lonely now that Carl is gone. And I am lonely just the same. I wish you would write more often. I am on the point of joining a correspondence club if you don't.

A Triumph. I am learning to chew tobacco, not the lowly star, but the lordly bootjack, a bit under the tongue you know and swallow the spit. I find I like it.

It is snowing again. Confound it will the winter never be over. I crave to have the solid ground under my feet. You cannot understand that craving if you have never lived in a country where every step is unstable. It is very tiresome and tiring to walk and have the ground give way under you at every step.

I am finishing the Henry mss out of duty [revision], but I have no hope of it any more. I shall probably pack it in Limbo balls and place it among the lost hopes in the chest of the years. Good bye Henry. I thought you were heroic but you are only, as was said of you, a babbler of words and rather clumsy about it. . . .

My soul is not a little white bird. I haven't any soul, nor much of agonized ambition any more. I shall go ahead, but I wonder whether that sharp agony of words will occur to me again. I wonder whether I shall ever be drunken with rhythms any more. . . . I shall write good novels but hereafter I ride Pegasus with a saddle and bucking pads, and martingale, for I am afraid Pegasus will rear and kick, and I am not the sure steady horseman I once was. [2/25/28]

Much of this, of course, should not be taken too seriously, especially such things as getting up "courage enough to blow out my brains." As in many early letters to Sheffield, he has struck a romantic pose in order to entertain himself, here exaggerating his disappointment. He did have some post-manuscript depression, but not enough to stop him from starting to plan a new novel or to inhibit his drive toward getting *Cup of Gold* published. He spent several weeks reworking the manuscript, sending it to various friends for comment and suggestions—receiving with mixed emotions a rather lengthy list of suggestions from Toby Street. After he made some changes, he got in touch with Ted Miller in New York to see if he would act informally as his agent.

Miller not only agreed to take the novel around to New York publishers, but also helped to arrange for the typing of the final copy. He had run into Kate Beswick, an old girl friend of Steinbeck's, and she volunteered to type the manuscript without charge. Katherine Beswick had been a French major at Stanford, who after graduation had worked as an assistant to the Dean of Women. John had met her through the English Club and thereafter they had had an extended affair. With a certain amount of male pride, John felt that he had provided a successful antidote to the attitude that a disillusioned Margery Bailey was trying to push onto her—that sex was a degrading and thoroughly disgusting activity. Not only were they lovers, but they were interested in each other's writing. John read and discussed at length his writing with her, and she, for her part, was a poet whose work he genuinely admired.

Kate had been in New York when John had been there, but through a series of mixups—including a spiteful deception by a third party—he had never been able to locate her. After Ted Miller told her that John had finished his novel, she wrote to him at Tahoe, offering to type a finished copy for him. She had not only cared for him as a person—not always an easy task during his college years—but had become devoted to her vision of his potential as a writer. He was very appreciative of her offer, since he had no money to pay for his manuscript to be typed, and he wrote back:

> I remember your sonnets at school. You have the sense of lovely English. You will see that in a rough way, I have made some attempt at nice English. In short, would you kick the lame sentences into shape? . . . I know no one on earth besides yourself with whom I would trust my sentences. Bad as they are I am jealous of them. And it is only because I know so well your love of words and sentences and your exquisite sense of sound, that I want you to do it. Parts of the book sing, Katherine. Will you kick out the discords for me? . . .
>
> You ask about old stories of mine. Everything was turned over to the agents Brandt and Brandt on Park Avenue with orders to do anything they wanted with them as long as they didn't use my name. They sold about two thirds of them and I received checks from the agents so I haven't the least idea where they appeared, nor do I want to know. That was stipulated. I am ashamed of them Katherine. In a month or so I shall be ashamed of this. . . . You ask about the old story the Olive Wood Cross. After making the rounds of every publisher in the country it was finally lost.

They began a correspondence in early 1928 that lasted four years. Several times they talked of the possibility of John going back to New York, and he tried to talk her into coming to California. But Kate had had a blowup with her parents and was reluctant to come near them again. In one letter, during the course of trying to talk her into coming home, he revealed more specifically than he ever had before his feelings about his own parents:

> When this nightmare is over, couldn't you come back home again? Would you sacrifice so much pride to your family? I cannot judge, for there are few parents like my own—tolerant, broad and kindly and understanding. My father is the finest gentleman I ever knew. I worship him and fail utterly in emulation. But couldn't you come back? It is more gentle here.

In his letters to Kate while she was working on *Cup of Gold*, several bits and pieces of information about his writing techniques and attitudes emerge. He reveals that he had worked on the manuscript by reading it aloud to himself: "Probably the reason the book can be read aloud is that I talked it aloud as I wrote it. That is one reason why I have to work in the hills. I drive people crazy with singing my sentences, but I find it necessary for the sake of rhythm." It is a marvelous image to think of Steinbeck alone in his cabin during a winter of deep snow, dressed in his long johns, pacing back and forth in front of his pot-bellied stove and singing out to himself the sentences of his manuscript.

Once the enthusiasms of composition died down, his spirits, particularly during the early part of his career, sagged rather badly, and he looked back on his work with pessimism. His regrets regarding *Cup of Gold*, as expressed to Kate were typical:

> *The Cup of Gold*, while it has nice moments, is wretched structurally. If its structure were as good as some of its scenes, I should have no doubt. But this book will be turned down on its lack of handling. Its technique is immature and clumsy. The death of Coeur de Gris is one instance. I have not learned enough restraint to let him die quickly. No, I had certain things which I thought nice and I wanted him to say them, so I let him suffer long enough to get them out of him and as a result made a dragging scene.

He did not see those faults that really disqualified the book from serious consideration—its romantic conception and materials, and its overly lyric style. But he was right about the novel's structure, providing early in his career a prediction of troubles ahead. His greatest talent (beyond the more restrained lyric style he would eventually develop) was the ability to create visually stimulating, interesting, often provocative scenes; his worst fault was to let his characters talk too much. He didn't really care for the novel form and never mastered it—even his best novels appear to consist largely of scene strung onto scene—and every time he wrote a long novel, he went through seven varieties of hell trying to work out the design.

In one letter to Kate he mentions, no doubt to underline his loneliness, that he had "just finished being drunk for three days." Kate wrote back that sometimes a little wine seemed to help her with her poetry. He replied, "I am sorry I cannot agree with you there either. When drinking, my writing is invariably in bad taste, over-emotional and somewhat pornographic. My head must be very clear before I can write. My intoxicated work is utter slush." In response to some speculation on her part about the ability of men writers to know what is in the heart of a woman, he opined:

> Most of our literature was written by men, and I am inclined to believe that they have given us other men a highly erroneous idea

of the sex. There is Cabell who has only known one woman and so he would tell us that all are like the one he knows. There is Conrad who never knew any and S—— [illegible] who knew three and D. H. Lawrence who only knew his mother. At least Katherine, I play safe. I use only the outward manifestations of some *I have known*. I make no attempt to enter their minds except where their thoughts have been obvious to me in some given experience.

Katherine did type his manuscript for him and, as the letters would indicate, did some editorial work on it as well. She was so taken with him that she proposed that he should be the father of her children, and that they would have to get together some time in the future for that purpose. And she was so taken with his work, that she offered several times to quit her own writing in order to go to work to support him, at long distance if need be. To her proposals, he replied:

No, I do not see how we can arrange your support of me. . . . If it were money, I should take it, because one can make more money, but I will not let you gamble with your art which seems to me a finer art than mine. There is no question of masculine posturing here. . . . I am delighted to have been chosen as the father of your children, or child, as the case may be.

When she asked him what he looked like now, whether he was getting handsomer over the passing years, he replied:

No, I am not becoming handsomer. My body just now, is nearly perfect. It really is beautiful, but my face, well, you see, there was so little for beauty to work with. It gets more and more Irish looking, and I have never heard anyone say that the Irish are a handsome race. The cheek bones become more accentuated, and the accumulated frostbite and sunburn of the last two years is rather deep, and my skin will never be anything but leather, I am afraid.

Although they made plans to see each other, meeting in either California or New York, they were never to meet in person again.

After Kate finished the typescript, it took nearly eight months of intense activity on Ted Miller's part to find a publisher. He literally took the manuscript under his arm and went door to door, trying to make friends with the editor, taking him to lunch, pressing for a reading, and then pressing for a favorable reply. In the meantime, at long distance, a frustrated Steinbeck sent a steady stream of suggestions, usually mentioning a publisher whom Miller had long since seen.

At the same time that Steinbeck was involved in getting his manuscript ready and finding a publisher, a number of important changes
were going on in his life. He changed jobs, met the girl he would
marry, and then moved out of the mountains to San Francisco. After
Carl left in the winter of 1928, his life returned to an uneventful routine, for the most part, of writing, working outside when he could, and
waiting for the mail, and he determined that he had had enough of
caretaking. He didn't like being off by himself as much as he thought he
would, and he wrote to Shebley to see if he couldn't arrange a job for
him at the Tahoe Hatchery. Bert West, no doubt with some misgivings,
agreed. Steinbeck would go to work for the hatchery in June. His job
with the Brighams would end the first part of May when the Ebrights
arrived for the summer. As far as Steinbeck was concerned, his new job
would be more or less permanent. He would have enough privacy to
get his writing done, and at the same time, he would not be completely
isolated: he and Shebley would be sharing a house at the hatchery, and
Tahoe City had some inhabitants throughout the year.

During both winters that Steinbeck had worked for the Brighams,
there had been some damage to the main house. The incidents had no
direct bearing on his leaving his job, although the story was spread
later, perhaps by Steinbeck himself in a moment of melodrama, that
one or the other had caused him to be fired. During December of the
first year, one of the trees near the house fell, and one of the limbs broke
through the roof. When he told Bob Cathcart of the incident the following summer, Bob wanted to know why he didn't rush out and, like Paul
Bunyan of the North, catch the tree on the way down. Steinbeck felt
guilty because he had been asked by the family to cut down the trees
near the house because they were getting old and dangerous. But after
it happened, the family forgave him since similar incidents had occurred on more than one occasion before.

Neither did they blame him when, during the second winter, a sudden heavy snowfall caved in a good portion of the roof. The fault was in
the design of the house, which had a sharply peaked roof that sloped
rapidly down to an almost flat area covering the porch on each side of
the house, providing a large cup on either side to collect the snow.
Early one morning while it was still dark, he was awakened by that
terrible sound of snapping timbers and the crunching, scraping groan
of a building being forced to the ground. He dashed out in the snow in
his long johns and bare feet, but could see nothing. Moments later,
dressed and with a lantern, he made his way into the house and began
to clean up as best he could. His first thought was for the books in the

living room, which he pulled from the snow, wiped off, and laid out on the tables and floor of the dining room and kitchen to dry by the heat of the wood stoves. He then struggled most of the day to move what things he could away from the moisture and to cover the openings through the roof, now hanging to the floor, with canvas and chunks of firewood. The family was grateful to him for doing as much as he did.

Another, and less calamitous, event broke into his routine during the early spring of 1928 when Bob Cathcart wrote asking for advice. Cathcart had been given the part of Rufio in a Stanford production of Bernard Shaw's *Caesar and Cleopatra* and wanted to know how Steinbeck thought he should play the part. His letter was delayed by the bad weather, and Steinbeck took his request seriously enough to spend the money to send him a telegram in order to get his suggestions to the actor in time for opening night. He advised Cathcart to play Rufio as a "blundering mouthpiece," a foil for Caesar's cleverness, who is "self-conscious in the face of splendor and breeding [;] confident when mad and so forces his anger" and suggested that his friend pantomime "convincing fierce gestures" [4/12/28].

He followed his telegram with a letter in which he discussed the playwright at some length, an analysis which indirectly reveals his own goals as a writer and presents his views as to what role a writer should take. He did not approve at all of Shaw's public posing and constant search for personal publicity.

Shaw occupies a peculiar place in the minds of reading people. I have no doubt that a few generations will show him up as a charlatan. One could say of Hardy "His divine coincidences are at times absurd" knowing that it didn't make the slightest difference what one said of Hardy, either to the man or to his reputation. He was always the artist and never the charlatan. His greatness bored him. But Shaw—he feeds upon plaudit. He has been the self-advertizer [*sic*] always and his advertizing [*sic*] has been taken for greatness. Rather than the greatest writer of the day, I should say he is the greatest press agent. As soon as he is dead, as soon as his paragraphs stop appearing in the newspapers, as soon as those anecdotes "your body and my mind and the like" which were never true of Shaw, are transferred to a newer popular writer, I think Shaw will disappear. And such a thought would be very galling to Shaw. Please don't think I derogate his work. His work is fine; but it is not as fine as is generally considered. It appeals to the very young mind, such as my own when I was seventeen. His wit is so dazzling that we never stop to consider that he has never said anything very important. . . .

Now, when I read Shaw, even the best of his work, I cannot clear my mind of the picture of a clever man pretending to be a genius, and pretending with such force that he convinces himself first and then other people. I hope that Shaw is not found out in my time, I like him. He is a pleasant theatrical figure and one very charming. He loves to refuse to have his picture painted and then gradually to relent and to give a grudging consent. [3/14/28]

At this time, of course, Steinbeck had no way of knowing that Shaw would continue to be Shaw for another twenty-two years. But the point for us is not so much the criticism of Shaw—a lot of people were saying much the same thing—as it is the insight provided by the passage into Steinbeck's view of what a writer should be and do. Earlier Steinbeck had acted, on a limited scale and among his own circle in college, very much like Shaw, and in light of his admission in the letter that Shaw had an impact on him when he was seventeen, one wonders just how much his behavior may have been actually prompted by the playwright's example.

But while Steinbeck might still behave outrageously in private, his view of the public role of the artist had changed markedly: if a writer is an artist, he stays in the background and lets his work speak for itself. From this point on throughout the remainder of his life, he struggled to preserve his integrity according to this vision of his proper role. He seldom allowed his picture to be taken, even by friends. (He hated photographs of himself. When he was in his early twenties, he discovered that it was his parents' custom to show off his baby and childhood pictures—some of them nude—to visitors. One day when they were gone, he took many of his photos out of the family album and burned them.) He would not cooperate with publishers by providing photographs or biographical sketches. Biographical reference books, reporters, and graduate students could get nothing or nothing of consequence from him. He always hesitated and usually refused to have his name used for public purposes to generate money or endorse a cause. And he never, except late in life and under very special circumstances, granted a full-scale or formal interview. (When he was abroad, he broke his rule of "no interviews" because he thought that to refuse too often might be rude, and he felt that Americans overseas should go out of their way to be courteous. And when he received the Nobel Prize, he felt that this forced upon him an obligation to talk to the press.)

Even though some of his work was as controversial as Shaw's, he withheld himself from those controversies. Again, only late in life, when he had the notion that he was defending his country's honor, did he enter into any kind of public argument. With only a handful of exceptions, he avoided all public speaking. (Once, when the chore was simply unavoidable, he got up from his chair, delivered a sentence, and sat down again.) He admired the fiction of his near-contemporaries Hemingway and Faulkner, but felt that they had lost some of their integrity by working so hard at becoming public figures. While there are a few apparent contradictions to this stand, this was the role he defined for himself from the very beginning of his professional life and stuck to, regardless of opportunities and provocations.

His idea of the proper role of the artist was formed not only by principle, but by his own peculiar personality. He was genuinely shy, and nothing illustrated the effects of that shyness more than his continuing problems in his relationships with women. Like many shy people, he tended to overcompensate in his relationships with the other sex, putting up a front of aggressiveness and confidence that frequently backfired. Further complicating his relationships was his romanticism, which led him to try too hard and to expect too much: on the one hand, he would try to be very gallant and make his dates too much of a production; on the other, he might try to compensate for his romantic tendencies by becoming callous and crude. His crudeness would also seem to have been prompted by his revolt against respectability. In short, his feelings were very mixed, and the loneliness of two years in the mountains with very little female companionship increased the tension of his emotional muddle. Nourished by his isolation, his romantic expectations soared while his sexual needs, impacted, throbbed. It was a volatile mixture that promised disaster. In May 1928 he left the Brighams' to take a vacation before starting his new job. During his vacation and the months at the hatchery that followed, he would have several experiences with women, only one of which would reflect very much to his credit.

Steinbeck and Shebley, stocked with dreams born of a long winter, planned their trip together. Shebley had written ahead to get them dates with two girls he had met while they were on a winter vacation near Tahoe City. One bright, clear, cool day in the middle of May, they left the mountains in the 1915 Dodge open roadster that John had just purchased and headed down through Sacramento to San Francisco.

The two men arrived in the city in the afternoon, just a few hours before they were to pick up the girls. They went to the Hotel Turpin, at Powell and Market Streets, since it was the only hotel that Shebley knew in San Francisco. As soon as they got to their room, they ordered the bootleg whiskey for that evening. Four pints of Old Crow arrived within minutes, the labels still damp and the caps not yet hardened. They knew that the girls both worked at United Fruit Express, so Steinbeck proposed that they send over two corsages that afternoon. They had two five-dollar orchids sent to their girls' office in order to really impress them and to set them up with their co-workers. Steinbeck was on a very tight budget, and Shebley was overwhelmed by this sudden shift in attitude. But there was more to come. Since they had come out of the back country with no decent clothes, Steinbeck suggested that they go out and buy some. They walked down Market Street to Roos Bros., where each picked out a suit—Steinbeck fancied a tweed which he began to call his "courting suit"—then begged the tailor to do the alterations before closing, and went back to their room to pace nervously until, at the last moment, the suits were delivered.

They parked the car on a hill in front of the girls' apartment building, and took the elevator to the third-floor apartment where they were to pick up the girls. The girls were dressed in their finest, and with the corsages and the sparkling appearance of the young men, they expected to be carried away in a limousine. They couldn't hide their dismay when they looked down at the street from their window and discovered instead a rather dilapidated old roadster without a top.

They went to North Beach, to a place that had booths with curtains, ordered a bowl of ice, and drank and danced. Later in the evening, worried that their corsages might be wilting, the girls took them off and put them in the bowl of ice—John thought they were tired of them or didn't care for them any longer. A man dressed in a gorilla suit had been hired to go around the place and entertain, and he suddenly pulled back the curtain to the booth, to frighten everyone. Steinbeck quickly reared back and with both feet shoved the gorilla onto his rear into the middle of the dance floor. Rather than being impressed by this manly defense, the girls were startled and embarrassed. John's shyness and oversensitivity had led him to add up one small thing after another into a thoroughly miserable evening: his "new" car had been scorned, his corsage rejected, and his heroics unappreciated. What had been overplanned and overdramatized in his mind turned out in reality to be a complete bust, and he had spent nearly all his money for nothing.

John and Lloyd continued their vacation by heading south, first to Palo Alto to visit Lloyd's parents and then to Salinas to stay with John's. At the Shebleys', the atmosphere was strained: Lloyd's parents very obviously did not care for their houseguest. The young men moved on. Before seeing his parents, John asked Lloyd to assume "ownership" of the car and coached him on what to say and not to say. He particularly warned him not to mention anything concerning drinking. The visit was a short one. They had barbecued lamb for dinner and stayed overnight in John's old bedroom at the top of the house. Their winter dreams spent, they returned to Tahoe the next day.

By the end of May, Steinbeck and Shebley had moved into the bachelor quarters at the Tahoe City hatchery, a little house with a kitchen and living room downstairs and two bedrooms upstairs. John staked out part of the kitchen as his own, setting his typewriter and dictionary on the kitchen table. Over the next few months, this writing area would spread throughout the downstairs, as books and stacks of paper accumulated here and there. But Shebley was an easygoing, accommodating sort, and neither the stacks of papers strewn about nor the constant clatter of the typewriter at night seemed to bother him very much.

The hatchery at Tahoe City was housed in a large rustic-looking building with a stone foundation and a tall, sloping, wood-shingle roof with dormers peeking out near its top. The building looked to be a large summer home, but inside there was one large room with an open-beam ceiling. The floor was concrete, with large rectangular ponds recessed below floor level, which in turn were connected by a system of canals and spillways for running fresh water through the fish tanks. One of Steinbeck's main duties was to feed the fish. Shebley remembers watching him walking absentmindedly around the tanks, shaking the strainer of curdled milk or chopped beef liver without paying any attention to what was going where.

In those days, the hatchery was a tourist attraction that drew a lot of visitors from vacationers at the North Shore resorts, and for their benefit John put up a sign on the door of the office partitioned off from the tank area—"Piscatorial Obstetrician." He would conduct solemn tours with a running commentary in double-talk that impressed some of his visitors so much that, to his delight, they addressed him as "doctor." He had fond hopes that one day a beautiful, unattached woman might wander in. His thoughts were not on romance, however, so much as they were on sex. He had ingeniously designed a way of preserving fish skins for prophylactic use, and spent a lot of time while he was supposed to be working, finding the right shape glass tubes around the hatchery, cutting them to size, and finding the right size corks. The fish skins would be put into the tube with a preservative solution, corked, and then placed in a shirt or coat pocket ready for the proper moment.

Bible-reading Samuel Hamilton would never have understood the uses to which his grandson had put his inheritance of mechanical invention.

However, no potential subjects for the experiment entered the field of observation. John and Lloyd attempted to extend the field by occasionally visiting the local dance pavilions, but these were populated largely by married couples. Once, after scouting the situation at Emerald Bay, insult was added to disappointment when they left the dance only to find that they couldn't get their car up the extremely steep grade to the highway. They had to resort to the remedy of automobile folklore and use the lower gearing of reverse to back up the narrow, winding road in the dark.

Then it happened, just as John had daydreamed it might: one afternoon two attractive girls walked into the hatchery. He was taken aback momentarily when they asked to see Lloyd Shebley, whom they had met the year before while vacationing in the area, but John explained that Shebley would be gone all day planting fish in nearby streams and asked if he couldn't show them around the hatchery. As he gave the young women the tour, he found out that the two were sisters, Carol and Idell Henning, on vacation from their jobs in San Francisco. They began to feel they had something in common when he discovered they were originally from San Jose and he told them he was from Monterey (a small lie)—girls from San Jose traditionally preferred to go out with Monterey boys, and vice-versa. As they walked around, not paying too much attention to the fish and the plumbing, John found himself trading gibes with one of the sisters, Carol, who was the more outspoken of the two. She was tall and had a handsome rather than pretty face, long brown hair, and a way of smiling and looking directly at you. She found John's manner amusing and laughed freely at his spiel about his role as midwife to lady trout.

When Shebley returned in the early evening, he found his friend agitated and enthusiastic. Did he remember two sisters from last year by the name of Henning? Did he recall the taller one, the one named Carol? Wasn't she something? Well, (John continued) I fixed us up for tonight with the two of them. They're staying at McKinney's down the road. I told them we'd pick them up at seven-thirty.

It was already late when they started off in Steinbeck's old Dodge, and two miles from the hatchery, not one, but two tires went flat. There was nothing for it but to take off their suit coats and wrestle with the tires in the dark. Nearly an hour later, with one wheel changed and the other tire patched, they started off again. Not more than another mile further down the road a third tire went flat. For Steinbeck, the situation became almost unbearable. Their clothes were dirty, their hands greasy, and they were already so late that the girls had probably given up on them. Out again in the dark, in a frenzy they pulled the tire off its rim, found the leak, glued a patch, and struggled to pump up the high-pressure tire. When they got to the resort, two hours late, sweat was still dripping down their faces.

Their appearance, however, confirmed their story and they were forgiven. After the men washed up, they went out for a late dinner, and following that, went to one dance pavilion after another until closing. Dancing by the water and under the stars, John and Carol become totally engrossed in one another. For the remainder of Carol's ten-day vacation they spent every possible moment together. John arranged a signal with Lloyd: if the light was on in the hallway, Shebley was not to come into the house.

For a change of scene, John and Lloyd took the sisters into Truckee, a small town fifteen miles north of Tahoe City, on the transcontinental rail line. This railroad-mining town was rough, a throwback to the frontier towns of a half century before, and had the best bootleg whiskey in the area. When they took the sisters into one bar, the owner was so complimented that they had brought some nice girls into his place, that he brought out his best liquor, gave them the best booth in the house, and even invited them home to dinner. The bar had a blind piano player who would play for any drink or dope that was available. For some further excitement they decided to take the girls to a really rough bar, called familiarly by the townsfolk the "Bucket of Blood." Here, too, the owner was complimented by having nice girls in his place for a change, but he worried about the consequences and loaned John his revolver for safety.

When Carol and Idell left on the Fourth of July, John was heartsick. He promised to write and to get to San Francisco somehow as soon as he could. The same day, Dook arrived for a short visit, but he might have saved himself a long trip—John hardly knew that he was there. The situation did not move toward the normal routine at the hatchery for some time. Shebley recalls that John was so incapacitated that he had to stay in bed for nearly a week.

John then wrote to Kate Beswick to tell her that he was in love. There was something very touching about the relationship that had developed between these two young people, separated by thousands of miles, as they supported each other in the terrible struggle to become an artist. Their letters, from Tahoe to Greenwich Village, seem to flash warm messages of understanding from one dark planet across endless space to another dark planet.

To his news, Kate replied;

My dear:

I shall write this, but God knows when it can be mailed. I have no money and no stamps and the monthly remittance from the family can scarcely arrive before the 2nd of August. So be it!

Your news letter of the 26th has just come, and I am so awfully relieved to know that nothing more catastrophic than a love affair is responsible for your silence. And why, dear, should I hold it against you that you are "so damned Irish"? It is, rather, that you're so delightfully Irish. I should be infinitely disappointed in you, I think, if you failed to go on, from one love affair into the next, so long as the power is on you. It's one of those things which just must be, and which is wholly delightful and desirable. . . .

And you must have gathered that my love for you is of a somewhat peculiar brand. It would be battered and broken by double-dealing and disloyalty—but otherwise it is singularly undemanding.

Why should you have thought yourself too old to be stricken? It is not only women who "go on forever." The damned, delightful Irish male has a very similar tendency. But it is true, as you say, that one does find old age an impediment to haste. I am thrilled that you can cast it aside for a long enough time to be in love. I am afraid I can never again be capable of a violent and romantic love affair—and it is very sad. I have a disturbing tendency to look at myself and laugh—and that rather wet-blankets the more romantic aspects of an affair. . . .

However, when you are a bit calmer, I do wish you would tell me about everything—the lady herself, for instance, and the progress of the affair. I am by way of being a bit renowned for wisdom and sympathetic understanding. . . .

Personally, of course, I am a little opposed to your marrying although, as I have prophesied, I think it inevitable within the next few years. It has a tendency to spoil things a bit; one can never be quite so free with a married man. However, I leave the matter entirely in your hands. . . .

I shall get more writing done, I think, now that I am not consumed with a desire to be going places and doing things. I am unendingly grateful to you and Henry Morgan for bringing me once more to the consciousness that I really can do something. I am convinced, now, as I used to be years ago, that I shall do something good eventually. Life is a very sound investment—in other words, I am happy. . . .

I really can't think of another thing that wants saying right now.

I shall go out and have adventures so that I shall have much to tell you if I am to carry on this unilateral episode for an indefinite period.

Always I love you, dear,
Katherine

Sensitive in his relationship to Kate, he could at this age still be a terrible lout in response to others; romantic in response to the idea of love, he could also be very biological in the pursuit of sex; and mystical in his view of life and the process of artistic inspiration, he could be pragmatic, even crude, in attempting to get what he wanted. All such contradictions in his personality seem almost natural in comparison with the ludicrous picture of this strapping young man retiring to his bed for a week while suffering from lovesickness.

His recovery, although perhaps not complete, came eventually, however, as best evidenced when he returned to a practice of taking notes during the course of a date, much to the distress of his companion once she realized what he was doing. Allan Pollitt, former Fish and Game employee, remembers coming into Tahoe City with a load of fish from the Mount Shasta Hatchery and meeting Steinbeck, who suggested they go out on a double date. Throughout the evening, Pollitt watched Steinbeck make "numerous notes . . . which he stuffed into the glove compartment of his car." When he was not emotionally involved, this kind of use of other people seemed to him to be perfectly justified in the pursuit of art—a sort of artistic field trip wherein people are treated as specimens, much as some of the characters in his fiction are handled as the objects of scientific curiosity. When his odd behavior was questioned, he told his companion "that he would write a book some day."

Nor was he so smitten romantically by Carol that he wasn't motivated, after a time, to chase seriously after other girls once again. Rather than drawing his complete devotion, Carol would seem to have cracked the lid on a pressure cooker. He was no longer satisfied by "dates," even when he could take notes. With rather poor timing in respect to Steinbeck's condition, Polly Smith, John Breck's daughter, showed up with a girl friend.

There had been a sort of love-hate relationship between John and Polly for some years, most of the attraction felt by John and most of the repulsion by Polly. Nevertheless, she was in the Tahoe area for a vacation and decided to stop by and see him at the hatchery, thinking that since he had sponged off her mother for so long, perhaps she could turn the tables and get a free meal or two. It turned out to be a very bad idea, as one unfortunate episode followed another. Polly, who was in her early twenties now, was small, pretty, athletic, and very sarcastic. John liked witty, sarcastic women. After an evening of drinking, John made a pass at her, and she made it very clear that she didn't want to have any physical contact whatsoever. Thinking that she had been teasing him, he hauled her to the second-story window of the bachelor quarters and, in a rage of drunken frustration, grabbed her by the ankles, hung her head down out the window, and began shaking her. He yelled at her and she screamed at him until Lloyd rushed upstairs to see what was going on and made the rescue.

Polly left quickly, and Shebley spent several hours sobering up his friend and telling him what an ass he was. Later that night, touched with remorse, Steinbeck realized that with one slip of the hand he could have killed the girl. To make amends, he sent Shebley as his emissary to apologize and to invite the girls, who had taken a cabin at the far other end of town, to dinner and then into Truckee for dancing. Shebley was very likable and persuasive, and the offer was accepted. When they arrived that evening, Polly was amazed to see John in a brown herringbone suit, the first time that she had seen him in anything other than his worn cords and a sweater. John drove them in his old Dodge into Truckee, where they stopped to pick up some local color at the same disreputable bar, the Roma, where the young men had taken the Henning sisters. Polly immediately began calling it the "Aroma" because it stank so badly. They had several drinks while they listened to Blind Frank play the piano.

After a time they went on to a basement speakeasy that had a small band. They were dancing on a small, crowded dance floor when suddenly Polly smelled something burning and saw smoke curling up from the back of John's suit jacket. "My God," she said, "you're on fire!" A little guy with long greasy black hair and a glazed look in his eye had been dancing around the floor with a cigarette in his hand and had bumped into Steinbeck, burning a hole in his coat that was starting to spread. Steinbeck turned livid—his "courting suit" was his pride and joy—and reached into his jacket and pulled out his revolver. He spun around looking for the fire bug, presumably to shoot him. Polly yelled "No!" and there was a great deal of screaming and confusion. Shebley once again came to the rescue, wrestling the gun out of John's hand, and hustling him back to the car and quickly out of town. Perhaps Steinbeck's wildness was another example of his confusion at times of life with art, since earlier that summer he had borrowed a complete set, some thirty-six volumes or so, of Zane Grey's novels from his boss, Bert West.

As one might imagine, the shocking appearance of the gun was enough for Polly, and even though she and her friend stayed on for a few more days in the Tahoe City area, she would have nothing more to do with John. She got to know several members of the band at the Tahoe Tavern, college boys, and started hanging around there in the evenings, talking to them during their breaks and listening to them play. This made John furious, and he promptly wrote to her mother that she was misbehaving and suggested that she be ordered home. The letter was a foolish gesture, since Polly's mother was more dependent on her daughter than the other way around.

While his outward life was often thwarted, degenerating at times into the grotesque, the inner life—the life of imagination, which he could reveal only in his writing and in rare moments to his closest friends and to children—continued to flourish. Some indication of the path of fancy his mind was taking is revealed in a story that he told Bob Cathcart that summer. The previous spring, when he and Shebley had been up on Taylor Creek at a weir where Shebley was stripping the eggs from the big trout as they came up the creek to spawn, an Indian suddenly appeared at their side. Both Shebley and Steinbeck recognized the Indian who stood near them, and John said, "Hello, Fred, how are you doing?" and Fred said, "Mr. Steinbeck, may I have one of the fish you've trapped?" and John replied, "Of course." The Indian started to pull off his clothes. There had been something in his manner that made them ask, "What is it, Fred?" And he said, "My father is quite sick, and the medicine man at Linden said that if I went to Taylor Creek, got a fish, took it up to Lake Aloha, and gave it to the lady at Lake Aloha, my father would get well."

He took off his clothes—it was March, very cold, with snow still on the ground—went into the river, and caught a fish with his hands. He laid it on the snow, put his clothes back on, and started out for Lake Aloha, ten miles into the back country. They saw him a few days later and asked, "Fred, did you take the fish to Lake Aloha?" and he replied, "Yes, my father will get well now." They asked, "What happened at Lake Aloha?" He said, "The lady came out of the lake, I gave her the fish, and she went back into the lake with it."

The lady of nature figured prominently in Steinbeck's imagination as he struggled to establish the plan for his next novel. The "new novel preparing," about which he wrote Dook in February, was the beginning of *To a God Unknown,* now called "The Green Lady" after Toby Street's play. The advantage of working from the play was that it gave Steinbeck some ideas from which he could work, ideas that fit very nicely into his own strange mixture of the mystical and the biological. Yet, the premise of the play had already stumped one author, and the second, working in the longer, more detailed novel form, was equally at a loss as to how to resolve the many conflicts that the plot set in motion. Steinbeck still had in mind the conclusion he had worked out earlier with Toby—the father's beloved forest is engulfed in flames and he walks, as a gesture of both sacrifice and union, into the fire. Not happy with this resolution and hoping that in the writing other possibilities might occur to him, Steinbeck plunged ahead on the first part of the novel, the part that roughly paralleled the completed section of the play.

He did feel compelled, however, to make several major changes. One of the most important was that of the setting. He had never been to Mendocino County, so he changed the locale to one with which he was familiar—the Nacimiento River Valley, just west of King City and the lower end of the Salinas Valley. This, then, is the beginning of John Steinbeck as "local color" writer. In connection with the change of setting, he changed the time, going back to "Andy Wane's" father, "Joe," and altering the family name so that it becomes "Wayne." As in the final version of *To a God Unknown,* Joe Wayne comes from Vermont, and once he is settled on his ranch, he sends for his relatives in the East. Near the end of Book I (the 107-page segment of "The Green Lady" that Steinbeck completed), Joe dies and Andy is married in a scene very reminiscent of the fiesta in the final version. Another major change in addition to those involving the setting and time is the introduction by Steinbeck of the drought into his narrative, a central aspect of the published version of the novel. As Book I ends, Andy is forced to sell off his father's land because of the drought and is preparing to move north to take up land in a wetter climate.

This draft, which he started during the summer of 1928, dropped for another project in the fall, and continued to work on during the winter that followed, reads very well. Its style is very close to Steinbeck's mature style—relatively short sentences, very detailed expositions, and a harder, tighter use of figurative language—a style that eschews the vagueness and ornamentation that marked the more poetic *Cup of Gold.* But although the draft was a good one, he, too, found himself baffled as to how to continue. One of the major stumbling blocks was Andy's impending move to Mendocino County, an area still unfamiliar to Steinbeck. In order to write about a man in love with a forest, he had to know the forest. So in order to try to solve this problem, in the late winter of 1929 he and Toby took a trip to the Mendocino area, about a hundred seventy-five miles north of San Francisco. But the trip still did not allow him to become comfortable with the setting, and that winter he gradually dropped the project in favor of a group of short stories he had been thinking about for several months.

There are so many elements in this unfinished manuscript that come into use later in various stories and novels, that the draft is almost like a small prediction of his writing career to come. Joe Wayne, modeled in part after Steinbeck's own father, is the prototype of all the taciturn country men in Steinbeck's work who have a deep feeling for the land and who tend to be overshadowed by their loquacious and assertive wives. Beth, Joe's second wife, takes that role. Modeled in part after Steinbeck's mother, she prefigures a wide range of Steinbeck women characters, ranging from the young, unmarried school teacher Molly Morgan in *The Pastures of Heaven* to the matriarchal Ma Joad in *The Grapes of Wrath.* Joe's third wife in "The Green Lady," Carry, is an early appearance of Bible-reading, secretly sipping Lizzie Hamilton in *East of Eden*, a caricature vaguely patterned after Steinbeck's maternal grandmother. And young Andy Wayne has some characteristics in common with Jody in *The Red Pony.*

In short, rather than the somewhat exotic locale of *Cup of Gold*, the setting of this new novel is familiar territory near the Salinas Valley. So concerned was Steinbeck that the setting be close to home, he was unable to complete his manuscript draft when the plan called for the action to move elsewhere. A major aspect of the novels that were to come was not only a knowledge of their location, but a feeling for it. Scene and setting would assume a far heavier burden of meaning in his work than in the fiction of most other novelists. His characters, rather than being imaginative extensions of figures from history and myth, would be patterned after relatives, friends, and the people he had observed while he was growing up. His subjects would be farm families, farm workers, drifters, subcultures within farm communities or small towns; and his themes would turn on conditions endemic to these settings: loneliness, alienation, oppression, and man in harmony with or in conflict with other men and nature. While he still hoped to achieve some measure of the greatness he had admired in such giants from the past as Milton, the location of Paradise had changed and its loss brought nearer home.

CHAPTER IX

uring the latter part of the summer of 1928, while Steinbeck was working on the early chapters of "The Green Lady," he began to think more and more of the possibility of leaving his job and trying to find something in San Francisco, where he could reestablish his relationship with Carol Henning. When Lloyd Shebley decided to leave, his inclination was turned to resolve.

A motion-picture company had been filming on location near Cascade Lake most of the summer, and Shebley had been offered a screen test. Since he was the third generation of his family to work for the Department of Fish and Game, the decision to leave his job and a rather certain future was a difficult one, and he turned to his friend for advice. Steinbeck was by no means an authority on Hollywood, but sometime after his return from New York he did make a brief try at becoming a script writer. A friend from the English Club at Stanford, Charles McNichols, had a job in the office of one of the studios but was unable to help him. From this wealth of experience, John advised Lloyd to take his chances—he was photogenic and had a good voice; he might just make it. So about the middle of August, Shebley left for Paramount, and Steinbeck was left to handle the work at the hatchery alone.

Although he didn't know it, his days at the hatchery were numbered anyway. Bert West, the superintendent, didn't like Steinbeck very much and had thought of him as irresponsible ever since he caught him one evening lying in his bunk with a bottle of gin and shooting holes in the roof of the Tallac Hatchery bachelor quarters with his revolver. He claimed to be ridding the place of packrats. The final straw came that summer when West sent Steinbeck and a seasonal worker named Tom Hunkins to Sacramento to haul a load of fir and pine boughs to the State Fair for the Fish and Game exhibit. They took West's pride and joy—a new, bright green State pickup truck.

They were supposed to stay overnight and then with an early start be back to work at eight the next morning. At six, they banged on the door of the superintendent's house, woke West up, and told him that they had wrecked his truck. The tie rod broke, they said, and they were lucky to be alive. West stood in the doorway for nearly three minutes, cursing Steinbeck, Hunkins, fate, and the Dodge Motor Company. He got the Tahoe City wrecker to retrieve the truck, which was down an embankment, on its side, off the Truckee–Tahoe City road. The mechanic checked the wreck and told West that the tie rod had not broken—it had been knocked loose with a hammer, and a cotter key had been pulled out. West decided at that moment that Steinbeck must go, but he waited until the season was over before telling him.

On the first of September, John wrote to Kate Beswick:

I'm going tomorrow. I'm terrified at my impending poverty. Such things as clothes—I haven't any of them. But why go on. I'll buy a pair of corderoys and pretend to be a college boy. But the girl, I rather hate to embarrass her. I'm really very fond of her. I intend to live with her, and the trouble is that she makes three times as much money as I can hope to. . . . Anyway she's a nice girl and doesn't mind my poverty in the least.

The new opus is going to begin just about as quickly as I can find a typewriter table. I'm pretty sure that the Green Lady is definitely shelved in favor of more biography [speaking here of *Cup of Gold* as biography]. I think it will be five biographies in fact, of five Saints. My research is barely started. I am very much interested in the subject. I'll see what I can do with it.

He came down the mountain for the last time the following day. His plans were to check in at home, spend a few days in Pacific Grove in the sun, and then go to San Francisco and with some luck find a job. He didn't fully realize what a good situation he'd had at the Brighams' and at the hatchery. At both jobs his time was pretty much his own, the work was easy, and no one, not even Bert West, hung over his shoulder telling him what to do. The salary in both cases had been small, but there would come a time at the depth of the Depression, a few years later, when even that small amount of hard cash would look awfully good in retrospect. He even thought about taking his wife back to the mountains with him, but decided that the Brighams probably wouldn't want a caretaker with a wife. Of course he hadn't figured that his wife would have to have been several steps beyond starvation before she would have agreed to any such thing.

In Pacific Grove he had the little house to himself and he spent his first few days sleeping. Then he began to wander about, getting reacquainted with the bay front and the wharf in Monterey. There, he was well known as "John Steinbeck from Salinas," whose father was the weights-and-measures man. As always, there were plenty of fish to be had for the asking, usually salmon too small to sell. Then walking began to pall, and when his parents came to visit, he asked them if they had anything new around the house to read. His father took him over to the library and asked for an application for a library card for this son. As John was filling out the form, he paused and asked his father what he should put down for "Occupation." After thinking about it for a moment he decided, "I'll put down 'bum.'"

By the end of the month, he had settled down in San Francisco for what he later called his "tour of duty as an intellectual Bohemian." It was a tour that was broken into two parts, reminiscent of his half-year stays at Stanford. He was in the city during the fall of 1928, lived most of the following winter, spring, and summer in Pacific Grove and Palo Alto, and then in the fall of 1929 was back in San Francisco again.

He didn't have as much trouble finding a job as he thought he would. His sister Mary had married Bill Dekker, a wealthy young man she had met at Stanford, whose family owned a considerable portion of the Bemis Bag Company, one of the larger manufacturing concerns in the Bay area at that time. And so Steinbeck spent much of his first season of Bohemianism working as a warehouseman. Bemis made a wide range of containers, from paper bags to gunnysacks, the raw materials for which came in by ship. Steinbeck's job, along with others, was to lift the bales (usually jute or hemp) with a hand truck and cart them into the warehouse, move them from one stack to another in storage, and then cart them back out again to the loading dock when they were needed by the factory.

As in New York, he found that hard physical labor and writing don't mix very well, and the longer he found himself in a condition where he was too tired to write, the more despondent he became. He reported his situation to Kate Beswick:

> For eight hours every day I push about trucks on which are bales of jute which weigh about eighteen hundred pounds. I have been at it only a week, and gradually I seem to be getting slightly used to it. But for this week anyway, I have come home in an aura of the most complete exhaustion imaginable. So much for literary effort. It just ain't possible yet. Perhaps it will be more possible later. And

I am making a wage which will feed me if I eat in the wrong places [but] by which, by no stretch of the imagination, or the wage, will clothe me. It is peculiar. The jute mill terrifies me, but one must live, I guess. . . . My goil frendt's mother has come to stay a month with her making my love life almost devoid of interest thank god. If I had that to keep up to, together with the work, I think I couldn't very well stand it. So much for hell. [9/28]

A couple of weeks later he wrote: "I fully intended to go to the library, but the tiredness was too great. . . . San Francisco is very lovely now. I wish I could see some of it. But I work in a basement and it is nearly dark when I get home." And at the end of September: "Am almost convinced that one cannot do eight hours of heavy labor and write, too. There isn't enough energy to go around. This knowledge brings with it an inevitable despondency which is nothing but the eating away of a bad conscience. . . . Just now, I want the time or rather the energy to write more than anything on earth."

Then at mid-October:

I don't know. I am approaching thirty. I shall be twenty-seven in February. Not the desire but the consciousness of an ability to write is slowly dying out of me. It is being pushed out by simple fatigue. I am making one last try to get words on paper, this try to last until Christmas, and if it prove as futile as the attempts of the last two months, I am resolved to follow my own advice. It would not be a bad thing.

Nothing in his other letters would indicate precisely what advice he is referring to here, but he was clearly at the end of his rope, and whatever course of action he was considering, it would appear to have been something drastic. From the time he was fifteen, he had been determined to become a writer. Now, he found it physically impossible to go on.

It is remarkable how many images in memory from this period in San Francisco match those from his previous stay in New York. Lloyd Shebley came up to visit Steinbeck that fall and remembers climbing one flight of stairs after another until he came to a small, dark room at the top, a "real garret." He recalls John working at a warehouse near the waterfront, a huge, dim, cavernous basement that echoed with the noise of the workers, but an echo swallowed up immediately by the size of the place, like a book dropped at the center of a large public library. John himself had memories of "a dark little attic on Powell Street. It was in the best tradition [of Bohemian living] with unsheathed rafters and pigeons walking in and out of a small dormer window. Then there was a kind of cave in North Beach completely carpeted wall to wall with garlic." He remembered coming back after a night out, to a "room with narrow bed, straight chair, typewriter and naked electric bulb with two sheets of copy paper pinned around it to shield the eyes." A small room with a cot, a table, chair, and typewriter—whether in Palo Alto, New York, San Francisco, or at Lake Tahoe—had been his lot for a long, long time.

But his life was not made up entirely of long hours at the warehouse and faltering attempts to fend off his weariness while sitting at his typewriter. There were also nights of celebration that years later he looked back on fondly:

Saturday night with five silver dollars laughing and clapping their hands in your pocket. North Beach awakening with lights in a misty evening. Perhaps a girl with you, but if not then, surely later, Dinner at the Cafe Auvergne! I don't remember its real name but I remember the long tables clad in white oil cloth, the heaped baskets of sour bread, the pots de chambre of beautiful soup de jour [sic], then fish and meat, fruit, cheese, coffee, 40 cents. With wine and that means lots of wine, 50 cents.

And after dinner to the shining streets again with more wine to carry in your hand, superior wine not rot gut, a half gallon 38 cents. And then a night of Bacchic holiness, love perhaps behind a bush, and a streetcar ride to the Beach and lying breathless and dry mouthed in the shelter of a rock while the fog-dancing dawn came up over you.

After a time, it was not just any girl, but always Carol. Carol was working in the advertising and circulation department at the *San Francisco Chronicle*, training, she hoped, for a career in advertising. She and John began going steady soon after he got his job, although since they were both working long hours, six days a week, for small salaries, the courtship was not a very extravagant one. Besides, John was trying to save money, living in the least expensive rooms he could find and eating "sardines and buns and doughnuts and coffee." But they walked the streets and absorbed life, talked and argued, and looked longingly at the sidewalk flower stands.

In October he wrote to Ted Miller: "This, if you will remember, is the grandest time of the year in S.F. The weather is perfectly swell. Yesterday we walked all after noon in Golden Gate Park."

They could go to a movie for a dime, or for a nickel take the streetcar out Geary Street to Ocean Beach, to Playland and the penny arcades or to Sutro Baths with its half dozen hot saltwater pools. And it didn't cost much to window-shop at Hale's, The White House, or The Emporium.

Near the end of Powell Street was a neighborhood of small apartment buildings mixed with laundries, garages, and corner grocery stores. In an attic room at the top of one such building, dressed in an old V-neck sweater and baggy corduroy pants, Steinbeck would prop his feet up on the grate of his coal burner and read aloud the last completed chapter of his novel-in-progress to Carol and Idell Henning.

Steinbeck's tour of "intellectual Bohemianism" was relatively solitary. San Francisco was not Paris. There were plenty of artists and would-be artists around, but few places to gather in those days of Prohibition and speakeasies. Looking back, he wrote:

> We of that period might, or should have been called, the Unfortunate Generation because we didn't have a Generation nor the sense to invent one. The Lost Generation, which preceded us, had become solvent and was no longer lost. The Beat Generation was far in the future. But we did have one thing they had. We were just as broke as they were, and we hated it just as much, and we gloried in it insofar as we were able. An acquaintance with money was fair game. We tried to trade our dubious talents for love and understanding and amazingly enough sometimes we succeeded. We pounded away at our deathless prose and even worse poetry, but if we had ever tried to read any of it aloud in a bar we would have been given the quickest A and C on record. Bars were for drinking, fighting, arguing and assignation, not poetry.

If there were any gatherings, they were usually very casual—a few friends on a weekend evening sitting on the floor of the living room of a small apartment with a couple of candles and a half gallon of wine on a coffee table. Occasionally they were on the floor of a larger living room up on Telegraph Hill; ostensibly a gathering of "Socialists," it was usually, in fact, a core of very serious people surrounded by the curious, the skeptical, and the needy: a woman émigré from Eastern Europe, a professor from Berkeley with a Vandyke beard, a little round man who owned a bookstore on O'Farrell Street, a writer who was working temporarily for a Jewish newspaper, a bald-headed Irishman who had some office with the Longshoreman's Union. The conversations, even the announcements, were all very earnest, very hushed and conspiratorial. Steinbeck, who had heard it all before, sat in a corner drinking his wine out of a jelly glass and watching the people, mumbling an aside every now and then to Carol, until he couldn't stand it any more. Muttering under his breath, he would grab Carol by the arm and move, stumbling over legs and bodies, though the semi-darkness toward the door.

By mid-December he had made a decision. Despite his resolution he still had not been able to get any writing done. Kate, anxious about his despair, had first offered to support him somehow, and then, when he turned her down, had sent him money. He had decided to quit his job, move into the beach house in Pacific Grove, and write until the money ran out. He wrote to Kate:

> Your letter came tonight. I am sitting in the lobby of the Trinidad Hotel on Broadway, doing my corresponding. You see I have a fire place at home, but nothing to put in it. And the nights are very bitter. . . . It is warm in here. . . .
> This is Monday—on Saturday I shall go home for Christmas. And immediately afterward I shall go to P.G. and start writing. I have $30 left of the $50 you sent. Perhaps I can stretch it over a month. Perhaps—I arrived at this decision last Friday. I haven't the least idea what I shall do when the 30 runs out for there are no jobs in P.G. But the moment I had decided, everything changed, and since then I have hardly been able to keep from throwing the bales through the roof. I shall write and write and write. . . .
> Good Lord! I'm excited. I think I shall really write an awfully good book one day. Isn't the change remarkable. I'm going to bust, for I can breathe in the old garden in the rockeries and pull up the weeds and walk by the ocean. And I can have time and time and time.
> I shall start two books. Not the Saints—to hell with the Saints. I'm going to dive into the Green Lady for day work and the Woolworth Jewelry for night life. [12/28]

He quit work, "purchased" Carol's Buick from her for a few dollars, and moved to Pacific Grove. During Christmas with his parents he found out that his father had decided not only to let him have the vacation house on 11th street in Pacific Grove rent-free, but that he had decided to loan him $25 a month to live on while he pursued his writing. It would be sort of an advance against future royalties. On New Year's Eve, John took Toby with him to San Francisco to Carol's apartment. Toby got very drunk and ordered Carol not to marry John because, he said, "You are not as important as his work." Carol was hurt because Toby didn't realize that she had as much interest in John's writing as he did.

For two months John worked very hard on "The Green Lady." There were inspired periods when he worked night and day, nearly without sleep. At the end of January, Carol came down and stayed with him for a couple of days, and he reported to Kate that they "caught crabs for salad and played tennis and broiled chops over coals in the yard." His parents did not know that he had been living with Carol off and on in San Francisco or that they were sleeping together on occasion in the Pacific Grove house whenever Carol could get off work to visit. One day, while the two of them were in bed, John's parents arrived suddenly. Getting no response when they knocked on the door, they began pounding on it, calling out John's name, and peeking in and tapping on all the windows. With hearts pounding, John got dressed while Carol slipped into the adjoining garage with her clothes. Then, pretending to have passed out from too much whiskey, John let his parents in the door.

When Kate wrote to ask if he thought he might marry Carol, he replied that he didn't think so. He wouldn't make her happy.

> That woman is fairly lucky who has me for a lover but I would curse no woman with me for a husband. She satisfies me in many ways for she is lovely and clever and passionate, but wives—well, I do not much want wives. I would anger a wife and then become angry because she was angry. You see, dear, the mountains did things to me. The long hermitage put an uncontrollable irritability very near the surface. I am pettish and small, and sullen. The mountains are not supposed to do this but they did. And when I am working, I know that I am unbearable. So I guess marriage is not for me. [2/29]

Early March brought an early spring, and an embarrassment of time caused him to relax. In words that forecast theme and subject in later writing, he reported: "My garden is wonderful. It's very wild you know and full of weeds and the flowers bloom among the weeds. I detest formal gardens. There are three big cats that hunt gophers in my garden every morning, big wild tom cats. They are pretty much untameable." He watched his garden, walked the beach, and soaked up the rare sun of Pacific Grove. He lost the momentum of his work. Once again, despite his trip with Toby to Mendocino to look at the novel's setting, the complications of plotting "The Green Lady" overwhelmed him.

In March he wrote to Bob Cathcart, who was in Palo Alto:

Many excuses for having failed to answer your letter. None of the excuses are worth a damn, but I offer them for what they *are* worth i.e. weather which is nize, flowers which are about to do exciting things, the weighty laziness of spring time so often adequately extolled by poets, the ocean which maketh a beat on the rocks, the tiny denizens of rocks and holes, cranies and tide pools which carry with them an amusing quality together with their shells. All rather deistic excuses, you see. I draw no moralistic, pious or philosophic conclusions from nature, I just like it when it is like this. It satisfies me. . . .

Like a great number of young writers (me for instance) you are very much, almost too much interested in paradox, aren't you? When analysed, paradox holds water with difficulty as a theme literatesque, and yet the bulk of modern writing grabs it and will not let it go. It has the same hold on modern writing that coincidence did on that of the period just finished. Eventually you will come to the conclusion that there is no such thing as paradox just as you are convinced that there is no such thing as metaphysics, that paradox is a manner rather than an effect. It doesn't make much difference anyway. The main thing just now with all of us is to get just as many words on paper as possible and then to destroy the paper. . . .

I think you may be a good playwright in time, even a very fine one, basing this idea not on anything you have written but on the number of your enemies. Friends and well wishers mostly strangle a person, but enemies more often pull the best there is out of him. . . .

I wish you could come down pretty soon. I need busting out of this slumbrous springtime. I am just sleeping away the months, only vaguely bothered over the fact that I am not getting much work done. Let me hear from you very soon. Don't take lessons from my behavior.

john [3/1/29]

II

In this letter to the younger writer, Steinbeck makes a revealing statement about his own writing procedures that shouldn't be overlooked: "The main thing just now with all of us is to get just as many words on paper as possible and then to destroy the paper. The unfinished and inexpert and naked writings which are being published are immoral. They show the workings of the writer too clearly. There was a time when a man did not publish until he could conceal his practicing." Throughout his career, Steinbeck did much to "conceal his practicing." Indeed, one might go so far as to say that he seemed to plan very deliberately what unpublished material would survive and what would not. Those manuscripts and drafts he wanted to survive he gave to friends (who would surely preserve them as gifts), and those he did not, he carefully destroyed. He was not, as are some writers, an accumulator. He occasionally held on to a manuscript for several years until it was eventually published (and in a few instances he let items that he would have destroyed get away from him), but if he realized that something was, after all, not worthy of publication, he burned it. When he died, he left no filing cabinet or trunk of unpublished material, no drafts, outlines, or story fragments—only the unfinished King Arthur manuscript, which he could not give up. It is important to realize that what we have of his unpublished or preliminary work is largely what he intended us to have.

At first glance, the surviving manuscript drafts and typescripts give the impression that he did very little revision, that he wrote out a manuscript in longhand, which, with only a few minor changes, was typed and then published. In truth, he did a great deal of rewriting and revision throughout his working life—nearly every book was written with a good deal more anguish than one might think. Even *Journal of a Novel,* which purports to be a record of the writing of *East of Eden,* is misleading. It is, in fact, a semipublic rather than private journal that seldom discusses writing techniques or problems very specifically and that only dimly suggests the terrible struggle he had with the novel and the extensive revisions he was forced to make.

He clearly did not want a record of his revisions, his "practicings," to remain after him, to be analyzed, compared, and classified. This concern, which was adopted long before he had any reason to believe that anyone would want to analyze his writing processes, was not an expression of ego so much as it was a part of his creed of professionalism. Later, as he sensed that his work might well become the object of intense scrutiny, part of his motive for concealing the progress of his books was no doubt a desire to preserve the magic of the final effect. Like Hemingway, Steinbeck often spoke in his letters and journals of secret narrative strategies, and also like Hemingway, who talked about his fiction in terms of an iceberg—only one-eighth of which shows above the surface—Steinbeck became convinced that there was a good deal more to his fiction than critics would ever be able to perceive in his lifetime or in the short term thereafter.

He held the familiar theory that the full depth of his work might be *felt* by the sensitive, ordinary reader, but that the critic, working primarily by intellectual analysis, would tend to miss the full dimensions of it. He hoped that the sense of life—which he always thought of in universal terms (just as he usually thought of his novels as having a very broad application to the world as a whole)—would transcend the words, just as the effect would transcend the magician's apparatus. And this magician had no intention of being caught with any cards up his sleeve.

"The Green Lady" is one of the very few preliminary manuscripts that we have, but circumstances strongly indicate that is by no means a first draft. It is much too polished, for one thing, and for another, it tells a somewhat different story from the one that finally emerges in *To a God Unknown*. He had been working on "The Green Lady" for the greater part of a year, starting in the spring of 1928. A year later, he wrote to Bob Cathcart:

> My own abortion of which I am already bitterly ashamed [*Cup of Gold*], because I am still growing rapidly, will not be out until the Fall list. Anyway it is going to have a nice dust cover. The Lady is growing very slowly and in some ways satisfactorily. But it is an awfully hard job and I have acquired a desire to hurry up from some undesirable place. It is a grand story but I am not afraid of it now as I was a month ago. It has people in it and that is always a dangerous innovation to try to include in a novel.

After about nine months of work he had 107 pages of finished manuscript, whereas the following year, from late spring 1929 to early summer of 1930, he would have produced more than 500 pages. The discrepancy suggests that he was doing a great deal of practicing during this period and that, as he claims, he was indeed "still growing rapidly."

The quality of prose in "The Green Lady" suggests further that a major preoccupation during these months of getting words on paper and then destroying the paper was a honing of his style. His prose had not yet achieved the leanness or clarity so remarkable in such works as *The Red Pony* and *Of Mice and Men*, but it was a cleaner, more precise prose, nevertheless, and his lyrical excesses—which had no doubt contributed to the shame he now felt for *Cup of Gold*—had been largely restrained. Despite his earlier cry of despair, in looking back over his first novel, that his disappointment would no longer allow him to "be drunken with rhythms," a "saddle and martingale" was precisely what his Pegasus required. The major problem he faced in the development of his style was to harness his impulse toward the poetic, to use it rather than letting it run away with him.

This was not a problem unique to Steinbeck, but rather one that tied him to his age. Much has been written about the colloquial as a key element in modern prose style, yet, the characteristic that appears to be most commonly shared by the most distinguished writers of prose fiction in English during the first half of this century is the essentially poetic nature of their prose. The effort to harness the poetic in the service of prose might be seen as the fundamental problem in the early development of writers as dissimilar in philosophy and technique as James Joyce, D. H. Lawrence, William Faulkner, and Ernest Hemingway.

Oddly enough, while many modern poets were seeking to give a new vitality, a more durable and harder texture to their poetry by embracing what Ezra Pound called "the prose tradition," fiction writers began turning in ever increasing numbers to stylistic devices more commonly associated with poetry. In the works of such Americans as Faulkner and Hemingway, style itself became a medium for conveying meaning—the rhythm, sound, and shape of language was being molded by novelists with as much care as a poet might shape a sonnet. The writer of fiction gave metaphorical significance to action, scene, and character; he wove language into complicated patterns of motif and imagery that subtly conveyed emotion or states of being; and he wrote with an elliptical style traditionally associated with poetry. What he didn't say might convey as much as what he did.

Steinbeck's basic difficulty in carving out a style of his own to fit the age may have been that he loved words too much for themselves. He collected, treasured, and caressed them. As his subject changed, moving from the past to the present, the challenge to his style became more and more intense: the music he treasured had to be composed with more subtlety, had to be made more organic. After *Cup of Gold* he had to move from the old poetry to the new, to a music less decorative and more functional. That he was successful eventually in composing a more subdued lyric is confirmed by the number of readers who have mistakenly classified Steinbeck's style as similar to Hemingway's. The two styles are quite different, but though both are poetic, Steinbeck's, no matter how lean and hard it may occasionally become, always sings.

For Steinbeck, one of the most important ingredients in writing was sound. It was the main reason he insisted on reading his work aloud—he wanted to hear what he had written. His concern with sound had a very wide range, from the accumulative impact of sounds in sections that developed into a pattern for the entire work, to the musicality of individual words as they created sequences within sentences. On a large scale, he wanted to create overall musical impressions that would carry out or reinforce the dramatic sequence, setting, or theme. Early in his career he was interested in trying to imitate the structure and movement of specific musical compositions, as well as more generally trying to imitate certain musical forms. At various times while working on *Cup of Gold*, he would listen to Dvorak's Symphony No. 5, "From the New World," using it both as inspiration (he felt the emotional tenor of his novel should be similar to that of the symphony) and as a pattern for structural development.

Steinbeck's own musical education was both formal and informal. In his adolescence, he took piano lessons, along with his sister, Mary, from Edith Brunoni in Salinas, who remembers that while he was willing to learn and practice every classical piece that she gave him, he also wanted a popular piece to learn at the same time. While he never went very far with his piano study, he did seem to enjoy it more than most children who are forced over that particular cultural hurdle. From his piano study he learned to read music and gained some musical vocabulary. He added to that vocabulary and acquired a knowledge of the history of music through reading when he was older.

The title of a novelette written during 1930 and 1931, "Dissonant Symphony," suggests that his interest in using musical forms as patterns for writing prose continued, at least for a time. After this manuscript failed to find a publisher, it was destroyed, but one could speculate that the theme—the diverse personalities of a single individual as seen through the eyes of his family and friends—might well have been carried out in a contrapuntal arrangement of the various points of view. The intricate patterning of a novel such as *Cannery Row* (as well as his use in this novel of music as a major metaphor) suggests that this interest in musical forms may have continued until late in his career, although the subject comes up again only rarely in letters or conversation.

Sometime before the summer of 1929, Steinbeck abandoned "The Green Lady" and began a second version of the same story, which he eventually called "To an Unknown God." He wrote to Kate, "The Green Lady has had a renaissance. I have started over again with a bang and am filled with the old enthusiasm. I think it will be quite a decent book—different from anything I have ever done. Summer is coming here."

During the summer Dook saw Steinbeck frequently and for periods

of two or three days at a time. As Steinbeck worked on the new manuscript, he not only read portions of it aloud to Dook, but went over
troublesome passages with him, so that Sheffield was able to witness
first-hand Steinbeck's writing and revision processes. Steinbeck trusted
Dook's judgment in literary matters—the only other people during the
first half of his career whose opinions of his writing he came to trust as
much were Carol and Ed Ricketts. All three had this in common: they
told him exactly what they thought, good or bad. He might get moody
and nasty if he didn't get praise, but if you always praised him, you lost
his trust.

As Steinbeck worked over this particular manuscript, Dook was surprised to see what care he took in going back over his work to review
the phrasing, the rhythm, and the sound of each sentence. He would
sound out the vowel sounds of a sentence to isolate the effect, making
changes where necessary, and then he would review alliteration in the
same way. In all of this he seemed anxious to check himself against excess, to make sure that the song in his head that had inspired the flow of
his writing had not carried him away.

One of the problems with his style that he was becoming more aware
of was the degree to which it was influenced by other writers. Steinbeck had been a great reader, but one who was wide-ranging and uncritical in his choice of material, and unfortunately, his ear had
absorbed sounds and rhythms both good and bad.

Aware at last of the deleterious effect on his prose of Donn Byrne
and James Branch Cabell, he determined to avoid conscious imitation
of them. They were not equally bad, but the wordiness that each manifested in his own way made them both equally bad for Steinbeck. Still
working on "To an Unknown God," he wrote to Grove Day at the end
of 1929:

> I have not the slightest desire to step into Donn Byrne's shoes. I
> may not have his ability with the vernacular but I have twice his
> head. I think I have swept all the Cabellyo-Byrneish preciousness
> out for good. The new book is a straightforward and simple at-
> tempt to set down some characters in a situation and nothing else.
> If there is any beauty in it, it is a beauty of idea. I seem to have
> outgrown Cabell. The new method is far the more difficult of the
> two. It reduces a single idea to a single sentence and does not allow
> one to write a whole chapter with it as Cabell does. [12/5/29]

And he included this note at the end of his letter:

I am engaged to a girl of whom I will say nothing at all because you will eventually meet her and I think you will like her because she has a mind as sharp and penetrating as your own.

The girl with the sharp and penetrating mind was, of course, Carol, who had detected the influences on *Cup of Gold* just as Grove Day had perceived them, and who urged Steinbeck to abandon what she scornfully termed "Irish blarney." That Steinbeck turned so strongly against this kind of writing was no doubt due in part to her influence—not only was she very bright, she was also "sharp" in the sense that she had a talent for poking holes in anything pretentious or over-inflated.

His statement that if there is any beauty in "To an Unknown God" it is "a beauty of idea" is misleading. He was still enamored of sound as he spells out quite clearly in another letter to Grove Day written only a couple of weeks after the first one:

I want to speak particularly of your theory of clean manuscripts, and spelling as correct as a collegiate stenographer, and every nasty little comma in its place and preening of itself. "Manners," you say it is, and knowing the "trade" and the "Printed Word." But I have no interest in the printed word. I would continue to write if there were no writing and no print. I put my words down for a matter of memory. They are more made to be spoken than to be read. I have the instincts of a minstrel rather than those of a scrivener. There you have it. We are not of the same trade at all and so how can your rules fit me? When my sounds are all in place, I can send them to a stenographer who knows *his* trade and he can slip the commas about until they sit comfortably and he can spell the words so that school teachers will not raise their eyebrows when they read them. Why should I bother? There are millions of people who are good stenographers but there aren't so many thousands who can make as nice sounds as I can.

I must have misinformed you about my new book. I never never read Hemingway with the exception of The Killers. I have not lost the love for sound nor for pictures. Only I have tried to throw out the words that do not say anything. I don't read much when I am working because novels have a way of going right on whether you are writing or not. You'll be having dreams about it that wake you up in the night, and maybe you'll be kissing some girl the way she expects it, and all the time your mind will be saying, "I'll do the thing this way, and I'll transpose these scenes." A novel doesn't stop at all when your pen is away.

Steinbeck's adamant protest here about the possible influence of Hemingway is interesting because it comes so early. Steinbeck's announcement of a new, more controlled approach to his writing apparently led Grove Day to think almost immediately of Hemingway. As Steinbeck's style evolved during the early and middle thirties, becoming more restrained, this comparison would be made more and more frequently. That Steinbeck should sense this comparison, resent it, and try to fend it off—before he had any reputation at all and while Hemingway was still becoming famous (he had in the fall of 1929 just published *A Farewell to Arms*)—is a bit surprising. It suggests that Steinbeck, in reading Hemingway for the first time in 1929, realized that what this author was doing in his prose was very close to what Steinbeck was working toward—as if another writer had preempted his own future, and that his growth would inevitably lead him into the trap of being thought of as some kind of disciple. The sadness of this realization at this particular time lay in the fact that he had managed to shed his early models and was just now working hard toward establishing his own voice.

Carol recalls the encounter. Steinbeck had vaguely heard of Ernest Hemingway—Hemingway was at that stage of his career where he was being discovered; literary people around the country were talking about him; reader recommended him to reader. Someone—perhaps Carol herself—had recommended that Steinbeck read Hemingway's short stories because they were really very good. Steinbeck read "The Killers." When he was through, he was stunned. He told Carol that this "was the finest writer alive" and declared that he would never read him again. He protected himself with this declaration all during the 1930s. Perhaps as the result of having securely established his own reputation with the publication of *The Grapes of Wrath*, he felt free later in life to break his resolution. He eventually did read more of Hemingway's work and admired it, but then that admiration, openly expressed, led to the terrible scene when the two authors met, for the only time, late in their careers.

III

At the beginning of 1930, *Cup of Gold* found a publisher—Robert M. McBride & Company, the same outfit that several years before had Steinbeck thrown out of their offices. Ted Miller liked the manuscript very much himself, and he found that nearly every publisher he brought the manuscript to was intrigued with it. In his letter notifying

Steinbeck of the acceptance, Miller reported that McBride & Company had expressed enthusiasm for the project. "They have taken the fatal leap without any reservations, and with the idea of making an all-fired success of it, instead of merely accepting it as just over the 'publishable' line." Furthermore, holding out the bait of an illustrated first edition by Mahlon Blaine, they hoped to land a book-club contract. In any event, Blaine would do the dust jacket, and McBride promised publication by early fall. Best of all, Steinbeck was promised a payment of royalties on the pre-publication sale, a payment that might be as much as $400. All of this sounded very good—particularly the arrangements with Blaine, who had agreed to do the dust jacket as a gesture of friendship. Steinbeck began to generate once again some enthusiasm of his own for the publication of the book.

After spending the spring in Pacific Grove, seeing Carol only occasionally, Steinbeck worked out a new plan for the summer. Dook and his wife had taken a house in Palo Alto while he once again took up his M.A. degree studies at Stanford. John arranged with Dook for him and Carol to meet at the Sheffields' on the weekends, John driving up from Pacific Grove and Carol coming down on the train from the city. It was not exactly a "love nest"—John was always first a writer and second a lover, and if he could combine the two, so much the better. These were the weekends during which John worked over his manuscript in progress with Dook, and Carol was drafted to service on Dook's typewriter.

In August Carol had some vacation time coming so she and John decided to go camping together. They took the Buick and started up Highway 1 on the coast looking for a place in the redwoods, and found a campground near La Honda in the hills southwest of Palo Alto, about eight miles from the ocean. In a wooded area near a creek, their accommodations included a one-room cabin, an outdoor fire pit, and a tent platform (without a tent during the summer) with cots—they slept outdoors on the cots.

In the mornings John wrote and Carol relaxed and read. In the afternoons they took walks, or they went swimming in the nude—when visitors arrived, they would have to rush to get dressed in order to become respectable.

And they did have visitors. Mary Ardath, the *Greenwich Village Follies* chorus girl who had left John to marry a banker, showed up at camp with her little girl, looking for John, and Dook and his wife came over from Palo Alto to spend a weekend with them. Dook recalls that

John was writing. It was there that he would start out in the morning wearing nothing but a pair of jeans and some shoes, and he found a redwood stump that served just fine for a desk. He would go silently and then come back with his eyes just dancing, all happy, and say, "I did 3,000 words."

Dook remembers also that a bit later, when Steinbeck was living with Carl Wilhelmson in San Francisco and would say something like that, Carl would say, "But what kind of words?"

Although Steinbeck protested in his letter to Grove Day that he was not a scrivener, he looked very much like a scrivener in very peculiar circumstances. He had, when he was younger, taken to writing in the blank pages of his father's old account books; now he purchased new ledgers for his writing. There he was, in the midst of a grove of trees on a hillside, with his straight pen, pen points, bottle of ink, and ledger, sitting cross-legged at a stump with the dew still wet on the wild grasses around him, writing about a man in love with a forest. He dipped his pen into the ink and then formed the words with the small, neat handwriting more characteristic of a cloistered accountant than a brawny outdoorsman. He wrote with the spirit of a fine cabinetmaker or woodcarver. And if he walked back into camp, his face beaming and his ledger held on high, it was to celebrate the product of careful craftsmanship that had turned out well.

On the first morning after the Sheffields' arrival, the camp was awakened by a strange noise, a "beee, beee, beee . . ." descending the scale. After dressing and scouting around for the source, they discovered that some Italians who were having a picnic across the creek had caught some crayfish, and the noise came from the crayfish as they sank into a big bucket of boiling water. That gave him an idea. That afternoon, as Dook recalls,

> we went out and caught us some crayfish and got us some miner's lettuce and made ourselves a fine salad. John and Carol had managed to pick up, for twenty-five cents, a burlap sack full of slightly mature corn. So they had that, and beans and bacon squares. [Bacon squares were from the back bacon, and at times you could get it for two pounds for a quarter.]

There was pleasure in doing as much as possible with very little. These were times to look back on.

At the end of their weeks at La Honda together, John and Carol found themselves in limbo. The Sheffields would be leaving for southern California, and John and Carol would no longer have their rented house in Palo Alto to use as a meeting place on weekends. John had become weary of Pacific Grove. Dook urged them to come to Eagle Rock; he and Maryon could put them up as long as necessary before they found a place of their own. This would mean, of course, that Carol would have to quit her job, and under the circumstances, that was something she was reluctant to do. She realized that some firm course of action had to be set: she didn't actually propose to John, but she did tell him that he would have to make a decision. He decided in favor of marriage and they became engaged.

Carol would stay at her job until Christmas, so as to save up as much money as possible. After a week or two, John would move to San Francisco and stay with Carl Wilhelmson; then after the first of the year, they would move to Eagle Rock. They decided they would be married in southern California—neither of them could stand the thought of a large family wedding.

In late September John moved in with Carl, who had a little apartment on Fillmore Street, not very far from where Carol was sharing an apartment with her sister. (He used Carol's apartment as his mailing address, and Carl recalled that he spent as much time at Carol's as he did on Fillmore Street.) As much as John liked Carl, he still found it difficult to live with him. Carl had a habit of dinging his typewriter bell while he was sitting at his desk thinking; it drove John crazy. Then, too, Carl had dark moods of depression just as John did, and neither was capable of cheering the other when hard times came. In addition to Carl's restlessness and moodiness, his fondness for eating fish upset John. In fact, the presence of fish became a Wilhelmson trademark—the apartment smelled terrible. Once, when Steinbeck couldn't stand the smell any longer, he began searching desperately for the source and finally found on a windowsill an open can of sardines that had apparently been there for weeks.

While John and Carl were living together, John brought Carl over to Carol and Idell's for a visit. John decided to use Carl's infamous habit as a calling card. When the women returned to their apartment after work, they discovered that every one of the spikes on the wrought-iron fence around their building had been decorated with a herring. As for Carl, he took John's displays of temperament with a grain of salt. "Oh, that John," he'd say and shrug his shoulders. He thought John to be rather unpredictable and strange.

Steinbeck wrote to Grove Day in October about his situation and activities:

At present Carl Wilhelmson and I live in the upper story of an old house here in S.F. It is a good life and very cheap. Like a squad of fleas, ferocious and very serious, we still make forays and dignified campaigns against the body of art. It is funny and a little sad (to the onlooker) and lots of fun (for us). We take our efforts to write with great seriousness, hammering away for two years on a novel and such things. I suppose in this respect we have changed less than any one you knew in Stanford. It is funny too. We have taken the ordinary number of beatings and I don't think there is much strength in either of us, and still we go on butting our heads against the English Novel and nursing our bruises as though they were the wounds of honorable war. I don't know one bit more about spelling and punctuation than I ever did, but I think I am learning a little bit about writing. The Morgan atrocity pays enough for me to live quietly and with a good deal of comfort. In that far it was worth selling. I have a novel about finished and Carl has finished two and is about a third through his third. It is an awful lot of work to write a novel. You know that because you have done it. I have been working on the present one nearly a year and have not completed it. The final draft will not be done before April I'm afraid. We don't do much else nor think much else.

The "Morgan atrocity" had been published in August, but the publisher neglected to send even one copy to Steinbeck, and he got his first glimpse of it on the shelf of the book section in a department store in San Francisco. He was immediately disappointed by the dust cover designed by Blaine, and he complained of its garishness to Ted Miller. He told Dook that the picture, which colorfully depicted a pirate in full dress, was more appropriate for a boys' adventure story than a serious work of art. In succeeding weeks he complained also about the way the book was being handled—it appeared to him that advertisements for it and reviews were non-existent. He wrote to Kate Beswick;

The reason there have been no reviews is that no review copies were issued. I did not even get a copy for my folks. Naturally I could not afford to buy it. I know nothing about publishing but what little I know about psychology would indicate that they did practically everything wrong. There are orders placed two months ago that are unfilled. All of the department stores seem to have it but none of the book stores. I suppose it didn't merit pushing, but I should have thought the business instinct would have prompted them to put it on publishing lists, a thing they neglected. . . . The jacket would have been swell without those ghastly colors—in dark brown or lighter brown it would have been effective.

As it turned out, the book sold fairly well—more than his next two books would sell combined. A good number of the 1,500 copies printed were sold during the Christmas season (during which time Steinbeck went periodically into bookstores and department stores to see how the book was doing and was gratified to find that every store sold out its stock). The dust jacket that Steinbeck objected to was probably responsible for the book selling so well as a Christmas gift. One has to wonder how many little boys were lost in the swamp of Steinbeck's prose as they tried to follow Henry Morgan's trek across Panama.

Once Carol and John's engagement became known, Steinbeck's parents came up on the train every two or three weeks for a "family get-together." They would take John and Carol out to a good dinner and then to a show or concert. Despite the fact that there was some strain during these outings—both John and Carol felt compelled to don a mantle of respectability—they were welcome opportunities to sample some of the life the engaged couple could not afford. Both Steinbeck's parents had aged; his father thinner and quieter and his mother a bit heavier, and, if possible, even more assertive. Assertive herself, it was very difficult for Carol to be subdued for very long, and one of the things that had motivated Carol and John to begin their married life in southern California was a feeling that they needed to get away from their families in order to be themselves.

As far as Steinbeck's friends were concerned, he had found what was for him the nearly perfect mate. No one could visualize him married to the stereotype of the "pretty young thing," empty-headed and passive. Carol was attractive, but intelligent and very independent. Like Steinbeck she had a great sense of fun, quickly saw the absurdities of any situation, and was inclined toward a very healthy skepticism. In a letter to Grove Day written only a couple of weeks before their marriage, Steinbeck wrote: "I'd like you to know Carol. She doesn't write or dance or play the piano and she has very little of any soul at all. But horses like her and dogs and little boys and boot blacks and laborers. But people with souls don't like her very much." If this description is reminiscent of Steinbeck's later, well-known description of Ed Ricketts, it is because in both instances he said the best things he could think of to say about someone.

John and Carol were quite different, but since their differences complemented each other, they developed a symbiotic relationship of sorts. Whereas John was shy and mumbled, Carol was outspoken and aggressive; whereas John tended to be sentimental, Carol could be hard-nosed and sarcastic; and whereas John tended to be self-involved, Carol had a very strongly developed social conscience. When John's spirit was cast down, Carol, who was usually up, tried her best to raise his mood. In certain things, however, they were very much alike—in their iconoclasm, their stubbornness, their humor, and their independence. While they fit together very well, they also fought together beautifully. On a visit to San Francisco that fall, Ted Miller was with them as they stood waiting for a bus on a street corner. John was seething, irritated with Carol beyond measure:

John: "I can't hit a woman in a public place."
Carol: "I have no public place."

PART THREE

Poverty
and Success

CHAPTER X

It was a bright, cold day at the end of December when John and Carol headed south along El Camino Real in the Buick, the back seat and trunk filled with boxes and layers of Carol's clothing. Last-minute packing and delays had made John grumpy, and he grunted monosyllabic answers first to Carol's rambling speculations about the future and then to her angry offers to call the whole thing off. The future did lie somewhat dimly before them. Steinbeck's feelings about marriage were, as he admitted later, somewhat "tentative." Their finances were, to say the least, shaky.

Steinbeck's father had promised them a small monthly income of fifty dollars until they got established. Carol hoped that she would not have to get a job, at least not right away. She had developed plans with some friends of John's from Pacific Grove, Tal and Ritch Lovejoy, to start a home manufacturing outfit that would make three-dimensional portraits and department-store dummies out of plastic. It was a wild scheme that had evolved during wine-stimulated discussions inspired by Ritch Lovejoy's enthusiastic discovery of a plastic casting process that had just come on the market. John and Carol looked forward to finding a place of their own, planning to stay only temporarily with the Sheffields, but where that place would be or whether they could even afford to pay rent was another part of their uncertainty. The stock market had crashed, and the worst of economic times was under way. But like so many others at the end of 1929, they were so filled with their own plans and problems that they had almost no realization of what was happening to the country.

Perhaps as a warning of things to come, they had driven only a little way beyond Palo Alto when the Buick began to make peculiar noises. John nursed it into San Jose and stopped at Carol's parents' home, where John determined that the car's condition was terminal. He was able to sell it for junk and went out looking for a replacement. He

was proud of his knowledge of old used cars and thought himself a
pretty good backyard mechanic, but pride doth often lead us into
temptation, and a custom-made Marmon, purportedly driven at one
time by Barney Oldfield, captured both his imagination and a good part
of his cash reserve.

It was a very high-class automobile, a five-passenger touring car with
a solid aluminum head and a slightly worn, but still luxurious interior.
The Marmon made it to Los Angeles, and for a month gave style to
their lives. Then the differential gave way, and Steinbeck and Sheffield
spent days canvassing the junkyards of Los Angeles County, the
junkyard capital of the world, trying to find a used but serviceable ring
gear. It took John nearly two weeks to install the gear, and he apparently did not do so properly, for after only twenty or thirty miles of
driving the differential failed again. Discouraged and certain that there
was not another ring gear in southern California, John sold the Marmon
and bought a dilapidated '22 Chevrolet, which, because of the resemblance, they began calling "the bathtub."

There is no large moral to this tale of pride, but it does point once
again to Steinbeck's fondness for, and familiarity with, things mechanical. To really learn about cars, inside and out, you have to be too poor
to afford a mechanic, and Steinbeck was poor for a very long time. Poverty on the road also teaches you about hitchhiking and hitchhikers, the
efficacy of prayer, and the kinds of people—always poor—who will
stop and help when you are broken down. While he wasn't always expert, he did know what the inside of a carburetor looks like. This kind
of knowledge and experience, largely ignored by those who have
viewed Steinbeck only in literary terms, has been part of the conduit of
sympathy that Steinbeck has established with his readers. He gives a
great deal of attention to small things which have meaning for ordinary
people, and it was such small things that provided much of the foundation for the success of a novel such as *The Grapes of Wrath*.

Starting a few days before John and Carol arrived and continuing for
more than two months afterward, the Sheffield household was in almost continual uproar. As one measure of the chaos, we might start
with the arrival of Tal Lovejoy's sister, Nadja, the first of the "Steinbeck contingent" to arrive, a lovely girl whom the Sheffields didn't
know and weren't expecting.

Out of the blue the Sheffields got a telegram, "Arriving six p.m. S.P.
please meet," and signed "Nadja." They didn't know what it meant,
but they thought they'd better go downtown to the Southern Pacific
station and meet whoever it was who was arriving. From the name,

they decided to search for a Russian-looking woman who appeared to be lost. They met the train, but were unable to spot anyone who matched their mental picture. Back at home, they found the door double-locked, and a strange woman behind the door wouldn't let them in and violently motioned them to go away. After many gestures and shouted explanations, the Sheffields finally made their way into their own house; Nadja had gotten a ride from a fellow passenger and had moved in, thinking it was the Lovejoys' house.

Next to arrive were the Lovejoys. After John and Carol were married and during those times that they lived in the same vicinity as the Lovejoys, the two couples were in each other's company continually. John had met them earlier in the year as a result of having renewed his acquaintance with Jack Calvin, a writer from Stanford who now lived in Carmel. Calvin was a writer of children's stories, a photographer and illustrator. He had married Sasha Kashevaroff, one of six daughters born to a Russian Orthodox Bishop in Juneau, Alaska. Ritchie Lovejoy, a former student of Calvin's, came to Carmel to visit his old teacher, met Natalya Kashevaroff, and eventually became Calvin's brother-in-law.

Although Calvin and Steinbeck did not care much for each other (which was awkward, since not only was Calvin Lovejoy's brother-in-law, but he was also a good friend of Ed Ricketts), Lovejoy and Steinbeck got on well very quickly. Lovejoy had that sense of humor, that creative sense of fun (as did his wife, Tal) which seemed to be one of the most attractive qualities in a person for Steinbeck—most of his close friends over the years had it. Once, for example, when the two couples were staying together and it was Ritchie's turn to do the dinner dishes, he put off doing them, stacking them dirty in the sink and leaving them until morning. The next morning he had disappeared when the others came into the kitchen to make coffee. The dishes in the sink were covered with ants. Lovejoy had left a professionally lettered sign nearby: MEN AT WORK.

Lovejoy was younger than Steinbeck and was an aspiring writer, illustrator, and cartoonist. Clever and enthusiastic, he was a man whom most people liked almost immediately. Part of his relationship with Steinbeck was no doubt built on the admiration of the younger man for the older, and later, when the relationship began to turn sour, it was probably due in part to jealousy of Steinbeck's growing success. Multi-talented, Lovejoy never had enough talent or drive in any single direction to get very far.

With the arrival of John and Carol, the Sheffields' one-bedroom house had nearly reached capacity, with guests sleeping on the porch and in the living room. Other less permanent visitors arrived, slept on cushions on the floor wherever there was room, and departed, adding further to the confusion. Sheffield, who made his own beer, found that his brewing capacity was strained to the limit and had to start rationing the household to two gallons a day. During the day, there was sunbathing in the nude in a "pavilion" of canvas screens set up in the backyard; in the evening, rambunctious games and endless discussions; and at night, a steady procession to the bathroom, punctuated by the grunts of those tripped over or the cries of cats stepped on.

Steinbeck wrote to Ted Miller:

> Received your letter this morning and hasten to express regrets for situations. . . . In this community we make beer, much beer, and it is both cheap and pleasant to induce a state of lassitude intershot with moments of unreal romance. I have only in the last two weeks been wooing that state. Before that some foolish asceticism kept me at the pad and pen. Which would seem to prove that I am quite unintelligent and have all the racial ambitions and fetishes which deal with ambitions. Anyway the beer is here and the rooming here and the sun is here and if things get too tough you can soon become a lotophagus along with the rest of us. [1/30]

The occasion for this gathering of talent was nearly forgotten for a time. A most important order of business was the selection of a name for the new company. The final choice suggests the Lovejoy-Sheffield-Steinbeck brand of humor: The Faster Master Plaster Casters. The "corporate" table of organization was equally elaborate: John didn't want anything to do with it; Dook didn't want anything to do with it either, but ended up supplying much of the funding; Lovejoy was the head technician, his wife, Carol, Nadja, and Maryon supplied technical assistance and unwanted technical advice; Mahlon Blaine, who had come West to work in Hollywood, was appointed art director; and a friend and former student of Dook's, Archie Strayer, was given the job of business manager.

They spent quite a bit of money and had, as Sheffield tells it, "all sorts of fine ideas." Unfortunately, very few worked. First, the plastic raw material, priced to sell to hobbyists, was extremely expensive. (The plastic was applied to the subject over a protective cream. After it set, it was removed and became the mold, which was then filled with the plaster.) They found that they were using huge amounts of plaster as they experimented, trying to refine the process by practicing on each other. They also found that the plaster sometimes shrank, and that the plastic mold was too flimsy to hold the plaster and thus they needed to design a way of bracing it. The most perplexing problem, one that they hadn't counted on at all, was that the busts were too realistic. A photograph can be made flattering by lighting and retouching, but a three-dimensional portrait taken directly from life was uncompromisingly accurate. No amount of clever painting by Blaine seemed to ameliorate the shock.

Their business manager, with their money, got himself an apartment and was given an expense account—as a matter of fact, as Dook recalls, he got himself a lot of things—but no business. Stores simply weren't interested. Then they got the idea that Hollywood stars, being notably vain, might want such a portrait. The trouble was that no one, certainly not the business manager, knew any Hollywood stars. Finally, somehow, Lovejoy was able to find an aspiring starlet, and she came over with her boyfriend. While the technical aspects of the portrait-making went without a hitch, the bust was so unflattering that the couple walked out without paying. This was probably the high-water mark of the enterprise.

While all of this was going on, John and Carol had taken out a marriage license. They were reluctant to go any further, postponing the wedding several times, until Dook's wife took it upon herself to make definite arrangements. On January 14, a little more than two weeks after they arrived in Eagle Rock, they were hauled by the Sheffields to the courthouse in Glendale, where they were married by a judge in his chambers. Dook recalls that they didn't even make it back to the house before, as a result of the strain and the shock, they were sniping at each other again.

John and Carol had been looking around for a place of their own to live in. Dook lived on a hillside on the edge of Eagle Rock in a section that was sparsely settled, but the Steinbecks did discover a rundown shack not too far away and were able to make arrangements to rent it for fifteen dollars a month. The shack had been vacant for some time and had been badly vandalized, and it took the Steinbecks, along with occasional help from the Sheffields, nearly a month to make the place liveable. Its best feature was a large living room, and after they had cleared away the rubble, they decided to refinish the floor. They did this by getting down on their knees and sanding the planks by hand. Then John got some old crankcase oil, which they spread around as a stain and finish. But the oil just sat there on the surface, and they had to bore holes in the floor to drain it out.

To restore a house that has been badly used is difficult in any circumstances—nearly every new discovery is depressing—but to try to do it with hardly any money is an act of valor. John visited the local junkyards in order to get hardware, glass, and pipe at rock-bottom prices. His greatest achievement was replumbing the gas line and installing a used water-heater that he had rebuilt himself. The house had no furnace, but there was a fireplace and plenty of downed trees up in the hills to supply fuel. They did have some furniture, mostly Carol's, which they had shipped down from San Francisco when they left. To these few pieces they added what was absolutely essential from a used-furniture store. With a coat of barn-red paint and a flower bed in front, the transformation, according to those who witnessed it, was on the order of a minor miracle.

Regardless of the problems and disappointments, and there were many (just getting enough to eat at the end of the month was one), they had a spirit of gaiety that carried them along and made this among the happiest of times. In contrast to the chaos at Dook's, they lived rather quietly. Their worst offense against the propriety of the neighborhood was that Carol walked their dog while she was wearing a bathing suit, but the outrage did not continue very long, since the dog died after a couple of weeks. John dug a large hole in the backyard, and, in a forecast of something he used later in *The Grapes of Wrath*, he wrote a note, put it in a bottle, and buried it with the dog.

About this time he wrote to Grove Day:

Why can't you pack up and come down here to see us for a few days. We have a separate bedroom with a three quarters bed in it and there is an oriental divan in the atrium on which I receive my concubines but which could be converted into a fairly uxorious impliment if one were to conjure it with the proper state of mind. I should like you to see the Royal Tomato Chamber and the Bed Room Bean, and Bruga the North West Mounting Police Dog. I just went in and looked and the Bed Room Bean has put on a new leaf. Carol is busy preparing her Spring Poem. How well I remember her last year's Ode. It was a lovely thing beginning, "Carbon has no known solvent—" [3/30]

Somehow, through it all—the plaster-casting, the visitors and partying, the marriage, and the renovation of the house—Steinbeck had been writing. During the previous year he was rewriting "The Green Lady," and by early spring of 1930, he had finished it and started on revisions. In March he reported on his progress to Carl Wilhelmson:

I do not know how long it is since I have written to you. Every-thing has been in a haze pretty much for the past three weeks. I have been working to finish this ms and the thing took hold of me so completely that I lost track of nearly everything else. Now the thing is done. I started rewriting this week and am not going to let it rest. Also I have a title which gives me the greatest of pleasure. For my title I have taken one of the Vedic Hymns, the name of the hymn—To the Unknown God, as

TO

THE UNKNOWN GOD

You surely remember the hymn with its refrain at the end of each invocation "Who is the god to whom we shall offer sacri-fice?" Don't you think that is a good title? I am quite enthusiastic about it.

Carol is a good influence on my work. I am putting five hours every day on the rewriting of this one and in the evenings I have started another [Dissonant Symphony]. I have the time and en-ergy and it gives me pleasure to work, and now I do not seem to have to fight as much reluctance to work as I used to have. The start comes much easier. The new book is just a series of short stories or sketches loosely and foolishly tied together. There are a number of little things I have wanted to write for a long time, some of them ridiculous and some of them more serious, and so I am putting them in a ridiculous fabric. It [torn—probably reads "will not be the"] series on Salinas at all. I shall not do that yet. I am too vindictive and harsh on my own people. In a few years I may have outgrown that.

"The series on Salinas" refers to an idea he had had in the back of his mind for some time, a series of stories and sketches satirizing several of the leading citizens of Salinas. But not only did his "vindictiveness" make such a work a poor artistic proposition, his consideration for the feelings of his parents made it impossible while they were still alive. Several years after their deaths, however, he did take up the project and work on it, and as strange as it may seem, this idea was really the origin of *The Grapes of Wrath*, at least in the sense that it led to the prelimi-nary manuscript.

Near the end of his letter to Wilhelmson, he talks in more detail about his revision of "To the Unknown God" (a title which shortly af-terward changed to "To an Unknown God"):

I guess that the ending of this novel [Andy Wayne's self-immolation in his burning forest] was melodramatic but I don't care. The book required such an ending. I am cutting several things out in the new draft namely that stuff about the girl in the university. Completely uncalled for. Also all of that throw back about the childhood of Carrie will be dropped because of its leading off the interest from the main theme. I think it is a better book than I have done though that is not much to say for it. Certainly it has more effort in it than I have ever put in anything. In the draft that is finished there are three hundred and seventy pages and in the final draft there will be a few more I think even though I do cut out those parts because there are certain places that need amplifying and clarifying. [3/30]

The comments about "the girl in the university" and "the childhood of Carrie" suggest that the first half of the manuscript was essentially an expansion of the part of "The Green Lady" that he had completed before giving up on it. Most of his writing during the previous year had apparently been devoted to the second half of the novel, what might be called the "case history of Andy Wayne" after he leaves the drought-stricken Jolon area to move north to Mendocino. Here Steinbeck determined to leave out the material relating to the girl in the university (Susie, in Webster Street's short story and play), and later he would decide to leave out most of the early material still included in part one. In proceeding this way, what he was really doing was gradually eliminating his original source, Street's play, and moving more and more to a fiction that was entirely his own. The real tragedy, if we can call it that, of his five-year effort to produce this novel was his bondage to someone else's ideas, ideas that never were very clearly developed and with which Steinbeck never was able to establish compatibility.

The story of Andy Wayne, who is developed in this draft as a psychological case history, becomes the basis for the story of Joseph Wayne, who in the published novel is developed as something close to a fertility god. From the very beginning in Street's play there was some ambiguity as to whether the central character was mad or was simply displaying a rather special religious feeling for the land. And although this ambiguity persists to the end, it was apparently a major stumbling block in Steinbeck's own mind, possibly, along with problems with the setting, the main factor that kept him from finishing "The Green Lady." He felt that he must give primary emphasis to one pathology or the other. As made clear in the passage below from a letter to Ted Miller, his first choice was to emphasize insanity.

I'm twenty-eight years old now and I must have at least one book a year from now on if I can manage it. The next one will be short as can be and shouldn't take as long as the last. This one offered too many problems, not only psychological but anthropological, to be done quickly. I had to do too much research and consult too many psychiatrists and physicians and alienists. I hope the thing doesn't read like a case history in an insane asylum. My father was very funny about it or did I tell you this? He was terribly interested from the first but quite disgusted at the end. After my careful work in filling the book with hidden symptoms of paranoia and showing that the disease had such a hold as to be incurable, my father expected Andy to recover and live happily ever after. I explained to him that with the ailment gone as far as it had, he must either turn suicide or homicidal maniac but that didn't make any difference. The American people demand miracles in their literature.

His reference to having to "consult too many psychiatrists and physicians and alienists" is probably an exaggeration (he knew one psychiatrist); still, he did do a great deal of research in both theoretical and clinical psychology, and this would become part of his "clinical approach" to characterization throughout his career. Even a character such as Cathy in *East of Eden*, who would be thought of by literary critics as implausible, was carefully drawn to have psychological validity. Since man was an animal, a special kind of animal with mental and emotional characteristics, Steinbeck felt it was essential for him as a novelist to have scientific knowledge of those characteristics.

McBride had an option on his next two manuscripts as part of the contract for *Cup of Gold,* so that when he finished his revision, he would send it to Ted Miller, who would take it to the publisher. While the revised manuscript was still being typed, he wrote to Miller about his mixed feelings upon being without a manuscript under way for the first time in many months:

I have been gloating and sorrowing in my freedom. It seemed good to be without the curse of a literary foetus and at the same time I have had a feeling of lostness, much I imagine, like that felt by an old soldier when he has been discharged from the army and has no one to tell him what time to brush his teeth. Bad as novels are, they do regulate our lives and give us a responsibility. While this book was being written I felt that I was responsible for someone. If I stopped, the characters died. But now it is finished and the words of it are being put down in nice black letters on nice white paper and the words are spelled correctly and the punctuation is sitting about in proper places and most of the foolishness has been left on other sheets with blue marks through it. And I am beginning to hate it entirely because I never wrote anything in my life that was spelled correctly. I use punctuation marks to keep my hands busy while my brain is keeping up with my chirography. And, so I shall be embarking on a new piece of work very soon.

"To an Unknown God" was sent to Miller in the late spring of 1930 and was almost immediately turned down by McBride. Steinbeck, who was still very disappointed by the way that McBride had handled *Cup of Gold*, was not unhappy to see it go elsewhere, but he did begin to fret when it went elsewhere, and elsewhere, and elsewhere. Meanwhile, he began his new work. Though it is unclear as to exactly what occupied him, in his correspondence he mentions at least two different projects he was working on at the same time, a novel and a collection of interconnected short stories—and he may have been working on as many as three.

The one thing that his wife and friends remember him writing at the time was called "Dissonant Symphony," yet the recollections about the nature of "Dissonant Symphony" seem to vary and are, in turn, contradicted by some of the descriptions in the letters. Part of the confusion may be due to the possibility that the novel itself was composed of stories or segments and that there may have been several false starts, the works in progress changing as time went by. Three things about this material seem certain: it was all very experimental as far as Steinbeck was concerned; there were at least two major drafts of the novel; and while some pieces may have been salvaged in later work, none of the writing from this period was published.

If one adds the failure of "To an Unknown God" to the failure of these other manuscripts (and the failure, as Steinbeck saw it, of *Cup of Gold*), the picture during these years seems to be very bleak indeed. Fortunately, the full impact of these failures taken together did not fall on Steinbeck at any one moment. By the time he realized that "Dissonant Symphony" was a mistake, he had completed *The Pastures of Heaven*. And while *Pastures* sold poorly, at least it was published, and in the long run it turned out to be a book to be proud of. The fact is that all the years up to the publication and warm reception of *Tortilla Flat* in 1935 were difficult years artistically, but the years 1930 to 1932 seem to have been particularly difficult and certainly crucial to his development as a writer. He was in the process of reforming his style, and he was, in a sense, a writer struggling to find out what it was he wanted to say—he had no subject of his own, no clearly defined philosophy, only ideas, interests, and attitudes, which, floating here and there on the sea of his enthusiasm, were occasionally given direction by the tide of his will.

Yet, during the spring and summer of 1930, he thought his writing was going well. He was pleased to be trying new things and confident, in a fundamental way, that his work would take form, that good books would be written. During the late summer he wrote to Carl:

> I have uncovered an unbelievable store of energy in myself. The raps of the last couple of years, i.e. the failure of the Cup, and the failure of my other things to make any impression, seem to have no effect on my spirit whatever. For that reason, I have high hopes for myself. Of course, the hundred page ms. flopped heavily. Just now I am busy on another one. Eventually I shall be so good that I cannot be ignored. These years are disciplinary for me.

He had a sure knowledge that he was a writer and would continue, come hell or high water, to be a writer. He never gave the impression to anyone that he was conscious of the possibility that he might ultimately fail and would have to turn to selling insurance or painting houses in order to make a life for himself. Those around him during the worst years sensed this certainty, sensed that this was an exceptional man who was in the process of gaining some measure of greatness. It is an attitude that seems very strange when viewed in retrospect, since there was almost no concrete evidence at the time to support it.

Although his writing did not worry him, their physical circumstances began to cause the Steinbecks more and more concern. With the low rent on the house, they were just able to get by, but then they lost the house. They had been settled for only two months when the landlord, who lived out of town, came by to see what they had done to his property. Their feeling was that by fixing the place up, they had proved to be ideal tenants and that any landlord in his right mind would let them stay indefinitely. But the landlord had a son who had just been married, and he decided that this house in its present condition would be perfect for his newlyweds. So the old newlyweds found that they would have to vacate within the month.

With that, the backbreaking labor and all the money they had scraped up to put into the house were lost. Not only was the order to vacate a terrible blow to their morale, but it hit them hard financially as well. They found that no house was available as cheap as the one they had. Forced to go somewhere, they settled briefly in a dingy little house on the edge of Glendale (just west of Eagle Rock) and then went on to a larger, old frame house in the unincorporated area called Tujunga (north of Eagle Rock). Here they were out in the country with few neighbors, surrounded by the Angeles National Forest. ("Forest" is a bit misleading; it is an area of foothills and canyons, with some oak and scrub pine, but mostly brush.)

Despite a higher rent, the house would have been perfect, except that the place was haunted. And this was not the kind of quiet, gracious ghost that John had claimed to have seen in Brooklyn, or the gentlemanly visit of old Dr. Brigham, whom John swore he saw on several occasions at the door of his cabin in the Sierras. This, they believed, was a poltergeist, noisy and destructive. They had to put up with more than just the usual creaking and snapping noises of an old house. In the middle of the night, doors slammed, hard. Pictures fell off the walls. Dishes spun across the kitchen and broke on the other side of the room. While it gave them something to talk about to their friends, it was not quite an environment for contemplation.

With new strains on their very tight budget, Carol decided that she must get a job. She thought that she would have little difficulty, since she had a number of business skills and experience as an executive secretary (to "old man Schilling" of the Schilling Spice Company in San Francisco), but day after day, week after week, looking all over the Los Angeles area, she was able to find nothing. It was only then, as she recalls, that the meaning of the Depression finally came home to them.

II

In addition to the fifty dollars a month his father was sending him, John had to borrow more money and this made him feel guilty; his father was doing enough already for them. Finally, there was nothing they could do but move to Pacific Grove, where the little house was available to them without rent. At the end of August, they packed the Chevy, said good-bye to the Sheffields, and headed north.

While the use of the Pacific Grove house was one of the main things that allowed John to keep writing without a break during the next few years, it was not without its disadvantages. For one thing it brought them back into the sphere of their parents—both sets—and diminished their sense of independence (of course, they had not been truly independent in southern California either, but they had felt as if they were). Their proximity meant that John and Carol saw them frequently, and their lives were structured by obligations. John's parents considered the house their second home, even while John and Carol were living there. The elder Steinbecks came, as before, to stay on weekends, and the younger Steinbecks did not have the use, at any time, of the bedroom. No one was allowed to sleep on "Olive's bed," and John and Carol were forced to use the sleeping porch, even during the winter. In effect, they were guests, a particularly difficult position for a new wife to maintain month after month.

And the house itself was difficult to live in. Like many beach vacation houses it was small and flimsy, built of batt-and-board, single-wall construction, with no insulation and no fireplace or heater. Although the climate of Monterey–Pacific Grove is temperate, it can get close to freezing at night in the winter, and in the summer the constant low overcast or fog is both damp and chilly. The Steinbecks suffered with colds and bundled up as best they could. John spread his work out on the kitchen table, and when necessary, in the early mornings, he used the heat from the oven.

Over the next few months John and his father worked together on several projects to improve the house and yard, the first of which was to build a small fireplace at the end of the living room. Although it took a long time to complete, it drew well and became for John a great source of pride. Under Steinbeck senior's care, the yard was already attractive—the climate in Pacific Grove is perfect for fuchsias and tuberous begonias—but John needed a vegetable garden and his father had always wanted to put in a pond. So they brought in a load of black loam to mix with the sandy soil, built a tall fence around the yard to keep out the neighborhood dogs and children, and excavated for the pond, buttering the hole with hand-mixed mortar. The elder Steinbeck provided the lilies and John provided the turtles.

As hard as it may have been at times, the young Steinbecks were not exactly engaged in a grim struggle for survival. They did have two main advantages, as Steinbeck pointed out in an article recollecting the 1930s that he wrote for *Esquire*:

> The Depression was no financial shock to me. I didn't have any money to lose, but in common with millions I did dislike hunger and cold. I had two assets. My father owned a tiny three-room cottage in Pacific Grove in California, and he let me live in it without rent. That was the first safety. Pacific Grove is on the sea. That was the second. People in inland cities or in the closed and shuttered industrial cemeteries had greater problems than I. Given the sea a man must be very stupid to starve. That great reservoir of food is always available. I took a large part of my protein food from the

ocean. Firewood to keep warm floated on the beach daily, needing only handsaw and ax. A small garden of black soil came with the cottage. In northern California you can raise vegetables of some kind all year long. I never peeled a potato without planting the skins. Kale, lettuce, chard, turnips, carrots and onions rotated in the little garden. In the tide pools of the bay, mussels were available and crabs and abalones and that shiney kelp called sea lettuce. With a line and pole, blue cod, rock cod, perch, sea trout, sculpin could be caught.

Food gathering was a major activity, carried out with an ingenuity and light-heartedness that at times brought it very close to a game. John and Carol bought a small, battered sailboat, and fishing with a drag line, they caught blue fish and, occasionally, a yellow tail. Once in a while the director at the Hopkins Marine Station let them park their boat overnight in the "no parking" area of the wharf, where they would drop nets, and in the morning they would have a good haul of small fish. They also dropped crab nets off the main pier in Monterey and left them overnight.

The fishing and the garden were helpful but not totally reliable. Store-bought food was mostly beans and hamburger, but although humburger was ten cents a pound, they didn't have the money to buy it very often. Once, before they got the boat, they had to apply for welfare food—two cans of peaches, one pound of cheese, and a can of corned beef a week. During the summers, they would try to get out to the nearby farms—sometimes walking for miles when they didn't have the money for gas—to hunt up what produce they could beg or buy cheap. And there were times when there was nothing in the cupboard at all, and John would take a walk downtown with his cane on an evening or Sunday. With his back to the grating in front of a closed produce market, he could reach in and pull out an acorn squash or a couple of apples.

Moments of complete desperation were rare, however, because Carol was able to get some work. Her jobs never paid much or lasted very long, but when they had her income, they were better off than most. If they lived on the ragged edge much of the time, not knowing from day to day where the next few meals were coming from, it was more often the result of their generosity than their lack of resources—they were completely open-handed with everything they had.

John was intense about his writing, and everybody around them knew it. He bluntly discouraged visitors until the late afternoon, and if someone showed up before then, unless it was a close relative or a visitor from out of town, he could be very unpleasant. But after four, the Steinbecks had open house. They always asked anyone who dropped by to stay and share their food, whatever they might have. When Carol came home from work, she never knew how many she might have to cook for, two or thirty-two, or whether there would be anything in the house to cook. On a lucky day they might have enough fish and crab to feed thirty. Someone would bring a couple of thirty-five-cent gallons of red wine, and someone else a couple of loaves of sourdough.

There were wild times, happy times:

> There was a fairly large group of us poor kids, all living alike. We pooled our troubles, our money when we had some, our inventiveness, and our pleasure. I remember it as a warm and friendly time. . . .
>
> For entertainment we had the public library, endless talk, long walks, any number of games. We played music, sang and made love. Enormous invention went into our pleasures. Anything at all was an excuse for a party: all holidays, birthdays called for celebration. When we felt the need to celebrate and the calendar was blank, we simply proclaimed a Jacks-Are-Wild Day.
>
> Now and then there came a bit of pure magic. One of us would get a small job, or a relative might go insane and enclose money in a letter—two dollars, and once or twice, God help me, five. Then word would fly through the neighborhood. Desperate need would be taken care of first, but after that we felt desperate need for a party. Since our clothing was increasingly ratty, it was usually a costume party. The girls wanted to look pretty, and they didn't have the clothes for it. A costume party made all manner of drapes and curtains and tablecloths available. . . . A wind-up phonograph furnished the music and the records were so worn down that it could be called Lo-Fi, but it was loud.

As one might imagine, this kind of crazy activity, sometimes people dancing in the street or parading up and down the streets in costume singing Christmas carols in July, did not sit well with those neighbors who were part of the staid, old-time Pacific Grove community. Perhaps it didn't happen often, but it did happen, just as in *Cannery Row*, that the police came, calmed things down a bit, and stayed to join the fun.

I remember one great meat loaf carried in shoulder high like a medieval boar's head at a feast. It was garnished with strips of crisp bacon cut from an advertisement in *The Saturday Evening Post.*

One day in a pile of rubbish behind Holman's store, I found a papier-mâché roast turkey, the kind they put in window displays around Thanksgiving. I took it home and repaired it and gave it a new coat of paint. We used it often, served on a platter surrounded with dandelions. Under the hollow turkey was a pile of hamburgers.

John and Carol were at their best together when they were poor; poverty was the occasion for their invention, for their enthusiasm. But it was Carol's spirit, more than anything else, that carried them through. She was the one who cut the pictures of food out of magazines; she was the one who got up the costume parties, who invented the crazy days of celebration. In describing Mary Talbot in *Cannery Row*, Steinbeck was really describing Carol (with a touch of Carol's friend and co-conspirator in generating gaiety, Tal Lovejoy), and Mary's support of Tom was pretty much the way that Carol tried to keep John going when times were bad:

> She could infect a whole house with gaiety and she used her gift as a weapon against the despondency that lurked always around outside the house waiting to get in at Tom. That was Mary's job as she saw it—to keep the despondency away from Tom because everyone knew he was going to be a great success some time. Mostly she was successful in keeping the dark things out of the house but sometimes they got in at Tom and laid him out. Then he would sit and brood for hours while Mary frantically built up a backfire of gaiety.
>
> One time when it was the first of the month and there were curt notes from the water company and the rent wasn't paid and a manuscript had come back from *Collier's* and the cartoons had come back from *The New Yorker* and pleurisy was hurting Tom pretty badly, he went into the bedroom and lay down on the bed.
>
> Mary came softly in, for the blue-gray color of his gloom had seeped out under the door and through the keyhole. She had a little bouquet of candy tuft in a collar of paper lace.
>
> "Smell," she said and held the bouquet to his nose. He smelled the flowers and said nothing. "Do you know what day this is?" she asked and thought wildly for something to make it a bright day.
>
> Tom said, "Why don't we face it for once? We're down. We're going under. What's the good kidding ourselves?"
>
> "No we're not," said Mary. "We're magic people. We always have been. Remember that ten dollars you found in a book—remember when your cousin sent you five dollars? Nothing can happen to us."

Carol was important to Steinbeck the writer in a host of subtle ways. She pulled him up when he was down, revived him when he was out. As he got older, Steinbeck tended to lose some of his ability to enjoy; occasionally, his sense of humor faded under the strain. Carol brought humor back to his consciousness; she wouldn't let him feel sorry for himself.

She spent hours and hours typing his manuscripts, and when she was working, this meant typing all evening and sometimes into the night. When he was working under a deadline, there was sometimes more pressure on her than on him. He hated to concern himself with such details as spelling and punctuation. So Carol corrected his spelling, arranged his punctuation, and made other minor editorial changes for him.

His most fundamental writing problem was unity, tying various aspects and parts of his work together. Steinbeck's talent was not intellectual so much as it was perceptual and instinctive. He wrote in bursts of feeling and insight; he had a gift for sensing the implications of relationships and for describing the conditions of people within certain situations and environments. He seems to have had very little sense of plot, particularly over the duration of a novel—possibly because it just wasn't important to him.

Many of his works have almost no plot as such, but instead tend to focus on one situation after another. When he does try to use a strong plot, as in *East of Eden*, the novel becomes very labored and one has the feeling constantly that he is following a plot reluctantly and that what he really wants to say has very little to do with a sequence of cause and effect, an evolving pattern of events that build to a climax and resolution. He didn't think that way. He was unable to see situations as having resolutions—to him, life and the difficulties of life were ongoing (as witness for example, the ending of *The Grapes of Wrath*). Therefore most of his novels aren't novels in the traditional sense so much as collections of scenes or sketches.

Plot, of course, is the great unifier of fiction. Without it the writer must depend on other devices to give his work shape, direction, and interest. Carol was aware of John's tendency to plow ahead without much concern for the work as an artistic whole, and she made suggestions to help him bring things together—for example the use of the Arthurian backdrop for *Tortilla Flat*.

Another great weakness of his work, as we have already noted, resulted from his tendency to get carried away by his emotional responses—to overreact to his own involvement with his characters and to overwrite. He never thought of himself as a realistic writer, even in his writing of *In Dubious Battle* or *The Grapes of Wrath*, which to many readers seem very journalistic. He recognized his tendency toward sentimentality, and he was defensive about it, but it was intimately tied to his talent, and he accepted the fact that he could never escape it or control it entirely.

It was part of the force that led him to write in the first place; it was the opposite side of the emotional coin from what "Salinas" and "Republicans" meant to him. The two together were the rage and the love that drove him to pen and paper. Carol sensed this, too, and she did what she could to correct or stem his excesses. Not very many people could confront this emotional man bluntly. He seemed to overwhelm nearly everyone by his size and by the power which, although usually contained, seemed to leak out from some glowing core at the center of him. Carol was one of the few who could read a piece of his work, look him in the eye, and say, "God damn it, that's just a bunch of bull shit."

Of all the people Steinbeck came to know during the course of his life, the one who most influenced his thinking and writing was Edward F. Ricketts. The two men knew each other for eighteen years, from 1930 to 1948, when Ed was killed in a train accident. The friendship really had three stages—from 1930 to 1936, when John was in Ed's company frequently; from 1936 to 1941, when John had moved to Los Gatos and saw Ed only occasionally; and from 1941 to 1948, when John lived most of the time in New York and saw Ed only rarely.

Ed Ricketts was a remarkable and complex man, and largely because of Steinbeck, he has become a legend, making it very difficult to discern the quality of the man himself behind the legend. Also clouding the reality of the man are the almost universally favorable reactions of those who knew him, reactions that sometimes approach idolatry. If one were to ask about Steinbeck among those who knew him in Salinas, he would find that he was very commonly disliked; ask about him in Monterey and the feelings are mixed—some liked him, while others thought he was a son-of-a-bitch. Ask about Ed Ricketts, and one hears only praise.

Furthermore, because of the positive feelings for one man and the often negative feelings for the other, there has been a tendency to overestimate both the importance of Ed as a thinker and of his thought on Steinbeck's work (the impact itself is unquestioned). The coincidence of time has contributed to this tendency: almost all the books considered by critics to be Steinbeck's major works were written during the time of the friendship, the most important of these either during or shortly after the period when Steinbeck and Ricketts were very close and saw each other constantly. Thus a very questionable syllogism has been set up by both literary scholars and friends of the two Ed in one way or another—through his ideas, his criticism, or his inspiration—was responsible for Steinbeck's success.

All of this is too easy and simplistic. Regardless of the contribution Ricketts made to Steinbeck's work, good or bad, large or small, the ultimate responsibility for the work in its entirety is Steinbeck's. Being an influence, inadvertently or intentionally, doesn't make you a partner. Those who give too much credit to Ed fail to realize the full range of Steinbeck's indebtedness to other people and other sources. He was, as his first wife has described him, a "lint-picker"; like most successful writers of fiction, he picked up what he thought might be useful from every experience he had, every person he met. His most important novel, *The Grapes of Wrath*, grew out of a wide variety of sources, both people and written documents, and out of his exposure to the work and thought of one man, in particular—but that man was not Ed Ricketts. If there is any single element in this novel that can be directly related to Steinbeck's discussions with Ricketts, it is what a number of critics have referred to as the rather fuzzy-headed philosophy of Jim Casy.

Indeed, one could probably build a better case, though equally fallacious, for the proposition that Ricketts's influence was more destructive than helpful. The talky, flabby parts of Steinbeck's work—the abstract philosophical speeches of Casy or the houseboy Lee in *East of Eden*, for example—which have so irritated readers and seriously weakened the narrative fabric of several novels, could be blamed on Steinbeck's admiration for Ricketts. A pernicious abstractionism, so uncharacteristic of his best early work, yet so characteristic of Steinbeck-Ricketts discussions and metaphysical games, seems to have increased in Steinbeck's fiction in the years just before Ed's death and after. Couldn't we just as easily, therefore, blame Steinbeck's decline on Ed as give him credit for his success?

Rather than focus on questions of credit or blame, let us concentrate on the sufficiently difficult questions of who Ed Ricketts was, what the relationship between the two men was, and in what ways the relationship may have affected Steinbeck's writing.

II

Steinbeck met Ed Ricketts in October 1930. In a biographical essay called "About Ed Ricketts" attached to the separate publication of *The Log from the "Sea of Cortez,"* Steinbeck says that he met Ricketts in the waiting room of a dentist, but in his autobiographical essays and articles, Steinbeck is not always literally accurate and it is just as possible—and more likely—that he met Ricketts for the first time at Jack Calvin's house.

Occasionally, Steinbeck would meet and warm up to someone almost immediately, but more often he would observe someone for quite some time, perhaps on several occasions, before he would even say anything to the person. His first ploy in a relationship was often a gruff ironic comment addressed to no one in particular. If the bait was picked up and the rejoinder was sufficiently provocative, a discussion or argument might ensue. If you were interesting without being arrogant (it didn't matter whether Steinbeck agreed with you or not) and showed you had a sense of humor and were not overly respectable, the relationship might continue.

Ed was a natural object for Steinbeck's interest. He was self-contained and self-possessed without being arrogant; very competent at his work; knew things that Steinbeck didn't know, but would like to know; was quiet, yet not completely withdrawn; and was a nonconformist with philosophical ideas, diverse interests, and vibrant enthusiasms. He was the kind of person who, without being famous, inordinately physically attractive, or assertive, somehow stands out from the crowd. Yet, like Steinbeck, he was always a bit of a loner, not the sort that people crowd around at parties. The friendship that developed between the two was extraordinary, for although fundamentally different in many ways, the two operated on the same wave length.

Ed was five years older, and in contrast with John, he was a city boy, born and raised in Chicago. His father was from Lexington, Kentucky, an accountant for his brother, who was part-owner of an art gallery. His mother was from Boston and judged everything by proper, upper-middle-class Boston standards. Feeling that they might become contaminated by the rough children of the neighborhood in Chicago, she isolated Ed and his younger sister, Frances, as much as possible. They sat and watched other children from the window, and since they didn't have any playmates until they were well along in school, they got into the habit of reading.

Ed was unobnoxiously precocious, and because of his extensive early reading, he acquired an unusually large fund of general information for a child. In school, without malice or mockery, they called him "the dictionary." Always very quiet, yet very likeable, he could correct the teacher in grade school without causing resentment. And even though he grew up in a very protective environment, he was always himself. He didn't rebel or fight the restraints placed on him, he simply maintained an inner self-sufficiency, a total independence of spirit that transcended his captivity. Steinbeck quotes Ed in regard to the silly rules of his childhood: "Adults, in their dealing with children, are insane. . . .

And children know it too. Adults lay down rules they would not think of following, speak truths they do not believe. And yet they expect children to obey the rules, believe the truths, and admire and respect their parents for this nonsense. Children must be very wise and secret to tolerate adults at all."

He never told jokes as a youngster or adult, but he did have a wry sense of humor that for all his gentleness was often pointed. It was an understated, spontaneous wit that penetrated the occasion. Once he put a nickel in the baking-powder box after emptying it for use in his childhood chemistry experiments, because his mother had been upset before when he used up such things. The nickel was an expression of a "Here we go again" sort of humor. He had a great curiosity that extended far beyond the things that children are supposed to be interested in, and he had the ability to talk about his discoveries in such a way as to make the most trivial things interesting.

Often his enthusiasms simply baffled his parents. From the eighth grade through high school and into his first marriage, he had a fascination with guns, though his horrified parents knew nothing about them whatsoever. He admired their accurate mechanics, which he studied, and enjoyed target practice, which he took in the basement of their house. On one occasion when his sister was in the basement with him, a shot ricocheted around, frightening her considerably. He said, "Don't worry. I know what went wrong, and I'll fix it. It won't do that again."

The one break from Chicago came when Ed was about ten and the family moved for a year to a small town in South Dakota. Looking back, his sister has said, "It must have been wonderful for Ed, who, besides making his usual warm good contacts with people, collected butterflies on a big scale and birds' eggs a little too avidly. Ed also raised what I thought were enormous flocks of pigeons, and was in love with the rector's daughter, a very advanced, vivid girl named Victoria."

Two of his most precocious interests were animals and girls. His concern for animals was unusual in that he didn't care about them as pets, but instead investigated them with an intense scientific curiosity. An uncle recognized this bent toward natural science and encouraged it; Ed is quoted by Joel W. Hedgpeth in an article called "Philosophy on Cannery Row": "At the age of six, I was ruined for any ordinary activities when an uncle who should have known better gave me some natural history curios and an old zoology textbook. Here I saw for the first time those magic and incorrect words 'coral insects.' " Among the curios was a collection of birds' eggs, which later stimulated his own collecting in South Dakota.

His sister remembers an incident that happened when they were quite young and were taken to the natural-history museum. Ed was dressed in his grade-school outfit—knickers, long socks, black shoes, and a blue serge Norfolk jacket—and his sister watched him slowly circle a dinosaur, gazing intently at every detail, walking around and around it for what seemed to her hours. Then he stopped and offered to explain it to her.

When he got into high school and was granted more freedom by his parents, he roamed the streets, walking all over Chicago. It was partly a rejoicing in his freedom and partly a voyage of discovery. Steinbeck quotes Ed, after Ed had read James T. Farrell's *Studs Lonigan*, as saying, " 'This is a true book ... I was born and grew up in this part of Chicago. I played in these streets. I know them all, I know the people. This is a true book.' And, of course, to Ed a thing that was true was beautiful." In high school he did well in his studies, taking all the biology and zoology that the school offered.

Most learning problems came easy for him, except for those mechanical, but because he was interested in mechanical objects and wanted to do jobs that required mechanical skills, he deliberately set out to learn how to use tools, take things apart, and fix them. This determination to master that which was difficult for him was typical. His notes and journals from his adult years suggest that he went through a series of self-improvement programs of his own design. Like Benjamin Franklin, who graded himself weekly on his virtues and vices, Ed was very self-analytical, and he seemed to be constantly working to better understand himself, to eliminate or moderate bad habits, to improve his knowledge in certain areas.

Art, music, literature, philosophy—the fact that the humanities were as much a part of his life as the natural sciences was a great part of what made Ed Ricketts so unusual. Indeed, his basic approach to life and to the problem of understanding it was one of synthesis; his approach to biology was often as much philosophical as it was scientific. He wanted to see each marine animal along the shore within the scheme of the shore as a whole, its total environment of physical conditions and other creatures. His mind stretched from the tidepool to the music of the entire universe, and he saw the arts and sciences as all of one piece.

There is nothing too unusual about a young boy who, by the time he is eleven or twelve, has filled a bookcase with books, who has read all the boys' books, and all the books by authors usually advised for children, such as Kipling. But it is fairly unusual for a teenage boy to become deeply involved in serious poetry. Ed's fondness for Whitman led him to quote from his poetry often during his late teens, and in a list of great works jotted down in his notebook only a few months before his death, he includes both "When Lilacs Last in the Dooryard Bloom'd" and "Out of the Cradle Endlessly Rocking." As Steinbeck mentions in his biographical sketch, Ed was so fond of Goethe's *Faust* that he studied German so that he could read the poem in the original.

His interest in philosophy also began early and continued throughout his life. His sister told Joel Hedgpeth that "our early life was spent rather in the shadow of a small Englishy Episcopal church which our parents were pillars of." Much of his impulse toward philosophical speculation can be traced back to the need to escape from the respectable religiosity of his parents. The challenge of "breaking out" of this stultifying theology was transformed later in life to one of "breaking through" (a phrase he used frequently) to a comprehension of the interrelatedness of the whole picture.

Ironically, his concern to break through appearances to an ultimate vision of reality, to achieve a "deep participation" with the essential character of the whole, was motivated by what would ordinarily be described as religious impulses. If one combines these things with his character, in which such traits as goodness and innocence shone forth so prominently, it becomes obvious why so many people perceived him in a religious light, even though they might not have been consciously aware of it or would have been extremely reluctant to use the word "religious."

But one must qualify this immediately, lest the wrong impression be given. Ricketts was no prophet, guru, or cult figure. He had no spiritual aura, made no claim of special revelation, and certainly held no brief for organized religion or religious dogma of any kind. If he was good, it was not the conventional goodness of the pious or those conforming to "community standards." If he was innocent, it was the innocence of a person who lacks cynicism and sophistication and who is very open and accepting and vulnerable. No—in most ways he was an ordinary man with weaknesses and problems, certainly no saint. He held the common prejudices of his times, drank a lot, was often very slothful in his personal habits, and had numerous affairs with married women, which were usually messy and sometimes sordid. Those who disliked him, and there were a few, found him unreliable, careless, self-indulgent, and even sullen.

Ricketts's college career was sporadic and similar to Steinbeck's—he had to work his way through and never finished. His parents had consulted their rector about their son's future college, and he suggested a small school, so they sent Ed to Illinois State Normal University, in those days primarily a teacher-training institution. Ed spent a year there, did only average work, and apparently felt that the atmosphere was too restrictive. So he took off to see something of the world, and his wanderings led him to Texas, where he ended up working as a book-keeper for a country club outside El Paso. By this time, late 1917, the United States was in the war, and over a period of several months, Ed tried to enlist. Much to his embarrassment, he was repeatedly rejected for flat feet. Finally, he was drafted, serving a little more than a year in the Medical Corps as a clerk.

He was discharged several months after the armistice and was ready to go back to school. He entered the University of Chicago in the summer of 1919, and over a three year period attended seven quarters. Two of these were summer sessions, and during the regular school year, he was seldom able to take a full program. He began school living at home, but at the age of twenty-two found this difficult, so after six months, he moved into an apartment on the South Side, which he shared with two roommates. His independence forced him to go to work and to cut back on his studies, and he took a number of jobs, sometimes more than one at a time, including filling-station attendant, rail-yard switchman, grocery clerk, and furnaceman for an apartment building. For a year he worked extremely hard—his grades were good and he received "Honorable Mention for Excellence" in his lower-division work.

In his essay, Steinbeck quotes Ed's summary of this period in his life:

"I don't know when I slept," he said. "I don't think there was time to sleep. I tended furnaces in the early morning. Then I went to class. I had lab all afternoon, then tended furnaces in the early evening. I had a job in a little store in the evening and got some studying done then, until midnight. Well, then I was in love with a girl whose husband worked nights, and naturally I didn't sleep much from midnight until morning. Then I got up and tended furnaces and went to class. What a time," he said, "what a fine time that was."

But the pace, and complications with the "girl whose husband worked nights," led him to skip the following autumn and winter quarters at the university and once again take off, this time on a walking trip into the South.

Steinbeck uses the trip in *Cannery Row* to describe Doc's love of true things and to contrast this love with the resistance most people have toward the true, the unusual, or the purely aesthetic. Ed got on the train in Chicago and took it to Indianapolis, where he donned a knapsack and began walking through Indiana, Kentucky, North Carolina, and Georgia. He observed and talked to many people in many places: he "walked among the farmers and mountain people, among the swamp people and fishermen. And everywhere people asked him why he was walking through the country." He said that he wanted to see the country, to savor it, to touch and smell the grass and trees, and to meet and know more about people, but this explanation sounded vague and evasive to his listeners, and they became suspicious and suggested that he move along.

So he stopped trying to explain. Instead, he started telling people that he was walking to win a bet. This seemed to win nearly everyone's confidence and admiration, and they couldn't do enough for him. This experience should have given him sufficient warning of the low tolerance most of us have for the truth, especially if it is a truth that doesn't somehow fit into our vision of reality. Yet, throughout his life, Ed was probably too frank, too open for his own good. People simply could not cope with that honesty, and it added considerably to the pain of his very complex relationships with women.

Similarly, Ed had a vision of individual freedom that also greatly complicated his life. He felt that people should be free to act as they truly felt and that they should not be restrained either by convention or by the demands or expectations of others. He felt that in love, as in friendship, two people should come together in freedom, without demands, obligations, or forms, to establish such mutual bonds as each might desire for as long as both might consent. Unfortunately, as he suggests in his journals, it was not uncommon for him to be pursuing someone who had no desire to share anything with him at all. And as active in matters of love as he was, it sometimes also worked the other way—at least one woman pursued him with a persistence that in reverse circumstances would have matched or exceeded his own. Too tenderhearted to confront her and declare his principles of individual freedom, he very uncharacteristically resorted to hiding or taking long collecting trips until the coast was clear. For a time it became one of the major comedy attractions on Cannery Row.

After his walking trip, Ed returned to his studies in the spring of 1921, and also began working as a clerk and lab assistant in a small biological supply house, Anco Biological Supplies. One additional quarter of full-time college work was apparently all he could stand, for he took only a single course that summer and another during the autumn of the following year. In all he completed the equivalent of two and a half years, yet in that time, in addition to various general education courses, he managed to complete ten quarters of zoology (three at Illinois State and seven at Chicago), half of which could be called advanced work. There is some irony in the fact that just as he was winding down his college career, he encountered the professor who would have the most influence upon him, W. C. Allee, biologist and ecological theorist, who in 1931 would publish *Animal Aggregations*, an important early study of the nature of animal associations, and in 1949 would collaborate in the publication of one of the great classics of ecology, *Principles of Animal Ecology*. Allee joined the science faculty at the University of Chicago in the summer of 1921, after five years as a biologist at Woods Hole, a marine study facility (later the Woods Hole Oceanographic Institution) on Cape Cod, Massachusetts.

According to Joel Hedgpeth,

> for several years before he came to Chicago, Allee had conducted a significant project at Woods Hole, and at the time he joined the faculty at Chicago he was engaged in writing this work up and without a doubt discussed it in his classes. [Ricketts took "Animal Ecology" from him in the fall of 1922.] For every summer from 1915 through 1921, Allee and his students had made systematic collections from characteristic areas of the shore in the vicinity of Woods Hole. The principal physical factors controlling distribution were analyzed, and some of the common associations were recognized.

The significance of this project was that it was not something that had been done very often, particularly with an ecological inquiry as its objective: systematic observations were made year after year in the same geographical location, providing rather exact data in regard to the relationship of intertidal animals to specific conditions of environment and of animals to other animals.

Allee was searching for some basic ecological principle as demonstrated through the nature of animal associations. In his *Animal Aggregations* he concludes that there is what he calls a "mutual interdependence, or automatic cooperation" which is a fundamental trait of living organisms. In layman's terms, he demonstrated that social behavior (as we see it) among the lower animals is not the result of conscious decision (as we would call it) based on a perception of need, but something characteristic of living matter itself.

Ed Ricketts was profoundly impressed by these and other associated ideas. Ed's sister recalls that he always spoke of Allee with great reverence as "the last word," and in a letter to the critic Richard Astro, Jack Calvin remembers that Ricketts and other former students of Allee always "got a holy look in their eyes at the mention of his name." Allee's ideas became the foundation of Ricketts's philosophy, which was composed of several concepts that might be called "extensions" from Allee's thought, and was not something that Allee himself would have necessarily agreed with in toto.

Some of these extensions have to do with what Ed called "non-teleological thinking," that is, thinking that eliminates man-centered concepts of the nature of reality. Man seems determined to explain the world and events that take place in it on the basis of cause and effect. If he cannot see the cause, he is likely to turn to the supernatural and invent one; if he can see the cause, he is likely to attribute human motives to it, or, if that is too difficult, interpret conditions or events totally in terms of human welfare. This kind of behavior obscures man's ability to see things as they are, to pursue "is" thinking, as Ricketts called it. To go back to Allee for a moment, animals do not cooperate because they are friendly, or because harmony is one of God's laws, or because they see the need to cooperate in order to survive and therefore act on that perception. They do so because it is what they do; it is part of their nature to do so.

Since in Ricketts's view all of nature, including man, operates on an "is" basis, the question "why" becomes irrelevant. This leads to another extension—"acceptance." Not only is man overly concerned with causes, he is also overly concerned with cures. If conditions or situations do not match his mood, his desires, his comfort, man determines that he must change the situation. He usually calls this change "progress." Although there is some contradiction here with Ricketts's own efforts to improve himself, he felt that in general and for the most part it was best to leave people and conditions alone, to let people be as they must be and conditions develop as they must. The pattern of nature was far too large and complex for man to comprehend, and too often changes turned out in the long run to be more destructive than constructive.

It remains to be demonstrated that Ricketts was a profound or impressively original thinker, but it is evident from his writings and from the testimony of those who talked with him at length that he was a serious thinker, a man who was not an academic, but who in ordinary life, day by day, considered questions of metaphysics, ethics, and epistemology—and that is rare enough. W. C. Allee provided a philosophical foundation and a direction for a man given to speculation, analysis, and synthesis. Unfortunately, by failing to get an advanced degree, let alone finish his undergraduate work, Ricketts found himself throughout his life at a disadvantage in attempting to publish his ideas or address them to academics.

While there is no simple explanation for Ricketts's withdrawing from college, he may have felt that at twenty-five he was getting a bit old to be an undergraduate. There is also some evidence that he was both bored and rebellious. The University of Chicago, while prestigious even in its youth as a result of a distinguished faculty, was still in some ways a "small, Baptist college." There were many things about it that would be galling to a freethinker trying to escape from a religious and regimented childhood, not the least among them compulsory attendance at chapel.

However, with Ricketts, as with the paperback detective working on a homicide, if you seek a motive, *cherchez la femme.* At about this time, when he was taking his last course with Allee, he met Anna Macker, who would soon become his first wife. Having no resources, he was forced to live with his wife at his parents' home until their baby was born. In the meantime, his former roommate, Albert E. Galigher, had gone to California to start a biological supply house in Monterey. As soon as Ed was able to leave Chicago, he joined him as a partner, sending for his wife and child several months after he was settled.

A year later Ed and his partner had a falling-out (Hedgpeth says it was a conflict of interest in the same woman), and Galigher moved to Berkeley with the part of the operation that dealt in prepared slides. Ed became the sole owner of Pacific Biological Laboratory, and the house on the waterfront in New Monterey, surrounded by the sardine canneries, became his place of business and, after the first couple of years, his home.

III

The impression that Steinbeck gives of Ed in his biographical sketch of him and in his depiction of him as Doc in *Cannery Row* and *Sweet Thursday* is misleading. Ed is made too colorful and his condition is sentimentalized. We see him through Steinbeck's eyes as a rather lonely bachelor (he was living with his wife and family for two years after Steinbeck met him and with his son, off and on, after he separated from his wife) who spends much of his time going for beer, counseling misfits and prostitutes, chasing girls, and partying. He did all of these things, but the emphasis is wrong; Steinbeck's portrait says as much about Steinbeck as it does about Ed. He spends a great deal of time describing Ed's peculiarities and those things that proper society might find disreputable. The former seems to illustrate once again Steinbeck's taste for the odd and the grotesque—no detail of this sort seems to escape his eye, whether it is Ed's distaste for the smell of old ladies or his odd bathing habits. The latter suggests that one reason Steinbeck liked Ed so much was that so many things about him would have been offensive to Steinbeck's pet hate, respectable society.

It also may have been that Ed was a sort of living example of the theorem Steinbeck tries so often to demonstrate in his fiction—that the people condemned or looked down upon by society are often the best people. Ed/Doc is thoroughly good, in a humanistic sense, but his way of life, habits, and opinions would strike many people as disgraceful or corrupt. That such a sinner could be so loving, innocent, kind, and generous might have been for Steinbeck the greatest joke of all on "the spirit of Salinas." Steinbeck needed to throw his friend up against the world as an "example," and thus while Doc may not have been the Ed that everyone knew, he was certainly the Ed that Steinbeck thought he knew.

Similarly, Cannery Row folklore, fed by recollections adapted from the novels and spread by a growing number of good friends of Ricketts, concentrates on the bull sessions and parties in the lab, the characters on the Row, and on Ed's eccentricities. In actuality, Ed was a serious, energetic man who spent most of his time working.

What Ed did for a living was to collect, prepare, and ship animals to schools to be used for exhibition, experiment, and dissection in high school and college biology and zoology classes. Some of these animals he purchased from collectors or fishermen, but most he gathered himself in the intertidal areas of the shoreline near Monterey. His catalogue offered primarily marine creatures, from microscopic organisms to somewhat larger animals—rays, octopuses, hagfish, starfish, jellyfish—although he also dealt in such laboratory staples as rats, cats, and frogs.

The lab was concerned in part with keeping certain live animals (a population that varied considerably in size and type)—rats, turtles, snakes, lizards, and some marine forms—in cages and tanks, maintaining and in some cases breeding them. In addition to the zoo function of the lab, there was the more important chemical-surgical function, in which animals were killed, partially dissected, preserved, and treated with dyes. Also, Ed gathered minute materials—microorganisms, tissue, sperm, ova—and mounted them on slides (he began to offer slides again several years after Galigher went to Berkeley).

In some ways he was a good businessman. He was honest and, despite what Steinbeck has said, kept good records. He knew how to run such a business—how to keep books, bill, pack, and ship—but he sometimes got behind, and the business would get muddled. Part of the problem was that he just didn't care about such things and put them off, and part of the problem was that there was just too much for one man to do. Although he did have help during various periods from his sister, his father, and Carol (who worked for him as a part-time secretary for several months), he needed a full-time secretary-bookkeeper and a lab assistant, but he couldn't afford them.

The lab was located just as it is described in *Cannery Row*. But in the novel the presence of the whorehouse, the grocery, and the men Steinbeck describes as hanging around the vacant lot across the street gives the impression of quaintness and activity. In fact, except for those periods during which the canneries were operating, the Row was usually vacant, almost ghostly in its quiet. There seem to have been only two kinds of days on the Row—gray days of low overcast and the bright, sharp days of spring or fall, when the wind cut through the sunshine. The former were more common—days when everything was gray, and soft and dismal, and the beating of the wind and salt spray reduced pilings, fences, and buildings to the same indeterminate color.

Inside, the lab too was rather dark, battered, and lacking color. Masculine, shopworn, with clutter all around, it was a little reminiscent of the badly maintained office of an impoverished rural newspaper. It had been a small, one-bedroom house built out over a basement-garage. The front door led into an entry hall, which Ed had turned into an office. Crammed into a rather small space were a rolltop desk, filing cabinets, and a safe, which was used for keeping cheese and canned sardines. Around on the walls were shelves, which held dusty jars of the sort of specimens offered for sale by the lab. To the left of the office, also in the front of the house, was what had been the living room, now a combination bedroom for Ed and gathering place. During the period when Ed's son was not living with him, the rear bedroom of the old house was used as a nursery for white rats, and the former kitchen, also in the rear of the house, became a slide-preparation room, with microscopes, trays, slides, glassware, and chemicals. There were stairs on the outside in both the front and the back, but none inside.

The real "lab" was in the basement, which, with pine shelving tacked to the studs and workbenches along the wall, looked much like anyone's cluttered basement workshop, except that there was more of everything and the hundreds of jars on the shelves didn't contain bolts and screws. Here the animals were processed, packed, and shipped. Outside, back of the house, there were holding tanks for live marine animals. When Ed moved into the house to live as well as work there, he simply added a bed he made himself, a sort of nautical bunk made of a redwood frame crosshatched with rope, and put some food in the former kitchen. He liked the arrangement of the place so much, that when it burned down in 1936, he had it rebuilt with exactly the same floor plan.

Steinbeck lived only a few blocks down and inland from the lab. By midafternoon he usually had finished his quota of a thousand words and was feeling restless, so he'd get up from his work at the kitchen table and take a brief tour of his little garden. Then, dressed in sweatshirt and work pants, he'd stroll down to the ocean. With Carol usually at work and no neighbors about, he craved someone to talk to. He started stopping by to see Ed for a few minutes now and then, and gradually it became a habit. If Ed was busy, sometimes John would stand by and watch. As they got to know each other better, John might help with some task that was under way, and occasionally he would go out with Ed on a collecting trip. After a while, he brought his daily writing with him, and if there was an opportunity, read it aloud. John began to spend a great deal of time with Ed and they talked:

> Very many conclusions Ed and I worked out together through endless discussion and reading and observation and experiment. We worked together, and so closely that I do not know in some cases who started which line of speculation since the end thought was the product of both minds. I do not know whose thought it was.
>
> We had a game which we playfully called speculative metaphysics. It was a sport consisting of lopping off a piece of observed reality and letting it move up through the speculative process like a tree growing tall and bushy. We observed with pleasure how the branches of thought grew away from the trunk of external reality. We believed, as we must, that the laws of thought parallel the laws of things. In our game there was no stricture of rightness. It was an

enjoyable exercise on the instruments of our minds, improvisations and variations on a theme, and it gave the same delight and interest that discovered music does. . . .

Always our thinking was prefaced with, "It might be so!" Often a whole night would draw down to a moment while we pursued the fireflies of our thinking.

But the talk did not always soar. There was discussion, too, of neighbors and friends, of women and sex, of tasks put off and projects contemplated, of current events and what happened the other night.

When John first met him, Ed did not have the mustache or the mustache and beard that he cultivated later. He was clean-shaven and rather ordinary-looking, of medium height and slender build, his longish dark-brown hair brushed straight back. His most distinctive features were his hands and eyes. He had the hands of a surgeon or artist—long fingers, with a gentle, but firm touch that matched his personality, which was also gentle with a sinewy toughness underneath. He had a wide, full mouth, which gave his face an air of sensitivity, a prominent, straight nose, and dark eyes. Carol thought that there was something a bit Svengali-like about Ed, perhaps referring to his charm, which almost seemed to put a spell on people, but the comparison may have also come from the arresting quality of his eyes. In some of his photographs, his eyes seem to capture you, and there is a penetrating, soulful quality about them that is reminiscent of Valentino's eyes in his publicity photos.

As the months and years went by, the two men became extremely close, closer than most good friends and closer, without any sexual implications, than most husbands and wives. What brought them together originally was probably a mutual interest in biology. What kept them close friends for so long was that each discovered that the other had a boundless curiosity about almost everything, and that their personalities meshed so well.

The key to Steinbeck's personality was his overwhelming drive to write, a drive that if anything became stronger during the 1930s and the period of his closest ties to Ricketts. To some extent the drives of these two men complemented each other: John the sender and Ed the receiver. In contrast with John's need to give was Ed's need to receive, to break through to understanding. Ed made listening an art, a creative thing. John usually restrained himself in situations where he might disagree, whereas Ed could partly give up being himself in order to join in spirit with others.

While Steinbeck could still be an agreeable companion and maintained a sense of fun and humor, as time passed, he became distinctly more serious, more intense. The thirties, the decade of his greatest achievements, was also a period of ever-increasing strain. Among the most telling factors was the pressure of work—the material he was trying to shape became more and more difficult for him to handle, and his success, when finally achieved in mid-decade, added to the pressure rather than relieving it. His involvement with the migrant workers became an extremely emotional one, and the social outrages he witnessed aroused a profound anger and compassion within him, pulling him in one direction, while his commitment to artistic achievement pulled him in another. And, perhaps the most important factor was the chaos and conflict of his personal life. His relations with Carol gradually deteriorated, causing them both intense pain.

Near the end of the decade what had been seen by Steinbeck's college friends as youthful iconoclasm and the development of a creative personality was now more often perceived as a sort of contained rage. The containment of self-discipline had always been a part of the Steinbeck personality. Unlike Carol, who could pull the cork in public and let out both joy and anger—and throw things to express either—John always remained, in this one sense at least, middle-class and inhibited. He kept the lid on so tightly that the internal struggle was not apparent to everyone who knew him. To some he seemed simply quiet and reserved; to others who glimpsed something of what was going on inside him, he could be intimidating, even frightening. Still, withal, he was a man who could sit and talk very agreeably to a fisherman or mechanic for hours over a cup of coffee or a beer, without any hint of antagonism or criticism, regardless of what sentiments the fisherman or mechanic might espouse. And with all his contained anger, he was a man who could care very deeply for others, could be very loyal, very sensitive to their feelings, and could be very sentimental if touched in the right place.

Ed Ricketts's personality could be judged as very nearly the opposite in most ways. Indeed, one basis for the friendship might have been that Ed's personality acted as a tranquilizer for Steinbeck's rage. He was very loving and accepting, almost completely without malice, yet he had a kind of sure, inner toughness that contrasted with John's sentimentality. His acceptance was remarkable. Whereas John, among close friends, could be very prejudiced and opinionated, Ed usually accepted people's foibles and didn't reject people because of them. (John might put up with them temporarily and then boil over later.) Whereas John could put people off, Ed had an enormous charm, neither phony nor superficial. Toni Jackson, who took Ricketts's name and lived with him as his wife for seven years, recalls that

> there would be a discussion or something, and he would agree with someone who was saying something that I knew Ed didn't agree with, and I couldn't understand it. To me, at first, it seemed like hypocrisy, and then I realized that it wasn't, that the relationship with the person was the important thing, that it came first. Ed was very conscious and very aware of relationships. He talked about them a lot. . . . Ed used to say that when two people are related there are actually three entities involved, each of the persons and the third entity which is the relationship. He was terribly aware of that relationship . . . as a third entity. So always with John he was very aware of the relationship. If John did foolish things or said foolish things . . . Ed would just laugh and say, "Oh that funny John." You know, he didn't resent it. He understood it and went along with it.

Joel Hedgpeth cites Ed's son as saying that his father had, as Steinbeck did, the tendency to identify the interests of others as his own, at least if he loved the other person. John and Ed shared a love for music and for poetry, and they tended to adopt each other's taste and share the delight that each had in response to various works of art. Once when Steinbeck had suffered "an overwhelming emotional upset," he went to the lab to stay with Ed:

> I was dull and speechless with shock and pain. He used music on me like medicine. Late in the night when he should have been asleep, he played music for me on his great phonograph—even when I was asleep he played it, knowing that its soothing would get into my dark confusion. He played the curing and reassuring plain songs, remote and cool and separate, and then gradually he played the sure patterns of Bach, until I was ready for more personal thought and feeling again, until I could bear to come back to myself. And when that time came, he gave me Mozart. I think it was as careful and loving medication as has ever been administered.

Steinbeck may have been unfortunate in many things during the long uncertain struggle over the years of the 1920s and early 1930s, but he was fortunate in his friends.

CHAPTER XII

There are certain times in the life of an author when he appears to have come to a crossroads. During the period 1930–1932, Steinbeck's work could have gone in any one of several directions, and that he chose the direction he did may have been due in large part to the failure of several manuscripts. Two of these, an unnamed novel and "Dissonant Symphony," were destroyed—and thus provoke our curiosity—but in addition he also wrote, during roughly the same period, *The Pastures of Heaven* and a pulp detective-mystery novel, *Murder at Full Moon*. Of the four, only *Pastures* found a publisher, but one has to wonder what would have occurred if one of the other works had found success instead.

We can speculate, on the one hand, that if his experimental works—the unnamed manuscript and "Symphony"—had gone well, the shape of his career might have turned out quite different. On the other hand, if his attempt at making money with a speedily composed pulp novel had succeeded, his career might also have taken a different course.

What kind of experimentation was he involved in? The indirect evidence suggests that he was trying out various ways of dramatizing the subjective nature of experience. Since Steinbeck's fiction has been considered to be notably exterior in its approach, seldom using, for example, interior monologue, just the possibility that he seriously considered other forms holds some interest for us. What he was doing may have been experimental for him, but not for fiction as a whole.

The twenties was a period of great ferment for all the arts, but particularly for literature. Forms, perspectives, and techniques were evolving, interacting, and changing with an energy and rapidity that most observers at the time could hardly keep up with. And no one has yet, even with the perspective of time, been able to unravel the complex interaction of ideas and movements of the period. It was as if a great wind carried a host of yeasty spores across Western culture—French post-impressionism and symbolism, Einsteinian relativity, Freudian subjectivism, and a dozen other "isms"—which settled here and there and combined in one permutation after another. Spreading from art form to art form, genre to genre, and artist to artist, the very air seemed heavy with budding possibility. A strain might be identified and labeled, but by then new species had developed, new patterns and combinations had formed, multiplied, and passed on.

Achievement in poetry or fiction seemed to be no longer gauged by how well a writer had fulfilled a set form, but by the affective power of the form itself. Writing fiction became concerned less with telling stories and more with devising inspired vehicles by which the writer could get the reader to perceive reality from a new vantage point. Concern for the nature of reality and the ways in which we perceive reality became more than ever the province of the writer as well as the philosopher.

How did Steinbeck become infected by this new spirit? Probably not directly, since he was motivated strongly toward independence and was isolated from other writers and the main centers of artistic activity. He may have been prompted toward experiment by the fiction of others—John Dos Passos's *Manhattan Transfer* (1925) and *The 42nd Parallel* (1930) are the most likely choices, although he also read James Joyce's *Ulysses* (1922) sometime during this period. However, after discovering, with some embarrassment, the extent to which his early models, Byrne and Cabell, had captured him, he became cautious about his reading of contemporary fiction and its possible influence on him. For the rest of his life, he was more likely to read classics than recent novels, nonfiction than fiction. The most probable sources of a stimulus toward a more subjective approach in his writing, therefore, came from poetry—Whitman, Yeats, and Jeffers—and from his extensive reading in philosophy and psychology.

What kind of experiment was "Dissonant Symphony"? Dook Sheffield remembers the discussions in Eagle Rock that led to the writing of the manuscript. Steinbeck had become interested in the way that personalities are formed and altered by interaction with other personalities, and he was also intrigued by the fact that sometimes the smallest event or circumstance, something that would ordinarily seem negligible in its importance, can lead to profound changes in a person's course of action. In an interview with Nelson Valjean, Sheffield also recalled Steinbeck's concern "that personalities are not fixed and stable, but subject to and influenced by the interpretations of the observer, almost as if the two were chemicals interacting on each other."

Dook remembers that Steinbeck intended to pattern the central character of his manuscript after his father, and perhaps it was Steinbeck's thinking about his father that as much as anything prompted the experiment. Steinbeck apparently saw his father, rightly or wrongly, as a man under severe restraint, both as a result of a lifetime of habitual self-discipline and as a consequence of the pressures from his wife's and society's expectations of him. Steinbeck let his imagination play with the idea that without these restraints, his father might have been quite different; and his actual father was left behind as he thought about a respectable figure resembling his father who might have a secret life or lives.

The writer determined to use for these purposes a structure that critics have called "The Ring and the Book," after Browning's poem, in which the central character would never be seen directly, but only through the eyes of those around him. Each of these narrator-observers would not only see the character differently, but the character would, in effect, become a different person in response to each observer. In addition, time would assume a subjective character in relation to the meaning and relationship of events in the observer's mind. Apparently Steinbeck also planned to use, in the manner of Dos Passos, materials from diaries, newspapers, and other written documents to enlarge the perspective and give further weight to the contrasts between the public and private man, his outside and inside dimensions.

In a letter to Carl Wilhelmson postmarked October 1, 1930, Steinbeck writes about his experimental work, although it is not clear which manuscript he is referring to, the "unnamed novel manuscript" or "Dissonant Symphony":

> It is so long since I have heard from my novel ["To an Unknown God"] that I have nearly forgotten it. Harper's had it the last I heard. In all probability it must be put away and rewritten in a few years. I think it is well worth rewriting. I am slowly working on a new novel now which is more leisurely than any I have ever attempted. The subject is not new or even recent. I rely only on the expression of the theme to give it any value at all. But in it I hope to get deeper under the surface into the black and sluggish depths of people than I ever have before. I want to show not necessarily why people act as they do, but to show the psychological steps which precede and clear the way for an act. There is material for a novel in the fact that a man goes to town to buy a blue necktie. My novel is by no means that delicate but it does move around among the tender searching roots of human beings. I think as I get older, things grow far more complicated. There is no end to the ramifica-

tions of every speech every movement of the hand. My time element grows shorter and shorter and months crop out of every crevasse of expression and gesture of people I see. The difficulty of this method lies in the fact that it is impossible to explore people below a certain level. It is as though a scientist, investigating an electron, said, "I cannot see this thing but it reacts thus and thus when I apply such and such. Now if I were that electron, why would I so react?" You see where it leads us—beyond the point where we can actually observe people, we have only ourselves to experiment with, and the probability of our being wrong is tremendous. . . . The series of stories about one man is a fair manuscript but of course it has no possibility of publication. It is just another of my experiments.

This letter serves to confuse the picture of his work in progress—both his description of his "new novel" and his comment about the "series of stories about one man" correspond with Sheffield's memory of his plans for "Dissonant Symphony"—and the picture is further confused by a comment in a letter sent to Wilhelmson only a few weeks later: "Last night I read over the first forty pages of my new novel and destroyed them—the most unrelieved rot imaginable" [10/30/30]. The "new novel" mentioned in both letters seems to be the untitled manuscript referred to a number of times in the correspondence of this period, and though separate from "Dissonant Symphony," it would seem to have had a similar experimental direction, as indicated by the references to psychological exploration, the effect on character of small actions, and changes in narrative time.

The comment about the "series of stories about one man" suggests the existence of yet another manuscript beyond what we have already accounted for, although he could have been referring in this way to "Dissonant Symphony." My guess, again, is that this *is* a different manuscript, and possibly the first attempt at the series of stories that later became *The Pastures of Heaven*.

Steinbeck reveals in this letter a heavy emphasis on the importance of observation as a basis for writing and an almost scientific approach to the analysis of character. This is one of most explicit indications of a significant change of direction from his previous writing, in *Cup of Gold* and "To an Unknown God," which had depended heavily on written sources—myth, history, and other literature. Furthermore, this emphasis indicates that Steinbeck's attraction to a scientific approach or basis for his work precedes the years of his closest association with Ed

Ricketts. In saying that he wants "to show not necessarily why people act as they do, but to show the psychological steps that precede and clear the way for an act," he appears to be referring to a process very similar to Ed's concept of "is" thinking—one should not ask "why" or look for causes, but instead look to see what things are and how they work.

The letter also indicates that in his experimentation, his struggle to find new forms, he had encountered a conflict between his attempt to enter the subjective area of human experience and his devotion to observation as the basis for truth. When we go beyond the point where we can actually observe, not only is there a high probability of being wrong, but we are actually involved in a form of dishonesty. In his letter he continues: "I know the modern escape is 'To be wrong is nothing. To be unconvincing is the one crime.' I cannot bring myself to this opinion. Somewhere in the creative mind there is a passionate desire for truth which has absolutely nothing to do with religion or ethics. The man who will distort the truth may be an artist who distorts for a given compositional purpose, but a liar turns out invariably to be a charlatan." That is, to project something you don't know to be the case was to him a form of professional quackery. Thus it is understandable, with such doubts under way, that only a short time later he destroyed a large section of his novel as "unrelieved rot."

What came of all this experimentation? In the battle between the subjective and the objective, the subjective lost—it didn't fit either his philosophy or his talents. From this point on, he thought of himself as an "objective writer," as he makes clear in a letter sent the following year to the writer George Albee:

> It is a gray day with little dusty spurts of rain. A good day for inwardness. Only I doubt that I have many guts of my own to look inward at. . . . That is one of the great troubles with objective writing. A constant practice of it leaves one no material for introspection. If my characters are sad or happy I reflect their emotions. I have no personal nor definitive emotions of my own. Indeed, when there is no writing in progress, I feel like an uninhabited body. [1931]

His personality had really made a subjective approach impossible for him from the start. He would have been distinctly uncomfortable if his emotions had been expressed in his characters—as attested to by his lifelong loathing of personal publicity. He could never have brought himself to expose, even indirectly, his inner feelings and thought process to public scrutiny—a fate far worse than having your photograph taken (and he was camera smasher on occasion in his prime). He recognized through his experimenting that (to use the words of his letter) "beyond the point where we can actually observe people, we have only ourselves to experiment with."

Throughout his career, Steinbeck focused on the discovery of and interpretation of what "is." Yet, while he thought of himself as an objective writer, oddly enough he never thought of himself as a "realist." To him, truth was the product of poetry, and the kind of poetry that produced truth was the kind that came out of a close and inspired observation of life. No other writer would write more closely from personal experience than Steinbeck, and yet no other writer could have been, at the same time, less specifically autobiographical. In another letter to George Albee, commenting on a manuscript Albee had sent him, Steinbeck wrote (in 1933): "I can't tell which of the endings you should use. The second sounds very Dostoievsky, and after all you never saw a prisoner flayed. You may argue that your reader never did either and so how can he tell. I don't know, but he can."

II

John didn't mind being poor, except on those rare occasions when he and Carol ran out of money completely and had nothing to eat for two or three days, but he did hate to be in debt. When he had gone into debt to his father while they were living in Eagle Rock and Carol couldn't find a job, he looked around for a way he could make some money fairly quickly. He decided on a dual course of action: one part of his plan was to enter a writing contest for novella manuscripts being conducted by *Scribner's*; the other was to write a pulp detective thriller that would sell easily and make money. In the advertising for the contest there was the suggestion that even if an applicant's story failed to win a prize, there was some possibility that it might be published in *Scribner's Magazine* anyway and paid for at the usual rate. The manuscript that he submitted to the contest was "Dissonant Symphony," which was tailored for the 30,000-word length requirement. After a long wait, during which he began to build up his hopes, he got his manuscript back. He did some rewriting and sent it out for consideration of other publishers in August of 1931.

The other half of his one-two punch—experimental novel to the head and potboiler to the stomach—was "Murder at Full Moon," which he sent to Ted Miller at the end of the year (1930):

> Conrad said that only two things sold, the very best and the very worst. From my recent efforts, it has been borne to me that I am not capable of writing the very best yet. I have no doubt that I shall be able to in the future, but at present, I cannot. It remains to be seen whether I can write the very worst.
>
> I will tell you a little bit about the enclosed ms. It was written complete in nine days. It is about sixty two or three thousand words long. It took two weeks to type. In it I have included all the cheap rackets I know of, and have tried to make it stand up by giving it a slightly burlesque tone. No one but my wife and my folks know that I have written it, and no one except you will know. I see no reason why a nom de plume should not be respected and maintained. The nom de plume I have chosen is Peter Pym.
>
> The story holds water better than most, and I think it has a fairish amount of mystery. The burlesqued bits, which were put in mostly to keep my stomach from turning every time I sat down at the typewriter, may come out.

Anyone who has tried to write commercial fiction can testify that it is not as easy as it looks, and it is especially difficult if all the while one is holding one's nose. By using Peter Pym as his pseudonym and by breaking into the narrative to tell the reader that all the elements of the book—murders, clues, and investigation—follow the prescribed rules of mystery-story writing, Steinbeck tries to send a message to the reader that he is above it all and a far more knowledgeable fellow than this kind of writing would indicate. While there are a few funny items in the novel (the first of two protagonists is a small-town reporter who has been kicked out of a California college for drunkenness, an echo of what could have, and some say should have, happened to Steinbeck), there is not enough good burlesque to make the book truly comic and too much self-conscious parody to allow it to be entertaining as a detective story.

Clifford Lewis has written an article analyzing this nine-day wonder from the point of view of Jungian psychology, and his analysis has validity in that even in this genre Steinbeck reveals what was of interest to him at the time. Ever since he began doing research for poor Andy's case in "The Green Lady" and "To an Unknown God" several years before, he had been thinking about "the black and sluggish depths of people." His concentration on the psychological in the mystery would seem to tie it to the subjective experimentation of his other work, giving some support to the theory that it was reading in psychology that triggered his experimenting, rather than exposure to someone else's subjective fiction.

"Murder at Full Moon" has its setting near Cone City, one hundred miles south of San Francisco (presumably modeled after Castroville, which advertises itself as the Artichoke Capital of the World). The coastal marshlands of the area, with their dense fogs, not only set up a *Hound of the Baskervilles* atmosphere, but provide a sort of primal soup. It is not some weird biological mutant that comes dripping out of the muck to commit the murders, as suggested by the young reporter, but a very nice old man who, by the primitive call of the full moon, is turned into a psychotic murderer. To give this Jungian-flavored mumbo jumbo some legitimacy, a psychiatrist from the big city is called in at the denouement to explain that the culprit is suffering from schizophrenia (the same disease that drives Andy in "To an Unknown God" to commit suicide). The full moon awakens the unconscious of the murderer, taking over his personality and forcing him to kill the people he loves.

Carol and Dook Sheffield both testify to the fact that it was indeed Jung that captured Steinbeck's interest, not Freud (whose theories, Carol recalls, he tended to reject). Aspects of Jungian theory, particularly the collective unconscious, found fertile ground in Steinbeck's previous interests in myth and evolutionary biology. However, it is clear from his work that he had also been reading abnormal psychology. While he took little care with Mac, the murderer in "Full Moon," he did take great pains with Andy's case in "To an Unknown God," trying to make it in every detail as clinically accurate as possible. This brings us back to what we noticed earlier as his concern for "truth" in fiction, a rather peculiar concern when one considers the near-fantasy of many aspects of *To a God Unknown* or the poetic license exercised in works like *Tortilla Flat*.

After writing "Murder at Full Moon," he went back, at the beginning of the new year (1931), to "working slowly on the novel [he] was doing before. The three generations of men" [JS/TM 1/7/31]. Meanwhile, in the fall of 1930 Carol had landed a job as secretary to the Secretary of the Chamber of Commerce of Monterey. She was hired to assist with special projects, such as a beauty contest and the Fiesta de las Rosas, and, as part of a survey being conducted by the Chamber, she worked for several weeks interviewing Mexican laborers. Her boss, however, was—to quote Steinbeck—"a drunken beast" and she had to quit before the end of the year.

During this work she had gotten to know Elizabeth Ingels, a young woman who had had some experience in newspaper work and in advertising, and Carol and Beth decided to start a business of their own. Steinbeck wrote to Ted Miller in January:

> Carol and another girl have just opened [an advertising agency] in Monterey. They have a number of accounts, no competitors on the peninsula, and they seem to be raising hell with business proceedings on the peninsula. And, to refute the inevitable anti-feminist propaganda. I am nominally the head of the firm. But I don't know a thing about advertising although now and then I do have a little idea they can use. . . . Both of them have had extensive experience in both advertising and publicity. Their most amusing account is with a local poetess. $10 a month retainer—heavy space rates for publicity stories and 25 percent of any increased sales in the lady's four volumes of poetry. I think that is sufficiently amusing. A pair of cutthroats they are. [1/7/31]

A major project was the creation of a directory. For three months they walked house to house, putting together the first directory of Carmel and Carmel Woods, and then sold advertising in the directory to businesses. When the time came to publish, they went to the print shop and gathered and bound the pages themselves in order to save money. Unfortunately, for all their work they cleared only $125 apiece, and the advertising agency collapsed from sore feet and fatigue.

It was about this time, the winter and spring of 1931, that Beth Ingels supplied, inadvertently, the idea for *The Pastures of Heaven*. Beth had been raised in a little valley in the hills west of Salinas called Corral de Tierra, and several events she witnessed there struck her as good material for short stories. She planned someday to write them and gather them together in the fashion of *Winesburg, Ohio*—tales of strange people whose fates influenced the emotional development of a young girl and the interaction of people in the small, confined valley.

Beth and the Steinbecks saw each other frequently—at the 11th Street house, at the lab, and at Jack Calvin's in Carmel—and at these gatherings, Beth told her stories. Such talk in front of another writer is usually a mistake, something that Carol reminded her of on several occasions, but she persisted. After the publication of *The Pastures of Heaven*, a small scandal ensued, based on the accusation that Steinbeck had stolen Beth's stories. But it was not Beth herself who complained; she and John remained friendly following the publication of his book, and in succeeding years she wrote several very complimentary articles for the Monterey paper about John and his work. All of which suggests that he had gotten some kind of permission from her, just as he did on every other occasion when he consciously borrowed material from those around him.

But the idea that the entire *Pastures of Heaven* was born whole from Beth Ingels's mouth is absurd to those who know anything about Steinbeck—too much of the book is too typical of him. Molly Morgan, for example, who figures in several stories is clearly modeled after Steinbeck's mother; Tularecito is one of many mentally handicapped characters in his work who are misunderstood by society; the story of the Lopez sisters was originally included in shorter form in "The Green Lady" (Steinbeck's manuscript); Junius Maltby reads Steinbeck's favorite literature and illustrates a favorite Steinbeck theme—the best among us (and the best in us) is often misunderstood and defeated by an insensitive society. In addition, the comment in a letter to Ted Miller about a manuscript dealing with "three generations of men" suggests that the stories dealing with the Whitesides (three generations) may well have derived from the aborted novel. Most of the stories themselves would seem to have been Steinbeck's.

But regardless of which ideas may have come from Beth, certainly the major unifying device for the volume did—the Munroe family and the curse they bring to the valley. However, according to Carol's memory, in the beginning Steinbeck did not see the Munroes as serving the function they later did. *The Pastures of Heaven* really began as an idea for a volume of interconnected short stories. Steinbeck wrote to Ted Miller from Eagle Rock early in 1930: "I have thought of a series of short stories which I have wanted to write for a long time. They might be tied together Decameron fashion or something. Most of them are not fit for magazines and maybe for nothing else. At any rate, I am contemplating them." References in other letters—as usual, unfortunately vague—indicate that he did write at least a half dozen stories during the year that followed.

The setting was also prepared for the writing of *Pastures* by Steinbeck's interest during these years in family history, continuity, and inheritance, particularly in father-son relationships and in primogeniture. Carol has said that he read the Bible a great deal at this time, underlining passages in the Old Testament describing the relationships between generations, such as the story of Jacob and Joseph which would figure so prominently in his rewriting of "To an Unknown God."

What first attracted Steinbeck to Beth's conception was the location, the small valley as a microcosm of interaction between families, which provided, as he put it in one letter, "aspects of American life." He seems to have thought of the name of the valley almost at once, and its thematic and ironic possibilities excited him. His original plan, as indicated by a projected list of contents for the first draft, was to begin with a description of the valley, go on to the stories that would deal with the histories of nine or ten families, then introduce the Munroes, and conclude with several more stories showing the Munroe influence. As he wrote the first draft, however, he began to have difficulties tying the stories together, and altered his plan, introducing the Munroes earlier. Finally, after discussion with Carol, he decided to give the Munroes the prominent place that they assume in the final version, bringing them into the book in the first chapter, following the introduction to the valley.

When the plan finally fell into place, he was so pleased with its possibilities that, uncharacteristically, he detailed it for others in at least three different letters. To Ted Miller he wrote, in May of 1931:

> As I may have mentioned I dropped the long work for a few months to rest from it. I am doing a thing called The Pastures of Heaven which takes its name from an enclosed valley in the mountains named by the Spanish discoverers Las Pasturas del Cielo. This is a mythical place but it is only mythical in name. The place is the Corral de Tierra and I would keep that name except for the fact that I am writing about actual people who live there. Now this is a series of related stories each one dealing with a family in the Pasturas. I had intended to write a three hundred page mss but perhaps it would be better to do a two hundred page one and combine it with the other ["Dissonant Symphony"]. The stories are entities in themselves and average somewhere near fifty pages apiece. The plan is simple and strangely enough true. Corral de Tierra, up to ten years ago was known as the Happy Valley because of the harmony and contentment of the people who lived there. They agreed on everything. The community parties were delightful. It became a place of almost mythical happiness. Then, about ten years ago a new family moved in. Their name was M——s [here he gives the actual name] (this is all true). They were just common people, they had no particular profundities or characters except that a kind of cloud of unintentional evil sur-

rounded them. Everything they touched went rotten, every institution they joined to broke up in hatred. Remember, these people
were not malicious nor cruel nor extraordinary in any way, but
their influence caused everybody in the valley to hate everybody
else. The place broke up into factions. One school teacher has
committed suicide and there have been two murders and numbers
of people have left the valley, and all of this can be traced indirectly
to the influence of the M——s. That is a true account of it. I am
simply taking a number of families and showing the influence of
the unconscious evil of the M——s. You see each family will be a
separate narrative with its own climax and end, and they will be
joined by locality, by the same characters entering into each and
by this nameless sense and power of evil. Do you think that is a
good plan or not. At any rate, that is what I am working on, and I
think the ironic name The Pastures of Heaven and the nebulous
parallel of the M——s with the Miltonian Lucifer is fairly good.
However I should like your opinion. Perhaps I shall cut the number of stories to five or six and combine them with the other. It
would make a very readable book, I think.

As the letter indicates, he was thinking of combining the novella-
length "Dissonant Symphony" with the *Pastures* stories to be published in one volume, but by the end of the summer, he had changed his
mind and sent off the novella separately. He then went back to the
three-hundred-page plan, adding the Pat Humbert story and the rather
substantial account of Richard, John, and Bill Whiteside. This latter
story, as I have already suggested, may have been a condensation of the
long work in progress that he described as dealing with three generations. Some evidence for this is given in a letter to George Albee written in December, just before he sent the manuscript to his agents:

Sometimes I think these stories are very fine. There's material for
ten novels in these stories. That was the method, you remember. In
the last story of thirty pages I covered three generations. You can
see how packed they must be. I should send them to you and to
Duke if I had time. I'm fairly convinced that I can't get a publisher
for them. They make too much use of the reader and readers don't
like to be used.

The year 1931 was largely devoted to work on *Pastures.* Unlike the
previous year, which had been eventful and filled with activity, his life
was almost stagnant and he often felt imprisoned and cut off from the
world. Even when the old Chevy ran, which was not often, they seldom

had the money for gasoline so when he had the urge to go some-where—to Palo Alto, to San Francisco, or down to Los Angeles to see Dook or George Albee—he couldn't. Only his walks to the lab and Sunday drives with his parents broke the monotony of his daily writing routine.

A major source of frustration that added to his feeling of isolation was the constant waiting to hear about his manuscripts. No one who hasn't been through it time and again can understand how the waiting can undermine a writer's morale. You wrap up your manuscript and send it off in the mail and a considerable part of your life goes into the hands of strangers. Every day begins to revolve around the coming of the mailman. As the days run into weeks, it's as if the manuscript, like Kipling's Morrowbie Jukes, rode off one day, only to fall into a dark pit of permanent quarantine, with little hope of communicating with the world of home and sunlight ever again.

What made the wait a little bit harder was that the publishers were communicating with Ted Miller, but Miller was not writing very often to Steinbeck. Miller would accumulate rejections and then, after several months, send him a letter reporting all the places that had turned a manuscript down. Steinbeck never received any commentary, any rea-sons. That's not because Miller was holding back, but because the re-jections were perfunctory—very polite form letters. But Miller became the scapegoat of Steinbeck's impatience, poor Miller, who was per-forming his duty out of friendship. He was struggling to place "To an Unknown God" and "Murder at Full Moon"—not an enviable case load—when Steinbeck heard of the McIntosh and Otis agency from John Breck (Elizabeth Smith).

Steinbeck had been in touch with Breck over the years; in fact, she was living on Telegraph Hill in 1929 at the same time he was living in North Beach. In the fall of 1930 she heard of a new literary agency in New York (perhaps from Carl Wilhelmson, who was a client) run by two women who appeared to be very helpful and quite honest. Breck sent them her most recent manuscript, a novel about early railroading, and in short order they sold it. Delighted with this success, she enthusi-astically recommended two young writers to them, John Steinbeck and George Albee. Steinbeck, who thought that Breck knew much about writing but whose own writing had never impressed him, believed that these two women must be miracle workers—he wanted these agents working for him.

Mavis McIntosh and Elizabeth Otis were two college girls (Wisconsin and Vassar) who had met while working for a literary agency during the mid-twenties. It was, as they found out, a crooked agency which took fees from would-be authors and made promises it could not fulfill. The two women left their jobs together, with the determination to start a legitimate literary agency of their own. By 1928 they had incorporated, and by the early thirties they were well on their way to becoming one of the most reputable and successful agencies in the business.

Steinbeck first made application to them in early 1931 and had Carl Wilhelmson write a letter of recommendation for him. By early spring he was hinting to Miller that perhaps representing him was becoming too much of a burden, and a month or so later he had Miller turn over "To an Unknown God" and "Murder at Full Moon," with a record of their rejections, to McIntosh and Otis. By August, Steinbeck withdrew the "Unknown God" manuscript, as he was convinced it would not find a publisher until it was rewritten, and had Miller pass along "Dissonant Symphony." Then during the summer and fall he sent several short-story manuscripts directly to McIntosh and Otis.

Even though they were not able to do much with these early manuscripts, both women at the agency were very impressed by Steinbeck's writing and from the beginning had great faith in his future. Elizabeth Otis remembers that it was his style that made the deepest impression on her—those sentences that in everything he did had their own distinctive rhythm. For nearly forty years (as well as after his death) the agency represented him, acting through the years as much more than agent. They did much of the editing that might be needed prior to publication, so that every manuscript was nearly ready to go to the printer when it was submitted. When Steinbeck became famous, they protected his deep need for privacy, blocking reporters and others who requested his time, screening his letters, and answering much of his mail. Elizabeth Otis in particular became his steady friend, standing by him as sounding board and tactful counselor in matters literary and sometimes in matters personal.

But in the spring of 1931 it wasn't just the waiting to hear about his manuscripts that had him down in the dumps, but the lack of an encouraging word from any direction. About the time that he was ready to switch over to McIntosh and Otis, he wrote to Miller:

I know it is hard to write when you don't know what I want to know. Rejection follows rejection. Haven't there ever been encouraging letters? Perhaps an agent with a thorough knowledge of markets would see that the mss were not marketable at all and would return them on that ground. You see the haunting thought comes that perhaps I have been kidding myself all these years, myself and other people—that I have nothing to say or no art in saying nothing. It is two years since I have received the slightest encouragement and that was short-lived. [4/31]

In the same mood he wrote to Kate Beswick:

By this time Little, Brown will have bounced the God [the last in a long series of rejections]. I guess it is due to fail. I'll probably write the missing 35 years sometime and try again. I'm feeling a little low. Carol's mother was down yesterday. She turned loose on me about why didn't I try for the S. E. Post, and make some money. The woman is a devil. Thank God we practically never see her. [5/31]

Throughout the previous decade he had managed to put up a bold and defiant front. Numerous times in letters he claimed to be surrounded by people who didn't like him or his work, but he was, he decided, glad of it: admirers can ruin an artist, whereas enemies and detractors help make him better. But often in the past he had had someone nearby—another writer or friend whose taste he believed in—who could, without being an obvious flatterer, tell him that this story or that chapter was really quite good. Now he had no one like that. Carol's encouragement was not enough, and Ed had not yet become the trusted friend and sometime critic he would later be. The best he could do was to write to Dook and to George Albee.

Albee, whose name I've mentioned in passing, was a young writer of articles and short stories whom Steinbeck met while he was living in Eagle Rock. He was genuinely captured by Steinbeck's work and believed in it so much that once when Steinbeck complained of lack of money and a shortage of food and clothing, Albee offered to buy him a pair of shoes and send them to him from Los Angeles. He was a man of passionate allegiances and vibrant enthusiasms. He, too, became a client of McIntosh and Otis, and apparently his letters to them were more often made up of praise for Steinbeck's possibilities than the actualities of his own struggle. Steinbeck wished with all his heart that Albee lived in Monterey.

Dear George:

Your letter arrived yesterday. I have written to you several times. If you don't believe it, I enclose one of the letters. Decipher it if you can. I have been filled with a curious cloying despair. The kind of thing that hampers mental movements as a wet silk robe hampers the legs. The origin of this is not simple. Probably the failure to entice an audience into my theatre is the main basis. . . .

There are a number of reasons why I wish you would live up here. We have literary acquaintances in Carmel—paper pulp and juvenile. They hate me and despise me because I can't "sell" anything. I haven't heard a word from any of my manuscripts for over three months. It is nerve wracking. I would welcome rejections far more than this appalling silence.

My new novel slumbers. I doubt myself. This is a very critical time. Carol's business is growing nicely. She gets prettier all the time. I'm more in love with her than I ever was. Sometimes I waken in the night with the horrible feeling that she is gone. I shouldn't want to live if she were.

I wish you would come up. There are so many things I want to talk to you about. Tillie [the Steinbecks' dog] is fine and nicer looking than ever. She jumps into the ocean when I tell her to now. We are just as broke as ever. More so, if that is possible. Money would probably kill me as too rich air would.

I shan't send this today. I haven't a stamp and probably I shall want to write some more tomorrow.

It didn't go tomorrow nor anywhere near it. And I must get it off this time.

John [6/31]

The "literary acquaintances" in Carmel were Jack Calvin and friends, who met informally over wine to discuss books and writing. These people were mostly younger, many of them had been to Stanford, and a few, like Calvin, wrote children's literature or had published pulp adventure novels. Steinbeck apparently brought to these gatherings a "purer than thou" attitude which inevitably aroused hostility. In late 1930, he had written to Carl:

We went to a party at John Calvin's in Carmel last week. These writers of juveniles are the Jews of literature. They seem to wring the English language, to squeeze pennies out of it. They don't even pretend that there is any dignity in craftsmanship. A conversation with them sounds like an afternoon spent with a pawnbroker. Says John Calvin, "I long ago ceased to take anything I write seriously." I retorted, "I take *everything* I write seriously; unless one does take his work seriously there is very little chance of its ever being good work." And the whole company was a little ashamed of me as though I had three legs or was an albino.

One can understand Calvin's baiting as a response both to Steinbeck's snobbery and to his attempts to displace Calvin's influence over such younger writers as Ritchie Lovejoy, but the full measure of Calvin's hostility was expressed in his conviction that Steinbeck had stolen Beth Ingels's stories. Steinbeck would come back from Carmel fuming. That he returned again and again is some measure of the isolation he felt and the need he had for some kind of literary companionship and feedback.

CHAPTER XIII

For a time in the middle of 1931 Steinbeck was cheered by the encouragement of Mavis McIntosh's letters. He wrote to Albee that "if I had not known her method of doing business, I should be very suspicious of her boundless enthusiasm." She was optimistic about placing "God Unknown" and even suggested that following its publication as a novel Steinbeck should try, with a collaborator if necessary, to make it into a play (since, as he had told her, it started as a play). She also asked for some short stories, and Steinbeck sent her what he called his "grand old unpublishables," which he thought "should damp her ardour to some extent." In fact, they did, for McIntosh and Otis found that nothing he had sent them could be sold, and thus there was very little encouragement they could offer.

The Sheffields again went to Palo Alto for the summer, but this did little to lift his morale, for he was so pinched for money that he couldn't get up to see Dook. Finally, the two families were able to arrange a trip together in the redwoods a week or so before Dook and his wife had to return to southern California. He wrote to Carl:

> I reread the Unknown God and was horrified at its badness as a whole. However I think I can make it pretty decent by working on it and by cutting, but these Corral stories must be finished first.
>
> We went camping in the redwoods by La Honda for a week. It was very pretty but I itched rather badly and made rather a spectacle of myself with my bad temper. . . .
>
> The world seems to be crumbling. It's about time. The old values were worn pretty thin. We may yet see Methodists dying on barracades in our cities. People are making communistic speeches to enthusiastic audiences here in P.G. Can you imagine that? And in the churches too. I really must take a paper. The times are too interesting to avoid. [9/1/31]

This sudden reference to the times is almost shocking, making us realize how ingrown he had become—or, perhaps, had always been. His letters tend to be dominated by references to his writing or writing problems, small talk about the weather, his dog, or his garden, or philosophical disquisitions on general topics, and seldom does he mention, as here, politics or current events. Despite the fact the country had plunged to the depths of a terrible depression, one has the feeling in reading his letters that his battle was separate, that he was having his own private depression. Indeed, his situation suggests that even if the country were prosperous, he really wouldn't be that much better off, in money or morale, until he made some progress in his own artistic struggle. It is strange at this point to think ahead and realize that in a few years he would be so thoroughly drawn into the times that afterward his work would be used to typify the decade.

Steinbeck also felt an increasing pressure to produce *something*. There was nothing definite, no dramatic accusations or confrontations, but his parents, through it all outwardly supportive, began to betray some doubts about his future. And he had the feeling that neighbors and friends thought of him as a failure, a would-be writer who couldn't make it and didn't have the sense to realize it. Nevertheless, he pressed on, story by story.

Although it was a bit tattered, he continued to put up a brave front. He told Carl, "I should have my volume of connected stories done by Christmas. Some of them are pretty good things. These years of leanness are probably the best things on earth for me. I am as concerned as ever that eventually I shall do very fine work" [5/1/31]. He took his mind off his problem with little things. As he reported to Albee, they bought two mallard ducks for the garden. "The drake has an irridescent green head. They are beautiful. They swim in the pond and eat the bugs in the garden. We are pretty excited. They cost our amusement quota for this month but are worth it. Named Aqua and Vita." They had pleasure in watching them for a time, and then he had to sell them to buy paper for his stories. Later they bought a two-dollar chess set, which they hoped would "eat up the winter evenings."

By late fall he was revising his *Pastures* manuscript, by the first of December Carol had the remainder of the manuscript typed and was waiting for him to finish working over the last story, and by the middle of the month the manuscript was in the mail. It would go to Miller, who would then deliver it to McIntosh and Otis. Steinbeck gave his benediction to the stories in a letter to Miller:

The Pastures of Heaven I sent off last Saturday. It should be there by the time you receive this. If the reader will take them for what they are, and will not be governed by what a short story should be (for they are not short stories at all, but tiny novels) then they should be charming, but if they are judged by the formal short story, they are lost before they ever start. I am extremely anxious to hear the judgment because of anything I have ever tried, I am fondest of these and more closely tied to them. There is no grand writing nor any grand theme, but I love the stories very much. [12/31]

With the manuscript completed, it was a happy, albeit lean Christmas, and Toby Street and Grove Day came down the next weekend for a celebration. After the rush to meet his self-imposed deadline in *Pastures*, Steinbeck decided to rest before going on to a rewriting of "Unknown God." By rest he meant doing a couple of short stories that had been "bothering [his] dreams" for some time. Still worried about money, he wrote to Miller, asking if he had any bibliophile friends who might be interested in buying a first edition of Pierce Eagan's *Life in London* (1821) with illustrations by the two Cruikshanks. At the bottom of the letter he listed recent auction prices for the volume, indicating that it should sell for three hundred, but that he'd take a hundred [12/31].

McIntosh and Otis received *Pastures* with little outward enthusiasm. Perhaps they felt that they had built up Steinbeck's hopes through too much flattery and encouragement in the past, only to disappoint him when the material did not sell. McIntosh warned him that short-story collections were very difficult to place, especially for an author who was not well known. Privately, however, both the women at the agency were pleased with the manuscript. There was no question in their minds as to whether it was publishable or not; the only question was, whom should they give it to? They decided on Robert O. Ballou at Cape and Smith, a publisher they felt had good taste and a reputation for being concerned with literary quality.

On his thirtieth birthday Steinbeck received a telegram: the manuscript had been accepted—it was the first good news he had had in years. Later he got the details by letter. In rather restrained fashion he reported his triumph to Albee:

The Pastures has been curiously fortunate. Cape and Smith accepted it with some enthusiasm within three days of its submission to them. According to M. & O. they showed a nice enthusiasm and intend to feature it on their fall list. I am very glad, more for my folks' sake than for my own. They love it so much. Dad's shoulders are straighter for it and mother beams. I am no longer a white elephant, you see. [3/32]

Yet, for all his pleasure in the acceptance of his stories, he was anxious to get back to "Unknown God." One might think that with all the trouble he had had with the novel, he would have abandoned it, but he had the idea to rewrite the manuscript in the back of his mind for over a year; it was, as he told Miller, too good a story to drop. In a sense, *Pastures* was only a recess from his work on what he considered a really major project. His mind and emotions had been steeped in the material for a long time, and the mythology (primarily from *The Golden Bough*), psychology, and segments from the Old Testament that he had been reading over the past several years had been percolating in his head like a witches' brew. It had thrown a spell over him much like, and probably connected with, his fascination with the *Morte d'Arthur*.

Previously, in the late fall of 1930, having sent off the manuscript of "To an Unknown God" several months before, he had written Carl Wilhelmson these curious lines, which give some indication of how the "Unknown God" material continued to work on his imagination:

Yesterday I went out in a fishing boat—out in the ocean. By looking over the side into the blue water, I could quite easily see the shell of the turtle who supports the world.... Our brains are rooted in some black mysterious murk like the great depths which occur in the sea. Somewhere in the bottoms of our brains there are hideous fishes, blind and slow and hungry. Some of them seem to carry little phosphorescent lights and others are known only by their bulk and by their movement.... I for one and you to some extent have a great many of the basic impulses of an African witch doctor. You know the big pine tree beside this house? I planted it when it and I were very little. I've watched it grow. It has always been known as John's tree. Years ago, in mental playfulness I used to think of it as my brother and then later, still playfully I thought of it as something rather closer, a kind of repository of my destiny. This was all in amusing fancy, mind you. Now the lower limbs should be cut off because they endanger the house. I must cut them soon and I have a very powerful reluctance to do it, such a reluctance as I would have toward cutting live flesh. Furthermore if the tree should die, I am pretty sure I should be ill. This feeling I have planted in myself and quite deliberately I guess, but it is none the less [strong] for all that.

In light of the fact that the relationship described here was to become a major aspect of the novel (in *To a God Unknown* a large oak houses the spirit of the protagonist's father), one might conclude that he was inadvertently rewriting the novel in his head while he was working on "Murder at Full Moon" and planning for *Pastures*. But he was also very deliberately thinking about how he would restructure it. "Restructure" is the key to his conscious plan for the novel during his year's recess from it, for when George Albee wrote to him about a publication opportunity in the fall of 1931, Steinbeck answered, speaking of his novel in the metaphor of a dismantled automobile engine:

> If the Unknown God were well done it might be submitted, but it is torn down like a Duzenberg having its valves ground. And it won't be rebuilt for nearly a year and a half. I thought I could finish the Pastures of Heaven by Christmas and I could too if the damned things wouldn't get in each other's way. Then I'll start rebuilding the Unknown God. It will be good to have a single entity to work on again. I don't think I like to write shorts very much. Still it was a change.

At about the same time, he wrote to Carl Wilhelmson, after rereading the manuscript and deciding that, as bad as it was, he might be able to fix it by "working on it and cutting." Later in the fall he told Albee that the title would have to be changed and that the story would have to be "cut in 8 pieces and the pieces refitted and changed." By the time he turned his full attention to the rewriting, in mid-January of 1932, he had decided that a patch job wouldn't do. Instead, as he wrote to Mavis McIntosh, he could "cut it in two at the break and work only at the first half, reserving the last half for some future novel." With the material of the first half of the manuscript, he would make a new story. Three weeks later he mentioned in a letter to Miller that he changed "the place, characters, time, theme, and thesis and name."

By eliminating mad Andy among the trees in Mendocino, which was the second half of "Unknown God," he had virtually wiped away the last vestiges of Toby Street's play, and his reworking of the first part was so complete that it would have to be considered a new novel. The rather dreary rancher Joseph Wayne is transformed into a central character of larger-than-life dimensions, part Old Testament patriarch, prophet, and priest, and part demigod from the vegetation myths; a new cast of supporting characters enters the drama, many of whom gain vitality from traits borrowed from the Steinbecks' friends, acquaintances, and relatives; and each character now demonstrates in some way an aspect of man's relationship with the mysteries of nature. The setting, too, comes to life, now almost totally confined to the familiar areas of Jolon, the Nacimiento River Valley to the west, and the adjacent coast below Big Sur.

The central plot device becomes the drought, a marvelous hook upon which Steinbeck can hang all his thoughts about man's relations with nature. Writing to Mavis McIntosh about his plan for the novel, he explained:

> Do you remember the drought in Jolon that came every thirty-five years? We have been going through one identical with the one of 1880. Gradually during the last ten years the country has been dying of lack of moisture. This dryness has peculiar effects. Diseases increase, people are subject to colds, to fevers and to curious nervous disorders. Crimes of violence increase. The whole people are touchy and nervous. I am writing at such length to try to show you the thing that has just happened. This winter started as usual—no rain. Then in December the thing broke. There were two weeks of downpour. The rivers overflowed and took away houses and cattle and land. I've seen decorous people dancing in the mud. They have laughed with a kind of crazy joy when their land was washing away. The disease is gone and the first delirium has settled to a steady jubilance. There will be no ten people a week taken to asylums from this county as there were last year. Anyway, there is the background. The new novel will be closely knit and I can use much of the material from the Unknown God, but the result will be no rewritten version. [1/25/32]

When he asks "Do you remember?" he is not depending on McIntosh's knowledge of California weather patterns, but referring to his use of the drought in the previous manuscript. The idea of using the drought was not new, but one that over a course of a year's thought and with the stimulation of current events came into focus as the basis for a new plot. Worth noting also is that it is not so great a leap from a homicidal maniac set off by the full moon to curious nervous diseases caused by dryness and insane joy in response to rain.

Another major element that Steinbeck brought to this final version of the manuscript was a second plot or subplot concerning inheritance, or the passing-on of property or authority from one generation to the next. Originally inspired, perhaps, by biblical stories, the theme finds its first expression in the unnamed novel manuscript Steinbeck was working on in 1930. Then, adapted from the novel, the theme is used in the story of the Whitesides in *Pastures*, and again in *God Unknown*. In both the story and in *God Unknown*, the theme of inheritance is tied to the themes of Westering (the movement west to California) and the Garden of Eden, a combination that would recur several times in his fiction, most notably in *East of Eden*.

During the first month his writing of *To a God Unknown* went "rapidly and well," as he wrote Albee, another indication that a good portion of the novel had already been written in his mind. Actually, the entire novel took a little over a year to write, and although there were the usual number of problems and delays, the writing went rather smoothly throughout, considering this was probably Steinbeck's most complex work of fiction to date.

As he began work, an amazing coincidence occurred: here he was writing a book based in large part on myth and Jungian psychology, and who should move in next door to Ed Ricketts's home (not the lab) but Joseph Campbell, who was becoming one of the foremost authorities on mythology. Campbell, who as a young man had been wrapped up in reading and research for years, had decided to see something of the world and ended up broke and without any resources in Monterey. In those dark days, the Red Cross and Salvation Army occasionally helped those who were destitute by boarding them in private houses in return for whatever gardening or other maintenance work they might be able to do, and the man who lived next to Ed took in such boarders.

Steinbeck seems to have lost no time in discovering who Campbell was and getting acquainted with him, for Campbell remembers Steinbeck reading the first page of *God Unknown* to him just shortly after he arrived. Carol recalls Campbell as an extraordinary man, extremely well-educated, who could talk with knowledge about almost any subject. He was frequently at the lab and at the 11th Street house, and, according to Carol, her husband picked up a good bit of useful material from him.

Yet, although Campbell was the mythologist, he feels he may have learned more from Steinbeck about the relevance of myth than vice versa. He soon discovered that as far as the fiction writer was concerned, nature power was the generator of myth. Later, in reading Steinbeck's fiction, he had the impression that some of the mythic images in it may have come out of their discussions, particularly in *In Dubious Battle* where the Madonna image was used.

There were also three-way conversations among Campbell, Ricketts, and Steinbeck, usually at the lab, about books and ideas—never about political or sociological problems, perhaps because their discussions were a form of recreation and escape. Campbell was reading Eddington's books on the new physics and Goethe's *Conversations with Eckermann* and talked about them to the others. He loaned Steinbeck the first volume of Spengler's *Decline of the West,* and he read some of it, but returned it, saying he couldn't finish it (although Sheffield remembers Steinbeck reading Spengler years earlier). Steinbeck was using Gibbon's *Decline and Fall of the Roman Empire* as a "pillow book" at the time and there was some talk about it as well.

This was the period in which Steinbeck, although he didn't know it, was beginning to gather material for *Tortilla Flat* and *Cannery Row.* The adventures of various *paisanos* were commonly talked about as a sort of contemporary folklore, the tales added to and elaborated as they made the rounds of the waterfront and bars of Monterey. What added a bit of spice to the stories was that several of the *paisanos* were sons of well-known families. Since everyone was out of work, a "bum" was not necessarily someone who didn't want to work, and Campbell recalls that Steinbeck knew many of the local characters and most of the bums on the Row and passed the time with them now and then.

Campbell feels there was one memorable party at the lab that might very well have been the primary model for the successful party at the climax of *Cannery Row* (there were, however, a great many such parties over the years, and they were very much in the same pattern). It was cooked up by Ed and John to be Campbell's first drinking party. Ed made the drinks with his lab alcohol, and at dawn they got into Ed's car and drove to the place where, as in the novel, the flagpole skater was doing his little dance on a platform high in the air.

During the winter and spring of 1932, what had been a cordial relationship between John and Ed grew into a very close friendship. Indeed, the whole atmosphere around Steinbeck had become warmer, busier, friendlier. Perhaps the success with *Pastures* had improved his outlook and made him more receptive, but his circle of acquaintance was also becoming larger, and among the more notable additions were Evelyn Ott and Francis Whitaker. Ott was a Jungian psychoanalyst who had a practice in Monterey. Considering what Steinbeck was working on, this, too, would seem to have been a fortunate coincidence. But Carol recalls that although there was some general discussion among the regulars at the lab, including Ott, of racial memory and so on, there was a reluctance on Ott's part to talk shop.

Francis Whitaker was a blacksmith and metal sculptor who lived in

Carmel. He and his wife were political radicals, leaders in the local John Reed Club, and they worked hard during the early and mid-thirties to convert John and Carol to a socialist point of view. It was through Whitaker that Steinbeck was later able to meet people active in the farm-labor movement. Although Steinbeck remained skeptical of Whitaker's politics, he admired him as a craftsman and as a man, and used him, twenty years later, as one of the models for the grandfather, Samuel Hamilton, in *East of Eden*.

In late February Ed Ricketts hired Carol to work for him half days as a bookkeeper-secretary, and Carol was delighted to be able to get back to work. Several times she and John accompanied Ed on collecting trips to Olema, near the Point Reyes lighthouse north of San Francisco. Once when Ed had gone collecting by himself, several boxes of turtles were delivered to the lab, and Carol typed out labels that said, "The turtle lives 'twixt plated decks," until she couldn't type any more. Then she and John pasted them on the top of the shells of the turtles and let them loose in the lab and office. On another occasion, they took a two-foot-long iguana, strapped a roller skate on it, and led it around town on a dog leash.

II

Not only did Ed and John share ideas and their experiences with music and literature, but they shared the same group of friends. The composition of the group changed as the years went by, but there was always a gang that dropped by the lab. The gatherings were irregular and impromptu—no one was sure who would show up or when. Sometimes there were three or four people sitting around the office or in the living room–bedroom, relaxing on a late afternoon: Ed sitting cross-legged on his bed, nursing a quart bottle of beer; John leaning back in the swivel chair, one foot on a packing case; and Ritchie Lovejoy hunched over the back of a straight chair, squinting through the smoke of roll-your-own cigarettes. A few more people might show up later— Carol, Tal Lovejoy, Bruce and Jean Arris—and put together dinner. If even more people came by, the gathering might turn into a party. Occasionally there were planned parties, which almost always lasted until dawn—and on a few renowned occasions, for two or three days.

The lab was a kaleidoscope. Everyone who was there remembers it slightly differently, probably because it was different at different times. The occasion gained its character from the number and kinds of people who happened to come together, and the number and kinds of people shifted from day to day, week to week, and year to year. At its best (from a literary or artistic point of view), the lab could be an exciting place, full of conversation, experiment, and discovery. Its potential was similar to that presented to the observer of the tidepool as described by Steinbeck:

> There are good things to see in the tidepools and there are exciting and interesting thoughts to be generated from seeing. Every new eye applied to the peep hole which looks out at the world may fish in some new beauty and some new pattern, and the world of the human mind must be enriched by such fishing.

This all sounds very serious, but in spirit it wasn't that way at all—it was fun prompted by intellectual curiosity. Some who have written about the lab have elevated its gatherings to a sort of unofficial branch of the American Philosophical Society, but nothing so exalted or romantic took place.

Virginia Scardigli remembers the atmosphere of the lab as 'Let's dig,' let's find out—a spirit which was in large part generated by the presence of Ed. For instance, one evening they were gathered listening to an African drumbeat recording that had come out of one of the Osa and Martin Johnson expeditions and someone got the idea that it might be interesting to find out just how many different rhythms were on it. So for hours they sat listening to the record and collecting rhythms. Somebody would say, "Stop! I've lost it. Go back and start that part over," and Ed would move the tone arm back and they'd go through it again. At the end of a long evening, they had determined that the record contained fifteen distinct beats.

Mrs. Scardigli remembers the atmosphere of the lab as "Let's dig"— let's look, find out, get involved. And this spirit was in large part generated by the presence of Ed. Steinbeck tells us in his essay about Ed that

> in conversation you found yourself telling him things—thoughts, conjectures, hypotheses—and you found a pleased surprise at yourself for having arrived at something you were not aware that you could think or know. It gave you such a good sense of participation with him that you could present him with this wonder.
>
> Then Ed would say, "Yes, that's so. That's the way it might be and besides—" and he would illuminate it but not so that he took it away from you. He simply accepted it.

Much music was played on Ed's phonograph, many songs sung, and a lot of poetry and prose read aloud. In a time without television and without money for other kinds of entertainment, there was a constant enthusiasm for inventing games, trying out activities. They could be almost anything, from automatic writing or a séance, to group composition of dirty limericks, or a costume party that parodied the dress and affectations of the wealthy. Joseph Campbell remembers that they had "let's get together and read a book parties." Someone would check out a new novel from the public library, or dig out an old classic, and everyone would sit around and take turns reading aloud from the book until late into the night.

The books read and talked about during these years varied widely, from the essays of Jung, to poems by Jeffers, the latest Huxley novel, or stories by Saroyan. One summer in the late thirties, the *San Francisco Chronicle* book critic Joseph Henry Jackson and his wife, Charlotte, came to stay with the Steinbecks for a few days and brought with them a copy of James Joyce's recently published *Finnegans Wake*. The group decided that the only way to tackle this book was to read it aloud. So, in a brave attack on its pile-up of syllables and words, each person took a turn reading for as long as he or she could until running out of breath.

Reading Joyce was not, however, a typical Steinbeck occupation. The farther he progressed in his career, the more likely he was to choose to read something for escape. During the ordeal of writing *The Grapes of Wrath*, after saying good-night to some guests, he turned to them with a book in his hand and said, "The only book worth reading in the whole damned house," and showed them *The Patchwork Girl of Oz*.

In the early days of the lab much of the informality, people dropping in and leaving, came from the fact that no one had a telephone and hardly anyone had a car. If something was planned, it might be talked about for days until the word got around—and sometimes the word got around too well. For an anticipated event, everyone chipped in what food and drink they could. The wives would bring their little balsawood cigar boxes with cigarette makings inside, papers and Bull Durham. As Steinbeck recalls,

> There were great parties at the laboratory, some of which went on for days. There would come a time in our poverty when we needed a party. Then we would gather together the spare pennies. It didn't take many of them. There was a wine sold in Monterey for thirty-nine cents a gallon. [Mrs. Scardigli says that Steinbeck always, in

his writing, gets the price of Lottie's wine wrong—it was thirty-five cents for the ordinary and fifty for the special.] It was not a delicate-tasting wine and sometimes curious things were found in the sludge at the bottom of the jug, but it was adequate. It added a gaiety to a party and it never killed anyone. If four couples got together and each brought a gallon, the party could go on for some time and toward the end of it Ed would be smiling and doing his tippy-toe mouse dance.

And toward the end of many parties, as in *Cannery Row*, there was a reading of "Black Marigolds."

Steinbeck writes of a party at the lab on his birthday which lasted four days, but the record, perhaps, was one that lasted two weeks, moving from house to house. No one wanted it to stop, so it didn't.

Besides the Steinbecks, who were frequently but not always at the lab (John more than Carol), the group's core could be roughly described (various people appearing at various times during the thirties and early forties) as made up of Ritch and Tal Lovejoy, Bruce and Jean Arris, Dick and Jan Albee, Ellwood and Barbara Graham, Remo and Virginia Scardigli, Toby and Peggy Street, and Toni Jackson. But there were many, many others who were there off and on, people like Joe Campbell, Jack Calvin and his wife, Francis Whitaker and his wife, Beth Ingels, Evelyn Ott, Tal's sister Xenia and her husband the composer John Cage, and even, a few times, the writer Henry Miller.

Most of these people had some connection with writing or the arts. Ritch Lovejoy, Dick Albee, Beth Ingels, Virginia Scardigli, and Toni Jackson, for instance, were all at one time or another with newspapers or local periodicals. Bruce Arris and Ellwood Graham were painters; Ritch Lovejoy was an illustrator; and Francis Whitaker was a metal sculptor. Although almost all were political liberals, and several were socialists, politics was seldom discussed at the lab. While there was political talk at the 11th Street house, politics and social problems were not topics that Ed cared very much about, and Ed was to some extent the mediator and moderator of discussion at the lab.

One could turn the kaleidoscope and see in the lab a collection of sages and explorers, artists and philosophers spinning in their orbits of curiosity and enthusiasm about the nucleus of Ed Ricketts's acceptance. Turn the kaleidoscope again and the lab might resemble nothing so much as a neighborhood bar, a place for people who were too poor to go anyplace else to get together to drink and talk, joke and tell stories, and sing.

Evenings at the lab commonly included a review of all the old songs. John in his deep voice sang the melody an octave lower than those who carried it, and while Ed couldn't carry a tune, he could harmonize. Toby Street sang an excellent bass, especially with something like "Swing Low, Sweet Chariot." His singing was so loud, however, that they had a hard time controlling him so that visits from the law could be kept to a minimum.

Steinbeck usually did not say very much, but among a small group of close friends, after a bit of wine, he could be outgoing—usually in spurts, from out of silence back to silence again. He was fond of shaggy-dog stories, the shaggier the better. Rolf Bolin, who, along with several of the scientists from nearby Hopkins, was an occasional visitor to the lab, remembers one story in particular that Steinbeck liked.

It concerned a Spanish-American War veteran, who, being handicapped by his wounds and destitute, was hired, as an act of charity by the town council of his small community, to clean and polish the cannon in front of the courthouse. Each day, day after day, week after week, he came every morning to polish the cannon and earned just enough money for him and his wife to survive. After many years, the Depression struck and the town council decided with regret that they could no longer afford to support this man, and they fired him. He went home in great despair to tell the terrible news to his wife. "Don't worry, dear," his wife told him. "For all the time we have been married, I've wanted to get you a gift, to buy you something special to make you happy. Every week I've managed to put a little money aside, a nickel here and a dime there. Finally, after all these years, I was able to get together enough money to go out and buy you a Cadillac."

Toby Street recalls Steinbeck's technique: "He would begin very slowly, and as he reached the end, he got faster and faster and faster. He'd be sitting, you know, and as soon as he got [to the punch line], his face would turn red, and he would get up and walk around, and scratch his rear, and kind of come back and sit down like a little kid. It was very funny." In conversation his voice rumbled out of the side of his mouth, sometimes with such poor enunciation that it was hard to catch what he was saying—very intimidating to new acquaintances who hardly knew what to say next, since they had missed what he had said. He was not the sort of person you'd ask to speak more clearly.

If you said something that he questioned or disagreed with, he'd look at you sideways, his right eyebrow arched up into the wrinkles of his forehead, and then turn toward you, his eyes boring in like the high beams of an approaching car coming at you after making a left turn. If he was perplexed about something while talking or something occurred to him that he disliked, he would make a face. When you said something that required an answer, he'd raise his head slightly, look up and off in the distance, and open his mouth. Then he would come back very quietly, look at you, and say, "Well, that's because of . . ." Occasionally, during a discussion, "he would throw his head up and act as though he was thinking about it, but I knew damn well he was just doing it for effect. He was trying to impress you that what he was going to say came after great reflection. But Christ, he could say it right off the top of his head. He was a ham."

In trying to deal with the possible influences of Ed Ricketts's ideas and those generated within the climate of the lab on Steinbeck, we encounter several difficulties in addition to the general problem of tracing and documenting influence. One is the difficulty in trying to separate those ideas Steinbeck may have had before meeting Ed from those he acquired after. Another is the problem of separating Ed's influence from a host of others Steinbeck was subject to during the same period.

The popular image of both Steinbeck and his fiction seems to belie the possibility that he was a man of ideas. We don't think of him as an intellectual, but as a rather large, good-hearted man, perhaps a bit gruff at times—a man of the people, who wrote either humorous accounts of simple folk or journalistic reports of the struggles of working people. We like his heart, we admire his eye, but we are a bit suspicious of his mind.

Perhaps the biggest strike against Steinbeck's intellectual power, in the minds of critics and academics, has been his failure to write very much really serious nonfiction. They perceive Steinbeck's output in this area as a large number of very lightweight articles and essays that tend to deal with trivial subjects or with serious subjects superficially.

Another grudge concerns his emphasis on the physical nature of man, his "animalism" and "materialism," as if somehow a writer who sees man as basically an animal can't be very bright. Even his fondness for simpleminded and mentally retarded characters has been held against him as further evidence that the author is rather simpleminded himself, lacking the intellectual depth and vision necessary to present fully developed "human" characters who can operate on high levels of human intercourse.

Among those who have judged Steinbeck, there are those who have wrongly assumed that he wanted to join them in being considered an intellectual, but that he just couldn't manage it—the fraternity assumption. On the contrary, he had no desire to apply—by writing criticism or philosophical essays, or by appearing at universities—and refused to wear any badges or carry any banners that might lead people to believe that he had aspired to or assumed such an identity. Indeed, he bent over backward to make sure that no one would ever make such an association.

While he was scholarly, he refused to look scholarly; while he frequently talked about intellectual concerns, he hated to talk about such things under any circumstances that made the discussion self-consciously "intellectual." In addition, the role came to have certain public aspects that his shyness could not have supported: he could not make speeches, refused public appearance, and if wild horses had pulled him into a studio, he would have made the worst guest ever to have appeared on a talk show.

For the most part, he was suspicious of and disliked professional intellectuals and was too individualistic to join what he considered to be simply another establishment. He identified the intellectual as a self-promoter who sacrificed truth and feeling to the advancement of his own reputation. While he took himself extremely seriously much of the time, he couldn't, as a rule, stand other people who took themselves so. He thought of intellectuals as destructive of creativity and saw their dress, speech, snobbery, and search for status as the quintessence of the very things he hated most in society. For him, the tweedy intellectual and the pot-bellied, hypocritical businessman were fraternal twins.

His vision of his role was writer as artist. As artist he had a reluctance to deal with ideas directly and publicly. Part of this came from a realization, born out of genuine modesty, that he had no great, original ideas to contribute nor much talent for dealing with ideas outside his fictions; part from a certain amount of insecurity in regard to his own intellectual stature; and part from a deep conviction that as an artist, his ideas should be expressed in his art.

For all his talk about his work in his letters and other private documents, he really tells very little about what he is thinking, what he is aiming for, and what he means. Throughout his career he had his secrets, and he kept them rather well from even his closest friends. He felt that art should be a mystery, and that mystery should not be diluted or dissipated by outside discussion or explanation. Rarely, as in his notes to Sheffield about *To a God Unknown*, does he violate that code. In short, one of the main reasons that he said little of importance outside his fiction is that he feared it might contaminate his art and weaken its integrity. His art was not a by-product of his ego, but had a separate, important existence of its own. The code baldly stated is, no matter how many people misunderstand or how often, an artist must keep his mouth shut. If he is going to talk, let him talk about the weather or the price of eggs.

But in contradiction to the public role that Steinbeck assumed, if we define an intellectual as one who is interested in ideas for their own sake, then surely he was an intellectual. The paradox is extended further when we realize that for all his general suspicion of academics, he was really a scholar himself: the drive to study and discover led him to spend a good portion of his life doing research, in written documents and in the field. Furthermore, he had an extraordinary devotion to what he considered to be "truth"—fiction need not be realistic, but it must be true. And, finally, he was almost alone among important fiction writers in this country of his generation in his interest in formal philosophy.

Unfortunately, Steinbeck's reading of philosophy was a private matter; he did not talk about it with his college roommates, his closest friends (up to the time that he met Ed), or his wife and family. As a result, this, too, becomes part of the secret, and we have only a very sketchy notion of what he read and how this thought evolved.

Because we have had only dim indications as to the sources of Steinbeck's thought, we have been led into a good deal of speculation after the fact. Working backward from fiction to an underlying philosophy from a specific source can be dangerous work: the critic is going to see in the background those sources he may be familiar with, not necessarily those which may have shaped the thoughts of the writer. Teachers of American literature may see American writers and thinkers—Jefferson, Emerson, Thoreau, and Whitman—in the background of *The Grapes of Wrath* and then extend this perception to place Steinbeck's thought, as a whole, within the American tradition. But despite Casy's speech at the beginning of *The Grapes of Wrath*, that "maybe all men got one big soul ever'body's a part of," Steinbeck was not, even in part, a Transcendentalist.

Although Casy's words are deliberately Emersonian (to give further emphasis, along with the novel's title, to the American, rather than foreign, roots of the revolution described), there is no evidence that Steinbeck was particularly fond of Emerson. He did share with Ed Ricketts an admiration for Whitman's poetry, particularly its lustiness and celebration of the natural, but the sentiment behind Casy's words was more likely inspired by the novelist's reading of Jung and Boodin (an influence I'll come to later), and his ideas about the human community in *Grapes* probably came less from Jefferson than from the tradition that inspired Jefferson.

If there is any evidence that Steinbeck was deeply involved in any national or cultural tradition of thought, it was not the American, but the ancient Greek. Unlike Ricketts, who rebelled against the Episcopalianism of his family, Steinbeck appears to have simply ignored it, never finding it particularly relevant. Instead, he developed almost intuitively a companionable relationship with nature, probably stimulated in part by the real, rather than the professed (Christian), attitude of his parents toward the natural world. It was a relationship that made him particularly receptive to the Greek concept of nature, first as a boy who had the Greek myths read to him, then as a teenager who read about the ancient Greeks, and as a student who studied Greek civilization in college.

B. A. G. Fuller, in summarizing the Greek concept of nature, has written:

> We have been accustomed to think of a universe, composed of dead matter and inhabited by a few living beings, which has been created out of nothing to serve as the staging and scenery for the all-important drama of human life. But to the Greek mind nature was living and companionable through and through. . . . Hence man found himself on a familiar and friendly footing with the whole of nature, at home in the world. . . . It is very difficult for us with our conditioning to enter into this fellow-feeling for the universe. The imaginative child perhaps still enjoys it.

In this respect, as in others, Steinbeck remained an imaginative child throughout his life. He always saw nature in an intimate relationship with man, often presenting a reflection of man's emotions and desires. While his thinking was often inductive, scientific, there was also something deductive in his acceptance of nature on its own terms and in his refusal to make nature a secondary reflection of something else. His continued reading of Greek history and philosophy long after college suggests a strong sympathy for the ancient Greek world view.

When a young man of middle-class family rejects or ignores the religion he has been brought up in and then goes to college, it is not unusual for him to search for alternate answers to the ultimate questions in his classes. Such was the case with Steinbeck when he encountered a course in the history of philosophy. He was attracted to the teacher, Harold Chapman Brown, because, like Margery Bailey, he was a maverick—independent-minded, skeptical of systems and movements and dogmas. He lived his life the way he wanted to live it, insisted on teaching only certain hours and only certain classes, and devoting most of his professional energies to teaching rather than publication. Unlike Bailey, who loved to bait students, Brown was very popular. Handsome, a good speaker, in fact a showman, he was what his colleagues would have referred to as a "popularizer."

Margaret, Steinbeck's Stanford coed on a pedestal, recalls that he spoke of Brown in glowing terms, talking more about him than about any of his other professors. Although he attended some of his other courses rather irregularly, he would never miss one of Brown's lectures and even attended his lectures during those quarters when he wasn't taking a class from him. Dook Sheffield remembers Steinbeck's admiration for Brown and his spending many hours at Brown's house discussing issues brought up in class.

Brown did not publish a book, but he did write several articles, two of which are revealing for our purposes in that they are rather generalized and appear to present a summary of Brown's own philosophical views. There are a number of items in these essays that parallel statements in Steinbeck's writing, but there is no way of telling whether or not Steinbeck read these essays, published in 1920 and 1925. But it doesn't matter. The kinds of things said in these writings were probably things that were said, with dramatic emphasis, a number of times in Brown's lectures.

For Brown, modern philosophy must work hand in hand with science. Science discovers and describes the characteristics of the physical universe which, in turn, philosophy tries to fit together into a larger picture and make relevant to man's position and condition. Man is but a physical object among other physical objects, an integrated whole existing with other integrated wholes, and within the larger integrated whole which is the physical universe. All that exists, exists in nature and is therefore ultimately subject to discovery by science. "Beauty, character, and thought itself, together with its products, must be viewed as part of nature." There is no separate world of the spirit, of the mind, or of the ideal. "The distinction," according to Brown, "between organic and inorganic matter is merely one of complexity and kind . . . life is the name for a delicately organized dynamic balance in complex molecular structures." In short, Brown, in his 1925 essay, "This Material World," argues for a scientific materialism.

These ideas, with some later modification, became fundamental to Steinbeck's philosophical perception of the universe. From this base, he would become, to use a term more familiar to those involved in literature, probably the most thoroughgoing naturalist among modern writers. Furthermore, what we see here in Steinbeck's early exposure to (and in my view, adoption of) the premises of scientific materialism is the beginning of a lifelong philosophical attachment to science, an attachment that brings us to an important difference between Steinbeck's thought and that of Ricketts. While Steinbeck, the artist, constantly looked toward science for enlightenment, Ricketts, the scientist, was more inclined to look toward art. In other words, Steinbeck was really more of the "scientist," at least in attitude and expectation, than Ricketts, and possibly more the scientist by temperament as well. This reversal would appear to be another aspect of the commensal relationship which bound the two men so closely together in friendship.

Brown writes well—lucidly, persuasively, and with very little jargon. His 1920 essay, "The Problem of Philosophy," looks to be an expansion of the kind of material he gave to his undergraduates as an introduction and an attempt to make the study of philosophy applicable to their lives. Although his bias here, as in his later article, is toward materialism-naturalism, his emphasis is on attitude and procedure. In a very commonsensical way, he treats the problem of building a personal philosophy, one that will stand the tests of experience and remain useful.

While he does not come out against systems of philosophy, he advocates that if a system is developed, it be open-ended rather than narrow and closed. The young person, especially, who brings such a closed system into life, may find it constantly undercut by experience. Along with the system that he has worked so hard to develop,

> he also brings narrowed vision. Not only does he fail to understand what does not fall within his scheme but he actually does not see the rest of life. Vision is not the mere act of looking but involves preparation, as every one knows who has looked through a telescope, a microscope, or been present at a dissection in a biological laboratory. Such a philosopher will see nothing that does not fall within his scheme of things and deny whatever threatens to wreck it.

Brown goes on to say that "the best situation is one in which the background for our judgments remains somewhat plastic while the details of its implications are worked out and tested by life. For the thinker, his metaphysics can not be first established and then his programme of life unfolded, but the two grow together into an integrated coherent whole. His philosophy is then inductively and not deductively established." Considering this approach to life in the background of Steinbeck's thinking, it cannot be a coincidence that the most common failure of his fictional characters is a failure of vision, nor that his most persistent theme is that of perception.

In his own life, Steinbeck tried to maintain an openness to experience. He was, in effect, always a philosopher "in progress." He seemed to operate during most of his life in two modes—writer or learner. A series of still photographs taken throughout his life might very well show that his most characteristic posture was that of a man, sitting or standing, near a campfire, at the counter of a coffee shop, aboard a ship, or hunched over in a chair in someone's living room—listening. By the same token, closed systems of thought, whether cultural, religious, or political, inevitably aroused his opposition or scorn.

The communist pitch made him shake his head in disbelief; the prune-faced fundamentalists of Pacific Grove gave him heartburn and indigestion; and the ignorance and superstition of rural Mexico, scene of *The Forgotten Village*, which allowed people to die needlessly of preventable diseases, aroused his anger. This last item presents striking confirmation of Steinbeck's role as scientist, while at the same time illustrating a basic difference between his thought and that of Ricketts. The script for the movie, which was made in Mexico in 1940, deals with a boy in a rural village who sees the sickness and death caused by contaminated water and realizes that the superstitious remedies applied by the village folk are of no value whatsoever. He determines to leave the traditions of his people and go to the city and become a doctor so that he can return and fight ignorance with knowledge. By this time in Steinbeck's life, he had seen not only the health problems in Mexico, but similar problems in the Hoovervilles and migrant camps of his own country, and he had been deeply touched by those easily remediable conditions.

In the film, he allowed himself to become a propagandist for science, something he was reluctant to do in *The Grapes of Wrath*. While Steinbeck in his work does not give blanket approval to progress (he has very mixed feelings about technology and industrialism) nor does he always advocate action (often in his writings things are as they are and there is nothing that can be done), here, in regard to health, the situation seems clear: science and education are the way out of disease and the pain of grinding poverty. Ricketts, from a philosophy composed of Eastern mysticism and eighteenth-century Western romanticism, disagreed. He wrote an "anti-script" as a counterargument to Steinbeck's screenplay, in which, rather strangely for a biologist, he advocates that the noble primitives be left alone in their disease. To quote from Richard Astro's summary of his argument (in his book on the Steinbeck-Ricketts friendship), Ricketts

> points out that an emphasis on "change, acquisition, and progress," symbolized by "high-tension lines, modern highways and modern schools," belongs "to the region of outward possessions" as opposed to the more important "region of inward adjustments." He observes that although "in an inward sense, the Mexicans are more advanced than we are," the powerful virus of "the present U.S. mechanistic civilization" can easily corrupt "the deep smile," the rich "relational life" enjoyed by so many Mexican people.

Since Steinbeck's script came out of several years of observation of needless suffering and represented something about which he felt very strongly, there was some strain in the relationship between the two men. Although this rather graphic illustration of their differences in philosophy came late in their relationship, I think it is a difference that existed from the very beginning. And I don't think it was a difference between someone who advocates progress and someone who doesn't, as Astro seems to suggest, but a difference between someone who believed deeply in science and someone, despite the fact that he was a scientist, really did not.

Confirmation of Steinbeck's attitude early in his relationship with Ricketts comes out in *To a God Unknown*. Although the last draft was written during the first years of their friendship, so much research and thought had gone into it beforehand that it probably is safe to say that Ricketts's contribution, if any, was minimal. Many readings of this novel by critics suggest an attachment between the novelist and his central character, Joseph Wayne, and a use of myth in the novel which represents a mystical-mythical approach to nature on the part of the author. While Steinbeck did enjoy writing about myth and seemed to like to "pretend" within its schemes of thought and values, *To a God Unknown* can be best thought of, perhaps, as a catalogue of superstitions, as a text on the skeptical scientific philosophy of Herbert Spencer and on Spencer's contention that God is unknowable.

The real "hero" of the novel is nature, an organic whole, which has its own being apart from man's vain attempts to control, influence, or understand it deductively. An entire spectrum of relationships between man and nature is presented, from the narrowly conventional to the bizarre and absurd—a variety of response to nature constructed out of Steinbeck's readings in the Old Testament, Frazer's *The Golden Bough*, Jessie L. Weston's *From Ritual to Romance* (1920), and Robert Briffault's *The Mothers: A Study of the Origins of Sentiments and Institutions* (1927). The point of the novel is that none of them mean anything, ultimately, although there is much conflict, prejudice, and suffering generated by man's delusions and the competition between various closed systems of belief.

Although there is no direct advocacy of science here, there is an exposure of the futility of the non-scientific, a criticism of closed, man-centered philosophies, an attack, generally, on the blindness and self-deception of religion. Even modern man (at the turn of the century) retains his primitive responses.

To a God Unknown also brings forward another aspect of Steinbeck's thinking prior to his acquaintance with Ricketts—the idea of the cosmos as an organismic whole. All of nature in the novel is interconnected—plants, animals, rocks, dust, and water; the moon and sun; the cycles of weather and the cycles of life. On two occasions, significant in themselves as they seem to punctuate crucial points in the life cycle of man, Joseph Wayne's body is identified with the whole of the natural world, and, conversely, the whole of the natural world is seen as one organic body. The identification is first made just after Elizabeth's death and before Joseph's intercourse with the earth mother, Rama. As he sits in a chair, drowsiness overcomes him and his arms and hands, resting in his lap, seem to change to mountain ranges, valleys, farms, and people:

> High up on a tremendous peak, towering over the ranges and the valleys, the brain of the world was set, and the eyes that looked down on the earth's body. It lay inert, knowing vaguely that it could shake off the life, the towns, the little houses of the fields with earthquake fury. But the brain was drowsed and the mountains lay still, and the fields were peaceful on their rounded cliff that went down to the abyss. And thus it stood a million years, unchanging and quiet, and the world-brain in its peak lay close to sleep. The world-brain sorrowed a little, for it knew that some time it would have to move, and then the life would be shaken and de-

stroyed and the long work of tillage would be gone, and the houses in the valleys would crumble. The brain was sorry, but it could change nothing.

In this very peculiar metaphor, there is no communication between the world-brain and the people and no possible comprehension on the part of the people of their place in the whole. Their fate rests on no reason they could comprehend, and whatever happens, happens because it must—not even the world-brain can alter the course of events.

The second identification of Joseph's body with the whole of nature is at the moment of his death:

He lay on his side with his wrist outstretched and looked down the long black mountain range of his body. Then his body grew huge and light. It arose into the sky, and out of it came the streaking rain. . . . Then a lancing pain shot through the heart of the world. "I am the land," he said, "and I am the rain. The grass will grow out of me in a little while."

Earlier in the novel Joseph had said, "Everything seems to work with a recurring rhythm except life. There is only one birth and only one death. Nothing else is like that." But at the end of the novel, at his death, he realizes that he was wrong, that all life is one and that birth and death in life are simply part of another cycle.

Steinbeck's vision of nature as whole takes us back once more to his college days and to the influence of another teacher. As I mentioned earlier, in the summer of 1923 he enrolled in an elementary zoology class at Hopkins Marine Station, and, as Richard Astro has discovered, his teacher for that class, C. V. Taylor, was in some degree a disciple of the ideas of William Emerson Ritter. Taylor was a doctoral candidate at Berkeley, and Ritter, while not Taylor's advisor, was an important philosophical force in the department.

The convincing evidence is that in an interview with Astro, the Hopkins biologist Rolf Bolin remembered Steinbeck telling him, years after taking the zoology class, that the one thing that stuck with him from that summer session was Ritter's concept of super-organism. It is possible, since Steinbeck was familiar with Ritter's name, that he was assigned part of Ritter's *The Unity of the Organism, or The Organismal Conception of Life* (1919) to read that summer or that his interest in the idea led him to read it later.

Ritter was one of those rare phenomenons in academe: he could combine, as he often did, writing about biology with philosophical discourse without losing his reputation as a scientist. His philosophy, to a large extent, appears to be part of the movement so prominent in the twenties that sought to reconcile science, particularly Darwinism, with religion and the humanities.

The most useful summary of his organismic ideas comes in an article, co-authored with Edna W. Bailey, called "The Organismal Conception: Its Place in Science and Its Bearing on Philosophy" (1928):

> The idea of unification and unifiedness with its concomitant idea of wholeness was never more alive and potent than it is today. So far as human society is concerned, the most explicit and influential manifestation of the conception has been the theory of society as an organism, as set forth by Herbert Spencer and others. . . .
>
> In the natural sciences the idea has become established on numerous masses of objective reality highly diverse in character and remote from one another. . . .
>
> The present writing is an effort to bring into one field of view the results of investigations in different departments of nature which justify the conclusion that, in all parts of nature and in nature itself as one gigantic whole, wholes are so related to their parts that not only does the existence of the whole depend on the orderly cooperation and interdependence of its parts, but the whole exercises a measure of determinative control over its parts.
>
> This idea of wholeness involves the recognition that a unit exists and is possible only through the existence of parts, or elements. . . . A natural whole stands in such relation to its parts as to make it and its parts mutually constitutive of each other. Structurally, functionally, and generatively, they are reciprocals of one another.

This statement reflects the essential message that Steinbeck got, directly or indirectly, from Ritter and which he brought into a philosophy already sympathetic to such a holistic perception of nature. The perception was further refined and modified in discussions later with Ricketts, who held a similar view, and by other reading in evolutionary philosophy.

Beyond an attachment to nature, a scientific outlook, an inductive approach to experience, and an organismic conception of nature as a whole, there is one other aspect of Steinbeck's thought prior to meeting Ricketts that should be examined in some detail—Steinbeck's adherence to non-teleological thinking. "Teleology" is one of those words whose meaning easily slips away and whose applications always seem a bit fuzzy. It comes from the Greek *telos*, meaning "end" or "purpose." We most often use the word to refer to design or purpose in nature and the existence of "God's plan." In the words of *Webster's Third New International,* we use the term to describe "the fact or the character of being directed toward an end or shaped by a purpose—used of natural processes or of nature as a whole conceived as determined by final causes or by the design of a divine Providence." Teleological thinking is goal-oriented (often linked with the idea of progress), usually associated with religious interpretations of the universe, and frequently tied to the idea of free will. Non-teleological thinking, in the traditional sense, is thinking that is mechanistic. One event leads to another, and what happens is dictated by physical laws. There is no possibility of free will—all events are determined—and there is no way of knowing whether or not there is a divine Providence, an overall design.

A great part of the difficulty with the term comes out of the circumstances that our culture, including our literature, operates on the basis of causal and purposive assumptions, and our very language has teleological implications. If one applies the term "teleological" very strictly, it is very hard to escape from it—in other words, to speak totally non-teleologically. Further complicating the problem is that Ricketts—the term "non-teleological" is his, not Steinbeck's—like so many self-educated men, attached his own meanings to words, and his use of "non-teleological" is partially his own. But it is a major word in his vocabulary, involves a concept much under discussion by the two men, and has become a key term in Steinbeck criticism of recent years. It also marks the place where Richard Astro, the most informed writer on Steinbeck's philosophy, sees the most significant conflict of ideas between Steinbeck and Ricketts.

It would appear that from very early, from his high school days or before, Steinbeck was, in this traditional sense, a non-teleological thinker. The precise source of these ideas in his life is impossible to trace. We can guess that it was probably a mixture of influences and events: a rejection of Christianity, because it represented for him middle-class respectability and because it seemed irrelevant and untrue; his early fondness for such writers as Mark Twain and Jack London; conversations during his college years with men in the fields who advocated a socialist-atheist point of view; and exposure to the materialistic philosophy of Harold Chapman Brown.

Whatever the actual combination, Steinbeck presented almost from the beginning of his published work a world that was mechanistic and independent of the desires of man and the presence of God. There may be enough immediate physical cause to provide some logic, but by and large, there is the pervasive sense that things just happen. People who act by their dreams are defeated; people who try to change things are usually unsuccessful. The best that man can hope for is to be able to adapt to what is and to survive. There is even a natural selection in his work. The weak, the deformed, the deficient—Joy in *In Dubious Battle*, the red pony, Lennie in *Of Mice and Men*, the grandparents, the Wilsons, and Noah in *The Grapes of Wrath*—do not survive. The healthy, amoral poor who deal with life on a biological basis are usually the people who can, like the *paisanos* and Mack and the boys, adapt the best. The middle class has been duped by a teleological value system that tends to make it easy prey either in the natural jungle or in the social jungle. To quote from Harold Chapman Brown: "In religion we hold to our dogma, extol the humble and praise the unworldly, yet, in practice, the humble are trampled upon, and the unworldly are neglected or merely the objects of a somewhat cynical wit."

Perhaps in William Emerson Ritter's organismic whole there is, technically, a sense of internal teleology. But if "the whole depend[s] on the orderly cooperation and interdependence of its parts," the only teleology for Steinbeck in this is the cause and effect of the gears in a machine. We don't know why one gear bears against another, or why this lever goes this way and another goes that way—it just does. Nor do we know if the whole machine has some purpose or overall design, nor can we suppose that there is some Great Mechanic in the sky. Man can never really change the operation of the machine in any significant way; all he can do is try to understand what aspects of the machine may be available to him to examine. For Steinbeck, looking and understanding are always the keys, and thus each man must be a scientist. In Ritter's words:

> The comprehensive study of nature when man is fully included in nature must be pursued with a mental technique adequate to conceive individual objects (of which the conceiving human being itself is one) and all objects to be so related to one another as to constitute the general order of nature, the universe. . . . The results [of Ritter's study of various biological processes] imply that all men should be naturalists, in the sense that they should be sympathetic in their feeling for nature, painstaking in acquiring knowledge of nature, eager in identifying their whole selves with nature, and critical in examining their own mental and physical processes in order to validate both their feelings and knowledge.

Of course, Steinbeck was not alone among American authors in presenting man as a small speck in an indifferent universe (Crane and

Twain), or as victimized within a society characterized by social Darwinism (Sinclair and Norris), or as subject to the harsh laws of nature (London), or as controlled by the physical-chemical scheme of a mechanistic universe (Dreiser). But his affection for the alternative to an anthropocentric view of life is unique. He was the only major writer within the American tradition of naturalism who reacted to science in a positive way, embraced a scientific perception of the universe with enthusiasm, and really knew something about science.

Because of his attachment to science, his approach tends to be more neutral, less dominated by irony and disillusionment. In realism-naturalism, one sees clearly and therefore is led to reject traditional or personal projections onto reality. One would like to believe in romance, in poetic justice, in a grand design and in a personal God, but in light of the evidence, one cannot. The resulting disillusionment, as in the case of the correspondent in Stephen Crane's "The Open Boat," often leads the individual to the anger of someone who has been swindled. By contrast, if the individual fully assumes a non-teleological point of view, he rejects traditional and personal projections so that he *can* see the truth. The fiction of such writers as Crane, Norris, and Dreiser often suggests that the dream is better than the reality, but that the dream is impossible to hold on to. Steinbeck's more thoroughly non-teleological perception leads to a fiction in which things simply are as they are. The real bitterness lies in man's attempts to divorce himself from nature and in his attempts to conceal or avoid reality.

In Steinbeck's work the revelation that the values of a man-centered universe are false—what he came to call the "non-teleological breakthrough"—is not an occasion for melancholy so much as for celebration in response to a fuller understanding. I suspect that Steinbeck's own lack of ego made it easier for him to accept the relative unimportance of man and turn instead to a calm and even joyful realization of man's interdependence with the whole of nature. Compare this response to that of Dreiser, a naturalistic author with a very large ego, who was almost destroyed by his reading of Thomas Huxley and Herbert Spencer.

Steinbeck's non-teleological approach is most apparent in his fiction of the mid-thirties and beyond, beginning with *In Dubious Battle*. In this novel Ricketts's influence would seem to have overt expression in a character, Doc Burton, who is modeled after Ricketts and who in speech and behavior reflects Ricketts's philosophy. Through Burton the author clearly sets up a non-teleological frame through which the action of the novel is to be viewed. This figure, although compassionate, remains detached. He declares that his main concern is to see, to try to get the whole picture, and this, in turn, is the concern of the book itself, to present the whole picture of men with narrow vision in conflict with each other and to do so without attaching praise or blame. The question is, is Steinbeck reflecting Ricketts's ideas here, or is he using a Ricketts-like figure to enunciate his own perspective because he found that the biologist in life was a demonstration of those ideas?

I think the latter is probably more true—*In Dubious Battle* does not mark a new direction in Steinbeck's thought. In his early fiction we also find a non-teleological point of view, but expressed more indirectly.

The world of *The Pastures of Heaven* and *To a God Unknown* is a mechanistic one in which there is no ultimate cause or design. While Joseph Wayne's life in *To a God Unknown* demonstrates the futility of man's vanity and the emptiness of his search for ultimate purpose in nature, there is, nevertheless, much about Joseph's character which expresses a non-teleological philosophy. As observed by the critic Lester Jay Marks, Joseph is in several ways a predecessor of the scientist figure or "Doc" character.

Although Joseph personally rejects the rigmarole of formal religion, he is concerned that each man follow his own belief. His only stipulation is that, since he will not interfere in the religious practices of others, they not interfere with his. Not only is he tolerant and accepting in this regard, but he refuses to condemn or be punitive in response to the killing of his brother Benjy, or to the girdling of his tree by his brother Burton. For Joseph, as for Casy in *The Grapes of Wrath*, "There ain't no sin and there ain't no virtue. There's just stuff people do." Furthermore, as Marks points out, there is in Joseph "the same kind of wide vision that is typical of Steinbeck's later [non-teleological] heroes." When he observes the ritual performed by the old hermit on the ocean cliff, he is not repulsed, he does not condemn— he is interested. He observes, "This man has discovered a secret."

Connected to his breadth of vision is his isolation from humanity. In Steinbeck's work the non-teleological hero—Doc Burton, Casy, and Doc in *Cannery Row*—is always something of an outsider, and by being so, he can observe more clearly the entire pattern outside of the small preoccupations of individuals. Joseph is never part of the group; he is always somewhat distant, preoccupied with larger concerns than the people about him. After his wife Elizabeth dies, Rama tells him, "You didn't know her as a person. You never have known a person. You aren't aware of persons, Joseph; only people. You can't see units, Joseph, only the whole."

This was the author's primary concern and a major theme throughout his fiction—he wanted the reader to discard the blinders of teleology and to see the whole as it really is. Even in short stories, such as "The Chrysanthemums" or "Flight," he is not just telling us about the frustrations of a rancher's wife or the tragic initiation into manhood of a Mexican-American boy, he is also—and for him, more importantly—defining the nature of reality.

The character of Joseph Wayne, so long in the making prior to Steinbeck's relationship with Ricketts, suggests that the role of the non-teleological observer was in progress and created without the input of Ricketts's philosophy. Indeed, what apparently attracted Steinbeck to Ricketts was that the biologist fit the role he had already created, and as the friendship progressed, Ricketts became more and more the living model for the role, which in turn was altered to fit the man, so that by *Cannery Row*, the role and the man had become nearly identical. Or at least identical in Steinbeck's mind—there is the further possibility that he did not always see his friend very clearly, but in "using" him, idealized him by exaggerating in his mind those qualities he valued most.

The two men did not always agree, of course, but even in seeming to agree, they sometimes were talking about different things. One of the most acute perceptions of the relationship between the philosophies of the author and biologist has been offered by Richard Albee, George Albee's younger brother, who came to live in Monterey in the mid-thirties. Having been recently involved in the study of philosophy at U.C.L.A., he became a participant in the serious discussions of ideas that usually involved only Steinbeck and Ricketts. He remembers sitting in the lab many times and listening to the two men discuss a subject in very similar terms. Yet, as Albee observed, although they might be talking about the same thing and using similar language, and might even feel that they were agreeing with each other, they were in actuality, Albee feels, talking in parallel, each within his own frame of reference.

The truth of the matter seems to be that both men came into the relationship with well-established philosophies, and neither dominated the other intellectually. One could just as well ask, "How did Steinbeck influence Ricketts?" as ask the question the other way around. They used each other, as friends should, and one would be hard pressed to say who got the better of the bargain. I don't think that any of the major ideas that find expression in Steinbeck's fiction originated with Ricketts, but most were developed and nurtured in the rich soil of their mutual enthusiasm for exploring ideas and their implications. They were like two trees of the same species but different varieties, which grew together, side by side.

Their ideas and interests often overlapped, but their needs were different. Steinbeck found a deep participation by writing; Ricketts looked toward some mystical breakthrough to a sense of a totally integrated reality. In his essay on Ricketts, Steinbeck described his friend's malaise and his search, which often seemed to be tied up with his relationships with women:

> There was a transcendent sadness in his love—something he missed or wanted, a searching that sometimes approached panic. I don't know what it was he wanted that was never there, but I know he always looked for it and never found it.... I think he found some of it in music. It was like a deep and endless nostalgia—a thirst and passion for "going home."
>
> He was walled off a little, so that he worked at his philosophy of "breaking through," of coming out through the back of the mirror into some kind of reality which would make the day world dreamlike. This thought obsessed him. He found the symbols of "breaking through" in *Faust,* in Gregorian music, and in the sad, drunken poetry of Li Po.

Part of Ricketts's mysticism, in apparent conflict with his Faust-like search, was an Oriental acceptance of the many manifestations of reality, whether beautiful or ugly, just or unjust. For Ricketts, acceptance (to quote from one of his unpublished essays) meant "not dirt for dirt's sake, or grief merely for the sake of grief, but dirt and grief wholly accepted if necessary as struggle vehicles of an emergent joy—achieving things which are not transient by means of things which are." Such acceptance, which seems passive, was not in his mind in conflict with the struggle toward enlightenment. On the contrary, the two must operate together: "Intense struggle is one of the commonest concomitants to a great emergent.... [But] where there is refusal to accept the hazards of grief and tragedy, as occurs more frequently than not, I should expect to see the struggle belittle rather than deify, since whatever *is* has to be taken and accepted in order for development to proceed."

In speaking of one such breakthrough, Ricketts describes a miner's wife at the scene of a mine disaster, talking on a company phone to her husband, who was one of the survivors down below. She talked to him all during the night as workers dug through the cave-in to reach those trapped on the other side. At last the rescue was made, and when her shocked and emaciated husband was hauled out of the shaft, dirty, unkempt and unshaven, she broke through into illumination. For years she had been repelled by his untidiness. She had blunted herself and him by nagging reform. Now suddenly all that seemed not very important. The fault was still there. If she paused to look she could realize it now more clearly than ever before. She was actually less blind than at any time in her life, only now she saw things in their relation to a far larger picture, a more deeply significant whole. She genuinely liked him she realized now, neither in spite of nor because of it; it was sufficient simply to face the fact that that trait was him whom she loved. She had accepted fully and without evasion the burden of anxiety, and something new was born again out of the ashes of struggle.

In such passages as this, the religious quality of Ricketts's thought becomes clear. To acceptance and the struggle toward spiritual enlightenment add his philosophy of nonacquisition of material goods and a belief that the pain and turmoil of daily life are only apparent, hiding from us the true harmony of reality, and you have assembled the elements of a doctrine shared by several Eastern religions. Ricketts did not convert his friend to a religious point of view—Steinbeck remained an agnostic and, essentially, a materialist—but Ricketts's religious acceptance did tend to work on his friend, moderating, as I have mentioned, his rage and persuading him in his daily life to take a larger perspective.

By his own impetus, Steinbeck did express a degree of acceptance, but it was of a variety different from Ed's. For him, people were the products of their environments, and he was curious about the equations expressed in individual lives. The inductive search became a habit of life, and he cultivated the ability to get along, even blend in, with a wide range of people. However, he could not forgive certain kinds of behavior, and he could not reach that "tower beyond tragedy" (to use a phrase that Ed adopted from Yeats) that would allow him to ignore injustice as ultimately unimportant.

Just as his personal acceptance was motivated in part by a scientific habit of mind, so the acceptance expressed in his writing was motivated by an effort toward scientific impartiality. In his writing there are no heroes or villains (even Cathy in *East of Eden* is simply a product of nature, part of the statistical extreme; indeed, it is out of the statistical necessity for such sports that myth is often generated—as in response to "giants"), not even the romanticized victims we call anti-heroes, just people caught in the web of nature.

A striking early example of Steinbeck's brand of acceptance appears in the first pages of *To a God Unknown*. Joseph Wayne encounters a wild boar eating a little pig. At first Wayne is angered by the sight: " 'Damn you,' he cried. 'Eat other creatures. Don't eat your own people.' " He pulls his rifle from its scabbard hanging from his saddle and almost shoots the boar. But with a sudden realization of the absurdity of his reaction, he laughs and tells himself, "I'm taking too great power into my hands.... Why he's the father of fifty pigs and he may be the source of fifty more." His realization is that man must accept events in nature that contradict his values, since the pattern of nature is not only beyond his comprehension, but it is also beyond his power to alter significantly.

This passage is also a good example of Steinbeck's "traditional" type of non-teleological thinking. By contrast, Ed's version, inspired by his struggle to "break through," assigned all temporal and material phenomena as perceived by man to the apparent, to the outward, teleological mask over the eternal and real. What was non-teleological was the permanent harmony beyond appearances. Thus Ricketts almost reverses the traditional meaning of the term.

In his discussion of relationships between the philosophies of Ricketts and Steinbeck, Richard Astro, using Ricketts's definition of non-teleological thinking, finds that of the two men, only Ricketts's thought was truly non-teleological. While this assessment may be accurate according to Ricketts's use of the term, it is also confusing. And misleading—since in order to appreciate Steinbeck's unique achievement in fiction, it is necessary to understand just how extremely naturalistic and non-teleological it actually was. Astro goes on to argue that "throughout his career, Steinbeck celebrated man's singular ability to pursue significant goals and achieve meaningful progress.... [He] consistently put the highest premium upon action, conflict, and change." Again, this is only the case if we judge Steinbeck within the context of Ricketts's ideas, and is misleading. The fabric of Steinbeck's fiction as a whole tells a somewhat different story.

Seldom in his work does action ever achieve anything or is progress actually made. In many of Steinbeck's novels a philosophical character with whom the author's essential sympathy lies is paired with a man of action. The philosophical character seldom acts, while the man of action does not usually act very effectively or very well. Steinbeck's point seems to be that you don't act to gain results—a teleological formulation—you look in order to understand.

Seeing, for Ricketts, was a matter of spiritual enlightenment, of moving toward that "deep thing" which takes man beyond the negative into a sense of the whole as more than a sum of its parts. Similar, but not the same, was Steinbeck's concern as expressed in his fiction that man overcome his personal prejudices and predilections, as well as cultural projections onto reality, in order to see things as they are. His hope for man was much more limited—that he see clearly so that he can survive, not by being the most ferocious animal in the jungle, but by exercising his "proven capacity for greatness of heart and spirit." For Ricketts, life seemed to be something like a long dark tunnel with a promising flicker of light at the end, where man might reach at last the peace that passeth all understanding. For Steinbeck, life was not a struggle toward anything, but a constant process in it. That dark tunnel, if that's what it is, is all we have, and in it man must wage an "endless war against weakness and despair." The only light we have is the light we create for ourselves by our courage, compassion, and love.

Bunkhouse door on the ranch formerly owned by the Williams sisters, Gonzales area, Salinas Valley. (© 1983 Richard L. Allman.)

Spreckels Sugar Refinery,
Salinas area.
(© *1983 Richard L. Allman.*)

Chemistry lab at
Spreckels Sugar Refinery.
Steinbeck worked here
as a bench chemist.
(© *1983 Richard L. Allman.*)

Workers waiting for train
to Spreckels, 1922:
John, far right;
next to him,
classmate Eddie Johnson.
(*Courtesy L. E. Johnson.*)

Steinbeck at Stanford, circa 1924. *(Courtesy Carlton A. Sheffield.)*

Frosh–Senior "Tie-Up," 1919. First row, center, without shirts: George Mors, left, and John, right.

Carlton Sheffield

Carl Wilhelmson

Mary Steinbeck

Katherine Beswick

Frank Fenton

Stanford Quad photographs, 1924. *(Courtesy Stanford University Archives.)*

English Club photo in 1926 *Stanford Quad*. From left, middle row, Grove Day, Dean Storey, and Webster Street. Third from right, front row, Margaret Gemmell. (*Courtesy Stanford University Archives.*)

The Ebright summer home (from the rear) on Lake Tahoe, 1925.
(Courtesy H. R. and Katherine Ebright.)

Caretaker's cabin (covered with bark) where Steinbeck lived on the Ebright Estate, 192
(Courtesy H. R. and Katherine Ebright.)

John: portrait,
sitting in chair,
early 1930s.
*(Photo by
Sonya Noskowiak, courtesy
Arthur F. Noskowiak,
The John Steinbeck
Collection, Stanford
University Libraries.)*

Carol, rarely photographed,
brushing her hair near the
swimming pool at second
Los Gatos home, 1941.
*(Courtesy Richard Albee,
John Steinbeck Library,
Salinas, Steinbeck Archives.)*

Children at entrance to Ed Ricketts's lab, 1941. *(Courtesy Peter Stackpole.)*

Ed Ricketts in lab with ray,
Ritchie Lovejoy pointing
over his shoulder,
preparing illustration for
Between Pacific Tides.
*(The John Steinbeck Collection,
Stanford University Libraries.)*

Natalya "Tal" Lovejoy
(in lampshade) at costume party.
*(Photo by Ritchie Lovejoy,
courtesy, © 1983
Iennifer Lovejoy Kelly.)*

CHAPTER XV

I f life was process, then that process for man, as far as Steinbeck was concerned, was largely a matter of learning. It was the major "action" for both his life and work. In his fiction, characters sometimes learn and adapt; sometimes the burden of what they learn is very heavy and they suffer greatly; sometimes they refuse to learn or cannot, and they perish. It can be a traumatic experience, as it is for Jody in *The Red Pony*; comic, as it is at times for Danny in *Tortilla Flat*; tragic, as it is for Kino in *The Pearl*; or heroic, as we follow the Joads in *The Grapes of Wrath*.

In his early life, the pressure toward learning never waned. He seemed to be always on the move, especially after he got enough money to travel, always reaching out to new experiences and new people—providing they were ordinary people in their own habitats. He would have done well as one of those gentle, persistent scientists sent by *National Geographic* to study primitive tribes in New Guinea.

What amazed many of those near him over the years was the delight he found in his personal discoveries by observation of little things. Both his personality and his work seem bound by this affection for detail, a capacity to be amused, even engrossed by the peculiarities of things—a word or phrase, the expression on a woman's face, the coloration of a leaf, the functioning of an unusual piece of hardware—that most of us would consider trivial. If there are two kinds of people in the world—those who say, "Look at that!" and those who say, "So what?"—Steinbeck was the former.

In this regard, perhaps the greatest gift Ricketts gave him was getting him involved in the day-to-day work of the lab and in the specifics of science. There is no exterior record of the many collecting trips they took and the time they spent consulting reference books and working over specimens, but there is little doubt that in an offhand way, as part of their shared experiences, Steinbeck received a fairly extensive course in practical zoology. He even took to wearing a field magnifying glass, and in private, Ricketts laughed and shook his head at his friend's pretensions to expertise.

During the spring and summer of 1932, Carol was also in the lab quite a bit, working part-time for Ed. Even in those days, fifty dollars a month for half days of skilled work was not much of a salary, but Ed was not a demanding boss, and there was sometimes almost as much fun at the lab as there was work. Steinbeck wrote to Albee: "Carol is working now and loves it. She has two rattlesnakes and about 200 white rats to love. She introduced Tillie [their Airedale] to the rats and they ignored each other. Like Omar and the garbage bear—one of my oldest stories but far from a good one."

In a dramatic moment during that spring, he decided to dispose of most of these old stories. He wrote Albee, "The other day I burned a pile of stories a foot and a half high. At least sixty or seventy of them and all waste in a way." On this occasion (witnessed by Joe Campbell), as well on several similar occasions later, he took a perverse pleasure in purifying his oeuvre. It wasn't done out of despair, since work on *To a God Unknown* was going forward very well. In fact he mentioned in a letter, "I'm really writing too fast I suppose, but that's the way it comes and I see no reason to put on the brakes" [JS/GA]. Later, after his work had been interrupted, he wrote, "I have got back to my novel with all the old relish. The days are ecstatic and the nights delirious. What the thing will be I don't care. The unspeakable joy of merging into this world I am building is more than enough" [JS/GA].

But from the world outside, some unhappiness began to rush in upon him. He began to halfway join with his mother in her superstitious fear of March as a month of disaster. In a tragedy that saddened the whole family, his sister Beth's son died, and Steinbeck drove to Fresno as quickly as he could to be at her side. At almost the same time, he learned that Jonathan Cape, his publisher for *The Pastures of Heaven*, had gone into bankruptcy. Part of his previous joy had come from the fact that he thought that he didn't have to worry about publication for some time: he had been given a contract that he thought guaranteed, sight unseen, the acceptance of the two books beyond *Pastures*.

Abruptly, he was thrust once again among the thousands of would-be writers, each trying to make his voice heard above the others. At such times, one feels he would have been better off if he had been left in the water than pulled out, given comfort, and then pushed back in. Fortunately, his frustration was short-lived. He got word that Robert

Ballou, his editor at Cape, was going to a new firm—Brewer, Warren, and Putnam—and wanted to take Steinbeck with him on the same terms. Steinbeck, who had formed a high opinon of Ballou on the basis of reports from McIntosh and Otis, accepted. The manuscript went to Putnam in May, and production went ahead on schedule.

Also in May, Steinbeck forwarded to his agents the manuscript of "St. Katy the Virgin," probably the most peculiar of all his published short stories, a farcical history of the religious conversion and eventual canonization of a fourteenth-century French pig. It was first written at Stanford as a verse parody, based on literary conventions and cultural practices of the Middle Ages that he had gleaned from a course in European civilization. The story's subject matter and its manner are very reminiscent of Twain, and it is filled with sly humor of the sort that Steinbeck enjoyed enormously: "Daily at four o'clock, Katy emerged from the gates and blessed the multitudes. If any were afflicted with scrofula or trichina, she touched them and they were healed."

His attachment for the story can be measured by the fact that it was one of the few things (in its preliminary form) that he kept out of the manuscript fire of the previous spring, and by his persistence in trying to get it published. After several years of submissions without a nibble, he had finally arranged with his book publisher at the time, Covici-Friede, for separate publication as a gift book. Then he insisted on including it in his story collection *The Long Valley*, even though it is so different in kind from the other items that the reader hardly knows what to make of it.

Also, perhaps because Mavis McIntosh had suggested that he adapt his novel when it was finished for the stage, he was experimenting with play writing. In one of the few things he would have normally burned, which survived by accident (operating on Depression economics, Carol rescued a child's composition book from the trash and used it as a scrapbook for newspaper clippings), he wrote a "practice play" called "The Wizard." His accompanying notes suggest that it was his first attempt at the form.

Whereas only a few months before he had complained that "there is no companionship of any kind here. Carol and I are marooned," he now wrote to Albee, during the summer:

We are having a fine time now. We have a group with different major interests and similar minor interests. We are infesting the country. I'm getting about eight pages a day done. The book is nearly half finished and I am filled with excitement when I contemplate it. The plan is working so far and the pictures—as I see them at least, are sharp and deep. If I can go on I'll be finished in two months. But I'm working harder than I know. Sometimes I feel an incipient exhaustion. If I can keep that down for two months everything will be clear. Every book I say I have the most fun with. I'm surely having the most fun with this one. We're going down the coast this evening—six of us to have dinner forty-five miles down on a cliff. Last week we found a haunted house on top of a mountain at midnight. And it was really haunted. A grisly white house on a round peak and the whole world lying around at its feet. This is the good time. I've borrowed a lot of Bach to play on the phonograph. And I've just cleaned my pipes with alcohol and they taste wonderful.

Yet, in midsummer the Steinbecks decided to move back to southern California. It was clear that they had been in Pacific Grove only because they didn't have the money to be elsewhere, and over the past year, John had written to both Dook and George Albee expressing the desire to get away, to move closer to them so that he would have someone to talk to about his writing. Then in July, Carol lost her job with Ed, and that, in combination with the advance that would be coming for *Pastures*, prompted them to move, almost on the spur of the moment, back to the Montrose area, just north of Eagle Rock.

Carol lost her job because Ed could no longer afford to pay her. As John explains in the letter to Albee cited above, Ed's "wife just left him taking all the available money and leaving a lot of debts. . . . We'll feed him until he has money. He is a very good man. His wife left him because he was interested in things other than bridge and kiddies. I've seen her jaw muscles bulge with rage if his conversation ever turned from those two." Not exactly a fair assessment, but among the many problems that separated the two, there was apparently a feeling on Nan's part that her husband was growing away from her, a feeling not entirely free of jealousy in response to friends, including Steinbeck, and interests she did not share.

In the meantime, John had received the galley proofs for *Pastures* and a request from Ballou for biographical material for publicity and dust-jacket copy. In a response typical of him throughout his life, he was embarrassed and uneasy. "I can't say how much I wish this kind of thing weren't necessary." He claimed that although he had no reluctance to write the "unreticent story" of his life that Ballou had asked for, he ran into a problem of emphasis:

> Things of the greatest emphasis to me would be more or less meaningless to anyone else. Such a biography would consist of such things as—the way the sparrows hopped about on the mud street early in the morning when I was little—how the noon bell sounded when we were writing dirty words on the sidewalk with red fuchsia berries—how teddy got run over by a fire engine, and the desolation of loss—the most tremendous morning in the world when my pony had a cold.
>
> What you undoubtedly want is about two paragraphs of facts. I've forgotten so many of the facts. I don't remember what is true and what might have been true. It hasn't been a story to write about, you see. Nothing much has ever happened. [6/10/32]

Yet it became a story to write about, after all. Either Ballou's request started his mind working on the past or he had already considered using his early experiences as the basis for a story. His next project would be the first of the stories that would make up *The Red Pony*, a story that would use the very kinds of childhood impressions he lists in his letter.

When John and Carol arrived in Eagle Rock, they stayed with the Sheffields once again, until they were able to find a place of their own. Once again, the southern California sun evoked a kind of madness. Maryon and Carol decided to talk John into peroxiding his hair, and the result was the most electrifying orange that anyone might imagine. The next day the two couples had a date to meet Steinbeck's sister Mary at the beach. The Chevrolet, an open touring car, was not in very good condition, numbering among its disabilities a leaky radiator. Someone had told Steinbeck that cornmeal would stop the leak, and he put some in the radiator.

At eleven o'clock the next morning the sun was so hot it seemed to turn the air into a hot, sticky screen that enclosed the car. According to Sheffield,

> we were driving down Sunset Boulevard toward Santa Monica, and I am sure we caused wrecks, because people would see that hair and suddenly turn around. Then in the middle of it, the radiator started spouting, spouting cornmeal all over the windshield and then all over us. We eventually got to Santa Monica and here was Mary, all neatly set out on a rug on the sand. . . . she had children

by that time, a couple of babies I think. She took one look at John and refused to have anything to do with him. She wouldn't let any of us sit on her rug. She didn't want to let on that she knew us. As for his hair, it took weeks. . . . I think he finally gave up and dyed his hair black. And that was almost as bad as the orange.

A few weeks later Francis Whitaker was at the lab in Monterey drinking with Ed, and sometime after midnight, they started out in Ed's old Packard to take Francis home. It was a beautiful moonlit night, and one of them said, "It's a shame to go home on a night like this." And the other: "Yes, it really is a beautiful night." "What shall we do?" "Let's go down to Los Angeles and see John." The first thing that Sheffield knew about it was when he got up in the morning and found the two of them asleep on the couch in the front room.

The next afternoon everyone had had quite a lot of beer, especially Whitaker, when John decided to take the new arrivals over to Hollywood to see Mahlon Blaine. Whitaker was enjoying the sun so much that he had stripped naked and was lying on top of the Packard. Ed and John got in the car and drove to Hollywood with Whitaker sunbathing on top. They went in, saw Blaine, came back out, and drove home, with Whitaker still nude, still sunbathing on top of the Packard. After four days the two men had to leave, and as they shook hands, Whitaker said, "This is a wonderful place to visit, but God, I couldn't stand the pace down here."

The Steinbecks found a house to rent in Montrose, but as the fall progressed, lack of money became a severe problem. Part of the plan was for Steinbeck to write some sketches of local interest to sell to newspapers, but he was unable to find anyone who would buy such free-lance material. The income from this was supposed to tide them over until the check came from Putnam at the end of October. By the end of September, they were in such bad shape that he had to borrow a hundred dollars from Albee, which he secured, in the words of his I.O.U., with "the slightly questionable collateral of a contract held by me from Brewer, Warren, and Putnam." Brewer, Warren, and Putnam, predictably, went bankrupt right after publishing *The Pastures of Heaven*. He did eventually get some advance against royalties, but as might be expected under the circumstances, the book came out without any advertising and with only catch-as-catch-can distribution. His total income from *Pastures* was meager—and what was worse, he had spent much of it before he got it. All in all, neither his fame nor his fortune was advanced much by the publication he had worked so hard for.

His parents forwarded enough money for them to go north for Christmas, but on their return to Montrose, they found themselves in the deepest financial hole they had ever been in. The money given to them every month by John's father wasn't enough to cover the rent and food, let alone other expenses, and their schemes for making a little extra money to get by on had all turned sour. They lived on hope—hope that more money might come in from *Pastures,* hope that one of John's stories might sell. In desperation he even turned again to "Murder at Full Moon," writing to Mavis McIntosh:

> We live in the hills back of Los Angeles now and there are few people around. One of our neighbors loaned me three hundred detective magazines, and I have read a large part of them out of pure boredom. They are so utterly lousy that I wonder whether you have tried to peddle that thing I dashed off to any of them. It might mean a few dollars. Could be very much cut to fit, you know. Will you think about it? It would be better than letting it lie around, don't you think? [1/33]

By mid-February 1933 their situation had become impossible. He told Ballou:

> Apparently we are heading for the rocks. The light company is going to turn off the power in a few days, but we don't care much. The rent is up pretty soon and then we shall move. I don't know where. It doesn't matter. My wife says she would much rather go out and meet disaster, then to have it sneak up on her. The attacking force has the advantage. I feel the same way. We'll get in the car and drive until we can't buy gasoline any more. [2/11/33]

They did pack up the car and drove south, not knowing where they would stop or what they would do when they got there. As the Chevy chugged along the coast highway, overheating and threatening collapse, they must have felt very much as the migrants felt making their way along Highway 66 to California.

They got about a hundred miles before they stopped at the resort-retirement community of Laguna Beach, where they found a little shack with tar-paper roof in the poor part of town below the Arches, which they could rent by the week for only a couple of dollars. Shortly after they arrived, Polly Smith stopped by to find them in good spirits but completely broke. John was glad to see her because Carol had finished typing *To a God Unknown,* but they didn't have enough money to pay for the postage to send it to his agents. John had climbed up to the roof of the house and cut off two overlapping flaps of tar paper and had used them to bind the manuscript, but Polly bought him a proper cover that weighed a half pound less, and paid the postage and registration.

Another visit was more peculiar. During the time of the Los Angeles earthquake of March 1933, John was awakened and saw a woman standing in the room where they were sleeping. She was someone both John and Carol knew. He tried to wake Carol quietly, but was unable to do so. Later, they saw the woman in Sausalito, and without a word from the Steinbecks, she asked, "Did I get through to you?" The explanation they tentatively settled on was that somehow the earthquake must have disturbed the vibrations enough to allow some kind of astral projection.

Such phenomena, as we have already seen, were not uncommon in Steinbeck's life, particularly during his youth, and they seem to pose an odd contradiction in a person attached in so many ways to science and scientific thought. Still, such reports do remind us that above all Steinbeck was a poet. He loved strange occurrences enough, perhaps, to will himself in some way to experience them. Obviously, some of his ghosts and visitations were just talk, an inheritance from his mother, talk that he indulged himself in as he had earlier talked about his leprechauns. Others may have been actual hallucinations, produced by combinations of hunger, fatigue, and alcohol. But not much stimulus is necessary for an imaginative man who half believes that nearly anything is possible: if he spends his day summoning vivid images to his mind, an image or two may very well come on occasion unbidden.

Robert Ballou, still holding to his agreement with Steinbeck, had pulled together the pieces from the last bankruptcy and this time had formed his own company. After forwarding *To a God Unknown* to McIntosh and Otis, Steinbeck wrote to him a covering letter—it was one man who couldn't pay his electric bill writing across the country to another man who was afraid he couldn't pay the printer:

> I shipped mss. to Miss O. this morning. You should get it before very long. I hope you will like it. The book was hellish hard to write. I had been making notes for it for about five years. It will probably be a hard book to sell. Its characters are not "home folks." They make no more attempt at being sincerely human than the people in the Iliad. Boileau (much like your name) insisted that only gods, kings and heroes were worth writing about. I firmly be-

lieve that. The detailed accounts of the lives of clerks don't interest me much, unless, of course, the clerk breaks into heroism. But I have no intention of trying to explain my book. It has to do that for itself. I would be sure of its effect if it could be stipulated that the readers read to an obbligato of Bach. [He listened to Bach while composing the novel.]

Ballou should be given credit for standing by Steinbeck at a critical time, and the irony of his loyalty was that it didn't last quite long enough. If he had been able to stay with Steinbeck for one more book, he might well have recovered his losses and gone on to share in Steinbeck's success. Nevertheless, he was one of the few who backed Steinbeck during the bad times.

Another, of course, was Dook Sheffield, whose continuous support was an important factor in enabling Steinbeck to survive. In acknowledgment of this, Steinbeck later gave Sheffield the ledger in which the handwritten manuscripts of both *The Pastures of Heaven* and *To a God Unknown* were contained. Inside this gray cloth account book with red reinforcing on the cover, in addition to the manuscripts, there were a series of notes addressed to Dook written at various times during the composition of *To a God Unknown*. Among the entries are these expressions of Steinbeck's affection and gratitude:

> When I bought this book, and began to fill it with words it occurred to me that you might like to have it when it was full. . . . I should like you to have this book and my reasons are all sentimental and therefore, of course, unmentionable. I love you very much. I have never been able to give you a present that cost any money. It occurs to me that you might accept a present that cost me a hell of a lot of work. . . . I wonder if you know why I address this manuscript to you. You are the only person in the world who believes I can do what I set out to do. Not even I believe that all the time. And so, in a kind of gratitude I address all my writing to you, whether or not you know it.

With these notes and the writing of the manuscript for a specific person, Steinbeck initiated a new approach to his work, a method of personalizing a large audience familiar to anyone who has taken a course in public speaking. As Elaine Steinbeck and Robert Wallsten note in their *A Life in Letters*, this was the first time "he directed the entire concept and approach of his work, not to a faceless and generalized audience, but to a single person." It was, as they also note, a prac-

tice he continued for the rest of his life. In later years, on those rare occasions when he gave advice to aspiring writers, he usually mentioned
this technique as the one "secret" he had that might be of some use to
them.

He did not, of course, continue to address his work only to Sheffield,
but he did always have someone in mind. The ledger he gave Sheffield
was only one of several that had similar journal-like notations. As in
this manuscript book, the others contained entries set down on an irregular basis, but they tended to be even less organized, amounting at
times to little more than doodling. The only exception to this was the
journal written to Pascal Covici during the composition of *East of
Eden,* which was published after Steinbeck's death as *Journal of a
Novel.*

One more reference to the notes that accompany *To a God Unknown* should be made, to a passage that underlines once more Steinbeck's view of his own work as far broader and deeper in intent than we
usually have conceived it to be. He writes:

> This story has grown since I started it. From a novel about people,
> it has become a novel about the world. And you must never tell it.
> Let it be found out. The new eye is being opened here in the
> west—the new seeing. It is probable that no one will know it for
> two hundred years. It will be confused, analyzed, analogized, crit-
> icised, and none of our fine critics will know what is happening. . . .
>   There are things in my mind as strong as pure as good as any-
> thing in the structure of literature. If I do not put them down, it
> will be because I have not the technique. The story is too big,
> Duke. I am so afraid of it sometimes. . . . Joseph is a giant shoul-
> dering his way among the ages, pushing the stars aside to make a
> passage to god. And this god—that is the thing. When god is
> reached—will anybody believe it. It really doesn't matter. I believe
> it and Joseph believes it. The story is a parable, Duke. The story of
> a race, growth and death. Each figure is a population, and the
> stones, the trees, the muscled mountains are the world—but not
> the world apart from man—the world *and* man—the one insepara-
> ble unit man plus his environment.

He saw himself, particularly in regard to his long novels, as a writer
searching out the essential drama of man in nature. He was not in his
own mind a local-color writer or recorder of the times; rather, he felt
that he was using Western American experience as a special window
by which he could lead us to rediscover man's identity in respect to

his environment. He was descended, in vision and intent, from the Greeks, rather than American transcendentalism or American realism-naturalism; he thought in terms of the *Iliad*, not in terms of *Sister Carrie* or *The Octopus*. If he had labeled himself at this point in his career, he probably would have called himself a "symbolist." In mid-1933 he wrote to Carl Wilhelmson and said, "I don't think you will like my late work. It leaves realism farther and farther behind. I never had much ability for nor faith in realism. It is just a form of fantasy as nearly as I could figure" [8/9/33].

II

In *Journal of a Novel*, at the beginning of the entry for March 30 (1951), he writes: "Well, March is nearly over—the month my mother dreaded so is nearly over. Mother never drew a carefree breath in March. All of her tragedies happened in March." In March of 1933, his mother fell ill and was taken to the hospital. A short time late she suffered a massive stroke, which left her almost totally paralyzed.

When it became clear that Mrs. Steinbeck's condition was serious, John and Carol returned to Salinas and moved into the family home. At first, there was some hope that his mother might recover, and John spent seven or eight hours a day at the hospital. Since he was the only one of the children who was free to tend his mother—his sisters were all permanently located elsewhere with family responsibilities—it became primarily his duty. He hated it. Throughout his life he had an abnormally strong repulsion to sickness, and what was happening to his mother made his knees buckle and his stomach turn over. He was overcome by emotion as he watched the strongest person he had known become helpless. Each day he sat by the side of his mother's bed, helping the nurses, ushering in visiting relatives, and placating her as her mind wandered to urgent problems long forgotten.

For several weeks he gave up writing altogether, afraid that the scratching of his pen would disturb his mother. He recalled that when he had been seriously ill, the slightest noise could give him pain. However, when her condition worsened and the doctors advised that not only would she not recover, but she might remain paralyzed and bedridden for several years, he looked forward to an "indefinite sentence" that he could not face without his work. He began writing again, fitfully at first, a little at home in the evenings and then at odd moments in the hospital. Looking back on his writing during this period, he declared that "if it has any continuity it is marvelous." His new project had probably been taking shape for some time in his mind before he put pen to paper, but in retrospect his work on a long story about childhood seems only fitting as part of the ongoing drama. Certainly, *The Red Pony* gains an extra measure of poignancy when placed within the circumstances of its composition.

At this point he was writing only a short story; the other stories, which would be brought together with the first and published as a novel, would come later. To George Albee he wrote, "If I can write any kind of a story at a time like this, then I can write stories." It was, he felt, a simple narrative

about a boy who gets a colt pony and the pony gets distemper. . . . This may not seem like a good basis for a story but that entirely depends upon the treatment. The whole thing is as simply told as though it came out of the boy's mind although there is no going into the boy's mind. It is an attempt to make the reader create the boy's mind for himself. An interesting experiment you see if nothing else.

Later, after the story was completed, he wrote, "It is an unpretentious story. I think the philosophic content is so buried that it will not bother anybody."

In contrast to Steinbeck, whose environment had shrunk to little more than a hospital room and who was creating one of his best stories from a comparatively small incident out of his childhood, George Albee wrote to complain that his environment was sterile and that so little had happened to him that he had no material as a basis for his fiction. He felt that he needed to move to the East Coast or to Europe to find a richer soil for creation, where he might witness or become involved in those things that he associated in his mind with "Literature." These, of course, are common feelings for a young writer, and Steinbeck's reply is a sort of classic—a statement that should be clipped out and pasted to the wall behind the typewriter:

Your continued talk about your lack of background worries me. I wish I had the temerity and the consciousness of my own rightness to train you. I think I should use the method of a Piece of String. In other words I would set you a situation and make you write it. I am convinced that a story is not particularly a matter of background at all, but of the ability to see together with the ability to arrange, together with an inventive strain. I should like to set you the story of the lean boy with the funny name who had money, or of the next door neighbor who bought the piano so she could put the music on it. These are stories. You insist on being a social critic and historian, ok. You will never find a place where social history is more in the making than in Los Angeles. . . .

I wish to god you would take my word for it. You have a richer field of story than I have, you know it thoroughly and you have a sense of its drama. There is no reason to believe that Cape Cod is more literary than Universal City. Remember that Paris was just as garish as Hollywood if you wanted to see it that way. . . .

Perhaps there is some comment on the efficacy of passionately felt and eloquently argued advice in the fact that George Albee only a few months later moved to New York.

While the "pony story," as he called it, progressed during the spring of 1933, there was some turmoil concerning the publication of *To a God Unknown*. Robert Ballou's option on the manuscript had run out while he was still trying to line up enough financial backing to publish two books, one of them Steinbeck's, in the fall. In the meantime, McIntosh and Otis began sending the manuscript to other publishers, and three expressed interest, including Simon and Schuster, which made a firm offer. McIntosh and Otis wrote to Steinbeck urgently, asking for a decision by telegram. At the same time Ballou wrote telling him that he thought he had the money but wouldn't have confirmation for two weeks. Steinbeck demonstrated some loyalty of his own by turning down the sure thing and taking a chance on Ballou.

By the middle of June, his mother's condition had stabilized enough so that it was considered best to take her home, but Steinbeck began to worry about his father. He had not told him at the beginning that the doctors held little hope of recovery, and now that his father realized that she would not get better and that she had, in effect, come home to die, he began to unravel under the strain. The situation was also difficult for Carol, who was working at temporary secretarial jobs, mostly in Monterey, and then had to come home and cook and wash for the family. They had hired two practical nurses to take care of Mrs. Steinbeck, but they would cook only for themselves and for the patient, so Carol ended up cooking for everybody.

Steinbeck took an almost permanent station at the dining-room table, just outside his mother's door. It was somewhat easier to write now, since he didn't have to be constantly concerned that he might disturb his mother, but the situation was still awkward and distressing:

I am typing the second draft of the pony story. A few pages a day. This morning is a good example. One paragraph—help lift the patient on bed pan. Back, a little ill, three paragraphs, help turn patient so sheets can be changed. Back—three lines, nausea, hold pans, help hang bedding, back—two paragraphs, patient wants to tell me that her brother George is subject to colds, and the house must be kept warm. Brother George is not here but a letter came from him this morning. That is morning. One page and a half typed. You can see that concentration thrives under difficulties since I have a fear and hatred of illness and incapacity which amounts to a mania. But I'll get the story typed all right sooner or later and then I'll correct it and then Carol will try to find time to finish it and how she is going to do that I haven't any idea. [JS/GA]

The horror and confinement of Steinbeck's situation for most of the year strangely stimulated both his mind and his work. After his initial hesitation to write while tending his mother, he immersed himself more and more in his work, perhaps more deeply and continuously, by the latter part of the year, than he ever had before. His immersion confirms what he had reported while writing *To a God Unknown* about the "unspeakable joy of merging into this world I am building." Writing had always been in part for him an escape; now escape became a way of surviving. As a result the period proved to be one of his most productive. He wrote the better part of two short novels and several stories, including some of his best, and, as appears to have become his habit, he was thinking well into the future about new projects. In the spring he wrote to Albee, "I think I would like to write the story of this whole valley, of all the little towns and all the farms and ranches in the wilder hills. I can see how I would like to do it so that it would be the valley of the world."

About mid-May of 1933, he wrote in another journal (this one kept in a ledger along with the manuscripts for most of the short stories that would appear in *The Long Valley*):

Tonight there came the first installment of galleys from T.A.G.U. I read a few pages and found them fairly effective. The detached quality is there undoubtedly. . . . But I was not cast down by the prose. It is ambitious. . . .

Today also I dispatched to my agents a rather mawkish story about a pony. Mawkish in effect, not in method. I saw to that. Now it is night—the only time left in which to work. Mother lies helpless downstairs. It is fight enough to stay out of her mind—to know the sorrow in it and to feel it not in myself but in herself. And this is the new theme.

The "theme," as he calls it here and elsewhere, was a sudden perception of the synthesis of the many associated ideas—mythic, psychological, and naturalistic-scientific—which he had used to shape the final version of *To a God Unknown*. Further refined, these same ideas would form a bridge from his early work, poetic and visionary, to the so-called sociological works of the middle period, from *In Dubious Battle* through *The Pearl*. The story of how this synthesis, this theme, came to him is reminiscent of the experience of a religious disciple, who, through suffering, has attained a highly sensitive state of awareness and who receives a vision—except that Steinbeck's vision was one based on science.

His mind was extraordinarily active, especially during the early weeks of his mother's illness, when there was very little he could do but sit and think. For years, in response to his reading and observation of patterns of life around him, he had been evolving a theory regarding the gestalt of animal groupings, particularly man. "The process," he wrote to Dook, "is this—one puts down endless observations, questions and remarks. The number grows and grows. Eventually they all seem headed in one direction and then they whirl like sparks out of a bonfire. And then one day they seem to mean something." The day came as he was sitting by his mother, struggling to justify the pity of her condition after a stroke had paralyzed her left side. His realization was that "half of the cell units of my mother's body have rebelled. Neither has died, but the revolution has changed her functions. That is cruel to say. The first line on this thing came from it though. She, as a human unit, is deterred from functioning as she ordinarily did by a schism of a number of her cells" [6/21/33].

That insight, which helped him give rational shape to the horror that had possessed his mother, gave him a key. In his morbid state of awareness its significance expanded, and he began to see it as a key to social movements, historical events—"the reasons of migrations, the desertion of localities, the sudden diseases which wiped races out, the sudden running amok of groups" [JS/CS 6/21/33]. As he began to see the multiple and widespread applications of his idea, he began to get very excited. He felt that he had discovered not something new, but rather had come across a common denominator that tied together the ideas then current within many different disciplines and expounded by a variety of thinkers and scientists. In his excitement he broke away from his duties in Salinas to discuss his thesis at length on several occasions with Ed. Then in June he wrote a long letter explaining his discovery to Dook, a series of letters on the topic to George Albee, and a short, formal essay, called "Argument of Phalanx," in which he summarized the basic principles of what he also called his "theme."

For once, his excitement allowed him to break through his reticence about discussing his philosophy in writing. Yet, through it all, he displayed some embarrassment, repeatedly qualifying his position as neither professional scientist nor trained philosopher. He was aware, always, that his argument and his examples were inspired by his enthusiasm and might well be shown, on closer examination, to be overdrawn or oversimplified. He told Dook, "I am ignorant enough to promulgate it. If I had more knowledge I wouldn't have the courage to think it out." And to Albee, "Of course I am interested in it as tremendous and terrible poetry. I am neither scientist nor profound investigator. But I am experiencing an emotional vastness in working this out. The difficulty of writing the poetry is so great that I am not even contemplating it until I have absorbed and made a part of my body the thesis as a whole." His ultimate concern, he told his friends, was not to write a philosophical tract using this material, but to think it through and then find the fictional symbols that would act as a vehicle for it in his creative writing.

In his journal, he mused over how his theme might be utilized, and noted, quite rightly, that our literature had become so divorced from our scientific discoveries and the changing perceptions of the universe held by our major thinkers that it was in a somewhat antiquated world of its own. Much of his excitement came from his determination to become the writer who would change this. But he must express these things fictionally, indirectly, and he worried about finding the forms and the symbols in our literary tradition that he could adapt to his purpose:

I don't know how this thesis and theme are to be worked. I don't like to cast about for new forms, but the old forms seem inade-

quate. Such things as character, single stream, the mind of man—
are out for this book is not about them. This book [must tap] the
great ocean of the unconscious. How am I to do it. On what point
can I stand to see the world—or more important, to make the
world see itself. Literature of all ages has celebrated the finest
thoughts of its time. Not so ours. Our magnificent conceptions of
physical structure are untouched except in monographs. No great
poetry has evolved from our great dream of atoms and of interstel-
lar space, of the quantum and the great snaky spirals of worlds—
god in a winding sheet. Where can I find symbols dignified and
simple enough to make it clean and lovely?

The most succinct statement of his thesis came in a letter to Sheffield: "All of the notations I have made begin to point to an end—that
the group is an individual as boundaried, as diagnosable, as dependent
on its units and as independent of its units' individual natures, as the
human unit, or man, is dependent on his cells and yet is independent of
them" [6/21/33]. Part of the background for Steinbeck's thought here,
as suggested by his language, came out of discussions with Ed about the
theories of W. C. Allee, the University of Chicago biologist. In the
same letter to Sheffield, Steinbeck mentions that "Ed Ricketts has dug
up all the scientific material and more than I need to establish the physical integrity of the thing," indicating how important it was to him that
his thesis have scientific, as well as historical-social validity.

But despite the obvious connection with Allee, the single most
important source for the materials of his thesis was George Albee's
younger brother, Richard, who was a philosophy major at U.C.L.A.
For several years Albee's youthful excitement added fuel to the fire of
the Steinbeck-Ricketts passion for ideas. It was he, for example, who
brought Saint John of the Cross and Novalis to Ed's attention, as well
as introducing Ed to "Gregorian" music. To John he brought his enthusiasm for the philosophy of one of his professors, John Elof Boodin,
a philosophy that would make a deep impression on Steinbeck and his
work. Indeed, Boodin would seem at about this time to have taken over
from Harold Chapman Brown as the central pillar in Steinbeck's philosophical pantheon.

Boodin was another of the many philosophers of the time who
sought to reconcile science, particularly evolutionary theory and scientific methodology, with humane values and the concept of an imper-
sonal God as a controlling principle. He shared Brown's enthusiasm for
scientific method, and his pragmatism, but differed from the materialist

in that he also wrote of a "cosmic idealism" in which matter responds to the control of Form (that is, God), which coexists with matter. What most interested Steinbeck were Boodin's ideas concerning the juncture of individual minds brought together to form a larger whole with properties of its own.

These ideas first came to John while he was visiting Dick Albee at his home in Hollywood during the winter of 1932–33, when Dick shared with him reprints of Boodin lectures on such subjects as "The Existence of Social Minds" and "Functional Realism." (John went on immediately to read two of Boodin's books, *A Realistic Universe* [1916] and *Cosmic Evolution* [1925] and he read others later.) Albee also showed John his class notes, and they had a long talk about Boodin's major ideas and about the great, mysterious movements of man, such as the Mongol hordes. Albee recalls that

> by the time I came north for my spring vacation, Ed Ricketts had already been contributing biological data to further excite John's interest, and when the three of us got together, I too was more stimulated than ever, for that was the first time I had heard about Allee's *Animal Aggregations*. We talked together more than once, but it was after one transcendent session that John produced his account of the social (and ultimately cosmic) theory under the symbolic title of "Phalanx."

At the beginning of summer, Dick was on another visit to northern California and stopped by to see Steinbeck, who was sitting at his typewriter. He reached into his desk and pulled out a couple of pieces of paper and handed them to Dick and said, "Is this the thing that you've been talking about?" What he gave him was the short essay entitled "Argument of Phalanx," which began:

> Men are not final individuals but units in the creator beast, the phalanx. Within the body of a man are units, cells, some highly specialized and some coordinate, which have their natures and their lives, which die and are replaced, which suffer and are killed. In their billions they make up man, the new individual. But man is more than the total of his cells, and his nature is not that of the sum of all his cells. He has a nature new and strange to his cells.
> Man is a unit of the great beast, the phalanx. The phalanx has pains, desires, hungers and strivings as different from those of the unit man's as man's are different from the unit-cells'. The nature of the phalanx is not the sum of the natures of unit-men, but a new

individual having emotions and ends of its own, and these are foreign and incomprehensible to unit-men.

Some time later, John asked Dick to carry a message to Boodin: "I
hadn't realized that one of the world's greatest philosophers is not only
living in my own time, but nearby in my own state." Following this,
Boodin reported to Albee that he had received a letter from the novelist
which had complimented him extravagantly and had gone on to ask his
permission to use some of his philosophy in his own work. "My," Boodin exclaimed to Albee, "he is modest, isn't he? He asks my permission!"

Dick Albee and Steinbeck shared a love for ancient history, and it
was from Greek history that Steinbeck got his idea of using the term
"phalanx" for his men-units. Invented by Philip of Macedon, refined
and made famous by Alexander the Great, the phalanx was a close-
order battle formation, twelve to sixteen ranks deep. When the men
pulled their shields together and advanced in lockstep, they became one
moving "animal," something like a modern tank in its advance on
enemy positions. After reading Steinbeck's essay, Albee commented,
"Did you know the Romans called the phalanx a tortoise? It's a wonderful symbol." Steinbeck quickly agreed, pointing out that it is like a
shield, of course, as a whole, but also the formation looks like a turtle
shell, which is like a lot of little shields put together. There was no
doubt in Albee's mind, when the turtle appeared in The Grapes of
Wrath, that it grew out of Steinbeck's perception of the phalanx as a
tortoise or turtle as a result of his suggestion.

In recalling the background for "Argument of Phalanx," Albee has
also noted the importance of the fact that the early thirties was a time
when mass movements were much discussed. Capitalism as rugged
individualism was seen by many as having failed, and some form of
socialism was thought to be almost inevitable. Many watched and discussed the progress of the Soviet Union and thought of it as a possible
model, and at the same time, of course, Hitler was leading another mass
socialist movement in Germany. Here, strikes, veterans' marches, protest rallies, and other mass demonstrations were commonplace news.
That Steinbeck was now keenly aware of all of this activity, at home
and abroad, is clear from his many references to such movements in his
letters of the period. The transformation of Germany was perhaps one
of the most dramatic contemporary examples available to Steinbeck,
and he wrote Dook: "Think of the impulse which has suddenly made

Germany overlook the natures of its individuals and become what it has. Hitler didn't do it. He merely speaks about it" [6/21/33]. In retrospect, it is interesting to think of Joseph Goebbels as one who, in Steinbeck's words in his "Argument," learned to "direct the movements" of the phalanx after analyzing "its habits under various stimuli."

Steinbeck went back to the many sources from which he had taken notes and followed leads to other possible confirming authorities in order to establish the integrity of his thesis. He wrote to Dook in a follow-up letter:

> The investigations have so far been gratifying. I find that in Anthropology, Doctor Ellsworth Huntington, in History and cultural aspects, Spengler and Ouspenski, in folk lore and in unconscious psychology, Jung, in economic phases of anthropology, Briffault, in biology, Allee, and in physics, Schondringer, Planck, Bohr, Einstein, Heisenberg have all started heading in the same direction. None has gone far, and none apparently is aware of the work of the others, but each one is headed in the same direction and the direction is toward my thesis. [6/30/33]

As the summer passed and he had assured himself that his ideas had support elsewhere, his investigations tapered off, and he turned to finding ways of bringing his thesis into his fiction. At this point, as his thesis became theme, it was no longer a matter for discussion. It would appear in one guise or another, without comment or explanation (most directly in *In Dubious Battle*), in nearly all his novels written during the next decade and a half. Almost immediately he brought it to *Tortilla Flat*. In the beginning of that novel he talks of Danny's house, which he says is not to refer to an old frame dwelling, but rather to a group of people, a "unit of which the parts are men." This, he says, is the story of "how that group came into being, of how it flourished, and ... in the end ... how the group disintegrated." To those readers who did not react moralistically to the *paisanos'* activities, the novel was a charming, folk-flavored comedy, but beneath that comedy, Danny and his friends were a particular kind of phalanx, related to each other as one cell to another in a single body. No view of life could be more naturalistic, more deterministic—it was, after all, based on a biological analogy.

CHAPTER XVI

"**L**ord," he wrote in mid-August, "how I wish we could spend at least a weekend on the beach." The days wore on with very little change. Outside, the walks, fences, and white frame houses reflected the muggy glare of the hot sun; inside, he sat at the black pedestal table under the dim light of the dining room chandelier. The quiet order of dying had taken over. It was as if he were the bell captain in a very efficient, but nearly deserted resort hotel, sitting in the lobby and waiting for the only resident to ring.

> Mother gets a little stronger but not less helpless. There are terrible washings every day. 9–12 sheets. I wash them and Carol irons them. I try to sneak in a little work, but mother wants to tell me something about every fifteen minutes. Her mind wanders badly. This story which in ordinary times I could do in four days is taking over a month to write and isn't any good anyway. Carol is working like a dog. She stays cheerful and makes things easier for all of us. It's hard to cook for nurses. If I can have two good days, I'll finish this darn story. It really isn't a story at all. [JS/GA]

As if things weren't bad enough, near the end of the summer the burden of worry became too great for his father and he collapsed. He recovered, but not totally, and John was forced to fill in for him at the county treasurer's office. This is something that he had done before for short periods of time and had learned to hate. He wrote Carl Wilhelmson: "Isn't it funny, my two pet horrors, incapacity and ledgers and they both hit at once. I write columns of figures in big ledgers and after about three hours of it I am so stupefied that I can't get down to my own work. . . . Once this is over, I shall starve before I'll ever open another ledger" [8/33]. His father remained largely incapacitated with heart trouble and a troubled heart for nearly a year. By late fall, Steinbeck began to think that his mother, as seriously ill as she was, might outlive his father, who was stumbling and fumbling badly with shattered nerves and failing eyesight. Steinbeck found it a dreadful thing to have to stand by and watch. "Death I can stand," he wrote Ballou, "but not this slow torture wherein a good man tears off little shreds of himself and throws them away" [11/20/33].

There are vignettes to consider in this heart-rending business. Of Steinbeck's father, stiff and proud, carrying around a copy of his son's new book to show off to friends and neighbors. Of him walking indignantly into the local bookstore, which had refused to carry any of his son's books, and demanding to know why. Of parents patiently sending money, month after month, backing their son in his long struggle, defending him against the sneers of relatives and even the epithets of an irritated sister—"bum," "fake." Of a mother who brought her son's new book into her club meeting, only to meet snubs and a refusal to add it to the reading list—"We will only consider decent books"—and the courage it took to go back, head high, with book in hand. And of a mother dying who talked to her nurses, too much it seemed to them, about her son, who was becoming a great writer, and who pressed his book on them to read.

The effect of the mounting dread was to drive Steinbeck not only into philosophy and into an intensive period of writing, but also into introspection. In his thinking about life and death as part of process, he was able to give it some order. But what about his own life? What order did it have? What meaning? There are times in the experience of nearly every person when diabolical forces act, as in some Edgar Allan Poe story, to push apart the floorboards of one's life to reveal a gaping black pit. Everything a person thought was true about himself seems wrong, suddenly, and everything he had depended on, damaged or missing. Under the circumstances, one retreats to the minimum basis for continued functioning—that, or gives up.

Steinbeck struggled with his sense of his own importance, realizing that as more and more demands had been made upon him, that sense had become unduly inflated. He described his basis for continued functioning to Carl Wilhelmson:

I work because I know it gives me pleasure to work. It is as simple as that and I don't require any other reasons. I am losing a sense of self to a marked degree and that is a pleasant thing. A couple of years ago I realized that I was not the material of which great artists are made and that I was rather glad I wasn't. And since then I have been happier simply to do the work and to take the reward at the end of every day that is given for a day of honest work. I grow less complicated all the time and that is a joy to me. The forces that used to tug in various directions have all started to pull in one. I have a book to write. I think about it for a while and then I write it. There is nothing more. [8/9/33]

It was as if he had decided to stop striving and simply be—to take a non-teleological position in regard to his own life. He had decided to focus on creation, rather than on himself as creator, concentrating on function rather than on ends. Only the desire, he wrote Albee, to rid himself of the consciousness of the suffering of his parents made him conscious of himself as a unit. Just as he relieved himself by depersonalizing his mother's paralysis, thinking of her rebelling cells as a phalanx within nature, so he sought to release himself from disappointment and failure by submerging the unit "me" into the larger whole. "I spread out over landscape and people," he wrote, "like an enormous jelly fish, having neither personality nor boundaries. That is as I wish it, complete destruction of any thing which can be called a me. The work is necessary since from it springs all the other things" [3/34].

This was not simply a low period in his life, a passing mood. Although an exaggeration—he was obviously not able to excise all ambition from his consciousness nor rid himself entirely of ego for now and the remainder of his life—the sentiments here get to the heart of Steinbeck as an artistic personality versus the usual driving of egotistical assertion toward success. To understand this now is to understand in advance how it could be that the success of *The Grapes of Wrath* later in his career could almost destroy him. Failure he could deal with, but success, which focused controversy and attention on him as a person, he could not. It also helps to explain, from another angle, why his fiction was a necessary mask—why underneath that mask, his fiction is always and truly Steinbeck, and why as himself, ego, his nonfiction so seldom is anything deeper than friendly conversation.

In the same letter to Albee, he declared: "I never come up to the surface. I just work all the time." For more than a year, from the spring of 1933 to the time when he began work on *In Dubious Battle* in late August of 1934, he devoted himself to short fiction. However, as he wrote Mavis McIntosh, he always started out to write stories and then "they invariably grow into novels," so that two longer works grew out of the shorter.

The stories that he wrote during this period can be divided into three groups: the four stories that eventually made up *The Red Pony* (printed first as part of *The Long Valley*); the remaining stories included in *The Long Valley* collection (except for "St. Katy," which had been written earlier); and the stories that were collected and became, after unifying revision, *Tortilla Flat.*

Since he was working on stories in one group and then another, sometimes working, apparently, on more than one story at the same time, the chronology of composition is difficult to settle exactly. This was such an intense period of work that it has been impossible for Carol or anyone else close to him at the time to remember which story was written before or after any other. Even the documentary evidence is incomplete and to some extent confusing. Nevertheless, despite such uncertainties, we do know that two of the earliest stories were "The Murder" and "The Chrysanthemums."

"The Murder" is a strange story, a sort of gothic Western, about a rancher who marries a Slavic girl who is very animallike in her behavior and in her responses to her husband. Inspired by the peculiar characteristics of the wife of one of his friends, Steinbeck places a caricature of her into a plot derived from a bit of local history (a husband who kills his wife and her lover) and uses as his setting a picturesque local landmark. The location is a ranch in a canyon off the road to Corral del Tierra, walled on one side by sandstone cliffs called "The Castles" because of their uncanny resemblance to a medieval fortress (the cliffs are pictured in one of the prints in George Vancouver's *A Voyage of Discovery* [1798]). The abandoned ranch buildings described in Steinbeck's story still stand at the foot of the cliffs.

In each of these stories Steinbeck was trying for some kind of special effect; he considered them, as he did so much of his writing, "experiments." After he had sent "The Murder" to George Albee and Albee responded to the story, Steinbeck told him: "I think you got out of the murder story about what I wanted you to. You got no character. I didn't want any there. You got color and a dream like movement. I was writing it more as a dream than as anything else, so if you got this vague and curiously moving feeling out of it that is all I ask." About "The Chrysanthemums," which he had also written during the fall of 1933, he wrote Albee: "I shall be interested to know what you think of the story. . . . It is entirely different and is designed to strike without the reader's knowledge. I mean he reads it casually and after it is finished feels that something profound has happened to him although he does not know what nor how. It has had that effect on several people here. Carol thinks it is the best of all my stories."

Phrased one way or another, the idea of striking "without the reader's knowledge" was an aim commonly expressed by him during these years, as if he plotted a channel of communication in each work that somehow bypassed or circumvented the brain, giving the reader an experience which then generated an emotion. His discussion along these lines indicates that he felt that the best fiction was that which brought its theme to the reader subliminally, and that the problem with criticism was that too many critics were insensitive to experience, operating too much by intelligence directed by expectation.

The former Carol Steinbeck remembers well the days of her mother-in-law's illness, the ironing and the cooking, the long evenings of typing. She remembers, too, her husband's work on "The Chrysanthemums" as he sat at the table outside his mother's door or upstairs in his old bedroom, and his work on "The White Quail" several months later as she helped out at the Salinas house while the health of her father-in-law was declining. In all, it was a very difficult time for her as well as for her husband, a time in which she gave much in order that he might have the time to write and succeed. During this latter period, in May 1934, John wrote in his journal:

> Time must be put in. If Carol can work over in that gloomy house for me, I must work enormously for her. There are certain new things I want to try but they must be done at night or not at all. The daily work time must be devoted to the end of a little security, to a trip some place and to time and time enough to work out the phalanx book. [*In Dubious Battle*]

Carol has always felt that the central women characters of these two stories, Elisa Allen and Mary Teller, were patterned in some degree after her. From an outside perspective, it is hard to see how the rather cold, rigid, and prim Mary Teller could in any way reflect a warm, volatile Carol, except in the conflict between a woman trying to bring order to her world and a husband who was often very untidy.

Elisa Allen in "Chrysanthemums" does, however, resemble Carol, even physically. They are both strong, large-boned, and competent; both wear masculine clothes (Carol wore jeans and sweatshirts that nearly matched her husband's). Both are seen—Carol by those who knew her at the time—as handsome, rather than pretty: Elisa's "face was eager and mature and handsome; even her work with the scissors was over-eager, over-powerful. The chrysanthemum stems seemed too small and easy for her energy."

But it is in Elisa's emotions and in her situation that her resemblance to Carol is most telling and revealing. "The Chrysanthemums" is probably Steinbeck's finest short story, and its excellence lies in its delicate, indirect handling of a woman's emotions. Like most outstanding stories, "The Chrysanthemums" can be taken a number of different ways, but one major theme, certainly, is that of the difficulty of the woman in finding a creative, significant role in a male-dominated society. Of the forces aligned against Elisa's freedom to be what she is capable of being, perhaps the most subtly destructive are, on the one hand, the basic understandings held by a society of a woman's presumed limitations—a force that seems to permeate the atmosphere of the story—and, on the other hand, the misguided sympathy and kindness offered by the husband. It is the latter that is so terribly defeating and—what is the feminine equivalent of "emasculating"?

The story indicates very strongly that Steinbeck was aware of and sympathetic to his wife's frustrations. She was, after all, a very intelligent, capable, creative person, happiest when she was able to make use of her talents and initiative beyond the role of part-time secretary or clerk, which she was usually forced to take. Beyond that, it was not easy being married to an artist, a man consumed by his work in a deeply emotional, totally committed way. The product of their marriage, to a large extent, was his books—not their books. Until near the end of the marriage, Steinbeck was not an unloving or unkind husband. Yet, as in the story, love and kindness can be, even inadvertently, subjugating, and great talent seems almost to act on its own to subjugate. People of immense talent don't viciously devour those around them like barracudas—not necessarily; more often they unknowingly absorb them, like an amoeba surrounding a particle of nutrient.

II

About the same time as Steinbeck was working on these stories, he was also working on *Tortilla Flat* (summer through fall 1933). One of the ironies of his career was that this book, written rather quickly and casually and published almost by accident, was the book that raised him out of obscurity. Written under the shadow of his mother's illness and his father's decay, it is, strangely enough, the most comic of his novels. "Its tone, I guess," he wrote a friend, "is direct rebellion against all the sorrow of our house [JS/EW-11/23/33]. The book began in somewhat the same way that *The Pastures of Heaven* began, with an idea to write a group of short stories, and like *Pastures*, the book got its main impetus from material derived from a friend. As the material came together, its shape changed from a collection of stories to something more like an episodic novel.

Until mid-1933, his idea was to write up some incidents he had heard concerning Mexican-Americans (and Mexican nationals in California), a collection of anecdotes that dated all the way back to his days at Spreckels Sugar. He wrote Mavis McIntosh at the beginning of 1933 that "there are some fine little things that happened in a big sugar mill where I was assistant chief chemist and majordomo of about sixty Mexicans and Yuakis taken from the jails of northern Mexico" that he planned to use. While still working on "The Red Pony," he began to look for more Mexican material and went to see a friend, Susan Gregory, who had told him many such stories in the past.

Sue Gregory was a Spanish teacher at the high school in Monterey. Steinbeck had met her several years earlier through mutual friends, who had introduced her as a poet. She came from a very old and distinguished California family, one branch of which went back to the Spanish land-grant days, and her grandfather was W. E. P. Hartnell, who founded Hartnell College, the first college established in California. She was a woman of charm and dignity, with large, liquid brown eyes. A woman of great compassion, she had become, in Carol's phrase, a sort of "Mother Superior" to a community of Spanish-speaking people who lived in the semiwooded outskirts of town. (It doesn't matter precisely where Tortilla Flat was, since the bulldozers of builders have completely altered the terrain.) She loved these people, helped them, laughed and sang with them, and collected amusing stories of their exploits. They were called *paisanos* because not only were they made up of Spanish and Indian blood, but many of them were also part Italian or part Portuguese.

Steinbeck saw Sue Gregory frequently when he went to visit Harriet Gragg. Hattie Gragg was another remarkable woman, probably in her seventies at the time that Steinbeck knew her, whose family had settled in California in 1837. When she was a child, she had to learn Spanish to survive in the schoolyard, since almost all the other children spoke English only in the classroom. She was the kind of woman who, in her seventies, nailed shakes on the roof of the Monterey Civic Club, which she had helped establish. Clarinda, Hattie's maid, was the model for one of the women characters in *Tortilla Flat*.

Both Hattie and Sue were good storytellers, excellent sources for Steinbeck for local color and historical background, as both were closely attuned to the speech, customs, and values of the *paisano* community. Julia Breinig, Hattie's daughter, recalls a time when Sue, Hattie, and John were invited by Clarinda to a party at her home in Seaside (a small town just north of Monterey). All three were dressed in their best clothes, the two women in beautiful long gowns and John in a dark serge suit. Julia, who had been to Clarinda's, was fearful that Sue might ruin her dress and warned her that the boards of the house were rough and the furniture in not very good repair. All three explained to her that it was necessary that they wear their very finest—they could do no less.

Writing *Tortilla Flat* was not, however, simply a matter of talking to Sue Gregory and then writing a novel using her stories. The bulk of the material came from her, but perhaps even more important, it was her influence that led Steinbeck to focus on the *paisanos* of Monterey. Yet, there were other sources, too. One of the stories came from Carol, who got it from the doctor who was tending Steinbeck's mother. Three of the incidents had been collected earlier from Steinbeck's work in the fields and lab for Spreckels: the story of the ex-corporal and his baby, the story of the old man who hangs himself, and (as discovered by Nelson Valjean) the story of Sweets Ramirez and her sweeping machine. And Toby Street has suggested that some of the most colorful material for the novel came from John's conversations with Monty Hellam, who was then chief of the Monterey police.

And Steinbeck himself was acquainted with several of the town characters, whom he brought together as Danny and his friends in the novel. Their adventures became, even while they were happening, a sort of living folklore that was passed around and became common knowledge. All the major characters in the novel had their real-life counterparts, although they were not all part of one group, as indicated in the novel, nor did they live in Tortilla Flat. They tended to drift here and there, sometimes living on the beach, sometimes in the canyons above the town. Steinbeck's invention of the houses inherited by Danny is a masterful stroke which brings these diverse characters together in one place and gives them a basis for interacting among themselves and with the community.

The most notorious of these men in life, Pilon (Eddie Ramirez), has left a legacy of legend that has made him a sort of folk hero (a backhanded fulfillment of Steinbeck's prophecy in the novel that Danny would become the subject of a myth). Part of the time, he and a friend, Eddy Martin, lived in a cave in Iris Canyon, twenty feet up the bank, which they called their summer home; Pilon called the county farm his "rest home" and went there regularly to dry out.

Although once in a while some of the *paisanos* worked in the sardine canneries, characters such as Pilon made it a point of honor never to do anything more than collect bottles or chop a little wood if wine could be obtained in no other way. Sometimes a chicken disappeared, but more often good things, although second-hand, were passed out the back door of a restaurant. Although Pilon did not, as Danny does in the novel, inherit a house, he did inherit $600, which, through prodigious effort, he managed to spend in one weekend, taking taxis everywhere and showering gifts on everyone he knew.

A couple of the *paisanos* came from good families, including one of the men who was probably the model for Danny, who had a habit of selling off everything from his former life of respectability, piece by piece, in order to get wine. Once he was apprehended walking down the center of the Salinas-Monterey highway at three in the morning, wearing little more than the jacket of a custom-made tuxedo. He had apparently been able to find a buyer for his shirt and his pants, but for some reason not his jacket.

Tortilla Flat is a tour de force. In retrospect it is hard to think of any other American writer getting away with it—it reflects Steinbeck's personality so perfectly. It is the kind of book, deceptively simple, that is invariably underestimated and leads one to think, I could write a book like this one. There isn't that much to it. It took Steinbeck fifteen years of practice to make a book look that easy, and behind that relaxed manner is a world of experience with and sympathy for his subject.

Steinbeck had a special affinity for Mexico and the Mexican people, whether in this country or in their own. The *paisanos* were a special variety, a subculture within the Mexican-American community, and the characters that he so enjoyed writing about were not meant to be thought of as typical of that community. Yet, they were of it, so that the idiom and the manner must be mastered, and even though the book is a fantasy, a modern folk tale, extensive real experience must be there to back it up and make it work. Only someone who truly loved and knew these people could have so successfully exaggerated and stylized their lives.

As I have already noted, from childhood Steinbeck was close to Spanish-speaking people, was brought almost as an adopted son into several families, and worked and played with them as a young man. Twice he had tried to go on extensive trips into the back country of Mexico: he had planned a trip by horseback with Dook in his college days, and just a few months before writing *Tortilla Flat*, when he was living in Montrose, he had tried to arrange a trip to be financed by selling travel sketches along the way. When he did finally get some money, one of the first things he did was to go to Mexico.

Although it may be obvious, it should be mentioned that a third of his published fiction has some degree of connection with Mexican or Mexican-American subjects. If one adds *The Log from the "Sea of Cortez"* and the two screenplays, *The Forgotten Village* and *Viva Zapata!*, to that roster, then the extent of the special appeal these people had for him is given even more weight. They seemed to him to provide the perfect counterbalance of looseness and enjoyment of life to Salinas and everything up-tight and narrow that it stood for in his mind.

When winter came, Steinbeck had completed a first draft of *Tortilla Flat* and turned back to the stories of his other two groupings, the "pony stories," as he called them, and the stories that would be gathered later into *The Long Valley*. First, however, he wrote the only surviving story from these months that was not used in *The Long Valley*, a story he had had in his head for a long time, called "How Edith McGillcuddy Met [Robert Louis] Stevenson."

This was based on an incident told to him by Max Wagner's mother, Edith, who as a child had traveled on the train from Salinas to Monterey to attend a funeral and met the famous author (she didn't know who he was at the time) by accident after wandering away from the ceremony. Mrs. Wagner had taught school with Steinbeck's mother, and as we have already seen, John spent a lot of time in her kitchen. She was one of several adults that he cultivated while in high school: he read his stories to her, and she told him stories of the Salinas Valley and of her years in Mexico when her husband was an official with the railroad there.

In late 1933, she had written to him to tell him that she liked *To a God Unknown*. Her letter triggered the memory of the story she had told him many years before, and he started writing it shortly thereafter, so that in February he told her in a letter that he had been "doing some short stories about people of the county. Some of them I think you yourself told me." Later, when he sent the story to his agents, he also sent a copy to Mrs. Wagner.

By a strange coincidence, she had herself written up the story only recently and was trying to get it printed in *Reader's Digest*. When Steinbeck heard about this, he wrote to apologize: "I'm terribly sorry if I have filched one of your stories. I'm a shameless magpie anyway, picking up anything shiny that comes my way—incident, situation or personality. But if I had had any idea, I shouldn't have taken it"

[6/4/34]. He withdrew the story from his agents, but Mrs. Wagner was unable to get her version published, and after several years, with her permission, he had his agents send his story out again. In 1941, Mrs. Wagner was old and crippled, and he thought publication of the story might help cheer her up. When the story was sold to *Harper's*, he sent the money to her.

A bit earlier, while writing "The Red Pony" (the first of the series, later called "The Gift"), he had written to George Albee in response to a suggestion Albee had made, "I don't need publication so why should I send it to *Story* which pays nothing. If I can't hit a paying magazine I'll put it away for the future collection that everybody dreams about." He had published two novels and a third would be published shortly, yet, as far as his stories were concerned, he was still fighting the battle for recognition—a tricky business in the always tight short-story market. High-paying, mass-circulation magazines that publish quality work seldom buy stories from unknowns, and Steinbeck, for all practical purposes, was an unknown. Like Hemingway, he was not able to crack this market until his novels had established his reputation. Such magazines, after all, do not build reputations; they feed on them.

By the end of the summer of 1933, however, McIntosh and Otis had been able to place his first two pony stories in *The North American Review*. Although it may not have been quite the placement he had been hoping for, still, this was his first such sale in a long, long time, and he needed both the money and the reassurance. Looking back, he wrote that he had been unable to find a publisher for "The Red Pony" until "at last a brave editor bought it . . . and paid ninety dollars for it, more money than I thought the world contained. What a great party we had in celebration!"

The North American Review was a prestigious monthly (in the December 1933 issue he appeared with Richard Lee Strout writing about the Supreme Court and Dalton Trumbo on the movies as art) and it did pay. The money was important to him, because he didn't have any, but the prestige meant little—throughout his career he seemed to give little thought to the literary reputation of a periodical. (He once commented, "If a story of mine is as well done as I am able to do it, and if it is not aimed at a magazine in particular, I wouldn't give a hoot if it were printed in Captain Billy's Whiz Bang.") His main reservation about the *Review* was that, with a limited circulation, it wouldn't be able to give him the kind of exposure that might ease acceptance by other magazines.

Nevertheless, he had found at least one fan. The managing editor, William Alton DeWitt, went on to purchase five of his stories in all, at rates of forty-five and fifty dollars apiece: "The Red Pony" and "The Great Mountains" appeared in November and December of 1933, "The Murder" in April 1934, "The Raid" in October 1934, and "The White Quail" in March 1935. The money was gratefully received; yet, when one thinks of the time and effort involved—as well as the quality of the stories—it becomes a convincing argument against pursuing the writing of short stories as a career.

In the late fall of 1933, the Steinbecks received a visitor at the house in Pacific Grove, a young man named Martin Bidwell, an aspiring novelist who had obtained an introduction from one of Steinbeck's neighbors. Of Steinbeck's work Bidwell had read only *Cup of Gold*, which he admired, and he came to Steinbeck in order to get advice from a successful writer of historical novels. His impressions of that visit, which he recorded and later published, are valuable as the fresh reactions of an outsider and as a sensitive contemporary account of the Steinbecks' manner of living.

Bidwell could not call first, because the Steinbecks had no phone. "Phones cost too much," Carol told him, greeting him at the door in a black silk dress. He saw her as "a young woman, tall, athletic-looking." He followed her into the living room:

> It gave an impression of gloominess. The only light came from glowing coals in a brick fireplace, and from two candles that had been stuck into empty liqueur bottles. . . . The unsteady flames trailed after sudden air currents and cast shadow fragments on the beaverboard walls of the room.
>
> "Come in and sit down," the young woman said. She picked up a loose tumble of magazines and books, and I sat on a straight chair. "My husband will be back in a few minutes." The books and magazines disappeared somewhere in the shadows. She sank into a chair by the fireplace, slumped down, and crossed her sturdy legs.
>
> "It's awfully nice of you to let me in on such short notice," I said, fidgeting a little.
>
> There was a friendly smile in her eyes. "We're usually at home in the evenings," she replied, "without very much to do. We count on our friends and—"
>
> In the middle of her sentence the door opened, and a large, tousle-headed man appeared. He wore sneakers, corduroy trousers, and a cotton sweat shirt. . . . I noticed how ruddy his face was, that a thin, dark mustache shadowed his upper lip, and that he didn't

wear any garters. His woolen socks had fallen down. His ankles looked as firm and sculptured as marble. In fact, as John Steinbeck sat in the wicker chair he looked massive and rough all over, like one of Rodin's statues. . . .

In answer to my hesitantly put questions about the difficulties of writing historical fiction, he began to talk, slowly, gravely, only after deep thought. Behind him was a series of shelves. Books spilled over them into mounds on the floor. Where the beaverboard showed through, it was stained and warped by rain. Cobwebs laced themselves up the corner of the room into shadows on the ceiling.

Steinbeck mentioned that they were thinking about going to the Sierras for the winter, where they'd been offered a cabin, or they might possibly go to Mexico, since the living there might be cheaper. Bidwell countered by suggesting Tahiti, where the living was very reasonable. In order to interest Steinbeck, he mentioned the names of several well-known persons whom he had met when he was there. Steinbeck scowled and said that if he ever went to the South Seas, he certainly wouldn't concern himself with well-known people. "Isn't it possible to get to know the Tahitians themselves?" he asked. "Because the truth about a country can be learned only from its common people."

He then reached over to a pile of books, pulled out *Crime and Punishment*, and absent-mindedly began to leaf through it. Lost for something to say to break the silence, Bidwell ventured, "So many of Dostoevsky's characters seem abnormal." Steinbeck sat up straight in his wicker chair and leaned forward:

"That isn't true!" he declared. "His characters are the essence of mankind. There's more psychological truth in one page of Dostoevsky than in most books! Every beginner should realize that. If he doesn't he'll never be able to write anything." . . .

His wife got up and put a stick of pine wood on the glowing coals. One candle had sputtered itself out. She stuck another into the bottle neck and went back to her chair.

Slowly he began to speak. Before, his ruddy face had been grave. Now, as if he spoke of something sacred, it was reverent.

"A man's a writer because there's a craving inside him that makes him write." His eyes came around to me. The heavy brows above them were thunderous: "A man writes to get at the bottom of some basic fact of life." His voice sank. There were overtones of contempt in it. "But writing never pays. Nobody can ever expect to make himself rich by it." . . .

"What kind of trouble are you having with your novel?" he asked. There was a look of weariness in his eyes.

"I couldn't sell it," I explained. "My agents want me to change the main character. It seems he isn't admirable enough."

"To please the publishers?" Steinbeck's expression tightened. "Don't you realize that you're the one who should be pleased— that you're writing solely for yourself?" His words crackled with scorn. "What anybody else thinks or says about it doesn't matter. That's why you're having trouble. You're selling yourself out. You're being dishonest! . . .

"My wife and I live in this house on almost nothing," he went on. "We never have any money. We can't go out to dance, or to the theater. But that isn't important. I'm writing as I know I should write. Nothing will ever stop me!"

A disciplined force of will, a tremendous self-confidence, glinted in his eyes. The dim room was too small for such determination. John Steinbeck seemed remote, elevated. His wife was little more than part of the shadows. I didn't count at all.

Despite the recent publication of two stories, Christmas of 1933 was sad, an extension of the pain of the previous year. Steinbeck, nearly twenty years later, called it "the most terrible wrenching scene" that he had ever witnessed, as his father bravely tried to recreate Christmas as it had been before his wife's illness: "We decorated a tree in her room and had presents and tried to make the Christmas jokes. And I remember her eyes—cold as marbles but alive. I don't know how much she could see or understand. But it breaks me up every time I remember how hard my father tried." His mother was close to death and died only a short time later. She was buried on the same day, and although he would have preferred not to, he served as a pall bearer—it was a family custom.

In late winter and early spring of 1934, he wrote the second pair of stories that would eventually make up *The Red Pony*, "The Promise" (which was turned down by *The North American Review*) *and "The Leader of the People." All four stories are to some extent about death and dying, and apparently the writing of them acted as a catharsis for the grief, the fear, and the pity of the situation that had held him captive for so long.*

In May 1934 he wrote in his journal:

I have written five stories in the scene. It would be well now to start bending the thing into one piece. But how. I've thought of that often enough. Five stories have been written about Jody or in which Jody was the eyes. After the story of the ghost house, why not switch to Billy Buck—to Mrs. Tiflin, to Carl Tiflin. It wouldn't be a bad exercise to make a volume of short stories all about one family. I suppose it has been done. I can think of a number of books and series, but always the emphasis lay in the incidents—not in the family.

It appears that a fifth story using Jody, never referred to in the correspondence, was written and then discarded (although it could have been written only in his mind). Following this entry in his journal, he outlines the "story of the ghost house," which has Jody and his mother seeing the ghost, but Carl rejecting the experience. It is against "the law" (Steinbeck's words), and Carl can't stand to think about it.

He went on in the spring to write "The Raid," his first fiction dealing with labor strife. By this time, he had already talked to some of his sources for *In Dubious Battle*—a matter I'll get to in some detail later—and this sketch, drawn from these sources, was a sort of preliminary exercise for his oncoming labor novel. From "The Raid" he went on in close order to produce "The Harness" (first called "The Fool"), "Flight" (first called "Manhunt"), "The White Quail," and "Johnny Bear" (first called "The Sisters").

According to Carol, the central character in "The Harness" was patterned after a real person who lived near King City, a man who went against everyone's advice and succeeded. Steinbeck got this story from gossip, but there may also be a tenuous connection with Steinbeck's perception of his father, particularly of his condition after Mrs. Steinbeck's death.

For a while, Steinbeck's father lived with John and Carol in Pacific Grove. Despite all the compassion he had for his father's condition, John wanted badly to have some time away from him. Never had the urge to get away been stronger, and one of the reasons he was pushing himself so hard in his writing was the hope that they could get enough money to take a trip and get a change of scene. Some relief came in the middle of March when he and Carol were able to accompany Ed on a collecting trip to Laguna Beach for a week as Ed had received an order for octopuses from New York. A few weeks after they returned, Steinbeck's father asked two old friends, Mr. and Mrs. Hargis, to move in and take over the Salinas house. In exchange for rent, he boarded with them, and they, in effect, looked after him for nearly a year.

Mr. Steinbeck seemed to do little more than go through the motions.

He got up early, went to work, came home, ate dinner, listened to the nine o'clock news on the radio, and went to bed. He was still weak, however, and distracted, and so Carol was made "assistant treasurer" to help with the backlog of work at the office. She remembers that she got along with him very well, but that he was rather a stern old man. As before, whenever he had to go out of town on county business, John would also come into the office to fill in until his return.

Every Saturday John and Carol, both dressed in baggy work pants, would come over to Salinas to use the old Maytag washer and the huge Simplex mangle to do their clothes. Once in a while during the week, John might stop by the house, and Mildred Hargis would ask him how the work was going. He would talk about the difficulty of maintaining his discipline. He tried to put out at least one thousand words a day, but it seemed to take him longer and longer as time went by to fill up the pages because his handwriting, for some reason, kept getting smaller and smaller.

Mrs. Hargis remembers that it was just about this time that the growing influx of Dust Bowl migrants in Salinas was becoming obvious, with more and more jalopies stacked with furniture moving around and occasionally through town and a Hooverville called "Little Oklahoma" already established on a hill just outside the city limits. As one such home-made truck drove by, she said to John, "There's a story in that somewhere." John watched the ragged family drive by and nodded.

In June, he wrote in his journal:

> There is too much work to get out. This Monday afternoon must be given to working out of this week's story and perhaps beginning it. . . . The bottom of my stomach is dropping out with accumulated loneliness—not loneliness that might be mended with company either. I think Carol is the same way. There's a haunted quality in her eyes. I'm not good company to her. I can't help her loneliness and she can't help mine. Perhaps this is a good thing. It may preserve some kind of integrity. Maybe it is exactly that kind of hunger that keeps us struggling on—I must get on to work. I'm wasting time now. Only work cures the gnawing. Maybe the work of last week wasn't good ["Flight"] but the doing of it was good.

His next story, "Johnny Bear" (called on first publication "The Ears of Johnny Bear") combined some local gossip with a character that Steinbeck had "collected" on a trip with Toby Street. According to Toby:

We were coming back from Palo Alto on the way to Salinas and we stopped for a beer at a bar just outside Castroville. We were sitting there talking, and suddenly we heard the bartender speaking to somebody wearing bib overalls. We listened for a while. The bartender said, "And then what did you do?" and the guy went through all sorts of motions. He didn't talk with his fingers as in sign language; rather he illustrated what he did. He was mute; he could hear but could not speak.

As Toby recalls, the mute was a very large man, sort of clumsy and powerful-looking. His gestures were awkward and anxious, as if he was very concerned that he please his audience. In the car as they drove away, Steinbeck turned to Toby and said, "Did you pay attention to that fella, the guy in the overalls? You know, he could do a lot of harm, that guy!"

But the story did not start, as one might suppose, with the figure of Johnny Bear. According to Steinbeck's notes, the seed was, instead, the secret that the impaired young man discovers: "I seem to be on the beginning of a story called The Sisters," he wrote on June 14. "And I have thought of an objective point of view who might be valuable in a number of stories—the half-wit Indian boy who lives in Castroville." The "sisters" refers to a piece of local scandal that Steinbeck had picked up, concerning two prominent Salinas women, sisters, one of whom had, as in the story, an affair with an Oriental man (a great disgrace in the California of that period).

If, as seems likely, the mute observed by Toby in John's company and the "half-wit Indian boy" are the same (unless there were two such strange figures in the small town of Castroville), we may have the model not only for Johnny Bear, but for Lennie in *Of Mice and Men* as well. In the writing of the story, of course, the focus shifts to the "half-wit" and his desire to communicate and to earn his drink, which becomes a marvelous metaphor for Steinbeck's own condition. Like Johnny Bear, the writer must try to break out of his inarticulate loneliness, and, anxious to please, mimics the voices of others in order to reveal their innermost secrets.

But Steinbeck was still not doing very well in earning his "whiskey." Just before starting work on the story, he received yet another piece of bad news, as he noted in his ledger:

both P. of H. and T.A.G.U. are to be remaindered. In as much as this was one of the considerations—no remaindering, I am surprised. . . . Ballou can make books but he can't sell them. . . . Anyway I'm a little upset by it. It means somewhat a new start to be made. I've been making new starts all my life. . . .

So far I've kept one [story] ahead of the number set and I have one extra written—making 6 in four weeks. . . . The bad thing will be if nothing turns out. If everything should flop then we'll have a bad period to overcome. I wonder in the long run, how many disappointments we can weather. An infinite number I guess. There doesn't seem to be any limit to our endurance.

The stories in all three of the groupings seemed to have two things in common: they had some relevance to his personal emotional condition—to his struggle to write and publish, to the terminal illnesses of his parents and the death of his mother, and to his relations with Carol; and they demonstrated some aspect of his philosophy, including, but not limited to, his phalanx thesis. In respect to his philosophy, the *Red Pony* stories seemed to act as a moral fulcrum. These stories, with their child observer, examine the nature of life and of death and the relationship of the individual to the whole. On each side of this foundation hang in balance two versions of adult life—the tight, rigid, and often frustrated pattern of middle-class living in the valley, and the relaxed, loose, and usually loving pattern of the lower-class *paisanos* on the coast.

Man, Steinbeck declared on several occasions in his writing, is basically a lonely animal that spends its life looking for love, in one form or another. Nearly every major character in *The Long Valley* wears some kind of harness, whereas in *Tortilla Flat* nearly all the characters, rather than frustrated in their search, express their emotions and make connections freely. But more than this, the *Long Valley* people lead teleological lives, whereas none of the *paisanos* look for causes or cures—they simply live and accept. Thus, Mary Teller's teleological garden of good and evil in "The White Quail" stands in implicit contrast to the weed-covered back lots of *Tortilla Flat* and their broken-down chicken coops.

The part of his philosophy that he called his "thesis" also found expression in all this work: in *Tortilla Flat*, as I have already explained; in the last of the Jody stories, "The Leader of the People"; and finally in the story that gave him the most trouble during the spring and summer of 1934, "The Vigilante."

From the beginning, in early June, it was for him a special story, just as the oncoming novel, which he was working out in the back of his mind during these months, was for him a special novel. Both, he thought, required careful thought and delicate treatment, for he intended that they express in fictional form the heart of his thesis. When the basis for "Vigilante" first came to him, he noted in his journal, "One story which occurred to me last night is so delicate and different that I don't feel justified in taking regular work time to do it. If I do it, it will be at night on my own time. There is too much work to get out. This is not a time for experiments on ~~my own~~ [sic] company time."

Nevertheless, a paragraph later he turned back to the idea that had come to him during the night and wrote it down:

John Ramsey—hated the war and misses it. Came home to the quiet, the lack of design, for the war was a huge design, wanders lost on his farm looking for a phalanx to join and finds none. Is nervous and very lost. Finally finds the movement in a lynching. War shock not so much war as the easing of war drive. Hunger for the group. Change of drive. What does it matter. The mob is not a wasteful thing but an efficient thing.

Not long after writing this, he tried his hand at the story itself, which he called "Case History." In this draft the phalanx is specifically discussed and the lynching plays only a minor part in it. It was not very effective, and certainly not very delicately handled. At the end of the month, he made three attempts to write the story, but failed. After the second false start, he wrote, "Wrong again, all wrong. What the hell's the matter with me."

Then he began once again, but this time he shifted the emphasis. Just as in the writing of "Johnny Bear," where he shifted the emphasis from the story observed to the observer, in this story he changed from the feelings of a man looking for a phalanx to the feelings of a man just deprived of a phalanx. The difference is only a matter of timing, since the central character in both cases is looking to re-establish connection with the group, but in the final version, which was called "The Lonesome Vigilante" on first publication, Steinbeck lets the very specific experience of having participated in a lynch mob dominate the story, rather than trying to use the vague and general feeling of having participated in the war sometime in the past.

The lynching on which the story was based occurred at the end of November 1933, in San Jose, when two suspects in a celebrated kidnap-murder case were taken from their cells and strung up in trees outside the jailhouse. The case and the vigilante action that accompanied it were front-page news in northern California newspapers for nearly three weeks.

Experimenting with his focus, Steinbeck avoids most of the obvious drama of the lynch scene itself and instead concentrates on the mob's emotion in retrospect. We follow one member of the newly dissolved phalanx away from the scene, to a bar, and to his home. As the title suggests, now that he is no longer part of the whole, he feels strangely empty, let down, and alone. Steinbeck builds on the man's feeling of emptiness, suggesting at the conclusion of the story that the life of this particular phalanx has paralleled the course of emotions during the sexual union of a man and woman.

His next story, "The Snake," speaks of another kind of vicarious sexual union. A woman watches a snake eat a rat and in the process has something like an orgasm. Although complex and well written, the story was so bizarre that Steinbeck could not get it published except in a local newspaper (although it appeared later in *The Long Valley*). It is notable in the history of Steinbeck's work as containing the first appearance of Ed Ricketts as a fictional character. Ricketts fed his rattlesnakes regularly, and there must have been a woman present on several occasions who reacted strangely to the feeding, since about a half dozen people feel certain that they witnessed the event which was the genesis of the story.

The most detailed account is that offered by Toby Street:

> That snake thing took place in Ed's laboratory. He had two big rattlesnakes in a cage in the lab, and he had a bunch of white rats running around. He went in and got a white rat and put it in the cage. A girl who was one of the dancers from a local vaudeville team that was passing through Monterey was there. She was just fascinated by the whole thing but she didn't say a word.
>
> The little rat went in there, and the snake waited and pierced the rat behind the ear. The snake pulled back and the fang caught and pulled him over to one side. The rat ran around for a little while, unconscious of the fact that he was mortally wounded, and he finally died and the snake took him. That girl never said a word, and when it was over, she just got up and left and we never saw her again. Now John, I am sure, made that episode into the story of the snake and gave it sexual implications which you could not help doing if you had seen that girl.

Asked on several occasions later what the story meant, Steinbeck always gave a "Robert Frost answer": that it meant just what it said—it was just something that happened and he didn't know any more than anyone else what its implications might be.

By August 1934 all but one of the stories from this period had been written, typed by Carol, and sent to the agents. The only good news that he had had since "The Red Pony" and "The Great Mountains" had been accepted and published was that "The Murder" had been selected as an O. Henry Prize story for that year. But this gave him only the slim hope of some kind of chain reaction of future acceptance, not the income that he needed so badly:

> Still we have no money. I've sent off story after story and so far with no result. Both of us are beginning to worry. I thought there might be a loss of one out of four but the loss seems to be all of all. Curious. Maybe this O. Henry selection might create some interest in my stories. I hope so. Esther says I am getting gray. Alice C [Cohee] says I look forty years old and I am 33. This year has done it. We've lived twenty years of pain in a year. Maturity came—not gradually, but like coal down a chute. I only hope early maturity may last awhile. I don't want to be old so soon. . . .
>
> The pen feels good to my hand. Comfortable and comforting. What an extension of self is this pen. Once it is in my hand like a wand, I stop being the confused, turgid ugly and gross person. I am no longer the me I know.

The final story written of the three groupings was the sketch, "Breakfast." Often thought to have been a warmup for his work on *The Grapes of Wrath*, its composition preceded by two years the earliest research and by three years the earliest writing that Steinbeck did for *Grapes*. Actually, this very moving and very real scene—it is little more than that—came out of his preparation for *In Dubious Battle*. To get to the origins of this novel, we have to go back a few months to the beginning of the year 1934.

Steinbeck was always on the lookout for a story and seems to have remembered in detail nearly everything he saw or heard. In this sense, too, he was Johnny Bear. A chance for a story came his way early in 1934 when he heard about two men, strike organizers, who were starving in a garret in the nearby town of Seaside. They were fugitives, hiding out in fear that there were arrest warrants out for them. Two of their comrades, strike leaders Pat Chambers and Caroline Decker, had already been arrested under California's anti-union criminal syndicalism law.

A young woman friend of Steinbeck's brought him to Seaside to meet the fugitives, and since they were destitute, Steinbeck made arrangements with them to buy their story. His idea was to write a first-person narrative, an "autobiography" of a communist labor organizer.

So it was that almost by accident, Steinbeck started down the road of concern with migrant farm labor, something he certainly had been familiar with himself in years gone by, but which he hadn't thought to write about recently. It was a road that would lead him to three of his greatest novels, *In Dubious Battle, Of Mice and Men,* and *The Grapes of Wrath,* and to the fame and fortune he didn't expect, didn't want, and learned to regret.

Personal problems, finishing *Tortilla Flat*, and writing several short stories consumed most of Steinbeck's attention during the fall and winter of 1933–34. In the meantime, a new context was developing around him. The thirties in California had brought not only the Depression but also an era of severe labor strife. Most of the trouble was on the docks and in the packing sheds and fields, and of these battles, the one between the growers and the farm laborers would shortly have a profound effect on the direction of Steinbeck's career.

While the production and value of agricultural goods climbed during the early thirties, wages dropped to all-time lows. At first, protests by workers were spontaneous reactions to wages too low to live on; between 1930 and 1932 there were some forty-four agricultural strikes, most of which were quickly squashed by local authorities working with employers. Unconnected to the traditional labor movement (which spurned farm labor) and for the most part unplanned and without experienced leaders, these strikes were doomed almost before they began.

In late 1932, however, the Communist Party moved to fill the void, organizing the Cannery and Agricultural Workers' Industrial Union. (Use of the word "industrial"—as in the I.W.W.—was like waving a Red flag in front of the employers.) They supplied experienced leaders, first on an ad hoc basis wherever a strike had started and later operating in a more deliberate way as they learned how to anticipate strike conditions. The skill of the C. & A.W.I.U. took the growers by surprise. For a year there were more victories (usually modest gains in hourly wages) than defeats. While the organization had weaknesses—it was always short of personnel and money, and it was badly split between the doctrinaire party leaders in the cities and the pragmatic organizers in the field—it did have the great strength of being able to mobilize support, moral and material, among those sympathetic to the farm workers' plight.

Several of Steinbeck's friends and acquaintances were involved in gathering support for the efforts of the C. & A.W.I.U., as well as for other labor-organizing and strike efforts. Chief among them was Francis Whitaker, who was very active in behalf of a wide variety of liberal causes and was, as I have said, a leader in the John Reed Club. He brought speakers into the community; raised money and collected food and clothing; and helped publish leaflets and posters necessary to gather support. It was through Whitaker that Steinbeck met a number of people associated with leftist politics and farm-labor organizing. Among others, Whitaker introduced him to James Harkins, a young man who was a lettuce grower, but who also became a worker leader-organizer active in the Imperial Valley strike of the winter of 1934 and the Salinas lettuce strike of 1936. Harkins became a major source for Steinbeck in checking such details as habits of speech among the strikers and strike leaders. Also, through Whitaker, Steinbeck met Ella Winter, Lincoln Steffens, and the band of young radicals who had attached themselves to them.

Carol remembers that these young people, many of whom had been helping with strikes near Watsonville, in the Santa Clara Valley, and in Salinas, started dropping by the Steinbeck cottage in Pacific Grove on almost a regular basis. They came to talk and to be fed—they always seemed to be half-starved. They glowed with a spirit of holy mission, something that Steinbeck found interesting, if not admirable. Since you were either for them or against them—there was no compromise—he did more listening than talking. Most of them used aliases and were members of either the John Reed Club or the Young Communist League.

Occasionally Ella Winter was with them when they dropped by (and sometimes Anna Louise Strong and Mike Gold, two other famous figures in the radical Left). Ella Winter and her husband, Lincoln Steffens, lived in a large house overlooking the ocean in nearby Carmel, and though Winter and Steffens did not become close friends of Steinbeck's, theirs was an acquaintance that he did cultivate, often stopping at their house to chat with Steffens during the years before he died in mid-1936. Steffens had won wide notoriety in 1902–03 with a series of articles in *McClure's Magazine* exposing corruption in various city governments, a series later collected as *The Shame of the Cities*. With these and similar articles that followed, he became one of America's foremost social critics, a force for reform, and a man who somehow seemed to have met nearly everyone worth knowing, even prominent capitalists and business leaders.

In 1931 he came back into public notice with the publication of his two-volume *Autobiography*, and as two decades before when he had been the most famous of the muckrakers, he was once again swamped by invitations to lecture. Then in the fall of 1933, shortly after Steinbeck had met him for the first time, Steffens was stricken by a coronary thrombosis and was confined by doctor's orders to his bed. Nevertheless, his fame and wide acquaintance seemed to draw the world to his bedside. Here Steinbeck encountered, as he did at home, Ella Winter's band of farm-labor activists. Here also he met George West, editorial writer for the *San Francisco News*, who would several years later start him on his road toward *The Grapes of Wrath* by asking him to do a series of articles on the Dust Bowl migrants, and Lawrence Clark Powell, scholar and librarian, who would become his first bibliographer. And it was through Winter and Steffens that a link was established between the Carmel-Monterey area and the union official who became Steinbeck's primary source for *In Dubious Battle*.

On the surface, it is hard to think of what these two very different men, Steinbeck and Steffens, would have in common. The older man was small and frail, and with his "little gray beard and metal-rimmed glasses had a certain resemblance to King George V of England." The younger man was, in Ella Winter's eyes, "excessively shy, a red-faced, blue-eyed giant." Steffens was a gentleman—courteous, witty, urbane, widely traveled and well connected—and Steinbeck, an outdoorsman only slightly domesticated, was by comparison a foot-shuffling provincial. Yet they were both Californians; both as children had swum in its rivers and ridden horseback across its sun-baked valleys. And both were essentially suspicious of "good" people, of capitalists, of politicians. Yet, for all that Steffens found wrong in this country, excesses of nearly any kind in Russia seemed to him justified, and it was here that Steinbeck parted company with him and his wife, although Steinbeck made no great issue of it with them.

This split in point of view between Steinbeck and Steffens and Winter reflected a larger split between doctrinaire, establishment liberals and those liberals, Marxist or non-Marxist, who viewed Russia with skepticism or outright distrust. It was a split that, as the years passed, would significantly affect the course of Steinbeck's literary reputation.

Steffens and Steinbeck did, however, agree on one thing: the importance and value of observing and discovering. Among the many visitors to Steffens's bedside were journalism students from Stanford and Berkeley who had been assigned Steffens's *Autobiography* and had heard of his accessibility. When Steffens would tell them what was going on right around them that wasn't being reported in the papers, they'd ask, "Is that really true?" And Steffens would tell them, "Don't take it from me, don't accept what I say, look for yourselves. Go to the strikes and watch the trials yourselves." As advice repeated frequently in Steinbeck's presence, it reinforced Steinbeck's own resolve to look into these matters for himself. Over the next few years, he spent more time looking, and looking carefully, at the California farm-labor situation in its various aspects than anybody else, except, perhaps, for a handful of government and academic experts.

In early 1934, however, although surrounded by the genuine concern of many near him for the misery of the farm worker and migrant, he remained emotionally uninvolved. As usual, he was concerned primarily about his writing, and the charged atmosphere told him that there was a story somewhere. The importance of the story "The Lonesome Vigilante," written during this period, may be that it was the first time he had written about something that was a contemporary event. Most novelists write in retrospect of events that happened at least several years in the past; it may be that this story taught him that fiction about present events was possible and made him ready when his opportunity came.

II

Sometime during the winter of 1934, two men who had helped with a strike in California's San Joaquin Valley made their way to the house of a local farm-labor leader in Seaside and holed up in his attic. They used the names Cicil McKiddy and Carl Williams, and of the two, McKiddy was the key figure—little is known about Williams. McKiddy was a likable, twenty-four-year-old Okie who only a few months earlier had made the trek to California with friends. They ended up, as most Dust Bowl migrants did, looking for farm work in the area near Bakersfield and when the cotton strike of 1933 broke out, McKiddy volunteered to help the union. The leaders discovered that he could type and had some ability as a cartoonist, so they made him secretary-treasurer of the C. & A.W.I.U. local in Tulare.

The storefront headquarters in Tulare served primarily as a message center, and McKiddy worked as a typist and errand boy, putting out leaflets (usually written by Caroline Decker) and carrying messages from one migrant camp to another. A brief picture of McKiddy at work is given in passing by Ella Winter in her autobiography. She had come to the Central Valley with a "task force" of her activist friends to check on the conditions of the strikers and to see if she could help get strike leader Pat Chambers out of jail:

> I went to "Strike Headquarters," a small room with bare floor and one bench. A quiet spoken boy in a turtle-neck blue sweater pecked at a typewriter, and some Mexican women, their hair in matted plaits, sat around suckling their babies. Bits of paper tacked on a soiled board had ill-spelled messages in English and Spanish, and a list of names was printed in uneven letters on a gray cardboard from a Uneeda soda cracker box. There were flies and a smell of sweat.

McKiddy served the union during the cotton strike, probably the largest and most successful strike of farm laborers in the United States before World War II. After the strike, the union leaders thought that it might be good for McKiddy to be exposed to intellectual people, and so he was asked to go to the house of Ella Winter and Lincoln Steffens in Carmel and stay with them. When he got to the coast, however, he was sent into hiding, most likely as a result of information that there might be a warrant out for his arrest. He was, after all, one of the most visible "officials" of the union during the strike, and union organizing could be interpreted as illegal under California's criminal syndicalism law, a law that was used instead of vagrancy statutes to get rid of union leaders, because the bail could be set very high.

Several people in the Monterey area, backers of the C. & A.W.I.U., knew where McKiddy and Williams were, and a young woman named Sis Reamer took Francis Whitaker and Steinbeck to Seaside to meet the fugitives. Her motive was twofold: to get the first-hand story of the strike to as many influential sympathizers as possible, and to gather some material support for the two men, who were destitute and nearly starving. Steinbeck was fascinated by what he heard in his initial meeting. McKiddy was a good source—even though he had not been a principal in the strike, he had been in a position to know about nearly everything that had gone on—and Steinbeck got the idea that he might be able to help the men and at the same time help himself. He would pay them for their story, and since much of McKiddy's information was about the strike leader Pat Chambers, he would write a first-person narrative from Chambers's point of view—a sort of diary of a communist labor organizer.

This was the seed from which Steinbeck's first major novel would grow. In mid-1934 he wrote to Mavis McIntosh to tell her of his idea, and she, in turn, wrote back to urge him to use his material as the basis for a novel instead. It would not be the last time in his career that he would start with an idea for a nonfiction narrative and end up writing a novel. As he thought about the possibilities for fiction, the project began to get bigger and bigger. He was particularly excited about the applications to his material of his phalanx thesis. While *Tortilla Flat* had given him a limited opportunity to express the thesis, his new manuscript, involving conflict between groups of men, seemed to him, the more he thought about it, tailor-made for it. His excitement drew him into one of the most concentrated periods of writing in his life: in a little over five months from the time he started on the manuscript in early September, he turned out something over one hundred and twenty thousand words.

Steinbeck had talked to McKiddy for hours at a time over the course of several weeks, questioning him in great detail. I should add, however, that although McKiddy was Steinbeck's major source for *In Dubious Battle*, he talked to other men involved in farm-labor organizing as well. Also, he had, of course, his own background in farm labor (there had been talk of organizing even in those days, as the influence of the I.W.W. swept down from the Northwest), and he went out himself, during the summer of 1934, to the migrant camps in the Salinas area to listen to the workers talk. (It was on such a foray along a county road that he had picked up the material for "Breakfast.")

There has been over the years a good deal of speculation among Steinbeck readers as to what particular strike or strikes the novel might have been patterned after. Writing in response to one critic's statement that the model for the place was the Pajaro Valley, near Watsonville, and that the strike was one that occurred near Fresno, Steinbeck said,

> I have usually avoided using actual places to avoid hurting feelings, for, although I rarely use a person or a story as it is—neighbors love only too well to attribute them to someone. . . . as for the valley in *In Dubious Battle*—it is a composite valley as it is a composite strike. If it has the characteristics of Pajaro nevertheless there was no strike there. If it's like the cotton strike, that wasn't apples.

Despite the suggestion here, without evidence of McKiddy's connection with Steinbeck no one would think to look twice at the cotton strike as a possibility as its general circumstances seem so very different from those of Steinbeck's fictional strike. He switched the geography around, borrowing the physical setup and a few aspects of an earlier strike (the peach strike on the Tagus Ranch in Tulare County in August 1933) and combining them with the major events of the cotton strike of October 1933. As he indicated in his letter, he had indeed created a composite.

I don't know whether Cicil McKiddy took part in the peach strike or not. Circumstances suggest that he did and that it was at Tagus where he met Pat Chambers, who then took him on as a sort of apprentice for the cotton strike. He may, however, have simply heard about the strike from Chambers. Whatever his basis for knowledge, McKiddy was able to report on the peach strike in some detail, for Steinbeck not only used aspects of the strike for *In Dubious Battle*, but used the Tagus Ranch as the model for the Hooper Ranch, an important setting in *The Grapes of Wrath*.

In the earlier novel Mac and Jim, the two organizers (the former, experienced, the latter, an apprentice), hop a freight and travel south from the city (presumably San Jose, where in reality the C. & A.W.I.U. headquarters was located) a hundred miles and then east another hundred miles or so. This would put them, roughly speaking, in the vicinity of Tulare. But there are several problems when one tries to match Steinbeck's fictional map with the real landscape of California. For one thing, there is no rail line running east from the coast south of San Jose into the Central Valley. (Francis Whitaker and Ed Ricketts loved to catch Steinbeck making up his own rail lines, valleys, highways, or mountains, and they would jokingly accuse him of tampering or ignorance. With assumed hauteur, he would claim the privilege of putting any railroad anywhere he damned pleased into his own novel.) For another, there is no self-contained little valley anywhere near Tulare (although the Torgus Valley does sound a bit like the real location of the Tagus Ranch). And finally, the climate in the Central Valley is too temperate for apple growing.

However, in the novel, when Mac talks about the Torgus Valley, he says, "When the apples are ripe the crop tramps come in and pick them. And from there they go on over the ridge and south, and pick the cotton. If we can start the fun in the apples, maybe it will just naturally spread over into the cotton." In life, the heart of the California cotton country is south of Tulare, and the peach strike did spread into the cotton fields and was a major factor in encouraging the cotton strike.

Although it was not in a small apple-growing valley dominated by a few large growers, the Tagus Ranch did have a similar environment.

Off Highway 99 below Fresno, about six or seven miles above the town of Tulare, the ranch spread over four thousand acres, much of it planted in peaches. The ranch was divided into a half dozen sections, each with a camp for migrant workers, mostly Mexicans plus Dust Bowl migrants. The ranch had a company store and issued company tokens, and Pat Chambers claims that they had people working there for three or four seasons who had never seen any cash paid out by the ranch. To insure careful handling, most fruit picking was paid for by the hour, whether apples or peaches, and the price offered by the management of the Tagus Ranch in the summer of 1933 was identical with that offered by the Growers Association in Steinbeck's novel—fifteen cents an hour.

Just as Mac in the novel has a contact in town, a sympathizer who owns a diner, so Pat Chambers had a friend who owned a store in town who was able to fill him in on the situation and direct him to the camps. Tagus had company guards with rifles staked out all around the camps, and so Chambers had to crawl along a drainage ditch and under barbed wire in the middle of the night in order to slip into camp. The initial contact was easy, according to Chambers: all you had to do was slip into camp and put up a union sign someplace. This, in contrast with the rather devious opportunism of the novel wherein Mac ingratiates himself with the strikers by delivering London's daughter's baby, a process he knows little about.

Pat Chambers's philosophy was very similar to Mac's in *In Dubious Battle*, except that it was less cynical and more concerned with the immediate welfare of the workers:

> Plant an idea and let it grow. Let the situation develop and take advantage of opportunities. Don't come on like a great strike leader—stay in the background (the growers are smart and they know enough to get you if you become famous). Talk to people on their own level and let the ideas about what to do come from them. . . . The essence of leadership is not to portray yourself as some sort of know-it-all, but your ability to develop the people you are working with so they themselves can take the initiative and do the organizational drive.

Even in 1933 a wage of $1.50 for a ten-hour day was cruelly designed to provide nothing more than the food for one day purchased at the company store, leaving little for other necessities, such as clothing, car repairs, medical care, or even gasoline to get to the next job. When workers arrived at places like the Tagus Ranch, they had usually exhausted their resources just getting to the job, and once there, they were at the mercy of the employer. Wages could be kept low and living conditions in the worker camps could remain miserable because with the Dust Bowl migrants entering the state in large numbers, joining the already more than sufficient Mexican and Filipino workers, there was a large surplus of farm labor. Many of the Dust Bowlers were so desperate that they would work for almost nothing, so that if one person or even a group wouldn't work for low wages, there were always others who would. The power of the growers' organizations, nearly always supported by local authorities, was nearly absolute, and that power, in combination with an almost inexhaustible supply of scabs, made union organizing extremely difficult and dangerous.

Nevertheless, the workers were being driven to desperation. They began to adopt the attitude that if they couldn't live on what they were making, what did they have to lose if they struck? Within such a climate of anger and frustration, a midnight visit from a union organizer was welcome, and as the pot boiled over, it was easy for Chambers to spot the natural leaders in each of the camps. Chambers recalls, "We knew that the first thing they'd cut is food supplies, so we stored up food in advance. Timing was all-important. We had it set up so that one morning everyone was suddenly on strike before the grower knew what was happening. One day or even a few hours could make the difference between success and failure." The careful timing here is at variance with the start of the strike in the novel, which is set off by accident. By showing the workers becoming a mob in response to old Dan's fall off a ladder, Steinbeck chooses to ignore his model in favor of developing his ideas concerning the behavior of the group animal.

The strikers asked for thirty cents an hour. At first Tagus resisted. Then, after two days of continuing unity among the strikers, the ranch offered to increase the hourly wage from fifteen to seventeen and a half cents. The offer was rejected. Chambers figured that they could hold out for seven days. But peaches must be picked right away, and the strikers didn't have to hold out that long. With the help of the State Department of Industrial Relations acting as mediator, a settlement was reached on the fourth day: Tagus agreed to a twenty-five-cent hourly wage and pledged reemployment of the strikers without discrimination. Another important choice Steinbeck makes is to reject the successful outcome of his model in order to emphasize the dubious nature of the conflict he is describing. Tagus, by the way, was so angered by having to give in to the strikers that it ripped out its peach trees and planted cotton.

III

While Steinbeck was able to use some aspects of the general situation and a few of the details from the Tagus strike, he derived most of the major events of the novel from McKiddy's account of the strike that followed. In contrast to the concentrated conflict of the peach strike, the cotton strike took place in an area that ran 120 miles long by 30 to 40 miles wide through the heart of the lower San Joaquin Valley. It involved twelve to fifteen thousand workers in five counties and lasted twenty-four days. Pat Chambers, in recalling the situation, said, "I'll be the first to admit, as far as the cotton strike was concerned, I was leery of it from the very beginning. I never did find out how many growers we were dealing with."

The cotton strike boiled over from the peach strike, almost starting by itself. The Agricultural Labor Bureau of San Joaquin Valley, a grower organization, set a standard wage for chopping and picking cotton throughout the area. The bureau was controlled by the large cotton-growing and -ginning companies, which in turn were often controlled by, or operated in association with, utilities and finance companies. Independent farmers found it impossible to set their own wages because of financing and marketing pressures that kept them "in line." Wages for picking had been dropping from well over a dollar per hundred-weight in the late twenties to forty cents in 1932. At its annual wage-setting meeting in Fresno in September, the Labor Bureau, sensing labor unrest, raised the rate to sixty cents for 1933, but this was far short of worker expectations. What really made the workers angry, however, was the arbitrary way that the wage was imposed on the entire industry.

Fortunately for the workers' cause, the cotton harvest was about two weeks late, which gave them time to organize. The C. & A.W.I.U. sent Caroline Decker down from San Jose to join Pat Chambers. They were the chief professionals on the scene—a thirty-one-year-old ex-construction worker, who had been working with the union for three years, and a twenty-one-year-old woman, who had had some organizing experience with the miners' union in Kentucky. It was not, however, the organizers who made the strike possible as much as it was, in Decker's words, "the development of leadership from the ranks, from the bottom up." What Chambers and Decker asked in late

September of 1933 was, according to Chambers, "How in hell do you handle thousands of people when you have nothing?" The answer was that you "place responsibility on the strikers."

Nevertheless, for anyone who has some sympathy for the cause of the farm workers during this period, the activities of Chambers and Decker would have to be thought of as heroic, especially when one thinks of the odds they faced, the danger they were in, and the fact that when it was over, they were both sent to prison for activities that today would be considered legal. Steinbeck deliberately avoids casting his characters in such a heroic mold, and in doing so he makes his story more believable. To recognize the actual heroism of his models would have been impossible—too many Marxist melodramas had been written over the years that automatically cast the labor leaders as heroes and the capitalists as villains. Anything that smacked of this same routine would have been perceived as propaganda. Indeed, the book's reputation for realism rests to a considerable extent on the author's relatively harsh treatment of its labor-leader characters. On the whole, they are rather unpleasant—one, Mac, coldly calculating and manipulative of other people, and the other, Jim, a young fanatic. While they are motivated by concern for the welfare of poor working people, they see that welfare in terms of a long-range political abstraction, not in terms of the immediate well-being of specific individuals around them. Both Chambers and Decker were much more caring, much more concerned about the workers and their present needs. Chambers felt that as far "as human beings go, I don't think you'll find many better than farm workers. . . . The overriding purpose was conditions; wages were a part. . . . To achieve that, you had to create unity. After that, if any organization came, that was a bonus. Your first consideration was the needs of working people. You ask nothing from them. You don't try to build an organization at their expense."

If Chambers and Decker spent little time on Marxist indoctrination, they did work hard to encourage unity and cooperation. Unity, always essential in labor activities, was especially important for the farm workers in California, who were frequently at odds with one another in a surplus-labor situation. One of the tactics used by the California growers was to set one group against another, often one race against another. The Mexicans, for example, might be given a "sweetheart" contract to come in as scabs to take over from striking Filipinos or whites, or the other way around. In the cotton strike, at one point, growers planned to import hundreds of black pickers from the South and Mexicans from

Los Angeles. According to one black leader during the strike, "Whites, Mexicans, and colored people all worked together just like brothers. They tried to get us to split just like they always do, but we wouldn't."

In reviewing the novel after it was published, both Chambers's and Decker's main objection was the emphasis on the calculated manipulation of the strikers as a mob, rather than an emphasis on the actual spirit of brotherhood and mutual support that made the strike possible and produced eventual success. Not only does Steinbeck alter the spirit of the strike, or at least the spirit as the strikers themselves perceived it, but he omits any reference to race or the race-relations aspects of the strike. Although three-quarters of the workers on both the peach and cotton strikes were Mexican, all the workers in *In Dubious Battle* are white. Since he had just finished *Tortilla Flat* and wrote frequently about Mexicans and Mexican-Americans during these years, the omission of any reference to them is puzzling—at least initially. However, it simply confirms that our interest in this novel, which has been usually connected to its realism, was not his main interest; he did not consider himself a realist, and his mining of his sources for convincing detail was not an end in itself but a means by which he could construct a more powerful metaphor.

The most explicit statement of the intent by which he selected from and altered his sources for this novel is made in a letter to George Albee in mid-January of 1935, only a few weeks before he sent off the manuscript:

> I don't know how much I have got over, but I have used a small strike in an orchard valley as the symbol of man's eternal, bitter warfare with himself. I'm not interested in strike as means of raising men's wages, and I'm not interested in ranting about justice and oppression, mere outcroppings which indicate the condition. But man hates something in himself. He has been able to defeat every natural obstacle but himself he cannot win over unless he kills every individual. And this self-hate which goes so closely in hand with self-love is what I wrote about. The book is brutal. I wanted to be merely a recording consciousness, judging nothing, simply putting down the thing. I think it has the thrust, almost crazy, that mobs have.

Indeed, the book was a scientific exploration of the stimulation and reaction of the mob. If Steinbeck's organizers are cold, it is because the author was cold.

Once the cotton strike got under way, Chambers thought that the growers would follow a strategy similar to that used at Tagus and act to isolate the pickers on the various ranches. He anticipated a situation in which communications would become nearly impossible to maintain. Fortunately, the growers did just the opposite, kicking the striking pickers off the ranches, often unceremoniously packing their belongings and depositing them in the middle of the nearest county road. According to one government account of the strike:

> The response of the growers and their sympathizers to the strike was immediate. Their first move proved to be a boomerang. As the walkout spread from ranch to ranch, individual growers followed a policy of evicting all those who refused to work at the prevailing rate, hoping thus to eliminate "agitators" and deter other pickers from striking. The result was to drive thousands of evacuees into large "concentration camps," where they could be more easily mobilized and dominated by C. & A.W.I.U. organizers. Large emergency tent colonies, as in Corcoran, McFarland, Porterville, Tulare, and Wasco, served as homes for strikers, centers for mass meetings, and bases for guerrilla picketing, thus facilitating the conduct of a strike involving pickers from more than a thousand scattered ranches.

Of these emergency camps, the one at Corcoran was the largest, containing about three thousand persons. Just as in Steinbeck's novel, where the land for a similar camp is donated by a sympathizer, this land was given for use by the strikers by a small cotton farmer and gas station owner named Morgan. His property was a vacant four-acre tract of land on the other side of the railroad tracks on the eastern outskirts of Corcoran, a small valley town a few miles southeast of Tulare. The camp began as a refuge for a handful of Mexican pickers who had been evicted at the start of the strike, but within a week the property had filled with people, and the leaders organized the camp by arranging the makeshift tents in rows and dividing the rows by dusty streets.

As reflected in Steinbeck's fiction, the growers and their sympathizers began to agitate almost immediately for the breakup of the camp, using as an excuse its dangers to the health of its inhabitants and the surrounding community. Various local officials at various times issued ultimatums to the camp demanding ten fly-tight toilets, fly-tight garbage cans, and a complex water system involving a tank, pipe lines, and numerous faucets. The irony of this sudden concern for worker health was that never were the facilities provided on the ranches subject to such scrutiny. Morgan helped with the toilets, but neither he nor the union had the money to pay for the pipe and faucets. Caroline Decker, who had already sent one S.O.S. to Ella Winter for money to buy gasoline, now sent another urgent request for help. Winter and several of her friends drove down the next day and met Decker guarding the gates at the Corcoran enclave. (Somewhat like Jim Nolan in Steinbeck's novel, Decker began to take over more and more authority as the strike progressed, particularly, of course, after Pat Chambers was arrested.) After a tour of the camp, one of Winter's wealthy friends, Noel Sullivan, wrote a check to cover the cost of the pipe. The union had already brought in someone to oversee sanitation at the camp. His name, as in Steinbeck's novel, was Doctor Burton.

In life, as in the fictional version, the law was usually on the side of the growers. "We protect our farmers in Kern County," said an officer. "They are our best people. They put us in here and they can put us out." Indeed, few if any of the strikers were voting residents. Many of the Mexicans were aliens, and many of the whites had come in recently from out of state. An "us versus them," or those-who-belong versus the outsiders, psychology was operative, and there were continual calls for deporting the aliens, sending the Okies back home, and getting rid of the "paid foreign agitators."

The lawmen, the county sheriffs in particular, were intent on eliminating, one way or another, the "agitators" in the belief that if the organizers were gone, the source of the trouble would evaporate. Like the growers, many lawmen came to believe that most of the strikers were being held in camps against their will and being coerced by the "Reds" into striking. One character in the novel says, "There seems to be a bounty on labor leaders," and so it appeared in life. It was not wise for either the organizers or the workers' leaders to go anywhere alone or even separate themselves from the protective ranks of the workers.

One of the workers' leaders, Leroy Gordon, who as the leader in charge at the Corcoran Camp may have been the model for Steinbeck's character London, was arrested three times during the course of the strike. During one confrontation with Sheriff Buckner of Kings County, when Buckner and his deputies were threatening to evict the workers from the camp, the sheriff announced over a loudspeaker that he wanted to talk to the camp leaders. When, after shouts of "We're all leaders!" Leroy Gordon presented himself during this presumed truce, he was arrested. This incident has its rough counterpart in the novel when Mac and Jim call a truce to talk to the deputies on the road in front of the camp and are arrested.

Perhaps most demoralizing for the strikers was the constant surveillance by police, often in large, intimidating numbers. They stood by, twenty-four hours a day, at the gates of the camp, and wherever groups of strikers went, the police were sure to go. Since the area of the strike was enormous, some 4,000 square miles, the only way it could be covered and scabs discouraged was for the strikers to use caravans of cars and trucks to drive to the fields where picking had been reported. Because their pressure was more effective if they were not accompanied by police, they tried everything they could think of to lose their escort: keeping their destination secret, dividing the caravan along the way, and even having everyone travel separately and then assemble at the destination.

Steinbeck uses this "mobile picketing," except that his strikers are not so successful with it. In life, the cotton strikers were spread out in too many locations for the police to hem them in completely. When a caravan found pickers in the fields, they would usually first try to talk them into joining the strike, and if that failed, they would shout and threaten, trying to shame or frighten the pickers into leaving their work. If the pickers were too far away to hear their shouts (growers, warned in advance by telephone calls from their neighbors, would move them away from the roads), the strikers stood on their trucks and blew bugle blasts at them. There was occasional violence, of course, especially if the strikers were able to lose their police escort. According to one newspaper report:

> Leaving the Corcoran strike camp this morning the strikers went to the Peterson ranch and drove pickers from the field. Arriving at the Guiberson ranch later in the day, they met opposition and a hand-to-hand fight followed with both sides sustaining bruised heads and faces. Pickers gave up the fight when several cotton-picking sacks were slit. Considerable cotton acreage was reported trampled down.

But the growers and various vigilante groups also contributed substantially to the violence: strikers were beaten, gassed, and shot, and if they needed help from the authorities, they were unlikely to get it. In fact, while the growers and their friends carried guns, the strikers did not, yet it was the strikers who were almost always disciplined by the police. Farmers felt that if a striker set foot on their land or even so much as touched one of their fence posts, they were justified, under trespass law, to shoot him (or her—in life, women and children also rode in the strike caravans). In one instance, a power-company truck tried to run some pickets off the road and right of way onto private property so that the farmer, who stood by with a rifle, could shoot them. In two instances, strikers were shot and killed. These occurrences and their aftermath are the basis for two of the most important narrative segments in *In Dubious Battle*, the killing of Joy, the old union activist, and the pageant made of his funeral.

The shooting scene in the novel was adapted from incidents that occurred in Arvin and Pixley during the cotton strike. Near Arvin, a small town twenty miles south of Bakersfield, a confrontation between strikers and armed growers resulted in one striker dead and several wounded. Nine strikers were arrested, according to the strange theory that a striker, acting as a sniper, had been aiming for a deputy sheriff but missed and hit a fellow striker instead.

On the same day, October 10, in Pixley, a town south of Tulare, a group of strikers assembled to protest the arrests of sixteen pickets, who had been apprehended on private property by armed growers. They gathered in a vacant lot across the highway from their headquarters and near the railroad tracks, and as Pat Chambers addressed the crowd, urging continued unity and resistance in the face of threatened grower violence, a group of angry farmers, armed, came into town and began to surround the strikers, taking up positions behind parked cars. As the meeting was breaking up, the farmers fired into the strikers, and the strikers scattered, many running into the union hall for shelter. After the strikers had found shelter, the farmers continued firing at the door of the union hall and through the windows. When it was over, two strikers, a man and a woman, lay dead and eight were wounded.

The aftermath of these killings was used by Steinbeck as the basis for the funeral parade in his novel. As Joy's funeral is used to create an event to boost the workers' determination, so in life the funeral of the two strikers killed at Pixley was used by the union as an occasion for a demonstration to unite the strikers and advertise their grievances:

> Assembling in the city park adjacent to the Southern Pacific tracks, strikers formed an orderly line of approximately a thousand persons and marched down Kern Street [in Tulare] to the church. The members were segregated into groups representing various local chapters of the Union, with captains in charge of each corps.

Banners and placards evenly distributed along the ranks of marchers advertised the policies and demands of the strikers, while marchers from each district carried a placard giving their location.

The cotton strike, like the peach strike before it, ended as a result of government mediation and pressure on both sides of the dispute to accept the settlement. A fact-finding committee recommended that the rate for picking a hundred pounds be raised from sixty to seventy-five cents, and the growers reluctantly accepted the wage hike. On October 24, the strike was over, but bitterness was still felt throughout the southern San Joaquin. Many of the leaders and the more active strikers were blacklisted, and the notorious Associated Farmers was founded, an organization of growers and their corporate allies dedicated to making sure that no such strike would ever again be successful in California.

Despite what seemed to be a rather small gain for so long a period of conflict and sacrifice, the organizers of the strike were, on the whole, pleased. In the face of such overwhelming odds, it was, according to Caroline Decker, "a great victory." She adds, that what they usually got in those days was "just smashed picket lines and disintegration." A few months later she and Chambers and thirteen others were charged with criminal syndicalism in connection with the C. & A.W.I.U. support of the San Francisco longshoremen's strike, and later convicted and sent to prison. After their release, both Decker and Chambers left the party. The C. & A.W.I.U. gave up the ghost after the mass arrests and imprisonment of its leaders, and the party reverted to a policy of working within established labor organizations.

IV

Steinbeck talked to McKiddy in the early spring of 1934 but did not use the material right away. In the meantime, he worked on short stories and worried about the fate of the "Tortilla Flat" manuscript. In light of the prejudice against publishing short-story collections, his agents were concerned about fragmentation of the novel, and, indeed, Robert O. Ballou, who had a contract to publish Steinbeck's next book, read the manuscript in disappointment. He felt that it lacked the depth of the author's previous work, and contract or no, he backed out. Steinbeck felt he had an ace in the hole, however. Louis Kronenberger had written to him, expressing admiration for his work, and on Steinbeck's instructions, McIntosh and Otis sent the manuscript to him at Knopf.

But he, too, turned the book down, and at this point, McIntosh and Otis suggested that he might want to do some revision. This hurt his feelings, and he wrote to Mavis McIntosh to protest that the book did have a definite theme and an integrated structure and that he thought these were "clear enough." But if they weren't, he continued, "What do you think of putting in an interlocutor, who between each incident interprets the incident, morally, esthetically, historically, but in the manner of the *paisanos* themselves?"

On second thought, he decided he didn't want to change it, so he put it at the bottom of a trunk. There it stayed for several months, until, at the end of a party one night that summer, he got it out on a whim to read to the few remaining guests. They found it hilarious, and in response to Steinbeck's morose admission that he couldn't get it published, the group urged him to send it off again. Apparently still stung by his agents' lack of faith in the book, he sent it off to Mahlon Blaine, once again living in New York, and asked him to make the rounds with it. The manuscript was read and rejected by five or six additional publishers and then returned to the bottom of the trunk.

As for his next novel, he gave up the idea of an "autobiography" of a communist about the middle of the year, but it took him two more months of thought before he was able to get into the actual writing. During this period of preparation, he talked often with James Harkins and later read passages of drafts to him. He asked "about things the Okies did or didn't do or how they lived; how they talked; whether certain things he would say [were correct in regard to] what you would call atmosphere. He tried to tell me these things to see whether they sounded right." Harkins, although only in his early twenties, had spent a lot of time in the company of the Okie workers in the Salinas area, who had been taking over more and more of the jobs in the packing sheds. Just the previous winter he had been active in a strike involving both field and shed workers in the Imperial Valley, in the company of an older organizer named Shorty Alston.

Alston was well known among workers in the Salinas area as a leader of the "fruit tramps," as the packing-shed workers called themselves. He had received his training as a youngster with the Wobblies in the woods of the Northwest, and he became involved in a series of Salinas strikes, running from 1933 through 1936, as well as strikes in the Imperial Valley and Arizona. Like Pat Chambers, whom he resembled physically, he was by this time a canny veteran, capable, in Harkins's words, of organizing and running a strike "out of his hip pocket." No one seems to know whether Steinbeck knew Alston or simply knew of him, but whatever the case, he is a likely candidate for having contributed something to the characterization of Mac, just as Jim Harkins probably gave something to the character of Jim Nolan.

It also seems likely that the Imperial Valley strike, as reported by Harkins and others, contributed something to Steinbeck's fictional account. This strike, as in the novel, was a losing proposition from the beginning. It was also a more violent strike than those in the San Joaquin, providing examples for Steinbeck of leaders who were beaten, abducted, and murdered. And if any place was "organized like Italy" in California agriculture (as Mac says in the novel about the Torgus Valley), it was the Imperial Valley, where growers and police did just about anything they wanted to do to the strikers. Several incidents of vigilante violence here suggest that the strike was also the basis for Steinbeck's story "The Raid."

By late October of 1934, Steinbeck was well along in his manuscript and enthusiastic. It was "getting a drive in it," he wrote Albee. "I feel swell when I'm working so hard and so completely." He may have been discouraged by his lack of success with "Tortilla Flat," but once he was writing again, deeply involved in a novel, he was happy. His joy came from the process, not from anticipation of fame and fortune. "It's like living a great many lives instead of one," he wrote.

Aside from the fact that he was worried about his father, who was running for reelection and was likely to lose (and did), other things were also going well for him. Carol had a job as a reseacher for the State Emergency Relief Administration, while he was going to pick up a few dollars by serving on the election board and volunteering for jury duty. At the end of the year, he wrote Albee again:

> If red tape had not interfered we could get this book out this week. I was taking Carol's job and doing it while she did typing. But the bureaucracy stepped in and said we couldn't do that, so the book is to be delayed a few days because Carol can't type more than twenty pages after work. But it goes along. I hope you will like it. It has three layers. Surface story, group-psychological structure, and philosophic conclusion arrived at, not through statement, but only through structure. I guess the first is all that will be seen though and it doesn't matter a damn. . . .
>
> I have a great deal of proof reading and correction to do and besides that I am doing the house and the cooking and bedmaking. So I'll sign off. But I am pleased with *Not in a Day* [Albee's novel

which had just been published], very well pleased. And Carol, whose judgment I respect much more than my own says it is the most amusing book she has read in years and the only one that has made her break down and howl. I think that it will make a free man of you. Don't let it make a slave of you. I mean, if it sells well, people will want another just like it, and don't let them have it. For right at that point of capitulation is the decision whether the public is going to rule you or you your public. [1/35]

In sense it was prophetic advice, for although it was the farthest thing from his expectation, his own manuscript, on which he had just about given up, was shortly to become a best-seller.

CHAPTER XVIII

I t is rare that a fan's admiration for a writer directly helps forward that writer's career—but this is what happened when Ben Abramson recommended Steinbeck's work to Pascal Covici. Abramson, the owner of the Argus Book Shop in Chicago, had been an avid Steinbeck booster for several years; when Steinbeck's early novels were remaindered, he bought a considerable amount of stock and thereafter spent a lot of time pushing these novels with great enthusiasm onto his customers. One day in late 1934 Pascal Covici, of the publishers Covici-Friede, was in Chicago on a selling trip and stopped by Abramson's bookstore, where he heard the proprietor shouting at a customer, "What kind of collector are you? You've never heard of Steinbeck? He's the coming author." Covici had never heard of him either. Who, he asked, was this writer that Abramson was so excited about? The bookseller answered by giving him copies of *Cup of Gold* and *The Pastures of Heaven* to read.

Covici stayed up all that night reading the two books and was impressed enough so that when he returned to New York, he began to make inquiries. He found out that Robert O. Ballou was Steinbeck's most recent publisher, and he called him on the phone. No, Steinbeck was no longer under contract, and as a matter of fact, he had just recently turned down a Steinbeck manuscript. He gave Covici Mavis McIntosh's name and phone number. "Five minutes ago," she told him when he called, "I got the manuscript back with a rejection slip for the fifth time." Two weeks later, Steinbeck reported to Albee, "I had a letter from Covici which sounded far from overenthusiastic. I liked it. It gave me some confidence in the man. I like restraint. Covici says, 'I am interested in your work and would like to arrive at an agreement with Miss McIntosh.' My estimation of him went up immediately."

Although he offered little flattery, Covici did offer a very favorable contract, which brought negotiations to a quick conclusion. *Tortilla Flat* would be brought out right away, Covici-Friede would take an option on future manuscripts, and Covici promised to reissue Steinbeck's earlier works as soon as economically feasible. (Apparently what Covici had in mind was not a reprinting, but buying up what stock remained of *To a God Unknown* and *The Pastures of Heaven* and reissuing the novels under his own imprint.)

At the same time that Steinbeck's agents were reaching an agreement with Covici, Steinbeck continued to revise *In Dubious Battle* and Carol continued to produce twenty pages of finished manuscript copy every evening after work. Also during January, Carol had her first publication. Her uninhibited sense of humor had found expression over the years in light verse and cartoons, which had been sent out on homemade greeting cards and pasted to the walls of various rooms in the houses they had lived in. The previous year a collection of her light verse, inspired by the sort of thing that appeared in the "Post-Scripts" page of *The Saturday Evening Post*, had been laboriously "published" on her typewriter and distributed to friends. These poems were then printed in several issues of the *Monterey Beacon*, appearing under the pseudonym of Amnesia Glasscock, a humorous use of the name of the California "poet laureate" Carl Burgess Glasscock.

Shortly after signing with Covici-Friede, Steinbeck received a letter from Ben Abramson in which the bookseller told the author of his admiration for his work and revealed the part he had played in bringing that work to the attention of Covici. Steinbeck replied, "I am extremely grateful to you for the things you have been doing for me. . . . I am glad you like my books. Not many people did." He went on to say that with the advance for *Tortilla Flat*, he and his wife were planning to go to Mexico in late April. They had been defeated in these plans so many times before that Steinbeck closed his letter by asking Abramson to pray for them so that "no one of the several factors which might keep us at home will develop."

As he told Mavis McIntosh in a letter just before sending off *In Dubious Battle*, he was very tired. He was clearly worried about the book's reception:

I hardly expect you to like the book. I don't like it. It is terrible. But I hope when you finish it, in the disorder you will feel a terrible kind of order. Stories begin and wander out of the picture; faces look in and disappear and the book ends with no finish. A story of the life of a man ends with his death, but where can you end a story of man-movement that has no end. [4/2/35]

He had labored hard over the speech of his working men characters, but was worried that it might be too harsh for publication. When he sent the manuscript off in mid-February, he told McIntosh:

> I should like the speech of the men to remain intact if that is possible. A working man bereft of his profanity is a silent man. I have used only those expressions that are commonly used. I hope it won't be necessary to remove them. To try to reproduce the speech of these people and to clean it up is to make it sound stiff, unnatural and emasculated.

He had carefully weighed every phrase, every intonation, checking the language against his own ear and often double-checking with James Harkins. He was tired, he told Albee in a letter, of reading the words of supposed working men in novels who sounded like "junior college professors" [1/15/35].

But trouble with Covici-Friede began at the end of the month with a request for material to be used for publicity. They had sent the usual questionnaire and request for a photograph, but Steinbeck refused to fill out the questionnaire and refused to be photographed. He asked Mavis McIntosh to talk to Covici in order to get some kind of agreement that would allow him to escape from such requirements. He wanted publicity for his books, but not for himself. "Please get this point over," he wrote, "with enough force to make it stick for some time. Let me assure you again that this request does not grow out of any desire to be enigmatic. Good writing comes out of an absence of ego, and any procedure which is designed to make a writer ego-conscious is definitely detrimental to any future work."

Then near the end of March, he received a three-page letter from Covici-Friede turning down *In Dubious Battle*, with a long explanation for why they were doing so. According to Mavis McIntosh, the manuscript had been put in the hands of Harry Black, an editor at Covici-Friede, while Covici was away on business. Black was strongly rooted in Marxist ideology and was certain that the book was inaccurate and that Steinbeck didn't know what he was talking about. McIntosh went in to see Black to discuss the rejection, and Black wanted changes made in the manuscript that she was sure that Steinbeck would never agree to. As it stood, Black was positive that the book would have no audience, since it managed effectively to offend everyone, whether on the right side of the political spectrum or the left.

Steinbeck was furious, not so much that the book had been rejected, but that some "cocktail circuit" communist back in New York had accused him of being inaccurate when detailed accuracy was exactly what he had prided himself on in preparing the manuscript. He suspected that Covici-Friede must be inhabited by a strong communist influence and that the rejection had come because he had not followed the party line. In answering the criticisms in a letter to McIntosh, he said that the complaint that the ideology was incorrect "is the silliest of criticisms. There are as many communist systems as there are communists." As far as the criticism that the book would be attacked by both sides was concerned, he had anticipated such a reaction and had tried to make it as unbiased as possible. He went on:

> Do you remember when Mac took out a list of sympathizers and studied it? One communist scoffed heartily at that, saying that no communist would ever carry anything incriminating in his pocket. And at this very moment Carolyn Decker is being sentenced under the Criminal Syndicalism law of this state, the evidence having been gained because she did carry just such data about with her. That is the trouble with the damned people of both sides. They postulate either an ideal communist or a thoroughly damnable communist and neither side is willing to suspect that the communist is a human subject to the weaknesses of humans and to the greatnesses of humans [4/35].

He mourned the fact that he would now have to cancel, once again, his plans for the Mexican trip. He had also hoped to gain some capital to tide them over for a long time so that he could start the "big book," a book that "would be a very grave attempt to do a first-rate piece of work." The "big book," something he talks about off and on for some time after this, turned out eventually to be *The Grapes of Wrath*.

In the meantime, Steinbeck's father's condition worsened; forced into retirement, he seemed to lack any incentive at all for going on. His son and daughter-in-law visited him regularly in Salinas, even during the period of the big push to finish *In Dubious Battle*, but he had become so ill by the end of February that he had to be moved to daughter Esther's house in Watsonville, where he could get constant care. After another month it seemed clear that he would soon die: Steinbeck's plans for Mexico would have had to have been canceled even if *In Dubious Battle* had been accepted immediately.

The uncertainty over the publication of *In Dubious Battle* lasted for several months. Complicating the picture was the strange circumstance that Steinbeck had suddenly become a "hot property." Although he had really done very little to arouse any commercial enthusiasm, he was getting letters from publishers asking that they be allowed to consider his next manuscript. Houghton-Mifflin and Random House each wrote once, and three letters came from Knopf; Macmillan called several times and ended up sending an editor to try to recruit him. But McIntosh and Otis had sent the manuscript to Bobbs-Merrill, which promptly accepted it.

At the same time, Pascal Covici had returned to New York to find that Steinbeck's book had been rejected, that the author was very angry with his firm, and that due to the rejection of the manuscript, the entire contract with his newly discovered author had been voided. One of the reasons Covici had been away from his office was that he was busily promoting pre-publication sales of *Tortilla Flat*, and, needless to say, he was very unhappy on his return. He fired the offending editor and sent a letter to Steinbeck apologetically offering to publish the manuscript after all, if he wished them to. Elizabeth Otis wrote to ask Steinbeck to make the decision, and John decided to stay with Covici.

Steinbeck's father died near the end of May, and after the funeral, John wrote to his godmother, Elizabeth Bailey:

> I should have preferred no service at all for Dad. I can think of nothing for him so eloquent as silence. Poor silent man, all his life. I feel very badly, not about his death but about his life for he told me only a few months ago that he had never done anything he wanted to do.

Five days after the death, *Tortilla Flat* was published. It was almost as if, with the passing of his father, the first part of his life also passed away. From this point on, he would become a successful author. The days of innocence and poverty, of fun and improvisation, of anonymity and publishing problems were nearly over. As if to symbolize the change, Steinbeck took some money sent to him by his godmother, bought some used lumber and building materials, and with the help of his brother-in-law converted the garage into a workroom, adding a floor, window, and stove. He would no longer be writing at the kitchen table, warming himself by an open oven door.

About this same time, Dook Sheffield wrote to his ex-wife, asking that she send him his collection of Steinbeck material. Instead of sending it to Dook, however, she gave it to Steinbeck, and at Steinbeck's insistence, Dook joined him one evening in front of the fireplace. They sat there late into the night, reading and remembering a decade of letters, sketches, and poems written in the early morning hours in the chemistry lab at the sugar factory, and drafts of early stories. Except for a very few things that Dook managed to hold on to, the pages came off the pile, were read, and then fed sheet by sheet into the flickering fire.

II

From the beginning, fame was "a pain in the ass" (as John expressed it, muttering protests under his breath). Since *Tortilla Flat* was set in Monterey, there was a great deal of publicity and talk about the book, its characters and location. Summer tourists wandered around trying to find Tortilla Flat, looked for real *paisanos,* and searched for the author's house. Steinbeck wrote to Elizabeth Otis:

> Hotel clerks here are being instructed to tell guests that there is no Tortilla Flat. The Chamber of Commerce does not like my poor efforts I guess. . . . The publicity on TF is rather terrible out here and we may have to run ahead of it. Please ask CF not to give my address to anyone. Curious that this second-rate book, written for relaxation, should cause this fuss. People are actually taking it seriously. . . . I'm scared to death of popularity. It has ruined everyone I know. That's one of the reasons I would like In Dubious Battle printed next. Myths form quickly and I want no tag of humorist on me, nor any other kind. [6/13/35]

With the first whiff of success he was besieged by a number of people who sought to become his business representative, and who, without knowing anything about his present arrangements, tried to convince him that they could make him a lot more money than he was now making. Publishers continued to pursue him until it was announced in *Publishers Weekly* that Covici-Friede had signed him to a new contract binding them to publish all his books through 1942. The author of the article also compared Steinbeck to Robinson Jeffers and quoted Steinbeck as saying that he had never met Jeffers and hardly dared to "because his poetry is perfect to me, and I don't think one should get the man mixed up with his work." The article, the first sketch of Steinbeck in a national publication, also spread the misinformation from an earlier biographical sketch that the author was born in Florida.

Another profile of him had been written by Ella Winter and had been published in June in the *San Francisco Chronicle*. Winter came to him to ask permission, which he gave, providing that she talked only about his work. When the article appeared, he wrote to Otis that "Ella Winter . . . doublecrossed me in the matter of publicity, promising to lay off the personal and then pulling out all the stops and playing with her feet in the *S.F. Chronicle*. So I trust no one any more." According to Winter, when she asked him why he was upset with her, he told her that she had not stayed with his work. "What did I say that was so personal?" she asked him. "You mentioned that I had blue eyes," he replied.

With fame he also began to receive, directly and indirectly, inquiries from magazine editors about his short stories. At least two people mentioned to Steinbeck that Arnold Gingrich at *Esquire* wanted to see some of his work, which struck Steinbeck as an interesting sign of his new status, since he was almost certain that *Esquire* had already seen and turned down some of his best stories. The previous year, "The Murder" had been chosen for the *O. Henry Prize Stories of 1934*, but aside from that reprinting, he had had no luck with any periodical except *The North American Review* (which in March of 1935 had published the last of the series of stories it had purchased—"The White Quail"). He reminded McIntosh and Otis that they had eight or nine of his stories, some of which he liked very much, and that now might be a good time to send them out again. When *The New Yorker* made an inquiry, he told Otis that if she had "anything of mine *The New Yorker* could use, fine . . . but I have never written 'for' a magazine and shan't start now."

As further evidence of this somewhat inverted pride, he reported at the end of July a sale of his own. He gave the *Monterey Beacon*, the local journal that had published his wife's poems, his story "The Snake," which Elizabeth Otis had returned to him as "outrageous" and presumably unpublishable. The *Beacon* was run in conjunction with a stable, and Steinbeck told Mavis McIntosh that they took the story "in return for six months' use of a beautiful big bay hunter anytime I want him, day or night. I send you the title page of the story and guarantee you ten per cent of six months' riding but you will have to come here to get it" [7/30/35].

He was beginning now to get some critical attention, and with very few exceptions the critics were complimentary. Although his favorite epithet for reviewers and critics was "lice," over the next few years he became friendly with several of them, including Lewis Gannett of the

New York *Herald Tribune*'s "Books" section (Gannett's wife did the illustrations for *Tortilla Flat*), Wilbur Needham of the *Los Angeles Times*, and Joseph Henry Jackson of the *San Francisco Chronicle*. Although there may have been some concern for self-promotion in his friendliness, he did feel, in these early days of critical attention, an obligation to those who seemed to have a genuine interest in his work. He cooperated with bibliographer Lawrence Clark Powell, corresponding with him, sending him material, and going over Powell's checklists for him. He also cooperated with Harry Thornton Moore, professor and critic, who wrote the first critical book on Steinbeck's work.

The Steinbecks and the Joseph Henry Jacksons became good friends. Jackson was probably the best-known and most widely respected book reviewer in the West, and Steinbeck liked him because he was his kind of intellectual—he had enough of the hardheaded newspaperman in him to make his brightness palatable. He and his wife, Charlotte, lived in Berkeley, and because of his job, often had out-of-town visitors in and often invited the Steinbecks. At the Jackson parties, Steinbeck met other authors, publishers, artists, Hollywood people, and occasionally academics from the nearby university. Steinbeck was usually fairly animated—the parties were small—and had a large stock of humorous stories and limericks (usually about some poor Portuguese or Mexican being put upon).

One evening, however, the Jacksons invited H. L. Davis, who won the Pulitzer Prize in 1936 for *Honey in the Horn*. Steinbeck was apparently determined not to "sit at the feet" of the better-known writer, and the better-known writer would be damned if he was going to go out of his way to enlist the younger in conversation. So although they had a lot in common as Westerners who had worked on ranches and as survey hands, Steinbeck stayed in one corner, Davis sat in another corner with his guitar, and the two spoke not a word to each other all evening.

The Steinbecks and the Jacksons lived sufficiently far from each other so that when they visited, they usually stayed overnight or for the weekend. Steinbeck would bring his own coffeepot with him, and after a party the night before, he would get up at five in the morning, make coffee, and read. During the several years that the two couples saw each other regularly, Steinbeck nearly exhausted the Jackson bookcase.

The Jacksons were with John and Carol when they met Pascal Covici for the first time in mid-August 1935. Covici was coming to San Francisco on business and decided that he'd like to meet Steinbeck and at the same time deliver the first *Tortilla Flat* royalty check to him. Covici was a short man, always impeccably dressed in clothing that had a slightly European flair. His features were well defined and classical, and his hair was graying at the temples, so that he gave the impression of being distinguished but at the same time sensitive. Long afterward, Steinbeck wrote to him: "I well remember one of the first times I met you. You had a black Borsalino hat and a brown brief case and you stayed at the Sir Francis Drake. I remember you coming through the lobby and paying your bill." John and Carol, wearing work pants and sweatshirts, were in the lobby. Covici said that he had no trouble recognizing them immediately from their clothing.

John and Carol brought Covici down to Pacific Grove, where he spent the night on the sleeping porch, and the next day took him around to see the sights and to the lab to meet Ed. The check, almost three hundred dollars, made it possible for the Steinbecks to reactivate their plan to go to Mexico, and only two weeks later, at the beginning of September, they left in their Model-A Ford sedan, which Carol called "antsi-tansi-dan." Before they left, they made arrangements to meet the Jacksons in Mexico City the following month.

Their original plan was to go to Puebla, south of Mexico City, stay there for two or three months, and then spend several months touring the country, but after stopping in Mexico City on their way to Puebla, they were so taken by the city that they decided to stay there and use it as a home base. They took a flat just off the Pasco de la Reforma near where it enters Chapultepec. Steinbeck wrote Albee:

The city is increasingly fascinating. We just stroll about the streets and get bathed in life. There has been too much death about us. This well of just pure life is charging us up again. We don't go to see things. The other day we saw some fine huge bronze doors and went inside. It was the National Museum. We're *not* getting material. Just getting life back in us and I'm beginning to lose the terrible dreams of constant death [10/35].

They took a number of side trips, some for a day and some for several days, to Caluca, Cuernavaca, Xochimilco, Valles, and Acapulco. At the beginning of their stay, John had planned to gather material and then write some kind of book on Mexico or his experiences there. But his intentions were vague—he looked for inspiration to come during the trip—and the relief at being away was so great and being in Mexico gave them so much pleasure that his plans gradually evaporated.

Carol was taken by the costumes and customs, the names of things, and the contradictions, such as modern apartment houses with wood-stoking bath heaters in the backyard. She was also stirred by scenes of social progress. She wrote to the Albees about attending a symphony for workers: "It is free and they get passes from their unions. We got in through a friend but the crowd was *thrilling*—half in jeans, had come directly from work. The symphony is undramatized and rather inferior, but by god there was another far more thrilling symphony being played by that crowd."

For his part, Steinbeck was taken by the dogs of Mexico. He found them very amusing, and for all the mentions of them in his letters, he must have spent a good deal of time watching them. He wrote Wilbur Needham:

> In the village of Tamazunchale there was a dog lying on a door-step. In his family there were two pigs and four chickens. And all up and down the cobbled street lived other pigs and other dogs and other chickens. Now our dog whom we shall call Corazon del San Pedro Martin de Gonzales y Montalba was content when his own pigs ate garbage in the street in front of his house, but let any outland pig, say from next door, come into his zone, and out charged Corazon, etc. and bit that pig. There would be screams and a scuffle and in a moment Corazon would trot back to his doorway, having satisfied his sense of propriety and private ownership. But one morning when I sat in one doorway and Corazon sat in his—a completely foreign pig from a half a block down trespassed on half a rotten cabbage. And this was a very big old pig. Up jumped Corazon del San Pedro Martin de Gonzales y Montalba. He made a slash at that pig's buttocks but that pig turned and took off a piece of Corazon's ear. Corazon after one howl, walked sheepishly back to his doorway. He glanced over to see whether I had noticed, and when he saw that I had, he bit hell out of one of his own chickens. [11/35]

There is something very "Steinbeck" about this little anecdote—the amusing inflation of that which most people would find unpleasant or beneath notice. With all the art and culture around him of a very picturesque people, that he should be watching the behavior of dogs somehow defines him.

Carol and he consciously tried not to do too many of the tourist things, but instead simply strolled about, largely governed by whim, glorying in their freedom and soaking up the atmosphere. "The air down here has a feel," he reported, "you can feel its texture on your fingertips and on your lips. It is like water" [JS/GA–11/35]. They seemed to have been blessed for the duration; none of the usual tourist disasters overtook them, although they ate anything and everything.

Wherever they went, out of a crowd, the beggars always chose Steinbeck, and they were right—he couldn't resist their appeals. At the marketplaces they took delight in the game of bargaining. He wrote, "When Carol bargains, a crowd collects. Indians from the country stand with their mouths open. The thing goes from gentle to fury to sorrow and despair. And everyone loves it. The seller as much as anyone." They found the prices incredibly low, but tried to restrict their buying to things they could use—a few serapes for rugs in their house and pottery for the kitchen. When they finally met and spent several days with the Joseph Henry Jacksons, they all went to Toluca to buy some serapes, and as the Jacksons were trying to bargain and get the price down, they saw John mouthing *"muy burrato"* ("selling too cheap") over their shoulders.

III

While still in Mexico Steinbeck got a telegram notifying him that *Tortilla Flat* had been sold to Paramount for four thousand dollars. It was not something he was particularly proud of, he reported, but he would take the money and invest it in government bonds for the lean times he was sure were ahead. He also heard from his agents that *Tortilla Flat* had reached the bottom of the national best-seller list. He expressed the hope that *In Dubious Battle* would sell well enough to make some money for his agents, who had worked so hard on his behalf without much return, but thought, or perhaps hoped, that the sales would be low enough to establish once again that he was not a popular author.

He had not done any serious writing since the previous February, and once it became clear that he would not be able to write in Mexico, he became increasingly anxious about his lack of activity. He had a puritan streak in regard to money and time, and he tried to rationalize his time there, first as research and then as a necessary rest and opportunity to clear his brain. But after three and a half months, he decided he'd had enough, and they cut their visit short of the planned six months. They took a long detour on the way home in order to go to New York to sign the *Tortilla Flat* film contracts and returned to Pacific Grove just before Christmas of 1935, exhausted after two weeks of driving and a hectic forty-eight hours in New York.

With the film money, the royalties, and his share of his father's estate (as well as the sale of the house in Salinas), the Steinbecks had far more money than they had ever had before. It gave them enough security so that John could plan ahead to spend three or four years on a major novel, and it also gave them the opportunity to do something about their house. Now, with the possibility of changing it, its smallness became almost unbearable, and rather than returning to his writing, he spent several weeks making alterations, including incorporating the sleeping porch into the living room and replacing the beaverboard walls with paneling.

At about the same time, he was notified that *Tortilla Flat* had won the annual Gold Medal of the Commonwealth Club of California for the best California novel of the year. He refused to go to the awards ceremony. He explained in a letter to Joseph Henry Jackson that he had worked hard over the last several years to get rid of a sense of self; if he were to allow himself to become a public personality, he might lose his ability to immerse himself in his creations. "I hate to run away," he wrote, "but I feel that the whole future working life is tied up in this distinction between work and person" [1/36].

In Dubious Battle was published in mid-January 1936 and had a moderately good sale (*Tortilla Flat* was still among the top five bestsellers on the Pacific Coast). The reviews were almost universally good, the striking exception a very nasty piece by Mary McCarthy in *The Nation*. McCarthy, who had just gotten out of Vassar, was of the same mold as the young man in the Covici-Friede office who had originally turned down the Steinbeck manuscript and of the same type as the Party know-it-alls in Los Angeles who wrote the handbooks for Pat Chambers to tell him how to run strikes (full of "bullshit," as he recalls, which he ignored). They all had the cocksure certainty of the parlor theoretician who never got his hands dirty.

Steinbeck, McCarthy felt, did not know enough about labor and didn't keep his eye on what was important—class warfare. If a revolutionary general, such as Trotsky, had written the book, the result might have been exciting, but Steinbeck, "for all his long and frequently pompous verbal exchanges, offers only a few, rather childish, often reiterated generalizations." He may be a natural storyteller, "but he is certainly no philosopher, sociologist, or strike tactician." He is interested in crowds, but doesn't say how a crowd is different, or why: "That the legitimately dramatic incidents of the strike should be subordinated to such infantile verbalizations is unfortunate."

Still, Steinbeck was surprised that almost all the other reviewers on the left had been generally complimentary. They liked the pragmatism displayed by the organizers and the lack of doctrinaire stereotyping in the novel. What surprised him even more, however, was the favorable reviews from conservative publications. He wrote to Otis, "I think the reception IDB seems to be getting is very funny. Instead of being fought by both sides it seems both sides are claiming and protecting it. . . . Out here it is getting editorial as well as critical notice and I expect a storm of abuse any moment" [2/4/36]. He was right in part of his pre-publication prediction, however—almost all the attention given to the novel was political. By April, he was writing Carl Wilhelmson, "I'm glad you liked the Battle. I knew what it was about once, but I've heard so much about it that I don't know now. And I still think that most 'realistic' writing is farther from the real than the most honest fantasy. The Battle with its tricks to make a semblance of reality wasn't very close" [4/1/36].

Although Steinbeck was not yet overwhelmed by people seeking him out, assaulting his door, trying to get interviews, he was more psychologically upset by the popularity of *Tortilla Flat* than one might imagine. Poverty and anonymity had given him and his wife a secure position—philosophically, politically, and socially—from which they could view the behavior and values of others. They were proud of being poor; they had learned how to function within very severe limits, and yet at the same time, they were free to act, dress, and do certain things because of their poverty that would be absurd if they had money. What Steinbeck sensed, correctly, was that he was losing his freedom, and he was desperately afraid that the changes that he saw coming would, in turn, subtly force a change in perspective.

In response to these worries, he started a new manuscript in January. He explained to Ben Abramson: "I guess there is no worse thing for a writer than to get an idea his work is important. It seems to me it would make for an 'important' or pompous tone. I don't know whether it has got me or not but I'm working on something now that certainly isn't important and yet is very difficult, a little study in humility." At the same time, he wrote Wilbur Needham that he was writing "a little study in humility for my own benefit in case I should be impressed with some fancied importance. That is the trap" [2/12/36]. He told Abramson that he was writing this book for children:

I want to recreate a child's world, not of fairies and giants but of colors more clear than they are to adults, of tastes more sharp and of the queer heart-breaking feelings that overwhelm children in a moment. I want to put down the way "afternoon felt" and of the feeling about a bird that sang in a tree in the evening. . . . You have to be very honest and very humble to write for children. And you have to remember that children aren't gay. [2/36]

The manuscript that he started turned out to be, eventually, *Of Mice and Men*. Although the finished novelette does not seem appropriate for children—that intention was obviously abandoned—the simplicity of its style and the clarity and precision of its imagery may well have been prompted by this original purpose. His anxiety about maintaining his identity in the face of fame seemed to lead him to reprise. From the recreation of his childhood feelings at home and on the Hamilton Ranch, he went on to his college-age experiences on the Spreckels Sugar Company ranches and his observation of the bunkhouse life of the bindlestiff.

The book was certainly an exercise in humility. For an author who lived through the lives of his characters, he was reminding himself on the gut level what it was to have nothing, truly, and very little hope for anything. His recent exposure to the never-ending struggle of the landless poor in Mexico to gain a piece of land may also have contributed to his choice of subject. Later, he would return to Mexico and learn enough about his theme in a Mexican setting to write the screenplay for the film *Viva Zapata!*

After several false starts during January and February of 1936, he began the first full draft of his book in March. He talked about the manuscript as a "flock of experimentation"—he was trying several different things at the same time. Paramount among his experiments was the attempt to write a novel that could be used as a stage play "as it is" (in words recalled by Dook Sheffield, who was visiting him during the period of composition). This renewed interest in play writing came to him in part through the film sale of *Tortilla Flat* and the realization that anything he wrote might well be dramatized in one form or another now that his books were beginning to sell. Almost immediately after publication he began to consider *In Dubious Battle* from this point of view and decided that it shouldn't become a movie, "with its usual tract," but "it might make a play." Another aspect of his interest in the theater was the realization, prompted, one suspects, by Carol, that the books he was writing, that is, novels, were not getting to the people he was writing about.

Working men didn't read novels. But he was aware of the fact that a theater troupe, the Aztec Circus, performed nightly for the workers at the Corcoran camp during the cotton strike, and he saw the workers in Mexico, poor and often illiterate, at concerts and theatricals. While working on *Of Mice and Men* he wrote to Needham:

> Between us I think the novel is painfully dead. I've never liked it. I'm going into training to write for the theatre which seems to be waking up. I have some ideas for a new dramatic form which I'm experimenting with. Of course I don't know yet whether I am capable of writing for the theatre. Just have to learn. [5/26/36]

Although a play, adapted from the novel, did get to Broadway, that was not his initial or primary target. His idea was not just to write a novel as a play, but to expand the audience of the novel.

In an extension of his previous effort, in *In Dubious Battle*, to present a conflict without taking sides, another experiment had to do with the attempt to write from a completely non-teleological standpoint: no cause and effect, no problem and solution, no heroes or villains—just, as he first called his manuscript, "Something That Happened." In this effort he was no doubt encouraged by his association with Ricketts, which had become extremely close both during the summer before his trip to Mexico and during the months that followed.

Another experiment that also extended from his work on *In Dubious Battle* was to try a different kind of symbol for group man. In the previous novel (as well as in *Tortilla Flat*) he had written about groups of men who, in response to one stimulus or another, had been transformed into a single entity. *In Dubious Battle*, he wrote Harry Moore, "was an attempt to make some kind of pattern out of the half articulate men." In his new manuscript, half-articulate mankind as a whole would be represented in a single character, Lennie.

In the middle of April he reported, "I'm working rapidly now. Pages are flying," but at the end of the following month, he had what he called a "minor tragedy." After their return from Mexico, John had acquired a setter puppy, one in a long line of dogs called "Toby." He recounted to Elizabeth Otis that his pup, "left alone one night, made confetti of about half my mss book. Two months work to do over again. It sets me back. There was no other draft. I was pretty mad but the poor little fellow may have been acting critically" [5/27/36]. He didn't want to punish Toby severely, since what was the use of ruining "a good dog for a mss I'm not sure is good at all."

Also that spring his agents had taken up the idea that *In Dubious Battle* might make a play, and the rights were sold to producer Herman Shumlin, who in turn contracted with the novelist John O'Hara to write the script. O'Hara stopped by on his way to San Francisco to meet Steinbeck and discuss the project. Years later O'Hara recalled the meeting on a warm afternoon in the Steinbeck cottage, "with some Mexican dish cooking on the stove, an English saddle hanging on a peg, your high school diploma on the wall, and you trying to explain about phalanx man" [11/29/62]. Steinbeck, who didn't know anything about O'Hara or his work, was impressed by him, but O'Hara soon afterward dropped the project. Whatever difficulties he may have encountered in dramatizing the novel, fruit bums striking in a California orchard was not really his cup of tea.

During the period in which Steinbeck was working on *Of Mice and Men*, he and his wife were in the process of building a new house. Although the cottage in Pacific Grove had been partially remodeled in January, it was still not very satisfactory. It was not a house that they had chosen for themselves, and they had returned to it time after time only through necessity. They both hated the cold, damp summers in the Grove and had long agreed that whenever it became possible, they would somehow arrange to spend their summers elsewhere. Carol, who suffered from sinus trouble during the summers, wanted to leave the area permanently, but John was somewhat reluctant. He was leery of property ownership, and he didn't want to try to crank out stories for *The Saturday Evening Post* in order to support a mortgage. Nevertheless, in early May they began to build a small house in an area of forested hills just west of Los Gatos, about fifty miles north of Monterey.

Carol went up to supervise the building while John stayed behind to continue work on his manuscript. The house was being built on two acres on the side of a hill and would overlook a canyon of oak and madrone, with a wet-weather creek at the bottom. Because of the increasing interruptions at their Pacific Grove house, they had chosen this spot for its isolation—there would be, at least for the time being, no phone service or electricity. The house itself, as planned by Carol and built almost in its entirety by a carpenter-contractor, was inexpensively constructed of board and batt. It ran along the canyon below the road, with a modest-sized living room with a central fireplace at one end of the house and a tiny workroom for John at the other. The workroom was just large enough for a desk, a stove, and a cot. Since adding his workroom to the Pacific Grove house, he had taken the notion that he should sleep in his study alone while he was deeply involved with a manuscript.

IV

Back at the Grove, John went on a six-day trip with Ed Ricketts to the Baja California coast below Ensenada to get baby octopuses, and on his return set out to rewrite his destroyed manuscript. In the early summer, Ben Abramson sent him a book to read. He thanked him, but wrote to him that he wouldn't be able to read it until he had finished his manuscript in progress:

> I can't seem to read anything at all except very dry treatises when I'm working. Just now it is Hallam's Middle Ages and a more desiccated bit of history was never set down and I love it. It takes so much effort to swing me into work that [to get] going I just steam roller through, dreaming the story at night and writing it in the daytime. That's the unfortunate part of having a single track mind. [7/36]

In the meantime, Covici had held to his word about reissuing Steinbeck's earlier works and keeping them in print. He bought up the remaining unbound sheets of both *The Pastures of Heaven* and *To a God Unknown*, and after tipping in his own title page and binding them, brought the books out in the fall of 1935. In April 1936, he requested permission to bring out *Cup of Gold*, a request relayed to the author by Elizabeth Otis. Steinbeck replied: "I am not particularly proud of C. of G. Outside of a certain lyric quality—there isn't much to it. I rather wish it had never been published. But as long as it has, it can't be recalled and further printing can do no harm" [4/15/36]. Since there were no sheets for *Cup of Gold*, photo-offset plates were made from the first edition, to which Covici added a preface written by the critic Lewis Gannett.

The publisher also brought out two special limited editions of Steinbeck items in 1936. In midyear he published, through Pynson Printers, 370 copies of a small book called *Nothing So Monstrous*, made up of the Junius Maltby story from *Pastures of Heaven* plus a short epilogue written by Steinbeck. And at the end of the year he published *Saint Katy the Virgin*, much to Steinbeck's delight, in an edition of 199 copies, which Covici used as Christmas gifts to his clients and as advance notice of Steinbeck's forthcoming *Of Mice and Men*. Covici was far more active in behalf of his author than any other publisher had been, and it was a new experience for Steinbeck to have a publisher who kept his word.

In Los Gatos, the Steinbeck house was supposed to be ready by the end of June, but it was not completed until the end of July. And while moving out of the Pacific Grove house, John and Carol found an item that had been missing for some time. Shortly after completing "The Red Pony," John had set down the manuscript on something, forgot where he had put it, and then couldn't find it. He and Carol had torn the house apart trying to find it. Finally Carol told him that he would just have to forget it and write the story again. Now, as they were moving, they found the original manuscript, which had fallen down behind an old Spanish trunk, and out of curiosity, they stopped to compare it with the second version that John had written. They found that it differed by only seven words.

Carol decorated the new house with the serapes, masks, and pots they had brought back from Mexico. The atmosphere was definitely rustic. Visitors recall that Steinbeck was so busy with his "Of Mice and Men" manuscript, that he didn't have time to chop wood—logs were pushed as they burned, from outside the fireplace-pit into the center. Steinbeck found it was very hard on his eyes to write by kerosene lantern, so he began a routine of getting up at dawn, writing until dusk, and then going to bed every night by nine o'clock.

Once they had taken up full-time residence in the new house—for several months it was very close to camping out—he went back to the "Long Valley ledger," in which he had sporadically kept a journal the year before. He reread his notes, in which he had so often worried about getting some money, and then wrote:

For the moment now the financial burdens have been removed. But it is not permanent. I was not made for success. I find myself now with a growing reputation. In many ways it is a terrible thing. . . . Among other things I feel that I have put something over. That this little success of mine is cheating. I don't seem to feel that any of it is any good. All cheating.

Then he turned his attention to his manuscript in progress:

Now let me get to a discussion of the work. For this, after all is to be the test of the new house. It is a little short novel to be called— something that happened. It is an experiment and I don't know how successful. It is two thirds done. There are problems in it, difficult of resolution. But the biggest problem—is a resolution of will. The *rewards* of work are so sickening to me that I do more with the greatest reluctance. The mind and will must concentrate again and to a purpose. This has been a long haul. . . .

The little novel could be fine if I could find the beauty to put into it. I know the way. Every morning I must come into this little room and settle down and put in my time. For awhile nothing will happen but after a little the matter will begin to crawl down the pen all over again. It always has.

There are subtleties in this ms. There's the [wall?] of background never stated. I say they are in it. What I mean is that I am trying to put them in it. Just now my mind is fat and sluggish. It hasn't emerged into the picture-making state so necessary. . . . This is an unexpected play. People I hope will act with all the unexpectedness of real people. The idea of building too carefully for an event seems to me to be doing that old human trick of reducing everything to its simplest design. Now the designs of lives are not so simple.

Today it seems almost shocking to read that someone of real talent confessed such a sense of unworthiness. And the nausea of success came as a strange and sudden reversal from the years of anxiety in response to poverty and rejection. Yet he would continue to be haunted by these feelings, as well as by the conviction that his success was a fluke and only temporary.

Progress on his novel (by which he would measure the worth of his new house) was rapid, since it had remained firmly in his mind despite the partial destruction of the first draft. In the above journal entry he provides some tantalizing clues as to his concerns while writing: his desire to find beauty to put into the manuscript; his perception of material included in the novel, but unstated; and his concern for the unexpectedness of actions, carrying out the non-teleological approach suggested by the title "Something That Happened."

There is also the reiteration of a theme that would run from the beginning to the end of his career—the consciousness that he was involved in an "experiment." He was always trying something new, taking a risk that might or might not pay off. And then in the notes there is the marvelous line about his mind not having yet "emerged into the picture making state" necessary for composition. Since his recent work was markedly different in style from his earlier work, does this indicate a shift in emphasis from sound (a concern he never abandoned entirely) to the acuteness of sensory detail?

He completed the second writing of *Of Mice and Men* about the second week of August. Earlier in the month he had had a visit from George West, chief editorial writer for the *San Francisco News*, who asked him to write a series of articles for the *News* on migrant farm labor in California. West wanted Steinbeck to go into the agricultural areas of the state and observe living and working conditions for himself, to report on these and to focus particularly on the Dust Bowl migration and attempts by the federal government to ease the problem by constructing sanitary camps for the migrants.

In preparation for his trip and in order to travel among the migrants as inconspicuously as possible, Steinbeck bought an old bakery truck, a "pie wagon" as he called it, and outfitted it with blankets, food, and cooking utensils. Then in late August he went to San Francisco to talk over his assignment with the editors at the *News* and to get a briefing from federal officials at the Resettlement Administration regional headquarters. He talked to Fred Soule at the Information Division and was able to gather most of the general background and statistical data he needed for his articles. The Resettlement Administration was having a hard time selling its program, and the possible favorable publicity that might come from Steinbeck's series was given high priority. He then left for a tour of the San Joaquin Valley, accompanied by ex-preacher Eric H. Thomsen, who was Director in Charge of Management (of the migrant camp program) for Region IX.

Driving down through the Central Valley, the two men sought out and stopped at several squatters' camps. Thomsen wanted to show Steinbeck the contrast between how the migrants lived on their own and how they lived at the sanitary camps provided by the government. Steinbeck had had some experience with hobo camps and labor camps, had seen the Hoovervilles that dotted the countryside and the slum outside Salinas called "Little Oklahoma," but the poverty and filth of these encampments appalled him. And the people—beaten down, scorned, without hope, and terrified of starvation—he couldn't get them out of his mind.

He later wrote about one family he had seen that had built a house by driving willow branches into the ground and wattling weeds, flattened tin cans, and paper against them. A man and wife and three children slept on the ground under a dirty old piece of carpet. The youngest child, a three-year-old, had a pot belly caused by malnutrition and a gunnysack tied around his waist for clothing. Steinbeck pictured him sitting in the sun in front of the crude hut, fruit flies crawling up his nose and seeking the mucus at the corners of his eyes. The child, who had had no milk for two years, was very slow in his reactions and only weakly reached up on occasion to brush the flies away.

In the articles he wrote for the *News*, Steinbeck continued his description:

> He will die in a very short time. The older children may survive. Four nights ago the mother had a baby in the tent, on the dirty carpet. It was born dead, which was just as well because she could not have fed it at the breast; her own diet will not produce milk.
>
> After it was born and she had seen that it was dead, the mother rolled over and lay still for two days. She is up today, tottering around. The last baby, born less than a year ago, lived a week. This woman's eyes have the glazed, faraway look of a sleepwalker's eyes.
>
> She does not wash clothes any more. The drive that makes for cleanliness has been drained out of her and she hasn't the energy. The husband was a share-cropper once, but he couldn't make it go. Now he has lost even the desire to talk.
>
> He will not look directly at you, for that requires will, and will needs strength. He is a bad field worker for the same reason. It takes him a long time to make up his mind, so he is always late in moving and late in arriving in the fields. His top wage, when he can find work now, which isn't often, is a dollar a day.
>
> The children do not even go to the willow clump any more. They squat where they are and kick a little dirt. The father is vaguely aware that there is a culture of hookworm in the mud along the river bank. He knows the children will get it on their bare feet.
>
> But he hasn't the will nor the energy to resist. Too many things have happened to him.

Steinbeck hadn't taken this trip because he was interested in becoming a journalist, nor did he need the money. He had gone to get away from his own preoccupations, to get ideas, and to find new material. Previously he had no idea what his major project, the "big book," was going to be about. Now, whatever he wrote, it was somehow going to be about this family.

CHAPTER XIX

The family Steinbeck was writing about was actually a composite of several families he had encountered in visiting one squatters' camp after another. The sheer number of such people, destitute and desperate, was as appalling as their condition. These were what Californians called "Okies," people who had been small farmers, sharecroppers, or small businessmen in the Dust Bowl states until they had been blown out, tractored out, and foreclosed. An extended drought and constant winds had robbed millions of acres of farmland of topsoil, converting the area to a desert of blowing, shifting dust. It became a continuing nightmare of dark days, wilted, stunted crops, and dying animals. Hundred of thousands of families who had lived on this land for generations had to sell off what they could, pack what they could, and go somewhere else—they hardly knew where. They didn't emigrate just from Oklahoma, but also from Arkansas, Texas, Kansas, Colorado, and a half dozen other adjacent states.

The mass migration of poor farm people to California, their hostile reception, and the shame of their misery became, largely through the continuing popularity of *The Grapes of Wrath*, a well-known story. For many Americans born since the thirties, it symbolizes the Great Depression, but that was not the case at the time. Americans were too caught up in the misery of the Depression as a whole to pay much attention to one small part of it. There was only one major article in a mass-circulation national magazine on the Dust Bowl migrants and their problems in California, and that appeared near the end of the decade. California, which had absorbed so many migrations before, didn't even realize what was happening until long after this migration started.

It might not have noticed at all except for the fact that these people could be identified as a group, and as a group they eventually became irritating. By their speech, their dress, and their manners they identified themselves not only as poor whites, but as primitive, rural, backwoods poor whites. Despite all of California's agriculture, the Okies had really entered an industrial society where even the farmers walked like city folk.

Their exodus from the Dust Bowl started in 1930 and increased every year, so that by 1935–36, 87,302 entered California that year. The total number of Dust Bowl refugees that entered during the decade has been estimated at three to four hundred thousand, an overwhelming number, considering that the total number of farm workers throughout the state prior to the influx was something over 200,000. They came with the vague idea that by heading west they might be able to get a new start, perhaps get some land. But there was no land, and there was already a surplus of farm labor. At the end of Highway 66 in the Central Valley of California, they encountered an agricultural region that was probably the most industrially organized and most highly mechanized of any such area in the world.

There these fiercely independent small farmers found themselves looked down upon. Refugees from the Bible Belt, whose strict fundamentalist Christianity was an important part of their culture, they found themselves pilloried as having loose morals. A proud people who had scorned those who accepted "charity" found themselves starving for lack of government relief. Texans who had had no use for Mexicans found themselves competing with skilled Mexican field-workers for jobs, such as fruit picking and vegetable harvesting, that they knew very little about.

The big ranches and corporate farms that controlled wages and working conditions treated their laborers, by and large, as serfs. Jobs were hard to come by, and once a man got a job, his wages were so low that he could barely feed his family. In 1932 farm-labor agents advertised for hands at fifteen cents an hour, and in 1933 wages went as low as twelve and a half cents. Conditions in the squatters' camps were miserable, but conditions in the labor camps on the farms were often not much better. On the smaller farms the accommodations (usually all the small farmer could afford) amounted to a place to park and put up a tent, a spigot, and an outhouse. For those who got harvesting jobs on the large farms, they likely found that a one-room shack cost them a dollar a week (deducted from their pay) and that they were forced to buy food at inflated prices at a company store (also deducted from their pay). They ended up working the next day to pay for the day before. On an average a single shower (cold) and a single chemical toilet served one to two hundred people. Since farm management had long held the idea that their workers were very close to animals—dirty, untrustworthy, and uncivilized—there was no attempt to keep these camps clean, and vermin and insects were prevalent. The most common story in the Central Valley regarding farm labor was about the misguided farmer who tried to be nice to his workers by putting in toilets and washbasins, only to find his workers urinating in the washbasins.

There were several major incidents of mass starvation or near-starvation. In 1935, 1,200 workers showed up at Nipomo to pick a pea crop that required only about half that number, to find the crop ruined by rain. Having exhausted all their resources getting to the job, the workers were stuck in the rain and mud, without gasoline to move or food to eat or fuel to get warm, until after many days the government brought in food. In 1937, 70,000 migrants assembled in the San Joaquin Valley. As Carey McWilliams reported in his book *Factories in the Field,* "Lured to the valley by announcements that 25,000 additional workers were required to harvest the 1937 cotton crop, a vast army of transients had assembled there to starve." As cited by McWilliams, Harold Robertson, National Field Secretary of the Gospel Army, observed that "people are seeking shelter and subsistence in the fields and woods like wild animals, and that children were working in the cotton fields for 15 and 20 cents a day."

Aside from the Salvation Army and a handful of volunteer liberal groups, the public response to this wholesale destitution was largely apathetic, and positive governmental response was meager. Since the growers held political power both locally and statewide until 1939 (when Governor Olson took office for the Democrats), law enforcement, relief agencies, and employment bureaus all tended to take a hard line toward the migrants, cooperating with grower demands, and even in several instances cooperating with vigilante actions directed against the "Red threat" of union organizing.

Local government efforts to "solve" the problem ranged from turning the migrants back from California at the state line to evicting them from areas where they were no longer needed, either by force or by gifts of gasoline, to a policy of constant harassment in the hope that migrants would somehow disappear, become someone else's problem, or go back to where they came from. An example of the hard line taken by local officials toward migrants can be found in the words of Dr. Lee Alexander Stone, a health officer for Madera County, who set himself up as an authority on migrants because of his own Southern background. In a speech before the Junior Lions Club of Fresno on September 14, 1938 (as reported by the *Fresno Bee*), Dr. Stone characterized the migrants as unmoral, lazy, and "incapable of being absorbed into our civilization." He proposed this solution: "You cannot legislate these people out of California, as some are trying to advocate, but you can make it difficult for them when they are here."

One of the few bright spots in the government's relations with the migrant workers was the sanitary-camp program. Paul S. Taylor, an economics professor and consultant to the State Department of Rural Rehabilitation, first perceived that the state was involved in something more than the typical kinds of migrations California had experienced before, and recognized that it was really the wholesale displacement of a large percentage of the population of one region and its movement to another. In 1934 he recommended that the state build a series of camps throughout California in order to house most of the migratory farm workers. The plan was approved and scheduled to go into effect in the spring of 1935, when it ran into stiff resistance from the "agricultural establishment"—the College of Agriculture, the Extension Service, the rural press, and, of course, the growers. The growers feared that the camps would become "hotbeds of Red activity" and that once the workers were out of their control, they might organize.

The plan might well have been aborted except for the fact that Rural Rehabilitation was taken from the state and made part of the federal Resettlement Administration in May 1935. The plan was then taken to Washington, where it was sold to Rexford G. Tugwell, the head of the R.A., and in the early summer of 1935, construction began on the first camp, located near Marysville. However, the program continued to run into opposition—this time, from a hostile Congress—and in 1936 the idea for a chain of camps to house most of the migrants was scrapped for the more modest concept of a limited number of "demonstration camps." The number of demonstration camps in California was to have been twenty-five, but even this goal was eroded through lack of funds, and the pace of building during the late thirties slowed. By 1940 fifteen camps had been completed or were still under construction, and in addition, three mobile camps were being operated, allowing the government to locate facilities wherever the need was greatest.

While well intentioned, the camp program had only limited success. Because of their locations, some camps were fully utilized only a few weeks a year. Some growers refused to hire workers who lived in the camps, and some insisted that their workers live in the labor camps on the farms. Nevertheless, the camps did provide some security for workers who had recently come into the state, and they became a buffer between migrant families and complete destitution and degradation. But when destitution turned into wholesale misery, as it did when tens of thousands of migrants were caught in the torrential rains and floods in the San Joaquin Valley during the winter of 1938, the camps became almost irrelevant.

If the idea of the demonstration camps was that the facilities would be used as blueprints by the growers and local governments for construction of their own camps, then the camp program was a failure, for no such emulation occurred. Yet the camps did offer a demonstration, but of a somewhat different sort from that contemplated by government planners. Through the work of a remarkable man named Tom Collins, the first camp manager, and other capable managers who followed, the camps demonstrated to various localities in California that the stereotype of the Okie, painted by Dr. Stone and others like him, was false. By providing decent treatment and a chance for Dust Bowl migrants to regain their health and self-respect, the camps made a dent in the prejudices of a number of farm communities by showing those communities that the migrants could be as industrious, moral, and law-abiding as the "natives" around them.

Tom Collins became another of those talented but relatively unknown people Steinbeck had the good fortune to run into during his career who helped him by providing material for his writing. Collins was deeply interested in all the details of migrant life that he observed around him, and he not only collected instances of migrant misfortune—they were common enough—but also became a living repository of the humor, the gossip, the folklore, and even the songs of those who had migrated to California from the Dust Bowl. It was this repository that Steinbeck tapped as a basis for much of what he wrote in *The Grapes of Wrath*; the second part of the novel's dedication, "To Tom, Who Lived It," was a grateful acknowledgment of Collins's help.

II

After Steinbeck and Eric Thomsen visited a number of squatters' and labor camps, talking to the people and surveying conditions, they continued down the Valley through Bakersfield to Arvin. After opening and running the Marysville camp for several months, Tom Collins had been sent to the other end of the Central Valley to set up the Arvin Sanitary Camp, more familiarly called "Weedpatch." Of their arrival, Steinbeck later wrote:

The first time I saw Tom Collins it was evening, and it was raining. I drove into the migrant camp, the wheels of my car throwing muddy water. The lines of sodden, dripping tents stretched away from me in the darkness. The temporary office was crowded with damp men and women, just standing under a roof, and sitting at a littered table was Tom Collins, a little man in a damp, frayed, white suit. The crowding people looked at him all the time. Just stood and looked at him. He had a small moustache, his graying, black hair stood up on his head like the quills of a frightened porcupine, and his large, dark eyes, tired beyond sleepiness, the kind of tired that won't let you sleep even if you have time and a bed.

In the crowded camp of two thousand people, an epidemic of illnesses had broken out in response to the wet weather—measles, whooping cough, mumps, pneumonia, and throat infections—and Collins was trying to cure everything himself. He had to, since there was no one else, and the migrants didn't have the knowledge. Collins took Steinbeck back to his little shack for a cup of coffee, but he had no more than poured the coffee when a man ran up to report that there was a riot in the sewing room. The room was being used to quarantine the children with measles, and on Collins's orders, a large woman, bare arms folded, stubbornly guarded the door, much to the outrage of family and friends, who had always visited their sick. Collins explained the nature of infection, and the riot was temporarily abated, but there followed a disturbance in the sanitary unit. Contrary to regulation, a woman new to the camp was standing on a toilet seat. Berating her was a group of women who had only recently learned not to stand on toilet seats. All evening the pattern continued:

A man beat his wife. New children came down with the measles and had to be separated from their parents and taken to the sewing room. Nerves were on edge in the pouring rain. Fights started out of nothing and sometimes ended bloodily. And Tom Collins trotted back and forth explaining, coaxing, now and then threatening, trying to keep peace in the miserable, wet slum until daylight should come.

Like Ed Ricketts, Collins had a great deal of love to give to people and a very large capacity for acceptance. His background was that of a man who had trained for a time for the priesthood and then quit to become a teacher. After teaching for the Navy in Alaska and Guam, he started his own school for delinquent boys, and when that enterprise went bankrupt, he found a job as head of the Federal Transient Service

Facility (the Depression era "soup kitchens") in Los Angeles. He was an idealist, a utopian reformer, a romantic, yet also a good administrator, a compassionate man, and experienced enough not to be too surprised at the foolish and stupid things that men do to themselves and each other.

After leaving the Federal Transit Service, he worked for the Resettlement Administration and Farm Security Administration from 1935 to 1941. He was very good at this work, and this period no doubt became the high water mark of his life. Although he was not an administrator who could make decisions about the camps as a whole, he probably had more impact on the camp program than any other individual for he was the first camp manager and designed the way the camps would actually operate. After his tenure at the Marysville camp, he became so well regarded by his superiors that he was assigned to open most of the camps as they were built and to train new managers.

Collins made the camps work by giving most of the day-to-day responsibility for running the camps to the residents. He established a simple democracy, in which the camp was governed by a camp committee made up of one representative from each of the sections of the camp. Each unit elected its representatives to this town council, as well as electing representatives to various operating committees that dealt with fire, recreation, children's playground, and children's welfare, and to the governing board of the Women's Club. (This club—which figures prominently in the government-camp section of *The Grapes of Wrath*—was later called the "Good Neighbors Society.") The camp committee at Weedpatch had the primary responsibility for setting up the rules and enforcing them, a job it took very seriously. It met once a week, acting on suggestions by other committees, handling complaints, and dealing with problems ranging from the overuse of toilet paper to severe violations of the rules.

Tact is probably the key quality that made Collins so successful as a manager. He was extremely conscious of the fact that those who came to the camp had been pushed around, insulted, and looked down upon, and he made every effort to allay their natural hostility and suspicion and restore their sense of self-worth by treating each resident with dignity. Milan Dempster, who came into the camp program as a manager in 1937, recalls that both Collins and Robert Hardie, who replaced Collins at Weedpatch, were extremely sensitive to the temper of the people in the camps, constantly cultivating a sense of their instincts and ways.

Taking charge of the initial planning and organization for one camp after another as each opened, Collins would usually work with two hundred to a thousand people, many of them ignorant of basic sanitation, many of them either hostile and suspicious or worn out and desperate, to help them mold themselves into a cohesive, self-governing society. Even though this was a society of migrants, a society whose members were always changing, the residents achieved a continuity, always passing on from the old residents to the new the spirit of what Collins called "the good neighbor." It was an old-fashioned virtue that both Collins and his Okies could believe in.

Steinbeck spent several days with Collins, carefully observing the operations of the camp, following Collins in his work, mingling with and talking to the campers. He attended a camp committee meeting, watched the Good Neighbors Society welcome new arrivals, and went to one of the camp dances on the weekend. Since it was part of Collins's job to keep track of conditions at nearby squatters' camps, Steinbeck also accompanied him on these trips and visited nearby farms, where he not only gathered material for his *News* articles, but also stored away bits and pieces of material that he would later use in *The Grapes of Wrath*. Dewey Russell, a manager at Weedpatch after Collins, has said that Collins told him that the model for the Joad family was that of Sherm Eastom, chairman of the camp committee at the time Steinbeck visited Weedpatch. Collins also told Russell that the model for Tom Joad was "the son [of Eastom] who was a fugitive, lived under another name, out in Lamont." (Lamont was a small town just north of Arvin that had a squatters' camp.)

The chances are that Eastom's son was but one of the ingredients in a composite character, just as the Joad family itself was probably a composite. Another model for Tom, perhaps the major one, would appear to have been Steinbeck's source for *In Dubious Battle*, Cicil McKiddy. Unfortunately, we don't know whether McKiddy became a fugitive because he hit a deputy or because the growers of the San Joaquin were convinced that his union activities made him a criminal syndicalist, but in any case, he was a young Okie who became radicalized, became a fugitive, and was forced to leave his adopted family. Like Tom, he was inspired through the suffering and persecution that he witnessed to commit his life to the cause of the poor and oppressed, joining the Communist Party following the cotton strike. He was killed during the Spanish Civil War. Because of Steinbeck's anti-Marxism, Tom Joad's commitment is, of course, much more generalized, even "Americanized" by having Tom speak in Emersonian terms. When he leaves the family and Ma asks him how she is going to know what happens to him, Tom tells her: "Well, maybe like Casy says, a fella ain't got a soul of his own, but on'y a piece of a big one. . . . I'll be ever'where—wherever you look. Wherever they's a fight so hungry people can eat, I'll be there."

McKiddy's family in California was that of W. A. Hammett. "Uncle Bill," as McKiddy called him, had come from Oklahoma almost a decade earlier. An ex-preacher and practiced public speaker, Hammett had been a farm laborer for many years when the cotton strike began, and he emerged from the ranks of the pickers as one of the worker-leaders of the strike. This history and Steinbeck's knowledge of it suggest that the ex-preacher might well have been the primary model for Casy. Although Hammett was not killed during the strike, he was one of several who tried to disarm the farmers as they assaulted the union hall in Pixley. Yelling at the farmers that there were women and children inside, he and another worker were trying to twist a gun out of a farmer's hand when the other worker was shot. That the Hooper Ranch and the strike involving Jim Casy were based on the Tagus Ranch and McKiddy's description of the peach strike would indicate that the seed for *The Grapes of Wrath* was planted at the genesis of *In Dubious Battle*, two novels and four years before the final draft of *Grapes* was composed.

In the words of one witness who saw Steinbeck on his return from his trip to the Valley, Steinbeck came back with "a pile of material" given to him by Collins "on the Okies and the government camp he managed, with observations and dialogue." This stack of material was composed of copies of Collins's camp reports, a rich vein of detailed information that had already been mined by the *San Francisco News*. Howard Hill, of the Division of Information of the R.A., had sent a number of the reports to the *News*, which had printed excerpts from them, one appearing under Tom Collins's byline, called the "Human Side of the Migrant Camp," in midsummer of 1936. The reports would also be used by Steinbeck for his *News* articles and in *The Grapes of Wrath*, as well as by Carey McWilliams in his discussion of the government camps in *Factories in the Field*.

These reports, which were sent in to the Resettlement Administration sometimes weekly, sometimes biweekly, were often very long, running to twelve, fourteen, even twenty pages. They included observations, statistics, and anecdotes covering almost every aspect of camp life, as well as some information about migrant life outside the camp. In the reports there are many discussions of the kinds of items one would expect—of the physical facilities and what was needed (at Weedpatch it was spraying equipment for the insects, and shade trees), of supplies (they were always running short of toilet paper), of efforts at make-do (Collins showed the baseball team how to make a baseball out of an old golf ball he had), and of social activities (the weekly dances are frequently mentioned).

But there was also a great deal of material that one might not expect. Collins apparently fancied himself a social scientist, for he presents numerous surveys, lists, polls, and investigations. He seems to have counted everything countable, including the number of campers per bed each month. There are classifications of campers by occupation and state of origin and lists of the kinds and years of cars in the camp. He kept a log of all the visitors and took surveys of work opportunities, attitudes of nearby farmers, and conditions in local squatters' camps. He counted the sick, those who had jobs, and those who caused trouble. He also investigated (by inviting himself to dinner) the diets of the campers.

In addition to the lists and statistics, which are probably more interesting to us today than they were to the officials at R.A. headquarters who had to read them, he told of his own experiences with various campers, sometimes at great length. He also included the words to some forty songs sung by the migrants, ranging from "It's the Wrong Way to Whip the Devil" to "The Lily of Hill Billy Valley" and "Why Do You Bob Your Hair, Girls?" But of all the miscellaneous matter that Collins put into his reports, the most interesting items, as well as the most useful to those such as Steinbeck who tapped the reports for material, are the narratives. These run from short anecdotes, which Collins usually included at the end of the reports under the title "Bits of Migrant Wisdom," to long stories with their own titles ("A Bird of Prey," "A Romance," "We Commit a Mortal Sin"), which might run to several pages. Collins had an ear for voice and intonation, for colorful dialogue and sayings, and each anecdote almost invariably had at least some dialogue, phonetically spelled to reproduce migrant dialects:

"All wimen shuda be in bed and tucked under by 8 oclock. Aint no good womn afoot and aloose after that air hour less she be agoin tu cherch."

"Kaint see how cum folks kinda hate us migrants. The Good Book says as how Jesus went from place to place when he wus on erf. Aint it so Jesus wus a migrant?"

"Gawd is good to us farm lab'rs. When we aint got wuk and every' thing luks blue he sends us a new baby ter keep us happy."

In writing *The Grapes of Wrath*, Steinbeck used Collins's reports as a kind of handbook of migrant attitudes and behavior, describing as they do ways of speaking, patterns of reaction, and conditions of life and work in various settings. In the novel there are names, characters, incidents, and pieces of dialogue that have direct ties to the reports, and bits and pieces of Collins's color are sprinkled here and there. For example, Gramma's "ancient creaking bleat," in the first part of the book, "Pu-raise Gawd fur Vittory! Pu-raise Gawd fur Vittory!" when she hears of Tom Joad's return home from prison, is taken exactly from Collins's report of the favorite expression of a woman that he employed as his housekeeper. This woman, called the "Holy One" by Collins, appears to be the model for the woman in the novel who causes so much grief to others through her religious fanaticism.

Quite naturally, many of the anecdotes adapted from Collins's reports appear in the section of the novel (roughly a hundred pages) that is set in the government camp. And many of these relate to the sanitary facilities of the camp, which were new and strange to most of these people who, by and large, had grown up and lived all their lives on subsistence farms without flush toilets, showers, or modern laundry tubs. Less directly, almost every major scene or incident that appears in the camp section of the novel—such as the Joad arrival in the camp, the camp committee meeting, and the dance—has its roots in one or more descriptions in the reports.

Beyond such connections between Collins's material and Steinbeck's novel, there were deeper influences flowing from the camp manager to the author, influences of spirit, emotion, and attitude, which are difficult to measure or locate precisely. Although Collins never became a close personal friend of Steinbeck's, the two had several important traits in common, which formed a conduit of sympathy between them: both had a knack for getting close to ordinary people and winning their confidence, and both could sense other people's states of mind and perceive the areas where others might be sensitive.

While both were considered "radical" by conservative standards of the time, they both had faith that our democratic institutions, through the pressure of an enlightened citizenry, could and would correct the inequities that appeared to be tearing the fabric of society apart. Although they hated the abuses of capitalism and favored labor unionizing, they really didn't see the problem in political terms. They saw it as a matter of attitude. Perhaps this was due to what can only be called a "religious streak" in each of them, although neither of them had any use for formal religion.

But most important, at least when assessed from the point of view of *The Grapes of Wrath* and its qualities, both Collins and Steinbeck had an idealized view of the common man and attributed somewhat more dignity, wisdom, and courage to the migrants than they actually as a whole probably possessed—or at least more than most observers would be inclined to assign to them. While Steinbeck's idealism was usually moderated by a rather skeptical view of individual human nature, Collins often lapsed into an uncritical sentimentality.

Collins's camp reports reveal a vision of the migrants as a sort of displaced American yeomanry, blessed with old-time American virtues, but misunderstood and abused for a rural simplicity that clashed with the sophistication of their new surroundings. There was no doubt more truth in this view than in the contrary position which held that the migrants were little better than animals and need not be treated any better. Nevertheless, Collins's position in reaction to the abuse of the migrants, which he resented so deeply, was in its own way extreme: seldom do the reports ever mention migrant misbehavior that was seriously reprehensible. All migrant misbehavior seems to be of a minor nature, and always it is subject to treatment by education. By and large, the reports picture a people who are quaint: they are the salt of the earth, the charming subjects of a study in folklore. Over and over again Collins notes that once they can get themselves clean and settled, they are happy, and their happiness is stabilized and their dignity restored by participation in the representative government of the camp.

Collins had a great faith in a kind of basic Jacksonian democracy, which he felt was not only the natural preference of the migrants but also the natural condition toward which all men aspired or should aspire. The problem was that society at large was in error insofar as it did not emulate the society that he had helped to create in his camps. For Collins, the camps were indeed a "demonstration." They gave flesh to his vision of man's possible social perfection, wherein all men were "good neighbors," responsive to each other's needs, and responsible citizens in a democratic society that was responsive to the general welfare.

Some of these ideas held by Collins no doubt rubbed off on Steinbeck, for good or for ill, although there is no way of telling how much, and there is little in Collins's vision that was original except in its application to the migrants. What we are dealing with here is not so much influence as the transmission and reinforcement of feelings and attitudes by the man who Steinbeck felt was closest to the Dust Bowl migrants. In this sense, the most important contribution by Collins to *The Grapes of Wrath* may well have been to the spirit at the heart of the novel, rather than to the details and color of its surface.

III

When Steinbeck returned home, he had much to think about and much to do. His long-range goal was the "big book," but it was perhaps just as well that he had several other tasks, including his journalism for the *News*, to perform first, for the depth of his anger and anguish was so great that over the next many months it threatened to incapacitate him as an artist. He simply could not achieve the proper distance from his material.

He wanted to lash out against the suffering and injustice that he had seen. As he wrote his agents sometime later, after coming back from another trip to the Valley, "Funny how mean and little books become in face of such tragedies" [2/38]. He struggled for many months with the temptation to satirize and attack those who, through their greed and indifference, made such widespread suffering possible, and then he struggled with the sense that his subject was just too big, too emotionally overpowering, for him to handle. He wasn't able to write *The Grapes of Wrath* until he was able to contain his anger—and that took almost two years.

Further contributing to his emotional muddle was his discovery on the way back from Weedpatch that his hometown was enveloped in an orgy of vigilantism. The Salinas lettuce strike of 1936 had started just before the first of September, and bullyboys—drugstore clerks and insurance salesmen—were marching around town with ax handles, determined to defend the honor of the community against the onslaught of "Red revolutionaries." The major growers had conspired with local officials to place the town's police and judicial powers in the hands of a retired army officer, who declared his own version of martial law and formed a local militia to resist the strike and scatter the strikers. Civil rights were voided and an internment camp was set up, and neither county nor state government interfered to any significant extent in one of the largest vigilante actions ever to take place in California. For Steinbeck, who took it all very personally, the scene was sad and painful, and it served, in light of what he had just seen in the Central Valley, to stir up his anger further.

The one positive thing that stuck in his mind from his experiences of the past weeks was the sanitary camp at Arvin. Almost immediately after his return to Los Gatos he wrote to Collins: "I want to thank you for one of the very fine experiences of a life. But I think you know exactly how I feel about it. I hope I can be of some kind of help. On the other hand I don't want to be presumptuous. In the articles I shall be very careful to try to do some good and no harm." He enclosed a small check to be used, anonymously, to start a fund so that the campers could raise pigs "without any charity." He would also contact some charitable organization with the idea of obtaining some books to send down to the camp for the children.

In mid-September his short summary of the migrant situation in California appeared in *The Nation*. Written before he had left for the Valley, it was based on the background information he received from George West and the R.A. Division of Information. During the last weeks of the month, he finished his series for the *News*, which he called "The Harvest Gypsies." Detailed and persuasive, the articles are excellent examples of investigative, advocacy reporting, calm and carefully presented. There were seven in the series, each dealing with a different aspect of the problem. He traced the background of migrant labor in California, identified the new migrant from the Dust Bowl, described the living conditions in the squatters' camps, discussed the large, corporate farm structure of much of California's agriculture and the relations between the large growers and migrant labor, examined the government camp program, and made recommendations for the future.

At this same time Steinbeck was involved in yet another project. While going through some of Collins's reports while he was at Weedpatch, Steinbeck had been so impressed that he told the camp manager that the reports should be published. Although he detested collaborations (even though he would be involved in several during the course of his career), he offered to edit the material and submit it for publication. He had four of the seven *News* articles written when he wrote to Collins about their joint venture:

I've been thinking a great deal about the collaboration work. Been reading such of your reports as I have. They are a magnificent collection. So fine that I couldn't hope to equal them. Consequently, I should like to present the following plan for your consideration. That I take these reports—edit them, rewrite some but keep them consecutive—cut out the private matter and the figures—maintain and include the human stories. There is drama and immediacy in these things. I should reduce them almost to the form of a diary; iron out any roughnesses—write an explanatory preface and see to publication. It would make one of the greatest and most authentic and hopeful human documents I know of. . . . I can act as editor or possibly in a sense as synchronizer. And I can get it a hearing. That is the main thing my name can accomplish.

At the end of September, not long after sending this letter, he made another trip to Weedpatch and again came back through Salinas. He wrote his agents, "I just returned yesterday from the strike area of Salinas, and from my migrants in Bakersfield. This thing is dangerous. Maybe it will be patched up for a while, but I look for the lid to blow off in a few weeks. Issues are very sharp here now. . . . My material drawer is chuck full." He also wrote Albee and described California as a bomb ready to explode. He reported that he had done an article for *The Nation,* was editing "a complete social study made of the weekly reports from a migrant camp," and had completed a series of articles for the *News* on migrant labor. "But," he added, "the labor situation is so tense just now that the News is scared and won't print the series. Any reference to labor except as dirty dogs is not printed by the big press out here. There are riots in Salinas and killings in the streets of that dear little town where I was born."

But the *News* did print the series, in consecutive issues from October 5th through 11th. Steinbeck relieved his anger regarding that "dear little town where I was born" by writing a satirical allegory called "The Great Pig Sticking," which he threw into the stove. Unfortunately, this did not release enough steam, and his satirical mood carried into his work on his large novel, which he began in the late fall. This manuscript, eventually titled "L'Affaire Lettuceberg," could be called the first draft of *The Grapes of Wrath,* although it apparently had little in common with the finished novel. Still captured by his hatred of Salinas, he wrote what his wife had described as "a series of cartoons caricaturing Salinas fat cats." The manuscript was later destroyed and we can only guess from his activities and hints in his letters that the Okie migration was involved in some way, possibly in contrast to the smug and wealthy Salinas citizens, and that the lettuce strike may have been the central event. Carol hated the project from the beginning—she didn't even like the title.

In the meantime, the reception given his "Of Mice and Men" manuscript was mixed. His agents expressed some disappointment that the subject wasn't as large as it could have been and Shumlin rejected it as a play, but Covici liked it as a book. In February 1937, the month prior to its publication, Steinbeck was notified that it had been picked by the Book-of-the-Month Club and that a very large sale was thus assured. In a letter to Elizabeth Otis he called the selection gratifying, but also frightening:

> I shall never learn to conceive of money in larger quantities than two dollars. More than that has no conceptual meaning to me. But a part of the money will be used for a long trip this spring. . . . The new book has struck a bad snag. Heaven knows how long it will take to write. The subject is so huge that it scares me to death. And I'm not going to rush it. It must be worked out with great care. That's one fine thing this selection will do. It will let me work without a starvation scare going on all the time. This may or may not be a good thing. [1/27/37]

The weather during the winter of 1936–37 was colder than Steinbeck could ever remember, and it rained almost constantly. Yet he was in good spirits when he wrote to Albee in January: "I guess I told you we have a phonograph now and are gradually getting a few records together. A definite extension of life. It is a very fine instrument. There is lots more rain here than in the Grove. Our stream is running and the grass is coming up and the fleur de lys are sticking up. Plenty of wood and we have big fires at night and music." Toby Street had helped Steinbeck build the phonograph, which in those days was a matter of taking a 78-rpm record player, adding large speakers, and putting it all into a homemade cabinet. Toby remembers that, as a hangover from the old days, Carol was still watching the pennies very carefully, and there was quite a row for a time between John and Carol about spending the money for the phonograph materials.

Although their location was somewhat isolated and they very seldom went into town, they still saw quite a few people. During the fall and winter, there was a steady stream of visitors—Wilbur Needham, Lawrence Clark Powell, the Joseph Henry Jacksons, and Tom Collins, who came up from the Valley twice to visit and discuss his collaboration with Steinbeck. They were also starting to get other, less welcome visitors, and so Steinbeck put up a very high fence around the front of the house. The fence was so high—eight feet—that old friends speculated that John had either become paranoid or "gone Hollywood." There had been a rustic sign out front, "Steinbeckia," which he changed to *"Arroya del Ajo."* "Garlic Gulch," besides being an attempt at anonymity, was a reference to their Italian neighbors, who made a good homemade wine, and whom the Steinbecks on the whole found more desirable than their neighbors in Pacific Grove.

The Steinbecks also found a circle of new friends in the Los Gatos area, including Martin and Elsie Ray. Ray was a professional vintner who at one time owned the Paul Masson winery, and Steinbeck, although he complained about the prices, bought a case from him whenever he thought he could afford it. The Steinbecks were also close to David and Lavinia Tolerton. Tolerton had known the author when he was still living in Pacific Grove, and Steinbeck had been up to Los Gatos to visit a couple of times when Tolerton had labor leaders or organizers as guests. Tolerton had friends in liberal and labor circles in San Francisco as well as in the Monterey-Carmel area. By profession a sculptor—his wife was a painter—Tolerton was sometimes needled by Steinbeck, who called him a "silver-spoon intellectual." Through the Tolertons, the Steinbecks also met Reginald Loftis and Roger Condon, and together they formed a sort of liberal caucus within a highly conservative community.

At parties with these friends there were often heated discussions of labor and poverty, the New Deal, and the possible onset of war in Europe. After several glasses of sauterne—which for some reason became the drink of choice during this period—Steinbeck, his hair and face red, would thump the table with conviction. Loftis remembers him as a man determined to live his philosophy, a very persuasive and powerful arguer. His trips to the Valley had made him an impassioned advocate of labor, but also a man so certain of his cause, on the basis of firsthand experience, that he could not tolerate disagreement. Like a soldier who had been on the front lines in company with soldiers who never left the barracks, Steinbeck treated his friends with a tinge of scorn. He told Loftis, "You wouldn't understand it [the migrant situation] in your gut, only intellectually."

Although Steinbeck had not "gone Hollywood," as some of his Monterey friends feared, Hollywood was after him. There had been a considerable amount of pre-publication publicity regarding *Of Mice*

and Men, and when it came out, it hit the best-seller lists almost immediately. Both Hollywood and Broadway were quick to see the novel's
dramatic possibilities, and according to Joseph Henry Jackson, Hollywood came after Steinbeck very hard. He was, reported Jackson, offered six thousand dollars for six weeks of work on the screenplay, and
he almost gave in because he "knew exactly where he could put his fingers on three thousand agricultural workers down in the Valley who
didn't have two dollars apiece to pay their union fees. If Pascal Covici
hadn't flown out to the Coast to talk him out of it, he'd have gone, too,
and for just that reason."

In the meantime, a stage production of the novel had been arranged
by Annie Laurie Williams, the agent associated with McIntosh and
Otis who handled film and stage contracts. She had shown the novel to
Beatrice Kaufman, the East Coast representative of Samuel Goldwyn
Pictures, who in turn recommended the novel to her husband,
playwright-director George Kaufman. Impressed by the novel, particularly the way it worked naturally in play form, Kaufman enlisted Sam
H. Harris as producer, and they planned to get the show ready for production in the fall. Steinbeck was to write the script, working from
suggestions made by Kaufman.

There was another, earlier presentation of the novel that matched
more closely the original intention of Steinbeck's experiment than the
fall Broadway production. In March, David Tolerton talked Steinbeck
into submitting his novel to a labor theater group in San Francisco that
Tolerton had worked with and helped support. The Theatre Union, as
it was called, had started in 1934, performing outdoors to boost the morale of striking workers on the San Francisco docks, much as the Aztec
Circus had performed for the strikers of Corcoran. Thereafter, the Theatre Union presented plays that fit in generally with a socialist-worker
philosophy, moving from one small, makeshift theater to another,
until it found a more permanent home in the Green Street Theatre in
North Beach.

Steinbeck went to San Francisco and read aloud from his novel to the
group (which seems very much out of character—he must have been
very concerned that his experiment run its course). The novel-as-play
was selected by the Theatre Union as its first presentation in its new
theater and opened on May 21, 1937. In reviewing the performance,
John Hobart of the *San Francisco Chronicle* said, in part:

When George Kaufman produces "Of Mice and Men" on Broadway some time next fall, his version will be more sharply dramatic,

more resourceful in its use of theatre values. The Theatre Union's dramatization follows the novel closely; the dialogue has been lifted straight from the book and transferred to the stage with hardly a single change. Since Steinbeck was writing primarily for readers the result is a play that seems slightly ill at ease in the theatre.

The play ran for sixteen performances, on Friday and Saturday evenings, in the first part of June and then through July. Steinbeck did not witness any of the performances but on the basis of reports considered that his experiment had "flopped." "By that I mean," he said later, "when I came up against a practical man of the theatre like Kaufman I found that I had to do a lot of extensive rewriting." With the first exchange of letters with Kaufman in early March, Steinbeck had dropped his work on the long novel and started his stage revision of *Of Mice and Men*. At first he thought he might have the script ready by the end of the month, but there wasn't enough time.

News in February of the book-club selection had immediately sparked the Steinbecks' interest in further travel, this time to Europe. They planned to go to Ireland ("to my home place," he wrote Ben Abramson), Sweden (where there was a good deal of interest in his books), and Russia. By the time they heard of Kaufman's interest in the dramatic rights to *Of Mice and Men*, they had already booked passage to Philadelphia for March 23rd. Matching their rather unconventional first-trip-to-Europe itinerary, Steinbeck had arranged for them to travel to the East Coast aboard a freighter via the Panama Canal—perhaps as a reenactment of his first trip to New York, but this time armed with fame and money. On April 15, the Steinbecks arrived from out of the West on the S.S. *Sagebrush*.

CHAPTER XX

The Steinbecks' departure for the East and Europe was largely motivated by a need to escape. If Steinbeck thought he'd had problems with intrusions before, they were nothing compared to the attack that was mounted after the publication of *Of Mice and Men*. The offers, deals, and requests came by car, by letter, and by phone—he had to go into town to a friend's house to answer his phone messages. He put a lock on his front gate, and the lock was broken.

Biographer Nelson Valjean describes the time an ambitious mother dragged her little girl into Steinbeck's front yard. And when Steinbeck appeared, she shoved her daughter forward claiming that she was a natural-born movie star. " 'Dance for the man, Mildred!' the woman commanded, 'Dance!' " The rather ragged girl with a runny nose shuffled around the yard, a horrible parody of Shirley Temple. It was all too much for Steinbeck. He wrote his agents, "This ballyhoo is driving me nuts." He wrote to Covici and asked him to stop releasing his picture to the press. "I was recognized in S.F. the other day," he told his agents, "and it made me sick to my stomach."

The requests for interviews or information from well-known journalists or critics were the most difficult to handle, particularly for a man like Steinbeck who was not good at being diplomatic. He was not so secure in his fame that he felt he could ignore inquiries from a man like Alexander Woollcott, especially since Woollcott was a close friend of his new collaborator, George S. Kaufman. Woollcott was doing radio broadcasts as "The Town Crier," a program on which he discussed books and plays, among other things, and he wanted to do a program about Steinbeck. He got in touch with McIntosh and Otis, asking for background material about the author, and the agents relayed the request to Steinbeck, who almost plaintively asked that they try to get Woollcott to "soft-pedal the personal matter" and instead talk about his work. He added, "Unless I can stand in a crowd without any self-consciousness and watch things from an uneditorialized point of view, I'm going to have a hell of a time" [3/19/37].

Steinbeck's trip to New York was a case of going toward the heat, rather than away from it. As soon as he arrived by train from Philadelphia, where the freighter had docked, Covici began working on him to go to a dinner that evening honoring Thomas Mann—an engagement Steinbeck had already refused by mail. That Covici was able finally to talk him into going points to a key element in Steinbeck's problems with publicity and the public life. One of the reasons he had so much trouble is that under pressure he had difficulty holding the line. He couldn't be adamant with people he liked, and it was hard for him, except when he had been drinking, to be rude.

Throughout his life as a celebrity he was unable to develop that tough outer skin that seems to be necessary for a public figure's emotional survival. So Covici talked him into it after all, a banquet with speeches, possibly the one thing he most hated to be a part of in all the world. He didn't have a suit, so someone in Covici's office lent him one, and to make him feel better, no one in the Covici party wore formal clothes that evening. Joseph Henry Jackson reported the results:

> He managed to sit through the first two or three addresses, but that was all. Friends found him afterward in the hotel bar, staring fixedly into a double brandy-and-soda, still embarrassed and ashamed that men and women who could write so well could stand up in front of an audience and talk such stuff.

Covici, a kind and generous man, had rung up quite a bill of indebtedness for Steinbeck over the previous years. He had sent Steinbeck gifts, including a beautiful book reproducing the work of Diego Rivera, whom Steinbeck had met in Mexico, and had published all of Steinbeck's work, including the key to his secret heart, *Saint Katy the Virgin*. It must have been for Saint Katy that Steinbeck reluctantly consented to his second publisher-arranged ordeal, a press conference. Armed with a bottle of brandy, which must have become the new drink of choice, he crossed his legs behind a desk in Covici's offices and gave up little information: he liked Thackeray, didn't like Proust because Proust wrote his sickness, and hated speeches, photographs, and press conferences. His shyness reduced him at times to grunts and strange mutterings. But the photographers, as Harry Thornton Moore has pointed out, "had a big day getting pictures of Steinbeck sitting there with the bottle looming so large beside him." It was this bottle in a widely distributed photo and the heavy emphasis on wine in *Tortilla Flat* (the only novel beside *Of Mice and Men* that most had read) that probably started the public's association between Steinbeck and heavy drinking. (Later, the legend seems to have been in large part responsible for that strange blurring-together in the public consciousness of the Hemingway and Steinbeck personas.)

Although the legend had only periodic confirmation in reality, heavy drinking did exacerbate whatever strains there were in the relationship of Steinbeck and his wife. When he drank, as I have mentioned, he tended toward anger, becoming abusive and critical. Carol, on the other hand, became gay and uninhibited, even wild. It was a volatile mixture. At the end of one fight in New York, Carol stormed off into the night, and when she didn't come back after several hours, John began checking the hospitals and police stations. Since he had to involve other people in his search, his main emotion seems to have been not so much worry as embarrassment. The episode became a major item that he added to a list of grievances regarding Carol's behavior, grievances that appear to have been mostly offenses against Steinbeck's sense of propriety.

Steinbeck was inwardly and personally very conservative, and like so many middle-class Americans, his personal conservatism was supported by an underlying puritanism that was exposed only when he was emotionally threatened or wounded. Anything extreme in his personal life threatened his privacy and the equilibrium that he felt he needed to function as a writer. This is why he was rather more controlled in his drinking than many people thought he was and probably why, unlike many of his famous contemporaries, he never became an alcoholic. He tended to put his writing in an Old Testament context; drinking and sex were temptations away from the purity of his goals. His worry about publicity was partly a moralistic worry about the damage that could be caused by pride. His retreat from the Thomas Mann dinner was partly a moralistic judgment on those who were indulging themselves there and somehow diluting or wasting their talents.

In this respect, his description, later in life, of his second visit to New York is revealing, particularly in its choice of metaphor:

Whereas on my first try New York was a dark hulking, frustration, the second time it became the Temptation and I a whistle-stop St.

Anthony. I had become a fifth-rate celebrity. People in a narrow field went out of their way to be nice to me, invited me places, and poured soft and ancient beverages for me. And I, afraid I would lose my taste for 29-cent wine and red beans and hamburger, resisted like a mule.

As with most St. Anthonys, if I had not been drawn toward luxury and sin, and to me they were the same thing, there would have been no temptation. . . . So I shut my eyes and drew virtue over my head. I insulted everyone who tried to be kind to me and I fled the Whore of Babylon with relief and virtuous satisfaction, for I had convinced myself that the city was a great snare set in the path of my artistic simplicity and integrity.

Occasionally during their two and a half weeks in New York, Carol's exuberance overcame her husband's reluctance. Shortly after arriving they got the figures on *Of Mice and Men,* and felt rich, so rich! They went to Woolworth's and spent the whole day buying everything that they wanted and even some things they didn't. On another occasion they went to Macy's, and went up and down, up and down the escalators; every time John got to the sporting-goods section, he went over and touched a boat.

Coming east they had taken a freighter, and for several weeks they had worried about a load of lumber that shifted back and forth all during the journey. Now, as they embarked for Europe, they took second-class passage on another freighter, the S. S. *Drottningholm,* and once more found themselves in somewhat peculiar circumstances. Their cabin was at the bottom of the ship, and they felt as if they were trapped in the bowels of hell as they looked up, what seemed miles, to a spot of daylight way above them.

Aboard ship, Steinbeck wrote to his agents to thank them for a *bon voyage* gift of a bottle of wine. He reported that the day after they had sailed, they were invited to a party in honor of the King and Queen of Sweden, a rather stuffy affair with toasts and speeches. Most of the passengers were Swedes, but they had two Norwegians in their mess, and they learned that May 17th was the Norwegian Independence Day.

Immediately Carol and I felt a surge of patriotism. Spiritually we felt Norwegian. And your bottle of wine was the nucleus. With only two Norwegians and Carol and I as kind of auxiliary Norwegians we turned the ship into a fury. We made speeches, wine, beer and brandy ran like water. All evening. We toasted everything we could think of. Gradually the Swedes began to feel a certain love for Norway. At two this morning the riot was still going on. Carol sprained her ankle and has it bandaged today but she is happy. She says it is little enough to suffer for Norway. The Swedes are jealous but admiring. Even the two Norwegians don't know how it happened. . . . And your bottle of wine started it. I know you will be glad that your gift was the node of new international brotherhood. I know you will. And I bet you never heard 40 Scandinavians rise with their glasses in their hands and solemnly sing:

> Sent Looisss Voomans, vit you diment rrrings
> Chessed det men aground be deck ehpron strings

By taking a Swedish ship, they had given up their plan to stop off at Ireland. They landed at Göteborg, where they were met by newspaper editor Martin Rogberg and taken to his country home for several days. They then spent the first part of June in Copenhagen, saw some castles, and went to Elsinore to see a production of *Hamlet*. Steinbeck wrote to Covici that "somehow the pale pansy English actors with their sweet flat voices seemed a little out of place in the strong background of that castle." He could have predicted, he wrote, what they had found politically: "It must be the same all over the world. The business men admire Hitler and wish for a fascist regime and all the intellectuals are communists. This in spite of the 'socialistic' tendencies of government" [6/7/37].

They went on from Copenhagen to Stockholm, where they became friendly with the Swedish painter Bo Beskow, whom Steinbeck had met briefly in the Covici-Friede offices the previous winter. They also met, in Carol's words, "a marvelous Jew by the name of Buckhalter and travelled with him. He lied and got us into all kinds of places. We also did crazy things like cooking spaghetti for the Swedes." From Sweden the Steinbecks traveled to Helsinki and then on to spend the middle of July in and around Leningrad and Moscow. Their time in Russia was too brief for them to get any clear impressions except a general sense of poverty and backwardness and suspicion. The trip back across the Atlantic was on a small freighter with few passengers, and Steinbeck reported that "we played poker with the master and the steward all the way to New York."

II

Back in New York, there was still the unfinished business of the play script for *Of Mice and Men*. It was not something that Steinbeck really wanted to do (earlier in the year he had turned down an offer from

Shumlin to write a play script based on *In Dubious Battle*), and he had been procrastinating. On his return from Europe, Annie Laurie Williams cornered him and insisted that something be done, since the play was scheduled to go into rehearsals in only a couple of weeks. He agreed with her to go to her country place, an old stone cottage in Connecticut, and do the necessary work. When he arrived at the cottage, the first thing he did was to put his own coffee pot on the stove. After coffee, he went outside to look around. An hour later, Annie Laurie found him playing with the neighbor's children, and she had to call, "John, come in here and get to work." He came in, sat down at the kitchen table, and protested, "But I don't know how to write a play."

"Of course you do—you already have," his agent assured him. As it turned out, his reluctance was due to his not knowing very much about the mechanics of the form. So Annie Laurie sat down with him and, from her experience as a reader of plays and as a frustrated actress, showed him where to set in the stage directions and mark the entrances and exits.

When the script got to Kaufman, he had a delicate problem: he knew how much work the play needed. Annie Laurie remembers when the two men met:

> When I introduced him to Kaufman, they just sat there. They were sitting on the steps of the theater, and I was determined that one or the other of them had to talk, so I just walked off and left them. There they were, the shy city man and the shy boy from the country. . . . When I came back, they were talking. But that was the only way that I could do it, because as long as I was there, John would look at me and Kaufman would look at me, so I just got out of the way.

Kaufman invited the Steinbecks to come to his farm in Pennsylvania, and there, during a week of intensive work, Steinbeck molded the final script under Kaufman's guidance.

Although the story was changed slightly, the script lived up to the quality and dramatic potential of the original. But Steinbeck was uncomfortable and out of his element—he wanted to go home. He waited until the casting had been done and then announced that since they didn't need him any more, he was returning to California. Kaufman and Jed Harris, the producer, expecting him to stay at least through the initial rehearsals, were perturbed, but to their objections Steinbeck simply replied that Kaufman could do anything he thought necessary, and besides, Annie Laurie would be there to represent his interests.

Steinbeck was anxious to get back to his "own" work, apparently feeling that in regard to *Of Mice and Men* as a play, he was only an accessory in someone else's project. He had written Tom Collins:

> Your letter was waiting when we got in [to New York from Europe]. Be home in about a month. Then in the house about two weeks and then I'm going to visit you for a while. Let me know where Gridley is and how to find you. I've got to get the smell of drawing rooms out of my nose. A squatter's camp is a wonderful place for that. So I'll be seeing you pretty soon and will be very glad to.

Although he had not done any work on his long novel for several months, his previous *modus operandi* suggests that he had been busy planning. He had been stalled before his trip to Europe because he didn't know enough; now he planned to take an extensive tour among the migrant workers, living and even working with them to get the kind of material he needed to go on. As part of this plan, he went to the Farm Security Administration headquarters in Washington, D.C., where he talked to Dr. Will Alexander, deputy administrator of the agency. The visit is recalled by C. B. Baldwin, Alexander's assistant:

> Steinbeck told us he wanted to write a novel about migrant workers but, as he expressed it, he needed the experience of a migrant worker if it was to be a realistic story of how they actually lived. He asked if we could give him this opportunity and said he would need the help of migrants or at least someone with whom he could work as a migrant. We were impressed, and because of the intense opposition of the Farm Bureau and the Associated Farmers in California this entire program was threatened, we were anxious to cooperate. I called Jonathan Garst [Director of Region IX for the F.S.A.] and he suggested assigning Tom Collins to work with Steinbeck. Tom responded enthusiastically. As a result, Tom Collins and Steinbeck became a two-man team, both working in the Imperial and San Joaquin valleys as migrant workers for some months.

Baldwin apparently did not know that Steinbeck already knew Tom Collins, and he has the length of time wrong, since the time that Steinbeck and Collins traveled and worked together could not have been more than a few weeks. Yet, this was the groundwork for Steinbeck's famous trip to Oklahoma and back—which turns out not to have been made to Oklahoma after all.

The Steinbecks purchased a red Chevrolet in New York (having gotten rid of their old car prior to going to Europe) and started home, stopping by Chicago to visit John's uncle, Joe Hamilton, and Ben Abramson. (Abramson had offered a bloodhound puppy to the Steinbecks, which they were supposed to pick up and take back with them.) They continued their trip, following Route 66 through Oklahoma, but according to Carol, John made no conscious effort to do any research for his book along the way. Still, it would seem he deliberately chose that route, and he must have gathered some impressions. Otherwise, he would have taken the more direct interstate to northern California through Salt Lake City and Reno.

In the meantime, Covici-Friede brought out the first edition of *The Red Pony*, a collector's edition of 699 numbered copies, printed on handmade paper in special type, and each copy signed by the author. When Lawrence Clark Powell wrote to him, wondering why he was coming out with such an expensive book, Steinbeck answered:

> I was expecting a howl about the price of The Red Pony. I wouldn't pay ten dollars for a Gutenberg Bible. In this case, I look at it this way. Covici loves beautiful books. These are old stories reprinted and they don't amount to much anyway so if he wants to make a pretty book, why not? The funny thing is that they're oversubscribed, about five hundred. I didn't know there were that many damn fools in the world—with 10 bucks I mean. I don't let Covici dictate one word about how I write and I try never to make a suggestion about publishing to him. [8/23/37]

Time magazine took the occasion to publish its first essay-review of Steinbeck and his work, called "Steinbeck Inflation." The article began with an unflattering comparison between the recent high prices asked for Steinbeck's work—including *Saint Katy*, which originally had been distributed free—and the price of calves' liver, once given away by butchers and now eighty-five cents a pound. *Time* noted that some readers might be baffled by the "famine-price" set on the eighty-one-page *Red Pony*, a remarkable price, the magazine thought, in light of Steinbeck's proletarian themes. It was a tone, once established, that the magazine would elaborate on and refine through subsequent years.

During the summer one of his best stories, "Flight," had been rejected by *Scribner's* and *The Saturday Evening Post* (it never was published separately), but Arnold Gingrich at *Esquire* bought two stories that the magazine had previously rejected: "The Ears of Johnny

Bear" came out in September and "The Lonesome Vigilante" in October. And the money kept coming in from *Of Mice and Men.* He was in a jubilant mood when he wrote to McIntosh and Otis in mid-October:

> Dear All:
>
> Acknowledging another check. Since I took your course I have sold!!! Yesterday a check from *Love Dreams.* Anyway, do you want a testimonial? . . . I'm going away tomorrow but Carol will know where I am and can reach me. . . .
>
> Thanks,
John
>
> P.S. Annie Laurie—will you send two mice, assorted sexes?

The trip he speaks of in his letter was the major trip taken in research for his novel. Once again he packed blankets, food, and thermos into his pie wagon and set off, heading east to Stockton and then north through Sacramento to Marysville. Dook Sheffield was working as a reporter for the Marysville newspaper, and Steinbeck stopped off to see him. Steinbeck was sorry to see that his friend, whom he considered to be the most talented of all the friends of his youth, was stuck as a reporter on a small paper in a small town. The two men went out to dinner, and then, as part of his job, Dook stopped by the police station to see if there was any news. After they left the station, Steinbeck asked him with some irritation and disappointment if that was now the highlight of his life, to be able to call the local cops by their first names. "For god's sake," he exploded, "I've got some money now. Let me finance you. Let me give you the money so that you can go back to school and get your doctorate. I'll send you anywhere you want to go—to Oxford, or wherever you want."

It was a painful scene for Dook, who wanted to carve out his own life and who was hurt by his friend's scorn, and for Steinbeck, who had that delusion of the newly wealthy and newly eminent that he could pack up his friends and carry them with him. And to be turned down at a moment of such sublime generosity and nobility was embarrassing. One could blame money and fame for the separation that ensued between the two men, but it might be better accounted for by a moment of insensitivity generated by good intentions.

The next day Steinbeck went on to the F.S.A. migrant camp at Gridley, California, where Tom Collins was the manager. Collins had been given a leave of absence from his duties, with pay, to accompany Steinbeck. It took Collins a day or two to wind up his affairs, and the author stayed in town, coming into the camp to visit with Tom and talk to the campers. Then the two went out together for several days in the Gridley area to work in the fields and to stay the night on a ranch and then in a squatters' camp. It was during this period that Steinbeck wrote a card posted from the Gridley camp to Larry Powell:

> I have to write this sitting in a ditch. Carol forwarded your letter. . . . I'll be home in two or three weeks. I'm out working—may go south to pick a little cotton. All this—needless to say is *not* for publication—migrants are going south now and I'll probably go along. I enjoy it a lot.
> Very flattering article—thanks.

Unfortunately, we have no way of knowing precisely where Steinbeck and Collins went on this trip, except that they started at Gridley and, as suggested by the postcard, stayed at or near Arvin at the other end of the Valley. There are, however, two other possibilities. Gwyndolyn Steinbeck, Steinbeck's second wife, overheard her husband talking to several old friends one evening, and one of them joked with Steinbeck about his so-called "Oklahoma trip"—leading everyone to think that he had gone to Oklahoma when, in fact, he had only made it as far as the Nevada state line. And a second possibility is suggested in Baldwin's letter—the Imperial Valley (probably Brawley, California, where there was another F.S.A. camp). This sketchy evidence suggests the following route: Gridley, down Highway 99 to Stockton; Stockton to Fresno; Fresno to Arvin; Arvin to Barstow; Barstow, on Highway 66 to the state line or Needles; Needles to Brawley, by way of Blythe and El Centro.

One possible reason that Steinbeck did not go to Oklahoma, as he may have planned to do, was that with Collins along, he had only a limited amount of time before Collins's leave was up. Then, too, there would have been ample opportunity to observe the migrants on the road and by the roadside as the two men traced the Dust Bowl migration in reverse over the long stretch of highway from Bakersfield to Needles. Just why Steinbeck chose to tell everyone except his wife that the trip was made to Oklahoma is a mystery. He occasionally indulged himself in schemes of personal melodrama, and he may have considered this some kind of secret mission in order to escape publicity. I suspect, however, that the misinformation was passed out at least in part as a practical joke on his friends, and perhaps on the critics and biographers. Several years later, when acquaintances mentioned the Oklahoma trip,

Steinbeck would only smile without comment. Many years later he began to talk of the trip with the migrants from Oklahoma as if he had actually made it.

He came home from the south, stopping by to see his sister Esther in Watsonville. The broken-down pie wagon was a bit of an embarrassment—his brother-in-law was a conservative farmer. When he got back to Los Gatos, at the end of the first week in November, there was a tremendous party to celebrate his "return from Oklahoma." Friends from Monterey and Los Gatos were included, and Toby Street and David Tolerton ended the evening doing their best to sing loud enough to drown out Steinbeck's phonograph.

He went back to work on what turned out to be the first version of the "big book," writing steadily in ink in a large bookkeeping ledger through the winter. The first night for *Of Mice and Men* on Broadway was November 23, 1937, and he and Carol spent the evening near the phone at a neighbor's. He wrote to Elizabeth, Annie Laurie, and Mavis:

> You don't know how good it was to hear your voices and how sweet it was of you to take the trouble to phone. It was a pretty exciting night even for us, what with Pat [Covici] sending wires after every act. I didn't feel it at all until about six that evening and then my stomach began turning loops of stage-fright. I was very glad when it was over and the audience hadn't stoned the cast and mailed poison candy to me. A wire from Kaufman says it seems pretty good but he can't tell yet how good.... I'm glad it had a good opening and I'll be very anxious to hear the little sidelights that you people can tell. We were all so hysterical over the phone that there wasn't time for much but squeaks of joy. [11/24/37]

The play featured Wallace Ford as George, Broderick Crawford as Lennie, and Clare Luce as Curley's wife (a role that had been expanded for the play). It was a success, a distinct hit of the season, an award-winner, and ran for 207 performances at the Music Box Theatre.

Steinbeck wrote a very gracious, flattering letter to George Kaufman: "To say thank you is ridiculous for you can't thank a man for good work any more than you can thank him for being himself. But one can be very glad he is himself and that is what we are—very glad you are George Kaufman" [11/37]. Kaufman, for his part was pleased with the play, but was disappointed that Steinbeck had not chosen to work more actively for the play's success and was hurt that he had not come to New York for the premiere. It was a hurt that was aggravated by time, as Steinbeck never did see fit to come East to view the production.

In an article in *The New York Times* on the play and its author, based in part on the interview Steinbeck had given to the press the previous September when he was in New York, the author is quoted in regard to the inspiration for his characters:

> "I was a bindle-stiff myself for quite a spell," he said. "I worked in the same country that the story is laid in. The characters are composites to a certain extent. Lennie was a real person. He's in an insane asylum in California right now. I worked alongside him for many weeks. He didn't kill a girl. He killed a ranch foreman. Got sore because the boss had fired his pal and stuck a pitchfork right through his stomach. I hate to tell you how many times. I saw him do it. We couldn't stop him until it was too late."

It is possible. But then again this was something that he had never mentioned before, to anyone, and it is also possible that he was giving them a little bit of the Wild West.

While one play had hatched successfully, another was in the incubator. Jack Kirkland, who had written the script for the extremely successful Broadway production of Erskine Caldwell's *Tobacco Road*, had taken an option on *Tortilla Flat*. He sent a copy of his adaptation to Steinbeck, and Steinbeck wrote to Joe Jackson that "Kirkland's dramatization of T. F. just came in and we are going over it and Carol has the skitters and it makes her even more emotionally unstable than she ordinarily is. The play is funny as the devil, not my play but I don't care." But although the play was funny, he had misgivings, and he wrote a letter to Kirkland making several detailed suggestions and enclosed his own version of a scene in the last act.

The problem was that Kirkland was trying to write another *Tobacco Road* using *paisanos* rather than poor Southern whites, not knowing anything at all about *paisanos*. The comedy of the novel is rather delicate, depending a good deal on nuances of language, mannerism, and custom, and Kirkland ran roughshod over these things in order to reach for easy laughs. Even though *Tortilla Flat* is a folktale peopled by semimythic characters, its effectiveness comes from a strong undercurrent of truth and sympathy.

As Steinbeck put it in a letter to Annie Laurie after his initial misgivings began to grow:

> These are little things but I have a feeling that unless they are taken care of, the play is not going to have any sound of authen-

ticity. You can argue that it doesn't matter because no one in the
east ever heard of these people anyway. Just remember some of the
phony dialect in pictures and you will see that it does matter. No
one believes that, in fact scorns it. [12/9/37]

With each reading and successive draft, the play seemed to get worse,
and it became harder for Steinbeck to maintain his distance as an interested bystander. He tried several times to get Kirkland to come to
the Coast so that together they might mend the play's deficiencies, but
Kirkland pressed ahead in New York, hoping for a Broadway opening
on Christmas Eve.

The Steinbecks had Thanksgiving with the Joseph Henry Jacksons.
Jackson had published the best early portrait of Steinbeck and his work
in the September 25, 1937, issue of *Saturday Review*, and although he
liked the article, Steinbeck found it strange to read about himself, like
looking into the mirror while shaving—"the invariable reaction is 'Why
you god dam liar.'" The two families saw a great deal of each other
during the period. When the Jacksons had moved into a new house, the
Steinbecks brought a large, hand-forged fireplace fork (the work of
Francis Whitaker) and a madrone tree as housewarming gifts. Later
when the madrone died, John delivered a long lecture to the Jacksons
on the evils of artificial fertilizers. The old-country German was still in
him.

He was always very good with other people's children and established a good rapport with the Jacksons' daughter Marion. One evening
he came in from the garden to tell Charlotte that he had seen her daughter make a magic circle around a lemon tree and her girl friend, Jackie,
couldn't step through it. He also insisted, to children and adults alike,
that his dog Toby was in tune with the spirit world and one evening
had alerted him to a clearly visible apparition. The Irish was still in him
also.

Although he tended to enjoy nearly any kind of celebration, he had
come to dislike Christmas. He found that it made him sad, he said, "like
watching little boys in a parade." Nor, at this point in his life, did the
idea of getting together with relatives, particularly his in-laws, fill him
with joy. So the day before Christmas, John and Carol went with Ed on
a collecting trip, driving north of San Francisco to Olema and spending
Christmas there.

A few days later Carol left for New York to attend the opening of
Tortilla Flat. John wrote Joe and Charlotte Jackson:

By now you probably know what happened to *Tortilla Flat*. It was, says Carol, the worst thing she ever saw. The lines were bad, but the directing and casting were even worse. The thing closed after four performances, thank God. We are really pretty happy about the whole thing because we think this may be so discouraging to Paramount that they will not try to make a picture at all now.

Kirkland added a final dollop to the bad taste that was already in everyone's mouth by swinging at one of the critics who had panned the play and getting tossed out of a New York café for his trouble.

"I get sadder and sadder," Steinbeck continued in his letter to the Jacksons. "The requests and demands for money pour in. It is perfectly awful. WPA worker in pencil from Illinois: 'You have got luck and I got no luck. My boy needs a hundred dollar operation. Please send a hundred dollars. I will pay it back.' That sort of thing. Getting worse everyday." A number of unpleasant things were beginning to add up. Prominent among them was another consequence of fame—a paternity suit, or at least the threat of one, from a woman whom he had known when she was a child and who was now, in Steinbeck's opinion, somewhat demented. While Steinbeck was unfaithful to Carol at the end of their marriage, he was not guilty in this particular case. He considered it an attempt at blackmail at first and was very disturbed and angry, but it finally appeared that the charge came out of a woman's desperate unhappiness rather than malice. She was talked out of the suit by her family, and the accusation never reached the newspapers.

Another disagreeable situation that developed was a growing antagonism on the part of George Albee. Albee, partly out of artistic jealousy, and partly out of a general, gnawing discontent, had begun to snipe at Steinbeck some months earlier, making cutting remarks about his work to mutual friends, and, most painful of all, using confidences out of Steinbeck's letters as ammunition in his attack. Steinbeck tried to withdraw gradually and gracefully from the relationship, but the sniping continued until he felt he had to bring his resentment of Albee's behavior into the open and make a clean break:

This has been a difficult and unpleasant time. There has been nothing good about it. In this time my friends have rallied around, all except you. Every time there has been a possibility of putting a bad construction on anything I have done, you have put such a construction. . . . I've needed help and trust and the benefit of the doubt, because I've tried to beat the system which destroys every writer, and from you have come only wounds and kicks in the face.

What hurt particularly was that Steinbeck had made Albee his literary alter ego, thinking that of all his friends, Albee's experiences were the closest to his own literary struggles and would therefore produce the greatest sympathy and understanding. Although the two did not see each other very often, living apart most of the time, Steinbeck's letters to Albee constitute almost a literary diary and probably served to some extent that function—as a warm-up to his writing and as a way of clarifying his thoughts and emotions.

"I've tried to beat the system which destroys every writer." Like so many others, Steinbeck knew in advance the kinds of things that might happen, but couldn't seem to be able to do anything about them. It was like having a nightmare, then finding yourself, wide awake, drawn inexorably through the very events you had predicted in your dream.

But Steinbeck's personal problems, as acute as they appeared to him at the time, were about to be swallowed up as insignificant within the appalling sea of human misery he was about to witness. As I noted earlier, 70,000 migrants gathered in the San Joaquin during the summer of 1937. Most of these people found themselves stuck in the Valley with no opportunity to work and no resources by which they could either continue to live in the Valley or move elsewhere. They roamed the countryside like wild animals, trying to find some means of subsistence.

As usual, there was little general interest in the fate of migrants and little newspaper coverage. Eventually an alarm was sounded, by the *Los Angeles Times* and others, and some temporary help was provided, but no one seemed to give any thought to the future. As Carey McWilliams pointed out, the transients were herded about like cattle and

were permitted to eke out an existence in the fantastic hope that they would ultimately disperse, vanish into the sky or march over the mountains and into the sea or be swallowed up by the rich and fertile earth. But they did not move, and with the winter season came heavy rains and floods. Soon a major crisis was admitted to exist, with over 50,000 workers destitute and starving.

The people at various social agencies knew what was happening but were frustrated by an inability to act. After beating back the temporary challenge of union organizing in the early and middle Thirties, the large growers and their corporate allies had once again assumed almost absolute power in the state's agricultural industry. By putting tremendous pressure on both the state's administration and the Congress, they were able to have their opposition to any sort of government aid to the migrant workers carried through into a "go slow" policy. They were afraid that help for the migrants would encourage them to stay where they weren't needed, and they opposed aid on the grounds that it would give the workers enough independence so that they might try once again to organize.

At the height of the floods around Visalia, the Farm Security Administration was called in to provide relief, but for many, it was too little and too late. For the frustrated F.S.A. administrators, it was a heartbreaking struggle. Conditions were so bad that field-workers trying to get food to the migrants and to rescue the sick couldn't get the supplies in where they were needed. In the sea of mud that confronted them, they couldn't even find the stranded and half-buried enclaves of migrants who had hidden themselves here and there across thousands of square miles of drenched farmlands to escape the wrath of local authorities. F.S.A. realized that it was not only fighting the elements in order to save lives, but it was fighting a political battle as well. To make any progress with the problem over the long haul, it would have to rally public opinion.

Steinbeck had letters from Fred Soule, at F.S.A. Information, and Tom Collins describing the situation in the Valley. Soule asked him if he couldn't go down to the flood area and help them by reporting what was going on. As Steinbeck described his mission to Elizabeth Otis:

> I must go to Visalia. Four thousand families, drowned out of their tents are really starving to death. The resettlement administration [actually, the F.S.A.] of the government asked me to write some news stories. The newspapers won't touch the stuff but they will under my byline. The locals are fighting the government bringing in food and medicine. I'm going to try to break the story hard enough so that food and drugs can get moving. Shame and a hatred of publicity will do the job to the miserable local bankers. . . . Talk about Spanish children. The death of children by starvation in our valleys is simply staggering. I've got to do it. If I can sell the articles I'll use the proceeds for serum and such. Codliver oil would give the live kids a better chance. [2/14/38]

Collins had been pulled away from his camp-manager post to join other F.S.A. personnel in the stricken area who were administering relief. After receiving his letter, Steinbeck wrote back: "Will you write as soon as you get this letting me know where you can be found at various times of the day or night? And Tom—please don't tell anyone I am coming. My old feud with the ass[ociated] farmers is stirring again and I don't want my movements traced." One of the reasons it has been so difficult for scholars to discover the details concerning Steinbeck's trips among the migrants is that he worked hard at the time to conceal them. From the time *In Dubious Battle* and "The Harvest Gypsies" were published until after the publication of *The Grapes of Wrath* and his move to New York City, Steinbeck had a genuine fear of retribution by the Associated Farmers for his pro-farm labor writings. He had seen what he believed to be evidence of intimidation by violence, blackmail, and extortion on the part of the Associated Farmers and other grower organizations and believed that they were capable of anything. He was particularly worried about a conspiracy designed to discredit him, and he half believed for a time that the paternity suit threat was part of such a frame-up.

In mid-February Steinbeck went to Visalia and spent about ten days in the company of Collins, helping in whatever way he could. As he wrote his agents, "I've tied into the thing from the first and I must get down there and see if I can't do something to help knock these murderers on the heads" [2/38]. In an unpublished autobiographical novel, Collins described their experiences:

> When we reached the flooded areas we found John's old pie truck useless, so we set out on foot. We walked most of the first night and we were very tired. . . . For forty-eight hours, and without food or sleep, we worked among the sick and the half-starved people, dragging some from under trees to a different sort of shelter, dragging others from torn and ragged tents, floored with inches of water, stagnant water, to the questionable shelter of a higher piece of ground. We couldn't speak to one another because we were too tired, yet we worked together as cogs in an intricate piece of machinery. [At two o'clock in the morning they both just collapsed in the muddy fields and slept.]
> . . . I found John lying on his back. He was a mass of mud and slime. His face was a mucky mask punctuated with eyes, a nose and a mouth. He was close beside me, so I knew it was John. How long we had slept in that mire we knew not. . . . [It began to rain again. Ahead of them, some yards away, they spied another tent.] We frightened the little children we found in the tent, the two little children. . . . We must have looked like men from some far-away

planet to those two children, for we frightened them. And the bulging eyes of those two children, the sunken cheeks—the huge lump on the bed—they frightened John and me. Inside the tent was dry because it was on high land, but it was an island in a sea of mud and water all around it. Everything under that bit of canvas was dry—everything—the make-shift stove was without heat; all shapes of cans were empty; pans, pots and kettles—all were dry. Everything, for there was not a morsel of food—not a crumb of bread.

"Mommy has been like that a long time. She won't get up. Mommy won't listen to us. She won't get up." Such was the greeting cried to us by the two little children.

Mommy couldn't get up. She was the lump on the old bed. Mommy was ill and she hadn't eaten for some time. She had skimped and skimped so that the children would have a bite. . . .

"How far is it to the nearest store? Is there an old car near here? Is the store East or West?" But the children only stared as John threw the questions to them. Well did he know that the big food trucks could never get off the roads and travel two miles or more over the muddy, drowned fields to that tent! So John faded into the early morning. . . .

[Sometime later John returned.] John and I sat on the dirt floor. We sat there and the five of us ate the food which John had obtained from the little store some muddy distance away. We sat there and ate a bite—a bite that was a banquet. . . .

Then names and ages of our new-found friends for delivery to the government agency which would succor the isolated family, and we were off again to find other mothers and children out there in that vast wilderness of mud and deep water.

Steinbeck went home for two days at the end of the month and then returned once again to the flood area. On the return from this second trip, he wrote to Elizabeth Otis:

Just got back from another week in the field. The floods have aggravated the starvation and sickness. I went down for Life this time. Fortune wanted me to do an article for them but I won't. I don't like the audience. Then Life sent me down with a photographer from its staff and we took a lot of pictures of the people. They guarantee not to use it if they change it and will send me the proofs. They paid my expenses and will put up money for the help of some of these people. . . .

It is the most heartbreaking thing in the world. If Life does use the stuff there will be lots of pictures and swell ones. It will give you an idea of the kind of people they are and the kind of faces. I break myself every time I go out because the argument that one person's effort can't really do anything doesn't seem to apply when you come on a bunch of starving children and you have a little money. I can't rationalize it for myself anyway. So don't get me a job for a slick. I want to put a tag of shame on the greedy bastards who are responsible for this but I can best do it through newspapers.

But *Life* didn't print the article, apparently because he wouldn't let them edit it and some of the language was too liberal for the editors to swallow. But the photographs, by *Life* photographer Horace Bristol, appeared twice in the magazine. They appeared the following year, in connection with a short article on *The Grapes of Wrath* as a best-seller, and they were used a second time the year after, alongside stills of the movie, to show that it was not an exaggeration.

In his efforts to get newspapers to print a version of the *Life* article, he had the help of Pare Lorentz, whom he had met just before leaving for Visalia. He and Lorentz had a number of acquaintances in common, including people with the F.S.A., such as Will Alexander and Dorothea Lange, and the critic Lewis Gannett, who admired the work of both men. Lorentz had been a well-known film critic but more recently had built a reputation as an artistic and innovative maker of documentary films, including *The Plow That Broke the Plains* and *The River*, the first artistic documentaries to be financed by the federal government and aimed at informing the general public. The whole concept of such films was constantly under fire from various members of Congress, who saw the films as propaganda for a particular political point of view, and from certain members of the film industry, who looked upon such an activity as unfair competition. During Lorentz's five years with the government, it took the personal intervention several times of President Roosevelt to keep his projects afloat.

One thing that brought Lorentz and Steinbeck together was that they were both, essentially, New Deal Democrats. They knew the experience of being attacked by both the right and the ultraleft, managing in their work to go "too far" and "not far enough" at the same time. They both were concerned about unemployment, poverty, the dislocation of people, and both were interested in the New Deal farm programs. While Steinbeck was in the middle of a novel about Dust Bowl migrants, Lorentz had done *The Plow That Broke the Plains*, a documentary which traced the history of the Dust Bowl, showing the effects of misuse of the land and following the migrants to a government camp in California. They had a lot to talk about. For his part, Lorentz showed interest in *In Dubious Battle* and *Of Mice and Men,* thinking that in some way he might help to see that they were filmed properly. Steinbeck, on his side, was becoming more and more interested in film technique (as the final draft of *The Grapes of Wrath* makes clear) and told Lorentz that he would like to work with him sometime, possibly after his novel was finished (he thought at that time) in the late spring.

At Lorentz's invitation, Steinbeck went to Hollywood, just after completing his flood article, to meet with people who Lorentz thought would be sympathetic to the point of view of his novels, including producers King Vidor and Lewis Milestone. Lorentz thought that Steinbeck should take a more active role in searching out the right kind of filmmaker, rather than sitting back and waiting for the most lucrative offer. Lorentz was in complete agreement with the viewpoint expressed by Steinbeck in his recent article, and with his connections, tried to syndicate the newspaper version. It was offered to the Scripps-Howard chain, including the *San Francisco News,* but they would not carry it. Disappointed, Steinbeck was finally able to arrange printing in the April 15, 1938, *Monterey Trader,* under the title "Starvation Under the Orange Trees."

While in Hollywood, Steinbeck and Lorentz talked to Jimmy Cagney, who wanted to be part of an *In Dubious Battle* production—he had his eye on the role of Mac, the experienced labor organizer—and the director Mervyn Le Roy, who asked Steinbeck to work for him, but Steinbeck refused. Le Roy told him that he had wanted to do *Of Mice and Men* and had a wonderful idea to change the plot so that Lennie does not kill the girl but instead is just accused of it. That way, Le Roy pointed out proudly, sympathy is kept with Lennie. Commenting on the incident to Elizabeth Otis, Steinbeck wrote, "I think that is wonderful. I build a job for two hundred pages and he destroys it with a turn of the hand and thinks he has improved the thing."

"Here's another thing," Steinbeck went on:

> Myron Selznick called me again while I was down there. The word had gone out that I was down to take a job. I told him I wasn't. He said again, "Why not?" I said, "Well, I like it the way I am. I write 'em and Covici prints them just as I write them." He said, "What you're asking is that you be writer and director and producer," and I said, "Sure, and front office and Hays office too." "But you can't do that in pictures," he said. "I know," I said. "That's why I'm not

working in pictures." He hung up promptly so I think I finally got over the idea that I don't want to work in Hollywood. [3/38]

About the time of his return from Hollywood, Helen Hosmer, head of the Simon J. Lubin Society, came to him to ask if he would let her have the series of articles that he had done for the *News*. She wanted to reprint the articles as a pamphlet, sell copies, and use the money to help finance the society's efforts to aid the migrants. Steinbeck readily agreed and threw in "Starvation Under the Orange Trees," which was added to the other seven articles as an epilogue. Hosmer gave the pamphlet the title *Their Blood Is Strong* and wrote a preface. A short introduction was provided by San Francisco newspaperman John D. Barry, and photographs of the migrants on the front and back covers of the pamphlet were done by Dorothea Lange.

Hosmer had met Steinbeck in the fall of 1936 through Fred Soule. She had worked as Soule's secretary at the Division of Information until she couldn't stand the bureaucratic inaction any longer. She decided to form her own private organization, and with the help of friends and donations from her colleagues at the F.S.A., she started the Simon J. Lubin Society, naming her organization after the man who, as Commissioner of Immigration and Housing, had been one of the few early voices to take the part of the migrant laborer in California. Hosmer kept extensive files on migrant problems in the state, and while Steinbeck was preparing his series for the *News*, he made much use of them. Hosmer also kept close track of the activities of the Associated Farmers, publishing a pamphlet of her own, a muckraking exposé of the growers' organization. She wanted Steinbeck to write this one also, so that a big name would be attached to it, but Steinbeck refused. He was already writing what he thought of as his own exposé, of the Associated Farmers and similar groups, in his novel.

CHAPTER XXI

W hat had been a relatively simple life was now becoming more and more complicated. Old friends reappeared and his circle of new acquaintances was expanding rapidly. Dick Oliver in New York and Ritch Lovejoy in Pacific Grove were suddenly out of jobs; he tried to put in a good word for the one and help place a short story for the other. Writer Louis Paul, whom he had been corresponding with since they appeared together in the *O. Henry Prize Stories of 1934,* was having problems, and Steinbeck recommended him to M. & O. as a new client. He was trying to get Tom Collins's collection of camp reports published and had sent them to Annie Laurie Williams, who promised to try to do something with them. Ed Ricketts's lab had burned down in 1936 and the insurance company would not make the loss good, so Ed had to borrow money in order to rebuild. Now the loan repayments had become so burdensome that Ed was about to go under financially, and Steinbeck paid off the bank loan and became a "silent partner" in Pacific Biologicals. The Steinbeck house, which had been so isolated, was suddenly in the middle of a housing tract, as a half dozen houses were being built nearby. The racket and commotion was, as he complained, "driving him nuts." And to top it all off, he got word that Pascal Covici was in financial trouble and that he was counting on Steinbeck's new novel to bail him out.

He had begun his novel almost two years earlier with the idea that he had achieved enough security so that he could take several years to write a long, complex novel which he would attempt to make an important work of art. Soon afterward, however, he was pulled by his sympathies toward launching a satirical attack on those responsible for the horrors of migrant life and the terrors of vigilante violence. For many months he was drawn by his emotions in one direction and by his artistic aspirations in another, yet he was unwilling to recognize that he could fulfill one goal or the other but probably not both. Throughout his career, every time he attempted a long novel, he seemed to get caught in a similar tug of war between conflicting goals—it had been true of *To a God Unknown* and would again happen while he was trying to write *East of Eden*.

There was also something in his makeup that seemed to make it impossible for him to slowly plan, develop, and then deliberately write a long work of fiction. The pressure of material and emotion built up in his mind, so that once his direction had finally been determined, he took off like a sprinter rather than a long-distance runner. When at last he did get into the writing of the final draft of *The Grapes of Wrath*, he made it a long sprint, rather than a marathon run, and the strain very nearly destroyed him.

In March 1938 he still had confidence that he could combine art and propaganda. In response to Elizabeth Otis's inquiry (he had said little about the book in progress during recent months), he wrote:

> Yes, I've been writing on the novel but I've had to destroy it several times. I don't seem to know any more about writing a novel than I did ten years ago. You'd think I would learn. I suppose I could dash it off but I want this one to be a pretty good one. There's one other difficulty too. I'm trying to write history while it is happening and I don't want to be wrong. [3/23/38]

A month later he appears to have come to a crisis; realizing that he would have to make a choice, he chose propaganda: "New book goes very fast," he wrote his agents, "but I am afraid it is pretty lousy. I don't care much. It has a job to do and I don't care how it does it"[4/26/38].

A week later he had finished the draft of his satirical novel, which was still titled "L'Affaire Lettuceberg." In a letter to Otis, he explained and justified a piece of work about which he was obviously ill at ease:

> The day before yesterday I finished the first draft of this book. Now just the rewriting but a lot of it because it is pretty badly done. It is short just a few thousand over sixty thousand words. We'll finish it and send it on and if you think it is no good we'll burn it up and forget it. The book has a definite job to do and I don't know yet whether it does it nor not. We'll just have to see.
> The name of it doesn't seem satisfying at all. Carol is at work thinking of a better one. I hadn't thought about the difficulty of pronouncing it and the trouble with the apostrophe. Anyway, we'll

get a new name for it before it is ready to send out. It should be with you inside of a month I should say. I'm a little sorry that Pat publicized it because it might well go up the flue. I don't care about its literary excellence, understand, only whether it does the job I want it to do. In fact if it could be vulgar, would like it. Vulgar in the true sense I mean. It is written not for intellectuals at all but for people who make up vigilance committees. It explains in easy words how the committees are formed and for what purpose. I should like anyone reading it to be hesitant before he takes up arms for good old Tom Girdler not on the grounds that it is wrong but on the grounds that he is being a sucker. So much for it. It is a mean, nasty book and if I could make it nastier I would. [5/2/38]

In the meantime, in a final vote of twelve to four over Thornton Wilder's *Our Town*, the New York Drama Critics Circle awarded its prize for the best American play of the season to *Of Mice and Men*. In its citation, the Circle praised the play "for its direct force and perception in handling a theme genuinely rooted in American life." Unlike fiction critics, who have often complained of the novel's alleged sentimentality, the drama critics cited the play for "its bite into the strict quality of its material" and for "its refusal to make this study of tragical loneliness and frustration either cheap or sensational." Steinbeck sent off a slightly facetious telegram of thanks to the Critics Circle, perhaps suggesting to some that he took the award too lightly. His failure to attend even one performance of the play had become something of a scandal, a common item in newspaper columns. He couldn't understand why there was such a fuss about it—"I'd like to have seen the play but I wouldn't go six thousand miles to see the opening of the second coming of Christ. Why is it so damned important?" [5/38].

He and Carol did not spend a month revising and rewriting "L'Affaire Lettuceberg." It took him only about a week of reconsideration and review of the manuscript to decide that he would burn it. Near the end of May he wrote to Otis and sent a copy to Covici:

I would be doing Pat a greater injury in letting him print it than I would be destroying it. Not once in the writing of it have I felt the curious warm pleasure than comes when work is going well. My whole work drive has been aimed at making people understand each other and then I deliberately write this book, the aim of which is to cause hatred through partial understanding. My father would have called it a smart-alec book. It was full of tricks to make people ridiculous. If I can't do better I have slipped badly.

Because Covici was in financial trouble and because (against Steinbeck's wishes) he had already announced the publication of the book and had begun to publicize it, the decision was painful. With his strong sense of loyalty to Covici, it would have been easier and almost more typical for Steinbeck to say, "Ah, the hell with it," revise the manuscript, and go on to something else. But a number of influences had gathered and, coming to a critical mass, had made him change his mind. Most prominent among them was Carol's intense dislike of the manuscript. And he trusted her critical sense more than he did his own. There was also his recent exposure to the work of Pare Lorentz, which presented to him a vision of an alternative direction, a treatment of similar materials, but artistically and with far more depth. And there were his recent experiences among the migrants during the San Joaquin flood. Collins seems to have felt that Steinbeck's involvement in this scene of abject misery was somehow cathartic, leading him beyond his rage and frustration, perhaps into something close to a sense of tragedy.

The most persuasive argument would not have been possible damage to his reputation, but, following his traumatic struggle to save lives in the mud of the San Joaquin Valley, that a cheap treatment would not do justice to the dignity of his subject. His use of the flood in his finished novel as the final setting, pitting the human spirit, *in extremis*, against the murderous indifference of society and nature, suggests just how deep a mark the experience had made on him.

So he began all over. But this time the book would focus on the migrants themselves, rather than on his hatred of those who had persecuted them. By the first of June, he was on his way again, pleased with his progress but a bit worried that he might be writing too fast. He decided that, for a "plodding, crawling book," he should limit his output so that his pace would be slow and steady. He wrote to Elizabeth that "it is a nice thing to be working and believing in my work again" and "I don't yet understand what happened or why the bad book should have cleared the air so completely for this one. I am simply glad that it is so" [6/1/38].

Although the withdrawal of the manuscript was a blow to Covici and the financial picture was not good, he was still afloat and even planned to bring out a collection of Steinbeck's short stories in the fall (*The Long Valley*). Annie Laurie Williams had been unable to do anything with the Collins manuscript, so Steinbeck had sent it on to Pat. Covici, preoccupied as he was with his own problems, might not have been the right person to consult about the publishability of the Collins material. Steinbeck wrote to Collins to give him the bad news:

I knew that I was not a good editor, so I sent your reports to the best editor I know, Pascal Covici. His reply disheartens me a great deal. He says that no eastern publisher will touch the reports, first because they are sectional and not of general interest, second because to give them the completeness they would need to be of social significance would cost so much, and third because no house could sell enough copies to break even. Were it any man but Covici I should say bunk and go on with the plans. But Covici is the head of the only socially minded publishing house in the country. . . . I wish I didn't believe it but I do. . . . The thing that hurts me is that I had hoped that from this piece of work which I still think is the finest social study I've seen, you could make a little money to carry on with. [6/38]

Rather suddenly the "collaboration" was ended. As seems clear from the letter, Steinbeck had postponed work on the reports and had done little if anything with them. In his letter he went on to suggest that Collins try to "utilize the material in other forms." Inspired, perhaps, by Steinbeck's example, Collins turned to the novel form, using fiction as a platform from which to express his philosophy and to describe his experiences with the migrants (Steinbeck later wrote a preface, a three-page narrative introducing Collins and his work, for the novel). He worked hard over a period of several years, producing three or four versions of the same novel, one of which was accepted for publication by a West Coast publisher who, as the result of poor advance sales, reneged on the contract.

There is a strange parallel between Collins and Ricketts, two men who contributed so much to Steinbeck's work, both directly and indirectly. Both were very unusual, very talented men, and each had that inspired, idiosyncratic, highly individualistic approach to life that often marks the man of genius. Both had writing aspirations, but neither was a very able writer. Aside from Ricketts's text *Between Pacific Tides* (which was in part a collaboration), neither was able to publish anything on his own. Steinbeck collaborated with each on writing projects, trying to get them published through the use of his name. He owed something to both, and he tried in this way, and in others, to pay his debts. Covici opposed both collaborations. Those who knew Covici have suggested that he may have been afraid that Steinbeck would dilute his talent and his marketability. Furthermore, removed from the scene, he seemed to feel that these men, among other people, were trying to use Steinbeck.

From the last few days of May until the first part of December 1938, Steinbeck worked on the manuscript for *The Grapes of Wrath*. It was a remarkable period of work. Although he had vowed to go slow, the pace gradually quickened until, during the last months, he was working day and night. In six months he wrote a 200,000-word novel that was highly complex in structure, detailed in fabric, and quite varied in tone and style.

At first, while he was trying to pace himself, he was in good shape and pleased with his task. In mid-June he wrote Elizabeth that there was "beautiful weather here and the work continues and I am happy." By the end of July, however, all kinds of pressures seemed to converge on him, and his life and writing became more and more of an ordeal, until in the final months he was working himself into a state of nervous and physical exhaustion. During the period of composition he kept an irregular journal which tells the story:

6/3/38 Margery Bailey coming down.

6/17 Doc Bolin here yesterday.

6/19 Mrs. Gragg and Julia came.

7/18 Went to Salinas for rodeo.

7/20 Wire last night that Pat is in trouble. Today I must get the family split and perhaps Tom and Casy to Santa Rosa or Tom at least for the part.

8/1 Brod Crawford came for the weekend. Nice fellow, but what a time to come. My nerves are very bad, awful in fact.... Don't know who will publish my book. It's just like slipping behind at Stanford. Panic sets in. Can't organize. And everybody is taking a crack at me. Want time want to use me.

8/3 There are now four things or five rather to write through, throat, bankruptcy, Pare, ranch, and the book. If I get this book done it will be remarkable.

8/10 Letter from Tom [Collins]—worried about this committee.

8/11 Did ever a book get written under such excitement? Well two got written while mother and dad were ill and if that could happen anything could.

8/17 Dan James and Chaplin coming up this afternoon.

8/23 I've always worked under some kind of pressure. TF while mother was ill, IDB while Dad was ill, M & M while this house was going up.

8/26 Yesterday we bought the Biddle ranch.

8/30 Mabel Ferry and Frank Fenton want to come down.... Carol is typing ms and I'm losing my thread.

9/3 Carol got the title last night *The Grapes of Wrath*. I think that is a wonderful title. . . . The book has being at last.

9/7 Fred Soule phoned yesterday to ask me to go on the radio concerning migrants. Trying to get out of it because it would be deadly to my life. . . . Would start a million fights.

9/23 The book is beginning to round out. I think they go to Shafter.

9/26 Anyway Francis [Whitaker] and Ritch and Tal and Ed were all up here and it was a terrific week end and it left me rather limp and raggy.

10/12 Letter from Sis [Sarah Reamer Elber]. La Follette people are here. That may raise hell.

10/13 The mail is full of requests to use my name. Another request to be a clay pigeon. . . . Now these two things are constantly working at me. Criticism of me is very strong and will grow bitter but I must remember the one and ninety-nine. And I must not stampede.

10/19 I'm on my very last chapter now. The very last. It may be fifteen pages long but I can't help that. It may be twenty. [One page in his manuscript book was equivalent to about three typewritten pages.] The rain—the birth the flood and the barn. The starving man and the last scene that has been ready so long. I don't know. I only hope it is some good.

The notation "throat" on August 3 refers to a severe strep infection that had been making Carol's life miserable for weeks. Although her husband tried to be helpful and compassionate, it was a time of strain. Carol felt even worse for the fact that she couldn't help him and because she was afraid her condition would hinder his progress. At the end of July she entered the hospital and had her tonsils removed. Steinbeck wrote Elizabeth Otis:

She is home now and recovering rapidly. And although she doesn't know it, I did lose a couple of days' work this week. Concentration wouldn't work through all of it. Don't tell Carol. It would worry her. She sets store by this book and sometimes I do too but other times it seems very lousy indeed. Maybe it will be all right. Particularly worried whether all of it is getting over. I'm nearly a hundred thousand words now. Nearly half through. I'm surely making up this year for last year's laziness. [7/28/38]

Carol had become very attached to the concept of this new novel, and indeed, she was so firmly behind it and helped so much with it that he thought of it later as "her" novel. In his dedication he spoke of Carol "who willed this book," and to a large extent, she had done just that.

After her operation, it took nearly six weeks before the infection subsided enough for her to get back to work, but when she did, she contributed more to the completion of her husband's manuscript than she had to previous books. As John reported to Elizabeth Otis:

> Carol is typing ms (2nd draft) and I'm working on first. I can't tell when I will be done but Carol will have second done almost at the same time I have first. And—this is a secret—the 2nd draft is so clear and good that it, carefully and clearly corrected, will be what I submit. Carol's time is too valuable to do purely stenographic work. [9/10/38]

Carol was in fact writing the revision, that is, correcting errors and editing for contradictions and awkwardness, while John was doing the first draft. Near the end, Carol had caught up, and off and on for more than a month the two worked together, John writing and then Carol typing and correcting what he had composed that day. The pace during these last weeks was punishing.

Definite word about Covici's bankruptcy had come at about the time Carol had gone to the hospital. Immediately Steinbeck began to get wires from other publishers. Although he referred all offers to his agents, the constant bombardment of blandishments was unsettling. He liked Covici and felt bad about what was happening to him. He offered to do whatever he could to help (and it was not an empty gesture—he eventually did a great deal), but he was also concerned, professionally, about his own position. He was losing an extremely generous and supportive publisher and stepping back into the uncertainty of early days.

Adding to his upset was the bankruptcy procedure itself. Like a piece of property, he was given over to a printing firm as part of the settlement of Covici's debts. Furthermore, the royalties owing to him evaporated as the printer, having first claim to assets, took whatever money there was on hand. The fact that authors could be treated like cattle and that they were the last to be considered in such matters made him furious. In his anger he developed a plan to break his contract in order to keep the printer from "tying my affairs in this miserable manner." He would write five books in five weeks. He would dictate them to a secretary, and they would be complete gibberish. Then he would find the worst handwriting possible and have the manuscripts copied by hand.

Upon submission, he would demand the down payment due each of them as specified under his contract. The more elaborate his plan became, the more his mood shifted from anger to a perverse sense of joy.

Fortunately, he did not have to resuscitate "Murder at Full Moon" and other condemned miscreations (another part of the plot) in order to win his freedom. Within a month the entire mess was resolved when Covici, with Steinbeck's backing, accepted a job as an editor at The Viking Press, taking Steinbeck with him into the fold. Covici sent a telegram:

> I shall never be able to repay you for this magnificent support you gave me and now you are with me at the Viking where with no financial worries to harass and embarrass me I shall continue as your honored and happy publisher love to you both. [6/12/38]

Viking not only rescued Covici and made up Steinbeck's royalties, it also took over the publication of *The Long Valley*, bringing it out in September.

Back in June, at Covici's request, Steinbeck had sent to him the magazines that had published his short stories, and presumably the texts of these stories in the collection were set in print from the magazines. The writer also called Covici's attention to that "other one of the Jody series," yet unpublished, "The Leader of the People." And so, in such casual fashion, was one of Steinbeck's best known "novels" put together for the first time, when the last of the Jody stories was joined to the other three and printed in sequence at the end of *The Long Valley*. (*The Red Pony*, containing all four stories, was published in 1945.)

While *The Long Valley* did not sell as well as *Of Mice and Men*, it did make the best-seller lists and overall did much better than a short-story collection was expected to do. Steinbeck was particularly gratified that this book was a success: he had not done as well previously with his short stories as he had hoped, and this time he had shown up very well against the competition. Earlier he had written to Covici: "I'm a little worried about the Long Valley. Understand it will have to compete with Hemingway's short stories. I am convinced that in many ways he is the finest writer of our time."

In addition to Covici's bankruptcy and Carol's illness, there were any number of other distractions and problems that made his life hectic. His journal indicates only some of the people who actually came to visit. There had been times in the recent past when the Steinbecks had gone for weeks seeing hardly anyone, and now his work, something like the scent of a large feast, seemed to attract nearly everyone he had ever known. In addition there was some emotional give and take in regard to the road production of *Of Mice and Men*. Kaufman, by Steinbeck's abdication, was supposed to come up with a script altered to suit the sensibilities of Middle America and then send it to Steinbeck for his approval. There were delays, probably due to Kaufman's resentment that Steinbeck was not taking a more active part in the work. Another troublesome loose end involved Pare Lorentz, who, simply by his vagueness and lack of communication, seemed to have established some sort of hold over Steinbeck's attention. Steinbeck had agreed to work with Lorentz on a film version of the radio play *Ecce Homo!* But Lorentz was constantly promising to visit, call, or write, and Steinbeck waited while nothing happened, wondering what Lorentz was up to.

In the fall, a Hollywood agent called and, talking to Carol, told her that he had an order to buy *The Red Pony*. Carol said, "Goody—for Freddie Bartholomew, I bet—no thanks," and hung up. Although her husband's attitude toward the Hollywood establishment remained skeptical and suspicious, he was gradually changing his mind about film as an art form. He had enthusiasm for trying new things, and he began to think he'd like to learn more about film technique. Eventually, he would establish probably the best record for quality films of any major American novelist, both in films made from his novels and stories (which he sometimes worked on and sometimes did not) and those made from his original screenplays.

His changing attitude was partly due to Lorentz, but also due to the influence and example of a new acquaintance, Charlie Chaplin. Chaplin, who had read Steinbeck's books, simply drove up to Steinbeck's house one day—in a large, black chauffeured limousine—jumped out of the car, extended his hand, and introduced himself. Steinbeck was suddenly presented with a short, incredibly handsome man, wearing a black, turtleneck sweater that contrasted with a thick mop of curly gray hair. Steinbeck's shock is understandable when one remembers that Chaplin was at that time one of the two or three most famous people in the world—and he didn't look anything like the Charlie that Steinbeck had seen in the movies.

Chaplin had rented a house in wealthy and exclusive Pebble Beach, near Carmel, and within a few weeks he was drawn into the community's social life. There was some irony in the circumstance that, whether Steinbeck knew of this or not, during the summer when he got to know Chaplin, the actor was romantically involved with Geraldine

Spreckels, the daughter of the family whose factories and farms had provided Steinbeck with most of his employment during his youth. In addition to playing with the rich, Chaplin sought the company of the two most accomplished artists in the area, Robinson Jeffers and Steinbeck. He got along better with the latter—unlike Jeffers, Steinbeck could match Chaplin's sense of fun and mischief. When he wasn't in a melancholy mood, discussing his artistic and romantic troubles, Chaplin loved to mime the stuffed shirts of Pebble Beach and the pseudo-artists of Carmel for John's amusement.

They also tended to see eye to eye politically. Although both were considered "dangerous radicals," neither had very clearly defined political ideas. In his memoir of Chaplin, Alistair Cooke points out that the comedian-filmmaker's "much abused 'radical philosophy' was no more than an automatic theme song in favor of peace, humanity, [and] 'the little man.' " A similar song could be attributed to Steinbeck. But while they both approved of the New Deal, they did disagree about Russia, which Chaplin, like so many Hollywood liberals of the time, saw as a model for salvation.

According to Chaplin's son Charles, Jr., his father "was fascinated by Steinbeck's books and used to drive around the countryside where his stories were laid, trying to place the characters in the books in their proper locations." He became a fairly common visitor to both Steinbeck homes in Los Gatos over the next two years, even after he ended his sojourn among the elite of Pebble Beach, and he was so taken by the Los Gatos area near the second Steinbeck home that he tried to buy the adjoining property. The townspeople of Los Gatos considered the Steinbecks undesirable bohemian types and did their best to ignore them, but they were impressed by some of their visitors, as when it was reported in the local paper that Steinbeck had been seen with Charlie Chaplin and Spencer Tracy, standing on a street corner watching an organ grinder at work.

Steinbeck became acquainted with an increasing number of Hollywood people during the late thirties and early forties, mostly actors, but Chaplin was one of the very few with whom, for a time, he had any kind of close relationship. This growing acquaintance with film personalities roughly coincided with changes in Steinbeck's personal life, particularly after the publication of *The Grapes of Wrath*, and several of his old friends attributed these changes to Steinbeck's having "gone Hollywood," but in fact the changes came from a variety of causes, the least of which was influence by the film capital.

One thing that did contribute to a change in Steinbeck's style of living was the new home that he and his wife moved into just before he completed his long novel. Carol's father was in real estate and was able to find a fifty-acre ranch, about five miles out of town, that provided the privacy they wanted. It came complete with a spring, a large pond, a forest, and a broken-down ranch house. They decided to construct a new house and remodel the old for use as guest quarters. At first their plans were shelved when they heard of the Covici bankruptcy, but they went ahead with the purchase of the Biddle property, as it was called, near the end of August 1938, and the foundation was laid for the new house in early September. The construction coincided with the stretch drive of Steinbeck's composition, and once again, as with *Of Mice and Men*, he had the added distraction of trying to write while managing the building of a home.

The earlier house had been built with a reluctance to get involved with anything as materially weighty as a home: it was functionally designed, inexpensively built, and simply furnished. This second one was far more elaborate. A swimming pool was put in as the house was being built, a gift to Carol, who had always wanted one, and a dedication to her on a brass plate was set into the diving board. In giving in to such a house, although it was by no means a mansion, it was as if the Steinbecks had made a conscious decision on the direction of their lives— almost an abandonment of principle. They could no longer pretend to be poor, or think of themselves as only temporarily fortunate, prepared at any moment to pack up and go back to the spartan life of earlier days.

As noted earlier, at the beginning of September Carol had come up with a brilliant idea for the title of the new book: the title, "The Grapes of Wrath," gave the book a dynamic focus, and the words of the hymn it referred to could be applied in numerous ways to the novel's contents. John was delighted, and he wrote to both Covici and Otis to ask them how they liked it. A week later he wrote to Otis:

About the title—Pat wired that he liked it. And I am glad because I too like it better all the time. I think it is Carol's best title so far. I like it because it is a march and this book is a kind of march— because it is in our own revolutionary tradition and because in reference to this book it has a large meaning. And I like it because people know the Battle Hymn who don't know the Star Spangled Banner. [9/10/38]

He particularly liked the title because it gave an American stamp to his material. From previous experience he knew that there would be those who would try to smear the book as foreign-inspired, and he wanted to blunt such an attack from the outset because he felt very strongly that what he was describing was an American phenomenon. For several years, as we have seen in his letters to Albee and others, Steinbeck had expressed the belief that the country was undergoing a kind of revolution. Although he appears to have been vague in his own mind as to what form the conflict would eventually take or what would be its ultimate results, he saw the movement as a phalanx of little people in our society, workers and small farmers, too proud and independent to be pushed around indefinitely by those who had grabbed a disproportionate amount of the country's wealth and power.

After the publication of *The Grapes of Wrath*, Steinbeck wrote a radio interview script (never aired) in which he provided both questions and answers, the major subject of which was this movement in American society as the theme of the novel. In response to the question, "In the growing American literature there was no such cleavage between so-called classes as seems to be at the core of present day writing. Can you account for this?" Steinbeck answered, in part:

> Before the country was settled, the whole drive of the country by both rich and poor was to settle it. To this end they worked together. The menaces were Indians, weather, loneliness and the quality of the unknown. But this phase ended. When there was no longer unlimited land for everyone, then battles developed for what there was. And then as always, those few who had financial resources and financial brains had little difficulty in acquiring the land in larger and larger blocks. . . . This condition left the great people in their original desire for the security symbol land but this time the menace (as they say in Hollywood) had changed. It was no longer Indians and weather and loneliness, it had become the holders of the land. . . . Now, since the people go on with their struggle, the writer still sets down that struggle and still sets down the opponents. The opponents or rather the obstacle to the desired end right now happens to be those individuals and groups of financiers who by the principle of ownership withhold security from the mass of the people. And since this is so, this is the material the writer deals in.

Later he describes this struggle in biological terms:

> The human like any other life form will tolerate an unhealthful condition for some time, and then will either die or will overcome the condition either by mutation or by destroying the unhealthful

condition. Since there seems little tendency for the human race to become extinct, and since one cannot through biological mutation overcome the necessity for eating, I judge that the final method will be the one chosen.

He saw the Okie migration as a smaller phalanx within the larger, and he also notes in his "interview" that in writing *The Grapes of Wrath*, "I have set down what a large section of our people are doing and wanting, and symbolically what all people of all time are doing and wanting. This migration is the outward sign of the want." It was a movement, both literally and figuratively, that for the purpose of this novel could be used as a metaphor for the social revolution as a whole. And just as the larger movement had, in his mind, its antecedents in the American Revolution, so too the Dust Bowl phalanx had its earlier parallel in the movement West of the settlers. In an interview with the *San Jose Mercury* during the composition of *The Grapes of Wrath*, he said, referring to the Okies: "Their coming here now is going to change things almost as much as did the coming of the first American settlers. . . . These people have that same vitality . . . and they know just what they want."

Knowing the American small farmer and worker better than either the capitalists or the communists, he was certain that the conflict, whatever forms it might take, would be made on our own terms, in terms of the "Battle Hymn of the Republic," rather than the "Internationale." And to underscore the point, he decided he would like to have the hymn, words and music, printed on the endpapers at the front and back of the book. When the idea came to him, he sent a wire to Covici, and followed up the request several times in letters. He was insistent, knowing that publishers do not take very seriously authorial suggestions regarding format. He wrote Covici in January:

> The fascist crowd will try to sabotage this book because it is revolutionary. They will try to give it the communist angle. However, the Battle Hymn is American and intensely so. Further, every American child learns it and then forgets the words. So if both words and music are there the book is keyed into the American scene from the beginning. [1/10/39]

When he got the proofs in February, Covici had given in to the extent of printing the first verse as a sort of prologue quotation to the novel. Steinbeck wrote, "I mean Pat to print *all all all* the verses of the Battle

Hymn. They're all pertinent and they're all exciting. And the music if you can" [2/8/39]. Covici obliged.

To his credit, Covici sensed from the beginning that this was going to be a blockbuster novel, in terms of both significance and sales. When he went to Los Gatos for a weekend in early November, what he saw and heard of the manuscript convinced him that he was right. Steinbeck, afraid that Covici was going off the deep end and might hurt himself with Viking, tried to calm him down. Disturbed by what he thought was his publisher's excessive enthusiasm, he sent off a warning to Elizabeth:

> Look Elizabeth I want to make something very clear and I want you to help with it. Pat talked in terms of very large first editions of this next book. I want to go on record as advising against it. This will not be a popular book. And it will be a loss to do anything except to print a small edition and watch and print more if there are more orders. Pat is darling and of course his statements are flattering but he is just a bit full of cheese. Anyway will you please see that this opinion is registered in the Viking office. [11/38]

Even after a large early advance sale, Steinbeck was still convinced (perhaps wishful thinking) that the book would not be a popular success and continued to warn Covici about overextending himself on a first printing. By the publication date in April, however, the advance sale had reached an enormous ninety thousand copies.

Near the beginning of November, the old house was sold while the new was still being built. For over a month the Steinbecks camped in the kitchen of the rundown farm house on the new property while they waited for completion. Their situation was so chaotic, with furniture and possessions stacked here and there and workmen coming and going, that for a time Carol had to give up trying to type and edit. The stretch drive took place while they were living partly in the farmhouse and partly in the new house. Then at last, after plowing through and around nearly every kind of disturbance and disruption that one might imagine, they completed the manuscript during the first week of December. Carol was ill and John in a state of collapse. He said later that he never would have thought that he could write himself into physical exhaustion, but he had.

But the problems with the manuscript were not yet over. Elizabeth Otis had planned for some time to make a visit to Los Angeles in early

January and had agreed to meet the Steinbecks and return with them to Los Gatos for a few days. In the meantime, the manuscript had gone on to Viking, where there was much concern over the novel's language. It was felt that if some passages were not changed and some words altered, bookstores would simply refuse to handle the book and it would be banned throughout much of the country. The problem was a delicate one. Viking would not censor the offensive language, yet the editors were quite aware that Steinbeck would not willingly alter anything, especially for reasons of placating an audience or insuring sales. So when Elizabeth came to the West Coast, what was to have been a vacation turned into a mission of mediation.

For a "terrible two days," she recalls, they worked together on the passages where Viking had made suggested changes. She sat at a desk, while Steinbeck, exhausted and fighting off the pain of an infected leg, lay on a couch. Each item involved a measure of trauma. Elizabeth fought to get the book in a condition in which it could be successfully published, and John fought to maintain what he considered his artistic integrity. He insisted that if changes had to be made, the rhythm of each passage involved must be absolutely preserved. Sometimes he balked entirely, refusing all alternatives, and the language remained as written. At other times Elizabeth and Carol ganged up on him and made him compromise.

When at last the ordeal was over, Elizabeth had to telegraph the results of their work marathon to the publisher. The agreed-upon language had to be sent in that very day, since on the next Viking would go ahead and print the original. She dictated the substitutions over the phone to the Western Union operator, specifying which obscenities should be replaced and with what. At the end of the long dictation, the operator told her, "I don't think I can accept that telegram." Elizabeth argued with her until she finally gave in.

Steinbeck was weary and angry. He needed to make his point with someone, so he lashed out at Covici:

> Elizabeth and I went over the ms and made some changes. I made what I could. There are some I cannot make. When the tone or overtone of normal speech requires a word, it is going in no matter what the audience thinks. The book wasn't written for delicate ladies. If they read it at all they're messing in something not their business. I've never changed a word to fit the prejudices of a group and I never will. The words I changed were those which Carol and Elizabeth said stopped the reader's mind. I've never wanted to be a

popular writer—you know that. And those readers who are insulted by normal events or language mean nothing to me. Look over the changes and I think they will be the ones you made. The epithet shit-heels used on the people in the hamburger stand, I will not change. There is no term like it. And if it stops the reader—the hell with him. It means something precise and I won't trade preciseness even if it is scatological preciseness.[1/13/39]

Steinbeck's relationship with Viking was not what it had been with Covici-Friede. Although Covici had been assigned to remain as Steinbeck's editor, he was a new man in the firm and decisions were no longer his alone to make. He had seldom made suggestions in regard to the writer's actual text; if he had tried to pressure Steinbeck, it was almost always in matters of publicity. Now there were others to satisfy—Harold Guinzburg, the president of the company, and Marshall Best, the senior editor, who was used to taking a more active and authoritative position in regard to Viking's authors. As far as he was concerned, Steinbeck was just another author, and authors can run astray without an editor's considered judgment. Throughout Covici's tenure at Viking, Marshall Best stood in the background.

About the same time as the language matter was being settled, another objection to the manuscript surfaced. When Covici diplomatically brought it to Steinbeck's attention, he made it sound as if it had been a group judgment:

> Nobody could fail to be moved by the incident of Rose of Sharon giving her breast to the starving man, yet, taken as the finale of such a book with all its vastness and surge, it struck us on reflection as being all too abrupt. It seems to us that the last few pages need building up. The incident needs leading up to, so that the meeting with the starving man is not so much an accident or chance encounter, but more an integral part of the saga. [1/9/39]

The suggestion was stupid, despite all the controversy stirred up by the ending after publication, and it is highly unlikely that it came from Covici. Yet Covici had to take the brunt of Steinbeck's understandably irate reaction:

> I have your letter today. And I am sorry but I cannot change that ending. It is casual—there is no fruity climax, it is not more imporant than any other part of the book—if there is a symbol, it is a survival symbol not a love symbol, it must be an accident, it must

be a stranger, and it must be quick. To build this stranger into the structure of the book would be to warp the whole meaning of the book. The fact that the Joads don't know him, don't care about him, have no ties to him—that is the emphasis. The giving of the breast has no more sentiment than the giving of a piece of bread. . . . I know that books lead to a strong deep climax. This one doesn't except by implication and the reader must bring the implication to it. If he doesn't, it wasn't a book for him to read. Throughout I've tried to make the reader participate in the actuality, what he takes from it will be scaled entirely on his own depth or hollowness. There are five layers in this book; a reader will find as many as he can and he won't find more than he has in himself. [1/16/39]

Whether or not Steinbeck knew what he was doing, he did what he did—which is about all one can say in the wake of a masterpiece. He really did not care all that much for the novel form, and he was bound and determined to use the form rather than the other way around.

Predictably, the next argument was about publicity. Because he was now with Viking, he had to go through the whole rigmarole of declining and explaining once again, and by the time the galleys came in early February, he was thoroughly sick of the whole business. "I'll be glad to be done," he wrote Covici. "I always have a strong reluctance toward going back into a finished story. Carol is going over it too and maybe we'll catch everything. It's hellishly long" [2/6/39].

The writing had taken a heavy physical toll. In September he wrote, "I'm desperately tired but I want to finish. And meanwhile I feel a though shrapnel were bursting about my head. I only hope the book is some good" [JS/EO-9/10/38]. As the next two months went by, he began to tire easily. Just before the manuscript was completed, he began to feel a dull ache in his leg. As the pain in his leg got worse, he found it difficult at times to walk. Apparently he, too, had picked up a strep infection, but with his generally good health and strong physique, the infection had taken a long time to manifest itself. And when he simply caved in, after the manuscript was sent off, it wasn't clear what was wrong with him, just that he was exhausted.

In January he had some tests, which showed that his "metabolic rate [was] shockingly low," and he was confined to his bed for two weeks because of "neuritis." When rest failed to bring any improvement to the pain in his leg, he went back for more tests, and this time X rays showed two ulcers on the base of one of his teeth. The tooth was extracted, and that seemed, for a time, to reduce the infection in the leg, but the pain came back, and the leg continued to hurt him, sometimes severely, for most of the year. During the spring and summer he was treated for tonsilitis, and his doctor removed his tonsils in July. It was the first time in twenty years that he had been seriously ill, and the chronic, indeterminate nature of his illness was both frightening and maddening. During the periods of remission he was sure that he had the problem licked. Then the pain would return.

In addition to his illness throughout much of 1939, the year also marked the beginning of the end of his marriage. The very foundations of his life seemed to dissolve under the continuing pressures of fame and under the erosion of a growing paranoia. Threats, both real and imagined, by individuals and groups antagonized by the publication of *The Grapes of Wrath* preyed on his mind and forced him to alter his manner of living. He became guarded and cautious about whom he saw and where he went. He spent the first part of the year looking for a way to escape and the second part looking for some direction or project by which he could restore some sanity and order to his life.

The satisfied reader puts a book down, happy with his journey, and waits for another just like it; the writer, having abandoned ship, is lost in the turbulence of the departing wake and tries desperately to take new bearings. Critics and literary historians have speculated about what happened to change Steinbeck after *The Grapes of Wrath*. One answer is that what happened was the writing of the novel itself.

CHAPTER XXII

Steinbeck had met the producer-director Lewis Milestone (*All Quiet on the Western Front*) through Pare Lorentz during the previous spring, 1938. Milestone expressed his great admiration for *Of Mice and Men* and told Steinbeck that he was going to try to get the screen rights. Steinbeck was lucky that not only had his work attracted a producer of Milestone's caliber, but also that Milestone cared about the project enough to work out a deal with Hal Roach (who was obligated to him as a result of a lawsuit settlement) whereby he maintained complete control of the picture.

Early in 1939 Milestone and Steinbeck met to talk about the project, and Milestone asked him if he would be willing to go over the script with them when he and his writer had finished. Steinbeck agreed. Then Milestone mentioned that Nicolai Remisoff was going to be his art director. Steinbeck said, "That's wonderful. You're going to do *Of Mice and Men* with a Russian art director, and you're of Russian extraction, and what the hell am I mixed up with?" Milestone thought that he took it as a big joke, but he was, in truth, becoming very sensitive about such things.

During February Steinbeck waited, but heard nothing further from Milestone. The composer Edgard Varèse wrote to tell him that he wanted to do "a work of great scope" based on one of his books, and John replied that he thought that *Grapes* might make a good theme for a symphony. He found the proposal flattering, especially since Varèse was the first person who had recognized that he used the mathematics of musical composition in his writing.

Charlie Chaplin had written to say that he wanted to come up to the ranch "to get clean" before shooting *The Great Dictator*. He and John had talked about the possibility of making the movie script of *Dictator* into a book, and John was enthusiastic, having gone over the script with him (there was a rumor, unconfirmed by either man, that John had helped him with the long final speech of the movie). He was willing to edit it, preface it, or whatever, just to get what he thought was a great screenplay into book form, but he heard nothing further about the matter from Chaplin. He had expected, before the first of the year, to be working with Lorentz on one or more of his documentary projects, but Lorentz remained as absent and as mysterious as ever.

A month before the official publication date of *Grapes* in April, Steinbeck began to hear rumblings that the Associated Farmers was out to smear him before the book appeared. He heard of printed material put out by the growers' organization that labeled him a communist and claimed that he was a friend of Harry Bridges. He reported to his agents a strange occurrence which added to his growing unease:

> In Monterey there is a bookshop run by a Miss Smith. She says that two weeks ago a group of people came in and asked a lot of questions about me. When she asked why, they said they were investigating me for Mr. Hoover—that Mr. Hoover considered me the most dangerous subversive influence in the West and was going into my past thoroughly. Since they were middle-aged people and prosperous, Miss Smith didn't think it was a joke. Since I have heard a number of things I began to wonder if a sex crime—a drunk driving charge or something like that might not be in the offing for me. You must understand that the Associated Farmers absolutely control the sheriff's office in this state. I went to my attorney and he said there was no way of stopping a charge but advised me to keep a diary containing names of people I saw and when so that I could call an alibi if I had to. I don't think they would dare attack me but they have done as bad. But it does no harm to take precautions. . . . Please keep this letter with the dated envelope. This group is the same that put Mooney and Billings and McNamara in prison for life on trumped up charges. They are capable of anything. I have seen their work on the migrants. [3/4/39]

At the end of the month he learned that local businessmen in counties all over the state were turning in the names of neighbors who were liberals to their sheriffs' offices and that his name had been turned in as a "Red" to the sheriff. In an effort to "start a backfire" that might discourage any plot, he began telling his friends what he thought the Associated Farmers and similar groups might try to do to him.

During the early spring he took several trips to Los Angeles to check on the rehearsals for the L.A. production of *Of Mice and Men*, find out from Milestone how the movie was progressing, and see Chaplin. The gathering storm made him increasingly restless, and despite the recurring pain in his leg, he began to travel much more than he had in the past. The rehearsals in L.A. depressed him: "Wally [Ford] is an actor. He wants to yell and posture. They are screaming their lines. No Kaufman to hold them down so they're just playing their heads off. The hell with it. I've asked Wally to keep his voice down three times but he's an actor."

At the end of March he received his copies of *The Grapes of Wrath* and he wrote Covici:

> The books came today and I am immensely pleased with them. . . . I think the way you laid in the Hymn on the end papers is swell. The pageage is less than you contemplated, isn't it? And I'm glad. 850 pages is a frightening length. You know I would like to see the New York reviews. Would you please save them for me? I understand Joe Jackson is going to do it for the Herald Tribune. I'm glad of that. I guess that is all. I just wanted to tell you how much I like the book. [3/31/39]

Two weeks later he began to get the first reviews. In regard to the first batch, he commented, "Amazing that these critics don't seem to know what that last chapter is about. One says superficial and another sentimental, and it is neither. Well, I know that some people do understand it and that's enough." [JS/EO-4/13/39] As further reviews came in, he thought he detected another pattern: "Do you notice that nearly every reviewer hates the general chapters? They hate to be told anything outright. It should be concealed in the text. Fortunately, I'm not writing for reviewers. And other people seem to like the generals. It's interesting. I think probably it is the usual revolt against something they aren't used to." [JS/EO-4/17/39]

But the vast majority of the reviews from important publications were favorable, many exclamatory in their praise. The literary world was won over; the denunciations, which were somewhat slower in reaction, would come from editorials, and from the podium and pulpit. But those who had demands, requests, and offers did not lag behind. "The telegrams and telephone," he wrote to Otis, "all day long—speak . . . speak . . . speak, like hungry birds. Why the hell do people insist on speaking? The telephone is a thing of horror. And the demands for money—scholarships, memorial prizes. One man wants 47,000 dollars to buy a newspaper which will be liberal—this is supposed to run with a checkbook" [4/18/39]. In the same vein, he told Dook Sheffield,

"Everybody in North America wants something from me." And he added wryly, "Remember when I used to like mail so much that I even tried to get on sucker lists? Well, I wish them days back" [6/23/39].

At about the time that Steinbeck's novel appeared, Ricketts's text, *Between Pacific Tides*, was put out by Stanford University Press. Although Ed had had help and encouragement from many friends over the seven or eight years of its preparation—and Jack Calvin is listed as coauthor—the book was essentially his and was a major achievement for him. It began, according to Joel Hedgpeth, as "a sort of cottage industry" among a group of people who frequented the lab in the early thirties, and at the outset it was intended to be a little book for beginners. But it grew, and after publication became, in the words of Richard Astro, "a definitive sourcebook for studying marine life on the Pacific Coast and is still used at oceanographic research centers from Scripps to Friday Harbor."

The book was different in that it dealt with the marine invertebrates of the shore and tidepools of the Pacific Coast inductively instead of by phylogenetic classification. Animals were observed in their manner of living, discussed as part of an ecology. In late March of 1939, Steinbeck wrote to Joe Jackson:

> In another package I'm sending you Ed Ricketts' new book. It is unusual and I think valuable. There have been handbooks describing the marine life of the littoral, none has been like this. The receptions of the book in scientific and university circles has been very fine but it strikes me that it is valuable to those people who just wander along the beach and wonder what that thing is. This book not only shows the thing's picture but gives its common name, its enemies, housing habits and food. Anyway, I think it is a good and a valuable book.... Could you, please, Joe, have it reviewed in the Chronicle?

The timing of Ricketts's publication has some importance for the course of Steinbeck's life, for he was deeply involved in the biologist's hopes for the book and suffered with him through the difficulties of preparing it, getting a publisher, and seeing the book through press. The successful conclusion of the work signaled to them that other projects were possible, and early in 1939—Steinbeck was making trips to Monterey as well as to Hollywood—they had already begun to discuss other, similar texts that they might work on together.

For the time being, however, Steinbeck simply wanted to get away from the telephone. Just as he had vastly underestimated the sales of the novel, so he misjudged the intensity and length of time of the uproar and controversy caused by its publication. He thought that if he could disappear for just a few weeks, everything would blow over. His main hope for disappearing lay with Pare Lorentz, who seemed to be pretty good at it himself. In March he had gotten messages from Lorentz describing the difficulties he was having filming *Ecce Homo!* The film was to include a number of scenes at various manufacturing plants, and he was having trouble gaining access. The word was that the National Association of Manufacturers was trying to stop the film by lobbying in Washington and advising its members to close their factories to Lorentz's cameras. Lorentz promised to send for him soon.

Then in mid-April, Steinbeck wrote to Dook:

> I told you I was going away. I don't want it known where I am going or what doing, so please don't tell anybody. I'm meeting Pare Lorentz in Chicago next week to go to work on a picture. The value of it to me is two fold. I'm going as assistant director but actually I'm going to work on script, carry lights, learn camera angles and direction under the man I consider the best in the country. I'll know something about pictures when I get through. I'm terribly interested. . . . I don't know how long I'll be away. A month or so anyway. But maybe I'll be in and out all summer. It serves a valuable purpose too—gets me out from under the mess of this book and I hear that it will be quite a mess with considerable name calling.

II

At the time Steinbeck knew him, Pare Lorentz was in his early thirties. He was a well-built man of medium height with brown hair parted on the side, who had that clean-cut, slightly pudgy appearance of a graduate student at a Midwestern university. Like Steinbeck, he had left his college, the University of West Virginia, without taking a degree, but unlike the novelist, success came to him early in his career. By the time he was twenty-five, he was an established New York film critic and had published a book on movie censorhip. By the time he was twenty-nine, he had syndicated a film-criticism column, been the movie critic for *Vanity Fair, Town and Country,* and *McCalls,* and contributed articles to such periodicals as *Harper's* and *Scribner's.* He had also published a second book, *The Roosevelt Year: 1933,* which traced in pictures and words the significant events of the first year of Roose-velt's first term.

This book got him a job as a sydicated political columnist for King Features, and in one of his early columns he praised Secretary of Agri-culture Henry A. Wallace and the New Deal farm programs. This gave Lorentz something in common with Steinbeck—both had been fired from a Hearst publication. The difference was that while Steinbeck had been discharged by a city editor, Lorentz was fired via a telegram from San Simeon.

Because of his Roosevelt book and his interest in doing a film on the Dust Bowl, Lorentz was hired as a film consultant to the Resettlement Administration. Rexford Tugwell had in mind doing a series of shorts to inform his staff, but Lorentz talked him into doing a longer film, a quality movie that would be good enough to win commercial distribu-tion and thereby educate the public about farm problems and the work of the R.A. to solve them. With no filmmaking experience, Lorentz set out to put together a crew to make a movie about the Great Plains— their settlement, misuse, and the resulting erosion of soil. Because he had so little money to work with, he ended up doing nearly everything on *The Plow That Broke the Plains* except hold the camera.

Despite the movie's success, both artistically and as a vehicle of in-formation, Lorentz had had enough of government bureaucracy and tightfistedness (he'd had to pay for part of the movie out of his own pocket). He went to Tugwell to quit, but instead took on a new project, somewhat better financed, a film about the Mississippi River and its in-terrelationships with the land and people. *The River* found a commer-cial distributor, and it was widely seen in this country and in the United Kingdom as well; it also won the first prize as best documentary at the Venice International Film Festival of 1938 (it was declared ineli-gible for consideration for an Academy Award).

Lorentz's next project was *Ecce Homo!*, a picture that would deal with unemployment from the point of view of men being displaced by machines. CBS had gotten in touch with him about doing a radio show, and although they could not agree on a regular program, the network did suggest that he might want to use the "CBS Workshop," a show-case for experimental work, to try out some of his ideas. Lorentz de-cided to adapt his script for *Ecce Homo!* to the format of a half-hour radio show, thinking that the broadcast could be a proving ground for the development of the film he wanted to produce.

In a book on Lorentz and his documentaries, Robert L. Snyder ex-plains how the radio show grew out of Lorentz's previous movies:

There are many similarities between the broadcast of *Ecce Homo!* and the sound tracks of *The Plow* and *The River* in the lyrical quality of the narration, the realistic sound effects, and the use of music as counterpoint to the narration. The broadcast was conceived, like the films, in the form of successive, short sequences. But a new element had been added—the element of people, of human interest—through dialogue. In the program, four men meet under a tree at a filling station on the Kansas prairie. They tell stories of being displaced by machines and speak of hopes and plans for finding work elsewhere. Lorentz based his material on interviews with applicants for relief.

There are several things in this description that may sound familiar to readers of *The Grapes of Wrath*—the musicality of the movement and structure, a succession of short sequences, the lyrical quality of narrative, and, of course, the displacement of men by machines. As I mentioned earlier, I think it is significant that Lorentz visited Steinbeck at the end of May 1938 and played for him a transcription of *Ecce Homo!*, just at the time the novelist was reconsidering "L'Affaire Lettuceberg." Joe Jackson wrote about this visit, that Steinbeck

talked to Pare Lorentz . . . and listened to him expound his theory of the technique of the documentary film, heard a play-back of the radio drama, *Ecce Homo!*, that Lorentz had done for the Columbia Workshop, unconsciously absorbed many of the Lorentz principles, as the merest glance at the "inter-chapters" in *The Grapes of Wrath* will show.

But perhaps more than anything, Lorentz's dramas gave Steinbeck a sense of a style and tone by which he could approach his material—seriously, lyrically, documentarily—material he previously had wasted in a lightweight satire.

Earlier Jackson had written of Lorentz's influence in a review of *The Grapes of Wrath*, and Steinbeck had responded by saying, "It is interesting the Lorentz angle. Because I had laid out the inter-chapter method before I saw *The River* or [heard] *Ecce Homo!* Where I see the likeness now is in the chapter of the route where the towns are named. I have little doubt that the Lorentz *River* is strong in that. But the other—maybe influenced by Dos Passos to some extent but not Lorentz." The full extent of Lorentz's influence was probably not recognized by the novelist, but was rather a matter, as Jackson suggested later, of unconscious absorption. And more was involved than inter-chapters. *Ecce Homo!*, and perhaps *The Plow*, gave Steinbeck a place to start in his revision, a set of images and an opening theme, and *The River* may have provided the rhythm, the sense of epic motion, by which to continue. There is too much of motion-picture technique in *The Grapes of Wrath*, a novel composed in sharply visual, filmlike segments, for the reader to think that the author did not have film on his mind as well as music.

Lorentz had stopped by to see Steinbeck in late May 1938 during the period when he was traveling around the country using his recording of *Ecce Homo!* to try to drum up support for a film production of his script. He planned to expand the radio program into a two-hour movie, and he was trying to interest various government agencies in sponsoring the film and to enlist the aid of whatever influential people he could to support him. He was unsuccessful until President Roosevelt intervened to order the establishment of the U.S. Film Service in August 1938. During the period of the fall and winter of 1938–39, when Steinbeck was wondering where Lorentz was and why he didn't get in touch with him, the filmmaker was busy shooting sequences of *Ecce Homo!*, primarily at dam construction sites, and struggling with the bureaucracies of the federal government and private industry.

At their initial meeting in February 1938, Lorentz had expressed (or at least that was Steinbeck's impression) interest in some kind of collaboration, perhaps based on something Steinbeck had already written. Lorentz brought the novelist together with producer Lewis Milestone for the making of *Of Mice and Men*, but as Lorentz's career with the government progressed, especially with the formation of the Film Service, he was prohibited from any independent project, and Steinbeck's position slipped from a possible collaborator to simply someone interested in Lorentz's work who was willing to help out. In the spring of 1939, with the publication of *Grapes* imminent and the pressures of publicity and controversy mounting, Steinbeck was eager to use any excuse to get away.

The "call" finally came in mid-April when Lorentz wired Steinbeck to meet him in Chicago. The project was not *Ecce Homo!*, as the novelist supposed it would be, but a new film, *The Fight for Life*. Only a few weeks earlier, President Roosevelt had asked Lorentz to drop *Ecce Homo!* for the time being in favor of doing a movie on public health that would illustrate the need for a comprehensive health bill, which the President planned to present to the Congress. Lorentz was directed to see Dr. Paul de Kruif, who offered the film rights to any of his books. The filmmaker decided on de Kruif's latest book, *The Fight for Life*, and on the first section of the book, which was concerned with the hazards of childbirth.

De Kruif's discussion of efforts to reduce the rate of infant mortality in this country focused on the work of the Chicago Maternity Center. It was there, on April 25, that Steinbeck joined an advance crew made up of a researcher, a location scout, and a still photographer. Their job was to do research on the functioning of the center and to map and photograph the institution and the slum areas surrounding it. (The location of the center made it possible for Lorentz to combine the theme of the fight for medical progress with the theme of the need to fight poverty and ignorance.) Research involved extensive observation of the institution's activities and interviewing of the doctors and staff. The crew also interviewed patients at length in an effort to get a full picture of where and how they lived and how the services of the center affected their lives.

Upon his return a month later, Steinbeck wrote Covici that "Chicago was horrible" and that "I never worked such long hours in my life." Nevertheless, he committed himself to continue with Lorentz, and when the shooting crew came to Hollywood that summer to do some difficult interior scenes, he promised to join them, and spent several periods of two or three weeks each there during the course of the next few months. He was often not feeling well and he hated the long drive or train ride, but he went anyway.

Earlier I mentioned that the publication of Ed's book brought Steinbeck and Ricketts back together again and stirred up plans for joint projects in the Future, but Steinbeck's experience with *The Fight for Life* and a developing friendship with its author also played an important part in turning his interest back toward science. It was a direction that would take him to the *Sea of Cortez*, *The Forgotten Village* (which seems to have sprung directly from his work on *The Fight for Life*), and, a bit later, *Cannery Row*. As his life began to break apart during the year that followed the publication of *The Grapes of Wrath*, the study of science became a sort of sea anchor with which he tried to ride out the storm and maintain some kind of stability. Once more he regularly sought out the company of Ed, and near the end of the year he was spending much of his time in Monterey at the lab. Even before going to Chicago, he had written in his radio script interview prepared for Joe Jackson: "Boilleau said that kings, gods, and heroes only were fit subjects for literature. The writer can only write about what he admires. Present day kings aren't very inspiring, the gods are on a vacation, and about the only heroes left are the scientists and the poor."

III

After leaving Chicago he made a hurried trip to New York and Washington, D.C., and then tried to return to Los Gatos in secrecy. He felt that he might maintain a fiction for a time that he was away—somewhere, vaguely, in the East. By the time he got home, his novel had sold over 200,000 copies, the screen rights had sold for $75,000 (at that time one of the largest sums ever paid), and he had more mail stacked on his desk than he had ever seen in one place before. Acting as a buffer was taking its toll on Carol, but nevertheless, after only a week or so at the ranch, he left to spend most of June in Hollywood.

Having been warned not to stay alone in hotel rooms, in case a rape or assault charge might be set up against him, Steinbeck rented an apartment to use when he was in Hollywood. His quarters at the Aloha Apartments were small but moderately well furnished in dark, over-stuffed apartment-durable. The apartment had a small kitchen with a chrome dinette set at one end, a bedroom with a bulging, black mahogany highboy, and a pink-and-lavender tile bathroom. Against one wall in the crowded living room he'd placed a large black diathermy machine—he was, in June 1939, going through a period of crippling pain, so bad at times that he had to be helped up and down stairs or getting in and out of cars.

For a time he tried to use a fictitious name at the apartment, and he used Max Wagner's house, nearby, as a mail drop. He had corresponded off and on over the years with Edith Wagner, Max's mother, and on one of his earlier trips to L.A. had looked her up and become reacquainted with the whole family. There were four brothers, all of whom worked in one capacity or another in films, and everybody in Hollywood knew the "Wagner boys," a hard-drinking, fun-loving, sometimes wild group. Apparently it was not unusual for Edith to get out a quart of gin on an evening for her and the boys to share, and then open up another. She had been the scandal of Salinas because she smoked cigarettes and typed, and so naturally Steinbeck had been drawn to her. He talked of her in his later years as his first writing teacher—more likely she was one of the few people he had read his manuscripts to while he was in high school who didn't complain. Her oldest son, Jack, was an assistant director who had started out with Mack Sennett. Next oldest were the twins, Bob and Blake, who had both been cameramen, Blake also starting his career in the silent days with the Hall Room Boys Comedies. Max, of course, had been a close childhood friend of Steinbeck's and was now a bit player and extra.

A year earlier, Max had met a young, attractive girl by the name of Gwyndolyn Conger, a radio and band singer who was trying to break into the movies by working as an extra. She lived with her mother and grandmother right around the corner from the Wagners, and Max began to see a lot of her, sometimes taking her to her job or her music lesson, sometimes out to eat after she was through singing at a night club. Some girls, while waiting for their call when working in a picture, would embroider, or knit, or flirt, trying to get an extra day's work out of the assistant director, but Gwyn read to pass the time. When Max saw her reading Steinbeck, he told her that he had gone to school with him.

When Steinbeck moved into his apartment that June he had cut himself off from people, and he was lonely and depressed. He felt the way he had a few months earlier, when he had written in his journal:

The people with panaceas of all kinds. Will you lend your name to this and to this. . . . "I seen about your luck. I got no luck. Send one hundred dollars." "Luck"! He thinks it is luck. He is poor and he thinks I am rich. And he seen about my luck. In the cheap welter, he seen about my luck. He seen about my destruction only he couldn't understand that. The Greeks seem to have known about this dark relationship between luck and destruction.

Max was shocked when he saw John's condition. He went to Gwyn and told her that "his friend"—he wouldn't use "Steinbeck" out of consideraton for John's concern for secrecy—was "hiding out" and needed help: "My friend is in town. A lot has happened and he's holed up with a bad back, and he's awfully sick and I told him I had someone I knew who could keep her mouth shut. Would you make some chicken noodle soup and go over and keep him company for awhile?" She made the soup and took it to his apartment. He introduced himself as "Mr. Brooks." When she got back home, she told her mother, "I have just met the most marvelous man with the most wonderful voice you have ever heard. He is just terrific. He isn't very handsome, but there is just something about him." And her mother, ever skeptical, replied, "You're not trying to give me the old chemical story, are you?" Gwyn said, "Yes, more or less." In Gwyn's memory, she and John fell in love sitting at the dinette table in his dim, crowded kitchen, over a bowl of chicken soup.

But it was more complicated than that, just as Gwyn herself was more complicated than she appeared to be. She was about 5'6", with shoulder-length dark-blond hair, a pretty face that would have been beautiful except that it was slightly too round, and a full, nearly perfect figure. The most common adjective applied to her was "sexy," yet she didn't act sexy. She wasn't a flirt; she didn't act coy. Her manner was open, gentle, friendly. She listened well and laughed easily, and she could be witty.

When Steinbeck met her, she was not yet twenty-one, some eighteen years younger than he. (At the beginning of their relationship she spelled her name "Gwendolyn," but I have used the latter form throughout to avoid confusion.) She had started singing professionally when she was fourteen with Ben Bernie, Bobby Meeker, and Ted Weems at the College Inn in Chicago. During high school she also went to the Chicago Conservatory of Music and at the same time sang at a local radio station. She broke off her schooling to come to Hollywood with her mother and grandmother, and she worked hard, taking singing lessons three or four times a week, working as a staff vocalist for CBS in the daytime and singing in clubs at night. She got a contract with M.C.A. and was booked for singing dates here and there around the country. "Then," she recalls, "I got a job at Columbia Pictures. I did extra work—God, I would ride the horse off in the distance. You needed every dime you could get in those days to pay for your lessons, your evening clothes, your makeup, your hairdo, your traveling expenses. In those days, they didn't pay for those things."

Along the way she had gotten help from people who were kind to her, people like Max, who escorted her and watched over her, and like Claude Thornhill, the bandleader-composer, who helped her with her singing style and phrasing. She also had run the Hollywood gauntlet and had endured the propositions and the ogling, the tawdry clubs and shabby hotels, and the inevitable drunks. At twenty, she still looked innocent and fresh, yet inside, she was very self-contained: she had seen it all and had calculated her chances; she knew precisely what she wanted to do and what she wouldn't do. In matters of the heart, Steinbeck was the teenager and she was the adult.

For Steinbeck's part, the relationship evolved slowly, tentatively. There was something about him in his early relations with Gwyn that smacked of the bashful boy in courtship. He and Max would go to Brittingham's, a cocktail lounge that everyone called "Rick's," where they would watch Gwyn sing and talk to her between shows. During his later trips to Hollywood that summer, he and Gwyn went out more alone or in the company of other friends—not many: Pare Lorentz, Lewis Milestone, and Frank and Lynn Loesser—Frank was a composer and lyricist who would eventually write *Guys and Dolls* and other Broadway musicals. The first four times John took Gwyn out alone, he forgot to bring any money, and he fumbled and mumbled. On the fourth date he asked her how she felt about him; she said that she liked him very much.

Lynn Loesser was also a singer and had the same coach—Sandy Oliver—as Gwyn, and the two singers became close friends. Eventually Gwyn revealed that she was dating John, and the two couples started going to each other's apartments for dinner. As Mrs. Loesser remembers, when they went out, they went to second-rate bars—

you know, really dumps. . . . Disinfectant poured over the smell, tile walls. You know, that sort of thing. But the booze was good, and the price was right, and Louella Parsons and the guy on the *Hollywood Reporter* didn't haunt those places, and nobody asked who you were. It wasn't that they were that crafty; it was just that truly John didn't have any interest in fancy places.

When he got back from his trip to Los Gatos in late June, he found that the situation was as chaotic as before he left. He seemed far more concerned about his own discomfort than Carol's—and it had been Carol whom he'd left behind to take the brunt of the assault. He wrote to Otis:

This whole thing is getting me down and I don't know what to do about it. The telephone never stops ringing, telegrams all the time, fifty to seventy-five letters a day all wanting something. People who won't take no for an answer sending books to be signed. I don't know what to do. Would you mind phoning Viking and telling them not to forward any more letters but to send them to your office? I'll willingly pay for the work to be done but even to handle a part of the letters now would take a full time secretary and I will not get one if it is the last thing I do. Something has to be worked out or I am finished writing. I went south to work and I came back to find Carol just about hysterical. She had been pushed beyond endurance. There is one possibility and that is that I go out of the country. I thought this thing would die down but it is only getting worse day by day. [6/22/39]

At the same time he reported to Dook that

I've been all over hell since I wrote last, to New York and Washington and Chicago and back to the south [Los Angeles]. I've been working with Lorentz in the U.S. Film Service. I wanted to know how pictures were made and didn't want to get the training in Hollywood so I've been carrying lights and working in every possible field even to the cutting room. I've learned a lot but not enough. So I've got to go back. I wish you wouldn't mention this much because all the administration stuff is under fire anyway and my connection might be just an added pain in the neck. So I come home for a little rest and find a stack of mail to be gone through about half as high as I am. Well it is all done now. And there were some screwey ones. Phoneys and real ones. [6/23/39/]

In addition to the requests that made up the bulk of the mail, there was also the inevitable harvest of messages from cranks, crooks, and madmen. No one ever gets used to such letters, reminding us as they do of the irrationality that lies just outside our gates, not even those who are in the limelight for most of their lives. For Steinbeck, who had never experienced such a downpour of incoherence and rage before, it was just another element among the dark forces that gathered around him.

Steinbeck took one such message seriously enough to turn it over to the F.B.I., which seems strange in light of his having heard only recently that he was being investigated as a subversive. (Although he may not have believed that to be true, he found out later that he had in fact been investigated by some Washington agency.) His faith is revealed further in the remainder of the letter to Dook:

Yes the Associated Farmers have tried to make me retract things by very sly methods. Unfortunately for them, the things are thoroughly documented and the materials turned over to the La Follette Committee and when it was killed by pressure groups all evidence went to the Attorney General. So when they write and ask for proof, I simply ask them to ask the Senate to hold open hearings of the Civil Liberty Committee and they will get immediate documentary proof of my statements although some of them may go to jail as a result of it. And you have no idea how quickly that stops the argument. They can't shoot me now because it would be too obvious and because I have placed certain information in the hands of J. Edgar Hoover in case I take a nose dive.

Even allowing for it being a private letter, and in that sense just talk, there is something terribly naive and unreal in all of this—the plotting, the melodrama, and the expectation that, like "Gangbusters," the federal government stands ready to stem the tide of evil. Despite a broad, Mark Twain–Will Rogers sort of distrust of politicians, he had at the same time an almost childlike reverence for American institutions, and he shared with other New Deal Democrats who had little practical political experience an inordinate idealism about America and an extraordinary faith in the possible efficacy of federal action. He was, alas, a patriot.

While he was in Hollywood, Steinbeck had made arrangements to review the screenplay for *Of Mice and Men*, and when Lewis Milestone and Eugene Solow, who had worked on the script, arrived at the ranch house in Los Gatos, they found Steinbeck, with his bad leg, stretched out on the couch in his study. He told them that he wasn't feeling very well and asked that the script be read to him. Solow read it aloud while the producer watched John for his reactions. Milestone recalls:

> He didn't say a word. He [Solow] read the whole script. He [Steinbeck] sat up and said, "It's fine. What do you want me to say?" I said, "Come on. Don't get lazy now. It's nice to hear that you are pleased with the thing, but there is a little more than that, because there are a couple of things I did without you, and I want you to go through it very carefully and make sure it is your own." He said, "All right." So he got up, and he sat at the desk, and I looked over his shoulder. He was going through the dialogue changing the punctuation, and then he would change an "if," "but," "and," and whatnot, and before my very eyes the whole thing was being changed and became Steinbeck's writing. It didn't take very long. When he finished, he said, "Well, that's it," and I said, "Well, that's better than it was," and we were ready to go into production.

A month or so later in Hollywood when Milestone mentioned that he was going up north to scout locations for the movie, Steinbeck offered to show him some typical ranches. The two men drove down into the Salinas Valley in Steinbeck's car to reconnoiter. As they approached a little bridge just outside of Salinas, John stopped the car and said, "Do you see that little bridge ahead of us?"

Milestone said, "Yes."

He said, "Notice that the bridge is kind of enveloped in a peculiar sort of cloud."

"Yes."

He said, "There are more plots in that cloud. That's where I get all my material."

After they had visited several possible locations, Milestone noticed that each time Steinbeck drove onto a ranch, he'd never stop. He'd just drive around the circle in front of the ranch buildings and back out again. The producer couldn't see anything that way, so he asked him why he didn't stop and let him get out and look around.

John said, "I can't stop."

"Why?"

"Because I'd get my ass full of rock salt. They hate me around here."

"Well," Milestone said, "if that's the case, I don't need you. I'll find my own locations and I can stop. Nobody wants to shoot me with salt. So you go home and I'll check with you later."

Of Mice and Men starred Burgess Meredith as George and Lon Chaney, Jr., as Lennie. During the shooting (most of the location work was done, ultimately, in the San Fernando Valley) Steinbeck visited a few times and started what became a very close friendship with Burgess Meredith. Milestone recalls it was very difficult to get Steinbeck to come onto the set; he didn't want to interfere. As soon as Milestone had finished the film, he invited Steinbeck to see it. The author told him that he was very pleased with it and he'd like to ask a favor: would Milestone call up Mrs. Wagner and arrange for her to see the picture? The producer said that he'd do better that that, he'd send a car for her, bring her over to the studio with any friends she wanted to include, and put them in a projection room by themselves.

Since Steinbeck liked the film, Milestone asked him to write a little blurb for it. The author agreed and sat down and wrote, "The English language is very strange and every once in a while we lose a word that used to be very popular in usage. I wonder whatever happened to the word 'good'? Everything is sensational, stupendous, tremendous, and whatnot, but whatever happened to the word 'good'? So all I have to say about the picture is that it is good." "That," Milestone recalls, "was the blurb. That is the one we used."

During this period Steinbeck also talked several times to Nunnally Johnson, who had been hired to do the screenplay for *The Grapes of Wrath*. Johnson swore that he was going to do it "straight" and that there would be no watering-down of the story. He also told Steinbeck that there were so many people working on the picture who cared about the message of the novel that there would be no cop-out—they'd scream their heads off if the studio tried to pull any shenanigans. Nevertheless, there were rumors that Darryl F. Zanuck would never complete the movie, or if he did, that it would avoid the truth. Annie Laurie Williams was particularly hurt because people were saying that she had sold John down the river by selling the rights to Zanuck. The next time Zanuck was in New York, she confronted him with the rumors. According to Annie Laurie, he got so angry that he went out and stayed with the migrants and was inspired to make the best picture that he'd ever made. Later, Nunnally Johnson told Steinbeck that the experience of making the movie had changed Zanuck's political point of view. John replied that he'd want to see some direct evidence of that before he believed it.

Despite Annie Laurie's belief that Zanuck went to check on migrant conditions himself, another story, as reported in the *New York Post* sounds more like the producer. At a meeting prior to production, Steinbeck told Zanuck that he was going to put the $75,000 paid for the rights to the novel into escrow, and that if the movie was watered down or its perspective changed, he would use the money to sue him. Impressed by John's vehemence, Zanuck assured him that the movie would reflect the novel—he'd seen Nunnally's script, hadn't he? Yes, John replied, but anything could happen in the cutting room. Well, don't worry, Zanuck told him—I believe in the story—I had the accuracy of the script checked out in the field by a detective agency. "And what did they find out?" asked Steinbeck. "That conditions are much worse than you reported," replied Zanuck.

Not long after John and Nunnally first met and had their initial conferences with Zanuck at Fox, they had dinner at Chasen's, along with Doris Bowden (who would play Rosasharn in the movie and who would become Mrs. Johnson), Gwyn, and Max Wagner. Mrs. Johnson recalls that Nunnally and John got along beautifully; their senses of humor meshed perfectly, and they fed each other lines and anecdotes all evening. The wine flowed and spirits ran high, and there was a lot of singing, mostly by Gwyn, who was doing Irish ballads—there was much ado, at some length, in the early morning hours, about cockles and mussels.

Johnson was one of several Hollywood people whom Steinbeck came to trust implicitly. He was a great screenwriter and was completely honorable, and knowing this, Steinbeck took the right course when he told him, in effect, "A novel and a screenplay are two different things. Do whatever you wish with the book. I've already made my statement. Now it's up to you to make yours." This gave Johnson the kind of freedom he needed and released him from that terrible burden the scriptwriter sometimes carries of having the novelist, in spirit, if not in fact, hanging over his shoulder. (Sometime afterward, Johnson told his wife that Steinbeck was only the second novelist he had worked with who would still speak to him.) Later, when Johnson did the adaptation of *The Moon Is Down*, he asked Steinbeck if he wanted him to take any particular line or if the novelist had any ideas about how the story should be developed for the screen. John's reply was simply, "Tamper with it."

Regardless of his trust of Nunnally Johnson, Steinbeck was still conscious that there can be many a slip between script and screen, and he continued to be concerned about the studio's courage. Steinbeck told the production people at Twentieth Century-Fox that if they wanted to get some realistic locations, they should get in touch with Tom Collins, and he sent a letter to Collins clarifying his position regarding the filming:

> I did sell it [the rights to the novel] but only after thinking it over very carefully. I think they are going to do an honest job. I will see and check the script but meanwhile if you can show them examples, etc., it will be good. Don't go out on a limb until we see the script, but good people are working on it. My thought is that if they can get 10% on film it will be worthwhile.

A bit later he reported to Otis, "They sent a producer into the field with Tom Collins and he got sick at what he saw and they offered Tom a job as technical assistant which is swell because he'll howl his head off if they get out of hand" [6/22/39].

Collins received $15,000 for working as the technical advisor for the film, and it was in part due to his influence that so much realism was maintained in location, dress, and manner. A good portion of the film was done at the Weedpatch government camp and at other locations around the Arvin-Lamont-Bakersfield area. During the filming, Steinbeck received regular letters from Collins reporting on the picture's progress and then at the end a note expressing general satisfaction with the film as a whole. At the end of the year, Steinbeck wrote to Elizabeth Otis:

> We went down in the afternoon and that evening saw Grapes at Twentieth Century. Zanuck has more than kept his word. He has a hard, straight picture in which the actors are submerged so com-

pletely that it looks and feels like a documentary film and certainly it has a hard, truthful ring. No punches were pulled—in fact, with descriptive matter removed, it is a harsher thing than the book, by far. It seems unbelievable but it is true. [12/15/39]

When he got back to Los Gatos, he sent a short note to Tom Collins: "Saw the picture and it is swell. . . . Been away 10 days and there must be two hundred letters to go over. You did a wonderful job on Grapes."

Sometime after this note and probably after Steinbeck and his wife had separated, Collins dropped by the Steinbeck home in Los Gatos, but the house was closed, and no one knew where the Steinbecks were or when they would be back. Collins never saw Steinbeck again.

IV

In the spring of 1939, the Golden Gate International Exposition opened on Treasure Island in San Francisco Bay. One of its biggest attractions was the "Cavalcade of the Golden West," the story of the Western movement, featuring covered wagons and a lot of square dancing, a reenactment of the discovery of gold, and, at the climax, two real steam locomotives, which met in the center of the stage for the driving of the golden spike marking the completion of the transcontinental railroad. There were also exhibitions by countries and companies and the usual array of carnival attractions (including the dancing of Sally Rand) and rides.

Steinbeck wanted to go immediately. As he wrote Joe Jackson, "I'm nuts about fairs even County Fairs. Just an extension of steam shovel watching and no one ever watched an excavation with more energy than I." He loved the music, the pageantry, and the come-on, but most of all the displays of technological gadgetry. He was a sucker for the magic vegetable slicer, the tempered-glass knife, and other marvels of the midway. Steinbeck went to the fair several times over the next few months, the first time in June with Carol, his sister Beth, the Joseph Henry Jacksons, and Paul de Kruif. The major mode of transportation was the rickshaw, and the group managed somehow to have drag races with each other in their rickshaws, plunging up and down the crowded streets of the fair.

In July John took Carol with him to Hollywood. During his trip to Chicago, Carol had her mother come and stay with her at the ranch, but during his other trips, she had been alone, left to cope with the turmoil that he had escaped. It was hard duty, and she scandalized the locals by coming into town alone to have a drink at the hotel bar and by using language in public that they used only in private. As the pressure on John increased, he became more restless and prone to travel. Having him home was not always a pleasure; his unhappiness and pain often put him in a foul mood. In Hollywood when they were invited to a home in Beverly Hills for dinner, Carol wanted to stay and talk with the men after the meal, but the Hollywood convention was that the wives would depart upstairs to discuss "woman" things—gossip, hair-styles, and new clothes. Carol would get upset, drink too much, and in her frustration end up insulting everyone.

Finally, the situation became unbearable and Carol left. John wrote to Elizabeth:

> This is a very hard letter to write because I don't know what to say in it. To tell you what has happened would be to know it myself and I'm not sure what it is. Briefly . . . Carol went hysterical in Los Angeles and pulled out. I was pretty sick, in fact hadn't slept for a long time with pain. You will remember that she did this in New York one time. I have no doubt that I am to blame for this. I have a very great sense of failure about it. I was in bed for two weeks after she left and as soon as I could get up at all I came here to Pacific Grove. I have no plans at all. Always before I have tried to do something about it and that hasn't worked and this time because I am tired and sad I am doing nothing about it. Perhaps this is wrong. I don't know. And always before I have tried to analyze the thing. And my analysis has apparently been worthless. The simple fact of the matter seems to be that Carol doesn't like me and that she suppresses that feeling until such times as the pressure of her dislike (usually when she has been drinking) breaks free and comes out. I don't know what she will do or not do. I haven't heard from her since she pulled out, but I do know she is on the ranch. I would rather you didn't mention it to her or to anyone. I want her to be, if not happy, at least a little contented and it seems that I personally am not able to make that true.
>
> Immediately, I shall stay here and try to recover my nerve and my health or at least until something else occurs to me. If you have written and I haven't answered, it is because I haven't had any mail for three weeks.
>
> This may clear up, but there are things that can happen to one that are so awful that the whole life system turns to water and that takes some recovering from. [8/20/39]

He thought at the time that the separation might be permanent. When he felt well enough to leave L.A., he went to the lab to stay with

Ed. There, Ed ministered to him, as he recalled in his essay "About Ed Ricketts":

> Once, when I had suffered an overwhelming emotional upset, I went to the laboratory to stay with him. I was dull and speechless with shock and pain. He used music on me like medicine. Late in the night when he should have been asleep, he played music for me on his great phonograph—even when I was asleep he played it, knowing that its soothing would get into my dark confusion.

John had not realized before how nearly completely dependent he was on Carol; he was the kind of man who needed to be married—to a strong woman—in order to survive emotionally. But although the separation was mended shortly after his letter to Elizabeth, his marriage to Carol was never the same.

CHAPTER XXIII

Their affair, as Gwyn put it, was "off again, on again, Finnegan." John simply could not make up his mind what he wanted to do. He wanted to stay on the ranch in seclusion—he wanted to get away; he wanted to reestablish a life with Carol on some basis or another—he wanted to be with Gwyn.

He tried to use the ranch as a retreat from the public furor over *Grapes*, the requests and the threats, but although his mail was screened and his phone number unlisted, word still filtered through somehow and he felt constantly pressured. And though he claimed to want peace, he was incapable of remaining quiet and establishing a defensive position. He became restless in seclusion and would invite people to the ranch whom he would later complain about as unwanted guests. He would call Gwyn or use some film business as an excuse for running down to Hollywood to look her up.

Following Carol's stormy departure from a Robert Benchley party in early August 1939, Steinbeck moved from the Garden of Allah Hotel into the Aloha Apartments, alone. Ill and depressed, he waited until he was recovered enough to travel and then moved in with Ed at the lab. A little over a week later, he was back with Carol at the ranch, feeling that Carol might be insane and that there might be a physiological cause that could be treated with medical help. Whatever her problems may have been, she was certainly no Zelda. The chances are that she had behaved as she had always behaved, precipitously and directly—when she was fed up, she was fed up. Despite taking the "blame" in his letter to Otis, her husband had no clear sense of having contributed to her unhappiness and was seemingly unaware that his own personality had undergone a change. More than ever before following the publication of a book, he was intolerant, impatient, and at loose ends.

Early in the summer, the Steinbecks had thought about escaping to Europe, but they changed their minds and vaguely planned a boat trip, perhaps to Mexico or Hawaii. After their reconciliation, Steinbeck wrote to Covici that they had decided to just get in the car and drive somewhere, "away from every pressure of every kind." They didn't even know yet in what direciton they would go, but he promised, "Will empostcard you on the way." As it turned out, they headed north, through northern California, Oregon, and Washington. "Just driving and stopping and sleeping," he wrote to Elizabeth Otis, adding "Good and restful and we're seeing a part of the country neither of us know" [9/7/39]. They spent several days in Seattle, took a trip with John Cage and his wife, Xenia (Tal Lovejoy's sister), to Vancouver, and then returned home.

Shortly afterward, in mid-September, he wrote to Elizabeth:

We go to Chicago Friday—Carol for the first time in a plane and she's pretty excited about it.... Isn't there a quality of insanity about most of my mail? The lady named Irma who writes every day. One old lady who claimed she was 88 wrote to me and I acknowledged her letter and she wrote me three letters a day for two weeks. It's kind of nuts. Everything is nuts. That thing from Paris kind of scared me yesterday. Commentator just said a Frenchman—whom he compared to me—had just been imprisoned for "defeatist attitudes." I expect I'd better entrench myself in some way because—when and if we go to war and the General Staff, the du Ponts and the American Legion take over the country I will be one of the first to be sent to prison and I don't like jails.

In Chicago they saw his uncle Joe Hamilton, and John checked in with Pare Lorentz and Paul de Kruif, who were still at work on *Fight for Life.* On their way back from Chicago, de Kruif drove his car in a cross-country race with the Twentieth-Century Limited—while in the back seat John clutched a bottle of whiskey and offered encouragement.

There were still wild times and times when John and Carol enjoyed each other, but to most of their long-standing friends, it seemed that things were not right with the Steinbecks and not getting better. There were occasions when John would verbally abuse his wife in front of other people, and he had gotten to the point where her unpredictable and sometimes outrageous antics, which he used to enjoy and even encourage, made him uncomfortable. They seemed to go out of their way to irritate each other. On one occasion, for example, when Bob Cathcart was visiting, he and Carol went into town late in the evening to pick up some liquor, and Carol invited two deputy sheriffs whom they saw near

the store to come back to their house with them. John was visibly chagrined to find himself suddenly playing host at eleven-thirty at night to
two men whom he and his wife barely knew.

Their manner of living, the whole atmosphere of the house appeared
to change, decline, even become corrupt, during the months that followed the publication of *Grapes* and on through the succeeding year. It
was as if John's worst fears about fame and money were coming true,
inevitably, like a long-dreaded disease that comes at last and spreads as
you know it must. Except for a period during the summer when his illness became so acute that he turned to drinking only buttermilk, both
John and Carol's consumption of liquor increased, especially on weekends, when drinking sometimes began in the morning. There were
fewer old friends around—they felt ill at ease, even unwelcome, in the
new atmosphere—and more new acquaintances and celebrities, people
like Charlie Chaplin, Spencer Tracy, Robert Benchley, Burgess Meredith, Aldous Huxley, and Gerald Heard. Some of the celebrities—
Meredith and Chaplin, for example—he got to know well and liked,
and Benchley, inventive and amusing, was a kindred spirit. It was his
invention that wine bottles be placed at the bottom of the swimming
pool as a test: if you drowned while retrieving a bottle, you had had too
much to drink.

But there were others—wives, mistresses, hangers-on, friends of
friends—that Steinbeck hardly knew and often didn't want to know.
To his old friends he complained about what he called the "swimming
pool set," which he felt was a cancer on his life and work that was
nourished by his wife. Someone he had known for many years recalls:

> He said that she was all for joining the swimming pool set. He said,
> "My friends now who are showing up here aren't my old friends."
> "You don't want to come any more, do you?" he said to me. He
> said, "You don't feel the way you used to about coming here, do
> you?" And I think I was candid and said, "Well things are differ-
> ent." . . . This was a very tormented, tortured time. . . . He once
> said something like, "Carol wants us to join the swimming pool set,
> and you know I'm not one of the swimming pool set and never will
> be." He said, "I want my old friends and don't want the sort of
> people who are dropping in on me, to have a drink. More and more
> of them all the time. They interfere with my work. That's Carol's
> swimming pool, not mine."

He was already beginning to feel the nostalgia for Monterey that
would motivate some of his writing in the future, and he was beginning

to realize, although he would resist knowledge of it for a time, that he couldn't go back. Relationships had changed. He had learned that spreading his good fortune to others—which he usually did bashfully and apologetically—was not always successful. He found that fame seemed to make strained relationships inevitable. If he helped he was damned, and if he didn't he was damned. As he once pointed out, if he went to a gathering of old friends, as he had in the old days, with a gallon of red wine, then he was thought cheap. If he brought a bottle of Scotch, he was thought a snob. So he shrugged his shoulders and said, "What the hell," But it hurt.

Not all of his attempts to help others turned sour. A couple of years earlier he had met a young painter, Ellwood Graham, and when he found out that Graham was strapped for money after moving to the Monterey area, he gave him a job putting a roof on the 11th Street house. The money from that job enabled the painter to start building a house of his own. Steinbeck became very interested in his work and assumed a fatherly concern for his survival, warning him of various problems he would encounter both in trying to succeed and in dealing, later, with success.

The hardest thing, he told him, was to paint or write as you thought you ought to, without regard to the expectations or opinions of others. For Graham, who felt he was about the only abstract painter in the West in those days, the path was not easy. Steinbeck prepared him for such things as "people coming up on the street and just being abstractly mad without really saying anything . . . just because I was painting something different than their Republican minds approved of. He had warned me about all these things, which was kind of paternal and at the same time he felt a little bit shy about doing it."

John commissioned Graham to go to Mexico to paint, and he gave him travel money and enough to live there for several months, on condition that he give Steinbeck his choice of paintings when he returned. When Graham's first child was due to be born, he went to the hospital to make arrangements and found that Steinbeck had already paid the bill. When he went to the doctor, he found that his bill had been paid also. During the period following the publication of *The Grapes of Wrath*, Steinbeck introduced him to Hollywood people, who purchased his paintings, and later in New York after the war, he took him to dinner with editors from *Life* magazine and to various nightclubs and introduced him to the famous and affluent. Throughout, John insisted that he tell no one of his efforts to help him. When Graham felt he was in a position to repay him, Steinbeck refused: " 'No, just pass it along.' There again looking down, shying away, afraid that he would echo the magnificent obsession or something like that."

II

The uproar over *The Grapes of Wrath* did not die down after a few weeks, as Steinbeck had hoped, nor did it die down after a few months. The novel was the number-one best-seller for 1939 and remained among the top sellers for the following year. Its huge sale was somewhat surprising, for as Joseph Henry Jackson pointed out in his essay for the Limited Editions Club, it was not the sort of novel that should have become a best-seller. The very fact that it did, reaching a large audience unused to a book of its kind, was a major reason for the intensity and duration of the controversy. The novel found tens of thousands of

> readers who had never been exposed, for example, to the Jameses, Joyce and Farrell, readers who had grown up through the magazines as far as *Gone With the Wind*, perhaps, or *So Red the Rose*, and who honestly felt themselves betrayed when a best-seller turned out to harbor anything from a turtle which frankly wet the hand of the person who held it to a new mother who shockingly gave her breast to a full-grown man.

Charges of filth against the novel were widespread and led to bannings and burnings in several localities, including Buffalo, New York; East Saint Louis, Illinois; and Kern County, California. (Since these early responses, the book has remained among the most frequently banned, as reported by school and library associations.) But this aspect of the controversy didn't bother Steinbeck nearly as much as the one that was essentially political (although, as Jackson noted, some of the charges of obscenity were no doubt politically inspired).

In light of Steinbeck's almost pathological antipathy toward being personally tied to his work, it was ironic that so much of the attack was directed toward him as an individual, rather than as a critique of his novel. Few novelists have been the recipient of so much personally directed hatred, and of all novelists, he was probably the least able to shrug his shoulders and let the venom run off his back. A variety of epithets were applied to him, describing his character, motives, and ancestry, but the most common were "liar" and "communist." Typical were the comments made in Congress by Representative Lyle Boren: "I say to you, and to every honest, square-minded reader in America, that the painting Steinbeck made in his book is a lie, a black, infernal creation of a twisted, distorted mind." A related charge made by many (including Representative Boren) was that the heart and soul of the book was its obscenity, which had obviously been included in such generous measure in order to sell more books and make more money for the author.

Soon after publication, a large luncheon was held at the Palace Hotel in San Francisco to protest the novel and denounce its author. Presiding over the luncheon was Steinbeck's neighbor in Los Gatos, Ruth Comfort Mitchell. She was the wife of Republican State Senator William Sanborn Young, a shining light of Peninsula society, and a prominent clubwoman, and author of numerous short stories, poems, and novels—all written from what used to be known as a "woman's point of view." She promised to write a reply to Steinbeck's libel of California and set the record straight. Thus when Joe Jackson asked Steinbeck if he would be willing to let the *Chronicle* Sunday magazine do a feature on him and his home, Steinbeck naturally declined but suggested to Jackson, "Tell your man to take the life of Ruth Comfort Mitchell. She is writing a book proving I am a liar. And I'm pretty sure you could work up a nice series in her garden and among the pen women." When Mitchell's novel *Of Human Kindness* appeared, it turned out to be a sentimental depiction of a California farm family that seemed to be based more on low-budget Western movies than on any perception of the problems that had prompted Steinbeck's novel. Her book was really a very sad announcement that neither she nor others of her ilk within the California Establishment had the slightest concept of the misery of the migrants that had been taking place right under their noses.

Throughout the summer and fall after release of his book, Steinbeck's correspondence revealed a continuing consciousness of the attack. At the end of June, for example, he mentioned to Dook that "the Associated Farmers have tried to make me retract things by very sly methods. . . . They have gone to a whispering campaign"; and in July he told Elizabeth that "the Associated Farmers are really working up a campaign. . . . The articles written against me are all by people who admit they haven't read Grapes, indeed wouldn't dirty their minds with it"; in August he reported that "the pressures on me are pretty much. I don't know whether you are seeing the inspired California press on me. I think we will take a long ocean voyage"; and a week later he added, "The Associated Farmers have begun an hysterical personal attack on me both in the papers and a whispering campaign. I'm a Jew, I'm a pervert, a drunk, a dope fiend. They are terrified of the La Follette Committee which will be here soon" [8/28/39]. During the controversy over the novel, "whispering campaigns" were particularly vicious, since they avoided any problems with libel laws. One rumor that gained great currency among conservatives and farmers in California was that Steinbeck was a Jew who was acting for Zionist-communist interests in deliberately trying to undermine the economy.

By the following year, the rumor had spread throughout the country and was apparently believed by many. In May 1940 he received a letter from Reverend L. M. Birkhead, national director of the Friends of Democracy, who described his organization as one devoted to "combatting the pro-Nazi and anti-Semitic propaganda so widespread throughout the country." His group had had inquiries regarding Steinbeck's nationality, Birkhead wrote, and he wondered if Steinbeck could help him refute the charge that *The Grapes of Wrath* was Jewish propaganda.

Steinbeck replied:

I am answering your letter with a good deal of sadness. I am sad for a time when one must know a man's race before his work can be approved or disapproved. It does not seem important to me whether I am Jewish or not, and I know that a statement of mine is useless if an *interested* critic wishes to ride a preconceived thesis. I cannot see how The Grapes of Wrath can be Jewish propaganda but then I have heard it called communist propaganda also.

It happens that I am not Jewish and have no Jewish blood but it only happens that way. I find that I do not experience any pride that it is so. . . .

Yours is only one of many letters I have received on the same subject. It is the first I have answered and I think it is the last. I fully recognize your position and do not in the least blame you for it. I am only miserable for the time and its prejudice that prompts it. [5/7/40]

Although there was a good deal of name-calling and much hysterical oratory and rumor-mongering, actual attempts to refute the substance of the novel in fact were few. Ruth Comfort Mitchell's novel, for all her promises to deal with the situation "without kid gloves," simply ignored the Dust Bowl migration. A promised production by the Associated Farmers, "Plums of Plenty," never materialized. A couple of crackpot pamphlets out of Los Angeles and a statement circulated by the Citizens Association of Bakersfield did little more than deny the truth of conditions pictured in Steinbeck's work.

The most serious attempt at a substantial refutation came in an article published in *Forum* in November 1939 by Frank J. Taylor, called "California's *Grapes of Wrath.*" Taylor's credentials would suggest that he had tried to get at the full truth of the matter (he was a former reporter for the Associated Press and Washington Bureau manager for Scripps-Howard), but although he adopted a tone of calm objectivity, his article followed the line set down by the Associated Farmers. He pointed with pride at the F.S.A. sanitary camps, yet failed to mention that the large growers fought their establishment tooth and nail. Never, apparently, had the farmers and their allies been guilty of callousness or vigilante brutality. On the contrary, Taylor's account was filled with examples of growers' and local officials' kindnesses and Okie ignorance and ingratitude.

The same distorted "facts" used by Taylor were repeated, in briefer form, over and over again in the press, as part of an orchestrated effort to produce what appeared to be a grass-roots rejection of the implications of Steinbeck's novel. A common item in the newspapers of the period was a testimonial letter, purportedly from an Okie or someone who claimed to have worked closely with the migrants, which denied that any of the things pictured in the novel took place. The letters testified to friendly treatment by growers, clean living conditions, and an opportunity to work for anybody who really wanted to work. Even those who identified themselves as Okies were inclined to blame "other" Okies for giving the migrants a bad name by preferring welfare to hard work.

Although this campaign was constant and persistent, the campaign that hurt Steinbeck the most was the rumor spread in the newspapers that the Okies really hated him and had threatened to kill him for telling lies about them. In response to these letters there were others, from California and Oklahoma, that supported the novelist. Some of these made their way to Steinbeck, but few were printed in a predominantly conservative Hearst-Chandler-Copley press.

Since the preponderance of public testimony was against Steinbeck, the general public probably was inclined to believe that the material in the novel was exaggerated, if not deliberately falsified as part of a plot to defame the state or the nation. Though public backing for the novel was meager, Steinbeck did have some help. The publication in mid-1939 of Carey McWilliams's *Factories in the Field* gave indirect comfort to the Steinbeck position by documenting many of the kinds of conditions and events used in the novel. Steinbeck read the book, en-

LIFE

dorsed it as "a complete and documented study of California agriculture, past and present," and sent a statement to his agents, telling them that they could forward it to McWilliams's publisher for use as a blurb. *Life* published a series of Horace Bristol's photographs taken during the trip with Steinbeck to Visalia during the 1937–38 flood, as a way of illustrating the factual nature of the book. Backing also came from Pearl Buck, who praised the novel in a speech to the League of American Writers, and from Eleanor Roosevelt, who testified to the novel's veracity on several occasions.

It was probably Mrs. Roosevelt's statements that produced the most clamor in the press and were most effective in raising the credibility of Steinbeck's work in the public mind. In April 1940, after visiting migrant camps in California, she was asked by a reporter what she thought of the novel's accuracy in depicting migrant conditions, and she replied, "I have never believed that *The Grapes of Wrath* was exaggerated." Steinbeck wrote to her: "May I thank you for your words. I have been called a liar so constantly that sometimes I wonder whether I may not have dreamed the things I saw and heard in the period of my research" [4/24/40].

The most convincing evidence, however, came too late to help Steinbeck—and too late to help the migrant workers. Enough controversy had been generated regarding violence used against striking farm workers in California to interest Wisconsin Senator Robert M. La Follette, Jr., a leader in the passage of the National Labor Relations Act and active in investigations into violations of workers' civil rights. Under his chairmanship, the Senate Committee on Education and Labor held a series of hearings in California starting in late 1939 and continuing through the early part of 1940. The committee's report,

> based on testimony and records from the Associated Farmers, government and law enforcement officials and others, detailed the "shocking degree of human misery" among farm workers and thoroughly exposed the violent tactics used by the Associated Farmers in carrying out the organization's openly admitted policy of taking the law into its own hands.
>
> The committee charged the Associated Farmers with "the most flagrant and violent infringement of civil liberties," through use of espionage, blacklisting, strikebreaking, brutality and "sheer vigilanteeism." It concluded that because of the activities of the organization and local law enforcement officers, "The civil rights of strikers, unions, union organizers, outsiders and many of the agri-

cultural laborers in California to speak, assemble, organize into unions and bargain are repeatedly and flagrantly violated."

Unfortunately, the report, which recommended that the Labor Relations Act be extended to include farm workers, was not issued until October 1942. By then, World War II was under way and most of the American farm workers either went into the Army or to jobs in the San Francisco shipyards or the Los Angeles aircraft plants. The controversy over the migrants was forgotten and replaced by concern for the growers, who lacked the work force to produce food essential to the war effort.

To meet this need, the bracero program was initiated in 1942, bringing hundreds of thousands of Mexican nationals every year into California and the Southwest to work in the fields and then be shipped back to Mexico. The braceros were supposed to form a supplemental work force, but in fact, since they were so easily controlled, the growers made them the primary work force, displacing U.S. citizens, both Chicano and Anglo, who would be more inclined to demand better pay and working conditions. For twenty-two years a total of four and a half million braceros were brought across the border, and when the program was ended in the mid-sixties, the effort to organize farm workers had to begin all over again from the beginning. Nothing had changed. Organizers for Cesar Chavez went into the white middle-class community in an effort to drum up support for the Delano grape strike. They mentioned *The Grapes of Wrath*, as historical evidence, trying to revive old passions for a new battle.

III

Steinbeck's reaction to the long controversy was not only outrage and extended depression, but a growing repugnance for the whole topic and everything connected with it. It wore him out, even though he refused to participate actively, and drove him to despair—he began to believe he might be through as a writer. On October 16, 1939, he wrote in his journal,

It is one year less ten days that I finished the first draft of the Grapes. Then we came up here to the ranch and then my leg went bad and I had ten months of monstrous pain until the poison from the infection was gone. This is a year without writing (except for little jobs—mechanical fixings).

And on October 19:

> The last two days I have had death premonitions so strong that I burned all the correspondence of years. I have a horror of people going through it, messing around in my past, such as it is. I burned it all. I think now I have left no vestige of writing except the few notes scattered through the ledgers and my work.

There was no great "turning point" in his work. Even if he had not been subject to so much personal abuse and publicity, he still would not have continued with the same subject matter. But the pressure on him did make it difficult for him to right himself so that he could take another tack. He worked hard to extricate himself, feeling that if he could withdraw his name from circulation, he might be able to escape. With only two exceptions (one was the preface to Tom Collins's book, which was never published), he adamantly refused to be connected to the migrant problem or to any of the hundreds of other liberal causes that asked for his endorsement.

The other, and most important, exception that he made to his rule was the "John Steinbeck Committee" formed by Helen Gahagan Douglas and other Hollywood celebrities to raise money for migrant relief. To aid their cause, he had ten copies of *Grapes* leather bound with an extra page tipped into the front that said, "This book, one of an edition of ten, made and bound at the request of John Steinbeck for presentation to ————." After the books were auctioned off at a banquet, he filled in the name of the purchaser and signed his own. Burgess Meredith recalls that Steinbeck attended several fund-raising dinners during this period, but on no other occasion did he allow his name to be used.

In a way, his reaction to those who sought his support was like that of a child who had touched a hot stove. But there was a conscious concern, beyond the worry that his ability to write might be somehow compromised or destroyed, that he would be dragged into a political thicket against his will. He hated to be branded or categorized, and above all, he feared being labeled forever as a social-political writer. He was particularly wary of attempts by the Marxists to adopt and use him. In the fall of 1939, Helen Hosmer, the head of the Simon J. Lubin Society (which had published from his *News* articles the pamphlet *Their Blood Is Strong*), came to visit Steinbeck at the ranch. She brought with her the Marxist-radical Anna Louise Strong, who, although she had met Steinbeck briefly in earlier days, had expressed a desire to Hosmer to arrange an interview so that she could talk to him at length.

Hosmer called and Steinbeck said, yes, come along. When they arrived, Hosmer recalls suddenly realizing that

> he was under terrific restraints—nervous as hell and incensed about her being in his house. He had closed up and didn't want to talk anymore. . . . His wife, Carol, underwent a deep sea change in this period. She had taken her piano and painted it shocking pink, and she was doing kind of crazy things and talking about the big times they had. Anna Louise Strong was bitterly disappointed in the interview because the one thing in the world he didn't want to be identified with was the Reds. He suspected me of being a Red and he knew she was, and as I say, he was a jittery man that afternoon. . . . The whole time Anna Louise Strong was trying to coax information out of him, and he was resisting every inch of the way. He was terribly glad when we left. I could see relief all over his face.

One might have thought that if the reactions to *Grapes* had been more generally positive and if there had been less personal abuse, he might have enjoyed what many others in the same position would have considered a great success. But he hated the very idea of being a best-selling author, and when *Grapes* fell from first place on the weekly lists, he celebrated. Thus at the height of his "success" as a novelist, he was plotting to turn away from it completely and study science. There was no fame or money to be gained from writing about invertebrates: one western regional text was published only because of the subsidy of a grant; another, Ricketts and Calvin's *Between Pacific Tides* came out in an edition of only a thousand copies and went out of print three years later (a second edition came out in 1948). Collecting sea animals was the sort of activity that might have been prescribed by a doctor to relieve Steinbeck's ragged state of mind and emotions, but he did not approach it as a temporary change of scene or as a hobby. He was serious. This was to be his new work, and for him, the work itself and its integrity was everything.

The first thing he felt was his ignorance. He wrote to Elizabeth Otis in October, "The last year has been a nightmare all in all. But now I'm ordering a lot of books to begin study. And I'll work in the laboratory." When Pat Covici came to visit in November, Steinbeck explained his plans for the future. Covici became increasingly more polite, as he tended to do whenever it was necessary for him to hide disappointment, but nevertheless, he was supportive enough to suggest that the writer order his books from now on through him, since he had a large discount on their purchase.

Steinbeck changed his mode of living. He stayed in Pacific Grove and worked at the lab during the week (sometimes Carol went with him), and spent the weekends on the ranch. In mid-November he wrote to Dook about the new direction he was taking:

> It's pretty early in the morning. I got up to milk the cow.
> I'm finishing off a complete revolution. It's amazing how every one piled in to regiment me, to make a symbol of me, to regulate my life and work. I've just tossed the whole thing overboard. I never let anyone interfere before and I can't see why I should now. This ultimate freedom receded. I'm keeping more of it than I need or even want, like a reservoir. The two most important [freedoms], I suppose—at least they seem so to me—are freedom from respectability and most important—freedom from the necessity of being consistent. Lack of those two can really tie you down. Of course all this publicity has been bad if I tried to move about but here on the ranch it has no emphasis. People up here—the few we see—don't read much and don't remember what they read, and my projected work is not likely to create any hysteria.
> It's funny, Dook. I know what in a vague way this work is about. I mean I know its tone and texture and to an extent its field and I find that I have no education. I have to go back to school in a way. I'm completely without mathematics and I have to learn something about abstract mathematics. I have some biology but must have much more and the twins bio-physics and bio-chemistry are closed to me. So I have to go back and start over. I bought half the stock in Ed's lab which gives me equipment, a teacher, a library to work in.
> I'm going on about myself but in a sense it's more than me—it's you and everyone else. The world is sick now. There are things in the tide pools easier to understand than Stalinist, Hitlerite, Democrat, capitalist confusion, and voodoo. So I'm going to those things which are relatively more lasting to find a new basic picture. I have too a conviction that a new world is growing under the old, the way a new finger nail grows under a bruised one. I think all the economists and sociologists will be surprised some day to find that they did not forsee nor understand it. Just as the politicos of Rome could not have forseen that the social-political-ethical world for two thousand years would grow out of the metaphysical gropings of a few quiet poets. I think the same thing is happening now. Communist, Fascist, Democrat may find that the real origin of the future lies on the microscope plates of obscure young men, who,

puzzled with order and disorder in quantum and neutron, build gradually a picture which will seep down until it is the fibre of the future.

The point of all this is that I must make a new start. I've worked the novel—I know it as far as I can take it. I never did think much of it—a clumsy vehicle at best. And I don't know the form of the new but I know there is a new which will be adequate and shaped by the new thinking. Anyway, there is a picture of my confusion. How is yours? [11/13/39]

Steinbeck's plan, which had been in the back of his mind at least as far back as the writing of the final draft of *Grapes*, projected two investigations, which would result in two books. The first object of study would be the littoral of the San Francisco Bay area. This would lead to a high-school-level textbook that could also be used by the layman-collector. John and Ed's idea was that this project would serve as the "laboratory" part of John's education. The book would be primarily Steinbeck's, produced under Ed's tutelage, and also serve the purpose of establishing John's credibility in the eyes of the scientific community. (This part of the plan was naive in respect to the intense snobbery of many professional scientists. Biologists at U.C. Berkeley didn't even consider Ed a professional, but referred to him as a "collector.") Following this project—which amounted to a "degree program" to give John an education and credentials—a larger and more sophisticated investigation was planned for the Gulf of California. The book resulting from this expedition was the major target, a publication which they hoped would be an important contribution to basic scientific knowledge. They also talked of other areas for investigation, beyond the Gulf of California, and as far as Steinbeck was concerned, his career in science stretched out indefinitely.

During the late fall of 1939 and the winter of 1939–40, he spent most of his time reading and studying, helped Ed with the routine lab work, and worked on the equipment for their field trips. During November and early December they took several brief collecting trips to the Bay area and planned a major trip of several days for the end of the month. With the work, Steinbeck's spirits began to revive. He wrote to Elizabeth in the middle of December:

Now—the collecting. I got a truck and we are equipping it. We don't go to Mexico until March, but we have the handbook to do first and we'll go north in about a week I guess for the solstice tides.

It will be a tough job and I'm not at all sure we can get it done by March. And I have a terrific job of reading to do. Ricketts is all right but I am a popular writer and I have to build some trust in the minds of biologists. This handbook will help to do that. The Mexican book will be interesting to a much larger audience, and there is no question that Viking can have it.

Yesterday we went to Berkeley with a design for our traveling refrigeration plant and it is being built. Also ordered a Bausch and Lomb SKW microscope. This is a beauty with a side bar and drum nose piece. Primarily a dissecting microscope. My dream for some time in the future is a research scope with an oil immersion lens, but that costs about 600 dollars and I'm not getting it right now. The SKW will be fine for the trip. But that research model, Oh boy! Oh boy! Sometime I'll have one. It may interest you to know that business at the lab is picking up. I can't tell you what all this means to me, in happiness and energy. I was washed up and now I'm alive again, with work to be done and worth doing.

It is clear that getting back to work was not the only thing that was making him happy—as ever, he was the enthusiast in response to tools, gadgets, and working equipment of all kinds. He found particular joy in outfitting the truck that he and Ed were going to use on their expeditions, another in that series of research vehicles that stretched from the bakery wagon of *Grapes* to Rocinante of *Charley*. This truck also had a name, of sorts, which reflected his current enthusiasm:

Last night [he wrote to Covici] we had our Christmas with Carol's parents and tomorrow we set out north on a verification trip, the solstice tides being right for five days. So Xmas will find us in rubber boots and slickers, in the littoral north of San Francisco.

And the equipment of the truck goes on, beautiful equipment, a tiny pump, a small refrigeration plant, small aquaria, and a beautiful new microscope, bookcases and typing stands. All mounted in the truck. Very pretty. Insignia is $\sqrt[7]{-(R+S)^2}$. Don't think about this too much. It will drive you crazy. We don't want any publicity on any of this. It would be wrong. [12/22/39]

After finishing their work of collecting the most common species of "marine invertebrates occurring between extreme high and extreme low tide levels in the area extending from the northern tip of Tomales Bay to Half Moon Bay on the coast of California," John and Ed drove the truck straight through to Monterey and began the tasks of identifying and writing up the specimens. Ricketts had tentatively outlined the text as 200 to 250 pages long and containing three sections: a series of essays on general principles, a detailed description of animals, and an annotated bibliography. During the last part of December and throughout January of 1940, both Ed and John wrote material for the book—John, a preface and 3,000 words for the essay section, and Ed, 5,000 words for the essays. Apparently, John was to combine his contribution to the discussion of general principles with Ed's, just as he actually did later in writing *The Log*, and then go on to write the animal descriptions for the second part of the text. In his working notes for the project, Ed had written, "Jon [*sic*] can make better descriptions than have ever been made."

Steinbeck's draft for the general essays has not survived, but we do have copies of what he called "Second Try of Opening Preface." Handwritten on eleven pages of ledger paper (and unfinished), the manuscript established several basic tenets of what might be called the Ricketts-Steinbeck philosophy, which were subsequently carried on through *The Log from the "Sea of Cortez"* and *Cannery Row*. After his introductory paragraph, he begins a discussion of the relativity of observation, writing in part:

> All observers viewing external reality through eyes set in a conditional thinking pattern will of necessity bring some residue of that pattern to the reality. Such a process however it may distort the object is never the less a creative association between observer and object, and such a process far from being limited to the naive, is, with relative intensity, of course, the inevitable product of all human observation.

The "creative association between observer and object" may remind us of the essential spirit behind the composition of *Cannery Row*, in which the author introduces us to that microcosm, that "tidepool" community, which can be either a stinking industrial slum or a poem, depending on which "peephole" the observer happens to be looking through.

As the preface continues, Steinbeck's recent reading in the history of science becomes apparent when he points to the misconceptions of earlier biologists whose expectations structured their vision: "With the coming of the microscope, good scientists, knowing in advance that humanoids were completely formed in sperm or ova, saw them there and drew them seated comfortably, with crossed legs and with gentle anticipatory smiles on their tiny faces." He concludes the first part of his preface by reminding the reader that he must "realize deeply that human knowledge is relational, as fluid and changing as the reality it refracts. . . . Under 20th century pressures, economic and sociologic, what nonsense may not some of our scientists be setting down."

If his purpose with the book was to establish his credentials with the scientific community, perhaps it was just as well that this material was never published. He may have been overly optimistic when he wrote to Covici that he thought the introduction he was writing was good, and "while there are heresies in it, I think they will all stand scrutiny by any except the crustiest minds" [1/20/40].

The second part of the preface introduces the ecological whole and the associational pattern within the whole, comparing the interrelationships in the tidepool to those established in a large city. Too often, he declares, the observer, frightened by the complexity of the entire picture, has picked out only one small group for study and thus becomes the specialist. Such a narrowing of focus, however, is like picking out one family in New York for study, but, he says, "there remains the city as a whole." Consciousness of the entire pattern and its inner associations has not been traditionally a part of the instruction for the beginning observer and has been probably the least investigated aspect of biology. He concludes:

> In this handbook the attempt has been to list and describe the common animals within their associational pattern. The picture cannot be very complete but its arrangement is intended as a suggested view point from which the student while seeing the family will not lose sight of the city. This is valuable as well as interesting for, just as a man's life is closely bound up in the material and social life of his city, with its climate, its water supply, its swamp or altitude, its politics, factories, its food supply and transportation, so is the life of each individual in the tidepool inextricably relative and related to every surrounding environmental factor.

Joel Hedgpeth has suggested that work on this text may have been abandoned because a competing text, S. F. Light's *Laboratory and Field Text in Invertebrate Zoology*, was published in 1941. However, another possibility is brought out in a note Steinbeck sent to Covici at the end of February:

> In a letter to Elizabeth, I passed the word for you to forget the hand book until it is in your hands. It is a long and painful job.

When and if we get to Mexico, we'll put it away for the while. Very difficult work, for every little part must be checked again and again. Our permits to go long the Mexican coast have not come yet so we do not even know whether or not we can go.

As they considered the "Mexican trip" more closely, they came to the conclusion that it would be impossible to survey the Gulf shore by truck and that the survey would have to be made by boat. Considerations of weather made it imperative that any seagoing expedition in that area be conducted in March and April, and further work on the handbook was necessarily postponed.

And although he wrote, "This difficult work is good for me. The discipline is good," there is the suggestion in his letters that he was becoming impatient. He felt under pressure to make his descriptions extremely accurate—otherwise the credibility he was trying to achieve would be lost. And while collecting expeditions and the equipment appealed to him, the routine of very demanding, close study rather quickly lost its attractiveness. Like all designs for self-improvement, it held more pleasure in contemplation than in execution.

Nevertheless, in his writing for the handbook he made for the first time an explicit commitment to an ecological view of the world and man's place in it, a commitment that had been implicit in his writing from almost the beginning. He became the only major literary figure of his time to embrace and bring to his writing one of the most—if not *the* most—important concepts of the twentieth century, a concept that has changed radically the way man views himself and his relationship to his environment. As a novelist, he was entering uncharted territory: in those days, it was an approach and philosophy endorsed by relatively few biological scientists; and as far as the literary world was concerned, it could have been a Martian religion. He didn't realize—nor would he have cared, if he had—that he was on the road to offending nearly everyone. He had already offended the "decency," the local pride, and the political convictions of much of Middle America. He was now on his way toward offending all those religionists who insisted on the central role of man in God's plan, as well as all those, such as the intellectual humanists, who simply insisted on man.

In this sense we could consider him a radical: he was an individualist who ignored the appetites, expectations, and prejudices of his potential audience to pursue those truths presented to him through his experience. Like one of his favorite literary characters, Don Quixote, having been beaten about the head and shoulders by his enemies, he had suffered more for lack of a new quest than from his wounds. When he needed inspiration, Ed Ricketts gave him not only something to think about but something to do with his hands. During his internship with Ed, his generalized, holistic view of the universe was given specific biological substance, as Ed convinced him that ecology was both an important and a much-neglected truth—perhaps the key to the future.

As Steinbeck wrote to Dook in November 1939, "Communist, Fascist, Democrat may find that the real origin of the future lies on the microscope plates of obscure young men, who, puzzled with order and disorder in quantum and neutron, build gradually a picture which will seep down until it is the fibre of the future." As he would suggest in various works over the next decade and a half, the best way to understand man may be, paradoxically, to look not at man but through microscope or telescope—or in the tidepool. In his essay for the proposed text, Ed had written: "Who would see a replica of man's social structure has only to examine the abundant and various life of the tidepools, where miniature communal societies wage dubious battle against equally potent societies in which the individual is paramount, with trends shifting, maturing, or dying out, with all the living organisms balanced against the limitations of the dead kingdom of rocks and currents and temperatures and dissolved gases."

These and other ideas from the aborted handbook were carried over, to be expressed first in the *Log* of the Mexican trip and then in *Cannery Row* (and in several later novels). In a sense, the material written for the Bay area text could be considered a first draft for the *Log*, and the *Log*, in turn, became the foundation for the novel. *Cannery Row*—that strange, neglected, often misunderstood little book—may be the only thoroughly non-teleological novel ever written, and certainly the only one to use the ecology of the seashore as its central metaphor.

CHAPTER XXIV

lthough there was serious work for much of every day, in the late afternoons and evenings the life of the lab was much as it had been in the old days, and the Row, or "Ocean Front Street" as it was called at that time, still had its characters who tried to con Ed out of a bottle of beer or money for a drink. In order to escape them, he had taken to getting into his car and backing across the street to Wing Chong's to buy his beer. If he ran out late at night, he simply walked directly across the way to Flora's, where the bar was open twenty-four hours a day. Sometimes he and Steinbeck would go over together to sit and drink beer and talk to Flora and her girls. Although later criticized for sentimentalizing Flora and her establishment, Steinbeck was right on the mark in showing her as kind and generous, and her girls were young, pretty, and "nice." Perhaps there is another kind of sentimentality in thinking that prostitutes have to be hard and nasty.

Many of the same people dropped by the lab, plus Barbara and Ellwood Graham and, occasionally, one of Steinbeck's more recent friends, Burgess Meredith or Lewis Milestone. They sprawled about in Ed's office or in the living room/bedroom/library/music room next to it, drinking wine or beer, swapping stories, and listening to records. Such serious discussion as there was tended to gravitate toward world affairs, particularly Hitler's takeover of Europe.

Every evening at news time they gathered around the radio. The newscaster, Gabriel Heatter, ended each program with a prediction, and for the honor of the clan, it was necessary that someone get to the radio and turn it off before the prediction could be made. They would be lounging in various positions, mostly on the floor, when suddenly the voice in the box would intone, "I . . ." and everyone would screech, "Aieeh! The prediction!" and catapult themselves toward the radio, grasping for the knob.

Current events provided other diversions. There were two or three very serious Party members who came by regularly and with evangelical zeal attempted, by argument and interpretation of world news, to make what converts they could. They seemed particularly anxious to enlist artists, and they never seemed to give up on John, whom they considered a major catch. Although most of those who frequented the lab had some sympathy for socialist principles, none could take seriously the Moscow line with its jargon about "international banking" and its constant shifts of position. The line changed so often during this period of the Hitler-Stalin Pact and the invasion of Finland that any poor salesman who came around could be easily baited. The group would pretend that it didn't know about the change, and going back to what he had argued a week or two weeks before, they would very earnestly tell him, "Pete, after thinking it over, we've decided you were right after all." Then they would sit back and watch him squirm.

Steinbeck gave money to the cause of "Little Finland" (earlier he had given for Republican ambulances in Spain), probably to combat the constant editorial charge that he was a "tool of Moscow." This action earned him the outrage of such acquaintances as Ella Winter ("Little Finland, indeed!"), who could clearly see Finland as a fascist threat to socialist democracy and who had no difficulty in rationalizing the division of Poland.

There were other unwelcome visitors. Even before the publication of *The Log* and *Cannery Row*, which made the lab an unwilling tourist attraction, there were the curious, usually women, respectable members of the establishment of that day, who had heard that it was "quaint." Perhaps because the lab was ostensibly a place of business open to the public, they would come by and expect to be given a tour. Ed would let them in and they would walk about, saying things like, "How charming!" in affected Boston accents. Then, almost inevitably, they would notice one of Ed's specimens which was mounted over the door. "Oh, what's that, Mr. Ricketts?" they would ask. "Oh that's the foreskin of a whale," he would reply. But no matter what he said or did, he seemed to have an incredible attractiveness for women, who appeared to flock to him by the dozens. Perhaps it was the somewhat incongruous combination of gentle innocence and vital sensuality that brought them to his door. From Flora's across the street, the girls had a picture-window view of the activity at the lab, and they marveled at the number and variety of expensive cars that drove up and parked at all times of the day and night and the well-dressed ladies who came calling. Here, certainly, was a man who had no need for their services—on the other hand, they had to wonder, how many of these ladies' husbands were patrons of their establishment just across the street?

The group at the lab also did not much care for the person who came there carrying his talent on his back. It was an unspoken rule that no one should, in the evening, get too serious about what he was doing during the day. If one spoke about his work at all, it must be self-deprecating and in jest. There were several running jokes about the handbook in progress. One had to do with inventing names appropriate to the characteristics of new species (and sometimes inventing species to fit a good name). Such a playful discussion produced the name *Proctophilus winchellii*, (after Walter Winchell, a radio commentator who specialized in sensationalism and gossip), which, as Steinbeck explained in *The Log*, was "a new species of commensal fish which lives in the anus of a cucumber, flipping in and out, possibly feeding on the feces of the host but more likely merely hiding in the anus from possible enemies."

Ellwood Graham recalls that Steinbeck, only very occasionally, would take him aside and gruffly ask, "What are you working on now—something I can see?" He didn't want Graham to talk about it, just to show it to him when he was ready. But Ed and John did keep track of Graham's paintings, and if they talked about them at all, it was to select appropriate titles. One they named "My Dog Rover, My Dog All Over." Another, of a naked blonde on a couch, they called "Northwest Passage." Graham kept the titles, but when a museum in the East hung the picture of the girl, the curator changed the title to "Nude Reclining."

As March approached, work on the San Francisco handbook stopped altogether as preparations for the Mexican expedition intensified. Since John was financing the trip, he had taken over the responsibility for most of the arrangements and the purchase of equipment and supplies. One needs to think of one's own preparations for a long summer vacation, and then multiply that a hundredfold, in order to appreciate the planning, the list-making, the packing, and the running back and forth to purchase last-minute-realized necessities. Two of the most important aspects of the preparations remained in doubt until only a short period before they had planned to leave: for quite some time he was unable either to find a boat or to get the necessary permits from the Mexican government. Acquiring the permits became an extended struggle with government bureaucracy, as Ed and John wrote to the U.S. State Department, the Mexican Consul in San Francisco, and to friends in Mexico. Eventually the red tape was cut by a friend who knew the Mexican ambassador in Washington, D.C.

Locating a boat also required persistence. Although the sardine season was over and there were nearly a hundred purseiners tied up at Monterey, none of the skippers could find it in his heart to risk unfamiliar waters for so frivolous a reason as the collection of seashore animals. John asked Toby Street to look for a boat, and after he had talked to twenty-five or thirty owners without success, John began to worry. Finally, he went to the boat owners' association and was referred to Tony Berry, a captain who had only recently come down from Washington with his boat, the *Western Flyer*. Berry was not yet a member of the association and needed the work; furthermore, he had sailed in Mexican waters, although not the Gulf, and had no great prejudice against marine scientists, having worked with them before.

Nearly new and well-maintained, the *Western Flyer* was a clean, good-looking boat. What drew Steinbeck's admiration was that the engine and engine room were spotless and the tools, something that always caught his attention, were all polished and hung up, each in its place. The engine was an Atlas Diesel, a 165-horsepower six, which was fairly small for a seventy-six-foot boat. Topside, there was a wheel forward, with a flying bridge and another wheel above. Behind the wheel was a little stateroom, normally used by the captain, followed by two sleeping compartments and the galley. Aft of the deckhouse was the fish-hold hatch (the fifty-foot-long hold below would be used to store the specimens after they had been pickled and ticketed) and near the stern was the roller and turntable for the net.

There were, all together, bunks for twelve, although only seven would be needed for the expedition. In addition to John, Ed, and the captain, there were three crew members and, even though she is not mentioned in her husband's narrative of the journey, Carol. For the crew they first signed Tex Travis as engineer, a tall, deliberate, down-to-earth Texan who had learned about diesels as a teenager while working at the power station of a small Texas town. Unpretentious and thoroughly competent, Tex was the kind of man that Steinbeck could take an immediate liking to, and Tex, in turn, became genuinely fond of the writer, even forgiving him for being "some kind of half-assed communist." "John and I," he recalls, "was partners of the boat. I mean we was real partners."

They both bunked in the engine room and shared the same watch.

On their shift, in the middle of the night, Travis would check the engines and then come up on deck, where John was at the wheel, standing in the green glow of the compass and peering out at the blackness ahead through the smoke from a cigarette clamped in the side of his mouth. During the long hours they talked to pass the time. John told him about Salinas, about going to college, and about working for Hearst in New York and getting "canned." And, putting on a bit about being an old sailor—a role he relished throughout his life—he talked about his time as a workaway on the boat from New York to San Francisco.

Some time toward the end of the trip, John told him, "Well Tex, you and I are going to buy a boat together." They made plans to get the boat, and they talked about how Tex would manage it. Most of the time the boat would be used for commercial fishing, but such a boat might be fitted up in such a way that it could be converted to a laboratory to be used for expeditions such as the one they were on. John wondered how a boat could be so designed as to serve such a dual function, for another of his several roles was that of inventor.

Most of the things he invented were little devices, conveniences, easily fashioned for his own use or the use of his friends. A special bracket for holding something, a pouch and strap for a cigarette lighter, a different kind of frame for reading glasses. Usually, the big things, like a dual-purpose boat, he only dreamed about.

But a rather ambitious project that he spent much time on prior to the trip was the invention and construction of a portable laboratory office. Among the items most lovingly described in his account of the voyage in *The Log* are the equipment, supplies, and books that were packed on board, and the "strong, steel-reinforced wood case" that he had designed as a field library-office to be used in a truck or on a boat. Its main value was "its compactness, completeness, and accessibility"—virtues that were usually on his mind as he attempted to organize his immediate environment, whether writing room or workshop. In a sense his own mind was organized like his steel-reinforced wood case or like an old-fashioned rolltop desk, with secret drawers and odd-shaped compartments and pigeonholes in which he stored experiences and sensations, bits and pieces of information, and words and phrases. Years after acquiring something, he could roll open the desk, reach in, and find precisely what he needed.

His field office had a front that hinged down to form a desk, which could hold a drawing board or portable typewriter. At the back there was room for twenty large books and two filing cases, and around the sides and top there were various cubbyholes for stationery, rolled-up maps, and a card file. Unfortunately, the unit had been designed prior to the charter, and as it turned out, there was no place on the *Western Flyer* to put it so that it could be used—no tabletop or bunk would hold it. So it ended up lashed to the top of the deckhouse and covered with a tarpaulin. Nevertheless, it was a noble invention, one that suggests Steinbeck might have been quite content to change places with Robinson Crusoe, at least until the living quarters, tools, and equipment had been provided for.

The rest of the crew consisted of Sparky Enea and Tiny Colletto, both hired as seamen, although Sparky's classification changed as the voyage got under way. Enea was a short, heavyset, garrulous Italian (who later became Tony Berry's brother-in-law). Men named "Tiny" are usually huge, but Colletto, a workaway for the trip, was five feet two. He was tough and outspoken—an ex-boxer. Once Steinbeck had secured a boat, the project seemed to catch the imagination of the whole community, and not only were there sailors, like Tiny, who were willing to go without pay, but a variety of acquaintances, artists and businessmen—some even with sailing experience—who wanted to go for the adventure of it. Many would have paid in order to go, but they weren't asked.

Carol was to come as cook, and she ran into problems almost immediately. Used to scrimping and saving for years, she ordered hardly enough food to last for a week—she planned on small, economical meals to be supplemented by fish that would (she hoped) be caught along the way. When the crew got on board to settle in, the Steinbecks almost had a mutiny before leaving port. Berry wanted to fire Carol as cook and hire Sparky, who had cooked previously on tuna boats, but Steinbeck said no, just have Sparky buy the groceries. Instead of one hundred dollars' worth, Sparky brought on board more than eight hundred dollars' worth of groceries, and Carol flew into a rage. Berry consoled her by promising to buy back from her everything over fifty-dollars' worth that might be left over. As it turned out, if they hadn't restocked in Guaymas, they wouldn't have made it.

Captain Berry was, as Steinbeck indicates in his narrative, a very serious young man. Above all he cared about his boat, and he judged the others on the trip as they related to its welfare and the efficiency of its operation. Of the crew members he particularly approved of Tex, and of the passengers, John. He liked Steinbeck's attitude and skill, and his obvious special regard for boats. "A boat," John notes at the beginning of his account of their journey, "more than any other tool [man] uses is a little representation of an archetype. There is an 'idea' boat that is an emotion, and because the emotion is so strong it is probably that no other tool is made with so much honesty as a boat."

Steinbeck's deep affection for both the boat as machine and the sea and shore as a "garden" unspoiled by technology or technological wastes is indicative of a deep schism in attitude or feeling, of which he seemed largely unconscious, although it is reflected in much of his writing. Like Mark Twain, he was enamored of the natural river, of the power and symbolic implications of the steamboat, and of the technical skill of the pilot—and did not necessarily or always perceive these as contradictory. In part the schism was bridged by Steinbeck's sense that the tools of science were simply extensions of man's attempt to see better. The boat was to him in function like a microscope or telescope. He appears to have drawn a distinction in his attitude between the technology of discovery and the technology of exploitation, and he does not seem to have been particularly concerned with the usual process whereby one leads to the other. A further link was provided between his own internal order (as we have seen reflected in his carefully designed field office), a similar order imposed by the function of the boat, and the order that he had set out on this trip to discover in nature.

Once the trip began, it became apparent to all who was in charge. Berry recalls that Steinbeck had the whole trip figured out in advance—time of year to go, temperatures they would have, and sailing times. As far as the captain was concerned, Steinbeck was the backbone of the voyage, the main push: "If not for him," he recalls, "we wouldn't have collected anything." The writer would tell Berry, "Be at so and so place by such and such time." He would remain sober while others were drinking, and he often took Ricketts's watch with Berry in addition to his regular turn with Tex. The captain was impressed that Steinbeck already knew how to steer, knew the compass and the stars.

The writer insisted before, during, and after, that the trip was "for Ed," but in fact it was a voyage he had to make for himself. He needed to bring his life and his work back into focus, to refurbish them through the cleansing agents of discipline and nature, and he approached the task with a fierce determination fueled by the messy, painful, dislocating experiences of recent months. He transmitted to the others a sense that he knew what had to be done, they were going to do it, and by God he was paying for it. And, whether he was totally conscious of it or not, he was fulfilling a pattern established in recent years of obtaining material for writing on the basis of the observations of a field trip, rather than mining personal experience. It led to the objective sort of writing he was most comfortable with.

Although Steinbeck's determination and competence won Berry's approval, most of the others did not fare so well. The captain, as Tex remembers him, "was a very hard man to please," although Tex managed to do so most of the time. Tiny and Sparky, though nearly the same age as the captain, were treated by him somewhat like wayward teenage sons—with some affection but a good deal more concern. Carol, as the lone woman and a wife of one of the men on board, he viewed with apprehension, and he had no use for Ricketts whatsoever—he didn't pull his weight and was soused most of the time. "If Ricketts had had his way," the captain judged, "he would have gone down and anchored for six weeks and had a vacation." The crew was more charitable. They didn't know quite what to make of Ricketts but found him pleasant enough. Tex had the idea that he was some kind of professor who had been fired from Stanford, and so when Ed did rather eccentric things, like sit in a tub taking a bath for two or three hours at a time out on deck, Tex viewed them as activities that might be habitual for a type unfamiliar to him.

The departure of the *Western Flyer* was a much-celebrated event. The entire stock of hard liquor, whiskey that had been purchased for the stores against the possibility of some dire medical emergency far away from civilization, was all consumed in port, as relatives, friends, and a few complete strangers crowded on the boat prior to sailing. Stories were told for years afterward about the quantities of booze consumed that day, and there are some who will swear that as the *Western Flyer* left harbor, dozens of bottles trailed in its wake marking its passage past the breakwater out into the open sea. There were even those who, out of an overdeveloped sense of the picturesque, imagined the trail extending further, to the very top of the Gulf of California. Much of the community had joined the expedition in spirit, and many of the tales of orgy and excess which have become attached to the trip can be attributed to the wishful thinking of those left behind.

The local newspaper even sent a reporter and photographer to record the departure for the men and women who missed the party. When a group photo was taken of the voyagers (plus Berry's wife and minus Ricketts), Steinbeck stood in back and hid behind his wife. This behavior mystified Sparky, who was glad to become famous, and he asked the writer what he was doing. Steinbeck explained that he did not want his face known any more than necessary. If his picture was readily attainable, it could be used as a way of identifying him for blackmail purposes. Throughout the voyage, he made sure that whenever still or moving pictures were made, he was either taking the picture or behind the camera.

As soon as they left Monterey—on March 11, 1940—Carol locked herself in her private stateroom for a day and a half, and Sparky took over the cooking until they arrived in San Diego. Toby Street had come with them that far—a participation he wished he could have extended—and there was another, more minor and more subdued farewell party and steak dinner. As they fueled the boat and took on fresh meat, ice, and a new supply of beer, they noted the extensive preparations by the Navy for war. The sight of ships and planes, bombs and torpedoes, being readied for inevitable conflict, to a certain extent set the tone for their final departure. It became a last-chance trip, a precious time before some kind of curtain would fall and things would change forever. Suddenly, as John wrote, "This little expedition had become tremendously important to us; we felt a little as though we were dying."

II

To enter the Gulf of California is to enter another world, a strange, nearly deserted area, lost in time and largely cut off from modern commerce. Its warm temperatures, ultra-blue water, and sudden, often violent storms are reminiscent of the tropics, but for the most part, the vegetation is sparse, dry, and stunted. Here and there, near a spring, a ramshackle ranch, a tiny village of one-room makeshift houses, a palm tree flourishes, but aside from these, the Baja peninsula seems to be without trees. Although there is heavy rainfall at times in the barren mountains, there are no rivers, as such, and very few all-season creeks. More generally, rivulets dry up before the rain has stopped, and springs, sometimes hot out of the bowels of the earth, trickle down rock ledges and through sharp ravines, only to disappear into the sand and dust below.

Airplanes bring tourists to La Paz, near the end of the peninsula, and to Guaymas on the mainland, but the gleaming white hotels of a new Waikiki or Riviera have been slow to materialize. Elsewhere Indians fish the deserted waters of the upper Gulf, a few Mexicans resist the easy money of Tijuana or Calexico to scratch out a bare living from the land, and American oil and tire companies sponsor races down the peninsula, "the toughest test of all."

The shoreline is ragged and rocky in some places, matching the land; in others, yellow or nearly white sandy beaches stretch for miles, smiling and friendly, belying the harsh landscape beyond. It is a shock in such lonely waters to encounter the fierce multitude of creatures in a tidepool littoral, a host of life that on the edge of a desolate and harsh land has fought and struggled, eaten and been eaten, multiplied, and for tens of thousands of years on this shore, has survived. Although most of the trip was hard work for Steinbeck—his hands were cut, scraped, stung, and sore; his back ached from bending over rocks on shore and stooping over pans on deck; and his eyes were weary and bloodshot from trying to spy small specimens in the early dawn and trying to read catalogues and labels by flashlight at night—despite all that, the experience for him was profound and moving. For a man who all his life had felt a part of nature and who thought of nature as *All*, collecting in the Gulf was a little like the sudden hearing for a time of the heartbeat of the universe. Later, joining his own perceptions to those of Ricketts, he wrote:

> Our ... interest lay in relationships of animal to animal. If one observes in this relational sense, it seems apparent that species are only commas in a sentence, that each species is at once the point and the base of pyramid, that all life is relational to the point where an Einsteinian relativity seems to emerge.... And it is a strange thing that most of the feeling we call religious, most of the mystical outcrying which is one of the most prized and used and desired reactions of our species, is really the understanding and the attempt to say that man is related to the whole thing, related inextricably to all reality, known and unknowable.... It is advisable to look from the tide pool to the stars and then back to the tide pool again.

The aesthetic experience, however remembered and recorded in tranquillity, is seldom so uncomplicated at the time. Lewis quarreled with Clark, and John Wesley Powell's men, caring nothing for science, bitterly resented being held up on their journey by measurements and observations. And the *Western Flyer* also had its share of emotional conflicts and domestic confusion. Some was due to a lack of appreciation by the captain and crew of the expedition's objectives; some to Ricketts's tendency to let everything but the collecting and preserving go by unattended; and some to Carol's presence and the strain in relations between her and her husband.

After the boat left San Diego, Carol resumed cooking and served three straight meals of hamburger, and then, after having had too much to drink, made a mess of trying to cook chicken cacciatori. "I'll get the hang of it," she said, but unused to cooking in a galley and subject to the scrutiny of the crew (including a former boat cook), she became more and more frustrated. When Sparky and Tiny caught some bonito, Sparky asked her how she wanted to cook it. "You cook it," she said and stormed back into her stateroom.

John simply shrugged his shoulders and let Sparky take over the cooking for the rest of the voyage. Carol had, in effect, signed on as one of the boys, and her husband was inclined to treat her as just another member of the ship's company for the duration. For her part, after she recovered her spirit, Carol helped with the collecting, mopped up around ship, and became in Captain Berry's judgment "a pretty good sailor." Perhaps in retaliation for her husband's remoteness, she began to carry on periodic flirtations with Ed and with Tiny—nothing serious (though Tiny, irritated with her behavior and in his cups, called her "a cheap bitch"), but not something designed to improve the atmosphere in the cramped quarters aboard a relatively small boat.

The aesthetic and philosophical dimensions of the trip were anchored in other ways to domestic reality—accommodations for the scientific work were entirely makeshift. Although Steinbeck only briefly mentions some of the problems in a matter-of-fact way, lack of facilities made the work more difficult and tiresome than it would have been ordinarily. Equipment and material were stored in awkward, inconvenient places. After tiring hours among the rocks and reefs on shore, the pans, jugs, bottles, and labels had to be set out, then put away again before the boat could move any distance. Books and other reference materials had to be dug out of the field office on top of the deckhouse. Pumps didn't work, the cooling unit was too small, and, above all, the "Hansen Sea Cow"—Steinbeck's pseudonym for the much-hated outboard motor—was balky and completely unreliable.

The Sea Cow almost becomes the leading character of Steinbeck's narrative. Throughout his account he scrupulously maintains the plural "we," as he, his wife, and Ed remain anonymous, and although the captain and crew are introduced in graphic strokes in the beginning, their personalities begin to fade during the course of the account, as impressions, observations, and thoughts take over. Out of this increasingly objective fabric, the comic perversity of the Sea Cow seems to triumph, perhaps a warning to man not to put too much faith in himself and his machines. In actual experience, however, the failure of the outboard was not very amusing: to row half a mile in a dead calm can be pleasurable, although time-consuming; to row even a quarter of a mile against wind and tide (both in and out) can be an exhausting, frustrating experience.

The first failure of the Sea Cow came at the very first collecting station, near Cape San Lucas at the tip of the peninsula. It was the first time, also, that Sparky and Tiny had gone collecting. No one had thought it necessary to explain to them what was to be done or why. They brought John and Ed ashore and stood amazed as the other two men, in rubber boots, pockets bulging with paraphernalia, clambered over and around rocks, busily peering here and there—as in some silly childhood game—dipping their nets, prying up specimens, and filling jars and tubes. Tiny lifted his arms and dropped them to his sides and shook his head. Sparky shook his head in agreement, thinking, "Jeez. They're crazy. We got mixed up with a bunch of crazies."

As they followed them around, they began to see what the other two were doing and tried to lend a hand, although in the back of their minds they worried that they might be observed by someone else while they were doing something very foolish. With some explanation as to what was wanted and another trip or two in to the littoral, collecting became a part of their regular duties. Along with Ed, John, and Carol, they made a five-person team, able to accomplish a good deal more than if only Ed and John had gone alone, as originally planned. (Tony Berry came out once, took a look at what was going on, and decided to retire to his boat and recharge the batteries.)

But five people in a small boat is too many, and some of the problems with the Sea Cow can be traced to the frequency with which it was doused with sea water. The *Western Flyer* carried two boats, a big twenty-foot row boat and a ten-foot dinghy. The collecting team always insisted on taking the smaller boat, probably because the outboard couldn't be fitted to the larger and because hope that the outboard would run sprang eternal. Overloaded, the dinghy barely had freeboard, and if someone stood up or a swell caught them at the wrong time, the boat would swamp, the motor would go under, and Tex, cursing under his breath, would be forced to spend half a day taking the motor apart, drying it out, putting it back together, and testing it in a barrel of water on deck. Since this happened over and over, no one developed as much hatred for the outboard as Tex.

The collecting and related processing were harder work and more time-consuming than Steinbeck had anticipated. He had hoped to set down a series of notes and impressions along the way, not only for the purpose of the projected book, but also as a basis for a series of articles he wanted to write to help finance the trip. He even thought he might write some of the articles on board ship between collecting stations, but these plans were scuttled under the weight of actual experience. After two weeks, he wrote Elizabeth: "We've been working hard collecting, preserving, and making notes. No log. There hasn't been time. It takes about eight hours to preserve and label the things taken at the tide. We have thousands of specimens. And it will probably be several years before they are all identified" [3/26/40]. And in a letter to Pat he added, "It leaves little time for sleep. Haven't heard a news report in nearly three weeks and it is a relief. It is a good thing to be in a world not dominated by ideological insecurities. The verities of hunger and repletion are here, but little else" [3/27/40].

As the voyage progressed, the ship's company was brought closer and closer together—one might even say inspired—by the purpose of the expedition. Steinbeck did not expect the crew to contribute much to the scientific work of the trip, and he was pleasantly surprised by their wholehearted involvement, a matter, really, of their volunteering extra work for the duration. Sparky eventually became so enamored of the collecting idea that he collected twelve gunnysacks of shells for himself. Tiny, a young man with a very fiery spirit, became personally committed to the hunt through an accident. As Steinbeck notes in his narrative, Tiny, leaping forward to try to capture Sally Lightfoot—a very elusive little crab—slipped and fell and hurt his arm. From that moment he conceived a vendetta against them, doing everything he could think of to destroy them. It was probably not true—a literary exaggeration—that Tiny considered poisoning them, but Sparky does remember his friend chasing them, club in hand and a wild noise deep in his throat.

Sparky and Tiny, Tex and Tony—these were Steinbeck's kind of people, not Ed's, and the biologist may have felt some resentment at being moved aside in the wake of the easy camaraderie quickly established between the writer and the men around him. The men agreed with Tony that John "was just like the rest of us. If I was just coming into money like he was, I would have had a big head. But he didn't." Not only was he working hard, but he enjoyed these people and was having a very good time. Sparky and Tiny's escapades, Tex's battle with the outboard and his attempts to escape doing the dishes, Tony's fretting and literal-mindedness—all these were subjects for good-natured joking.

In the evening, if there was no work or if the epsom salts, formaldehyde, and pans had been put away, there were long bull sessions on deck. Anchored in the flat calm of the Gulf, a deep darkness all around the boat, they sat in warm, still air that seemed to join the water so that it was all one element enclosed by the hemisphere of sharp stars that ran from horizon to horizon. It was pleasant, but at the same time almost frightening, and comfort came from the sounds of their own voices and the occasional clatter as Sparky put away the dishes and pans in the galley.

Depending on the mood or who was out on deck, they talked of serious things or trivial. Sometimes the awesome closeness of the stars got them talking of the size of the universe and man's place in the scheme of things. Sometimes they went over the legend and lore they had heard about the Gulf—pirates and sea monsters, the Indians who were cannibals, and the island inhabited by nothing but rattlesnakes. But just as often they discussed other boats and other trips and recalled the ports and whorehouses they had known. Man to man, Steinbeck speculated with Sparky and Tiny why it was that a woman like Paulette Goddard (currently attached to Burgess Meredith) was chasing after him.

If challenges and gibes filled the air during the day when the men worked together, the man most likely to accept any challenge was Tiny Colletto. He had a very combative spirit in a small, muscular body and was inclined to turn any situation into a personal test of manhood, and it was through the leadership of his spirit that the group was brought into several of the most memorable adventures of the voyage.

One such Colletto-inspired adventure was really a continuing saga: Tiny against the sea monster. It began with the sighting of the first giant manta ray, which roused a mild curiosity among some on board to examine one more closely. From the time of this first encounter at Puerto Escondido, when a giant ray passed directly under the skiff with Tiny as its sole occupant, to the time when he ran out of any kind of gear by which to hunt them, it became Tiny's ambition to satisfy any curiosity anyone may have had by hauling one aboard. His combativeness aroused the supportive instincts of those around him, including Steinbeck, and molded them into a team, a strike force. Several attempts to harpoon a large ray with ordinary line failed. With the frustration of defeat, Tiny's ambition grew to obsession—an "Ahab complex," as Carol termed it, watching Tiny poised at the prow of the ship, harpoon in hand and a coil of rope at his feet.

South of Guaymas Tiny spotted a number of the big rays, some according to Steinbeck's report as large as twelve feet between wing tips. Sparky got up into the crow's nest to direct Tony at the wheel, while John stood by, ready to assist Tiny, who stood at the bow, with harpoon fixed to a one-and-a-half-inch hemp line. At Sparky's direction, the engine was stopped (Tex scrambled up on deck to watch) and the boat coasted up over one of the mantas. Tiny drove the spear home with all his strength. Two hundred feet of line slipped out from the coil, almost unbelievably smoothly and quickly, as the monster angled down and away from the boat. The line came to the end, sang a deep note for a moment, and snapped free.

Tiny's frustration, leavened by his amazement at the tremendous power of his quarry, was expressed only in a cold silence and a long stare in the direction of the animal, out of sight, below. His purpose had infected everyone else, however, and the team reorganized for a new assault. This time Tex brought on deck a long, heavy trident spear and attached a three-inch hawser to it. With grim determination—there were no jokes now—he took Tiny's place at the bow. The action was repeated, as the *Western Flyer* once again coasted over a giant ray. According to Steinbeck, the line went limp and only a hunk of flesh was hauled aboard when the trident was recovered. According to Tex, who shakes his head in memory of it, the three-inch line—tough enough to tow a fishing boat in a heavy sea—parted somewhere in the middle as the manta sounded. Perhaps, somewhere, still, a giant manta ray trails a length of tattered hemp, the way a mountain trout—the one that got away—trails a foot or two of broken leader.

For the most part, however, contacts by the *Western Flyer* and its company with nature tended to be harmonious and, in terms of the goals of the expedition, successful. It was in port that relationships became ragged, as copious amounts of strong drink clouded the atmosphere. In La Paz, during a party, Carol jumped overboard completely clothed and with a three-hundred-dollar watch on her wrist—it was the watch that shocked the crew, since it was worth twice what they were getting for six weeks' work. Tiny and Sparky were just returning from shore leave when Carol began defiantly to strip off her wet clothing. Deciding that they had rather not get involved in a scene that promised some conflict, they turned around and went back into town. In Guaymas the two men went into town and visited six or seven whorehouses in a row, and when they got back to the boat, they were chagrined to find a party going on, full blast: music, liquor, and two beautiful Mexican girls. It was useless to compete for the girls, although they made a few gestures in that direction. Later during the party, Tony and John got into a fight, short-lived, but fierce in intentions.

The confusion that accompanied port celebrations followed them all the way back to San Diego. The trip home was so rough that nearly everyone was sick at least part of the time, and Carol and Ed, all the time. So miserable were these two that they decided to get off the boat at San Diego and travel the rest of the distance by land. Sparky also re-members that as they were heading home, news came over the wireless that Germany had invaded Norway, and during most of the rest of the voyage, John had his ear to the radio and a pad of paper at hand on which he was taking notes.

Since Ed and Carol were leaving, John planned an "end of voyage" party. That evening after arriving in San Diego, he took everyone, in-cluding Max Wagner, who had come down to meet them, to a hotel for a steak dinner. Then the party continued at a series of bars. Tiny's girl had come from Monterey to meet them, and she joined the crowd at one of the later stops—an addition, Sparky recalls, that did not please Carol. At another stop they picked up two more girls, but when they insisted on getting Steinbeck's autograph, he called for a couple of taxis and hustled everyone off to a new bar, leaving the girls behind. Ed got sick and then ended up with Tiny's girl in the back seat of someone's car, while in the meantime Max, sitting cross-legged on the floor in the back room of the saloon, was entertaining anyone still alert enough to listen with Hollywood stories.

CHAPTER XXV

The *Western Flyer* docked in Monterey on April 20, 1940. John paid the crew, told them that they had done a good job, and gave Tiny, the workaway, $100, with words of appreciation. Tony was happy to get his boat back to port intact and in time to go fishing, although he became a little disgruntled later when he found that many of the specimens were being sold—if he had known that, he would have asked for a cut of the profits. But the end of the charter did not signal the end of camaraderie; the entire bunch was invited to Los Gatos on several occasions, and Sparky and Tiny dropped by on their own, both in Los Gatos and later, after John had moved to his new house in Monterey. Dook remembers visiting the Steinbecks that summer at the ranch and "half the crew was up there drinking wine and just visiting. They delighted in John." And through the next few years, whenever Steinbeck was in the area, they usually ran into him in Segovia's or Brucia's taverns in New Monterey. One of the things they talked about was Cannery Row—Sparky and Tiny knew it intimately.

After the Gulf trip, it was Steinbeck's intention to retire to the ranch, where he hoped to continue to escape from public scrutiny and the hullabaloo that was still being generated by the publication of *Grapes*. He was still reeling from the psychological impact of it, still a bit beaten down and confused about the future, although he continued to hold to two thoughts: he did not want to write anything that might become popular, and he thought that his future work should be connected to science—particularly science as discovery, as a mode of perception.

Of immediate concern was the narrative portion of the *Sea of Cortez*, although upon his return he would put this aside—very briefly, he thought—in favor of a film project in Mexico. On a back burner were simmering several more ideas for films, and beyond that—perhaps almost unconsciously—he was adding to a pot of images about Cannery Row. (What seemed to stimulate his early ideas for a book was the perception of a situation as a microcosm that could be developed into a self-contained metaphor for whatever ideas had current sway over his thinking—in this case, the perceptual and biological.) The fire had not gone out. The burning core, if anything, had become harder, hotter, and more intense, but deeper, too, under the accumulating ashes of what he felt more and more to be a "messy" life.

His interest in film had never been greater. Lorentz had asked him to write the narration for *The Fight for Life* and had discussed with him the possibility of writing a script for a new work, *The Land.* But Steinbeck was determined to make use of his training with Lorentz by developing a film of his own, preferably a documentary, and working without the constant pressure of government interference and confusion that followed Lorentz. All of Hollywood, at least according to *The New York Times*, wanted to bring Steinbeck into some project or another, but he was, as he had been, very wary. He was willing to sell his novels, usually on a selective basis—if he couldn't control the product, at least he could select the people who would. But offers to work on a movie, directly, never involved any degree of artistic control whatsoever, and he had no faith in the "typical" Hollywood producer.

It was in this sense—as commercial and predatory—that he viewed Howard Hughes, so that when he got word that Hughes wanted to meet with him to discuss a picture, he never even considered getting involved, regardless of the subject or the money. Yet, he was curious about Hughes, who was already a legend, and wanted to see what he was like, so he agreed to meet him at 6:30 p.m. at Chasen's, but arranged a rescue with Gwyn and Max (Gwyn was at this point his L.A. "girl friend," and they still used Max as a cover)—he didn't want to get stuck with Hughes for dinner. At a convenient moment, he would excuse himself to go to the men's room, dial the number of Max's apartment, and let the phone ring twice. At the signal, Max and Gwyn would rush over to the restaurant and come in and say, "Well, darling, we are waiting for you at the party."

That evening the two of them got dressed to the teeth—dinner jacket for Max and evening clothes and jewelry for Gwyn. After Gwyn arrived at Max's apartment, Max asked, "Do you suppose we ought to have a drink?" "Oh no," Gwyn said, "we've got to do a scene, you know." They settled down to wait. And they waited, and waited, and waited. They got hungry, and they got thirsty. Then they started playing Robber's Casino and betting their next week's salary. After another hour Max said, "Let's call the liquor store. For God's sake let's have a drink. Maybe Hughes sold him on something."

Another hour later they had gone two-thirds through a bottle of Scotch, still without anything to eat, and they were becoming angry. "I'm going to fix that son of a bitch," Max said as he looked at the clock for the tenth time in the last ten minutes. Gwyn agreed that they ought to do something to get even. After another drink and some deliberation, they decided that maybe John's friends shouldn't look so beautiful, after all. And they went to work with the makeup. Gwyn blacked out her two front teeth, and Max decided it might be effective if he had something hanging down out of his nose. So they set to work at the bathroom sink constructing a very large, long dewdrop out of shredded Kleenex and clear nail polish. There they were—a beautiful blonde in black crepe evening gown and a tall and very handsome Irishman in dinner jacket, both drenched in cologne and every hair in place, Gwyn humming with the creative joy of her vengeance and Max periodically complaining that the nail polish was terrible to inhale.

When the call finally came, sometime after ten, it was John who was suffering: "My God, come and get me. This guy never lets up. I feel like I've been through a wringer." Max: "Well, we'll try to get over there." John: "Is Olivera Street still open? I thought maybe we could stop by there or maybe go to Mike Romanoff's." Max: "Well, we'll try."

Neither John's air of martyrdom (a fairly common ploy when he was in the wrong) nor his bribe could sway the two from their plan. They arrived at Chasen's in Max's turtleback Oldsmobile, with dented fenders and only one working headlight, turned the car over to the attendant, and entered the exclusive restaurant with an attitude of elegant disdain that only bit-part players from 1930 movies could have pulled off. When they approached the booth in the back, John stood up and introduced them. "How do you do, Mr. Hughes," Gwyn said, and flashed a toothless smile. John gave them one of those "what have you two been up to?" looks and they all sat down. During the conversation that followed Max leaned over the table to hear what was being said, and every time he exhaled, his dewdrop vibrated. John did a double take and then began a series of furtive signals to his own nose when he thought no one else was looking. Every time he signaled, Max gave him a look of studied innocence and asked, "What John? Did you want to say something?"

Steinbeck never did catch on to the performance, so that when they got outside the front door, he turned to both of them and exploded— "Jesus Christ!" The two looked at him, wide-eyed. "Why, what's the matter?" "Max," he said, "your *nose!*" "Here," said Max and handed him his makeup. John erupted with laughter that echoed up and down the street, and laughed until tears came to his eyes.

Rescuing John from awkward social situations became one of the duties he thrust upon his female companions. Perhaps one of the differences between those who have been raised in a middle-class family, as had Steinbeck, and those raised in the upper classes is that the former are taught to be polite, but not how to be politely rude: Steinbeck had great difficulty in fending off bores, cutting off phonies, and extricating himself from the company of those that he disliked. Of all people, he disliked phonies the most, yet when buttonholed by one he would simply get red in the face, mutter, fidget, and turn, this way and that, looking for an escape. All of his wives were outspoken, counterbalancing his reticence, and this may have been one of the main things that initially attracted him to them.

During a party in Hollywood when he was first dating Gwyn, they were both captured by a director, who started off on a long, self-serving spiel designed to win Steinbeck's approval and set up the basis for a deal he was promoting. Finally after a piece of embarrassing self-flattery, Gwyn simply exclaimed "Oh, horseshit!" From then on, Steinbeck would give Gwyn a certain look, and she would respond on cue with some well-chosen epithet. Steinbeck loved the shock treatment—but he would always get Gwyn to administer it, and afterward he would pretend as if he hadn't heard a thing. He also dreaded gossip columnists. Louella Parsons had a technique whereby she would greet you, reach out her hand, and then as you shook hands, keep your hand or arm as she guided you into a corner. At this point, Steinbeck behaved something like a hooked trout; his head would bob here and there as he tried to catch Gwyn's eye, and he would begin circling the room, trying to avoid the corners until Gwyn could position herself for a rescue.

II

The film that Steinbeck decided to work on as his own was that which was eventually called *The Forgotten Village.* Its genesis had come months earlier when producer-director of documentaries Herbert Kline approached Steinbeck with an idea to do a film about a poor Mexican family caught up in the turmoil of revolution. The writer liked the focus on a peasant family but suggested, in line with his concern with science, that instead of revolution the conflict come out of the attempt to bring modern medicine to a backward area. This was a theme that had been in his mind for some time, ever since his encounters with the problems faced by public health nurses in attempting to deal with the prejudices of Okie and Mexican migrant workers, and it had been stimulated further by his work on *The Fight for Life* and periodic discussions of the topic with Paul de Kruif. *The Forgotten Village* evolved into precisely the kind of picture, a semi-documentary (that is, real people acting out familiar roles) with a social message, that he had been in training with Lorentz to make.

A company had been formed, announced in early April while Steinbeck was still on the Gulf, with the writer as one of the directors and money coming from a number of sources, including Steinbeck himself, his publisher, Harold Guinzburg, and his editor, Pat Covici. Steinbeck would go to Mexico, where the picture would be filmed in its entirety, visit locations and do research, and then write the screenplay. He had intended to leave right after his return from the collecting expedition, but he couldn't get Pan American reservations until the twenty-third of May. He and Carol stopped over for a few days in Hollywood, primarily so that he could get together with Lewis Milestone about arrangements to film *The Red Pony*, arrangements that had dragged along for months.

The evening before they flew to Mexico City, the Steinbecks went to a party at Milestone's with Max and Gwyn (which may have been the first time the two women had met, although Carol did not know at the time what Gwyn's relationship to her husband was). Charlie Chaplin was there, and he and John got together for a long talk, their first in months. Later in the evening someone began warming up at the piano, and Max, who as usual had had more than his share to drink, loudly demanded, "Who is this guy?" which was followed by a sudden silence throughout the room. John jabbed him in the ribs with his elbow and whispered, "That's Horowitz." The pianist went on to play from memory a transcription of the then unpublished Shostakovich *Seventh Symphony*.

At the same time as the Steinbecks were getting ready to go back to Mexico, John got word via a phone call from Joseph Henry Jackson that he had won the Pulitzer Prize in fiction for *The Grapes of Wrath* (earlier in the year he had won the National Book Award). The big news, however, was that William Saroyan, who had won the prize for drama (*The Time of Your Life*), had turned it down. The wire services and a host of reporters called asking for Steinbeck's reaction to Saroyan's refusal. Steinbeck, who had met Saroyan on several occasions but didn't care for him much, wrote to Jackson:

> I'm not going to make any statement about that. Bill knows what he wants to do and I don't see that it is anybody's business. His motives and his impulses are his own private property. Do you want a quote from me. I suppose I must say something. If you want to print it, fine. Might go something like this.
> "While in the past I have sometimes been dubious about Pulitzer choices I am pleased and flattered to be chosen in a year when Sandburg and Saroyan were chosen. It is good company." That's the end of the quote. And it is one of the few times when tact and truth seem to be side by side.

Steinbeck gave the prize money, a thousand dollars, to Ritchie Lovejoy so that he could take time off from his job as publicity man for Holman's department store to finish a novel manuscript he had been working on for some time. In signing the money over, he commented that when he was young, his father had given him a thousand dollars so that he could continue the struggle to get published.

The Steinbecks moved into a huge house in Mexico City, "like a club," and shortly after he wrote to Elizabeth:

> We got down here two days ago and since then have been on the run. Have seen many people, bought some equipment and tomorrow we start on a location trip into Michoacan. We'll probably be about ten days on it so will not write you before then unless something important comes up. As we drove out to the airport from the ranch, your letter with the check was in the mail so we were able to bring Herb his money. We found them fine and the situation popping fairly but not dangerously [probably a reference to the upcoming Mexican elections]. We'll cover the country on this trip, find the place we want to shoot in. [The location they selected was Pátzcuaro.] Then I'll come back and begin on fairly detailed story and we'll pick up things as we go along. It is fine here. I like it even better than I did before. . . . By the way, if I get a minute or so, I am going to try to get out an article or two while I am here. There are such interesting things and I'd like to get them down on paper. [5/40]

Every time he took a trip during this period of his life, he planned to write some articles—often to help cover expenses—but he never was able to take the time to do them. This trip was no exception.

At Steinbeck's invitation, Ricketts came to Mexico, arriving in June after the Steinbecks had been there for about two weeks. Overtaken by enthusiastic bursts of good fellowship and hospitality, John had a tendency to invite people either to his home or along on trips (he had invited Elizabeth Otis to Mexico also) without thinking of the consequences. When Ed arrived, John was tied up with the complexities of trying to make arrangements for a business enterprise in a foreign country and had started work on his script.

Ed detected a "feeling of coldness and hecticness" in the Steinbeck household, and when he was left to his own devices, felt left out: "A new experience," he wrote Ritchie and Tal Lovejoy, "for me being the poor cousin." And as Richard Astro has pointed out in his discussion of the relationship between the two men, Ed probably was also disappointed that John had not stayed in Monterey to work on their book. Relations between them were strained further when the thematic direction of John's screenplay became clear and Ed expressed open disapproval of it, writing his "Thesis and Materials for Script on Mexico" as rebuttal. It is not particularly inspiring to a writer to have someone nearby who is expressing disapproval of what he is writing about, so that it is little wonder that Ed was not invited to dinner every night at the Steinbeck house.

Perhaps because of the circumstances, Ed's hurt feelings and Steinbeck's preoccupation with a project other than their own, Ed's "anti-script" was an overreaction. As Astro summarizes Ricketts's argument, the biologist expresses concern for "the inward things," pointing out that

> an emphasis on "change, acquisition, and progress," symbolized by "high-tension lines, modern highways and modern schools," belongs "to the region of outward possessions" as opposed to the more important "region of inward adjustments." He observes that although "in an inward sense, the Mexicans are more advanced than we are," the powerful virus of "the present U.S. mechanistic civilization" can easily corrupt "the deep smile," the rich "relational life" enjoyed by so many Mexican people.

Although he was perhaps less extreme in his views, there is much in this that Steinbeck would agree with—never in his work, in *The Forgotten Village* or elsewhere, does he express a single-minded devotion to "mechanistic civilization." In his discussions of rural electrification under the New Deal with Pare Lorentz and Paul de Kruif, he was the one who expressed reservations about the unmixed blessings of "high-tension lines." As fascinated as he was with new technology, he never saw it as a substitute for humane values and often saw it as dangerous and destructive.

Those who have taken *The Grapes of Wrath* as a hymn to human progress and have seen *The Forgotten Village* as a follow-up in the same direction are wrong. The novel may celebrate man's best qualities—his courage, his willingness to sacrifice for others, and his capacity for love—but nowhere does it indicate that these qualities will triumph and lead to a more just society, a better race, or more rational world. Steinbeck's view was too historically broad, too biologically deterministic for him even to consider these as possibilities. Indeed, his perception of man's nature includes the idea that not only is real progress impossible, but that too much perfecting of man and too much taming and regularizing of his environment might well destroy him or change him into something that we wouldn't like.

He made his thoughts on these matters clear in a letter to Pascal Covici at the end of 1940, thoughts stimulated by the new year and continuing news of Nazi "invincibility":

It is cold and clear here now—the leaves all fallen from the trees and only the frogs are very happy. Great cheering sections of frogs singing all the time. The earth is moist and water is seeping out of the ground everywhere. So we go into this happy new year, knowing that our species had learned nothing, can, as a race, learn nothing—that the experience of ten thousand years has made no impression on the instincts of the million years that preceded. Maybe you can find some vague theology that will give you hope. Not that I have lost any hope. All the goodness and the heroisms will rise up again, then be cut down again and rise up. It isn't that the evil thing wins—it never will—but that it doesn't die. I don't know why we should expect it to. It seems fairly obvious that two sides of a mirror are required before one has a mirror, that two forces are necessary in man before he is man. I asked Paul de Kruif once if he would like to cure all disease and he said yes. Then I suggested that the man he loved and wanted to cure was a product of all his filth and disease and meanness, his hunger and cruelty. Cure those and you would have not man but an entirely new species you wouldn't recognize and probably wouldn't like.

There it is—It is interesting to watch the German efficiency, which, from the logic of the machine is efficient but which (I suspect) from the mechanics of the human species is suicidal. Certainly man thrives best (or has at least) in a state of semianarchy. Then he has been strong, inventive, reliant, moving. But cage him with rules, feed him and make him healthy and I think he will die as surely as a caged wolf dies. I should not be surprised to see a cared for, thought for, planned for nation disintegrate, while a ragged, hungry, lustful nation survived. [1/1/41]

There is no endorsement of socialism or technology here—in fact, from a political point of view and with a misreading of Steinbeck's intent (since politically he was a New Deal Democrat), the Republicans could take the latter part of this as a prologue quotation for a platform for the nineteen-eighties.

The Forgotten Village is a small thing (the handwritten script is thirty-six pages), and it would be a mistake to give it too much importance. Still, it can be seen as a logical evolution out of earlier work, *In Dubious Battle* and *The Grapes of Wrath*, and a forecast of things to come—*The Log* and *Cannery Row*. The village is a victim of primitive forms of teleological thinking, and the film script can be seen as an essay on perception. A boy, a family, a village have a choice—to deal with the world on the basis of superstition or to deal with it on the basis of scientific observation. If they wish, the people can look into the microscope and see the animals in their water that are killing them, or they can continue to depend on the *curandera* and her magic. There is no reason, in Steinbeck's view, why Mexico cannot have both its "deep smile" and clean water. The great irony of the dispute between Steinbeck and Ricketts, if it can be called that, is in recent years high-power lines have spread out to much of Mexico, but sanitary water has not.

A lot more was going on in Mexico than Ed apparently understood. John liked the country and admired its people, but under the circumstances of this trip, he wanted to get home as soon as possible. He had encountered a good many more problems setting up the operation than he had anticipated, and the script, although relatively short, was difficult to write because much of it had to be tentative. He was worried that the Mexican elections, and the possible violence that might accompany them, would make the filming difficult or dangerous. And, odd as such a perspective may seem in retrospect, he was worried that the United States might enter the European war and the film project would go down the drain. Loss of his part of the $35,000 investment would not have hurt him, but he did not want his friends, who had invested on his advice, to lose any money, whether they could afford to or not.

On June 20, 1940, Steinbeck wrote to Elizabeth from Mexico City: "I've finished my script and am ready to go. So . . . the day after tomorrow . . . Carol and I are flying to Washington. We'll be meeting my uncle there and trying to find out a few things. . . . we'll see you before we go West." One of the things he wanted to find out was whether war was likely to come soon and "upset all applecarts." His uncle Joe Hamilton was working in Washington as an information officer for the W.P.A., and Steinbeck hoped he might give the writer some sense of how the country was going. Another concern came out of his experiences in Mexico, where he found that the country was being deluged with Nazi propaganda that the people were all too willing to believe. The things he heard upset him so much that when he got to Washington, he wrote to the President directly, and Roosevelt gave him twenty minutes in order to present his views. Steinbeck advocated a more effective propaganda effort on our part in Central and South America, lest we lose their support completely in the coming conflict.

As Herb Kline has reported, the *Sea of Cortez* project was on Steinbeck's mind throughout the time he was in Mexico working on the film. However, his decision not to work on it immediately was not, as Ed apparently thought, a matter of shoving it aside to work on something else that, for the moment, was more interesting. Instead it was a typical pattern in Steinbeck's work—he needed the time to let the ideas develop. *The Forgotten Village* took only a few weeks more of his time—in the late fall he returned to Mexico for part of the filming—but he did not actually start the physical process of writing *The Log* until the following January.

As it was, the Steinbecks spent most of the summer and early fall at home, ostensibly to rest and pull their lives together, but ended up entertaining a stream of visitors. This was the summer during which Steinbeck complained most vehemently to his friends about Carol and her "swimming pool set" and during which he stewed and fretted about not getting anything done. It was also a time when he began to complain about Carol's drinking, although in retrospect Carol insists that she was not drinking all that much. Carrying over the mood from Mexico City, it was largely a hectic and unhappy time for both of them.

At the beginning of the summer, Steinbeck got a letter from Dook Sheffield, the first in several months. Out of a job, he had applied at the *Chronicle*, but without success. Steinbeck offered to use whatever influence he might have and to lend him money if he needed any. Dook asked about the ranch, which he had never seen, and Steinbeck answered:

> It was good to get your long letter. I've been too raddled and confused to write letters for a long time. But with the decline of the

pressures on me I'm feeling better and if it weren't for the coming war, I could look forward to a good quiet life for a few years anyway. You know my nature and my old prospects so you must know what a terrible experience this last two years has been.

You ask about the ranch and whether it is an estate. If we were going to sell it, the description would surely sound like an estate. But I'll try to give you some idea of it. At the Greenwood Road place we were finally surrounded with little houses and right under my work room window a house was built by a lady who was studying singing—the mi-mi-mi kind, so we finally went nuts. Carol's father found this little ranch far up the mountain. It is forty-seven acres and has a big spring. It has forest and orchard and pasture and big trees. It is very old—was first taken up in 1847. The old ranch house was built in 1858 I think. So we came up, built a four room house for ourselves, much like the Greenwood road house. There had been an oil well on the place and we used the big timbers and boards for our house. Then we refinished the inside of the old ranch house for two guest rooms and a big winter playroom where one can have parties. So far in our ad we have "two houses—four bedrooms." . . .

Then we have a Japanese boy who cooks, gardens, and looks after the place when we are away. And in the summer I have an Okie boy by the day to work around mainly because he needs the money so dreadfully. So there's a staff of servants. You see it really is an estate. But it is one of the most beautiful places I've ever seen. And I hope you'll see it soon now that we have something of a normal life again. [7/9/40]

The houseboy, Joe Higashi, did not just cook, garden, and look after the place when they were away—he ran the place. Carol, who depended on him a great deal during the time when the house was frequently filled with guests from New York or Hollywood, did have one complaint—he insisted on serving dinner exactly at six. As a result, Carol recalls, you'd have to start cocktails in the middle of the afternoon. John marveled at how during a time of crisis when the phone would be ringing all the time (although it was unlisted), Joe could unerringly select the calls the Steinbecks wanted to receive. John suspected that behind that formal Oriental reserve and efficiency lurked a man of great perception and, possibly, charm, but a man that they, as his Occidental employers, would never see.

III

The off-and-on relationship with Gwyn had been "off" for several months. Although Gwyn, in retrospect, has thought of their early dating as the first part of an extended love affair, it is probable that Steinbeck took it less seriously, thinking of her as a friend and pleasant companion, a fine date when he was in Hollywood alone. Most of their time together was spent with other people—with Max, whom they invariably took along to any parties they went to, and with the Loessers—and their relationship, up to now, had been more or less "proper." However, the combination of a hectic life on the ranch and Gwyn's absence changed his attitude toward her during the summer of 1940: he had apparently worked out his romance in his mind before acting, much as he worked out his books before writing. He perceived Carol as the cause of his malaise and Gwyn as the one person who could give him peace.

While Steinbeck had been away in Mexico, Gwyn had been asked by CBS to sing at the San Francisco Fair, where the network had a display called "Coast to Coast," which demonstrated how a nationwide broadcast was put together and transmitted. Gwyn and an orchestra were isolated in a glass booth surrounded by an audience. Five times a day, the orchestra played and Gwyn sang, while an announcer explained to the crowd at the fair how the transmission worked and the circuits were put together. Several weeks after she had started the job, when she was on the air, she got a message to call an operator number. She called, and John said, "I heard you singing on the radio. I have to see you right away."

In the months that followed, they saw each other as often as they could, and in between, Gwyn left messages for him at the lab. John went to San Francisco, where Gwyn was staying with her mother, as often as he could find an excuse, and on at least one occasion, he brought her to Monterey to stay the weekend. At the beginning of this weekend, John picked her up at the train station and drove her to the San Carlos Hotel so that Gwyn could check in and freshen up. He promised her a very special steak dinner, which he described in detail, and suggested that they eat early because he had some things he wanted to talk to her about. He had picked out a place in Carmel where he thought he could go without being recognized.

They arrived at the restaurant about five and went into the bar for a drink before dinner. An hour later they were still drinking, telling stories. John, Gwyn recalls, "thought I had a terrific sense of humor, and he loved to have me tell stories about my family and my relatives." Four hours later the bartender had joined them in telling stories, and they were surrounded by people, drinking and laughing. Gwyn kept saying, "I've got to get something to eat," and started reaching over and behind the bar for the green olives, ripe olives, and pickled onions. Twice the manager came in to tell them that the kitchen was closing. Finally, a little after two in the morning, the bar closed. Gwyn said, as they were walking toward the car, "I've got to get something to eat," but the only all-night restaurant in the area was the one place where John was sure he'd be recognized. "I have some wolf dust at the cabin," he said. "Let's go there." ("Wolf dust," according to Gwyn, was a "Wagner-phrase"—what you keep in the house when you have a lot of money for the day the wolf might be at the door when you don't have any more money.)

The cabin was near the beach down the coast. Owned by John's sister Esther, it was a convenient retreat, one that he used later frequently with Gwyn when they wanted to be alone. When they arrived, he lit a fire and went into the kitchen to see about the food. As she sat in front of the fire, he was laughing and singing, opening up cans: a can of chili, a can of beans, a can of ravioli, a can of tamales, and a can of mushroom soup. He threw it all in a pot and heated it up, adding salt, chili pepper, and raw onion.

They sat in front of the fire on a daybed that John had pulled over from across the room, spooning the hot mixture out of bowls and burning their tongues because they were trying to eat too quickly. If anything should have warmed them, that food should have, but Gwyn had her coat over her shoulders and was still cold. She asked for coffee, and John made it ranch-style, boiled with an egg, and put the pot right on the fire. "You stay here," he told her. "I don't mind the cold. I have a sleeping bag, and I can sleep in the bedroom."

Despite his promise to keep the fire going, it was out when Gwyn woke in the morning. She was still in the same position, paralyzed, as if she had been embalmed and laid to rest, not a hair out of place, her shoes still on her feet. John made some more ranch coffee and mixed it with brown sugar and canned milk, then drove her back to the San Carlos. As they walked through the old lobby, her powder-blue skirt somewhat wrinkled, there were some curious glances from the people at the desk. John whispered out of the side of his mouth, "I think your reputation is lost." When they got to her room, she begged for time for a bath, and he said, "Well, I'll pick you up in a couple of hours for lunch," and added, "We'd better go back to that place and pay the tab." As usual, the previous evening he had forgotten to bring any money with him, and he didn't want to sign anything because he didn't want anybody to know who he was. When they returned to pay the bill, they found that they had each consumed twenty-seven martinis the night before.

When he went to San Francisco to see Gwyn, he took elaborate precautions for fear the press—particularly Herb Caen, whom he thought of as his archenemy during this period—would find out what he was up to and expose him. Whenever Caen did spot him, which happened on two or three occasions during these months, Steinbeck would talk unwillingly and then break off their conversation with "Don't turn me in, kid." One evening when Carl Sandburg was in town (on meeting him for the first time, Steinbeck wrote in his journal, "A good thinking man. I liked him and got a nice feeling from him") they went to the Top of the Mark for a drink together. Sandburg was dressed somewhat eccentrically in flowing tie and a very wide-brimmed black fedora. They were seated at a small table near the window overlooking the city, and Carl was telling John a long story. The waiter came up, interrupted, and said, "Sir, your hat." Carl looked up at him for a moment and went on talking. A few minutes later, the waiter came over again, and then a third time he interrupted, "Sir . . . your *hat.*" Carl looked at him for a moment and said, "Quack, quack, quack, quack," and went on with his story. From then on all the rest of his life, when somebody nagged him or badgered him, John would respond, "Quack, quack, quack," and many years later, he began wearing the same kind of hat himself when he dressed up to go out on the town.

Later, with Gwyn and Pare Lorentz, who had just flown in from the East, they all went to dinner. Gwyn recalls: "John asked me to dance. He danced beautifully and tangoed very well, but they had been drinking all afternoon, and he went slow motion right over backward. I never will forget it, I was so embarrassed." Gwyn had to go back to work and left the men, still drinking.

Late that night Gwyn's mother got a phone call from John. He had signed into a hotel earlier that day using a pseudonym, and now that he was ready to go to bed, he couldn't remember what the pseudonym was and there weren't any other rooms available. He couldn't find Pare, because Pare was in another hotel and he couldn't remember which hotel. Finally, at Gwyn's mother's invitation, he spent the night on their couch. To avoid the problem in the future, he adopted the name Joseph Duckworth, and from then on, whenever he wrote to Gwyn or gave her anything, he signed with the drawing of a duck.

In mid-August, he wrote to Dook that he had been taking flying lessons at the Palo Alto airport and loved flying:

There's something so god damned remote and beautiful and detached about being way to hell and gone up on a little yellow leaf.
It isn't like the big transports at all because this little thing floats
and bobs and yet is very steady and—there's no sense of power at
all but rather a sense of being alone in the best sense of the word,
not loneliness at all but just an escape into something delightful. I
think you used to get it after you had had a lot of guests and they
all went home and the house was finally cleaned up and you could
turn on the radio and cook your own kind of stew and read and
look up and know god damned well that you were alone. And
there's something about seeing a cumulus cloud way off and going
over there to see what it is like. [8/12/40]

His description here suggests an allegory for the condition he imagined
at this point in his life as most desirable: all the guests would go home
(and stay home) "and the house was finally cleaned up and you could
turn on the radio and cook your own kind of stew." The ranch, as relatively isolated as it was, had not fulfilled his dream of peace, and he
began to refer to it as "Carol's ranch," the way it was "Carol's pool"
and "Carol's crowd." Yet, many of the guests were *his* guests, and
Carol was suffering from the hectic life nearly as much as he was. Even
with the work of the houseboy, Joe, it was Carol's responsibility to take
care of their guests, and it was wearing her out.

Flying was his dream of peace, as was Gwyn, and he managed to
bring the two together, since his frequent trips to Palo Alto (sometimes
overnight) provided the perfect cover for seeing her in San Francisco.
He gave Carol a car (they now had twin Packards), one of a series of
expensive gifts that he may have been using to salve his conscience. "It
will give her a lot more freedom," he wrote, and indeed, it set her up on
an equal basis to lead her own life. He reported that the

day before yesterday after my stretch in ground school I and a
bunch of young pilots went to a bar to discuss wars. Five hours
later and about seven bars we were in San Francisco. So I spent the
night. Carol was in Monterey anyway so that was all right. Last
night when Carol called up she said her conscience was hurting her
because she had done some bad things in a bar, so I said I had done
a lot of bad things in bars and she said, "Thank God," and hung
up. [8/20/40]

The situation between them seems to have developed into one of extreme tolerance on both sides. During August the Steinbecks gave a

party for the captain and crew of the *Western Flyer*, Ed, the pilot who was teaching Steinbeck how to fly, and fifty or sixty other people. There was a pit barbecue in the afternoon and drinking and dancing all night. Sparky recalls that John made it clear that a beautiful blonde, dressed in a blue pajama suit, was his date (not Gwyn—this girl had an accent), while Carol spent a lot of time with Tiny down by the pool, until someone turned on the pool lights. Spencer Tracy, who would be playing Danny in the movie of *Tortilla Flat*, showed up with his agent the next morning when the party was nearly over, and Sparky made spaghetti for all those who had held on to the end.

What little room in his life he had for thoughts of work at this point was given over to concern for the various films that were in the works, two of which were Hollywood movies. Milestone was still having trouble working out the financial arrangements for *The Red Pony*. His backers were disagreeing among themselves and bickering with Annie Laurie, while Milestone was running back and forth, trying to iron things out, his only concern to do the script. Steinbeck was impatient and couldn't understand why there was so much confusion. As for the others, he told Elizabeth:

> I wrote to King Vidor who is going to direct Tortilla Flat and I had an immediate answer. He hadn't seen the script but said before he started making it he would come up to Monterey and meet me there. I'd like to see a little bit of that shooting if I can. . . .
> There hasn't been much word from Herb [working in Mexico on *The Forgotten Village*]. They are shooting story now the last I heard and that should take about all their time so I am not thinking about it. When it is done it is done and that will be time for me to stew about it. [8/20/40]

Another movie matter had come to his attention involving Chaplin's *The Great Dictator*, the picture whose script he earlier had wanted to help Chaplin make into a book:

> This is off the record. I got a secret message from some people inside the Chaplin Studio begging me to happen in and look at the film. They say that there is seven minutes of solid sermon at the end of the picture and it is awful and they are afraid the film will be ruined by it, and all the friends are stooges. And they say that if I would come down and see it and say it is too long . . . that he might cut it out for me. Isn't that funny and sad? I don't know anything about film at all but I do know that seven minutes of sermon

isn't good and an audience won't sit through it. So if I do go down I'll certainly look at it and see what I can do. [8/20/40]

He did go to Hollywood, see the film, and recommend changes. Chaplin's son, in his biography of his father, suggests that Steinbeck may have had a hand in rewriting the ending, but the length of the "sermon" remained the same.

Also in August Steinbeck wrote to President Roosevelt once again, this time asking for an interview for himself and Dr. Melvyn Knisely, professor of anatomy at the University of Chicago:

He is a remarkable scientist and an old friend of mine. Discussing with him the problem of the growing Nazi power and possibilities for defense against it, he put forth an analysis and a psychological weapon which seem to me so simple and so effective, that I think it should be considered and very soon. I would take it to some one less busy than you if I knew one with imagination and resiliency enough to see its possibilities. . . .

Please forgive this informality, but frankly, I don't know anyone else in authority whom I can address informally. [8/13/40]

Carol and John once again flew to Washington, and on September 12, 1939, John and Dr. Knisely presented to the President their plan to use the resources of the U.S. Bureau of Engraving to produce exact copies of German paper money and then drop large amounts of it by air over Germany, Italy, and the occupied countries. Several months later, Steinbeck commented in a letter to Archibald MacLeish that "a friend and I took a deadly little plan to Washington and the President liked it but the money men didn't. That is, Lothian and Morgenthau" [11/13/40]. It may have been that the contamination of anybody's money, even the enemy's, was too terrible a thing, by their gods, to even contemplate.

The Steinbecks went on to spend two weeks in New York, where they saw everybody they knew and went out on the town at every opportunity, returning to California on September 27th "as the compositions say, tired but happy. . . . I bet people are very glad to see us go after one of these splurges." Their Los Gatos friends had planned a party for them on their return. A story known to their friends was that when John originally asked Carol to marry him, he had pleaded theatrically, "Marry me and you will be swathed in furs, have your own swimming pool, and your name up in lights"—all of them the furthest things from possibility he could think of at the time. Now, the pool at the second Los Gatos house had Carol's name on it, and while in the East, John had purchased a fur for her. So their friends got together and had a neon sign made. At an appropriate moment during the party, it flashed on over the pool: CAROL. It was the fulfillment of an ancient promise. It was perhaps also an omen of the closing of the circle.

IV

The hectic social activity of the summer seemed to reach its apex in their New York splurge. What followed was a period of let-down and brooding. In one of his rare entries in the journal he had started while writing *Grapes*, Steinbeck seemed compelled to record his malaise:

> Emotionally I am pretty much messed up too. The old trouble of restlessness. . . . Carol feeling lone and lost. . . . My own change of temperament seems pretty radical.

> Strange thing honor. The most sapping thing in the world. Oh Lord how good this paper feels under this pen. I can sit here writing and the words slipping out like grapes out of their skins and I feel so good doing it. . . . Here is a strange thing—almost like a secret. You start out putting words down and there are three things—you, the pen, and the page. Then gradually the three things merge until they are all one and you feel about the page as you do about your arm. Only you love it more than you love your arm.

Almost all his letters throughout the fall and until after the first of the year reveal an uneasiness, even foreboding about the future, mixed with a sense of lassitude. He saw the discord of his own life, and the paralysis that prevented him from resolving it, as in a way parallel to the discord that was ripping apart the world of nations and the apparent paralysis of the United States as it was being drawn closer and closer to chaos. While the fate of the country, indeed of the whole world, was in doubt, it seemed little use to go ahead full speed on any of his own work. Instead, for months, he seemed to be treading water in slow motion, looking about, doubting his condition, and despairing of the situation in general. In all of this, looking and trying to understand where he was and what was going on seemed to him his only course, and he continued to grasp science to him like a life preserver, thinking also that science might save mankind.

Although there are some hints that he may have made one or more false starts on the *Log* during this period, almost all his writing was confined to letters. A long letter to Wilbur Needham, written just after his return from New York, reveals how his mind was working:

I am trying to do about four jobs and shall probably do none of them well. Because in the formulae of the present there seemed to be factors still unannounced, it has recently seemed to me silly to try to solve the equation. So I went back to biology where the factors are at least observable if one has the eyes. That work has been of some solace. The world of men is fit now mainly for satire but a ghastly satire of the insane—the rolling head and laughing tongue and glassy eyes. The voices spoken by all sides—left-right, center, fascist-communist, Willkie are nonsense words having no relation to an obvious change and movement of the species. Coming up occasionally from the observation of invertebrates particularly in an ecological sense I have found myself looking at my own species with the same eyes. And it makes a great difference. Lemmings have been observed at fairly regular intervals, to come charging down out of the Norwegian mountains, to burst into the sea in thousands and to swim until they drowned. And man has been observed at fairly regular intervals to break into groups which destroy one another. We do not know the reasons for either phenomenon. The reasons given—economics, etc., surely are not adequate to describe the sudden mutation in the group psyche which makes lemmings and men react in such an interesting way.

The word "defeatist" is tossed about now like a small grenade. And like most of the word-bombs, it has no meaning. My own defeatist attitude has resolved itself to this—In the thinking of the present, there is a lot of nonsense, a lot of word and conception bondage. Very well let's tear the thing down and start again with a new Cogito ergo sum. Dead word and litter accumulates so rapidly in the thinking patterns. All this sounds like a lecture. It isn't. I'm trying only to tell you the direction my poor puzzled mind has been taking. I have found so little that is satisfying in the thinking of the non scientific men of the present. It has been hard to stay clear of politics but I've done it and made many enemies thereby. But I am clear and at least I am capable of approaching the "Cogito."

I wish I could see you. I live such a messy life now though that I never know when I'll be here and you would have to know in advance. The invertebrate book [*Sea of Cortez*] is not done yet. It is a long hard job but I think a good one. It too will resolve itself into a plea for observation and that in this time is a meaningless plea. But one does what he does. I'm going to fight in this war as hard as I can, not because I believe there are any solutions in it but because

I am beginning to see it as a part of a species pattern, perhaps a mutation process the results of which are unknown to the individuals. Reasons and causes are then merely symptoms, little flashing lights which do not show causes but merely indicate that the blind tropic movement is underway. When mould gets in a bee hive, the bees sometimes grow very angry and sometimes sting each other and if there were bee minds and bee speakers I have no doubt they would be saying that there was an unequal division of honey or that the present queen was leading them into crackpot alleys.

I'm talking a hell of a lot.

So long

John [9/29/40]

Has anyone ever come up with a more peculiar reason for fighting in a war? Strange—that he was, on the one hand, such a patriot, writing to Roosevelt about his concerns for his country's well-being in the face of the Nazi threat, and was, on the other hand, so totally detached. There is a similar paradox of thought in the filmscript for *The Forgotten Village*. On one side he shows compassion for the villagers as their children die; on the other, he is objective, fatalistic, in showing the villagers, as a kind of phalanx inspired by fear and superstition, rejecting the remedy of modern medicine and driving the public-health doctors away.

Perhaps the answer is that he cared about persons as he cared about his country, but he had little faith in people, less in political discourse, and none in the prospect that people would rationally determine their own fate. The answers he proposes—to purge the language and thereby clean out the thought processes, and to get men to look beneath appearances to see themselves in a different way—ecologically—were solutions that he knew would not be adopted. But he would write about them anyway: "One does what he does."

PART FOUR

To New York

By mid-October of 1940, he realized that he would have to go back to Mexico. The film crew was far behind schedule, and he thought he had no choice but to go down and stir things up. He wrote Elizabeth: "I imagine I will raise a little hell with the crew in Mexico. I know if I had gone through the discouragement and the work of making a picture and then someone fresh, not knowing all the trouble that had gone into it came along and criticized [it] would not get the best treatment out of me." But he went reluctantly. The fall was his favorite time of year on the ranch, and thanks to Joe, the gardens were beautiful, among them, "a field of chrysanthemums so beautiful they would make your head swim, about eight inches across each one." A few days before he left he wrote to Dook and recalled the days when they used to think of Mexico as something golden and how they thought that they would never get there. Now, he told Dook, he was going there again and again, but not particularly wanting to. This time he left Carol behind.

After he had been there for a few days, he discovered that the main difficulty was finding good light. He wrote to Max and Gwyn (who was not in Hollywood): "Herb cannot learn that a Mexican answers what you want to hear. He asked if the October sky was clear and of course they said yes. . . . You see, this is not like a studio picture. We have to wait for light and catch it as we can." He was working very hard, going out at daylight and coming back after dark. "But," he told them, "we're getting a picture on film—one of the first times a Mexican pueblito has been photographed. I hope it is good. I know it is true—so true that in direction we don't say 'Do this!' but 'Do as you always do.' And what natural actors they are. When the film gets to Hollywood I'll show it to both of you right away" [11/1/40]. When he came back during the third week of November, he left the crew still filming.

A production aspect of the film would cause him first embarrassment and then deep anger, during the course of the next two months. The film people who had their money in the production wanted Spencer Tracy to do the narration, for his name would add considerably to the film's chances for commercial success. Tracy was willing, but he was under contract, and it appeared that there would be no chance that his studio would allow him to do it. As a result, Steinbeck asked Max Wagner to narrate. He was a natural, since he had grown up in Mexico and would do a fine job, as Steinbeck said, "through love." But Tracy cared about the subject of the film also and worked out a deal with MGM whereby if he did a movie for them that he didn't want to do (a new version of the Jekyll and Hyde story), they would allow him to do the narration for *The Forgotten Village*. So the writer, for fear that his friend would think he'd been pushed aside for a bigger name, wrote an anguished, apologetic letter to Max, explaining what had happened.

But just after Tracy began recording the narration, while at the same time working on the Jekyll and Hyde movie, MGM told him he couldn't do the narration after all, "knowing," as Steinbeck surmised, "he wouldn't stop a picture already in production." The writer was furious. He wrote Elizabeth, "Perhaps you do not think revenge is good but I would like to teach those bastards they can't double-cross me with impunity" [2/7/41]. He devised two plans: one, "to blast their production of Tortilla Flat with everything I have," and two, to take them to court and get an order prohibiting them from using anything in their production of *The Yearling*, the name of the boy, Jody, and any story elements that might infringe on *The Red Pony*. He gave up both plans after he had cooled off.

His depression carried over into the new year. He had written Dook in October that although it might not have seemed so when Dook had visited him at the ranch, the loneliness and discouragement of earlier days had not been dissipated by success. "In fact," he wrote, "they seem to crowd in more than ever. Only now I can't talk to anyone much about them or even admit having them because I now possess the things that the great majority of people think are the death of loneliness and discouragement." In December he wrote to Toby, "I get so dreadfully homesick I can't stand it and then realize that it's not for any home I ever had." And at the end of January, although he had begun to write again, he told Elizabeth, "I seem to have a lot of writing energy now but it is so bound up in sadness and solar plexus longings that I don't trust it." He still had his restlessness, he continued, and he supposed he always would.

Once again his depression was accompanied by physical illness, as both he and Carol were struck by a serious flu attack while in Hollywood just before Christmas. He was forced to drive home in the rain with a 104-degree temperature, the trip becoming a nightmare as he struggled with the pain and weakness. They hired a nurse to take care of both of them for a week, although both cases hung on for some time and Steinbeck's turned into a kind of "walking pneumonia." He chose to ignore it, returning to Hollywood after the first of the year to finish the film with Herb Kline. He made arrangements to meet Gwyn, writing to her through Max and using a code in his letters because "the heat is on the mail."

One of the causes of his depression, of course, was his longing for Gwyn, and the one thing that seemed to revive him and bring fun back into his life was being with her. Gwyn's voice coach and friend Sandy Oliver saw the two of them often during those times they were in Los Angeles and watched the relationship develop. The couple would stop by at her little cabin in Laurel Canyon—John liked it because it was off the beaten track. Gwyn, Oliver recalls, was a

> very attractive girl, full of life, full of mischief. And I really felt, as I look at it later, that this man [Steinbeck] had never really learned to play. And he was ready for some serious playing. And they played. Had gads of fun together. They used to show up at my place dressed as though they were going on safari. And he would call Chasen and say, "We are up in a lookout, and we have been doing our duty, and would you please send up some ribs?" So up would come the caterer's truck and there was no street, just teeny-weeny steps to go up to the place. And he would send up a man to serve and then clean up in my modest little place, and then people would come over and we would talk.

Steinbeck sometimes came alone. He "sort of used the canyon apartment as a hideout when he was doing some writing. He didn't want anybody around, and so he would come up and get my rocking chair with the breadboard in his lap." And occasionally he would have friends up, while Gwyn was off somewhere else. One evening magazine writer Alva Johnson and Pare Lorentz were there, and the three men began teasing Sandy about her love of Thomas Wolfe:

> I said, "Well gentlemen, who is your favorite writer?" And to a man they said Hemingway. And I said, "Good." Then I said . . . "In the music world we are very lucky that there are no language barriers. . . . Here you guys are very good writers, isn't it possible

for you to write in such a simple fashion that your words can be translated into any language without loss?" And they just looked at me like I was insane. John said, "Well, what do you think we are trying to do? There's only been one book and that's the Bible. But that's what we are trying to do. So just rest assured that just one day maybe we'll make it."

Although he thought of it as "a good competent picture," the end of his work with *The Forgotten Village* left him with a bad taste in his mouth, and he was determined that he would make "no more of these little cooperative films." In looking back, he felt that none of them had had any knowledge of how to make that kind of picture and that there had been too many cooks—everyone kept contributing story ideas, to the point that he had almost given up. Once he had the problem of the narrator resolved (he finally got Burgess Meredith to do it), his only concern was that the film be properly distributed. He thought because of the low cost, it might make a lot of money.

In mid-January he wrote a preface for Tom Collins's semiautobiographical novel, "They Die to Live," and the copy for a word-picture story, to be published in *Life*, that would reveal what Tortilla Flat was really like. During a second trip to Hollywood that month, he talked to Zanuck and others about the distribution of the film. Pat Covici, who was in Los Angeles without Steinbeck knowing about it, located the writer in a nearby hotel, and Steinbeck showed him the Collins preface and outlines for the Gulf book. At the end of the month he finally got to Monterey and began the actual writing. He planned to stay at the lab during the week, returning to the ranch on weekends.

His work plans were changed, however, when Carol left for a vacation. She still had not recovered from the flu, and he had tried to talk her into going to the desert for a couple of weeks to get some sun, but she refused. After another week of cold rain, alone at the ranch while he was in Monterey, she agreed to take a trip to Hawaii. He was genuinely concerned about her—she had lost weight and her spirits were very low—and though he had not intended to get rid of his wife so that he could see his girl friend, that, as it turned out, is what happened. Several years later he recalled this period in a letter to a friend:

When I wrote the text of the Sea of Cortez, Gwen and I were hiding in the pine woods in a cabin and she would sleep late and I would get up and build a big fire and work until noon when she woke up and that would be the end of work for the day and we

would go walking in the sand dunes and eat thousands of doughnuts and coffee. I worked very hard.

In recalling the period Gwyn, too, talked about "hiding out" in the
cabin. It was a delicious time, a sort of forbidden honeymoon (as odd
as it may seem in today's moral climate, this was probably the first time
they had had sexual relations), but it was not, for Steinbeck, entirely a
good time.

Unlike in his youth, in his middle life he found difficulty in doing
something forbidden and enjoying it. He was a man with a conscience
in respect to the people who were close to him, and no one had become
closer than Carol. She was now a permanent part of his life, and during
the sequence of the final breakup of their marriage, he felt much more
than guilt. His letters suggest indecision, remorse, and deep concern
that Carol, who seemed to him lost, lonely, and unhappy—in the process, even, of breaking apart—might break apart entirely and not survive if he did not stand by her. The great paradox of her personality
was that she was so very strong, so individualistic and assertive, and yet
so vulnerable.

On the one hand, she angered and upset him; his life seemed in constant turmoil; he was cruel to her and she retaliated. On the other,
when he was honest with himself he regretted his cruelty and felt a re-
morseful responsibility for her condition. His situation seemed to him
intolerable, yet his conflicting feelings toward his wife kept him almost
paralyzed. He did invite Gwyn to stay with him while Carol was away,
and he did precipitate the final crisis by declaring his love for Gwyn.
But at the same time, he seems to have just drifted, depressed, indeci-
sive, tortured, through the whole process, as if it were all too much for
him.

Carol's suspicions were aroused when, after wiring her that she
should stay two additional weeks, he wired her that since she was having such a good time, she should extend her vacation even longer, but,
ironically, the extension urged by Steinbeck was from his concern for
her health and well-being—Gwyn had stayed for three weeks and had
already left. What had led to Gwyn's visit in the first place was that although Steinbeck wanted to be near Ed and the lab while he was writing the *Log*, he couldn't stay at the lab because Ed had a new live-in
female companion. After John had arranged to stay in the cabin and
had lived and worked alone for several days, the idea came to him—
why not have Gwyn come up and stay for a while? Now that Gwyn

had gone back to Hollywood, he solved the problem of finding a place to write in Monterey, where he could work in peace and yet not be completely alone, by hiring Ellwood Graham to paint his portrait. He was also doing a favor to the painter, who needed the work.

Graham asked him if he could take some photographs to work from, but Steinbeck said no, couldn't he just come every morning and write while Graham painted him? Having revolted against the ranch as part of the pattern of his unhappiness and now determined to sell it, he arranged to buy a little, run-down house on Eardley Street in Monterey. Every morning he got up, had his coffee, and then walked up the hill to Graham's studio, where he spread out his materials and notes on a card table. Holding his pen with four fingers, he wrote on his lined yellow pad or stared out the nearby window like a boy in school waiting patiently for recess. Graham sketched him in various attitudes, trying to get the sense of the man and his emotions.

He told Graham to go ahead and do any kind of portrait he wanted, and that he'd pay him when the painter was satisfied with what he'd done—he didn't even have to show the picture to Steinbeck if he didn't want to. The writer's "queer manner" of holding his pen, Graham recalls, seemed so incongruous with "the impression of a large, athletic, florid face. . . . These were some of the qualities I tried to bring out, with the tenderness behind." The resulting impressionistic portrait is not a favorite with the Steinbeck family. The overall feeling is of a huge man, innocent and vulnerable; with cleanshaven face and T-shirt, he looks like a big boy, a man who hasn't grown up. The moon-shaped head with large nose and ears sits low on massive shoulders. The lines etched into the forehead and around the mouth suggest both weariness and sensitivity—the expression seems to be that of resigned anguish.

Just before Carol came home from Hawaii, Mavis McIntosh arrived. John picked her up at the airport and brought her to the ranch (he was, she recalls, the wildest driver she ever had known in her life, taking the road through the Los Gatos hills at about 60 m.p.h.). He seemed sick with worry and talked to her at great length about his problems: he wanted to get out of his marriage, but was at a loss as to how to handle it. After a couple of days of this kind of discussion, he took Mavis to Monterey, introduced her to his friends, and showed her around the peninsula. He continued to go over the situation with her, even as he showed her the sights and took her twice to the lab for long and wild parties. Then he drove her to Los Angeles, where he was going to meet Carol's boat and where Mavis had business, and gave her messages for

Gwyn. When they picked up Carol, Carol gave no hint at all that she knew what was coming.

Carol had returned about the first of April, and what followed for the next few days was a series of terrible confrontations. Typically, she would not give up or let go, and her will, stronger than his because of his guilt, put him in a position where he was trapped. True, he had an obligation. True, they had gone through much together. True, it might just be an infatuation that might not last. True, she was far too young for him. But he wanted out. He called Gwyn, and hoping, perhaps, that she might somehow rescue him, asked her to fly up. When she arrived, Ed met her at the airport and drove her to the Eardley Street house in Monterey.

When Gwyn walked into the house, she remembers, John and Carol were sitting on a dirty-ragged couch drinking pink champagne, and it was obviously not the first bottle. "He did a very funny thing which I should have realized was a peculiar insight into his nature. He said, 'I want you two gals to talk this out, and the one who feels she really wants me the most, gets me.' So it was rather a painful three or four hours there in that crumby little house." John left the room, and Carol turned to Gwyn. "Carol was always very tough, a very masculine woman, and so she tried to have at me, and she continued to, but I said, 'Well, look, you are his wife, I just . . .'—you know—so she said that I would regret it and that she'd make my life miserable." At the end, John and Carol were arguing in the living room while Gwyn was crying in the car. John came out eventually and drove her to the house of some friends, where she spent the night.

In Gwyn's version of these events, John's reaction seems very callous, when in fact he found himself in a situation where he was paralyzed, unable to make a decision, because the emotional claims on each side were too strong. He was playing a kind of psychological poker in which the stakes were his sanity, and he was being whipsawed by two players who held all the cards and who seemed determined that, regardless of which of them won, he would lose. The final raise—as he reported to Mavis McIntosh—which had caused him to throw in his hand was the claim by each woman, one after the other, that she was pregnant. The ace in the hole, as always, was guilt, and he decided that he was unworthy of either woman, but since Carol held more aces than Gwyn, she won the first hand—he decided his duty was to stay with her regardless of his own feelings.

A few days later, John wrote to Mavis McIntosh:

This has been a hell of a time and I'm pretty shaky but at least I'll try to give you a small idea of what happened. My nerves cracked to pieces and I told Carol the whole thing, told her how deeply involved I was and how little was left. She said she wanted what was left and was going to fight. So there we are. All in the open, all above board. I'm staying with Carol as I must. I don't know what Gwen will do nor does she. Just as badly tied there as ever—worse if anything. Carol acting magnificently. I don't know why in hell anybody would want to bother with me. Anyway, Carol won the outside and G the inside and I don't seem able to get put back together again. . . .

Guess I was pretty close to a complete crack up but probably have passed it now. We're camping down here really now. And I'm trying to pull myself together but pretty bruised as everyone is. Funny thing. All looks hopeless now but I suppose time will fix things. And at least no more whispering is necessary. [4/16/41]

A week later, near the end of April, John and Carol were separated. The separation would prove permanent. In the middle of May, he wrote Elizabeth Otis:

I've been very raddled and torn out by the roots. Nightmared, etc. In many ways I have more of a sense of peace than I have ever had and am working hard but I get the horrors pretty often. It's an awful thing to me to be cruel. I don't do it well. Meanwhile, as you know, I am having my assets gone over very carefully and will give Carol half and her interest in my contracts will probably make it more. . . .

I'm putting an awful burden on you. Came very close to cracking up and I guess did but not finally. Getting stronger now though. The work saves me a lot. If only Carol can be happy and whole, it will work. I don't know.

He continued to live on Eardley Street and sent a thousand a month to Carol until the property settlement of the divorce. Despite the cheerful letters she managed to send him throughout the separation, the situation was much harder for her to deal with than for him. She had given her life to him and to his work, and now she had neither. She had not been well, either physically or emotionally, so that it was probably the worst possible time for her to try to cope with such an ordeal, and her family blamed Steinbeck for abandoning her when she needed him the most. With the onset of the war, she went into mechanics' training school at nearby Fort Ord and ended up at the top of her class, winning an award as best mechanic. The challenge of this training, as she looks back now, probably saved her.

II

"The work saves me a lot," Steinbeck wrote Elizabeth Otis, and in another letter continued, "I suspect that I am in such turmoil that I won't have anything to do with myself for a good long time. I don't have to as long as there is work to do. And after that there will be more work to do" [6/24/41]. The narrative part of the "Gulf book," as Steinbeck called it at the time, or *The Log* as it was called later, took from the last week of January through the third week of July to complete, covering the worst part of the ordeal of the break-up. It was amazing, in light of what was happening, that he was able to get any writing done at all (although Gwyn claims that in a perverse way his work very often thrived within an atmosphere of emotional upset and conflict), let alone writing that was reflective and thoughtful and expressed such a calm, objective approach to life in its leisurely pace. Yet there is no doubt that his work on the narrative, which talks a good deal about ways of looking at things, acted as therapy, helping him put his own difficulties into a larger perspective. At one point he told Covici that he thought he could now look objectively at himself, and he had to laugh.

As usual near the beginning of a project, he was enjoying the work enormously. "I hope," he wrote Elizabeth, "others will as much. It has everything in it. Kind of like a letter containing everything that happened and was discussed and thought about. Formless it would be if there weren't the physical form of the trip to hold it in bounds. But it is fun" [2/17/41]. He was writing it so that it would appeal to a larger audience than just the scientific one, but was convinced—and thankful—it would have only a very moderate sale. At about the time that Gwyn left and before Carol came back from Hawaii, he reported that he was producing more than 2,000 words a day and had reached a total of about 45,000, and now the writing had become "by far the hardest work I've done." He anticipated that it would cause some antagonism in scientific circles, "for we are attacking some of their sacred cows. But it is always good natured and never didactic. . . . Its main attack is on didacticism in fact. As far as I know it's the first really accurate and complete account of an expedition" [3/23/41].

By mid-June, after he had been separated from Carol for almost two months, he reported that the end was in sight: he had only seven more collecting stations to cover, although these were extremely important ones and would require quite a lot of words to deal with adequately. He was getting a bit weary: "The work never stops and I will be ready for some kind of rest when it is done." And he no longer perceived the work as nearly formless, as in the beginning; instead, it was now "carefully planned and designed," as he wrote his editor, with "four levels of statement in it." Few readers, he thought, would follow it down to the fourth level. Still, he told Elizabeth at about the same time, the book had "quite a bit of fun in it . . . a tricky book . . . full of traps—intellectual traps as well as jokes" [6/24/41].

In reviewing the progress of the manuscript, we may find difficulty in remembering that it was, after all, a collaboration. Steinbeck himself seems to have had a hard time remembering, sometimes talking about the manuscript as a joint effort and sometimes referring to it in very personal terms, as in these references in a letter to Elizabeth just after he had finished the first draft:

> We're really putting a lot of work in. I hope you are not too disappointed in it. Perhaps it is a little crazy but it is a good clearing out of a lot of ideas that have been working on me for a long time and they do fit into the loose framework and design of such a book. I've even tried to use normal techniques of change and climax . . . in this case the climaxes are ideas. [7/9/41]

Even though the original purpose of the expedition and subsequent report was to promote Ed and his ideas, Steinbeck seemed to get so wrapped up in the project during the writing that he began—at least at times—to think of it as his own. He even saw it as having a place in the pattern of his work as a whole, writing to Covici that "when this work is done I will have finished a cycle of work that has been biting me for many years and it is simply the careful statement of the thesis of work to be done in the future" [6/19/41].

Yet when Covici, understandably confused, suggested that on the title page Steinbeck be given credit for the narrative and Ricketts for the catalogue, Steinbeck was furious. "I not only disapprove of your plan," he wrote back, "but forbid it." As a result of this kind of pressure to feature Steinbeck's name, the authors sent a joint memorandum to Viking describing the collaborative procedure used in the composition of the narrative:

Originally a journal of the trip was to have been kept by both of us, but this record was found to be a natural expression of only one of us. This journal was subsequently used by the other chiefly as a reminder of what actually had taken place, but in several cases parts of the original field notes were incorporated into the final narrative, and in one case a large section was lifted verbatum from other unpublished work [from Ricketts's "Non-Teleological Thinking," which makes up much of Chapter 14, the so-called "Easter Sermon," in *The Log*]. This was then passed back to the other for comment, completion of certain chiefly technical details, and corrections. And then the correction was passed back again. [8/25/41]

During the voyage of the *Western Flyer*, Steinbeck had not kept a journal, although he had intended to—he was just too busy. Captain Berry had recorded the sailing data in a ship's log, and Ed had kept a journal of collecting data and experiences, so while Steinbeck wrote *The Log*, Ed's journal, Ed's essay on non-teleological thinking, and an outline-plan that Steinbeck and Ed had developed together were spread out in front of him. Thus there is no doubt that Ed's contribution to the narrative was substantial, yet for many years after *Sea of Cortez: A Leisurely Journal of Travel and Research* was published, it was wrongly assumed that Steinbeck was wholly responsible for the first part and Ricketts for the second, a misconception continued and encouraged by the separate publication in 1951 of *The Log from the "Sea of Cortez"* as a work by John Steinbeck.

Steinbeck critic Richard Astro, who discovered and first published the memorandum quoted above, has probably gone too far the other way by stating that "Steinbeck composed the narrative almost entirely from Ricketts' journal," as if Steinbeck merely rewrote what Ed had originally written. Until that terrible day when someone attempts to analyze the work line by line, attributing this idea to Steinbeck and that to Ricketts, it might be best if we view the collaboration, as Steinbeck originally intended, as seamless. He had wanted to make the account a true reflection of the joining of their two minds—primarily his descriptions and perceptions as an underlayment for ideas they shared and developed together and, to a lesser extent, for ideas held by each that were, if not in actual conflict, at least complementary.

Sea of Cortez was a very different kind of book for Steinbeck, not only as a collaboration, but as a nonfiction work that, since part of it was technical and specialized, could expect only a limited audience.

The Viking editors seemed suspicious of the collaboration and reluctant to invest in the illustrations and special typefaces required for the catalogue, so there was much correspondence back and forth during the summer of 1941 about these and other details of publication.

Even Covici, who liked very much the first portion of the book once it had been completed, seemed uncomfortable with the project and apparently did not grasp until later the significance of the narrative as a key to Steinbeck's thinking. While the writer was working on the narrative, Covici urged him to go back to another manuscript, a work of fiction called "God in the Pipes," which Steinbeck had started in Mexico the year before and which may have dealt with subject matter related to *The Forgotten Village*. In the middle of July, once his work on the Gulf book was nearly completed, he decided to return to it, if for no other reason than to keep busy. He wrote to Elizabeth:

> But now it [the *Sea of Cortez* narrative] is done—rewrite work is not really work any more than wood chopping is. I must get to work again and right away even before this rewriting is finished. I have a kind of instinct that says that in the integration of disciplined work there is some kind of safety for me now. So I think I'll go on with the Pipes even if it is no good. Being another little story in technique like Mice, that is an attempt to make a small novel that can be played, it will require the greatest of integration. I hope I can do it. I'll try. I've abandoned it several times but this time I'll start at the beginning and try to carry it through. It would be good to do for the discipline of the form if for nothing else.

In the meantime, Carol had moved to New York, and although relations between them were still cordial, Steinbeck had a feeling that it was but the calm before the storm. He told his agent:

> I am of course holding my breath about C. I know so well her basic violence and if she becomes vindictive you are quite right, anything may happen. . . . I wish I could get over the horrors about her. It comes back and back in a blind blackness that is awfully sharp. There is only one possibility for me, only one in all of them, and that is that she should meet someone whom she could fall in love with, someone who is good and strong and good to her. If that doesn't happen the haunt is not going to be laid ever. . . . Throughout all of this people say and think that if I had just done so and so and if Carol had just done so and so it would have been all right. But there was no trick that would make it whole. It was a basic disagreement that went even into our cells. [7/18/41]

By the end of August, the ranch had been sold, and the houseboy, Joe, came down to the little house in Monterey to take care of Steinbeck. Toni Jackson, who was living with Ed, became John's secretary, answering letters from admirers and doing much of his typing, starting with parts of the "Sea of Cortez" manuscript. John and Ed both were writing to Viking during this period, trying, among other things, to convince the publisher that the book would be an important one scientifically since the expedition had been "almost unique" and "thirty-five new species [had] already been determined." It was as if they still didn't believe that Viking was taking the book seriously. Steinbeck had barely started work again on "Pipes" before he heard from Milestone that the contract was finally set (with RKO) and he was ready to start on the script of *The Red Pony*. He immediately dropped everything else and sat down to do a synopsis: "I have mapped the whole thing out and think I see a way to make it carry the dramatic load and one which might work." And then he began to fret as he waited for the director to show up in Monterey: "Milestone had better hurry up or I will go to my play and postpone his picture. I can't do the actual writing without him because it works best if techniques are worked out together" [8/31/41].

"Milly" arrived just after the first week of September and the two of them set to work, first on the overall treatment, then on the narrative, and finally on the script itself. From their previous experience on *Of Mice and Men*, they had learned to respect each other's judgment and the work went smoothly, although it took longer—through the first of October—than Steinbeck had expected. But the script presented many more problems than the previous one, since in this case they were really working with three short stories, which did not have plot continuity. They changed the order of events, moving, for example, Jody's attack on the vulture from early in the stories to a later, more climactic moment (the scene was filmed with young Peter Miles on one side of a big piece of plate glass and the camera and vulture on the other). They also added a fourth story, "The Leader of the People," from *The Long Valley* (not added to the published version of *The Red Pony* until the 1945 edition) and featured the role of the grandfather, played in the movie by Louis Calhern.

While John was working on the script, he got a letter from Carol saying that she had decided to come back to the West Coast. He decided to leave for the East. "If I got out of the way," he wrote Elizabeth, "she would be able to come here and see her friends. I would be frankly avoiding trouble. There was enough for a lifetime and I won't take it again if I can avoid it. I just want a little peace and work for a while until I'm all well again" [9/14/41]. And it was on this basis, primarily, that he made the decision to live in the East and abandon the native soil that had been so important to his work. He was not, of course, conscious at the time of making any kind of final decision to leave California, but as it worked out, he was to spend most of the rest of his life either in or around New York City or abroad.

His "continuing decision" to live elsewhere points up an important difference between how he viewed himself and his career and the way he has been viewed by critics and literary historians. Although the latter have placed great importance on his connection with his native surroundings, it is doubtful that he perceived his own situation in those terms. He had no conscious plan to write about rural central California other than the normal use of his own early experiences in his work. The course of his career, at least as he saw it, had been largely accidental— he had simply written about those things that had come to hand that had stimulated his imagination and provided metaphors for his ideas. In this regard, he was in his own perception much more a cerebral writer than one who exposed native customs and settings.

One of several reasons he was pleased with *Sea of Cortez* was that it ran counter to the pattern that reviewers and critics were beginning to build in order to categorize him. His oft-expressed irritation with the efforts of critics to pigeonhole him suggests that consciously or unconsciously he was driven to break the pattern that had developed, in order to escape being stereotyped. He did have a conscious desire not to repeat himself, to make each work different—even disturbingly so, if possible.

III

A contributing factor to his decision to leave the West may have been Gwyn's generally negative feelings about Monterey as too small, too cold, and too isolated. And as the "new woman," she would face the awkward task of fitting into old relationships and the ordeal of being judged by old friends. With all her poise, she was still very young, and the challenge of such a social adjustment was apparently too much for her. On one occasion, a friend of the Steinbecks from Los Gatos dropped by the Eardley Street house at John's invitation to meet Gwyn, and John went to the bedroom to tell her that they had a visitor he wanted her to meet. He told the friend that she would be right out, but when after an hour it became clear that she was not going to appear, the visitor decided it would be prudent to leave.

Just as the parties to an auto accident may begin with apologies and self-recriminations and after a period of thought work themselves into self-justification and mutual accusation, so too the parties to a divorce seem inevitably drawn, after a time, into rancor and distrust. This stage began with the Steinbecks after Carol had had enough time to add up her grievances, which were real enough, and brood about them. What had set her off was a report from a friend that Gwyn was sleeping in the house on "her" sheets. The coming storm added further fuel to Steinbeck's determination to leave the area, and in order to establish a buffer between him and his wife, he hired Toby Street as his attorney with instructions to work toward a settlement with Carol and in the meantime let her have anything in the houses that she wanted. John suspected that Joe had been a bearer of tales and so sent him back to the ranch, which was still in escrow.

After he had made his decision to go East, he flew to Hollywood to ask Gwyn if she'd go with him. When she agreed, he then consulted her family, asking their permission to take Gwyn to New York to live with him until the divorce. After the divorce was final, he announced, they would get married. With the mention of marriage, Gwyn's mother and grandmother breathed great sighs of relief and gave John their blessing.

John and Gwyn flew back to northern California together, and since he figured he might have a month or so before they'd have to leave for the East, he arranged for them to stay at the 11th Street house in Pacific Grove, which for the moment was without tenants. He wrote later about this period to Toby: "Do you know that the little time in the Grove is the only time since she was a little girl that she ever had a home? And oddly enough it is the only time I ever had one either." The weather was fine, and John was doing some of his writing on the play-novelette at a wooden picnic table on the patio. One day a fierce wind came up suddenly while John was inside making himself some coffee and lifted sixty or seventy pages of manuscript into the air, spreading them around the neighborhood, in the streets, on lawns and hedges, and even carrying a page or two into the trees.

Some children playing in a yard two or three houses away saw the papers fly up in the air and out of curiosity retrieved one or two sheets. When they saw the sheets had writing on them, they combed the neighborhood, gathering all they could find except those up in the trees. Several hours after they had delivered the pile of paper to Steinbeck's house, he wandered over to the yard where they were playing and thanked them. They had an electric train set up on the ground to run around a tree, and he sat down to watch the train. As he petted their dog, he explained that dogs really like to be stroked along the furrow between the eyes.

The children told him that their dog was a mystery dog. Every year the dog, well-groomed and with a collar, appeared in the late spring, stayed with them through the summer, and then disappeared at the beginning of the fall. This was the fourth year this had happened, and none of them had ever seen the dog anywhere around the neighborhood any other time of the year. The next day Steinbeck came back to the yard and sat down once again to watch the train. Overnight he had invented a story, and as he sat on the bench next to the tree watching the train, he told them where it was that their dog went during the winter and why he came to them in the spring.

John and Gwyn left somewhat more abruptly than they had planned after John received a request to attend a conference in Washington, D.C. It was a request that amounted "to a command," he wrote Elizabeth, and added mysteriously, "I had made certain suggestions" [9/30/41]. These were the suggestions he had made to F.D.R. the previous year regarding setting up a propaganda office that would use radio and film "to get this side of the world together" in opposition to the effective Nazi propaganda he had witnessed in Central America.

Steinbeck had not been the only one to make suggestions along these lines. A similar proposal had been strongly urged by William J. Donovan, who had made several "unofficial" fact-finding missions for the President to England and the Middle East. Donovan was a World War I hero, a former assistant attorney general under Coolidge, and an unsuccessful candidate for the governorship of New York. His nickname, "Wild Bill," was misleading and unfortunate. He was mild-mannered, soft-spoken, and conservative—a Republican Irish Catholic who was shrewd, controlled, and totally competent. Yet, both in his political campaigns and in his administrative work for President Roosevelt, his nickname was effectively used by opponents to suggest irresponsibility.

As the result of an earlier recommendation by Donovan to Roosevelt, fifty mothballed Navy destroyers had been transferred to the British, bypassing a reluctant Congress by an executive order that exchanged them for bases on British territory. Now, Donovan proposed that the President establish an agency which would counter Axis propaganda, act as coordinator and clearinghouse for all intelligence-gathering organizations, and engage in training for spying and sabotage. Roosevelt agreed and persuaded a reluctant Donovan to become head of the new agency, misleadingly called Coordinator of Information (later, the Office of Strategic Services). It may be that Steinbeck's conversations with the President had been a contributing factor in the decision to create such an agency.

An excellent administrator, Donovan acted quickly during the summer of 1941 to organize the agency and bring in the best talent available. Among the several units created was the Foreign Information Service, headed by Robert E. Sherwood, the noted American playwright and long-time friend and advisor to Roosevelt. Just as other units were enlisting the help of prominent social scientists, businessmen, and scientists, so too did Sherwood recruit for his F.I.S. not only well-known journalists and radiomen but also important novelists and dramatists such as Thornton Wilder and Stephen Vincent Benét. It was to a meeting of a group within the F.I.S. that Steinbeck was summoned in early October of 1941, a meeting designed to elicit suggestions from people in communications, the film industry, and the arts as to possible future activities for the newly created propaganda unit.

Only one item in O.S.S. files mentions Steinbeck: he was offered a job with the C.O.I. and turned it down. Yet it is almost certain that he did work for the C.O.I. The most likely explanation is that he worked as an unpaid consultant and that such things were arranged on an informal basis and not recorded for the files of the fledgling agency. This would be the first of a series of such unpaid jobs for Steinbeck during the war years, for he later worked for the Office of War Information, the Writer's War Board, and the Air Force. To put his work for the Coordinator of Information in as dramatic terms as possible, he wrote his next novel, *The Moon Is Down*, on assignment for the agency that eventually became the C.I.A.

In 1963, looking back on the composition of *The Moon Is Down*, Steinbeck recalled the circumstances:

In the Office of War Information I began to know and to associate with escapees from the occupied nations. They spent their agonized energy trying to help the underground organizations which kept a steady and heroic resistance to the occupying Germans. And I became fascinated with these organizations which refused to admit defeat even when Germans patrolled their streets.

The experiences of the victim nations, while they differed in some degree with national psychologies, had many things in common. At the time of invasion there had been confusion; in some of the nations there were secret Nazi parties, there were spies and turncoats. Quisling has left his name as a synonym for traitor. Then there were collaborators, some moved by fear and others simply for advancement and profit. Finally there were the restrictive measures of the Germans, their harsh demands and savage punishments. All of these factors had to be correlated and understood before an underground movement could form and begin to take action. And as the war progressed these silent figures had to be advised, encouraged and supplied with materials and weapons to carry on what must often have seemed a hopeless struggle.

Gradually I got to know a great deal about these secret armies and I devoted most of my energies in their direction. Then it became apparent that each separate people had to learn an identical lesson, each for itself and starting from scratch. I did not and do not believe people are very different in essentials. It seemed to me that if I could write the experiences of the occupied . . . such an account might even be a blueprint, setting forth what might be expected and what could be done about it.

Steinbeck's autobiographical writing is revealing of the motive and spirit within a situation, but frequently confused about facts and chronology. He was not yet working for the Office of War Information (*The Moon Is Down* was published in March of 1942; the O.W.I. was created in June), but for Robert Sherwood's unit of Donovan's agency. After his conference with that unit in early October, he and Gwyn took up Burgess Meredith's offer and moved into the house on Meredith's farm near Suffern, New York.

He had planned, once he got to the country, to start again on "God in the Pipes," but his discussions with the Foreign Information Service people, together with testimony from European refugees, led him to another subject, a theme compelling in its currency, yet timeless—foreign occupation and resistance. So he started in a new direction, but kept the same form, although he began writing the manuscript as a play and added novelistic elements to it later. The play (as I shall call it for the time being) would also be written in service to the nation, for it would dramatize the possibility that "it could happen here." The first draft had for its setting a medium-sized American town, showing that America, with its own collaborators and resistance movement, would react very much as towns in various countries of Europe had reacted to the brutal force of an invader.

Living on the farm, Steinbeck worked on his play through October and into November, while at the same time writing broadcasts for the F.I.S. He traveled frequently to Washington, D.C., and New York City, where Sherwood had opened a branch office of the F.I.S. In November Donovan's agency started up a new unit, the Foreign Nationalities Branch, which brought together both foreign nationals already in the U.S. and newly arrived refugees for the purpose of gathering information on the populace and its attitudes in various occupied countries. It was at this point, while interviewing the people in this unit for material for his overseas broadcasts, that Steinbeck began to put together the information that would enable him to write the final draft of *The Moon Is Down*, which had its setting in an unnamed occupied European country.

By mid-November he and Gwyn had moved to a two-bedroom-and-kitchenette apartment in a residential hotel, the Bedford, on East Fortieth Street in Manhattan (recommended by Annie Laurie Williams, who lived there). Despite living out of suitcases, and the cold and rainy weather, he was in good spirits when he wrote Toby Street:

> I have seen Shumlin one day and Serlin another day and I'm seeing another producer this afternoon. None of them have read the play yet. No one may want it. And I really don't care very much. There's no imminence. I have now four irons in the fire. The Play—which has no name yet, The Forgotten Village, The Red Pony, The Sea of Cortez, and one new one. All of them may crash for all I know. But I feel singularly free and a little wild. I don't know why. Something in the air, something crazy. I might even go and buy a suit and a red dress for Gwen. [11/17/41]

Yet, he was having problems with nearly all his projects. *The Forgotten Village*, which was supposed to open in New York, had been stopped by the New York State Board of Censors as "indecent" and attacked by the America First Committee as an endorsement of socialism. Concerned that the America Firsters would find further ammunition for their attack on Steinbeck in certain passages in *Sea of Cortez*, McIntosh and Otis suggested several small changes, which Steinbeck agreed to make in the galley proofs. Viking seemed to be going ahead very slowly with the production of the book, and production of the film of *The Red Pony* was held up once again (in fact it would not be filmed until 1949, backed by yet another studio, Republic). And Steinbeck had submitted his play to the F.I.S. for its approval, only to have his bosses there (presumably including Robert Sherwood) turn it down because, as Steinbeck recalled later, "many people might think this an admission that we might be defeated, and this would have a devastating effect on morale."

The suppression of *The Forgotten Village* in New York, after all he had gone through to push the picture to completion, was a terrible blow. If they were unable to show it in New York, they were bound to have trouble all over the country. Furthermore, favorable reactions from the New York film critics would be very important in the attempts to sell the picture to exhibitors and the public. Steinbeck had several requests from wire services and newspapers for his response to the banning, and after some thought, he decided to issue a statement. He wrote Elizabeth that "when the Grapes was giving such trouble everybody wanted a statement and I found it was much better just not to have anything to do with it. In this case it seemed better finally to do so."

The film had been suppressed by the Board of Censors because of a scene showing the birth of a child, and another that showed the mother nursing the child. In his response, Steinbeck said, in part:

> The board had been set up to protect children from the more bitter and suggestive factors of life. No doubt it has been largely successful.
>
> In the picture there is no nudity. No suggestiveness and no actual birth is shown. The indecent fact which seems to have upset the board is that child birth is painful and in primitive communities where there is no medical care, not only painful but dangerous. The Mexican government is not upset about this film because it is trying with every resource at its command to remedy the situation.
>
> The Hays office has passed on the picture. In Mexico we found courtesy and intelligence. This censorship is inspired by neither.

He also said that in terms of our relations with Mexico, the ban had come at a very unfortunate time and should be repealed "if only as a matter of policy." Later that fall at a hearing, which Steinbeck attended as a spectator, the ban was lifted. He had feared all along that the U.S. entry into the war would push the picture aside, and with the censorship delay, that was essentially what happened. It made good marks with the critics but did not get very wide distribution. Twenty years later he spoke with great pride of *The Forgotten Village* to his children's tutor, who was an aspiring playwright—"I wish there was some way you could see it," he told him.

The decision by his bosses at the F.I.S. against publication of the play-novelette hurt—it was another in a line of vetoes of things that he had tried to do to help his country. He had been very enthusiastic about what he thought was really a very good idea—to show foreign occupation of an American town—and he thought it would wake America up and at the same time build a sympathy for what many peoples were going through abroad. Following the decision, he found that

> my friends from the various resistance groups, Norwegians, Danes, French, Czechs, who had furnished me with the details and who had read my manuscript, were outraged at the decision. At that time no account of the process of occupation and resistance had been written. Why not, my friends suggested, change the scene to an occupied country? The book might hurt American morale, they said, but it would be very good for the morale of the resistance men. And so I placed the story in an unnamed country, cold and stern like Norway, cunning and implacable like Denmark, reasonable like France. The names of people in the book I made as international as I could. I did not even call the Germans Germans but simply invaders.

Life in the little hotel apartment was not easy, especially for Gwyn. John was frequently away, busy seeing producers or going to the F.I.S., and when he was home, he spent most of the day by himself writing. Gwyn knew no one in New York, had nothing to do and no place to go. Later, when the Loessers came to the city for a time from Hollywood, Gwyn went around with Lynn Loesser to the shops, to the theater, and to various social affairs. One evening after she had gotten home after a particularly long party, she found John furious. "If you want to stay with me," he said, "you are going to have to give up *that* woman." Gwyn dutifully stayed home and sat in the living room reading. Steinbeck wanted to be alone and not be bothered while he was writing, but he wanted to be alone in company.

When he turned to the problem of revising his play (*The Moon Is Down*), he did something he had never done before. The first draft was in longhand, and he went through it making notes. When the notes were completed, he had a court reporter come in with her machine, and he went through the manuscript, reading it aloud and making changes as he read, sometimes trying a line several different ways aloud to hear which sounded the best.

The reporter was a great fat woman, very severe-looking, who came every day to the apartment and without a word put her machine on the table and sat down on a little wooden chair, great bulges of fat hanging over on both sides. As the days went by, she seemed to become more and more hostile, her expression changing from disapproval to something that appeared to be very close to outright hatred. Every morning she thrust a stack of typed pages at her employer, the transcription of the dictation from the day before, and in the afternoons, after she had gone, he would go over the typing, correcting errors and making further changes. Gradually, he became aware that there were differences between what he had dictated and what she had typed. At first the differences seemed minor and he thought that she was simply making mistakes; then it became clear that she was making changes and deleting whole passages on her own. After he fired her, he made inquiries and found that she was attending German Bund meetings.

In the meantime, Steinbeck's relations with his wife hit rock bottom. Carol was, according to him, on a rampage of threats and recriminations, talking "of nothing but money and revenge" everywhere she went. She raided Burgess Meredith's files while he was gone in order to recover her husband's letters, and she told Elizabeth Otis that her books better be accurate because she was going to have an accountant go over them. In an effort to put things on a more even keel, Steinbeck wrote a long letter to her. As he explained to Toby, "I wrote to Carol in your care. I tried to tell her why it was and what had happened. I don't expect it to do much good. She will digest out of my letter only what she wants. She will scream liar at me as she has so often before. It was a very hard letter to write. I did not take all the blame as I have done before so that she could feel easy" [11/1/41]. He was right—the letter did not help. It would be a long, long time before Carol would be able to forgive him for wrongs she felt she had suffered from him, and there were some that she never would forgive. If she had any consolation, it would come later, when her husband suffered from another the same treatment that he had accorded her—and reacted in very much the same way.

Eleventh Street house, Pacific Grove. (© 1983 Richard L. Allman.)

Ed Ricketts and Natalya
"Tal" Lovejoy on outing.
*(Photo by Ritchie Lovejoy,
courtesy, © 1983
Jennifer Lovejoy Kelly.)*

George Albee. *(Courtesy Richard Albee, John Steinbeck Library,
Salinas, Steinbeck Archives.)*

Hayfield, Corral de Tierra
(locale of *Pastures of Heaven*).
(© *1983 Richard L. Allman.*)

Salinas River, southeast
of Soledad: possible locale,
Of Mice and Men.
(© *1983 Richard L. Allman.*)

Cotton-strike leader Pat Chambers and worker leaders. *(Courtesy The Bancroft Library.*

Cotton-strike leader
Caroline Decker, at strike
headquarters in Tulare.
(Courtesy The Bancroft Library.)

John in his early thirties
in the Pacific Grove house.
Fireplace that he built
is to his left.
(Courtesy Peter Stackpole.)

Claire Luce as
Curley's wife and
Broderick Crawford
as Lennie in the
Broadway production,
Of Mice and Men.
(Courtesy Peter Stackpole.)

Gate plaque made by Steinbeck ("Arroyo del Ajo"), Greenwood Lane house, Los Gatos. (© 1983 Richard L. Allman.)

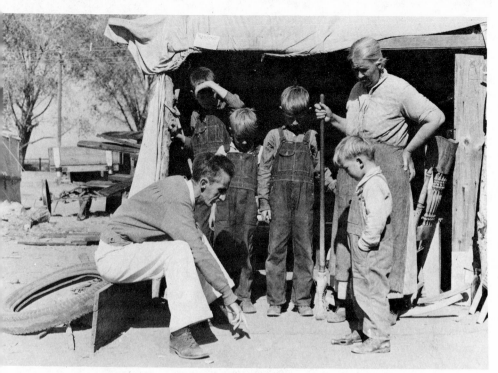

Tom Collins at Weedpatch (Kern County Migrant Camp, F.S.A.), 1936.
(Dorothea Lange, courtesy Library of Congress.)

Garden plots at Weedpatch. *(Dorothea Lange, courtesy Library of Congress)*

Crew and passengers on board the *Western Flyer* before sailing. From left to right: Horace "Sparky" Enea, Travis "Tex" Hall, Mrs. Anthony Berry (did not go on trip), Anthony "Tony" Berry, Carol Steinbeck, John, Ratzi "Tiny" Coletto. Missing: Ed Ricketts. In alternate shot, published in newspaper, John is hiding behind Carol. (*The John Steinbeck Collection, Stanford University Libraries.*)

CHAPTER XXVII

After a month in the East, Gwyn was "going crazy for something to do" when an opportunity came for her to sing. Elizabeth Otis had invited John and Gwyn over for the evening and had also included a singing group of her acquaintance. The group specialized in American folk music and in a few days was going to Washington to sing at a "Fight for Freedom" rally. Gwyn joined in the singing with "Johnny Has Gone for a Soldier," one of John's favorites, and the group asked her to perform the song at the rally. Dorothy Thompson, one of the organizers of the event, then contacted John and talked him into giving a short speech, along with other notables, including Archibald MacLeish and Henry Wallace.

John and Gwyn flew to Washington and checked into a hotel, where Gwyn put on her costume, a Martha Washington type of outfit, with pantaloons and hoop dress, pink and silver, and a white wig with dangling curls. But John decided that he could not go through with the speech and instead wrote a message to be delivered for him. Worried about Dorothy Thompson's ire and embarrassed by his reneging, he made arrangements to leave Washington that evening. The rally was held in conjunction with the opening of Maxwell Anderson's play *Candle in the Wind*, and when John took Gwyn back to the hotel after the rally was over, he told her he was going to go see a little bit of the play, but she should not even get out of her costume—he'd be back shortly.

Gwyn packed her street clothes and waited in the lobby of the George Washington Hotel for nearly three hours. John arrived and announced that they would have to hurry—leave the baggage to be sent later—or they would miss their plane. The play had gone badly, and he'd been in a bar drinking Stingers and commiserating with the star's (Helen Hayes's) husband, Charles MacArthur.

By this time it had begun to rain, and as they made a mad dash for the plane, Gwyn had her own raincoat on, was holding John's over her head, and with the other hand was pulling up the hoops of her skirt so that she could get up the steps of the boarding ramp. Once aboard, John sat next to the window, squirming because he hadn't had time to go to the bathroom, and Gwyn sat on the aisle, her dress covering part of John's seat and much of the aisle next to her. "If you could only see yourself now," John told her, "with your wig hanging down, your glasses fogged up, and your mascara running down your cheeks." They began to get the giggles. The plane taxied to the end of the runway, revved the motors and stopped. It sat at the end of the runway for almost a half hour, and John was getting desperate. Finally, a steward announced that they were overloaded with mail and would have to return to the terminal to unload some of it. A man in front said "What?" and Gwyn told him, "We're overweight!" There was a pregnant silence, and then John said in a soft voice that somehow carried throughout the plane, "Well, if they'd just let me take a *pee*, we could take off!"

Gwyn was asked on several occasions to perform, but John would not allow it. He insisted that she give up her career entirely and stay at home, perhaps clues to the breakup of his previous marriage as well as to his intent to establish a different pattern for his relationship with Gwyn. His marriage to Carol, most of their friends agreed, had been combative and competitive, and her uninhibited behavior, which he had delighted in at the beginning of their marriage, began to wear on him. Both of them were domineering, and neither was easily dominated. His desire for "peace" during their last years together would seem to have been to a large extent a longing for a more traditional marriage, one in which he would be clearly dominant, with a wife whose main concern would be to cater to his needs. He was supported in this longing by his streak of personal conservatism as well as a romanticism that allowed him to dream of a domestic life as painted by Norman Rockwell. It was, indeed, a Rockwellesque softness of focus that he longed for, a very feminine wife who would maintain a very conventional home for him that he could roam from and retreat to, like an island. In this, he was not so much a male chauvinist as he was a weary sentimentalist.

He was building a dream of life around Gwyn that had little to do with what Gwyn was or what she wanted. He wrote to Toby in the middle of January 1942:

> Gwyn is well. This suitcase life is not very satisfactory to her. She wants some place to light but there is none in sight. She doesn't

complain at all though. And when I do get called I don't know where it will be—maybe Washington, maybe not. The new little book [*The Moon Is Down* in short novel form] will be out the end of Feb or early in March. Viking Press thinks it will sell a lot of them. The Sea [of Cortez] is moving very slowly and it will never make any money. . . .

Anyway the physical clearness of my own personal life should come out in or within two weeks. Then I'll let you know. Meanwhile Gwynnie sits on a bag of dynamite, but she is good about it. I think she wants security more than anyone I ever knew. Carol thought she did and didn't. But Gwyn who has never had any has really a gift for it—an inner security which would make an outer one if given half a chance. And so far she hasn't had that chance. If we could even take a house or an apartment in Washington that's all she wants. She wants to cook. She doesn't talk about any of these things. . . .

After the war is done, if I can, I know what I want if my domestic difficulties and my finances will permit it. I want about ten acres near the ocean and near Monterey and I want a shabby comfortable house and room for animals, maybe a horse, and some dogs and I want some babies. Maybe I can't ever get that but it's what I want. And I'm pretty sure it's what Gwyn wants too. Then maybe I want a small boat. I suppose there isn't a chance in the world of having these. Something will come up but I'm going to try and get them just as soon as the war is over. And I may not even wait for that to start getting the babies. I know now that Gwyn can run a hospitable house where I am welcome. That's why our houses were so doleful. There was no hospitality in them. It is curious that I sit here and plan what is probably an impossible future. My earning years in terms of money are nearly over. Not that I won't work and probably do good work. But the years of a writer financially are very few. And there will be no chance of picking up another reserve. But that is all right too. We'll get along. There's love in the house even here.

There was love—a different, softer, more intimate kind than he had ever experienced before. He delighted in a wife who was dependent on him, one he could take care of. She got into the habit of sleeping late, and he would get up early and do his work while she was still in bed. She would make a brunch or lunch about noon, and unless he was in the middle of developing an idea, he would join her, then return to work for part of the afternoon. Sometimes he would bring her breakfast in bed, and at night he would read to her or tell her stories.

Often during these first years together, before they had established a circle of friends in New York, they were cut off from much social activity and Gwyn became a great reader. When they did meet people, they were often people in the arts or in journalism, bright, articulate, well-informed people who gave her a slight sense of inferiority. She had enough natural intelligence and wit to survive, and with her reading gained a sort of proxy education. And while Steinbeck seemed to value her in part because of her dependence on him, his frequent absences during these years of the war led her to develop a tougher fiber. Thus a collision course was set from the beginning between what he wanted and needed her to be and what she was and, out of circumstance, became. The potential for tragedy was even greater than in his first marriage because he invested so much more emotion in this one. He had determined that she was the romantic love of his life and embodied all the answers to all the vague longings and dissatisfactions that had haunted him for so long. She was, now that he was nearly forty, all that he had missed.

II

The statements that Steinbeck never wrote anything worthwhile (or that "his powers declined rapidly") after *The Grapes of Wrath*, or after he separated from his first wife, or after he moved to the East and no longer saw Ed Ricketts on a regular basis have had wide currency in encyclopedias and other glib summaries of his career. It would be more accurate to say that the widely respected work of his early and mid-career, from *In Dubious Battle* to *The Grapes of Wrath*, was more often praised by reviewers for its presumed political liberalism and social realism than for its themes, which were seldom perceived. Once the subject matter changed (as society itself was changing) and his themes became more apparent, the critical response was much more divided. A good deal of the negative response to Steinbeck's work throughout his career would seem to have been politically motivated.

For over thirty years *Time* magazine expressed its antagonism toward him as a "proletarian" writer and never gave him or his work a kind word until it wrote his obituary. On the other hand, the Marxists, who tended to applaud his early writing and who tried to use him for their own purposes in whatever ways they could, scolded him when he turned away from the subject of farm labor. One must wonder, in retrospect, how much of Steinbeck's alleged decline in quality following *The Grapes of Wrath* was real and how much simply the expression of a lack of interest in Steinbeck's new subjects by critics who were disappointed that he didn't write the same book over and over again.

Once Steinbeck's work was noticed he got his share of bad reviews, although on balance, the reactions to all his writing up through *Sea of Cortez* had been favorable. The author had expressed the view on several occasions, however, that some of his work had been overpraised, particularly *The Grapes of Wrath*, and after *Grapes* his letters suggest that he was waiting for the critical ax to fall. Too much praise made him nervous, for he thought that it might well lead to an automatic rejection of whatever else he might produce of a different kind.

With the publication of *The Moon Is Down* in March 1942, and increasingly with the books that followed, it became clear that the reviewers had indeed categorized him, just as he feared they would. Gwyn recalls that one newspaper review of *The Moon Is Down* expressed great disappointment—apparently expecting another *The Grapes of Wrath*—that Steinbeck had produced a "slim volume," rather than a substantial one. It became a joke between Gwyn and her husband. "Well, honey," John would say, "what should I write this time, a thin book or a thick one?"

That is not to say that he always took a philosophical view of his critical reception. There were times when a particularly snide or stupid review sent him into a tantrum. Like a wounded bull he would rage through house or apartment, stopping only to string together litanies of misbegotten lineage or promises of terrible revenge. But just as often he agreed with negative assessments of his work—he was never satisfied with what he wrote—and in the long run what seemed most imporant to him was that he try different kinds of things, even if he had to acknowledge later that the attempt had failed.

Many years after the event, Stanley Edgar Hyman wrote in *The New Leader* that the publication of *The Moon Is Down* caused him to lose interest in Steinbeck's work because the novel signaled a shift in the author's "social commitment." And it would seem, for the intellectual left at least, that this novel, with its allegedly "soft" treatment of German fascists, was the beginning of the decline of Steinbeck's reputation, although at the time the attack on *The Moon Is Down* was not stated in political terms.

Having previously published in *The Grapes of Wrath* what was already recognized as one of the most accomplished novels of the decade, perhaps of the half-century, he was writing for an audience whose expectations were naturally very high. He wrote to Toby that "the new book is doing frighteningly well. Prepublication it is outselling Grapes two to one. In trade edition there will be a prepublication sale of 85,000 and Book of the Month Club is ordering 200,000" [1/20/42].

But the book was not a major effort on his part. In contrast with the narrative for *Sea of Cortez*, which had been written slowly and with great care, the play-novelette had been written in some haste and partly by dictation. (After having revealed to Burgess Meredith in the late forties that he had used dictation while writing several of his books over the past few years, he swore him to secrecy—but he seemed always to be swearing people to secrecy about one thing or another and then, more often than not, giving away the "secret" himself.) *The Moon Is Down* was not executed as a work of art; it was, in his view, a job he was doing for the F.I.S., a contribution to the war effort. "I had thought," he wrote later, "I was doing a good and patriotic thing."

That was precisely why the criticism hurt so very much. If they had said only that it was below the standard set by his best work, it wouldn't have bothered him; or if he had been attacked on the usual political grounds that he was a socialist or communist or sympathizer, he was used to that; but the harshest criticism of the novelette, the accusation that he could not handle, was that in writing the book he had, in effect, given aid and comfort to the enemy. The injustice of it rankled for years afterward.

The most violent attack was launched by James Thurber in *The New Republic*, and when Marshall Best, editor in chief of Viking, took the unusual step of protesting Thurber's review in a letter to the editor, Thurber replied, "Mr. Best is quite right when he says that we might yet lose the war. Nothing would help more toward that end than for Americans to believe the Steinbeck version of Nazi conquest." In response to Best's assertion that Thurber's review was "a slap in the face for all the decent people who have been moved by the book's shining sincerity," Thurber replied that he was sorry about that slap in the face. "I didn't realize my hand was open."

It was very nasty stuff, and Steinbeck quite properly labeled the attacks "hysterical." In the novelette he had applied the spirit of biological objectivity that he had developed with Ricketts in *Sea of Cortez*, along with certain aspects of his theory of the phalanx, to the war situation in Europe. While the conquered had become soft (like the property owners in *Grapes*) and were bound to fall in face of the efficiency and single-minded ferocity of the oppressor, the oppressor would eventually fail, for the conquerors were herd men, lacking the flexibility to adapt. "It is always," he says in the novelette, "the herd men who win battles and the free men who win wars." Such an argument was completely alien to the perception of his reviewers, who had no inclination during the darkest days of the war to view German might and Nazi atrocities from such a detached, philosophical point of view.

According to his critics, Steinbeck's dangerous romanticism included not only making his invaders too human and taking a too optimistic view of the war and its outcome, but also advocating, by implication, resistance to the Nazis by the occupied peoples. Such resistance would surely be useless and play into the hands of the Germans by giving them further excuses to terrorize and kill their victims. However, history proved that his critics were wrong on nearly every count, except that the book was artistically not among the writer's best. Twenty years later, Steinbeck took the occasion of having received in the mail a beat-up, paper-covered mimeographed manuscript of *The Moon Is Down*, put out by the Danish resistance in 1942, to review his motives in writing the book, the attack on the book, and its subsequent history in the European underground.

He pointed out that his friends in the resistance did not find the book overly optimistic—that if they didn't think that they would win eventually, they would have surrendered long ago:

> The little book was smuggled into the occupied countries. It was copied, mimeographed, printed on hand presses in cellars, and I have seen a copy laboriously hand written on scrap paper and tied together with twine. The Germans did not consider it unrealistic optimism. They made it a capital crime to possess it, and sadly to my knowledge this sentence was carried out a number of times. It seemed that the closer it got to action, the less romantic it seemed.

The book itself became a romantic, but true story. At most it gave support to the courage of many people in desperate circumstances; at the very least it gave evidence of our faith in them and their cause at a time when faith was a very precious commodity. As a novel it lacked the rich texture and interesting characterizations of his other work, but it was a brilliant idea, and it was remarkable that an American author who had never lived under an occupying army could strike so close to the hearts of those who were. In years after, Steinbeck was decorated by the King of Norway for his contribution to the morale of the Norwegian underground.

The play *The Moon Is Down* opened on April 8, 1942, on Broadway, starring Otto Kruger as Colonel Lanser and Ralph Morgan as Mayor Orden. The controversy over the book spread to the criticism of the play: Was Steinbeck too easy in his characterization of the invaders? Was the play too hopeful too early in the war? This time he took the criticism with a good deal more equanimity, writing to Toby:

I'm sending you the reviews and as you will see they are almost uniformly bad [an exaggeration—the response was mixed]. Furthermore, they are almost uniformly right. They don't really know what bothered them about the play, but I do. It was dull. For some reason, probably because of my writing, it didn't come over the footlights. In spite of that it will probably run for several months. It is too bad it isn't better. I don't know why the words don't come through. The controversy that has started as to whether we should not hate blindly is all to the good and is doing no harm. What does the harm is that it is not a dramatically interesting play. [4/10/42]

From an attack on the novelette and play, the activity gradually shifted to a battle between critics, which Steinbeck followed with interest and some amusement, particularly when critic tangled with critic. In regard to one critic, he wrote to Toby, "I think his article when he went right on past me and attacked Plato is wonderful" [4/30/42].

III

In the meantime Carol was taking her revenge in bitter revelations concerning John's idiosyncrasies and in her settlement demands. In March, she filed the papers for divorce on the basis of mental cruelty, one of the few times that the California law had been used with such accuracy. There was a waiting period, so John and Gwyn would have to wait a year for the final decree. The filing of the papers made him reflect, "I am sad at the passage of a good big slice of my life. It could have been ecstatic. That was the age for it. But I still have energy and I am still capable of loving a woman very much. So it isn't really too late for either of us. It's the first divorce our family ever had and it makes me sad" [2/14/42]. The first divorce our family ever had—again that streak of personal conservatism: several years later he would make Gwyn swear that she would never reveal to their children that they had had sex before marriage.

They found a house to rent at Sneden's Landing, across the Hudson River from the city, about twelve miles from the George Washington Bridge, and moved in on the first of April. He continued to work for the F.I.S., writing overseas broadcasts, and wrote to Toby, "I go on every night and in the day time. Not I, of course, I send the stuff in. [He would compose in the morning and then drive five miles to Nyack and send in his material by wire.] I had my voice tested the other day and it was just as I knew it would be. My enunciation is so bad and the boom in my voice is so bad that I can't be understood" [4/8/42]. He found any form of public speaking extremely unpleasant and was glad that he had been eliminated as a broadcaster. In terms of the course of his career, his tenure with the F.I.S., and later the O.W.I., provided an introduction to people in the industry and to broadcasting technology. The idea of its possibilities fired his imagination and led him, after the war, to a disastrous attempt to enter the broadcasting business.

Although he felt he was doing something good for his country, his work for the F.I.S. was temporary and unpaid, and he was anxious for some kind of permanent assignment. He was getting his first taste of the bureaucratic confusion that he would be caught up in for the next year—F.I.S. would not take him on officially, but neither would they release him to do something else. By the middle of April and after several months of such delay, he was becoming very restless, a constant state by now, which for him was a sort of chronic "disease" of the nervous system, and he and Gwyn decided to take another vacation trip to New Orleans—they had previously spent a week there over the Christmas holidays with old friends of John's, Howard and Margery Hunter. Upon their return from this latest trip, John reported to Toby that their hostess had "summed the party up in immortal words when she said happily one afternoon, 'If all the horseshit I've heard in this room for the last three days were only on the roses, how the garden would bloom this year'" [4/21/42]. Margery Hunter was a woman after his own heart, an urbane woman of the soil.

He had sent to the West Coast for his work clothes and boots and was now spending many of his afternoons trying to revive and reshape the neglected garden of their rented Rockland County house, but his heart wasn't in it, since he had no idea how long they would be living there. After the near isolation of their first few months in New York, they began to entertain occasionally and to go out on the town, especially once John began to realize that the city was full of celebrities and that no one, except for the maître d's, cared who he was. They had moved to Sneden's Landing because the Paul de Kruifs lived nearby, and they soon also became friendly with neighbors Maxwell Anderson, whom Steinbeck had known casually before, and the painter Henry Poor. Burgess Meredith, who was technically in the Army but still performing (without being able to keep his wages), dropped in on them now and then.

Their closest friends during the war years were probably Frank and Lynn Loesser. John objected to Lynn only when she kept Gwyn away from home, and in Frank he had found a kindred spirit. Neither of them was much interested in sports or games, and so for recreation they sat around inventing outrageous schemes or crazy things to do. Seldom were their pranks carried out; the fun was in thinking them up and in projecting possible reactions. Early one evening they had been talking about the gift boxes that the large talent agencies, such as M.C.A., were sending to their clients who had gone into the service. The boxes contained very expensive items, such as cologne, that would be of no use whatsoever to anyone actually fighting in the war. The absurdity of the whole thing got them laughing, and they ended up drawing up an elaborate contract specifying what each would send to the other when he got to the front. Frank drew it up on a great big piece of cardboard in impressive formal lettering, sketched in a beautiful, official-looking design at the top, and attached a seal with a ribbon at the bottom. The final clause was that if either of them broke this contract, the person who did so would be honor bound to write the life of Eddie Cantor.

They also planned other, more serious, projects, but few of them reached fruition. John arranged for Frank to do the lyrics for the music in the film of *Tortilla Flat*, and they talked about making the book into a Broadway musical. (They also planned another musical, to be called "The Wizard of Maine," which they worked on after the war, but it was never completed.) And John was responsible for Frank's writing several of his war songs, including "Praise the Lord and Pass the Ammunition," which John wanted the Office of War Information to use as a sort of unofficial anthem for their broadcasts.

During this period John met Burl Ives, and Lynn Loesser remembers John's delight in listening to the original, uncensored versions of old folk songs as sung by Ives. These were also the months during which John got to know radio comedian Fred Allen and his wife. The three couples, Lynn recalls, would "start out with cocktails and end up going to God knows what kind of places, tootling around in taxicabs, singing together, telling jokes. I remember one night a cabdriver slowed down the cab and turned around and said to John and Fred, 'Can I tell one now, please?' " Allen wanted to write a book but was afraid he couldn't write, so that it became a "cause" among them, particularly John, to try to prod Allen into it. They nagged and nagged until finally John said that if Allen would try to get something down on paper, he would edit it and make it publishable. Allen agreed to start on it and fourteen years later *Much Ado About Me* was published with a preface by John.

One of the effects of the divorce was to take away all of Steinbeck's savings. When he and Gwyn had moved to New York, he began to worry about money for the first time in a long time. Not that he was close to being broke, but he was concerned that he no longer had a cushion for the day when his books stopped making money—a day he was confident could come any time—and for someone who had struggled through many years of the Depression without money, just the idea of having something in the bank was very important. So he was very much relieved when, at the end of April, he was notified that *The Moon Is Down* had sold for the largest sum ever paid for a story by the movies. The announced figure, $300,000, was over twice as much as he would actually net over time, but it was more than enough to restore his sense of security.

Early in May he wrote to Toby Street:

Already people who think I have got 300,000 dollars in my pocket are writing, hundreds of them and my mail is pretty horrible as it was after the Grapes. . . .

Believe it or not, I'm doing a short story every day. A five hundred word one but it is a job to do one every day and two other things besides. It makes for work. . . .

Tomorrow . . . we are going in town to see Nunnally Johnson [who would be doing the screenplay for *Moon*] and then later we are going to meet Paul and Rhea de Kruif for dinner and very late we are going to pick up Mildred Lyman and bring her back to the country. [Mildred Lyman was on the McIntosh and Otis staff.]

The short stories, really just finger exercises, underlined his growing frustration with the uncertainty of his future.

His situation was made even more uncertain by events at the F.I.S. The section was about to be taken from the intelligence agency, the O.S.S., and along with other information and propaganda programs run by the government, be combined into one agency, the Office of War Information. He was offered a permanent job with the O.W.I., but in signing the papers, he would be submitting himself to a security check. Several of the people in the section had been dismissed from government service because they, like Steinbeck, had given money for ambulances for Spain or had, again like Steinbeck, been accused of being a communist or socialist because of something they had written in the past. None of these people who had been fired had as big a name as Steinbeck, and so he was asked by his colleagues to become a test case, or as Steinbeck put it, a "clay pigeon." He warned Toby that he could expect a visit from the F.B.I. and "they will probably ask you a lot of very funny questions and they may attack me on my morals which god knows are just as bad as I can make them." If Steinbeck was refused, the office planned to quit en masse and appeal to the President and the courts. The writer apparently did not have enough experience as a clay pigeon to realize that such solid moral support often evaporates under pressure.

At just about this time, mid-May of 1942, he was offered another temporary assignment. Gwyn had gone to the West Coast to visit her mother, and Burgess Meredith was visiting at the time the offer came. The job was to write two books for the Air Force, and Steinbeck was very dubious about it, since the books were obviously designed as publicity for the service and as enlistment bait—he didn't know whether he wanted to lend his name to something like that or not. It was typical of him that in this he was not worried about the possible cheapening of his literary reputation, but rather that he didn't want to be responsible for someone going to war and being killed. Meredith felt he had talked him into it as a job that he could do thoroughly and honestly and then let the chips fall where they may.

John described his mission for Toby:

I'm going to write a book for the Air Corps on bombers and bomber crews. Beginning Monday I am going from one training camp to another and I'm going to live with the kids and find out what the air corps is about and then do a book with pictures in it. If the first book is successful and well done I shall go on with it into a second volume which will be the task in combat areas.

It was this last thing that appealed to him more than anything else. Meredith recalls that while he wanted to stay as far away from the fighting as possible, John wanted to get to the action.

It was part of another paradox. On the one hand his instincts were largely pacifistic and he perceived war intellectually as futile—a biological racial spasm generated out of the unconscious. He had no lust for blood and battle, no need to certify his manhood, which he always had deemed self-evident. On the other hand, he had a very strong sense of duty. When he wrote Gwyn about doing the books—"It's a tremendous job I've taken on and I have to do it well"—the tone was the deep bass expression of national determination right out of a "March of Time" newsreel. He had also developed a need to be on the scene, where things were going on—it was part of his restlessness—which was similar to the compulsion, or perhaps addiction, that some journalists have to rush to the eye of the storm.

In time he would think of himself more and more as a journalist, and with some pride he would carry his press card with him wherever he went. It was another role, like that of the old sailor (he wore his bush jacket for the one and his sailor's cap for the other), which gave him a special status and air of experience. Perhaps they were both assumed as an unconscious rebuttal to the belief held by many in our society that there is something either effete or effeminate about the man who is writer as artist.

In the purest sense, however, he never was a journalist. From his first reporting, in New York for the *American,* to his last, in Vietnam for *Newsday,* he was always the novelist, commenting on the meaning and emotion of what he saw, focusing on its drama. Yet following *The Grapes of Wrath,* more often than not it was things happening that stirred the writing juices, rather than, as early in his career, things imagined or recalled. As he grew older his appetite for travel and experience increased with his means and opportunity, and there was a constant battle within him between the part that found comfort and convenience at home (in old clothes, planting, and carving) and the part that drove him outward to new knowledge. Other major writers, such as Hemingway and Faulkner, refused assignments such as *Bombs Away,* but Steinbeck took it as his duty and because he wanted to know what it felt like to fly in a bomber.

He went to Washington to be briefed and bought some Army shirts and pants. He met General "Hap" Arnold, and he went to a dinner party with more generals, where he was taken aback by the heavy drinking (we drink, he told Gwyn, but not like that). He also met John Swope, who would accompany him on the mission as photographer. He liked Swope, even though the photographer thought it was amusing to take pictures of Steinbeck waking up, walking naked to the shower, and sitting on the can. At the briefing he learned he would fly in just about every type of aircraft the Army had, from trainers to the largest bombers, and his trip would take him to Texas, New Orleans, Albuquerque, Phoenix, Las Vegas, Los Angeles, San Diego, Sacramento, Illinois, and Florida, and then back to New York—about twenty thousand miles and twenty different locations in thirty days.

The trip was hectic and exhausting, but at the same time boring, since he spent a lot of time just sitting in a slow airplane looking down at Texas. His routine involved getting up at five in the morning, going out on a flight, coming back and attending classes and training sessions, and then going to the local commander's quarters for dinner. He and Swope usually shared a room, and he had almost no time to himself. He wrote Gwyn:

> It's seven thirty in the evening and we're flying back from Ellington field to Kelly Field and then to Randolph to sleep. It has been god awful hot today near the gulf. I'm still soaking wet. We went up with a formation today and followed it around taking pictures of it from all angles. Then to a number of classes for the demonstration. I'm hot and tired and burned and lonesome. [5/42]

He followed the training of the pilots, the navigators, the bombardiers, and the gunners; flew with them on training flights in the cockpit, the nose, and the tail; took some of the tests that they took and worked with their equipment; and went with them at night to the roadhouses and bars and watched them play the jukeboxes and dance with their girls. And then he went home to write his book.

His last stop had been Florida, and back in New York he wrote to Toby, "I haven't one inch on my body that isn't mosquito bitten. I never saw such bugs as there in those Florida swamps" [6/18/42]. He had a deadline of August 1, and near the end of June he reported:

> I'm dictating a book into the ediphone now for the airforce. My first experience in this kind of dictation but much preferable to doing it to a stenographer. I always have a feeling that I am keeping a steno from going home and doing what she wants to. But this machine is a slave and has no rights nor any home. . . .
>
> I'm working very hard now doing about four thousand words a day. I hope they are good words but I'm afraid that they are being done too rapidly. [6/25/42]

He worked through July and August, missing his deadline in part because the Air Force didn't get material to him that he needed for the book—while at the same time demanding that he get the manuscript in. He had to remind them several times, he told Covici, that he simply would not do shoddy work. Then several weeks after he had submitted the manuscript, he got a long telegram from Covici saying that the Air Force wanted the book to end with a final chapter showing a bomber crew on an actual combat bombing run. At first the writer agreed, but the more he thought about it, the less he liked the idea. He had never been on a real bombing mission, he wrote Covici, and he refused to fake it.

Near the end of September, he and Gwyn moved to Sherman Oaks, California, in the San Fernando Valley, into "a pleasant little house with a big garden," so that he could start to work on the movie version of *Bombs Away: The Story of a Bomber Team*. But, to use World War II jargon, the picture was snafu from the beginning. When Steinbeck showed up for work, he found his boss was away in England, that nobody knew who was doing what or why, but that everybody was going ahead and doing it anyway, and, as he wrote Elizabeth, "that everything they wanted me to do was not only being done, but being done ad nauseum." [9/23/42] So he decided to try to promote his own idea for another picture, a reversion to the original concept for *The Moon Is Down*—the invasion of a small American town. Only this time, it would be by the Japanese, rather than the Germans, and they would follow their usual tactic of bypassing heavily defended areas, in this case the West Coast, and attacking where it would be unexpected—somewhere in the middle of the country (Steinbeck thought he might have them drop by parachute). "This kind of thinking," he wrote Elizabeth, "was sharpened by crossing the country and seeing the kind of greed and apathy of the country inside the mountains."

Nunnally Johnson and Twentieth Century-Fox liked the idea, but it was vetoed, as the earlier version had been, by the head of the picture division of what had been the F.I.S., now the O.W.I. At about the same time he was trying to get this idea through, he was asked to do some writing about our Alaskan defenses, but the O.W.I. stalled on giving permission for that. It seemed as if everything he tried to do or planned or was offered was being cut off at the nub, and it was driving him crazy. To avoid just sitting in Sherman Oaks twiddling his thumbs, he started making notes for his own version of *The Good Soldier Schweik*, which he thought he would write after the war was over.

Even in the doldrums of bureaucratic confusion and his own forced inactivity, he was able to find some humor in the ups and downs of his semi-career in government. When he and Gwyn visited Sandy Oliver, he revealed how he got involved in *Bombs Away* in the first place. He had heard about the project but was dead set against it when he was called in to see President Roosevelt. Having seen the President in action before, he knew that he would have to have great determination to stick to his guns and not get involved. So when he got to the White House, he set his jaw and kept thinking to himself, "I am not going to do this. They will have to get somebody else. I am not going to do this."

He went into the Oval Office, and there sat this very affable man, just oozing charm, puffing on a long cigarette. They never discussed anything but Roosevelt's interest in his writing. Then suddenly at the end of the interview, Steinbeck was taken aback, he recalled, when the President suddenly said, "Now John, you are going to do what I want you to do—what I want you to do, John." John told Oliver, "Then I found myself saying, 'Yes, Mr. President, I am,' and that was it."

Then John brought out a copy of his travel orders. He told Sandy Oliver, "You've got to set them to music. This is the funniest document I've ever seen." She and Gwyn sat down at the piano and worked out a musical accompaniment for his orders:

> Under the authority of the Secretary of War, dated November 21, 1941, John Steinbeck, Special Consultant, will proceed by rail, or by military aircraft or by commercial aircraft, or by privately owned automobile on or about July 13, 1942, from his proper station, Washington, D.C., to Nyack, New York; thence to New York, New York; thence to Mitchel Field, New York; thence to New York, New York; thence to Nyack, New York; thence to New York, New York [and so on and on in the same vein].

"This particular rendition of music," Oliver recalls, "suited John's sense of humor exactly. He liked things like that."

But the situation got progressively worse, more and more confused and more and more frustrating. From October through March of the following year, he was bogged down in a mess of delay and bureaucratic haggling and conflict. He was supposed to be released from the O.W.I., taken out of the hands of his draft board, and commissioned as an officer in Air Force intelligence—all this after he finished work on the film. Since he never really got to work on the film, he asked to be released from that job, and when he got no word about being relieved of his film duties, he wrote to Washington asking that he be detached from the Air Force and returned to duty with the O.W.I. Washington notified him to sit tight; they would put through papers for a commission and in the meantime get him a temporary deferment from his draft board.

What happened next can be readily believed only by those who have had some experience with the arrogance sometimes displayed by small-town draft boards. Toby had attended the hearing during which the board considered the request by General Henry H. Arnold for a thirty-day deferment for Steinbeck, and he sent a special delivery letter reporting to the writer that "the members of the board couldn't figure how you who had always written trash could write anything that could be of any benefit to the Army." They denied General Arnold's petition.

One can well imagine Steinbeck's expression while reading that letter. He wrote back immediately: "I had your special delivery letter this afternoon and am answering it now. I love the draft board as literary critics. I love also their taking it upon themselves to know better than the commander of the air force to know what he needs and who can supply it. . . . Arnold likes to think that he knows what he wants and he will not be pleased with the literary critics of Monterey County" [11/7/42]. He fired off a telegram to Washington telling them that he was fed up and wanted to enlist. Word came back that he was not to do anything, just hang on and wait.

Winter passed and Steinbeck wasn't drafted nor was he commissioned. In December a presidential order setting up a national manpower pool put Steinbeck in a category where he was unlikely to be drafted, but at the same time he got a letter from the Air Force telling him that new regulations made it almost impossible to give any further commissions to civilians; nevertheless, it was going ahead anyway. But his interview, done in New York, and his recommendations had been misplaced somehow—would he go to the Federal Building and have himself interviewed again? Meanwhile, Steinbeck, who had tried to turn the royalties from the book of *Bombs Away* over to the government, was finally able to arrange to give the royalties to the Air Forces Aid Society, but he had to pay taxes on the income first.

The battle of Hollywood was grim, and he had very little stomach for it. Some of the studio executives had been commissioned and were parading around in their uniforms, and Steinbeck was surprised that they didn't require that he salute. Colonel Jack Warner, he wrote Elizabeth, "is running this thing as though it were his private war and someone might steal it from him." He wrote to Pat Covici at Viking that his "desire to help in this war does not include sitting in Hollywood for the duration," and noted that this had been the longest period of non-work in his life. In order to keep his sanity, he was planning books, even if he couldn't write them: "a very large work is beginning to take shape in my head—something that will take a couple of years to do and that can only be done after the war."

In December he started writing a training film for the Air Force. (In none of these jobs, by the way, was he paid. He was rankled by the fact that he had come to Hollywood to work on *Bombs Away* and then sat around doing nothing, while he had paid for the move from New York and was paying all his own expenses. In the meantime he watched people like Gene Autry, along with two colonels, fly across the country at government expense in order to change the hour of the Autry radio show—something that could have been done by letter or by phone.) During December he was also involved in an effort to raise money to buy Christmas presents for the children, some eight thousand of them, whose fathers had been killed or captured on Bataan. He wrote to all his friends and relatives that this did not seem to be a Christmas for usual gift-giving, and that all his gift money would be going elsewhere. In mid-December, Jack Wagner, Max's brother, came to him with a picture idea. Depressed, Steinbeck said so what? I may be in the Army tomorrow or be sent to Washington next week. But Wagner persisted. It was a great idea, but he needed help to write the script. Steinbeck finally agreed, but only on condition that when they sold it, the money would go to Wagner's mother. Over the next few weekends they produced the script for *A Medal for Benny*.

In the middle of January, he wrote to Toby that they were moving out of the house in Sherman Oaks (expecting to be in Los Angeles only temporarily, they had taken only a three-month lease) and were going to stay with the Wagners in Hollywood:

> I think I am blocked in fact black balled for the army although they say not. I imagine that you have had an investigator by now. They really seem to think I am a communist. So I'll work at other things and still be subject to call. I'm working on a story now for 20th Century at the request of the Maritime Commission. Hope to finish it before I go. It is pretty interesting I think. At least I feel pretty good with it so far. I think it could be very good. . . .
>
> Jack Wagner and I wrote a movie about three week ends ago—a kind of vicious comedy. I don't know who will make the film but every studio in town is bidding for it. It would make a pretty good picture too. Now at last I am at work I feel some of the old excitement in work. Maybe I'll get the whole excitement again. I have an exciting story sure enough. [1/11/43]

The story he was working on during the first part of 1943 was for the Hitchcock movie *Lifeboat*. According to Gwyn, John had begun a short story or novelette manuscript just after they first moved to New York (while still working on the first draft of *The Moon Is Down*), which dealt with the victims of a U-boat sinking. He was inspired by the number of sinkings reported almost daily in the newspapers and began to think of the possibilities for drama and metaphor in the inter-action between various strong, almost allegorical characters in a lifeboat (it was a similar metaphor of the world in microcosm adrift in the uni-verse that he would use in *The Wayward Bus*).

When Kenneth MacGowan of Twentieth Century-Fox asked him to do a script for a film requested by the Maritime Commission, he not only resurrected his earlier idea but was further inspired, again accord-ing to Gwyn, by the recent ordeal of Eddie Rickenbacker, who in 1942 was forced down in the Pacific six hundred miles north of Samoa and, along with seven other survivors, spent twenty-four days in rubber rafts before being rescued. John wrote Annie Laurie that if, as he devel-oped the story, it seemed to be working well, then perhaps "Hitchcock will go east with me and we will talk to some of the seamen who have been torpedoed" [1/8/43]. But Hitchcock, whom Steinbeck did not know at the time, had a very different idea about the movie, one that had little to do with Steinbeck's drive to base the drama on as realistic a recreation of that sort of ordeal as possible. There would be trouble ahead, the very kind that had made Steinbeck shy away from Holly-wood in the first place.

He finished the screenplay about the middle of February. In the meantime, he and Gwyn had moved back to New York. He had found an apartment on East Fifty-first Street with two fireplaces and a gar-den, and Gwyn was busy furnishing it. (Several weeks later he com-plained that there was still no place to sit down and he sent Gwyn out to buy at least *one* chair.) He wrote Toby that he was working for half a dozen different war agencies and that officially he was acting as "spe-cial consultant" to the Secretary of War. In March, he was notified that the final papers for the divorce would be filed, leaving the way open for him and Gwyn to get married. And there would be another change in his status: no longer would he allow himself to be pushed around senselessly from pillar to post, always waiting for someone else to make up his mind. He was going to take his destiny in his own hands. To Toby he wrote:

Everything in the government is so screwed up and complicated and mean that I am going to try private industry. It may not work but neither does the army nor the gov't. I run up against nothing but jealousies, ambitions and red tape in Washington. [3/15/43]

So he applied for a job as a war correspondent:

I want a job with a big reactionary paper like the Herald-Tribune because I think I could get places that way I couldn't otherwise.

I seem to have been finally rejected by the army. My record was completely cleared of all the slanders and then the Craig board rejected me on the ground that there are no more civilian commissions. It is a relief to me. From what I have seen so far, if I go into the army, I would prefer to be a private. The rest is very like the fraternity system at Stanford. [3/15/43]

He was hired by the *Herald Tribune*, but the job depended on whether he could get clearances from the War and State departments. He told Toby not to say anything to anybody until the job was settled, since so many things that had depended on government action had been pulled out from under him. Although he was told that he had been "cleared of all slanders," it is quite possible that he was told this to keep the Army clear of controversy. Certainly a large part of the delay had been caused by unproven accusations of Party membership or Party sympathy. His permanent civil service appointment to the O.W.I. had never gone through; the harassment at the hands of the draft board was politically motivated; and finally, according to his second wife, he was prevented for a time, again mysteriously, from getting his passport and had difficulties with the passport office all during the war years. Through all of this, of course, he was never apprised of the specific nature of his crimes, of the evidence, or of his accusers—indeed, he never knew for certain that all his troubles didn't stem from personal animosity and ineptitude.

Some of the evidence against him has been revealed, long after his death, through the agency of the Freedom of Information Act, as requested by his widow. There were apparently several files kept on him and more than one investigation made, but the only file still extant is one that summarizes an investigation during the spring and summer of 1943 conducted by Army Counterintelligence. This was a security check made for the purpose of deciding on his most recent, and last, application for a commission.

In some ways the investigation was almost funny. As John's widow commented after seeing the report, "If John were only here to see this.

He would especially like the witness who reported that the 'subject' was usually badly dressed and the agent who said he was a.k.a. 'Dr. Beckstein.' " But other aspects may have been ludicrous, though not very funny. Of the eight people interviewed, two didn't know him at all and two had had barely any contact with him. In fact the only really damaging personal report came from one of those who had never met him, the man who purchased the Los Gatos ranch. This gentleman read Steinbeck's second-class mail and found it "apparently communistic" and "very radical." On the basis of the conditions in the house when he bought it, the gentleman reported Steinbeck to be "very impulsive, eccentric, and unreliable socially."

Two derogatory bits of information came from a New York Air Force major, who had reported Steinbeck as having "communistic tendencies," and Naval Intelligence, which had recorded that "one John Steinbeck . . . was a subscriber to the *People's World* as of September 1939."

But the major source of negative material came from the American Legion Radical Research Bureau. It noted that Steinbeck had contributed articles to *Pacific Weekly* (which it cites as a "Red publication"), was one of the sponsors of the Assembly of Youth, was Chairman of the Committee to Aid Agricultural Organization (cited as a "Very Red outfit"), and, furthermore, that his book *The Grapes of Wrath* had been branded by a Jesuit priest, A. D. Spearman, as "Red propaganda." (This, by the way, was the only "critique" of the novel in the file.)

Despite the solid recommendations of all those interviewed who did know Steinbeck and the positive recommendations by both investigative agents on the case, the lieutenant colonel in charge found "that substantial doubt exists as to subject's loyalty and discretion."

In effect, throughout the war he was a victim of a form of blacklisting. Not that every problem he had with the government was part of a conspiracy, but he had been painted Red by people who didn't like what he had written and the color stuck. However tenuous the basis for the accusations against him, they had tremendous power—a man who knew many people in high places, including the President and the Commander of the Air Forces, was unable to get any kind of "permanent" official job with the government for the entire period of the war. In addition, he had been subject to continual harassment by several branches of the government.

The fact that he was not a communist, had no sympathy for communist doctrine, and didn't even like most of the communists that he had met made the situation that much more frustrating. What made it most painful was that he had such a strong sense of duty and such an intense desire to serve. Since there was no way that he could fight the slander any further than he already had, his instinct was to escape from it somehow, to put as much distance between himself and what he was accused of as possible. Working for "a big reactionary paper" was a step in that direction.

CHAPTER XXVIII

On March 18, 1943, Carol Steinbeck obtained the final divorce decree, and eleven days later, John and Gwyn were married in New Orleans in the courtyard of the French Quarter home of writer Lyle Saxon. The witnesses were former national administrator of the W.P.A. Howard O. Hunter and Paul de Kruif—none of John's family attended. Gwyn's mother, Mrs. Stanley Heuit, attempted to handle the bride's share of the wedding arrangements, but as far as she was concerned, the whole thing was an unmitigated disaster. To begin with, she disliked John intensely, and then everything that could go wrong did. It was a dark, damp, foggy morning. A strike had interfered, so she couldn't get the wedding cake delivered and she couldn't find any flowers; at last she discovered a place that had some calla lilies, had them tied with ribbon, and brought them to the ceremony herself.

The night before, John had a dream in which he lost both wedding rings, and it so worried him that he told Gwyn that he couldn't stand to keep them. "You take yours," he told her, "and I'll take mine." After Gwyn had dressed in her hotel room, she and her mother were unable to get a cab, but were finally able to hire a car; when they got to Lyle Saxon's house, Gwyn dropped her purse getting out of the car and the contents spilled all over the street. Inside, just before the ceremony was to start, she discovered that she had lost the ring. Terribly upset and thinking that John would never trust her again with anything, she dashed out to the street to look for it, then called the hotel to have her room searched. She couldn't find the ring, so she shut herself in the bathroom and wept. In the meantime, the minister had arrived and was waiting, impatiently, since he had another ceremony to perform that morning. In order to pacify him, John and his friends plied him with liquor, and by the time the search for the ring had been abandoned and Gwyn consoled and brought into the courtyard, the minister was tipsy.

The ceremony stumbled forward, John giving Gwyn his ring, several times too large, while Gwyn, with swollen eyes, smiled wanly at the spectacle of her husband-to-be with a silly grin that seemed to be permanently engraved on his face and of a minister who seemed to find the words of the marriage service unfamiliar and at times unpronounceable.

Mrs. Heuit had managed to get the wedding cake to the reception at the Hunters' by sweet-talking the hotel policeman into carrying it over. At the moment when John had his hand on the top of Gwyn's while cutting the first piece of cake, two mounted policemen burst in the front door, stomped over to the groom, and asked if he were John Steinbeck. John, still grinning, said, "Yes." They said, "We have a warrant for your arrest." "What for?" "There is a young lady outside who claims that you are the father of her child." John turned pale and muttered, "Well, that's news to me." Gwyn's hands were shaking, and Mrs. Heuit grew rigid, certain that her worst fears about John's character were being confirmed. "You're going to have to come along with us," the two men told John. There was a long moment of strained silence in the room, and then someone began to titter. After a moment more, the whole room burst into laughter and cheers. It had been a joke arranged by John's best man, a joke known to everyone except the wedded couple and bride's mother. The party continued at Antoine's well into the night.

After John and Gwyn returned to New York, he wrote Toby that they were "a little bit tired out," but that the wedding had been very nice and very sentimental. And to Nunnally Johnson, he wrote, "It would have wakened all of your latent romance. People cried and laughed and shouted and got drunk. Oh! It was a fine wedding." Beyond the blur of toasts, jokes, and loud music was the fact that after a very long wait—they had met four years before and he had proposed nearly two years earlier—they were finally married. Despite all the mishaps—and it was clear that John was not aware of everything that had happened—he, at least, had had a good time.

On his return he was greeted with the good news that the War Department had accredited him as a correspondent for the European theater. (Gwyn, physically and emotionally drained by the hectic experience of New Orleans, was less than thrilled to find that her husband would soon be leaving her. But for the time being, she hid her opposition by simply staying in bed for several days.) John became very excited and began to gather supplies and clothing for the trip.

He planned to leave in a week, since it seemed to him that something big was in the air, but he had not reckoned on the continuing hostility of Selective Service Board 119. He was not draftable, and the matter could have been handled routinely, but the board insisted that it be notified formally by the War Department. The War Department, however, did not operate that way. This was the last straw:

> If I seem a little bitter it is because I have never had any trouble with generals, with secretaries of departments, but a year and a half has been made horrible by little men with temporary authority who, armed with envy, have pushed me around, lieutenants and such who could put in secret reports they thought I would never see and so forth. I just get a little frantic at the mess. At my age, my only chance of getting near combat area is in the capacity I am working on, and now if I am cut off by these sons of bitches, shit. I get so god damned disgusted with stupidity. [JS/WS-4/9/43]

There was no basis on which the board could deny his request, but it managed to drag its heels as long as possible, through April into May, and when he had finally obtained clearance from the board, he had to wait another month in order to get a troop transport. Rather than flying to England, he wanted to share the soldier's experience of going overseas from the beginning. Throughout his wait, he maintained his enthusiasm for the new job, wondering what it would be like, what the problems would be, and whether or not he would be able to see clearly and write well:

> I'm going to try to see what is happening. Maybe I'll get some larger picture out of it. I have a good job with the Tribune. No strings at all and I can use my own judgement about what I send. I'd like to do a lot of work. . . .
> I hope I can solve the censor problem. I'll phone my stuff through but it will be censored. I'll just have to find what will get through and what won't. No one has yet put down what the army is like. Maybe I won't be able to either but I can try. [JS/WS-5/4/43]

While he was waiting to go overseas, he had another attack of homesickness—"home" to him now meant the Monterey area, not Salinas. He wrote to Toby that "all last week I had a strong nostalgia for the Peninsula. Got to dreaming about it. I wish I could go back. . . . I hope

when [the war] is over that I'll have a little money left so I can go back
to the Grove and spend a couple of years on a book I want to write"
[5/12/43]. He had planned to write so many different books once the
war was over that it is impossible to say whether or not he had his next
major work, *Cannery Row*, in mind. But thoughts of Monterey had
followed him and would haunt him even as he went to the war. In his
letters, he talked of wanting to settle near Monterey after the war, of
wishing he could drop everything and just go sit on a rock and fish in
the bay, of missing Ed and old times in the lab.

He and Ed wrote each other regularly, although we have none of
their letters from this period. Ed had been drafted and was now serving
as a medic at the Presidio in Monterey, doing blood tests. Early in 1943,
John wrote Toby that he had received a letter from Ed and that "as
usual in every experience Ed is getting a philosophical pattern of richness. I don't think he likes the army but he isn't closing his eyes to it."
Much later, several months after Steinbeck had gone abroad as a correspondent, he was in North Africa. It was hot, he had been bitten all
over by mosquitoes, he hadn't been able to take a bath for several days,
and sweat poured down his back as he sat in a little room in a French-
Arab hotel, writing a letter to his wife:

> Read a great deal of Shakespeare last night and perhaps because of
> the situation found great meanings in it. I liked it very well but it
> reminded me so much of the evenings in the lab with the gallon of
> wine on the floor and the music playing and the reading of poetry
> and drinking of wine and the people wandering in and out to look
> at the microscopes and the anoemones. [9/1/43]

The idea for Steinbeck to go overseas as a correspondent had been
generated in a conversation at a dinner party at the Lewis Gannetts' (he
was a friend from the early days and book editor for the *Herald Tribune*; she had illustrated *Tortilla Flat*). Steinbeck was telling his tale of
woe about his treatment at the hands of his draft board and the government bureaucracy and mourning the fact that he would never see anything of the war when Gannett suggested that he go as a correspondent.
In fact, Gannett exclaimed, why not go for the *Herald Tribune* and the
Hearst syndicate? He would talk to the editor himself, Gannett told
Steinbeck, and make the preliminary arrangements.

Through Gannett, Steinbeck met William L. Shirer, correspondent
for the *Herald Tribune* and CBS (and later author of such books as
Berlin Diary and *The Rise and Fall of the Third Reich*), who was

home temporarily from Europe. While he was waiting to go overseas, Steinbeck sought out Shirer several times to get his advice about what he should expect in his new job and what approach he should take. At the same time, Gwyn, who knew that her husband respected Shirer's opinion very much, went to the correspondent without her husband's knowledge to ask him to talk John out of going. She didn't want him to go; she thought it would be very dangerous. But Shirer refused; he told Gwyn the experience would be good for her husband and for his writing.

Steinbeck finished his wait for passage by getting his shots, which he pronounced worse than the diseases. He was sick for three weeks, delirious for several days. On about June 3 he departed for England (the exact date and the name of the ship were secret), taking with him his clothes, a typewriter, four quarts of Scotch, a large quantity of sulfadiazine, a hundred multicebrins (a gift from Paul de Kruif), and two pounds of pipe tobacco. He had packed for survival. On board he prowled around, watching and listening, already gathering material for his dispatches. The ship was packed with men, and Steinbeck wrote later:

> The major impression on a troop ship is of feet. A man can get his head out of the way and his arms, but, lying or sitting, his feet are a problem. They sprawl in the aisles, they stick up at all angles. They are not protected because they are the part of a man least likely to be hurt. To move about you must step among feet, must trip over feet.
>
> There are big, misshapen feet; neat, small feet; shoes that are polished; curl-toed shoes; shoestrings knotted and snarled, and careful little bows. You can read character by the feet and shoes. There are perpetually tired feet, and nervous, quick feet. To remember a troopship is to remember feet. At night on a blacked-out ship, you must creep and feel your way among acres of feet.

Although the scene of the troopship had been written about dozens of times (his detractors among the press corps called his writing about such subjects "trite"), this was an unusual view and typical of the kind of writing he was aiming for as a correspondent. He would not try to compete for the hard news but would work to see things that had been overlooked or to see differently things that had already been reported. He would become a correspondent of perspective, just as he had been a novelist of perspective—not telling us new, but seeing it new. In his concern for the commonplace and in his preference for the ordinary soldier, he became in many ways a correspondent much like the war journalist he admired the most, Ernie Pyle. In tribute to Pyle, he wrote in 1944,

> There are really two wars and they haven't much to do with each other. There is the war of maps and logistics, of campaigns, of ballistics, armies, divisions and regiments—and that is General Marshall's war.
>
> Then there is the war of homesick, weary, funny, violent, common men who wash their socks in their helmets, complain about food, whistle at Arab girls, or any girls for that matter, and lug themselves through as dirty a business as the world has ever seen and do it with humor and dignity and courage—and that is Ernie Pyle's war.

Steinbeck made it his war also, and since he and Pyle were interested in many of the same things—immediate experience on a small scale, rather than facts and figures as provided by military briefings—they even used similar techniques in gathering material. Neither took notes as a basis for his stories (Pyle did record the names and addresses of G.I.s for use in his column), but instead lived with a unit, observing the situation and talking to the men, and then came back to the rear and wrote several columns from memory of what he had experienced.

Although both used a great deal of detail, the similarity in their writing ends there. Pyle was a good newspaperman whose columns often sounded like letters to the folks at home. His use of detail was often encyclopedic: he moved from one close-up, to another close-up, to another, surveying the human components of an operation or battle that to other journalists would be largely a matter of numbers or generalized description. As one might expect from a novelist-turned-correspondent, Steinbeck usually marshaled his detail into a pattern, building his material up to a single effect. He referred to his columns and thought of them as "stories," not so much in the newspaper sense of the word as in the sense of "short story." Although they were not fiction, they were fictionalized, employing many tricks of the novelist in order to heighten their impact and provide a sense of depth to a rather narrow focus.

Circumstances were not difficult for Steinbeck when he first got to England. His main problem seemed to be escaping magazine and newspaper reporters who wanted to interview *him*. He began by living at the Savoy but found that it was "a madhouse, with people drinking and talking too much," so he moved to a small apartment in Athenaeum Court, overlooking Hyde Park. It was not exactly the same as contending with trench foot in a muddy foxhole. He had a room and a bath, the room furnished with a chair, a sofa-bed, and a desk that ran across two wide windows overlooking the park. He wrote his wife that he looked out his windows and "all of London that I have ever read about is there. Extreme left is St. Paul's and next but further away London Bridge. Next and closer is Whitehall and next and even closer is St. James Palace. A little farther right is Big Ben, so close that I can set my watch by it." [6/43]

He was now famous nearly everywhere, certainly in England, where his books had had wide circulation and where Lord Beaverbrook was publishing his columns in the mass-circulation *Daily Express*. His status since publication of *The Grapes of Wrath* was confirmed by *Time* and *Newsweek*, which were reporting every major event in his life—divorce, book sales, marriage, and now, before he had even lived it, his life as a correspondent. His column stimulated a lot of mail (it was syndicated by the *Herald Tribune* to papers all over the States—except in Oklahoma—and in Australia, New Zealand, and South America), most of which was being handled by Toni Jackson in Monterey. However, his English mail, large piles of it, was delivered to his apartment. One letter, he reported to Gwyn, was from a

Czech woman who wanted to be my assistant. I imagined she saw me in a Guntherish atmosphere with tickers and stenographers and secretaries phoning like mad to generals instead of in a hotel room with a typewriter and a big pot of tea. She phoned me later and when I told her I had no secretary and probably wouldn't have one I think she had a great contempt for me. How the hell can you write without a staff, was her attitude. I finally told her that I could do everything for myself except one thing and I didn't think she could fill that job. She got huffy and hung up. [6/24/43]

Newsweek wrote that his fellow correspondents noted that his "cold grey eyes didn't miss a trick, that with scarcely any note-taking he soaked up information like a sponge, wrote very fast on a portable typewriter, and became haywire if interrupted." Some of his colleagues were indeed impressed, and some were kind enough to show him the ropes and even, since they were not in competition with the kind of story he was doing, pass on to him story ideas and leads. But others were resentful of his immediate success without, in their view, having earned his stripes. Without their struggle, he seemed to have it made: byline and syndication, freedom to choose his own subjects, and access to the highest governmental and military circles. He seemed both puzzled and hurt when one evening, as he wrote Gwyn, he was taken out to dinner and then to the Embassy Club and was confronted with an outburst of hostility:

> There were some young American correspondents there, quite drunk and consequently very brave. And then came out the thing I have heard about, the hatred of me. They really told me where I stood as a newspaper man and how my stuff stunk, etc., for a long time. It made me very sad because they were quite fierce about it. I'm not in any way in competition with them so I can't see why it should be. I suppose I can though. This island was sucked dry of material or so it was supposed and then I came over and found more stories than I could write, most of which had been lying under their noses all the time. [7/22/43]

He didn't seem to realize that someone would have to have his kind of talent and his level of reputation in order to write and get away with the kinds of columns he was writing.

He hated the disadvantages of fame, but seemed, very quickly, to take the benefits for granted. True, he had been a prisoner of his notoriety, particularly in California, but at the same time he had the freedom to do all sorts of things, in his work and otherwise, that other people could not. One of the benefits of his situation was that he was able to meet all kinds of people—cabinet members, generals, publishers, foreign affairs experts, and members of the aristocracy—although it must be said that he probably relished more his strolls through London's streets and parks, where he was unlikely to interview anyone with a rank higher than staff sergeant. As some of his columns testify, he spent more time talking to his driver, Big Train Mulligan, than to the brass Mulligan was assigned to ferry around. His experiences with the brass were often uncomfortable, as in the incident he reported to his wife:

> The other night I had dinner with nine generals and twenty-eight colonels. To my horror, I found that I was the guest of honor and was asked to speak by the commanding general. I have never spoken before and I don't think I will ever be asked again. Not that I said anything startling. I just didn't say anything. The horrid mouthings that came out of me are partly responsible for the greying of my hair. There was absolutely no way of escaping any of it.

But if you can imagine me in my boy scout suit without insignia weltering in all that brass. There was a certain grandeur in my nakedness. I was unique. The stars and eagles were shining and screaming. [7/21/43]

But he did enjoy associating with some of the most notable journalists of that time, journalists too good at their jobs to be worried about Steinbeck being on the scene—men like Quentin Reynolds, Ernie Pyle, William L. Shirer (who was now back in London), and Edward R. Murrow. He admired Reynolds, thought Murrow had a good head, a "rare product here or anywhere else, I guess," and got along well with Shirer, whom he probably saw more of than any of the others. Shirer was of the breed of correspondent that is part scholar, part newspaperman. He was extremely well read, knew several languages, and had had long experience in Europe, having covered the rise of Nazism in Germany and the onset of the war. Soft-spoken and thoughtful, he "wore well," Steinbeck thought, like an old Harris tweed coat.

They went out to dinner together, ran into each other at the Savoy bar, a gathering place for journalists, and occasionally went together to look for stories at military installations in England. Shirer remembers that Steinbeck wanted to meet some of the Labour people, although he was, in Shirer's estimation, "a very unpolitical guy." Shirer had met a number of men in his youth who were in the Labour movement and would later become ministers in the government, among them Aneurin Bevan, a great speaker who even during the war was debating Churchill. Although largely self-educated, Bevan was well read, talked to Shirer about Hemingway and Faulkner, and wanted to meet Steinbeck. Shirer invited them both to his room at the Savoy for a drink.

It was rather typical for Shirer and Bevan to get into very heated political discussions—Shirer was, to Bevan's mind, a bit too liberal. "Nye and I were practically coming to blows, shouting like hell, and John wasn't used to that kind of passion about politics, and I remember him getting rather nervous when Nye shoved me and we almost came to hitting each other."

There was not much war in England at the time, and the scene in London for correspondents had become stagnant and ingrown, a place of rumor, gossip, and too much drink. Shirer remembers that among several parties or gatherings they were invited to together was a backstage affair for Noel Coward. When the party got into high gear, Coward entertaining at the piano, the boys began to gather around him, tearing off their coats, shirts, and undershirts in a show of ecstasy. It was all too much for the provincial Americans Shirer and Steinbeck, who had never seen anything like it, and they had to leave.

Steinbeck tried to get away from the city and out to various kinds of military bases as often as he could. On the south coast he visited one of the many gun emplacements called a "mixed battery"—men and women working together on large guns used against marauding boats and planes. He also visited and wrote about Dover, which was being shelled from across the Channel, about the arrival of American G.I.s at their temporary home somewhere in the English countryside, and about the wounded in the military hospitals. He and Shirer went to the American bomber base that was sending Flying Fortresses over Germany and stayed ten days, watching the operation. When he got back to London, he wrote about nearly everything except the missions themselves—the names of the bombers, the superstitions of the men flying them, the mission briefings, the mascots, the work of the ground crews, and the hard wait for the planes to come home. During just a few weeks in late June and July, he wrote about an extraordinary variety of subjects, from British minesweepers, to G.I. vegetable gardens, and from shooting craps to the luck brought by an alcoholic goat. Everywhere he went his mind collected subjects like a vacuum cleaner, and with nearly everything he touched he made the ordinary interesting.

Except for the pace that he set for himself, his tour in England was not filled with hardship. His major problem, which would grow during the weeks and then months that he was overseas and at last would become unmanageable, was his worry over Gwyn. From the outset of his plan to become a correspondent, she had opposed it. When he refused to listen, almost possessed with the necessity of seeing the war for himself, she accused him of choosing the war over her. When that failed to dissuade him, she played her trump card once again: she claimed to be pregnant. Thus when he left for England, he was filled with worry and guilt. When he didn't get any letters for several weeks, he blamed it on the poor mail service, but he was getting letters from other people and became almost frantic with worry—sending cables, asking friends to call her. Finally, after six weeks, four letters arrived in a bunch, and he spent hours that evening reading and rereading them. It had turned out that she wasn't pregnant after all, but he never did realize that she had been punishing him. And the worst was yet to come.

Burgess Meredith, who was now in London also, remembers that

John seemed to talk of having children almost incessantly; he expressed deep concern about Gwyn's pregnancy and was worried about getting back to New York in time for the birth of his child. Even after he found out that she wasn't pregnant, his letters reveal how strong a hold domestic matters had come to have on his imagination. He thought much about making their apartment homelike and comfortable (until the end of the war, when they would move to a country house near Monterey). From a sweltering North Africa in August, his letters return again and again to Christmas in the apartment and the question of where to put the Christmas tree.

London was the crossroads for that theater of the war, and he ran into any number of old friends, such as Meredith, as well as making new ones. Meredith had an office right around the corner from where Steinbeck was living. They saw each other fairly often and occasionally John dropped by to help him with his work: "Yesterday which was Sunday I lent a hand in a picture Buzzy is making for the army. And today with all the other work I've promised to do a little dialogue for it. Always pictures and I don't even like pictures" [7/26/43]. He also saw Max Wagner, who was on his way home from North Africa for a medical discharge. Max, who was as inspired by duty as John, wanted to stay in the Army, and John, who was afraid his friend might relapse into heavy drinking from discouragement, tried to pull strings to keep him in, but to no avail. John tried to help with another problem when Annie Laurie Williams's husband, Maurice, was reported missing in action. John spent days trying to find out for her what had happened and whether there was any hope or not. Once he had gathered some meager information (some parachutes had opened after the plane went down), he had to argue at some length with the censor in order to get the message to Annie Laurie. The cable gave her some hope, which turned out to be justified when her husband was reported alive in Germany as a prisoner of war.

For several weeks, Steinbeck had tried to get to North Africa. He'd picked up clues to several possible stories there, and he felt he would be able to do more if he were closer to the action (although North Africa had fallen to the Allies in May, there was still fighting going on in Sicily). But it was difficult to get the necessary clearances:

Today I have been fighting the battle of permissions again. You never get that over with. It has to be done every time all over again. I guess a good half of my time must have been spent in offices getting permission. I get very tired of it because by now I can look at an officer and tell exactly what he is going to say. There are the difficulty boys to whom everything is difficult and who must make millions of orders of all kinds and who have to think over everything for twenty four hours. And then there are the sure it's easy boys, who agree to everything and then don't do anything. I get a frightful sense of futility sometimes. [8/15/43]

On a day during the second week of August he was told suddenly that if he wanted to go to Africa, he would have to be packed by three that afternoon and ready to leave by seven-thirty that evening. Algiers was not as comfortable as London. In a short time he found himself with diarrhea, bug bites all over his body, clothes soaked with perspiration night and day, and mild heat stroke. But he did have a room to himself, a miracle he accomplished by failing to check in with the Army to get an assigned space but instead, through ignorance, simply walking up to the desk in the hotel and asking for a room. Nobody had tried that before.

Seldom in his letters, from this period or any other, does he describe in any detail famous people he may have met or people who became his friends. Invariably the ones he describes are to him in some way unusual, not by their position, but by their manner or appearance. One such character attracted his attention just after he arrived in Africa:

I thought you might like to hear about my chamber maid here in this little dungeon. The room itself looks like a set for a Maxim Gorki play. It needs only water dripping from the walls to make it perfect, that and the screams of the tortured in some sub cellar. Anyway about the maid. She is Jewish and Arab and she has no teeth whatever. She rejoices in the name of Yvonne. My French is bad enough at best but listening to it spoken without teeth leaves me paralyzed with laughter. Anyway Yvonne did not appear yesterday and this morning she tried to explain to me why. I could not get her French at all, when suddenly she went into pantomime. She made what seemed indelicate gestures at me, highly suggestive ones, and I thought I was being approached and invited to participate in some Judo-Franco-Arabic perversion. And only gradually did her meaning emerge. Yesterday her nephew was circumcised and there was quite a party at this rite. She was trying to explain circumcision to me, using me as the chief party, since naturally she was not equipped to be the subject. Yvonne is a good sixty and you can imagine my alarm at her method of explanation. When I finally realized what she had been doing I lay on the floor and howled.

And now she thinks I am crazy. Her toothless French obviously with a strong Arab accent if there is such sounds very like Buzzy Meredith eating thick soup. The vowels are liquid and the consonants are the little pieces of meat and the whole thing is a little like water running down a clogged drain. [8/16/43]

When Steinbeck first got to North Africa, he got in touch with the *Herald Tribune* man there, John O'Reilly, who was covering General Eisenhower and SHAEF, then in Algiers. O'Reilly remembers that Steinbeck was rather overwhelmed, initially, by the situation he was suddenly thrust into. North Africa itself was strange to him, but with the confusion of the war, it was even more difficult for him to get his bearings. At night, the air-raid sirens would wail in preparation for the German bombers, which came in to hit the headquarters. Barrage balloons, as in London, were moored all around the city, which lay inside a cup of surrounding hills. As the enemy planes approached, large quantities of smoke were released, filling the cup, and batteries of ack-ack would open up, dotting the sky above the smoke with tiny orange explosions. Inevitably, two or three of the balloons would be hit by the antiaircraft fire and explode into flame. The Germans would usually avoid all of this and dump their bombs outside town.

The outside, which had the appearance of some eerily lit, smoke-filled inferno, matched rather well the dungeonlike atmosphere of his cell, and Steinbeck spent most of his first days in Africa in his room sitting morosely and wondering what he was going to do. O'Reilly urged him to get out and get around, and as he did so, John was able to pick up some background stories, but they were not as good as those he had done in England and mediocre compared to the work he would do when he got closer to combat.

After Algiers, he traveled west along the coast to Oran, then back, eastward, toward Tunis, stopping at several cities and making several excursions south into the desert along the way. A lot of his time was taken helping with a movie being made by the Army (Why do I always get caught up in movie-making and I don't even like movies? he asks again plaintively), a project that he found completely frustrating since it was constantly hampered by rank-happy officers whose only joy seemed to come from setting up barriers to the film crew's work. Furthermore, the big story that he'd heard about in England about food distribution didn't pan out as he had hoped. All in all it was rather a terrible time, without sleep, washing facilities, or news from home.

By leaving England he had cut himself off from the possibility of getting any mail for several weeks. What mail he had received before he left was not cheering—Gwyn had been ill and she was encountering a lot of problems. Although in Africa he did run into correspondents he knew from time to time—Quentin Reynolds, H. R. Knickerbocker, and the photographer Robert Capa, who would become his good friend—he was usually alone and lonely, getting more homesick and concerned about Gwyn with each passing day. He wrote Gwyn on August 19:

> Yesterday I traveled through country that looked just like that stretch between Moss Landing and Monterey, with sand dunes and then the sea. It was identical and the dust was just as thick and the growth on the sand hills was just the same. Of course it was hot. But the sea was the same blue as in Monterey and it made me very terribly homesick. And I wondered what has happened to the little house and how everyone is. I have stopped writing to anyone at all except you. I write to you nearly everyday and I wonder whether you get my letters. [8/19/43]

And a few days later:

> I remember best the coffee in the morning and the music at night and the dictionary sessions and the painting of chairs and where shall we eat tonight. Lets have a whale of a big Christmas and not only strung popcorn but also strung cranberries and also whatever tinsel we can find. Lets have a really Christmas. . . . I've thought and thought and it does seem that the corner in front of the lower bathroom door is the best place for the tree. [8/25/43]

He planned, now, to go back to London at the first opportunity and then return home. He told himself that he had, after all, accomplished what he had set out to accomplish, but he hadn't really—he hadn't seen any fighting close at hand. So when he got the chance to cover the invasion of Italy by General Mark Clark's Fifth Army, he couldn't pass it up, although it was very difficult for him to stay. He had received a small batch of letters, and he found them very disturbing. Gwyn complained that she was being approached by men, and that even his friends were making passes at her. She was very lonely, she told him.

Steinbeck began the Italian campaign by observing and writing about the invasion rehearsals on Algerian beaches and then the embarkation of the troops. Rather than join the troops on the convoy, however, he chose to join a special-operations unit and made the trip from Ferryville on the coast of Tunisia through the Tunisian War Channel to Palermo, Sicily, on a sixty-three-foot plywood PT boat. According to one of the officers on board, Jack Watson, the boat "bobbed around like an errant bath-tub. Everybody on board, including the skipper, parked his cookies in the drink. It almost cured us from ever going to sea again. The worst 110 miles of our lives . . . and it took all night." (Later, Steinbeck inscribed a copy of *The Grapes of Wrath* to Watson: "This is to prove I can still write after recent PT submarine mission. John Steinbeck, of the Philo phibious phorce.")

No one seems to know how he found out about it, but the unit that Steinbeck had himself assigned to was a super-secret commandolike outfit of the U.S. Navy whose mission was to deceive the enemy and cause as much confusion along the coast of Italy as possible. The unit had already been operating for some time in the Mediterranean when Steinbeck joined it, and at this point, just prior to the Salerno invasion, it was headquartered on the destroyer U.S.S. *Knight* and was operating with a half dozen PT boats, several British MTBs, and two Dutch gunships. Unknown to Steinbeck at the outset, the man in charge of planning for this group and the leader in its field operations was someone he already knew—Douglas Fairbanks, Jr.

Fairbanks had been in the Navy for two and a half years, and during part of that time, because of his family's friendship with Lord Mountbatten, he was the only American who participated in British Commando operations. As a result of this experience, he was asked to form an American version of the Commandos, specializing in tactical diversions, hit-and-run raids, and delivery and rescue behind enemy lines. In order to get the personnel he needed, Fairbanks went to various military installations and university campuses and, without being able to reveal what the job was, asked for volunteers with knowledge of electronics, navigation, ballistics and demolition, communications, and gunnery. Steinbeck, Fairbanks recalls, was fascinated with the expertise that had been gathered together into one group and with the gadgets and various tactical tricks that had been developed.

The job at the time Steinbeck arrived was to make the Germans believe that something big was developing north of Naples, in the hope that troops that might otherwise be used to repel the Allied invasion would be diverted (documents captured after the war revealed that in fact a whole division had been pinned down), and to make raids along the coast, cut communications, harass coastal shipping, and capture such small islands as they could. In deceiving the enemy, the tactic was to run in toward the coast with small boats—the number varied from one little trial boat, to six or eight, or sometimes as many as fifteen or sixteen, including a small destroyer with PTs and MTBs—pretending to be a large ship or a task force of large ships. The run, of course, would be made at night, and all kinds of false signals would be sent to make the enemy believe that it was dealing with heavy cruisers rather than PT boats. Balloons would be sent up on lines, carrying tin foil cut the proper size in order to project the radar image of a capital ship; the little boats carried the radio-transmission equipment of a cruiser and with deceptive power broadcast the code patterns typically sent out by an attack force and communicated with nonexistent airplanes.

Steinbeck was with Fairbanks's outfit just before and during the first couple of days of the Allied invasion, while it was working hard to keep German reserves from moving south. On September 11 he wrote home:

> As the British say—this is a good show. I haven't slept in three days more than an hour at a time and I haven't had my clothes off in four days and I smell terrible. Now I have a chance for a bath and a nap before the next show but I want to get this to you first only hoping that I do not communicate how I smell. But I'm not alone. And I'm a rose to the 300 people I saw the other night who have been living in a cave for three years. The cave didn't smell so good either.
>
> As soon as I get where I can, I'm going to start calling you like mad. I haven't heard from you since July 21.
>
> Wait up *good* for me dear. I'll try to get home before very terribly long. And will have happy fun. My eyes are closing and I just have to sleep.
>
> love to you, dear
> John

He broke off from the PT boats to join the fighting on the beachhead at Salerno. He had been under fire before, but always from a distance, and now that he would be with front-line troops, he wasn't sure how he would react. As he wrote about the green troops who were going in for the landing, "No one, least of all themselves, knows what they will do when the terrible thing happens. No man there knows whether he can take it, knows whether he will run away or stick, or lose his nerve and go to pieces, or will be a good soldier. There is no way of knowing and probably that one thing bothers you more than anything else."

But he had been more or less fearless in the face of physical danger throughout his life, so it was not a lack of courage that came to attack him, but a deep sense of the horror of it all. Perhaps he was too sensitive; perhaps, as his mother-in-law suggested later, he had gone to war too late in life. But the horror of it nearly overwhelmed him and stayed with him for months. There were those close to him who thought, when he returned from the war, that he had suffered a complete personality change—he was morose, despondent, and preoccupied; he seemed for a while unable to function, unable to get any enjoyment out of life. Whatever had happened to him, it seemed to hit him hardest after he got home; those who were with him in Italy detected little change in him at the time.

His experiences at Salerno prompted some of the most graphic and deeply felt prose found in his dispatches:

> His [the correspondent's] report will be of battle plan and tactics, of taken ground or lost terrain, of attack and counterattack. But these are some of the things he probably really saw:
>
> He might have seen the splash of dirt and dust that is a shell burst, and a small Italian girl in the street with her stomach blown out, and he might have seen an American soldier standing over a twitching body, crying. He probably saw many dead mules, lying on their sides, reduced to pulp. He saw the wreckage of houses, with torn beds hanging like shreds out of the spilled hole in a plaster wall. There were red carts and the stalled vehicles of refugees who did not get away.
>
> The stretcher-bearers come back from the lines, walking in off step, so that the burden will not be jounced too much, and the blood dripping from the canvas, brother and enemy in the stretchers, so long as they are hurt. And the walking wounded coming back with shattered arms and bandaged heads, the walking wounded struggling painfully to the rear.
>
> He would have smelled the sharp cordite in the air and the hot reek of blood if the going has been rough. The burning odor of dust will be in his nose and the stench of men and animals killed yesterday and the day before. Then a whole building is blown up and an earthy, sour smell comes from its walls. He will smell his own sweat and the accumulated sweat of an army. When his throat is dry he will drink the warm water from his canteen, which tastes of disinfectant.

He stayed at the front for a week and then returned to the command ship of the attack force, where the correspondents' pool was located, to write his stories. It was not much of a trade-off: the command ship was being bombed constantly, alerts sounding every half hour or so around the clock. He wrote to Gwyn:

I do know now those things about myself that I had to know. I know that I can take it as well as most and better than some and that is a reassuring thing to know. And there is no way of knowing until it happens. I've broken all the rules too, but I'll tell you about that when I am with you and if you want to hear about it. I hope I won't be that kind of a bore. In England they call them "bomb bores." [9/18/43]

He went back to stay with Fairbanks's outfit for several weeks. Nearly every night there was a mission, and Steinbeck went along on many of them. Fairbanks recalls that "John, to his everlasting glory and our everlasting respect, would take his foreign correspondent badge off his arm and join in the raid. If you are caught in a belligerent action without a badge and carrying a weapon, and you are a foreign correspondent, you are shot. You don't get any of the privileges of an ordinary prisoner. He took his risks rather than go along, saying grace as a war correspondent. We had great admiration for him." He would wait until he got on the boat, so there were few witnesses, and an extra tommy gun would be brought up and he would just pick it up.

Although he could not write about the secret deception tactics of the force, he did record in his dispatches several actions in taking small islands, sinking German ships, and downing enemy aircraft. In many of these raids, Fairbanks was the leading character, but out of respect for him and because of the need for security, Steinbeck changed the names, sometimes disguising Fairbanks's activities by making him two or three different characters in his stories. Such was the case in his account of the taking of Ventotene, an island just off the coast of Italy north of Naples, the subject of the last five of his dispatches reprinted in *Once There Was a War*.

They were told that the island, on which was a major German radar station, was defended primarily by Italians who were ready to surrender. The destroyer and several patrol boats stood offshore pretending to be a larger landing force, and over loudspeakers an American officer demanded the surrender of the island. After a delay of several minutes, the signal for the surrender came from the darkened island, and, as pictured in Steinbeck's story, "In the wardroom the commodore of the task force sat at the head of the table. He was dressed in khaki, his shirt open at the throat and his sleeves rolled up. He wore a helmet, and a tommy gun lay on the table in front of him. 'I'll go in and take the surrender,' he said, and he called the names of five men to go with him." The "commodore" was actually Lieutenant Fairbanks, who had also

planned the operation, and he took along with him on this initial landing party five Navy men and Steinbeck. It was an operation that Steinbeck would admit later had "scared the shit out of him," and
Fairbanks's bravery under fire and action against heavy odds would
win him the Silver Star. (Steinbeck was also recommended for the Silver Star, but since he was not a member of the armed services, he was
not eligible to receive it.)

The task-force officers felt it was important to get into the island as
soon as possible and accept the surrender before the enemy changed its
mind so Fairbanks took his men in a motor-whaleboat toward the harbor. It was completely dark—there were no lights on the island and no
moon. After some difficulty in finding the narrow entrance to the harbor, the whaleboat nosed in, and at that moment a large explosion went
off just behind them. There was no choice but to go ahead, and as the
boat approached the pier, it came under machine-gun and rifle fire. At
the pier, Fairbanks was the first ashore, and as he got to his feet, he
spotted a German warrant officer in the act of throwing a grenade at a
German patrol boat in order to sink it. Steinbeck writes, "One of the
American officers ran at him, and with one motion the German ripped
out his Luger pistol and tossed it in the water and then put both of his
hands over his head. The lancing light of a powerful flashlight circled
him. The officer who had taken him rushed him to the whaleboat and
put him under guard of the boat's engineer." Fairbanks brought his
men ashore, and as they started along the quay toward the town, a
crowd of Italians came down the hill in front of them, crying out, "Surrender, surrender!"

Steinbeck describes the scene:

> The five Americans stood side by side with their guns ready, while
> the Italian carabinieri brought their guns and put them in a pile.
> Everyone seemed to be confused and glad and frightened. The
> people wanted to crowd close to see the Americans and at the same
> time the ugly pig snouts of the tommy guns warned them back. It
> is not reassuring to be one of five men who are ostensibly holding a
> line against two hundred and fifty men, even if those men seem to
> have surrendered.

The Americans learned that the Italians, who had signaled, were perfectly willing to give up, but up in the hills, heavily fortified and well
dug-in, there was a large detachment of Germans who had no intention
of surrendering.

There ensued a very nervous period as the small group of Americans waited for a second landing of three dozen men, all the while thinking of those Germans. Steinbeck describes this second group as paratroopers, but in fact they were a special-operations unit made up of American Navy and British Army and Navy personnel—two of the American officers, Henry Ringling North (of circus family fame) and Jumpin' Joe Savoldi (Notre Dame All-America), were also O.S.S. After what seemed an interminable wait with their two hundred and fifty prisoners, they were reinforced by the second landing party. Still under sniper attack and mortar fire, Fairbanks led a patrol of men (as the official action report states) "through the village to the outskirts to establish pickets and to make sure that no enemy threatened the further debarkation of troops." All this in nearly complete darkness, on unfamiliar terrain, and in complete uncertainty as to what the situation on the island was. He did know one thing—not all the enemy were willing to surrender. The question was, Did the enemy have any idea how small a unit, even reinforced, they were?

It was clear that they could not attack the Germans in the dark and without artillery, and from what the Italians told them, they were certain that they were outnumbered by at least two to one (it turned out that there were ninety Germans on the hill). Henry Ringling North volunteered to try to talk the Germans into surrendering, acting on the assumption that the enemy had been fooled into thinking that the Allied forces, both at sea and on the island, were far larger than they actually were. With a bath towel to be used as a white flag of truce, North crawled up the hill to act as a forward listening post until morning. At first light, he walked toward the German positions, carrying the bath towel over his head, and was taken into custody by three soldiers, who brought him to their officers. The interview with the officers, which Steinbeck describes in some detail, was a touch-and-go affair for some time, but ultimately North's bluff was successful and the Germans were captured without a further shot being fired. For his courage, North also received a Silver Star.

In Steinbeck's account, of course, the identities of North, Fairbanks, and the others are concealed, and even the kind of troops used in the action is disguised. He also omits a few things, such as the continuing sniper fire by Germans who were outside the garrison and the very dangerous reconnaissance patrol led by Fairbanks, and he changes the location of the interrogation of the German officers, which took place on board ship rather than in the town jail. The powerful effect of this series of dispatches, however, comes out of the author's treatment, which is essentially fictional rather than purely journalistic. Technically, it is a beautiful piece of writing. The five dispatches that tell of the capture of Isola di Ventotene would, if joined together, make a fine short story, except that the events (even after he had moderated them) are so melodramatic as to be unbelievable. Sometimes the situations he encountered in the war were so strange that he didn't even try to write about them.

The usual practice for the torpedo boats when attacking coastal shipping (usually "Lighties"—slow-moving but well-armed German supply boats) was to fire off the torpedoes at a thousand yards or more, but one British captain followed his own rather unorthodox operating procedures. His name was Greene-Kelly and he was skipper of an MTB squadron attached to Fairbanks's unit. He sported a large, bushy black beard, and because of his daring, had become a sort of hero to the men around him. Steinbeck was very taken by him and went out with him on several missions.

When Greene-Kelly found his target, he would get in as close as possible before firing his torpedoes. Then, if the ship was not mortally wounded, he would come in with machine guns blazing, pull alongside, and board her—a strange bit of anachronistic madness—his men firing tommy guns and he swinging a cutlass. The coincidence of such a character operating within the same command as Douglas Fairbanks, Jr., was too much for any newspaperman to report (even allowing for the fact that Steinbeck's friendship for Fairbanks wouldn't have permitted him to mention his name). Fairbanks, who demonstrated his own brand of madness repeatedly throughout the war, was perfectly willing to leave all of his boat-boardings behind on the Hollywood set.

A strange postscript to the author's relationship with Greene-Kelly came to him in the mail more than a year later while he was in New York. As he described it to Dook:

I had a little school note book and one night we were off Genoa and I was below making some notes and an alert sounded so I went on deck and it was pitch black. Then all of a sudden a flak ship started firing on us and I hit the deck because tracers scare hell out of you and the boat started running and twisting. Well that was the last I saw of my note book. Recently it arrived in the mail from England. Sent by the Ministry of Information. I suppose it got stuck in the slats some place and the skipper sent it in. Now I remember that skipper. He was 26 and his name was Greene-Kelly. He was killed eight months ago when he attacked two E boats. He sunk one and crippled the other and then two more came down on him and sunk him. But my note book got back.

The Special Operations Unit had its headquarters on the destroyer *Knight,* which most of the time was anchored at Capri, after the island was captured in a bloodless battle which had Special Operations and attached units come in on one side while the Germans evacuated from the other. The Fairbanks people had to double up with the officers of the *Knight,* which still left the communications officer, Jack Watson, and Steinbeck, who had to bunk on the transoms, the leather divans at each end of the officers' wardroom. Watson remembers Steinbeck—his very ruddy, somewhat pock-marked face with usually about two or three days' growth of beard, stretched out on his temporary bed, trying to get some sleep after being up all night on one mission or another. Then "I'd see these guys in their jeans and white hats sneaking in there, being as quiet as they could, to take a look at this man sleeping. I followed one of these guys and asked him what's this all about? And he said, well, we just got it on the radio that Warner Brothers was paying John Steinbeck $300,000 for *The Moon Is Down* and we just wanted to see somebody who was going to get $300,000. I told Steinbeck about it later and he said I'd like to see that $300,000 myself."

Steinbeck typed out his dispatches on a little portable typewriter while sitting at the wardroom table, and all around him people were coming and going or sitting and talking in what was, in effect, the officers' living-dining room. Other correspondents came aboard and stayed briefly—Quentin Reynolds, H. R. Knickerbocker, and Lionel Shapiro of the *Montreal Star*—but Steinbeck stayed for about a month, really becoming part of the group.

Recreation was somewhat difficult, since the American Navy was stubbornly dry, so they made other arrangements as they could. Fairbanks recalls:

We luckily had a lot of British Naval associates, and we were always inviting ourselves over to the British. They had everything, you know, and they were very liberal with it, so we would try and repay with fresh fruits—wasn't quite a fair trade. The British ended up healthier than we did. And then we had a couple of Dutch boats, and they were very serious. They weren't much fun. The Dutch were more serious and kept their ships as clean as hospitals in the middle of the war, absolutely spic and span, but very little with the booze and gin, you know? . . . We used to love to go there except their hospitality wasn't as much fun as the British. Much gayer and took the war as a big game—making jokes in the middle of battle and so on. That amused John.

After visiting and taking the hospitality of other navies, or having made the rounds of the trattorias up in the piazza on Capri, the officers of the *Knight,* the Fairbanks group, and whatever other officers might be visiting at the time would on occasion gather in the wardroom to swap stories. One evening they were sitting around, as Jack Watson remembers, and the executive officer of the tin can led off, retelling a few wartime experiences. He was followed by a commander from the British Navy who'd seen a lot of action, and then by others who'd had strange or amusing experiences. Fairbanks joined in fairly frequently, encouraged by the group, since he was skillful at imitating a range of Hollywood characters—Chaplin, Barrymore, C. Aubrey Smith, and Errol Flynn. He didn't imitate David Niven, but he had what seemed to be an inexhaustible supply of Niven anecdotes.

But the real topper, according to Watson, was provided by Steinbeck, who told the story as he made it up about "The Dog That Got Religion." It was a long tale with vivid details, but in broad outline, as Watson remembers it, it concerned a dog who, having suddenly seen the Light, set out to reform the ways of the forest creatures around him. The dog who got religion was, of course, a mongrel.

Steinbeck returned to London on September 24. He began to feel his life with the Special Operations Unit, for all of its occasional excitement, was becoming repetitious, and besides, he had plenty of detailed material for his writing, perhaps even too much material. He needed time, he thought, to sort his experiences out. The writing he had done on the destroyer he brought back as notes to be rewritten, since there had been no opportunity to send his work out on a regular basis. He found London pretty much the same as when he had left it, and was very anxious to get back to New York and Gwyn:

I cabled the moment I got back and suggested that it might be a good idea if I went home to write this stuff and this morning got a frantic cable from Cornish [his boss at the *Herald Tribune*] asking me to stay here. I suppose he is right, but in answer to your question, I SHALL be home by Christmas if I have to crawl home. . . . I have a great number of stories to write and besides I have to finish the picture for SOS [the Army movie he had been working on with Burgess Meredith].... Such good stories if I can only write them well. I'm going to take a couple of weeks and just pound them out and try to get well ahead.... As long as they do not want me to go home now, I will fill out the six months which will bring me home about the first of December.... I do wish I could be with you in the fall though. I love that time so much. I saw Buzzy last night for a little while and he was getting pretty lonesome for his own red leaves. He is a little sad because he came to a war and the closest he has come to it is London and little chance that he will see anything else. Well anyway, your little friend here has seen enough war. Enough for him anyway. I don't want to be a glutton about it and I will give my share to anyone who wishes it. But it is strange how you must do it. No one can do it for you. And the dark gentleman was very near. I think I wrote you about one particular night when I felt his breath. [9/25/43]

He talked to Buzzy Meredith about where he had gone and what he had seen, and Meredith, bored in London, was envious. He talked of some of the people they both knew whom he had seen in Africa and Italy, among them Ernie Pyle. Pyle made him laugh, he told Meredith. He recalled that one day Ernie had become disgusted with the average soldier's limited vocabulary. Pyle told Steinbeck, "If ever I hear another G.I. use 'fuck' as an adjective, I will cut my fucking throat."

For a week or so after he got to London, John became very excited about the possibility of bringing Gwyn to England, for a British film company wanted him to do a film, and when he refused on the grounds that he had to get home to see his wife, the film people offered to bring Gwyn over as his "film editor." He wrote several times, imploring her to come and selling the beauty of England, but it all came to naught when he found out that the U.S. State Department opposed such arrangements on the basis that it would cause jealousy. On his return to England from Italy, he had picked up several letters from Gwyn that had been waiting for him, but since then he had sent two cables and a dozen letters and had had no reply. He did get a letter from Howard Hunter, who mentioned that Max Wagner was stationed in Newport News and "practically commuting to New York." The seeds of suspicion planted by Gwyn over the previous months began to bear bitter fruit once again, and, as he wrote to her, "I got a sudden rush of jealous rage. Not too well these last couple of days. Kick back from some of the Italian stuff I guess. Anyway it made me crazily angry that he could see you and I couldn't.... I've got a bad set of blues today. I don't like my work. I don't like sitting here doing work I could just as well do in New

York. . . . I feel a little crazy and bad pictures keep popping into my mind and I can't get rid of them" [10/1/43].

He didn't wait until his contract was up in December. He ignored the pleas of the *Herald Tribune* that he hold on in London for just a few more weeks and returned to New York in early October.

CHAPTER XXIX

When Steinbeck returned to New York and his wife, he was in poor shape physically and emotionally. While he had been on the beachhead at Salerno, our troops had undergone a prolonged and heavy bombardment by German 88s. At one point a round had come in nearby, blowing a stack of fifty-gallon oil drums every which way, one of which was thrown up in the air, hit the ground, and then rolling, slammed against his head, neck, and back. He had already badly twisted an ankle while jumping out of the landing craft onto the beach, and both eardrums had been burst, so that he could only barely hear. What was most frightening to him, was that he was subject to periodic blackouts and temporary loss of memory, but he never mentioned his problems to anyone.

Emotionally, in response to the horror he had witnessed—particularly the maimed children—and his own disabilities, he seemed to be in a state of prolonged shock. He became acutely aware of his own mortality. His blackouts reminded him of his mother's strokes, and he became obsessed with the idea that he was getting old (he would turn forty-two in February). This, in turn, tied in with the jealousy that had been engineered by his wife while he was overseas, so that he was more than ever conscious of their difference in age. He hated himself for being sick and worried about being man enough to hold his wife. He tried to ignore his disabilities and hide his pain and fear, but when, after several months, the various symptoms of his injuries did not disappear, he consulted doctors about them. He felt so depressed and exhausted that one doctor, at his request, administered shots of vitamins and male hormone. In light of his procrastination, there was some irony in the determination that none of his problems were subject to any kind of dramatic cure—only time could help.

Gwyn recalls that "one solid year after he came back from the war he had no sense of humor at all. He had a chip on his shoulder the whole time. He was mean, he was sadistic, he was masochistic, he resented everything. The great sense of play that he had, the wit, the kind of happiness that he had [had disappeared]." No one else, except perhaps Gwyn's mother, saw the change in John in quite such dramatic terms—and one must always take Gwyn's judgments about her husband with a grain of salt. Furthermore, the question arises, how much of his change was due to the war and to his injuries, and how much to the anxiety and jealousy that Gwyn, in part, provoked?

In October, he wrote to Toby Street:

I've been home a little over a week now and am beginning to breathe freely again.

I've got a lot of writing to do on the last show yet and I rather think I will stay with the paper because I like it. At least for a while I will. It keeps me working and it keeps me humble. I know I write a lot of crap but at least I write and I don't care about the other.

I am very glad to be home and in one piece. . . . Haven't been here three days when the Navy asked me to go to the South Pacific. I refused. I want to get my ears to hearing a little bit before I get shot at again. . . . I've found there are only two kinds of people who aren't afraid of tracers—liars and people who haven't seen them. A tracer has a way of coming right between your eyes and only turning aside in the last two feet.

I just want to stay here awhile and do some writing but not too hard and try to find out what happened to me in the last five months. I have some very curious ideas. Having it is very different from imagining it.

By mid-November he had nearly finished his writing for the *Herald Tribune* and was complaining that "the Navy is cutting the hell out of my stuff—even correcting my grammar" [11/18/43]. By the middle of the following month, he had started *Cannery Row*, "a funny little book that is fun." He and Gwyn planned to go to Mexico for a couple of months after the first of the year, Gwyn thinking that this would be the vacation he needed, and he that he would do research for yet another book. Ever since the trip to the Gulf, he had had in the back of his mind a story that he had heard in La Paz, "a true story, but . . . so much like a parable that it almost can't be," about an Indian boy who finds a large and valuable pearl. But instead of the blessing he thought it would be, the boy finds the pearl is a curse on his life and he throws it back into the sea from whence it came. The story had nearly all the elements that Steinbeck favored—myth, folklore, moral allegory, and folk wisdom—and he determined to make it into a drama-novelette, the form he had come to believe that for him was the most manageable.

In January 1944, he saw the movie *Lifeboat* and found that it differed in several respects from what he had written, enough so that he wrote a letter of complaint to Twentieth Century-Fox: "While it is certainly true that I wrote a script for Lifeboat, it is not true that in that script as in the film there were any slurs against organized labor nor was there a stock comedy Negro . . . instead . . . there was a Negro of dignity, purpose and personality" [1/10/44]. The more he thought about it, the more upset he became, and he sent a telegram to Annie Laurie asking her to get his name withdrawn from the picture's billing. (She could not do so.) He followed this with a letter in which he theorized that the slurs came from the fact that Hitchcock "is one of those incredible English middle class snobs who really and truly despise working people" [2/21/44]. Technical errors in the film bothered him almost as much, since they reflected discredit on his small-boat expertise.

In a featured review in *Time*, Hitchcock is given credit for the story idea, Steinbeck for the story, and Hitchcock and screenwriter Jo Swerling for the film script. Actually, Hitchcock's idea was to do a movie on the merchant marine—it was Steinbeck, long before he was brought into the project, who had the lifeboat idea, and it was he who wrote the original screenplay. His work was then doctored to make it slicker and less allegorical, and to reflect Hitchcock's prejudices. It was the kind of treatment that Steinbeck had originally expected from Hollywood, although it did not turn him against Hollywood or even Twentieth Century-Fox—it simply renewed his resolve never to let anything of his ever again get in the hands of a producer or director that he didn't know and trust. Hitchcock had been highly recommended; so much for high recommendations.

On January 11, 1944, the Steinbecks left for Mexico, stopping by Chicago and New Orleans on the way (through the Howard Hunters, the Steinbecks had developed quite a group of friends in New Orleans, and one of those friends had offered to take John fishing and show him the bayous). Once in Mexico, John had planned on continuing his work on *Cannery Row*, developing an outline for *The Pearl*, and at the same time writing articles (as always, a plan to pay for the trip). But, as he wrote Pat Covici, when he got there, his ambitious plans evaporated and his need for a rest overcame him:

We have been doing completely tourist things and I haven't wanted to do any writing. I'll get to work on the little book as soon as I get back. It is being a good rest here in a way and a mulling over of a lot of things. I'm doing more mulling than anything else. Went down to the ruins of Mitla and Monte Albán near Oaxaca. It was beautiful there. Tonight we are going to Cuernavaca for a couple of days and next weekend to a little town called San Miguel Allende where I have never been. . . .

It is very strange down here. Crowded with Americans because where else can they go for vacations. Besides there is no rationing down here so they go hog wild with steaks for awhile. People who don't even like steaks, eat them like mad. . . .

This is a new pen and I like it very much. I got it to finish the little book with because it is good for drawing. I have finished my jacket design and am sure you will like it very much. It has everything that you admire so much in my drawing. [Covici had had trouble in the past with Steinbeck's "art," which was on about kindergarten level, insisting that the author leave illustration and book design to others.] Also I have some new characters. I could sit down and do the book now [*Cannery Row*], but I want to let it mellow a little longer. Meanwhile I think of it a great deal.

The food is good here and I am sleeping many hours at a time— almost like a drugged sleep. Seem to have been more tired than I knew. Hear some music and now and then go to a movie and that is my social life. I was going to do some articles for the Tribune but just haven't wanted to. Can't get coagulated. Newspaper work is not natural to me. And while I could turn out the wordage, it wouldn't be worth printing, like so much of my work overseas. The rebirth of the individual is happening to me. Maybe that is good or bad but it is happening anyway.

He also did some thinking about *The Pearl* and some informal research, absorbing a sense of the place once again and reading some folktales in Spanish.

He renewed acquaintance with some of the film people he had met or worked with earlier, and as a result of several enthusiastic offers, worked out a deal to have *The Pearl* filmed entirely in Mexico by Mexicans with Mexican financing. As with *The Moon Is Down*, he would do the dramatization first and the short novel afterward. He would have complete control over the script, and a Spanish version and an English version of the movie would be made at the same time. In his irritation over *Lifeboat* and enthusiasm for the new project, he forgot his frustrations while making *Forgotten Village* and his vows never to make a movie in Mexico again.

Once again Gwyn announced that she was pregnant, and this time it was true. Since he had returned from the war, his letters were full of nostalgia for Monterey, the fog and the smell of fish—a strong emotion that was no doubt one of the major factors that led him to the writing of *Cannery Row*—and he talked frequently of moving back. His plan now was to wait until the birth of the baby, and then after the baby was old enough to travel, return to Mexico the following winter to make the picture. When he was through with the film, they would move to the Coast. If possible, he wrote Toby Street, he'd like to find fifteen or twenty acres on the Carmel River, perhaps straddling the river:

> It may take a long time to find what I want because this one is going to be fairly permanent. . . . I intend to take years on this one with a cement mixer and a dobe pit and never to get it quite finished. That seems to be a bad idea to get it finished. I even have a kind of a plan that will make it go on indefinitely. But I would like to be on the river and not too far from the ocean. [2/22/44]

They returned to New York in the middle of March and planned to stay until after the baby was born, although in the past they had sworn that they would never spend another summer in the city. He spent many of his mornings working on his novel at Viking, which provided him a small office, and in doing so, he got to know Pat Covici far better than he had before, having coffee and lunching with him frequently. In April, he wrote to Dook Sheffield for the first time in quite a while:

> You will laugh to think that for a year and a half I tried to get into the army but was blackballed from this largest club in the world. I am very glad of it now but at the time I was very sad about it. Had I succeeded I would either have been guarding a bridge in Sante Fé or writing squibs for the Santa Ana Air Force Monitor. As it is I've had a look at the war, too much of a look I guess. . . .
>
> We are living in an apartment at the above address [330 East Fifty-first Street] and Gwyn is going to have a baby in July which makes me very glad. Then I am going to make a picture in Mexico next winter and after that we hope to get back to California. I am very homesick for it. . . .
>
> Now I am back at work and working every day on a silly book that is fun anyway. We have here the lower part of an old brownstone with a yard and we have a sheep dog who is as crazy as all my dogs are. If in New York at all this is a pleasant place to live. [4/12/44]

But being pinned down in New York was difficult for him, and that "old restlessness," as he called it, returned once again to haunt him. He had dreamed for months of returning from the war to Gwyn and the apartment, but, when actually achieved, none of his dreams of domestic tranquillity were satisfying for very long, whether it was the ranch in the hills of Los Gatos, the garden apartment in New York, or the adobe he now dreamed of near Monterey. He was driven all his life to move. In New York, in the spring and summer of 1944, he would come home and tell Gwyn he couldn't stand it anymore—he had to get out. "Pack a bag," he'd tell her, and so she'd pack a bag and they'd go to the de Kruifs' for the weekend, or to New Orleans, or Chicago. He had just returned, but he couldn't wait to travel back to Mexico.

Gwyn and Lynn Loesser were pregnant together and compared bellies in the reflection of shop windows. As for John, having a baby was satisfying, but it was another domestic dream that was perhaps better as a dream—already a pregnant wife was more of an anchor than he would have desired. But even stuck in New York, he was constantly busy. He planted his garden, and went on long walks around the neighborhood. They went out frequently, and if Gwyn was too tired, he sometimes went out alone. Perhaps he wasn't quite as gay as he had been, but there was little evidence, as far as his friends were concerned, of the moroseness and meanness that Gwyn claims lasted nearly a year after his return from Europe.

If there had been a change in his personality, it had been a gradual one, not caused by war experiences alone, but by a series of events beginning with the extraordinary success of *The Grapes of Wrath*, continuing through the divorce, and then his displacement to the East into a strange environment and a new set of friends. To say that he couldn't handle success would be wrong. It wasn't that he couldn't handle it—it was as if he didn't know quite what to do with it, or how to take it.

In trying to adjust to a new status and a new social milieu, he was often defensive and insecure. As in the past, he got along easily with any workman he ran across, but with his peers, artistically or socially, he was awkward and shy, unless he knew them very well. The contradictions in his personality showed more dramatically when he was under social pressure. Usually a modest man, he could, for example, become a bumbling braggart in order to show that he belonged; in the presence of someone who he felt for some reason was "one up" on him (like Lyndon Johnson he was very uneasy around Harvard types), he could blurt out the most terrible hogwash in order to establish his equality. He wouldn't take honorary degrees, but when confronted with an Ivy Leaguer, suddenly Stanford became "his" or even "the" university.

If there was one outward change that was most noticeable during these years, it was his evolution into a more and more social creature (something Gwyn claims was a result of deliberate pressure on her part). He was more inclined to enjoy parties and to go to gatherings where he did not know everybody; he liked dressing up and going to the theater; the circle of his acquaintance grew wider and wider, so much so that it is not too much of an exaggeration to say that there was hardly a prominent figure from the Hollywood or New York of that day who didn't claim some acquaintance with him. Yet, he continued to insist that he was a very private person.

He had always detested gossip columnists, but he got to know and like Leonard Lyons and his wife, and went to many of Leonard and Sylvia's parties—though he made Lyons promise not to refer to him in his column unless he cleared the item with Steinbeck first. When he went to a large party, he still skulked in a corner, but at the same time, if he was not recognized, he was hurt. At times in company he seemed like an awkward, oversized teenager who, although ill at ease, was going to put up a good front. Nevertheless, he could be very sophisticated. Lynn Loesser says that she recalls no one, except perhaps Hitchcock, who could order from a menu at a fancy restaurant with more knowledge and aplomb than he.

Most of these contradictions came from his inability to decide whether he should embrace fame and its privileges wholeheartedly, or reject it all and withdraw from society, as he had tried to do at various times in the past. He liked people, he liked being recognized (he had cultivated a beard in imitation of the MTB crews that he had admired in the Mediterranean), and he enjoyed getting special treatment. He acquired his own table at "21," and it pleased him to be ushered in with deference among the elite. When on occasion he came in and the place was so crowded that they had seated someone at his table, he was furious, especially if he was embarrassed by having brought someone for whom he was trying to show off. But at the same time, he had a deep-seated feeling that there was something wrong, something corrupting about such pleasure—he still feared that such activity might ruin him as a writer.

Another measurement of his state of mind during these years was the change from open admiration of Hemingway to a sense of competition with him. During the summer of 1944 he met John Hersey, and Hersey recalls:

> I would meet him at places where writers gathered or where he just happened to hang out. I remember seeing him a couple of

times at "21" and at Costello's, I believe, a place where a lot of writers used to go. Hemingway was in town at one time when he was there. I remember a sense of competition between the two because they had both grown beards just a little before that. John was very proud for having a reason for growing his beard besides just trying to look that way. He had some sort of skin problem, he said, that obliged him to grow it, and that seemed to be points for him.

Throughout most of his life, Steinbeck was cautious and restrained in making judgments about serious writers who were his contemporaries. He really didn't talk much about writing, his own or anyone else's, in public or private, but of all the writers of his own time, the one he admired most was Hemingway. He had developed some scorn for the legend and his search for publicity, but he was almost in awe of the skill and care of Hemingway's writing. (By contrast, he liked John O'Hara as a man, but confided to his wife that he thought his work was sloppy.) Earlier, as I mentioned, he had been overwhelmed with admiration upon reading "The Killers," and years later he read a story that Hemingway had written about the Spanish Civil War called "The Butterfly and the Tank" and was so impressed by it he wrote a letter to Hemingway expressing his admiration. Apparently as a result of this letter, when Hemingway was in New York in the spring of 1944, he expressed a desire to meet Steinbeck, and a meeting was arranged at Tim Costello's on Third Avenue.

People seem to think that by bringing two great writers together, great things will happen—perhaps immortal words will be exchanged and recorded for posterity. In reality, such meetings have tended more often than not to be disasters—two people defensively eyeing each other, embarrassed by circumstances, and wondering what to say. The only meeting between Steinbeck and Hemingway was such a disaster. Furthermore, no one seems to remember very clearly what was done or said. There isn't even agreement as to how the meeting was arranged. Vincent Sheean recalls that he and his wife arranged the dinner party. But Gwyn is sure that it was Robert Capa, who, she recalls, spent weeks trying to make the arrangements while her husband was "playing hard to get." During the party itself, Capa, she remembers, clucked over the two of them like a mother hen.

There were quite a number of people present, including Sheean and his wife, John O'Hara, Capa, Costello, and John Hersey and his wife (who arrived late). The only memorable incident during the evening concerned Steinbeck only indirectly. Apparently several of the men were standing at the bar in the front room, and O'Hara was proudly showing Hemingway his walking stick, a gift from Steinbeck, which was a blackthorn that had been handed down from his grandfather. Hemingway questioned its authenticity—"That's no blackthorn." When O'Hara insisted that it was, Hemingway bet him fifty dollars that he could break it over his own head. O'Hara accepted. Hemingway took the stick by both ends and pulled it down over his head, breaking it in two. "You call that a blackthorn?" he said, and threw the pieces aside. O'Hara was mortified, while Steinbeck, who had withdrawn into himself for most of the evening, looked on and thought the whole thing was unnecessarily cruel and stupid.

Later after Hemingway had left, the Steinbecks noticed O'Hara, slightly wild, coming into the bar mumbling, getting a drink, and then going out again. This happened several times, and when the Steinbecks left, they found him standing out in the rain with his hands in his pockets and his coat turned up, shuffling back and forth, talking to himself. They saw immediately that he was waiting to pick a fight with someone. Gwyn turned to her husband and said, "John, John, for God's sake go in and get Capa. I'll go home and you two talk to him." Steinbeck went to get Capa, but Capa didn't want to leave. Then, as Gwyn remembers, she suggested that they take O'Hara home with them, since they lived only about three blocks away. Steinbeck looked at O'Hara weaving back and forth in the rain and said, "No, he's too drunk. He'll try to paste me in the nose if I get near him." And then, she remembers, her husband stopped

and looked at me, and I'll never forget his eyes, and he said, "The poor son of a bitch. The poor, poor son of a bitch. He has *really* fucked up his life." And with that he took my arm, and he took me home.

After that evening, Hemingway seemed to stick in his craw, and he worked up an enormous hostility toward the man and his work, which he maintained for several years, a competitive hostility that one would think more typical of Hemingway than of Steinbeck. But even in his hostility, there was something almost humorous in his capricious outbursts. One friend recalls one afternoon in Steinbeck's apartment, when

he would suddenly put down the bowl of onions he was peeling for the great chili he used to make. "Hemingway," he'd sneer, although nobody had mentioned Hemingway, and he would get up and go over and take *The Sun Also Rises* from a bookshelf. Then, sighing with satisfaction, he would read aloud, intoning the celebrated dialogue in a deliberately flat voice, without cadence, without caesura, and naturally it sounded awful. Then, pursing his lips and nodding, he would close the book and slap it against his knee. "God damn it. I don't understand why people think Hemingway can write dialogue." And for a little while he would be very happy.

And a few months later when he was in California at Ed's lab, Toni Jackson remembers being startled when out of a clear blue sky, like some rocket bursting out of the subconscious, Steinbeck suddenly exclaimed, "Hemingway . . . that shit!"

Gradually, as he gained more confidence in his own position, this sense of hostility and competition dissipated of itself, and he returned to his previous standard of not even mentioning other writers (except to talk about those he came to know very well in terms of their personal relationship), regardless of how he may have felt about them. There was only one further significant reference to Hemingway, which came as a kind of humorous coda to Steinbeck's period of professional jealousy. In 1948 Pat Covici passed on a remark overheard by a third person: "Hemingway said he could not read Steinbeck any more after the last scene in *Grapes of Wrath* wherein the starving man seeks food at the breasts of the dying woman. Hemingway said that 'aside from anything else, that's hardly the solution to our economic problem.' " Steinbeck wrote back to Covici, "Mr. Hemingway's analysis is not quite valid but very funny."

To a great extent John's malaise upon returning from the war was but a part, a more intensified episode, of a continuing battle with himself, the terms of which had been set down many years before when he determined that he could not write well unless he was able to rid himself of ego, a crippling sense of self. Of course, as he became very famous, the temptations increased and the problems of escaping from a sense of his own importance multiplied. He had an ego, and he was not always able to control it very well, but he tried. His continuing campaign against personal publicity was part of that effort, and he worked very hard to maintain a modesty that was for the most part genuine.

The contradictions so apparent in his character were the outward manifestations of this inner struggle for control. There were those whom he met during this period, such as George Frazier, who were baffled by the personality of this troubled man and thought such discrepancies symptoms of a basic dishonesty. Frazier was a magazine article writer and, at the time he met Steinbeck, entertainment editor for *Life* magazine. He was a habitué of all the "in" places, such as "21" and the Stork Club, a Harvard man, and a snob. As such, he brought out the worst from a Steinbeck besieged by insecurity. In a malicious article published the year after Steinbeck's death, he convincingly demonstrates his own superiority and insider status while showing Steinbeck up as a fool and celebrity-seeker. Nonetheless, he tells several anecdotes that ring absolutely true of the author at this point in his life and that illustrate the battle Steinbeck was fighting (and not always winning).

They both lived in the same East Side neighborhood—in fact, they met at midnight, each walking his sheep dog down First Avenue—an area that was almost like a small town in atmosphere, with its own shops, restaurants, and bars. One shop that Steinbeck frequented was the bookstore on the corner of First Avenue and Fifty-first Street, run by a literate and kindly man who used some of his profits to help indigent writers in the neighborhood. Whenever one of his customers published a book he would put up a window display with the sign LOCAL BOY MAKES GOOD. "He had done it," Frazier recalls, "for Russell Maloney and William Shirer and a lot of others, a courtesy that impressed Steinbeck when I told him about it."

Frazier decided to ask the owner to put up a display of Steinbeck's books with the same sign above. As Frazier tells it:

> The next afternoon, when I knew that it had been done, I phoned Steinbeck and suggested a walk. When we reached the bookstore, I stopped and feigned astonishment. "John! Look!"
>
> He studied the display for a moment and then began to blush. "God damn nonsense. I don't go for that stuff."
>
> "Yes, I know," I said. "He should know that. I'll tell you what I'll do. You can't do it because it would seem ungracious, but I'll get him to take it out of the window."
>
> He looked at me with something like terror. "Good God, no." He shook his head emphatically. "You can't do that. It'd hurt his feelings." And for weeks thereafter he would take anyone who dropped by his apartment over to the bookstore window to point out how no one could have any privacy in New York.

It was about this time, the summer of 1944, that he first got involved in a project called "The Wizard of Maine," conceived during one of those long evenings filled with madness when the Steinbecks were with the Frank Loessers and the Fred Allens. John and Frank got the idea of writing a musical for Fred. The story, which fit Allen's talent to a T, concerned a snake-oil salesman, a genial humbug who travels from small town to small town doing magic tricks—and doing good, although he pretends to be indifferent to everything but profit and expresses a cynical view of human nature. Steinbeck wasn't able to do much with the idea until the following year, but he did mention the role as a possibility to Burl Ives, and Ives was interested. The singer and writer had renewed their friendship as a result of meeting frequently at Café Society, where Ives was appearing on the bill with Jimmy Savo and Hazel Scott. Ives began to drop by the apartment now and then and

John would cook up some chili. He was a great chili man. There were only two things on the menu: there was chili and crackers and red wine. That was it, nothing else, and that was the whole evening. You had a little chili, a little wine—they went together you know. We'd sit up there till twelve, one o'clock and then Gwyn would chase me out, and sometimes later. But he was a remarkable man. He didn't talk a lot. I used to go over there and sing a couple of songs. He liked the ballad, so I'd sing a couple of ballads once in a while, and he'd tell some stories. But a lot of times we'd just sit there and say nothing. That was very nice.

Gwyn's claim to the contrary, John had not lost his sense of fun. One occasion that was always very special to him and provided a wonderful excuse to let go of his inhibitions was a birthday—it didn't matter whose. An important part of the ritual was to begin celebrating early and then go out and purchase the most outrageous, impractical gift possible. Once, years ago in Hollywood, he and Gwyn bought Max Wagner what Gwyn refers to as "a taxidermist's dream" of a Pekingese dog. On another occasion in Monterey, for Beth Ingels's birthday, John and Ritchie Lovejoy had quite a few rums, went out shopping, and came back in triumph with a single moose antler—just one side, with a little bit of the velvet hanging on it, badly scratched, with a couple of holes punched in it where the brittle horn had collapsed.

In New York in 1944, it was Abe Burrows's birthday, and John and Frank Loesser followed the pattern, going out in the late morning and visiting bars and shops, alternating from one to the other. Finally they came home at six, having purchased a very old and very badly put together model of a sailing ship, a male department-store dummy, and a stuffed swordfish, about eight feet long, so old that the skin was cracked and the stuffing was falling out. Gwyn and Lynn—in full evening gowns—struggled to find some way to wrap the gifts.

That evening in the middle of the party, the Steinbecks decided they wanted to liven up the celebration, so they removed the head from the dummy and placed it face up in the toilet bowl and carefully put the seat cover down. Gwyn claims the effect was dramatic, and John felt they had a smash hit with the head and decided he wanted to take it home. They extracted it from the john, dried it off, and Gwyn carried it under her arm, the dummy all the time showing that sweet, expectant smile that dummies have.

It was three or four o'clock in the morning when they got to the street, and it was raining hard—conditions that in New York make it almost impossible to get a cab. John and Frank whistled and waved, but with no results—the cabs just rattled and splashed by, soaking the two men from the waist down. Then Gwyn came out and said she'd get them a cab, and they said, "No, you can't," and she said, "just wait and see." With the head in her arms, she screamed at the passing taxis, "Stop! Stop! I've got to get to a hospital!" Sure enough, a cab skidded to a halt, the cabbie said, "Sure, lady. Sure, lady." She climbed in and they all piled in after her and sat in the cab, stroking the head and roaring with laughter. "Oh," Gwyn remembers, referring to John, "he was so proud of me that night."

In midsummer they were invited to spend the weekend with the John Herseys at Sands Point. John had brought with him a huge, yellow, war-surplus life raft of the sort made to hold an entire bomber crew. The night after they had arrived, John inflated it for use the next day. The harbor was full of fancy little yachts, as Hersey remembers, with

elderly bald gents with blonde girls aboard, and Steinbeck called them the "Twin Screw Set." I had a little dinghy, and that Sunday morning we went out on the bay before any of the "Twin Screw Set" were awake—they tended to have their lights on rather late at night—and we hitched his raft on behind my dinghy, and I sailed around in the harbor towing Steinbeck, Gwyn, my wife, and a sheep dog that they had at that point. And as we went by these boats, John would call out, "Candy, chewing gum, peanuts," to see if he could wake them up.

The boy who once went out on snipe hunts, smacking pine cones with a stick to arouse the protective zeal of wealthy property owners, was still alive.

In early July John wrote Toby: "I have been working madly at a book [*Cannery Row*] and Gwyn has been working calmly at a baby and it looks as though it might be a photo finish." He mentions that he had also been working for the Treasury Department and the Army, so that "it is kind of sneaking a book out." As was often the case with him, the projects seemed to line up, like freight cars on a siding, waiting their turn to be coupled to the engine and switched onto the main line. There was *The Pearl*, which he was thinking about even as he finished *Cannery Row*, then "The Wizard of Maine," and, in the back of his mind, a major project, which he refers to off and on in his letters, as in this mention to Dook: "Within a year or so I want to get to work on a very large book I've been thinking about for at least two years and a half. Everything else is kind of marking time" [9/27/44]. Perhaps he was thinking about the book that eventually became *East of Eden*. If so, a number of other cars would be switched onto the mainline first.

Near the end of July, when he completed the book before the baby was born, he won twenty dollars from Gwyn. He wrote to Ritchie and Tal Lovejoy: "I just finished a crazy kind of a book about Cannery Row and the lab, etc. All fiction of course but born out of homesickness. And there are some true incidents in it." He had by this time decided not to wait in New York until winter and then go to Mexico, but to move to California as soon as Gwyn and the baby could travel. He was not an Easterner, he wrote to several of his friends, and he just couldn't stand it anymore. No doubt he was right in thinking that much of his emotional discomfort came from trying to live up to what he thought were the expectations of the more status-conscious East. What companionship he could find at "21" had been a poor substitute for the lab. In preparation for the move, he bought a used station wagon. His plan, as he wrote the Lovejoys, was, "If Gwyn and the baby feel well enough, they'll go with me. Otherwise, they'll take the train and I'll drive Willie the dog and a load of stuff across." I'm coming home, he wrote, I'm coming home.

On August 2, Gwyn delivered a boy, whom they named Thom, and John wired Max and Jack Wagner, "Both doing splendidly." He was delighted, but chose not to play the doting father in too obvious a fashion. "It isn't mean or anything," he told Toby, "but he can't do anything. Just eats and sleeps. Be weeks before he can help around the house." Gwyn did not recover from the birth quickly, and their plans to go West were delayed. He could barely restrain his impatience. At the end of the month he wrote to Toby: "Gwyn is still a little peaked but is on the mend now. We're planning to go out there about the 1st of October. . . . Have lots of energy and a good desire to get to work. I think getting back will be good for me. . . . I have a good feeling about going back. Hope nothing overturns it" [8/25/44]. He was putting so much faith in the beneficial effects of going home that he began to worry that something might go wrong. He wrote to Dook that they had rented two small houses down the coast from Carmel, one to live in and one for him to work in, while they took time to look for just the right place for a permanent home. He added, "I've had a wonderful sense of going home but just lately I'm a little scared. Probably the same thing as your saying you aren't at ease with me. There must have been a change in me and in everyone else" [9/27/44].

With *Cannery Row*, as with *Tortilla Flat* and *The Moon Is Down*, he began by telling his friends that he was not working on anything terribly important—perhaps to ease the pressure of writing—and then once it was completed, he talked about the book's complexity. At the end of September, he told Dook:

> I finished the book called Cannery Row. It will be out in January. If Pat Covici sends me an extra proof I'll send you one. I don't know whether it is effective or not. It's written on four levels and people can take what they can receive out of it. One thing—it never mentions the war—not once. I would be anxious to know what you think of it. You'll find a lot of old things in it. I find I go back to extensions of things we talked about years ago. Maybe we were sounder then. Certainly we were thinking more universally. The crap I wrote overseas had a profoundly nauseating effect on me. Among other unpleasant things modern war is the most dishonest thing imaginable.

Unlike earlier work for which he claimed complexity—like *The Moon Is Down*, which really wasn't—this book was as complex as he was. In a way it was a summation of all his conflicts and contradictions, and all that he had learned. It was Steinbeck—funny and deadly serious at the same time, sentimental and coldly deterministic, loving and satirical, lyrical and yet very precise.

Perhaps it was another example of how excellence in his work had to be produced out of emotional turmoil. Nowhere else in his work is his poetry so well controlled, and nowhere else does he cut quite so deep. Out of the onrush of recollected experiences and emotions of a life once lived, of friends once loved, and of a place indelible in memory, he creates a mythical land:

> The word sucks up Cannery Row, digests it and spews it out, and the Row has taken on the shimmer of the green world and the sky-reflecting seas.

And mythical characters:

> Mack and the boys are the Beauties, the Virtues, the Graces. In a world ruled by tigers with ulcers, rutted by strictured bulls, scavenged by blind jackals, Mack and the boys dine delicately with the tigers, fondle the frantic heifers, and wrap up the crumbs to feed the sea gulls of Cannery Row.

And a mythical hero, unlike any hero ever imagined:

> Doc has the hands of a brain surgeon, and a cool, warm mind. Doc tips his hat to dogs as he drives by and the dogs look up and smile at him. . . . Doc would listen to any kind of nonsense and change it for you to a kind of wisdom. His mind had no horizon—and his sympathy had no warp.

The myth evolved during scores of evenings when he told his wife bedtime stories of Gabe (Mack) and the boys, of Flora's place and Wing Chong's, of Ed and the lab and the people who gathered there.

But the novel, if one can call it that, is connected to Steinbeck's life in a number of ways beyond the creation of a myth out of nostalgia. It is, although it doesn't mention war, Steinbeck's war novel. It was born out of the discovery in war of his own mortality, and out of the haunting question: why does a little girl have to be blown up? What is life, what is death, and what do they mean? He also asks, what are the most important things in life? The answers are simple: life is process; death is part of life; neither life nor death means anything—they simply are; and the important things in life are love and beauty, which bring joy to the process of living.

The answers are, of course, another presentation of the Steinbeck-Ricketts philosophy—probably the most sophisticated and convincing expression of it found anywhere in their writings. During the war and through the writing of the novel, it was not just nostalgia that was working on him; he was still filled with his experiences on the Gulf and with the ideas exposed briefly in *The Log*.

Steinbeck felt strongly that his expression of these ideas had been incomplete, partly because *Sea of Cortez* did not sell very well and partly because the medium, the narrative portion of the book, was not a satisfactory forum. The philosophy, which to him was the most important element, had to be subordinated to the progress of the trip and slipped into the account as digression. He came to realize that the best means of expression, in terms of both the nature of the material itself and his own talent, was poetic rather than expository, and that the power of Ricketts's philosophy resulted in large part from the appeal of Ricketts's unique personality. *Cannery Row*, therefore, is in a sense a fictional-poetic version of *The Log*, and Doc a metaphor for the spirit of Ed as Steinbeck perceived it. Part of the motive for writing the novel was the press on its author of unfinished business.

When Steinbeck moved West at the beginning of October, he was fully aware of the potential for disappointment: he might be looking for *Cannery Row* and find that only Cannery Row existed. He had driven across country while Gwyn came by plane. The trip for her and the baby had been terrible, and at the end they were marooned in Los Angeles. They found after they got into their rented house that because of gas rationing they were just too far from town, so they moved into the Eleventh Street house in Pacific Grove, all the while looking for a permanent place. John's dream had had two parts, an adobe and a piece of property in the Carmel Valley. The rationing crunch and the unavailability of any property on the river pushed them to look closer to town, and they ended up with just the adobe.

But it was a magnificent old house, a local landmark that, as John wrote to Pat Covici, he had wanted since he was a kid. The Soto House, as it was called, was built in the late 1830s, had a very large garden surrounded by an adobe wall, and was only four blocks from the waterfront in Monterey. He liked the privacy provided by the thick wall and gloried in the promise of the garden: it was eight city lots in size, plenty of room for walnut and almond trees and a vegetable plot. The only lack was of some private place for him to work, but he would remedy that by getting an office somewhere in town, going there, as he did to his office at Viking, for four or five hours every morning—"Four doleful walls and a ground glass door are about my speed, particularly if the door says 'accountant.' "

While they waited to get into their new home, there was time to check in with old friends. "Ed is fine," he wrote Elizabeth, "and Ritch is doing some nice little stories for the local paper. He doesn't seem to have time to clean them up but he should because many of them are quite good" [11/44]. And they had visitors: "Robinson Jeffers and his wife came in to call the other day. He looks a little older but that is all. And she is just the same"—a gracious gesture of welcome by the Jefferses, since Steinbeck knew them only slightly. Near the end of November he reported that "Gwyn is cooking a turkey for Ed and Tony and the Lovejoys. I think she is too tired but she wants to. It's a kind of second Thanksgiving. We spent the real one with Beth and Mary and my other sister came over too. So it was quite a gathering of the clan" [JS/PC-11/25/44].

The house that at first seemed to him to be in such good shape turned out on closer inspection to require a great deal of work before they could even move in. There were "millions of little things to be done ... broken pipes, broken windows, everything to be cleaned and painted," plus some replastering and a new roof. Just as he was beginning these tasks, John heard that his old friend from Tahoe days, Lloyd Shebley, was in town staying at a local hotel. Shebley was working as a fisherman, and since he was between boats, Steinbeck hired him to help with the painting and repairs on the house. The repairs didn't get too far, however, for lack of materials. It was still wartime, and boards and bureaucrats doled out such supplies. Steinbeck began to feel that he was having a harder time than most others around him getting things and suspected deliberate hostility. "I'm catching it from some of the local people," he wrote Pat. "They have never had any power over me and now they have and are they using it to the limit. All of the hatred and envy is coming out" [1/45].

In the meantime, he had been trying to find an office where he could retreat to do his writing. And, as he reported to Pat, he found out in yet another way where he stood with "official" Monterey, its businessmen and politicians:

In Monterey there is only one office building, owned by a man named Parsons. I tried to reach him for three days and this morning got him by phone. I said, "I want to rent an office for a couple of months." "Very well," he said, "we have some vacancies. What is your name?" "Steinbeck," I said. "And what is your business?" "I'm a writer," I said. There was a long pause and then—"Do you have a business license?" "No," I said, "none is required in my business." Another long pause, then "I'm sorry—we don't want people like that. We want professional people like doctors and dentists and insurance."

Isn't that wonderful? So I cleaned out the woodshed and set up a table and I'll work there. I just thought you'd like to know that I can't get an office in my own home town and that the building owner never heard of me. Sic transit or perhaps it never existed. [12/44]

But it wasn't just the ration board, the O.P.C., and the Parsonses of Monterey who were giving him trouble. He was also having a difficult time on a more personal level. Some old friends had moved away for the duration; others were in the service. He found that the circle that had once included him had changed, and he felt awkward, an intruder, even less comfortable than he had felt in New York. Among the thinning ranks of old friends—particularly with people like Ritchie Lovejoy who had ambitions in art—his very presence seemed a rebuke to their lack of achievement. Among new faces he was on the spot to demonstrate, immediately, some sign of greatness. He became an object of curiosity, a target for deflation. He had come to Monterey with his antennae extended, and the vibrations he picked up were not reassuring. He went ahead with the house, doing what he could, and he planted trees, rose bushes, and a vegetable garden. But, as he wrote Pat, he was only going through the motions of permanence: "Privately and deeply—I don't believe it. It's a series of gestures. But that is between us. It has nothing to do with anything except my own disbelief in permanence. And certainly nothing in the world happening now is designed to convince me otherwise" [1/45].

We are bound to think, as Steinbeck himself did, of Thomas Wolfe and *You Can't Go Home Again*. But in going West the problem was not that he had expected too much, although perhaps he had, or that people and circumstances had changed during the intervening years, although they had. His mistake was that in returning to Monterey he thought he could just ignore fame when he chose, and lead his life as he had before. And he still carried with him a heavy burden of dissatisfaction and malaise that no change in exterior circumstances could relieve him of.

Rather than with George Webber in Thomas Wolfe's novel, Steinbeck's condition might be better compared with one of Saul Bellow's middle-aged anti-heroes, perhaps Henderson, that bull of a man in *Henderson the Rain King* whose florid face and large nose give the signal of a fierce inner passion, a huge thirst for life. Steinbeck's dark moods, occasional wild shenanigans, heavy drinking, and rages against friends suggest, as in Henderson, a fundamental discontent, and his frequent moves, a quest for some form of grace by which he could learn to live harmoniously with himself. Throughout his remaining years, he gave nearly as much attention to the search for a way to live as he did to the continuing search for a way to write, and it may be that his writing suffered for it.

One of Gwyn's axioms about her husband was that he quarreled with every male friend he ever had and parted angrily from each of them. This is only partly true, but there is enough truth in it to reveal something of Steinbeck's darker side. He could be intolerant and sometimes showed a striking lack of charity and understanding. A somewhat truer axiom is that he often expected more from others—friends, wives, children—than he expected from himself. All these things would seem to apply to his breakup with Ritchie Lovejoy.

Lovejoy had failed enough times so that he realized he wouldn't become the writer he had dreamed of being. It was hard for him even to be around Steinbeck, and the fact that Steinbeck had given him his Pulitzer Prize money (widely announced in the newspapers) to finish a novel manuscript that was never published made it even more awkward for him. Rather obtusely, Steinbeck told Pat: "Ritch Lovejoy doesn't look well at all to me. He's had too long a stretch of bad luck and it is beginning to get him down" [12/8/44]. Rather than understanding Ritchie's situation, Steinbeck took his lack of enthusiasm for their relationship as a personal affront. Envy seemed to him to be a mean and unreasonable emotion. The final breaking point came when *Life* magazine asked Steinbeck to help with a spread it planned to do on Cannery Row. When, after discussion with Ed, Steinbeck decided against it, Lovejoy latched on to the job. It might have helped Lovejoy break away from a small-town newspaper into the big time, but Steinbeck saw it as a double cross—a betrayal of him, of Ed, and of the lab and all it had come to mean to all of them. It was a completely irrational reaction, particularly in light of what his own novel did to publicize Ed and the Row, but this "betrayal" was added to his growing list of grudges against Monterey and became a major factor in convincing him that he would be better off living elsewhere.

The only friend who seemed to him to remain the same was Ed. And it must be said that Ed, with all of his loving acceptance and complete lack of competitiveness, was the perfect friend for the man Steinbeck was at this point in his life. When John had first come back to Monterey, he had taken the typescript of *Cannery Row* to Ed to read, wanting to make sure he wouldn't resent being fictionalized. Ricketts was sometimes called "the Mandarin" because of his habit of sitting cross-legged on his bed and quietly nodding and smiling in response to whatever nonsense was going on in the room at the time. When John gave him the typescript and asked him to read it to see if he wanted John to make any changes, Ed sat on his bed and "read it through carefully, smiling, and when he had finished he said, 'Let it go that way. It is written in kindness. Such a thing can't be bad.' "

In order to try to pick up his life as it had been before, Steinbeck began taking long walks through the drizzle of the gray Monterey winter. He tracked the Bay, up and down, watched the seagulls, inspected the boats, and occasionally stopped for a cup of coffee or a beer along the way. He made it his habit, as in the old days, to stop by the lab in the afternoons, and he and Ed spent a lot of time together, drinking and talking. Ed was trying to revive his business, which John would once again subsidize. They even planned together selling off the property, which had become very valuable, and building a more up-to-date lab at another location (primarily John's enthusiasm). They also discussed taking another research trip, similar to the *Sea of Cortez* expedition, but this time northward (primarily Ed's enthusiasm).

Near the end of November, John began work on *The Pearl*, sitting in his unheated woodshed and writing by kerosene lantern—an echo of days long past. He had to endure the cold for only a couple of weeks, however, when Toby found him an office over one of the local banks. He wrote Pat:

> I'm still struggling away at the Pearl and it isn't going well. But with this new place to work I expect it to pick up. It gets me out of the house too which is probably good for both of us. Monday I'm going to start coming down early and finishing about one o'clock. Then I can go for walks and go fishing and work in the garden. It will be a good life maybe. [12/8/44]

About mid-December Max and Jack Wagner came up for a visit, Jack to consult with Steinbeck about the screenplay version of *The Pearl*, but despite the infusion of an outside perspective, he still couldn't get into it. He wrote Pat at the end of the month:

> I've gone into a slump on the Pearl and that bothers me even remembering that I always go into two or three slumps on every

book. But it always worries me. . . . You know I can inspect my slumps pretty well. I go grey in the head and then I begin to worry about not working. Then I get disgusted with myself and when this disgust grows big enough the whole thing turns over like an iceburg [*sic*] and I go to work again. It's always the same and it's always new. I never get used to it. [12/29/44]

In the meantime, although the official publication date was scheduled for January 2, thousands of copies of *Cannery Row* were being sold by booksellers as early as the first of December. Pre-publication orders and a book club contract indicated that sales would be enormous. Steinbeck had sent a copy of the galleys to Dook, who, after reading them, wrote: "I heartily approve of the book and can see your constantly improving technical skill." But, he added, he could forecast already how it would be received by the critics:

The consensus of the literary Petronii will be something like this: "The vagaries and minor felonies of brown-skinned indigents, naive, amoral, and lazy, can be entertaining, but the same formula applied to American Bums gets a little out of focus. 'Angels, saints, etc.,' forsooth—a bum is a bum, and we got a war on." Some of them will wickedly point out that you conscientiously got a couple of bad words in to assure its being banned in Boston, and sadly remark that the world marches on but Steinbeck wallows at the same old troth. [11/44]

When the first reviews appeared, Steinbeck wrote to his publisher that they seemed to bear out Dook's predictions exactly. "But," he continued, "there was something he forgot. There is a time in every writer's career when the critics are gunning for him to whittle him down. This is my stage for that. It has been since the Grapes of Wrath. . . . The criticism is good but what saddens me is the active hatred of most of the writers and pseudo writers around here. It will not be terribly long before we will be associating only with fishermen" [12/3/44].

Even Joseph Henry Jackson, who had been a Steinbeck booster in the very early years when it was unfashionable to be so, wrote a lukewarm, rather reticent review. Steinbeck reported to his editor that "the local cop hates Joe [Jackson] because he said it was a fantasy and the cop says it is literal truth. 'Why,' he says, 'I've taken them all to jail in my time' " [1/12/45]. He also reported with some amusement that Gabe, his model for the *Cannery Row* character Mack, came to him quite drunk and said that a lot of feelings had been hurt down on the Row—"The ones you left out," said Gabe.

But the reviews were so dismal that Covici, afraid that the accumulating bad news might send John into an emotional tailspin, wrote repeatedly in an effort to bolster his author's spirits:

> The small fry of writers and some of the academic ones will always be gunning for you. Were you to be merely a successful writer, like Fanny Hurst, Temple Bailey or Dr. Cronin, you would be occasionally patronized in an oily way but mostly ignored. But to be successful and command serious critical attention—that's too much. They can't stomach it and so they will take it out on you no matter what you write. Better start building a tougher protective skin around you. Poisonous javelins will be constantly coming your way. [1/8/45]

And then a couple of weeks later, he wrote quoting a favorable comment from a letter by Muriel Rukeyser: "That is what I like best in Steinbeck—just that range. It is a range that belongs in poetry, and that I mean to live with. It is a range in our people, and at our best we speak for it" [1/25/45]. And then Covici added, "I read 'Cannery Row' over again. It's a good book John. You poured a great deal of poetry into it. You give a good many reasons for living and for dying. And I am glad you were born and happy that you are alive" [1/25/45].

That the reviewers didn't like the book, thought it unworthy of his talent and a weak repetition of previous work, didn't bother Steinbeck as much as that none of them seemed to understand it. There seemed to be no comprehension at all of the novel's real themes, and the constant attack without understanding was making him angry as well as depressed:

> Commander Kremer, the man I was with so much in the Mediterranean was killed in the Pacific recently. That is sad, he was a good man but probably died at the right time. It strikes me that that is one of my critical crimes. I haven't died at the right time. It is interesting to me, Pat, that no critic has discovered the reason for those little inner chapters in C.R. You would have known. Mostly all lay readers know. Only the critics don't. Are they somehow the lowest common denominator? If in pictures, the thing must be slanted for the 9 year old mind, in books they must be slanted for the critics and it seems to amount to the same thing. Far from being the sharpest readers, they are the dullest. You say I am tak-

ing it philosophically. I'm not and I feel wonderful. Don't you remember the years when those same critics were sneering at every book—the same books incidently that they now remember with awe. No I feel all of the old contempt for them and it is a good feeling. I *know* C.R. is a good book. [1/15/45]

Pat answered, "If the reviews make you feel full of hell and arouse your energy, they have done a remarkable deed. When you finish Pearl . . . you can begin then on your big folklore novel. It is a good mood to begin anything in—I mean full of hell" [1/18/45].

CHAPTER XXX

Although not an autobiographical novel in the strictest sense, *Cannery Row* was very personal. It reflected closely the personality and imagination of the man who wrote it and dealt intimately with many of the people and ideas he cared about deeply. In addition, it was a very experimental novel. Nearly every element—language, form, imagery, and characterization—expressed a non-teleological view of the world. The novel was a great personal risk, and much of Steinbeck's hurt and anger came not from getting bad notices, but from the feeling that in the callous hands of uncaring and insensitive reviewers, the book's fragility and intimacy seemed to be constantly violated. *The Pearl*, by contrast, was a work of imagination which had extraordinary distance from its author. As such, it was another kind of experiment with another set of risks. But it was similar in that it, too, was fragile—in this case, a balancing act of tone, rhythm, and image. A wrong move and the carefully cultivated effect would come tumbling down into absurdity.

The slump that Steinbeck had slipped into before Christmas broke in the middle of January 1945, and he began to press hard to finish the manuscript. He wrote to Elizabeth that

> the Pearl moves ahead slowly. I should finish it in about ten more working days if nothing happens. . . . I don't know how it is. Gwyn was reading some of the beginning of the first draft last night. I'll ask her how it is when I go home today. It's a strange piece of work, full of curious methods and figures. A folk tale I hope. A black-white story like a parable. But we'll see. [1/26/45]

The Steinbecks had seen the Joseph Henry Jacksons several times since their move to Monterey from the East, and in a letter to Jackson he explained how the project got started:

I'm working on the Mexican picture now. The set up is this. Last year in Mexico I came on a curious combination. Indio [Emilio] Fernandez, an ex-cowboy actor, ex-revolutionary leader, started directing pictures. He had taken Delores del Rio, between us a passé actress who was never terrific, stripped the make-up, head dress, and eye lashes from her and made a good emotional actress of her. A Mexican camera man named Figueroa was doing remarkable things for them. There was a flavor about this work like some of the French people, like Renoir, etc. I told them a folklorish tale I picked up in La Paz about the Indian and the Pearl and we decided to make it—to make it straight without any concessions to Hollywood. . . . I think Indio will emerge as one of the great directors of the world. He is really an Indian Zapotec I think and he knows that level of life and is passionate about wanting to put it down. [1/45]

Despite Fernandez's passion, Steinbeck thought that there was a very good chance that the film would never be made. He had stayed with the story for the last months by convincing himself that he needed the discipline—he had had no word from Mexico.

About three weeks later he had finished a draft of the story, which he reported was about 125 pages long, and was ready for Fernandez to come to Monterey, where they would work on the shooting script together. He half thought that he would never hear from Fernandez again, but the director called from Mexico City, saying it was essential for Steinbeck to come down in order to help with the arrangements for casting, locations, and the music. Since Gwyn was to be in charge of the music, gathering and transcribing regional folk themes for the score, they left for Mexico together the second week of February, leaving Thom and his nurse with John's sister Beth in Berkeley.

When they returned in the middle of March, John reported to his agent that it had been a very successful trip and that they had finished a master script. They planned to go back in May at the start of production so that he could "ride herd" on the film: "It can be a very fine one and I want it to be." On their return they found their garden overflowing with produce—spinach, green onions, radishes, beets, lettuce, and carrots—"Things are shrieking they are growing so fast." Thom, too, had grown and gave every indication of becoming a huge child and a mountain of a young man. His parents decided to have Thom baptized in the Episcopal Church, just in case he might need it someday, and besides, John reasoned, it wouldn't hurt for him to absorb some of the litany.

Pat Covici was after him to edit a Viking Portable edition of Robert Louis Stevenson and had offered him a "bribe" of a beautiful set of Stevenson's works and a $1,000 government bond for "Red Tom" (in references of the Steinbecks and their friends, "Thom" and "Tom" would become interchangeable). Steinbeck replied that he could do the essay in his sleep, but he didn't think he wanted to spend the necessary time rereading all of Stevenson's works in order to make a selection. Perhaps, he suggested, Gwyn could make the selection and he could just write the introduction? The only reading that he had done recently, Steinbeck noted, was of the *Arabian Nights*. He was amazed, he said, how many Western stories appear to have had their origins in that collection. As far as writing was concerned, "since finishing the Pearl I've done nothing but write testimonials for Red Cross, War Bonds, Merchant Marine. A bunch of crap but it must be done" [3/45].

At the end of March Gwyn took Thom to Los Angeles to see his grandmother; she also wanted to consult her former music teacher, Sandy Oliver, about her work on the music for *The Pearl*. Left alone, John spent a good deal of time drinking Scotch with Ed, brooding about the hostility he'd felt in Monterey. He was fed up with Lovejoy. As he told Elizabeth,

> Ritch has us by the whatyoucallems because he needs money. It's funny because he would be the first to blame me if I did it. But of course if *Life* wanted to do it they could anyway. I don't know why they are so insistent. . . . Clever trick of theirs, wasn't it? Ed wouldn't have consented for any other reason than to help Ritchie. So there it is. . . . But Ritchie has an invariable method. When he thinks he has the sale he raises the price. And he may ask so much that they will give the whole thing up. *One's friends!* How he would have sneered if I did it. And that's that. [1/26/45]

It was the sneering that made the situation intolerable. Lovejoy, in Steinbeck's absence, had adopted the condescending attitude of his brother-in-law Jack Calvin. Neither had published anything of importance, but they were able to maintain their own egotism by insisting that Steinbeck's writing was flimsy and derivative—without Ricketts he would be nothing. To mutual friends out of Steinbeck's presence, Lovejoy had made sure that his attitude was well known, and he had gained a certain number of converts to his thinking.

At the same time, once her husband's attitude toward Monterey began to turn, Gwyn started to mount subtle pressure for a change.

Gwyn had been against the move from the beginning, saying nothing in the face of her husband's enthusiasm. She had felt rejected when she had been in Monterey before: she had not become part of the group at the lab, and she detected a certain coldness on the part of Steinbeck's relatives. Although they tried very hard to be kind, they had always had the feeling that Gwyn had seduced John away from Carol in order to gain his status and money, and some of John's friends had adopted more or less the same attitude. In New York Gwyn's situation had been quite different.

By the time Gwyn got back from Los Angeles, John had made up his mind. He had decided to leave for Mexico nearly a month early, and then after several months in Mexico, if he felt the same on his return, they would move back to New York. He explained his feelings in a long letter to Pat Covici:

This is a private letter really. We're going back to Mexico in a few days. And I'm glad to go. You remember how happy I was to come back here. It really was a home coming. Well there is no home coming nor any welcome. What there is is jealousy and hatred and the knife in the back. I'm beginning to think I made a mistake. I don't mind that, but I'm not going to let a mistake ride me on through. This is no new thing. I've tried to conceal it and explain it and analyze it and make a joke of it and to ignore it. It's much more than a feeling. Our old friends won't have us back—always except Ed. Mostly with them it is what they consider success that gets in between. And the town and the region—that is the people of it— just pure poison. I laughed about being refused an office. But the local gas board cut off my gas in spite of the fact that I had a job with the War Food Administration. Every business man in town has a "C" card ["C" cards provided a more generous allotment than most civilians usually got]. Ours is the first request to repair a house that has been rejected. (60 homes are being built for rent but we can't get a plank to replace a rotten board in the kitchen.) These are just two of many things. Gwyn has nothing to do with this. I hate a feeling of persecution but I am just not welcome here. And the bastards have power now due to the war but war or none it would be there. It is a very active and very vicious thing. Well it's here. And I'll be damned if I'll stay in it very much longer. The apt. in New York and the people on 2nd Ave were friendly people to us compared to this. You can't imagine the hostility. . . .

Some of the things are so dirty that I don't even want to think about them. Maybe you can figure something, but this I can tell you, I was happier in New York. Living is people, not places. . . . You see this isn't my country anymore. And it won't be until I am dead. It makes me very sad. There's no one to talk to or to associate with. And so I'm glad to be going back to Mexico and I'll probably be back in the East next winter. [4/45]

John took the train on the 5th of April, accompanied by Willie, the sheep dog. He picked up Jack Wagner in Los Angeles, and they proceeded on the train to Mexico City. Gwyn and Thom followed a few days later on the plane. They went to Cuernavaca (where Gwyn had relatives in the real-estate business) and rented a beautiful house: "a large garden and a sixty foot swimming pool and more darn flowers than you ever saw or heard of . . . 10 minutes walk from the plaza" [JS/PC-4/45]. Since work on the movie was not scheduled to start for at least another month, he and Jack spent their time working on "The Wizard of Maine" and on a short story set in Mexico.

It was a good life. John got up early and worked until one o'clock, then swam for an hour or so, followed by a long siesta. Every weekend houseguests came down from Mexico City. Thom was turning brown from the sun, and Willie had become a town character known to all the children as "El Oso." John reported to Toby that since the Mexicans had a habit of celebrating their religious festivals, which occurred frequently, with rockets, El Oso spent a good deal of time under Thom's crib. John was happy to be working again in good surroundings, although his work on "The Wizard" was more a game than anything else. He was certain it would never be published, and he had doubts that as a play it would ever be produced.

At the beginning of May he got word that the *Pearl* manuscript, which he had sent from Mexico on his previous stay months earlier, had finally passed through the censors and arrived in New York. He wrote Elizabeth:

Naturally I am very glad and frankly relieved that you like The Pearl. It was so full of experiments and I had no idea whether they would come off at all. Also the thing seemed doomed never to get there. It was all ominous. Gwyn and Sandy Oliver made some recordings of the basic music—the Family and Pearl themes. The Evil music is not finished. Gwyn is going to try to have a pressing sent to you. These themes are ancient Indian music long preceding the Conquest. And I think they are beautiful. Anyway, I'm terribly pleased that you like the story and that Pat does. I hope that you and he will consider very carefully whether another little book is a good idea. But of course you will know more about that than I. I can't imagine how Collier's could print it because of its length

but I wish they would. They are getting such a good reputation.
[5/3/45]

Covici had written, "I just finished 'La Perla' and I like it. . . . In this
parable you say there are only black and white things and no in-
between, but what rich blacks and what dazzling whites. . . . One could
also say . . . it has only three notes—love, hunger, and freedom from
greed. But again what infinite longings you put into them" [4/26/45].

But despite his encouragement, Covici was concerned, just as were
Steinbeck's agents, that the author had not tackled anything really substantial in years. They wouldn't say anything directly, but in their
hearts they felt that the movie was just another perverse detour from
the real use of his talent. And with yet another small book following
two that had been criticized for their slightness, they would have to
brace themselves for a real onslaught of negative criticism. Tactfully,
Covici suggested that perhaps the best course might be for Steinbeck to
develop the new Mexican story into a novelette and go back and finish a
previously attempted work called "The Good Neighbors," so that they
could bring out a volume of "three novelettes of Mexico." It would be
completely different from anything he had published and very likely
receive serious critical attention.

But "The Good Neighbors" (which, although set in Mexico, had
been written the summer before in New York) had turned sour, Steinbeck replied, and was beyond hope of rescue. He, too, thought that he
"had enough little books," but instead of the three novelettes, he proposed that he combine *The Pearl* with a longer version of the Mexican
story he had been thinking about. In fact the more he thought about the
story, the better he liked it and the more possibilities he saw in it, so
that it grew in his mind over the next few months from a short story, to
a short novel, to a very substantial novel. He called it at the beginning
"*El Camión Vacilador*," (which he later translated—only approximately—into "The Wayward Bus"), and he wrote the original synopsis in Spanish, thinking that he would publish the short story in
Mexico.

Living at the house in Cuernavaca was so easy that he was beginning
to get suspicious. He wrote Elizabeth that

this garden is full of incredible flowers most of which I don't know
at all. We're just beginning to get squared around in the house.
And it is quite a job. Gwyn is getting forced Spanish lessons since
she has to manage the house and none of the servants speak any

English. ... I'm working under a huge bougainevilleae in the shade. It is a little too beautiful I guess. But I like it. Tom is turning very brown and Gwyn is blackening up. Maybe it is good for us. I don't know. I'm always a little suspicious of places that are too nice. [5/7/45]

It was a long way from his preferred "four doleful walls and a ground glass door [which] says 'accountant.' "

In his Edenic garden, the itch of discontent gradually spread into a rash, as time went by and he waited for production of *The Pearl* to begin, not really accomplishing anything. The "Wizard" didn't count—"It is amusing but that is all and it keeps my pen point damp." Fernandez and the crew were working on another picture, work that seemed to extend on and on, as the beginning date for *The Pearl* was repeatedly set back, first until June, then July, and finally to August.

In the meantime, he had been approached by an outfit called Pan-American Films to do a film on the life of Emiliano Zapata. The idea excited him, since he admired Zapata very much, but he saw that there would be a great many difficulties in doing the kind of honest job on which he would insist. A major problem was that some of the men who helped to trick and murder Zapata were still alive and in power in Mexico. He wrote Annie Laurie that he'd have to have government assurance that there would be no interference: "This will have to be an iron bound agreement because Zapata could be one of the great films of all time as by a twist or a concession it could be a complete double cross of the things Zapata lived and died for" [6/26/45].

The idea so appealed to him that he went ahead on his own to start on an outline, while Gwyn, who was more and more becoming a partner in his enterprises, spent nearly a month, off and on, commuting to the National Archives and the library at the National University, doing research on the life of Zapata. It was work that further extended her rudimentary Spanish, although most of the time she found herself copying down things that she didn't understand at all. But real work on Zapata would have to wait until after *The Pearl* and *The Wayward Bus*. It was somehow typical of him, however, that while he was beginning to swear up and down about *The Pearl*—that the delays were driving him nuts, that he would never do another film script, and that he would never do another film in Mexico—he was getting very excited about doing another film, in Mexico. The possibilities that he saw in the potential of a project made the adrenaline surge, while the actualities—filmmaking was so very slow—he found deadening.

In the middle of May he reported to his agents that "the Wizard story progresses. Longest synopsis in the world. It is now nearly 20,000 words, and it gets crazier all the time. I'm pretty anxious to finish it so I can start on the Wayward Bus." By the middle of the following month, he and Jack Wagner got so weary of waiting for Fernandez, they started on the actual shooting script on their own, leading Steinbeck to decide to postpone work on the "Bus" until that winter. In early June he got an offer from the New York *Herald Tribune* to cover the proposed war-crimes trials in Europe. He wanted to do it, but he had no idea when he would be able to leave Mexico. He wrote Elizabeth and asked her, if the trials didn't start until he was through with the movie, "What do you think the Trib would think of us or me covering the trials, then going on to Denmark, Sweden, Norway and Russia and maybe doing some work on each? If Gwyn could go with me I would like that I think. It might be interesting to see them now, since I did see them before the war" [7/12/45]. Although he didn't cover the trials, as it turned out, the offer did plant the seed in his mind of making a return trip to Europe, this time with Gwyn.

He finished the "Wizard" synopsis and sent it on to Annie Laurie, and he and Jack Wagner finished the preliminary shooting script, but he still felt empty, as if he hadn't really been doing anything or getting anywhere. He needed a deep involvement, something he could get his teeth into. The death of the President, the end of the war in Europe, the sense that we were entering a new era—all contributed to his sense of dissatisfaction. He wrote of his feelings and hopes to Pat:

> I don't have the sense of rush I used to. In fact sometimes I seem to be waiting maybe for a design or a shadow or something to indicate a future. I don't know what it will be. I know the lines are down but the accidental historical direction is not sketched yet and no party line or theory is likely to give us the direction. Everything takes so long and I want to see everything and then I want to think about it and there doesn't seem to be time for all of that. . . .
>
> I am heartily sick of this picture now and there are stirrings in me for new work. This is like beating a down dog. I've never liked rehashing—but I'll do it this time and it is once for all. There's so much new work to do—to go over old. . . .
>
> The people down here are very kind to us. And I hope out of this stay to write a book that may be something for them to have. For the Wayward Bus could be something like the Don Quixote of Mexico. The more I think of it, the better I like it and the better I like it, the longer its plan and the wider its scope until it seems to

contain the whole world. From the funny little story it is growing to the most ambitious thing I have ever attempted. Not that it still won't be funny, but funny as Tom Jones and Tristram Shandy and Don Quixote are funny. And it isn't going to take a little time to write, but a long time and I don't care, for my bus is something large in my mind. It is a cosmic bus holding sparks and back firing into the milky way turning the corner of Betelguese without a hand signal. And Juan Chicoy the driver is all the god the fathers you ever saw driving a six cylinder broken down, battered world through time and space. I think the time of the hands is nearly done for awhile and maybe a new little time of the mind is due. If I can do it well the Wayward Bus will be a pleasant thing, and maybe we'll have coffee in Longchamps when I do it, and maybe the whole flower will open and the bugs will get in it. And that's why I'm sick of flogging this donkey of a moving picture. It will be a good picture but what of it. But I'll finish it as I said I would. [7/12/45]

Without having put anything down, he had done a great deal of writing.

Ill health plagued both of them, although Gwyn seemed to be suffering the most. They consulted doctors and the verdict was that they were still suffering the aftereffects of an earlier bout with food poisoning, and they were put on a strict diet. When the diet didn't help and Gwyn got even weaker, John, at the end of July, sent her, with Thom, to New York for treatment and rest. Later, from New York, Pat reported that "Gwyn seems cheerful enough, but rather weak," and then later in August, "I wish you would leave Mexico right now. You had enough of it. 'The Bus Story' is growing into epic proportion and it is not going to give you any rest until you buckle down to it" [8/26/45]. And in another letter he prodded further: "[I] dipped into *Grapes of Wrath* ... the overture essays ... what organ music they are. And I was thinking—please forgive me—when will you put your clarinet away (not that I don't enjoy greatly its lovely lyric music) and take up the organ once again. There is a time for each, I suppose" [8/19/45].

With Gwyn in New York, his discontent deepened and the only thing that kept him from sinking into complete despair was that work finally began, in earnest, on the picture. He went over the shooting script with Fernandez and was impressed: "Fernandez is a fine workman and I think we are going to get a really good picture. It will have a quality no other picture has had" [8/10/45]. Near the end of August, they had finished the revision of the script and had gone to Mexico City for further casting. There would be a break in activity before the shooting began in Acapulco, and so he flew up to New York "to do some business and to see Tom and Gwyn," he wrote Toby. "She is much better and may be able to come back to Mexico with me in a few weeks. I have so much to do here that I am running crazy. The show to set up and another script to write before I go back to Mexico" [9/11/45].

He was referring to "The Wizard of Maine," which was beginning its long history of abortion. The summer before when he and Frank Loesser had conceived the idea, Steinbeck got the inspiration, born out of drink or in the spirit of helpfulness, of offering the job of doing the script for the musical comedy to George Frazier, his entertainment-editor neighbor. Almost no one around Steinbeck applauded the wisdom of this—Covici asked, "I love and admire your loyalty and friendship, but is Frazier the man to do the stage version of your story?" [8/16/45] Steinbeck replied that "he can or he can't," and that it didn't really matter. It turned out that George couldn't. The attempt dragged out over a period of months, and since Steinbeck was not very helpful in their collaboration (aside from providing a 20,000-word synopsis), the friendship was ruptured, as George blamed his failure on Steinbeck. For the author, the "Wizard" was something to play with, in the same spirit which had given it birth; for Frazier, it was a more serious proposition—he had quit his job with *Life* to work on the play.

John returned to Cuernavaca in October, after spending more than a month in New York. There he thought he had made arrangements for the "book" of "The Wizard," he had purchased two adjacent brownstones (one for investment purposes), and he had learned that Gwyn was again pregnant. Back in Mexico, he moved from the house into the hotel where most of the movie people were staying. He was surrounded by characters—not just the movie people, who had their own intrigues and jealousies, but a bizarre assortment of international expatriates. Among them, Mrs. de V, who complained about everything: "Last night Jack and I made a bet. We had dinner with the de V's. She complained about 49 things in three courses and there were little half point complaints like cleaning her spoon violently with her napkin and puke looks about the mouth. We only gave things like that ½ point. And ¼ point for comparison complaints like 'It's better somewhere else.' She will make a Pollyanna out of me if she stays long" [JS/GS-10/45].

Then there was Mr. B, who drank so heavily in memory of Lupe Valdez that he was convinced he saw Steinbeck looking in the window at him while he was in bed with a socially eminent woman: "Then I got a photographer and had a picture taken of the two of them in bed. I had 700 copies made and gave them out in Mexico. B has to stop me and he has to collect all the pictures I have spread about. . . . But he has seen animals too and I'm afraid he is in for a time of it" [10/45].

Then there was the musical group which, when Gwyn had been there, they had christened the Banda Sinfónica de los Chiles Refritos and which, in jest, they had decided to use to provide the music for the picture, since they were so awful. John wrote to Gwyn that they "have learned to play too well. I'm in favor of not using them. They sound now like a bad German band. Their rendition of 'Sobre Las Ola' would turn your hair grey. There has never been anything like it. They have taken in a trumpet player who is afraid of nothing. He rushes in where even fools blanch and refuse" [10/45].

As if to make up for all the time lost earlier, work went ahead on the film at a punishing pace, from seven-thirty in the morning until ten at night. Since the first day, when Fernandez didn't show up until mid-afternoon, leaving Steinbeck waiting and leading him to tell the director that if it happened again, he would go home, Fernandez had become a model of the Yankee work ethic. The most exciting shooting came on location at the seashore. One scene required a shot of fishermen launching boats into the surf, and everyone was a little frightened because the breakers were so high and rough. "One man claimed to have appendicitis this morning so Emilio [Fernandez] told him to rest today and tomorrow he could go into the surf alone. He recovered almost immediately." The following day a Spanish actor "got tumbled and rolled by the waves so often that he was nearly dead. That night he said very sadly to me 'Why do you write these things for me to do? Please write for me a few scenes in bed.'" In addition to being on the set all day nearly every day, Steinbeck continued to work on the shooting script in the evenings with Wagner and Fernandez. His work, plus all the interesting sideshows around him, kept him so busy and diverted, that he had little time to feel blue.

In November Gwyn came back to Mexico for three weeks, but after she left John stayed for most of the rest of the filming, the last stages of which were done in Mexico City. The first week of December, he packed his car and, with Victor, the houseman, and Willie, headed for New York. The trip was a nightmare. He had paid to have his car overhauled, but it broke down one hundred kilometers outside Mexico City. Then, as he later reported to Jack Wagner "we pushed the car 1,800 miles before we could get a repair job. The whole country is frozen and we nearly froze to death" [12/15/45]. He was very glad to join Gwyn in New York in an apartment on East Thirty-seventh Street—not fancy, but *warm*—until the brownstones that they had purchased were finished being remodeled.

Aside from a feeling of being unsettled (many of their things were still in Monterey and would have to be shipped out), the only thing that marred their pleasure in being together once again and back in New York was that this pregnancy had hit Gwyn very hard. John had planned to go regularly once again to the Viking office to work, but Gwyn was so miserable that he tried to do much of his work on "The Wayward Bus" at home, setting up in the kitchen and trying to stay out of the way of the nurse and the houseman. At the end of January 1946, he wrote to Toby:

> Just had to toss out about 20,000 words. Wasn't any good. I don't know why I always have to do it. But it happens every time. . . .
>
> Our house is getting along fine and should be ready in another month. It is going to be a very nice house, and my cellar room is going to be a thing of joy. At last I'm going to have a place to work. Also a place for tools, etc. . . . Lock on the door and everything.

In the face of the abusive criticism of *Cannery Row*, he had reaffirmed an old defensive position—the most important thing is the writing process itself, not what comes from the writing. He was determined to ignore the critics and go on to do what he wanted to do, the way he wanted to do it, and to have fun in the process. When Covici urged him to go back to his "organ tones" of old, he replied that he did want to get into a major project and that the "Bus" might be that project, but that he wasn't going to sacrifice the enjoyment he would have in writing it just to satisfy everyone's expectations of significance. Enjoyment in writing for him involved trying something different, and that in itself, he believed, was enough to bring the critics automatically down on his back.

When he declares in his letter to Toby that he has had "to toss out 20,000 words," he is probably exaggerating. (Nathaniel Benchley, who would become his close friend starting in the spring of 1946, recalls that he would often write not for publication, but for what he called the "exercise." He would write a thousand words a day for two or three days and then believe that he had been writing a thousand words a day for weeks, telling friends what "good discipline" he had been imposing upon himself for so long. With Steinbeck, what he wanted to do or thought he ought to do often became, upon further reflection, what he actually had done.) Nevertheless, his new start on the "Bus" suggests a shift in strategy, probably a change in the story's setting.

It had begun as a story about a Mexican bus driver and his old broken-down bus carrying tourists along the treacherous mountain roads of central Mexico, a trip that Steinbeck had taken several times himself. For some reason, a reason that he apparently never mentioned to anyone, he decided to shift the setting from Mexico to California. My guess is that he reread *The Canterbury Tales* and realized that the parallel he had planned would not work unless each "pilgrim" had a different reason for his trip. These different reasons would not seem very convincing or urgent for a busload of tourists going to see Indian ruins. Furthermore, in picking out "specimen" Americans for his satire, he had chosen some, such as the salesman, whose presence on a tour bus would not seem likely.

His work on the novel, as so many times in the past, was complicated by building and moving into a "new" house and complicated as well by old business—"The Wizard" was still hanging on—and something new: a young child running around (or at least crawling very fast) and occasionally making very loud noises. As the weeks went by, Gwyn grew more and more uncomfortable, her pregnancy complicated by the ravages of dysentery (as the New York doctors ultimately diagnosed her illness to be), and John felt that he should be as attentive as possible. He had had a big buildup to getting back to serious work, and then found that circumstances were making it almost impossible for him to get anything done. In desperation, he moved into his workroom in the basement of the new house, even before the contractor was through with the remodeling. In mid-March he wrote Toby:

> Our house is nearly finished. I moved into the basement to work a couple of weeks ago and we should be in the house in about two weeks more. That is going to be such a relief. Just the process of spreading out is going to be a joy. Imagine being able to get away from the family and getting to the toilet without an elaborate plan and a time schedule.
>
> My working cellar is fine—grey concrete walls and cement floors and pipes overhead. A comfortable chair and Bill's desk and chair and filing cabinet [he had purchased the houses from "Wild" Bill Donovan] in which I hope to file bills so I can find them. All fine—no window, no ability to look out and watch the postman and the garbage wagon. I should get some work done here if I don't have to run upstairs too often to look at the garbage wagon.
>
> I'm tossing the musical comedy away. I didn't like it and didn't know what was the matter with me. I thought I just had a contin-

ual stomach ache from something else, but that was it. I'll go on with my book now. I hope I will anyway, and I will, but that won't mean I won't throw it out too. I might easily do that. . . .

I now have it fixed up so I do not have to go back to Mexico to cut the picture but will go to Hollywood. Maybe by the time they get it to Hollywood I can get a print sent out here and then I can stay home and take care of Gwyn which I should be doing anyway.

I have been feeling lousy in my mind but today there seems to be some break in the clouds and maybe the darkness will go away. It has been a period of blue despair such as I haven't had in quite a long time.

The second of the two houses that the Steinbecks had purchased on East Seventy-eighth Street had been promised, after remodeling, to a friend of John's, Charles Jackson (author of *The Lost Weekend*), but the Jacksons decided to live in the country, and it was rented instead to the Nathaniel Benchleys. Although John had known Robert Benchley, he had never met his son, and it was only by accident that the Benchleys became tenants and neighbors—they knew the remodeling contractor. He introduced Margery Benchley, who was also pregnant at the time, to Gwyn, and the two found an immediate rapport. Once they all moved in, in April 1946, the two couples became very close. Nat was fifteen years younger than John, and since he had just lost his father, he found in John—at least part of the time—a father-advisor. For John, Nat became a playmate, taking the place of Frank Loesser and others in John's life who liked to drink, talk, and invent impossible schemes and outrageous activities.

The close relationship between the two families lasted for about three years (although John was away a good portion of the time). They were in and out of each other's houses, ate together, raised their children together, and went out together. For the first year, Benchley worked for *Newsweek*, but thereafter as a freelance writer (becoming known in later years for his biographies and children's books), which gave him the time to pal around with Steinbeck in the afternoons, investigating the neighborhood bars and shops. Rapaport's Toy Bazaar, on Third Avenue and Seventy-ninth Street, had a particular fascination for them, and they stopped by regularly, once bringing home cap pistols as presents for their wives on Valentine's Day. John was a sucker for any new toy or gadget that came out; sometimes he would buy it to amuse a friend, and sometimes he would buy it to take home and play with it himself.

Both men were writers, but they almost never talked about other writers or writing. (Benchley does remember one instance when Steinbeck told him that in order to write well about something, you either have to love it very much or hate it very much.) Instead, they were more likely to escape from their work and the problems of the world by cooking up some project. For example, once while contemplating the electric train that the Benchleys had set up in their basement for their son Peter, Steinbeck suggested that it might be made more exciting if they made a tunnel for it. He recalled reading somewhere that a good way to make papier-mâché was to mix shredded paper, warm water, and flour in a Waring blender. After they got the ingredients together and started mixing, they found that they had to push the stuff down into the blender with the top off, and as they pushed down, the blades splattered the material upward onto the walls, the ceiling, the kitchen cabinets. After a good deal of effort, both constructive and destructive, they finally finished the tunnel. The only problem was that Peter didn't like the train, even with the tunnel.

But Steinbeck always had ideas, always some new project. In the heat of the summer he thought of a swimming pool for the common back yard, an idea only a Californian in New York might have. He got a big army water storage tank and set it up, and it was a source of fun for both families—as well as an unusual topographical feature—until one of the children almost drowned in it and they took it down.

Not all the ideas were actually put into practice. The yard was surrounded on all three sides by apartment buildings. The neighbors knew everything that was going on, sometimes made loud comments out the window, or threw trash into the garden. In plotting some kind of revenge, as Benchley recalls,

> we thought at one point of getting either a small gallose [gallows] or guillotine and setting it up at the bottom of the garden and renting a lot of folding chairs. Set them up in rows and then have "A-H," "J-M," "Reserved for Press," and all this, and then in the middle of the night take it down very quietly. And the next morning people would be saying, "I told you to watch the window, God damn it! I can't watch it all the time! What the hell happened? We missed it!" But like so many things, we didn't do it.

In rebounding from the antagonism of Monterey, Steinbeck was becoming (to use Lynn Loesser's phrase) a "devout New Yorker." He had written Jack Wagner earlier in the year: "New York is a wonderful city. I'm glad to be putting down some kind of roots here. It is going to be the capital of the world. It isn't like the rest of the country—it's like a nation itself—more tolerant than the rest in a curious way. Littleness gets swallowed up here" [1/46]. He became convinced that it was the only place where his celebrity seemed to have more advantages than disadvantages.

One of the many bonuses of living in New York that he appreciated was the availability of good food and entertainment—theater and music. Although he was still attached to his classical record collection and occasionally went to concerts, he was now far more involved in jazz, and just as he would read anything he thought was relevant as background to what he might be writing, once he got seriously interested in jazz (which was about the time he started dating Gwyn), he read up on it. He knew its history and the names of all its major performers, and had mastered much of its vocabulary. In New York, he had the opportunity to see most of the jazz greats of the time, even meeting and getting to know some of them (that was where rank had its privileges).

The musician he probably knew best was Eddie Condon, the guitarist. He had met Condon in the early forties when he and Gwyn were living at the Bedford Hotel. He was introduced to the musician at Nick Rongetti's place in the Village by Bill Feinberg, an official in the musicians' union. Condon, who didn't place the name, thought for some time that he was "some kind of labor leader." In Condon's view, Steinbeck was the kind of person who, if "you hear him talk, you'd never think he was anybody. You look at him, you'd never think he was a writer." Their first long conversation, after Steinbeck's identity was straightened out, was in John's room at the Bedford. It was Election Day, and they couldn't get any liquor anywhere. Annie Laurie, also living at the hotel, didn't have any either, but she knew of a cocktail party for an English writer being given at the Bedford. John refused to go, regardless of the desperation of the situation, so Annie Laurie went, pinched a couple of bottles, and came back with them.

Condon and Steinbeck sat for hours talking about "the real American jazz." Then Steinbeck told him that he ought to be playing the banjo. As Condon recalls:

He said the banjo is the only truly American instrument and he went into the history of the banjo considerably. I said, I stopped playing the banjo when everybody else did, shortly after I left Husk O'Hare . . . around 1924. The last banjo I had some landlord wound up with. Couple of months later he said to me again,

Eddie, why don't you go back to the banjo? I said, John, the banjo went out with button shoes. He said, Eddie, button shoes are coming back.

During the period that John and Nat Benchley were living side by side, they often went to the Village to hear Condon, who now had his own place. Between sets, Condon came over to sit and talk, often bringing a musician to meet Steinbeck. Dick Carey, jazz great on half a dozen instruments, recalls several such visits: "If there's a quality I can remember at all—it's the one I call the 'no bullshit' quality." Max Kaminsky remembers Condon bringing him over and praising him to Steinbeck, and John saying, "It's true, Ed, but isn't it great about the marvelous name of Max Kaminsky," and going on about how great it was that he never changed his name. Condon remembers that "one time some of the boys and I were up at Commodore Records, cutting some sides, and we figured we better do something for this Steinbeck so we made up a blues—he likes blues best—called Tortilla B Flat. Next time Steinbeck and I ran into each other, he just grinned."

Since leaving Monterey the previous year, John had corresponded regularly with Toby and with Ed, and they had kept him informed as to what was going on with the old gang and on the Row. In the months after the publication of *Cannery Row*, Ed had been besieged by an ever-increasing flow of visitors—by students from Hopkins, fishermen, and other locals who came to receive and offer advice, and by tourists. As Steinbeck noted in his essay on Ed, "People stopped their cars and stared at Ed with that glassy look that is used on movie stars. Hundreds of people came into the lab to ask questions and peer around." Ed reported in April one extreme instance of tourist behavior. On a late Sunday morning he and Toni Jackson were relaxing, reading, and drinking coffee, not yet dressed, when a stranger walked in the front door and without a word started to enter their bedroom. Ed blocked him off and steered him out, while all the time the man was protesting that he wanted to bring his wife into the lab also. As Ed pushed him through the front door against his wife, the tourist's last words were, "Wait a minute, I want you to tell me what you did with all those frogs, those tom cats. Bothered by a lot of people coming in you ought to charge admission."

Ed usually concluded his letters with best wishes for Gwyn and the hope that this birth would not be as difficult as the last. At the beginning of May, John wrote Jack Wagner: "For two months I've been fighting the Bus and only now have I got a start which seems good. I've thrown away thousands of words. But I think it is good now. And at least it is moving. . . . Gwyn only has about a month yet to go and she is pretty uncomfortable and uncomplaining." A week before she was due, he told Toby, "Gwyn has not had a good time for a long time. She will be glad to be done with it." He was spending a lot of time with his son while his wife was going through her misery:

> Tom is getting to be a lot of fun and I am enjoying him. He has a fine sense of play and is a nice boy—very good with relationships, generous and not possessive. . . . I built him a box to stand on to pee, out of a Haig and Haig whiskey case. I was going to paint it and then didn't. Every time he looks down while peeing he sees those two proud if slightly repetitious names. What better training in good taste could he have. I only hope he can afford it. [6/5/46]

On June 12, 1946, their second son, John, was born, and for almost two months afterward neither mother nor child was very well. The atmosphere in the Steinbeck household had been strained for many months, and the continuing ill-effects of the pregnancy and birth made matters worse. Even in the best of times, Gwyn made it a practice to stay in bed much of the day, usually not getting up until the early afternoon. At first this was something that her husband liked, as it gave him the opportunity to get nearly a full day of writing in before family life began.

But then staying in bed seemed to become more and more combined with the symptoms of various illnesses—a cold, the flu, an allergy of one sort or another, and, most violently, asthma. John became suspicious of these recurring illnesses, and having little patience with the illness of others anyway, was half convinced that they were largely psychosomatic, possibly even voluntarily self-induced. It seemed to him as if his wife was sick all the time, lacking energy, and always unwilling to go anywhere or do anything without extensive urging on his part. As her lethargy increased, so did questions regarding the genuineness of her suffering—and when John was in a black mood, not an infrequent phenomenon, there were bitter words exchanged.

The second pregnancy had increased the tension. She couldn't complain that her husband was keeping her barefoot and pregnant, since she had wanted the children as much as he, but she did complain that her husband was repressing her career and her creativity, that she could become a writer, a composer, or a successful performer. There may be some truth to this (although his earlier request that she no longer sing professionally had been withdrawn long ago), in that he did have an unrealistic picture of her, at least in the beginning, as a wife who yearned for nothing more than domesticity. Still, she could have created, even performed, if she had really wanted to—her problem was that she simply didn't have the necessary drive and energy. Steinbeck thought afterward that she had invented this grudge because she could think of no other.

A month following the birth, largely because of the emotional strain at home, he gave up using his basement workroom and took an office at Viking that was vacated for three months by one of the editors. He no longer planned to take a long leisurely time on his novel but wanted to finish it before the three months were up. He barely got settled at Viking, however, before he got word that he would have to finish *The Pearl* in Mexico. (Gwyn, who hated his traveling, added this trip, so soon after the birth of their child, to her list of things to be resented.) He wrote from Mexico that everything was just as it had been—in a mess. The principals all seemed to be at odds with one another and the film in limbo. There was a fight about the music that Gwyn had worked on, and it would have to be changed; the narration would have to be redone; the cutting would have to be finished. He was going to try to straighten it all out as soon as he could and get home, but it took him over a month to do so.

Despite the birth of his second son, the illness of his wife, the confusion of moving into a new home, and a month lost working on the movie, his novel was progressing very rapidly. At first he was going to call it "Whan That Aprille," and when Benchley commented that that might be a bit obscure, he replied that "anyone literate would understand it, and I'm not writing for illiterates." At the beginning of September he wrote to Frank and Lynn Loesser:

> I'm doing about twenty-four hundred words a day but still there seems to be a little time left over. I guess the bus is about two-thirds through now.... I haven't any idea as to whether it is any good or not. No one has seen it except Pat Covici and Gwyn part of it. They both say they like it. But I know that Pat wants so badly for it to be good that he might just make a few excuses for it to save his own wishes about it. It is a curious book. There is no wishful thinking about it and it won't be a well loved book because things happen in it the way they would be likely to happen, not the way you hope they will happen. But the people in it are alive, so much

so that sometimes they take a tack I didn't suspect they were
going to.

As usual he was not a very good judge of his own work, either its quality or major features—the characters in *The Wayward Bus* are among
his least lifelike and convincing. He needed someone like Carol to tell
him, "This stuff is crap. You had better ditch it or start over." And he
was writing very, very fast.

CHAPTER XXXI

I nstead of taking until Christmas, his original intention, he finished *The Wayward Bus* during the first week of October, a little over a month after he returned from Mexico. It was the first time he had ever finished a work ahead of his own deadline. Although throughout his career he claimed not to do very much rewriting, he actually did, and sometimes corrections and rewriting pushed him to spend twice as long on a book as he originally projected.

The explanation was that he was using a new technique, or at least new in its application to work that he considered his own. During this period, as he confessed to Burgess Meredith, he was dictating his work. It began, he said, as a way of correcting his manuscript. He would read it into the machine (he had, Meredith recalls, "a very nice flat voice without an actor's interpretation" that he would use for such reading), and then lean back with his eyes closed and listen to himself, sitting up to make corrections on the manuscript as needed. This gradually changed to a process whereby he began with dictation, had the dictation transcribed, and then read the transcription to himself on the machine and made corrections.

Apparently Steinbeck's use of dictation had been prompted in part by his fascination with gadgets and new techniques and in part by a temporary inability to find a secretary who could transcribe his handwriting. It was then developed, as it appeared to Meredith, as a calculated experiment. But one must wonder whether the experiment was not also prompted by haste or laziness. At some point, either because of conflict in his personal life that sapped his enthusiasm or because the idea basic to the novel did not jell sufficiently to enlist his full commitment, he simply gave up on it as something that could be made into an important work.

Ironically, the name of the stenographer who worked on the novel manuscript was Emaline Mechanic. He wrote to her on October 10,

1946, to thank her: "I know what the difficulties were. But I think in the future they will be less because both of us know how to work the equipment better. . . . I'm sorry nothing happened in the book but that was the way it had to be. It actually did happen of course but nobody knew it happened and that's the way it is in living." It may seem odd that he should feel compelled to defend the manuscript to his secretary—but then nearly every letter he wrote during this period contained such a defense, perhaps an indication of some uneasiness about what he had written.

The following day he sent a letter to Joe Jackson, writing once again a kind of apology for the novel and announcing his plans for the immediate future:

> Beth [Steinbeck's sister] will have told you that we are going on a little junket for five weeks to Scandinavia. Looking forward to it too. I like cold weather and so does Gwyn and we want to see something different from Mexico and there isn't anything more different. I just finished my book last week and am ready for a rest and god knows Gwyn is too. The proof reading all done yesterday and I don't know whether it is a good book or not. It is what I wanted to say and I think it is in there for anyone who really wants to find it and there's a top story for those who don't. But whether it is effective or not I haven't the slightest idea. It will be called simple character study and that is only the littlest part of what it is. Well anyway it's done and as well as I can do it. I'm going to drink some snaps [sic] and do a little loud singing for a few weeks and then come back and go to work again.

During the period when he was finishing his manuscript, he and Gwyn had started to become more socially active again. As they had occasionally done in the past, they took in Fred Allen's radio show and then went out to dinner with Fred and Porty afterward. (When young John was born, Fred had agreed to be his godfather.) And they saw a lot of the Benchleys. On one occasion they went over, set up the electric train, and played with it while drinking gin and tonic until three in the morning. Another evening they played with the Benchley camera equipment, taking joke pictures: Gwyn as the Valkyrie in men's long underwear and John as "the man of distinction"—straight, except there was a mouse in his glass. Willie, their sheep dog, was cast in a show being readied for Broadway by Abe Burrows, but, as John reported to the Loessers, it "closed out of town and we haven't mentioned it at all. We just don't speak of it. And Willie is very brave. He pretends that the whole incident never occurred." Just before they left for Europe on October 18, the Steinbecks gave a party for eight or nine couples, the first since they had moved into their new home.

They sailed on the S.S. *Drottningholm* for Sweden, the same ship that he and Carol had taken almost exactly ten years before. He wrote Toby that he was looking forward to the eight days at sea and doing "nothing whatever most of the time." Their itinerary was to spend a week in Copenhagen, ten days in Stockholm, a few days in Norway, and a week in London. *Time* magazine reported their arrival as a "hero's welcome": "Reporters and cameramen woke him at 4 A.M. the morning after his arrival in Sweden; reporters stuck with him on the seven-hour ride by train and ferry to Copenhagen; more boarded the train at every stop. Cried one Copenhagen paper: 'John Steinbeck, all of Denmark is at your feet.'"

At the end of the month, Steinbeck wrote his agents from Copenhagen:

> We are ensconced in the Hotel and Gwyn has a sore throat and we have been considerably pushed about. Coming in there were about thirty cameramen with flashlights and it was dreadful. The phone starting calling while we were still at sea and the only way I saved myself from complete hell was by seeing all the reporters yesterday morning. I didn't know anyone treated writers like this. It is the sort of thing that would greet Lana Turner if it became known that she was going to come into Grand Central Station without any clothes on. And it is all so kind and well meant but it is very embarrassing. Every morning there is a mound of books to be autographed, and presents. Went to a night club last night and the orchestra leader played Stephen Foster in my honor. We've seen old friends and new ones, have had millions of toasts and the trip over was a dream. [10/30/46]

In a formal ceremony on November 15, Steinbeck was awarded King Haakon's Liberty Cross for his writing of *The Moon Is Down*. The medal had been previously given only to heroes of the Norwegian resistance. Before the ceremony, a friend had given him a phrase to say in Norwegian when the King gave him the medal. Steinbeck asked him what the phrase meant. "It means 'Thank you. How much did this cost?'" the man replied, which delighted Steinbeck almost as much as the medal. While he was in Norway, he was feted by former members of the underground, various groups inviting him to dinners and receptions. He was getting rather weary by now, but he felt obligated to go to as many of these events as possible. Always during the evening the resistance people would ask, "How did you know what we were doing, all those tricks we played on the Germans? We thought that it all was secret." And John said, "I guessed. I just put myself in your place and thought what I would do."

After arriving in Copenhagen, the Steinbecks went on to Paris. Whether it was the strain of the trip, which was far more hectic than they had anticipated, or, as John thought later, his wife's resentment of all the attention that was being showered on him, Gwyn had complained of illness and insisted on staying in Paris while he went to Norway to receive his medal. On his return to Paris, she began to argue for returning home because she was worried about the children. So they skipped England and came home a week early. John wrote "as Goldwyn would say, a bon voyage letter" to the Loessers the morning after they arrived, exclaiming "Jesus, New York is a pretty town. I wouldn't live here mind you if you gave me the place" [11/20/46].

New York was fine. There was, he often said, energy in the air. In the mornings, early, he would head for the kitchen in his robe and start making coffee, and since the nurse was getting up with the children, he would pour her a cup, too. He'd drink half a cup, standing at the kitchen counter, surrounded by new appliances. The new washing machine, he claimed, was "the smartest thing in the house." Refilling his cup, he'd pad down the stairs to his workroom, turn on the little heater, and put on his slippers. At his large desk, stacked with yellow pads, stenographer's notebooks, and bound manuscript books, he sat and smoked and drank coffee. On one wall there was a display of masks; on the other, guns and fishing rods, and an old dagger. After a while he would thumb through a stack of letters, and turning to his new electric typewriter (it was great, he told Frank Loesser, except that it grabbed the letters from your fingers), spend an hour writing to friends.

In mid-December he wrote to Bo Beskow, who had painted a second portrait of him while he was in Sweden. Beskow was having marital problems, more advanced than Steinbeck's:

I have not gone back to work and that bothers me. I shouldn't take these long rests. They aren't good for my soul or whatever it is that makes you sick. I make myself think that I will go back to work right after Christmas and maybe I will. I think Gwyn and the children will go to California for a month or six weeks about the first of February to let the children see their relatives. But I will just stay here and get back to work. Marital vacations are sometimes good things. Not that we need them very much. But just as the trip to Europe made us love our house so we get to liking each other with a little time spent apart.

Relationships are very funny things. I've wondered what I would think if this one were over and I think I would only be glad that it happened at all. I don't think I would rail at fortune, but then it is impossible to know what you would do in any given situation unless you have experienced it. It was and would be silly of me to make any sort of judgment about your difficulty because I do not know all the factors. But you'll never get out clear no matter which way you go. A man going on living gets frayed and he drags little tatters and rags of things behind him all the rest of his life and his suit is never new after he has worn it a little.

The week before Christmas the Steinbecks had their tree-decorating party, an annual event for John ever since he and Carol had taken the idea from Elizabeth Otis in the mid-thirties. They invited just about all the people they knew and liked—about fifty or so—and John made a "monster bowl of punch" and Gwyn set out an incredible spread of food. Gwyn was at her best as cook for special occasions and as a hostess, and John found Christmas that year particularly enjoyable, since Thom was old enough for the first time to get and play with real toys. Shortly after the holidays John got an idea for a new project from Burgess Meredith.

Meredith and Paulette Goddard had been married just after the war, and a friend of Meredith's, head of the Abbey Theatre, had invited the two to Dublin to do a play for them. Meredith gave John a title and an idea:

> The title was "The Last Joan." The idea was that there are always Joan of Arcs who hear voices. This has to do with witchcraft. And that in a modern sense we better heed what the present Joan tells us of the atom bomb, because it's the last time that we'll have a Joan to tell us what to do.
>
> I remember that he enthused to this in my house, still in Rockland County, and he thought that he could write a play for us and promised to do so. . . . Just parenthetically, I don't think that John did anything good when anybody gave him an idea. I think it had to come out of him. . . .
>
> He was up to my house, and we were talking about it awhile . . . he talked to Paulette and myself. He said, "Have you got an *Encyclopaedia Britannica*? I'd like to look up the life of Joan." I didn't have one. He said, "I wonder if Max Anderson would have one?"

And we said, "Well, John, we can't very well go and say we're writing a play, you know."

The idea appealed very much to Steinbeck's pride in his Irish background and his interest in Irish mysticism. He was also excited about doing a play for the Abbey Theatre, the scene of so much controversy and theatrical ferment, and an Irish audience. It was a connection that he longed to make, for he still felt, as he would tell an interviewer that spring, that his gift for writing was based on his sensitivity to sound, a gift, of course, that he believed came to him through his mother's family.

The interview, given during the period when he was working on "The Last Joan," was possibly the first lengthy one-on-one interview he had given—to Robert van Gelder, writing for *Cosmopolitan*—and one of the very few he gave during his lifetime. He even allowed himself to be quoted directly and to be photographed. Van Gelder heard him mention the phrase "the craft of writing" several times and asked him what he meant by it. His answer suggests that even at this point, relatively late in his career, he still adhered to the philosophy of composition that he had developed at the beginning:

"It is the art of penetrating other minds with the figures that are in your own mind." He feels that the human mind is a very complicated machine and that there are none too many entrances into it. In making his own entrances into other minds, he said, he puts trust in the sound of words, in a kind of lulling with syllables. Sound prepares the way for the impact of ideas. When he was young, Steinbeck was influenced by two writers, Donn Byrne, the author of "Messr Marco Polo," and James Branch Cabell, whose best-known book is "Jurgen." "The words don't have to mean much," says Steinbeck. "These men were specialists in sound— and that's what I was after. When I'd got what they had to give, I knew what I wanted to do."

Although his use of a Dictaphone was no doubt an attempt to put his theories into practice in a somewhat different way, he returned to pen and yellow legal pads for his work on the play. (He showed van Gelder his dictation machine, described his method on his last novel, and told him that *The Wayward Bus* had taken forty-eight sides of record discs, twelve hours of playing time—a strange, detailed explanation to make publicly for a man who had just sworn Burgess Meredith to secrecy.)

He had found someone at the Viking office who could read his hand-writing and would transcribe for him.

During the winter the Steinbecks had a visit from Gwyn's mother, Mrs. Stanley Heuit, which did not contribute to their domestic harmony. She and John had never gotten along well (he called her "Birdeyes" or sometimes "Big Gwen"), for she was domineering, opinionated, and almost continually outspoken. Early in his relationship with Gwyn, John had found her mother so objectionable that he had insisted, for a time, that she break from her. Mrs. Heuit, for her part, thought her son-in-law the most wicked man she had ever met. She thought of him as very lower class because of the language and people he used in his books and because when he was living in Monterey he associated with fishermen and ne'er-do-wells in bars.

Mrs. Heuit brought with her a little yip-yip dog, pampered and spoiled, which in itself caused problems. Steinbeck despised small, female-pampered lapdogs and was very critical of this dog as a poor excuse for a dog, poorly trained. All his life he had at least one dog and took great pride in what he thought was his knowledge of dogs and his ability to handle and train them. But at this point he had Willie, who, as Lynn Loesser had observed, was one of the few dogs she had ever known that needed a lobotomy. He may have been born somewhat deranged, but certainly the confused atmosphere of the Steinbeck household did not help, nor did Steinbeck's rather inconsistent treatment (after the dog had been originally raised as a puppy by Gwyn).

The truth was that Steinbeck's dogs were never particularly well behaved, regardless of his belief otherwise, since he tended to let them have their own way, according to their nature, except in certain things at certain times. Yet when his rules were broken, he could be very severe, although up to this time never brutal, with them. In general he thought of dogs as animals that should be treated as animals and if need be conditioned as animals, rather than as something akin to human beings. Indeed he liked to show off his lack of sentimentality in dealing with his dogs.

In Willie, though, he was completely frustrated. The sheep dog was totally irresponsible and could not be intimidated. Whenever Steinbeck tried to show off his dog lore, Willie inevitably embarrassed him, which in turn led Steinbeck to lose his temper and whack the dog on the rear, sometimes harder than he should have under any circumstances. Such beatings, totally contrary to a life-long kindness and respect for animals, seem to underline the severity of Steinbeck's own emotional derangement during this period. This was one area where he had thought he had maintained some mastery, and even it, in a sense, had failed him.

Mrs. Heuit and her dog made a bad situation even worse. Here was his mother-in-law whom he hated and her dog which he despised, yet every time she called "Come to Momma," the dog came to Momma. It could also sit up, lie down, and stand on its haunches on command. Willie, on the other hand, had his own brand of talent. He could sneak into the kitchen when no one was looking, stretch up to the countertop, and with a front paw hook a chop, or given enough time, a whole dinner of chops.

The final dose of salt was administered to Steinbeck's wounds by his abrasive mother-in-law one evening when her dog probably saved the house from burning down. John had cleaned out the fireplace before retiring, bundling the ashes with the rest of the trash which was put under the stairs to be taken out the next morning. Before going to bed, Big Gwen claimed to smell smoke, but Steinbeck walked around the house sniffing and couldn't detect anything. In the middle of the night, the little dog was running up and down the stairs and barking in the hallway. John yelled from his bedroom, "Do something about that son-of-a-bitching dog of yours before I wring its neck." Big Gwen tried to get the dog in her room, but it kept running back down the stairs until she followed it. At the bottom of the stairs was a haze of smoke. "Fire!" she called out, "Fire!" and John, with only his pajama tops on, rushed down the stairs to see what was happening. "I told you so," Big Gwen said, "I told you so."

"Be quiet," John said, and, turning to Gwyn, who was now downstairs also, said, "Get some water, and I'll get this box outside." "Shouldn't we call the fire department?" interrupted Big Gwen. "Good God, no," he yelled on his way to the door, "we don't need the publicity." He got the front door open, carried the smoldering box out into a New York snowstorm, dropped it in the gutter, whereupon it burst into flame, illuminating the lower part of his anatomy for the edification of Seventy-eighth Street.

In the meantime, carrying pots, pans, and teakettle full of water back and forth from the kitchen, the two women were fighting the fire which was threatening to burn through the floor into the crowded basement below. For several minutes, they covered the area with water and scraped the charred edges of the wood. They had forgotten all about John, who was standing on the front porch pounding on the front door (the doorbell had been removed), which had swung closed and locked him out. When they had surveyed the damage and caught their breath, turned off the water in the kitchen, they began to wonder where he was. They opened the front door and there he stood, partially dusted with snow, blue and shriveled with cold, and certain that he was going to die of pneumonia. Big Gwen never let him forget how smart and well trained her dog was.

In February he became forty-four years old. He still looked strong, but he had put on weight, on his face and waistline, and his hair had receded, so that two deep widow's peaks outlined the reddish-brown hair combed straight back from the middle of a high forehead. He had looked something like a farmer, in his plaid shirt and cords, or like a construction foreman, in khaki shirt and pants, shirt pocket bulging with pens and scraps of paper, but now, as he appeared more often in suit and tie, with a pencil-line mustache over his wide mouth (he had shaved off the beard), he looked like a nightclub manager, or, as Douglas Fairbanks, Jr., has suggested, the new tenor at the Met.

He had developed the mannerism of jutting out his chin, abruptly, and talking with his lower teeth set out in front of his upper teeth, making his gravelly mutterings even more difficult to understand. It was a gesture, Burgess Meredith thought, that was kind of an assertion of masculinity. Although he didn't parade his masculinity, he seemed to be always conscious of his size and of the strength his size suggested (although he had almost no exercise nowadays except walking) and was mortified when one evening in a cabaret he was bested three times in a row arm wrestling with a Broadway actor.

The "ham" that Toby Street had observed in him years ago was still there. Fairbanks, who from time to time dined or had a drink with him during these years, recalls that he sometimes tended to take on the somewhat exaggerated tones and mannerisms of an old-time stage actor, so that after a drink or two, you'd think you were talking to John Barrymore. (Lewis Milestone recalls that Steinbeck also sometimes assumed a *paisano* accent: Milestone—"Why are you talking like that, John?" Steinbeck—"Like what?" Milestone—"With a Mexican accent." Steinbeck—"Was I? I don't know.") Fairbanks sometimes tried to tease him out of it, when he seemed to become entranced by the timbre of his own voice, but he was careful, knowing that he could be very sensitive: "Some people, no matter how close you are, you can go on and pull their legs and so on and they don't mind it. But with John, you felt there was a touchiness underneath—that you could only go so far without making him angry—or hurting his feelings. Which was worse."

And apparent to those near him during these years, there was still that sense about him of strong outward control battling an inner force straining to come out. Meredith remembers that

> he would sometimes seem to be just bursting, with what he was saying, inside. His eyes would kind of glow and so forth and his face would get scarlet and still out of his mouth would come a kind of quiet tone . . . [and inside there was] some sort of secret excitement and some sort of secret boiling. . . . I think he liked to get out of himself as much as he could, and couldn't always. Almost like somebody else inside of him, you know.

The Wayward Bus was published in early February, 1947, and received what might be better called "contradictory," rather than "mixed" reviews. For example, Bernard De Voto in the New York *Herald Tribune Books* gave the book high marks and was particularly happy about Steinbeck's apparent turn toward a harsher, less involved treatment of his characters: " 'The Wayward Bus' is almost entirely unsentimental and faces directly away from the lovable polyps with whom Mr. Steinbeck has recently been too much preoccupied." By contrast, Ben Ray Redman in *The American Mercury* thought that the great weakness of the book "is that it holds no characters who enlist Steinbeck's full sympathy." While detachment can claim great literary triumphs, he concludes, up to now, at least, "sentimental warmth and emotional involvement have best served John Steinbeck and his readers." The contradictions were so sharp that the first State Department broadcast to the Russian people featured the controversy, apparently as an implicit comparison of American freedom of discussion with Russian enforced uniformity.

Steinbeck gave his reaction to all of this to Jack Wagner: "I should never read reviews, good or bad. They just confuse me because they cancel each other out and end up by meaning nothing." [2/16/47] To Mrs. Maxwell Anderson he wrote: "The trouble with Max and me is that we've been around too long. Critics get to resenting people if they don't die or go to pieces. They just get sick of us." [2/19/47] In the long run, what bothered him, as with *Cannery Row*, was the failure of the reviewers to get the point. And this failure of the critics to address the real issues of the book—which he saw as conceptual and philosophical—further eroded his confidence in the reader and undermined his strength of purpose. These doubts did not dominate his thinking or erase his ambition, but they did eat away at him more and more as time went by. He had always been a troubled, restless man; now he was on his way to becoming a troubled, restless—and unsure—writer.

Work on "The Last Joan," begun in January, continued on through February and into the spring. In February he wrote Ritch and Tal Lovejoy and told them of his progress:

> I'm working on a play or a novelette or whatever you want to call it, at least in that form I did a couple in before. It is going great guns and almost keeping ahead of me so that I seem to be dragged after it. This is usually the kind that stinks to high heaven. But I hope it is good because if it is good enough Meredith will open it in Dublin this summer where he has a schedule run. That would be opening out of town farther than any play I ever heard of. But it has to be awfully good for that and I don't know whether it is or not. I had four false starts and just finished the first act. . . .
>
> Gwyn is going to California on the twenty-fourth of this month. She will probably spend about a week on the Peninsula. I would go with her but I have to get this thing in shape. I hope to pour it on and maybe join her and that will be in Los Angeles. Then maybe I can back track and see you all for a few days before I come back and get to work again. . . .
>
> I hope you will get to work on something a little longer than columns. . . . If you are thinking of a play let me give you this kind of advice—few characters, few and cheap sets with particularly not tricks like revolving stages, and as few scene shifts as possible. That way you save stage hands and with few people you can get more expensive ones. . . . Then cut your lines to the bone. And keep your message under wraps. If it is there, make the audience discover it. There have been dozens of shows that closed this year because the actors advanced to the footlights and lectured the audience and it never works. You've got to make them think they thought of it themselves. [2/10/47]

He had not only spent some time reading about Joan of Arc in preparation for doing his play, he had also been talking to people about the theater—about what worked and what didn't and why. He freely confessed to people that he knew, like Abe Burrows, that his first success, with *Of Mice and Men*, was entirely due to the work of George Kaufman. Working on his own, Steinbeck thought *The Moon Is Down* did not play very well, and so he felt he needed to know more about dramatic technique and more about practical theater. Some of this he was passing on to Ritch Lovejoy.

He told the Lovejoys that he had "a cellar to work in now. It is lovely. There are no windows and no air, nothing to distract you. I can't see out and get gradually poisoned by carbon dioxide and in that semi-suffocated state I work like hell." Not long after he wrote this, he again felt compelled to move out of the house to do his work elsewhere, taking over Annie Laurie's apartment at the Bedford in the daytime while she was at work.

He told van Gelder in the *Cosmopolitan* interview that he gave up drinking while he was working on a book, and he told the Lovejoys and others in letters during this period that he was not going out very much. Neither assertion is entirely accurate. The bar at home was open on the weekends, starting Friday afternoon, and he did drink when he went out during the week, which was not uncommon. "Getting out of himself" usually involved sitting around somewhere and drinking and talking. Burgess Meredith recalls, "I can see him sitting in '21' where he had his favorite table . . . glowing red like a ruby and with a high flush on his cheek bones and being a center, a cynosure to anyone who came in there, and surrounding himself with his buddies." There was one late afternoon when he got out of "21" and caught a cab to go home. He settled back in his seat, and when the driver said "Where to?", he replied, "Murray Hill 4-3685." The driver turned around and said, "That's north, isn't it?" and John said, "Yes," not realizing what he had done until they had gotten all the way up to Ninetieth Street.

And they were going out quite a bit, to the theater, to the Village to listen to jazz, and to parties. It was a great period for parties. Nearly anything served as an occasion to celebrate. "Jacks-Are-Wild Day" was sometimes celebrated twice a year; when Abe Burrows left for Hollywood, someone had a "Abe Burrows Memorial Party"; and Nat Benchley and John planned a "Rites of Spring Festival," during which they would sacrifice a virgin—Kitty Carlisle was John's prime candidate. The parties were lively affairs, with nearly everyone standing up to do something—impressions (sometimes complete with improvised costumes), blackouts and sketches, comedy routines, readings, and stories. Abe Burrows would sit down at the piano and do a medley of his songs, such as "Walking Down Memory Lane Without a God Damn Thing on My Mind" or, with the help of Dorothy Parker, "If I Had to Do It All Over Again, I'd Do It All Over You." If the Loessers were in town, Frank and Abe would sit down together at the piano, sometimes to outdo each other at improvising, sometimes to run through Lindsay and Crouse. Steinbeck seldom did anything, but was an excellent audience—occasionally laughing so long and hard he'd almost fall off his chair. Once in a while he would tell a story, about the trappers up at Tahoe, about the hallucinations of the bums on Cannery Row after drinking canned heat, about the seagull over the Monterey picnic. Another, which became a Steinbeck classic, concerned a little boy, shunned and ignored in school because he wasn't good at anything, who became a hero after he had deposited in the school toilet the largest feces ever seen by his admiring classmates. Bathroom humor was a favorite with John and Frank and Fred Allen.

Early in 1947, Nat Benchley was fired from his job at *Newsweek*. It was a severe blow, and Steinbeck did his best to pull him out of the dumps, sympathizing and boosting his ego. The day after Nat was fired, John met him at the Bedford, where he had been doing his writing, for lunch. They never did get to lunch.

> Between 12:30 and 7 that evening, we had, each one, 14 Suissesse's—with the white of an egg. At the end of the time, the Bedford was stuck with 28 egg yolks. John signed an autograph for somebody who hadn't asked for it, and I think I spilled an ashtray. We kept calling our wives and saying, "Don't worry. We'll be right home," and then they began to worry that we might be home. There was somebody else at the bar who for some reason taunted John as being a cowboy, so John left him tied to the bar. We then went home and literally threw our hats in the door.

John had his own reasons for tying one on. Each of the Steinbecks had at one time or another confided in the Benchleys that their marriage was in trouble. One time Nat found John down in his basement office, obviously depressed after some kind of friction with his wife. John shook his head and looked up, "Well, there goes that experiment. I wanted to be part friend and part lover, but I guess that isn't going to work out." There were few screaming arguments, as Gwyn recalled later, but rather a constant tension—irritability, sulking, and retaliation. Each was trying to outdo the other in flirting with others, feeding with jealousy the mutual antagonism that was building between them. Gwyn's trip to California at the end of February was really a temporary separation that they hoped might help straighten things out. She took the children to see Beth in Berkeley, their friends in Monterey, and her family in Los Angeles.

A month after she left, John took the plane to join her. They had made arrangements to stay with the Loessers in Hollywood for two weeks, and when John got off the plane he reached into his pocket and pulled out a hamster, which he presented to Lynn as a hostess gift. There was a wild round of activity, including dinner at Mike Romanoff's with Humphrey Bogart and Lauren Bacall and an opening at the Los Angeles Philharmonic, as well as the usual practical joking that went back and forth when the two families got together.

On their return to New York, nothing had changed between them—if anything, their relationship had deteriorated even further. Burgess Meredith recalls a rather incredible episode that suggests the state that they were in. He had entered a bar where he happened to find the two of them seated and joined them. As they sat there talking, Meredith on one side of Gwyn and John on the other, to Meredith's astonishment Gwyn began to whisper to him. "This is from me to you," she whispered, taking off her ring and pressing it into his hand, "I want you to take this for what it means." Meredith didn't know what the hell it meant, since he felt no attraction for Gwyn and had never made any advance in that direction. But it seemed to be some sort of message—perhaps in alcohol—and so he slipped the ring into his pocket and tried to go on with their conversation. A little bit later, she apparently told John what she had done, because (as Meredith recalls) "he said with a fury with his jaw out that he didn't like me taking the ring from her, he didn't like the whole business at all. . . . When emotions played on him they played with a loud chord, you know, like a 32-foot pipe organ." Many years later Gwyn told Meredith, "He never got over my giving you that ring until his dying day. He never got over my giving you that."

John had tried a half dozen different treatments of "The Last Joan" and none of them seemed to work. In April he wrote to Frank Loesser:

I have finally faced it. The play is no good and I have thrown it away and have so warned Buzzy Meredith. It just didn't come off and I would rather destroy it than to have it destroyed by others. I think I will go to Europe in the near future but I will tell you about that when it matures. . . .

We had a big picnic yesterday with twenty fried chickens up at Sneeden's Landing and Gwyn has a cold today and so has Tom. It was bitterly cold and so was just what a picknick should be. The food was fine and we all had a very fine time. We went to Henry Poore's afterwards and continued with the picnic a little while.

Today they are sanding the floor over my head and it is fairly noisy and I am trying to write a review of the new book got out by Yank. It is a very fine book and the review is no trouble to write but the noise is deafening. . . .

Gwyn's new potters wheel and oven are here finally and I guess she will go to work with them just as soon as she gets over this cold. She is staying in bed today.

For some time Steinbeck had had it in his mind to take a trip to Europe—longer in duration and more leisurely than the one he had taken a few months earlier with Gwyn—and write a series of articles for the New York *Herald Tribune* in order to finance the trip and give purpose to his travels. In March, over drinks at the Bedford Hotel bar, he had talked of his plans to Bob Capa and explained that his main idea was to focus on the changes in Europe as the result of the war and reconstruction. He talked of his trip before the war and said that he would particularly like to see what had happened in Russia. Capa pointed out that no one from the West had been allowed to tour the countryside, since newsmen, like Western diplomats, were pretty much confined to Moscow. Perhaps, Capa suggested, the two of them could somehow get permission to talk to and photograph the common people of Russia as they were today—ignoring the news and political controversy. After a conference with Gwyn, it was decided that John and Gwyn would go to France—both of them wanted to see Paris—and spend several weeks there. Then Gwyn would come home, while John and Capa went on to the Soviet Union.

Robert Capa was a wild, audacious, funny man, a perfect companion for Steinbeck, although sometimes even he found Capa's craziness too much to bear. At the same time, of course, he was one of the great photojournalists of the midtwentieth century. Completely devoted to his art, he would do or say nearly anything to get his picture. In his youth he had talked his way from Berlin to Copenhagen without a visa in order to get some pictures of Trotsky who was speaking there. Trotsky did not want to be photographed, and all photographers were prevented from entering the auditorium, but Capa, a small Leica in his pocket, joined some workmen carrying long, steel pipes into the chamber and got his pictures.

Born Andre Friedmann in Budapest in 1913, the man later called Robert Capa invented himself. In Paris in the mid-thirties, he and his girl friend, Gerta Taro, who worked in a picture agency, made up an imaginary rich, talented, and famous American photographer, Robert Capa. Since Capa was so rich, Gerta would refuse to sell his pictures for less than three times the prevailing rate. The scheme worked for several months until young Friedmann, in a ragged leather jacket, was spotted on an assignment at the League of Nations by one of his major customers, the editor of the French illustrated journal *Vu*. But Capa kept his name nevertheless.

Thereafter, he became best known for his war photography, covering the Spanish Civil War (where Gerta, now his wife, was killed), the Japanese bombings of China, the "phony war" in Europe, and then the European theater of World War II. With a combination of almost reckless courage and a complete involvement in his work, his trademark became the closeup view of battle. Capa and Steinbeck met in London in 1943. According to Steinbeck, he was at the bar in the Savoy Hotel when he

> overheard a Chicago *Tribune* man snort: "Capa, you have *absolutely no integrity!*" That ... remark, says Steinbeck, "intrigued me—I was fascinated that anybody could get so low that a Chicago *Tribune* man could say such a thing. I investigated Capa, and I found out it was perfectly true."

He ran into him in North Africa, the Mediterranean area, and on the beach at Salerno, and in the course of time they became good friends. John Hersey has described Capa as "short, swarthy, and carrying [himself] as if braced for something, with a spaniel's eyes, a carefully cynical upper lip, and good luck in the whole face." He was one of those men who, although completely dedicated to his art, disdained to appear so. Except when in a funk in response to bad weather or the mishandling of his negatives, he was joking, light-hearted, casual. On the other hand, as on the day Allied troops recaptured Paris, there were times when tears blurred the faces in the viewfinder of his camera.

John was impatient to go as soon as possible, since with the collapse of the play he was at loose ends and felt he needed a change of scene and a new direction. But before the arrangements could be made, he was involved in a serious accident that threatened to force him to cancel, or at least indefinitely postpone, his trip. He and Gwyn had been sitting in the living room on the second floor of their house when someone came by and cleared his throat. John thought it was Benchley, so he went to the window and out on the balcony, leaned down the railing, and said, "Is that you?" Just then the rail gave way, and he fell. As he went down, he reached out to protect himself from the iron spikes of the wrought-iron fence below, pushed away from them, and landed on his hands and knees. He had broken a kneecap, badly sprained a foot, and suffered a number of bruises and scrapes. The railing had been only recently removed in order to bring a piano into the house (so that Gwyn could start work once again on her music) and had not been re-placed securely.

The knee required an operation. Early in the morning in the hospital, they woke him up to get him ready. A mild-mannered male nurse came into his room and told him that he would have to shave him, including his pubic hair. Steinbeck protested that his pubic hair was a long way from his knee. The nurse explained that he was only following orders. Steinbeck refused to let him touch him, explaining that he had once had his privates shaved, and that it was very painful growing out, and he could see no reason to have them shaved for an operation that would take place two feet away from that area. The nurse shrugged his shoulders and said that he'd have to report this, and Steinbeck said, "Go ahead. Tell them everything."

The nurse reported to the head nurse, a large woman who came in breathing fire. She did her best to intimidate him into submission to the rules of the hospital that made no exceptions, even for people who thought they were important. Steinbeck stubbornly resisted, even though his knee and back and foot hurt like hell and he was beginning not to care much about anything one way or the other. After she had gone out, furious, he called the chief of surgery on the phone, and after a time the male nurse came back and shaved him around the knee.

After the operation, Steinbeck asked Covici to go to Tiffany's and get one of their fancy boxes and a piece of ribbon. He clipped off a piece of hair, tied it with the ribbon, and sent it in the box to the head nurse with a note: "You wanted some of Steinbeck's pubic hair—here you are."

From the hospital, he wrote to Frank and Lynn Loesser:

Sitting up the first time today and it feels good but is tiring, sur-prisingly so. I think by the end of the week I might be getting around on crutches and then it isn't long if I am just careful. Just have to wait for the knee to heal. Otherwise I seem to be all right. . . .

Gwyn is doing some awfully good songs and I think she's going some place with them. Besides it is very good for her to get to work. And the stuff is really good. . . .

Gwyn and I are going to France between the 15th and 20th of June. We'll be gone a month or rather Gwyn will. I'll go on from there and she will come home.

Fred and Porty [Allen] were up the other day. They look really well. He's on a vegetable diet and very funny about it. Half starved all the time. He awakened Porty the other night to ask her if she had a carrot.

Although he would go forward with the trip, he would have to walk with a cane and suffer a great deal of discomfort from his knee the entire four months he was abroad.

As the most popular American writer in France, Steinbeck received almost as warm a reception as he had the previous year in Scandinavia and once again was showered with gifts and invitations and besieged by reporters and photographers. For a man who enjoyed wine as much as he did, one gift was particularly touching. A French farmer had come to Paris to see Steinbeck. He was a little man and old, dressed in an ill-fitting suit and work shoes, and he had brought with him on the train eight bottles of his own wine packed in straw. When he arrived at the Hotel Lancaster early one morning, the desk clerks tried to discourage him, but he insisted that he would see Steinbeck—he had come a long way especially to see him, and he would wait all day if necessary. After a time, perhaps in order to end the embarrassment of his presence, they rang the room to ask what they should do. John told them that by all means they should send him up. When the old man came in the room carrying his wine, he blushed and explained through Capa that he had come to see Steinbeck because he had read that he had a ranch in California and bottled his own wine. John rang the floor valet and got a corkscrew, and he, Gwyn, Capa, a photographer friend of Capa's, and the old man sat around tasting the wine.

After a few minutes the others had to leave, and John, still dressed in his robe and pajamas, poured himself some more wine, even though he was supposed to meet with several journalists and critics that morning. At one o'clock that afternoon, Gwyn and Capa returned to find John and the old man still together. The author's cheeks and nose were as red as the farmer's, and he had his arm around the man's shoulder. Despite the fact that John could not speak French, they had apparently had a long, and presumably animated conversation in sign language. The journalists and critics had been stood up. John asked Capa to tell the old man that the wine was excellent, perhaps the best he had ever tasted, and that he would always remember his visit to France because of his gift.

He wrote to his agents in New York, "If you think we haven't been going about eating and drinking things, you are very wrong. We have.... Paris seems to be coming back rapidly. The food expensive but wonderful, the wine as always.... I should have come here 20 years ago. It is a shame" [7/47]. He also reported that an edition of *The Grapes of Wrath* was being published while he was there, something like 50,000 copies, the largest first edition imprinted in France. They did some sightseeing, mostly by car since his leg was not yet well, and celebrated Bastille Day. After several weeks, he began to feel guilty: "I feel something of a mess. This is the first time I have ever played for so long a stretch. And I can't take it" [7/17/47]. Gwyn returned to New York on July 18, and on July 21 he and Capa flew to Stockholm for a week and then went on to Russia.

Steinbeck and Capa's arrival in Moscow was somewhat different from Steinbeck's in Scandinavia and France—the reception was nonexistent. No one met them at the airport (although they had wired ahead), and no taxis of any kind were to be had in the rain. They caught a ride with the French embassy courier only to find when they got into the city that they had no hotel rooms. The *Herald Tribune* bureau chief was out of town, and when they called on the American ambassador, he wasn't in. They found that "officially" they didn't exist. To tour Russia, they had to be the guests of some group or another, but no group was anxious to claim them.

They survived the first few days through the generosity of several American foreign correspondents who put them up in their hotel rooms and loaned them money so they could eat. Eventually they got their own room and began trying to get adopted. They were directed to VOKS, the Cultural Relations office, where they found that the chief of the office was "a critic of English literature, and he doesn't care for it very much." The young Russian who interviewed them told Steinbeck, "Your own most recent work seems to us cynical." Steinbeck tried to explain that his job as a writer was to set down his time as he understood it, then he went on to try to make clear where writers stood in America. "They are considered," he told the Russian, "just below acrobats and just above seals."

On the first of August they received permission to travel, first to the Ukraine, then to Stalingrad, to Georgia, and back to Moscow. Steinbeck found Moscow very different than it had been in the thirties, much cleaner and with thousands of new buildings—about double the size that he remembered. The people were not well-dressed, but they were not ragged as they had been during his earlier visit. As they toured the city during the days while they waited to leave for the Ukraine, Steinbeck began the practice of getting up very early to write notes about what he had seen, to expand and refine the things he had written down the night before. "I carry impressions home," he reported, "like eggs and write them quickly before I forget them." He told Gwyn that

> Capa is straining at the leash to get going with his pictures. As for me my notes go on just the same. I don't need light. I just set down details, little stories, prices, etc. So rain doesn't matter so much to me. But Capa is getting camera happy. He has about 7000 exposures and he hasn't exposed any of them. Indeed his permit to photograph has not come through. There is no permit for seeing. Another reason why my trade is more satisfactory. [8/2/47]

They found the Ukrainians very hospitable, full of laughter. One of their toasts, he reported, was "Let us drink so that the people at home may be happy." They ran into an old woman working in a cucumber field who told them that there were two very fine things in the world— women and cucumbers—and then she threw back her head and howled with laughter. At one farm they took papers of salt and walked through the fields, picking and eating ripe tomatoes. As they walked, they noted

> two little boys . . . watching us with wide eyes. Finally one said to the other with a tone of wonder, "Why—the Americans are just like us." It had never occurred to them that this could be so. The farm people gave us a big dinner with toasts and it was very gay. We had pepper vodka. Our most successful day for material so far. . . . Capa is quivering with pictures and I have to get up very early in the morning to keep my notes up. [8/10/47]

There was one image that stuck with both men. In nearly every farm-house they visited they found a little room of whitewashed plaster with handmade chairs and benches. On the walls there would be homemade paper flowers, with an icon in the corner, a small religious picture canopied in homemade lace. And on the walls elsewhere, photographs of the sons and the fathers who had died in the war, the strongest and most needed.

Back in Moscow, before continuing their journey, Steinbeck reported to his wife, "My leg still kicks up a little now and then and the muscles tend to get tired. I still use a stick but gradually it gets better. Great changes of climate are painful to it and I am still pretty clumsy. . . . I know about ten words of Russian now which seems to be my saturation point" [8/19/47]. At Stalingrad, they found the descriptions of destruction had not been exaggerated. It had been destroyed "not by bombing, but by shell fire and the houses pitted and carved by machine gun fire. This town was the turning point of the war and it looks it. Every single building is hit. Factories in ruins. The rebuilding is everywhere. This must have been the greatest fight of all time" [8/20/47]. The Commandant of the city, who had fought in its defense, gave them a tour of the areas that had seen the bitterest fighting, and they visited the location where a motion picture company had set up to film a documentary of the battle of Stalingrad.

It was getting close to the time when they would return, and John wrote Gwyn asking her to arrange to rent a room at the St. Regis for him to do his work when he got back. It would be better for everyone for him to work outside the house, and besides, he got more work done if he shaved and got completely dressed and went somewhere deliberately to work for a certain length of time. Gwyn had been looking for a country place for them to go to in the summers and had found a farm in Connecticut near the ocean that sounded good to Steinbeck. It would be a shame, he told her, if the boys were to grow up without boats—they were the most exciting things in the world to him when he was young, and still were.

"Capa," he wrote, "is an ideal man to work with. He gets along with people and seems effortless, yet gets a tremendous amount done when it is available" [8/25/47]. To John's letter, Capa added one of his own:

Dear Homefront, it is a month now that I am sharing not only John's royalties [the rubles that had accumulated in Russia as payment for their editions of John's books] but nights and he already is beginning to have fickle thoughts and says that your cooking is better than mine. Also he admitted bearing some illegal children and talks about X-mas trees, farms, and other homely by-products.

Now we are sitting in this poor man's Lancaster without wicked girls and bloody maries and are becoming ardent letters from home readers and are filled with the kindest thoughts toward you poor people stewing in good hot luxuries. . . .

Our sinless life is disimproving my disposition and John helps out waking me up around seven in the morning asking me questions about history and geography.

The remainder of their trip was spent in Georgia and then Moscow again. "Georgia," John reported, "is the paradise Russians like to think they will go to when they die. The climate is wonderful, the fruit tasty, the wine strong and the people handsome" [8/27/47]. They saw churches and castles beyond anything that Steinbeck had seen before, "perfectly beautiful." And all the time, their guide, Svetlana ("Sweet Lana"), hustled them along from one place to another, one event to another—from a football game, to an amusement park, to a boat trip, and to factories, farms, orchards, sanatoriums, summer camps, fairs, and village celebrations. They were seeing so much so quickly they had "mental constipation" and could no longer take it all in. Returning to Moscow, they had to spend a day just getting their eyes clear. Their itinerary was planned so that they would be in the capital city during the first week of September, when the theater and ballet seasons opened, and as an added bonus, they would also be able to witness the city's 800th anniversary celebration.

Steinbeck's knee hurt from tramping around, his head hurt from evenings of compulsory toasting with warm vodka, his shoes were wearing out, and his patience growing thin. And about half way through their journey, he began to get homesick. It was a familiar pattern: when he was home, he longed to get away; when he was away, it didn't take long before he started dreaming of home. By the time he got to Georgia, he was writing Gwyn:

> I am quite violently homesick. Nothing to do about it but I am. I would like to head my way home now but it would be criminal not to use this opportunity. It is almost unique. No one has had this chance in over ten years—no one. It is strange to be in a city of 800,000 [Tiflis] where you are the only foreigner and where most of the young people have never seen a foreigner and where American has about the same connotation as Martian. [8/30/47]

Another familiar pattern also emerged in his letters home. As in the letter above, he was defensive of being away from home, worried about his wife's growing hostility to his absence. Reminiscent of his correspondence during the war, he repeatedly sought to justify his work abroad: "But Lord, darling, we are getting so much and stuff that has never been got. Much as I want to be home, I know that this is important and that it is the best thing for me to be doing now" [8/27/47]. And there was another note in his letters, sad and somewhat strained, of assurance for the future. In talking about the farm in Connecticut, he told Gwyn that they didn't have to make up their minds now, that they had plenty of time: "We have some really fine years coming I think."

He and Capa left Moscow in the middle of September and spent a week in Prague and another in Budapest on their way back to New York. Once back home, Steinbeck confided in Benchley that while he still liked Capa, and admired his work, he didn't think he'd want to work with him again. In order to take pictures of people when they were reluctant, Capa would promise to send them things from America, cameras or anything else they might fancy, and then when he returned to the United States, he, of course, forgot all about such things. This made John angry, and he felt that he had to make up for Capa's broken promises and send them himself.

He took up a working residence in his hotel room office. He had a lot of writing to do, and it had to be done rather quickly. In mid-November he wrote to Toby Street about where he was going and where he had been:

> It was a good trip and I will tell you about it sometime. I'm doing a series for the Herald Tribune which paper we went over for. . . . Anyway it is a book too and I am about two thirds through with it and working like a dog. I would like to get it done early in December because I have not had a rest in a long time and I want one very badly.
>
> I have a great deal of work to do this year and I would like to get it all done by this summer because then I would like to stop everything to do a long novel that I have been working on the notes of for a long time. It seems to me that for the last few years I have been working on bits and pieces of things without much continuity and I want to get back to a long slow piece of work. I need to go out there for a lot of research so I may be out in California this summer. I'd be glad if I could for a little while. I'm living too hectic a life but then so are you and so is everyone. . . .
>
> My kids are thriving and are becoming very interesting to me now. The oldest one is beginning to reason and is lots of fun and the youngest who is a clown by nature is very gay. He may not have much brains but he is going to have a hell of a wonderful life if he keeps the disposition he has now. That's about what it takes, a good disposition. I never had one and that is the reason for the kind of life I lead, I guess, although my disposition is better now than it ever was. . . .
>
> I had a wonderful time in Paris. I had never been there you know and I wish I had been there years ago. Gwyn didn't like it terribly much but I did and I'm pretty sure I have not seen the last of it. There is something there, there is really something there.
>
> Winter is coming and that is the season I love in New York. I feel wonderful when it is cold. I guess I was never more healthy in

my life than the winters I spent at Tahoe. I am just a cold weather kid and I am miserable in heat. Luckily I missed New York this summer.

I may be coming out to see you before too long. I would like to. I would like to just sit with you for a few days without any rush. I don't know what the hell I'm rushing about. There is some terrible kind of urgency on me and that is a bunch of nonsense. Maybe I'll get over it when I get this deadline piece out of my system. I hate to write to deadline but I have to on this. I'm going to try to stop it before it is too late though.

My typing never gets any better. I guess it is never going to get any better. That is one of the comforting things about the middle age I am in. Always before I could promise to reform and now I know I'm just never going to do it so I don't bother. The only thing I can really do is work and I might as well face it. I don't have any other gifts but I can work and if it doesn't amount to a damn it was still hard work.

Anyway I am going to plan within the next year to sit with you a while if you still want to. It wouldn't be bad to take some kind of inventory—not that it will change anything because you aren't ever going to change either and the joke is that if we had only known it, we never were from the very beginning. Maybe the self-kidding is part of the process. Maybe I couldn't have stood myself as I am when I was younger and so had to make all the plans about changing. . . .

I've got to get back to work. I have a hundred pages to get out before Thanksgiving. Christ, I remember when an eighteen page story threw me for weeks. Maybe they were better then but I don't even care about that. The Hell with it. I'm doing the best I can with what I've got. [11/17/47]

This is a letter that perhaps says as much by its tone and what it doesn't say, as by what it does. It does suggest in a quiet way the pressure that was accumulating year by year to "live up to the promise of *The Grapes of Wrath*," as the critics were expressing it, and produce another book of real substance. And he had given too much attention to the critics in his years of success to ignore the general drift of their opinions about him now. He felt more and more that something major must be done in order that he redeem himself, as if he somehow had not fulfilled his obligations. His "bits and pieces" had been a kind of temporizing to fill the need for work, but they had also been most recently a form of procrastination.

As he approached a new long work, he encountered artistic difficulties that provided additional pressures: he had lost contact with the only setting he could properly use for a long novel; he was not very good at organizing a long work of fiction—his work had always been, in a sense, "bits and pieces"; and perhaps most important, whether he was conscious of it or not, he had lost some of his confidence. He really did not have enough ego to carry him to true artistic greatness. Too many people had told him for too long that he was not very good. Overly sensitive and too modest, perhaps, for his own good, he tended to believe them, forcing him to withdraw to that position he defined for Toby: "The hell with it. I'm doing the best I can with what I've got."

What the letter doesn't say was that his personal life was falling apart. Gwyn did not give him a particularly warm welcome on his return home from Russia, and his idea of going to California to gather material for a new novel did not please her at all. She was beginning to feel that she was making real creative progress on her own, and she refused to be uprooted again just because he couldn't sit still. Both children were very lively now, and even though they had a full-time nursemaid, Gwyn felt the burden of dealing with them was too much on her shoulders, especially with her husband gone most of the time.

When the nurse left for the holidays at the end of the year, John was under extreme pressure to finish his Russian articles, but at the same time, Gwyn was once again ill and stayed in bed most of the day. All hell broke loose when John found himself having to take care of two small children while trying to make his writing deadline. Because of Gwyn's condition, there was no tree-decorating party; instead, they went to a Christmas party at "21" and had a miserable time. The children now were becoming for him a positive nuisance. As Nat Benchley has observed, Steinbeck simply didn't know what to do with humans so young they could not yet reason. (Thom, at three, may have seemed more reasonable than John at two, but in terms of the noise and confusion, the difference was slight). He would have preferred that both the boys had been born age twelve.

If in 1946 Steinbeck resembled a Saul Bellow protagonist, perhaps a Eugene Henderson full of rage and questions and contradictions, then in 1947 he was a Saul Bellow character in an Edward Albee play. "Fun and games" by the Steinbecks, with the Benchleys and the Loessers, were sometimes an escape, sometimes a cover, and sometimes the covert expression of domestic bitterness and private jealousies and frustrations. In the next act, Steinbeck took part in a more complex drama, somewhere between soap opera and tragedy.

CHAPTER XXXII

I n response to his difficulties with Gwyn, he decided not to wait until the summer to go to California, but to leave as soon as possible. He wrote to the editor of the *Salinas-Californian*, Paul Caswell, and got permission to go through the files of the old Salinas *Index*. To Lynn and Frank Loesser, he wrote:

I finished all the Russian stuff which starts in papers on the 14th of January. I don't know who is doing it in L.A., if any, but it has full syndication.... Then I finished the U.N. children's appeal stuff. Now I go over the Cannery Row script with Buzzy. Hope to get it done by the 15th.

About the 1st of February I want to go to Monterey for awhile. Have to do some research and get my batteries charged. I want to go collecting and go to the mountains and ranches I used to know. I'll probably be there about 6 weeks. Gwyn will come out toward the end and we will both go down to see you before returning. I'm going to start a long book this summer and I want to find out many things first. [1/2/48]

Near the first of the month he flew to Los Angeles where he spent two days talking to Lynn about his troubles with Gwyn, and after getting it all off his chest, he rented a car and drove to Monterey. Instead of staying with friends, he decided to take a cottage at Casa Munras, which would allow him to come and go as he pleased. In his rented Buick he began to travel about the country, visiting scenes from the past and trying to steep himself in color. After a week and a half, he reported to the Loessers that he had called Gwyn several times:

I don't know when Gwyn is coming out. They are tearing up the first act of their play and starting it again. Maybe she will never get out. But I hope she does. And maybe I shouldn't have blown, but I'm glad I did. You get to eating yourself up inside. I'm getting rested up and all full of reserve strength so that will be all right now. I didn't realize how tired I was. [2/11/48]

The play was "The Circus of Doctor Lao," which Gwyn was writing with Nat Benchley. Some time later, when it was finished, it had a short run in Chicago with Burgess Meredith in the lead.

In addition to his worry about Gwyn, Steinbeck had other problems on his mind. He had made arrangements with Lewis Milestone (who after a delay of several years had just finished filming *The Red Pony*) and Burgess Meredith to do a film of *Cannery Row*, and now one Bernie Byrens was filing a million dollar breach-of-contract suit, alleging that he had acquired the film rights to the novel in 1945. Of concern to Steinbeck also was his participation in a new company called World Video. The company had been formed late the previous fall as a result of conversations between Steinbeck and Harry S. White, a distinguished-looking, smooth-talking promoter and ex-radio executive who had impressed John with his show business contacts and his talk about the potential of television. Always easily excited about the possibilities of a new technology, Steinbeck was readily convinced, and decided to invest both his money and his time in the new medium, believing, as White had suggested, that it might very well make books, movies, newspapers, and other forms of communication nearly obsolete in the future.

Joining Steinbeck and White in the venture were Bob Capa and RKO Vice President Phil Reisman. The company was incorporated in January of 1948 to package and film shows for sale to the TV networks. Steinbeck wanted to produce a wide variety of high-quality programs, for he reasoned—not very accurately, as it has turned out—that the new medium would demand better material than radio:

> People become literate only by exposure to fairly literate things. We're making no soap operas at all. . . . When the radio's on, people only half-listen, but when your eyes are centered, your attention is centered . . . the quality must be higher.

Television seemed to nearly everyone around Steinbeck the wrong thing for him to get into. At the end of the previous year, he had hired Toni Jackson (who had broken off with Ed Ricketts) as secretary–office manager for World Video, and as soon as she understood the setup, she did her best to try to talk him out of participating. Annie Laurie, who acted as his agent in show business matters, was against it, and Gwyn warned him if he tried to provide material for television, he would be "ground up like hamburger." He hated deadlines, hated writing trivia, and yet he found himself in January writing copy for the first World Video show to be aired—"Paris: Cavalcade of Fashion."

By March, it became clear that Harry White was a dynamo. Dozens of arrangements were being made and contracts signed with performers, writers, and various other collaborators (some, such as Elia Kazan, the *Herald Tribune*, and folksinger Alan Lomax, had signed as a result of contacts made through Steinbeck or the use of his name), as some sixty ideas for shows were being developed. But as it turned out, it was all built on paper and very few things were actually done. Before long, the whole structure of words, ideas, and agreements would collapse into an incredibly tangled and sticky mess.

Despite all the things that weighed heavily on his mind, Steinbeck found pleasure in revisiting the scenes of his childhood, quietly and alone, in preparation for his novel—he had been "going around the country getting reacquainted with trees and bushes." He wrote Bo Beskow from Monterey: "I think through fatigue and other things I have been down near the insanity level lately and it is odd how I can feel the tensions roll away from me. I sleep about twelve hours every night and every night it is better. . . . One of the best things is being alone" [2/12/48]. He took long, leisurely walks around Pacific Grove and Salinas; he visited the old Hamilton ranch; he found the old stage coach road and drove over it to San Juan Bautista.

In his enthusiasm for his new project, he was regaining his confidence. "It is," he wrote Beskow, "what I have been practicing to write all of my life. Everything else has been training. . . . I wouldn't care if it took all of the rest of my life if I got it done." Every book that he deeply cared about was for him a new beginning, and in the risk of such things perhaps also the end. His ambition soared, but the letter he wrote Pat Covici sounded suspiciously like the one, also brimming with ambition, he had written earlier while planning for *The Wayward Bus:*

> I've been into the river beds now and on the mountains and I've walked through the fields and picked the little plants. In other words, I have done just exactly what I came out here to do. What will come out of it I don't know but I do know that it will be long. There is so much, so very much. I've got to make it good, hell, I've got to make it unique. I'm afraid I will have to build a whole new kind of expression for it. And maybe go nuts doing it—and pay the

price for doing it and climb on it and tromp on it and get my nose rubbed in it. I hope I have the energy to do it and without accidents. I think I have. The yellow pads will catch hell for the next few years and nobody better try to rush me because I will not rush this one. I'll make a living at something else while I am doing it. But it's the whole nasty bloody lovely history of the world, that's what it is with no boundaries except my own inabilities. [2/48]

But this time there was a good deal more determination—"It may be my swan song," he wrote his wife, "but it certainly will be the largest and most important work I have or maybe will do" [2/17/48].

It had to be very large. He had been told so often that the short books he had done didn't really count, that this one had to be very long. And it had to be important. He had been accused of being trivial so often that this time he somehow would have to get at the heart of life and what the world was about.

In Salinas he visited the newspaper office and went through old issues dating back to the turn of the century, and he made arrangements to have a certain number of them, at intervals of six months or so, photographed so that he would have a reference library on the daily life of the community. He went around the area talking to old friends of the family, to people like the Williams sisters and to Mrs. Gragg, who had been living in Monterey nearly a century, and found that not only were the memories of events at odds with the newspaper reports, but that the attitudes that grew out of events were often twisted away from what one would have expected.

In passing, he also discovered that a whole mythology had evolved regarding his own childhood and youth, based on incidents involving others or apocryphal stories now accepted as fact. "There is one," he wrote Gwyn, "by a grocer about how I engineered the complete cleaning out of his store. Actually I was a very law abiding little boy" [2/17/48]. Another tale was being circulated by a former neighbor who claimed to have seen Steinbeck as a child walking down the street in an overcoat lacking all its buttons and being held together by a huge horse-blanket pin. "Poor mother," John lamented, "who was so proud of how well she dressed us and how neat she tried to keep us."

While in Monterey he also spent time with Ed at the lab and on several occasions went collecting with him. During this period John also became acquainted with a relatively new friend of Ed's, a man named George Robinson, who after the war had come to work as personnel manager at California Packing, one of the canneries near the lab. Ed was doing chemical analysis work for the cannery, and he and George had established a daily ritual of having coffee together in the morning. One evening the three of them went to the movie together. The picture was *Treasure of Sierra Madre*, and they ended up staying to see it three times (which caused Ed a bit of discomfort when halfway through the second showing he would have liked to have gone out to get a beer). On leaving, they agreed among themselves that it was the finest film they had ever seen.

John and Ed also made plans to take the trip to the north coast that they had been talking about since 1944, when John was living in Monterey. In 1945 and 1946 Ed had made collecting expeditions first to Vancouver Island and then to the Queen Charlotte Islands off the coast of British Columbia. And in 1947, with endorsements from Steinbeck and The Viking Press, he had applied for a Guggenheim grant in order to finance further expeditions (his application was turned down). All of this was in preparation for a final trip that Ed and John would take together, which would result in a book "The Outer Shores," with a narrative portion written by Steinbeck. Ricketts saw the book as the completion of a trilogy, the first parts of which would be *Between Pacific Tides* and *Sea of Cortez*, that would deal with marine animals of the coast from the tip of Baja to the edge of Alaska.

They decided to go that summer to the Queen Charlottes, and Steinbeck would finance the voyage, Ed's share of the expenses to be paid back out of royalties. Although John knew that he would still be doing preliminary work on his new novel, taking a break from it, he thought, would give him a chance to think. He wrote to Ed that he planned, for now to

> work at the structure and method of The Salinas Valley and then to cut it off completely while I work with you. I think that will throw it back into the unconscious where it can be judged and evaluated so that when I go back to it, maybe it will be screened and the good saved and the bad rejected. That, anyway, is my plan. [4/14/48]

After he returned to New York in mid-March (Gwyn never did come to California to join him), Ed sent him some of the notes he had taken on his previous northern expeditions. At the end of the month, John wrote the Loessers: "I am going to the Queen Charlotte Islands sometime early in July and Gwyn now thinks she might like to go with me. Maybe even take Tom. It will be a rough trip but fun. Necessary to go for collecting of marine animals and for the book The Outer Shores."

In April he went into the hospital to have varicose veins removed from his legs. He had been warned by doctors for years that the burst places held the potential for embolisms, bringing to his mind the specter of his dying mother, the image above all others from the past that he found the most terrifying. Death he could face, but the idea of lying in bed like a vegetable for a year or more, he could not. At just about the time he got out of one hospital, Gwyn went into another for treatment of a severe sinus infection. "Struggling down and getting to the other hospital and then home to see the kids and then back here to sleep is about all my legs will take right now."

During his recovery he took a room at the Bedford, since he was not supposed to climb stairs. But his stay there was also part of his continuing separation from Gwyn who at this point was very depressed, very unhappy about their relationship. In the face of continuing domestic difficulties, as well as worry over a lawsuit, his own health, and a struggling new business enterprise, he latched on to work, as he had before during his breakup with Carol, as the one thing that could save him. He wrote the Loessers on May 1st:

> Zanuck wants me to do a picture for him. About what I don't know but Gaz [Elia] Kazan is coming to talk about it and he is a good man. The possibility of doing it are remote. However, I'll talk to anyone. But my big book is going to be started in the fall and in spite of anything. It is going to take a very long time to write and I am looking forward to it. Before that I shall do the Outer Shores with Ed Ricketts about the Queen Charlottes. My work is really cut out for me but that is good. Otherwise insanity.

At twilight on May 7, Ed Ricketts got into his old Packard, drove down Cannery Row, and then turned on Drake Street to go across the railroad tracks and into town. The old car was noisy and the crossing was blind without any signal. He ran into the Del Monte Express coming in from San Francisco. The train demolished the car and dragged it several hundred feet along the tracks before the engineer could stop, and then it was some time before Ricketts could be extricated from the wrecked car. His last words on the scene were, "Don't blame the motorman." Critically injured but still conscious, Ed was taken to the hospital, where he refused to let one doctor operate and requested another. At least twenty people gathered in the corridor as word spread from one disbelieving person to another, along the Row, the wharf, and in town. He hovered between life and death for four days, but the internal damage was too severe and he died on May 11.

By the time Steinbeck was notified, it was certain that Ed would die. The evening before he was to fly to California, he told Nat Benchley tearfully that, "The greatest man in the world is dying and there is nothing I can do." The trip was a nightmare of delays and missed connections, including a maddening enforced stopover in San Francisco— so close, and yet so far—while he waited hours for a flight to Monterey. He was in very poor shape when he was met at the Monterey Airport late on May 11 by Alice, Ed's new wife, and George Robinson. Ed was already gone.

The funeral was held in a chapel above the ocean, and a crowd including most of those who had come to the lab over the years, gathered outside. At the appointed time for the service, John and Virginia Scardigli broke away from the group and walked toward the chapel, Ritch and Tal and the others trailing behind. John pushed open the double swinging doors, and stopped. In front of them, at the foot of the aisle in the darkened chapel, they saw a gray coffin, with an ugly, purple artificial wreath. After a moment they turned, stepped out of the way of those following, and started walking. They walked almost aimlessly at first, and then they began to follow a path down the hill. Some of the crowd continued into the chapel, but others also stopped and turned away, following, straggling, down the hill. One by one, they came and found a place to sit, and without a word, they sat and watched the water flow into and out of the tidepools.

That evening most of those closest to Ed went to a small Mexican restaurant in a home on the hill above the Row. It was a formal dinner, and Ed's place was set at one of the tables. John sat during the meal without speaking or even moving, completely rigid with grief and drink. A day later, John went with George Robinson to the lab to go over Ed's things, the boxes of letters and stacks of notebooks, journals, and records. His letters to Ed he burned, but the manuscripts he saved, thinking that sometime he would edit and publish them. As he and George went over the journals, they discovered that right in the midst of biological notes there were entries describing Ed's affairs with prominent Peninsula matrons. They edited the journals on the spot, tearing and slicing out what they could, although in some instances leaving compromising material rather than destroy what seemed to be valuable notes.

As usual, there was very little inside the huge safe, but there was an inside door that was locked, and none of Ed's keys would fit. "What should we do?" George asked. Steinbeck shrugged, "I guess we'd better have it opened." So, at some expense, they had a locksmith come out from downtown Monterey and pick the lock. Inside the compartment they found a little pinch bottle of Haig & Haig and a note, dusty and yellowed. It said, "What the hell do you expect to find in here? Here's a drink for your trouble." John and George matched a coin to see who got the little bottle, and John won. Some of Ed's materials and notes went to Hopkins, other things were given to Ritchie Lovejoy, and some items, including some of Ed's books, were, for some reason, burned by Alice on the beach. Alice, who turned out not to have been really married to Ed after all, shortly afterward pulled up stakes and disappeared. John took Ed's microscope with him.

With that sense of timing that only someone with show-business experience could have developed, Gwyn confronted John upon his return from California and told him that she wanted a divorce. She gave familiar reasons: he was gone too much, and he was smothering her creativity. She added a new, more painful reason: she had not been in love with him for several years. The request for a divorce was not totally unexpected, but the combination of the two events together with the announcement that she had not loved him for years was devastating. He still loved her; he still had hope. But he moved into a room at the Bedford, this time on a more or less permanent basis. A few days later he wrote to Ritch and Tal:

> There's been a lot of thinking to do. By some intelligence greater than our own, we were able to stay drunk enough or withdrawn enough during the immediate thing. But that comes to an end and I have been sitting alone in my hotel room for some days now. Impact is not sharp now—all dulled out. It would be interesting if we all flew apart now like an alarm clock when you pry off the mainspring with a screw driver. Wouldn't it be interesting if Ed *was* us and that now there wasn't any such thing or that he created out of his own mind something that went away with him. I've wondered a lot about that. How much was Ed and how much was me and which is which.
>
> And another strange thing, I have a great feeling of life again. It's not the same but it is vital and violent. Almost as though I were growing new tissue. Do you feel that at all? There were times of cold terror about doing it alone but now the prop is out and I have a feeling that I can. It won't be the same but it will be done. Do you feel that at all? You know how sometimes in candle light, the

room darkens and then lights up again and seems to be brighter. It's kind of like that. I haven't yet got used to the unreality of this new reality but I am sure now it is going to be all right. I remember Ed's words for it even—"This species has experienced channels for all pain and sorrow and all happiness possible. They are ready when they are needed."

Then there's another thing. The rock has dropped in the water and the rings are going out and God knows where they will go or for how long or what patterns they will change obliquely. I have to tell this to someone and I guess you are the ones to tell. Nothing about me is the same. It is all changed. Tightening up now but in a different way. Almost a relief to be alone. As though some kind of conscience were removed and a fierceness I haven't had for many years restored. I'm going to work now as I have never worked before, because for the time being anyway, that's all there is. [5/27/48]

Despite the appearance here of a man who is already beginning to make some adjustment to what he called in an earlier letter "the ring-tailed, doublebarrelled impact" on him of these events, he was really a man cast adrift about to enter a long crisis of the soul. He had had such crises before, but never as severe as this one. Only a couple of weeks earlier he had been determined as a writer to pull himself up by his own bootstraps; now, that effort would have to wait while he tried to save himself.

II

In June the Benchleys and several other friends came to visit John in his room at the Bedford. He had a bowl of tobacco for make-your-own cigarettes, a bottle and some bathroom glasses, and in his window, between the burlap curtains that he'd hung, was a sweet potato he was training to climb a stake. They sat around discussing what they were going to do in the summer, whether they were going to New Canaan or the Cape or for one reason or another would have to stay in town. Finally, after everyone else had shared his plans, John said, "Well, I promised my sweet potato we're going to do what it wants to do this summer."

In fact, while Gwyn took the children to Los Angeles to spend the summer with her mother, John spent most of the summer in Mexico, with a few weeks between trips at an office that he rented on Fifty-eighth Street in New York. After grief and shock, came calm, then anger. As he wrote to Bo Beskow in June, "I am out of sadness and into fierceness now. That is natural to the organism that feels under attack I guess" [6/19/48]. He decided that he was not ready to begin his novel; instead, he accepted Kazan's offer to do a movie. He wanted to plunge into something immediately, so thoroughly that he would not have time to think. At the beginning of June and again at the end, he went to Mexico, ostensibly to "set up research on the life of Zapata," but in reality to brawl and womanize his way through two long lost weekends.

Alarmed that his friend might be slipping off the deep end, Pat Covici wrote to John in Cuernavaca, using a stern tone that he had never used before in their correspondence:

> I hope while you are in Mexico that you will do some tall thinking and wake up to yourself and your own peace of mind. It isn't simple, nor is it pleasant to look at the smashed pieces of something that you wanted to build and have. . . . It seems to me that a quick clean-up is the less painful, and a sober realization of what is sterling and what is not is creating values that one must have. [6/29/48]

After a week in New York again, he went back to Mexico through the first part of August. He was still drinking heavily, but now he was also doing some work. He tried to find out what censorship problems there might be, and he scouted filming locations. Much of his time, however, was devoted to gathering material on Zapata, and since the man had become a legend, getting authentic information was no small task. On July 25, he wrote to Gwyn, "Going to Cuautla to talk to people there. I will just about have to cover the state." Throughout the summer he had written to Gwyn regularly, sending a telegram to young John on his birthday, but had no response from his wife.

He returned from Mexico via Los Angeles, stopping to stay overnight at the Loessers. That evening the Loessers gave a dinner party, which included among others the Ira Gershwins and Lewis Milestone. After most of the guests had gone, John went upstairs to his bedroom and brought down a little wooden box in the shape of a coffin, which he opened to show the Loessers and Milestone; inside was a dead bird. He said that it had been given to him years ago by a witch woman in Mexico. When Lynn reached out to touch it, he told her, "No! Don't touch it! If you touch it, three weeks from today you would have some terrible bad luck, some calamity." Lynn just looked at him unbelievingly, and with a childish impulse, reached out and put her finger on it. John, as Lynn recalls, "slammed the box shut and went up stairs, almost in hysterics. He said, 'I love you, I love you, and I don't want anything bad to happen to you! Why did you do that?' And Millie and I just stared. I felt awful. And Millie said, 'That's a side of John you don't realize.' "

While he was in Los Angeles, John confided in the Loessers that he still hoped that somehow he and Gwyn could patch things up. Indeed, he had hope for a reconciliation up to the time of the divorce. All his overtures were rebuffed, however, and Gwyn told him in Los Angeles that she had made up her mind and didn't want to discuss it anymore. From New York, in mid-August, he wrote to Bo Beskow, confirming what he had hinted at in their correspondence for several months:

> After over four years of bitter unhappiness Gwyn has decided that she wants a divorce, so that is that. It is an old story of female frustration. She wants something I can't give her so she must go on looking. And maybe she will never find out that no one can give it to her. But that is her business now. She has cut me off completely. She feels much relieved now that she has done it and may even be a good friend to me. She will take the children, at least for the time being. And I will go back to Monterey to try to get rested and get the smell of my own country again. She did one kind thing. She killed my love of her with little cruelties so there is not much shock in all of this. And I will come back. I'm pretty sure I have some material left. But I have to rest like an old dog fox panting beside a stream. I have great sadness but no anger. In Pacific Grove I have the little cottage my father built and I will live and work in it for a while. Maybe I'll come to see you next winter and we'll "sing sad stories of the death of kings"—with herring. [8/16/48]

It was a very restrained letter that did not reveal what was really going on or the actual depth of his feeling. The "little cruelties" were not so little. What Gwyn had told him—and what he did not tell his closest friends for some time—was that she had not loved him for years, and had been unfaithful to him for years. While this was true, she also tortured him with other revelations, all false but all calculated to cause him pain and create suspicion in his mind concerning their married life.

Although the seed of doubt had been sown, he was at first skeptical of all this and thought of it as talk that had come out of Gwyn's anger, which was designed to hurt him. But over the next several months, in his growing bitterness and depression, he began to believe her entire "confession." Such belief had unfortunate results, of course, on his state of mind and on his relations with his children—and, once he was able to pull himself together, it very dramatically influenced the direction of his writing.

Always cautious about references of a very personal nature in his letters to friends, he seldom referred to the real causes of his breakdown, and then in the most indirect terms. Perhaps the most explicit mention came in a letter to Pat Covici more than a year after he had talked to Gwyn in Los Angeles (and even here his reluctance to write about it is signaled by the use of her initial). Pat had seen Gwyn and found her lonely and distraught, and he suspected that she might be regretting her decision. John replied to Pat's suggestion of a possible reconciliation:

> As to the G. matter, I would prefer to discuss that with you when I see you. But I assure you that it seems utterly impossible that anything in the world could heal that. Three years and more of treachery, consistent and careful are not got over. And the treachery continues even now. I'm afraid I built a person who wasn't there. I'll tell you about that some day. Not wanting to know, I didn't know. The anger and the evil have grown greater—not less.... Life seems to be flowing back into my veins—didn't realize how hard hit I was but it was pretty bad When one's whole pattern of thinking proves untrue it seems to cause a seismic shock. [12/49]

To understand what happened to him and the dark night that he went through during the fall, winter, and spring of 1948–49, one has to appreciate the depth of the love he had for Gwyn. He was an intensely passionate, feeling man, and every ounce of feeling that he possessed, he had invested in her—or at least in the image that he had created of her. Carol had been lover, friend, partner—as well as critic, adversary, and even, for a time, enemy. But she was flesh and blood. Gwyn was an ideal. Only by reading his love letters and the dozens of love poems addressed to her can one comprehend the extent of his adoration. She complained of his neglect, when in fact he doted on her, babied her, worried about her, and constantly courted her. He tried to serve her in all things. When she was sick, he hated it, but he fretted about her and waited on her. When she wanted something, she nearly always got it— he went through a fortune during these years, and much of it was spent on her and in satisfying her desires in regard to their style of living. By making her part idealized object of his love and part child, he spoiled her completely. When he went away on a job, he went as a knight-errant to slay dragons in her service. While he was gone, he wrote to her nearly every day and inevitably became heartsick after only a week away from her. She stayed home and sulked, and when he got home, she punished him.

For Steinbeck, romantic love was part of the magic, the myth, and the emotional intensity that was also literature. From early childhood on, he had been conditioned, through music as well as through reading, to consider love the noblest of emotions, a powerful force that can elevate the soul, overcome all obstacles, and even transcend death. Malory, Shakespeare, Petrarch, Verdi, Wagner, and his mother had told him so. The greatest experience of living was to find one's own true love, to have an all-consuming romantic obsession, to suffer for it and to be faithful to it until the end. By her flirtations and threats Gwyn made him suffer, and in her frequent illnesses she had developed a means by which she could keep him at a distance, reward and punish him, and make their relationship platonic and charged with frustration and longing.

Gwyn's tragedy was that through his idolatry, in combination with her own self-centeredness, she became a kind of monster in John's mind. He gave her the tools by which he could be manipulated or tortured, and he seemed to expect that she would use them. He denied her as a person and made her a character, and in order to become a person again, she apparently thought that she had to destroy him. He had cast her as his "Lady" in his play, and she always seemed to get most ill or have the least enjoyment of those times, as in Paris on the trip to Norway, when the spotlight, so often on her in their domestic life, shifted in public to him. In those situations, she became the leading character of a supporting cast, and she hated it. She wanted to star in her own play. When he came back from the war, she accused him of sadism and masochism, but in fact their relationship through its course reverberated with the sadomasochism of the courtly-love tradition. She was his Guinevere—but in the end he turned out to be Arthur, rather than Lancelot.

It is difficult enough to be oneself, to maintain a strong identity as the spouse of a famous and accomplished person, but the burden on Gwyn was enormous. The vast majority of Steinbeck's friends and relatives have indicted Gwyn as villainess, siding with John and seeing him as her victim. Yet, in all such things, the assignment of blame is not so simple. The sadness of Steinbeck's plight was that he had brought a literary inspired passion to his writing, and it drove him to success, but when he brought it to his life, it nearly destroyed him. There was further irony in the circumstance that one of the major themes of his writing had been the destructiveness of myth when it is used as a pattern for living.

He was very fond of Petrarch, of the poems written to Laura, the fourteenth-century poet's unobtainable, idealized love. While Ed Ricketts might finish a long evening of drink and talk and music with a reading of "Black Marigolds," Steinbeck often turned to Petrarch's sonnets. With one or two guests left, very early in the morning, over a final brandy in the darkened room and sitting amid the disorder of dirty glasses and overflowing ashtrays, something would lead Steinbeck to the bookcase. In a simple, low voice, almost expressionless yet full of emotion, he would read from the sonnets. And there was one sonnet that he could never finish.

Part of one of these sonnets sounded the doleful anthem for the months ahead:

> A rain of bitter tears falls from my face
> And a tormenting wind blows with my sighs
> Whenever toward you I turn my eyes,
> Whose absence cuts me from the human race.

III

At the first of September 1948, he moved back to California and into the little house on Eleventh Street in Pacific Grove. It was, he wrote Pat Covici, "a full circle with 20 years inside of it," and he was back where he had started. "There are moments of panic but those are natural I suppose. And then sometimes it seems to me that nothing has happened. As though it was the time even before Carol. Tonight the damp fog is down and you can feel it on your face. I can hear the bell buoy off the point."

He had come away with very little more than the clothes on his back. His journals, correspondence, books, phonograph records, recording machine, electric typewriter—nearly all his personal possessions were still at the house in New York. Some of the things he would have liked to have retrieved, particularly his books that he used for reference, but Gwyn would give up nothing. He couldn't understand why, if she were going to depend on him for her income, she refused to at least allow him the tools of his trade. The house in Pacific Grove was a shambles. A series of non-rent-paying tenants had almost stripped it of furniture; even the pots, pans, dishes, knives, and forks were gone. The garden was unkempt, and the house itself in disrepair. He was also nearly broke—his savings were gone and he owed money on his taxes. Incoming royalties would not be enough to pay the alimony and child support over the long haul, and so for the first time in many years, since the early days with Carol when he tried to write a pulp detective novel, he would have to write specifically to get money. Everything considered, it was like starting all over again, only worse.

He did have a car, and he did have the help of Neale, an ex-Navy steward who had gone to work for the Steinbecks as a houseman several months before. The two men batched as best they could, taking turns with the cooking and working around the house together. There wasn't much to batch with—when the Joe Jacksons sent Steinbeck some Mexican dishes, he accepted with pleasure, noting that he only had three mugs in the house and if more than three people ate dinner, someone would have to eat out of the serving dish: "I think Neale is a little ashamed for me. I told him one had to be very rich to have no money" [11/30/48]. Pat Covici sent him *Casserole Cookery.* "Now that you will enjoy the simple life," he told him. Covici also sent a carton of yellow writing pads.

Steinbeck spent the first month and a half working to restore the house, cleaning and painting and doing repairs, and working in the garden, trimming all the overgrown and neglected shrubbery, mulching and fertilizing, and then planting. He did these things almost automatically, depending on the hard physical labor to help bring his life back into equilibrium. He wrote Pat that although he was planting things, he probably would never see them flower "either because I won't be here or I won't be looking." But moving rocks around made his hands and arms ache, and that felt good, and checking his garden each day, noting the new buds and fighting off the pests, gave his mind occupation. He put off all thought of writing again until the house was finished: "There will be only one test of this and that is whether any good work comes out of it. I am not going to touch paper for several weeks yet. I want this damp sea fog to get deeply into me and the fine wind over the kelp on the rocks" [JS/BB-9/19/48].

During these months, his letters were often filled with reassurances—don't worry about me, I'm fine, I'm doing the things I want to do. Every once in awhile, however, word leaked through his line of defense. To Covici, who kept up a steady stream of supportive letters during this period, he wrote in September, "You are right—I do get the horrors every now and then. Comes on like a cold wind. There it is, just a matter of weathering it. Alcohol doesn't help that a bit. I usually go into the garden and work hard" [9/19/48]. Covici was deeply concerned. A very intuitive, sensitive man, he didn't need any admissions from his friend to know precisely what he was going through. Forced by circumstance to try to help only at a distance, he was going through a measure of hell on his own, frustration mixed with worry, sympathy, and concern. He was also a little angry that John should have to endure such treatment at the hands of others. To his mind, Steinbeck was always being taken advantage of:

> It is difficult to get rid of poison which has permeated your whole body and mind for so long. You could never say "No" to any second-rater who forced himself upon you. . . . By nature shy and retiring and almost uncommunicative, you never would go out of your way to meet the people of your choice, but the second-raters, who never wait, forced themselves on you and you, being also very compassionate and human, made easy companions of them when at heart you really didn't want them and much preferred to be alone. In other words, you had plenty of bastards and bitches clinging onto you. Your secretary I understand is also claiming your soul, the little bitch. Just because you are a writer doesn't mean you have to be milked. There are two places that proved poisonous for you—Hollywood and New York. As far as you are concerned they are good to visit but not to take to heart. [9/23/48]

Visitors to the little house reported Steinbeck as by turns silent, irascible, and absent, or garrulous and manic in rationalizing a style of living that featured a hermitlike defiance of the world and a rejection of his previous habits of regularity. One visitor, an old friend from Los Gatos, found the atmosphere bizarre, with Steinbeck in a kind of melancholy stupor and Ed Ricketts's microscope enshrined under glass and set in a position of reverence in the center of the room. But it wasn't just the loss of Gwyn and of Ed, the hurt and the loneliness that haunted him, it was also his inability to write. He told Pat in a note that "gradually my energy is coming back a little at a time. It is so strange that I could lose it so completely," and he meant that he seemed to have lost his will to write, and that frightened him [10/18/48].

George Robinson was a frequent visitor during these months. It was of some comfort to have a friend of Ed's about. George was a good-hearted, liberal-minded fellow, who had no artistic ax to grind, but instead had something of the rough directness of the working man. On the other hand, he had, like John and Ed, a taste for classical music and knew a great deal about it. He was the kind of person that John could sit with of an evening, sometimes without talking for long periods, or sometimes talking about things in general and nothing in particular.

George recalls that John had fixed up the Eleventh Street house so that as you entered, there was a huge aquarium, about four feet by five feet, which John used to divide the entrance from the front room. He recalls that John's bed was in the front room, covered with a corduroy bedspread. It seemed to be John's "corduroy period," in that he wore corduroy pants, corduroy shirts, and had a corduroy jacket. When Robinson commented on this, John said, "I love the feel of it—it's not a snob material." John still had some humor, although not much about himself. Once when George brought over some books from friends to have them signed, he mentioned he also had some books for author Ann Fisher. John put down his pen and turned toward George with raised eyebrow. "Do you know Ann Fisher?" he asked. "Yes," George replied. "George," John said, "I understand an unautographed book by Ann Fisher is a collector's item."

He had determined to go to Mexico on the first of November in order, he claimed, to dig up more material on Zapata. Mildred Lyman, from McIntosh and Otis, came to visit him, and she wrote back to Annie Laurie:

> He is deeply disturbed and frightened about his work. If it doesn't go well in Mexico I honestly don't know what will happen. The fact that so much time has elapsed without his accomplishing anything to speak of worries him a great deal. He has a defense mechanism which is constantly in action and it is hard to get behind that. What John needs more than anything right now is discipline. I'm afraid that he wanted to get to Mexico for reasons other than writing. I heard quite a bit while I was with him about the gal, and I don't think that bodes any good. She's a tramp. [11/48]

Just before he left he wrote Pat that he would be leaving for Mexico shortly: "I'm working on the life of a very great man but primarily a man. It would be good to study him closely. His life had a rare series— beginning, middle and end, and most lives dribble away like piss in the dust" [11/1/48].

He stopped at Hollywood and met Elia Kazan, and the two flew on to Mexico City. He found the city sad, empty of tourists and the hotels dying, and after a few days they moved to Cuernavaca. Kazan was a sympathetic companion, and Steinbeck liked and was impressed with him: "Kazan takes to this country very quickly. I guess this maleability is one of the great traits of the Greeks. I think he will understand very well what I am talking about—more than any other American director and surely better than any Mexican director" [11/12/48]. Steinbeck had come to Mexico the way a person lying in bed, racked with pain, thinks that by getting up and doing something, the pain might be lessened. But the diversions he had counted on were not there, and he found that he hurt worse than he had in Pacific Grove. His "tramp" was occupied with someone else, and when he tried to force himself upon her, he was thrown out and threatened with the police. In a rage, as he reported later to Bo Beskow, and in complete despair he "wanted to kill some one or be killed, even to the extent of walking alone at night in Mexico with a bare machete in my hand but the challenge did not work. I was avoided like that mad dog I guess I was" [11/19/48].

Like the invalid who tries to walk too soon, he had had a bad fall and it left him shocked and shaken. He wrote Pat, "The sickness has been worse than I have been able to admit even to myself. Must be getting better because now I am beginning to be able to see that it was there at all. At my advanced age I have to go back to some kind of childhood and learn all over again" [11/14/48]. He had returned from Mexico two weeks before he had planned on leaving. He told Pat, "You must not worry about me. I am all right. This is the worse season and I am still all right and it will get less bad. That anyone can depend on. That's the law."

His work on his movie script went badly, and the more false starts he made, the more frightened he became. He was going out very little and writing mostly at night, living, he reported, almost as he had done years ago at Lake Tahoe. Those who did stop by to see him were probably sorry that they did—both Toby and Duke Sheffield took some abuse from his ill temper, while he wondered what it was that he had ever seen to like or admire in either one of them. Thanksgiving came and the whole family gathered together—the only ones missing to make the occasion complete were his boys. The full impact of his separation from them was beginning to come upon him, to add further to his woes, and he worried about them growing up in the city with only a female parent. "The impulse of the American woman," he wrote Beskow, "to geld her husband and castrate her sons is very strong" [11/19/48].

Following the family get-together, he reported to Pat, "I did Thanksgiving very well but Xmas I will not try. I will get a gallon of wine and the prettiest girl I can find and I will forget Christmas this year" [11/29/48]. Much of his time was taken with going over and over again his relationship with Gwyn and what had happened. Sitting in front of the fire late at night or staring out the window at the rain, he tortured himself by reviewing events in detail, constructing speeches and dramas, and theorizing about the nature of man and woman and love and American culture. He constructed many theories and philosophies, as if some intellectual formalization of what had happened would somehow release him and set him free. At the end of November, he wrote to Pat:

My shell is getting pretty hard now and it doesn't come off very often. I'll be very glad when it can come off like a bandage and there won't be any wounds underneath. That will happen in time if there is only the time allowed for healing. I try not to be hopeful but I do feel some kind of surge. And I am understanding some things that perhaps are better not understood. It is not a matter of disillusion at all but probably the illusion of a lack of illusion. One thing we Westerners have which is probably not so with Orientals and some Europeans. We feel that other people are nicer, kinder, more virtuous and wiser than we are. This individual guilt and humility is put in us very early and maintained by group lies. And when we find that this is not necessarily true we suffer what we call disillusion. Disillusion is that emotion we feel when any of our safe patterns are disturbed. It is actually a kind of anger that we have been wrong. The things or people have not changed—only we have and so we are upset. With me the idea that Gwyn is not all wise and kind and beautiful and unselfish is distasteful. Therefore I am angry because my pattern is broken not because reality has in any way changed. My error was in permitting the pattern to establish in violation of all realities. [11/29/48]

During her visit to Steinbeck, Mildred Lyman had written that he "has very peculiar ideas of women these days." As part of his defense, he had generalized from his experience to condemn all American women, who, as he wrote Beskow, were "part man, part politician—they have the minds of whores and the vaginas of Presbyterians. . . . American married life is the doormat to the whore house" [11/19/48]. He decided he could love Mexican, Chinese, black, or European women because they were content to be women, rather than trying to be men. He had always had conventional views about women and had acted throughout his life more or less on the basis of the typical double standard of the American male: there are women you put on a pedestal and marry, and there are women whom you go to bed with but don't marry. Having had his goddess fall off her pedestal and onto his head, he turned now to the "other kind" of woman for solace, with what he called a "goat-like lust," reaching out in all directions. It was a kind of revenge for what he now looked back on as his humiliation at the hands of Gwyn: "I guess I wasn't a man or I wouldn't have put up with it. But I am a man now and I don't think I will surrender that nice state. I like it and the others can lump it."

Another part of his defense was a conscious attempt to be tough and uncaring. He wrote of this decision a number of times and reported with satisfaction his progress in becoming nasty. He told Pat, "I am tough and mean after quite a house cleaning. My closets were full of dust, of little feats, of half felt emotions. If I am to be a son of a bitch, I'm going to be my own son of a bitch. I've kicked out the duty emotions" [1/22/49]. He took a perverse pride in behaving, as he noted in another letter, like a "crabbed old hermit," turning visitors away and even kicking out young women before the night was over (a lascivious old hermit). He had almost no money, so he found he could turn down requests for loans with ease and even call in a few I.O.U.s.

During the latter part of November he made another attempt to write his script. This time he worked several weeks on a long introduction, which, although perhaps necessary to an understanding of the script to come, stretched out to the point where he realized that he was procrastinating. Having finished that, he wrote Pat that he was going to "flog" himself into the opening scene. But flogging did not help, and once more, even after having launched himself with the momentum of his introduction, his effort to get into the drama failed. Everything, including the script, seemed to fall apart over Christmas. The holidays, he wrote Elizabeth Otis, "were quite the worst I have ever had bar none" [1/5/49].

In December he had been notified that he, along with William Faulkner, Mark Van Doren, and the painter Leon Kroll, had been elected to membership in the American Academy of Arts and Letters. Usually when he received such an honor, he reacted with refreshingly candid delight, but in this instance, as an indicator of his mood, he found it to be "a little like a premature embalming job—a very empty thing." What he needed, he felt, were returns of a more substantial nature. Very little money was coming in and there was no prospect of it until after *The Red Pony* was released sometime in early 1949. He still maintained the fiction that he could live on practically nothing, taking his food from the sea, but he needed money to pay his alimony. The alternatives were either jail or fleeing the country, and, as he wrote in a moment of exasperation, he might well end up doing one or the other.

He told Pat so often that although he was broke he wasn't going to worry about it, that Pat started to worry. Covici wrote him, "Indeed, I know you are broke. I checked up your February statement and I couldn't believe it. You will have to start all over again and you will, and I am sure there is nothing to worry about. Only it is a shame to have pissed away two fortunes in so short a time" [12/21/48]. In order to relieve some of the strain, Covici helped to arrange for John to sell his rights to *The Wayward Bus* to Viking. And if only John would finish "Zapata" or if Covici could have convinced him to drop it in favor of "The Salinas Valley," he would have gladly arranged an advance for as long as it would take to write the novel. But Steinbeck was fixed on "Zapata," as if writing it finally would mean the redemption of his soul, and he didn't want to take an advance. Covici reminded him that it was a little like the old days, when John didn't have enough money while writing *Grapes* to travel to Oklahoma and Pat offered him $250, and John refused. Steinbeck did not like writing against an advance, and he had not done so since the very early novels (which did not make their advances). An advance, as far as he was concerned, was just another debt, like back taxes, and he didn't need any more debts.

Over New Year's he went to Los Angeles and stayed with the Loessers, and while he was there, saw *The Red Pony*: "I think it is good. It will be no smash because of its pace but I think it will play for a long time. Surely it is faithful to the script. And it is the first color film that has looked like this country to me" [1/5/49]. (One of the aspects of film that he seemed most conscious of was "pace." Gwyn recalls that while he was watching *The Pearl*, early the year before, he shrank down in his seat and nearly died of mortification, the pace of the movie was so excruciatingly slow.) On his return he went in to have his eyes checked. The verdict that he needed glasses for reading and writing was good news: it had put at least part of his difficulty in writing on a physical basis. He reported, "I have my glasses now and print jumps out of the page at me. It has been creeping up on me for years and I didn't know it. I only knew that it was getting increasingly difficult to work. I thought I was getting lazy and old and ill and now I think it was mostly eye strain" [1/22/49]. It wasn't, but thinking so did make him feel better.

Whether it was the glasses or simply the workings of time, by the end of January his letters began to indicate a genuine recovery. There were definite stirrings of life:

> I have some new snapshots of my children. They are growing so rapidly and they look fine. We shall have great fun this summer. I think I have located a boat for us to go cruising in. I told them we would sleep and cook our dinner on a boat and that seems to excite them very much just as it excites me still. What better thing is there than that?
>
> Pat, I'm getting the old ecstasies back sometimes. Thinking about a boat made the hair rise on the back of my neck. You say a good piece of writing does that to you. . . . [Life] still has some savor and what more could I ask of it. Women are still beautiful and desirable and things smell good and sometimes the flame burns jumping the nerve ends like little boys jumping fences. [1/22/49]

He decided to go back to Mexico, this time to stay until the script was finished. What was needed, he thought, was the inspiration of the place itself: "I need the country and the language in my eyes and ears." But he found Mexico lonely and depressing and returned in mid-February, after staying only two weeks. It had been a final impulse toward procrastination, and at long last, he sat down very deliberately to get his work done. "I don't know what has happened," he reported to Pat in late February, "but the dams are burst. Work is pouring out of me." He stopped drinking and started to regulate his life, getting up early to work as he always had before his breakdown. At the end of the month he wrote Pat again, "I am grateful to you for sticking by in the dark time when everything was tottering and falling away. I for one, never expected to get out of it."

In March he reported, "I think this script must be excellent. The dialogue has a good sound to me. I am putting some of it on record for typing now. And the speech sounds like talk." He had the old excitement again and he was "writing like a fiend." Not only was he making progress with the script, but he was also writing short stories and making notes for the novel that would eventually become *East of Eden*. He commented to Pat at the end of March, "My critics (as evidenced in the letters you forwarded) are still waiting for me. They are going to be very angry with The Salinas Valley because it will be even more unlike Mice and Men."

During the spring he saw Alice Jackson several times, telling her that the only women he had been able to remain friends with throughout the years were she and Elizabeth Otis. Still bragging about his sexual activity (and still overstating it), he told her that he had been going out with so many women that he couldn't even remember their names. "Why," he asked, "do you think I painted my house stud red?" He took great interest in Alice's youngest son, and talked to Alice about his own boys. He told her that he saw Cain and Abel in their relationship and saw it also in the characters of Alice's two boys. He told her that he wanted to settle down and that he was preparing to write the great book of his career.

It was about this time that he began seeing Paulette Goddard on a regular basis. He had known her since the days when she had been living with Charlie Chaplin, and during the time she was married to Burgess Meredith he had had, in Meredith's words, "eyes for her." She was a very beautiful woman, but also impulsive and quite often flirtatious. Now that she was separated from Meredith, it was all right with him if John wanted to play with her, but he warned him that she might be more than he could handle. Indeed, there was something in the relationship that made one think that a country boy might be suckered in a league out of his depth. But John knew what the game was. Max Wagner remembers him talking about Goddard and her love of expensive trinkets, and in order to satisfy and amaze her, John and Max went shopping at several five-and-ten-cent stores in the Hollywood area, where John purchased, in today's money, about a hundred dollars' worth of rhinestone necklaces, bracelets, and rings. It was his intention to gather it all together in a large chamois bag or an impressively decorated chest, and when he and Goddard were alone, to get down on his knees, protest his love passionately, and then open the chest and pour all the sparkling junk jewelry at her feet.

His relationship with Goddard made all the gossip columns and it was widely reported that he was drinking heavily ("People always want to believe the best of you," he commented), even though he had stopped drinking entirely in January. The romance with Goddard was a temporary thing, a matter for amusement on both sides, and came to an end when John met someone else. For many artists, the ability to love would have come first, and the ability to work would follow. For John, being able to write again allowed him to gradually discard his shell and reach out to love once more.

CHAPTER XXXIII

That new love was Elaine Scott. She was attractive and well tailored—New York sharp and Texas soft—and like his other wives, she was intelligent, outgoing, and had a sense of humor. Unlike the others, she seemed to have a sure sense of who she was and what she could do. She not only had the capacity to love, she had the capacity to be loving.

Elaine Anderson had grown up in Fort Worth, Texas. The daughter of an oilman, she had gone to the University of Texas, and was studying drama production there when she met Zachary Scott, an aspiring actor and son of an Austin, Texas, doctor. They were married, had a daughter, and when Scott got his degree, went off to seek their fortunes in the New York theater world. Soon after they arrived, she and Zachary got jobs at the Westport Country Playhouse, and he went on to roles on Broadway, alternating with work in summer stock, while Elaine went into production, getting a good job that first winter with the Theatre Guild. She eventually worked her way into becoming a full-fledged stage manager, a job which up to that time had been seldom performed on Broadway by a woman.

In 1943 Scott signed a contract with Warner Brothers and went to Hollywood, and in the spring of the following year, Elaine and their daughter, Waverly, joined him. She had given up her job reluctantly, since there was no job in the movies that she had been trained for, but Scott became a star, and he and Elaine soon became totally involved in the life of the colony—Hollywood in those days was still Hollywood. By the spring of 1949, their marriage was nearly all but officially over.

In April of the same year, Steinbeck had finished the first draft of the master script, and he was pleased with it. He had written to Pat at the end of March, "There are some great scenes in the Zapata script. I don't know whether they will ever get on film but they are there." His longing for his children increased, and on an impulse, he made a quick trip to New York to see them, and was sorry that he did—all the bad feelings he thought he had gotten rid of seemed to rush in on him again, and he left New York in a funk.

After returning, he wrote three stories inspired by his feelings after seeing his children again. Two of them he destroyed, and the third, "His Father," he sent to Elizabeth Otis: "I don't know whether you will like or approve of the enclosed. It is what happened anyway. Maybe it isn't good to even think of printing it. But it occurs to me that if Nat Benchley can write the things that didn't happen in my family, perhaps I can write some that did" [5/6/49]. (He was referring to several stories Benchley had written, published in *The New Yorker* and other magazines, which were later collected and published as *Side Street*.) Near the end of the month he got notice from Elizabeth that she had sold the story to *Reader's Digest*. He wrote back,

> You know darned well you done good with the little five-page story. What a price! It is next best to Air Wick. Very good news. . . .
>
> In the same mail with your letter, one from Ralph Henderson assuring me that they bought the story because they like it and not because of my name. Apparently you cut them deeply by asking for money as well as the honor of being published. In the light of this $2500 for four pages—do you remember when you worked for months and finally got $90 for the longest story in the Red Pony series and forty for the shorter ones? I hardly made $1000 on my first three novels.
>
> Thanks for your letter. I'm going to have some more little stories before long now. They are good practice in a form I have not used for a long time. [6/23/49]

But he would not have time to do any more short stories during the weeks immediately ahead—his boys would be coming for the summer, a visit he had long anticipated, and the stage was set for meeting Elaine Scott.

Whenever anyone at a dinner party asked him how he met his wife, Steinbeck would raise his glass and propose a toast, "Here's to Ava Gardner!" and then tell this story:

> I came down to Hollywood to work on "Zapata," and Zanuck gave me an office roughly the size of the Taj Mahal, where I couldn't possibly work, so I got myself a suite at the Beverly Hills Hotel and started to work. Doris Johnson [Nunnally Johnson's wife] called and said, "Are you free to come to dinner tomorrow night?"

and I said, "Yes." And she said, "Do you know Ava Gardner?" and I said, "No." "Well," she said, "will you pick her up and bring her to dinner?" and I said, "All right." Then she called back and said, "Ava is sorry but she has a date. Do you know Ann Sothern?" and I said, "No," and Doris said, "Well, you pick her up and bring her to dinner." I did and we got along fine.

I went home to Pacific Grove and started to get lonesome, so I picked up the phone, called Ann, and said, "Will you come up here and we'll have some good Italian food and drink some wine and have a little fun?" And Ann said, "Yes," but being a cautious soul, she brought a chaperone, Elaine Scott. The first night we all went out to dinner together. The second night we all went out to dinner together. The third night, Ann said, "I'm terribly sorry, I have to go out with some other friends for dinner tonight. Will you take care of Elaine?" And I did, and I have, and I always will! So, here's to Ava Gardner!

Ann and Elaine had come up over Memorial Day weekend and stayed at the Pine Inn in Carmel. Steinbeck took them around the Peninsula and showed them the Row and Ed's lab, the wharf, and the coastline, fed them at his favorite restaurants, and took them to Sonny Boy's, a roadhouse hangout that he had used a couple of times as a setting in his books. Elaine found the weekend rather peculiar—although he had invited Ann, not her, and although she was a married woman, he began, as the weekend passed, to concentrate on her in an odd way. He took her to meet Toby Street, as if, she felt, this was the start of a process wherein she would be introduced to all his friends. He took her to meet his sister Esther in Watsonville, and it was clear at the time that this was something unusual, something he had not done before. Ann had a new camera and was taking pictures constantly; John and Elaine were in most of them, and at one point Ann stopped and said, "Hey, this is going to look like a record of a romance between you two."

Right after the two women left to go back to Hollywood, he wrote to Annie Laurie to inquire about Elaine, knowing that she had worked with the Theatre Guild in New York: "I kind of fell for the Scott girl. Who is she—do you know? . . . Can you give me a report on her?" Louella Parsons, Hollywood gossip columnist, got a tip on the Ann Sothern–Steinbeck rendezvous and reported it on her radio show. In his letter he added, "Annie Sothern just called to ask if I was embarrassed by the Parsons thing and I had to tell her that I was only complimented. Now P.G. [Paulette Goddard] will call to rib me about it" [6/7/49].

In his excitement he didn't wait for Annie Laurie's report, but wrote to Elaine only a few days after her departure:

Dear Miss West Forty-seventh Street
  between Eighth and Ninth:
Am a widower with 10,000 acres in Arizona and seven cows so if you can milk I will be glad to have you give up that tinsel life of debauchery and sin and come out to God's country where we got purple sage. P.S. Can you bring a little sin and debauchery along? You can get too much purple sage but you can only get just enough sin. . . .
I was sad when you two bugs went away. Now I haven't even a half-assed reason for not working.
I am told that darling Louella tagged Annie and me last night. This will henceforth be known as The Seven Days That Shook the Pine Inn. Running naked through the woods with flowers in your hair is against the law and I told you both but you wouldn't listen. Sometime during the summer I will drift down your way. [6/6/49]

"Sometime" turned out to be a week later, and he didn't just "drift down" to Los Angeles, but came at full speed. He came ostensibly for conferences on his script (and as a sort of "cover" saw Ann Sothern once or twice), but in fact, since Elaine felt the same excitement he did, they saw each other for nearly a week as often as she could arrange to be absent from home. He took her to meet Max and Jack Wagner (although Max still had connections with Gwyn, Steinbeck trusted him not to say anything, and he didn't) and took her to out-of-the-way places where they wouldn't be recognized.

Although he had been enormously attracted to her almost immediately, he had no other motive at this point than the pursuit of a charming woman who was willing to be pursued. He had arrived at an antiromantic, almost biological formulation earlier in the spring which was a codification of his minimum requirements for survival. He repeated it over and over again in letters to various correspondents, including John O'Hara: "For myself there are two things I cannot do without. Crudely stated they are work and women, and more gently—creative effort in all directions. Effort and love. Everything else I can do without. . . ." [6/8/49]. He was also holding fast to the idea that it would not do for him to get married again. As he expressed it to Bo Beskow, "I find that I am a very good lover but a lousy husband and that is something I might as well accept since I do not think I will change at my time of life" [6/9/49].

While for the most part these conclusions were self-limiting and would pass in time under the pressures of circumstances and emotion, he had come up with other formulations during his recent ordeal which would turn out to be much more durable. In his letter cited above to John O'Hara, written at about the same time that he met Elaine, he stated as explicitly as he ever would the direction that both his life and work would take, in tandem, in the years to come:

> Being alone here has allowed me to think out lots of things. There is so much yapping in the world. The coyotes are at us all the time telling us what we are, what we should do and believe. The stinking little parasitic minds that fasten screaming on us like pilot fish that fasten on a shark, they contribute only drag. I think I believe one thing powerfully—that the only creative thing our species has is the individual, lonely mind. Two people can create a child but I know of no other thing created by a group. The group ungoverned by individual thinking is a horrible destructive principle. The great change in the last 2,000 years was the Christian idea that the individual soul was very precious. Unless we can preserve and foster the principle of the preciousness of the individual mind, the world of men will either disintegrate into a screaming chaos or will go into a grey slavery. And that fostering and preservation seem to me our greatest job.

His greatest weakness had been that he was too easily affected or hurt by the opinions of others. He gave the impression of being strong and sure of himself, but he was often full of doubt about his work, doubt that grew with exposure and with fame. Steinbeck looked upon writing as a very private act, and he put too much of himself in his work to ever be happy about public discussion of it—particularly if that discussion personally connected his work to him. He truly was not competitive as a writer, because competition with other writers didn't have much to do with his motives for writing, but he did hate to be compared or have his work classified or categorized in respect to other people's work.

The one thing that he insisted on was that he was an individual and his work was individual. Now, as he emerged from a long night filled with nightmares of self-doubt and self-deprecation, both of his own worth and the value of his work, he was determined to be strong, and he rededicated himself to defining himself. He would insist on his own beliefs and maintain them regardless of the many pressures to conform and compete within the arena of the tastes, values, and modes of thinking and expression set up for him by others. And when his life was over, there would be men and women themselves sometimes referred to as great, who would find in these remaining years of the writer's life a measure of greatness to admire, in his independence of mind and his stubborn insistence on being himself.

Although in his previous work he had not ignored the unusual individual, he had most often been concerned about the formation and behavior of groups. Now out of his own struggle to maintain his sanity and individuality, his focus turned toward the social role and ethical dilemmas of the single person. During these months he was reading *Don Quixote*, and perhaps it reinforced his conviction that only by ignoring fashionable opinion and social pressure could a true nobility of mind and heart be achieved. In his major work to come, in *Zapata*, *East of Eden*, and *The Winter of Our Discontent*, the lonely individual strives to find out himself, to survive as himself, and to do what is necessary. Steinbeck's life, his themes, and even the process of writing were tied together in this, as becomes apparent in another passage in his letter to John O'Hara:

> I've been practicing for a book for 35 years and this is it. I don't see how it can be popular because I am inventing method and form and tone and context. And of course I am scared of it. It's a cold lonely profession and this is the coldest and loneliest because this is all I can do, and when it is done I've either done it or I never had it to do.
>
> I've re-read your letter and this is another day. You know I was born without any sense of competition. Consequently I have never even wondered about the comparative standing of writers. I don't understand that. Writing to me is a deeply personal, even a secret function and when the product is turned loose it is cut off from me and I have no sense of its being mine. It is like a woman trying to remember what child birth is like. She never can.

II

There was one other element, however, that was required before he had achieved enough stability in his emotional position to go on. For all his talk of independence and despite his protestations and biological formulations, he needed not just a woman, or women, but a wife, someone to stand by him and support him. He needed someone by his side who was strong, loving, and faithful; if he had that, he could stand at the bridge and hold off the whole world.

During the summer and early fall of 1949, John and Elaine tried to see each other as much as possible, not always an easy task, since Elaine was still married and they had to keep their relationship a secret. He came to Hollywood several times in June and once in July, staying the first time at the Beverly Hills Hotel and thereafter checking in at a more anonymous tourist court. During one week in June he had to testify at the *Cannery Row* breach-of-contract trial, and Elaine drove him to court every day. Often Steinbeck took her to see the Wagners, and to see Eugene Solow. Solow, an old friend of John's who had done the final scenario of *Of Mice and Men*, was now working on a script for *The Wayward Bus*, and Steinbeck was helping him as well as conferring with people at Twentieth Century-Fox about "Zapata." He hoped that with two movies in the works, he would soon be able to free himself financially so that he could go to work on his novel.

Early in July the Scotts gave a dinner party at their house in Brentwood, inviting John along with Ann Sothern, Ann Sheridan, Caesar Romero, and John Emery and his wife, Tamara Geva. Several people at the party, as they told Elaine later, sensed that there was something between John and Elaine, but these were close friends and nothing was leaked to the gossip columnists. John was still taking Ann Sothern out occasionally, and when Joan Crawford asked Elaine to go on a vacation with her and Elaine agreed providing they went to the Monterey Peninsula, Ann Sothern called and asked Elaine not to introduce Crawford to Steinbeck, not yet having caught on to the relationship between Elaine and John.

The two women went during the latter part of July, taking a cottage at the Pebble Beach Hotel. As soon as John came by to see them, Joan Crawford got the idea and gamely went along with the situation, even though it meant that she would be left to herself a good part of the time. It was a dangerous gamble on Elaine's part because she really wasn't sure how much she could trust Crawford not to say anything, but Crawford was understanding and completely close-mouthed about it, and later gave herself credit for bringing the two of them together.

During those times when John and Elaine were apart, John wrote nearly every day, usually combining several entries in each letter. It was a journal-like correspondence, similar to the one he had had with Gwyn during the war and more recently with Pat Covici during the aftermath of the divorce. Even in writing, there was a necessity for subterfuge, and with what Elaine has called "his penchant for drama and intrigue," John addressed his letters to "Belle Hamilton," using his mother's maiden surname, and sent them in care of Max and Jack

Wagner—what he called the "hollow oak tree." Since as always he was somewhat bashful and reticent about expressing himself either in person or on the telephone, he bombarded Elaine during this period with "nearly a ton of letters," which contributed much to the rapid, serious advancement of their relationship.

In the meantime, Steinbeck's houseman, Neale, who was a pilot, had flown to New York, took a vacation there, and then at the beginning of July, flew back again with John's two boys. John had all kinds of plans for them, as he explained to Bo Beskow:

> I have my boys the two months this summer and I am going to give them some manness—by that I mean they are going to help me do things, physical things, they are going to be let to wander if they want. They are going to eat when they are hungry and sleep when they are sleepy. As much as possible they are going to be responsible for their own actions. They are going to associate with men and animals and they are going to be treated with respect—their ideas listened to and included. Maybe it is bad but it will give them some cushion against the winter and the Eton collars and showing off at parties. They can have hammers and nails and boxes to build with. Thom is old enough to take the dual control of an airplane so he can learn to fly as he learned to talk with an automatic reflex sense. And he can drive my jeep on country roads. And in a very few years, if I can afford it, I'll begin taking them to different places in the world, to Stockholm and to France and to Italy and Mexico. [5/23/49]

Like most divorced fathers separated from their children, he had developed a rather romantic view of their natures and their capacities (Gwyn threw up her hands in despair when she heard of his plan to have Thom drive the jeep—she didn't know about the airplane), a view that would be quickly shattered in the reality of coping with a two-year-old and four-year-old. One was still a baby and the other nearly so, and yet he wanted so badly for them to be big enough so that he could play with them.

His plan for the summer was a script that had been polished over and over again in his mind, like a teenage boy fantasizing all the action and dialogue of a first date. His youngest seemed attracted to boats, and to enlist his enthusiasm for coming to him during the summer, Steinbeck promised not only would they ride in a boat, they would eat and sleep in one, so he had purchased an old boat and worked during the spring to refurbish it. He and Neale tried to build a hut from a kit for the boys to play in, but they couldn't get it to go together properly, so they settled for putting up a tent. And despite his comparative shortage of funds, he managed to buy a small trailer for the boys to stay in and hired a nurse.

The nurse that the boys had during the first few weeks of the summer, however, was one that had come with them from New York (her name was Cathy, and John disliked her intensely). She reported to Gwyn those things she disapproved of, which led to open disagreement between the parents as to how the boys should be raised, one among several factors that led to a generally unhappy period of growing up for the children. There are those, like Gwyn's mother, who have stated that Steinbeck hated children, and there are many more others who have said that Steinbeck was very good with children, but did not handle his own very well. The truth seems to be that although he loved his children and tried to do the right things, he wasn't a very good father. Like many parents, but particularly those who are divorced, he was sometimes too lenient and sometimes too strict. There were times when things were too organized and too much effort was given toward having a good time; but there were more times when he just didn't pay much attention to them. John was very often consumed by the problems of his writing and having the boys around served as an irritant.

Like his own father, Steinbeck found it difficult to express his affection for his children directly, and a great deal of the love and concern he had for them was put into his work. And many of his concerns were so personal and so deep that they come out only in his work—he wouldn't talk about them. Many of the nagging doubts about their family and life together Gwyn had planted in his mind. There were fears he had in regard to Gwyn's influence over the boys while they were primarily in her custody. He worried that they wouldn't have the experiences outdoors that he had had as a child; that they would be too citified, too pampered, and too dependent. But his deepest fear was that they would grow up to be like their mother. He thought a lot about genes, heredity, and environment, and about what it is that formulates character, and the more he thought and worried about these things, the more of an intellectual problem they became, so that they were almost divorced from the immediate welfare of the real-life children themselves.

It might not be too far wrong to say that his children had almost a separate existence inside his head, the way a novel developed in his mind. So many of the plans, projects, and remedies that he created for them, as for that first summer they would be together, came out of thought about what would be good for them (in light of their circumstances as he perceived them), rather than out of contact and communication with them.

Early in August he wrote to Elaine a letter in which in a paragraph he discussed his ideas regarding discipline and punishment, a discussion that reveals this tendency to intellectualize his relations with his boys. There is also the suggestion that his attitude toward them was formed in part by the idea that they are essentially biological entities—an idea confirmed in later correspondence when he celebrates their apparent release from the citified and feminine influence of their mother to become, under his tutelage, "healthy animals." (There is in this attitude a parallel with his philosophy about dogs.)

In the letter he writes,

I don't approve of punishment. I never knew it to help anyone. Discipline is during and before the fact but punishment is later and it is like criticism to a writer. By the time he has it, it is too late even if it is valid. Last night Tom didn't come when he was called to dinner. I didn't want to punish him but I had to make him listen to a call since I am sure he didn't really hear. So I put him under room arrest for two hours this afternoon. There was no punishment in it. But it was so he will listen for a call. He just took a powder but he said he would listen when he was called. I told him I hoped so because the arrest was doubled tomorrow and was automatic if he didn't hear. I think that way it isn't punishment but just a natural sequence. And there's neither justice nor anger in it. In the emotional naughtiness I think anger is necessary but not in such things as not coming in from play. Anyway he seems to feel good about the room arrest because he got neither a sense of shame nor a loss of dignity from it. He said he thought about listening quite a lot while he was in limbo. That's the name of it. But I don't want even disapproval to be part of it. Just a sequence. You do this—and this happens. And it's nobody's fault. [8/8/49]

Over and over again during the first few years of the divorce and Gwyn's custody of the children, John expressed the view that she would eventually do something so terrible that she would be disqualified from custody. He wanted them, and he thought that he would get them eventually.

III

During the summer John and Elaine told each other that they loved each other, but they had no plans—they didn't know what was going to happen. John knew that early in August, Elaine would be going to New York with her husband and daughter—Zachary was going on location for a movie—and that he might not see her for some time. Near the end of July he wrote to her,

> Do you know when a plane flew over today I was four feet off the ground following it? Must watch that.
>
> One fault of such closeness is that words no longer convey much. Before—words can stimulate the senses and the understanding but after—they are pretty weak vehicles. Wherefor words are properly the tools of loneliness and rarely of fulfillment—the conveying of loss and frustration but no triumph like the closing of fingers on fingers or the pressure of knee on knee or the secret touching of feet under a table. Do you realize that language reaches its greatest height in sorrow and in despair—Petrarca for Laura, the Black Marigold. The fierce despair of Satan in *Paradise Lost*. L'Allegro is not nearly the poem Il Penseroso is. I suppose that what the human soul says is—"If one finds it—there is no need for words."
>
> I want to send you some records. How can I do this? Shall I send them in care of Jack? They are the recordings of Monteverdi—these have some of the passion in music that the Black Marigolds have in words....
>
> Oh! and I have a present I want to get for you one day but it will take a very long time. But all good things do take a long time. The engagement ring my father bought for my mother, a good quarter of a carat, took him several years to pay for. But when he had done that he had something. I suppose that one of the troubles with having money is that beautiful things are available without effort and so the things have not the same value. I suppose nothing in the world was ever so valuable as that quarter carat diamond....
> [7/25/49]

Elaine and her daughter, Waverly, returned from New York about the third week in August, leaving Zachary behind to finish his work in New York. John, in order to be near her, rented a small house on the beach in Malibu, and he, the children, Neale, and a nurse that he hired lived there until the children had to be sent back to Gwyn. Elaine came down almost every day from her home in Brentwood, usually with Waverly, and they all went to the beach. The boys stayed with their father into September, longer than originally planned because of an outbreak of polio in New York. Then there was a repetition of the "conference," what John called "the old tough one":

"When are you coming home to New York?" "I don't know."
"You aren't ever coming back, are you?" "That seems correct."
"Why not?" "I honestly don't know." "Do we have to go back?"
"Yes." "Why?" "I don't know." "Why can't we stay here? We can
stay in the tent—we would like it there." And Catbird [John,
Jr.]—"I *like* the tent." Catbird underlines all words. There are
bad times when I can't tell them anything and still am not willing
to lie to them, and they are not old enough for the truth because it
wouldn't make any more sense to them than it does to me. I'll have
to make this start home an awful lot of fun or there is going to be
bad heartbreak.

According to his plan "to take these months to learn about the boys
and maybe to have them learn a little about me," he claimed to have
done no work during the summer except to help Solow with *Bus* and to
confer on "Zapata." Although he had not set pen to paper, he had been
"writing," as he hinted in a letter to Pat Covici early in October:
"There was word from Kazan when I got back here [Pacific Grove]
that he did want to go on with Zapata. So I guess I will be working on
that for a little while. I do have something really jelling and want only
to get clear or half clear to get into it. And I think you might like it too."
He wrote Elaine a week later:

Everyman [an early title for *Burning Bright*] continues to grow in
my mind. My Christ! it's a dramatic thing. Now it has beginning,
middle and end and that's what three acts are and that's why there
are three acts. The 5-act play is still three acts. And the form was
imposed by the human mind, not by playwrights or critics. This
doesn't mean that external reality has beginning, middle and end
but simply that the human brain perceives it so. This letter is
growing pedagogic, isn't it? [10/11/49]

It was a very dramatic story for him because it was based on his
story. He had taken Gwyn's unpleasant revelation, the divorce, and his
own breakdown and spent the summer mentally transposing the elements in order to universalize his experience and create a modern allegory. It had been an expiation of pain and doubt and anger through
daydream.

Burning Bright would repeat several of the aspects, such as the use of
character types, which had been so severely criticized in his previous
allegory, *The Wayward Bus*. Regardless of the criticism, in his present
work he would press on further, leaving realism even farther behind as

he sought to develop a special language for his play, lyrical and essentially literary, rather than colloquial.

He had in mind a modern morality play, patterned after the fifteenth-century *Everyman*. In its model the play may have been old, but it was ahead of its time in its overall impressionism, its bizarre transplanting, for example, of the same characters into three entirely different settings—the circus, the farm, and the sea—with accompanying changes of identity, but in roles having the same relationship. It was a daring piece of writing for a writer who had gained prominence largely as the result of the supposed "realism" of *Of Mice and Men* and *The Grapes of Wrath*. Indeed, such a play was the kind of thing a writer who didn't care whether he retained his popularity or not might do.

In many ways the play (and its novelette form) was among the author's worst efforts—yet there is much that could have been said for his courage and his willingness to experiment—could have been said, but for the most part wasn't. There is bitter irony in the circumstance that with *The Wayward Bus* through *Burning Bright* to the end of his life, he did not lose his audience, while at the same time, he would be rather viciously attacked as an author who had lost his integrity by writing potboilers to please the public and make money.

One of the most acute comments about the play-novelette was made by Peter Lisca when, in talking about the language, he noted that "the closest thing to it in Steinbeck's works is found in the language of his first book, *Cup of Gold*, and indeed some of the images are taken right out of that early book." (Since *Cup of Gold* had just been reprinted in a new paperback edition, it is quite possible that Steinbeck took the occasion to reread the book and, consciously or unconsciously, "plagiarized" his own work.)

Like *The Wayward Bus*, only more so, his new work seemed to be a return in several ways to the beginnings of his career—in the emphasis on sound, in the use of a more obvious allegorical form, and the reference to historical-mythical materials. Why? First, because he had rededicated himself to being himself and setting his own artistic goals. Second, because he had always been convinced that the path to great literature seldom coincided with the modern mode of writing called Realism.

In writing *Burning Bright* he was operating almost totally in the mind, which gave him tremendous freedom, but he was also writing without the outside controls that had given discipline to his work and had moderated his excesses, often making them virtues. One control had been setting—time and place—which had been abandoned in part in *The Wayward Bus* as he turned from Mexico to a California valley created from archetypal California features. Here, and more dramatically in *Burning Bright,* in the attempt to universalize his depictions, setting provides control not only for character and event, but for language, the aspect which would cause him the most trouble in his play-novelette and, as he drew away from California permanently, cause difficulty for the remainder of his career. His correspondence in these years returns again and again to the problem of finding an appropriate language for his work—which may have been only an outward symptom of a deeper sense of displacement.

Another control had been the model of exterior situations. By using events and circumstances outside himself, he was bound to some degree to specifics; he was forced to use the specific as a means of reaching the universals he was always grasping for. Even though he loved ideas, his curiosity had provided a kind of journalistic counterbalance to his impulses toward the abstract and the poetic. His writing had been for the most part objective and exterior in its direction, but now, apparently because of his ordeal and long period of introspection, his direction had changed.

And he no longer had the control of the marketplace. Editors and publishers did not turn down his books, and no one said, "Go back and do it again." Pat Covici tried to bring the best out of him by encouragement, rather than criticism, but he was so conscious of the debt he felt he owed the writer and so painfully aware of the ordeal that the writer had been through, that he probably could not have been tough with him even if he thought he should be.

Elizabeth Otis could be tough, but he had been separated from her influence since the time of his divorce. And, of course, there was no Carol, Dook, or Ed around, willing to evoke his ire by being honest with him. Indeed, he did not want to be criticized, reined in, or interfered with. Buoyant with new health and exhilarated by the rediscovery of love, he wanted to charge unimpeded into the citadel of literature. The first time he sat down with Elaine to read from his manuscript to her, he paused and she offered a comment. "I don't want a critic," he told her, "I just need an audience." That was probably his ideal—no critics, just a small, intelligent audience.

There was another control on Steinbeck's fiction that was missing in *Burning Bright,* and that was the tension of counterbalancing between a scientific or naturalistic view of the world and a poetic-idealistic one.

About the only aspect of the play which might be thought of as offsetting the poetic-idealistic qualities of its form, setting, and language was its theme, sterility. As Frederick Bracher has stated, "When Steinbeck goes beyond the simple biological virtues, it is a set of values equally non-humanistic: the mystical. Steinbeck oscillates between two poles: the tide pool and the stars; and of the area between the animal and the saint, which most novelists have taken for their province, he has relatively little to say."

This is partly because he is a "romancer," in Hawthorne's sense of the term, rather than a novelist, since his work is always more or less allegorical. In writing about *In Dubious Battle* he said, "I'm not interested in strike as means of raising men's wages, and I'm not interested in ranting about justice and oppression, mere outcroppings which indicate the condition." The same was true of *The Moon Is Down*, when Thurber accused him of damaging the war effort by being too soft on the Germans. Steinbeck was interested in examining a certain mentality and a certain human condition—herd man in conflict with free men. He was no more concerned in this particular work with Nazi atrocities than he was in *In Dubious Battle* concerned with strikes. These were but "outcroppings" of a deeper conflict. Thurber thought the novel was a sentimental fantasy, when, in fact, it was a biological allegory.

The novelist's oscillation between "the tide pool and the stars" also came from a split in the author's view of reality. His was not the traditional New England–Puritan split of the antagonism between good and evil, but rather a complementary split between the natural and the ideal, between the material and the spiritual. But as a materialist-naturalist, the ideal and spiritual had reality for him only as manifested in nature—to be observed and measured in human behavior.

IV

As Steinbeck moved more and more obviously in the direction of overt allegory—"declaring his true colors," so to speak—the critical reaction was at first somewhat bewildered and then increasingly hostile. And once the hostility began, it never let up. It seemed to have little relationship to the quality of the work involved, since artistic successes such as *The Pearl* and *Cannery Row* were treated with as much, and in some cases more, scorn as his partial successes, *The Moon Is Down* and *The Wayward Bus*. (And his failure, *Burning Bright*, was given very little recognition for the experiment that it was.) The author himself chalked the reactions up to the tendency of critics to want to categorize everything, and their anger, he felt, was a response to his unwillingness to let himself be categorized. But the motives would seem to have been more complex than that.

Attacks on him in the late thirties and following the publication of *The Grapes of Wrath* had come mainly from the conservative popular press, and it was slow to forgive or to give up its labeling of him. But now, in the late forties, he would be squeezed from the other side, from the intellectual left, by writers in such periodicals as *The New York Times Book Review* and *The New Republic*, who held up his years of glory, the *Grapes* years, as a constant reproach to his later degeneration. One of the major dramas of the last two decades of his life would be played internally, as he battled to maintain his artistic and emotional equilibrium in the face of a growing and very intense critical hostility by the intellectual establishment. It was a painful battle because while he could fight or disregard sniping from the right, he held a number of the same values as the intellectual left.

It hurt him very much to be scorned as a popular author, since he had not wanted popularity. He had never written serious fiction for money, he considered himself an artist, and despite his common touch and for all his modesty, he had some snobbery himself in this regard, looking down on others whom he considered "best-selling" writers as being in a different category altogether. His only remedy was to follow his own lights, and there is some mystery as to why the public followed him through so many changes and experiments, whereas the critical establishment displayed so little tolerance.

Beyond a kind of knee-jerk reaction of hostility toward the popular writer, there was also the need, particularly on the part of academics, to declare their superiority by finding convenient targets for condescension, and Steinbeck became, just as Thomas Wolfe had been for years, the goat of those who find satisfaction in playing the role of the cool, detached intellectual. Steinbeck's lyricism, his emotional warmth, his humor, as well as his lack of pretentiousness, contradicted many academic critics' neo-classical, new-critical preference for a prose and approach that was "hard and dry," and they were easily persuaded that his work was sentimental.

A good deal of the growing antagonism would seem to have had political roots. Although in such books as *In Dubious Battle, Of Mice and Men,* and *The Grapes of Wrath* he wrote about the working poor, these were not propaganda novels that called for social justice and exposed the evils of capitalism, although they were often interpreted by both the right and the left as such. The intellectual left, the dominant force in the literary criticism of the thirties, was, for the most part, willing to praise Steinbeck to use him, but either refused to see Steinbeck's real themes or chose to ignore them. When during the war and thereafter his subjects changed and his themes became more apparent, its reaction was predictable.

Part of their deep hatred for the novelist came out of the peculiar conviction that he had once been a Marxist himself and had now turned traitor, although it was they who had made him a Marxist, something he had never been. It got to the point that during the Vietnam war Peter Collier in *Ramparts* would compare Steinbeck's support for American troops in the war to Ezra Pound's "aid and comfort" to the enemy during World War II.

Much of the abuse, although at least in part politically motivated, was clothed as aesthetic criticism, since it became unfashionable after the thirties to criticize literature directly on political grounds.

Their particular targets have been Steinbeck's philosophy and his use of allegory. Instead of examining his philosophy in detail and then disagreeing with it for reasons given, their practice has been to dismiss it out of hand. Prominent Marxist and liberal critics have been standard in their claim that *nothing* following *Grapes* (or at most, *Sea of Cortez*) has been of any value. Of this group only Edmund Wilson seems to have had any idea of what the novelist was talking about, but even he, without reasons, dismissed "the philosophy of Mr. Steinbeck" as "obviously not satisfactory."

Steinbeck's usual practice of developing several levels of meaning (a matter, usually, for congratulation in the work of other writers) irritated these critics enormously, and they referred to it as "fuzzy mindedness" or as a deplorable tendency toward "allegorizing," which somehow suggested that the author was moonlighting and not paying enough attention to his main job. What they wanted Steinbeck to do was to stay in the Long Valley and write about poor people; what they valued in Steinbeck's work was the realistic surface of the early novels which from their point of view dealt with "important things."

What seems to have bothered Edmund Wilson and some others was Steinbeck's thoroughgoing naturalism. While earlier naturalists mourned man's condition as a feeling, thinking animal set adrift in an indifferent universe, Steinbeck celebrated it, and this celebration was totally antithetical to the humanism that many social literary critics endorsed. What they could not forgive him was not that he denied God, the more typical naturalist's sin, but that he denied the relative importance of man. Not to see man at the center of the universe struggling with good and evil, but instead, to see him through non-teleological glasses as a special kind of animal that may survive only if he adapts was for some readers as unthinkable and heretical as Galileo was in respect to the dominant opinions of his day.

Steinbeck's early bypassing of the question of good and evil, to endorse "the love and understanding of instant acceptance" of things as they are, has seemed to some readers sentimental and an evasion of "responsibility." And his devotion to non-teleological thinking seemed simply a convenient way of begging the question. Among those who strongly objected to Steinbeck's thought on these grounds was Professor Blake Nevius, whose article, "Steinbeck: One Aspect," was sent to Steinbeck by Pat Covici in the summer of 1949. Although Steinbeck did read his reviews, usually sent to him by his publisher, he did not usually see academic articles, but after reading it and, typically, brooding about it for a bit, he wrote Covici that Nevius's article didn't make much sense,

> as most arguments do not when they are this specialized. All of the "moral critics" are shocked about illusion. They conceive it as a disease or an accident whereas a reasonably good psychiatrist could tell them that man is born with a built in mechanism of illusion, closely tied to his glands and his cortex. The form it takes may vary but illusion is as general as people. And the ones most caught in it are those (like this critic) who attempt to rationalize himself out of having them. He is the lost man. Actually, it is just as Ed and I always found, the shock of the concept of non-teleological thinking sent people into a thoughtless rage of attack. It is like the effect of abstract painting on a certain type of mind. . . .
>
> He is surely right about my preoccupation with illusion. It is probably the most important cerebral happening. Having no basis in reality it is the product of the human. He creates it and so illusion takes its place in reality because it exists and I know no other definition of reality. It can be trapped, isolated, measured and forecast and what more of reality is there. Actually the argument is only that I have used certain kinds of illusions instead of this man's illusions of good, evil, responsibility, etc. Far from evading, I think I have merely extended the boundaries. . . .
>
> This doesn't mean to be an impassioned letter but that is what it seems to turn out to be.

Back to critics—I have known for a long time that they are building their own structures which have little reference to mine. So I'm afraid I will go ahead and do my own work in my own way. There seems to be screams of pain at my moral life too. And actually it is highly moral because I am a moral person.

This letter was sent at the end of August, and at the beginning of September 1949, Covici sent him the gift of a new edition of *Don Quixote*, commenting, "I hope that when you read *Don Quixote* you go right through the second part which I never read until now. . . . I never knew that at the end Cervantes completely blends the character of Don Quixote with that of Sancho—illusion and reality becoming interchangeable." And he added, "You've been doing that for a long time."

A month and a half later John wrote Pat that he was still in the second volume of *Don Quixote*—"You know how slowly I read"—and that certainly this section of the book was the best of all. To Elaine he wrote that he could feel the second volume coming to an end

and with such grandeur and mature sadness. Nothing can take away the dignity then. He stands him up naked. He pins placards on his back (literally) and the enormous childlike dignity is still there. It is as though he said—"You see, if there is greatness no smallness has any effect." And suddenly it turns out that the book is not an attack on knight errantry but a celebration of the human spirit. [10/14/49]

CHAPTER XXXIV

I n the fall of 1949, Elaine was at home in Brentwood and John was in Pacific Grove, still struggling with "Zapata"; he kept working and working, yet could not come up with a script. Nearly all his writing time over the past few years had been spent on "Zapata," yet he had received no money for it, and he needed the money to bail himself out from the divorce and to settle his taxes. In addition to the money and the importance that he placed on the subject matter of the story, he also seemed to feel, as I pointed out earlier, that completion of the script was somehow connected to his personal and artistic survival. Zanuck was understandably impatient for the writing to be completed, but despite the earlier help of Elia Kazan, who had provided a three-page outline on what direction the script should take, Steinbeck was absolutely stuck.

At Zanuck's request, he sent what material he had, and then Zanuck handed it over to his assistant, producer and scenarist Jules Buck, to see if Buck could figure out what to do with it. Although Buck did not know Steinbeck, he was an admirer and collector of his works, so the material was put into sympathetic hands. Still, he was taken aback when he was given a stack of paper some three or four inches thick. He read through all of it. "It was," he remembers, "a very definitive breakdown of the revolution, the causes—it was magnificent—and of Zapata, the history. A master's degree is what he had, together with a Ph.D. Except it wasn't a screenplay." Not only had John researched every aspect of the revolution, he had gone in great detail into the nuances of Zapata's character. There was far, far more background material than could ever be used as a basis for a screenplay.

Zanuck asked Buck if he could get a script out of Steinbeck in about four weeks. In four weeks? Buck replied. Zanuck looked at him, and Buck said, all right, four weeks. That evening, John, who had been "in hiding" somewhere in Hollywood, and Jules met and liked each other immediately. John told him that it would take him about a week to gear up for the writing, to get into his own work rhythm. Jules, his wife, and his secretary traveled to Pacific Grove where they found motel rooms and settled in for the duration. For a week the two men talked about the material, going through it theme by theme and breaking it down into component parts. Jules would make suggestions, and John would accept or reject them, and if he rejected something, he gave his reasons why.

Then one morning, Jules came to Steinbeck's house. "I said, 'Okay John, today's the day.' I typed 'Zapata,' and then I said, 'Give me the words,' and by God, he gave me the words. No problem in copy, none." Jules sat at John's battered old IBM typewriter, while John alternately sat, paced the room, or retired to a corner to think or work something out. Every once in a while, he'd say, "Wait, let me rewrite this," and he would sit down with pencil and yellow pad.

> He would write in this very meticulous closed handwriting, and he would dictate into a recording machine and listen to a playback, listen to the flow and the rhythm of the words. And he would say, "No, that's not right," and he would do something, and then he would say, "How does this sound?" [And I would say] "Wonderful, great," whatever, you know, or "No, John, try it again." But anyway, he would always come up with something that, you know, really sparked. Or he would take an idea and say, "No, that's no good, but you gave me something else that I can use." . . .
> If he didn't understand something in his own mind, he'd say, "Wait a minute, I want to draw how the scene should be played."

And he would actually draw on a piece of paper the setting and the location of the characters in a scene. Buck recalls him doing this several times, but remembers specifically John diagramming the courting scene, wherein Zapata, the peasant, has to face Josephina's middle-class family.

During his work with Buck, he wrote often to Elaine, reporting their progress and his feelings about what they were working on at the time:

> I have been working alone tonight. It was a dialogue scene and a strange one. I think it is effective. I surely hope so, because it is a very important scene to the picture. It dam well *has* to be effective. It sounds all right in my ears. But how in others. Tomorrow more battle stuff which bores the shit out of me. All such stuff is generality and I like the particular. Battle is just faces seen for a moment that then disappear. [11/15/49]

And the next day:

> Today another tooth puller—montage. I hate it. It is a base trick
> and a lousy one. This is the only time I have used it and the only
> time I will but I guess it is necessary here to telescope material that
> has to be in and yet which cannot be permitted to take up footage.
> But the dialogue scene is pretty good and I managed to reduce a
> speech—or a scene of some charm in which a speech is got over
> without making a speech. . . . If there is anything I hate more than
> general war scenes and montage—it is a speech. [11/16/49]

He and Buck worked well together, and their progress was very rapid.
While, as Buck told him, in the studios they might average two to four
pages a day, the two of them were working so intensively that they
were averaging twelve.

They would begin at eight in the morning and break for lunch
around twelve thirty for a half hour. In his little Mexican corner fireplace, John would have a pot of stew simmering, and they would have
some of that and a little wine, and then go back to work until six. When
they were finished for the day, they would pour themselves a couple of
stiff drinks of whiskey, and Jules would return to the motel, give the
pages to his secretary, who would type all night, and the following day
present beautiful copy to John, who'd say, "My God, we couldn't possibly have gotten through all of that." In fact, they finished a first draft
in eleven days. When they were through, John looked at the title page
and said, "No, no, that's wrong. It should be put down by John Steinbeck *and* Jules Buck." "No, now just a minute, John," Jules said. "You
are the writer. I am the producer. . . . These are your words. I've only
done what a producer should do."

Before Jules left Pacific Grove, John talked to him about another
project. He had the idea that the real story of the Alamo and the Texas
Revolution had never been told, and he said to Jules, "As long as we are
going to be out of the country, why don't we do it?" His hero was not
Jim Bowie or Davy Crockett, but Santa Anna. He had come to this peculiar perspective after studying the history and having been impressed
by the Mexican side of the story and by the circumstance that they, by
this time, had freed their slaves, while we had not. It was perhaps just
as well that the project was never pursued, since he was about to marry
a Texan.

On November first, while John was still working with Jules, Elaine
called to tell him that the break from her husband had come. Earlier,

John had told her that he would never do anything to break up her marriage, but if it happened, he thought that Zachary would do it himself. "When it happens," he told her, "then you tell me right away. I will take charge completely, and I will be by your side for everything, and you will not have to worry about anything." There was something a bit strange about going out with a woman and then telling her that you would not do anything overtly to break up her marriage; nevertheless, he was trying to act as honorably as possible under the circumstances. Elaine had been separated from John for several weeks, and the situation was beginning to depress her. Her husband asked her what was wrong—a mistake—and she told him that she loved John and wanted a divorce. Zachary asked her to go up to Pacific Grove and talk the whole thing out. "I know Steinbeck's reputation," he told her, "and I think when you tell him you are going to be free, he will walk out on you."

John made arrangements for her to stay at a little family hotel near him in Pacific Grove, and they spent the weekend talking about what they should do. When she returned, she told her husband that she was going to start divorce proceedings and that afterward she and Steinbeck were going to live in New York. The divorce hearing was held on the first of December in Malibu in order to attract as little publicity as possible, and a week later Elaine, her daughter, her dog, and a maid moved to New York. In the meantime, John had finished his work with Jules Buck, and at the end of November had gone to New York and taken a room at the Plaza to wait for Elaine. They went out to look for a building where they could rent two apartments near each other and found what they wanted on East Fifty-second Street, a large apartment for Elaine, Waverly, and company, and on the floor above, a small penthouse for John. They had a "good and noisy festival" with the children Christmas eve. Just before Christmas, he wrote to Bo Beskow:

New York is exciting now. The air is crisp and cold. I walk a great deal. Indeed, from my little apartment I can walk nearly any place in the town very quickly. And it's a good town for walking. Last Christmas was a bad one without my boys. But this year I will have them on Christmas eve. Gwyn has all my books and all the money and the house and the pictures—except for your portrait of me. And I have one little room and a tiny kitchen and a bed and a card table and that is all I need with yellow pads and boxes of pencils. This she cannot nor ever will understand. But my new girl understands and likes it and so there we are.

Just after the first of the year, John started the actual writing of the play-novelette that he had been thinking about since the previous summer; its title, originally "Everyman," was now "In the Forests of the Night" (a line from the same Blake poem from which the ultimate title, *Burning Bright*, was taken). Thoughts of writing his novel seemed to fade even further into the background, as he became more and more enamored of plays and the idea of playwriting, and he started thinking of writing three plays rather than just one. (He had an idea for adapting *Cannery Row* for the stage; the subject of the third play was never mentioned.)

No doubt part of the reason for his enthusiasm was his exposure during these weeks to numerous friends of Elaine's who were connected in one way or another with Broadway, people like Richard Rodgers and Oscar Hammerstein whom Elaine had worked with on *Oklahoma!* Early in the year Elaine asked John whether he wanted her to work or not, and he replied that he would rather that she didn't take a job for now, but since he was going to be working on plays, perhaps she would be willing to act as liaison between him and the production of his work. He had always been stagestruck, he told her, and wanted very badly to do a play on his own that would be successful. He talked to her about *Of Mice and Men* and said that he had always regretted not having come East to see the play. He didn't realize until it was too late that he had made a mistake—a practical mistake in not being closer to the production where he could have learned something, and also a mistake in depriving himself, needlessly, of something that would have been pleasurable.

John spent the month working very hard on the first draft of his play, and it was a very happy, busy time for him. They had moved to New York primarily because of Elaine's affection for it, and he wrote to Elaine's sister, "I am sure that she belongs here rather than in that despondent paradise of Hollywood. She strides along the windy street cutting a swath of light as she goes. She is excited all of the time and she is near to the people and work she loves best of all." Her happiness infected him, and he was at peace with himself as he had not been for years. "One thing has happened to me," he wrote Bo Beskow. "I am not as shy and frightened as I was. I realize now what did it. Both of my wives were somehow in competition with me so that I was ashamed of being noticed. I am not a bit ashamed now. Elaine is on *my* side, not against me. The result is that I am more relaxed than I have ever been" [1/24/50].

He was meeting Elaine's friends and was introducing her to his—the people at McIntosh and Otis, the Pascal Covicis, the Harold Guinzburgs, the Maxwell Andersons, Burgess Meredith. At the end of January he wrote to his niece Joan (daughter of his sister Mary), and her husband, David Heyler, Jr.:

With fingers crossed I am finishing my play today. That's pretty fast since I started it on Jan. 9. But that doesn't take into consideration the months of thinking about it of course. Naturally we haven't done very much else but that's not entirely true either. We saw Hepburn in As You Like It and that was a really beautiful show. I had never seen it before although of course I've read it many times. Then Saturday we went to a big party for Ethel Barrymore whom I had never met. She is charming and sharp but old and a little sick. The guest list was very strange: Bernie Baruch, Abe Burrows, Saroyan, Ray Bolger, Margo, John Ringling North with a tomato (why does he do it), Frank Loesser, Leonard Bernstein, Lillian Gish. Can you remember a crazier guest list? Anyway it ended at six in the morning with a dance contest between Bolger and Margo—she in classical Spanish and he in classical Bolger. A real good party. That's the only late one I've been to since I started. Friday we're seeing Caesar & Cleo with Hardwicke and Lilli Palmer and The Happy Time, Monday, and The Cocktail Party, Wednesday. This is more theatre than I have seen in years. And I'm loving it. If I am going to do plays I'll have to know about them.

Through February he was polishing "In the Forests of the Night," reading the dialogue into a Dictaphone in order to refine it and achieve the effect, as he described it later, or a "universal language," a language that "did not intend to sound like ordinary speech, but rather by rhythm, sound, and image to give the clearest and best expression of what I wanted to say." He was trying "to lift the story to the parable expression of the morality plays." He was also making notes for his next project, which would be the dramatization of *Cannery Row*; he talked to Frank Loesser about possibly making *Of Mice and Men* into a musical play; he even entertained the idea—very briefly—of reviving "The Wizard of Maine." At the end of the month, however, he was pulled back into the never-ending "Zapata" project. He wrote Gene Solow:

Next week I have to go out to talk to Zanuck about Zapata. I'll probably get out there late Sunday night and will be staying at the Beverly Hills Hotel. I'll call you. It's a quick trip and I hope only to be away from here for a week. But conferences seem to be in order. Let us have a conference also—shall we? There's nothing like a good conference. You bring the whisky and I'll bring the communist. [2/20/50]

He and Elaine flew to Los Angeles, where they met Kazan, and the three of them drove to Zanuck's house in Palm Springs. Part of the next two months would be spent with Kazan in New York, putting the finishing touches on a script that had already been so long in the works that Zanuck was convinced he had written most of it himself.

In March, Rodgers and Hammerstein purchased "In the Forests of the Night" and made plans to produce the play in the fall. John had been talking for several months about the possibility of spending the summer in Sweden, taking Elaine and the children, and visiting Bo Beskow, but the sale of the play and the possible bad publicity for Elaine (who would not have her final decree until the end of the year) made him change his mind. He and Elaine did go that spring to Texas to meet her family, which was somewhat skeptical about John who, through frequent appearances in various gossip columns, had acquired a rather gamy reputation. (He told Covici that if only half the things they printed about him were true, he would have had a very exciting life.) Elaine had been married to Zachary Scott for thirteen years, and his family had been very close to Elaine's. Just before Elaine had filed papers, the Scotts, with the knowledge and approval of the Andersons, had come to Los Angeles to try to talk Elaine out of the divorce.

So when the time came, Steinbeck was extremely nervous, and Elaine's family was nervous—here suddenly in their living room was a very famous, and by some accounts, very strange man. He said, "I've never been so nervous in my life," and everyone relaxed.

As Elaine recalls, "He knew he had to please an aunt who was the matriarch of the family, and he knew he had to please her because we all adored her. He knew my aunt was sort of a frontierswoman so he talked cattle and grass to her and completely captivated her."

When they returned in early April, he went back to work with Kazan on "Zapata" and part of the time he worked on the play version of *Cannery Row*. He wrote to Frank and Lynn Loesser,

We miss you. I think you should never have left this city. Oh! I know you have high toned friends out there with beautiful houses. But can you get a *good* hot pastrami sandwich? No. Or raw meat at five in the morning? No.

I went up to see the boys yesterday and they were fine. Next week is Tom's vacation. Gwyn says she can't afford to take them to Florida, so I'll take them to the country. They are quite excited about it.

I can't go to Sweden this summer. I must stay with this production and I just can't leave the country this summer. I am going to try to get a place in the country about an hour out where I can take my boys and we can have fun and at the same time be available for work here. [4/50]

By mid-April, "In the Forests of the Night" was at the printers, and by the end of the month he breathed a sigh of relief, thinking he had finished with "Zapata" once and for all. He had also started a new project, as he reported to the Loessers:

I am half way through a sketch of Ed Ricketts—quite a long one to go in the front of a new edition of the Sea of Cortez. The sketch will be nearly a hundred and fifty pages long. And the phyletic catalogue will be left out. Some of the sketch is very funny.

Then I am going to make Cannery Row into a play. I have it just about laid out. I think that properly done, it will make a very good play. However, we will see. [4/22/50]

For the summer, Steinbeck rented a house from Henry Varnum Poor (which of course they called the "poorhouse") in Rockland County, near where years before he and Gwyn had lived in the house borrowed from Burgess Meredith. Meredith was still living there, Maxwell Anderson lived next door to the Poors', and the cartoonist Bill Mauldin had a house just across the road. The Poor place was a charming old stone house filled with beautiful things—antique furniture and art objects. One room was tiled with tiles Poor had made (and there was a piano in the room on which, during the summer on one occasion, Frank Loesser played the score of *Guys and Dolls*). Outside there was a pretty garden with a little stream that ran by a terrace with a table for al fresco dining.

John worked in the mornings, usually until midafternoon. He had hired a tutor-companion for the boys, a Columbia University undergraduate who kept the children out and away from the house while their father was working. Since John was concerned primarily with "toughening them up," the tutoring was primarily in swimming, rowing, football, and softball. By the end of the summer, John found them "hard as nails due to constant exercise" and looking "as wild and brown as range ponies." As far as his wife-to-be was concerned, he wrote to Bo

Beskow, "My Elaine is a wonderful girl. I can write with her sitting in the room with me and that's the best that can be said about her calmness and benignity. It is the first peace I have had with a woman" [7/50].

It was, as Elaine recalls, a marvelous summer of fun and activity, of lots of comings and goings of friends and family. There were picnics with the children and evenings of songs and poetry. (They taught the boys poems to recite, among them "The Walrus and the Carpenter" and "The Lion and the Unicorn.") It was the first time that John and Elaine had lived together and they spent time, often in the late evenings, talking about what they were going to do. John thought that he would finish the second play by late August, and after that, both plays would be in rehearsal, "Forests" in September and "Cannery Row" in October. Then that winter he would work on the big novel, and if he could get a big chunk done by spring, perhaps they could go to Europe together.

They were close enough to the city so that their friends came out to see them, and they went in to parties and to the theater. John's sister Mary came to visit for several days, and they took her to see *Peter Pan*. She didn't like it, which nonplussed John, who had enjoyed it enormously. She did take to Elaine, however, and Elaine may have been the only one of John's wives whom she thoroughly approved of. In mid-July "Zapata" came back to haunt him once again, as he and Kazan decided it needed more work. Then in August he wrote to Kazan:

Last night Elaine read me parts of the script. She liked it very much and I must say I did too. It is a little double action jewel of a script. But I was glad to hear it again because before it is mouthed by actors, I want to go over the dialogue once more for very small changes. Things like—"For that matter." "As a matter of fact"—in other words all filler wants to come out. There isn't much but there is some. I'll want no word in dialogue that has not some definite reference to the story. You said once that you would like this to be a kind of monument. By the same token I would like it to be as tight and terse as possible. It is awfully good but it can be better. Just dialogue—I heard a dozen places where I can clean it and sharpen it. But outside of that I am very much pleased with it. I truly believe it is a classic example of good film writing. So we'll make it perfect.

But his main work during the summer was on "Forests," sharpening it up for production, and on the biographical sketch of Ed Ricketts. To-

ward the end of July John reported to Pat Covici that none of the people connected with the production of the play liked the title—it was too
long and a bit too literary. Rodgers and Hammerstein suggested
"Burning Bright," which John liked, but he didn't know what to do
about the fact that the book was already in page proof at Viking. With a
bit of uncharacteristic irritation, Covici accepted the change, although
he still liked the original better: "However, your producers should
know and I would not argue against their decision. . . . We will sell the
book under any title" [7/26/50]. Also, about this same time, Covici
received a note from Carl Sandburg about a collection of Ernie Pyle
columns, and he passed on to Steinbeck Sandburg's comment: "I am
sorry there was never a book of the Steinbeck newspaper pieces during
the war. I clipped some that still are good reading." Covici added, "So
there you are," thus apparently planting the seed for the publication
eight years later of the collection *Once There Was a War* [7/20/50].

By the first week of August Steinbeck had decided against going
ahead with the dramatization of *Cannery Row*. He told Covici, "I have
finished that whole phase," and wrote Gene Solow, "I'm not going to
go over old things any more." Apparently he had also abandoned his
plans for the third play. Covici was almost ecstatic about the news that
John would not be doing any more plays: "Really exciting—I don't believe you can possibly realize how exciting it is to me that you will start
on your novel. I must admit that I am not really perturbed or disappointed that you are not going on with dramatizing *Cannery Row*"
[8/2/50].

These had been hard times for Covici, and for Viking, in regard to
the progress of their star author. There had been the period of the
breakdown, during which Covici was very supportive, but following
John's illness, rather than turning to the fiction he had planned, there
had been this constant preoccupation with "Zapata," which went on
and on, driving Covici, with all his patience and kindness, almost to
distraction. These movies and plays were, as far as the editor was concerned, a great waste of Steinbeck's talent. *Burning Bright* was a disappointment to Covici, not as measured by anything negative he said
about it, but by the fact that he said so very little about it.

By the first of August, John had submitted to Viking a draft of his
profile of Ed Ricketts, a rather impressionistic memoir, rather than the
factual, biographical introduction the editors apparently expected. Covici wrote, "I still feel that you should do a paragraph or two telling
why the profile, why the journey and Ed's influence in the undertak-

ing" [7/28/50]. Marshall Best thought that the profile appeared to be painting a portrait of a man who wasn't a success sexually and who was overcompensating. There wasn't, Best thought, enough indication in the sketch that Ricketts really knew marine biology. This criticism, which was somewhat unusual, suggests a subtle shift in attitude of the people at Viking toward Steinbeck's work, an attitude that in recent years had been rather passive and that now was becoming more critical.

As the time approached for rehearsals of *Burning Bright*, which would begin just after Labor Day, Steinbeck was still working to polish the play. Burgess Meredith, who lived nearby and dropped over to see John frequently, remembers that during the summer John was struggling with the ending for quite some time before, with a sudden inspiration, he came up with the key line, "I had to walk into the black to know—to know that every man is father to all children and every child must have all men as father." It was the line by which the central character, Joe Saul, indicates his ability to accept as his own the child born of his wife but fathered by someone else.

Meredith also remembers that despite John's general happiness during the summer, he was still smarting at the terms of the settlement with Gwyn. Meredith recalls saying to him, "Why in hell are you getting so angry about it?" as John went into a kind of tirade about how broke he was. "Listen, I know why," he replied. "It's because I'm a shrewd farmer and I like to make good deals."

During the summer Toby Street had taken a long vacation in Mexico and had written several long letters to John. At the end of August, John wrote back:

Did you find you could stand leisure? I can't very well. I go into a restless unhappy coma. It isn't that I want to work but that I don't want to not work. If that makes any sense. I am conditioned with a pencil until it has become a nervous tic. I can give the best advice about relaxing and not take any of it. I don't think I have ever been relaxed in my life—not for one single minute. That might be the secret of my failures. Too much tension always.

The summer is almost gone. We have one more week here. We start rehearsals on the 5th of Sept. . . . It's a good play, strong and simple and basic with no smartness. It will either strike with a smash or not go at all. It is a morality play, completely timeless and placeless.

As a short novel—it has been turned down by every magazine in the country. The Book Clubs would not touch it. This makes me proud of them and of me. This is a highly moral story and they are afraid of it. It also gives me reason to believe that I am not writing crap. Indeed I think it might start a new trend in the theatre— partially going back to old and valid thinking and partially something entirely new. I feel some of my old vitality and courage coming back. And I do have the electric courage of a confirmed coward. [8/30/50]

The play seemed to have every chance to succeed. It had some of the best people available—Rodgers and Hammerstein as producers, Guthrie McClintic as the director, and a cast of Kent Smith as Joe Saul, Barbara Bel Geddes as Joe's wife, Mordeen, Howard da Silva as Friend Ed, and Martin Brooks as Victor. On the day rehearsals were scheduled to begin, John wrote to Frank and Lynn Loesser (Frank's *Guys and Dolls* was set to try out in Philadelphia at the same time John's play was in Boston):

I won't know anything about how this play is going to do before it opens. One nice thing is that everyone connected with it is very enthusiastic about it. That gives me a good feeling. I am going over the lines a last time before rehearsal this labor day weekend. And of course there will be other word changes during rehearsal. Elaine is pleased because she is a fire horse and this play is her baby fire. That's a real professional. She walks on air. [9/5/50]

After rehearsals started, however, he changed his mind and decided to stay away for a while, thinking that a rest from the play might help him see it more clearly. He was an inconspicuous observer during the final rehearsals—the cast didn't even remember him being there—but when the show was taken on the road to try out, first in New Haven and then in Boston, he became an integral part of the process of solving the problems brought to light by playing in front of an audience.

The run in New Haven was brief, but they discovered at once that the play sagged in the middle. From the Ritz Carlton in Boston, John wrote Annie Laurie: "I know you will be wanting to know how things are going. I have been working on the second act. The new build and curtain goes in tonight and the opening [in Boston] on Monday. I think we have a tight and dramatic second act now but I'll know more when I see it [in rehearsal] tonight. They have practically chained me by the leg to the hotel radiator" [10/6/50]. The run in Boston was two weeks, long enough to test the play thoroughly and alter its details considerably. Steinbeck, along with Rodgers, Hammerstein, and McClintic, took notes on their own reactions and on those of the audience both during the play and intermission (eavesdropping on lobby conversations).

John worked very hard in Boston trying to save a play that already appeared to be in trouble. Aside from the usual number of lines that once on the stage simply sounded wrong, they found that lines that were meant to be straight were getting laughs. Applying his theory of the group-man to the phenomenon, he wrote later that "we found . . . to the average audience the whole subject of sex is funny if the audience is permitted to find it so. Sentences which had seemed clean were dirty to an audience although on test the same sentences were clean to an individual. . . . The group mind of an audience is very different from the minds of the individuals who compose the audience." Since the entire play dealt directly or indirectly with the subject of sex, and since it was a very serious play, problems of wording were commonplace and the remedy often difficult to find. McClintic, the director, was a man with insomnia, and he practically lived with John and Elaine, who had adjoining rooms at the Ritz, while they went over the play and John did the rewriting. By the time the run was over in Boston, the play was running smoothly and holding its audiences well—all concerned thought that they now had a play.

But according to the New York critics, who reviewed its opening on October 18, they did not. There were two favorable notices, one mixed, and, as John reported later, "a series of negatives—from a decisive no through a contemptuous no to an hysterical and emotional no, no, no." Because everyone connected with the play was so devoted to it and because it was so well directed and acted, John had come to have very high hopes. Add to this the long series of disappointments he had gone through in recent years, and it is easy to understand why the failure of *Burning Bright* was a hard pill to swallow. He wrote to Gene Solow two days later;

The critics murdered us. I don't know how long we can stay open but I would not think it would be long. And it really is a good show and audiences like it. But there you are. I've had it before and I will survive. In fact I've had it every time. But a book can wait around and a play can't. . . . We are disappointed but undestroyed.

Now I'll get to work again. One good thing about these things— they keep you from getting out of hand but they promote no humility in me. I'll not change my address.

The experience did not embitter him, however, and shortly afterward, after thinking it over and talking about it with people like Abe Burrows, he came to realize that the play was a flop, that he had not been victimized by the critics, and that the failure was his fault. He realized, as Elaine recalls, that it was written wrong—that the audience was ahead of the play all the way through. There was no dramatic suspense, no surprises.

That he was able to shrug off his failure in a relatively short period of time was testimony to a new strength, which was probably due in large part to his relationship with Elaine. The experience of working on the play and with its production had been, despite its eventual demise, pleasurable and exciting, and there were no hard feelings among the people involved. After only a short period of recovery, he began to look forward to his marriage, a new home, and new work—or, more precisely, since it was "The Salinas Valley," old work confronted at last.

He continued to write to Gene Solow who was still trying to get the film script they had written together for *The Wayward Bus* produced. Early in November John reported on his activities and plans:

I guess Elaine and I are going to buy a house. It is on 72nd St. just off third and is one of the most charming I have seen in New York. Not fancy but damned comfortable. It won't be available before Feb. 1st which will be just about right for us. I think you will like it. It is big enough but not too big. It has a little garden and some trees. Elaine is crazy about it. The main advantage is that it needs nothing, not even decoration. We can't afford to rent in these crazy times. . . .

Kazan is not back yet or if he is I haven't heard from him. I guess he had lots of censor trouble with Street Car. So I don't know anything about Zapata. . . . I am anxious to get to the large novel one way or another. That is not far away. I plan to start my false starts next week. Of course I do not know how many of them there will be. Maybe hundreds. But I do want to get on with it. [11/5/50]

Then on November 17 he added another piece to the letter:

Did I tell you that Elaine and I are going to be married December 28th at Harold Guinzburg's house? If you are here, we would like you to be with us. You surely sponsored us in unmentionable ways. Did I ever tell you the name I gave Joan Crawford who also did us some services? I called her Cover Girl. She loves the name. . . .

I have started my new novel. Have made three false starts in one week. I figure it will take about 10 false starts before it fixes itself. I guess we will not be making Zapata before next summer, which is fine for me. I can probably finish this novel by that time. . . .

We have been doing a little Xmas shopping but not much. We aren't going to do much of it this year. We need the dough for other things. For one thing we are going away for 10 days to a place unknown. This will be expensive and fine. . . .

The good part of the winter is here. The wonderful walking weather—the fine walking weather. I must have done five miles today.

The story of the composition of "The Salinas Valley," which became *East of Eden*, is a complicated and emotional one. Despite his renewed determination to be his own man, the nature of this new novel and its significance for him seems to have been dictated in large part by the expectations of others. There were pressures from all sides—from his audience, from the critics, and even from his own agents and publisher—sometimes unspoken, but felt nevertheless, to follow *The Grapes of Wrath* with a volume equally weighty and significant. Gradually the pressure was drawn from the outside to the inside and at last became an expectation that he held for himself. The delays had allowed the project to grow and grow in his own mind and assume an importance beyond what it should have had for it to remain emotionally manageable—for Steinbeck or any writer.

He described his emotional burden in a letter to George Albee, who had written him a friendly letter ending a long silence between them:

Of course I want the new book to be good. I have wanted all of them to be good. But with the others—all of them—I had a personal out. I could say—it is just really practice for "the book." If you can't do this one, the practice was not worth it. So you see I feel at once stimulated and scared. The terror of starting is invariable but I am more terrified not knowing more about technique than I did. [12/19/51]

He would also carry over and explore in more depth the emotions from his personal life, concerning his ex-wife and children, which he had used in *Burning Bright*, and the power and conflicting claims of these emotions would add considerably to the difficulty of composition. Just as his feelings had stimulated a structure of ideas that he used in his play, so too in composing his long novel he would become deeply engaged in evolving a philosophy that would allay his hurt and anger in respect to Gwyn and formulate a rationale for the salvation of his boys. This overriding concern once again for ideas would bring him into conflict with his own affection for the particular and natural and his previous plans for the novel, which had their concrete expression in a very large accumulation of notes resulting from his research on the social and economic history of the Salinas area.

During the decade of the forties, his work had seemed to waver from the more or less abstract and stylized presentations of *The Moon Is Down, The Wayward Bus, The Pearl,* and *Burning Bright,* to writing that was journalistic or very detailed descriptively, as in his war dispatches, *Cannery Row, A Russian Journal,* and *Viva Zapata!* This split, which was seldom total as expressed in the approach of any single work (even in his war dispatches there are occasional elements of the stylized and allegorical), was carried on into the composition of *East of Eden,* where the conflict between the two modes reached a sort of crisis. Rather than being resolved, the split was simply confirmed.

The conflict, whether it was ever fully articulated in his own consciousness or not, became so severe that as he approached the writing of the book, he was held in a kind of paralysis. He made more false starts than he ever had before, as he found himself going back and forth, from one approach to the other. At one point in his preliminary work, as Elizabeth Otis recalls, he had determined to write a nonfiction family history, but then he debated with himself about fictionalizing the family history. His work on *Burning Bright,* however, led him into thinking more and more about an extensive personal allegory. In the pain of the aftermath of his separation from his second wife, he spent a great deal of time brooding over questions that preoccupied him: why did she seem to work for the destruction of herself and others, and why did she seem to prefer deception, even when it accomplished nothing? Predictably, the answer he came up with was that "Why?" was the wrong question—she had no motive. She did what she did because that was the way she was. She was, to paraphrase his original title for *Of Mice and Men,* simply something that happened.

As he weighed his attraction for developing this line of thought in fiction (which had the advantage of dealing for the first time in his work with the problem of evil—the problem that Blake Nevius had accused him of evading) against the months of painstaking research he had done about Salinas and his long-standing commitment to write a detailed account of his home country, he found it impossible to decide which direction to take. His ultimate solution was to use both approaches, leaving them in suspension to balance and work one against the other. There were two schemes that he brought to his work that gave some unity to this combined approach—unity at least in his own mind. One was to use his children (when they were grown) as the audience he would write to: in each mode, realistic and allegorical, he had a story he wanted to tell his boys, one overt and the other covert. The other was the adoption of another literary model.

Elaine recalls that before his final attempt at the book, he began talking about using the true history of the Hamiltons and the Salinas area as, in his words, "intermediary chapters" between the chapters that developed the fictional history of the Trasks. He talked of this in terms of what he had already done in *The Grapes of Wrath*, but the structure of that novel was inspired by Dos Passos. *U.S.A.* could not provide a model for the kind of radical counterpoint he wanted to establish between dark allegory and "natural" history. For this he turned to one of his favorite novels, *Moby Dick*, which not only established a similar relationship between dissimilar materials, but which, in his view, espoused a non-teleological view of the universe. We cannot know which came first, thoughts of Melville or the name of the central character in *East of Eden*; nevertheless, his main character, who becomes as obsessed by the monster Cathy as Ahab does by the whale, was named after a family friend, Captain Trask, who was said to have been at one time the master of a whaling ship.

Although the combination of whaling fact and whaling allegory with biblical overtones worked for Melville, whether a similar combination is effective in *East of Eden* or not is still debated. But it wasn't just the structure of *Moby Dick* that made it a useful model, it was also that in the relationship between men and the whale there was a metaphor that gave a non-teleological answer to the theological question about the existence of evil. In a very approximate way, Cathy in *East of Eden* becomes Steinbeck's non-teleological white whale. Like so many other Steinbeck characters, she is a sport born out of nature who simply does what she does. The question is, how do those around her see her?

As he began his novel for the last time, even with his model before him, he still had grave doubts about bringing the two modes of writing together, and the complexity of the work that he had ahead of him must have seemed overwhelming. He wrote in his journal:

> Maybe I can finally write this book. All the experiment is over now. I either write the book or I do not. There can be no

excuses. The form will not be startling, the writing will be spare and lean, the concepts hard, the philosophy old and yet new born. In a sense it will be two books—the story of my county and the story of me. And I shall keep these two separate. It may be that they should not be printed together. But that we will have to see after the book is over and finished and with it a great part of me.

Contrary to the feeling that the novel was a departure in a new direction (a sudden emergence of his missionary ancestry, as one acquaintance of his put it), it was really, he felt, both an outgrowth of and a culmination to everything that he had written before. Basic to his philosophy previously and carried over into *East of Eden* are the beliefs that man is but a small part of a large whole that is nature and that this whole is only imperfectly understood by man and does not conform to his schemes or wishes. Furthermore, as part of nature, man often obscures his place and function and the true nature of his environment by putting on various kinds of blinders—whereas it is essential to both his happiness and his survival that he learn to see himself and his surroundings clearly.

In *East of Eden* Steinbeck adds a further element, prompted by his own recent struggle to survive and his concern for the future of his sons: in this materialistic, mechanistic universe, is there any chance for the individual to affect his own destiny? (For despite his using a biblical metaphor, the nature of the universe as he saw it had not changed.) His answer was a guarded "yes"—yes, to some extent under some circumstances. It remains a question still of whether man can see things as they are or not; if he can, he then has some freedom to act or at least to *be* different from what might be predicted on the basis only of genes and environment.

In other words, his boys might survive being raised by the mother who also gave them part of their blood heritage. They *need* not follow in *anyone's* footsteps. Once they see, they can choose, and to help them see, he would present in some detail another heritage, another set of genes, that to him seemed more blessed and even creatively heroic, that was also theirs. In giving his book to them, he was, in effect, leaving his last will and testament and, for whatever good it might do them, his blessing. In the back of his mind he feared that like his parents he would die relatively young; he felt very strongly that this novel might very well be the last major effort he would be able to make.

In late October of 1950, after his play *Burning Bright* had folded, John was moved to write an "apology" for it, describing his aims, the audience reaction and the critical reception, and his feelings about what happened. Obviously prompted by his disappointment, he nevertheless maintained a pleasant, objective tone, underlining his intent as not one of criticizing the critic, but rather one of describing a curious experience. Still, he expressed some surprise at the strident tone of some of the notices: "Most of the criticism seemed emotional beyond the importance and the danger of the play." With this overreaction (in his judgment) in mind, he concluded:

> I have had fun with my work and I shall insist on continuing to have fun with it. And it has been my great good fortune in the past, as I hope it will be in the future, to find enough people to go along with me to the extent of buying books, so that I may eat and continue to have fun. I do not believe that I can much endanger or embellish the great structure of English literature.

This was a public attitude that he maintained throughout his career as a means of self-defense—if he claimed little for himself, the critics could hardly attack him for not doing more.

The truth was quite different: while he often enjoyed writing smaller pieces and had fun with certain lesser works, he went through absolute hell whenever he attempted a long, serious work. Not one was started without a great deal of difficulty; not one was written without great anguish; and not one did not go through extensive and heart-rending revision. In each case he pushed himself as far as body and spirit would permit.

Thus beyond an opportunity to explain himself and relieve some bottled-up emotion, the article was also a way of relieving some of the pressure for the future. And despite some genuine modesty here (genuine because he expressed and acted such sentiments in private as well as in public), he still felt it was possible for him to write that one great book that would indeed embellish to some extent the history of English literature. He just didn't want to be held to that possibility by the expectations of others.

The last two months of 1950 were largely taken up with his attempts to get into the new novel. Then, on December 28, John and Elaine were married at the home of his publisher, Harold Guinzburg. The atmosphere was quite different from that of his marriage to Gwyn, which Gwyn's mother had described as a drunken brawl. This time there was more of decorous, family feeling to the occasion, as the Guinzburgs' young daughter, Carol, played "The Wedding March" on the piano and the couple exchanged vows in front of fifty or so close friends and family.

Henry Fonda and Susan Blanchard, Mrs. Oscar Hammerstein's daughter, were married a little later on the same day, and that night the Steinbecks were at the St. Regis and the Fondas at the Plaza. Both couples were relaxing and drinking champagne, and they called back and forth on the phone, checking up on each other periodically.

John and Elaine went to Bermuda for their honeymoon, staying at a resort bungalow at Cambridge Beaches, and while they were gone, Waverly and two of John's nieces decided they would give a party for John and Elaine's homecoming. Some of the couple's older friends advised the girls against it, thinking that perhaps they would not like to come home from their honeymoon and walk into a crowd of people, but the girls decided to go ahead anyway, and they put on a big fried chicken party and invited everyone who had been asked to the wedding. When John and Elaine arrived at Elaine's apartment on her door was a big sign: "Hell, said Mack, everybody likes a good party." And when they opened the door the place was jammed with people waiting to welcome them home.

The remainder of January was taken with a trip to Hollywood for further conferences on "Zapata" and to northern California to see family and friends. In Pacific Grove they visited with Ritch and Tal Lovejoy at some length, and John was quite taken with their young daughter Jennifer (although he insisted on spelling her name incorrectly), already an aspiring artist. On their return to New York, he wrote:

It was very good to see you. In fact Elaine and I had a very good time and we needed it because the Hollywood experience was pretty bad. But I did get the work done and I am glad of it. On the way home in the plane we made a change in a poem which may be permanent. It goes "I do not like thee Southern Cal, The reasons why I cannot tal, But this we know and know ful wal—etc."

Friday we move to our new house. . . . And this brings me to the real part of this letter which is to remind you to remind Jenifer that she has accepted a commission to paint a picture for our new house. But because I believe the rich should support art, I enclose the commission price. J. may need canvas and oils and brushes and sausages. As to the subject, we leave that entirely to her. One should never instruct an artist. Naturally, we would like to have it as soon as convenient but we do not want to rush her. Sometimes one has to think a long time before the actual work starts. . . .

In regard to the mss [of *The Log*] I promised to send you I find I don't have one. But I will send you a galley. . . . I hope you will like the account but I don't for a moment think it will be the Ed you knew. Actually I was trying to put down a feeling and an effect rather than a factual matter. The result will be of course that it will be much more effective with people who did not know him, for I am sure that Ed was as many people as he had friends. [1/29/51]

Enclosed was a card with a quarter and a dime taped to it and a note which said, "Jenifer—The extra dime is for artist's materials, postage, insurance, carrying charges, interest, and with what is left over, for just plain self-indulgence. J.S."

Several weeks later, after having detoured to two of his old addresses, the painting arrived. Steinbeck wrote, "Dear Miss Lovejoy (Jenifer): I like the painting very much. It is being framed now and in due course will hang in my library. It is a good painting. Tom on seeing it said, 'It's lots of mountains and I guess it surely is a great many mountains.' Thank you again for painting it. It is very fine. I hope to see you soon. Yours sincerely, John Steinbeck" [3/21/51].

He had timed the "official start" of composition of his novel to coincide with his and Elaine's move into their new home on the first of February, and had devised two procedures to help him focus on his work. The first was to direct his writing to his boys, and the second was to keep a daily journal while he wrote, which would take the form of a series of letters to his editor. Several years before, Pat had given him in the spirit of subtle encouragement a bound notebook of blue-ruled pages, slightly larger than those of the yellow legal pads that Steinbeck usually used. The writer planned to use this book, writing his daily journal-entry letter to Covici on the left-hand pages and the text of the novel on the right. In fact, the journal entries did not appear every single day, but for nearly every workday, and the first words of the novel were not set down until more than two weeks after the first Covici letter was written.

This initial letter, dated two days before they moved into their house on Seventy-second Street, expresses both the hope and the dread that he felt as he faced at last, without any further possibility of procrastination, the huge task that he had set for himself. Embodied in the entry is one of his best and most self-revealing statements about the nature of writing and what the writer should aim for. His aim was very high:

I am choosing to write this book to my sons. They are little boys now and they will never know what they came from through me, unless I tell them. It is not written for them to read now but when they are grown and the pains and joys have tousled them a little. And if the book is addressed to them, it is for a good reason. I want them to know how it was, I want to tell them directly, and perhaps by speaking directly to them I shall speak directly to other people. One can go off into fanciness if one writes to a huge nebulous group but I think it will be necessary to speak very straight and clearly and simply if I address my book to two little boys who will be men before they read my book. They have no background in the world of literature, they don't know the great stories of the world as we do. And so I will tell them one of the greatest, perhaps the greatest story of all—the story of good and evil, of strength and weakness, of love and hate, of beauty and ugliness. I shall try to demonstrate to them how these doubles are inseparable—how neither can exist without the other and how out of their groupings creativeness is born. I shall tell them this story against the background of the county I grew up in and along the river I know and do not love very much. For I have discovered that there are other rivers. And this my boys will not know for a long time nor can they be told. A great many never come to know that there are other rivers. Perhaps that knowledge is saved for maturity and very few people ever mature. It is enough if they flower and reseed. That is all that nature requires of them. But sometimes in a man or a woman awareness takes place—not very often and always inexplainable. There are no words for it because there is no one ever to tell. This is a secret not kept a secret, but locked in wordlessness. In utter loneliness a writer tries to explain the inexplicable. And sometimes if he is very fortunate and if the time is right, a very little of what he is trying to do trickles through—not ever much. And if he is a writer wise enough to know that it can't be done, then he is not a writer at all. A good writer always works at the impossible.

He called it "our little house," but every house that he had had that he liked he called "little" as a term of affection. In actuality their new home on Seventy-second Street was large enough to take in all the children (Waverly lived with them and the boys often came on the weekends) and to entertain a sizeable number of friends handsomely. It was a four-story brownstone, narrow and deep, and it had the two features John found the most desirable: a room upstairs he could use as a workroom and a garden in the back. At the beginning of his final assault on *East of Eden*, he sat and luxuriated in his pleasant surroundings. "At last," he wrote, in effect, to several people, "I have a room of my own!"—as if he had never had a workroom before.

He was delighted to have a drafting table to write on, something he'd always wanted (it was adjustable so that he could change his position while writing), and Elaine had bought him a comfortable swivel office chair. It was all so very pleasant that, of course, he began to worry. "I have never had it so good and comfortable," he wrote in his journal. "It does occur to me that perhaps it might be a little too comfortable. I have known such things to happen—the perfect pointed pencil—the paper persuasive—the fantastic chair and a good light and no writing."

The backyard, with partial exposure to the sun and full exposure to pollution, was from the beginning a challenge. The only access was through the house, and to his wife's dismay, all plants and supplies and tools went through the dining room and kitchen on their way to the yard—he inevitably picked the afternoon before a dinner party to leave a trail of cow manure through the house. During the years that followed, he fought poor soil, harsh weather, and bad air, trying one thing and then another in his efforts to get plants to grow where they weren't supposed to. Even with minimum success, he enjoyed it—it was an ongoing experiment in urban horticulture.

For a man who while writing could have a very short temper (in his journal he confessed, "Pat, there is so much violence in me. Sometimes I am horrified at the amount of it"), he could show extraordinary patience with cuttings, bulbs, seedlings, and unseasonable frosts. He could also become totally absorbed by some project, sitting for hours carving on a piece of wood or fashioning some new convenience for himself or the household. If what he was working on fell apart, one might hear "Nuts!" or "Rats!" or some other strangely innocuous expletive. Then, he would usually pick up the pieces, and quietly try again.

He would live in this house for thirteen years, longer than any other place since his childhood home in Salinas, and although he would continue to travel and occasionally live abroad for months at a time, he would become settled in this house as no other. The major reason for this was that Elaine created a loving, comfortable home and was willing to take charge of all the many details of day-to-day living—the bills, insurance, social obligations, and business appointments. Although once in a while her efficiency and management attitude infuriated him, he was very happy most of the time to be taken care of.

His life was assuming a different pattern, more domestic, more comfortable, and more conventional. He and Elaine spent much time decorating and furnishing their house—gradually, since there was some concern over money at this point—and the result was a home that was attractive and comfortable, but in no sense elegant or plush. Under Elaine's tender cultivation, all of his dormant domesticity blossomed, and in addition to helping her choose tables and rugs and bookcases, he assumed a role he loved as handyman and household inventor. He wrote in his journal during this period:

It is amazing how many things there are to do in a house, new house or old house. And for some reason I love to make the little repairs and improvements myself. A curious penuriousness comes out in me about paying a man twenty-five dollars for doing badly what I can do just as badly in less time. Besides I can improvise and most people can't. Give me a box of odds and ends of metal and wood and I can build dam near anything. But it isn't only penuriousness either. I love to do it. It gives me some kind of satisfaction. Now I have worked out a way of arranging plants on an old hat rack we bought. I think my method is wonderful but I had to invent it and I don't think anyone else would ever have thought of it. This gives me pleasure, believe it or not. [3/29/51]

He thought it would be amusing if by some quirk of fate he were re-membered not for his books, but for his inventions and innovations.

As he grew older he became increasingly more absent-minded and inadvertently sloppy, although consciously he wanted to be neat and organized. He liked to have everything in its place, particularly his writing materials and his tools, and it drove him crazy when he couldn't find something. His tendency to lose things was a major im-petus toward invention, so that it seemed as if he was forever thinking up various kinds of organizers, brackets, holders, and straps, so that he would find things when he needed them. But his unconscious habit of leaving small items about seemed to defeat his most ingenious inven-tions, and wherever he went in the house, he seemed to leave a trail.

Aside from his writing, the two things that he worried about during this early period of their marriage were his boys and money. Through the year that he worked on *East of Eden*, he depended on Elaine to take care of entertaining his children when they were with them, something they tended to resent. As we learn from *Journal of a Novel*, the post-humously published series of letters to Covici that accompanied the text of *East of Eden*, Thom was far more on his father's mind than John. Perhaps this was a result of a father's concern for his first born, but it also seems to have come from the perception that young John could take care of himself, while Thom always seemed very troubled. Thom's unhappiness hurt his father and caused him to identify with him: "I love him very dearly and I guess because of his faults which are my faults. I know where his pains and his panics come from. He can be ruined or made strong in this exact little time. And now is the time when I must help him—not by bolstering him up but by forcing here and making him learn to balance there." Thom had developed both emotional and learning problems, and it was left to Elaine to tutor him on weekends and during the summer—not an activity designed to put a new stepmother on the best footing with a new stepson. As Thom's problems continued, John senior worried, while Elaine, in response to her husband's concern, redoubled her efforts with them while continu-ing her care for John.

In addition, as time went by, there were the conflicts often suffered by the children of divorced parents between environments of softer and harsher discipline and between the desire in each home for primary al-legiance. In addition to a talent for warping the truth, Gwyn also had a talent for creating witty and caustic caricatures of the boys' father and stepmother. Starting when the boys were very young, she built up a picture over the years of events and character, flattering to herself and very unflattering to John and Elaine, based on supposition, reports from the boys, and her own need for self-justification, that she came to believe, as did her friends, relatives, and children. (For example, from a report to her from the boys prior to John and Elaine's wedding, which supposedly included the comment, "I don't know why he wants to marry her, mother. They've been living together for two years," Gwyn came to believe that her husband and Elaine were sleeping together prior to the time when she asked her husband for a divorce [which would put John and Elaine together nearly two years before they met]. She claimed that Elaine broke up her marriage, and that John deliberately threw her together with other men so that the way would be paved for John to divorce her and marry Elaine. She seemed to believe later that her action and statements to John were her only means to protect herself and insulate herself from John's neglect and his intention to dump her.)

On the other hand, although John and Elaine tried to guard against open criticism of Gwyn in the presence of the boys—particularly when they were very young—John could hardly disguise his antipathy for his ex-wife and in various ways sought to counteract her influence and arm his sons against her. Over the years he became painfully aware that Gwyn's version of reality was making more headway in the boys' minds than his, although there appear to be times when the boys said in effect "a pox on both your houses." Many of his closest friends have criticized him for not giving enough attention to his children; yet, references in his letters would indicate that he did as well as if not better than most divorced fathers in this regard and that his sons may have blamed him somewhat more than he deserved.

As far as Steinbeck's other worry was concerned, it does seem odd as we read through *Journal of a Novel* to find a man who buys a piano on impulse (though neither he nor his wife played) and who contemplates buying a Jaguar, also worrying about money. It would appear that such concern is endemic to the writer who has had some financial success. Steinbeck felt he had no guaranteed income (which was technically true, although book royalties and film percentages taken altogether had been paying him a substantial amount even during those recent years when he hadn't published a book), but with alimony and child support and a new household to finance, he felt he had guaranteed expenses. Steinbeck still felt that as an artist, however, what he wrote was independent of his need for money. He wrote to Pat in his journal:

You said this morning you had to sell x thousands of copies. I am sure, after all of our years together, you will not ask me to make one single change for the sake of sales except in terms of clarity. I am not writing for money any more now than I ever did. If money comes that is fine, but [if] I knew right now that this book would not sell a thousand copies, I would still write it. I want you to remember that, Pat. I have not changed in that respect even a little bit. [4/10/51]

On the other hand, he made a distinction in his mind between such serious work as he now was doing on *East of Eden* and other kinds of writing. Some things, such as journalism and motion pictures, he was willing to work on primarily for money and saw no contradiction in doing so. Indeed, as Elaine has testified, he thought of journalism, especially, as work of another sort altogether, having nothing to do with his art.

As the "shrewd farmer," he had no pangs of conscience in using his name to sell articles to make money, and he would write many pieces for a variety of periodicals in the decade to come. For the compulsive writer, journalism was a form of recreation and relaxation. Just as he had always written letters, either as a warm-up or instead of more serious work, he also had a habit of writing little articles or essays. Sometimes they involved bits of personal history; sometimes, observation on contemporary life; and sometimes they argued a point of view or proposed a solution to a problem which might be anything from what to do about reckless drivers, to how to achieve world peace. In the past, as random inspirations had come to him, he had written them down and then thrown them away, but now that there was a market for such pieces, he often had his agents try to place them. If he could get income from his recreation, so much the better. If the magazine or paper had an ultraconservative publisher—*Life* or *Reader's Digest*—he would tell Elizabeth to charge them as much as she could get.

In a more deliberate way, as I have pointed out before, he had often planned to finance his trips by writing travel sketches—a procedure with a long, honorable history in American letters—but usually had found himself too tired or busy to do the writing he had planned. Even in the spring of 1951, after deciding to spend the summer in Nantucket, he wrote his agents to see if they could arrange the publication of "a set of informal but informative articles about the Island . . . It has a fantastic history, its own language and it seems to have developed a culture and an outlook quite different from the mainland" [5/21/51]. He was trying to arrange this despite knowing that he would be spending most of every workday on his novel. In addition, he thought he would be through with *East of Eden* by the end of the year and planned a trip to Europe at that time. He already had his agents trying to line up a publisher for a series of articles to finance his travels there.

Once he had started his assault on the novel, he worked hard and steadily, although he tried to pace himself. "I don't want to get too tired," he wrote. "I want to take enough time so that I will avoid the rather terrible exhaustion of the *Grapes of Wrath*" [2/23/51]. He also felt that the pace of the writing contributed to the pace of the book as felt by the reader—*The Grapes of Wrath* had been, he thought, "headlong," and he wanted the felt pace of this book to be slow and deliberate. He figured that at a rate of two notebook pages a day, each running about 800 words, barring accidents, he would finish his draft by the first of November. By the end of March, he calculated that he was a little less than one quarter through; by the end of April, a little less than a third through a projected 200,000-word manuscript.

Very soon, after the first week or two of writing, the book began very nearly to take over his life. He depended more and more on Elaine to assume little household chores that he had performed, he became more absent-minded than usual, and he was often vague—Elaine found herself taking part in one-sided conversations. They cut back on their social life, and John stopped drinking except on weekend evenings. He seemed to immerse himself totally in the life of his novel and only pull himself partially out of that life during the intervals between writing. As he had before, he wrote in the mornings, started his journal about seven-thirty, and then continued with his work on the text until the afternoon. He tried to read in the evenings, but "I find I don't pay any attention to the script of the book because I am always thinking of my own" [7/5/51]. Many nights he lay awake all night thinking of his characters and planning the next day's work.

The totality of his involvement was no doubt due in part to the structures of "fictitious contact" that he had designed to help support him during the long ordeal, the letters to his two sons that he inserted periodically into the text (which were later removed and presumably never seen by his sons), and the daily letters to his editor. He wrote these letters as if Covici were reading them day by day, which of course was not the case, and the situation became confusing at times when he couldn't remember whether he had discussed something with Pat face to face or he had written it and Pat would not yet know of it. Nevertheless, the device was valuable in that it enabled him to be freer and more frank than he otherwise would have been.

There was an additional fictitious contact that he had not counted on: as he traced his family history, he began to live in it and with it. He identified very strongly with his grandfather, Samuel Hamilton— blacksmith, well-driller, and inventor, and told Pat, "I know you make fun of my inventions and my designs. But they are the same thing as writing. I come from a long line of inventors. This is in my blood. We are improvisors and will continue to be" [4/16/51]. Like the other Hamiltons who are featured in the novel, Samuel is a semifictional character made up of various component parts from various models: there is more in him of Steinbeck and of certain Ricketts characteristics that Steinbeck admired, than of the real grandfather as others remember him. Nevertheless, the writer believed that these *were* his people, and as he brought them back to life—his grandparents, parents, aunts, and uncles—it added for him another very emotional dimension to an already emotion-laden process.

During the course of writing, he had established contact with Pat Covici in yet another way, a process that he was afraid might prove more harmful than helpful. The editor had in the past on several occasions asked Steinbeck to submit his work to him a piece at a time in draft, but the writer had always refused. Steinbeck had a natural aversion to letting anyone see an unrevised first draft (although he would often read aloud from such a draft to his wife and others in order to test out his writing), but Pat was so persistent in his request that the writer finally, but reluctantly, gave in. Throughout the period of composition, therefore, every week either Pat picked up the week's work or Steinbeck sent it to him. Pat then had the manuscript pages typed, read them, and returned a copy of the typescript to John and kept one for himself.

Steinbeck developed very mixed feelings about this procedure. Pat, who wanted to help his friend achieve his best work, took the opportunity of his visits to the writer to discuss the work-in-progress and make suggestions. This John found intolerable, and for a time he felt he had made a great mistake. As he put it in his journal, presumably planning what he wanted to tell Pat in person:

I want to ask and even beg one thing of you—that we do not discuss the book any more when you come over. No matter how delicately we go about it, it confuses me and throws me off the story.

So from now on let's do the weather or fleas or something else but let's leave the book alone. In that way we'll have some surprises. . . . It is just too hard on me to try to write, defend and criticize all at the same time. [4/16/51]

But the following day, he had changed his mind: "I guess my note of yesterday was pretty silly. When one lives completely in a book as I do in this one the determination not to talk about it is a really futile thing." But in fact he did ask Pat the following weekend that they not talk in any detail about the book, and Pat obliged by confining his reactions to general enthusiasm and words of encouragement. This was what John had wanted anyway—week-by-week approval to help him keep going. But later, in a contradiction that was typical of him, he decided he would have to go elsewhere to get any real criticism of the book, since Pat had been too close to the writing to render an objective opinion. Several weeks into the writing he began sending his copy of the typescript to Elizabeth, who thought there might be some possibility of serializing the novel before book publication, and about the beginning of summer, Pat began passing on his copy to Harold Guinzburg at Viking. This would turn out to be the most read-in-progress of any of John's novels, although once Pat's mild suggestions had been silenced, no one would offer any real criticism of it until the first draft had been completed.

For someone so emotionally involved in a project, however, Steinbeck had a remarkably clear vision of what he was doing and where he was going, and was also aware of what many of the main criticisms of the book would be. In another journal letter he wrote:

The book does move along little by little. And it never moves back, that's one thing about it. It lacks tension and that is just exactly what I wanted and intend it to do. But it may cause trouble to you as a publisher because people have grown to expect tautness and constant action. It's like in the present-day theatre. If there isn't shouting and jumping around it isn't liked. For people seem to have lost the gift for listening. Maybe they never had it. Who knows. The admired books now were by no means the admired books of their day. I believe that Moby Dick, so much admired now, did not sell its first small first edition in ten years. And it will be worse than that with this book. It will be considered old-fashioned and old hat. And to a large extent it is—you have to look closely to see its innovations even though there are many. And in pace it is much more like Fielding than like Hemingway. I don't think the lovers of Hemingway will love this book. You may have noticed that young people in particular like only one kind of book. They cannot enlarge to like more than one. I myself have been guilty of this. [3/16/51]

But there were other problems he did not appear to be conscious of at all, and among these perhaps the most serious was that of language. While the artificial dialogue of *Burning Bright* might be overlooked or forgiven on the basis that it is stylized play language, the occasional stilted and overwrought wording of *East of Eden* would seem to have no such similar justification. Yet, the language was not a breakdown; it was deliberate. He felt that a certain nonidiomatic, literary sound was most appropriate to the effect he wanted to achieve.

In *East of Eden*, as in other recent works that displayed the same language characteristics, he had used a recording machine to work on dialogue, but it would be wrong to blame his use of a Dictaphone for what we may perceive as his stylistic lapses. His ear was still good; the machine helped him to get precisely the sound he wanted. If we fault his style, it is because his taste in sound was corrupt and his theories of how sound related to sense were wrongheaded.

His apparent misjudgment about Hemingway would seem to locate the source of his problem. Hemingway did not achieve tautness in his work through action or a fast-moving plot—in his work as a whole, there is comparatively little action or plot—but as a reaction to and contemplation of activity that has or will take place. The emphasis is on thought, not events, on suffering or shock in response to things that have happened or might happen. The tautness of his best work comes out of a language that is so perfectly appropriate that it convinces us absolutely that the suffering is real.

By comparison, Steinbeck's language, particularly in his very early and his late work, is artificial and too often unconvincing. His problem was that he was too damned literary. Hemingway broke from literature and the tradition of what one was supposed to say, to try to find the language of the "real thing." Although he was always conscious of the great literature of the past, he sought to compete with it by going beyond it—or as Carlos Baker has put it, "What he seeks to imitate is not the texture, it is the stature of the great books he reads." The "real" for Steinbeck, who had an ear trained by the Bible, Shakespeare, Milton, and, unfortunately, Donn Byrne, was what one reads rather than what one sees, what one hears by reading rather than what one hears by living. It was a tragic affliction. Too often his effort was not to find life, but to find what was literary in life or to make life like literature.

Having made the decision to include both the allegorical and the natural, his instinctive corrective for the literary was the inclusion of copious natural and historical detail. As he wrote to Pat, "I want the illusion of time passed between the happening and the story to keep it from the kind of immediacy I am trying to lose. And at the same time I want it to be believed as a record of a past truth" [5/9/51]. He found himself involved in a balancing act: the more obvious the allegory became and the more "literary" the language, the more detailed and specifically historically accurate he felt he must be about Salinas and its people.

In early April, he began taking the Salinas newspaper. Reading it gave him "a sense of closeness with the region" and kept the names of places fresh in his mind. He wrote to his sister Beth, who in turn talked to his other older sister, Esther, and between the two of them they answered his questions about family history. And in June, he hired the city editor of the Salinas paper, W. Max Gordon, to do further research for him and double-check information he planned to use: "In writing this book there are many matters of exact fact which must be accurate." He made a prodigious effort to be precise about dozens of small things that hardly anyone knew about; even the smallest references in passing to people and events went back to the real thing.

In the meantime during the spring of 1951, there had been a frustrating delay, frustrating particularly for Pat Covici, in bringing out the *Log* portion of *Sea of Cortez* with John's portrait of Ed Ricketts. The portrait had been John's idea—Pat regarded Ed as a hanger-on to John's success and all in all not a very good influence on John's work. He had been against using Ed's name as coauthor on the first book, and now that the *Log* would be published separately could see no reason to continue the coauthorship. John put up less resistance to this than he had to the earlier proposal to omit Ed, probably because Pat wanted so badly to do it his way and because Ed was no longer around to care one way or the other.

So Viking determined that with the new edition permission should be sought from Ed's heir for the single authorship. Ed had left his affairs in some confusion, and Toby Street tried unsuccessfully for several months to get some kind of agreement from the lawyers for the estate and then from young Ed. Finally, at Covici's request, John wrote a rather impatient letter to Ed, and Pat followed up by going to California to talk to him. Under this pressure, Ed, Jr., signed the agreement, with some unhappiness, in mid-June. Although neither Pat nor John had thought either had done anything wrong, the episode does not stand to their credit.

The episode does suggest, however, the extent to which John had drawn close to Pat over the last few years. He had always been fond of him, but the way Pat had stood by him through his ordeal following the divorce and the support he had unfailingly provided during the disappointments of recent years had caused fondness to grow into a deep affection. As a man of learning, sensibility, and taste, Covici might well have been able to offer some of the outside criticism that Steinbeck needed, but Steinbeck would not allow him to function in that way—as witness his reaction to Covici's attempt to offer suggestions for *East of Eden*. Instead, for a writer as troubled and doubt-ridden as Steinbeck had been, having someone always there who loved him and believed in him meant a very great deal. Covici may not have been an editor who contributed directly to the betterment of his author's writing, but he was an editor who helped his author survive in order that he could write.

It was of grave concern to John, therefore, when he found out in May that his friend had been ill and that the symptoms were similar to those of his mother's illness before she had suffered her fatal stroke. Almost in a panic, he insisted on taking Pat to see his friend Juan Negrin, a well-known neurosurgeon, in order to get a thorough, expert examination. After the examination, he wrote to Pat:

> I may have spent a worse day than yesterday but I don't recall it. And when I went over the record with Juan and saw no clot, no tumor, the relief was almost unbearable. . . .
> You must have been frightened. I would have been.
> I'm sorry if I was rough yesterday. I was wound up very tight and I'm afraid I would have been rougher if necessary.
> But there—now I can work. I told you it was a selfish matter. I couldn't stand it if anything happened to you.

He chose Pat to confide his great secret for the summer: he had purchased a small sailboat—an event that may have caused him more excitement than anything else in his life in recent years except, perhaps, his marriage. Then when they moved to Siasconset on Nantucket Island in the middle of June, his excitement turned to an equal measure of angry disappointment when a week had passed and the boat had still not arrived. By that time his secret—in the manner of most of his secrets—had evaporated in the expression of his anticipation and impatience. Accompanied by the boys, John and Elaine had taken an old, Victorian, two-story family beach house at the end of a row of widely separated houses that sat on top of a bluff near the San Katy Light. Below the bluff several trails crisscrossed down a long slope and through the swordgrass to the beach.

In June the mornings were gray, and the narrow roads across the sandy island and the wide beaches were usually deserted. Only here and there a parked station wagon near a house, the distant sound of a barking dog, or smoke from a chimney announced the presence of a year-rounder or early vacationer. At the Steinbecks, everyone was up at seven-thirty, and an hour later John was sitting at a cardtable in his room on the second floor, writing in his journal. Soon after they had arrived on the island, he wrote:

> I did not sleep last night and I look forward to those nights of discovery. I have one about once a week. And after everyone is asleep there is such quiet and peace, and it is during this time that I can explore every land and trail of thinking. Conjecture. . . . I split myself into three people. I know what they look like. One speculates and one criticises and the third tries to correlate. It usually turns out to be a fight but out of it comes the whole week's work. And it is carried on in my mind in dialogue. It's an odd experience. Under certain circumstances it might be one of those schizophrenic symptoms but as a working technique, I do not think it is bad at all. [6/19/51]

Elaine held school most every morning that summer. Thom had a reading block, and his school had asked her to teach him to read, loaning her books, charts, and other equipment to help her with her task. She worked with Thom an hour at a time, two hours in all, and John learned to read sitting beside them. They often sat outside later in the morning, and during recess if the children yelled and screamed, John would lean out his upstairs window and shout, "Can't you keep your children quiet?" After school was over, she would take them to the beach for a picnic or someplace where John couldn't hear them. The Benchleys had a summer home about a quarter of a mile away, and later in the summer after they arrived, she and Marge Benchley would take all the children on outings and to beach parties.

On July 7th, after they had been on the island for almost three weeks, John sent a "progress report" to Elizabeth:

The work goes well, I think, and there has been no loss of time. If this can only continue I will have a great gob of work done by the end of summer. The boat came and we have sailed it and it handles like a dream. Also we have bought rods and are learning to surf cast and we will be very good at it. I am getting hard and losing more stomach. We have discontinued hard liquor, except maybe Saturday nights, but we do drink beer at the family cocktail hour. . . .

It is cool—almost chilly here. It is such a wonderful place. We are falling in love with it. It is a nice quiet place but the air is filled with energy. Really a place to work as well as play. Without work I don't think I could stand it but then without work I can't much stand any place. We have no social life whatever and do not want any or at least very little. By going to work early I am usually finished by one o'clock and can then swim or sail or fish. The boys are getting brown and so am I, for even in the cool it is a burning sun.

The Lighthouse is a very good neighbor. I am sorry it is so long before you will be here. But, Lord, the summer is going fast. It will be over before we know. . . .

I stay fascinated with *East of Eden*. Never has a book so intrigued me. I only hope other people can enjoy reading it as much as I am enjoying writing it. Did you ever get the last pages?

"East of Eden" had become his firm choice as the title of his novel. In the late spring he had become dissatisfied with "The Salinas Valley," the title he had held for so many years in his mind as the name of *the* book he would someday write. The old title now seemed too narrow, and he wanted something that would refer to the Cain-Abel story, which was (as it had been for several years in his mind) the thematic framework for his own story. The new title had come to him in June as he copied out Genesis 4:1–16 from the Bible, carefully preparing for the scene in his novel (Chapter 22, section 4) where the Bible story is discussed by Adam, Lee, and Samuel as they search for names for Adam's twin sons. He wrote in his journal,

What a strange story it is and how it haunts one. I have dreaded getting into this section because I knew what the complications were likely to be. And they weren't less but more because as I went into the story more deeply I began to realize that without this story—or rather a sense of it—psychiatrists would have nothing to do. In other words this one story is the basis of all human neurosis—and if you take the fall along with it, you have the total of the psychic troubles that can happen to a human. [7/11/51]

As happened a number of times, he took these ideas which he had worked out in his journal and put them in his manuscript. The following day he wrote, as part of the section he composed, " 'Two stories have haunted us and followed us from our beginning,' Samuel said. 'We carry them along with us like invisible tails—the story of original sin and the story of Cain and Abel. And I don't understand either of them. I don't understand them at all but I feel them.' "

At this point his interest was piqued by the wording of the Lord's command to Cain regarding sin, Genesis 4:7, ". . . and if thou doest not well, sin lieth at the door. And unto thee shall be his desire, and thou shalt rule over him" [King James Version]. He compared the King James with two other translations, which gave him variously, "Do thou rule over it" and "Thou mayest rule over it." While the first two suggested prophecy and command, the last version suggested, he felt, the offering of free will: "Here is individual responsibility and the invention of conscience." This possibility excited him because it could give biblical authority to his theme of heredity versus choice, and he wrote Pat to ask him to get the original Hebrew word, which he planned to use in the book, and a scholarly discussion "both of its grammatical and etymological aspects."

Pat provided the word and also wrote to an authority to trace the word's background. In early July, Pat wrote to John:

> Your scholarly discourse I found fascinating but I am a little afraid that you are getting into deep waters. I just heard from Dr. H. L. Ginsberg of the Jewish Theological Seminary, one of our outstanding rabbinical scholars, and he told me that the word *tinshel* [*sic*], a pure future tense, means "shall." He translates the line as follows: "Thou shalt prevail over it," meaning assurance that he will do it. . . . I have written to one in Israel. [7/3/51]

There was further consultation with other authorities, both theological and linguistic scholars, and the future tense, "shall," was confirmed. However, there was disagreement over what the future tense implied, and there was some basis for interpreting it in the sense of "may" or "can," offering Cain a choice. In mid-July Pat wrote to him about a note which appeared at the bottom of the page of the Douay, 1812 Manchester edition of the Bible, referring to the passage translated as, "Thou shalt have dominion over it." The note stated, "This is a clear proof of free-will. . . . The whole discourse is about doing well or ill, and Cain is encouraged to avoid the stings of conscience, by altering his conduct, as it was in his power, how strongly so ever his passion might solicit him to evil." With this and other slim evidence that a choice might be implied and could be argued, John went ahead with his plans to feature a discussion of *timshol* (he had been misinformed—it was neither *tinshel* nor *timshel*) as a part of the central thesis of the novel, even though he was quite conscious that there would likely be some controversy about his use of the word when the book came out.

John also asked Pat to get the Hebrew characters for *timshol*—he had a secret purpose, he told Pat, that he couldn't reveal as yet. He was spending his evenings carving a box that would hold the manuscript of the novel and the accompanying journal, and when his work on the book was completed, he planned to surprise his editor by presenting the box and its contents to him as a gift. On the cover of the box, he would carve the title of the novel and below, the Hebrew word. It was a surprise he planned in great delight and anticipation, but when Pat and Dorothy visited them in Nantucket in late July–early August, he couldn't wait and showed them the box.

During July Pat's impending visit seemed to act as a spur to John's efforts, and he went through one of his most concentrated periods of writing ever. On July 16, Monday, he wrote in his journal:

> This year the weeks are padding along like ducks in line. And this one will be gone quicker than most. Saturday night Elaine and I sat up sedately drinking gin and tonic. And she read me some parts of E because I had never heard it except in my own voice and I was amazed at the charge of emotion in it. I hadn't realized it carried so much but maybe that is only to us. Wouldn't you think that on Saturday night I could get away from the book? But I couldn't.

Elaine contributed a great deal simply by being there. In the evenings, he might read from his manuscript, or he might talk out a problem:

> Eden moves along. Last night E and I went over it generally to see whether it is fulfilling its purpose and staying within the banks of its design. And it is. Amazingly enough it has openness and it has not gone out of the path I set for it. I do not see how I have managed to do this but I have. Maybe the millions of words [throughout his career] were not in vain after all. I like to think that anyway. [7/17/51]

On July 19th, Elizabeth Otis came up to stay with them for several days. The soul of discretion as a guest, she caused no changes in the household schedule on her account, and on Friday night, the day after she arrived, he added her to his audience while he read aloud the week's work, Chapter 24—the first part, dealing primarily with the Trask children. John had skipped from their infancy to eleven years old, and as Lee describes them to Samuel Hamilton, they bear a remarkable resemblance to Steinbeck's own boys (John was five and Thom almost seven). In words that the writer had used often to describe his sons and his reaction to them—Thom as troubled and Johnny as likable and self-sufficient—the character Lee says,

> "They're very different. You can't imagine how different."
> "In what way, Lee?"
> "You'll see when they come home from school. They're like two sides of a medal. Cal is sharp and dark and watchful, and his brother—well, he's a boy you like before he speaks and like more afterwards."
> "And you don't like Cal?"
> "I find myself defending him—to myself. He's fighting for his life and his brother doesn't have to fight."

As August approached and with it the Covicis' visit and then Thom's birthday at the beginning of the month and Elaine's in the middle, he began to tire. When the Covicis did arrive, there was more displacement, both physical and emotional, than they had experienced with other visitors. In the middle of their visit, he wrote to Elizabeth:

Last week was a particularly brutal one. I slept twelve hours last night in complete exhaustion and today feel better. I don't know whether the slight but constant pressure of Pat and Dorothy had much or little to do with it. I'll know next week when they are gone. I think there was a lot to it. But also there is an accumulated tiredness which must be operating. Tuesday of the week after next is Elaine's birthday and I think I am going to take Tuesday and Wednesday off. I think it would be good for me, and a kind of a sinful thing. . . .

It is hard to believe that next week we will have only one more month up here. I haven't missed a single day of work so far. God the book grinds slowly. But it moves along. And it tires me but does not bore me. That's good. I've never worked so long and with such concentration in my life. I'm glad I can do it.

Weekends are pretty much booked up from now on. I don't know whether that is good or bad. You are our favorite and ideal guest. Wanting to rest you brought a sense of rest with you, and you left us rested. Between us, the C's are leaving us tired out and I don't know why. I had to give Pat a bit of hell. He kept talking about increasing my work rate, of speeding up—telling me when I would finish. Part of it was a joke but I finally turned on him and he is contrite now and will not do that again for quite a while. [8/5/51]

Earlier, he had given Pat hell for counting words and pages, yet no one was doing any more counting, as *Journal of a Novel* makes clear, than he. Now Covici was talking about his word rate and when he would finish, which irritated Steinbeck, not because he wasn't conscious of his pace himself, but because he didn't want any outside pressure: "My first impulse on such a suggestion," he wrote, "is to stop entirely for a while and get my breath back. . . . A book takes so long that people get tired waiting. I know that. But I said at the beginning that this had to be written as though it would never be done. And if I lose that feeling for any reason, the book will go to hell" [8/3/51]. Once again he had become the long-distance runner. This time, in an effort to avoid trying to sprint the distance as he had while writing *The Grapes of Wrath*, he was trying to take it step by step and to ignore the finish line.

He had planned Elaine's birthday party for weeks. Birthdays were for him the most important holiday celebrations of the year, and his wife's birthday, through all his marriages, was always the most important of all. He loved to plot and plan, sending away for unusual presents (this birthday, among other things, he was giving Elaine a Swedish steel bow and a rack of arrows) and secreting them, working out the decorations and activities. He had written to Elizabeth, "We can't have Elaine's birthday without Japanese lanterns. Could about 1 doz. of them be bought and sent to me? Just the solid color kind in various colors. I would be awfully pleased if you could have this done. Elaine thinks she is not going to have any this year" [7/30/51]. They were, as he noted in another letter, "the birthday symbol and it would be a very sad thing not to have them." He had asked Pat to inquire for him at Abercrombie and Fitch about a small cannon used for starting yacht races, which he wanted so that he could fire a twenty-one-gun salute on her birthday. Put the information about how much they cost and so on, he told Pat, on a separate piece of paper so he could hide it from Elaine.

When Pat came to visit, he secretly brought the cannon with him, and the two talked privately of John's plans. Pat seemed to recall that although presidents and heads of state received twenty-one-gun salutes, queens and royalty received more. John asked him when he got back in New York to please look that up and send the information to him in an envelope marked "personal."

Tamara Geva, an old friend of Elaine's, and the Kent Smiths—he had played Joe Saul in *Burning Bright*—came for a visit shortly before Elaine's birthday. While the three women talked, John took Smith aside very secretively and said, "I want to show you what I bought for Elaine's birthday." He took Smith by the arm, looking furtively over his shoulder to make sure that Elaine was still engaged, and guided his guest out the door and around to the shed. After much moving of things about and digging under this and that, Steinbeck finally pulled out a small cannon. Smith just stood there for a moment with a blank expression on his face, and then recovering slightly said, "Gee, yeah, that's great. That's really nice." Steinbeck said, "There is only one woman in the world that rates a forty-one-gun salute and that's the Queen of England. Tomorrow morning on Elaine's birthday I'm going to get up at dawn and start firing that cannon. I'm going to fire it forty-one times." The next morning the cannon began to fire, with three or four minutes between each explosion for cooling and reloading. After more than an hour of this, the Coast Guard arrived and found a man dressed in blazer and captain's hat firing a small cannon out to sea. "What in hell is going on?" they asked. While reloading, Steinbeck explained that he was firing a salute to his wife on her birthday and that the only other woman who had ever had a forty-one-gun salute was the Queen of England. This seemed perfectly reasonable to the Coast Guard, who let him continue.

Elaine, in looking back on the year that John worked on *East of Eden*, has said that his work on the novel affected him deeply, but it is difficult to say precisely in what ways it may have changed him. Perhaps the best way to put it would be to say that it was the last stage in putting himself back together again after the years that had torn him apart. He had been stripped of his will, his confidence, his pride, and a large part of his sense of his own manhood; he had felt mean, and low, and was filled with self-disgust and hopelessness. Now, through his marriage and Elaine's uncompromising love, he had regained enough strength and courage to try, through the writing of *East of Eden*, to become what he thought he should be. With the successful completion of the novel, he became a whole man again. It was what might be called a "healing."

Seen in the context of his life, the sickness of his soul and the years of frustration in trying to write his big novel, and perceived with a knowledge of the incredible pressures on him that had accumulated month after month, year after year, the story told in *Journal of a Novel: The "East of Eden" Letters* is magnificent. Perhaps because of the intensity with which it was written and all the passion with which it was conceived, the novel *East of Eden*—despite what we see at the moment as its flaws—seems destined to be read and remain a part of our literature for some time to come. Yet, of the two books written at the same time, one consciously and the other, in a sense, unconsciously, it may be that the *Journal* will prove in the long run the greater of the two.

Of all the authors' journals, notebooks, and diaries that have been published, there is nothing quite like this completely honest and nearly unselfconscious exposure of the embattled self. Step by step we touch the thoughts of this modest and humane man as he tries to make himself whole again by achieving in writing more than he ever had before—"A good writer always works at the impossible." Day by day we feel this application of will, over sloth, illness, discouragement, weariness, and fear, and we gradually come to realize what it really feels like to be a writer. And in the end, there is a victory of will and thought and purpose, a small victory perhaps on the scale of victories, but a most genuine and moving one nevertheless.

After Elaine's birthday he took the rest of the week off, succeeding for a couple of days "in putting the whole book out of my mind," and then on August 20, he began the last section of the novel, Book 4. He wrote, "My mind is letting in all kinds of side things from the world of my life. That is how quickly discipline is lost. It happens very soon. And I must shake my spirit like a rag. And I will." He had little faith that all that he was trying to do would ever be known: (August 21) "I think when Harold says the book is ambitious he doesn't know how ambitious it is. Only you and I and Elaine know that. And maybe we are the only ones who will ever know it. It has things in it which will probably never come out because readers do not inspect very closely. . . . The hell with it. I'll just do my work and forget everything else." There were days of pleasure in contemplation of the work to be done: (August 22) "It is quite early. Elaine is going to take the boys to a movie this afternoon and then they are coming back and we are all going out to dinner. So I have all day at my desk and I like that. I feel so good today—just wonderful. I have a kind of soaring joyousness." And days of depression: (August 24) "Suddenly I feel lonely in a curious kind of way. I guess I am afraid. That always comes near the end of a book—the fear that you have not accomplished what you started to do." And so many days when he had to force himself to concentrate, push himself to the task: (August 27) "My brain just doesn't want to tackle it today and if I let it get away with it, tomorrow it will have another excuse. My brain is very treacherous and I do not dare to give it any freedom to wander."

And through it all, he had the sense of how strange it was to be a writer: (September 3) "Writing is a very silly business at best. There is a certain ridiculousness about putting down a picture of life. And to add to the joke—one must withdraw for a time from life in order to set down that picture. And third one must distort one's own way of life in order in some sense to simulate the normal in other lives. Having gone through all this nonsense, what emerges may well be the palest of reflections. Oh! it's a real horse's ass business."

Always there was the pressure of writing the book he had been "in training for all of his life" and always the pressure of self-doubt, the fear of failure: (September 6) "As to the work itself, only time will show whether it has been good. Sometimes it seems to me actually to have the high purpose I set for it, and at other times it seems pedestrian and trite. I know how much work must go into it after it is done but I have plenty of time for that and I am quite willing to do it. This is *the* Book still as far as I am concerned." Always, too, there was the pressure of reliving in his work the pain that had in part inspired that work.

After reading what became Chapter 38 in the published book, Pat Covici wrote to John:

> After I read the conversation between Cal and Lee, upon Cal's return from the whorehouse, I knew what had happened to you the week of your writing this chapter. All the ancient wounds were opened; disappointments and fears, and a kind of pain of what may come gripped your mind and heart. A terrible darkness must have been yours. The writing of it has great density and sharply compressed feelings. And again you hint at greater tragedy to come. [9/6/51]

John did not reply to his friend directly, but instead wrote in his journal:

> I was interested in your letter about the interview between Cal and Lee. You must never quite believe that I am putting myself down

on paper or if you do so believe, you must never say so. There are many things which must not be said but which must be translated into symbols. Robinson Jeffers once said that he wrote witches and devils outside the house in order to prevent their getting in the house. Maybe everyone does that to a certain extent. [9/10/51]

In mid-September the Steinbecks returned to New York. He took a week of rest with the move and then on September 24 wrote, "It will be hard to go to work today—hard to get back the rhythm and drive and direction—but at least I will have the energy for it. And I am looking forward to it very much. I can't work all the time but I should. The conditioned animal again. Always the conditioned animal." But as September ran into the weeks of October and the writing continued day after day, he began to tire once again: (October 7) "What a strange thing is a book. Sometimes I feel so close to it and sometimes very far away. Sometimes I love it and sometimes I hate it. I guess all of this is weariness. I dread the next scene very much. It is such a difficult one." [Chapter 47, section 1]

In October as the end of the book approached, many of the entries were short. It was as if a shortness of breath had come on and he was conserving his energy for the final lap. His pace began to quicken: (October 16) "I didn't tell you that I got up at four this morning to work on this final Cathy scene—but I did [Chapter 50, section 1]. Couldn't sleep for thinking about it and I couldn't see any reason to lie in bed waiting for daylight." And: (October 18) "If I were not so nearly finished with this volume, I would not permit myself the indiscipline of overwork. This is the falsest of economies. But since the end is in view I am permitting myself the indulgence. It is two o'clock in the morning and I can't stay away from my book" [Chapter 52, section 1].

In the final days at the end of the month he was writing largely on nerve and determination. He couldn't stop, but he was beginning to stumble: (October 27)

I feel weak and miserable today as though the sky were falling on me. And maybe it is. Weariness is on me, really creeping in, and I can't give in to it. I know that sounds strange. Rest is always supposed to be good. But it would take too long and it would be too hard to get back. So—I'm going to try to go on. Sometimes I think I'm a little nuts and sometimes worse than that. I'll shake this off as soon as I can. Sounds almost as though I were sorry for myself and I really am not. Yesterday's work was no good. I had to throw it out. I made a bad mistake in saying when I would be finished and now I find myself trying to make it when I said I would. I'll have to stop that—stop it cold. The book is more important than the finish. I'll try to re-establish in my mind the fact that the book is never going to be done. That way it will move smoothly to the finish. God knows how to do this. But yesterday's work was way off.

On November 1, he began the day, the day he predicted that he would finish, by writing, "Today I should be pretty close to finishing. . . . You can see it is going to be a tough day. But I'll do the best I can." Elaine was downstairs in jeans and sweatshirt late that afternoon, standing on a scaffold wallpapering the dining room. John came down the stairs and into the room and said, "Guess what? I have finished the book." He was exalted. They jumped and danced around the room and laughed and hugged and kissed. He said, "Let's get cleaned up and go over and read it to Pat." But first, they sat down and he read the concluding section to her. As she listened, she could feel her disappointment grow. She hated it. It was terrible, all wrong. But she said nothing of this, and they went over to Pat and Dorothy's. Once again John read his ending aloud, and Pat said, "Wonderful. Marvelous. That is a beautiful ending."

The next day, they took the manuscript to Elizabeth. She listened carefully, a small, tough-fibered woman with keen eyes. When he was through, she sat there a moment in silence, her back very straight, her lips compressed. In a voice in which a small waver of tone fought against the precision of her words, she said, "But John, that will never do."

"What do you mean?" he said.

"This is not the way to end this great big book. It's ridiculous. You certainly were in a hurry."

"No, I . . ."

"Go home," she said, "and sit this out."

PART FIVE

The Quest for New Directions

CHAPTER XXXVI

T he joy had temporarily gone out of his life, but still he granted the justice of Elizabeth's comment. He sat down at her dining room table and wrote the rough version of the present ending to the novel. Two weeks later he wrote to Bo Beskow:

> I finished my book a week ago. Just short of a thousand pages— 265,000 words. Much the longest and surely the most difficult work I have ever done. . . . I have put all the things I have wanted to write all my life. This is "the book." If it is not good I have fooled myself all the time. I don't mean I will stop but this a definite milestone and I feel released. Having done this I can do anything I want. Always I had this book waiting to be written. [11/16/51]

He still had in his mind that he would, after a year or two, write a second volume that would bring *East of Eden* from 1918, where he had left off, to the present.

In mid-November of 1951, he had thought that "correcting and rewriting" would take until about Christmas, but as it turned out, he was still working on it January 21 when he wrote Beskow to say, "The year moves frantically. I am working against time rewriting my long book. I have one third yet to go—and the hardest part." It was the kind of work he hated absolutely, and he had to force himself to do it. As far as he was concerned, the book was done. The more he had to work with it, analyze it, the more it became clearly a created thing. Later he described the process for Dook Sheffield as something "like dressing a corpse for a real nice funeral."

Although he talked about "correcting and rewriting," his idea of revision was primarily one of cutting here and there and then supplying new transitions. Whatever was involved, he "revised and revised and revised," according to Elizabeth. Whether he paid any attention or not, he got opinions from several people at Viking, from Elizabeth, and from a friend of Elizabeth's, Chase Horton, who owned the Washington Square Bookshop. He worked for nearly four months (not long enough in Elizabeth's view), by far the longest period that he had ever spent reworking a novel. When he was through, he appears to have lost his appetite for doing a second volume in the future. He wrote to Dook, "Now, I'm going to start fresh. I think this is all I am capable of in the novel. I'm going to try to learn about drama. . . . Just have to see about that."

About the time that Steinbeck was starting his revisions, John O'Hara's novel *The Farmer's Hotel* came out and received several condescending notices in the press. O'Hara, who took himself very seriously and thought that reviewers had falsely categorized him, was easily bruised by a bad press, and so Steinbeck hastened to reassure him:

> Don't let these neat, dry, cautious, stupid untalented leeches on the arts get you down. It's a hell of a good book. I wrote a letter to the Times differing with Miss Janeway.
>
> They just won't forgive originality and you'll have to get used to that. Have you found too that the same people who kicked the hell out of Appointment when it came out—now want you to write it over and over?
>
> Hoch der Christmas
>
> love to Belle,
> John
>
> I've got one hell of a rewrite job to do. [11/26/51]

There were any number of instances when bad reviews of what he considered good work by friends he loved, like O'Hara, seemed to distress him more than when he, himself, had been mocked or slighted. He wrote often to periodicals during these years, particularly to the *Times* and *Time* magazine, to protest unusually cutting or snide reviews, occasionally writing when the article was about a work he admired by an artist he didn't even know. He wrote so often, in fact, that *Time* began to comment sarcastically on his letters. Occasionally, although he was rather shy about doing so, he wrote letters of encouragement to younger writers.

Earlier in life he had avoided reading contemporary writing for fear that it would influence his own work, but since the war, his reading had been rather evenly divided between the old and the new. He found a lot to admire in the work of such writers as Bellow, Updike, and Styron, and when it came out in the early sixties Joseph Heller's *Catch-22* became one of his favorite books, one that he very much wished he could have written himself. The main sense of the war that remained with him was its terrible dishonesty. He often told a story that could have come out of the Heller novel, about an American Senator who came to North Africa while he was there. While working with an Army film crew, he witnessed this Senator at a cemetery for war dead posing in front of the graves, piously kneeling and calling out to the cameraman to be sure to get in a position so that as many crosses as possible would show behind him in the photograph.

But the writer he grew closest to was John O'Hara. On the surface, it was a rather strange combination, although both men were very complex, their lives and personalities filled with contradictions. O'Hara was usually dressed immaculately in tailor-made suits and had adopted the style and some of the mannerisms of an English gentleman. He wanted desperately the approval of his peers. He had known both Faulkner and Hemingway, and in his anxiety to be accepted by them, had opened himself up to their scorn and to rather shabby treatment by them.

He was terribly oversensitive and almost without humor about himself. Once he wrote a complaining letter to Steinbeck about getting a poor review in a Richmond paper, a review that he felt came as an act of revenge by his wife's ex-husband. Steinbeck wrote back, in jest, on a postcard, "You can't blame them for being resentful. We stole their wives." O'Hara took the card seriously and wrote a ten-page justification in reply. Steinbeck wrote a card back, "Well, I stole mine, anyway."

Every now and then O'Hara would take offense from something that Steinbeck did or said, usually without Steinbeck knowing what it was, and would not communicate with him for several months. Then just as suddenly, he would send Steinbeck a gift or invite him over for a drink as if nothing had happened. In the long run, he was among the most loyal of Steinbeck's friends. During the latter period of their friendship, O'Hara gave up drinking, and when John and Elaine went to O'Hara's house on Long Island, neither of them would accept the offer of a drink. Part of the reason for O'Hara's abstinence was that he had developed severe digestive problems, and in a typical O'Hara overreaction he became convinced that he could only eat one food without suffering. These foods would change from time to time, but once he became convinced that a certain food would provide his salvation, he would have it morning, noon, and night for months without variation. His wife, Sister, would call the Steinbecks and ask them to luncheon. "This summer we are eating egg salad," she would tell them.

The two Johns seldom talked much about what they were doing, although they occasionally wrote to each other about such things. O'Hara's concern was what he felt was his failure to make the "A list" of writers, to be mentioned in the same breath with Faulkner, Hemingway, Dos Passos, Dreiser, et al., and to be named in the press as a possible recipient of the Nobel Prize. To these anxieties, Steinbeck brought a comfortable common sense, arguing that a concern for immortality was futile and destructive, and urging that O'Hara concentrate on each individual book, getting as much pleasure as he could from each, and the hell with the rest of it. For several such friends as O'Hara, Steinbeck was loving, accepting, a gentle bear of a man.

O'Hara was grateful for the friendship. Just before Steinbeck and his wife left for Europe in early March of 1952, O'Hara sent him a gift, to which his friend responded:

> What a courteous memory you have. You did remember how I admired your hat. I shall wear the one you sent, and only it, on the jaunt through history we are about to make. Thank you. It should however have a plate on it and I think I will put one on, saying—
> THE JOHN O'HARA MEMORIAL HAT
> Thank you again. I'll wear a feather in the hat because you gave it to me.

II

As always, even while deeply involved in the problems of one project, he was thinking ahead to the next. In the middle of *East of Eden*, he had written to Pat Covici:

> I keep wondering what I will do when I finish this book. It will be a terrible jar to put down the last words. I'll have to have something very soon like right away to sop up the sorrow and something very different. I've thought I would write a play but strictly in play form this time—a comedy perhaps. I can do pretty good comedy I think. And it would be fun to write a straight play. If I seem to be anticipating, it is because it is necessary. I would hate to be left high and dry without anything when Eden is done. That would be awful. [7/51]

He did not, however, go immediately to writing a play when he finished his novel, but it was on his mind. There was a glamour about the theater for him which was constantly being fed by contact with playwrights, producers, and actors, and there was within him a need to master the craft of playwriting well enough so that he could make a play *work*. He thought of it as a challenge of learning a skill and technique, and to that end he both read up on drama and questioned, often rather persistently, his theater friends.

Among them was the dramatist Arthur Miller, whom he had first met during the war when the playwright, then unknown, was working on a screenplay about the life of Ernie Pyle. Miller and Pyle were taken by the heads of United Press to dinner at "21," and when they walked into the restaurant, Steinbeck invited them all—ten in the party—to join him at his table. The wire service men were hard drinkers, and by the time they had dinner and wine, the bill came to several hundred dollars—but Steinbeck insisted on paying it. Afterward, Steinbeck and Miller walked the streets of the city together and talked.

They saw each other rarely after that until they were both invited to a dinner party at the Covicis in January of 1952, during the time that Steinbeck was still working on the revision of *East of Eden*. Miller was now published by Viking, and during the decade that followed, they would get together from time to time either at the Covicis or at each other's houses. There were wide differences in their backgrounds, which may be one reason they found each other interesting. On one occasion, Miller was describing his boyhood in Brooklyn, and Steinbeck found it so alien that it was hard for him to understand, whereas the idea of Steinbeck riding around with a girl on a horse in his childhood sounded to Miller both very desirable and amusing—he used to kid him about it. The novelist, like most outlanders who came to the city, found more glamour, Miller thought, in New York than the natives and may have been more overwhelmed by it than he should have been. On the other hand, Miller longed for a life in the country.

Later, near the end of the decade and before Steinbeck would go on his journey with Charley, the two writers corresponded, and in one letter the novelist asked the younger Miller how he kept in touch. He seemed to feel that his generation was passing and that he no longer had a clear sense of what people were feeling and thinking. Steinbeck's move to New York and his growing sense thereafter of being cut off from those conduits of sympathy and knowledge on which a writer depends raises a problem, which, as Miller has commented in looking back,

transcends John, and that is the American writer and his relationship to any community in this society. I think what John suffered from was really a personal thing. We have an urban civilization, and John was not an urban man. He liked to think he was sometimes, and I, when I make various attempts at agriculture—which I have always done—every real farmer has a hard time keeping a straight face, as he would to anybody who wasn't born to the land. And I think one of John's problems is the same as mine or anyone else's in this country or maybe in this world where there is no continuity, or very much community. He was trying to find a community in the United States that would feed him, toward which he could react in a feeling way, rather than merely as an observer or a commentator. And I don't know if there is such a place left in the world. Faulkner tried to keep it alive, in Mississippi, but him apart, I don't know if it is possible.

Miller has put his finger on some key questions regarding the course of Steinbeck's career: Why did he leave his own land? Didn't he change and didn't his work suffer for it? If these questions imply that it was the move that altered him and that if he had stayed, he would have remained the same and written the same kinds of books, such assumptions have the cause and effect of the situation backwards. Because times had changed, Monterey had changed, and he had changed, had grown out of and away from Monterey and the Salinas Valley, he could no longer stay, even though he tried several times, as we have seen, to go back. California was not the same place and he was not the same man—whether he liked it or not, his roots had been cut away from him. But then, once a writer goes on to a new area, how does he write, a stranger without strong connections with the land and the people? This is not just a question of material—material is everywhere—but a question of motive, involvement, perspective, and impulse.

Steinbeck really did not "leave" California, in the fullest sense, until he had completed *East of Eden*. But now that he had left, how could he engage his soul? It was a question that would nag him for the rest of his life, and one that for him, as for so many other American writers, seemed without any satisfactory answer. Only a few years before his death he wrote to Dook Sheffield:

I really tried to go back to Pacific Grove to live after my breakup with my second wife. I stayed nearly a year or maybe more than a year [it was almost two years]. But it wasn't any good. I didn't belong there. I guess it was there or maybe not very long afterwards that I discovered what I should have known long before, that I don't belong anywhere. [1/14/63]

His dislocation was not only a problem of space and locale, it was also a function of time. In our society in our age, things change so rapidly that there is very little stability except in memory. In the years following *East of Eden*, the problem of turning away from the past to the present was of constant concern to Steinbeck. In the middle of the decade, he wrote to Pat Covici that he had decided he must pull away from memory: "I want to leave the past and the nostalgic. It is the disease of modern writing." Earlier in his life, themes came to him almost as an instinctive reaction to ongoing experience. Now, while he seemed to be interested in everything and concerned about a hundred things, nothing seemed to touch him deeply enough to provoke an extended fiction. Instead, the impulse to write was channeled into letters and dozens of little articles.

As time went by and he tried to push himself into serious work, he found that again and again he was drawn into a reconsideration of the past. He began to feel, on reflection, that perhaps his way of thinking about stories and his mode of writing were somehow joined to the use of memory. If he were to leave the past behind, it might be necessary for him to dismantle his style, to "tear it right down to the ground and to start over." He wrote to Elizabeth in 1954:

> When a writer starts in very young, his problems apart from his story are those of technique, of words, of rhythms, of story methods, of transition, of characterization, of ways of creating effects. But after years of trial and error most of these things are solved and one gets what is called a style. It is then that a story conceived falls into place neatly and is written down having the indelible personal hallmark of the writer. This is thought to be an ideal situation. And the writer who is able to achieve this is thought to be very fortunate.
>
> I have only just arrived at a sense of horror about this technique. If I think of a story, it is bound automatically to fall into my own personal long struggle for technique. But the penalty is terrible. The tail of the kite is designed to hold it steady in the air but it also prevents versatility in the kite and in many cases drags it to the earth. Having a technique, is it not possible that the technique not only dictates how a story is to be written but also what story is to be written. [9/17/54]

A few days later he wrote again,

> [What I wrote to you before] seems truer to me all of the time. And the necessity for a new start is also valid. I have thought and am

still thinking of the transition. Perhaps the hard discipline of play which does not have the advantage of the novelist's apology and explanation but only the iron discipline of form and the requirement that dialogue carry the whole burden not only of movement but of character. This is something I do not know and so would have to struggle with. But I have no idea in this of abandoning the novel but only starting fresh with it.

Turning away from earlier experiences, previous places, and even his habits of composition, he looked and hoped for a rebirth as a novelist during the fifties. Throughout the decade and even beyond, he planned to use the writing of plays as a way of cutting down and sweeping away what as a writer he had become, and providing the foundation for a new writer to replace the old. It was a nearly impossible challenge and one which, rather than helping him overcome his writing problems, probably made it more difficult for him to function. What was really necessary was not a rebuilding of the writer with a new technique, but rather finding a theme so engaging that it would challenge his technique to follow. As he himself pointed out to Covici in early 1956: "Technique should grow out of theme—not dictate it."

Nevertheless, he persisted in looking at the writing of plays as a means of purgation and renewal, even though during his remaining years he was never able to complete a "straight" play (by contrast to the play-novelette form he had used before). And despite a good deal of exposure to the theater, he kept a certain amount of naive awe in response to it and to theater people. There was almost a wistful quality to his dream of becoming a successful playwright, like the little boy who collects baseball cards, studies the batting averages and box scores, and aspires to be a big-league player.

For him, Arthur Miller, and others like him, were major leaguers, bigger than life. Miller recalls that when they saw each other from time to time during the early fifties, they never discussed what Steinbeck had done or was doing—"I never dared . . . you see he had a ferocious kind of self-modesty—a good quality—he was practically alone among writers in that respect." Occasionally they would talk about Stendhal, or someone like that, and very infrequently contemporary writing, but "the thing he loved to talk about with me was the theater, because John was a sucker for the theater, for actors, for acting, for directing . . ." He regarded Miller as the "old pro"—as if he never failed, knew exactly what to do at all times.

Perhaps, as Miller suggests, most successful novelists aspire also to be successful playwrights, but for Steinbeck there was something in it beyond simply the success of a second career. There was a compelling mystique and the attraction of a very special and demanding craftsmanship:

> [He] seriously ached to be what he conceived to be an expert playwright. He rather worshipped expertise in the theater. I know he loved Kaufman and Hart's comedies and musicals—some of them were wonderful, you know. . . . And he also had a tremendous respect for any craft whether it be carving wood, or being a mechanic, or an astronomer or a playwright. A playwright in his view of it at that time was a craftsman—maybe more so than most novelists would have to be. You see a novelist could get away with more. A play that is boring for more than a few minutes is done. We all know that there are many great novels that are boring for more than one-half the time. You can't say that about a play.

III

After completing the revisions on *East of Eden*, Steinbeck planned a trip abroad. It was to be a long vacation, except that he planned once again to finance the trip by writing articles. This time, possibly because his finances were still rather rocky, he was serious about the articles, and Elizabeth Otis had been negotiating with publisher Edward Anthony of *Collier's* for several weeks. The ultimate price, recalls managing editor Gordon Manning, was so steep that it threatened to throw the budget for those issues out of kilter—it was one thing to have a very attractive by-line for your magazine, another to have to try to compensate for the cost.

The articles were not to be serious discussions of politics or issues, but rather a gathering of personal impressions. It was to be Steinbeck-at-large, *Collier's* depending on Steinbeck's curiosity and ability to get close to ordinary people. As the editors considered the possible articles—Steinbeck talks to a blacksmith, winemaker, restaurant owner, or waiter—they considered how they would illustrate these things and decided they would have to have photographs. Since the Steinbecks were not keen on having a third person along, Elaine volunteered to take pictures, and the photo editor, Bill Stapleton, taught her how to use a Rolleiflex (later, in Paris, she would also take lessons from Capa).

This would be the first of several long trips abroad for John and Elaine—in fact, during the remainder of his life they would spend almost as much time outside the country as at home. Although he was

usually either writing or doing research for writing while he was overseas, his nearly insatiable appetite for travel—which could now be indulged, since he had both the means and a wife who enjoyed it—was
another factor that weighed against the accomplishment of serious
work during the last decade and a half of his life. Besides taking up
much of his time and energy, travel took him away from his natural
subject matter (which, if not California, was at least life among ordinary Americans in their native land) and contributed a great deal to his
later feelings of being out of touch. Although with *The Pearl* and *Zapata* he had written well of Mexico, his work in response to France
(*Pippin*) and his research in England (*Arthur*) were not, for differing
reasons, very successful. Like his travel, both projects were somewhat
self-indulgent—yet, as one of his friends commented in looking back,
"John was not an institution with institutional responsibilities—why
shouldn't he do what he wanted to do?"

By the time he had married Elaine, of course, he was already a sea-
soned traveler. While they were packing for this first trip to Europe,
Elaine was thinking in terms of style—what she could wear in various
climates—and John would interrupt to hand her a screwdriver, a pair of
pliers, a small hammer, and a container of assorted nuts, bolts, screws
and nails, saying, "Here, would you just slip this into one of your
shoes?" He was a good traveler in the sense that he was good at making
do when through the inevitable mishaps and confusion of travel things
went awry. When they were in big cities, however, he enjoyed staying
at the best hotels and wanted a lot of service and as much comfort as
possible. At such hotels they would usually take two rooms, so that he
would have one to write in.

It had become his habit in New York to get up early but to stay in his
robe during the morning, and he carried over this practice to his stays
in the luxury hotels of Paris, London, and Rome. Getting up around
seven, he would order coffee and the papers, sometimes having breakfast and sometimes waiting for Elaine, and during the remainder of the
morning he would write letters or work on his articles. He occasionally
received reporters for interviews, not that he liked being interviewed
any more than he had before, but he liked talking to local journalists
wherever he went. He became adept at providing a little information
about his recent work and almost no information about his personal
life, while at the same time milking the journalists to get the clearest
possible picture of local conditions and issues. In the meantime, Elaine
would go out and discover the city for herself. Later in the day, John

would dress—always in a suit, if they were in a city—and they would go out together.

Usually when they were in Europe, they traveled by car (purchased for the duration of the trip and then sold). When they were touring the countryside, moving from village to village, they would get up fairly early, have their breakfast together in their room, and then while John paid the bill at the inn and filled the car with gas, Elaine would go shopping for bread, sausage, cheese, tomatoes, and a bottle of wine; later they would find a pretty place to stop and have a picnic.

Elaine rapidly adapted to his mode: he wanted to go where he wanted to go and see what he wanted to see and "he really didn't give a damn about what anybody else wanted to see." On those few occasions when they tried to go with other people, the journey became chaotic and unpleasant. He did not sightsee casually. When he got to where he was going, he was slow, deliberate, and intense, and if they were with others, he would almost always be deeply engaged long after everyone else was tired and ready to move on. Wherever they went, he searched for the essence of the place; he wanted to rebuild the life of it in his imagination.

Although he was often preoccupied with his own goals while they were sightseeing, Elaine found in him an extraordinary guide. He enjoyed showing her the cities that he knew—Paris, London, and Stockholm, in particular—and he was delighted when, as a result of her reading, she could point out to him the landmarks. But it was usually he who did the pointing and reciting. He had an unusually extensive fund of knowledge about the historical and archeological sites of Italy, Greece, and England, as if he had been reading all his life in preparation for seeing them. Elaine recalls going to Hadrian's Villa outside Rome, during their first European tour: "It is a ruin that is not very complete. We spent most of the day, and he knew it so well that he built it back for me before my eyes."

In late March of 1952, John and Elaine left from New York on a freighter bound for Genoa, Italy and then Greece. In passage, however, the ship changed its destination, stopping first at North Africa. Elaine wrote to Pat Covici, "We are anchored in Casablanca harbor and we have just heard a donkey bray—the first land sound in 11 days. J and I stood on the forward deck for 3 hours, from the first moment of spotting the mainland till we dropped anchor—we came into port at sunset and now the city lights are all around us and the sky is full of stars."

From Casablanca they went to Algiers and to an all-night party at the palace of the French general of the air force, with "oceans of champagne, singing and dancing and fun," and from there they took a boat to Marseilles. They rented an old Dodge with an American driver and motored down the east coast of Spain, then in from Valencia and through Granada to Seville.

John had never been in Spain before, and he reported that it was very different from what he had expected. "Seville is *wonderful!*" he wrote back home, and "Spain excites me as I have rarely been excited" [4/10/52]. They toured the city and examined the Moorish architecture, spending a lot of time at the great cathedral and the Giralda, and they did the tourist things such as watching the Gypsies and the flamenco dancing. But John also took at least an hour a day to go to the museum on the Guadalquivir River to read the Christopher Columbus letters there. These were, for him, the great connection with history, the essence of the place.

In Madrid they concentrated on the art, going to the Prado and then to Toledo to see the El Grecos. As was his habit when he came to a major city, Steinbeck dropped his card off at the American Embassy. From his early days as a volunteer with the F.I.S. at the beginning of World War II, he had supported the American information services, now the U.S.I.S., performing whatever small tasks they would ask of him. Quite often he would be asked to a reception at the American library to meet with young writers and students, would help the libraries with lists of books, or would sometimes be taken by the American mission to a nearby university to talk informally with students and faculty, or to accompany the agronomists or other American technical experts to villages and farms. Such activities on behalf of his country were expressions of his old-fashioned sense of duty—although he never talked or thought about these activities in those terms.

He had begun to worry about doing the articles he had promised to *Collier's*. After two or three days in North Africa, he had written that he had found nothing suitable for the sort of articles he had in mind, and now, after being in Spain for several weeks, he was feeling very guilty: "I seem silly to myself having said that such oceans of copy were going to pour out and then nothing. I do hope this won't continue too long but there is no question that it will at least for another week" [4/18/52]. By early May he had outlined several possible pieces, including one on the bullfighter Litri: "I think of doing a story on him from childhood with pictures—not Hemingway but the story of a man.

I'll talk to his mother and father and friends if I can—go to his birth-place which is two hours away. He is pure courage and a kind of pure genius." He and Elaine were going to the bull fights in Seville every day. They "leave us," he reported, "with the breathlessness that comes of hearing great and moving music" [4/52].

By accident they had acquired a very good guide to the fights, a hap-penstance that he later recounted in a letter to Barnaby Conrad, after Conrad had written to thank him for praising his book *Matador:*

> I liked Matador for a number of reasons chief of which was that I believed it. I am not informed enough to be an aficionado but that has nothing to do with it. If I had never been near a bull ring I would still have believed it. That makes it good to me. . . .
>
> You will be amused at something that happened to me last year. I had very good seats for the week at the Feria in Seville 2nd row sombra right with the newspaper critics. A nice little business type man in a double breasted suit sat next to me all week and he was very kind in explaining many things. My questions were extremely naive and he was very nice to us. Only afterwards did I discover that the little business man was Juan Belmonte. [12/29/52]

Although he had intended to start writing while he was still in Spain, he wrote: "I must say I am anxious to get to work but such are the paradoxes here that it will take some doing to clarify them in my own mind" [5/3/52]. On May 10 they took the train to Paris, and two days later he got up early and began work on his first article on Spain. Gor-don Manning had sent some suggestions regarding things he might cover in such a piece, and Steinbeck dutifully tried to include com-mentary on all, though it was difficult to do in a mere 5,000 words. Prodded by a guilty conscience aroused by a month without writing, he pressed himself very hard to do the kind of job that he thought *Collier's* wanted.

There was time enough, however, to see Paris, and for Elaine it was the first time. He wrote Pat:

> Paris is always wonderful—both recognized and new everytime. This time the chestnuts are blooming and the trees are in full leaf and it is the core of spring. We walked for three hours this after-noon—from the Arch to the Concorde and to the river and back. Sunday and sun and everyone was out walking. The Champs was crowded with people all walking and not going anyplace just as we weren't. [5/12/52]

And he added in a letter to Elizabeth that "Elaine is on fire with Paris. She will know the city better in a week than I will ever learn it" [5/12/52]. At the Lancaster where they were staying they ran into Darryl Zanuck, as well as Frank and Lynn Loesser, and later they discovered that Jules and Joyce Buck were also in Paris.

Buck recalls that Steinbeck felt he owed him something for his help with *Zapata*—"He didn't owe me a damned thing. On the contrary, I owed John."—and John thought that he could repay Buck by collaborating with him on another movie project. His idea for a script was to adapt and rewrite one of Ibsen's early and nearly unknown plays, *The Vikings at Helgoland*, which, as he wrote Dook later in the year, struck him as "a roaring melodrama, cluttered and verbose but with great dramatic construction and character relationships." References in other letters indicate it was a project that he had had in mind for several years.

After talking to Buck about the possibilities in the play, Steinbeck spent several days trying to track down a copy, finally locating one at Shakespeare & Company. He gave the play to Buck and said, "Here, read this." When he asked, "Well, what did you think of it?" Buck said, "I think it is bloody awful." "What do you mean," John replied, "it's fucking terrible. But it might make a really good picture." Steinbeck spent most of May, part of July, and August working on his articles and planning the script. At the end of August he wrote to Pat Covici from Paris:

> If we weren't so busy now, we would be very itchy because we want to get home. But we are busy. Elaine is shopping for the last things and I am devoting this last week to writing a complete picture script dialogue and all. And I must say it is pretty good. But I haven't had on clothes for days. I get up, go to work in a bathrobe, eat in the room and when I can't work any longer fall into bed only to wake up and go to work again. It is a little rough but I must admit that it has one advantage. When I finish it, the day after tomorrow or Sunday morning, it will be done. [8/28/52]

When it was completed, Buck thought it was quite good, but for various reasons (including another movie called "The Vikings" that went into production not too long after this) the picture was never made. Before leaving Paris, Steinbeck gave Buck a package, saying, "Here—I'm giving you the source material for all stories. You'll have no problems after this." Buck said, "What is it, John?" "The Bible."

He had sent the first article, on Spain, to *Collier's* on May 17, but despite a great effort on his part to give them what he thought they wanted, he was notified a week later that the magazine had rejected it. Frustrated and angry, he wrote Elizabeth:

> Your letter this morning with Collier's reaction to the first piece. This first piece was written to order. I won't make that mistake again. I enclose the wire specifying the kind of piece required. If you can see how I could have covered all of these fields in a whole nation in 5,000 words by any other method I'll eat it. Maybe I could have done better but not much different. It may turn out that they don't want my stuff at all but Collier's stuff with my name on it. As for its not being my kind of stuff, that's balderdash. One wants Tortilla Flat and another [*Collier's* editor] Grapes of Wrath. I write all kinds of stuff. I will not again follow their rules. They can accept or reject, but I will not work it over and over until it sounds like Quent Reynolds. [5/26/52]

In addition, people at home were writing him that he should do this or that, go here or there. When the Steinbecks by the end of May had spent several weeks in Spain and several in Paris, Covici wrote to John, your "continental trip is beginning to puzzle me"—a euphemistic way of expressing his irritation that John had not focused on what he, Covici, thought most important. In his letter to Elizabeth, cited above, John continued:

> It is certain that we have changed our plans. We changed them to match conditions we didn't know about in advance. Pat writes saying I should go to Israel, Manning thinks I should go to the Slovak border. I am going to the Jura. If they think I am hanging around Paris too long—let them. I have been gathering a sense of Europe here. I know where to go now and what for. I could not have known without coming here. This is not a city desk assignment.

He had decided to go to the Jura, the mountains which separate France from Switzerland, at the invitation of a schoolteacher in the village of Poligny. Most of Steinbeck's mail was of course screened by his very protecting agents, but interesting letters were often passed along, including, several years earlier, a letter from Louis Gibey, the teacher, which had led to a small correspondence. A comment in one of the teacher's letters had even prompted Steinbeck to send, through Elizabeth Otis, several bare-root fruit trees to him. And now, having read in the papers that the writer was in France, Gibey had written to invite him to stay at his home. He warned that he had a toilet, but no water, and three daughters: "They have many friends whom I hope will not bother you." Steinbeck saw it as a wonderful chance to see French farm life.

The Steinbecks had found renting a car in Spain "ruinously" expensive and so through his French literary agent, they bought a good second-hand car, which Elaine, picking up her husband's predilection for naming things, called "Aux Armes O Citroën." Very near the end of May, they drove from Paris, stopped in Dijon for the night, and arrived in Poligny the next day. The village lies in the pass that leads upward through the mountains to Switzerland. It is an old village, probably dating back before the time of the Romans, and a tower and part of a wall are left from the Middle Ages. The area is known for its fine wines, and Louis Gibey not only taught English in the local school, but raised grapes as well.

His neighbors were the peasant farmers of the district. Tough and independent, many of them fought with the *maquis* against the Germans, and a good number bore the marks of wounds or of the suffering of the concentration camps. Gibey lived in a very old house on a dirt street, "no plumbing, no inside toilet, three little girls, two hunting dogs, flies, crumbs, bees from the hives in the yard, shouting of neighbors and birds, street full of cows, a fine dust of manure over everything." Living conditions were primitive, and the region had not yet recovered from the war, but food was plentiful, the wine, excellent, and the Gibeys would not hear of the Steinbecks staying at a hotel; they gave them the best room in the house, newly replastered in their honor. And the children had new shoes for the occasion: "But the shoes had been bought for glory rather than comfort and hurt the little girls' feet. Mostly the shoes were left off but kept on display, thus preserving both grandeur and comfort."

Not long after the Steinbecks were settled, they were introduced to the major concerns of their host and his neighbors: wine, hunting, and politics. Of these, wine was by far the most important. They were taken to the wine caves and to the partially destroyed church which, since it was cool, had been converted to use as a winery. Hearing of the visit of the American author, people from all around the area came to visit the Gibeys', and the Steinbecks were taken to visit one home after another. At each, as Steinbeck described their experiences in his article, the host brings a crusty bottle up from below ground. His wife rushes wonderful cheese to the table. A little girl lugs in a loaf of bread approximately as big as she is. The bread has a fine crisp crust and the sour taste of great French bread. Now you are ready for business.

Your host handles the dusty bottle as tenderly as he might move a flask of nitroglycerin. A silence falls on the room as he slowly twists the corkscrew in. There is a tiny squeak as the cork comes out. Your host looks at the cork, turns it over, smells it and then passes it to his guests.

The wine is poured, savored, and discussed at length. The glasses are refilled, and in the meantime, a neighbor has slipped home and returns with a dusty bottle from his own cellar. The talk goes on, about wine, and these people "are like all country people. They boast that their wine is the finest in France and yet they find fault with every bottle they open."

With all of their marvelous hospitality, the French were watchful, curious about their guests, and every now and then, in one way or another, they tested the Americans. As Elaine recalls, at one home, a very striking-looking man strode in. He had dark piercing eyes and a great scar across his face, and was dressed in a pair of American paratrooper pants. As he passed, John asked him, "Where did you get the pants?" In a very rough, challenging voice the man said, "I had to kill me an American to get them." John never changed his expression or shifted his eyes. He said, "That's funny, in America we kill just for fun. But never for pants." The man threw back his head and laughed, and they became friends.

They stayed five days at Poligny and were taken by their hosts to several of the other villages and small towns in the area. Everywhere they went the Steinbecks were given gifts of wine to take with them on their travels. From the Jura they motored to Geneva. The contrast was striking. In Paris they had met Faye Emerson, who had stayed at the same hotel in Geneva that they were staying in now, and she had said about it, "Remember how you always heard of a place where you could eat off the floor? Well, I've just seen it." After the Steinbecks arrived, they began taking baths—one bath after another. The hotel was immaculate, and the entire staff spoke English, a relief after straining for days to understand in a language not their own. It had been a particular strain on John who, through the generous flow of wine and local idiom, was trying to catch and remember every word of the conversation that he could. Reflecting on the contrast between the two places, John wrote to Elizabeth that while it was pleasant to have a hot bath, "I like both things, though."

During the several days they were in Geneva, they managed to rest, see the sights, and work. Elaine was busy arranging their Italian itinerary and accommodations, as well as with trying to get their clothes back in shape. John wrote his article on what they had seen and heard in the Jura; it would be called "The Soul and Guts of France" and was the first of his articles written in Europe published by *Collier's*.

Collier's had shown good taste. There is no telling what the two articles on Spain were like, but this, certainly, was very well done, combining good journalism with those things that were "Steinbeck": genuine interaction with ordinary people—drawing them out; an uncanny recreating of the feeling of the place and its people that goes far deeper than the usual reporting; and a touch of the novelist Steinbeck who is willing to take the risks of sound and sentiment that other writers will not take.

IV

From Geneva, they took two weeks to drive over the Simplon Pass through Milan, Verona, Venice, Florence, and then to Rome. In Venice John was asked by the American Consulate to open an adjunct of the Venice Art Exhibition, at which would be displayed sixty-five reproductions of famous paintings depicting life in the United States. The Steinbecks met Peggy Guggenheim at the opening, and she invited them to her villa on the Grand Canal to see her collection of modern art (one of the finest in the world), then loaned the Steinbecks the use of her gondola, with her gondoliers dressed in her livery, for the duration of their stay in Venice. Their report of their adventures prompted Pat to write to them, "It wouldn't surprise me at all if you were soon to be elected Duke, and Elaine, Duchess, of Venice."

In driving from Venice to Florence, in the Tuscan hills, they had a very upsetting experience. As they were climbing up into the pass, a motorscooter almost hit them head-on and then went on to crash into a stone wall. They carried the injured Italian couple fifty miles to a hospital in Florence, the couple in the front seat of the Citroën with Elaine in the back crouched on top of the luggage. In Rome, after the shock had worn off, John began to think of the experience, as writers will, as the lead to a possible story. He was suddenly aware of the little scooters everywhere, and he thought they might be changing the way of life in Italy as much as the Ford changed America. He wired *Collier's* to ask if the editors would be interested in such a story.

This was but one of many ideas for stories that fill his letters of the period. He had had an idea in Paris to do a humorous article on high fashion from the man's point of view, and he talked about doing an article on possible future trends in Italian politics and about doing one in the manner of his piece on the Jura about a peasant community in Italy. He started some of them, completed a few, but by the time he had gotten to Rome, he had been in Europe more than three months and had not yet had an article accepted, let alone printed (he had not yet been notified that *Collier's* had taken the Jura piece).

He began to worry terribly about the dual problem of his failure to produce and lack of money. He had earned no pay for his writing and he felt guilty that he had not even earned his expenses. Near the end of June he wrote to his agent:

> I have a kind of desolate feeling of failure in this whole trip. I wish I could talk to Mr. Anthony again. I like him. Maybe you will talk to him. I hesitate to have the things I would like to tell him read all over the Collier's office. I have not heard from him as yet about the scooter story but will probably tonight or tomorrow. But what I would like to tell him is that when you have finished a long piece of work any work seems easy. It was easy for me to promise that I would turn out copy in an unending river. It always seems too easy to me when I am not doing it and you know as well as I do that I have never turned out a really easy piece of copy in my life. [6/23/52]

And, as always, there was the worry about the boys, and this worry too was tinged with guilt. He felt that by being away from them for the summer, when he usually took them, he was abandoning them to the unrelieved negative influence of their mother. By being abroad, he had put himself at her mercy, and Gwyn used this opportunity to punish him to the fullest, not writing or cabling him as to where the boys would be, as she had promised, and then writing brief news to Elaine, rather than to him. Later in the summer, she refused to answer his letters of inquiry: How were they doing at camp? Did John's birthday presents arrive in time? What plans did she have for sending them to school in the fall?

During the period when they were traveling between Paris and Rome, John was concerned that his agents be able to get in touch with him, not so much for business reasons as to make sure that he was available, if needed, by the children: "I know there is no great need to keep in touch. But it does bother me. I guess it is largely the constant and never-changing sense of impending tragedy concerning the boys. I wish I could lose that. But I never have" [6/2/52]. Staying with the Gibey family, with their children and animals, had given both John and Elaine a good dose of homesickness, and failure to hear about his own children made John's case even worse. As was his custom quite often when he was depressed, he would stay in bed all day, occasionally getting up to sit long periods in a hot bath brooding and thinking.

And he had other thoughts of home during this period. *East of Eden* was in production and much on his mind. As he did so often, he refused to have the galleys sent to him, wanting to leave the whole thing behind him as he sailed to Europe, but once there, he changed his mind and wanted them sent to him as soon as possible. He always talked about a book leaving him once it was written, so that it was now a stranger which had no further interest for him. But although he no doubt believed this, it wasn't true. He loved to see his work in print, to read it and savor it. When the galleys finally got to him in Paris, he told Elizabeth:

> Last night I read from the galleys of East of Eden and it is better than I thought. It is amazing how much of it I had forgotten. I find I like it. I had my galleys bound because they break up so.
> Doesn't print make a great difference though? [6/2/52]

As far as publication was concerned, there was good and bad news. The good was that there had been an advance sale of 100,000 copies: the bad was that so far no book club had been willing to take it—Covici reported that Book of the Month could not stomach Cathy and the whorehouse. John replied, "Do you remember when I argued that the book clubs were bound to be burdened by the prejudices of so many readers? When the reader tells you what to write and publish, you can't have very good books. Maybe that is our trouble now. Writing for readers instead of ourselves." As the summer passed, a suspense built as he waited to see the published novel and to hear about its reception:

> I am getting anxious to see the book now and to hear about it. I have been away from it long enough now to lose the initial disgust that comes right after finishing. So let me have little bits of news about what is happening. I do hope the book will do well. . . . I

would really hate it if it were beaten to death by the sneers of our critics but I would hate it more if people didn't read it. [JS/PC-6/4/52]

Viking went all out in promoting a book that it felt would certainly be the most important publishing event of that year and perhaps of that time. As part of its promotion, Viking published a special edition of the novel just for booksellers, and it stimulated a great deal of advance publicity and as much book talk as possible.

In early June Covici reported to his author that at Viking's sales conference Marshall Best had read excerpts from Steinbeck's daily journal, ending with the passage which begins, "The writers of today, even I, have a tendency to celebrate the destruction of the spirit ..." Covici continued his description:

When this was over there was absolute quiet in the room—I could hear a little fly buzzing over the ceiling. It seemed to me as if somebody were going to burst out crying. No word was spoken for I don't know how long. Never in my 30 years attending sales conferences have I ever experienced anything like it. Here we were assembled to talk about an important book and without saying a word, in complete silence as if in prayer, we all felt and thought alike. [6/6/52]

When John and Elaine got to Rome, they found this letter from Pat waiting for them. John wrote to Elizabeth that he had gotten a good long letter from Pat: "He told about the sales meeting and made it sound like high mass at St. Peter's."

CHAPTER XXXVII

Pennants waved, bands played, and police lined the route as General Ridgway's procession made its way to the heart of Rome. Near the end of the parade was a little Citroën containing Mr. and Mrs. John Steinbeck. The inclusion was accidental, although it later proved to be symbolic. Elaine had carefully plotted their route from the highway to the hotel on a street map, but once they turned onto one main street, they found that they were prevented from turning off. Of course, if they hadn't joined the parade, they wouldn't have been able to get through the city at all, and since Ridgway was staying at the same hotel, they got where they wanted to go, eventually.

Rome had been prepared for communist rioting as a result of the general's visit (he was replacing Eisenhower as NATO commander), and the hotel was protected by layers of heavily armed soldiers. As John stood in his room, drinking a beer and looking out his window, he decided that he had never felt safer in his life. But shortly after their arrival, John was presented with a Roman newspaper on the front page of which was a sizeable article entitled "An Open Letter to John Steinbeck." Since Steinbeck and his work were well-known in Italy, and since he had been greeted by pleasant articles about him when he had arrived in Venice and Florence, he at first thought nothing about it.

When he expressed his pleasure in regard to such a greeting to the friend who had given him the paper, the friend replied, "Are you kidding? This is the biggest Red paper in Italy. And this is no compliment." The writer, Ezio Taddei, had taken the opportunity of the coincidental joint arrival of Ridgway and Steinbeck as a vehicle to attack Ridgway, NATO, the United States, American soldiers, the U.N. effort in Korea, and finally Steinbeck himself. There was a charge of germ warfare and the accusation that American soldiers, degenerates all, were using the bodies of little children as a roadway for their tanks. And all this was Steinbeck's fault because he would not denounce the commander-in-chief, who had organized and ordered these crimes, and his own country which would sanction such crimes against humanity. What, the author lamented, had happened to the man who had written *The Grapes of Wrath*?

Since this kind of attack, or variations of it, would be used against Steinbeck both abroad and at home for the remainder of his life, it is worth examining. It assumes that Steinbeck was once a Marxist, that he had become corrupted in some way by money and fame, and that as a result of this corruption, he had become a fascist (which is what Taddei calls him in a later article—perhaps becoming the first in a long line to do so). The same assumptions are reflected in the view of Steinbeck expressed from the other end of the political spectrum. The incident was reported by Henry Luce's *Time* magazine and refers to Steinbeck as "the Reds' favorite U.S. proletarian novelist," and calls Taddei's attack "a haunting voice from his past," although Steinbeck "is now an outspoken anti-communist."

For *L'Unità*, the Italian paper, and *Time* one is either a communist or a fascist (although *Time* is careful not to call the writer a former communist, the implication is quite clear). Steinbeck's dilemma with this polarization was that since he was, roughly speaking, in the middle, he was always wrong. Throughout his life he was left of center in many of his political beliefs and rather conservative in many of his personal values, but his attachment to classical literature and his scientific view of the nature of the world cloud the picture considerably and make him extremely difficult to label.

For example, his use of the "Argument of Phalanx" in *In Dubious Battle* and *The Grapes of Wrath* was a philosophical interpretation of the human position and human events, yet it was interpreted by both the Left and the Right as an advocacy of collectivism, with favor from one and disapproval from the other. One can state almost categorically that Steinbeck, in his *fiction*, is never an advocate, always a describer of what is—the writer who searches for the essential condition, from the perspectives of history and science. The temptation to read *The Grapes of Wrath* as a hymn to political progress can be checked by reading it in the context of *In Dubious Battle* and *Of Mice and Men*.

For the Old Left, especially in foreign countries, it was impossible that any writer who showed such sympathy for the dispossessed and poor could be anything less than a sympathizer with international communism. For the New Left, it was impossible that anyone with middle-class values, especially a fundamental patriotism and a sense of individual responsibility, could be anything less than a reactionary.

A fairly accurate way of describing Steinbeck, perhaps even more accurately than a New Deal Democrat with middle-class values, is as an independent who valued individuality and strived for independence from any kind of system of thought that obscured his attempt to see the world as it actually was. He wanted to be an individualist; he admired individualists; yet he also had a strong social conscience and a strong sense of right and wrong.

He distrusted "givens" of all sorts—political, social, or personal—yet he had a rather rigid code of personal morality (which did not match conventional morality of the narrowest sort). His code appeared to be partly drawn from his favorite reading—the chivalric code as seen in the *Morte d'Arthur* and *Don Quixote*—and partly from what upper middle-class parents in the West at the turn of the century were likely to tell their male children as they grew up was the "gentlemanly" thing to do. A man must have courage, not just physical courage, but the courage to do the "right thing" even though everyone else around may not understand or approve. A man must have loyalty to country, family, and friends, a responsibility to all those who are weaker or less fortunate than he.

All of these values were tied to his appreciation for independence. His "anti-communism" came largely out of an awareness that it squashed individuality. He saw it among the young communists in the thirties in California, and he saw it in Russia, and was appalled by the thoroughness and brutality with which all traces of independent thought were tracked down and purged. (Indeed, he was to become a kind of expert on Russia, visiting there three times—two trips lasting for several months each—and seeing more of the country and talking to more of its people than most diplomats and journalists who were stationed there.)

When he was in Rome, he called to find out the condition of Ingrid Bergman and offer his love and support. Bergman was at the time the source of a great scandal—not so much for Europeans as for Americans—because she had left her doctor husband and family to live, unmarried, with Italian moviemaker Roberto Rossellini. She was the occasion for much titillating gossip in American Sunday supplements and tabloids, and roundly condemned by the general press and many public figures. While a number of movie people were being blacklisted for political reasons, she was banned from Hollywood for "moral" reasons—a great hypocrisy and injustice.

As a result of his call, John found out that Ingrid was expecting the birth of a child momentarily, and three days after the birth, Rossellini drove into town and brought the Steinbecks out to visit her. As John leaned over her, she looked up and said, "I came to Italy to make a film and made three babies." Afterward, the novelist reported to his agent that Ingrid "looked well and the babies, non-identical twins, are big and blooming. Both she and Rossellini are very sad and upset about the dirty thing that is being done in Hollywood. I wish I could help them" [6/22/52].

The "dirty thing" upset Steinbeck as well, and the lack of support for her among public figures aroused his sense of gallantry. A short time later he decided she should star in the movie that he and Jules Buck had been planning, and as tangible evidence of his public support, sent her a proposal:

> I am going to make the Ibsen play The Vikings at Helgoland in Stockholm next summer. It will make a very fine picture.... Hjordis is one of the really great women's parts. Would you be interested, Ingrid? Besides being a good part and a good picture, it might give you the chance to kick the pants of some of the people who have been kicking you in the pants for a long time. We will have a major release but the money will be private money so there will be none of that tampering with the script. Let me know whether you might be interested.... We're glad to have seen you. I think you have some of the things licked now. And you are rapidly breeding a private army which may protect you in the future. Love to you both. [7/23/52]

In the meantime, in the States, another friend, Elia Kazan, was being pilloried by a different group for very different reasons. During the aftermath of John's separation from Gwyn, when Steinbeck was suffering intense pain, Kazan had spent many a night, all night, with him at the Bedford Hotel, helping him live through what had seemed to be the breakup of his whole world and the loss of the great love of his life. Since then, they had become, in Kazan's words, "like brothers—he was always my friend, no matter what, and I was always his friend, no matter what." While Steinbeck was often silent with people, even people he knew well, he could talk freely to Kazan.

The Kazans moved into a house only three doors away from the Steinbecks, on Seventy-second Street. The two families became close—some of their children were the same age—and Kazan came by often to sit and talk with John in his workroom on the top floor of the house or, in the summer, out on the terrace that John had built. They were very frank with each other. "He'd tell me everything about his life," Kazan recalls, "his troubles and anxieties. He was not what he appeared to be, a great strong guy, but he was also a strong man— both."

As a director on Broadway, Kazan had been both strikingly innovative and remarkably successful, artistically and commercially, and he had repeated this success in his Hollywood ventures. He had become a kind of show-business legend at a relatively young age, and so it was a shock to many when, in response to a summons by the House Un-American Activities Committee, he decided to cooperate and answer all the committee's questions. He had struggled with the problem for several months, talking it out with John before the Steinbecks had gone to Europe, and though Steinbeck had an utter contempt for the committee, for all it stood for and all it had done, he respected his friend's decision and, when almost no one else would, stood by him. Kazan and Lillian Hellman appeared before the committee at about the same time. Kazan talked, Hellman refused, and almost immediately Kazan became the arch-villain and Hellman the arch-heroine of American intellectual circles.

Steinbeck was in Paris, their first visit there that summer, when he heard about Kazan's testimony, and a short time later he wrote Pat Covici:

> Have not heard from Kazan. But I understand there is a great fuss and feathers over his statement as opposed to Hellman's. One can never know what one could do until it happens. I wonder what I would do. I'll never know I guess. And I don't even know what I wish I would do. Isn't that strange. I understand both Hellman and Kazan. Each one is right in different ways but I think Kazan's took more courage. It is very easy to be brave and very hard to be right. Lillian can settle snugly back in a kind of martyrdom but Kazan has to live alone with his decision. I hope I could have had the courage to do what he did. [5/28/52]

Several years later another friend of Steinbeck's, Arthur Miller, refused to testify. The only celebrity to come out publicly in his defense was John Steinbeck.

A great paradox of Steinbeck's personality was that sometimes, with very little provocation, he would almost fall apart. He was terribly afraid, for example, of catching pneumonia (a legacy, no doubt, from his near-fatal experience as a teenager), and after getting a chill, he might fall into bed and stay there. But if he were in a really rough or desperate situation, he would act with great determination and courage. If the car broke down in terrible country while it was pouring down rain, he would forget his pneumonia and get the job done. As a hypochondriac he was insufferable; as a truly sick man he was fine. It was somewhat the same thing when he was writing.

When he was greeted in Rome by the *L'Unità* attack, it could have been the occasion for depression, for two days in bed. Steinbeck liked being liked, especially in foreign countries. At first he thought it would just have to be something he would live with, for answering criticism, he felt, was a losing game: "You can answer a columnist once, but he has a column every day." But then he began to get mad, and the more he thought about the way he was being used, the madder he got. It was a challenge: if he didn't answer, the communists could claim that his silence indicated that he agreed with them.

Once he saw the attack as a challenge, his depression left him and he was inspired with purpose. Their hotel suite began to resemble a war room, as for the next three days Steinbeck gave up everything else to consult with embassy officials and his colleagues in journalism about the facts that contravened Taddei's fictions and the best tactics to use to refute the Italian's arguments. It was the embassy, for example, that supplied the information that the first mention of germ warfare by any nation was by Russia, which during World War II had announced that it was fully prepared to "use bacteriological warfare in retaliation against any enemy." As for the Italian's charges that Americans were machine-gunning Korean refugees, it was Steinbeck's idea to ask the question, "If we are so brutal to refugees, [why] do they always come to us, never to the communists?"

After Steinbeck had prepared his answer, he sent it to *L'Unità*, telling them that they must print it without altering or cutting it, or he would send it to another Roman paper to be published in full. After several days of silence, *L'Unità* sent two of its editors to Steinbeck's hotel to negotiate. They were embarrassed by the length of the novelist's response—it would take three columns, and no paper in Italy, they insisted, would consider printing so long a piece in one issue. When Steinbeck refused to cut it, the paper did so for him: "Every bit of information was deleted, and the paragraphs were rearranged so that the piece didn't make sense. It was a deadly job. But to top it, Taddei had written an answer to my cut answer. His letter ran more than three columns." Steinbeck lost no time sending a copy of the original to *Il Tempo*, which found no difficulty in printing the entire letter. Steinbeck's account of the exchange, written in part tongue-in-cheek and with just the right note of not taking himself too seriously, called "Duel without Pistols," became the second of his European articles published by *Collier's*.

The whole incident was exciting and interesting to him, and he enjoyed himself immensely. Afterward the Steinbecks went about their business (although the phone rang constantly with reporters asking for further comment) doing what Steinbeck called "churchifying and antiquitying." He wrote to Elizabeth:

> Good Lord but Rome is a big city. And the easiest place to get lost in. This is a strange trip. In some ways it makes me feel like a ghost. Every city we stop in sends reporters of all kinds. I have to see them and also they are interesting, but they know me so much better than I know myself that I feel like a stranger who is somehow eavesdropping on the talk of strangers. And if this is so with me, think how Gide must have felt, or even more, Shaw. It is almost as though you had outlived your time. They know all about me, what I have done and what I will do. I wonder whether East of Eden will give them any surprise. It will not make them happy if it does not coincide with what they thought I would write. [6/20/52]

He met and talked to some of the leading politicians in an effort to gather material for a piece on Italy's political future, and they drove to Positano, which he had seen under different circumstances during the war, for a period of rest on the beach. While they were there, he thought of doing an article on the town, which seemed to him, like the Jura, a kind of microcosm of southern Italy. "I find I have to write about little things," he confessed to Pat. "I can't write about big things. It never comes out good. But this little town I can understand." An active interest in skin diving, first with a snorkel and later with tanks, seemed to have begun in Positano. He reported, "I bought an underwater glass and I just lie on the surface and look down at fish. It has a breathing tube so I never have to come up for air. I can spend hours at it. The air is fairly hot but the water is just the right temperature" [7/4/52].

During the time he had known Elaine, he occasionally mentioned some of his exploits during the war, a few so wild that she began to refer to them as his "war stories," kidding about their authenticity. It got to be a joke between them, and to some extent, Elaine really did not believe some of the things he told her. So when they took a side trip to Capri and the shopkeepers and tavern owners came out to greet him with open arms, calling him "Liberator!"—she was properly abashed, while still somewhat unbelieving, and he was unforgivably smug.

They drove back to Rome for a day and then up the coast into France, arriving in Paris on July 13. They had arrived just in time for Bastille Day, and for the celebration they joined a whole group of people, including Bob Capa, John Huston, who was in Paris to film *Moulin Rouge*, Suzanne Flon, who was Huston's leading lady, and Jose Ferrer, who was playing Toulouse-Lautrec. They had dinner at the Eiffel Tower restaurant, while Capa photographed the fireworks, and they then went down to the street to dance until dawn. Steinbeck did not much care for nightclubs, but he loved street celebrations.

From Paris the Steinbecks went to London, the foreign city where he felt most at home and where he had many friends from previous visits. They stayed from the last week in July through the second week of August, and their time was filled with theater, dinner parties, shopping, and sightseeing. Among several plays, they saw Gielgud in *Much Ado About Nothing*, and John wrote two pieces about the London theater scene for the *Evening Standard* and the *Sunday Times*. He also had ideas for two articles to be done for *Collier's*: he wrote to the "Red Dean" of Canterbury and made arrangements with the U.S. Air Force to visit one of their permanent air fields. However, the Red Dean never answered his request for an interview, and although Elaine took a number of pictures of the air force facilities at the base they visited, John never found an approach for the story that he liked.

In Italy John's agent had arranged publication for several of his European articles, including—he hoped—two that had not been published in the United States, and now that he had met his British agent, Graham Watson, he hoped to get them all published in England. Watson was also interested in four or five essay-stories that John had decided to cut from *East of Eden*. John also wrote to Pat Covici suggesting that perhaps Viking might be interested in doing an essay-collection volume, containing all of these items and adding some of the best of his earlier essays, including several from *The Log*. Even though "they would need, as you say, considerable work," Pat replied, he liked the idea [6/25/52]. But it never went through; apparently Pat agreed with

John that "nobody ever buys essays" and instead Viking arranged an edition of Steinbeck's short novels. Nevertheless, Steinbeck, the prudent farmer, was working hard in Europe to sow as large a crop as possible.

During the last two decades of his life, Steinbeck was so often abroad that in those countries where his work was published, his publisher, his agent, and usually several people from the information section of the American embassy became his "family" in each country. (This also became true in the United States, where in New York Elizabeth Otis and her friend Chase Horton, John and Shirley Fisher [Shirley was also from McIntosh and Otis], Harold and Alice Guinzburg, and Pat and Dorothy Covici formed for him a kind of family group.) He was tied to all of them closely and saw them frequently, but they weren't necessarily—as in any family—closely tied to each other.

Of all the business connections abroad who became family to him, Graham Watson in England may have been the one with whom he established the warmest rapport. When Watson and his wife Dorothy met the Steinbecks for the first time in the summer of 1952, they had lunch together, and then the two women went shopping on Bond Street, while the two men, as Watson remembers,

> repaired to Hardy's—always his most important call in London. Here he bought a rather ridiculous fishing hat covered in salmon flies (the first of numerous bizarre purchases which we were to make together). A few days later I sent him a telegram to his Italian hotel. I cannot now remember the contents except that it was mildly insulting and I signed it "Angus of Old Muckie." By return I received an answer. It read, "Go home, Sasenach. Signed, Black Scone." . . . John loved acquiring sports clothes and no London visit would pass without his buying a new yachting cap or a pair of shooting boots or a heavy mackintosh.

Another favorite pastime with Watson was to lunch in Soho, and then play a game that consisted of each of them choosing a book in three categories: a current best-seller, a standard reference work, and a relatively obscure book that was not so rare that one could not reasonably expect to find it in some used-book store or another. Then they would start off together at the top of Charing Cross Road, going in one bookstore after another between there and Hatchards in Piccadilly. If one of the chosen books was in stock, the chooser won half a crown.

Just as John used Elizabeth and Pat in New York to obtain things for him, usually a present or decoration for a birthday party, so too he used Watson in London—and all of them delighted in their tasks. On one occasion John asked him to purchase bagpipes in Anderson tartan (for Shirley Fisher); other times he was asked to get a print of the foreign office and a stuffed hedgehog. The hedgehog was a challenge. After inquiring at many possible sources, Watson finally went "to Harrod's zoo department and, of course, they instantly agreed to help. But it would, they told me, involve catching a live hedgehog and then stuffing it. John wouldn't hear of it."

As mid-August approached and their time remaining in Europe became short (they planned to return home by the first of September), John sat down with Graham to plan their itinerary for Scotland and Ireland. As at the beginning of their trip when they decided to stay in Spain and skip the Mideast, they decided now that they would defer going to Stockholm, although John had promised Bo Beskow that they would try very hard to see him.

Before they left London for the north, John wrote Elizabeth:

I have not got to writing the military piece yet [the article on the U.S. Air Force base]. Want to think about it some more and there is one other reason. Or rather two other reasons. I am getting so confused about what Collier's wants and can use that I find it very hard to get down to anything. There are two distinct crafts, writing and writing for someone. The second requires a kind of second sight with which I do not seem to be gifted. In writing you put down an idea or a story and then see whether anyone likes it, but in writing for someone you must first, during and after, keep an invisible editor sitting on the typewriter shaking an admonitory finger in your face. It is a special business and one I don't seem to learn very easily. The third reason is that I have been far from well. The stomach disorder which began in Africa has by now become chronic and extremely unpleasant with considerable bleeding. I will have to go for a very serious check up as soon as I go home. Trying to soft pedal this just as much as possible so that Elaine's trip will not be interfered with but I just haven't felt well enough to do much work. A kind of sickish lethergy verging on a physiological despondency sets in with too great regularity. I will have a good internist go over me when I get back and see if I can find out what causes it. I am darned well sick of it. [8/11/52]

Some, perhaps a good deal of his "sickish lethergy" may well have come out of his anxiety about the *Collier's* articles and his feeling that he wasn't living up to his promises to the publisher. It was a common enough pattern in his life that when the writing dried up, he lapsed into illness. Part of his sick feeling may have come, also, from the anticipation of his trip to Northern Ireland, a trip he both desired and dreaded.

After visiting Scotland, the Steinbecks rented a car, an ancient Rolls-Royce "of sneering gentility, a little younger than Stonehenge and in a little better condition," to travel from Belfast to Londonderry. They found Londonderry a stark contrast to the rolling green of the nearby countryside—a dark, dour, unpleasant city to the visitor. There was no feeling of home or welcome in the "bleak hotel, that carried its own darkness with it." The woman behind the desk was determinedly stern, refusing to smile in spite of the best efforts of John and Elaine, and in the bar there was not a hint of gaiety. By the time they got to the dining room, it was two minutes after closing, and they could not be served. Nor could they get any clothes pressed, a London paper, a loaf of bread and some sausage, or a bottle of whiskey. It was after hours, and, as the porter explained, the rules of the hotel were very strict. As John looked out the window at the cold stone buildings and the locked shops and deserted street, his depression deepened and he wanted to go away quickly and forget the whole thing.

Elaine recalls that

John had said to me, quite a lot before we went, that every time he wanted to go to Europe, he wanted to go to his family's ancestral home in Northern Ireland, and Gwyn would never go with him, and how terrible it was. He beefed about it all the time, and he said, "All right, you and I will go." He made going to Ireland one of the big reasons we were going to take this trip. And when we got there, he just decided he didn't want to go. Of course, I expect that's what had happened before, other times he had gotten cold feet. And I said, "Oh now, this is Northern Ireland. You are not going to go home and wring your hands and say, 'I didn't get to go to Northern Ireland.'" We went on, and it really was a sentimental and wonderful trip.

He dreaded it because he felt that it could never meet his expectations. "I guess," he wrote later, "the people of my family thought of Ireland as a green paradise, mother of heroes, where golden people sprang full-flowered from the sod. . . . And at the very top of the glittering pyramid was our family, the Hamiltons." What he found was sad, and the experience was bittersweet, but it had been worth the effort. They took another car from Derry eighteen miles out into the countryside, past thatched cottages and hedged little fields, and after asking directions several times, found Mulkeraugh, which was not a town at all, but simply a small region with three or four farms on a hill. John had known from an uncle who had returned to Ireland that all that was left of the Hamiltons was two sisters and a brother, children of Steinbeck's grandfather's brother.

But by the time the writer had finally made his way to his mother's family's original home, all the Hamiltons were gone. None of his cousins had married, and the name had disappeared—a strange parallel to the gradual erosion of the Hamiltons in America as pictured in part in *East of Eden*. The family house had been sold to strangers, and worst of all, no one remembered his grandfather, the grandfather that John remembered as a "really great man, a man of sweet speech and sweet courtesy."

John's discovery of all this, with a bit of touching history concerning the fate of the two sisters and brother, became the third of his *Collier's* articles, "I Go Back to Ireland." Although it is autobiographical, it is also the story of everyone's mixed feelings in searching for his origins and finding, almost inevitably, that his roots have decayed or disappeared. As a restrained and effective re-creation of an emotional experience that nearly every reader can share, it is probably the most durable of the pieces he did for *Collier's* during this period. But each of the three articles was quite personal, and began a trend of first-person writing that extended through the journalism of the fifties and into *Travels with Charley* and his final novel.

Not only are *Travels* and *Winter* written from a personal point of view, they are both, fiction and nonfiction, extremely revealing of the person John Steinbeck and his private life—something that the earlier Steinbeck would have found intolerable. This trend toward the personal in his writing accompanies, and may even be in part the product of, the gradual emergence of a more public Steinbeck. The young man who felt he would be unable to gather material for his work if his face were known and only with extreme reluctance allowed himself to be photographed by anyone under any circumstances had gradually given way to the older man who grudgingly tolerated having his picture taken and published.

In this regard it is revealing to see the progression of photos accompanying his *Collier's* articles: in the first he is seen in a group of villagers in one photo among many; in the second a photo of him and Elaine is featured on the first page of the article; and in the third there are four pictures, each one of which features the author. When he received a request from Pat Covici for snapshots to be used for publicity on *East of Eden*, he wrote back, "I really don't like pictures any better than I ever have. Can't avoid them as much as I used to but I avoid them as much as I can." But he would do several public things in the years ahead that before he would have considered unthinkable. One, right after his return from Europe, was to be filmed for an appearance in a motion picture.

From Ireland the Steinbecks returned to London, went to Paris for a week, and on the evening of the last day of August, they flew back to New York. After six months abroad, Elaine was asked by friends about her trip: "I saw a lot of beauty," she said, "but I also saw every hardware store in Western Europe."

II

In mid-September, in a reflective mood, John wrote to Dook:

Fifty is a good age. The hair recedes, the paunch grows a little, the face—rarely inspected, looks the same to us but not to others. The little inabilities grow so gradually that we don't even know it. . . .

We had the grand tour—six months of it and I liked it very well. I'm glad to be back. We have a pretty little house here and every day is full. Very nice and time races by. When you really live in New York, it is more rural than country. Your district is a village and you go to Times Square as once you went to San Francisco. I do pretty much work and as always—90 percent of it is thrown out. I cut more deeply than I used to which means that I overwrite more than I used to. I cut 90,000 words out of my most recent book but I think it's a pretty good book. It was a hard one. But they're all hard. And if I want to know I'm fifty, all I have to do is look at my titles—so god-damned many of them. I'll ask Pat to send you a copy of the last one. To see if you like it or not. . . .

Have three more articles to complete for Collier's to finish my agreement with them. Then I want to learn something about plays, so I'm going to try to plunge into that form this winter. You may look for some colossal flops. But I do maintain that gigantic stupidity that will let me try it. . . .

Just read Hemingway's new book [*The Old Man and the Sea*]. A very fine performance. I am so glad. The obscene joy with which people trampled him on the last one was disgusting. Now they are falling too far the other way almost in shame. The same thing is going to happen to me with my new book. It is the best work I've done but a lot of silly things are going to be said about it. Unthoughtful flattery is, if anything, more insulting than denunciation. [9/10/52]

He didn't have to worry about an avalanche of unthinking flattery. While there were a few reviews of *East of Eden* that announced in effect that "Steinbeck had returned to his old form"—thus paralleling the reception given to Hemingway's novel—most of the reviews ran true to the form of his earlier predictions to friends: *Time* hardly even bothered with the book and, after condescendingly categorizing the author and his work in general, went on to say about his most recent work that it was "too blundering and ill-defined to make its story point." *The New Yorker* was snide and unpleasant in its consideration. In tones reminiscent of a forgiving Christian bewildered by the rage of a particularly ferocious lion he wrote about Anthony West, the reviewer: "I wonder what made him so angry—and it was a very angry piece. I should like to meet him to find out why he hated and feared this book so much."

Perhaps the most complimentary aspect of the novel's treatment was that whether positive or negative, most periodicals dealt with it as a serious major effort by a serious major author. Many, including *The New York Times Book Review*, New York *Herald Tribune Books*, and *Saturday Review*, ran interviews with the author or biographical sketches along with their discussions of the book. The interviews all appear to have been given on the same day at Steinbeck's house, with Pat Covici in attendance—possibly a way of making sure that the reluctant Steinbeck (who had a different view entirely of the necessity of interviews in his own country) would keep his appointments and manage to say something to the reporters that they could use. As usual, however, he refused to talk about himself or his just-finished book except to say that it had taken him a long time to write.

In *The New York Times* piece, by Lewis Nichols, there is a good description of the Steinbeck workroom:

This, he says, is the first room of his own he ever has had. Machinery of one sort or another crowds all but one small corner, where is placed the hot seat for literary endeavor. Sawdust from woodworking instruments lies thick on the floor, and when the master is in residence, a glum sign on the door proclaims, "Buzzard's Despair." When he goes out, he meets on his return the reverse of the sign, "Tidy Town," which shows that women have got in and tidied up the place.

It is a very quiet room. For companionship, Mr. Steinbeck

would like to get a myna bird. With a tape recorder he would teach this to ask questions, never answer, just ask. "Is that your wife with you?" "What are you doing here?" "Not looking so well today, are you, old man?" A quiet room where nothing ever happens.

Lewis Nichols appears to have been the only person to write on literary subjects for *The New York Times* who appreciated Steinbeck's corny, in-house humor.

For the most part, the author was gratified with the reception the novel received, for although he disagreed with a number of things that were said and was hurt by a few others, he found that many of the reviews considered the book very carefully. By November *East of Eden* was number one on the fiction best-seller list—an event that may have caused some of the academic reviewers to lower their estimation of the novel.

It is a book that seems to grip the reader in a special way, as John wrote to Dook, "I am getting flocks of letters and oddly enough, most of them have the sense of possession just as you do. People write as though it were their book." Several of those aspects that had aroused the most criticism became, in an odd twist, the very things that many readers found the most engaging: the intrusions of the first-person perspective, directly or indirectly, which told the author's family history; the character of Cathy (which, no matter how unbelievable, is unforgettable); and the blarney-philosophy of the Chinese houseboy Lee, which has become the particular target of academic sarcasm.

Above all, "Cathy the incredible" was to become a *cause célèbre*, and although Steinbeck never commented about her publicly, he did write to Dook:

> You won't believe her, many people don't. I don't know whether I believe her either but I know she exists. I don't believe in Napoleon, Joan of Arc, Jack the Ripper, the man who stands on one finger in the circus. I don't believe Jesus Christ, Alexander the Great, Leonardo. I don't believe them but they exist. I don't believe them because they aren't like me. You say you only believe her at the end. Ah! but that's when, through fear, she became like us. This was very carefully planned. All of the book was very carefully planned. [10/16/52]

Privately, he argued with several of his friends about Cathy. One of them, who remembers telling Steinbeck he was disappointed in *East of*

Eden because he couldn't believe in Cathy, was a young radio announcer named Allen Ludden.

Ludden, who later became known as the emcee for the TV game shows "College Bowl" and "Password," had gone to drama school with Elaine at the University of Texas, and he and his wife Margaret had been friends of Elaine's and Zachary's when they were married. As a young man doing a teenage radio show in Hartford, Connecticut, he was overwhelmed when he and his wife were invited to John and Elaine's wedding to find himself among so many celebrities, and then to go to a party at the Steinbecks and be in the company of Elliott Roosevelt, Faye Emerson, the Richard Rodgerses, and the Frank Loessers. But it was probably because Ludden was not a celebrity and not particularly literary, but simply an old friend of Elaine's, that John felt so comfortable with him. The writer also enjoyed his frankness, and since they disagreed about many things, they were able to have the kind of argument-discussions that John really liked.

Periodically the Luddens were invited down for the weekend. Elaine would cook dinner, and afterward they would retire to the bar off the library upstairs and sit and talk and drink all Friday night. He and Allen had long discussions about Allen's conversion to Catholicism, and about the Bible and Thomas Aquinas; both of the latter, as Ludden admits, John knew a great deal more about than he. Evenings of talk usually found Elaine and Margaret on the couch, John in a big, pull-back chair in the corner, and Allen on the ottoman. Deeply involved in their discussion, John would become angry when the two women on the couch, talking together, would suddenly burst into laughter. He would get angry, too, when as he talked, Allen would interrupt with "What?" because he couldn't hear what he was saying. The more he had to drink, the less intelligible was his speech, and the more Allen said "What?" the madder he got.

Steinbeck started bringing Allen up to his workroom (he never invited Margaret) during the time that he was working on *Burning Bright*, showed him his tools, his drafting-board writing table, his pencil-sharpening system (at the time he was rubbing the lead to a very fine point on a strip of carborundum paper), just as another man might show a male friend his workshop garage and his model ships. Ludden read the first two chapters of *East of Eden* one evening in John's room, and during the period of composition, when the Steinbecks were in New York, he listened to John talk about his family—his uncle, his aunts, his mother, father, and grandfather. "That life," Ludden recalls,

"I just pumped him on it. I was fascinated with it, because he just loved to be pumped on it. The drunker he got, the drunker we got, together, the more I wanted to go back to Salinas and hear about his country."

As a result of this talk, Ludden thought the book was going to be about Steinbeck's family, and when the novel came out, he was disappointed. "He knew that I was disappointed in *East of Eden*. I didn't know how to tell him, except to tell him that I didn't believe Cathy because she was all bad—there she was, the totally evil person. John said, 'How can you, with all your blind faith which allows you to become a Catholic—how can you believe in angels, believe that God has sent angels and not believe that the devil is able to send devils? Katie is a total representative of Satan. If you can believe in saints, you can believe that somebody can be all good, you've got to believe that somebody can be all bad.'"

Late in the evening, it was not uncommon for John to speak tearfully of Ed Ricketts, and the first autographed book that John gave to Allen was *The Log from the "Sea of Cortez."* "Here, read this," he admonished once when the topic of Ricketts and their adventures together had come up. It was a bit too scientific for Ludden who admitted one evening that he had never finished reading it, and John was angry with him for the rest of his visit.

III

In today's political arena it is difficult to believe that not too many years ago a man could be so impressed by a presidential candidate's words that he was converted to the office-seeker's candidacy. Steinbeck was an admirer of Eisenhower, the general, and then was vaguely attracted to his candidacy, but when he read Stevenson's speeches, he was converted and became not only a Stevenson supporter but, in the long run, he, who had once defined himself as a Roosevelt or New Deal Democrat, became a "Stevenson Democrat" and so defined himself for the rest of his life.

He was captivated by Stevenson's humor and his frankness, his refreshing lack of cant and sloganeering. When his admiration for the candidate's speeches became known during the campaign, he was asked to write a foreword to a collection of them that was published as part of the election effort. In the foreword, Steinbeck detailed his conversion and went on to declare: "I think Stevenson is more durable, socially, politically and morally. . . . As a writer I love the clear, clean writing of Stevenson. As a man I like his intelligent, humorous, logical, civilized mind."

In the fall of 1952, he had neither met the man nor heard him speak in person, but he and Elaine worked hard for his election. Elaine and two other women took over the job of "casting" all of the Stevenson rallies east of the Mississippi, and eventually, the women turned to John, who wrote a number of short speeches for the various celebrities who volunteered to appear. "Honey," she would say, "Hank Fonda is going to do the Washington rally for us, and he wants to know what he should say. Do you mind writing a five-minute speech for him to deliver?" In neither the 1952 or 1956 campaigns, however, did Steinbeck write directly for the candidate, as some accounts have alleged. In the later campaign, after he had gotten to know the Governor, he was sometimes asked to contribute speech ideas and did so on several occasions.

Besides speeches, the writer was also working to fulfill his *Collier's* obligation and to start his play. He wrote three articles, only one of which *Collier's* published, and two of the three were autobiographical. The *Collier's* piece was "The Secret Weapon We Were Afraid to Use," an account of his proposal to F.D.R. during the war that they use counterfeit money to disrupt Nazi Germany. The two others, "Making of a New Yorker" and "Positano," appeared in *The New York Times Magazine* and *Harper's Bazaar*. By the time he had returned from Europe he had given up the idea of writing a "straight play" in favor of going back to a project that he and Frank Loesser had discussed doing together several years earlier—making a musical out of *Cannery Row*. But by Christmas this too had changed. He told Dook, "You are right about the difficulty of transposing Cannery Row to the stage. I'm not going to do exactly that. I have a whole new story. It will simply be set against the old background. You know Dook—it never gets any easier. The process of writing a book is the process of outgrowing it. I am just as scared now as I was 25 years ago."

He was also involved in another project that fall. Earlier in the year Gene Solow had proposed to him that he write an introduction for an anthology of O. Henry short stories that Fox was to film that summer and suggested that John might want to narrate his introduction himself, on screen. John knew the director of the picture, Henry Hathaway, and he decided that it might be interesting and fun. But, he wrote Solow, he wouldn't be able to do it until he returned from Europe.

In early October, he wrote several drafts, reading each aloud to Elaine until he felt it sounded right. Then Elaine said, "Now you've got to learn it." "What do you mean?" he replied. "Why should I learn it? I wrote it, didn't I?" Then his wife explained that when the camera got on him, he would go dry. "You've got to memorize it," she told him. Elaine recalls that she had never seen anybody go through such agony: "It should have taken part of a day, and it took three or four, as I remember." The filming date had been arranged and they went to the studio:

> When the camera came on him, he just lost everything. The first day he was a pretty good sport about it, and then he just went all to pieces. It was a terrible experience for him. He said, "If you don't come and stay with me every second, I'll kill myself." And Hathaway was marvelous with him; everybody was marvelous with him. They finally got it, but we never saw it. He didn't want to see it and asked me not to, so I didn't.

In January of 1953 the Steinbecks went to the Virgin Islands for a winter vacation, the first of nine straight years that they "celebrated New Year" in the West Indies. Arthur Farmer, John's lawyer, had asked him, "Can you give me two weeks of your life?" John said, "Of course. What is it you want to do?" Farmer knew that he did not have very long to live and wanted the Steinbecks to go on a vacation with him. Arrangements were made for all to fly to St. Thomas, but Farmer died before the trip was made.

The Steinbecks decided to take the vacation anyway and went instead with Barnaby Conrad, whom they had not met until he came to New York prior to their leaving for the islands. *The New York Times Book Review* had polled several celebrities, asking them to list their favorite books for the year just ending, and John had included Conrad's *Matador* among his selections. Conrad wrote to thank him, and John wrote back, "I liked Matador for a number of reasons chief of which was that I believed it." When it turned out that Conrad was also just about to leave for the Virgin Islands, they made arrangements to go together.

When they arrived at their hotel on St. Thomas, they found it very disappointing. It wasn't on the beach at all, and they had planned a vacation of sunning, fishing, and swimming; besides the hotel itself was rather gloomy and the service uninspired. Elaine recalls that "John did what he so often did when he went anywhere—he just went to bed when he got there. . . . And he would say, 'Elaine go out and find us a better place to live.' " She tried to prod him into helping her, but he couldn't be stirred from his bed. Barney went with her, and they sur-veyed St. Thomas and then took a boat to St. John, where they found a hotel of cottages right on the beach at Caneel Bay. John was pleased with their choice.

CHAPTER XXXVIII

I n the fall of 1952 Steinbeck described himself to Dook Sheffield as

changed in some ways, more calm, maybe more adult, perhaps more tolerant. But still restless. I'll never get over that I guess—still nervous, still going from my high ups to very low downs—just short of a manic depressive, I guess. I have more confidence in myself now, which makes me less arrogant. And Elaine has taught me not to be afraid of people (strangers) so that I am kinder and better mannered I think. [10/16/52]

Although he had analyzed himself in similar terms before, friends agreed that after two years with Elaine he had become a happier, more confident, more sociable man.

For the Steinbecks, 1953 was one of the few years of their marriage that they spent most of their time, including the summer, in New York. While in general John was a more contented man, he still had his extremes of mood and he remained a great worrier, and their marriage was not without strife. If you are going to let someone manage most of the mundane details and arrangements for living, you have to expect to be bossed around a bit. John wanted the former, but resented the latter.

As Elaine recalls:

We were not often a very peaceful family. There were a lot of things to worry about, lots of troubles. . . . John's and my trouble came most all of the time over the children—mine or his, which is true in most marriages. Waverly was a problem sometimes between us. John was very jealous of her, and they always said they got along fine until I came into the picture. . . . And there was never any peace from Gwyn, never. He never had any peace from Gwyn.

To John, Gwyn seemed to make her dealings with her ex-husband as difficult and as irritating as possible. She would call and when Elaine answered, ask "Well how is father today?" in a way that suggested that she still held proprietary interest over the affairs of the entire family. Exasperated, Elaine could only reply, "He is *not* your father." Elaine's low voice provided Gwyn ammunition for one of her pet names, used with her own family and the boys, for her ex-husband's new wife— "gravel Gertie." Because she never remarried, maintaining her alimony and having custody of the boys, she had both the financial and emotional upper hand, and John felt she used it.

There were also the everyday frictions between a woman who was healthy and capable and a man whose depressions sometimes drove him into hypochondria and helplessness, between a woman who strove mightily to keep a moderately clean and comfortable house and a man who when he was preoccupied could be a terrible slob. His room was the depository of more than just woodshavings and sawdust. Mail often accumulated and was sometimes lost to sight forevermore; cups, glasses, and dirty dishes perched here and there. If he got hungry, he would go down to the kitchen, cook a can of beans in a pot, climb the stairs eating the beans out of the pot with a spoon, and then leave the remainder to grow moldy over a period of weeks sitting on the top of a bookcase.

His uniform during these years when he was round the house and not in his robe was khaki pants—loose-fitting enough to be comfortable for a man who sat a lot—and a long-sleeved sweatshirt that had pockets in the front and a drawstring hood. He also favored other clothing worn by yachtsmen—the shoes, the hat, and foul-weather gear—but though he was a man most at home under informal circumstances, he enjoyed dressing up. He began having his suits tailor-made abroad, usually in England (taking his lead from O'Hara), and he was a man on whom good clothes looked good, except that he felt they never remained as pressed and sharp as he would have liked. He had taken to wearing bow ties some years back, and he always had the impression that five minutes after he was out his front door, his tie had spun around three or four times to remain at an absurd angle and his collar was askew.

While other men might object to having to get into a tuxedo to go out, he enjoyed it, but when he was with someone, like Kazan, who complained about dressing in formal clothes to go to a theater opening, he would also complain, as if he didn't want to be left out of the boys being boys. The truth was that he would have loved to be able to cut the dashing figure of a Douglas Fairbanks, Jr., but while Fairbanks could wear a cape, on Steinbeck it seemed to be somewhat pretentious. As he grew older, his attire became more and more extreme—but unconsciously so. Once while walking down Third Avenue near their home in what by then had become his fairly common outfit of suit, cape, walking stick, and broad-brimmed, black felt hat, he took his small cigar out of his mouth, turned with dismay to Elaine, and seriously asked, "Why are people staring at me?"

II

In the early part of the year, John was busy writing his musical play, and the person closest to the writer throughout this project was Ernest Martin, of the production company Feuer and Martin. Steinbeck came to know Martin and his wife through the Loessers and Abe Burrows, and the two families saw each other for dinner periodically and during the summers. Steinbeck and Martin shared a love for ocean fishing, and they sometimes took their children with them on charter-boat fishing trips off the end of Long Island. It was through talking his project over with Martin that John decided to turn from *Cannery Row* and do a new plot against the old background. Martin recalls:

> The story of *Cannery Row per se* wouldn't make a show. It needed more. So we asked John to see if he could develop for us the basis of a musical play or actually write a libretto based on the characters of the Row, built around the character of Doc. . . . We had sort of a vague theme, but the form that we had in mind was to be a story about Doc and some woman—I mean there would have to be a love story in it, and then the rest of the people would be the bums and whores of Cannery Row, those that existed prior in the book and any others that he might want to invent.

After John returned from St. Thomas, he began to dictate the script and then send the tape to Martin's office to be typed. His dictation went on for almost two months, and then one day a tape came in, on which he told the producers that he'd tried, but that he just couldn't write in that form, he didn't feel adequate. He thought the best thing to do would be to make it into a novel and then he or someone else could adapt the novel to the stage. With all the buildup in his own mind for this attempt and with all his admiration for the playwright as craftsman, it was a terrible admission to have to make.

Before going on with the story as a novel, John took his boys for a week during their spring vacation to Nantucket, while Elaine went to Texas to visit her family. He wrote to Elaine, telling her that the days had been beautiful, but the nights cold, and they had been building big fires.

> Yesterday we went to town and I ordered a jeep to be delivered today. We will go out for driftwood for the fires. We made menus for the whole week. Boys make their beds and wash and wipe dishes. They do it pretty well—sometimes three times before perfect. But they do it. Tonight we wash clothes. Yesterday we walked to the lighthouse and back. Boys want to stay up late but what with the cold air and the exercise they conk out at about 8 o'clock and I about 8:30. There has been no talk of radio, television or movies. I made my justly world famous corned beef hash last night. A dead and properly mummified seagull on the beach is being reburied for the 8th time right now with a border of clam shells. This time he is being interred with his head above ground so he "can look out." I love you and miss you. [3/24/53]

A long hot summer in New York passed as John worked on his book, which he now called "Bear Flag" but which would be titled *Sweet Thursday* upon publication the following year. As the book was written, it was tailored to the idea of its eventual conversion to a musical comedy, which may be one of the most peculiar frameworks of development ever used for an American novel. In September the Steinbecks rented a house on Long Island for a month. They had been looking for a place to go during the summers, and the Ernest Martins, who lived during the summer in East Hampton, found them a big, old house to rent in nearby Sag Harbor, which would allow John to consult frequently with Martin about the book in progress.

By the middle of the month the first draft was completed. Despite John's commitment to the musical, he really wrote the book for the fun of it, a bit of self-indulgence that he felt he was entitled to after the rigors of *East of Eden*. Nevertheless, he was somewhat defensive about it with Elizabeth.

> Elaine is in New York with Waverly this week and I am alone out here. The fall is coming quickly, a chill in the air and a hoarse wind

blowing over the water. This is my favorite time and I couldn't be in a better place for it. . . .

I have enjoyed writing this book the B.F.

There is a school of thought among writers which says that if you enjoy writing something it is automatically no good and should be thrown out. I can't agree with this. Bear Flag may not be much good but for what it is, I think it is all right. Also I think it makes a nice balance for the weight of Eden. It is kind of light and gay and astringent. I think that right now it is kind of healthy. Practically nothing funny is being written and I think B.F. is funny. The New Yorker humor (practically the only humor today) is bitter, smart and despairing. At least B.F. is none of these. It may even say some good things. . . .

I'll be sad to finish Bear Flag. I have really loved it. I am reluctant to start into the last two chapters. But I will. I do hope you love this book a little, self-indulgent though it may be. Try to like it. [9/14/53]

The problem with his work on the musical was that it gave him license to do the sort of writing that amused him but which didn't meet the standards he had usually set for himself. He had indulged himself rather shamelessly in fantasy, whimsey, nostalgia, and sentimentality—all the things that from the time of his early days with Carol he knew could be destructive to his work—and now he came to Elizabeth Otis, who had always been for him a kind of stand-in for Edith Mirrielees, and asked to be forgiven: "Try to like it." Elizabeth, however, did not like it. She felt very strongly that he was going over the same ground, writing out of nostalgia, and she told him so.

However, in the same letter he noted:

As I have been writing it, story after story has come up . . . I have held them back for next year of short stories. . . .

I keep thinking of the European trip next year and coming up with new ideas for things to write while there. I wouldn't be surprised if this should be one of the most productive times of all. It is time for me to do short things—but short things I like. I'm making a list of them. The Alhambra for instance—kind of revisited as it hasn't been since Washington Irving. Does that sound interesting to you?

Indeed the next few years would be among his most productive, matched only in quantity by the mid-thirties. From late 1952 through 1956 he would write most of the articles that he would publish during his career, and for the first time since the thirties he would write and publish several short stories. Much of this production—including *Sweet Thursday*—seems to have been prompted by an urge to dwell on his own past, as if one of his reactions to finishing *East of Eden* was an attack of nostalgia. "I Go Back to Ireland," in January 1953, was followed by "Making of a New Yorker," which recounted his early experiences in New York. In the middle of the year, "A Model T Named 'It' " was published, one of those pieces culled from *East of Eden* which retold the anecdote, famous in the Steinbeck family, of John's mother being sprayed with an explosion of oatmeal that her son had put into the leaky radiator of his car. The strain of personal memory continued to hatch with, most notably, an article about Salinas and a short story about his Salinas childhood, both written during the summer of 1954; he even considered writing an autobiography.

After returning from the rented house in Sag Harbor at the beginning of October 1953, John's spirits began to sink. The aftershock of finishing *East of Eden* had been allayed by his trip to Europe, but now, having finished the first draft of "Bear Flag," disappointment in himself over failure to write a play as he had planned to do for so long, continuing trouble with the children, and unhappiness in response to friction with Elaine all seemed to pile up on him. And a bad experience in making a record for Columbia deepened his depression.

The record was part of an album in which each of several contemporary authors was given an hour to read from their own works, and Steinbeck chose "Johnny Bear" and "The Snake." When he had recorded things for the United Nations or for U.S.I.S for broadcast overseas, he did them at his leisure at home on his own machine, and they came off very well. But for this record he was asked to come to a studio, and under the pressure of technicians hovering around him, and a bombardment of time cues and suggestions, he became unsettled and confused. Both he and Elaine thought he did very poorly. Along with the earlier motion picture debacle, it was his second failure "before the public" in a year.

Later that month he went into Lenox Hill Hospital with what he thought was pneumonia, the first of many stays in the hospital during the time that he was married to Elaine. At first alarmed, Elaine visited every day and expressed concern, but as she saw him sitting up in bed, eating copiously, and having great fun kidding with the doctors and nurses, she became angry. "There's really not a lot wrong with you," she said, "I can see that." Her "lack of sympathy," reminiscent of

Gwyn's hard-heartedness and failure to mother him when he was down, was apparently the final blow that knocked him into a deep depression.

On the recommendation of Elizabeth Otis, he began seeing Gertrudis Brenner, who was not a formally trained psychologist or psychiatrist, but who was a skillful counselor, effective in helping him recover his equilibrium. He went to see her several times a week for about three months, not making a secret of it from Elaine, but not talking about it either.

III

They took a longer than usual winter vacation that year, staying the whole month of January at Caneel Bay on St. John. The resort was uncrowded (they were the only guests in the hotel for a time) and right on the beach near beautiful water. After a week John wrote to Elizabeth that he had lost track of time: "This is the laziest I've ever been and that's a record anywhere." Elaine worked hard to get a tan, while John spent a lot of time in the water, first with a snorkel and then with an aqualung. He reported, "The sea is so beautiful here that it is heartbreaking. I am going to do more and more diving. That is the greatest thrill since flight" [1/54].

Their isolation was broken when the John Kenneth Galbraiths arrived—he was teaching as a visitor at the university in Puerto Rico. On meeting Steinbeck, Galbraith found him "a shrewd and perceptive man, much interested in politics and contemporary anthropology and not only droll but very, very funny. He was a large man, still clean-shaven, exceedingly homely, and in 1954 looked older than I imagined or he was." The Galbraiths, both of them witty and charming and interested in the same things as the Steinbecks, made good companions.

Whatever they might be doing during the day, the two couples usually got together in the late afternoon for what John called "Milking Time," a time for talk and banter, tall tales, and political speculation. Galbraith recalls Steinbeck's serious recounting of the activities and misfortunes of a woman who was a frustrated circus performer, who hurt herself while stepping out a window onto a badly secured clothesline.

More seriously, they talked of Stevenson, whom they shared a regard for, and of Joe McCarthy, who was at the height of his influence. Steinbeck, Galbraith recalls, didn't think McCarthy would last: he seemed vulnerable to the bottle, for one thing, and "to exercise power through fear [Steinbeck thought] required commanding intelligence and great diligence." Joe, he felt, had neither. (John took McCarthy more seriously later, writing, among other things, a marvelously innocent bit of mockery called "How to Tell Good Guys from Bad Guys" for *Reporter*. Although it was hard to get an anti-McCarthy or anti-HUAC piece published, he felt after McCarthy's fall that he should have written more and yelled louder, especially when writers and artists were being attacked.)

Originally, John had left the matter open as to whether or not he would do the adaptation of "Bear Flag" for the stage. But when Frank Loesser withdrew as the composer for the musical, and Oscar Hammerstein expressed interest in the project, taking a copy of the first part of the first draft with him to Europe in the early fall of 1953, Steinbeck, weary after working on the book, was happy to see it taken over by someone else. And taken over it was. He had suggested the title be "Palace Flophouse," thinking it might give the swanky Palace Hotel in San Francisco some much needed publicity—they might even sue, he hypothesized gleefully; then "Bear Flag Cafe" was the frontrunner, but finally, he heard while at Caneel Bay that all those concerned were beginning to favor "Sweet Thursday"—especially since Rodgers and Hammerstein were in the process of writing a song with that title. In a way, the change in title from "Bear Flag" to "Sweet Thursday" was a prediction of change in emphasis from the novel to the musical, a softening of focus, and a forecast of the production's fate.

On their return from the Virgin Islands, the Steinbecks had only a few weeks to get settled and make arrangements before they would be off again on another long trip to Europe. This time they had more definite plans as to where they were going to go and what they wanted to see. They would start in the south and "follow the spring," as John called it, moving through France, and ending up in Scandinavia. They would do almost all of their traveling in their own car, and John had already made arrangements to pick it up in Gibraltar. To avoid the pressure he had had two years before, he made no firm commitments about his writing, although he planned to write a variety of short things, both fiction and nonfiction. He had, as he told Elizabeth, "made a list."

At the end of February he wrote to her (a letter written for tax purposes):

Remember the book I told you I want to write next year—the one that parallels Don Quixote? In Spain I am going to make a detailed (and photographed) expedition through La Mancha to all of the places Cervantes wrote about. Incidentally, in addition to the basic material for my book, don't you think such a thing might not make a very good article? Footsteps of Don Quixote—with pictures? The country has not changed much. The windmills are still there and the castles. You might query Holiday on this. It is the kind of special article they like sometimes. [2/24/54]

In a covering letter with this letter, he indicated that he was pleased with himself—not only had he set up a basis for deducting his expenses in Spain, he had come up with a writing possibility that wasn't half bad.

At about this same time, John wrote a letter to Arthur Miller. He had been very disturbed by the political conflict between friends and co-workers in the arts that had been generated by the witch-hunting of the HUAC and aggravated by the hysterical paranoia of producers, backers, and patrons. In particular he was much grieved by the split that had developed between Miller and Elia Kazan. In effect, the letter said, "It's none of my business, but I think you are really suited as writer and director, and you mustn't let all this politics get in your way." As Miller recalls:

> It was a very moving letter. Then I met him afterwards; in fact, I think we met that evening at George Kaufman's. And as soon as I walked in, he moved over to me and grabbed me and said, "I'm sorry I wrote that. I understand you feel as you do," and I said, "Why are you sorry?"
>
> That man was always so moved with everything. That was so precious about him, he really was. He agonized about everything—he never knew how to handle all that. He always reminded me of an adolescent. . . . And he could blush—one of the few people I had ever met who could blush. His sensitivity must have been driving him crazy. That's what I mean, too, by saying that there was something of a country boy about him. I don't mean literally that he had to be a rural person, but there was a blessed naïveté here. . . . He was not inured by life, I thought.

IV

On his first trip to Spain two years earlier, he had been full of misgivings, having the same negative feelings about Franco that most liberals had, and their extended stay there had been more or less accidental. Now Spain seemed to be uppermost in his mind. He had written to Dook several months earlier: "I'm going back to Spain in the Spring. I feel an affinity there. . . . I feel related to Spanish people much more than Anglo-Saxons. . . . They have kept something we seem to have lost" [11/2/53].

The Steinbecks sailed for Europe in mid-March 1954, arriving in Lisbon on March 26. When they got to Gibraltar, their car had not yet arrived from England, so they visited Tangier for a couple of days. The car was a black Jaguar sports roadster, and Steinbeck bought a wicker basket just the right size to fit the luggage rack in back and sprayed it black. In addition, he had purchased at Abercrombie and Fitch just for this trip an auto horn that sounded like a bull—he was going to give the cattle on the roads some of their own medicine. It was a smart-looking outfit, and they decided to call themselves "the Joads in the Jag."

Wherever the Steinbecks stopped in Spain, small boys would suddenly appear and swarm all over the car, coming up over the hood and luggage in the rear just like flies. No matter what he said, he couldn't seem to get them off. Finally, he developed a technique to deal with the situation. He would contort his face into a demonic mask full of rage and bark out, "Animal Crackers! Animal Crackers!" Then half rising and looking as if he was just about ready to cut their throats, he'd growl, "Go butter your toast!" The kids would scatter.

One of their first stops was in Torremolinos, whose one hotel at that time had three beachfront apartments—one taken by MacKinlay Kantor, one by the Steinbecks, and one, when he arrived third, by Joseph Bryan III. Bryan had been the editor of *The Saturday Evening Post*, had written a biography of Admiral Halsey, and was now freelancing, gathering material for magazine articles. He was a tall, bespectacled, rather severe-looking Southerner who had a great sense of fun and humor, and the first time he had met Steinbeck, several years earlier, they had laughed and joked together all evening. This first night together in Spain was a repetition, except John had a new wife and Joe had not yet remarried. Bryan recalls John telling him about the first time he saw Robert Benchley. He was sitting with a Hollywood friend on stools at Dave Chasen's bar in Beverly Hills when a man came in, and John said, "That man has a very interesting face—who is that?" The friend replied, "Oh, that's Bob Benchley. I don't think you'd care for him. He drinks." At that moment John's friend passed out, slipping off his stool to the floor. That evening in Torremolinos, Bryan and the Steinbecks lived up to the text of John's story during a long boisterous night. The next morning, very late, Bryan stopped by the Steinbecks' apartment to see if they would like to go for a walk. On the door he found a sign: SICK ARAB.

Joe Bryan was a very pleasant and witty drinking companion, and the party was continued two nights later. Hearing the general hilarity, a man who had been a fellow passenger aboard ship with the Steinbecks came over and asked if he could join them. They all sat at the table talking, and then, out of the blue, the man turned to John and said, "I suppose you know that your wife was sleeping around with half the men on board?" John looked at him coldly and said, "You son of a bitch," got up, and was in the process of dismembering him when Joe Bryan barely managed to pull him off. It was a rare moment in a life almost totally without personal violence—the man had touched the right nerve.

In response to the continuing stream of news regarding Senator McCarthy during this period, John had written an article-story the previous fall called "If This Be Treason," which he was unable to get published, and now in Spain he wrote a little poem. He sent a copy to Elizabeth and shortly thereafter received word that Harold Guinzburg, his publisher, was upset by it and asked that he not publish it anywhere. John replied to Elizabeth that he was shocked "that Harold should be so afraid of McCarthy re the poem." Each of the stanzas began, "Schine and Cohn and Tailgunner Josephine/Dancing on the Senate Green" and ended "Let Trumpets wail and eagles groan/Josephine and Schine and Cohn." A few days later he wrote again to Elizabeth:

Of course Harold and Harry [Buckman—Steinbeck's lawyer] are right. The verse is pure libel even if it's true. Josephine is not likely to sue. That would bring it into the open. I think Harold believes he would try one of the oblique attacks. The Roman method of classical purity would be to post it on the forum walls (read Capitol) during the night. I believe this was done in England in the 17th century. [4/21/54]

With Joe Bryan the Steinbecks went to Seville for Holy Week, and as before, found themselves exhausted at the end. On this visit they had met a number of Sevillanos, and were able to get a glimpse of the inner life of the city. He reported to Pat:

Holy week was beautiful and strange. I am trying to find the meaning behind the meaning of it. Sometimes I almost have it. These people grew up with it and so they understand it without knowing it or vice versa. I think it is very important and, Pat, important to my next book *Pi Root*. I have to understand unconscious dedication on all levels before I am ready to write that book. Have been rereading Cervantes with a new eye. I wish I could spend this whole year without writing one single word. I won't of course but I wish I could—just kind of rest this process so that something fresh might come when I start again. For I feel that I am becoming hackneyed. I am dissatisfied with my efforts. I am desperately afraid that tricks are creeping in and that I am utilizing technique rather than creation. And increasingly a disgust with myself arises. I want to write well of course but I want much more than that and I don't even know what it is that I want—except that it is a light over a hill. I can see its light in the sky but no matter how many hills I climb—it is always over the next hill. And I am afraid of the time when I will not have the strength to climb any more. [4/22/54]

Before leaving for Europe, he had taken a physical examination as part of an application for life insurance, and now he learned from Elizabeth that his application had been turned down. He decided that when he got to Paris, he would find a specialist and get his opinion, but in the meantime he wasn't going to allow himself to become panicky: "I will not permit myself to become one of those heart cripples who spread their psychopathy around. It has been a good heart to me and I won't insult it now by being kind to it" [5/5/54]. From Madrid (where they celebrated Joe Bryan's birthday) he wrote that his plans were to leave Spain on May 8, and, stopping wherever something interesting caught their eye, arrive in Paris on May 14. "I have decided," he told Elizabeth, "to become a royalist. That is the only thing I have not been accused of. How about Mamie for Queen? Besides, royalists can and do remain in complete ignorance of any reality—a highly desirable state I am beginning to believe" [5/5/54].

On their way to Paris, John had what Elaine is now sure was his first episode of heart failure. They had been driving all day in the hot sun with the top down on the Jaguar, and as they pulled up to their hotel in Blois, Elaine could see that her husband was flushed and drenched with perspiration, about ready to pass out. Suddenly his eyes rolled back, and he completely blacked out, limp. With help she got him to their room, and minutes later a doctor arrived, a kindly man with a celluloid collar and tea-stained mustache. Then a young man came in and said, "I hear there is an American couple here in some kind of trouble." He was the local librarian, and when he heard that the man who was ill was John Steinbeck, he was nearly overcome. The doctor and the young man stayed with the Steinbecks all night, and in the morning the doctor pronounced the writer fit enough to travel again. He called the attack sunstroke.

When they got to Paris, John went to bed, and this time, in Elaine's view, he had good reason. They were met in Paris by Marlene Gray, a bright, very accomplished young woman they had met two years earlier in Spain, who would act as John's secretary. While John stayed in bed at the Lancaster, Elaine and Marlene scoured the city and its environs for a suitable house to rent. Although he was determined not to get up or get involved until the house had been secured, Pat and Dorothy Covici arrived in Paris, and John had to make some effort to be with them. Still, he frequently begged off because of illness, and Elaine wound up escorting them alone.

By the third week of May, Elaine and Marlene had located a rather spectacular rental, a five-story town house that had once been the servants' quarters for a larger house across a covered courtyard. Next door was the Rothschild mansion, and across, the President's palace. On the lower floors there were rooms for all the children (who would be joining them for the summer); above the kitchen on the third floor was a salon and dining room (the food came up on a dumbwaiter); and above that was the master bedroom and a small library which John could use as a writing room, overlooking the Rothschild gardens. Adjoining the upper stories was a rooftop terrace on which the Steinbecks made a garden (satisfying, John said, his "farming instincts"), fixing trellises, training vines, and planting flowers in the plant boxes. About three blocks away, near the river, there was a small fair or carnival—ponies to ride, carousels and balloons, and children playing.

It was delightful, and John began to get well. His French publisher, without his knowledge, arranged a reception for the publication in France of *East of Eden:*

> When I said I was sick he said he had invited only a few influential people. Well I went and there were at least five hundred influential people and twenty cameras and radio microphones. I saw I was stuck but I did it and do you know I didn't mind at all and in fact rather enjoyed it and I think did it well. I attribute this entirely to Brenner's work. I think one whole block of shyness has disappeared. And I will never be afraid of such things again. Pat was there and he was horrified. Kept saying I would never do it in New York. It violated a picture he had built up in his mind and shocked him I think. I'll be interested to hear his report to you. It will be hysterical. Anyway I must have signed at least a hundred books including those of all the waiters. It was a bang. Afterwards we came back and drank a bottle of champagne and went to bed. Today I am going to make some tape for French radio and see

some of our Embassy information people. And tonight we are going out with Art Buchwald. Faye Emerson is in town and he is giving a little party for her.

Last night before I went to sleep I started one of the little stories I want to write just in anticipation of having a room to work in. And after the lights were out I designed two more. I am really champing to get to work. Hope something comes of it besides talk. Really hope so. So many things I want to write. I'll never get one tenth of them done. [5/22/54]

The stories he was writing in his head were to be an interconnected series based on experiences that he had had as a youngster growing up in Salinas. (Only two or three were ever put on paper, and only one, "The Summer Before," was published.) At about this same time, he got an idea for a format for a series of articles—he had known he would do some articles, but he had been unsure what he was going to write about and for what periodical.

You know [he wrote Elizabeth] I have had an idea in the back of my mind for a long time. Here in France I get interviewed all the time. I spend hours with journalists helping them to make some kind of a story and then when it comes out it is garbled and slanted and lousy. I wondered why I did not write my own interviews and charge for those hours of time and have it come out my way. In other words, why should I not write 800 words a week for one French paper, simply called something like an American in Paris—observations, essay, questions, but unmistakably American. . . . Hoffman [his French agent] will sell them to one of the big Paris papers, perhaps Figaro. [5/27/54]

From early June through early September, Steinbeck wrote a short article every week which was published in *Figaro Littéraire*, a weekly newspaper magazine roughly similar to *The New York Times Sunday Magazine*. In his first article, he began:

At first intemperate thought it seems presumptuous for an American to write about Paris. So it did seem to me until I reversed the positions. How would I feel about a Frenchman writing about America? Then I remembered that the very best account we have of America of the late 18th century was written by a traveling Frenchman. He set down details of life of that time so usual to Americans that they did not bother to record them and now the French report is the only way we know what people ate and how they conducted themselves. You do not record what everybody knows and in a few years no one knows it.

"I will offer you Paris, " he continued, "perhaps not as it is, but as I see it." It would be a challenge to write of Paris for Parisians, and, he concluded modestly, he hoped he would not fail too miserably.

Marlene Gray would type from John's handwritten copy and then take it to the American Embassy's information office for checking. This bothered Marlene, since it smacked of censorship, but it was something that John wanted to do, both as a matter of courtesy and as a way of making sure that he didn't, inadvertently, put his foot in his mouth. After the Embassy opined, she would take the copy to be translated.

Initially there were problems in finding a good translator. Marlene, who had been in part hired by the Steinbecks because she had just graduated from the university in Geneva as an interpeter, tried several translators suggested by the editor at *Figaro*, but she felt in each case that the results were inadequate. She told John, "We've got to find another writer, someone sympathetic to your work to translate these. This is not you in French. Anyone can take your story and write about it, but it's the way you write about it."

Time was running out. The last translator had been the daughter of a brilliant French writer, but the translation had come out sounding like a high school composition. When Marlene went to the newspaper office to tell the editor that it just wouldn't do, he was extremely angry: "But I've got to have that copy. I've got to go to print. What are you doing?" Marlene was only twenty-two and beginning to feel out of her depth, but she said, "You can't print this. Do you really want this kind of French in your newspaper?"

When Marlene got back to the Steinbeck house, Elaine was furious. The editor had been on the phone. "You're going to make my husband lose his job," she said. "They have to have that copy right away." By chance, Marlene's professor at school, who was also a translator at the U.N., was in Paris at the time, and Marlene knew he admired Steinbeck. She took the first article to him, and asked if he would be willing to translate this, and, if it were accepted, the other articles of the series. He agreed, and was able to get into the spirit of what the writer was doing very well. In one article, John wrote about the house he was living in and the muse in the stables. As Marlene tells it:

Stables can be translated two ways—one is for horses and one is for cows. So Jean-François, very tongue-in-cheek because the entire piece was rather tongue-in-cheek, translated it into French as cow stables, and the Count and Countess in the big house were so furious. John thought this was the funniest thing ever. He got such a big kick out of it.

For a time both John and Elaine had been exasperated with her, not feeling as she did the crucial importance of translation, but over time they grew very close, and the Steinbecks called her their "European daughter." After he had settled into their house, Steinbeck was again dedicated to his writing, and once explained to Marlene that to be a writer, as far as he was concerned, a person had to practice every day like a musician. "Not a day goes by," he told her, "that I don't write at least a page of something—it doesn't matter what it might be—something."

Of all the aspects of the household, the one that impressed Marlene the most was the relationship between John and his wife. She thought of him as very possessive of Elaine, but not possessive in the sense of jealousy. "It wasn't like that," she recalls. "He just liked to have her in the house. When he was working in the study, no one ever disturbed him, but he liked to know that she was in the house. Once a week she would go to have her hair done. It was quite close—several blocks away, but she loved to walk. She'd walk there and back. If she was five minutes late, he'd come downstairs, saying, 'Where's Elaine?' And I said, 'She's on her way back. She'll be back. Don't worry about her.'"

During the summer Waverly and a roommate from school rented a car and went for a holiday in Venice. They had an accident on the way, so Elaine went down to help. John, Marlene recalls, was like a tiger in his cage. One evening, he told her, "You know, I really know one thing about myself—I am a one-woman man. And when I have that woman, when I finally think I have found *the* woman, I want her here all the time."

V

It may be that his possessiveness of Elaine was not usually inspired by jealousy, but this early summer he had been suffering an acute attack of it. On shipboard on their way to Europe, Elaine had had a very superficial flirtation with another man, and it plunged him into a tremendous internal turmoil that probably contributed to his poor physical condition throughout their early weeks in Europe and to his lengthy stay in bed once they reached Paris. It explains too his violent reaction to the drunk in Torremolinos who took a wisp of truth and magnified it into a forest fire in order to be as obnoxious as possible.

In mid-June in a letter to Elizabeth, he reflected on his previous condition and recovery in general terms:

> I had a good and long letter from Brenner. What a good woman she is! I kind of needed it too because I had taken a deep relapse. Got crowded by all the extra-marital facets of marriage and achieved a "what the hell" feeling that was like old times. Sometimes I do seem to pay a lot for marriage. But I suppose maybe I don't give enough—only all I have. And I'm sure I'm a thankless, ungrateful son of a bitch for even thinking this. I just don't have any place to run to, it seems sometimes. Anyway, the remarkable thing was that just when I hit bottom the letter came from Brenner telling me to be not too worried if I took a dive because it was perfectly natural. She must know by the quality of progress about when it will happen—like a drunk who falls off the wagon. Anyway, it gave me hope that the backslide was not permanent. [6/13/54]

But Elaine's flirtation was not the only blow that he had to absorb. One of the reasons that they had come to Paris was to see Bob Capa, who had been in Vietnam—wherever there was a war, Capa would be there, and he would always be in the middle of the action. The Steinbecks were expecting him to meet them in Paris after his "tour" in Indochina was over, and Marlene remembers that they were counting the days, talked about him all the time: "Wait till you meet Capa. He is so funny, so full of life." But only a few days before he was to arrive, the Steinbecks received word that he had been killed, blown up by a landmine. It didn't seem possible, Capa who had seen a half-dozen wars, who had taught John how to survive under fire. Capa, the charmer, the man without any money who knew everybody. Capa, the survivor.

After he received the news, John simply went out and walked all over Paris for fourteen hours. During the last decade and a half of his life, John suffered several losses of friends, but Capa's death seemed to hit the hardest of all. They were pals, almost brothers. They had fought each other and stood up for each other and understood each other. There was a service for Capa in Paris, where photographers and artists mixed with celebrities, jockeys, and bartenders, and, later, a wake conducted by John Huston in Capa's favorite bistro.

One of the things that pleased Steinbeck most about being a writer in Paris was the high regard in which the French hold writers, a regard that contains both respect and a measure of warmth in the relationship of reader to writer. It was very gratifying for him, and came through most vividly when he was asked to serve at the Kermesse aux Etoiles, a charity fair held out of doors. Celebrities of various kinds are invited, each holding forth in a booth from which, for a fee donated to charity, they dispense conversation and autographs.

When Steinbeck arrived, he found himself being introduced to the entire crowd over a microphone in such glowing terms that he wished some of his American critics who had said unkind things about his work could have been there to hear them. As he was conducted through the throng to his station, he heard applause and an occasional "hurrah." But, as he wrote of the experience later,

> The natural balance was soon restored. I distinctly heard some hisses. And I remembered that in the last century there was a French writers' club made up of men who had been hissed in Paris. Tourgenieff applied for membership and was rejected. He had never been hissed in Paris. He protested that he had been not only hissed but stoned in Moscow and St. Petersburg, but his claim was disallowed. It was not good enough. Until he was hissed in Paris he had no standing. And now I had been hissed in Paris and it made me very proud.

At the writers' booth, he sat among most of the leading names in contemporary French letters. *East of Eden* had just been published in France and an incredibly long line of people of all descriptions bought the book (receipts from this, too, went to charity) and asked him to sign it. Flustered by the length of the line, John began scribbling his name as fast as he could, then looked to his left and saw André Maurois working very slowly and deliberately. "There is no hurry," he said. "Take your time." And so John slowed down and began to look at the people and talk to them. "Where do you come from?" he would ask, or ask the youngsters where they went to school and their names. When the young girls broke into smiles when he misspelled their names on the book, he smiled with them.

Most bought their books, but when a young paratrooper just back from Vietnam came up, John gave him a copy. In return, the soldier offered him a piece of camouflaged silk, all he had with him to give. The people began to tell him about themselves:

> "This is my daughter. She is to be married next week."
> "My mother could not come. She is ill. Will you dedicate to her?"

"I was hurt in the resistance. My leg is artificial."
"I am a poet but unknown." . . . "As yet," I reply.

Marlene, who sat with him and helped when his French failed him completely, found herself in an embarrassing position. After giving the book to John, many of the people passed it on to Marlene for her signature. She would close it and pass it back, but they would say, "No, please write in it." She would say, "But I'm nobody," but they would insist. By this time the line had backed up, and John asked her, "What's happening?" She explained. "Sign," he said. "Don't be an idiot—sign 'Dame Edith Sitwell' or 'Greta Garbo' or whatever." Marlene protested, "But that would be dishonest!" He raised an eyebrow and looked at her. "They just want a signature, Marlene. Go ahead and sign it."

For a man who had always hated and avoided public occasions, he was coming to enjoy them more and more. There had always been a streak in him, perhaps related to his romanticism, that liked fancy dress and ceremony, although, as he told Elaine a number of times, "I have the soul to wear a cape and plumes and carry a sword, but I have the physique to be always handed a hod." To a certain extent, like Miniver Cheevy, he mourned the loss of the elegance of earlier times, and couldn't understand why the American Academy didn't have the same pomp and circumstance in its dress and occasions as the European academies. Several years earlier he had written to one of the operating officers of the Academy, saying that he was tired of "seeing Marc Connelly parading in regalia to make a peacock squirm while I remain as undecorated as a jailbird." "Will you," he asked, "please send to me at the above address, any regalia, buttons, ribbons, small swords etc., as are befitting to my academic grandeur?" [2/20/51].

When by return mail he learned that the only "regalia" authorized by the Academy were decorated buttons, he was dismayed:

Many thanks for your letter and I shall treasure the buttons when they arrive. I must say I am disappointed at the lack of regalia. The French Academy meets dressed in cocked hats, embroidered vests and small swords. The Spanish academicians wear pants made entirely of bird of paradise feathers. Why can't we do something as spectacular and for the same reason—to cover with finery our depressingly small talent? [2/23/51]

Now, in the summer of 1954, he had been invited to a dinner given in his honor by the French Academy, and he was frightened to death. He could have used a peacock feather or two to shore up his confidence, but he was forced to do with dinner clothes. And it was an affair to match all his dreams: gold service, crystal, great brass candelabra, and toasts to the guest of honor. He had no thoughts of a dinner long ago honoring Thomas Mann, an occasion that had filled him with disgust.

CHAPTER XXXIX

When he had come home from his long walk of mourning, he had written about Capa, out of his love for Capa. When he had returned from the charity fair in the Tuileries, he wrote of the warmth that was given him, out of love for the French people. He wrote about living in Paris, writing in Paris, being interviewed in Paris, and fishing in Paris, and about French-American relations. But because he felt that France was "hurt in its pride," he had not been quite as frank in his *Figaro* articles as he would have wished, and toward the middle of the summer he was tiring of "treading lightly." Nevertheless, for the most part he had written well, and his articles at their best had that effortless Steinbeck grace. He had written about small things, but, characteristically, it wasn't so much what he wrote about that gave his work value, as it was the quality of the man that he brought to the writing.

The short stories he had planned to write were another matter. They "languish," he wrote Elizabeth, although he had been "thinking about them a lot, heavens knows. I think maybe I might like to set down some of the thinking if it wouldn't bore you." He had been turning the problems posed by the stories over and over in his mind, and talking to various visitors about them in order to get their ideas:

It seems to me that most writers in America, and I myself among them, have gone almost entirely in the direction of the past. We are interested in setting down and celebrating old times. It is almost as though we wanted to define a past, which probably never did exist. The stories of childhood, the stories of the frontier, the novels of one's old aunts, etc. This is fine but there can be enough of it. There are very few American writers, notably writing for the New Yorker, who write about today or even today projected into the future. With something of a shock I realize that I have written about nothing current for a very long time. Even in my projected short stories it is that inevitable going back. The projected book "Pi root" is of course the present verging into the future, but I am not writing that now. I do want to write some short stories this summer. It has occurred to me that we may be so confused about the present that we avoid it because it is not clear to us. But why should that be a deterrent? If this is a time of confusion, then that should be the subject of a good writer if he is to set down his time. I must think about this. I wonder whether this might not be the reason there are so few good mss coming from the young writers. If it were so then it would be valid to inspect the scene for its salients, its character tendencies, its uncertainties, its probable effects on the future in terms of character making and warping of people now growing up. [6/17/54]

This was the second stage in his effort to find a new direction for his work after *East of Eden*—the first had been his aborted effort (a possibility he still held to in the back of his mind) to regenerate his thinking and technique by writing a play. His thinking now led him almost immediately to abandon his short story series, for as he had always done, he was looking to advance, to experiment, to become a better writer, and to cover old ground using the same techniques would not bring him any closer to that "light over the hill" that, as he told Covici, he was always striving for. His determination to focus on the present as "a time of confusion" with a "climate of fear and suspicion" would lead him eventually to *The Winter of Our Discontent*.

But first he had to solve "the problem behind the problem," the difficulty of gathering the necessary materials about the present out of a life that was peripatetic and generally, nowadays, led in a rather rarefied social climate. His answers were to avoid the problem and turn to fantasy, as in *Pippin;* to try to establish ties to a new community, Sag Harbor, which provided the material for *Winter;* and to look for material and try to get in touch with the fabric of ordinary life, which provided the material for *Charley.* The sadness of John Steinbeck, writer, during the last years of his life was that although he had the will to advance—a will that was almost superhuman in its determination—none of the solutions that he tried were very satisfactory.

He continued to complain about the harassment he was receiving in regard to requests for interviews. Since in his *Figaro* articles he thought of himself interviewing himself, he had tried to cut off all such activities on the basis that he was a working journalist who needed to mine his own ideas rather than giving them away. Then at the end of June, he told Elizabeth:

> I have now passed from the interviewing stage to the portrait stage. There are proposals to do me in every possible medium from terra-cotta to chicken wire. And I don't have a great deal of desire to be perpetuated in much of anything except strawberry ice cream perhaps . . . at least it would be in my natural coloring. [6/28/54]

In the meantime *Sweet Thursday* had been published in the United States, had reached the best-seller list, and was being reviewed. In sending the clippings, Pat declared that they were running about ninety percent in John's favor. After receiving a batch of the reviews, John wrote back:

> I am constantly impressed with the fact that reviewers do not read very carefully. They always seem to read with a preconception of what it might be or might have been. And I wonder why they are so obsessed with my immortality. They feel that I am letting them down by not giving a good god dam about it. And also they do not want me to have any fun. They say I enjoyed writing STH as though it were some kind of crime. [6/21/54]

A few days later he wrote again, this time reporting on his activities and those of the children, who had recently arrived with Waverly and her college roommate:

> I enclose in this the newest article for Figaro. An essay on fishing. I think it is true and hope you find it amusing. The boys have poles now and are ready to do some fishing in the Seine. And about time too. Catbird [young John] would rather fish than do anything in the world. It is the only thing that can hold his attention indefinately. Tom has conceived a passion for Napoleon and is making a scrap book about him with pictures of battles and things. We went to Invalides and he was fascinated. I guess the reason children and small people have this love for Napoleon is because of his height and because what he did was completely improbable.
> I was very much pleased with your last report of the reorders of S.Th. That, after all, is the best test of all. I wish just one critic would have found some of the very low keyed jokes which were placed for the highly educated. I suppose as usual, these will be only discovered by the illiterate.

Elaine and I have met Alice B. Toklas a couple of times and have succumbed to her charm. I guess she is the ugliest woman I have ever seen and within a few moments she becomes one of the most attractive. I have never seen anything like it. . . . Would you please mail a copy of the Short Novels to [her]? [6/23/54]

In mid-June Radio Free Europe asked John to come to Munich to look at their operation, and he and Elaine went the first week of July and stayed a week. Although it rained both going and coming and the whole time they were there, John felt that it was a very rewarding trip. They received an intensive tour of the facilities, met and talked to most of the key personnel, and watched various aspects of the operation in progress. When he got back, he wrote to Elizabeth about his thoughts in response to his visit:

I have been thinking of the Munich experience ever since I got back and the most frightening aspect of the whole trip is the gradual and deadly effect of the Soviet system on the minds of the people. We know what brain washing was able to do to our troops made prisoners in Korea. But the gradual suppression of people behind the curtain is horrible beyond thought. Even those people who, disliking the regime, have at great danger to themselves escaped, have been so conditioned that they are no longer able to think straight, words have changed their meaning and it is practically impossible to communicate with them. It is possible that our broadcasts behind the curtain are practically meaningless to the listeners, because the semantic tie has been broken. In addition the people have been subjected to a long series of frustrations so that their wills have been destroyed. If you subject a rat to twenty-four hours of frustration you can drive him insane or reduce him to a shapeless apathy. Reports from the satellites, even official reports, show that a general apathy has overcome the youth there. This is one of the penalties of the system. By destroying individual choice, they also destroy initiative. It is beginning to worry them very much. Actually what they have created is whole nations of neurotics who have lost the power of response. But also we have lost contact with them. [6/54]

While he was in Germany, Radio Free Europe asked him to do a piece that could be broadcast to the Satellite Countries, a short, personal statement outlining his position as a writer. The psychology of reaching these people interested him greatly, and he thought a long time about what he should say and how he should say it. He decided that he could be even more effective if he could deliver his message in the native languages of the countries involved—he planned to learn how to say his speech phonetically in each of four languages: Czech, Polish, Hungarian, and Rumanian.

Marlene remembers that after composing his statement, he had a Czechoslovak come to the house and write out an English-phonetic rendition of it as it would sound in Czech. Then hour after hour he practiced, working with the tape recorder and having Marlene critique his progress. He did not, Marlene thought, have a very good ear for languages, but with his usual drive toward perfection, he pushed himself to get it right, going over and over it, again and again. Finally, Marlene suggested diplomatically, "John, you sound so good in English, why don't you do it in English?"

He compromised by doing it in Czech and English, giving up on trying to pronounce the other three languages.

To my friends,

There was a time when I could visit you and you were free to visit me. My books were in your stores and you were free to write to me on any subject. Now your borders are closed with barbed wire and guarded by armed men and fierce dogs, not to keep me out but to keep you in. And now your minds also are imprisoned. You are told that I am a bad writer but you are not permitted to judge for yourselves. You are told we are bad people but you are forbidden to see and to compare. You are treated like untrustworthy animals, subjected to conditioning as cold and ruthless as though you were rats in a laboratory. You cannot travel, you cannot read freely and you cannot work at the profession of your choice. Your writers are the conditioned servants of a regime. All of this is designed to destroy your ability to think.

I beg you to keep alive the integrity of the individual, in his ability to judge and compare and create. May your writers write secretly and hold their writing for the time when this grey anaesthetic has passed as pass it must. The free world outside your prison still lives. You will join it again and it will welcome you. Everything around you is cynically designed to destroy you as individuals. You must remember and teach your children that they are precious, not as dull cogs in the wheel of party existence, but as units, complete and shining in themselves.

II

The first part of summer had been terrible—a deep depression, the death of Capa, and almost continuous bad weather, rain and cold—yet as time passed, it became a very good summer after all. John and Elaine were happiest when they were by themselves, but John got great satisfaction from doing his duty as a father. He frequently sent the boys out on their own in Paris, thinking to build up their self-reliance and independence (Gwyn would not allow them to go out unaccompanied), and he was pleased with what he perceived during the summer as their "progress."

It seemed as if nearly everyone they knew came to Paris that year, and they had a constant stream of visitors. Jules and Joyce Buck saw them several times, and Jules noted the change in his personality: "Elaine brought him out, brought out that side of him that was always trying to escape. He was bashful, and having gone through a very rough early period, a very careful man in many ways. But when things were going really well, my God the look on his face was pure happiness."

They enjoyed entertaining in their house, the most elegant "home" they would ever have. Elia Kazan and Burl Ives visited them one evening, and as they were leaving, walking down the street together, Kazan glanced back at the house and said, "God damn. I do hate the middle class." Ives, happy to see his friend had at last found a safe harbor, was somewhat taken aback. "What the hell are you talking about? If John wasn't in there, for Christ sake, he'd be out in the cold ... probably wouldn't be alive. He's comfortable. What the hell. Middle-class, my ass."

On occasion the Bucks walked with John through Paris, and they recall he seemed fascinated with everything. He could give you a biological breakdown of the composition of horse manure, could tell you what the horse ate two days earlier. He would talk to the pigeons, and they would talk back to him. One day they saw a rat crossing the street, and John said, "This rat shouldn't be here." "Why not?" Buck asked. "Because he's a Seine river rat—he's not a sewer rat," John said. Buck asked, "How do you know?" John said, "I can tell from its legs." "What are they, flippers?" "No, but look at that nose. He can poke it above the river." "So," Buck said, "you've been snorkeling." John said, "Yes." "And so you're trying to tell me that river rats go snorkeling?"

The Bucks also remember Elaine's birthday party that year, which John began planning three months in advance. For her presents, he gave her a painting and arranged to have Waverly's portrait painted. For the party, he decided to have it out of Paris at a house rented by a friend, the interior decorator George Stacey whose house was a huge

U-shaped chateau that had once belonged to the finance minister of Louis XV. When the guests arrived, they were greeted by the sight of candles burning in each of the windows of the chateau, and they were escorted from their cars by Thom and John dressed in livery and carrying torches. Inside they were conducted to the ballroom, illuminated by candelabra and firelight, where they sat down to a catered dinner and listened to an orchestra. "Truly," Joyce Buck recalls, "you felt you were back in the 18th century."

Shortly after this John wrote to his accountant, Sol Leibner, and to Marcia Ross, in charge of finances at McIntosh and Otis, in response to the news that he had only $4,500 in the bank. He told them that he didn't think it was a very good policy for them to scare him, since he had not spent any money he could have avoided spending—except, perhaps, for the car. But they wouldn't want him to buy an old junker, would they? He was getting to the point where he was feeling guilty if he just considered buying a pair of pliers. His glasses were mended with wire because he didn't want to spend the money to get new frames. In the time that he had spent worrying about this, he could have written three short stories—they were stifling his work and he was worrying so much that even though he was in the most beautiful city in the world he couldn't have any fun. He ended: "Love to all there and please don't take this too much to heart. But I also hope you will know how serious I am about it" [8/20/54].

As his association with *Figaro* came to a close—he was several articles ahead of publication by mid-August—he became involved in a variety of writing projects. He told Elizabeth and Pat that he had finished two-thirds of a long short story and had written part of a ghost story. *Holiday* had asked that he do an article about his writing in respect to his growing up in Salinas, and he told Elizabeth:

> I don't know what I can say for Holiday about writing in Salinas. Whatever I said would probably be a fake because I don't remember. What I could say is that I don't know whether I was influenced by the town except in so far as everyone is influenced by everything but that I do know there was always a sense of dark and violent drama there to influence me if I were influenceable. [8/17/54]

The article he eventually wrote, published in June of the following year as "Always Something to Do in Salinas," was one of his best, even though it ran counter to his resolution to get away from writing about the past. It was not entirely complimentary to his hometown and served to fuel antagonisms already ignited by the publication of *East of Eden*.

In August he met Carmel Snow, editor of *Harper's Bazaar*, who asked if he would write some articles for her. He gave her copies of the *Figaro* pieces, but also promised to do a short article just for *Harper's Bazaar* on a man's view of women's fashions (he had told her of the article he had planned to do for *Collier's* two years earlier). Also in August *Plaisir de Paris* asked him for an article, and when he refused, they offered to pay him the same price for an interview, and so he obliged. Late in the month he did a story article in "collaboration" with Catbird on bubblegum, an amusing fantasy (about which Catbird later had nightmares), and after it appeared, he reported to Elizabeth that "the mail on it is hilarious. A number of letters ask if it really happened. Some say they don't believe it and one man has taken it as an allegory for world philosophy."

At the beginning of September, John and Elaine sent the boys off to Gwyn, who was in Rome, and went to London for two weeks. There they met Malcolm Muggeridge, an editor at *Punch*, and he also asked John to do some writing for him. John told him that he had a piece on television in mind which he might be able to use, but when they met again at Muggeridge's house, John told him that perhaps he could contribute something like a monthly letter to *Punch*—but not to hold him to it since he wasn't sure he was up to it. As was their custom in London, the Steinbecks spent as many evenings as possible at the theater, one evening going to see *A Day by the Sea* with John Gielgud and Ralph Richardson. They stopped by backstage afterward to see Gielgud, and he seemed very pleased. Steinbeck wrote his agent, "I like the London theater so much. It is entirely different from ours. If I lived here I am sure I would want to be a playwright. Maybe I will want to anyway. Among other things I have thought it might be a good transition into the new thinking about writing. A play has less chance of having attitudes because there is no chance of editorial" [9/14/54]. They saw the Graham Watsons and went to see *The Boy Friend* with them. Watson also gave them a pile of books by young English novelists to read on their trip.

It was while he was in England that the thinking he had done about a new direction in his serious writing seems to have come to a head, and he wrote a little essay about it "to himself" and sent it to Elizabeth. It said in part:

Style or technique may be a straitjacket which is the destroyer of a writer. When it is said that he has ceased to progress, can it not be that he is held to a line by his own unconscious technique? It does seem to be true that when it becomes easy to write the writing is not likely to be any good. Facility can be the greatest danger in the world. But is there any alternative? Suppose I want to change my themes and my approach. Will not my technique, which has become almost unconscious, warp and drag me around to the old attitudes and subtly force the new work to be the old? I think this is true. . . .

Now the next problem is this—Can one dump his technique or has it become so much a part of oneself that it is like the shape of his face. I don't know. I want to dump my technique, to tear it right down to the ground and to start over. [9/17/54]

His drive to improve was a lonely struggle, one that had little to do with those motives that more commonly inspire the serious writer—appreciation, recognition, the hunger for immortality. It was simply something he had to do for himself, for what he was and what he had chosen to be. In childhood his father had told him, "If you are going to do a job at all, do it right." And John Steinbeck was going to do it right, never satisfied that he had worked hard enough. He wanted to relax after an all-out effort with *East of Eden*, to pace himself with short pieces about small things that caught his interest, but no matter how slight the occasion, he ended up trying to make the piece as perfect as possible for what it was.

He was caught between the compulsion to write and the impossibility of writing constantly at the level he insisted on for himself. Late the previous fall he wrote to Dook Sheffield indicating some awareness of the contradiction, although suggesting that his conflict was with the expectations of others:

It is a restless time for me between jobs. I look forward to it and then it comes and I don't know what to do with it. Once I was able to take up the slack by writing letters but that doesn't work any more. I write very few letters. There is a vast difference between writing letters and answering letters.

Then too, between jobs, the pressure is on me to write "short pieces" for this or that. It is generally considered that I can whip out a short piece—about anything you want. And damn it I can't. Or if I do it stinks. It takes just as long for a short piece as a long one. [11/2/53]

He was the one beforehand of course, who thought he could "whip out" a short article or two without any great strain, only to discover that he had been fooling himself about the amount of effort he would expend. If he had only put as much energy into discovering and developing his subjects—coming up more often with topics of real significance—as he did worrying about and working on technique, at least some of his articles during this period would have achieved a level beyond being simply well-written, and interesting or amusing.

But he didn't care about "significance"—he always paid more attention to "how" than to "what." It was a concern that had stayed uppermost in his consciousness from his earliest days as a writer when he was experimenting with sound as a means of communication. When he felt, as he did in the early fall of 1954, that his writing was not moving forward, he looked to technique as the source of the problem. Steinbeck shared with Hemingway the belief that any problem in writing can be solved by the application of heavier and heavier doses of self-discipline. But the idea of imposing a discipline on his choice of subject did not seem to occur to him—even though he was conscious that the subjects of both books of this period (*Sweet Thursday* and, later, *Pippin*) were self-indulgent. It may have been a virtue that he was not an egotist obsessed with his own importance and achievement of possible immortality, but it was also a major factor in allowing him to write books like *Sweet Thursday* and *Pippin* almost entirely for his own amusement.

At the same time, he was not totally unaware of "the problem behind the problem," the need to become inspired by and involved in new subjects and themes. Only a few weeks after he had written his "Essay to Myself" [my title] in which he had decided he must tear his technique down to the ground and start over, he wrote to Elizabeth, forecasting the trip he would take six years later in preparation for *Charley*:

> There is one thing I want to do. When I get home I want to sort of clear my mind and then do some work I have laid out but about the late spring I want to take a drive through the middle west and the south and listen to what the country is about now. I have been cut off for a very long time and I think it would be a valuable thing for me to do. New York is very far from the nation in some respects. And it isn't politics so much as the whole pattern. I have lost track of it I think. [10/6/54]

After going to Paris to close up the house, the Steinbecks packed up the Jaguar and took a leisurely journey through the south of France, headed for Florence. Just before he left, he did some readings of pieces selected from various of his books for a record to be loaned out by U.S.I.S. libraries and used by the Voice of America, and by the time they were on their way to Italy, they were both nearly exhausted, and John went into an emotional tailspin. They motored down to the Loire, through Bourges, Le Baux, and then to St. Paul de Vence. Here John emerged from the bathroom in their hotel room one morning, having shaved off his mustache, and Elaine screamed—she thought he was a stranger.

From Florence he wrote to Elizabeth in early October:

> I'll start a letter but don't know how far I will get at one sitting. We're going up to a lake for lunch and it is getting near time. We have had a busy time. I am finally getting to see the Florentine artisans at work, gold, silver, leather, wood, ceramics. They are simply wonderful. Every day we have done a little of museums but thank God not so much as before. Elaine has relaxed about this. She was frantic before. Now she is content with an hour or so a day which is all I can take with pictures and statues. Fall has come really. There was a snowfall in the Appenines night before last and it looks very beautiful from the Ponte Vecchio, and the golden autumn light is on the country, something unbelievable. . . . I'm having kind of fun not thinking about much of anything except how you make things out of leather. [10/9/54]

This was a major highlight of their trip for him—watching the artisans at work, particularly the leatherworkers who so fascinated him that he went into a phase that lasted most of the rest of his life of making things out of leather. He brought to it so much enthusiasm that friends of the Steinbecks developed a motto: Don't lend John anything or leave anything at his house smaller than a breadbox; otherwise, when you retrieve it, you will find that it is covered in leather.

After several weeks in Florence they went to Rome. There, the Embassy gave a reception for him, and although the guest list was long, including many dignitaries, by applying his new-found confidence as prompted by the work of Gertrudis Brenner, he found the experience pleasant and without strain. One thing happened that he thought was amusing, as he reported to Elizabeth: "They have about 70 volumes of various [of my] titles in the library. Not one was in and they couldn't get them in so they had to go out and buy a dozen copies. Pretty flattering but funny."

Clare Boothe Luce was the Ambassador to Italy at the time, and she invited the Steinbecks to a cocktail party and then to a small dinner party. John was anxious to meet the wife of the man who through his publications had expressed so much antagonism and scorn toward him over the years, but despite this background and a notable gap in their political perceptions, the Steinbecks came away with the opinion that she was a very remarkable woman. Later, however, Mrs. Luce sent a note to John asking him a question about something they had talked about at dinner, to which she had added a P.S. that said in effect, "My husband doesn't really hate you as much as you think." John wrote a note answering her question and added: "P.S. If either of your husband's publications ever gave any of my books a good review, I would reexamine myself for mediocrity."

At the end of October 1954, they left Rome with John McKnight, the head of U.S.I.S. in Rome, and his wife and took a Greek steamer to Athens. From there they chartered a small boat to tour the Greek Islands. He had dreamt of them all his life, and they were a fixture in his imagination—still, he was not disappointed. He reported in one letter that the day before they had gone to "Mycenae and Thyreus [Thívai?] where Hercules was born and also to the theater of Polychaetis and the great sanctuary of Aesculapius. We saw the tombs of Agamemnon and Clytemnestra and Aegisthus and the plain of Argos. . . . I am so full of impressions that it is going to take a long time to get them straightened out—almost frantic with the things I've seen. Greece is much more than I had imagined and I had imagined plenty" [11/10/54].

Back in Athens, they stayed a week and then sailed back to Amalfi and drove to Positano and then Naples. Earlier they had met Joe Bryan in Rome, and one evening the three of them went to Capitoline Hill with wine and sandwiches and sat there in the moonlight, looking out over the Forum, celebrating the anniversary of the night that Gibbon decided to write *The History of the Decline and Fall of the Roman Empire*. Now, in Naples, John told Joe of an experience he had had in driving up. Part of the road is dead straight for miles, on one side a broad canal, with a bridge crossing it every kilometer or so, and on the other side a screen of trees between the road and the adjacent farmland. John was bowling along in the Jaguar when he spotted a donkey starting to cross the highway. He slowed a bit to make sure he would pass behind the donkey, but the donkey was hitched to a horse and the horse to a wagon. He slowed a bit more, but then suddenly realized that the wagon was being trailed across the highway by a cow, tied to the back.

The whole line was about sixty feet long, crossing the road very slowly, and John finally had to slam on the brakes at the last moment. As he reached the caravan, the Jag, in a skid, spun out a hundred and eighty degrees. Somewhat shaken, John and Elaine just sat there while the dust settled. In the meantime, the driver, with a dark hat and a very large black mustache, had pulled up his wagon and sat looking down at them. He put down his reins and began to applaud: *"Magnifico!"* he shouted. *"Magnifico!"*

John and Elaine returned to America on the *Andrea Doria*, arriving in New York just before Christmas. And in January John met William Faulkner for the first time, a meeting that was as disastrous as his earlier one with Hemingway. As before, it was somebody's idea that the two men get together, and it was ultimately arranged by Elaine and Jean Stein, Faulkner's New York friend: Stein, Faulkner, and Saxe Commins, Faulkner's editor, would come to the Steinbecks' for cocktails and then all go out to dinner.

Although John had misgivings, they were overcome by his curiosity, and he and Elaine were determined to be gracious hosts and make sure that everything went well. When the three guests arrived, it was clear to the Steinbecks that Faulkner had been drinking heavily—he was stiff in his attempt to be steady and almost totally uncommunicative. The Steinbecks took them up to the library and offered the Southerner John's chair by the fireplace, which he stubbornly refused, instead finding himself a straight chair off by himself in a corner. The situation became very awkward. Every time a topic was brought up in the conversation, Faulkner refused to comment, and when asked a direct question, he just grunted. After a long pause, Elaine brought up something about one of his books, and he muttered, "Don't talk about my books." When they got into a taxi to go out to eat, Elaine, also a Southerner, thought he might like to talk about Southern cooking. When she brought the topic up, he rattled something like, "Oh, I eat anything they put down in front of me."

Later, through Stein and Faulkner himself, they found out that he had not wanted to come, had dreaded it, and consequently had tanked up to get through the evening. The first time they met after that fateful evening, Faulkner apologized and said that he must have been pretty terrible, and Steinbeck replied, "Yes, you were." But they were two writers who didn't like talking about themselves, other writers, or literature, so they established a cordial relationship talking about hunting, fishing, dogs, and horses.

The Steinbecks spent much of the late winter looking for a country place, a house that they could go to on weekends, yet far enough out so that they could get away from the city completely. At various times they had thought about Nantucket (too far away) and Rockland County (not on the ocean) and various locations on Long Island (usually too crowded with city people). Now after returning from Europe with a sense that he was losing track of the mood of his own country, John felt that he had to get out of the city and get in touch with people again. The search now was for something more than a weekend or summer retreat—a place where they might want to settle and live much of the time. They even thought of it as a search for a sort of Cannery Row East. On several occasions they simply got into the car and drove around, looking for a community that they liked. Both John and Elaine liked the ocean, and they found themselves returning to Long Island, and focusing on Sag Harbor, the town where they had rented a house for a month in 1953.

It had many advantages. It was so far from the city that it didn't even seem to be part of Long Island; its history, and the speech and attitudes of the people gave it a closer kinship to New England than New York. It was somewhat isolated, not being on either the rail line or the main highway, and it was nearly surrounded by water. For a time John and Elaine argued, John wanting to find a place inland so he could have trees and a garden, and Elaine wanting to be close to the ocean beach. Then Elaine decided she also wanted a garden, and they settled on looking for a place off the ocean, but near one of the several inland waters so that John could have a boat and be able to fish.

One day in late February they had purchased a local paper and noticed that a house on one of the inland coves was for rent for the summer. While they were being shown the house, John stopped, looked out the window, and pointed to a small peninsula with a little house sitting on the bluff above the water: "I don't want this house—I want that one over there." But that one isn't for rent or for sale, he was told. "Just check and see if it isn't," he told the agent. And it was, the owner having decided just that day to sell. Within two weeks they had purchased it, without ever having looked inside the door, but the condition of the house hardly mattered because the property it stood on was spectacular.

They had purchased two acres of a bluff in the shape of a pie-shaped wedge that pointed westward across the water. From the house which stood at the head of the point there was a view down across the oak trees and grass of the point and then across the water toward the village and the harbor a mile or so away. Around the point and below the grass and a border of shrubs, a fairly steep sandy bank dropped a dozen feet to the water. On one side, near the house, there was a boat dock, and although the water was not the ocean, but a large cove off the bay, there was an atmosphere of the ocean—ocean birds, salt smells, and sea borne weather. The feeling of the area was roughly similar to Pacific Grove, or at least enough so to give John some sense of being at home.

Steinbeck grew to love the place, both his home and the village, and during the years that followed, each summer their stay got longer and longer until Elaine had practically to drag him back to the city. The house, as they had suspected even before they examined it, was one of those odd, jury-rigged summer cottages that had been added to, altered, and fixed up in an incoherent fashion by a series of owners and handymen with varying levels of ability. Like the Pacific Grove cottage, this one had single-wall exterior construction and no insulation or heater, but it did have a large, impressive fireplace. His first work on the house was to winterize it, and in doing so, he turned the vaulted living room with fireplace into a combination library–game room–dining room and converted a screened-in porch into a small sitting room. Since the new sitting room was easily heated and adjoined the kitchen—the two were really one room with a bar separating one area from the other—most of their living was done there. Even after all the major work on the house had been done, it was still a rather strange, tacky little cottage, one that you could learn to love for its peculiarities if you owned it, but not the sort of place you would imagine as the primary residence for a world-famous, moderately wealthy author.

In fact, none of the Steinbeck residences during the last part of his life were particularly impressive—the address may have been good, the property expensive, but neither the townhouse, the apartment, or the Sag Harbor cottage presented either luxury or wealth in the way they were decorated or furnished. It was not their style to live in plush surroundings—interesting, comfortable, or attractive, but not plush. When John Fisher, the decorator husband of Shirley Fisher came by the townhouse to help out, the Steinbecks asked him to make sure that the house didn't end up looking as if it had been decorated. They spent most of their money on travel, and many of the decorations and appointments in their residences were gathered during their travels. Beyond travel, their money went into cars—they had a series of very good cars—and boats (John had a new boat almost every year after they had purchased the Sag Harbor house). For the most part, their style of living was very middle class.

Aside from recovering from his trip to Europe and looking for a country home, John had done very little in the two months since their return. As he put it in a letter to Ritchie Lovejoy,

> I seem to have been in a kind of state of suspended animation for quite a long time. Haven't done any work or any thinking or anything. Just coasting and kind of enjoying it. But there's a restlessness that goes with it too and when the restlessness gets too great, then I usually go to work. And maybe I've done too much writing rather than too little. Spring is going to break loose pretty soon and that is a very exciting time. I have a little point of land on a bay out on Long Island near a place called Sag Harbor. Used to be a sailing center and hasn't changed much. Anyway there's a little house and a pier and big oak trees and a little boat and good fishing and I'm pretty anxious to go out there. . . .
>
> Ritch, do you have, or can you get any photographs of Cannery Row—of the lab and Wing Chong's and Flora's, etc.? Jo Mielziner asked me. He is designing the sets for Sweet Thursday for next fall. I find I don't have a single picture. . . .
>
> My sister Mary is living in my little house in P.G. She rented her Carmel house and is using the cottage as a camp between trips. I miss that little place but have no idea when I will see it again. I want to stay in New York this year. All last year we were travelling and got pretty tired of it. I want to stay home and work this year—but I don't do any work. . . .
>
> How are Tal and the kids? They must be big. I see my boys all the time. They live only six blocks away and come over regularly. They are real good company and lots of fun.
>
> The picture of East of Eden is going to open next week. Big benefit and a mess. But its a real good picture. I didn't have anything to do with it. Maybe that's why. It might be one of the best films I ever saw. [3/2/55]

He didn't get much pleasure from writing letters anymore, and this was a tired letter from a tired man who for the time being had little more on his mind than a desire to go fishing.

Near the end of March he and Elaine went to the opening of Tennessee Williams's *Cat on a Hot Tin Roof.* Steinbeck had mixed feelings about Williams's work, and on occasion had referred to Williams and Faulkner, privately, as part of "the neurosis belt of the South," as writers who dwelt on sickness, decay, and abnormality (admitting, at the same time, that to a lesser extent he did the same thing). On the other hand, he admired and perhaps was a little jealous of Williams's ability to bring a lyrical quality of speech to the stage in such a natural way, and he also admired Williams's innovation and experimentation. When *Camino Real* ran into rough reviews in 1953, he wrote to drama critic Richard Watts, Jr., of the *New York Post*:

> At least twice a year, every critic, during the dead period, writes a piece bemoaning the lack of courage, of imagination, of innovation in the American theatre. This being so, it is my opinion that when a play of courage, imagination and invention comes along, the critics should draw this to the attention of the theatre-goer. It becomes clear that when innovation and invention automatically draw bad notices, any backer will be cautious of investment, and furthermore will not playwrights stop experimenting if their plays will not be produced? [4/7/53]

Cat on a Hot Tin Roof was a play that presented several outstanding performances by individual actors, but perhaps the most electrifying was the characterization of Big Daddy Pollitt by John's friend Burl Ives. A very dramatic moment in the play comes in the second act when Big Daddy, the large, overbearing patriarch, the embodiment of health, virility, and hedonistic self-gratification, is told suddenly that he has cancer. Ives' own father had died of cancer, and Ives had taken him to the doctor when he got the diagnosis. His father was a big, straight man, on the same physical order as his son, and when he came out of the doctor's office, Ives recalls, "he was now a little old man. He just was deflated; he had literally shrunk. He really had. My God, he was reduced in every way."

During the opening night performance of the play, when the boy tells him that the character he is playing has cancer, Ives cried out in anguish and deflated animal pride, a cry like a stuck pig, all the time thinking of his father. After the performance was over, John came backstage, pushed his way through the people, and said to Ives, "I just want to say one thing. That was the first time I ever saw a man shrink right before my eyes on stage." In looking back, Ives recalls, "That shows how penetrating his mind was—that's where my mind was. And I was really unconscious of it myself. But the essence of that got to that man. . . . He had it right on the nose."

In the spring of 1955 John began his long association with *Saturday Review*. The magazine, through Elizabeth Otis, had asked him on several occasions for contributions of a short article or "guest editorial," but he had always been busy with other things, and the opportunity had not appealed to him. Now, after his pleasant experience with *Figaro*, he decided it would be good to have a regular outlet in this country for occasional short pieces he might write. For its part, *Saturday Review* was one of the few Eastern literary periodicals that operated independently of the so-called New York literary mafia, and Norman Cousins, the editor, was an admirer of Steinbeck's work. Looking back, Cousins recalls:

> I think we held substantially the same literary values; namely, that the main purpose of the novel was to tell a story and not just to bare one's soul; that the obligation to readers was primary; that writing was a craft imposing stern requirements on the writer; and that cliques, like gangs, were as obnoxious in literature as they were in universities.

Steinbeck, who contributed both time and money to the support of the United Nations, was impressed by Cousins's staunch editorial support of that organization, and he shared with Cousins a broad liberal view of mankind's global interdependence. Over recent years they had lunch together occasionally and talked about authors, books, and sports. They found that they had had roughly parallel experiences during their visits to Russia, had gotten to know some of the same Soviet writers, and agreed that it was important to maintain direct contact with them and help them in every way possible.

During a P.E.N. (International Association of Poets, Playwrights, Editors, Essayists and Novelists) luncheon earlier that year, Cousins once more broached the subject of Steinbeck writing for *Saturday Review*, possibly on a regular basis. "It would have been an important triumph," he recalls, "for *SR* to have been able to publish him in every issue." Steinbeck was receptive, but he didn't feel that he could write a column on a weekly basis—he might be able to do something monthly, but he didn't even want to be held to that. With that understanding, Cousins added the novelist to the staff as an "Editor-at-Large" and developed a plan whereby his work would alternate on an irregular basis with other contributors. Two of John's first three pieces were categorized by the magazine as "editorials." One appeared at the beginning of April and was an anti-McCarthyism essay that reexamined the role of the "professional witness" and forecast his demise. Another, which

discussed the lack of family responsibility as a cause of juvenile delinquency, came out at the end of May. This latter essay again brought to
the surface two long-standing Steinbeck interests—society in the Middle Ages and group behavior. He concluded his second piece by saying,

> People need responsibility. They resist assuming it, but they can-
> not get along without it.
>   I know this will cause cries of pain from the doctrinaires of the
> individual. I'm one such myself. But also I believe that man is a
> double thing—a group animal and at the same time an individual.
> And it occurs to me that he cannot successfully be the second until
> he has fulfilled the first.

During the spring he and Elaine spent every other week in Sag Harbor. He had ordered a boat for fishing and could hardly wait for it to
arrive. When he was in the city, he was using Elia Kazan's office on
Times Square, writing for *Saturday Review* and for *Punch*. "When I
finish work," he told Toby Street, "I walk around in the streets for an
hour or so, looking in windows. I never get tired of that" [5/9/55].

By the first of June they had moved to the country for the summer.
One of the things that made Sag Harbor very attractive for them was
that they were able to become part of the community fairly rapidly.
They met Bob Barry, who owned one of the major marinas, Baron's
Cove, and the hardware store, and whose mother owned the dry goods
store and whose father had been mayor. Bob, a hearty man with a big
belly, took the Steinbecks under his wing, invited John to go fishing on
his boat (before John got his own), had John and Elaine over for
drinks, and introduced them to many of the locals. Soon after moving
to the cove, John developed a pattern of getting up in the morning, and
with Charley-dog next to him on the seat, driving into the village. He'd
get his mail at the post office, buy a paper, and sometimes stop in at the
hardware store to buy material for whatever building or crafts project
he was working on.

He soon got to know most of the shopowners and people who
worked on Main Street. Others who had heard that Steinbeck had
moved in came up and introduced themselves. Later, John often
stopped by to have breakfast with a gang of regulars at the local coffee
shop after he had done his errands, and sometimes later in the day after
work he'd stop by and ask Barry out for a beer at Sal and Joe's or the
Black Buoy. Once the two of them were in a bar, sipping beer and listening to Jake the Plumber, a local character, tell tall tales. Jake, who

did not yet know Steinbeck, turned to him and asked, "You believe me, don't you?" Steinbeck, who had hardly said a word, turned his head slightly to look at him, and after a moment growled, "Believe you? Hell, I invented you!"

There may have been some in the town who were hostile to the idea of someone famous moving into the area, and there may have been some who after meeting the Steinbecks decided they didn't like them, but there weren't very many. One afternoon John was shooting skeet off the point with the police chief and the mayor. A neighbor called the police, and when the officer got there, he wasn't quite sure what he should do. John handed the gun to him and said, "Here, try a shot." The officer did, and John said, "Now you're just as guilty as we are." But the neighbor was an exception; John was made to feel more welcome than he had ever felt, even in Pacific Grove or Los Gatos. It became a tradition that when tourists came to town asking where Steinbeck lived, no one could ever really tell them exactly where. The Schiavonis, owners of the local grocery store, probably paid John the highest compliment any native of a "New England" small town can pay an outsider when they said, "He should have been born here and shouldn't have been famous."

About the middle of the summer the Steinbecks invited nearly all the people they had met in Sag Harbor to an open house–housewarming, which John called the "Sag Harbor Yacht Club Dry Regatta." It turned out to be not so dry, and they ended up with hangovers that lasted two days; they decided that would be their last attempt at "Village amity" for some time to come. The boat arrived, and John was out nearly every day learning the coastal waters and trying to find the best places to fish. He was not, as measured by results, a very good fisherman, but he loved doing it. He wrote Toby early in July:

This afternoon, we are taking the boat off Montauk Point to fish for blues. They are fine fighting fish and wonderful to eat. . . . It is about a forty-five minute run in our boat which will do thirty-four miles an hour if it has to. It is a sea skiff, lapstreak, twenty feet long and eight feet of beam and a hundred horse power Grey marine engine. I could cross the Atlantic in her if I could carry the gasoline. Has a convertible top like a car so that you can put it up when green water comes over the bow. Also it only draws eighteen inches so we can take it into little coves and very near the shore if only we watch the charts for rocks and depth. This is fabulous boating country and fishing country too.

We bring them home alive and cook them while they are still

kicking and they are delicious.... The Atlantic is very much richer in varieties than the Pacific. Lobster, clams, crabs, oysters and many kinds of fish. I really love it out here. Am going to winterize this little house so I can come up when it is cold. My little harbor freezes over and then you fish through the ice. The house needs double walls and an oil furnace but I'll do a lot of it myself. I am actually losing some stomach working around here and haven't felt so good in years. [7/5/55]

He also told Toby, "I am starting a new play. Hell I have started it over and over again. Good god what an exacting medium it is and how tricky." But a week later, he wrote Elizabeth, "I don't seem to be able right now to get down to hard writing but maybe I will."

CHAPTER XL

The production of *Pipe Dream*, the musical comedy version of *Sweet Thursday*, had been delayed for nearly a year, but it was now scheduled to go into rehearsal on September 20, 1955. Although John was not directly involved—Hammerstein did the book for the musical—he did want to follow it through rehearsal and tryouts to opening night in New York, to see how a musical was put together and to have the pleasure of watching it grow. For him one of the attractions of the theater was becoming a part of a close-knit community and sharing with the company the sweat and hope of building a creative whole that either came together, and clicked, or did not. And he was very enthusiastic about the chance for success of this production. Just after the start of rehearsals he reported to Toby: "Lord! its a good show. Fine score and book and wonderful direction and cast."

He was so enthusiastic that he practically begged Rodgers and Hammerstein for a piece of the action, and they arranged after some delay (there were so many backers that they had a hard time working Steinbeck in) for Steinbeck to have a small percentage of the play. Steinbeck insisted that ten percent, or the regular agent's commission, of his share go to McIntosh and Otis. When Elizabeth Otis objected that she'd had no part in the arrangements and didn't deserve a commission, Steinbeck wrote a most touching declaration of his gratitude:

As for the percent in P.D. [*Pipe Dream*]—let us never mention it again. I love you very dearly and I have never been able to demonstrate it—perhaps due to a curious embarrassed stiffness on the part of each of us. Also I remember everything—*EVERYTHING* and I am thankful for all of it and all of you. And now I will draw back into the little house of shyness in which we both live. [9/17/55]

On paper, the show seemed to be very, very good. In putting it together, the producers had tried to be revolutionary by hiring a dramatic director, Harold Clurman, for a musical and by getting an opera star, Helen Traubel, to play the part of the madam. In addition, this was to be a new direction for Rodgers and Hammerstein, who had specialized in soft, romantic, "family" musicals. Feuer and Martin had talked to them about the necessity in this show to take a more realistic, tougher direction.

As the show continued in rehearsal, John started on some serious writing, working in the morning and early afternoon, and then went to watch the show being put together afterward. He reported to Toby:

> Rehearsals go on and the thing gradually pulls into shape. I am learning a lot about what you mainly *can't* do on stage. At least I hope I am. Abe Burrows told me the wisest thing about the theatre. He said it is the art of leaving things out. The audience is usually ahead of the playwright waiting for him to catch up, he said. And I believe that is true. I know it is true in the plays I have written. . . .
>
> I wrote three short stories this week. And that would sound boastful if you didn't know I had been thinking of them a long time. The writing of them was simply putting them down. I work until four and then go over to rehearsal. I can't sit in the theatre all day. Wouldn't want to. So I work in an office around the corner where they call me if they wanted to. I am one of the very few authors who doesn't interfere. This is a matter of rejoicing for everyone. [10/1/55]

However, later, when the show started to go sour and it became clear that it wasn't going to work, he did try to "interfere" to the extent of passing on a number of specific suggestions. Since he had no official role in the production, no one really listened.

His new attempt to write a straight play, which he had pursued off and on during the summer, was put aside, and at the end of September he began an experimental novel. The novel would, he hoped, embody the ideas he had proposed the previous year in his "Essay to Myself" and be the culmination of all the thinking about a new start that he had done since then. He told Elizabeth:

> I want to work this with an absolute minimum of description and exposition—perhaps none—except in so far as the protagonists themselves are able to describe and expose. Naturally I am scared of it, but it is excited scared. I've given it every bit of thought I can now and for a long time. I have held off with the same reluctance

one has for jumping into water of unknown coldness. But I'm being pushed into it finally by built-in persuasions. It's time. . . . What I propose to do is to tell story, setting, character and mood using absolutely nothing except dialogue. If I can't make the people and the situation clear instantly by this method I will have failed. But I'm sure going to give it a try. In the more than a year that I have been thinking, I have also been listening very carefully to speech. . . . They say that a life is written in the face but now it seems to me, after listening, that it is even more written in the speech. The background is all there and the fears, the nature of the man in his speech. [9/24/55]

He then went on to describe at length the way that speech is used to conceal feelings, kinds of speech patterns and their purposes, the way talkers can reveal group feeling, and how every individual has a rhythm and tone unique to that individual. Then he told Elizabeth that when he sent her some of his experiment to read, she must follow the pauses carefully because sometimes they will contain the meat of what is being "said." He planned to use what he called "pause symbols" extensively, ellipses and underlining to indicate the length and the rhythm of unspoken words. "I have given this," he told her, "a great deal of thought while I have been, as Elaine says—'vegetating.' I don't really think I have been vegetating. There's no way of painting a Men at Work sign on the brow."

He would work on this manuscript for nearly eight months, after planning it for over a year. There is no record of the day-by-day struggle, but since he was entering uncharted territory, we can assume that it was painful and difficult.

By the time of the tryouts in New Haven and Boston, he was certain that *Pipe Dream* was in trouble—he was afraid not so much of failure, as he wrote to Oscar Hammerstein, as of "half-assed success which . . . would be worse than failure." There were many problems, but the basic one was that contrary to the understanding reached before the show was written, Rodgers and Hammerstein did not take a tougher, more realistic line than they had before. Much of the show was simply conventional pap. As much as he liked the producers, what they had done made him angry. "You turned my whore into a visiting nurse," he told them. Or, as he wrote to Kazan later, "What really is the trouble is that R. and H. seem to be attracted to my kind of writing and they are temperamentally incapable of doing it."

But there were other, practical difficulties. Richard Rodgers went in for his first cancer operation just as the show was coming out of rehearsal. The casting of Helen Traubel was a mistake. Not only was her presence in a relatively small part disrupting to the balance of the play, but as it turned out, she had lost her ability to project her voice. Throughout rehearsals everyone said, "Don't strain your voice, Helen. We know that you can fill the hall when the time comes." When the time came in New Haven, she couldn't be heard beyond the orchestra, and everyone connected with the show went into a state of shock. And finally, the musical score was not particularly memorable. Usually a Rodgers and Hammerstein musical had several songs in each show that became hits—this show had only one tune to hum on the way out of the theater, "All at Once You Love Her."

In Boston, night after night, John took notes on his own reactions and the reactions of the audiences. He sent letters to Rodgers and Hammerstein, pleading with them to make certain changes and appended the notes he had taken with scene-by-scene, often line-by-line suggestions. According to John Fearnley, who had worked often with the two men and was casting director and production aide for this play, none of John's suggestions were ever seriously considered. They accepted them as a courtesy to the author of the original story, but they didn't do him the courtesy of really listening to what he had to say. It was too bad, for part of the greatness of the team was their usual willingness to listen and to judiciously adopt suggestions that made sense. They had really missed the point of the novel, the undercutting of romance and fantasy by reality, and stubbornly insisted on making the ready room of the whorehouse a family room and turning an ambiguous love affair into a conventional prince-meets-and-falls-in-love-with-a-pauperess situation. It was the worst show that Rodgers and Hammerstein ever did, and Steinbeck's disappointment was far greater than he let on: this failure on top of that of *Burning Bright* (failures that, particularly in the second instance, were not necessarily his own) stung him so deeply that he never made a serious attempt to write for the theater again.

In January of 1956 the Steinbecks flew to Trinidad, where they were joined by John Fearnley. They chartered a forty-five-foot sailing boat, with skipper and one crewman, and toured the Windward and Leeward Islands. John gave the three of them Calypso names—he took "Inside Straight," a good pun and, perhaps, a comment on his recent luck, and gave Elaine "Queen Radio," because there was an omnipresent singing voice heard over the air in the region called "King Radio." He had fun writing some Calypso verses for the occasion, one of which compared

"Old Style Elaine" (Sir Lancelot's Elaine, who in the Arthurian legends dies of a broken heart) and "New Style Elaine" (a verse written as "a happy wedding of the Trinidad and the Texas schools"). The last stanza ran

> Now *my* Miss Elaine got a new-style set,
> She a high-breasted deep-breathing growed-up brunette.
> She tuck her behind in and she walk real proud,
> Got a B flat baritone C sharp loud.
> Say, "Listen, you rounders, and you'll agree,
> I got me a man and he got me."
> She rustle up her bustle and the folks concur,
> That she branded her a wrangler and he earnotched her.

It was a relaxed, bathing suit trip, with everyone in and out of the water, and John snorkeling, taking turns at the wheel, and fishing. They trolled to get fish for food, and occasionally they pulled up an odd specimen about which John would expound. When they sighted an island, they'd stop or not (they stopped at fourteen), depending on how they felt, and when they went ashore, they stayed as long as they felt like staying.

One island they stopped at was Saba, which belonged to the Dutch. There was no place to dock, but skiffs came out to meet them, and they decided to go in and look at the capital. The city turned out to be Bottom, which was at the top of the island at the bottom of a crater, eight hundred feet above sea level—all of which they found very amusing. They thought they would have some time to themselves, but the governor, a black married to a Dutch woman, had heard that Steinbeck had arrived, and he insisted they come and enjoy his hospitality.

They were sipping a drink called "apricot nectar" in the governor's house, when he asked if they had had a chance to see any of the beautiful needlework done by the women of the island. They said no. Whereupon the governor's wife brought out a selection of her work that was obviously for sale. Out of politeness, Elaine selected a handkerchief. Out of mischief, she picked out one that was a singularly nauseous purple—perhaps the ugliest handkerchief that John Fearnley had ever seen. Several months later, the Steinbecks had occasion to give Fearnley a gift. It was a book inscribed by John, and as Fearnley looked through it, he found the handkerchief folded between the pages. He returned it later to Elaine, tied around the branch of a plant.

The nauseous purple handkerchief changed hands back and forth over the next few years. Each time one of them gave it, the other had the terrible certainty that he'd get it back, and every time one got a gift from the other, he had a sick feeling in the stomach that the purple handkerchief would be there somewhere. During Lyndon Johnson's presidency, when the Steinbecks were frequent visitors to the White House, Fearnley was able to smuggle the handkerchief in, with instructions, with the help of Mrs. Johnson's secretary. At three o'clock in the morning, Fearnley's telephone rang. It was Elaine. "Fearnley," she said, "do you know who gave me that goddamned purple handkerchief—the President of the United States."

Even though it was winter, they returned to the Sag Harbor house rather than going to the city, and John went to work again on his experimental novel. They found it pleasant to be isolated:

> Out here I get the old sense of peace and wholeness [he wrote Pat Covici]. The phone rings seldom. It is clear and very cold but the house is warm. Elaine is ecstatically happy out here. She cooks and sews and generally enjoys herself. You can't imagine the change in disposition and approach in both of us.
>
> And it seems to be getting into my work. I approach the table every morning with a sense of joy.
>
> The yellow pages are beginning to be populated both with people and with ideas. This book with its new approach is not going to be long. It is only a practice book because in the back of my mind there is arising a structure like those great cumulus clouds you see over high mountains. [2/56]

He persisted with the experimental work for another month and then worked with it off and on for a few weeks following. It did not hold his attention beyond that because ideas, not technique, stirred his imagination and enthusiasm, and while he was working on his experiment, ideas for stories began to flood his consciousness, demanding to be written. He reported to Elizabeth:

> I am constantly amazed and to a certain extent frightened by the vagrant tendency of my mind and writing direction. It seems so often to take its own direction—can be resisted but goes into a pout if it is resisted. An example of this was Mr. Hogan. I had no intention of writing him. He just started and came out. Now I am embarked on Pi Root. H was and is going well, but in New York— what with Cat [young John] being in the hospital and other complications, he got interrupted. Then a crazy little idea intruded and festered like a mosquito. I sat down out here to go on with Pi Root, and what came out is this other thing. I resisted for a while and

then decided that the only way to get rid of the mosquito was to write it. And that is what I am doing this week with great amusement. It is a long short story but in the form of an historical report. It hasn't any title yet although I think it might be called *All Your Houses.* Can't get it out of my mind without putting it down.

Mr. Hogan was "How Mr. Hogan Robbed a Bank," which was published shortly after completion in the March *Atlantic.* In several ways—character, plot, setting—the story was the seed for Steinbeck's last novel, written several years later, *The Winter of Our Discontent.* "Pi Root" was a project he had had on his mind for some time; no one knows what it was about, but he had intended to use the experimental manuscript as practice for writing it. The title was apparently one that tickled his fancy, since Joe Elegant, in *Sweet Thursday,* is said to have written a novel called *The Pi Root of Oedipus* (which contains a scene in which "the young man digs up his grandmother to see if she was as beautiful as he remembered").

The "other thing" that he had resisted for a while and then decided he'd have to write to get rid of was the first version of *The Short Reign of Pippin IV.* Elaine recalls that he first got the idea of a story about the return of the monarchy to France in 1954 when they were living across the street from the Élysée Palace and making trips to the chateau where her birthday party was to be held. The story as it evolved in the back of his mind concerned a political crisis wherein the French, unable to form a stable government, decide to bring back the Comte de Paris as the Bourbon King of France.

He began, thinking that he would work on it only on weekends, but by the middle of March it had begun to run away from him. There were so many rich opportunities for satire, so many things and people that could be parodied, so many possibilities for humor offered by the plot hypothesis, that his mind insisted on working with it all the time. Elaine remembers that he never had more fun in his life. She could hear him while he was sitting at his table in the spare bedroom, chuckling and laughing while he wrote. By the end of the month, what was to have been a short story, grew to a long short story, and then to a full length book.

When he finished the first part of his first draft he sent it to Elizabeth to read, and told her:

I find that I completely believe in it. Hope you get a few laughs out of it. It certainly shows very little mercy to anyone. As a matter of fact I rather think the French will like it. It is the Americans who won't, but then the Americans I am afraid have very little humor. This damn thing has almost a Kafka overtone but it is written as history which indeed it is. [3/14/56]

A few days later he reported:

The bourbon story continues. The darned thing is about sixteen thousand words now and I don't quite know how far it is going but I should think twenty or twenty-five. That is a very ungainly length but then it is a very ungainly story, and it is surely a self-indulgence, but I'm doing it anyway and that is all there is to it. [3/17/56]

More than a month later, near the end of April 1956, he had finished the first draft:

The French story completed only proved one thing—that it has to be done over again or not at all. But since I am interested in it I shall do it over again. It is more than just a clever idea I believe and should be given that dignity. The basic structure is there but it needs warming and softening and sharpening and, horrors, lengthening. Attempting to make it a satire on scholarship in addition to everything else, I am afraid I came too close to the thing I was satirizing. It was dull. I am going to try it again to see whether I cannot make it better. [4/20/56]

As he began the revision, he found that, suddenly, he had "dried up." His mind was racing ahead again with various changes and new ideas, but he couldn't get his hand to move beyond the first paragraph. In the meantime, he had made arrangements to cover both the Democratic and Republican National Conventions, starting in early August, and he began to worry about being able to finish the book, which he now planned to be 40,000 words, before he left.

Two years earlier he had met Mark Ethridge, the publisher of the Louisville *Courier-Journal,* on the *Andrea Doria* coming back from Europe, and in the course of the correspondence that followed he expressed a desire to attend the political conventions, noting that perhaps a fresh point of view of all the goings-on behind the scenes might make good material for a series of articles. Ethridge took him up on the proposal, hired him to report for the *Courier-Journal,* and put together a syndicate of almost forty other papers around the country that would also carry Steinbeck's convention coverage. Steinbeck met Ethridge and his editor-in-chief, James S. Pope, in New York in April to make the arrangements, and then Ethridge invited the Steinbecks to come to his home in Louisville for a house party during the Kentucky Derby.

The Ethridges had a big, rambling, old Southern plantation house, and there were about five parties each day, starting at eleven o'clock in the morning with a mint julep party and then going on all day and all night. In between parties they went to the track twice (John, who was not a gambler, lost on the Derby and won on another race, coming out even). One of the nights, while everyone else was dancing, Mark and John were drinking together and, in the course of their conversation about women and marriage, invented what they called the "Aggressive Agreement." Elaine can remember them telling her about it, Mark talking in his soft Southern voice and John mumbling:

> It goes like this [Elaine recalls]—you walk in and your wife says, "You're drunk." And you say, "You're damned right I am, and I'm going to get a lot drunker." And of course then she's got nothing to say. You agree aggressively to everything your wife says when you are in any kind of spot. It doesn't have only to do with drinking. It can be "You are not producing the work you are capable of." And you say, "You are so right and I may never work another day in my life." It really leaves the wife up the creek. They loved it.

The Steinbecks, by the way, had two months earlier given up drinking except on Saturday evenings and had substituted having tea before dinner instead. John had been concerned because he felt that his two drinks before dinner were contributing to his tendency toward depression, and he and Elaine were both concerned that on those occasions that the drinking continued into the evening, they were very likely to get into a fight. The two days of day and night partying at Louisville involved more drinking than they had done in a very long time, and John was pleased and surprised, since recently one party usually disabled him for as much as two days afterward, that he was able to handle it. Along with a number of other people that they met for the first time, they were introduced to Alicia Patterson Guggenheim and her husband Harry Guggenheim, an introduction that led to John's writing for *Newsday* several years later.

The summer of 1956 brought a season of domestic conflict, perhaps one of the worst continuing battles of the Steinbecks' marriage. The boys came to Sag Harbor when their school was out, and they always brought with them a parcel of problems. This summer they were both sickly, having been ill off and on for much of the year, and John was convinced that they were learning hypochondria from Gwyn—he was determined to turn them away from "goldbricking." At the same time, he was pressing hard to finish the rewrite of *Pippin* and it wasn't going well. With one interruption after another, he was often in a foul mood. (Sometimes, of course, he made the interruptions himself, blaming them on others, just to get away from the writing table. Nearly anything that happened around the house or yard could become the occasion for an interruption.)

But the main trouble was caused by Waverly's wedding. The affair was to be held in New York, and Elaine had to travel back and forth to the city to make the very complicated arrangements. Elaine remembers that "he hated every second of it. The little boys were out there, and he would train the little boys to say things like 'You love Waverly better than you love us'—oh, yes, this was John. John's jealousy was beyond anything. . . . He hated anything that took the attention away from him where I was concerned." He thought that a big wedding was stupid and criticized every aspect of it (while earlier he had thought that the big weddings of his two nieces in California were just fine). To Graham Watson in London he complained:

> Our daughter is getting married on July fourteenth, and this astonishing occasion is being produced only a little less splendidly than Billy Rose's Aquacade. You can't imagine how many clothes you have to put on a girl when the sole purpose is to get them off.
> Meanwhile I have been trying to finish a little book which could be amusing and could get me guillotined also, but the interruptions of more important, i.e. wedding things have made it very difficult. [7/2/56]

As the father of the bride, Zack had been in New York to help Elaine with the arrangements, and this probably added to John's sense of jealousy. Just before the wedding, Zack had to fly to London for a movie, but would return for the ceremony itself. The night before, John asked Elaine if Zack's plane didn't get in on time, could he walk down the aisle and give Waverly away instead? Elaine assured him that if that happened, he could, and he found that possibility very pleasant. At the wedding itself the next day, Zack did show up, but John behaved very well anyway.

With the purchase of the Sag Harbor house, he had run into a familiar problem: where could he find a place to write? The previous year he had had a garage built on the property with the idea that he would put his workbench and tools in there and also set up a table for writing. He found, however, that during the winter and spring, even with a little heater, it was just too cold to work, so for a time he moved into the house and set up a place in the tiny second bedroom. From there he could hear nearly everything that went on in the house, and every time there was a noise that he couldn't identify, he would come out to see what it was. When it got warm enough, he moved back into the garage, but the garage was full of temptations. There were all kinds of things on his workbench that needed fixing, and in a futile effort to bring order to his surroundings, he had become a compulsive labeler. Now that he was in the garage most of the time, he found himself spending more effort naming things and labeling drawers (one label on a drawer reads BLADEY THINGS), boxes, and bottles of screws, nuts, bolts than he was on his writing.

In late June of 1956 he wrote to Shirley Fisher of McIntosh and Otis of his new plan:

I'm still pounding away at my book and still holding to the frail hope that I may get it done before the conventions. You know how it is utterly impossible for little kids [not] to interrupt? Well, I've worked out something. I've built a work table which sits on the front seat of the station wagon and makes the second seat a work room. It is very comfortable and it will even hold a typewriter. So the first thing every morning I will drive out and park someplace and not come back until I've done my daily stint. It will not only save me from the kids but will save me from myself and all the things I think of that I should be doing when I should be working. I can park in a different place every day and it is really the most efficient little work room you ever saw. If it is cold, I can warm it up with the heater. And don't think I'm not going to use it for all occasions when there are guests or relatives. It's turning Texas time now and they will be here before long. So I will be spending many happy mornings out beside the sea in my traveling study. I love the idea. It makes me completely self-sufficient for work and no one has to be quiet for me, which should make them all happy.

Shirley never saw this particular work room, and when she later asked Elaine whatever happened to it, Elaine told her that his first parking place had been on the loose sand on the upper part of the beach; he had to be pulled out by the Long Island Beach Buggy Association.

The following year he tried to solve the problem another way. He still liked the idea of a portable office—as he wrote Toby Street about his station wagon equipment, he could go out by himself with "nobody to interrupt me for at least three hours or forever for that matter because no one knows where I am"—so this time he would put his portable office on his boat, rather than in his car. However, the boat he had was open to the sky and not very suitable for writing, so although he liked it very much he decided to get a new boat, about the same size, but with a snug little cabin sheltered from the sun and wind and a stove for making coffee.

He invited Shirley, who had become one of his fishing companions, to go with him to pick the boat up. They arrived at four in the morning at City Island, got in the boat, and began what they thought would be an eight- or nine-hour run to Sag Harbor. It was a cold and windy day with choppy water, which made the trip uncomfortable, even dangerous, for the engine kept conking out, and they had to drift in fairly heavy seas with boat traffic around them until John could get the motor started again. Once the engine quit in the middle of Plum Gut, and they almost foundered on the rocks at the old Bug Light. After fifteen hours of swearing at the engine and pumping out the bilge, they arrived at the dock at Bluff Point, six or seven hours late—but Elaine and John Fisher, Shirley's husband, were still waiting with pennants flying, and as the boat came in, they fired off a twenty-one-gun salute with the brass cannon.

With his new boat, John thought that he could "move out and anchor and have a little table and a yellow pad and some pencils . . . and put [himself] in position so that nothing else can intervene." Unfortunately, as Shirley has pointed out, there were all kinds of things to see—waves, and birds, and little minnows churning about, and occasional boats, and changes in the weather. In short, he realized that working on his boat at anchor wasn't very satisfactory either. But he did like the new boat.

The next year, 1958, he planned the little workroom house at the end of Bluff Point. In April of that year, he wrote to Elizabeth with his idea:

> This is really heaven out here. There is only one drawback to it. If there are guests or children here I have absolutely no place to go to work or to be alone. My stuff gets stuffed into closets and drawers and it sometimes takes me several days to find it again. . . . I am going to build a little tiny workroom out on the point, too small for a bed so that it can't be considered a guest room under any circumstances. It will be off limits to everyone. I can take electricity

out there on a wire which can be rolled up when we are not here. It doesn't need plumbing of any kind. I designed a cute little structure, six-sided, with windows looking in all directions. Under the windows will be storage space for paper on three sides and the other two will be a desk so that it will need no furniture except a chair and I will use one of our canvas deck chairs for that. It will look like a little lighthouse. I'm going to get to it right away because Elaine gets too lonely without guests and with no place to go guests throw any work I want to do sky high. I will build most of it myself and then with that and the boat I will have some semblance of privacy. One of its main features will be an imposing padlock on the door. I think I am going to name it Sanity's Stepchild. [4/6/58]

Once the structure was built, however, he called it "Joyous Garde," after the castle to which Lancelot took Guinevere, and put a sign with that inscription, hand-lettered in old English, over the door. One might think that having once achieved the perfect work place he might have been frustrated in any further attempts to use the problem as a means of escaping from work, but for the good writer, the resources for procrastination are endless. The challenge now was to arrange the inside, and he spent years refining the conveniences and appliances of his little house to make it as perfect for his needs as possible.

He made the room small enough so that only one chair would fit comfortably in the center—if anyone did happen to wander out to visit him, he would have no place to sit down. The chair, a director's chair with "Siege Perilous" lettered on the canvas back, was nearly surrounded by desk and countertop, so that papers and books could be spread out in all directions. He put a bookshelf all around the room over the windows, between the windows he put peg-board so he could hang things, and below the windows was a desk on the side facing the cove. The countertop, which extended on both sides of the desk around to the door, was desk-high, and below it were shelves. On the right of the desk, the counter and lower shelves were cut so that a typing table would fit next to the wall. He had a hot plate, an intercom, an electric pencil sharpener, and his adjustable drafting table with an adjustable fluorescent light.

Books were gathered into groups on the shelves above and below the windows. They were mostly reference works, including a twenty-four-volume set of the *Encyclopaedia Britannica*, a Bible, the complete works of Shakespeare, an English/Italian dictionary, a survey of twentieth-century American literature, and a collection of medieval and Renaissance poetry. Sitting on shelves or at the back of the desk or, in the case of some of the smaller items, hanging from hooks or large, spring-loaded clips, were such items as filing boxes, a variety of metal and wooden boxes the size of a cigar box, Dictaphone belts and tape reels, packages of pencils, staplers, tape dispensers, paper and leather punches, an eyelet maker, sewing kit, and three or four sets of glasses.

The eye glasses were all altered to fit Steinbeck specifications. He hated glasses that slipped down over the nose or hurt after they had been worn for a while, so each pair had liquid rubber applied to the nose bridge and ear hooks, as well as a piece of rubber, which looked as if it had been cut from an old innertube, attached from ear hook to ear hook so as to fit behind the head. Many of the boxes and drawers had labels, such as MATTERS OF RUBBER, EXTRAORDINARY THINGS, and WRITING STUFF. On the side of the desk with the wastebasket under it was the label LETHE.

The room gave evidence of a man interested in a wide variety of things. Next to two volumes entitled *Documents of American History,* there was a copy of Kafka's *Penal Colony,* and next to that, *Star Gazing with Telescope and Camera.* There were instruments that go aboard a boat, materials for dog care, tools for working with canvas and leather, books and items for the garden, and books, clippings, and instruments related to the study of nature. And although there were a number of devices to help bring order—hooks, clips, divided boxes, filing cabinets, cubbyholes—the room also gave evidence of a man who wanted to be neat and well-organized, but who was always fighting a losing battle.

Looking at the little house on the point long after its master departed from it, the feeling is less of joy captured than of a lonely tower, a place where a man was captured and sat in banishment in a strange land. As he sat in his six-sided house, he was surrounded by windows. He could look out through the trees to the main house, across to his vegetable garden, and out over the water toward the sliver of land that separated the cove from the bay. When he had finished building, he had acquired the perfect workroom at last, but he had somewhere along the line, somehow, lost his work.

Before going to the national conventions, Steinbeck wrote to the managing editors of all the papers that were to print his column, explaining that he had never been to such an event before, that certainly Walter Lippmann and David Lawrence had nothing to fear from him, but that he would do his best to give them printable copy. He had no sources—dependable or otherwise—but he would get what information he could from the wife of the alternate delegate from San Jose and tap what rumors came to him from the bell-hop who had just delivered a bucket of ice to someone who should know. He hoped the editors found his material amusing or illuminating—if not, they could back out without any hard feelings.

He also wrote to the journalism school at Northwestern asking for a student who would be willing to work as his gopher:

> I want a combination copy boy, telephone answerer, coffee maker. One who can type and file. I want someone who knows Chicago somewhat, an eavesdropper and peeping Tom, a gossip, and preferably a liar. . . . He must be able to spell better than I can but not enough better to make me self-conscious about it. His life will be pure hell. . . . He is the Patsy and I want him never to forget it.

He had fifty students apply to be patsies at two hundred dollars a week, but he ended up hiring Tom Deutchle, a Chicago press agent. Steinbeck explained, "He's a friend of a friend. How else do you get a job?"

He and Elaine left for the Democratic Convention in Chicago on August 10. A journalist at heart—he loved to be in the middle of the action and liked the companionship of the other journalists he had come to know over the years—he enjoyed himself enormously at both conventions, but particularly at the Democratic because the outcome was in doubt. (Eisenhower was already set to be renominated by the Republicans in San Francisco.) He prowled the floor hour after hour, eavesdropping and interviewing, trying to pick up any unusual tidbit of information that he could, and tracked the king makers to their lairs.

He had fun hunting material, but he was very nervous about his articles. After sweating over his first column, he and his leg man pushed very hard to get it phoned into all the participating newspapers as soon as possible. Then, as Elaine remembers, "At two in the morning we got a phone call from the Louisville *Courier-Journal,* asking, 'Where is the Steinbeck material?' He had filed with every newspaper except the one that had hired him. He told this on himself quite a lot, but it really did embarrass him."

Although Elaine and John had both worked for Stevenson in the previous campaign, they met him for the first time in Chicago at a small, political dinner party. From the time of this meeting, the Steinbecks and Stevenson became close friends, visiting each other often in the years that followed. At the convention, Stevenson grabbed Steinbeck, pulled him into a little room, and said, "Sit down. I need a drink." The two sat talking for a half hour, John telling him of the humorous things he had heard on the floor. Every time he got up to go, Stevenson asked him to stay. It was the first time in days, Stevenson told him, that he had had a chance to relax.

After the conventions, John sent speech material to the Stevenson campaign. According to John Kenneth Galbraith, Steinbeck was just one, however, of a number of writers deeply attached to Stevenson— Archibald MacLeish and Bernard DeVoto were two others—that sent drafts on one subject or another which, in turn, became the basis for further collaboration. Sometimes the phraseology and the language would survive; sometimes it was altered to fit the tempo of Stevenson's speaking. (Galbraith was, as he recalls, "singled out to do the anti-Nixon speeches. Stevenson thought I could do them because I had no instinct to be fair.")

From San Francisco, the Clift Hotel and the Cow Palace, the Steinbecks drove to Watsonville and Pacific Grove to see John's sisters, then flew to Hollywood for several days: "Five years absence have not changed my dislike for [it]," he wrote. "There is some terrible kind of gas here that makes people hate and suspect each other." They went on to Texas, where Elaine stayed to visit her family, and John continued to New York, picked up his sons, and took them to Sag Harbor to stay until school started.

At the end of the boys' stay, he decided to put them on the train to New York. He wrote Elizabeth:

> I want to stay right here and get into my work and kind of establish some kind of work rhythm again. I'll get to the Peppin [sic] thing first because I would like to have that done and off my neck. Also I think it is pretty good. Pat made me a little mad the other day. I am sure he doesn't like this kind of book but I'm pretty sure he was parroting Marshall [Best] about how many copies it would sell. Hell, there is no surety that any of my books will sell and a lot of them haven't. I agree heartily with the suggestions made, but I do not and will not agree with Pat that the historical date must come out because someone may not understand it. If the reader doesn't know what a Merovingian is, let him find out or buy some other book. Pat treated me a little like Mickey Spillane and I know that he simply wants me to write the Grapes of Wrath over and over. There is another thing you probably don't know. Pat had an idea for a book for me to write this summer. He thought about it a lot. It

is a sequel to the Pastures of Heaven. I was to repeat it as of this generation. And that is a lovely idea except that the people who used to live in the Valley don't any more. New people moved in. And besides, that's not my country any more. . . .

I live here and now and my next book is going to be about here, not a vague memory of Monterey County of my childhood. As a matter of fact, it is so changed out there that I hardly recognized it. And this country I am beginning to know, as a living place, not a memory. Between us, I have a feeling that Pat is slipping rather rapidly, but then maybe I am too, only I don't feel that I am. I'm full of life and interest and meanness. I've had my battle at home and have taken my stand and I'm going to stick with it, and that is that. I just damned well am going to get some writing done and the hell with the side issues which have been eating away all of my energy [9/15/56].

When he was fighting with himself, to get himself going, he sometimes pursued the tack of transferring his own inertia into the opposition of others—it was *their* interference, it was the constant barrage of *their* needs that made it impossible for him to work. His unhappiness spread in all directions, regardless of the actual causes of his distress, and what he was working on was not particularly good or important and he knew it, which made him even more defensive and prickly. Much of his distress was self-inflicted—he was the one who had volunteered for outside work, and more often than not, he was the one who invited people to visit them.

It must be admitted, however, that in an election year the requests for his time were unusually heavy. In late September he reported:

Alan Lerner called me frantically yesterday about the Kefauver speech so I did it late last night. I've finally got the room set up [in the New York house he was setting up his workroom in Waverly's old bedroom—it was larger] and should be ready to go before long but I seem to be married to Radio Free Europe, U.S.I.S. and the Stevenson campaign. No help for it I guess except meanness. [9/27/56]

And a few days later he wrote,

I get daily appeals from the Stevenson bunch. They rather shamefacedly admitted that my atomic fission thing was too hot to handle but they are going to have to face it sometime. . . . Everybody wants me just to turn out things. It is so damned easy you know. I really sweat blood over these things. Alan Lerner told me that everybody else promises and then doesn't do anything. He says that he and I seem to be the only ones working, at turning out copy that is. [10/10/56]

By the middle of October he was certain that unless the direction of his campaign changed, Stevenson was going to lose the election. Steinbeck felt that the campaign managers were taking a line that was too general and too bland: "It is their failure to say things straight and in the idiom, of refusing to name names or face issues that is going to lose." And he fired off a series of blistering letters to various people in the campaign in the hope that he might be able to stir things up. He also thought that Sevenson himself was too disdainful of anything that smacked of a little rabble rousing: "I wish to God they would let me write one violent fighting speech and then get it delivered. I may be too confident of my own powers but I bet you anything I could raise them out of their seats" [10/18/56].

Earlier in the year, Pascal Covici, Jr., who was at Harvard studying to become an English professor, had written to Steinbeck for advice about writing literary criticism. In his reply John mentioned several things that Pascal could write about that he couldn't, including what happens to writers after they receive the Nobel Prize. "It kind of retires them," he observed. "Maybe it makes them respectable and a writer can't dare to be respectable."

A considerable part of Steinbeck's own nonconformity was in his mind based on his decision long ago not to be bound by anyone else's expectations for him—not Elizabeth's, although he respected her opinion enormously, not Pat's, not the academics' nor the critics'. It was the kind of freedom that only a writer who valued his process of work in itself for itself more than outside approbation could achieve. As he told Pascal, he found Faulkner's and Hemingway's preoccupation with their own immortality ridiculous. "It is," he added, "almost as though they were fighting for billing on a tombstone."

There has been a tag applied to Steinbeck, particularly by leftist critics, that states that in his middle age he became middle class and respectable. "Middle class," yes—he was always middle class—but "respectable," no. Not that Steinbeck wouldn't have loved a kind word from *The New York Times Book Review* or, later, *The New York Review of Books,* but he wasn't about to go out of his way to try to get it.

He'd walk across the street to talk to a bum he knew, but he wouldn't tip his hat to get on the right side of the right people. In the rapacious tidepool of literary affairs, of favor and acceptance or sudden nonpersonage, commensal and parasitical relationships have often been the rule, and Steinbeck's kind of independence has been a rarity.

At fifty-four he still dressed and acted pretty much as he did when he was thought to be the disgrace of Los Gatos. There wasn't very much, if anything, about his life or his belongings that was designed to impress other people. Even in his loving to dress up occasionally for the theater in evening clothes, cape, broad-brimmed Italian hat, and cane, there was no motivation to impress anyone with his wealth or status. He did it the way a small boy likes to put on a cowboy or pirate outfit, for the fun of it.

Unlike his great contemporaries, he generally scorned publicity, refused to put his name to popular causes (although he worked privately for a number of things, such as the United Nations, that he believed in), avoided public appearances of all kinds, refused honors and speeches, stayed away from college campuses and literary gatherings, and turned down invitations to any number of society functions and elite parties. When they were invited to the party given by the Joshua Logans for Princess Margaret, an invitation other people would have given their eye teeth for, he declined—"That's not the way I live," he told his wife.

Yet, he was not totally predictable. By impulse or perversity, he would on rare occasions break from his rule or reverse the habit of years. In a year he would attend the P.E.N. congress in Tokyo for no compelling reason—a gathering that was very unlike him to attend.

He spent far more time with people that were "nobody" than with people that were "somebody." In New York he knew the couple that ran the newsstand, the man who ran the hardware store, the butcher, the bartender, the neighborhood characters. In Sag Harbor he knew Bob Barry, Jake the Plumber, the host of "ordinary people," including a couple of disreputable old men on the waterfront whom no one else in town would talk to. He spent time with people because they had humor, because they were interesting, or because they were comfortable and relaxing, not because of who or what they were. He came to know John O'Hara because he was a writer, but he was a friend of John O'Hara's because he was a kind and interesting man. He liked being with him so much that he didn't mind going without drink during the conversation (when he wasn't going through one of his periods of "not drinking," which he insisted was different from being on the wagon). Over the years he came to know a lot of literary people, but any kind of closer connection was always made on some other basis.

So when Joe Bryan came that summer to Sag Harbor, Bryan's status as an editor and writer was irrelevant. What was relevant was that he was a good man to talk to and have fun with. Bryan had married a French woman, and when they arrived, John had two flags flying from the pole near the Bluff Point house. One, at the top of the pole, was the flag of France, the other was a banner that read: WELCOME AMERICAN DENTAL ASSOCIATION. The gesture gave a certain charm to the beginning of the weekend.

In October 1956 Bryan visited the Steinbecks in New York, and taped to the back of the door of the medicine cabinet in his bathroom he found the following:

$$C_{15}H_{19} NO_2$$
Mandragora Iscariot (fecit in noctis)
$$C_{21}H_{33}NO_5$$
Diacetl Morphine (mainline with pin)
Aconite & Day
(for pure fun)
Eye of newt, powdered(bring to boil, strain & drink)
$$CH_3CH_2CHCH\text{-}VH\text{-}(CHO) N(CH_3) OH$$
Amanita Phalloides
(2 tsp at bedtime)
Elixir of Hemlock
1 cup as decreed
(chill & serve)
Graveyard dust, Hypochloride
(sprinkle on doorstep)
smutted spoon, candle, safety pin
KEEP THIS PLACE CLEAN
STERILIZE YOUR OWN NEEDLE
BAIL BONDS. OPEN DAY & NITE

Although this note may have been posted for the edification of any visitor who happened to use the guest bathroom, Steinbeck was perfectly capable of taking the time to compose and post it just for Bryan because he knew Bryan would enjoy it.

Even when he admired another writer's work a great deal, as he did, for example, Arthur Miller's, he put his admiration aside as he became absorbed in the personal connection. He was always interested in the quality of the man or woman, and his engagement with people while he was conversing with them or even just observing them was often almost total—usually more than they realized. He was, to paraphrase Henry James, one of those on whom very little was lost.

What slight connection he had with William Faulkner was carried on with little regard for the other's status, and his abhorrence for the public Faulkner did not extend to person to person contact. The southerner had become spoiled and very self-centered in his late years, and it was sometimes hard for those who didn't defer to him to get along with him, but by contrast with some writers who tended to treat Faulkner with a reverence that was embarrassing to witness, Steinbeck managed to talk to him in about the same way he'd talk to Joe Bryan or Bob Barry.

The only occasion when they were in each other's company for any extended period, after the unfortunate evening of their first meeting, was during the meetings of the writers' committee of the People to People Program. The program was the brain child of the Eisenhower Administration, essentially an effort to counteract Soviet propaganda and spread the doctrine of individual liberty overseas. To avoid the impression that this was a propaganda effort by the United States government (which it was), contact would be made by private individuals and private groups with their counterparts in commerce, the professions, and the arts in various other nations, particularly the satellite countries of Eastern Europe, so that the word could be spread on a personal, rather than institutional or official basis. In the spring of 1956, Faulkner had been asked by Eisenhower to serve as chairman of those writers he could enlist in the cause and form into a committee. When he was asked later why he would get involved in something like this, considering that he disliked literary groups and detested committees, Faulkner replied in terms reminiscent of Steinbeck's reply when he was asked why he got involved in *Bombs Away*: "When your president asks you to do something, you do it."

With the help of critic Harvey Breit and Jean Ennis of the Random House publicity office, Faulkner sent out a letter in September to a list of writers explaining the President's request and asking for suggestions. The letter also asked for volunteers to serve on the committee. Steinbeck was among the twenty writers who, by early October, had responded favorably, saying that he'd be glad to work with the committee after the elections were over. He, too, had a great distaste for any kind of committee and had always felt that committees never really accomplished anything, but the cause of communications with and help for writers behind the Iron Curtain had long been one close to Steinbeck's heart.

The committee had its first meeting on November 29, with Edna Ferber, Elmer Rice, Donald Klopfer, Robert Hillyer, Saul Bellow, and Donald Hall among the fourteen writers in attendance. Of all those in Harvey Breit's living room, it may be that Steinbeck was the most seriously concerned with the central issues of the program, having been involved in similar activities for U.S.I.S. and Radio Free Europe for a very long time. One of the issues that concerned him the most was our failure, in the wake of the Hungarian revolt, to aid and speedily admit to this country Hungarian refugees, many of whom had fought with sticks, stones, and bottles filled with gasoline against Soviet tanks. Our radio broadcasts—and he had been among the broadcasters—had urged the captive nations never to forget freedom and to work for its return in every way possible. We pledged our constant support in their effort. Yet now, after failing to support the uprising, we were hesitant to give aid and refuge to its victims. Steinbeck felt a little like a Judas goat and was both troubled and indignant. He brought with him to the meeting a Hungarian writer, George Tabori, in order to provide support for his proposal: an airlift of Hungarian refugees to the United States.

There seemed to be general agreement that something should be done to help the refugees, but some discouragement, since the group could do little more than recommend. As the meeting continued, however, it began to confirm Steinbeck's worst opinions about the workings of committees. The discussion became chaotic and diffuse. William Carlos Williams made a long and impassioned plea that they recommend to the government that Ezra Pound be freed; Steinbeck suggested that one of the best ways of describing our country abroad might be by the distribution of the Sears Roebuck catalogue, and also recalled the cheap paperback editions distributed to the Army during World War II—couldn't the plates for these be found and then thousands of these little books be smuggled into Eastern Europe?

Having led the discussion in regard to some of the more practical proposals during the meeting, Steinbeck was nominated to serve on a subcommittee, along with Faulkner and the poet Donald Hall, to put the proposals together into a draft report. According to Hall, who relayed his experiences to Faulkner biographer Joseph Blotner, when the subcommittee met the following day, Faulkner and Steinbeck chatted while waiting for a secretary at the Random House offices:

Steinbeck was as little interested in literary talk as Faulkner, and the two men swapped hunting stories [which shows Steinbeck's adaptability or imagination, since he had never been much of a hunter]. All that Hall remembered of it was their agreement that the Springfield was the best kind of rifle there was. When the secretary appeared, they dictated to her the recommendations about the Hungarian refugees and the dissemination of books. Then Hall suggested that they write in the proposal to free Pound.

"Oh, no," Steinbeck said, "no, that will just make people mad. That will make them all mad. You don't want to do that."

But Faulkner spoke immediately. "Yes, yes. You take this down, young lady," he said. "The government of Sweden gives the chairman of this committee its greatest award and the government of the United States keeps its best poet in jail."

With that, Steinbeck withdrew his dissent. His concern, thought Hall, was about tactics. He was not against freeing Pound; he simply thought it would outrage public opinion if they proposed it. And not just outrage public opinion, but endanger the adoption of their own proposals concerning the refugees and the dissemination of books, which he felt were more central to the work of the committee.

As far as Faulkner was concerned, once the report had been written, distributed for further comment, and then sent to the President, the work of the committee, and his role of chairman, would be blessedly over. Steinbeck believed, however, that if he pushed as hard as possible, something might actually be done about their proposals. To this end he wrote several letters to people he knew in government, among them a letter to Arthur Larson, who was Director of the United States Information Agency.

He wanted Larson to get the message from the Faulkner committee directly, particularly its concern regarding "our closed and suspicious borders" which "have not reassured our friends and have given our enemies magnificent propaganda fuel." The first act of a dictator, he noted, is to close his borders to travel and to the commerce of goods and ideas, and "it is always a matter of sadness, and of suspicion to me, when we close our borders to any of these." Such commerce, he added in his letter, "is not only the mother of civilization, but the teacher of understanding and the god of peace."

In his letter he went on to recount his experiences in Russia in 1936 and 1947, when he was asked over and over again to send back books. More recently he had received letters from East German students asking for books and giving Berlin addresses to which they should be sent.

His conclusion was that "the book is revered. The book is somehow true, where propaganda is suspected. A packet of books thrown over the barbwire fence and picked up by a border guard *might* be burned, but I swear it is more likely that the books would be hidden, treasured and distributed."

What kind of books? Any kind—poetry, essays, novels, and plays. But they must show us as we are, both the good and the bad. "The moment it is all good, it is automatically propaganda and will be disbelieved."

On November 19, 1956, John wrote Elizabeth to tell her that he had finished *The Short Reign of Pippin IV*: "There's a great unease about it at Viking, but there's an unease all over and maybe one thing transmits to another." "Unease" was an understatement. Marshall Best recalls that there were seven different readings of the manuscript and that it was the only book that Viking tried to persuade John not to publish. In large part because there was so much opposition to it—both Elizabeth and Pat had come to hate it—the book took a place close to his heart. It was an orphan, and just as many years earlier when another satire, "Saint Katy the Virgin," had met rejection at every hand, he was determined to defend it.

He thought part of the problem at Viking was that the editors did not think it would sell well, but he saw nothing wrong with a book that had a small printing and appealed to only a limited audience. Indeed, it would give him pleasure to escape from the "best-seller" category and be accused of obscurity. Although when it was published, it was criticized as too bland for good satire and rather superficial, he thought it arcane and rather nasty. When he signed a copy for Abe Burrows's wife, who was a museum curator and had had many conversations with him about history, he inscribed it as to someone who would understand, as if not many others would. When the Book-of-the-Month Club, against all expectation by him and by Viking, selected *Pippin*, he thought that it was the greatest joke in the world: on him, on Viking—and on the Book-of-the-Month Club.

Before he had finished *Pippin*, he had gone back to his experimental manuscript and reconsidered it. "I've thrown out the novel I was going to write," he announced in a letter to his niece's husband, David Heyler, Jr., "because it arose from a wrong premise. And because I must go on working because I get unhappy when I am not working, I am taking on something I have always wanted to do." [11/19/56]

Once again, as with *Pippin*, he would turn his attention to history and historical research—he had decided to work on a modern language version of Malory's *Morte d'Arthur*, to put it into simple, readable prose without adding or taking away anything from the original. At the beginning, this seemed a relatively straightforward task, involving little more than translating the obsolete words and simplifying the more convoluted sentences. But for various reasons, including his strong love for the original, which made it difficult for him to make changes, the task turned out to be one of the most complex and challenging of his career, one that dogged him, unfinished and seemingly unfinishable, for much of the rest of his life.

Although in his letter he declares that his new project is something he had "always" wanted to do, the stimulus that prompted him to start work on Malory at this particular time came from Chase Horton, owner of the Washington Square Bookshop and longtime friend and companion to Elizabeth Otis. As a bookstore owner, Horton had been aware of the continuing interest in Malory and the legends, and the many books written and sold on the subject (a bibliography of over two thousand books). He was also aware that the most recent updating of Malory had been done in the 1890s and that there was a need for a new "translation." Over the years he had talked to one author after another in an effort to convince someone to take on the project, but without success. After discovering the extent of Steinbeck's attachment for and knowledge of Malory's work, Horton talked to Otis and decided he would mention the project to Steinbeck.

Steinbeck had, of course, been devoted to the *Morte d'Arthur* since childhood. Not only had it been the first book he loved, one that generated his initial interest in literature and language, it was a book that had stayed with him on an intimate basis throughout his life. He had alluded to it, overtly and covertly, frequently in his work, he had named the things around him from it, and he even acted as if, at times, he saw it as a metaphor for his own life. He really did believe, with his whole heart, in Lancelot, and that Knight's nobility became for him both a model and a measure of the love, generosity, loyalty, and sense of duty that a man may bring to life.

Early in his work he wrote a personal introduction to the volume which would follow. As a young reader, he wrote, he found in this book

> all the vices that ever were—and courage and sadness and frustration, but particularly gallantry—perhaps the only single quality of man that the West has invented. I think my sense of right and

wrong, my feeling of noblesse oblige, and any thought I may have against the oppressor and for the oppressed, came from this secret book. . . . In pain or sorrow or confusion, I went back to my magic book. Children are violent and cruel—and good—and I was all of these—and all of these were in the secret book. If I could not choose my way at the crossroads of love and loyalty, neither could Lancelot. I could understand the darkness of Mordred because he was in me too; and there was some Galahad in me, but perhaps not enough. The Grail feeling was there, however, deep-planted, and perhaps always will be.

Elizabeth was anxious to bring Chase Horton closer into the "family circle," and John, partly because he sensed this and partly because in his initial enthusiasm for a project often wanted others to join him (as he had pulled Pat into *East of Eden*), proposed to her that Chase work with him:

Do you have a Caxton edition? I should like you—as you read my version—to compare it, so that recommendations can be made.

Next, what would you think of Chase as a kind of Managing Editor? His knowledge and interest seem to be great and he could be of help to me when I come a cropper. It would be good to have someone to consult with. And he might have an opening essay to precede mine. Let me know about this.

Let us keep this project to ourselves until I am well along. I don't want Pat or Viking nudging me. [11/19/56]

Thus not only Chase but Elizabeth as well were brought into the project at the very outset. Although Chase was of great help, doing much of the legwork, obtaining materials, and probing the subject in many different directions (he estimates that he put in about three thousand hours over the years of the project on the basis of a log that he kept), John always grew to hate collaborations of any sort, and there were times when he became very unhappy about this one. During periods of intense frustration with this work, he would first condemn himself for ever getting involved in a joint venture, then rail against Chase and Elizabeth. Chase's slow, methodical way of doing things heightened Steinbeck's irritation, which usually became the most acute in response to suggestions or criticism (often requested by him). He came into constant conflict with his feelings of obligation to Horton for his selfless hard work, and over the months and years of the project, the emotional strain of the personal relationships involved became one factor in persuading him to abandon it.

From mid-November through the winter of 1956–57, he spent much of his time reading and studying. "Just reading and reading and reading," he wrote to Elizabeth from Sag Harbor in early January, "and it's like hearing remembered music." He moved his card table from the bedroom to the big window in the library–game room, and set up his telescope beside it so that if anything happened outside, he could "tompeep" it. He wrote to his English publisher, Alexander Frere (the project had not been kept "to ourselves" very long), that "to read and read in one direction night and day . . . to pull an area and a climate of thinking over one's head like a space helmet—what a joy that is!" [1/18/57]. Using the Oxford edition of Malory, which was based on the Winchester manuscript, he compared it to the Caxton version. As he began work on a rough-draft translation, he found he preferred the Winchester, for it seemed to him closer to the original Malory, and, he noted, "there are lovely nuances in the Winchester which have been removed by Caxton."

Not all of his work was done at home. In December he wrote to the Pierpont Morgan Library in the city asking to inspect their Lancelot manuscript, as well as what "Frensshe" books they might have which Malory spoke of as his sources. One day, while sitting in the reading room of the Morgan, examining the rubric of the first known owner of the Lancelot with his sixty-power magnifying glass, he discovered, deeply imbedded in the ink, a perfectly preserved crab louse: "I called the curator over and showed him my find and he let out a cry of sorrow. 'I've looked at that rubric a thousand times,' he said. 'Why couldn't I have found him?' " He may be exaggerating the curator's disappointment, but certainly he found in this a moment of great pride. Ed would have been proud of him.

Out of the many books of literary history and criticism that he was also reading he developed a theory that Sir Thomas Malory had at one point in his life gone to Italy as a mercenary. And "since the economics of fifteenth century England were dominated by Florentine bankers," he determined to go to Florence that spring and search through the archives for some trace of Malory, as well as to review any Arthurian material he might find there.

In preparation for their trip, he and Elaine both took lessons in Italian from a teacher who came twice a week to their house in New York. He told David Heyler that "we are . . . getting nowhere but it is kind of fun and a kind of discipline which I am not used to these many years. . . . Elaine and I find ourselves fighting to recite when we know the answer and pretending to be busy when we don't. I guess you don't grow up at all" [11/19/56]. To finance the trip, he proposed to James S. Pope of the Louisville *Courier-Journal* that he write some mail pieces. Continuing the tradition set by his "inspired convention coverage," he would send in "reports on Europe comprised of lies, inaccuracies and whoppers. . . . Nothing of this caliber has been undertaken since Mark Twain wrote *The Innocents Abroad,* from which book I intend to steal unmercifully."

He assured Pope that:

they will have the breathless beauty of a letter to Aunt Emma. I went through the war without meeting a general, to the convention without meeting a candidate, and I think I can promise to comb Europe without contacting anyone of any importance whatsoever. . . .

I hope you will receive the proposition in the spirit in which it is offered, i.e., that you get something for nothing and I get very rich. This is the American dream.

On March 25, the Steinbecks, along with John's sister Mary, sailed to Naples aboard the *Saturnia.* In Florence they found it rainy and cold, so cold in fact that they had to go to bed just to get warm. At the request of the U.S.I.A., Steinbeck agreed to a press conference–cocktail party and to meet small groups of Italian writers, professors, and students at various times during his stay, though he was anxious to get to his research and so found these arrangements a bit onerous. But it was a two-way street; the U.S.I.A. was helpful in arranging contacts for him which he needed in gaining access to restricted scholarly collections. When the newsmen came to the U.S.I.A. reception, he warned them in advance that although they thought they had come to interview him, he was actually going to interview them—and did.

By the time he had been away three weeks, he had sent six "letters" to the *Courier-Journal,* some of them "pretty amusing, but the standard is not very high." At about the same time, he received a batch of reviews of *Pippin* from Covici, who was enthusiastic about the reception the book was receiving. John, however, sounded battle-weary when he told Elizabeth, "They follow exactly the old pattern I am so used to, celebrating old books which the same people raised hell with when they were printed. The book does do one thing that I think I also anticipated. It makes every reviewer a French expert" [4/16/57].

He also complained to Elizabeth that the Florentines were killing him with kindness. They were receiving too many invitations and seeing too many people, and while Elaine thrived on the activity, he was worn out. He thought that he might escape the hectic social scene by a trip to Rome to visit the Vatican libraries. From there he wrote Elizabeth and Chase: "The archives are the God-damnest things you ever saw, acres and acres of just pure information. I had a hard time tearing myself away. I have certain things to look for and the US Information Agency is going to get me someone to see if the material I want is in existence" [4/26/57].

Back in Florence at the end of April, John and Elaine made arrangements to meet Robert Wallsten at a cafe for a drink. Wallsten had been an actor, and in fact had known Elaine when she had been a stage manager, but in recent years he had turned to writing. He had first met Steinbeck at the opening of *Burning Bright*, with the novelist Katherine Brush. Elaine greeted him, and he said, "Do you know Miss Brush?" and Steinbeck said, "I've never had the honor of meeting her before." Wallsten recalls, "Considering the declining state of her reputation and the eminent one of his, I was deeply impressed with the kind of modesty and respect he showed to a successful novelist of a period before him."

Wallsten had seen the Steinbecks occasionally since then, at dinner parties and Elaine's birthday celebrations, and in Florence John had a present for him. He brought out a switchblade knife and said, "You'll find this very helpful if anyone attacks you." Wallsten was completely taken aback, then startled, as John pressed the button on the handle to demonstrate and the blade leaped out toward him. Although he kept the knife because John gave it to him, he could hardly wait to get back to the hotel and get the knife off his person.

It was an odd present to give, but for John not an unusual one. He gave a rare, antique walking stick that fired a small shotgun shell to Joe Bryan, and blackthorn walking sticks to John O'Hara and to Wallsten, whom he told, in a similar vein to his recommendation regarding the switchblade, "If you are attacked, you can always make a flashing gesture with it and it just rips the skin off."

He had a romantic attraction to weapons that was part attraction to novelty, part love of things mechanical, and part enthusiasm generated by an early reading of adventure novels and stimulated later by an admiration for historical and legendary heroes. Ernest Martin, among others, recalls coming to Bluff Point and finding him, often with his sons, at target practice with a variety of weapons that ranged from a crossbow, to a pellet gun, to a .22 rifle. John's son Thom recalls that they spent all one summer learning history by constructing medieval weapons, one of which he remembers as a catapult adapted from a rat trap. And John had a small collection of guns and other kinds of weapons—daggers, swords, bows, and spears—with the emphasis on the unusual, rather than the practical.

Attached to his love of weapons was some measure of boylike play acting, of adolescent daydreaming, and of a tough façade. The façade was a tricky business, since behind it was a man who really could be tough, but he used it to protect himself because of his shyness. Although he thought kindness and courtesy were essential to manhood, he wanted no man to mistake these traits for weakness. He was a peaceful, even gentle, man who would play the role of tough hombre, making belligerent faces and speaking roughly, talking to people about guns, self-defense tactics, and hunting.

Budd Schulberg recalls that "John looked tough. But he looked twice as tough as he acted, I think. I think he perfected that purposefully. John could really glare at people—I think it was rather a cover-up. I never had one hot word with John, and I never saw him really violent except when he was provoked—that was with the knife. I never saw a meanness in him." The incident occurred at a party in Elaine's apartment before she was married to John, and Schulberg remembers it as somewhat more melodramatic than it actually was.

John and Elaine were sitting at a table with several others, including a man who was making passes at Elaine, half-jokingly. John, who was bent over slightly working at some project with his pocket knife, looked up and glared at the man. But the man continued his flirtation, and John said to him, "Elaine is going to become my wife. I prefer that you don't do that." Again, the man continued. John, very coldly and deliberately, stopped what he was doing, reached over the table with his knife, and dropped it, point down, onto the back of the man's hand, nicking the flesh.

All of this seems far removed from the Steinbeck who sent speech ideas to Stevenson, supported the United Nations, and attacked the House Un-American Activities Committee. Or the man in Florence who was studiously pursuing clues to the life of Malory and the evolution of Arthurian legends, more and more caught up in the search. Chase Horton, in reflecting on this, has said, "Malory can be addictive. He captures the imagination. Steinbeck found himself going off on one tangent after another, particularly becoming interested in Malory himself—who is he?—a trap that many others had fallen into before him."

Indeed, the mystery of Malory had become his primary concern at this stage of his studies. An English mercenary by the name of Sir John Hawkwood had fought along what is now the Italian Peninsula—he is depicted in a fresco in the Duomo of Florence—and Steinbeck had found a connection between Hawkwood and Malory. He was convinced that Malory had also fought in Italy, and if he could confirm his belief, that would make a good deal of difference in the estimate of Malory's sources and possible influences on him. But although John found one clue after another that led him on, he was never able to find any definite evidence for his hypothesis in the papers in Florence or Rome.

The mystery of Malory preyed on his mind. From Rome on April 26th, he wrote to Elizabeth:

I have been reading all of the scholarly appraisals of the Morte, and all the time there has been a bothersome thought in my brain knocking about just out of reach. . . . Then this morning I awakened about five o'clock fully awake but with the feeling that some tremendous task had been completed. I got up and looked out at the sun coming up over Rome and suddenly it came back whole and in one piece. . . .

Malory has been studied as a translator, as a soldier, as a rebel, as a religious, as an expert in courtesy, as nearly everything you can think of except one, and that is what he was—a novelist. The Morte is the first and one of the greatest of novels in the English language. And only a novelist could think of it. A novelist not only puts down a story but he is the story. He is each one of the characters in a greater or a less degree. And because he is usually a moral man in intention and honest in his approach, he sets things down as truly as he can.

A novel may be said to be the man who writes it. Now it is nearly always true that a novelist, perhaps unconsciously, identifies himself with one chief or central character in his novel. Into this character he puts not only what he thinks he is but what he hopes to be. We can call this spokesman the self-character. You will find one in every one of my books and in the novels of everyone I can remember. . . . I supposed my own symbol character has my dream wish of wisdom and acceptance.

Now it seems to me that Malory's self-character would be Launcelot. All of the perfections he knew went into this character, all of the things of which he thought himself capable. But, being an honest man he found faults in himself, faults of vanity, faults of violence, faults even of disloyalty and these would naturally find their way into his dream character. . . .

And now we come to the Grail, the Quest. I think it is true that any man, novelist or not, when he comes to maturity has a very deep sense that he will not win the quest. He knows his failings, his shortcomings and particularly his memories of sins, sins of cruelty, of thoughtlessness, of disloyalty, of adultery, and these will not permit him to win the Grail. And so his self-character must suffer the same terrible sense of failure as his author. Launcelot could not see the Grail because of the faults and sins of Malory himself. He knows he has fallen short and all his excellences, his courage, his courtesy, in his own mind cannot balance his vices and errors, his stupidities.

I think this happens to every man who has ever lived but it is set down largely by novelists. . . . Now this is so. I know it as surely as I can know anything. God knows I have done it myself often enough. And this can for me wipe out all the inconsistencies and obscurities scholars have found in the story. And if the Morte is uneven and changeable it is because the author was changeable. Sometimes there is a flash of fire, sometimes a moody dream, sometimes an anger. For a novelist is a rearranger of nature so that it makes an understandable pattern, and a novelist is also a teacher, but a novelist is primarily a man and subject to all of a man's faults and virtues, fears and braveries.

Elizabeth wrote back: "Your letter about Malory this week is one of the most impressive letters that you or anyone else has ever written. Now you are back home. The creative process has started. I never saw it so accurately described. Time, place, feel. Enter novelist." A few days earlier, Pat had written to him: "What interests me most now is your delving into the life and times of Malory. I have been thinking about him quite a bit myself, recently and what a wonderful historical novel Malory could make. Now, don't be laughing your head off but just think about it. I have a funny suspicion that you have already been thinking about it."

Neither of them had much use for the *Morte d'Arthur* project in itself. Elizabeth hoped throughout his work that, as in his research on his family and the history of Salinas before writing *East of Eden*, the novelist would take over from the historian, but John had no intention of converting his work on Malory to a novel. By the time he had worked on the project for several years, Elizabeth could not bear to hear the name of Malory spoken in her presence.

In the meantime, in the States, Arthur Miller, who refused to answer the questions of the House Un-American Activities Committee, had been cited for contempt of Congress and was now standing trial. In addition to the by now familiar dilemma of the witness before the committee who is asked to inform on his friends and associates, thus possibly destroying them without a trial or hearing, there were other important aspects to the case.

The committee's intimidation in recent years had been applied particularly to those in the arts and communications industries. The purpose was to root out subversive influences among those who entertained or informed the public, but the effect of the committee's tactics, reinforced by industry blacklists, was to deprive hundreds of "suspects" of their work, some permanently, without due process of law, and to abridge the right of free speech and expression for those whose profession it was to speak, write, act, paint, direct, or produce. Some of the intimidation seemed directly aimed at those who had had the temerity to criticize the committee: Arthur Miller had recently written a play, *The Crucible* (1953), which recalled the Salem witch trials as an implicit parallel to the activities of both the House committee and the Senate committee of Joseph McCarthy.

Before he left for Europe, Steinbeck had written a well-reasoned yet impassioned defense of Miller, which he hoped would appear in print before the trial started and help persuade Congress to reverse its decision and provide public support for Miller in his cause. Unfortunately, its publication was slightly delayed and it appeared in the June issue of *Esquire,* after the trial had started. In his essay he wrote:

> Law, to survive, must be moral. To force personal immorality on a man, to wound his private virtue, undermines his public virtue. If the Committee frightens me enough, it is even possible that I may make up things to satisfy the questioners. This has been known to happen. A law which is immoral does not survive and a government which condones or fosters immorality is truly in clear and present danger. . . .
>
> We have seen and been revolted by the Soviet Union's encouragement of spying and telling, children reporting their parents, wives informing on their husbands. In Hitler's Germany, it was considered patriotic to report your friends and relations to the authorities. And we in America have felt safe from and superior to these things. But are we so safe or superior?
>
> The men in Congress must be conscious of their terrible choice. Their legal right is clearly established, but should they not think of their moral responsibility also? In their attempts to save the nation from attack, they could well undermine the deep personal morality which is the nation's final defense. The Congress is truly on trial along with Arthur Miller. . . .

If I were in Arthur Miller's shoes, I do not know what I would do, but I could wish, for myself and for my children, that I would be brave enough to fortify and defend my private morality as he has. I feel profoundly that our country is better served by individual courage and morals than by the safe and public patriotism which Dr. Johnson called "the last refuge of scoundrels."

My father was a great man, as any lucky man's father must be. He taught me rules I do not think are abrogated by our nervous and hysterical times. These laws have not been annulled; these rules of attitudes. He taught me—glory to God, honor to my family, loyalty to my friends, respect for the law, love of country and instant and open revolt against tyranny, whether it come from the bully in the schoolyard, the foreign dictator, or the local demagogue.

And if this be treason, gentlemen, make the most of it.

Through Pat Covici, Miller conveyed his thanks, noting that no one else had come to his defense. John wrote to Pat, saying, "When Artie told me that not one writer had come to his defense, it gave me a lonely sorrow and a shame that I waited so long and it seemed to me also that if we had fought back from the beginning instead of running away, perhaps these things would not be happening now. . . . Please give him my respect and more than that, my love. You see we have had all along the sharpest weapons of all, words, and we did not use them, and I for one am ashamed. I don't think I was frightened but truly, I was careless" [5/16/57].

In looking back, Miller has commented,

John had a fantastic and marvelous, the best kind of romantic streak, which a lot of people can mock. But I think it is an invaluable part of people, the kind of romanticism which makes really substantial gestures that can turn out to change the world, totally unreasonable, many cases self-defeating. You can only end up admiring somebody who is capable of that. And he was. John had that.

At the same time on a different front, Steinbeck was fighting another, but related battle. As one of a series of editorials that he had been writing for *Saturday Review*, he wrote "A Game of Hospitality" (a rather trivial-sounding title that disguised the seriousness of his purpose). The subject was the denial of visas to foreign writers, who, regardless of how distinguished their worldwide reputation, were not allowed to visit this country. In some cases moral or legal charges had been brought against them, often politically inspired by repressive governments, but it was more common that our immigration officials felt that a writer was dangerous because his work was tinged by leftist politics, or was thought, by hearsay or supposition, to be so.

He had been invited to go to P.E.N., the international congress of writers, meeting in Tokyo that fall, and in his naïveté had asked how long it had been since a meeting had been held in the United States. He was told "never," since there would be no way to get permits of entry for enough first-rate writers to hold one. He began thinking about the many people in history that under our present law could not visit this country, regardless of their genius or accomplishments, and in his article presented a list of more than fifty such names followed by the charges likely to be used in order to prohibit their entry, beginning with Socrates (contributing to moral delinquency of minors), Pericles (consorting with prostitutes), and Sappho (homosexuality), going on to François Villon and Jeanne D'Arc, and finishing with Washington, Jefferson, and Robert E. Lee—if the latter were out of the country trying to get in. He concluded that "a great majority of the desirable and creative men of all ages would not be welcome, or permitted, in our country."

The Steinbecks were in Florence and Rome through April and May of 1957, and as the weeks went by the pace seemed to John to get more and more hectic. He gathered material and Elaine took pictures for a projected *Holiday* article on Florentine craftsmen; he wrote an introduction for a volume of photographs for the U.S.I.S.; and he continued to write for both the *Courier-Journal* and *Saturday Review*. On May 19th, he sent two pieces for the newspaper to Elizabeth and one other article:

The other piece called The Short Rain I wrote after reading a mass of small town criticism that Pat sent me. Send it along to the Saturday Review if you like. [She apparently did not, since it was not published.] Elaine hates me to answer criticism. She feels that it is beneath my dignity but since I am not conscious of any dignity I find it fun. There was a time, a lustier time, when critics were answered and everyone had fun. Now the damned thing has got so sacrosanct that a kind of holy hush falls over everything. The hell with it. I am not bidding for honors and stupidity is stupidity wherever one finds it. Besides, I like a good fight. I find it healthy.

At the request of the U.S.I.S., he continued to see groups of Italians, but was finding the going very difficult—the same questions, the same stories, the same answers. Two nights before they were to leave Italy, they were guests of honor at the U.S. Embassy at a party for about fifty, and he talked to people for three hours. "That is my last duty for the jolly State Dept.," he wrote. "They have worked me pretty hard but they have done nice things for us too. Only sometimes I feel that if I have to talk to another intellectual I shall cut my throat" [5/28/57].

On their arrival in Paris at the beginning of June, he was completely worn out and collapsed into bed with the symptoms of food poisoning. By the end of the week, however, he was well enough to go to a party set up by his publisher as publicity for the forthcoming French publication of *Pippin*. The book had been serialized in *Figaro*, was receiving good reviews, and the expectation was that the hardcover version would do very well; indeed, there was much talk about doing a movie of it starring Fernandel. The party was given on a *bateau mouche* decorated as a royal barge, and as it progressed down the river, flying the royal standard of Charlemagne, a hundred guests sipped wine while an orchestra played.

From Paris they went to London for a week and then on to Denmark and Sweden. He was still very tired, and wrote to his agent from Copenhagen in mid-June, "I wish to goodness I could get out of going to Japan in September. Will you put your incisive mind to work on the problem of how to avoid going? Of course I can always get sick and it may be that this will be a truth rather than an excuse" [6/19/57]. When they arrived in Sweden, they went to a small farm owned by Bo Beskow near Löderup, and John spent another week resting. The one social event while they were there was a midsummer night festival put on by the local farm families, and he noted to Elizabeth, "They hadn't heard of me which was wonderful. I'm so tired, so desperately tired of being celebrated" [6/25/57].

While they were in Stockholm, John was surprised to get a phone call from the secretary to the Russian writer Sholokhov, who, the secretary informed Steinbeck, was presently in the city and would like to see him. When John and Capa had been in the Soviet Union in 1947, they had tried to see Sholokhov, whose books, *And Quiet Flows the Don* and *The Don Flows Down to the Sea*, they both admired, and who John thought might well be the best of the living Russian novelists. However, they were unable to get in touch with him—whenever they asked, they got the bureaucratic runaround; there were rumors that he had run afoul of Fadayev, the head of the Soviet writers' organization, and had been "disciplined" and sent into exile in the country.

Steinbeck invited the novelist and his secretary to his hotel room for a drink, and they arrived promptly at six and accepted Scotch and soda, without ice. In writing about the meeting later, Steinbeck described Sholokhov as "short and rather delicately made. His hair is thin and blonde grey and he has a mad and merry blue eye and several gleaming gold teeth. His secretary and interpreter is a dark and intense young man whose command of English leaves something to be desired but whose concentration on his job was something painful to behold."

Steinbeck was curious to find out what had happened to the novelist during the time he had tried to see him earlier, but the conversation had to follow the usual rules, rules that John had already learned in Russia. First, there were the obligatory compliments on both sides—Sholokhov expressed his great admiration for John's books, and John expressed his for the Russian's. He told him that he had tried to see him in Russia, but had been unable to. Sholokhov expressed regret: he had been in his village on the Don 130 miles from the nearest railroad. But he was glad to see Steinbeck now and wanted to tell him how much his books were admired in Russia. Departing from the rules somewhat, Steinbeck asked, how come they aren't being printed?

The Soviet writer replied that there had been a magazine that printed the works of foreign authors that had disappeared some years back but was now being revived. Steinbeck, now beginning to push hard, wanted to know if Mr. Fadayev had anything to do with the removal of the magazine? Sholokhov said that he didn't think so. Pushing harder, Steinbeck said that it had been rumored that Mr. Fadayev and Mr. Sholokhov had had some ideological differences—was there any truth to that?

This question was uncomfortable. Mr. Sholokhov said uneasily that he did not believe that this was so. I continued to break the ground rules by saying that I as an individual did not like Mr. Fadayev and that I did not consider him in a class with Mr. Sholokhov as a novelist.

He replied that this was probably because Mr. Fadayev had been very busy in organizational work with the writers of the Soviet Union. I said I thought it the purpose of writers to write, and Mr. Sholokhov asked whether I did not believe it a good thing for writers to get together for the exchange of ideas. He gave as an example the association of Tolstoy and Turgenev. I said it was my

belief that Tolstoy and Turgenev mostly fought, but Mr. Sholokhov said that perhaps a richness came out of their fighting. I said
that most American writers were kind of lone wolves who believed
that two good men could not write one good book.

Steinbeck found it significant that for some reason the novelist was
no longer in disgrace, but allowed to move about freely. Not only that,
but it was interesting that he should make a point of seeing Steinbeck,
since Steinbeck was now in great disfavor with the Stalinist writing establishment. But what was really going on, Sholokhov wouldn't say
and Steinbeck could only wonder.

In Stockholm they also saw their friend Dag Hammarskjöld, and Bo
Beskow painted his third portrait of John, one about every ten years.
After Stockholm the Steinbecks had planned to return home, but even
though he desperately wanted to go home and pull Sag Harbor up over
his head, John thought he'd better go to England to see Malory country. He would have to see it to write about it, and if he didn't see it
now, he would only have to come back another time.

In England, after a few days in London, they went first to Manchester, where John inspected one of the two existing Caxton first printings
at the Rylands Library and where he met for the first time Eugène
Vinaver, professor of French language and literature at the University
of Manchester and the world's leading authority on Malory. Earlier in
the year when he had been comparing the Winchester and Caxton versions of Malory, Steinbeck had used Vinaver's edition of Malory based
on the Winchester manuscript, and he had been encouraged to try to
meet Vinaver when, after sending one of his early attempts at translation to the scholar, he had received a very complimentary reaction to
his work.

In Elaine's words, "the relationship from the moment they met was
absolute magic. They just adored each other." John knew he had the
master, and Vinaver, a charming and rather shy man, was flattered by
the passion of John's interest and the extent of his knowledge—he knew
he had a very advanced student indeed. He offered Steinbeck any help
he might be able to give and opened his files and bibliography to him.
"He was very much excited by my approach to the subject," John reported to Elizabeth, "saying it was the first new approach in many
years" [8/7/57].

Armed with books, special maps, Chase's letters, and Elaine's cameras, they took a brief, but intensive tour of those areas which were rel-

evant to Malory's life and to the *Morte*. They rented a car and driver and visited Warwickshire, going to Malory's birthplace and the place where he was imprisoned, and then on to Alnwick Castle, Wales, Glastonbury, and Tintagel. During the journey, Elaine made an intensive photographic record of what they saw. It was John's aim to get a sense of the topography, particularly the relationship of one place to another, and as much as possible in a short time, to get the feel of what these places might have been centuries earlier. In fact he was only able to get enough sense of what he saw to interest him further, a taste that would lure him back and back again before he was through. The tour lasted only ten days, although he had stayed in Europe nearly a month longer than he had intended, and on July 25 they sailed on the *Queen Elizabeth* for home.

He couldn't remember what madness it was that prompted him to accept the invitation to attend the P.E.N. meeting in Japan; perhaps he had been seized with a momentary passion for seeing the Orient, or perhaps the sincerity of the P.E.N. agenda, those items concerning the free circulation of ideas and freedom of movement for writers, had so inspired him to join ranks with his fellow writers that he forgot he hated organizations and agendas, dinners and speeches. As September drew closer, he was sure he would be sick. But he wasn't. So he decided the next best thing would be for him to go there quickly, get it over with, and get home as soon as possible. In the meantime, Elaine could make her pilgrimage to Texas while he was gone, and they would be away from each other—or, to put it more precisely, John would be without Elaine—for only a few days.

He flew to Tokyo with John Hersey and John Dos Passos, two men he had known casually in the past and whose company he enjoyed, and found when he arrived the kind of reception he had come to expect and dread whenever he came to a foreign capital. The phone in his room at the Imperial Hotel rang constantly, and dozens of newsmen clamoring—politely—for interviews were ushered in and out of his room, singly and in groups, all day long. Almost immediately he was charmed by the Japanese. He found himself bowing so much that he was sure that he had already taken inches off his waistline: "It will take me months to get the smile off my face and this noon I caught myself bowing to a samovar in the dining room" [9/1/57].

His second day in Japan he was sitting in the bathtub reading the newspaper when he discovered, to his horror, that he was to make the closing speech of the opening session of the congress. Little else could have caused him more alarm and apprehension, but the news came so suddenly that he didn't have time to stew and fret, only to sit down and quickly write out something to say. On a stage illuminated with enough candle power to light up all of Japan, as he recalled later, he held on to the lectern as tight as possible, and in front of the gathered dignitaries and writers from all over the world, delivered an address that may have lasted two minutes. He said, in effect, "I have come here to listen and learn, and I hope you have too." After two hours of speeches by the Mayor of Tokyo, the Prime Minister of Japan, the President of P.E.N., and a long prayer intoned by a woman delegate from India, his speech hit just the right note. Tumultuous applause marked it as the highlight of the opening session, and he claimed that Japanese newspapers, which printed every word, compared it favorably to *haiku*. He was glad he hadn't had the time to compose a real speech.

The next morning, he collapsed: he had come seven thousand miles to catch Asiatic flu. Everyone sent doctors, including a medical colonel from the U.S. Embassy, and after a day or two his room began to look "like a combination of Forest Lawn and a garbage dump." The congress was over for him, after only one day, but by the end of the week, he was up and out a few hours every day, buying gifts for his family, sightseeing a bit, and talking to people. He found confirmation for his recommendation the year before to the Stevenson campaign that it speak out strongly against nuclear testing. He reported to Elaine:

the feeling about the bomb is something. It is strange and submerged and always present. It isn't quite anger and not quite sorrow—it is mixed up with a curious shame but not directed shame. It is an uncanny thing—in the air all the time. The typhoon rain is reported to have an all time high of radioactivity. Every bomb test is salt in the wounds. [9/9/57]

In his room, he began to accumulate flowers, presents, and mail— "The ones I have looked at begin, 'I are Japan girl higher student which like you bookings.' Mostly they enclose photos and pretty cute too. I could be a real heller with Japan girl higher student if I having impulse. But not soooo" [9/7/57]. Two days before he was to fly back to the West Coast, he wrote Elizabeth:

My first and last Congress is over. If I ever suggest it again I will take it kindly if you will shoot me. Some of the boys go to several of these things a year. There's a whole technique for it but I'm never going to learn it. The fixed smile, the generality, the open bowel. I'm just not a good organization man. I hope I have learned my lesson and on the other hand I wonder whether I am capable of learning anything. [9/8/57]

When he returned home, he knew what Elaine would think. So, before she said anything, he told her that he had asked the doctor, "Could this be psychosomatic? I hate making speeches." And the doctor, he told his wife, had said, "Well, it certainly would take a strong mind to raise a 103 degree temperature."

Back in Sag Harbor, he again took up the Malory. In England he had ordered a microfilm copy of the manuscript at Winchester College, and now Chase had purchased a reading machine for him so that he could work from the manuscript directly, as well as go over other film copies of rare materials. He was pleased that in the future he wouldn't have to spend so much time at a library table with a guard hovering at his elbow. During this period he was traveling back and forth from Sag Harbor to the city, staying a few days to confer with Chase and to go to the library, and then returning. At the end of October he wrote to Chase to tell him that

> right now I'm staying away from Malory. But when I go back to him I think it will be with a new dimension and that, my friend, is completely your doing. This work is collaboration, and don't think it isn't. The fact that I will do the final writing does not make the work less collaboration. Meanwhile I'm having a hell of a fine time with the books. And I'm going to take all the time I need—or rather, want. And I want a lot. I have even stopped writing letters except to you and Elizabeth. I want to forget how to write and learn all over again with the writing growing out of the material. And I'm going to be real mean about that. [10/25/57]

All around him he felt the pressure, unspoken, to get on to some serious work—as if the Malory had become his hobby horse.

It became a custom during these years that when the Steinbecks were in Sag Harbor, John and Shirley Fisher would spend Friday evenings at their house, and then the Steinbecks would go to the Fishers' in nearby Bridgehampton on Saturday evening. The Fishers were comfortable, unpretentious people, and an evening with them, at either house, was like an evening at home with the family. Shirley was one of the principal agents at McIntosh and Otis, although she was not directly responsible for Steinbeck's account there. A short, stocky Scotswoman (who on occasion wore the kilt that John bought her and played the bagpipes), she was articulate, opinionated, emotional, and just as much at home baiting a hook on board John's boat as she was talking to publishers over martinis at the Biltmore. Her husband, John, was quieter, easygoing and friendly. He was an interior decorator, but he looked more like a very relaxed English professor from a small New England college.

When they arrived at the Steinbecks, they usually watched the news on TV, and very often much of their talk was about the news and about politics. Steinbeck, as Fisher recalls, would drink whatever he had discovered that week to be a new drink, but as he got older he seemed to prefer what in John Fisher's opinion were really terrible things—pink grapefruit and vodka or strawberry soda and vodka. He liked sweet things. He ate a lot of candy and toward the end of his life discovered Hawaiian Punch, which he drank with or without vodka, depending on how he felt about liquor at the time. They would sit around in the evening talking, drinking, and cooking, but there was no compulsion to talk—sometimes they would read. Fisher usually put out the catalogues from the mail order houses that offer tools, gadgets, and garden supplies, and John would often turn to these as soon as he came in the door and become completely absorbed by them.

If they were talking, John's hands were never still. He was always fiddling with something, working on a gadget, taking it apart to see how it worked, fixing something, carving something, or working with leather. Often after he bought something, he would think about it for awhile and then try to redesign it or improve it in some way. They were little things—when he got a choke chain for the dog, he didn't like the way it worked and so altered it; when he got a timer, he worked out the time for all the things they usually cooked—eggs, coffee, and so forth—and then marked the dial with special colors for each item.

He paid a lot of attention to small things, but it was also, as John Fisher remembers, the small things that upset him. He hated to hear the phone ring, and when it did, he'd call out to Elaine, "I'm not going!" If the dog misbehaved, if a repair didn't hold, or if Elaine told him too pointedly or too often what to do, he would burn. When Elaine would take over, he'd say, "O.K., stage manager," and Elaine would answer, "Somebody has got to do something."

It was not unusual for Elaine to go to a social event and have to explain his absence. One such occasion came after Fisher had done the decorating for a large mansion. He told the Steinbecks about it, and Elaine mentioned that she'd like to see it. The owners invited them over for a drink, but on the way, John (Fisher thought predictably) suddenly got a headache and decided he couldn't go. Elaine and the Fishers went on and found that instead of just a drink, the owners had a full-scale cocktail party in progress, with neighbors and friends all gathered to meet Steinbeck. When Elaine explained his absence, a noticeable groan arose from the assembly, but Elaine carried on as best she could. John constantly deferred to Elaine in any number of ways in social situations. If they were at a dinner party, for example, and if some experience or anecdote came up in the course of the conversation, he'd often say, "You tell it, Elaine. You tell it better than I do."

Sometimes when Elaine was away, these two Johns would go out together, and occasionally when the two of them had been left to their own devices, Steinbeck would say, "I'm going to cook for you," and they would eat in the kitchen standing up. It wasn't very good, but it was served with affection. (His son Thom recalls that when they spent a week in Nantucket several years before this, without Elaine, his father cooked with great enthusiasm, but it was about the worst food that he and his brother had ever tasted.)

John Fisher recalls that Steinbeck got so much pleasure from corny little jokes, that Fisher got in the habit of making sure that he brought at least one with him when they came Friday for dinner. One that particularly tickled him surfaced when the names of the African leaders Joseph Kasavubu and Patrice Lumumba were often in the news: One of the Africans says to the other, "Isn't 'John Kennedy' a funny sounding name." But anything, serious or funny, that had to do with names, words, or sounds always seemed to evoke in John special interest or enjoyment. In his constant penchant for naming, it was as if he stood in a special, part humorous and part loving, relationship with all material objects around him. He even named his suits: "Burying Black," "Old Blue," "New Blue," and "Dorian Gray." The voice of Ethan Hawley, in *The Winter of Our Discontent*, which chants Latin, plays with rhyme, and addresses, while Ethan is alone in his store, the canned pears and piccalilli, must have been Steinbeck's own internal voice.

Sometimes the Fishers brought newspaper or magazine clippings that contained an odd bit of information or an unusual word or use of a word. The discussion of words nearly always led them to wonder where they came from or how they happened to be used in that particular way, and that in turn would lead John to the *Oxford English Dictionary*. He would carefully pick out the right volume, carry it to his chair, adjust his glasses, and read out loud the history of the word, peering through his bifocals closely, as his rumbling voice traced the journey of the word through time and country. He might pause over a foreign word, pronouncing it at last with relish, if not necessarily correctly, or might pause to look up over his glasses with satisfaction, if he had guessed right about the word's origins—as if he had won a bet with himself. He had many favorite books, but he could not live without the *O.E.D.*

In mid-November the Steinbecks moved in from the country to the house on Seventy-second Street. After a long lapse in their correspondence, John wrote to Toby:

> We spent a lot of time in Europe [this past] year and then a lot of time in the country at Sag Harbor. Last week we came into town and settled for the first time in seven months.
>
> Time is shrinking pretty badly, isn't it? My boys are big and practicing to be delinquents and haven't yet discovered that it is an overcrowded field. I am working on a very long and fairly scholarly work concerning the fifteenth century and am having a wonderful time with it and also am kind of pleased with the fact that it won't make a dime, and it may take five years to complete. Right now I am reading monstrously both in printed books and on microfilm. . . . I've had to reactivate my limping Latin, Anglo-Saxon and old French which for me is easier than modern French. But it is still a gambling game and what comes out is going to be a joyful game with the thin lipped faculty clubs of the smaller colleges. The great men in the field are invariably more tolerant and helpful than the little men who didn't get a boost in position last year.
>
> I read in the paper that Pilon died. He is about the last of the crowd I imagine. What a really successful life that was. One of the very very few who did exactly what he wanted to do and never got deflected. . . .
>
> [We] will probably run to the country after Thanksgiving. Then just before the first of the year we will make our yearly trip to the Caribbean for some sun and clear water and also for some information for future work. It is a pleasant way to start a year. And we always try to get out of town for New Year's Eve.
>
> There was a report in the paper that Gwyn was going to marry someone but our enthusiasm was premature. I don't think she can afford to marry anyone at these prices. If she marries, her alimony

stops and she isn't that big a fool. Besides the people she goes with aren't that solvent, or at all.

I wrote Marge Bailey a long and sentimental letter at the time of her retirement orgy which apparently made her sick to her stomach because I never heard from her. [11/21/57]

As during the previous year, he would spend the fall, winter, and into spring reading and studying. He continued to feel the pressure, and in December wrote a somewhat apologetic note to Elizabeth: "I still have a kind of stomach spasm about doing any writing yet. And I mean a real spasm. I'm just not going to do any for a while. I'm just not ready. Sometimes I think I never will be but I know that is not so." Involved as he was with Malory, however, there is evidence that the seeds of both *Charley* and *Winter* had already been planted and were beginning to take form in the back of his mind.

How does an author write a serious novel? Does he come up with some characters and a plot idea and start writing, using the stock phrases he has accumulated and throwing in a little description here and there? Does the felicitous sentence come by accident, do those small perceptions that so truly bring us into life come to him at the typewriter carried by the muse, and are those insights into the human condition at the heart of his work evolved out of the sudden inspiration provided by an approaching deadline and the need to pay the gas bill? Not if the writer is Steinbeck and not, I suspect, for any other author of similar stature.

It is rather simply a matter of living as a novelist twenty-four hours a day, every day, whether you happen to be writing a novel or not. Everything, EVERYTHING, is material, from your thoughts about your wife, your dreams and nightmares, to how your neighbor talks when he is embarrassed and how a friend looks at you when he wants something and what the local grocer does when he puts on his apron or makes change for a customer. Everything. Most of us could neither stand the burden or bear the exposure of our privacy.

The life of a novelist should probably really be a history of the constant gathering of bits and pieces of observation and insight, and the personal suffering and human concern which generates the pattern for the pieces and the need to express that pattern. For a novel such as *East of Eden* or *The Winter of Our Discontent* the novelist lives a preparation of years, accumulating hundreds, even thousands of small items. To describe the process from the outside is nearly impossible—even from the inside, as in the notebooks left by Henry James, it cannot be more than suggested.

But the writer does not just remember bits of information, sense impressions, interactions between people, ideas, conversations, and his own emotional reactions, he also notes the slight coloration of things, their manner and their tone. The year before, in 1956, he had taken the Long Island Railroad into the city from Sag Harbor, and in front of him sat a young woman, about college age, and an elderly gentleman in a tweed suit, smoking a pipe. The man said nothing, but the young woman kept yakking in his ear, and he would nod and puff on his pipe. They finally got to the first stop before getting into New York, and Steinbeck could hear the conversation at this point. When the train stopped, the old gentleman turned to the girl, obviously his granddaughter, and said, "My dear, you wouldn't worry so much about what people think if you realized how little they care." The writer remembered this, not only the precise words, but the entire coloration of the event, and four years later used it in *Winter*. Everyone can recall things from childhood, but to be almost sixty years old and to recall a small incident that had absolutely nothing to do with you from four years before, and to recall it precisely, that, as Henry James might say, is the great thing.

CHAPTER XLII

As Burgess Meredith remarked later, the whole thing was preposterous, but might be an interesting way to spend a vacation. A mutual friend of his and Steinbeck's by the name of Kevin McClory, a promoter on the fringes of show business who was trying to get a start as a producer, had received word of a Spanish treasure on the ocean floor near Nassau. He proposed that they all pay their own way to Nassau, rent a boat and diving equipment to locate the treasure, and if they found it, form a company to make a film while they recovered the gold.

Although he had already planned on going to the Caribbean during that period, Steinbeck took a somewhat dim view of the project from the beginning. He was suspicious of McClory, and his relations with Burgess Meredith had not been very close in recent years. Nevertheless, they all agreed to go, and McClory even talked diver-adventurer Peter Gimbel into joining the expedition and leading the underwater search. It turned out to be a very strange trip.

They arrived in the Bahamas to find the island gripped by a general strike, the first in its history. The party couldn't find a place to stay, there was no place to eat, and, more important, it was impossible to get the equipment that they had counted on. They went to another little island where they could rent a boat and made contact with a group of blacks who spoke mysteriously about knowing where the treasure was. The weather was constantly bad, with rain and fog much of the time, and Peter Gimbel was almost lost in the fog during a dive one evening—when they found him, he was surrounded by sharks.

As far as the gold was concerned, it was, Steinbeck came to believe, a salted treasure. The weather was bad, the expedition was poorly organized, and to top it all off, Steinbeck was certain they were being made fools of. He took a somewhat more sanguine view of his behavior than those around him when he reported to Elizabeth later, "I find that I have a tendency to become irritable with nonsense. Everything about this trip has been ridiculous including ourselves. But I think that Harry [his lawyer] would have been proud of me because I listened a great deal and didn't do much of any talking except to ask innocent and naive questions" [1/24/58].

In reality, he slid into a very black mood, or as Meredith put it, "A sea change took over, and he became maddened by the whole process. He just hated the whole thing ... lost his sense of humor ... and thought the whole bunch of us were outlandish and without purpose." In his anger, he lashed out so severely against Meredith that they were never friendly again. Meredith, saddened and shaken, went back to Hollywood; John took Elaine to St. Thomas, where they hoped to find a week of sun before returning to New York; and Kevin McClory stayed, met Ian Fleming, acquired the movie rights to the James Bond thriller *Thunderball*, and eventually became rich.

Right after they returned to New York in early February, Elaine was scheduled to go to the hospital for an operation. It was not highly dangerous, but John was so worried he could hardly function. Friends tried to have him over to dinner, but he refused to go out. Finally, after four days it was certain that Elaine would be fine, and he felt so relieved, as he told Elizabeth, "I could yell." When he came to the hospital, he was so obviously uncomfortable that Elaine wouldn't let him stay very long. They talked about her coming home; she would have to stay in her bedroom on the third floor of their house for a week or two.

It was typical of John that while other people would leave the problem in the hands of the ambulance attendants, he began to worry about how they would get Elaine up the stairs. For two days he fretted over the problem and planned one ingenious way after another, before he settled on a plan involving a sling, which he then manufactured. The night before Elaine was to come home, the Fishers came over to fix dinner for him. He got to talking about his plan, and then suddenly exclaimed, "Jack—you're about the same weight as Elaine. Let me try this rig out on you." Fisher testified later that when John slung him from his shoulders, across his back, and struggled to carry him up two flights of steep, frilly, old-fashioned stairs, he was absolutely terrified, certain he was going to die. Of course, when the ambulance came the next day, the two attendants got out, and without a word, took the chair apparatus that Elaine was sitting in, grabbed the handles, and carried her without any fuss to the third floor.

For John, life was full of problems that required ingenious solutions.

He never looked for the easy way, the normal way, but always had to find his own way. And while he brought this same spirit of inventiveness to moral as well as physical problems, he was particularly delighted when he had to think up a solution that involved some kind of apparatus.

In early March 1958, John sent a "progress report" on his Malory work, couched in formal language, to Elizabeth. The tone of the letter indicates that it was to serve also as a tax record if need be:

As you know, the research and reading and accumulation of knowledge has gone on over a long, long period now, and must continue to go on at least until the autumn [Elizabeth, while reading this, must have been gritting her teeth]. You will understand that I am pumped full of information, some of it possibly ill assimilated and perhaps being slowly digested. As usual it is the texture rather than the exact information which has the most profound impact on me, but even so a remarkable amount of factual material seems to be getting through to me. I have read literally hundreds of books on the Middle Ages and have literally a few hundred more to dip into before I shall be ready to start writing. The enormous accumulation of notes which Chase and I have made are necessary, even though they may not come to the surface in the work to be done. To proceed without the information would be to proceed without foundation. Last year I spent some time in England, as you well know, going to a number of places which will be referred to in the work, to absorb the physical feeling of the places. I thought that I had covered the field fairly well. It is only with continued reading that I find that there are gaps in my information. I shall find it necessary to return to England to pick up, or rather fill up the holes in my visual background. . . . And I must have the feel and look of all of these places, which are not only referred to but are parts of Malory's experience in the fifteenth century. . . .

I plan to spend the month of June in England picking up final topographical information and also consulting with certain authorities, such as Professor Vinaver of the University of Manchester, and others who are preeminent in the field of the fifteenth century. I shall return to America about the first of July and will continue the reading in the light of what I have found in this next trip into October. And if I can judge at all by my own state of information and mind, I should be able to start writing on this book this fall.

That March, while Elaine went to Texas, John and the two boys went to Sag Harbor for a week. Just as his feelings in response to his children and their mother had had a great deal to do with the motive for writing *East of Eden* and with its content, so also did his feelings about his children and his relationship to them during this period, through the late fifties, have an important part in the motive and content of *The Winter of Our Discontent*. His sons were going through their early teenage years (in March of 1958 they were 14 and 12), and when he wrote to Toby Street that they were "practicing to be delinquents," he was not entirely joking. They were exhibiting behavior fairly common to American children of that age—trying as often as they could to win as much independence as possible and get their own way. And, like most parents, Steinbeck was frustrated.

On the one hand, he tended to excuse them because he could look back and see that he had done many similar things. When the boys did very poorly in school, he would say, "But I wasn't much of a student either, so it probably doesn't matter." He was also conscious that they had a home life, as he wrote Toby, that wasn't very "peaceful—Gwyn isn't sober much anymore and when she is, she's sick." On the other hand, he knew that he hadn't done *that* badly as a student, and it seemed to him that they usually made no effort at all, spending more time and ingenuity in getting out of things than it would take to do them.

Over the years he believed that he had tried just about every approach he could think of to motivate them. He or Gwyn, or both of them together, had tried doctors, counselors, summer camp programs, and special schools. Time after time there had been a hopeful sign—a sudden interest in a subject, a good grade on a report, a sincere resolve to do better, or the promise of a new school, a new method, or a new teacher. Then the hope seemed to be blasted by some new rebellion, and each time hope became more slender, misgivings and doubt more ponderous.

Whatever blame for their behavior is assigned must be given in part to their father, who, although he worried about them constantly, gave them his attention in spurts and usually only when it was convenient. Despite his failures, however, John cared, cared deeply about them, and no matter what happened—and many things did— never gave up hope for them or stopped trying, in his own erratic way, to help them. But for us, the important thing is that it was out of the conflict of his love for his children with the intense frustration that they caused him that much of his later writing was generated.

Part of the novelist's difficulty as a father is that a large part of what he wants to say or do is siphoned off by his work. There he can control the circumstances, and his manner and speech can be measured and tooled true. The writer, by writing, acts on that part in all of us that plans the perfect interview or proposal in advance, or looks back to re-write a conversation, saying what we wish we would have said if we had thought of it in time. To some extent, the writer's persona can drain off the best in him, both motive and action.

In his letter in which he talks of Malory as a novelist, John speaks of what he calls the "self-character," saying that his own self-character probably expresses his "dream wish of wisdom and acceptance." Throughout much of his career, up to *Sweet Thursday*, that character was an identification with an idealized Ed Ricketts, but through his ar-tistic struggle in the fifties, wherein he consciously planned and at-tempted to make several radical changes in his writing, the largest and most crucial change may have come unconsciously as a result of a grad-ual change in his own personality. His "symbol character," as he also calls the persona, changes from others, Ricketts, to himself, an idealized Steinbeck. It was an act of reconciliation, of integration, that may be unparalleled in literature.

Steinbeck had learned, at last, to like himself well enough to speak as himself and to project a possible version of Steinbeck based on what he actually was, as well as what he would wish to be or become. In both *Winter* and *Charley* he is saying in effect, it seems to me: "This is what I am, both as I see myself and as I see the possibilities in myself. These are the things I do or could do; these are the thoughts I think or could think. You may find them strange, or funny, or false—but I am not going to be afraid to be truthful, to be corny or sentimental, if that is what I am. My aim is to reach the deepest truth available to the novel-ist, not the truth of proverbs, axioms, or generalizations, but the truth that all novelists must aim for and the only truth they are really quali-fied or able to present—the truth of my apprehension of life as I have experienced it."

At the same time as he was writing *Winter*, in 1960, he was also writing an article for *Holiday* called "Conversation at Sag Harbor," a "nonfiction short story." Although the editorial subtitle for the story, published in 1961, refers to conversations "last year," the story was really based on the visit of Steinbeck and his sons to Sag Harbor in March of 1958 (and Steinbeck changes the ages of the boys to 15 and 13).

After a description of Bluff Point in the winter and enough conversation and interaction to display the personalities and attitudes of the two boys and their relationship to their father, the talk after dinner turns to more serious topics, among them, the then current disc jockey "payola" scandal and the rising tide of juvenile delinquency. Since grade reports have just come out, at one point the discussion is interrupted by the periodic "father must give hell to the boys for bad grades and misbehavior" lecture, which both lecturer and auditors have dreaded but known to be inevitable.

"I have prepared a few remarks," the father begins. "At intervals, it becomes my duty, through the accident of being your father, to give you what for." The reports are bad. Do they have anything to say for themselves? Hasn't he given them good advice? Yet, they persist in their lives of "sin and gold bricking." He is at his wits' end, he tells them, "and I mean that literally. I've told you all I know and it isn't much but you've had it." So, after much thought, he has decided to do something drastic:

"I am going to give you your freedom."
"Sir?"
"I'm getting off your back."
"How do you mean?"
"I mean no more lectures, no more come-uppances. You are crowding manhood and you'll have to take some of the pain. You are free."
"How do you mean free?"
"I'll tell you. If you get a good grade, it's your grade. If you fail, it's your failure. That's what freedom means and it's awful." I think for the moment I had caught their attention.
"What's awful about it?" [John] asked.
"I'll tell you, but you'll have to find it out yourselves. Freedom is the worst slavery of all. No boss to cheat, no teacher to fool. No excuses that work. And nobody to bitch to."
"Do you mean it? About—getting off—our backs?"
"I mean it, all right. It's a lonely feeling, isn't it?"
I could feel their dishonest little minds scurrying about looking for a trick, and I answered their thoughts.
"It's not a trick," I said. "Of course if you get in trouble beyond your control, I'll stand by. But I want no more details. That part of your lives is over."
[Thom] said, "I'll bet the masters won't go for that."
"No, of course they won't. Neither will the cop, neither will the

judge if you come before him. But that's your business. Being a man is a good thing, maybe the best, but a man has to do his own time, take his own rap, be his own man."

"Yes," said [John], "but how about all those people on the couch or the drunks?"

"They're sick or they're children but they aren't men. I think the lecture is over; I think it's over for good. I've taught you everything I know. From now on we can only discuss."

He was not a philosopher, but he was always a man of ideas, and his urgent need to bring his ideas to the attention of others lay at the heart of his impulse to write. But especially, as seen in this interview with his sons, he was a man with ideas and theories about human nature—about freedom and responsibility, courage and conformity, private morality and public duty. For a man who at times was swept with romantic and mystical currents of feeling, he was strangely also a rationalist who observed a world full of problems, large and small, and considered many capable of solution—if he could just think of one. His creativity was largely that of the problem-solver, and like most men of genius, his solutions were usually unorthodox. Some were fanciful, some even ludicrous, and others might evoke the response given by the hero in so many B-movies: "That's crazy—but it's so crazy, it might just work."

At the beginning of June 1958, he and Elaine flew to England to spend a month reestablishing physical contact with the ground that Malory knew. "I have read until I am blind with reading," he wrote to Professor Vinaver. "Now, I must feel and taste some few more things—Colchester, Bamburgh, Cornwall. These are stimulations to intuition" [3/10/58]. They were met on their arrival by the Graham Watsons, who took them to Kent for a weekend in the country; then they spent the following week in London. It was sunny and warm, and they walked for miles. They went to the London Museum at Kensington Palace to see the models of the city through the ages, and with visions of the city as it had been, they went out, following the line of old walls, and attempted to reconstruct their visions. All you had to do, John reported, in order to see the city in all its periods was squint your eyes a little. Yet, as he told Elizabeth, "I am still stunned at being here at all. And maybe there is no real reason for being here but I think there is, or rather I feel that there is. The whole trip is a feeling matter rather than a thinking matter, and I find it very difficult to explain" [6/3/58].

After a trip of several days to Glastonbury, they returned to London to await Vinaver, who would be going with them to Colchester. Although Steinbeck was not sure in his own mind why he had come to England at this point, it would seem he had the need of some kind of final fix of inspiration before attempting a task that he had already come to believe might be impossible. He was frightened. Always before on a major project he had put so much pressure on himself through a constant escalation of expectation prior to composition, that it had been nearly impossible for him to function except in a kind of frenzy. Now he had tightened the screws so hard that he felt himself nearly paralyzed. He had read so much that he thought to himself, "If I go much further, I will know nothing." He wrote to Vinaver to ask if the Malory scholar would accompany him on a walk about the territory, hoping, perhaps, that the scholar's acceptance and companionship would provide the security he needed to go on.

Steinbeck and Vinaver were in many ways an odd pair—the rough, weathered Monterey pine and the cultivated fleur-de-lis. Steinbeck had in his late middle age adopted the style of the old sailor, and wind, sun, and constant work with his hands had roughened and spotted his ruddy complexion and had given his hands, shaped like those of a surgeon, the scars and calluses of a laborer. Vinaver, by contrast, was refined-looking and well groomed. On the short side and slightly plump, he was distinctly an indoor type, very quiet, very retiring, and very cultured. While John trooped about the countryside, slightly disheveled in his corduroy jacket and khakis, squinting over a small cigar and surveying the territory as if for battle, Vinaver, in his dark, three-piece suit followed along, nodding and polishing his glasses. In a gentle, slightly accented voice, he brought a ministerial assessment and caution to bear on his companion's bold speculations.

Following their trip together to Colchester and then to Winchester, to go over the manuscript once more, he wrote to Vinaver to tell him that many years earlier he had learned rather than address his work to a faceless reader, he would write his books to someone he knew. For his work on Arthur, which he was about to start, "I should like to hold you in image. . . . You would then be the focusing point, the courts, the jury. Also the discipline of your great knowledge would forbid nonsense while the memory of excited exchanges would keep alive the joy and the explorations. This would be very valuable to me. And I hope you will not forbid it" [6/22/58].

Vinaver's was a friendly face, and entering, as he was, new and potentially hazardous territory, John needed to keep the scholar's approval in mind to ward off the evil spirits. Although he was more secure now than he had ever been, discouragement, self-doubt, and dissatisfaction dog the writer's progress. He must have an extraordinary amount of courage to continue, or like Kafka's hunger artist, he must come to know that his art is his life, regardless of outside understanding or approval—his art defines him, and while the pursuit of his art may be the easiest thing in the world for him to do, it is also the hardest.

Since the artist exposes himself to the world, risking everything, harsh disapproval can be particularly painful, for such attacks can serve no useful purpose, can only work to encourage his self-destruction. Regardless of his defenses and regardless of the motive or form of such an attack, for the artist, whose functioning, and therefore survival, is at stake, the completely derogatory assessment of his art must always be among the most personal of all things that can happen to him.

While Steinbeck was in England, the critic Alfred Kazin came out in *The New York Times* with a broadside against him. Kazin had taken the opportunity provided by the publication of Peter Lisca's *The Wide World of John Steinbeck* to review the novelist's career. He began with the question, "What turned one of the most powerful of American writers to the banal propaganda of 'The Moon Is Down,' the self-conscious cuteness of 'Cannery Row'. . . ?" He then labeled Steinbeck a "pastoral writer" and mourned the failure of the writer's "intellectual and creative resources" in not allowing him to live up to Kazin's expectations for him in that category. This, of course, was a matter of sadness for Kazin, who would have liked to have seen the novelist find "new strength," rather than relapse, as he did, into "sentimentality."

The essay was a complete and damning indictment—the more so in its tone of sad condescension—based on half-truths and gross oversimplifications. Such an indictment—that nothing in Steinbeck's work after *The Grapes of Wrath* (or after *Sea of Cortez*) had any value, had been made before. The importance of Kazin's essay was that this simple-minded formula was now certified, on page one of *The New York Times Book Review*, and would become official doctrine, inevitably adopted by a number of other reviewers, critics, and professors. The formula had been written in stone.

The writer's response to belittlement and pity administered by a prestigious critic in a prestigious periodical must necessarily be mute agony and stomach cramps. Convention forbids the artist to reply to criticism, whereas practicality insures that the convention be adhered to. If one replies, there is scarcely any way that the tone of such a defense cannot further indict the author. He is automatically either self-righteous in his anger or a cry-baby in his complaints.

At first Steinbeck's long-practiced defenses were in place. When in a fury Pat Covici wrote to report the attack, John replied, "Don't be mad at Kazin. He describes himself perfectly in your quotations. What frustration the man must have, and what jealousies." But then he received another letter from an incensed Harold Guinzburg, and he began to feel his blood rising. "I have never seen Harold so angry," John wrote to Elizabeth. "He says it was a dirty deal—intentionally dirty." Even Vinaver wrote to John to express his indignation.

By this time, Steinbeck had become angry enough to write a reply, which he sent to Harold, leaving it up to the publisher's discretion whether to send it on to the newspaper or not. "I rather hope he does," he told Elizabeth. "I think I could take this boy apart." A brave hope, but there was no way that Harold was going to let him try, since he knew full well that any such attempt would only make the situation worse.

In London, John ran into John Kenneth Galbraith by accident. Galbraith's book, *The Affluent Society,* had just come out, and he was sitting at a table in the Dorchester reading a review of it in *Time* magazine (it called his book a "vague essay with the air of worried dinner-table conversation"). Galbraith recalls that he happened to glance around and there was John reading over his shoulder; he was a bit startled, not only by the circumstances, but because he hadn't seen the novelist with a beard before. He pushed the magazine away, because "the last thing in the world I wanted to see was the expression on his face as I read this lousy review. John said, 'That's all right, Ken. I've always said that unless the bastards have the courage to give you unqualified praise, ignore them.' "

John also saw Adlai Stevenson, who was on his way to the Soviet Union. Among several missions he had taken on was one in response to pleas from writers and writers' organizations to talk to the publishing officials in Russia in an attempt to persuade them to become party to the Universal Copyright Convention (a cause that John himself would press vigorously in Russia on his next visit). They talked about this over breakfast, and John explained that he had no idea which books had been published in Russia or how many had been printed—there was no way to find out. From publishing the talk drifted to politics, and they both agreed that the greatest danger to the Republic was Richard Nixon.

John and Elaine returned from England at the beginning of July and went to Sag Harbor. John determined to impose upon himself an "iron discipline" in order to get into a work rhythm once again. The work he had set for himself loomed so large—he thought it would probably be several volumes—that he dared not think about finishing it or else the despair would be too great even to start. He would work five days a week, and using both the Caxton first edition and the Winchester manuscript, he would do six to eight pages of translation a day. In addition, he would keep a working diary in which he would put down interpretive and background material drawn from his reading for each day's translation. He intended to write an introduction to each of the stories, using his working diary as a source for these as well as for a running commentary to be published either alongside the translation or as notes.

On July 7 he wrote to Elizabeth:

> I am aching to get to work after the years of preparation. And I'm scared also, but I think that is healthy. I have spent a great deal of money and even more time on this project. It is perfectly natural that I should have a freezing humility considering the size of the job to do and the fact that I have to do it all alone. There is no one to help me from now on. This is the writing job, the loneliest work in the world. If I fail there is only one person in the world to blame. But I could do with a small prayer from you and from others who feel that this should be the best work of my life and the most satisfying. Prayer is about the only help I can hope for now.

Although he expected several false starts, the next three months were very painful as he tried one approach after another. Nothing seemed to work; he couldn't find a language or style that was satisfactory in producing the effect that he wanted. In the middle of September he told Toby Street,

> I've been preparing for a very long and possibly climactic piece of work for a very long time. Now the preparation is complete and I am scared to start. I guess that might be because I have doubts that I can make it. Anyway I am fighting the start and it is fighting me with great success. Of course I always have trouble starting but

this time it is even worse than usual. In fact it is so bad that I can't remember what usual is like. One keeps wondering whether one's guts are gone or one's head worked out or one's juices dried up. That is perfectly natural I guess and perfectly unpleasant also. [9/15/58]

It wasn't so much that he was scared to start, as that he couldn't find a mode of translation that he could commit himself to. Since he had envisioned a very long work, added weight was brought to bear: the success of the entire project, years of preparation and execution, would depend on this initial decision. And it was made even more crucial in that he continued to believe that this, because of illness, death, or failing powers, might very well be his last major project. He talked a lot during this period about the *Arthur* becoming his insurance policy—it would not only be the climax to his career (a fitting one in his mind, since it emphasized his connection with the tradition of Western literature), but security for his old age—if he had one—and his legacy to his wife.

He had thought about it so much that he even wrote a short article about it for *Saturday Review,* called "The Easiest Way to Die," in which he argued that it might be just as well that he did not have insurance (omitting any mention that he couldn't get any). "I believe," he wrote, "that by far the greatest number of heavily insured men simply die because it is expected of them." But if a man is uninsured, his family is concerned that he live and continue to work, and the pressures on the man are for survival: "I realize, of course, that my own case is a little unusual. The best insurance I can leave is a long list of copyrights. Therefore it is to the advantage of my heirs and dependents to keep me alive and well and working. This is a happy state of affairs."

Near the end of September he gave the most recent of several attempts at the manuscript to Elizabeth and Chase Horton for their opinions—a step that was unprecedented for him. When they replied that they thought his treatment was dull and boring, he was furious. He stomped about the house at Sag Harbor in a rage and then went into a prolonged sulk—or "hibernation," as he called it later—during which he would not communicate with Chase and wrote to Elizabeth infrequently. He felt as if he were at his wits' end.

After several weeks, he decided that he needed both a change of scene and a change in work. He would go back to the house in New York more often, and he would start on another project, a "diversion," in the hope that it would take him out of his stalemate and allow him to come back to *Arthur* later with a fresh approach. He wrote Elizabeth to tell her:

> Sometimes it becomes necessary to break the siege for a time and to make a diversion against some less well defined position, after which he may find on his return that the castle is undefended against him. Your agreement that such a change of direction may be necessary, a course which I suspected, has opened the campaign and let in some light. I am starting the diversion immediately and may have some tangible evidence in the near future. [10/58]

The new work was "Don Keehan," which he referred to as a "modern Western," evidently a take-off on *Don Quixote*, but also related to his work on *Arthur*. For more than a year he had noted here and there in his letters the continuity of legend, running from ancient times, through Malory, up to the present. He was particularly struck, as he had mentioned in a letter to Joe Bryan the previous March, by the similarities between Arthurian legends and those that had evolved out of our frontier experience: "One thing grows out of another while keeping a great part of what it grew out of. The American Western is not a separate thing but a direct descendent of the Arthurian legend with all the genes intact and drawn to the surface by external magnets. Nor was the legend ever new" [3/15/58]. And in a letter to Vinaver he had made the point that our time, in his view, was better able to understand the fifteenth century than any other, "for we are as unconsciously savage and as realistically self-seeking as the people of the Middle Ages" [6/27/58].

But perhaps the most explicit statement of his thinking which led to the "diversion" came in a letter to Berkeley professor Joseph Fontenrose, a classics scholar, but one who had been working off and on for several years on an analysis of Steinbeck's thought and sources and had sent a copy of his manuscript to the novelist for comment:

> I hope you will forgive my delay in answering your letter and in reading your manuscript. It is a kind letter and a most careful and defensible manuscript, much the most penetrating I have seen. It might even be true. . . .
> Your work in the Delphic Myth is fascinating and I shall look forward to seeing your work in it. . . . My own work is not so far from yours. The myth seems always to be there 900 B.C. 450 B.C. 1450 A.D. 1958 A.D. The sleeping anlage seems to be brought to life

by needs arising from circumstances, usually external ones. Wyatt Earp, King Arthur, Apollo, Quetzalcoatl, St. George all seem to me to be the same figure, ready to give aid without intelligence to people distressed when the skeins of their existence get bollixed up. Surely the so called adult Western is blood brother to the Arthurian cycle. [8/26/58]

As both Elizabeth Otis and Pat Covici had hoped, he had become sidetracked from his translation work and was once again a novelist. But while Pat and Elizabeth had hoped that the novelist would respond to the rich detail of his research, he had no intention of writing a historical novel. Instead, he began to write a novel based not on experience, but on a conception that excited him, having to clothe that conception with people, places, and the texture of life out of his imagination.

By the middle of October he claimed to have written seventy-five pages. He was thinking in terms of making "Don Keehan" a novelette-movie combination, and during a visit of the Kazans to Sag Harbor, he read his pages to Gadg, thinking to interest him in the project. Indeed, just as he had visualized *Sweet Thursday* as a musical stage production, he was apparently writing "Keehan" projecting a motion picture in his mind. The picture on his mental screen starred Henry Fonda, as he made clear in a letter to Fonda sent in late November:

It is strange but perhaps explainable that I find myself very often with a picture of you in front of my mind, when I am working on a book. I think I know the reason for this. Recently I ran a 16 mm print of The Grapes of Wrath that Kazan had stolen from Twentieth Century-Fox. It's a wonderful picture, just as good as it ever was. It doesn't look dated, and very few people have ever made a better one—and I think that's where you put your mark on me. . . .

Now I am working on another story, and again I find that you are the prototype. I think it might interest you. . . . It seems made for you. In fact it's *being* made for you—let's put it that way. [11/20/58]

In other words, he had solved the problem of imagining the main character for his new manuscript by thinking of Henry Fonda—but not Henry Fonda in person; rather, he was thinking of Fonda as he was playing a character in a movie made from one of his own books. When one stops to think of the implications of all this, it is like entering a hall of mirrors, a very strange business indeed.

Having read the material to Kazan, he became dissatisfied with it and threw it out. He started again, wrote fifty pages, and then threw that away. At this point, he thought that he might have solved the language problem for his work on *Arthur* by using the language he had been using for "Don Keehan," present-day, idiomatic American. This seemed to him a bold idea. American, as it is spoken, had been used in dialogue and in first-person narratives, but "I don't think," he told Chase Horton, "it has been used as a legitimate literary language." Suddenly, he "felt as Chaucer must have felt when he found he could write the language he had all around him and nobody would put him in jail." He couldn't sleep at night for his excitement: "The myths keep flowing past my audio complex and the figures jump like chiefs over my visual complex" [10/21/58].

But his enthusiasm for idiomatic American as the vehicle for the translation lasted only a short time before it, too, palled under the pressure of actual, extensive use. Bouncing back and forth from one thing to another in frustration—as he had so often since finishing *East of Eden*, nearly a decade earlier—he dropped the *Arthur* and picked up the "Don Keehan" once again, beginning yet another draft of the Western in early November of 1958. He became increasingly restless. Unable to sit still in Joyous Garde, he roamed the point, examining his plants and finding innumerable little tasks to perform, stopping every now and then to stand looking out over the water.

Despite the emotional chaos of the year, the trip to England and the extended stay in Sag Harbor afterward, certain aspects of his life went on very much as before. He continued to write and publish short pieces, one of which, published during the summer, came out of his close relations with the people in his Manhattan neighborhood.

Two doors from them was a candy store–newsstand where they purchased their papers, magazines, and cigarettes. It was run by a hard-working couple and their two children, all four sharing in the nineteen-hour workdays. Over a period of several years, the Steinbecks had gotten to know them so well that the family kept a key to the Steinbecks' house and watched over it when the Steinbecks were gone. In his article, John described the difficult struggle of the Spivacks and how they had courageously made a life for themselves, without complaint or self-pity, and had managed, as a sort of miracle of dedication and frugality, to send their son to college and through medical school. (What he did not mention was that he had helped with the medical school expenses.)

Despite his attempts to isolate himself in Sag Harbor and to cut himself off from interruption in Joyous Garde, their social life went on, almost as before. Elaine's relatives had come from Texas that summer, just as he was starting in earnest on the *Arthur*, and he could hardly conceal his irritation. There had been weekend guests occasionally throughout the summer and early fall, and in August, a wild blowout of a birthday party for Elaine and Shirley Fisher—he had given a greenhouse to Elaine and bagpipes to Shirley. He swore that Shirley, whom he now called "Elfinheimer," had taken the pipes to bed with her at dawn and that later in the day, when they got in their car to leave, John Fisher turned to his wife and said, "That's going to have to go in the back seat. There are too many of us up here."

He had come to love Shirley very dearly, once telling her, as perhaps the highest compliment he could pay to anyone, that she reminded him of Ed Ricketts. She had become his most frequent fishing companion, and they went out together, usually on weekend afternoons, on his pride and joy, the cabin cruiser that they had shepherded home with a balky engine through heavy seas. John spent a lot of time plotting against the fish in his bay, gathering the latest scuttlebutt on location and technique and investing in new lures and fishfinding equipment. However, they usually came up with bottom fish, rather than the bluefish they were seeking, and for a man who considered himself an experienced sailor and fisherman, it was something of an insult, but he never gave up trying.

Shirley recalls that once John had started the engine, because of his deep voice and the cigarette butt that was always in his mouth, you couldn't hear him. If you happened to be facing the other way and he asked you to do something, you wouldn't know and it wouldn't get done—which sometimes led to confusion or to near disaster. Equipment failure, which he could not abide, caused him to go into a frustrated rage, and you couldn't understand what he was saying when he was yelling, either. "He hated it," Shirley recalls, "when things went wrong, and things always went wrong."

In New York, during those periods when they went in from the country, they went to dinners, parties, and openings. On a couple of occasions they had gone to the Covicis' for dinner with Arthur Miller and his wife at that time, Marilyn Monroe. It was a strange mixture: Pat, whom Miller has described affectionately as "an old Rumanian bandit"; Pat's wife, a gracious hostess but somewhat literal-minded; Arthur, relaxed, commenting with a dry wit that John delighted in;

Marilyn, girlish but sexy, trying to participate properly; Elaine, always at ease, supplying Texas charm and humor; and John, who wasn't an old Rumanian bandit, but who looked more and more like an old pirate. John and Marilyn seemed to be in awe of each other. She, because he was a real artist—she knew some of his books—and he, because she was glamorous, at the height of her fame, a fantastic movie star.

Through November John worked on "Don Keehan," reporting to Elizabeth, "I am pounding away . . . working much too hard and too fast, and maybe it is because I feel guilty about putting the Malory off" [12/7/58]. Indeed, despite his attempted "diversion," the Malory was still much on his mind. With his continued restlessness, he and Elaine decided it might be best to try to get away entirely, out of the country. He reported the making of the decision to Vinaver:

> Elaine the Fair who is good and loving but more wise than her cousin of Astolat, said very recently, "Are you troubled about not working on the Malory?" and I said, "Of course. Always troubled, even when I have explained it to myself."
> Then she, that wise one, said, "Could it be that the dissonance created by the clash of 15th and 20th centuries is making trouble?" My words but her meaning. And I said, "That is certainly part of it. Too many friends, relations, children, duties, requests, parties. Too much drinking—telephones—play openings. No chance to establish the slow rhythm and keep it intact."
> Then she said, "Would it be good to go away—say to Majorca or Positano?"
> "Yes."
> "Where would you like to go?"
> And I said, "One place. Where it happened—to Somerset." [11/30/58]

They planned to go in March, to rent a small farmhouse and a car, so that he could travel about and visit those places where he could establish connection with the ground and through it, the past. He wanted to "hear the speech and feel the air, to rub hands on the lithic tactile memories at Stonehenge, to sit at night on the untouristed eyrie at Tintagel and to find Arthur's mound and try to make friends with the Cornish fayries and the harsh weirds of the Pennines. That's what I want, so that my book grows out of its natural earth" [11/30/58].

He had not written in this vein since his letters to Carl Wilhelmson when he was in his early twenties. It was as if, having tried all else in his quest, he would turn to the half-believed magic and incantation of his youth. And perhaps it was not just his search for the inspiration to write the *Arthur* that was involved here, but, in some archetypal sense, he was bringing forth from deep in his throat the anguished cry of the poet in search of his muse.

The *Arthur* had many links to his life—to his childhood, to his close relations with his sister Mary, to his wife, Elaine, and to his sense of manhood and its duties—but more important than all of these, it was linked in his mind to the impulse that had led him to become what he had become and the feeling—the excitement and transfiguration by inspiration—that the act of writing had provided. It was, in short, a justification for all of it and a searching out, in late middle age, for the root of it all.

No other project could flourish or even survive in the shadow of such a soul-driven dream, and after two months of concentrated work on this last draft of "Don Keehan," he could no longer tolerate it. He wrote a letter to Covici that was similar to several he had written in the past, particularly to the one he had written on the occasion of the destruction of the first draft of *The Grapes of Wrath*:

> I do not intend to finish nor to publish the little book you have been reading parts of.
> It isn't a bad book. It just isn't good enough—not good enough for me and consequently not good enough for you. It is a nice idea—even a clever idea but that isn't sufficient reason for writing it. I don't need it. The danger to me lies in the fact that I could finish it, publish it, and even sell it. The greater danger is that it might even enjoy a certain popularity. But it would be the fourth slight thing in a series.
> It would bear out the serious suggestion that my time for good writing is over. Maybe it is but I don't want that to be for lack of trying.
> Frankly this is a hack book and I'm not ready for that yet. To be a writer implies a kind of promise that one will do the best he can without reference to external pressures of any kind. [12/26/58]

Just after the first of the year, he received a letter from an old friend from Monterey, Alice Jackson, who asked him what he thought about the direction in which the country was moving and in particular about nuclear power. He replied with a 3,500 word, "magazine-article" type of letter, in which he said that he thought, on the whole, we had managed atomic power fairly well, although in the long run it, or something similar, will prove our undoing: "Man will disappear and other species have the capacity to take over." He concluded that he had "learned to write and will not write anything more—just a history of King Arthur."

"The ranch," in second Steinbeck house in Los Gatos area. (© 1983 Richard L. Allman.)

John and Gwyn in Hollywood, circa 1940.
*(From the private collection
of Sandy Oliver, Hollywood,
California. © 1983 Sandy Oliver.)*

Gwyn and John,
wedding picture, 1943.
*(John Steinbeck Library,
Salinas, Steinbeck Archives.)*

Left to right: Frank Loesser, John, Margery Hunter, Max Wagner, Howard Hunter, Gwyn, Lynn Loesser; in Hollywood, circa 1945. *(Steinbeck Research Center, courtesy San Jose State University Library, San Jose, California.)*

Displaying captured
Nazi flag after
Ventotene engagement.
Top, left to right:
Lt. Comdr. John Kramer
(later killed),
Capt. Charles Andrews,
Lt. Douglas Fairbanks, Jr.
Bottom: Lt. Arthur Bryant
(later killed), John Steinbeck.
*(Courtesy Douglas
Fairbanks, Jr.)*

Ed Ricketts collecting in the littoral, 1945. *(Courtesy Peter Stackpole.)*

Webster "Toby" Street at the steps of Ed's lab on Cannery Row.
(Courtesy Peter Stackpole.)

John and Max Wagner in London, 1943. *(Courtesy Elaine Steinbeck.)*

Pier and buildings at extreme northwest end of Cannery Row, circa 1973; later destroyed by fire. (© *1983 Richard L. Allman.*)

John, Gwyn, and Jack Wagner in Cuernavaca, Mexico, 1945. *(Courtesy Max Wagner.)*

John, Willie, Thom, and Gwyn in the pool at house in Cuernavaca during filming of *The Pearl. (Steinbeck Research Center, courtesy San Jose State University Library, San Jose, California.)*

John, standing, left, and Gwyn, standing, center, at party in Mexico.
(*John Steinbeck Library, Salinas, Steinbeck Archives.*)

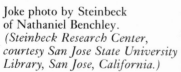

Joke photo by Steinbeck
of Nathaniel Benchley.
(*Steinbeck Research Center,
courtesy San Jose State University
Library, San Jose, California.*)

CHAPTER XLIII

rossing the Atlantic in late February, the Steinbecks met Erskine and Virginia Caldwell. John said, "I've taken quite a few compliments for *God's Little Acre* over the years," and Erskine replied, "And I've taken quite a lot for *The Grapes of Wrath*." At first neither man would say much—Steinbeck looked down and mumbled and Caldwell spoke shyly, quietly, and looked off into the distance—but after a day or so they warmed to each other. John claimed to dislike being around other writers, but when he was thrown together with one by circumstances, he usually enjoyed it. They both got up early in the morning and so established a routine, for the duration, of meeting at "early bird coffee" and then finding a place to sit and talk. Also in the morning, John would go to the navigation area on the bridge, check to see where they were, and "help" plot the course. He was usually happy and at home aboard a ship and had forgotten his previous resolution to fly to Europe and save time.

When they landed at Plymouth, they took delivery of a small Hillman station wagon and then drove to Somerset. Robert Bolt, whom they had met the previous year—a playwright and teacher at the local school—had arranged for them to rent a house near Bruton, Discove Cottage.

The cottage was the only one still standing of a group of peasant houses near an old manor house; made of thick rock walls and thatched roof, the cottage had been old when it was listed in the Doomsday Book. It was small, and although electrified in recent years, it was relatively primitive, with no water in the kitchen (it was plumbed in during their stay) and no heat except the fireplace and a coal cooking stove. Both the fireplace and the stove had to be fed constantly, for it was bitter cold and damp when they first arrived. The cottage had no refrigerator, but then, as John wrote his agent in mid-March, "Our landlord has put in a refrigerator named His Majesty's Voice. It must be his late majesty because it stutters" [3/17/59]. They soon learned how to live in the style of rural England, which was geared to a countryside where people didn't know cars. The wine and spirits merchant came once a week; the greengrocer, every other day; the baker, three times a week; and the postman delivered their mail by bicycle.

Inside the cottage there were narrow stairs at each end which went up to separate bedroom suites, one over the living room and one over the kitchen–dining room. Soon after they arrived, John purchased a lamp and card table and set them up in the room near their bedroom. From his upstairs window he could look out across the rolling hills of field and pasture dotted with ancient oak trees. He was in the middle of Arthur country, with the Roman fort, the traditional Camelot, ten miles away. He wrote to Elizabeth:

> The other night I discovered that fifty feet from our house, through a break in the trees, you can see St. Michael's Tor at Glastonbury. Elaine didn't believe it until I showed her and she is so delighted. It makes this house so much richer to have the Tor in sight. Am I in any way getting over to you the sense of wonder, the almost breathless thing? There is no question that there is magic and all kinds of magic. [6/17/59]

He immediately began work around the house, putting up weather-stripping and making other little changes for their convenience and comfort. Nearly every day he chopped wood, and he longed to get out into the garden, for there were no fresh vegetables available, but the garden was a sea of black mud for the first weeks. Then, when the ground dried out a bit, he sprang to the task of turning the earth with a cry of joy, planting beans and peas, almost too early. The gardener at the manor house, a hard-bitten, red-faced Somerset-born man, as John described him, became his tutor in English gardening: "When I asked to borrow a scythe he said cynically—'Thu be a scythe-hand?' 'Once was,' I said. Then he watched me use the scythe in the grass and his whole attitude changed. You can't fake it if you don't know the rhythm of the scythe any more than you can fake the clean use of an axe" [3/59].

He did not begin his writing until almost a month had passed, but once he started, it seemed to go very well. Getting up early, he would go out for a walk: "Sometimes for over an hour I do nothing but look and listen and out of this comes a luxury of rest and peace and something I can only describe as in-ness. And then when the birds have finished and the countryside goes about its business, I come up to my little room to work. And the interval between sitting and writing grows shorter every day" [3/30/59].

He found his medium, a hard, taut, economical English, without accent or locality, and he determined to use no words that would be beyond the knowledge of the general, educated reader. He planned to fill in where necessary for contemporary understanding and cut down on those things, particularly the repetitions, that the modern reader would find boring. In London he bought a battery-operated tape recorder and used it to check the sound of everything he wrote. Then he would give his manuscript to a typist, correct the typescript (sometimes recording and listening to it again), give it to the typist once more, and send a carbon of this final draft to Elizabeth and Chase in New York, chapter by chapter. This was, he felt, the best prose he had ever written.

But for all his confidence that he was on the right track at last, he found the work very difficult. He felt, at times, overwhelmed by detail: he had to make decision after decision while taking into consideration a dozen factors simultaneously—tone, sound, image, emphasis, perspective, narrative coherence, character development and consistency, and theme. Early in May he sent off a report to Chase that was representative of those that he was mailing regularly during this period:

Another week starting. Elaine and Mary [his sister Mary was one among several visitors they had that summer] off to Wells which gives me a fine long day for work. Start Torre and Pellinore, marriage of Guinevere etc. Half the typed Merlin came back. The rest early this week and I will get a carbon off to you and Elizabeth with strong hope that you will like it. After you have read it I suggest that you go back to Malory and see what I have done. You will instantly know why. I put the Balin on tape yesterday and listened to it back and it sounds pretty good. There will have to be lots of refinement of course in all of it but the essence is there and I can't find that I have missed much from the original. It is most painstaking work. You will notice that I have removed all of Merlin's prophecies having to do with future stories. They simply blow the point. Also Malory never could lead to a climax. He gave it away three times before he came to it. The harder work was the battle. Nothing will be that hard again—am removing the tiresome detail and at the same time keeping action and plan of battle. But there are such profundities in Malory sometimes hidden in a phrase. I have to be very careful not to miss them and sometimes to blow them up a little to make them apparent [5/4/59].

His conscientiousness led him to visit one site after another in the surrounding country, so that not only would he become inspired by the general atmosphere, but he would also search out specific locales as a basis for his descriptions. At the end of April, he had gone to Cadbury on a golden day when the apple orchards were in bloom. He climbed to the upper wall of Camelot and for the first time walked around the ramparts, looking down and across to the Bristol Channel, to the Mendip Hills and the little villages, and on the other side, Glastonbury Tor and King Alfred's towers. He found himself so moved by the sight and the feeling of being where he was that he wept.

He was concerned with exterior landscapes, with waterways, topography, colors, but also with interior scenes, which, in the case of ruins, required a mental reconstruction born of knowledge and intuition. The things he observed were often carried directly into his writing. Later in the summer, the Steinbecks, along with the Robert Wallstens, made a tour of several days through Wales, and there was one castle that was of particular interest to John. This was Caerleon at Usk (where John could not resist sending a telegram to Shirley Fisher, which read, "Happy Birthday to Yousk from Usk").

John and Robert went up the round staircases of the castle and peered into room after room after room and then at the top waved down to their wives, who were waiting in the courtyard below. When they returned to Discove very shortly after, John read to them a scene about Lancelot and Guinevere that he had placed in the castle they had surveyed, with its interior design described just as they had seen it.

These were very happy times for both John and Elaine. Their best times seemed to come when they were forced, in simple or awkward circumstances, to make do and cope, and here in Somerset they learned to cope beautifully: gardening, walking, talking, cooking on the coal-fired stove, and sitting in front of the fire at night. Elaine had written to Chase in April:

Jackson [a London book dealer] sent the two-volume *History and Antiquities of Somerset* by Phelps this morning, and we had to hide them for a day in order to get any work done. They will make fine reading for us. —John is working on "The Lady of the Lake" sequence today, and only comes up for air every two or three hours to get a cup of coffee. He is beginning to live and breathe the book.

In the evening he carves wooden spoons for our kitchen and talks about Arthur and Merlin. [4/11/59]

Their happiness made them reexamine their lives, and they thought about "pulling in, in terms of things—of having only what we use." So firmly established was their happiness, that it weathered a severe disappointment. Of the seven tales that John would write, he had by mid-May done at least a first draft of six of them. (In these seven he dealt with most of Books I, III, IV, and part of VI of the *Morte D'Arthur,* which contains twenty-one "Books," a "Book" being roughly equivalent to a modern chapter in length.) His version of Book I, which he called "Merlin," had been revised and typed, and he sent it off via air mail at the end of the first week of May to Elizabeth and Chase. He was very nervous about it and wanted their approval.

It was not to come. Instead, he received a very critical letter from them, primarily from Elizabeth, which said, in effect, "This won't do. It lacks life, interest. It is too fragmented. Rather than take this approach of sticking so close to the original, you need to take over and make the material your own. You must tell the story in your own way, but above all, tell a story." He was stunned, and on May 13 he replied:

Your comments and Chase's almost lack of comment on the section sent to you. I must think very carefully and not fall into obscurity in my answer. To indicate that I was not shocked would be untrue. I was. I wonder if the three thousand miles makes any difference. It is apparent that I did not communicate my intention but I wonder whether I could have if I had been there. It is natural to look for arguments in my defense or in defense of the work as I am doing it. Let me say first that I hope I am too professional to be shocked into paralysis. The answer seems to be that you expected one kind of thing and you didn't get it. Therefore you have every right to be confused as you say and disappointed. . . .

I know you have read T. H. White's *Once and Future King.* It is a marvelously wrought book. All the things you wished to find in my revision are superlatively in that. But that is not what I had wanted and think still do not want to do. . . .

White brilliantly puts the story in the dialects of present-day England. I did not want to do that. I wanted an English that was out of time and place as the legend is. The people of legend are not people as we know them. They are figures. Christ is not a person, he is a figure. Buddha is a squatting symbol. As a person Malory's Arthur is a fool. As a legend he is timeless. You can't explain him in human terms any more than you can explain Jesus.

I am not writing this to titillate the ear of the twentieth century. Perhaps I am overambitious, but I am trying to make it available, not desirable. I want the remote feeling of the myth, not the intimate feeling of today's man who in his daily thought may change tomorrow but who in his deeper perceptions, I am convinced, does not change at all. In a word I have not been trying to write a popular book but a permanent book. I should have told you all of this. . . .

You will understand that what saddened me most was the tone of disappointment in your letter. If I had been skeptical of my work, I would simply have felt that you had caught me out. But I thought I was doing well, and within the limits I have set for myself, I still do. . . .

Finally, and I won't labor the point after this, I feel that I am reaching toward something valuable. It doesn't sound like me because I don't want it to.

Elizabeth, of course, was still trying to push John into a novel, or at the very least a novel-like interpretation of Malory. And Chase, who was caught between Elizabeth and John, apparently felt that it would be best if he simply kept his mouth shut—to encourage John in the translation, in the manner he was doing it, would alienate Elizabeth, and to go along with Elizabeth, joining in her harsh criticism, might alienate him from John. John, as Elaine recalls, was sick at heart and walked around like a man in a dream. "We've made a mistake," he told Elaine. "We've got to go home—all of this has been for nothing."

On and on he raged in his despair. He had been so thrilled with himself and had been having so much fun with the project, and now he had been told, "This is terrible." The disappointment was killing, but he gradually recovered, and after some thought he was determined to go on. He knew what Elizabeth wanted him to do, and he was convinced that she was wrong, but she had so much influence over him that he did change his method, although not as completely as she would have wished.

If he had continued in the manner of his first chapter, would he have produced a worthwhile work of art? Possibly, although subsequent events suggest that without a word from Elizabeth, he would have become dissatisfied with it. Since "Merlin" is unchanged from when it was submitted to Elizabeth and Chase, the reader can decide for himself whether the ultimate result would have been worth the effort. What Elaine, Elizabeth, and others close to Steinbeck seem to agree on, in retrospect, however, is that the material written after he received the letter gets gradually better, through the revisions of Chapters 2–6 to the completely new final chapter, 7, which takes up roughly half the posthumously published book. This last chapter, "Sir Lancelot of the Lake," is written much more in his own style and contains a considerable amount of material of his own invention. To think of an entire work in this manner, covering what he wished of the entire Malory, suggests that Elizabeth may well have been right, although his struggle to gain some confidence in this work had been so long and painful, it is difficult not to think of Elizabeth as acting the villain here.

The seven chapters that have been left to us reflect the same quality of gradual improvement that John detected in Malory, as if Malory was learning how to do what he was doing as he went along. Steinbeck was not able to tolerate the same gradual change in his own work, however, and insisted that when he was through, it should be all of one piece in style and manner. His ultimate failure—his inability later in the year to continue with the project—came not so much as a result of outside comment or pressure, as from his inability to resolve his own internal struggle and meet his own demands.

As much as John and Elaine enjoyed the simple life, it sometimes got a bit complicated when they had guests. The stove fire, for example, might die down right in the middle of a roast. And the house was so small that it was hard not to run into people, the partitions so thin that it was nearly impossible not to be heard. Nevertheless, John invited people to come, issuing invitations right and left, and as usual regretting later that he had done so. He enjoyed having guests if they didn't make demands on his time and if they didn't stay too long, and he felt that Elaine would be happier with other people in the house now and then.

They saw a number of English friends, both at Discove and in London, where they retreated every few weeks to go to a restaurant and a show. Among others, Kazan and Adlai Stevenson visited from America, and John's sister Mary and the Robert Wallstens came to stay for several weeks each.

It was appropriate that Mary came, since John had already dedicated his book-in-progress to her. His close relationship with his sister, which had been strained at times by arguments during the period when he was writing of the misery of farm labor and she was part of what he called the "Carmel Republican crowd," had gradually returned to normal in more recent years as they saw each other more frequently. He was drawn close to her when she lost her husband, who was reported missing in action in Sicily while John was in the Mediterranean. He did everything possible, talked to all the brass he knew, and pulled every string he could, trying to get more information for her; then, he shared her grief when it was discovered that Bill had been shot down by our own guns.

Mary did not like Gwyn, but once John married Elaine, she saw her brother more often than at any time since they were at Stanford together. She usually came for several weeks at a time, visiting John and Elaine in New York and Sag Harbor, in Paris, in London and Somerset, and traveling with them in Italy and Spain. John also called Mary and his other sisters frequently. The usual procedure was for him to say, "Hello. I'm fine. Here's Elaine," and quickly hand that dreaded instrument, the telephone, to his wife. Whenever John was in the West, he almost always made a detour to the Monterey area to see his family, but although he looked forward to such visits, once he was together with his sisters and a few nieces and nephews and their children, it was only a short time before he felt closed in and restless.

He described one such visit in *Travels with Charley*:

> I arrived in Monterey and the fight began. My sisters are still Republicans. Civil war is supposed to be the bitterest of wars, and surely family politics are the most vehement and venomous. I can discuss politics coldly and analytically with strangers. That was not possible with my sisters. . . . Each evening we promised, "Let's just be friendly and loving. No politics tonight." And ten minutes later we would be screaming at each other.

Although Mary was far more conservative than John, and although she was more concerned about appearances and social status than her brother, they were in many ways alike—they had many of the same paradoxes of personality. Once she said to Elaine, "You must find it a great nuisance to be recognized by the name 'Steinbeck' everywhere you go," and yet some time later, Elaine saw that in her passport her name was given in the rather unusual form "Mary Steinbeck Dekker." She, like her brother, was fun-loving with a good sense of humor, and yet, also like her brother, she was a worrier and shared his moodiness, restlessness, and general sense of discontent. She could be practical and rationally thoughtful, yet there was in her, too, the Hamilton streak of mysticism and sentimentality.

Whether they disagreed about politics and social philosophy, whether they were separated or together, they seemed to have that kind of closeness of sympathy and understanding more typical of identical twins than of brother and sister. One of the archetypal pictures of Steinbeck is of him as a youngster leading his pony, with Mary riding bareback, across a field of wild oats and mustard weed under the warm sun of a Salinas afternoon. It was apparently a picture that stuck in his own mind, too, as reflected in his dedication to *The Acts of King Arthur:*

> When I was nine,
> I took siege with King Arthur's fellowship of knights most proud and worshipful as any alive.
> In those days there was a great lack of squires of hardiness and noble heart to bear shield and sword, to buckle harness and succor wounded knights.
> Then it chanced that squire-like duties fell to my sister of six years that for gentle prowess had no peer living.
> It happens sometimes in sadness and pity that those who faithfully serve are not always as faithfully recognized, so my fair and loyal sister a squire remained, undubbed.
> Wherefore this day I make amends within my power and raise her to knighthood and give her praise.
> And from this hour she shall be called Sir Marie Steinbeck of Salinas Valley.
> God give her worship without peril.
>   John Steinbeck of Monterey
>   Knight

And in the original, to cite just the last part:

> Wherefore thys daye I mak amendys to my power and rayse hir knyghte and gyff hir loudis
> And fro thys hower she shall be hyght Syr Mayrie Stynebec of the Vayle Salynis
> God gyvve hir worshypp saunz jaupardye
>   Jehan Stynebec de Montray
>   Miles

That the Middle English here clearly carries both more meaning and more emotion than the modernization gives some indication of the difficulty of the job that Steinbeck had set for himself. He didn't want to write his own version of Malory's stories because it wasn't the stories in themselves that he cared about. He was in love with the magical evocations of the language, the sense of being in history that the sound and the sight of the words conveyed. It was all tied together with the love he had for his sister, his family and parents, and the nostalgia for a world created in childhood. The task of bringing these emotions to the modern reader in modern language was impossible.

Robert and Cynthia Wallsten arrived in July. Elaine met them at a pub in Bruton and drove them to the cottage, where John welcomed them and then told them that they would be staying in the suite over the kitchen. Pointing toward the door at the bottom of the stairs, he said, "You just open that door." Robert did, and down on him and his wife came an avalanche of colored balloons that John had laboriously inflated then stacked in the enclosed stairway. Later in the summer the Wallstens were involved in the elaborate planning and execution of Elaine's birthday celebration. She had to sit in a room alone for what seemed hours while the processions and ceremonies were rehearsed with all the guests and the decorations were put into place. At one point during the celebration all the guests were to say at the same time, "Who would believe that Elaine had reached 45?" and then let air out of their balloons making a chorus of Bronx cheers.

With four of them together for several weeks in a small house, the situation was sometimes a strain for the guests, who found themselves tiptoeing about the house and whispering for fear of disturbing John while he was at work. Late afternoons and evenings were freer. Wallsten can remember sitting in the living room with John, listening to the two women, both of whom loved to cook, in the kitchen talking: "We would hear the sometime rather heated, though friendly disagreements about whether to stir something first or put herbs in, when and where, and that sort of thing, and John would say, 'Ah, there's a dame fight. Good. There's another dame fight going on.' This was a favorite expression of his—'a dame fight.' " Wallsten recalls John reading from his manuscript as they sat in the living room after dinner, and many passages, Wallsten thought, had great beauty.

One weekend Bob and Cynthia went to London, and Elaine decided to go with them. Although he had encouraged her to go, John was furious at being left alone and then felt lonely and abused once Elaine had gone. The next morning Elaine called him from London in an attempt to catch him before he had started work; she got him early enough to wake him. The phone was downstairs, and John, wearing an old-fashioned nightshirt, caught it on the gate on the top of the stairs that the previous tenant had installed to keep children from falling down. John slipped, fell, and scraped himself rather badly. By the time he got to the phone, which he hated to touch under any circumstances, he was in a towering rage. Elaine came back from the phone to tell the Wallstens, "I have to get back to Somerset. There is no question about that."

Despite some progress in his new direction with Malory, John continued to feel more frustration than satisfaction with what he was doing. He continued to believe that there was some magic key he was missing, some chord of inspiration that once apprehended would lead to a breakthrough. He didn't know whether it would come through research, through immersing himself in the physical environment, or through visiting and revisiting those sites most often associated with his material. But whenever his frustration reached a certain level, he felt he must do something different from what he was doing in order to encourage the breakthrough to occur. One is reminded of Joseph's search in *To a God Unknown* to find some belief, ritual, or mystical procedure by which he could end the drought. It was in this spirit that in early August John decided that the four of them should make a tour of Wales.

The Wallstens knew it would not be easy because John was nervous, depressed, and frustrated. Elaine had consulted a guidebook and had made reservations for them, and at one of their first stops at a country inn, Bob and Cynthia were taken to the marginally better of the two reserved rooms. The Wallstens insisted that they exchange rooms, but John would not hear of it, "Absolutely not. No, absolutely not." Yet he went into a terrible funk and sulked to such a degree that Elaine came to the Wallstens' room and, with tears streaming down her face, apologized for his behavior. The Wallstens were not seeing Steinbeck at his best, for in addition to the strain put on him by the Malory, there were two things he was absolutely selfish about—Elaine's company and travel.

He not only wanted his comforts when he could get them, but he wanted to see certain things and to come and go on his schedule. Robert recalls that "we were expected to be as interested in the King Arthur relics as he was, and it never occurred to him that there might be members of the party who didn't care that much."

Elaine and Robert were the kind of travelers who with dogged determination see everything they have set out to see, step by step, by the book. According to Elaine, if they went to see the Wells Cathedral, for example, "Robert and I are going to see it and we're going to read about it. Believe you me, we're going to see everything. Now Cynthia is going to take a sweeping glance and say, 'My, that's marvelous.' She'll admire the arches, and she's going to remember it the rest of her life. Then she's going to say, 'It's getting toward lunch. I think we all need a martini.' Now John's going to go in and use all his knowledge of medieval architecture. He sees where they were in the process of the perpendicular. He studies it very carefully, and he doesn't want Robert and me reading anything out of any guidebook. We were all standing on what is known as the North Porch, and Robert was reading a paragraph and I was reading a paragraph. And Cynthia says, 'I now know more about the North Porch than I care to know,' and John says, 'I knew more about the North Porch before we got here,' and off they go to the car, ready for their martinis and lunch, leaving Robert and me standing there."

When they returned to Somerset, the Wallstens and Elaine did as much local sightseeing as possible in order to give John time alone, but the guests still felt that they were a disturbing element, and when they told him they would move on to London John agreed with apparent reluctance but obvious relief.

As much as anyone who knew him, Wallsten felt the contradictions in his character. Once when he was at Sag Harbor and the two of them had been drinking late into the evening, John, without any cue whatsoever, slammed down his glass and said, "F. Scott Fitzgerald was a drunk," and went on to say that all this Fitzgerald-worshiping irritated the hell out of him. Wallsten had never heard him say anything before about Fitzgerald, nor did the topic ever come up again. During the summer the Steinbecks were in Somerset, after the Wallstens had moved to London, they took John and Elaine to visit some friends in Hampstead, where the host, a volatile actor, was behaving a bit like an "agent provocateur" by saying some unflattering things about Hemingway in an obvious attempt to draw John out on the subject:

> I remember John's face going off and freezing. My friend got nowhere. Not a word came out of John about Hemingway. He was not going to be drawn into the discussion, and there was a kind of feeling of craft loyalty which was in direct contra-distinction to the way he behaved with me about Fitzgerald. John was a character about whom you make a statement and immediately think of the contrary as being also true. He could be large spirited to a degree that was extraordinary, and he could be petty to a degree that was extraordinary.

By the end of August John had nearly completed the Lancelot section. He had incorporated what he had felt and learned in Wales into his writing, along with what was by now an extensive knowledge of the details of living in the early Middle Ages, so that the fabric of his work came alive with people, their manners and customs, their weapons and tools, their huts and castles, and the meadows, streams, and forests through which his knights traveled. It was good, but not good enough, and he wrote to Eugène Vinaver a letter that was a cry of anguish and despair:

> I have a dreadful discontent with any efforts so far. They seem puny in the face of a hideous subject and I use the word in a Malorian sense. How to capture this greatness? Who could improve on or change Launcelot's "For I take recorde of God, in you I have had myn erthly joye—" There it is. It can't be changed or moved. Or Launcelot's brother Ector di Maris—"Thou were the curtest knight that ever bare shelde! And thou were the trewest frende to thy lover that ever bestrayed hors and thou were the truest lover of a synful man that ever loved woman—" Good God, who could make that more moving? This is great poetry, passionate and epic and with also the stab of heartbreak. Can you see the problem? Do you know any answer? . . .
>
> This perplexity is like a great ache to me. You see a writer—like a knight—must aim at perfection, and failing, not fall back on the cushion that there is no perfection. He must believe himself capable of perfection even when he fails. And that is probably why it is the loneliest profession in the world and the most lost. I come toward the ending of my life with the same ache for perfection I had as a child [8/27/59].

His time in England was growing short, and he began to think of how he could best make use of the month before they would have to go back. He decided that a room in the cottage was very much like a room in New York and that rather than writing, he might better spend his time seeing so he would have a storehouse of impressions to draw on after he returned to America. After making his decision, he began to feel some panic, as if he must gather up as much as possible before it was too late. He wrote Elizabeth: "I feel a sense of rush. A few more side trips to make but just daily to accumulate as much as possible for the winter of my discontent" [9/18/59].

The apparently unknowing reference here to what would become the title of his next book points toward the connection that *Arthur* had with *Winter*: they were both part of the same drive, the same effort—one could even go so far as to say that in a sense, *Arthur* acted as a first draft for *The Winter of Our Discontent*. It was a first draft in the same way that "L'Affaire Lettuceberg" was for *The Grapes of Wrath*, although the two preliminary works in each case were very different from what followed.

Another dimension of Steinbeck's frustration in working on the *Arthur* was that he kept getting ideas for things he wanted to say. It was a situation he had experienced a number of times before; indeed, he had turned away from *Arthur* to "Don Keehan" largely because he had been distracted by ideas that seemed to cry out for expression. The idea that there were many connections and similarities between Arthur's time and our own and Malory's time and our own—the idea that had generated "Keehan"—would not go away. During August he had tried to bring these perceptions to his work on *Arthur*. His new direction involved not just an attempt to bring more life to his narrative and make the stories more his own, but to *use* the Malory to say what he wanted to say about his own time. He wanted to make the *Arthur* speak to us, just as Malory had used the legends to speak to the fifteenth century.

The key to the shift in his thinking from *Arthur* to *Winter*, although he didn't know it then, was his growing concern with the immorality of our time, the decay of such values as loyalty, courtesy, courage, and honor. This shift of thought was made clear in a letter to Joe Bryan:

> It doesn't march because it doesn't jell. If I knew less it would be easier. If I knew more it would be increasingly difficult. This has been a good time—maybe the best we have ever had—not wasted at all. But my subject gets huger and more difficult all the time. It isn't fairy stories. It has to do with morals. Arthur must awaken not by any means only to repel the enemy from without, but particularly the enemy inside. Immorality is what is destroying us, public immorality. The failure of man toward men, the selfishness that puts making a buck more important than the common weal.
>
> Now, next to our own time the 15th century was the most immoral time we know. Authority was gone. The church split, the monarchy without authority and manorial order disappearing. It is my theory that Malory was deploring this by bringing back Arthur and a time when such things were not so. A man must write about his *own* time no matter what symbols he uses. And I have not found my symbols 'nor my form. And there's the rub [9/28/59].

On the one hand, as we see in the letter to Vinaver, he simply could not solve the problem of how to preserve the poetry and emotional impact of the original language; on the other, he found that he had something to say, something that had been brought to him largely by the study of Malory and Arthur, but which he had discovered he could not use the Arthur itself to express. He had stopped his work on the *Arthur* at that point where Lancelot finds that his Courtly Love for Guinevere had become more carnal than Platonic. How could Steinbeck make his point about duty, loyalty, honor, and selflessness if the knight of knights, the exemplar of all that was worthy must be also shown to be the worst of men? Lancelot betrays his friend and his King, his knightly oath and his religion, to become both sinner and traitor, thus violating all moral order.

Steinbeck could identify with Lancelot's imperfection—perhaps he had always done so—but that only made it more difficult to advance his point through Lancelot. Just how close this identification was came to light later, and the discovery suggests yet another, more personal reason for his inability to continue with the manuscript.

Very soon following John's death, Elizabeth and Chase began to try to persuade Elaine to publish the work, but she had decided that this was the one thing she would not do. Since her husband had himself talked of publishing *Journal of a Novel,* her decision about that book was easily made, as was the decision to publish the letters of a man who put such stock in letter writing. But publication of *The Acts of King Arthur* was another matter. Not only was the manuscript unfinished, but the first part of what had been written seemed to Elaine, as she remembered from hearing it read aloud at Discove, not worthy of print. It seemed to her that the work would not add, but probably detract, from her husband's reputation.

But while she was editing the letters, she saw the subject mentioned again and again, and was forced once more to go through the anguish of his struggle. She decided that perhaps she should read the manuscript through—some of the last part she recalled as being very good writing.

Many years earlier, on the evening of the day that Elaine and John first met, they were in Ann Sothern's room at the Pine Inn. It was time to say good night, and Elaine spoke to Ann, left the room, and was in the hall before she realized she hadn't said good night to John. Why? It suddenly came to her that for some reason she expected that he would follow her. She was embarrassed, but went back in and asked to use Ann's bathroom. Departing for a second time, she said good night to John and told him that she hoped she'd see him again and left.

She went downstairs to her room, and in a few minutes he knocked on the door. He came in, and they sat and talked until dawn. As he left, he kissed her good night–good morning. That, for them, was the very beginning.

Now, as Elaine read the *Arthur* manuscript, she came to the very last part of it and stopped. She hadn't read this or heard this, nor was it anything from Malory:

> And Lancelot knelt down and took the king's beloved hand in both of his and kissed it. "Good night, my liege lord, my liege friend," he said, and then stumbled blindly from the room and felt his way down the curving stone steps past the arrow slits.
>
> As he came to the level of the next landing Guinevere issued silently from a darkened entrance. He could see her in the thin light from the arrow slit. She took his arm and led him to her dark chamber and closed the oaken door.
>
> "A strange thing happened," she said softly. "When I left you I thought you followed me. I was so sure of it I did not even look around to verify it. You were there behind me. And when I came to my own door, I said good night to you, so certain I was that you were there."
>
> He could see her outline in the dark and smell the scent which was herself. "My lady," he said, "when you left the room, I saw myself follow you as though I were another person looking on."
>
> Their bodies locked together as though a trap had sprung. Their mouths met and each devoured the other. Each frantic heart beat at the walls of ribs trying to get to the other until their held breaths burst out and Lancelot, dizzied, found the door and blundered down the stairs. And he was weeping bitterly.

In Malory there is no physical contact between the two here or elsewhere. Reading this, Elaine realized that her husband had brought his love for her together with his love for the *Morte d'Arthur*, and as a consequence, had written himself into a corner. Tears came as she put down the manuscript, and she thought, My God, why didn't you tell me you had written this?

In mid-October 1959 Steinbeck made his journey homeward from Somerset, suffering deep depression from what he conceived to have been another failure. His search for perfection, his own Grail, the final major work, was slowly destroying him.

* * *

For all those things one might complain of in terms of Steinbeck's shortcomings by ordinary moral standards—and he would have been the first to admit to them all—he was absolute in his sense of duty, in his sense of loyalty to family, friends, and country, and absolute in his sense of honesty. Robert Wallsten has made the point that one of John's favorite words about people was "probity," meaning honesty and integrity: "What I might have called integrity, he always used to say, 'Oh no, I believe him. He's a man of probity.' This was vitally important to him. He would always—I wish I could think of an example of the kind of surprisingly rigidly honest stands that he would take where somebody else might compromise a little. He would say, 'No, that wouldn't be honest.' "

Within this context, we can understand the pain he experienced that summer in England when he got word of what he considered Thom's "latest exploration of dishonesty," largely matters of carelessness that John felt should not be treated casually. But his pain was not just that of a father, but of a writer, social thinker, and citizen deeply concerned about the welfare of his country, who believed, with some justification, that Thom and John, Jr.'s values were those of a whole generation, a generation that was raised by example to believe that success was achieved by "looking out for number one."

He sensed a shift in values as reflected by the behavior of our media heroes and our political and social leaders from any concern for right or wrong, to the idea that if it works, then it must be good. (He had written to Toby in August, "The new Nixon bears out what I have thought. He has so few principles that he would even do a good thing if it suited his needs" [8/22/59]. Later he would take delight in the title of his new book because it was a quotation from *Richard III*, a play that he thought in any number of ways fit the times.) Selfishness and dishonesty, as far as he could see, had gradually become the accepted norm; the honest man was now a freak, an outcast.

These feelings were exacerbated by the move in October from England to the United States. When they were about ready to come home, he told Elizabeth that "moving from here is like closing up a life. I must say that right now I dread the rat race of New York. And the first cab driver who snarls at me is going to get my back up I think. There has been nothing here but the most kind and patient courtesy for a long time" [9/18/59]. And, in fact, the shock of encountering the commercialism, the rudeness, the occasional hostility of New York was like leaving a warm shower to get doused with a bucket of cold water.

After the pastoral simplicity of Somerset, they felt overwhelmed by the importance placed by Americans on things and the importance of buying things. All these concerns and impressions would become themes in his new novel.

To add to this stew, the Steinbecks returned just at the height of the controversy over the TV quiz show scandals. John had thundered against the idea of the programs from the start—it seemed outrageous that people would receive $64,000 for being able to recall the names of baseball players. In England they listened to a little Welsh radio station which had a running quiz that asked listeners very erudite questions. If you knew the answers, you got a pound ($2.80). It seemed to highlight further the unfavorable contrast between the two cultures and in particular America's superficiality and greed. The exposed dishonesty of the TV quizzes pointed directly, John thought, to the tumors growing in our heart and guts: the end always justifies the means and it is all right, in the name of productivity and progress, to appeal to people's worst instincts, since that is what they want.

Charles Van Doren's involvement in the fraud as a contestant was a particular blow to John. He didn't know the family, but had admired it, and Van Doren seemed to him to represent the best and brightest among us, the very kind of person who not only should be above the general corruption, but set the best sort of example. It was a bit like discovering that Sir Galahad had pawned the Holy Grail. But what really stuck in his craw was the all-too-prevalent feeling he detected in society in response to the exposed corruption, that the cheating wasn't so bad, that everyone did it, that it really didn't hurt anything, and that the real sin, after all, was being found out.

In Steinbeck there had always been a strong connection between mind and body, and his depression and the string of events that served to confirm rather than relieve his despondency led to a general physical malaise, which lasted several weeks and then descended into serious illness. He had to dictate his periodic letter to Gwyn about the boys from his bed: "Max Wagner's Second Law of Increasing Returns which says 'Everything happens more and more' seems to be using me as a guinea pig. After a month of feeling like a roupy chicken, I came down with something that my home diagnosis clearly indicated as late pregnancy entering labor—embarrassing as well as painful" [10/29/59]. It was a severe kidney infection, which put him down for the last part of October and through the first weeks of November. He had planned on going to the West Coast to see his family and then coming back to rest and study in preparation for yet another assault on the *Arthur* sometime after the first of the year, but the illness forced him to cancel plans for the trip.

Then something happened that changed all his plans. On December 3, he was feeling ill and had gone to bed, and at that point, Elaine

left him resting and went downstairs to the kitchen. Something impelled her to return to the third floor, where she found he had lost consciousness and dropped a lighted cigarette which had set fire to his pyjamas and sheets. She was able to put out the fire and send for help. By the time it arrived and Steinbeck was taken to the hospital, a brief impairment of speech and hand had passed.

She was not given an official diagnosis, but she was certain it had been another minor stroke, similar to the "sunstroke" he had in Blois, except that this time the consequences seemed to be more severe and the warning more imperative. He was in the hospital nearly two weeks, and then returned home to the Seventy-second Street townhouse to recuperate and think.

He was convinced that his great frustration in being unable to get on the right track with the Malory had been largely responsible for his heart attack or stroke, and this led him to consider, as he had so often in recent years, where he had been going in his writing and why. He decided, as he had on several occasions during the past decade, that his direction had been wrong and that he would have to start over again.

He felt that what had gone wrong was the result of a loss of control over his own work, a failure to follow his own instincts and allow others to take "command." This in turn was caused, he decided, by bringing his work from the inside to the outside—by which he meant sharing his work on *East of Eden* with Pat Covici and following very much the same path of sharing and following advice on manuscripts in progress all the way up through his recent work on Malory. As he told Elizabeth, writing from Sag Harbor after Christmas, "I . . . know I have to slough off nearly fifteen years and go back and start again at the split path where I went wrong because it was easier [not that he wrote easy things, but that he found it easier to share his burden than carry it alone]. True things gradually disappeared and shiny easy things took their place. I brought the writing outside, like a cook flipping hot cakes in a window. And it should never have come outside. The fact that I had encouragement is no excuse" [12/30/59].

If he thought *East of Eden* was not as good as it could have been—or that *Burning Bright, Sweet Thursday,* or *Pippin* should not have been published but were because of outside pressure—then he was missing the source of the problem once again. He apparently did not yet realize that his best previous work had been done under the critical "control," or at least the watchful, critical eyes of others, and was continuing to operate under the mistaken assumption that in recent years he had abandoned making his own critical decisions. A follow-up letter to Elizabeth in March would seem to confirm this:

> Once I trusted the persuasions of whatever force it was that directed me and it was easy because no one else gave a damn. But then I became what is called eminent and immediately many people took over my government, told me what I should do and how, and I believed many of them and gradually tried to be something I am not and in the process became nothing at all. It is a sickeningly common story. [3/60]

Actually, the story had been almost the opposite. In the early years he had been reined in by his wife and close friends, and more recently, since marrying Elaine and telling her that he did not want her criticism, he had gone very much his own way, with a great deal of determination not to be swayed by the opinions of others. It may be natural to look back on the good old days and think, mistakenly, that he did it all himself and that as an individual, isolated and pure, he had been able to find that which was true. What may have also been natural under the circumstances, but not very healthy, were the feelings of paranoia and self-pity that seem to underlie many of his letters during this period.

Whatever his reasoning and however accurate his conclusions, this period of thought and self-examination did, as subsequent events were to show, mark a dramatic turning point in his career. He was able to turn away from the indecision, constant self-questioning, and lack of direction of the previous decade. His determination was not so much to reach out for something entirely new—although with both *Winter* and *Charley* he did achieve precisely that—but to write, to produce and not torture himself so much with the possible consequences. He told Elizabeth, in the same letter cited above:

> I remember once long ago, I wrote you ten titles for unwritten stories and asked which one I should write, and you replied—"Write all of them." And that was correct. What's to stop me ex-

cept the traffic officers of criticism and I don't mean only the external ones. I should have written everything—absolutely everything. And it's back to that I must go. What have I to lose except sadness, and anger and frustration?

It was precisely in this spirit that he abandoned the *Arthur*—for good, as it turned out—and turned to *The Winter of Our Discontent*.

The stroke, the circumstances of the fire, and subsequent hospitalization of her husband had left Elaine badly shaken. Both she and John believed that he had come very close to death on more than one count, and both believed that there was a lesson to be learned by the experience—but each had a different lesson in mind.

For Elaine, John reported, "She, as do most people, considers this a warning to me to take it easy. And that's not the way it is at all. That's the thing which makes invalids. It's not taking it easy that matters but taking it right and true" [12/30/59]. Nevertheless, Elaine began to talk of John not going out on the boat without her, of him not trying to do so much and resting more. She felt he shouldn't be left alone. She talked to him in terms of having accomplished enough and blamed a society that asked too much of its great writers, never letting them retire in dignity, but always demanding something more, something better than before. He had no obligation, she insisted, to push himself so hard. All of this, needless to say, irritated John—his "stage manager" had moved into high gear. Suddenly he had the sense that everybody was watching over him and preparing to baby him—the smothering concern of womankind—and he couldn't stand even the thought of being treated so.

Since he had already decided that his writing had suffered from his dependence on others, the tendency of those around him to protect him simply added fuel to the fire of his determination to break free. The lesson to be learned from his experience, as far as he was concerned, was not to take it easy, let others take care of him, or to ease up in his demands on himself, but rather to get going, to assert his individuality, and to do as much as he could, the best that he could in the time he had. The decision to write a novel came, and then, as a sort of extended declaration of independence, he also made the decision to take the trip alone across the country, which led to *Charley*.

He did not wait very long to begin, and once he began, he really did not let up on work, travel, or on life until the illness that immobilized him just before his death. On January 16, they went to Caneel Bay for two weeks to complete his recuperation, but he was there only a day or two before he became involved in researching an article on the island for *Reader's Digest*. A friend had been assigned the article but couldn't do it, and so John, who had already done some research for such a piece, took over.

By late February, he had finished two articles meant for *Saturday Review*, including "Atque Vale," a meditative essay on the black man's burden in America and his courage and dignity, which was published in July. He was also well into a long article for *Esquire*, "A Primer of the 30's," published in June, and when he finished that, he started on "Conversation at Sag Harbor," the story about his granting freedom to his boys, which was published in *Holiday* in March of the following year. As he had written to Elizabeth after he got out of the hospital, "I will not take it easy. . . . But I will throw everything I possess against whatever world I can move in the effort to take it right."

CHAPTER XLIV

I t began innocently enough, and it was a good example of how he was constantly getting involved in one thing after another even though he did not intend to. He and Elaine were entertaining a guest, Lieutenant Wellesley of the Royal Navy, and they were sitting in the living room of their cottage in Somerset, having after-dinner drinks. Steinbeck later blamed the whole thing on the drink, a local product made from apples called "scrumpy."

Their guest was talking about his new assignment and complaining in a light-hearted way that his ship, a recently commissioned frigate of the Carnivorous Cat Class, had no mounted head of its namesake in the ship's wardroom. Alas, the H.M.S. *Tiger* had a tiger's head, the H.M.S. *Leopard*, a leopard's head, but his ship, the *Puma*, had nothing, and morale was certainly suffering because no one could find a puma's head anywhere. It may have been the scrumpy, but it seemed at that moment to everyone present that this was a very sad situation indeed. John sat thoughtfully, looking into his glass. When an idea came, he found it nearly irresistible—it had to be uttered. As he reported later in a newspaper article,

"Look . . . I come from Monterey County in California, and we have almost too many pumas there. We call them mountain lions. They are in bad repute because they kill deer and sheep and calves and sometimes cows. If they went after men it would be different, a sporting matter, but these cats interfere with private property and that will get anyone a bad name. . . . Maybe if I wrote to my home county they might dig up a head for Puma's wardroom. We're knee deep in pumas."

He wrote to Jimmy Costello of the *Peninsula Herald*, who in turn asked the readers of his column if anyone had or knew of a mounted puma head the owner would be willing to donate for the good of international relations. "Look in your attics," he advised. Presumably, his readers looked and looked, but either no one had a stuffed mountain lion head or if he did, he didn't care about international relations. However, it was discovered that a professional hunter near Paso Robles had a live mountain lion, and the cat was acquired by the King City newspaper, which had also joined in the hunt. The cat was named "Flora"—but no one knew what to do with her or how to get her to England.

Blissfully ignorant of the intensity of feeling that his simple request had stirred up, Steinbeck pursued his research, waiting for a moth-eaten relic out of someone's garage, when he got a cable: HAVE LIVE FEMALE PUMA NAMED FLORA FOR SHIPS MASCOT. PLEASE SEND SHIPPING INSTRUCTIONS. The author "went promptly into what an old mountain man used to call a catamouse state."

By this time, city and county officials and any number of public-spirited citizens had joined in the project—schoolchildren donated money toward Flora's food. Steinbeck, letting one idea lead to another, had also suggested that it might be a fine gesture if Monterey were to offer the British ship "freedom of ports." It was something that Monterey had never heard of, but it was willing. Not only was a resolution to that effect passed by both the city and the county, but the captain of the ship was made high sheriff of Monterey County. Not to be outdone, the city offered him a key to the city.

The situation became more complicated, however, when the *Puma*'s captain notified Monterey, city and county, of his gratitude, but indicated that he could not accept the hospitality and honor without permission of the Admiralty. As for the lion, perhaps it might be best to release it in the mountains, as sort of a living memorial to the friendship of the two countries. In the meantime, someone found a stuffed puma—not a head, but a whole cat, one of the largest ever bagged in the area. It was groomed and dusted, placed on a shiny new redwood plank, and, along with the warrants, proclamations, and key to the city, shipped by air to England.

The Admiralty gave its permission that the freedom of the port of Monterey be accepted, the captain became high sheriff, and the stuffed puma arrived just in time for Steinbeck to present it to the ship's company the day before he was scheduled to leave England. The crew named it Fauna, and it was placed under plexiglass in the ship's wardroom.

Unlike some who are famous and concerned about their image, who pick and choose their activities with care to make sure they are with the "right people" and on the "right side" of every issue, Steinbeck tended to get involved in situations or events, trivial or significant, in much the same way he tended to choose the topics he wrote about. He was attracted by whatever was nearby that caught his attention. It was difficult for him to be just a spectator of life, and to an extent, he was a man of impulse, usually generous impulse. Such impulses operated both in the public and private sectors of his life—indeed, he was a man of such convictions and passion that there really was no such division. He was the same man in all circumstances; he had no calculated public countenance except the fierce look he used to protect himself in his shyness. On his last trip to Russia in 1963, largely on impulse, he got up before an audience of five hundred teachers, critics, writers, and students in Moscow, and, as difficult as it was for him to speak to any group under any circumstances, gave a passionate endorsement of Ilya Ehrenburg. Ehrenburg had been recently denounced by Premier Khrushchev for gross ideological errors and was suffering from various sanctions brought against him. Steinbeck called him a "good and brave man" and told his audience that all Russians should be proud of him.

Beginning in February 1960, after the Steinbecks came back from the Caribbean, John began an intense period of activity that would carry him through nearly two years of work and travel, in a race against time, before he was forced once again by health problems to slow down. Through it all, the *Arthur* was not forgotten nor ever officially abandoned (periodically, he spoke of going back to it), but it was set aside. His work on it had provided more frustration than anything he had ever worked on; like a bad dream, it had eluded his outreached arms every time he had drawn close to it, and what he needed now was something he could embrace, hold on to, and finish.

What followed were a number of dramatic changes in direction. After the prolific years of the mid-fifties, he had retired into research and had almost given up writing articles the last two and a half years; now, he was busy working on one short piece after another. For many years he had spent most of his time either in New York–Sag Harbor or in Europe; now, he planned to break away from that pattern and establish a connection with his own country again. To that end, late in the spring he ordered a pickup truck with a camper that had been built to his specifications, and, most important, after ten years of indecision, he began once more a long, serious novel.

The pattern of its composition was similar to that of *The Grapes of Wrath* and *East of Eden*. As before, he had several false starts—in this case, both "Don Keehan" and his work on the *Arthur* served as preliminaries to the novel—and as before, he had written much of it in his mind.

He began *The Winter of Our Discontent* about the first of March (not Easter, as he claimed later) in New York, and his mood in attacking this novel was different from what it ever had been before. Now there was something almost of desperation in the way that he set out his task, and he changed his work habits rather radically. He had been through a severe trauma, physically and psychologically. Looking back on his hospitalization, he wrote:

I was pretty far out, regarding my disappearance with pleasure. The real battle they couldn't see nor test. It was whether I wanted to live and I knew I had the choice. One who has lived in the mind as much as I have does have a choice which he can enforce. When I closed the door, I knew it wouldn't open again.

When he began to think over his life and his work, he wrote Elizabeth:

In the hospital I must have hit bottom or at least a very low level. For one thing, I got over mourning for lost time because I grew to know that time can't be lost—only people can be. Also I seemed to survey all literature with clarity and to understand not only where I went wrong but where so many have in the last hundred years. [12/30/59]

Out of his anguish came a determination to set his course straight once again. As he began his novel, he was saying in effect, "The thinking is over. I've made all my mistakes. I don't need to lean on all of you. I can write a book, on my own and out of my immediate experience, about the present day, the present situation."

His habit in Sag Harbor, as we have seen, was to get up in the morning, have coffee, drive into the village with Charley, have breakfast and buy the papers, and then come back home and read them before going to work. Now, having moved to the country house in mid-April, he got up at six, listened to fifteen minutes of news on the radio while he drank his coffee, filled a Thermos, and went out to Joyous Garde and began work very early. Furthermore, the long period of warmup—the letters, the journal, or the articles—was largely eliminated. Elaine felt that he was pushing himself to write, that the novel was forced out of a need to prove himself to himself.

He cut himself off from nearly everybody. Although he did mention the novel-in-progress to Elizabeth, and later to Pat, he said very little about it. He wrote Elizabeth:

> The work I am on goes rapidly. I am letting it go because it seems to have a life of its own and vitality and to me a newness. That's about the best experience a writer can have. I don't know whether it will be sixty–seventy thousand words, more or less. I just don't know. It seems to me it grows in stature all the time. I am not showing it to anyone. Only Mary Morgan who types it from hand-writing has seen it and I have invited her not only not to discuss it but not to make any comments to me about it. I have never done this with a book. It seems to me it might have value. I have a ten-dency to talk too much about my work and sometimes I think I talk myself out of it, or, having said it, thought I had written it. But not this one. All the mistakes in this one are going to be my own. But it is going rapidly and if nothing of a vital nature interferes, I should have a book by early fall but for God's sake don't tell Pat that. He will get breathing down my neck and that makes me very nervous. I will show it to him whole and complete and not before. [3/30/60]

To ward off the inevitable question that everyone feels compelled to ask the writer, "How's the book coming?" he had little cards printed. When someone asked him about the book, he'd raise one eyebrow and silently hand the person a card that read, "I wrote ten pages today." The traffic in requests was very heavy during those years. A few years earlier, as a result of some conversations with Faulkner who shared the same problem, John had written an article for *Saturday Review* called "The Mail I've Seen," which in particular lamented the tendency of teachers to ask their students as part of an assignment to write to the author for a commentary on his own work. He had copies of this article printed, and McIntosh and Otis sent them out. Now he had a series of postcards printed with a message that covered such requests—if he stopped to answer all such inquiries, he would never get his work done.

Elaine was the only one who was close to the writing of *Winter*. At the beginning he talked to her about his concern in using Sag Harbor as his setting. He was afraid people might come to seek him out there (apparently forgetting that he had already described where he lived in several magazine pieces), and he was worried about inadvertently creating a monster, turning the village into another Cannery Row. He read aloud from the manuscript in progress only to Elaine, who thought at the time:

> It was awfully false and coy to me, but that was the one thing I couldn't say to John. I didn't like that at all. I wanted at the very beginning to say, "Oh, I know what you are trying to say, and I hope and I think it's valuable. And I think it's important. But please rethink the way you are saying it. But I simply couldn't— he'd asked me long before not to, and then he got into it so deeply nobody could correct it.

He was engaged in another radical experiment. Previously, he had tried over and over, by traveling over the territory, reading everything he could get his hands on, and even by living there, to make the legends of the past part of his own experience and thus give them life, but he failed. With *The Winter of Our Discontent* he would go full-bore in the other direction, making the novel immediate in every respect, more immediate, he felt, than any novel ever written.

Its action would take place from Easter to the Fourth of July 1960, at the time he was writing it. Day by day he used the weather as it actually was, and he used the environment of Sag Harbor very precisely. For characters, he had to change things a bit, but still managed to use himself, his wife, his children, and their friends, neighbors and acquaintances in Sag Harbor very closely. Most of all, he used himself, from the way he thought and spoke to himself in his own mind, to the way he talked and related to others around him. Among other things, the novel would attempt to reproduce the specific texture of consciousness and relationship within a specific frame of time and place. The flaw in all of this, of course, was that he had a very eccentric mode of thought and the texture of his life was by no means typical. Ethan Hawley, a small town shopkeeper, ended up with the fancies and sensibilities of a big-time writer.

The domestic scene—the affectionate relationship between husband and wife and the problems of parents in dealing with teenage children—had not been handled very well or even attempted very often by

American writers of Steinbeck's generation, and some critics appreciated this and gave the writer credit for breaking ground in difficult territory. But at the same time, many critics saw the language of affection, Steinbeck's actual language in life, as a major flaw in a novel with some virtues.

John used words of serious endearment infrequently, but as part of his love of language, he delighted in pet names and nicknames. The sound of certain names was so pleasing or amusing to him that he would use them over and over. An acquaintance of his from grammar school, "Skunkfoot" Hill, was mentioned often, as was the name Button Gwinnett—the signer of the Declaration of Independence whom almost no one has heard of; there were the nicknames he assigned to family and friends, "Catbird" for his son and "Toy Brunhilda" for Frank Loesser's second wife; and then pet names, such as "mouse" for Gwyn, which often changed depending on what the joke of the moment or circumstances between him and his wife might be.

Elaine recalls that while she called people "Honey" and "Sweetheart" and "Dear,"

> John was very sparing in his use of such words. When he said—very often to a child—"Dear, I want you to do such and such," it absolutely, always, broke my heart. "Dear" shouldn't be that passionate. He would say it to Gadg in a moment of excitement or of argument, and he'd say, "Now look, dear, I think you are terribly wrong about that" or something like that. And he said it to me, and it always touched me tremendously. But on the other hand, he used all kinds of funny endearments, constantly, and he thought that was his way of showing affection, light affection. So he used it in his books, and it is cloying to most people.

But the irritation with Steinbeck's language was not confined to his use of pet names and terms of affection. To some, the whole tone of the novel was offensive, especially to those critics whose sensibilities had been shaped by the harsh thrust of the neoclassical tradition into modern literary criticism. Evolving out of the anti-Romanticism of T. E. Hulme and his advocacy of a poetry of "dry hardness," and through the criticism of T. S. Eliot, the tradition has had an enormous impact on critics of nearly every philosophical persuasion, spreading a deep suspicion of emotion through academe and the critical-intellectual establishment.

The mainstream of reaction toward emotion in the novel among the critics has been that it must be severely controlled, suppressed, and understated—especially if it is one of the "tender" emotions. The early models approved of by many of these critics were the poetry of Eliot and Pound and the fiction of the early Hemingway (although, for various reasons, Hemingway has not been a favorite of the traditionalists). It has become a cool and tough standard, making it far easier to justify psychopathic hatred, for example, than simple day-to-day kindness in a literary text.

In Steinbeck's writing after *The Grapes of Wrath* and starting with *Cannery Row*, a tone of lovingness emerges more and more frequently and reaches a kind of climax in *The Winter of Our Discontent*. It is as if—and I think this is true—he himself became more and more loving as a person throughout the decade of the fifties, a quality accentuated by the increasingly more personal direction of his writing, both fiction and nonfiction. For some, this quality of love and affection has made his work more valuable, giving it depth, reality, and power. For others, however, the quality has been absolutely nauseating and has inspired an almost unbelievable amount of hostility.

Writing to Elia Kazan the previous summer from Somerset, Steinbeck spoke of emotion in literature and social values:

I have a letter from Elizabeth Otis after seeing Sweet Bird of Youth. She says—"I wonder what it would be like to live in Mr. Williams' mind. I don't think I would like it."

Well, a writer sets down what has impressed him deeply, usually at an early age. If heroism impressed him that's what he writes about and if frustration and degradation, that is it.

Maybe somewhere in this is my interest and joy in what I am doing. There is nothing nastier in literature than Arthur's murder of the children because one of them might grow up to kill him. Tennessee and many others would stop there saying—"There— that's the way it is." And they would never get through to the heart breaking glory when Arthur meets his fate and fights it and accepts it all in one.

The values have got crossed up. Courtesy is confused with weakness and emotion with sentimentality. We want to be tough guys and forget that the toughest guys were always the wholest guys. Achilles wept like a baby over Patroclus and Hector's guts turned to water with fear. But cleverness has taken the place of feeling, and cleverness is nearly always an evasion. [5/59]

The process of composition for the books he took most seriously, as versus the process used for the entertainments he wrote between times, was always a hectic one, in which he put incredible pressure on himself. And he took *Winter* seriously, although he never thought of it as a "big book" as he had *The Grapes of Wrath* or *East of Eden*. There seemed to be only one way that he could write such a book. First, there was a long period of collecting information and impressions, a process that was only partially conscious and that went on without his having any particular goal in mind. Then there was an emotional shock, a stimulus to ideas in response to something he had experienced—the misery of the migrant worker, the infidelity of his wife and loss of his children, or the awareness of dishonesty and greed both close at home and as a pervasive climate in society at large.

Third, as the ideas began to form a pattern, one idea leading to another, he began talking it out to himself and composing pieces of it as internal dialogue. Fourth, he saw the more immediate problem and conflict in larger terms of the flow of history and the tradition of literature, and made connections with previous events and with the literature he lived with—Shakespeare, the Bible, classical literature, and Malory. Also, much that he was reading just before and during the time of composition found its way, one way or another, into his writing. In the case of *Winter*, he had been reading, among many things, documents from American history, collections of American poetry, and the short stories of Kafka.

Finally, at some point, he was so filled with the excitement of ideas, their implications and connections, and so filled with the emotions that had generated the ideas, he would virtually explode. Then the process became a matter of trying to discipline the series of detonations that went off, so that the secondary explosions of insight and enthusiasm did not carry the writing process out of control. The intensity of his involvement was such that he walked around like a man sleepwalking, failed to answer when addressed by others, and became absolutely incensed when interrupted. When Waverly, Elaine's daughter, came for a visit that summer, he fumed. Even though there was two hundred feet of space and the wall of Joyous Garde between them, Waverly talked so much, in his opinion, and talked so loudly that it seemed to fill his consciousness whether he actually heard it or not.

Not all of his time was spent at his desk. He would write while tending the garden, write while checking out the pier and boat, write while eating and relaxing in the evening, and often stay awake most or all of many nights while ideas chased across his consciousness. He thought that very fast and intense composition often led to poor writing, so he tried to pace himself to write deliberately and slowly, but as we have seen before, he seldom slowed until physical exhaustion almost overcame him.

One thought that came to him was that he should, off and on, turn his attention to a short piece or two, which would tend to check the flow on the novel a bit. He had Elizabeth write to the *Courier-Journal* to make arrangements for him to contribute on an irregular basis—whenever mood or inspiration prompted him.

This was similar to the arrangement he had already with *Saturday Review*, but he had been unhappy about his relationship with that magazine, primarily because they paid so little. Then in May *Saturday Review* printed "Atque Vale," a piece that compared white behavior at Little Rock—a mob with "faces drooling hatred . . . brave only in numbers, spitting their venom at children"—with that of the black children, who carried such a heavy responsibility with such dignity. How many white children would have the guts to do the same? he asked, and how many white parents could show the restraint demonstrated by black families who were having their children spat upon every day? When he noted that some of the article had been altered and cut, he was very angry—some editor, he felt, had been at work "justifying his existence." He said nothing to the magazine; he just decided not to send anything to it again. The editor-in-chief, Norman Cousins, was under the impression that the relationship had simply faded out.

In the late winter and spring of 1960 a controversy erupted over a letter, made public, which John had written the previous November to Adlai Stevenson. Following his major concern at the time, John had mourned the "cynical immorality" he detected in his country on his return from Europe and reflected, "A strange species we are. We can stand anything that God and Nature can throw at us save only plenty. If I wanted to destroy a nation, I would give it too much, and I would have it on its knees, miserable, greedy, and sick" [11/5/59]. The letter, apparently passed on by Stevenson, was printed in *Newsday* just before Christmas, then picked up by the wire services and published in England, and reprinted in March in *Coronet* with an introduction by Stevenson.

The judgment John had passed was harsh, and it touched off debate both here and in Europe regarding American decadence. While a number of editorials agreed, others, along with some hostile letters to the editor, questioned the novelist's motives and his qualifications for passing such a judgment on the nation. Carl Sandburg came to Steinbeck's defense, stating, "Anything John Steinbeck says about this country— about us as a nation—is worth careful reading and study. His record of love for his country and service for it is such that what he says is important."

The release of the letter to the press may have been calculated to play a part in the Presidential primary campaign of that spring. Steinbeck found the two parties sounding very much alike, the issues superficial, the rhetoric empty, and the front-running candidates, uninspiring. He of course despised Nixon ("I liked him better when he was a mug"), but he didn't care much for either Kennedy or Humphrey, although his main objection was that neither of them was Stevenson. When some intellectuals began to drift into the Kennedy camp, he made a rare move to put his name on a public list to join with a group of writers and academics for the purpose of trying to draft Stevenson. Even more unusual, in itself some measure of his loyalty and concern, he became chairman of an advisory council to the Stevenson-for-President Committee of New York.

Work on *The Winter of Our Discontent* continued through March, April, and May. Early in June, he finished the first of two parts, without chapters, to emphasize the unities in the two divisions and to mark them for the reader as individual "things." In such few letters as he wrote, he made only occasional reference to his progress, but some indication of his thinking during composition occasionally came through his correspondence indirectly. At the end of May he had asked Elizabeth, in person, to think back to what sensory experiences she had as a child that remained strongly in her mind and asked what associations they had for her.

He followed this up in a letter in June:

Please try to remember to tell me whether you remember in your family some physical object—chair, book, picture or anything else which you felt was a symbol of the whole family, a continuity, a center, kind of penates, what the eagle was to the legion or the bulldog to Yale or the Khaabs to Islam. Do you remember such? How did you feel about it? Did you love it? Did you want to possess it? Did it comfort you? And do you remember certain sounds as meaning a mood or a state of being, good or bad? And odors? Were you deeply affected by smells, revolted by some, drawn by others? Does odor set off a memory sequence in you? Could you

smell people and tell them apart by their smell? Can you still?
Now that's quite a questionnaire.

Please ask Chase these questions and Shirley and anyone who
happens by when you are just talking. I want to know because I'm
using such things and I would like to know how wide the experience is.

Later he would speak of the manuscript as having images "peeking
out" all over it, and the "symbol of the whole family" he speaks of here
would become the family talisman that figures so prominently in the
ending. (Once again he would end his novel not with a plot event, but
with a symbolic scene, which, as with *The Grapes of Wrath*, would
baffle and frustrate a certain number of his readers.) But most often in
referring to the manuscript he would speak in general terms of its
strangeness—it was, he told his agent, "such an odd book to be coming
from me." And in a letter to the Loessers he noted, "It's a strange book
that is taking its own pace—part Kafka and part Booth Tarkington with
a soup-song of me."

In addition to the talisman and sensory memory, other indications of
what he was thinking about came in a letter to Adlai Stevenson at the
end of June. After talking about Nixon again, whom clearly he saw as
an ominous symbol of our time, he quoted:

"He was close and secret, a deep dissembler, lowly of countenance,
arrogant of heart, outwardly companionable when he inwardly
hated, not letting to kiss [not refraining from kissing] whom he
thought to kill; despiteous and cruel, not for evil will always, but
after ambition and either for the surety or increase of his estate."
No, it's not Poor Richard. It's Holinshed on Richard Crookback.
Perhaps it is an accident that the names are the same—but the
theme of Richard III will prove prophetic—Blood will get blood
and evil can only father evil. Damn it, those boys knew what they
were talking about. . . .

About every two years I rediscover the Sonnets with wonder.
Always fresh, always with increased meaning. May I suggest for
your refreshment and a kind of shining joy that you go alone and
read aloud to your listening heart #54.

Oh how much more doth beauty beauteous seem
By that sweet ornament which truth doth give!

or the great 29, "When in disgrace—" or 25, "Let those who are in
favor with their stars—" or 6 or 14. But as you know, it's like a dictionary, one leads to another. [6/29/60]

Shakespeare was part of the fabric of life for the Steinbecks. John had carried his own love for the poet since childhood, and had married a woman who was devoted to Shakespeare, so they read him, referred to his work, and quoted and misquoted him in jest to each other rather constantly (their line at the beginning of a picnic was "For God's sake, let us sit upon the ground and tell sad stories of the kids"). Elaine started reading the plays to the boys when they were very young, beginning with the more dramatic and gory, *Macbeth* and *Lear*, and then moving to the others as they got older. In 1961 they took the boys to Europe, and they all learned a sonnet every couple of days or so and recited them in the car as they drove through England, Scotland, and Wales. Sometimes they would do them as rounds, one person beginning one sonnet, another person beginning another, and so on.

Confirmation that the sonnets were playing a part in John's thinking during his work on *Winter* came in a letter to Elizabeth, one of the few explicit references to the novel's content during the period of its composition.

Now I am ready for the stretch. I'll take Sunday off to get my breath and then plunge on. I've made the final pause before the sprint. It must finish with enormous speed and then an envoie like a sonnet. In fact this whole thing is conceived in the sonnet form. Shake—not Petrarchian, I mean the tone and sequence. And that's a dreadful hard form. But what is easy? [6/25/60]

His use of the Shakespearean sonnet form led to several of the most serious objections to the novel. The speed with which the ending is reached and the ending itself, as a poetic, symbolic statement, left readers bewildered. And it was not just the terms of affection, the undertow of emotion, that offended the ears of many readers, but the "stepped-up" (to use Steinbeck's term) quality of the prose, a kind of introspective lyricism that was reminiscent of the sonnets. From the first to this, the last of his novels, he had resisted the modern mode of tough understatement. In his judgment, dialogue should sound like life, but in overall tone, literature should sound like literature.

One other indication of his thought comes out of the letters. Early in his work, in March, he reported that he had gone to an astrologer to have his horoscope told. Since the novel, like T. S. Eliot's *The Waste Land*, follows the pattern of a man going to a fortune teller, the fortune that is told, and the unfolding of that fortune, Steinbeck apparently wanted to have the actual experience and hear the language in order to write about the process accurately. In the novel, however, as in Eliot's poem, the fortune is told from Tarot cards, rather than from the stars.

The draft was finished in the middle of July, and when it was typed he sent a complete carbon to Elizabeth for her to make suggestions before he started the revision. He told her, "This little thing has turned into a major thing—to me at least. You won't find it like anything I have ever done. You may hate it, for all I can tell. But I have poured every ounce of energy into it, and what aging passion I have left." He was glad, he said, that she would be seeing it all at once, "because it is a unit, a whole thing in time, place, and direction."

She did hate it, just as Elaine had disliked it and Pat Covici would dislike it when his turn came to see it (although he proceeded in his usual diplomatic manner, beginning by telling John that he thought it was the best thing he'd done in years and ending up by saying that he didn't like this, he didn't like that, and he didn't understand the ending at all). For all their protestations to the contrary, Elizabeth and Pat had categorized him, in much the same way that the critics had: down deep, they also wanted repetitions of *The Grapes of Wrath*.

Some evidence for this, as far as Elizabeth is concerned, came during the period prior to his start on *Winter* when she suggested that he write about the Puerto Ricans in New York. She was confident that he knew Spanish well enough (he was, for instance, reading *Don Quixote* in Old Spanish at the time) to live with them and to get to know them. He could even go to Puerto Rico first and then trace their migration to the city and the problems of poverty and prejudice that they faced there. But John was not that confident of his spoken Spanish, and while the Mexican-Americans were, by love and adoption, his people, the Puerto Ricans were a very different culture. But his most important reservation was that, in his view, the problem of the sixties, unlike the thirties, was not deprivation, although certainly some still existed in this country, but the affluence of the middle class. Overall, it was not that Americans had too little, but that they had too much.

The Winter of Our Discontent was indeed a strange novel to be coming from him—but what novel wasn't? As book followed book, fiction and nonfiction, throughout his career, each was different, each was experimental—an attempt to broach a new subject, a new approach, a new form. Yet, he had become so categorized even in the minds of family and close friends that it is hard to think what novel he could have written at this stage of his life that would have satisfied his audience's appetite for more "Steinbeck."

Within the framework of Steinbeck's life, his final full-length book, *Travels with Charley*, can be best appreciated as an act of courage. From this point in his life onward, John knew, as did his family and friends, that the next attack might well be his last. They shared a sense, unspoken, that the end could come at nearly any time. It gave a special urgency to John's plan to tour by car and reacquaint himself with the feelings and concerns of the country. There was some urgency for him, too, in the need he felt to combat the atmosphere of care and caution that had been building around him since his hospitalization.

At the beginning of *Charley*, in describing the rescue of his boat from Hurricane Donna, he sets up a paradigm for the book as a whole, as well as dramatizing his motives for going. As the wind reached ninety-five miles per hour (he had a wind gauge, so this was not a guess), his boat, the "Fayre Eleyne," had been dragged by two other poorly anchored boats toward a neighboring pier, where she was in danger of breaking up against the pilings. Steinbeck rushed out into the blast of wind, and as his wife shouted at him to come back, pushed his way to the pier. Once there, he waded into the chest-high water on top of the pier, pulling himself from pile to pile while the wind slapped water into his face, until at last he could struggle aboard his boat in the half-darkness. He started the engine, cut loose the derelicts, and ran the "Fayre Eleyne" out into the bay, where he set anchor again. A hundred yards out, he jumped into the water and grabbed onto a tree branch that was skidding by. The wind and tide carried him rapidly toward shore, where his wife and a neighbor pulled him, still in his rubber boots, out of the surging water. It was quite an adventure for the "sick old man" he thought everyone now considered him to be.

Both Elaine and Elizabeth tried to persuade him not to take his trip. Elaine had been warned by the doctor that she shouldn't let John try to do too much, and regardless of John's resistance, she was determined to follow the doctor's instructions. One evening the Allen Luddens had come over, and they were all sitting in the townhouse library, drinking and talking, Allen and John on one side of the room and Elaine and Margaret on the other. John was mumbling to Allen that he would not stop doing the things he had been doing.

Just then he paused for a moment, and the two men could hear Elaine talking on the same subject, across the room.

"Of course, I am going to have to learn how to drive the boat," she was saying.

Sharply, John spoke across the room. "What do you mean you are going to have to drive the boat?"

"The doctor told me you can't go out . . . I can't let you go out in that boat alone. I'm going to have to go out and drive the boat or at least be with you."

"Bullshit."

"John . . ."

"Bullshit."

At that moment John turned to Allen to resume their conversation:

"I'll be God damned if I am going to become some kind of a cripple. She is not going to learn to drive the boat. I am going to get a truck. I am going to drive all of this country by myself. I am going to leave her here. I am a man, I will not be a boy, and she's not going to be taking care of me all the time. If you don't watch Elaine, she can do that, you know."

The Luddens were only one couple of many who heard a similar dialogue during that late winter and spring. Despite the opposition, he began considering his route and marking maps, as well as working out his strategy for remaining anonymous and unnoticed. When it seemed to Elizabeth clearly a waste of time to try to talk him out of it, she did her best to get him to go by bus and stay in motels. She argued this from the point of view of his purpose, that he would be able to mingle with and talk to more people along the way, but her thought was that if he went alone in a truck and had any sudden illness, he might very well perish either undiscovered or too far from help.

John realized that if he could get Elizabeth on his side, he would have a much better chance of getting Elaine to change her mind, and to that end, in June, he wrote a nine-page letter to his agent, defending his project as carried out on his own terms. He concluded:

> It is so seldom that you and I disagree that am astonished when it happens. Between us—what I am proposing is not a little trip of reporting, but a frantic last attempt to save my life and the integrity of my creativity pulse. An image of me is being created which is a humbling, dull, stupid, lazy oaf who must be protected, led, instructed and hospitalized. The play will have been stage managed out of existence.

Under that kind of pressure, Elizabeth had no choice but to agree, and John wrote back, "Your letter made a very great difference. Many thanks. . . . The thing isn't really Quixotic. . . . It undoubtedly is selfish but there are times for that too. . . . Elaine, with your backing, which in our house amounts to public opinion, was dead set against my going until your letter" [6/60].

When Elizabeth labeled the journey "Quixotic," what John up to now had called Operation America became Operation Windmills. Shirley Fisher found a book in the library that had reproductions of early-seventeenth-century Spanish manuscripts and copied the script to paint "Rocinante" on the side of John's truck. In the meantime John finished *Winter* in mid-July, and again, as with *East of Eden*, he went into a difficult period of revision. Since there was a good deal of confusion about the book at Viking, and since nearly everyone close to him disliked it, it was an emotion-laden time for him, with suggestions coming from all directions. Some passages were rewritten and some changes made—most notably, the deletion of the suggestions of incest between the Hawley son and daughter, one of several themes John had used to suggest the process of social decay. A few figures of speech were altered to make them fresher, and a number of person and place names changed (e.g., "Halsey" to "Hawley"), apparently to make them less identifiable. But the things most objected to—the terms of affection and banter, and the ending—John insisted on keeping intact.

Hurricane Donna interrupted his plans to leave as soon as possible after Labor Day. (The idea was to avoid the summer tourists and see the country in a more normal light, yet leave early enough to get through the northern states without snow.) Among the damage that had to be repaired was the sign on the truck, which had been worn down by the storm. Shirley came over and repainted it, and John was ready to go—except he procrastinated a bit longer. After arguing so hard to take the trip, he suddenly realized that it was going to be very difficult for him to leave his wife and home for three months. He knew he had to go; he felt it was crucial to his life and his work that he go; yet with a sudden chill he realized just how lonely he would be.

And this turned out to be the basic problem of the trip, which tended to undercut its purpose and which ultimately weakened the book that followed—he could not force himself to take the time that he really needed, by himself, to accomplish what he had set out to do. He took somewhat less than three months, rushing through the last half of the trip, when he probably should have taken six or eight months and stopped several weeks in various parts of the country to get a deeper sense of the country's mood. Nevertheless, eleven weeks is a long time to be on the road, and he pushed himself as hard as he could to stay with the trip. It was from the feeling of how hard it was going to be to leave his wife that he asked her if he could take her dog, Charley, along. And without the dog, of course, the book would have lost its imaginative center and much of its flavor.

What had interested him about the trip as much as anything was its planning and the opportunity to work out various ways of doing things. He thought of his trip as something like a sea voyage—he had even packed the camper as he would a boat—and the problems associated with packing and making his vessel self-sufficient and comfortable provided the kind of challenge he loved to deal with.

In addition there was the challenge of tactics. He determined he wanted to see people at home, not in motels or in transit, and by using a truck he felt he could go on back roads and get into the countryside. Concerning himself with the psychology of people meeting strangers, he decided that a truck, as a working vehicle, would be more readily accepted, and by being self-contained, he could also be at home and invite a man to come in and have a beer or cup of coffee. He also came up with the idea of carrying fishing rods and guns to allay suspicion, since this is one purpose that is never questioned and "causes instant recognition and sympathy," and he would wear khaki hunting clothes and a Stetson or sailor's cap, depending on where he was.

In a letter Elizabeth had advised him "not to go as J. S. novelist or journalist but as J. S. American." "What I really hope for," he replied, "and believe I can do is go as nobody, as a wandering ear and eye. And the means I have chosen is designed to make it unnecessary for anyone to ask my name" [6/60].

He had so many ideas for things to take along for every possible need or contingency that the overload springs on the truck sagged and groaned as he pulled out of his driveway early on the morning of September 23. He headed northeast, stopped to see his son John at boarding school in Massachusetts, and continued to the tip of Maine before starting west across the country. He called Elaine about every other day, and still he wrote, "I find I am terrible lonesome tonight. And so I won't go on about it. But I miss you dreadful. Been gone a week today. It seems like more" [9/29/60]. The driving was hard, over rough and twisting roads, and he found very few people to talk to. His main impression was desolation—"Maine seems a big empty place where people have been." When he got to the cities he found them surrounded by trash, miles of junked autos and machines, and the scene reminded him of the Christmas he had described in his controversial letter to Adlai Stevenson: "Presents piled high, the gifts of guilty parents as bribes because they have nothing else to give. The wrappings are ripped off and the presents thrown down and at the end the child says—'Is that all?' "

As he drove west he began to ask Elaine during their periodic phone conversations if she would join him for a few days, and so she flew to Chicago, where they stayed at the Ambassador East and then drove in the camper to see Adlai Stevenson and stayed overnight with him. Before leaving Chicago John made arrangements with Elaine to meet her once again, this time in Seattle.

He continued to search for opinions, but he found on the whole that people had very little to say. In the East and Midwest the talk was mostly of baseball, and the further west he drove, the more likely the talk would be about hunting. So far there seemed to be almost no talk about the approaching election.

Along the way he was writing a series of letters to Elaine, although it was difficult. He found that after driving all day, cooking his dinner, and cleaning up, he was exhausted. In mid-October, he reported to her:

> I'm past Missoula and about 60 miles from the Idaho line. It's a deep pine forest. Today I dropped down to Yellowstone—not for the big job which takes a week but just to wave a salute. And it's pretty remarkable all right. Charley saw his first bear and went mad. The jungle sprouted all over him. But I don't know whether he wanted to fight them or propose to them. The keeper or warden advised me to forbid him freedom. Some of those bears never heard of diplomacy.
>
> Of all the states I've seen I guess Montana impresses me most. [To Elizabeth at about the same time, he wrote, "I know how Columbus felt. But—good Lord! To have seen this country for the first time must have been an impact."] There's something so grand about it. Everything in the state is heroic. And the people are just as nice as they can be. . . . It's not nearly so cold tonight. Last night was a doozer, 22° only, but I felt it. It woke me up a couple of times and I turned on the gas for a bit. . . .
>
> The nice lady of 80 on whose land I'm camping just knocked to see if I was all right. What she really wanted was to see Rocinante. So I gave her the big tour, open ice box and all. Thank heaven I'd washed it.

It was about this time, during one of their phone conversations, that Elaine told him that she was enjoying his diary letters. She told him, "They remind me of *Travels with a Donkey* . . . I think of them as

Travels with Charley." He replied, "You've just given me my title."

Elaine met him in Seattle—he practically raced to the Coast from Montana to join her—and together they drove south, following the highway near the ocean, stopping overnight in the redwoods, and then staying in San Francisco for several days, where he was captured for an interview. In it he talked about his forthcoming book, *Winter*, and shed further light on its origins:

> A woman journalist in England asked me why Americans usually wrote about their childhood and a past that happened only in imagination, why they never wrote about the present. This bothered me until I realized why—that a novelist wants to know how it comes out, that he can't be omnipotent writing a book about the present, particularly this one.

When the *Chronicle* reporter asked what the subject of his book was, Steinbeck replied, "Immorality," which he defined as "taking out more than you are willing to put in." Expanding on this, he then made a statement that suggests that he was still thinking in biological terms:

> A nation or a group or an individual cannot survive being soft, comforted, content. The individual only survives well when the pressure is on him. The American people are losing their ability to be versatile, to do things for themselves, to put back in. When people or animals lose their versatility they become extinct.

This was just the sort of thing he was saying and writing in 1934–35, when he was working on *In Dubious Battle*. Perhaps the early and the late were not that far apart after all.

The day after they arrived in the city, he and Elaine were having drinks at Enrico's Cafe with Barnaby Conrad and Howard Gossage, an old friend and brilliant advertising man. Gossage was a charming companion, but stuttered terribly. At the same time, John, with his underslung jaw, always seemed angry. He thrust his words out, a phrase at a time, with what seemed great grunting effort. "Howard," he said, "look at that poor dog Charley over there in that corner. You know yesterday, we were out in Muir Woods, and he lifted his leg on a tree that was fifty feet across, a hundred fifty feet high and two thousand years old." He paused for a moment and looked around the table at his companions. "What's left in life for that poor dog?" He paused again for a moment, then shook his head in sadness. "What can he possibly have now to look forward to?"

There was silence around the table as everyone acknowledged the tragedy of a life empty of goals. Then Howard leaned forward, looked into his glass, shook his head in sadness, and said, "W—W—Well, J—J—John, you know, he can always t—t—t—teach."

John asked Barnaby Conrad where was a good place to eat, and Conrad told him that Trader Vic's was the best. A day or so later Conrad saw them again and asked John how he liked the restaurant. John said he couldn't get reservations. Conrad couldn't believe it. "You mean you told them you were John Steinbeck and they wouldn't give you a reservation?" And John said, "No, I didn't tell them I was Steinbeck," and Elaine added, "He doesn't like to do that." Conrad said, "Well what's the use of working your ass off alone at a typewriter and winning the Pulitzer Prize if you can't even use your name to get into a restaurant?" So Conrad called Trader Vic's himself and made them a reservation.

John and Elaine saw quite a bit of Conrad during the time they were in San Francisco and again after they drove south to Watsonville, to see John's family, and on to Monterey. Conrad had been drawn in as chief backer and producer of a film of John's story "Flight" by a young film student from Berkeley who had written a shooting script for the story, and had sent the script to Steinbeck, who liked it very much. He wrote back, "Your script of 'Flight' is the most exact translation of story to film I have ever seen. There is no softening, no sweetening, no attempt to sentimentalize." So he gave the rights to the young man for two years with the provision that he would take a cut later if the film eventually made money.

But in many ways the project was a disaster, since no one knew the larger aspects of how to organize and produce a movie; by the time Steinbeck got to San Francisco on the Charley trip, Conrad found himself in deep financial trouble. When John learned this, he asked Conrad if it would be helpful to him in selling the film if they filmed some shots of him acting as narrator. Conrad, who wouldn't have dared ask for such a thing, was delighted, and they agreed that the best place to shoot it would be near Monterey. John said, "My God, I haven't been to Monterey in twenty years," and he began to worry about going there, as well as about the narration.

On the way to look for locations they stopped at Cannery Row and got out of the car to look around. Elaine was full of curiosity about the place she had read and heard so much about, and in her excitement she pointed to this and to that. "Oh, isn't that Ed's lab over there? Is that where the Chinese grocery store was?" John was in shock at what he saw and, unaccountably, embarrassed. He couldn't bear to look—each time Elaine pointed, he turned away and involuntarily hid his face behind his hand. When Elaine insisted, he muttered reluctantly, "I suppose so, yes, I suppose that is." Elaine said, "Look! Look, there's a movie theater called the John Steinbeck Theatre! Can't we go in and see it?" And John said, "No, let's don't do that. I don't want to do that."

Driving down the coast they noted a seal in the ocean, and Conrad said, "I've always wanted to be a seal in the next life." He and Elaine talked for a moment of the next life, and Elaine said, "I've always wanted to come back as a seabird. They're so free and graceful. What would you like to come back as, John?" John, who still had not got over the shock of Cannery Row and who had been glum all day, grunted, "A bug, a chocolate-flavored bug." Barnaby and Elaine both laughed and said, "Why would you want to be that?" "Because," John answered, "Ed Ricketts found a chocolate-flavored bug once, and he could never find another one, and looked for it all his life." Elaine and Barnaby were nearly having hysterics by this time, which served to make John even glummer. "You mean to say," Barnaby asked, "that Dr. Ricketts ate bugs?" John glared at him. "I didn't say he *ate* them, just *tasted* them. The way a scientist tests things—he eats them, I mean he tastes them."

They found a spot near the ocean for the filming and came back with the crew the next day. Just as with the O. Henry film, John went through hell, repeatedly drying up and forgetting his lines, but he stuck doggedly to it.

Elaine flew on to Texas, where John would meet her later, and he repacked the camper and got organized for the return trip across the country. Before leaving, he and his sister Beth went out to eat at one of the tourist restaurants on Cannery Row, and an hour later they were both stricken with a mild case of food poisoning, which seemed to provide an appropriate coda to his homecoming.

He didn't want to go on alone, so he asked Toby to come part of the way with him, but once he got out of the city limits, he suddenly didn't want him and couldn't wait to get rid of him. It was another example of a strange aspect of his personality that went all the way back to Tahoe days, when he begged Carl Wilhelmson to come and stay with him, but once Carl was there, he couldn't stand to have him around. The same quirk was demonstrated in his invitations to people to come and join them in Europe and Sag Harbor. He would talk about the impending

visit for days, nearly driving everyone around him crazy with his anticipation, but an hour after the guest arrived, he wanted him to leave.
Often, when it seemed certain the guest would stay as invited, he
would go into a funk and become completely uncommunicative, much
to Elaine's embarrassment. It was almost as if—at least part of the
time—he liked people better in his mind, as memory or anticipation,
than he did in person.

This did not, of course, apply to Elaine. After leaving Monterey he
couldn't wait to see her again, and he drove as quickly as possible, seeing very little on his way to Texas. He met her at the ranch of her ex-
brother-in-law, outside Amarillo, in time to celebrate Thanksgiving,
and then the two of them went on to her sister's in Austin.

He had only one more thing, after confronting Texas, that he wanted
to see before going home, and that was the "cheerleaders." Late in 1960
a mob of stout, middle-aged women were gathering every morning and
evening to spit on and scream invectives at three small children, two
black and one white, being brought to and from a newly integrated
New Orleans school. They had become folk heroes of a sort to a certain
segment of the local population, many of whom gathered to watch and
cheer them on. The grotesque antics of these women were being featured in the newspapers and on television, and Steinbeck felt he had to
see it for himself.

It was not something he looked forward to with any joy: "I knew I
was not wanted in the South. When people are engaged in something
they are not proud of, they do not welcome witnesses. In fact, they
come to believe the witness causes the trouble." His description of the
scene was unforgettable, the dramatic centerpiece of his book, branding
on the minds of millions of readers the horror and nausea of the crowd's
demented cruelty and the theatrical degeneracy of "these blowzy
women with their little hats and their [newspaper] clippings [who]
hungered for attention." Every time one of them spewed forth her filth,
"the crowd behind the barrier roared and cheered and pounded one
another with joy."

But most unforgettable was his picture of the little black girl who, in
the middle of all of this, was being led into the school by very big marshals, whose size made her seem all the smaller. She didn't look at the
howling crowd, "but from the side the whites of her eyes showed like
those of a frightened fawn." The marshals with the little girl, dressed in
starchy white with new white shoes, moved in a procession up the walk
toward the school:

Then the girl made a curious hop, and I think I know what it was. I think in her whole life she had not gone ten steps without skipping, but now in the middle of her first skip the weight bore her down and her little round feet took measured, reluctant steps between the tall guards. Slowly they climbed the steps and entered the school.

CHAPTER XLV

T
he John Steinbecks were invited to attend the inauguration of John F. Kennedy on January 20, 1961; the night before John called John Kenneth Galbraith, and the two couples agreed to spend the day together.

One of the television networks had decided it would cover the proceedings by following four celebrities, Galbraith among them, throughout the day with cameras. Perhaps, since one of the worst snowstorms in memory had settled on the capital, they wanted to see how their subjects would respond to the challenge. When the television people found out that the Steinbecks had joined the Galbraiths, they rejoiced—it was, in Galbraith's words, "from the point of view of the producer, roughly equivalent to discovering Toynbee in the studio audience at the Johnny Carson show."

The Galbraiths and Steinbecks found themselves in the back seat of a Cadillac limousine, driver and camera in the front, and pictures were taken of them constantly, from the traffic jams getting to the ceremony to the traffic jams getting away from it. We might presume that when the producer wanted beauty, he cut to Janet Leigh; when he wanted reassurance that the American system was working, he went to Hubert Humphrey; when he wanted social notes, he went to Scottie Lanahan; but when he wanted irreverence and relief, he went to Galbraith and Steinbeck.

In a segment of the *Charley* manuscript cut from the book, John described the proceedings:

> I got us to our seats below the rostrum at the Capitol long before the ceremony—so long before that we nearly froze. Mark Twain defined women as lovely creatures with a backache. I wonder how he omitted the only other safe generality—goddesses with cold feet. A warm-footed woman would be a monstrosity. I think I was the only man who heard the inauguration while holding his wife's

feet in his lap, rubbing vigorously. With every sentence of the interminable prayers, I rubbed. And the prayers were interesting, if long. One sounded like general orders to the deity issued in a parade ground voice. One prayer brought God up to date on current events with a view to their revision. In the midst of one prayer, smoke issued from the lectern and I thought we had gone too far, but it turned out to be a short circuit.

As Galbraith recalls, to have a television camera on you all day "was an unbelievable mark of political status. We attracted attention second only to President and Mrs. Kennedy and well ahead of Douglas Dillon, Dean Rusk, or the Secretary of Commerce." Since he was there and receiving all this attention, Steinbeck was assumed by some in the press to be up for some job in the administration. When he was asked, on one occasion he said that he had been named Chairman of the Joint Chiefs of Staff, but he had not yet got his uniform fitted. To others, he replied that he was the new Secretary of Public Health and Morals and Consumer Education. When asked his reaction to the inaugural address, he said, for the television audience, "Syntax, my lad. It has been restored to the highest place in the Republic."

After it was over and they had made their way back to the Cadillac, John turned around from the front seat to ask Elaine what she liked best in the inaugural speech. Elaine said, "I like that line, 'Never negotiate out of fear, but never fear to negotiate.' " The way that the camera picked this up, it looked as if the answer had come from Galbraith's wife, Kitty. Five minutes after the program was aired two nights later, the President called Galbraith. Certain that the exchange between Steinbeck and what appeared to be Galbraith's wife was a set-up, he chided, "I've seen levels of self-advertisement in my life, but you outdid yourself on that one." The line in the speech that Elaine had quoted was Galbraith's contribution.

Because of his recent travels and the inauguration, the Steinbecks postponed their annual trip to the Caribbean to early February, and it was not until then that he began working on the *Charley* manuscript. This time they stayed at a "very British" hotel on Barbados, and John was not entirely happy with his surroundings, complaining in his letters that he would rather have been at Sag Harbor with the snow and fewer people around. He got his usual bug bites and sunburn, and the people, very wealthy and many with titles, irritated him:

It is interesting to watch the process of British colonialism dragging its anchor. These blacks are lazy, stupid people, they say, and they say it sitting on the beach with their big stomachs hanging out. And one day they are going to come out of their haze of rum and find they've lost it to those lazy stupid people who have long since stopped trying to communicate with them. [2/24/61]

He made the best of the situation by getting up early, working until noon, and then scuba diving in the afternoons. After more than a week of steady writing, he reported to Elizabeth:

Actually I'm kind of pleased with the form it is taking—a most relaxed and personal account, somewhat like an extended letter but exploring many fields. I've had to get used to a lack of privacy. Everyone at a place like this is a compulsive talker and it is impossible to get away from the endless prattle. I have only the porch to work on which draws all conversation like a magnet. And there is no escaping it. There is a time between seven and eight-thirty in the morning before the guests arise when there is a minimum of talk but they make up for it later. [2/21/61]

He continued to work steadily on *Charley* throughout his stay on Barbados, spurred by a desire to get as much of the manuscript done as possible before they returned to New York at the end of February, since he was scheduled to start on a new project in mid-March. The scientist in charge of Mohole, an expedition to explore the earth's composition by drilling a twelve-thousand-foot hole off the coast of Mexico, had asked him to come along as historian, and he was very excited about it. Right after he and Elaine had been married, he had been asked to go as historian on a survey of the Marianas and the Great Barrier Reef, but he felt he had to refuse. Now, as he told Elizabeth, he had another chance, and he wasn't going to pass it up: "Ed Ricketts would have loved it. The overtones will be that in the cores taken at this great depth there should be found the whole history of the planet from the time it cooled to the present" [2/24/61].

On March 1 he wrote in his journal:

Yesterday came letters and appointments from the Mohole Project. •
I had not understood the primary purpose. To bore through the crust and penetrate the core. Is it iron-nickel? Maybe we will know. I want to know the designer of the equipment. Those great outboard motors and the method for keeping the mole over the hole. Fascinating. . . . Maybe I'm too old, and surely I'm too ignorant but I'm the best they've got because my mind can look ahead. I can forsee what is ahead. I only worry that I get tired, that I am

plagued with little things. The little foxes are eating up the grapes and perhaps spoiling the vine. Despair is never far from me. This is not good.

A week earlier he had written to his agent, "Next week I'll be 59. Isn't that remarkable? I have to remind myself of it all the time. For so long I was too young and now I'm too old" [2/24/61]. And in his journal on his birthday he noted, "This is said to be my birthday . . . I am 59. Never expected to make it. In fact I never really believe such ages existed. It is expected of me to be gay today, to be glad that I was ever born at all. I shall try not to fail in this."

When they returned from the West Indies to their house in New York, they found Thom and young John waiting, sitting on the doorstep, asking to be taken in. They reported their mother had been throwing beer cans at them, but now, they were full of beer. From this point on, they would live mostly with their father and stepmother. Their father, who at least for the time being was pleased with this turn of events, spent a lot of time thinking about what he could do to break the cycle of failure, deception, and disappointment that had marked his sons' relations with him in the past.

For the moment, however, he hardly had time to do much more than unpack and pack again before he flew to San Diego, where the Mohole Expedition ship (really a barge) was being outfitted. The head of the project was Willard Bascom, and Bascom's wife, Rhoda, came to the airport to pick John up. She was worried that she might not recognize him—she had not seen him since fifteen years earlier, when she and her husband had met him at one of Ed's parties—but there he was, in his scraggly beard and foreign intrigue coat—the traveling journalist. You couldn't miss him. For two weeks John stayed with the Bascoms in La Jolla while last-minute preparations for the voyage were being made. His reputation had led the Bascoms to wonder what to expect—perhaps a rather rough, unmanageable type—but they found him to be kindly and rather quiet. Bascom and the other scientists, some of whom would drop by the house now and then to grab some sleep, were working around the clock. The National Academy of Sciences, operating on Washington time, would start calling at five or six in the morning. Noting everyone's exhaustion, Steinbeck would get up and answer the phone, but he was usually unable to answer the Academy's questions, so Mrs. Bascom would do so. "I didn't have any nightgown, so I was wearing Willard's old pajamas and vacuuming the floor. John was sitting there in his robe, which was as ragged as the pajamas, and he said, 'You know, we get along pretty well together, don't we?' And I said, 'Yes, we do.' I thought, we really haven't had the time to enjoy him, and yet we saw a lot of each other. He was just very easy to be with."

The day before they were scheduled to sail, John wrote to Elaine and his two sons from on board the *Cuss I*, the experimental drilling barge:

> I don't think you ever heard noises like those that are going on around me. Triphammers going and pounding on the steel hull with sledge hammers and the engines all running, hundreds of them. People rushing about with cables and bits of steel and new electronic equipment. We are supposed to sail at dawn and all this has to be cleared by then, and I don't see how in the world they are going to do it. Sailing is a laugh. We are going to be towed by a navy tug and when we turn across the waves we wallow like you couldn't believe. The crew aboard is as crazy as everything else— geologists, zoologists, petrologists, oceanographers, engineers of any kind you want to imagine, and on top of this the toughest crew of oil riggers you ever saw. They look like murderers and have the delicate movements of ballet dancers, and they had better have, because to lower drill string from a heaving ship takes some doing [3/23/61].

Bascom found him to be very observant and a good judge of character: "We would meet somebody and he would nail them with one shot. . . . Whatever you were, he knew what it was." John shared Bascom's compartment, and as John observed him working his tail off, he worried about him getting cold. So he went out and bought him a sweatshirt, one like his own with pockets and a hood. They all wore yellow hard hats, and as Bascom recalls:

> One of the boys on the ship went around painting little bits of names and symbols in a modest way on each hat. I've still got mine. . . . It shows a guy with a big brace and bit drilling a hole through the earth on it. And he made one for John, too. It was a nice little black symbol. John immediately took a piece of electrician's tape and pasted it over it—like he really didn't want to get identified as being special. It was sort of an unnecessary modesty, because everyone else was wearing one too.

Once underway toward their station, which would be 220 miles south of San Diego, Steinbeck roamed the ship, asking questions and getting to know the riggers, the scientists, and the engineers. He was writing an article for *Life* in order to pay his expenses, and found that he had to tie his chair to the stationary table legs in order to keep from rolling away from the typewriter. They reached their station on midnight, March 26, and even before the barge was in place, the drilling crews were out on the rotary table positioning the string of drill pipe. The bottom was about twelve thousand feet down. On March 28, the drill touched and started cutting into the sediment, but the next day, at three hundred feet, the corer cable kinked and parted, and they had to start all over again. Two days later they began getting samples again, and each time a core was brought up, John was ready with the magnifying glass that hung around his neck to examine it in detail. Then on April 2, at a little over six hundred feet, they broke through to the second layer, which no one had seen before. They brought up "a great core of basalt, stark blue and very hard with extrusions of crystals." "I asked for a piece," John wrote, "and got a scowling refusal and so I stole a small piece. And then that damned chief scientist gave me a piece secretly. Made me feel terrible. I had to sneak in and replace the piece I had stolen."

He left for home shortly after this, and at the end of April wrote to Willard Bascom:

> I know that it must seem to you that I dropped out of sight, and in one sense, so I did. I don't know whether you noticed on Cuss I, and when would you have found that time, that I was pretty much bent over a large part of the time. What happened was that I tore a large well defined hernia and there was considerable pain involved in all the climbing. . . . So that's where I have been, in a New York hospital getting my guts sewed back in. . . .
>
> I am glad that I was able to get the little piece off to Life before I went in. They were on my neck instantly when I got back but I did do one thing, I made them read it back over the phone so that I was sure that I had written what they printed. Therefore, whether you liked what I did or not, it can be blamed on no one but me. I still don't like Life or Arsenic and Old Luce but this is one time they did not change copy on me. Since then I have not heard a word from any of them but I am getting a large mail about the piece. And, do you know, what I wrote was as nearly true as language permits us to tell truth. [4/26/61]

In May the Steinbecks were back in Sag Harbor, where he would recuperate and pick up work on his travel book again. *Holiday* was beginning to run a series of excerpts from the first part of the manuscript in progress, and John wrote to Elizabeth, "We got the Holiday and I think it has a fine front cover. In the picture I look much more like Charley than Charley" [5/14/61]. But he could not recover his previous writing rhythm, and at the end of June, he told Pat:

> Every day I have fought it and with no sense of getting anywhere. This is not a new experience with me and it has a painful ally that comes at night. I lie in bed and in the dark try to work out the difficulty. Then other difficulties enter. The worries about John and Thom and Waverly and Elaine and her mother and her aunt—all matters impossible of solution but in the dark they grow to intensity until the skin of my mind begins to crawl and itch. And all sense of proportion disappears. Then I know there is to be no sleep that night. It is a kind of silent ballet of frustration. [6/28/61]

Most of the summer was spent in such a state. He reported again to Pat in July: "Somewhere there must be a design if I can only find it. . . . The mountain has labored and not even a mouse has come forth." In the meanwhile, *The Winter of Our Discontent* had been published, and by late June he was receiving the reviews. He hadn't seen the really unpleasant ones when he wrote to Elizabeth at the end of the month, but he found the complimentary ones were bad enough:

> The reviews of Winter have depressed me very much. They always do, even the favorable ones, but this time they have sunk me particularly. Of course I know the book was vulnerable. And I don't know why this time I feel so bad about them. But I do. Of course I'll climb out of it. Maybe as the future shortens, the optimism decreases. I don't know. I wish I did. [6/26/61]

His dejection during these months seemed almost total. There would be many reasons why he would never write another novel—failing health (which was not a steady decline, but fluctuated, although each "episode" and each operation became increasingly more serious), the press of family concerns, the demands on him from outside forces over which he had no control, and his continuing desire to finish the *Arthur*—but certainly the reception of *Winter* was the final blow that removed any lingering motivation to do so.

It seemed so damned hopeless, so damned useless to go on. It wasn't a matter any longer of whether critics liked what he was doing or not, but that they were so locked into their expectations for him that they couldn't even see what he was doing. In the reviews he read, he could find no appreciation of the risks he had taken or any apprehension of the enormous changes he had made in his approach and the many technical innovations he had attempted. Perhaps he had failed in these things, but he would have liked some perception of them at any rate.

Instead, what he wrote was always measured against *The Grapes of Wrath* (or *Of Mice and Men*, *Tortilla Flat*, and *In Dubious Battle*). He was frequently castigated, as in the blast by Kazin, for not growing, yet that was precisely what he had been doing. Apparently the only kind of growth that would be deemed acceptable was if he produced some kind of "super" *Grapes of Wrath*. In *The Atlantic Monthly*, in a very kind review, the reviewer concludes:

> John Steinbeck was born to write of the sea coast, and he does so with savor and love. His dialogue is full of life, the entrapment of Ethan is ingenious, and the morality in this novel marks Mr. Steinbeck's return to the mood and the concern with which he wrote *The Grapes of Wrath*.

That is to say, not that Steinbeck has moved beyond where he had been and should be congratulated for using some interesting techniques to diagnose our current moral sickness, but that this is a good book because it is somewhat like *Grapes*.

Most of the reviews in national magazines and major newspapers, whether positive or negative, followed this pattern. To gather all the available reviews for such a book as this—the first important publication by a major author in many years—and read them all together, an experience that approximates that of the book's author, is dispiriting. One realizes that, under the pressure of time and space, most reviewers appear not to have read very carefully nor considered very fully. A review, of course, is not just a communication to a periodical's subscribers, but also a message to the author, and the messages that Steinbeck had been getting for some time now, both complimentary and disparaging, had maintained an awful sameness no matter what he did or how he changed.

Although Steinbeck's career as a writer would continue for several more years, his career as a creative artist was largely over. It seems appropriate to ask the question, what does it take for an artist to continue, not as a young but as an old man, when it appears that he is locked into a kind of failure? Or to put it another way, does an artist have to be an egotistical bastard in order to survive? Without an overweening ego, Steinbeck had survived quite a long time on sheer grit, but having come to the conclusion that he had done all he could, that he would not be allowed to be other than what he had been taken to be, he decided to spend what capital he had of courage and ideas elsewhere. He had fought what seemed to be a losing battle as long as he could.

Now he was tired. He had written to Elizabeth the previous year, when she was opposing his trip around the country: "Frequently, of late, I have felt that my time is over and that I should bow out. And one of the main reasons for this feeling is that—being convinced in myself of a direction, a method or a cause, I am easily talked out of it and fall into an ensuing weariness very close to resignation" [6/60].

As he wrote to Pat during the period when the reviews from *Winter* were coming in and he was bogged down with the *Charley* manuscript, he had been whipping himself for a long time.

And I have had not one whip but several. First the whip of duty— this is more like a club or a goad than a whip. Second, the whip of inadequacy. I have always recognized that I did not have great talent but rather relied on the whip to make me over-leap my limitations. And third the whip of flattery. This is as delicate and painful as a limber buggy whip with a striker of sharp knotted string. It is applied to me by the wishes and the desires and even the needs of those around me who by expecting of me more than I am, force me to do better than I can. The only whip I do not think I am subject to is that of ambition. I don't think I have that. Vanity yes, but not ambition. . . .

When the invasion barges started for the beaches during the last war—full of huddled frightened men, the sergeants and officers did not address soldiers saying—"Go forth and fight for glory and immortality!" No, they said, "Hit the surf! Do you want to live forever?"

And it does occur to me that those critics who so belabor me for my inadequacies are trying to force me to want to live forever. And I don't. [6/28/61]

The Winter of Our Discontent was very different from anything, including *The Grapes of Wrath*, that Steinbeck had ever written. Perhaps its experiments, as in *Burning Bright*, were largely failures, but of all the books of that moment, it seemed to put its finger on the malaise of the American soul better than any other. Whatever its successes and failures, it certainly was not a potboiler written to please the public.

II

Despite his depression and despite the difficulty he found in pulling his travel manuscript together, Steinbeck managed to finish it by the first of September. He had imposed a deadline on himself because he had come up with an idea about what he could do for his sons. Eugène Vinaver was one of several people to whom he described his plans:

> In March, through a tragic and fortunate situation, my boys came to me permanently and unquestionably, badly battered and scarred. At about that time I went as historian with a project of the National Research Council with the attempt to bore into the Moho or outer crust of the earth where it is thinnest under 20,000 feet of sea off the West Coast of Mexico. I shall tell you about that some day. But on the drilling barge I thought of what I could do for the boys since my time is limited and also my resources. And I thought I might at least give them a glimpse of the world. They are 15 and 17. A good time to look around. Elaine concurring with enthusiasm, we made our plans in the loosest way. We engaged a young but very good tutor and the five of us plan to wander around the world, taking about a year to do it. On Sept. 8 we sail on the Rotterdam for England. We will be at the Dorchester for two weeks, then rent a car and tour through England. Then to France to move slowly south to Italy—no time—no schedule. Then to Greece, to the Islands, to Turkey, Israel, Egypt. Then through the Red Sea and to India, the East Indies, China, Japan and through the Pacific Islands slowly back to San Francisco and home.
>
> Our tentative time for this is 10 months but we will take more if necessary. The boys will have to study every day but it will be as nearly as possible with what they are seeing. This can't be wasted nor entirely resisted and at the end they will have seen the world rather than one small part of it. It is not the tour de luxe. We will travel by every kind of conveyance and stay any place available. I can find little fault with this plan and I have looked carefully for faults. It will not be easy or soft nor by any means all pleasant. But I think it is the best I can do for them. As with everything else, they will take from it what they are capable of receiving. Most important, it will be a marker between two lines. I don't think it will work magic but I do believe there will be some magic in it. [8/28/61]

The tutor they hired for the boys was Terrence McNally, a student at Actors Studio who would later become a well-known playwright. He went through a difficult interview, as John asked questions, mumbled through his underbite, that McNally could barely understand. Then it became even worse when John attempted to test him by conversing with him in mumbled French. Since the five of them would be spending a lot of time together, McNally was brought to Sag Harbor nearly every weekend that summer just "to see," as Elaine put it, "how we all felt about one another."

McNally recalls that

> when we left New York, I realized that for all those weekends in Sag Harbor we spent that summer, that in a sense we were sort of like three groups of strangers. There were the two boys, there was John and Elaine, and me in the middle because the boys had been living with Gwyn until shortly before I met them. One of the purposes of the trip, too, I think, was to kind of get John and Elaine and the two boys together as a family unit. So there was some kind of obvious strain.

The strain would increase before it abated. The boys were estranged from both their father and stepmother—he represented periodic outbursts of discipline and occasional generosity, while she represented tutoring and was the person who tried to keep them occupied while their father was working. For McNally they would be more than a handful.

They rented a Ford station wagon to tour the British Isles, and it was hardly big enough, considering the amount of luggage they had brought. Terrence, at John's request, began by having the boys read Malory, so that the father could go over Malory country with his sons, but beyond that, the tutor had worked out a curriculum of British literature and history to match their progress through the country. Very shortly, John reported, "Terrence is locked in mortal combat with Tom who has brought his great arsenal for resisting learning anything. . . . I don't know who is going to win but he can't escape a good try this time. But it's a sad thing to watch" [10/1/61].

Elaine remembers that they would start to leave an inn, the luggage packed in the station wagon, and

> then Terrence would come down and say, "We can't go. Not until Thom finds his paper he was supposed to write last night. He says he's lost it." Well this was resolved in turning everything upside down, people screaming and yelling, and Thom saying that

Johnny started it. It was murder. I handled it very badly. I lost my temper quite a lot. We had some good times and some very bad times.

By the time they had traveled through England, Wales, and Scotland, the station wagon had become very, very small.

After the first week of October, John confessed to Elizabeth, his literary conscience, "I can't yet bring myself to do any writing. It's just gone from me. It's not laziness but pure reluctance. Very strange. Somewhere I seem to have lost my soul" [10/9/61]. However, with some optimism, he observed:

It is interesting and terrifying to see the boys struggling with the world—trying desperately to hold onto this one they know. They are frightened by the new and they think they are rejecting it but they aren't. They can't. Terrence is making them memorize sonnets as we drive. At first they hated it, but the glorious words are working in. Each one has his own sonnet and feels pretty proprietary about it.

And from Gloucester he wrote,

I'm glad to be here—very glad. . . . The southing birds are gone or getting ready to go and the rooks are holding congresses, talking over the year. On the moors the merlins are hunting field mice. And the cows are all summer fat. In every church there's a harvest festival with marrows and tomatoes and giant carrots and the vicars go about with armloads of celery. On Dartmoor at Widdecombe in fact they were weaving little crosses of wheat with the beards turned inward like rays. [10/10/61]

After crossing the Channel, they drove to Paris, where it seemed wise to split up for a time. John and Elaine moved into the Lancaster, where they rested from family conflict and led their own lives for a couple of weeks, seeing such old friends as André Malraux, Art Buchwald, and Marlene Gray. In the meantime, Terrence and the boys were staying on the Left Bank, enjoying themselves by emulating the life of the Paris student. Marlene showed them around, and they had dates, but Terrence also kept them working. They studied conversational French and read French literature in translation (Terrence talked John

Senior into rereading *Madame Bovary*, something he hadn't looked at in many years).

As Terrence got to know more about John, some of the things he discovered rather surprised him. At Columbia, where Terrence had been an undergraduate, they had been quite contemptuous of Steinbeck's work, and from his own reading of the work, he had the impression of a man of feeling, almost anti-intellectual. John's scholarly interests and depths of reading knowledge came to Terrence as a surprise, as did John's tendency to seek out, as they went through Europe, intellectual company. He also discovered the impact that John's work had on readers overseas:

> Whenever people would find out who John was, they would come—these small places in Italy and France—with battered old copies of *The Grapes of Wrath* with tears in their eyes. You know, the attraction of those books to this vast audience I thought was very moving. He meant, especially I think to Europeans sometimes more than to younger Americans, his books just mean an awful lot. . . . He was in the best sense a "popular" writer.

From Paris they traveled through southern France, from Avignon to Nice, which was, as John told Elizabeth,

> a place I dislike almost as much as Miami Beach and for the same reasons. We are staying at the ———, a dismal hotel which required great genius to have everything in bad taste. To the worst of the 19th century they have added the worst of the 20th, stainless steel and plastic. We stopped so the boys could see Vence and St. Paul de Vence. . . . What a dreadful place this is. If Matisse hadn't stopped his wheelchair near here we might be in Portofino this moment. [11/23/61]

Paris had been expensive, and because of a minor auto accident in which Elaine had suffered a muscle injury, they were forced to stay longer than expected. By the time they reached the Riviera, John was beginning to worry about money—he had had no idea how much it would cost to support five people traveling in Europe—and was beginning to have grave doubts about continuing all the way around the world. Instead of sitting down with everyone to talk it over, as Elaine recalls, "He just began to get worried, and to stew and fret and to be upset and to get into depressions. And if I would bring it up, he would say, 'Don't worry about it. Let's let things take their course.' "

Just before Thanksgiving they took the train to Milan. They went to a hotel that had been recommended to them, but though it was cold, drafty, and very uncomfortable, instead of moving, they stayed, and everyone began getting irritable. On the way back from dinner one evening, the family was having a bitter quarrel about studying and about what should be next on the schedule. When they got back to their rooms, John lay down on the bed and suddenly was seized by an attack. Elaine began to scream at the children, and Thom, who was good in an emergency ("Why shouldn't I be? I've taken my mother through everything"), got a first aid kit and worked on him. Elaine recalls:

> Thom was the one who was cool and calm and brought his father back to consciousness. And we got doctors in the middle of the night and we got nurses.
>
> [Afterward] we decided to divide up and let the boys go on traveling in northern Italy. There's lots to see; there's Venice, all the hill towns. . . . Terrence was willing to do it and thought it was a great idea. So John and I stayed there.
>   These were scarey days for me, because I didn't really know how bad he was. The doctor didn't think we should take the risk of moving him. I stayed beside him every minute except I would take an hour's walk, from 5 to 6 every day in the fog, such terrible fog, and bring him back presents, funnies and stories about the live world, to keep him cheerful and happy.

After ten days he was well enough to travel, and Elaine hired a car to take them to Florence. A few days later Terrence and the boys joined them, and while John stayed in his room, they went on a tour of the city. Then they all moved on to Rome for Christmas, staying at the Hotel de la Ville in a suite with a sitting room, where they could all gather and put up a Christmas tree.

Despite the problems of the trip and John's illness, they had a very good Christmas. John asked Elaine to arrange for Kai Leslie and her two teenage children to join them. The Leslies were the owners of Discove Cottage, and this was the first Christmas after Mrs. Leslie had lost her husband. It was something John wanted to do, and it also gave them a big family for their celebration. John's Italian publisher had arranged for them to have an audience with Pope John XXIII, so at about ten o'clock on Christmas Eve they were ushered into the Pope's private chambers with about twenty others. Repeating his message several times in various languages, he wished Peace on Earth, Good Will to Men, and then blessed them. Afterward they went up on the Aventine to an ancient church and heard midnight mass, which was followed by Gregorian chants.

For a time, John was convinced that they should continue with their original plan. He was feeling much better, his morale was rising all the while they were in Rome, and the boys, finally, seemed to be making good progress. Furthermore, his stubbornness had been aroused—he felt as if the Angel of Death were haunting him. Not only had he had his own narrow escape, but since the trip began, he had been besieged by news of the death of friends and relatives—first Dag Hammarskjöld, whom he had learned to love; then Harold Guinzburg, his publisher; Allen Ludden's wife; and his sister Esther's husband. He took the death of Harold particularly hard, and he wrote to Harold's son Tom: "I hold no grief with stiff upper lip. This is a goddamned outrage." The string of bad news seemed to strengthen the resolve that came with his recovery. He might be surrounded but he would continue.

Yet, faced with the argument that worry about him might very well undermine the things he wanted to accomplish by the trip, he finally consented to a partial and temporary retreat. Perhaps by insisting, he conceded, he was guilty of the sin of pride. At a family caucus it was decided that he and Elaine would settle someplace (he decided on Capri) and Terrence and the boys would go on numerous trips around the Mediterranean, coming back to them occasionally at home base.

Even as he retreated, he was still defiant. He wrote to the Robert Wallstens:

> The last section of Travels with Charley has been giving the publishers trouble. It deals with some rough things in the South. Of course, Holiday will clean it up and even then think they will get cancelled subscriptions. But Viking wants to keep it tough and still not be sued. And I have been so bloody weak that I just don't give a damn. It seems to me that everybody in America is scared of everything mostly before it happens. I finally sent word that what reputation I had was not based on timidity or on playing safe. And I hope that is over. What I wrote either happened or I am a liar and I am not a liar. And I know that truth is no defense against libel. But there is no way of being safe except by being completely unsafe. And in the succeeding months I don't think that being careful

of my health is likely to improve it. Rather it will give me another sickness called self-preservation. And that's our national sickness, and I hate it. . . .

When work is not in me, I think it will never come again. It is always so and I've been in a black funk about it. My pencil has wavered and my hand has been shaky. I know it doesn't matter a damn whether I ever write another word but it matters to me. [1/9/62]

It was a bit strange to be going to Capri in January, but they had had enough of the fog and rain, and John thought there might be more chance of sun on the island, even in the winter. They wanted space enough so that when Terrence and the boys came, they would have rooms, too, so they rented the top half of a villa, up from the piazza in a small orange grove. There was a spectacular view of the sea, of Naples across the bay, and of Mt. Vesuvius, snow-capped, in the distance. The air was clean and clear, and the Steinbecks walked with great pleasure along the small, winding streets in the village where there were no cars, no tourists. Although there was sun, it was chilly in the daytime and cold at night, rather about the same temperature range, John thought, as northern California.

Like the natives, the Steinbecks would go down to the piazza around eleven, buy a newspaper, and drink strong coffee, sitting out in the sunshine in the little square. Then everyone would go home for lunch and a siesta, and later nearly everybody would gather once again for a drink at five. On overcast days when a cold wind blew across the island from the north, they would go into a cafe and sit and have their coffee or drink near the warm pizza ovens.

In mid-February he wrote to Chase Horton:

Today is a great blowy storm. The olive trees are wresting the wind like girls with their underskirts showing. And the tall pencil cypresses just chuckle and bow. No window in Capri is tight so that the wind moans like cats. . . .

Oh! It's a grim and wonderful day. Nearly everything clouds can do, clouds are doing. In a while there will come a burst of rain and then it will be over. The weather is very formal.

A card from Terrence in Siena says they will be here Monday or Tuesday. They will have been out a month. They will be well informed, well travelled and filthy. They are supposed to wash their clothes as they travel. Boys of that age smell terrible. We'll probably have to isolate them until they are clean. But they have had adventures, some of which we will hear. If all goes well, we'll let

them rest here for a week before we send them out again.
[2/13/62]

John followed the progress of his sons carefully for this was to be the all-out effort of his last years—to help them, as he saw it, to redirect their lives. He hoped that by being exposed to some of the greatest works and thoughts of Western man, they would acquire a grasp of history and come to sense their own possibilities. He was conscientious about considering the literature he recommended to Terrence for the boys' instruction, and often he and Elaine read the material along with them. He and Elaine also worked with Terrence to plot out the things that the boys should see and do in each city they visited—not just landmarks and historical sites, but art works, drama, and music. In England, Ireland, and France, they had gone to the theater, and now in Italy he had them go as often as possible to the opera, and, possibly because of the infectious enthusiasm of Italian audiences, the boys had become fans.

Reading to keep up with the boys led John into rereading a number of things he had not looked at in years. He read the classical historians, Toynbee, and Rousseau's *Confessions*, and near the end of February he wrote Elizabeth:

Did I tell you I had reread *South Wind*? I remember being deeply impressed with it long ago. But now I find it very thin and sophomoric, a man full of attitudes rather than true learning. Oddly enough, the real depth both of thought and style I have found lately has been in Plutarch. What a great man that was! And most of the people he was writing about were such children and he knew it. One of the nice things about this time is the rereading of the old things and re-evaluating. Some things I admired have fallen off but others have become far greater. Walter Pater, whom I used to adore, has slipped way back for me, while Thucydides has gone way up. They haven't changed. I have. [2/19/62]

Although he did a great deal of reading, he did almost no writing during these months; the only thing he produced beyond letters was a short preface to a new paperback edition of *Story Writing* by his old teacher Edith Mirrielees.

As in the period following his previous two attacks (or minor strokes—none of the three was ever definitely diagnosed), he spent much of his time in thoughtful reassessment of his life, work, family, and future. Much of his reading seemed to be part of his effort to place

his own immediate concerns in a larger perspective and to become more
accepting of those things, such as his own fate and the future course of
his sons' lives, over which he had little ultimate control. In response to
a letter he received from Chase Horton, which, in referring to Esther's
loss, stated that there must be a plan in nature of some kind, Steinbeck
wrote back to Elizabeth to say,

> Yes, there certainly is, and the one we can see and understand, as I
> said in my last letter, seems to deal in numbers and has very little
> interest in individuals except as units in the larger groups and spe-
> cies. In many cases we know of, Nature, which is another way of
> saying WHAT IS may sacrifice the individual for the good of the
> group. I suppose the greatest feeling of sad discrimination comes
> with the conviction that this Nature has very little concern with in-
> dividuals no matter what their virtues. More and more I believe
> with Ed Ricketts that the greatest, the only security lies in a com-
> plete sense of a lack of security. If that can be fixed, there is no
> longer any fear or confusion. [2/5/62]

In March, Allen Ludden came to Capri. He had lost his wife and was
in such a state he couldn't function; he didn't know what to do or where
to turn, but he knew he had to do something, so on impulse he flew to
Italy and took the boat to the island. That night Elaine went to bed, and
John and Allen stayed up talking. John told him he wanted him to talk
about Margaret, "to really talk about her, completely," and their life together, and they did so all night and into the next day. Then they all
walked around the island, and that night Ludden slept for the first time
in weeks, and the second night, and the third. The fourth day Ludden
returned to the United States, refreshed, and feeling that John was the
dearest man he had ever known.

The following month John was sent a script for *Cannery Row* (actually based on the *Sweet Thursday* material) by Otto Preminger. He
wrote to Elizabeth and Annie Laurie:

> I have now read the picture script of Cannery Row. To make sure,
> I read it a second time. All I can feel is a kind of weariness about it.
> It is a moving picture pronounced moompitcha. . . . In this script I
> find to my amazement in the end that she is a virgin [Suzy, now
> called Sweet Thursday], even though it is by a series of accidents,
> and furthermore I discover that Doc finds this important. Further-
> more, I find that my Doc, who in real life and I hope in my ac-
> counts of him, would have gone to bed with a two-headed calf if
> she were available, this same Doc has for years kept himself celi-

bate for some reason unstated. Do you blame me for being simply weary? . . .

That's the only story there is—a hooker who marries a middle-aged scientist. If that story is abandoned, what you have left is the stalest, untruest piece of old-fashioned romantic slime imaginable. It is Abie's Irish Rose on the West Coast. . . . Believe me, I have nothing against fairy tales. God knows I've written enough of them. My point is that no fairy tale is acceptable unless it is based on some truth about something. You can make it as light and airy and full of whimsy as you wish but down underneath there has to be a true thing. [4/7/62]

He suggested that they get out the copious notes he had written in Boston to Rodgers and Hammerstein in protest against their efforts to clean up *Pipe Dream* to make a family show of it and send them to Preminger, though he doubted that it would do any good.

As April passed and he seemed to be in good health, they decided to join the boys once again, first for a week in Positano at the end of the month and then for several weeks in Greece before returning home. A friend of Terrence's best friend was a teacher at the American College in Athens, and he begged Terrence and John to come and speak to the students—the young, beginning American writer and the established figure of letters. The students were all Greek, from impoverished backgrounds—many of them orphans—but the instruction was totally in English. Terrence worked on John and finally talked him into it. John insisted later that it was the only real speech he gave in his life. He was so nervous and shy that Terrence, watching him suffer so, was sorry that he had gotten him into it.

While the Steinbecks were in Athens, they went to the theater and later met the King and Queen. John and Elaine had known two of the leading actors of Greece, Katina Paxinou and Alexis Minotis, in New York, and with the children went to a performance by the two actors, which was also attended by the royal couple. Backstage, they were introduced, and John said that he knew that they knew Kazan. "If Kazan and I would do a movie," he asked, "would you sponsor us?" and they said, "Yes, certainly." Then he asked, "Will you give us an island to work on?" and the Queen said that she would. For years he had dreamed about working with Kazan in Greece.

Earlier, in Capri, he had written to Kazan:

I will go on working because I like to, but it won't be like any work I have done before. It won't be like the way-out theater either.

These people are blinded with a petty hopelessness that has built a very feeble despair—a kind of nastiness. I think I'll write a play or something to be said, because I don't know what a play is—dolls on strings mouthing incomplete sentences. Words should be wind or water or thunder. [2/19/62]

He thought Kazan was wasting his talent on modern trivia and that he should be doing Shakespeare or classical tragedy. Perhaps the two of them could do a modern version of one of the Greek tragedies—then the words could be wind or water or thunder—but like so many such things during these years, the movie and the play remained only dreams. He couldn't stop the ideas from coming, but he didn't seem to care enough to push them to reality.

The climax to the trip came with their visit to the Parthenon. In September in London, Terrence had taken the boys to the British Museum, where he had them spend an entire day studying the Elgin Marbles—making drawings, lists, and maps. Now Terrence took them up the Acropolis, as John and Elaine followed behind. Terrence said to the boys, "You remember that day last September at the British Museum? Now let's see if we can put those marbles in their places." And they did. Thom said, "That horse's head goes right there," and young John said, "That chariot we saw goes there," and they continued until each one had been put in its proper position. John and Elaine, standing in the background, watched and wept.

CHAPTER XLVI

In New York, Elaine was passing a newsstand when she spotted her husband's picture on the cover of a paperback, *John Steinbeck*, by Frank William Watt, a Grove Press Evergreen Pilot book. She brought a copy home for John, and as he began to read through it, he was fascinated. All the old mistakes were there, plus a few new ones, but if that was the way people wanted to think of him, what difference did it make? When he was through, he commented, "This book doesn't seem to be about me but it's pretty interesting about somebody."

In June he told Elizabeth that he had an idea for a play he was outlining from an item in *The New York Times*, which cited agreement among leading scientists that the amount of nuclear radiation sufficient to wipe out humanity would have little, if any, effect on cockroaches. John decided that his play, "A Colloquy of Bugs," patterned after Cervantes's *Colloquy of Dogs*, would involve a discussion between two or more cockroaches about how mankind went about destroying itself. "I don't see why," he told Elizabeth, "two cockroaches couldn't hold stage as well as two people in garbage cans or a woman buried in sand" [6/25/62].

It was a year, following his illness, in which he seemed to mark time by playing with any number of such fantasies, perhaps filling a need that he was unable to fill with serious writing. Earlier in the year, when John Kenneth Galbraith and Adlai Stevenson had been appointed ambassadors, the one to India and the other to the United Nations, he wrote letters to both, asking if they would use their influence to get Kennedy to appoint him ambassador to Oz. He thought that he might acquire several important secret weapons that would be useful to us, including Glinda the Good's mirror, which made all our listening and testing devices obsolete, and the melting down of the Wicked Witch, which was a process that might be beneficially applied to all sorts of people. In addition, Oz had a Wizard who admitted he was a fraud. Who knows what might happen to politics if such a principle were made popular? He also thought we might adopt the Oz practice of dyeing different countries different colors, "so that we would be able to know whether we hated them or not." When he didn't hear from the President, he decided, as he wrote Galbraith, that probably Senator Dirksen had got the appointment instead: "Maybe he can do the job better than I can.... It's just one more small heartbreak."

This was the period when bomb-shelter madness hit the country, and John developed several completely irrational schemes to meet the insanity of the times. One, as he explained to Galbraith, was to pry open a manhole cover at the first hint of a bomb. The great advantage of this shelter would be that the rats would be unlikely to draw a gun on him (there had been a great deal of hysteria about people arming themselves to protect the holes they had dug in their backyards and stocked with food). Later, he drafted a more comprehensive plan to accommodate all of those dear to him.

He decided that no matter what happened, Sag Harbor would be totally safe, the farthest from ground zero of any place in the Western or Eastern Hemisphere. Family and friends should make their way there, somehow. He instructed Shirley Fisher to attach Elizabeth Otis to her and then swim across the East River, where he would have stashed the first of a relay of cars or trucks along their route to Sag Harbor (map of their hidden locations to be supplied later). As they drove—or if they couldn't find the cars, as they walked—they were not to eat anything until they hit the Shinnecock Canal; after that they could eat absolutely anything, and it would be pure and safe.

From the time of their return from Europe in late May, John and Elaine had worried about Gwyn undoing all the progress they had made with the boys over the previous year, but the boys seemed to stay on course all summer, aiming to finish their remedial work and qualify to enter a good prep school in the fall. In late August, after they had returned from summer school, John wrote with praise of them to Elizabeth. They had changed, he was certain, and he was particularly pleased that Thom had apparently become a reader at last. However, as far as his own work was concerned, he didn't seem to be getting anywhere:

> I, of course, can escape out here to Joyous Garde. Already today I have started some work three times and thrown it away. That

seems to be the pattern now. It comes unstuck. It isn't good enough; more than that, it isn't good at all. Of course one always hopes but it doesn't take much of an eye or ear to reject it. Why, oh why does there have to be so much marking time? It would be glorious if I were simply lazy but I'm lazy plus work and so neither gets properly served.

He had tried to pick up the *Arthur* again and failed. Whatever other projects he had in mind, he was silent about.

In the meantime, *Travels with Charley* was published in midsummer, receiving very good reviews from nearly everyone. Even a Princeton professor writing for *The New York Times* praised it as "pure delight, a pungent potpourri of places and people interspersed with bittersweet essays on everything from the emotional difficulties of growing old to the reasons why giant Sequoias arouse such awe." Another reviewer saw it as "a book to be read slowly for its savor, and one which, like Thoreau, will be quoted and measured by our own experience." Many pointed to the relaxed and easy style, its thoughtful observation—even its wisdom—and its sharp perception of detail. An associate professor from Stanford, writing in *Saturday Review*, was one of the few who found it difficult to praise the book without a serious reservation. A certain note of what he perceived as false humility irritated him, yet he was willing to grant in his conclusion that "the novelist's eye, which sees the droopy, early-morning men at a roadside restaurant 'folded over their coffee cups like ferns,' makes this book memorable."

As a sort of one-two punch, along with the sharp moral vision and experimentation of *Winter, Travels with Charley* should have provided a triumphal conclusion to a long and varied writing career. Few modern writers had worked as long and steadily and with such integrity. Few had attempted and succeeded with so many different forms—short story, novel, novelette, article, column, nonfiction book, play (on two occasions), and movie. There had been many partial successes and a few outright failures—but then, who but Steinbeck had taken so many risks? What other writer of his time had been able to touch America's soul in both the thirties and the sixties?

Yet, for all its acclaim, it wasn't long before *Travels with Charley* was tossed, along with *Winter*, on that general pile of "second-rate" material published since *The Grapes of Wrath*. Once the enormous popularity of *Charley* was demonstrated (its initial sale was greater than any other Steinbeck book), a second round of opinion about the book began to surface. Reacting more to the sales, one suspects, than the book's contents, later reviews called what had been termed wise and perceptive, superficial.

On the morning of October 25, 1962, Elaine was cooking breakfast at the house at Sag Harbor, when John, dressed in pajamas and robe, padded over to the television set in the adjoining sitting room to turn on the news. It was the period of the Cuban missile crisis, and John wanted to see, as he muttered to Elaine, "if the world was still turning." The first words that came from the set were, "John Steinbeck has been awarded the Nobel Prize for Literature." John was thunderstruck—he had absolutely no idea that he had even been under consideration that year. He had first been nominated in 1945, and for several years in the forties and early fifties he had been mentioned in the press along with a list of other prominent writers as possibly under consideration for the prize, but as his reputation with the literary establishment faded, he was no longer listed, and the idea that he might get the prize had long ago left his mind.

Elaine was so excited that the first thing she did was to take her pan full of frying bacon and put it in the refrigerator. The phone began to ring. John wouldn't touch it, so Elaine began taking the calls. To each one she said, "Please hang up, so we can call our children." When she got a free line, she put a call in to John at his school in Massachusetts. When a woman answered and Elaine asked to speak to her son, the woman said, "Of course not. He's in class." So Elaine asked her to please send someone over and tell him his father had just won the Nobel Prize. Then she heard a "Whoop!" at the other end.

By this time John was so worked up that he had to do something. Terrence McNally recalls being awakened at some ungodly hour in the morning by an exuberant John calling to give him the news: "He was very happy and excited. He was very, very proud." But the press was beginning to get through on their unlisted number, and the Steinbecks realized that reporters might be showing up at their door at any moment. They knew they couldn't handle such an assault at Sag Harbor, so after a conference with Pat, it was decided that Viking would have a press conference early that afternoon.

They thought about flying to the city. But then John said, "No, let's just drive in. I want to sit there in the car with the radio on and hear the announcer say, 'John Steinbeck has won the Nobel Prize for Literature.'"

The press conference was held in the big reception room at Viking, and it was jammed with about a hundred and fifty people. Steinbeck came in with Elaine and Elizabeth and was conducted to the front of the room, where he sat in front of a map of the world. He was dressed in a gray pin-striped suit (his "Dorian Gray"), with a blue shirt and tie. His hair, thinning on top, was combed straight back. He had a mustache and short beard ("skunk-striped" was his description), and as he answered questions briefly in rapid order, he squinted over a small cigar.

What was his first reaction? he was asked. "Disbelief." Then what happened? "I had a cup of coffee." A reporter asked how he felt. "Wrapped and shellacked," Steinbeck muttered wryly. Someone in the rear called out, "Louder please," and a cameraman begged, "Look this way, Mr. Steinbeck." The questions continued to come, one after another. Who are your favorite authors? "Faulkner and Hemingway," he answered. "Hemingway's short stories and nearly everything Faulkner wrote."

"What do you mean when you said you felt wrapped and shellacked?"

"Ever see a fishbowl that's going to crack? You wrap it and shellack it. I don't feel very real."

"What happened when you turned on the TV set?"

"I was stunned and happy."

"I'm not clear about wrapped and shellacked. Could you explain?"

"When you've got a cracked fishbowl you wrap it with line and shellack it."

"What was your wife's reaction?"

"She loved it. So did I. . . ."

Before the hour was over a reporter asked, "Do you really think you deserve the Nobel Prize?"

If he had a little more ego, he would have lost his temper; if he had been more of a politician, he would have said that that was for the committee to decide; but being John Steinbeck, he looked straight into the eyes of the reporter and said, "Frankly, no."

The next morning *The New York Times* published an editorial:

The award of the Nobel Prize for Literature to John Steinbeck will focus attention once again on a writer who, though still in full career, produced his major work more than two decades ago. The award will bring back the vivid memory of the earlier books: the relaxed gaiety of "Tortilla Flat"; the stark force of "In Dubious Battle"; the anger and compassion of "The Grapes of Wrath," a book that occupies a secure place as a document of protest.

Yet the international character of the award and the weight attached to it raise questions about the mechanics of selection and how close the Nobel committee is to the main currents of American writing. Without detracting in the least from Mr. Steinbeck's accomplishments, we think it interesting that the laurel was not awarded to a writer—perhaps a poet or critic or historian—whose significance, influence and sheer body of work had already made a more profound impression on the literature of our age.

When Elaine put down the paper, her face was frozen. She couldn't talk. She went to the closet, put on an old raincoat and hat, and went out into the garden to work. She knelt on the wet ground at the edge of one of the flowerbeds. Her floppy hat buckled and fluttered in the wind, and drops of moisture ran down her chin and inside the collar of her coat. She held her mouth very tight and her jaw firm as she sank her trowel deep into the ground in front of her and then reached over with her other hand to loosen the wet clod that her trowel had pulled up. Then she reached forward to stab the ground again. Each time as she reached forward she said, "Damn," and each time she pried loose a new clod she paused for a moment and said, "Oh, God damn."

A few feet to her left, John stood watching her from the screen door. "Honey," he said, "it isn't important. It doesn't matter."

She wouldn't answer, but looked out over the darkened trees. "Damn," she said, and jammed her trowel back into the ground. "God damn," she said, her voice breaking a bit as she pried it loose again. At the screen door her husband stood and watched.

Storm clouds quickly gathered in response to the Nobel Prize committee's choice. As *Newsweek* had noted the year before when it reviewed *Winter*, "Any critic knows it is no longer legal to praise John Steinbeck," and about the only periodical to come out in his favor after the prize had been announced was the New York *Herald Tribune*. The rejection cut very, very deep—he would even make reference to it later in his acceptance speech—but he was determined to bear up with dignity, play his part with credit to his profession and to his country, and not apologize. After all, as he noted in one of his letters at the time, this honor was one of the few in the world that one could not buy nor gain by political maneuver. It was precisely because the committee made its judgment—choosing from sixty candidates—on its own criteria, rather than plugging into "the main currents of American writing" as defined by the critical establishment, that the award had such value.

Because of the opposition, he felt he was under particular pressure to come up with the best possible speech, and to that end he solicited suggestions, read up on the history of the prize, and read the previous speeches delivered by other recipients. On November 10, he wrote to Bo Beskow in Sweden:

> I suppose you know of the attack on the award to me not only by Time Magazine with which I have had a long-time feud but also from the cutglass critics, that grey priesthood which defines literature and has little to do with reading. They have never liked me and now are really beside themselves with rage. It always surprises me that they care so much. . . .
>
> All in all I could relax and go along with the little play acting were it not for this damned speech I must make. I never make speeches as you know. I haven't an idea of what to say. I've read Lewis' wild and ill-considered rambling and I've read Faulkner's which on many readings turns out a mass of dark egotism. But what am I to say? Maybe I'll ask Adlai Stevenson to write it for me. He makes the best speeches in the world today. It will be short, I know that. I should like to make it as near to the truth as is permissible. Do you have any ideas? The idea of having to stand up there and speak just scares me to death. If I could just get clear on what I wouldn't have a worry.

He wrote to Stevenson and many others, but could find no relief—the speech involved too personal a statement for anyone to help him except by general encouragement. He worried and fretted and stormed about the house, trying draft after draft. Allen Ludden, visiting the Steinbecks with his new wife, Betty, was there when John finished his first draft. He had been working all day upstairs at his typewriter, an unusual method of composition for him, and came down late with a typescript that he asked Ludden to read aloud. He was very worried about using a word too often, and in despair he cried out to Ludden, "With all your communications expertise, what the hell other word can I use for this? I have wracked my brain, but I can't come up with a single other possibility."

He told Elizabeth in late November that he was just about finished and that now he was "going over it word by word to see whether each word has the value and meaning I want it to have." He recorded it several times, trying to make sure that it had the rhythms he wanted and that everything was pronounceable. At last, a few days before they were scheduled to leave for Stockholm, he reported to Dook that the speech was finished:

> I wrote the damned speech at least 20 times. I, being a foreigner in Sweden, tried to make it suave and diplomatic and it was a bunch of crap. Last night I got mad and wrote exactly what I wanted to say. I don't know whether or not it's good but at least it's me. I even put some of it in the vernacular. Hell, that's the way I write. Now they can take it or leave it. Only I hope I get the money first. [11/28/62]

In addition to the speech there had been an avalanche of mail to attend to, and they were forced to hire a secretary, although John and Elaine answered hundreds of personal messages from friends by hand. Among them was a letter from Tal Lovejoy and a wire from Carol, who said, in effect, "Congratulations—I always knew that it would come to you someday." Also, he had to get fitted for tails, "a costume I have always found ridiculous," which he consented to buy rather than rent when Elaine convinced him that a rental would not fit well enough. "I'll buy it," he said, "providing I can wear it twice—once standing up and once lying down." And he got the idea that it would be therapeutic and give some pleasure to Harold Guinzburg's widow, Alice, if she were to accompany them to the ceremonies—she had remained crushed and withdrawn since her husband had died. John called on her and told her, "You must go to Stockholm with Elaine and me." And she said, "No, I can't. I can't possibly travel. It'll kill me." But John insisted, "You must come. Harold would expect you to."

John had heard that the only American literature laureate who had gone to the ceremonies and remained sober was Pearl Buck, which he recognized as a possible exaggeration, but he was determined that his conduct would be flawless in this respect. (He also had been irritated that the old, false slander that he was an alcoholic had been intimated once again in the recent press attacks on him.) He knew from previous experience in Sweden what the rounds of parties and the constant toasting could do to even the most reserved of drinkers, and so he decided with Elaine that they would not drink hard liquor during their stay, declining drink at the parties and accepting only wine at the dinners, where toasts would be offered. This does not mean, however, that there was no small bit of rebellion still left deep in his breast. There was something, perhaps something of the spirit of Mark Twain, that required that he show some signal of democratic independence in the face of aristocratic rigamarole.

On the evening of the presentation, the laureates were all seated on the podium. A speech would be made about each one and his contributions, and following the speech, the laureate would come down, the King would give him his medal, the man would bow to the King, and go back on the podium. Anders Osterling, Secretary of the Swedish Academy, finished his presentation address to Steinbeck:

Dear Mr. Steinbeck—You are not a stranger to the Swedish public any more than to that of your own country and of the whole world. With your most distinctive works you have become a teacher of goodwill and charity, a defender of human values, which can well be said to correspond to the proper idea of the Nobel Prize. In expressing the congratulations of the Swedish Academy, I now ask you to receive this year's Nobel Prize for Literature from the hands of His Majesty the King.

John came down, received his medal, bowed to the King, and then, as he passed Elaine, bowed to her on his way back to the podium.

The next night, once again breaking tradition, he began his acceptance speech, "Your Majesty, your Royal Highnesses, Members of the Academy, *mein vakra fru* [my beautiful wife]." . . .

I thank the Swedish Academy for finding my work worthy of this highest honor.

In my heart there may be doubt that I deserve the Nobel award over other men of letters for whom I hold respect and reverence—but there is no question of my pleasure and pride in having it for myself.

It is customary for the recipient of this award to offer personal or scholarly comment on the nature and the direction of literature. At this particular time, however, I think it would be well to consider the high duties and the responsibilities of the makers of literature.

Such is the prestige of the Nobel award and this place where I stand that I am impelled, not to squeak like a grateful and apologetic mouse, but to roar like a lion out of pride in my profession and in the great and good men who have practiced it through the ages.

Literature was not promulgated by a pale and emasculated critical priesthood singing their litanies in empty churches—nor is it a game for the cloistered elect, the tinhorn mendicants of low calorie despair.

Literature is as old as speech. It grew out of human need for it, and it has not changed except to become more needed.

The skalds, the bards, the writers are not separate and exclusive. From the beginning, their functions, their duties, their responsibilities have been decreed by our species. . . .

The Swedes did not stick entirely to protocol either. In addressing him at the presentation as "dear" Mr. Steinbeck, there was a special note of affection that reflected feeling of the Swedish public for him above all American writers. All over Europe Steinbeck on various occasions had come to feel that regard, and now in Sweden he felt it once again, but even more intensely as the Swedes made it clear that he, regardless of what others might say, was first in their hearts, the most popular choice that could have been selected for the prize.

This was made evident once more at the state dinner at the Royal Palace that marked the conclusion of the ceremonies. Attached to the Steinbecks throughout their stay were a young count and his wife, who asked especially to be assigned as the Steinbecks' guides. Before going into the palace, the count informed John that he would be the Queen's dinner partner, and he instructed him on what he would be expected to do. To Elaine he said, "I'm not sure who will be your partner tonight. But don't worry, the wife of the literature laureate has never been the King's dinner partner." Before dinner there was a reception, during which the laureates and their wives stood in a ring around the Great Hall, while the King and Queen passed before them, moving from one to the other offering congratulations.

At the conclusion of the reception, the Master of Protocol, in velvet britches and wig, came over and stood in front of Elaine. He stamped his staff on the floor and said, "Madam, will you please advance to the King, curtsy, and take his arm."

That night in their hotel suite, John and Elaine and Alice Guinzburg packed and, for the first time, had drinks. They celebrated the successful completion of all the ceremonies with some relief, as people came in and out and gifts and food arrived. It was a bit like a cast party after a successful opening night. Early the next morning they flew to London, where they saw all their friends and did their Christmas shopping.

Alice Guinzburg's daughter took them to the London airport to send them home. John turned to his wife, "Now, have you got the tickets,

Elaine?" Elaine reached into her handbag and pulled them out. "I've got them. Don't worry," she said. Absently, Alice reached into her purse and pulled out some odds and ends of paper. "I've ended up with some envelopes and some luggage tags and things," she said. "Well, I suppose I can safely dispose of them now." As she turned, Elaine said, "Wait a minute," and she reached across the table to pluck from her trash the Nobel Prize check. Alice turned so pale that they thought she was going to collapse. She hadn't known she had the check, and no one could remember how she got it. John said, "Wouldn't it have been embarrassing to have to wire and stop payment on it?"

II

"This prize business is only different from the Lettuce Queen of Salinas in degree," he had written before going to Stockholm, trying to believe that in order to put the situation into perspective. During the preceding years, when he had no idea of receiving the prize, he had always spoken of it as a kind of curse that made the artist into some kind of living monument. No one, except perhaps Shaw, had been able to produce anything of real value afterward—not Sinclair Lewis, not Hemingway, not Faulkner. He was determined that one way or another he would "beat the rap," regain his privacy, and return to the life of a working writer. He told Dook in a letter in mid-January, "I want to write a small rude book and right away to get the taste of prizes out of my mouth. I'm about ready to start it. Maybe I can next week. It is for my own enjoyment" [1/14/63].

From Sag Harbor, where they went for several weeks in January and February to rest and escape the telephone, John wrote to Pat at some length his thoughts about his own situation, after receiving the Prize, and on the current state of fiction. He was stimulated to such thinking by an issue of *Publishers Weekly*, sent to him by Pat, and by a review of his career in *The New York Times* by Arthur Mizener.

Publishers Weekly contained an article that discussed the rise in reader preference for nonfiction, and in his letter, John mused for several pages about the differences between fiction and nonfiction, wondering if "the present-day reader rejected fiction because the fiction is not good or because the reader has changed and the fiction has not?" Since fiction gave form to experience so that through the reader's involvement it can be understood, he wondered if it could be "that the present day reader *does not want* to participate—wants rather the things he reads set apart and aside for inspection but refuses to be involved or caught up in them." Possibly this was why the only fiction people seemed to be buying was that which dealt with material far separated from common experience. Or, it may be, he added, that "the form of fiction has taken us so far away from experience that we are no longer convinced by it."

In regard to his own situation, he wrote to Pat, this time in the country had been good for him, a good chance for him to recover his balance. It had also brought back his old restiveness to get back to work:

> I confuse pretty easily I guess, although the Stockholm experience is capable of confusing anyone. . . . When it comes right down to it, nothing has changed. The English sentence is just as difficult to write as it ever was. I guess a whole lifetime of direction can't be changed by one experience.
>
> But I have had to make a couple of drastic changes in the time past. Once I thought I could successfully divorce everything about myself from my work, I mean as far as the reader was concerned. I discovered that this, while it could be done if one had only written under a pseudonym, was impossible. So I had to split in two and establish two entities—one a public property and a trade mark. Behind that I could go on living a private life just so long as I didn't allow the two to mix. Now perhaps there must be three—the Nobel person, the trade mark and the private person. I don't know how many of these splits are possible. As far as I am concerned the only important unit is the private one because out of that work comes and work is to me still not only the most important thing but the only important thing.

The sadness of this was that for all that work and fiction meant to him, he was not able to gird himself for yet another assault on the novel. He was held in virtual paralysis for the rest of his life, not so much by getting the Nobel Prize, as by the outpouring of critical scorn that had accompanied it. If his frustration in response to the reception of *Winter* acted to close the door, the severity and near-unanimity of the Prize criticism put a lock on it, setting up an emotional barrier to any further creative effort more formidable than he was ever able to recognize consciously. He would write several hundred thousand words of journalism, but not another word of fiction.

One of the most brutal of the condemnations had come from Arthur Mizener in the *Times*. In his article, "Does a Moral Vision of the Thirties Deserve a Nobel Prize?" he finished a brief recapitulation of the atmosphere of the thirties that led us to have an affection for Steinbeck's work by saying, "After 'The Grapes of Wrath' at the end of the thirties, most serious readers seem to have ceased to read him"—an astonishing piece of condescension. He then goes on to dismember Steinbeck's career, mocking, faulting, or rejecting every single accomplishment of a lifetime. There are no qualifications or exceptions—even such works as *In Dubious Battle, Of Mice and Men,* and *The Grapes of Wrath* can be seen, in present perspective, as not having anything near the merit it was thought they had at the time. Mizener concluded that the Swedes had made a terrible error in judgment by honoring a writer whose "limited talent is, in his best books, watered down by tenth-rate philosophizing."

Coming as it did in *The New York Times,* the American newspaper of record, on the eve of the presentation in Stockholm, it acted to take away the Nobel Prize before it was even given. Steinbeck, in his letter to Pat, is far too generous in attributing Mizener's attack to a case of "bad manners." He asks:

> Does he say that there are no relationships between people which he would call sentimental? If this is his meaning his is wrong or inexperienced or unobserving. Or is he saying, "All right such things exist but they should not be written about." If he is saying this, then he is defining what reality should be written about and which should not. . . . It occurs to me that Mickey Spillane is writing for Mr. Mizener much more than I am. Never will he catch a Spillane character in such abominations as humor, love, compassion, or thought. What it boils down to is that everything exists, it is what you pick out of the grab bag of experience that matters. [1/28/63]

In January he and Elaine went to a dinner at the Waldorf honoring Carl Sandburg on his eighty-fifth birthday. John had known Carl for twenty years or more, and they were in many ways kindred spirits. Both were, on the one hand, sophisticated, learned, and intellectual, yet on the other, they had the common touch. They both sang of America and had a Whitmanesque feeling for the land and its people. They were fiercely loyal to each other: after Alfred Kazin had attacked Steinbeck, Sandburg thought unfairly, the poet-biographer refused to attend a reception at Kazin's home honoring some foreign literary figures who had asked to meet him, instead going alone to see the visitors at their hotel.

Whenever Carl came to New York, he came to see John and they talked and sometimes sang the night away. Now John, in as certain a proof of his love and loyalty as could be required, sat on the dais of the banquet room, blinking under the glare of television lights, and waited for his turn to give public tribute to his friend. When his turn came, he made his way, half-blinded, to the podium. "Damn those lights," he muttered, and then turning to Carl, he said, "Carl, all of us could learn from you and some of us did." With that he shook Sandburg's hand, whispered something in his ear, and returned to his seat.

After it was all over, and Sandburg had thanked everyone by saying that he would never forget that evening, "It will help me to live a little longer," the crowd broke up into groups and stood around, visiting. Mary Hemingway came up and spoke to John, and John asked her if they could drop her somewhere. Mary said, "I'm here alone—I wish you would." And then John looked at her and said, "No. No, we won't drop you at all. We are all going to go down to the bar and have some fun." They sat and talked for a very long time, and thereafter the three of them went to parties together and the Steinbecks had Mary over to the house and apartment on a regular basis.

In March the Steinbecks decided to move from their townhouse to a tower apartment in a building half a block away. The flights of stairs had become difficult, and because of problems in the neighborhood, they had come to realize that they would have to install a security system. John did not like the idea of looking out through barred windows.

John found that it was a lot easier to talk about shrugging off the effects of the prize and its controversy than to actually do it. He wrote Elizabeth:

> I have been so immersed in the mail and trying to keep up with it, that I have been able to give no thought to any writing. . . . Then there are the everlasting interviews. I have put them off and off. I have about three more I must do and then I am going to put a stop to that. It could easily happen that I would have no time for anything else. And I am really tired of the same old questions. It's a strange ballet of unmeant questions and ignorant answers. The whole thing must be brought to a stop or the effect will be just what I was afraid it might be—stopping being a writer and becoming a kind of public character. [3/1/63]

One request he could not turn down, however, was one from his President. Because of his attachment for Stevenson and his dislike for Joseph Kennedy, Steinbeck began with a distrust of John F. Kennedy, but the President's concern for the arts, his literacy and humor, gradually won him over. He met Kennedy socially several times during the year, and the President selected Steinbeck to receive the Medal of Freedom, although he did not live to present it to him.

At the urging of Ed Murrow, who was then director of the U.S.I.A., Kennedy suggested that John be invited to go to the Soviet Union as part of the cultural exchange program. John asked that Elaine be allowed to go with him and also suggested that playwright Edward Albee be invited to accompany them as a representative of a younger generation of American writers. The Steinbecks had met Albee through Terrence McNally the previous year, just after his great success with *Who's Afraid of Virginia Woolf?* Not only were they of different generations but of completely different backgrounds, with widely divergent visions of American culture, yet the two writers became good friends. Since Edward was scheduled to put on an adaptation of Carson McCullers's novel *The Ballad of the Sad Cafe* early that fall, the trip to Russia was scheduled for October.

In May the Steinbecks moved to Sag Harbor, but as he reported several weeks later in June, he still seemed to be marking time: "My days are absolutely full and at the end of each one I can't see that anything has been done." Pat wrote, urging him to break free of his inhibitions, to forget his instinctive desire to live up to the Nobel Prize. Just do something frivolous, he advised, and let your imagination run free. John was still fighting his internal battle, when fate once again took the situation out of his hands.

He awoke one morning and found that he could not see out of one eye, and was taken to the Southampton Hospital, where he underwent surgery for a detached retina. Afterward he was blindfolded and immobilized between sandbags for several weeks for the healing process. The hospital did not have a very good security system, and one afternoon, while he was lying in bed, a mother with her son entered the room. They came over to the bed and tried to talk to him, but he pretended to be sedated and made no sign that he was conscious. After a few minutes he could hear them going over his room, looking through his things, grumbling because he wasn't awake. The mother sounded furious as she told her son, "Well, at least you have seen him," and they stomped out, apparently very angry that they had been unable to get an interview.

He was surrounded by flowers and other gifts, but the best was given by John O'Hara, who drove to the hospital every day, about forty-five minutes through traffic he hated, in order to read to his old friend.

Steinbeck missed his companionship when at last he was able to move. He wrote O'Hara, "I got well before we got enough talking done. So many things I want to discuss with you—the general things that turn out to be personal and vice versa. If I pretended great pain—couldn't you come once again?"

For weeks after he left the hospital he had to wear first blinders with pinholes and then a series of prisms in order to gradually acclimate and train his repaired eye. He couldn't read or write and so dictated his letters, but he was determined to do as much for himself as possible. To that end he invented a number of gadgets, including a stick with an articulated hand at its end in order to pick up things, since he was not allowed to bend over. He trained himself so that he could do things like turn on the spigot outside, pick up the hose, and water the yard. When he got the prisms, he struggled to read, but it was "like peering through a knothole full of cobwebs."

Another present came from a friend, Danish writer Knud Meister, who sent a badly worn manuscript, *Maanen er Skjult, en Roman af John Steinbeck*, which had been run off in occupied Denmark in 1942. This hand-made copy of *The Moon Is Down* had been discovered among Meister's father's papers after his death, and it reminded Steinbeck of the circumstances of the book's composition and how in this country critics had accused him of something close to treason. Of all the specific criticisms he ever received, this attack for doing what he thought was "a good and a patriotic thing" seemed to rankle the most, and it gave him great pleasure in the article, "Reflections on a Lunar Eclipse," to point out that underground movements throughout Europe had published the book and that it had been so valued it was passed from hand to hand at the risk of death if discovered by the Germans.

Early in the fall John and Elaine and Edward Albee went to a series of briefings at the State Department, where they were given a list of Soviet writers they should try to talk to. They also had a long conference with Edward R. Murrow, who filled them in on some of his experiences in the Soviet Union and advised them to "kick up as much dust as possible" rather than being too polite, since the Soviets tend to respect those who speak out. John and Elaine were scheduled to leave first, spending six days in Finland, four weeks in Russia, ten days in Poland, and then several days each in Hungary, Czechoslovakia, and West Berlin. Albee, leaving three weeks later, would meet them in Moscow, travel in Russia with them, and then meet them again later in Prague.

The Steinbecks arrived in Helsinki on October 11, 1963, to begin what turned out to be an incredible ordeal, physically and mentally, of more than two months of constant activity. Every moment of every day was scheduled by their hosts in each country, with meetings, tours, luncheons, receptions, dinners, press conferences, or travel. Nevertheless Steinbeck retained his sense of humor and, despite the repetitions, worked to give meaningful answers to even the most trite or provocative questions. In Helsinki he found himself doing things like meeting with nine hundred booksellers at nine o'clock on a Sunday morning. On one day he was scheduled to accompany the American ambassador to pay a call on F. E. Sillanpää, the only Finn to win the Nobel Prize for Literature, meet with a group of university students in the afternoon, and dine with a group of local writers that evening.

It was in Helsinki, of all places, that *The New Yorker* magazine caught up with him for a somewhat belated interview concerning his winning the Nobel Prize. "Sending me on a cultural tour makes as much sense as a bank advertising that Willie Sutton is one of its cashiers," he told the reporter. "Jayne Mansfield is also in town," he added. "She's helping judge the Miss Scandinavia contest. You see, we're both spreading culture." *The New Yorker* asked him to recall the circumstances under which he heard the news of receiving the prize, and despite the fact that he had already covered the ground several hundred times, he retold it in good humor with Elaine's help.

The interview concluded with Steinbeck mentioning that he had received a letter several weeks earlier from a book dealer in one of the rural areas of Denmark, who said, "I feel you ought to know about this. A woman rowed in an open boat over eight miles to bring two chickens to my store to exchange for one of your paperback books." "Just think!" he exclaimed to the reporter, "rowing eight miles there and eight miles back—sixteen miles—to make a trade for one of your books! That is what you write for. That is as good a prize as you can get." The article in *The New Yorker* that resulted from this interview was one of the very few in any major American periodical that did not treat Steinbeck or his winning the Nobel Prize with sarcasm or critical disapproval.

The most difficult part of the Steinbecks' journey came in the Soviet Union. Journalists returning from the U.S.S.R. often report that it is almost impossible to describe just how closed and oppressive the society is, how little anyone except a few of the governing class knows about the outside world and the West, and how constantly the Soviet press drums on the theme of American villainy, its aggression and imperialism. They also report that we often have mistaken notions about so-called dissidents, that they are anti-communist and pro-Western democracy, when in fact many of them oppose only certain practices of the Soviet government and have almost no understanding of capitalism, as it is actually practiced, or of our democratic institutions.

Those like Steinbeck who have been sent to Russia during exchange programs have usually found themselves to some extent pawns in a game being played by two governments. The Americans hope to crack the Russian information blackout by spreading as much "truth" about the West as possible and to demonstrate that Americans are not monsters, that we do care about art and are not just concerned with making money, and that our people are free to criticize their own government, even abroad.

The Soviets, on the other hand, prefer to invite writers whom they see as "progressive," that is, writers who have been sharply critical in their writings of their own society. (This was their attitude toward Steinbeck because of *The Grapes of Wrath*, which apparently at one time had wide distribution in the U.S.S.R., although they had been very angry about *A Russian Journal* and had attacked him in more recent years as a "turncoat." Now, however, he was once again in favor because of *The Winter of Our Discontent*, which was published in part serially in *Izvestia*.) Their hope seems to be that by getting American writers to repeat their criticism of the United States in Russia, the writers provide confirmation of the Soviet line.

To this end, the Russian hosts do everything possible to structure and control the situations in which the foreign writer has contact with Soviet citizens—usually students and writers. They provide the guide-translators through whom everything the guest says must be filtered; they make sure that each gathering has at least one older official present to act as political chaperon; they sometimes stack the audience to make sure that certain questions are asked; and they report meetings and interviews by selecting and even altering what was said so that the newspaper report makes those points that they want made. Even the frantic schedule provided the visitor seems designed to lower his defenses through fatigue and make him less aware of being manipulated and watched.

Of course the American State Department is aware of all this, and the game is to break through these controls in whatever ways possible so that "real" contact, uncensored and frank, with younger writers and intellectuals is made. Having been in the Soviet Union twice before,

Steinbeck was familiar with how the game was played, and had several ideas of his own on how to counteract being used or manipulated. One was taking Elaine along, which gave a whole new dimension to the visit in that the wives of writers came out and a kind of closeness of relationship developed at times that wouldn't have been possible without her. Her presence also served to protect John from trumped-up charges of spying or moral degeneracy. Another idea was having Albee come along. He had a special appeal to the younger generation, and because he did not have John's celebrity, he had somewhat more freedom to contact students and young dissidents. When John and Edward went to events together, they were able to show that they agreed on some things but disagreed on many others, thus providing some food for thought for those in their audiences that had experienced little but uniformity of opinion.

Finally, John had the idea of insisting that an officer from the American embassy who spoke Russian should accompany them. Peter Bridges, the second secretary, was assigned, a young man who not only knew the language but was well-versed in Russian history and literature. The major interpreter from the Union of Writers, who accompanied them throughout their visit, was Frida Lurie, who acted as a guide and "control" as well as interpreter. A pleasant, well-educated woman, she got to know John's responses very well after they had been repeated time after time, and John got to the point where he would say, "That reminds me of a story—Frida, tell the story." And she'd tell it, and John would say, "You see—you got the laughs in the same places I did."

But Frida would also on occasion leave things out. John would talk in response to a question, Frida would translate, and then Peter would say, "Wait a minute. Frida, finish the translation," and she would reluctantly go on. Or sometimes Peter would nudge John and tell him that Frida had not translated the meat of what he had said, and John would raise a fuss with her and make her go back and give his complete statement.

Although John had tried to warn Elaine of what to expect, she didn't really believe some of the things until she experienced them herself. On one side there were the incredible extremes of generosity and hospitality—the food, the drink, the presents, and activities were overwhelming; on the other, the constant bugging, the searching of one's luggage and possessions, and the surveillance that was so clumsy and heavy-handed were equally unbelievable. When Elaine saw her first hotel room in Moscow, she exclaimed with dismay that if the Russians ever expected to attract tourists, they'd better start providing hangers, bathmats, and towels. The next morning after they returned from a visit, they found hangers, bathmats, and towels. It got to the point that whenever they got irritated about something, they made speeches to the lighting fixtures or to the little American flag at the center of their dining table.

One of John's intentions was to raise as much fuss as possible about the Russian piracy of Western books. On their second day in Moscow, the Steinbecks were invited to a publishing house. The publisher explained to John that he had published *The Winter of Our Discontent* in an edition of three hundred thousand copies, which sold out in a week. Then, with some ceremony, he called in his bookkeeper, who entered with a silver tray covered with rubles. The publisher said that although it was not required of him, he, through his generosity, was presenting Steinbeck with one thousand rubles.

With an air of indignation John said:

"If it's royalties, it's about ⅝ths of one percent; the lowest on record. If it's a bribe, it's insulting and as for generosity, how can a man who has stolen my property be generous?"

"Ah!" he said, "we do not have private property."

"No. But you sell books. You charge 90 kopeks a copy. Do the books belong to the buyer?"

"You don't understand."

"I do understand. If you're bribing me to overlook stolen property, make the bribe worthwhile."

He said, "It's against our law to pay royalties to foreign writers."

"Then change the law—you made it. And you do pay royalties to foreign writers, if they are communists."

John had discovered that there was a woman pickpocket in the seventeenth century named Sonja Goldenarm, and began introducing Elaine as Sonja Goldenarm, a name that the Russians knew as the English would know Robin Hood, and he would say, now I don't care about my royalties, but Sonja right here—she cares about royalties. The audiences would roar with laughter. Then he would hold up a stack of the rubles he had been given, riffle them so that they clinked together, and hand them to Elaine, "Here you are, Sonja." He would tell them that he'd been told he couldn't have royalties, but they sold his books all over the country. "When they start giving my books away, then Sonja won't expect any money for them." The officials of the various writers unions would declare that they didn't have anything to do with publishing and besides, it was a very complicated matter. But John persisted.

Because of her interest in stage management and production, Elaine asked to go to the Moscow Art Theatre, but when they got there, she couldn't believe her eyes. She had learned to read the Russian alphabet by this time, and she saw an announcement outside the theater that had something to do with "John Steinbeck." When they went in, they found that the company was in rehearsal for a play of *The Winter of Our Discontent.* John told them that there was no such play, and they said that they were making one. "Do you mean to tell me," John roared, "that you sons of bitches have not only stolen my book, but you have stolen my book and made a play of it?" The Steinbecks watched the rehearsal for a while, with some translation of the lines, and it seemed to Elaine that they were turning John's book into a Marxist interpretation of American history. This prompted her to protest to the producers, which in turn led to a long debate—a very strange one under the circumstances—over the meaning of *Winter.*

Near the beginning of their stay in Moscow, they went to lunch at Ilya Ehrenburg's, whom John had met during his visit in 1947. The Russian told John that he was working on a new volume of memoirs, and he gave him a list of Soviet writers he should see, including Aleksandr Tvardovsky. (The only other people at the luncheon were Raisa Davidovna Orlova and her husband, Lev Kopelev. Although no one knew it at the time, Kopelev was a good friend of Solzhenitsyn and had taken *One Day in the Life of Ivan Denisovich* to Tvardovsky and pressed him to publish it in his magazine.)

One of the reasons that John had been anxious to revisit the Soviet Union was that he had heard that the climate for writers had become much more liberal than when he had been there before. He wrote home about his lunch with Ehrenburg: "A fine lunch with lots of good talk. There is no question that the thaw is on—people—at least intellectuals—speak quite freely on almost any subject but of course they, from having no experience with the outside world, are fairly limited in some of their estimates" [10/18/63]. Although he would speak in letters several more times about the "thaw," it turned out that his experience at Ehrenburg's was not typical and that if there had been a liberalization, it had been reversed before the Steinbecks arrived.

On October 21 John went to a luncheon at *Izvestia* as a guest of

Aleksei Adzhubei, the editor, who was Khrushchev's son-in-law. The editor, Steinbeck, and an interpreter sat at the head of a U-shaped table surrounded by about twenty members of the newspaper staff. Adzhubei drank and talked a great deal during the luncheon, behaving increasingly like a boorish grand duke. When John suggested that perhaps he and the editor should allow some of the others present to say something, Adzhubei replied, "We have real democracy here—Adzhubei talks and everybody listens!"

When John mentioned that he hoped to meet Aleksandr Tvardovsky in Moscow, Adzhubei snapped his fingers and told someone to telephone Tvardovsky, explaining, "He works for us. We print his magazine" (*Novy mir*). The call wasn't put through. Then John mentioned that he hoped to see Aleksandr Korneichuk in Kiev, and Adzhubei ordered that a call be put through to Kiev, which led John to ask if perhaps they could telephone the moon just for fun.

At such functions several questions were invariably asked. One was, "Do Americans believe that peaceful coexistence is possible?" To which John always replied, "We thoroughly intend to exist, and we would be delighted if you could coexist, but when the price of your existence is our disappearance, then you can be sure that nobody will exist." He was also usually asked why he criticized his country so sharply in his books, to which he would reply, "Because I love it. If I did not, I would not bother."

Along with Frida and Peter Bridges and his wife, the Steinbecks went to Kiev from October 22 to 26 for a visit largely taken up with sightseeing and entertainment by a group of middle-aged writers, most of whom John had met in 1947. Chief among these was playwright and Central Committee member Aleksandr Korneichuk, one of the "old boys," as John characterized him, who had won his position under Stalin and who was now holding on for dear life in fear of being ousted by younger and more liberal men.

Steinbeck asked if he might meet with some of the younger Ukrainian writers, and so a boat ride on the Knepr River was arranged. Korneichuk ordered a fifty-foot launch, and, almost like setting up props for a play, he produced a half-dozen young writers who lounged about the boat very awkwardly, obviously intimidated by Korneichuk's presence. The young writers tried to be sociable, but would say very little. Later, a meeting at the Writers' Union palace was also arranged with some younger men in attendance, but with much the same atmosphere.

Ehrenburg had suggested that John try to see Viktor Nekrasov while in Kiev, and he asked his hosts about him several times, but each time there was a different excuse—you can't see him because he is sick, you can't see him because he is out of town, you can't see him because he is in the middle of a project.

By the time the Steinbecks came to the meeting at the Writers' Union, they had given up hope of seeing Nekrasov. The meeting was held in a very large hall, filled with 250 or 300 people, with long tables loaded with food and drink. The Steinbecks sat at a table in the center, facing the massive doors, and in front of John there was a microphone and several other microphones around the room. The Steinbecks noticed that behind them were several newsmen, who hadn't been served. Elaine asked, "Why aren't the newsmen served drinks?" and they were told that they were never served at such affairs. Elaine said, "At a press conference in America, the press wouldn't come if they were treated that way. I won't drink unless you serve them," and she and John pushed their glasses away.

At a point when the press conference-reception was about two-thirds over, the massive door in front of them suddenly opened, and a man stood in the doorway. As Elaine recalls,

Everybody stopped talking and looked. He was absolutely one of the most beautiful looking men I ever saw, very dark with a big scar across his face, very dashing and sort of like a peasant. The man strode across the room, stopped in front of John. He slapped his hand down on the table and said, "Nekrasov!" And John smacked his hand on top of his and said, "Steinbeck!" And the man said, "I heard you were asking for me. I've come out of hiding to see you." It was something. There was a deathly hush in the room, and John said, "Pull up a chair, my friend," and he looked at all the men he'd been asking about Nekrasov and said, "Please serve him a drink." John carried on the press conference as if nothing had happened, and when it was over, Nekrasov went with us back to the hotel, and he and John talked all night.

PART SIX

The Last Battle

CHAPTER XLVII

From Kiev the Steinbecks were scheduled to go to Yerevan in Armenia and Tbilisi in Georgia. Although American embassy personnel were usually not allowed to leave Moscow, except to go to Leningrad, the Foreign Office permitted Peter Bridges to accompany the Steinbecks to Kiev, though not to Yerevan. John wired the American embassy in Moscow, "Please cable the Writers' Union in Yerevan that due to Foreign Office interference, I shall not be able to accept their invitation." Permission for Bridges to go on to Armenia came through before John's cable could have been delivered in Moscow. He had "won one," but the Russians always seemed to keep score in such things.

In Armenia they were taken to the monastery of Etchmiadzin, where they met the *catholicos* of the Armenian Church, and near Yerevan they visited two churches that are carved out of the rock. They were also driven to a high plateau in the mountains, and a marvelous feast was spread out on the grass in a high meadow for a picnic. The car drivers were segregated behind bushes out of sight, and John asked, "Where are the drivers? In a classless society we should all have our picnic together!" The officials replied that they would get them, of course.

Many of the functions the Steinbecks attended—usually two or three things a day, along with sightseeing of various agricultural or building projects—were formal and stiff, although Steinbeck did his best to get together with individuals or small groups and to provoke genuine discussion. (Sometimes when he was successful, the discussions ended in shouting matches over the Berlin Wall or the Hungarian uprising.) But in Georgia there was a somewhat different atmosphere, more lively and less formal, perhaps because the Georgians are a different people from the Russians. One evening they were taken by the First Secretary of the Writers' Union, Irakli Abashidze, to a typical Georgian house on the outskirts of Tbilisi, where they had a large dinner that lasted for hours. It was the custom during such a dinner that the women stayed in the kitchen and cooked, while the men—there were about a dozen seated around the table—ate and entertained the guests.

After dinner there was a great deal of drinking. The Georgians appoint a toastmaster for such an event, and there followed one toast after another—for Khrushchev, for Kennedy, for Queen Tamara (the great medieval Queen of Georgia)—and on and on. They toasted the women, and the Steinbecks asked, Where are the women? Let's have the women come out and join us. So the women came out, blushing and smiling, and they toasted them again. Then they sang together, in four-part harmony, one song after another, the Steinbecks joining in when they could. It was a most pleasant evening.

But even after the most jovial of times there was still the constant sense of a dark bureaucracy, an edge that one dare not ignore, a presence that sees everything and forgives nothing. On the plane on the way back from Yerevan to Moscow, the Steinbecks were seated by blacked-out windows—they were certain it came as retaliation for threatening not to go to Armenia without Peter Bridges. John protested to the officials on the plane that he wanted his wife to see the Caucasus, but they replied that they were sorry, she couldn't. During the flight Elaine defiantly moved up to a seat where she could see out the window, and a big, burly airline hostess lifted her up bodily and carried her back to her original seat. Back in Moscow the Steinbecks had a private dinner with Yevtushenko, and John told him about the plane ride. Yevtushenko wouldn't believe him. John told him, "I know that it sounds insane, but it is true. Why would I tell you this if it wasn't true?" But when Yevtushenko wanted to talk privately to John, he took him out to walk on the street.

They also had trouble when they wanted to visit the grave of Boris Pasternak. Several times they asked their hosts at the Writers' Union if they would take them, but were refused. Pasternak had become a nonperson, and the Russians didn't want to talk about him at all. But John was determined, and he told Leslie Brady, the cultural attaché at the embassy who had set up the exchange, that he was going to go. Brady said, "I'll take you," and drove them over in a big, black embassy car. There was a little cup of flowers on the grave, and the Steinbecks added flowers of their own. Later they heard that the Russians had built a military installation nearby so that they could close off the whole area to foreign visitors. The Steinbecks may have been the last to make the visit.

Early in November the Erskine Caldwells, who were staying at the National Hotel on Red Square, invited the Steinbecks to dinner. The Caldwells were on one of several private trips they took to Russia "to spend their rubles." The Steinbecks dismissed their car and driver, told everyone they were going to bed early, and then sneaked out of the hotel and took a taxi to the National, where the Caldwells had a suite and served dinner in their room. They ate and talked and drank until it began to get late, and every now and then Erskine or Virginia would interrupt and say, "You are going to have one hell of a time getting back to your hotel." But John was having a good time, and he kept saying, "Don't worry. We'll be all right."

When they finally left the Caldwells and went outside, they found they couldn't get a taxi. John went back into the National to the Intourist desk and asked, "May I have a taxi?" The woman behind the desk looked up and said, "No." John said, "I'm John Steinbeck, and I'm here as the guest of the Writers' Union." The woman shrugged, "And so?" "I need a taxi to get back to my hotel." "I'm sorry, there are no taxis. I can't help you."

Then John asked, "Would you get the American embassy on the phone for me?" The woman said, "The lines are down." "Would you," John asked, "get Mr. Aleksei Adzhubei on the phone?" "No. I can't help you." John and Elaine went outside. It was very cold and it was snowing, and Elaine asked, "What are we going to do?" John replied, "I really don't know."

At that moment the Bolshoi Theatre, which was just down the way, broke, and people began to pour out on to the streets. John had on his big cape and his big fur hat, and as the people began to approach where they were standing, he walked out onto the square and sat down on the pavement. Elaine cried out to him, "What are you doing?" And he said, "If I sit down here, somebody is going to come and help me." He sat there, the snow coming down on him, and the people, thinking he was crazy, rushed by him. They didn't want anything to do with this madman, this foreigner.

Finally a very affluent-looking couple came up and stopped. The man looked Elaine over and saw that she was a foreigner and then went over to where John was sitting. As the man circled around him, John began crying, "Ooh, ooh, ooh." The man stopped, pointed at John, and, substituting the "g" for the "h" of a Russian speaking English, exclaimed "Gemingway!" John started laughing and then began to cry again, "Ooh, ooh, ooh." The man circled partway around again, looked, and said, "Steinbeck!" John nodded, and the man shook his hand and lifted him up off the pavement. The man knew a little English and asked, "What is your trouble?" John said, "My wife and I can't get back to our hotel." The man clapped his hands, and a pair of policemen came over immediately. He said "taxi" and three taxis suddenly appeared. John and the man kissed each other on both cheeks, Elaine and the woman kissed each other on both cheeks, and then they shook hands all around.

Also early in November John went to the offices of the magazine *Yunost'*, where he met with the editor-in-chief Boris Polevoi, Yevtushenko, and two or three other officials and editors. Yevtushenko, a regular contributor to the magazine, and Steinbeck conversed for a while in Spanish. (Later in the week when John and Elaine spent an evening at Yevtushenko's apartment, the Russian inscribed a volume of poetry to John in Spanish, to the effect that writers must fight hard for justice, but not *too* hard else the struggle would become a struggle for its own sake.)

Then Polevoi introduced Steinbeck to a group of about thirty regular contributors to *Yunost'*, including Aksenov, Rozov, Gladilin, and Akhmadulina. Steinbeck had asked to meet with them, since they were all younger writers, and as they sat around a large table in a sort of "board room," he tried (as he recalled later in notes made during his trip) to encourage them to talk about rebellion and innovation as expressed by young Russian artists. But no one would say much, and he could see that the presence of Polevoi was intimidating them. Finally, Bella Akhmadulina said with some sarcasm that Mr. Steinbeck should not imagine that simply because her young comrades did not speak that they were not the most fearless and intrepid sort of people.

Anatoly Gladilin remembers the occasion from the other side of the table. Now living in Paris, he recalls that the "thaw" that Steinbeck thought he felt was over:

> It was the end of 1963, the decline of Soviet liberalism. The famous exhibition in Manezh has passed, our Nikita Sergeyevich already has shaken his fist at Aksenov and Voznesensky from the Party Platform, newspapers unmasked a search of abstractionist painters and young nihilist writers. The hunt for witches in Moscow's organization of writers was on. Yes, the epoch of liberalism was coming to an end, but writers were not arrested, not expelled abroad, and we still hoped for something.
>
> And so, I received a call, from the magazine *Youth*, which said that Boris Polevoi wants to see me urgently. The editor-in-chief of the magazine meets me on the threshold of his office, taps me on the shoulder, "How is life, old man?" and so on. "What life?" I an-

swer. "Everything is closed up for me. The book is stopped in the publishing house, the play is banned in the theater, so I have written a letter to the Central Committee, to Ilichev." "We know that," says Polevoi, "I have my own entry to Ilichev. So, old man, don't fall into despair. I'm sure that the noise will fade and everything will come back to normal. And we will help you. Just don't tease the geese." "Well," I answer, "thank you, Boris Vikolaevitch for a kind word. . . ."

"By the way," says Polevoi, "John Steinbeck is here in Moscow and wants to meet with you, with you and with all the young ones. We'll come to the editorial office. But," Polevoi hesitated, "Steinbeck himself is a good man, and if he asks provocative questions, it won't be with evil intent, but thoughtlessness." (That's what he said, "thoughtlessness.") "But Steinbeck will be accompanied by two persons from the American Embassy. And these two," Polevoi winked, "I know exactly, are professional secret service men from the CIA. Those two will be trying. So, old man," continued Polevoi, "I rely on you. Don't let down—neither yourself, me, or the magazine. You know by yourself—we are hanging by a thread."

I naturally promised not to tease the geese.

In the cafeteria of the Central House of Writers, I meet Aksenov and it becomes clear that Polevoi has talked to him also and also asked him not to give way to provocation.

Preoccupied, Voznesensky runs by.

"Where are you hurrying, Andrey?"

"Well, Polevoi has called for something."

The matter is clear. Polevoi has done spade-work with everyone.

And so, all of us sit at a long table in the biggest room of the magazine *Youth*. I probably do not remember everyone present, but there was Voznesensky, Yevtushenko, Aksenov, Rozhdestvensky, Balter, Akhmadulina, Sarnov, Rassadin—in general, all of the most active members of the magazine, plus, of course, the editorial workers.

John Steinbeck—living classical writer of world literature, winner of the Nobel Prize—was at the head of the table. His novel *The Grapes of Wrath* we have read long ago, but *The Winter of Our Discontent* appeared recently in Russian translation and made a good impression. Steinbeck has a rather rough face, as the sailors have or as the people who like to put their hand on a drink. Next to Steinbeck, looking like an angel, a very young man with a stiff smile on his lips in a wonderfully made suit. We guess—"the secret service man" from the American Embassy. By the way, that young man hasn't said a single word. Where is the second spy? We don't know. Either he didn't come, or he is hiding under the table. You never know about the crafty designs of the CIA.

And Steinbeck runs his eyes along our faces and asks provocative questions, like, "How do you live, you people?" "I want to know about your troubles, about your problems. . . ." We drop our eyes, mumble something inarticulate, add more tea to each other's glasses, and nibble barankas. A samovar boils on the table, and the silence around us is broken only by the knocking sound of teaspoons with which the sugar is stirred in the glasses. But Boris Polevoi is in bliss. He even encourages us. He says, "Fellows, be more active, ask questions, otherwise I am myself, as an old goat, the answerable one." (The comparison with an old goat was Polevoi's favorite joke.)

Someone asked about relations of Steinbeck with Hemingway. Steinbeck answered briefly—they met only twice and what they talked about he doesn't remember because at both meetings they had a lot to drink. One time Hemingway paid; another time, Steinbeck.

I ask about John Dos Passos, and there is heard immediately the laughter of the critics Rassadin and Sarnov—they knew that Dos Passos was my favorite writer, and as it turns out, they have laid a bet beforehand between themselves whether I would ask about Dos Passos or not. Steinbeck answers about Dos Passos with reluctance, as though he had a car accident and hadn't been writing for a long time. Someone asked about something else, definitely not very interesting for our guest, and Steinbeck's questions jumped away from us, as from the wall. We knew that we were making an impression of idiots, but we can't tease the geese. We don't have a right to let down the magazine, we have promised. . . .

Only Polevoi has a good time and spouts with jokes about being an old goat. Two hours pass in this manner. Steinbeck's fingers nervously knock at the table. "Hey, you," says the winner of the Nobel Prize, "I was told about you, that you are young wolves with sharp teeth. I was ready to argue with you, to fight. . . ."

And then, the melodious voice of Bella Akhmadulina was heard. Very calmly, without raising the tone of her voice, even a little in the elegiac manner, not teasing the geese and avoiding risky comparisons, Bella Akhmadulina explained to Steinbeck the difference between his situation and ours. She hinted that Steinbeck would go back to a free America, but that we would stay here, and we have to live and work in this country. And right then, for the first time during all of the tea-drinking, Steinbeck's eyes flashed, and he smiled, and it seemed to me that his smile was somewhat awkward. He understood.

Steinbeck left with the silent Embassy angel in a huge American car. And we, the whole crowd, went to the House of Writers to drink. But not tea. And the hero of the day was Bella Akhmadulina.

II

Each situation seemed to have inherent tensions and conflict. The Steinbecks, and then Edward Albee after he arrived on November 4, were taken to luncheon after luncheon and dinner after dinner. The dinners, particularly, seemed to be tests of endurance and will. It wasn't always clear whether the hosts were being simply generous and enthusiastic, or whether they had purposely planned with overwhelming amounts of liquor and wine to try to lead their guests into some kind of indiscretion. The Americans had to constantly monitor what they said and agreed to, and this was not easy after hours of toasting. Steinbeck was certain that the Russians watered down their own vodka, but it may be that they were so used to the process that they didn't need to.

Albee recalls that there was one head of the Writers' Union who would begin the most awful kind of doctrinaire business, long sermons or lectures at every social event. At one dinner everyone was enjoying himself, when suddenly he stood up and announced that it was high time for everyone there to protest in solidarity all the West Germans shot by the West while trying to escape through no man's land to the East in Berlin. Steinbeck got up and responded, "No wonder the Germans were shot if they were running backwards into East Berlin."

Elaine remembers a less solemn occasion at a very large dinner party. John was sitting at one end of a big table and Elaine and Edward at the other. They had been through several nights in a row of dinners. Just as you started to put a bite of food in your mouth, Elaine recalls, someone would always stand up and make another toast to brotherhood, or peace, or love or something. Each toast ended with "To your health," which in Russian began to ring in John and Elaine's ears day and night because they had heard it so much. At this dinner John was tired and hungry, and there was yet another toast—"To peaceful coexistence—to your health!" When everyone sat down, John got up and looked at Elaine, raised his glass, and, as formally as he could, proposed, "Natchez to Mobile!" Elaine picked it up immediately and raised her glass, "Memphis to St. Jo!" Everyone stood to join in—"Natchez to Mobile! Memphis to St. Jo!"—except for Edward, who nearly fell under the table laughing.

Just as the Steinbecks had, Albee soon felt the constant pressure: "We knew we were watched and supervised and spied on. . . . You end up claustrophobic. . . . I actually came back after six weeks convinced I couldn't speak freely to friends in their homes, my home." He came to believe that there were plants at every single meeting. At one of the universities he and John were talking about writing in the United States to a group of students:

> One of them, a 45-year-old KGB type of student, asked John the question, "Mr. Steinbeck, you used to tell the truth about your country in your work. Why in the past 15 or 20 years have you been lying about the United States?" A really stupid question. And John gave a good answer, I thought. He said, "Changes—if I wrote what I did in the thirties, I'd be lying about the U.S. now." . . . He was hounded by that particular kind of thing.

Nevertheless, they both worked hard to bring questions into the minds of the students they talked to. They found that while Soviet students were learning a lot about the French Revolution, they heard practically nothing at all about the American Revolution, nor were they aware of the second American revolution of 1932.

Among the events that the Steinbecks attended in Moscow was a dress rehearsal of *The Moon Is Down*, and the anniversary parade in Red Square with the Kremlin reception that followed. On November 8 they left with Albee for four days in Leningrad. After they arrived, John, who had been going nonstop for nearly four weeks, turned green and collapsed. He was taken to the hospital, where doctors pumped him full of glucose and vitamins and told him he needed a two-week period of complete rest. The next day he was back on tour.

In Leningrad, as in other areas they had visited—more often when they were outside of Moscow—they had some unofficial contact with dissident writers and students, although John was quite concerned that such clandestine meetings were probably being observed and would get the Russians involved into serious trouble. On several occasions, two or three writers came to the Steinbecks' hotel room late at night. Very often during large meetings, someone would manage to smuggle a note to Elaine (it was always passed to Elaine as a bit of misdirection), asking John a question so that the asker could not be identified. In Leningrad one such note asked John and Edward if they would come to the university late that night if someone would come and fetch them at the hotel. They agreed and found themselves taken down dark little alleys and side streets to a student's room which was packed with about thirty people. John and Edward stayed until dawn, talking about politics and literature.

Only a day after their return to Moscow they learned of the arrest of Yale Professor Frederick Barghoorn on spy charges. Barghoorn had been traveling in the U.S.S.R. as a tourist when, without any apparent provocation, he had been arrested and was being held incommunicado. John called a press conference for Western correspondents at the American embassy and spoke of his anger. "The Soviet action is irresponsible," he said. "Such irresponsibility is too damned dangerous. Barghoorn is no spy. He's the least likely person you could find for such a thing." Unpublicized was his letter to Aleksei Adzhubei in which he called the arrest an outrage and expressed the hope that the editor would join him in his protest. The next day, November 15, the Steinbecks left by air for Warsaw. Writer Vladimir Maximov, who did not meet Steinbeck while he was in Moscow, nevertheless heard through his friends that while Steinbeck had been welcomed with great ceremony, "the leave-taking was more than cool. Evidently, the American guest did not fulfill the propagandistic hopes of the Union of Writers."

Leaving Moscow for Warsaw seemed to the Steinbecks like opening a door and stepping out into the fresh air. Later, Polish dissidents complained: "Why do they always do this, send us people after they have been in the Soviet Union. Anything looks free after Moscow, and of course we are not free." Still, although they assumed a schedule as demanding as that in Russia, they didn't feel as tired and their activities gave them more pleasure. It also added to their enjoyment to have as their interpreter Kazimierz Piotrowski, a well-known Polish writer who was also a translator and scholar of English and American literature.

Shortly after their arrival *Polityka* published an interview with Steinbeck, which included the following:

> There is no creative work without experimenting. I may not like the result of experimenting, but this is another matter altogether. And what about my failing to write something that might be called experimental in the popular sense of the word? Well, perhaps I am unable to do this, but to the question put to me here whether I would not prefer to remain unintelligible to my present readers for the sake of being intelligible to those who would read me in the year 3,000, I reply without hesitation—"I want to be understood today." . . .
>
> What are the virtues you appreciate most in people?
>
> Gallantry.
>
> Chivalry, courage?
>
> Yes, but this is not all. I also mean kindness, heartfelt kindness

besides chivalry and courage; and all that is genuine, individual and unique in men.

After two days of touring Warsaw and attending many meetings with various Polish writers at the capital, they were taken to the Mazurian Lakes District, where they visited Ketrzyn and the "Wolves Den," Hitler's eastern headquarters. They spent the night at a Forestry Hostel and had an evening of song and conversation with some Polish writers who were also hunters. The next day, John went on a wild boar hunt in the woods, and they saw five boar. John was quoted by the Polish press as saying, "They were running so nicely that I didn't have heart to take aim."

The Steinbecks' next stop was Krakow, where John found his tours particularly enjoyable because of his interest in medieval history and old armor. On the first day, following the obligatory luncheon with local dignitaries at the local chapter of the Polish Writers' Union, John was taken to the student club at the university where he was scheduled to meet with students of the department of English philology. However, a local paper had announced the meeting, and there were some two hundred fifty gate-crashers who did in fact break down the door of the hall in the crush to get in.

Some of the students were from a class in American literature being taught by an American exchange professor, Virginia Rock, and the quality of questions was very good. One, which John mentioned several times during the remainder of his stay in Poland, was: Please comment on the "moment of wonder," that creative moment at which an author conceives and gives birth to a novel. John replied that for him, the moment was the result of approximately three years of research and thinking about a book, which gradually built up in his head like a "tone," and could only be purged by putting it down in writing.

From Krakow the Steinbecks went to Wroclaw and then Lodz, returning to Warsaw on November 22. Late that night they were informed by the embassy that President Kennedy had been shot and killed. A deluge of calls and visits by correspondents wanting comments followed. In a state of shock, which was probably made more severe by their sense of isolation, the Steinbecks didn't know what to say. Their first instinct was to call home or to go home, but there was no way to get a call through, and after some thought, they decided they should continue the job that Kennedy had given them. They would attend the official meetings but cancel the social part of their schedule.

The next morning John and Elaine went to the embassy to help the personnel deal with the crowds of Poles who had gathered to express sympathy. Although it was the middle of winter, each person brought a flower, and, after placing it before a portrait of the President, the person would write his name and a message in the embassy register. The procession continued all day and all night. At each of the three official meetings remaining on his schedule, John spoke first briefly in tribute to the President, but refused to answer questions or comment further, since he knew no details of the tragedy.

The Steinbecks felt that they could not go on and asked the State Department if they could take a few days' rest somewhere on the other side of the Iron Curtain. After gaining permission, they went to Vienna and attended the funeral service held there for the President, rested, and then went on to Budapest. Elaine recalls that in Budapest a bookstore was under siege because it had announced that it would sell Steinbeck's books, and that Steinbeck would be there at ten o'clock on a Tuesday morning. John, who throughout his life had refused to attend an autograph party at an American bookstore, sat in this store all day and into the evening signing books. They also went to many private parties and visited many people in their homes. The men who had been in the revolt had grown beards at the time, but now were clean-shaven. When one of them met John, he would say, "It wasn't too long ago that I wore a beard," and John would embrace him.

From Budapest they went to Prague, and from Prague to West Berlin, where they found the visit was very difficult for them emotionally. After having spent nearly two months in Russia and Eastern Europe, the lingering bitterness of the people toward the Germans, the exposure to place after place that was stained with the memory of German atrocities, even the frequent discussion by the writers about the war as a subject for literature—all made their mark on the Steinbecks' consciousness. On the other hand, they felt as they toured West Berlin the very real threat by the East to close the city.

It had become a fad for visitors to Berlin to cross into the East, but John refused to go: "I am not an ambulance chaser. I don't go to the scenes of accidents. . . . It is an obscenity to me." But he did consent to look at the wall. At the Friedrichstrasse crossing point, he borrowed a pair of binoculars from an American military policeman and gazed at the other side and at the East German border guards who cradled submachine guns in their arms. John pointed his gnarled cane at the wall and said, "I'm amazed that anybody would confess so completely that he failed. . . . That's what this amounts to . . . a failure in competition, a failure in everything."

During their five days in Berlin, the Steinbecks went through another extensive series of planned events, which included a meeting with Mayor Brandt, lunch with the American commanding officer, General Polk, and a dinner given by the head of the U.S. Mission to Berlin, which was arranged for Steinbeck to meet and talk with such German writers as Günter Grass, Uwe Johnson, and Hans Scholz. He met with several large groups of students, intellectuals, and writers at the Free University, the Technical University, and at the Amerika Haus to answer questions.

Among them he was asked if the bombing of Negro children was a typical expression of the Southern white point of view. He replied that while the bombing made news, it did not make news that churches throughout the nation, including the South, held memorial services the following Sunday. Asked "Why have you turned from being a Marxist to a puritan," he answered, "I don't know what you mean. I've never been either. My novels of social reform were stories of people, not political treatises."

III

Before they left Poland, John had written to Mrs. Kennedy to express their sorrow and sympathy and to the new President, Lyndon Johnson, their support. Shortly after they returned home, on December 17, they went to Washington for three days of debriefing by the State Department, and on the last evening of their stay they were invited to a private dinner at the White House. Elaine had known Lady Bird Johnson at the University of Texas, so there was already a connection between the two families, and this dinner, given so that John and Elaine could report to the President on their travels behind the Iron Curtain, would lay the foundation for what developed into a warm and relatively close friendship between the two couples.

Elaine recalls that at the end of the evening, as they were leaving, "John said, 'Lady Bird, we have been debriefed for three days, and nobody asked questions as good as yours.' It was true." The Steinbecks started to go back to their hotel, the Hay Adams across Lafayette Square, but after they said good-bye at the elevator, the Johnsons got on and rode down with them. John said, "You don't have to see us to the door," but the President just ushered them all out the front door, the one that is seldom used except for state occasions, and continued to guide them down the walk out to the gate.

As Secret Service men in overcoats began streaming out of doorways and running this way and that, Elaine said, "Please, Mr. President, you don't want to do this." "Don't worry," the President said, taking Elaine's hand. "No one expects to see us walking out this way, so they won't pay any attention." He continued to walk with them, around the square and to the front of the hotel. It was, of course, a very flattering and moving gesture. This would be the last time the Steinbecks would stay in a hotel when visiting the Johnsons—from then on, they stayed in the White House.

At about the time the Steinbecks returned from Europe, Thom and young John came on vacation from boarding school to join their father and stepmother for the first Christmas to be celebrated in the new apartment. They came home with very poor grades, a great disappointment to John, for his hopes for the boys had never been higher—he had been certain that the trip and special attention and tutoring would help them turn the corner with their studies.

After New Year's they were sent back to school, but the following day John and Elaine received phone calls from the schools telling them that the boys had not arrived. The Steinbecks didn't know where they were, whether they had run away (they had done so on occasion before) or had been kidnapped or hurt. Their worry increased when they called everyone they could think of who might know of their whereabouts—relatives, girl friends, and friends—and still couldn't find out where they were. Eventually they found out that the boys had in fact returned to Gwyn—they had decided they were going to live with *her*.

In the meantime, John F. Kennedy's widow wanted someone to write a definitive biography of her husband, and she had thought Steinbeck the writer most suitable. She got in touch with mutual friends and made some inquiries and then wrote the Steinbecks to invite them to come and see her in Washington. When John and Elaine called on her, they could see that, although she had herself under control, she was still obviously in a state of shock. She talked to them about the kind of book she had in mind and very openly and movingly about the President and about her relationship to him. At one point Elaine began to cry, and Mrs. Kennedy said, "Please, Elaine, if you must cry, go in the bathroom and pull yourself together. I can't bear it now, and I'll go to pieces." Elaine did leave for a few minutes and then came back. Their visit stretched into a stay of several hours, as every time they started to leave, Mrs. Kennedy would beg them to stay—"I've nothing in the world to do."

Elaine feels that her husband recognized from the beginning that it wasn't his kind of book, a biography that would require extensive research, but that he didn't feel he could say this to Mrs. Kennedy at the time. Yet, there was a correspondence over several months between him and Mrs. Kennedy, as well as two other meetings, and his letters suggest that he may have, at least for a while, thought of the project as a serious possibility. But what he had in mind does not seem to have been an orthodox biography.

The connection between the metaphor of Camelot, which the press had attached to the Kennedy White House, and John's continuing preoccupation with Arthurian legend would seem almost inevitable. The book John thought about was apparently some sort of retelling of the legend using Kennedy's life. When he wrote to Mrs. Kennedy on February 25, eleven days after their first meeting about the book, he tells of his study of "this recurring cycle" and connects it with her husband:

> The 15th century and our own have so much in common—loss of authority, loss of gods, loss of heroes, and loss of lovely pride. When such a hopeless muddled need occurs, it does seem to me that the hungry hearts of men distill their best and truest essence, and that essence becomes a man, and that man a hero so that all men can be reassured that such things are possible. The fact that all of these words—hero, myth, pride, even victory, have been muddled and sicklied by the confusion and pessimism of the times only describes the times. The words and the concepts are permanent, only they must be brought out and verified by the Hero. . . .
>
> At our best we live by the legend. And when our belief gets pale and weak, there comes a man out of our need who puts on the shining armor and everyone living reflects a little of that light, yes, and stores some up against the time when he is gone. . . .
>
> In our time of meager souls, of mole-like burrowing into a status quo which never existed, the banner of the Legend is the great vocation.

"I shall try," he promised her, "to find a form for this theme," but of course he had been trying for years to do so, and the addition of Kennedy to the equation seemed to bring only further complication and emotion to an already too complex and emotional task. Yet, in March he wrote to Dook, "I am stamping the ground trying to get started on a new book that means a lot to me. I want it to be very good and so far I have the tone of it and what it is about and that is all. I'll have to kick it around for some time."

Apparently the idea of biography revived consideration of a project he had thought about once before—an autobiography. But he wanted, he tells Dook, to make it a "real one," that is, "since after a passage of time I don't know what happened and what I made up, it would be nearer the truth to set both down" [3/2/64]. But this, along with the Kennedy approach to Arthur, seemed to drift into limbo as he mulled them over in his mind, but never found solutions to the problems of form that they presented. Near the end of April he wrote to Mrs. Kennedy, "One day I do hope to write what we spoke of—how this man who was the best of his people, by his life and his death gave the best back to them for their own" [4/20/64].

But not now. Throughout the next months, he found, as he wrote to Pat, the pencil felt to him like a foreign instrument, and in a letter to his editor that summer, he confided: "I'm worrying because words seem to have lost their value for me. I've wanted to work and the words aren't any good. And they're just the same words that used to be in the dictionaries."

During the late winter and early spring of 1964, the two sons would neither see nor talk to John or Elaine. Then in March they were notified by their lawyer that Gwyn and the boys were taking John to court for additional support. For John, it was painful that the boys were joining with their mother in this suit, as he felt it demonstrated ingratitude and indicated they were siding with Gwyn against him.

John was totally depressed. He suggested to Elaine that it might be good for them if they went away over Easter, to Rome, to give their lawyer time to get things together and give them an opportunity to stand back from the situation and recover from the shock. From Rome John reported to Elizabeth:

> I guess we didn't know how . . . injured we were by the recent bestialities. The first of several nights I had nightmares—real screamers. But now things are kind of leveling off into a semi-benign stupor. We walk a great deal, everywhere, drink coffee and walk some more. [4/1/64]

They came back in mid-April to the trial, which was held in New York Family Court. It was an ugly and miserable affair. Gwyn's approach seemed to be to diminish John's contribution to the rearing of the children and to show that she had been badly treated, that she had worked very hard to raise the boys but had found it difficult because of John's interference and stinginess. John's lawyer countered that he and his clients were not going to put up with such unsupported allegations, and that if the court wished, he would be glad to supply testimony regarding her behavior.

Near the beginning of the hearing, the judge barred the sons from the courtroom. If this is going to be a fight between a husband and ex-wife, he ruled, then I'm not going to let the children come into the court. Of course, the "children," going on seventeen and nineteen, had heard it all before, many times. Gwyn tried to argue that since it was also the boys' suit, they should be there, but if they were excluded, Elaine should be excluded. The judge denied that, saying that Elaine was the boys' stepmother and had a right to be a part of the proceedings.

Following Steinbeck's testimony, which simply recounted what he had done or tried to do for his sons, the judge took the case into his chambers and talked to each of the boys, to Gwyn, and to John separately. The next day he announced his decision. Just because this is a very famous and well-to-do man, he announced, I will not have him abused. He gave a slight raise in alimony and child support to the plaintiffs to cover the increase in the cost of living. Bitterly disappointed, Gwyn went to the window of the courtroom to tell the boys, "Nothing. Nothing!"

Later, Thom and John told their father that the suit had been Gwyn's idea, but he felt they were old enough to know what they were doing. He forgave them, but was hurt by the thought that they had not yet come to the maturity he had hoped for.

Early in June John and Elaine moved to Sag Harbor, where Elaine involved herself in gardening while John took up the *Arthur* once more, reading, reviewing, and thinking. He tried to retreat into the habits of the past in order to recover something of what he was. For all his talk about how he no longer had or needed a home, just a place to store his books, he really did require a familiar location and friends in order to function. Now that the house was gone and the apartment still something like a large hotel suite to him, Sag Harbor became more important than ever before. Then too, there was still something of the farmer in him, and planting seedlings in boxes on window ledges in the apartment wasn't entirely satisfactory.

Once again he joined the life of the village, going down in the mornings for coffee, stopping by the hardware store and boat yard, visiting with shopkeepers, and occasionally having a beer with friends in the late afternoon. At home he raked, trimmed, and planted, and fiddled with his boat.

Now early each summer he was involved in the planning and work for conducting the Old Whalers Festival, a civic celebration to catch tourists and a long weekend party to raise the spirits of the locals. The festival celebrated the town's colorful whaling port past, and Steinbeck, who was fond of nearly anything to do with history and of nearly any kind of celebration, was happy to join in.

Since this was something like planning for a party, he became totally involved, coming up with one idea after another. The festival at that time involved little more than some historic displays and a parade down Main Street, and it was Steinbeck's concern that they bring some historical color and action to it. He suggested that they inaugurate an annual debate between Sag Harbor and Nantucket as to which port had the greatest historical importance, and having read in some depth about the history of the region, he acted for several years as the debate's moderator.

He also suggested that they hold whaleboat races, an event that led to another, the International Whaleboat Competition, started in 1966, in which crews from several nations raced each other, rowing in twenty-eight-foot double-ended whaleboats, in pursuit of a motorized "whale" target which had to be harpooned. John delighted in setting off the fireworks for the weekend, and it was also his idea that they have a grand finale. For a man who at sixty-two sometimes now talked of being old, it was an odd scene: his face under his yachting cap half-illuminated and sinister-looking from the torch he held in his hand, he would wait for the signal. Then with a grunt of triumph he would spring forward with his torch and rush down the line, firing off one rocket after another as fast as possible, so that whistling up into the blackness at nearly the same time, they would suddenly erupt in one gigantic, extended burst of thunder and fire.

As the summer passed, John went through the motions of writing, but nothing would come forth. Pat, as usual, wrote encouragement and advised patience:

Please relax and don't force yourself. It never works. The muse is a shy dame and will not be importuned. Besides, you are trying to ignore the terrible nervous and soul shake-up you recently had. Of course this, too, will pass away, but give it time and you will be a wiser man.

And then you can always go back to Sir Thomas Malory and work on your translation. I know of no better way to sharpen your pencil. I would also recommend reading The Tales of Boccaccio—they are an excellent anodyne. Best of all enjoy Elaine and your garden, and forget about writing masterpieces. They'll come when they come, and they will come. Your subconscious is working for you, never fear. [7/1/64]

Pat struck the same notes many times before, and as well-intentioned as they were, in the frustration of having failed for several years to write anything that gave him any satisfaction (he didn't much care for *Travels with Charley* once he had finished it), he found Pat's messages irritating.

He loved Pat, but Pat was always asking to see a bit of John's writing—even while John wasn't getting any writing done. And Pat was always telling him that everything would turn out just fine eventually, like a mother telling her son in the midst of disaster that every cloud has a silver lining. In response, like a son unwilling to hurt his mother, but bursting with irritation, John barely communicated with Pat, sending only the barest of "duty" reports.

Pat didn't know that it was the Malory that John was working on and so terribly discouraged about. His telling John that going back to Malory would be good for "sharpening his pencil" was like rubbing his nose in his failure, but worse, since Pat seemed to take the Malory work so lightly. What was unfortunate about the situation was that Pat, who was hurt by John's steadily increasing coldness and his reluctance to confide in him, was ill, but John didn't know it.

By the end of July the lawsuit still hurt and his attempts to write were still futile. To Elizabeth he wrote:

Today, Thursday, is HAIR DAY. Elaine is at Southhampton getting it bent and tonight being the night of HAIR DAY, we take Elaine's hair out to dinner. Makes it nice all around. Wasn't it interesting and typical that my charming children and their mother paid not the slightest attention to the court order and went about their usual practices and sent the bills to me. . . .

I hate to report that my work is not going well at all. It just won't get off the ground. I have been out here early and late and for many hours a day and it won't get off the ground. The words sound pretentious and sour and unreal. It just makes me sick. Maybe the fire has gone out. . . . Maybe it is because this subject has been tramped over by so very many people and is the property of so many. I hate to give up again but I am not getting anywhere. It's a damned shame because I have put as much work into this abortion as a whole book would take. . . . I just can't seem to do it. Even my translation seems lousy and uncalled for to me. The Morte is so much better than any pale imitation of it. Maybe I sold myself a bill of goods and can't make the payments. . . . Well, there's no reason to put it on your back either. And I don't bother Elaine about it. She worries so when I can't work. . . . I guess I will have to go back into the silence for a time and see what I can dredge up. There must be something in that mire. [7/23/64]

He was pulled out of his despondency by two events in August. Thomas H. Guinzburg, who had taken over from his father as head of Viking, came to John with a collection of photographs that he had commissioned to be taken all over the country. The collection was designed to distill the spirit of America and its people, to show Americans at work and at play, at repose and in action, and to picture all the various characteristic component parts of the land, East and West, North and South, urban, suburban, and rural.

The original concept was simply a picture book with captions, but Tom got the idea that Steinbeck might like to provide an introduction as well. John approached the project with the understanding that it would be a short "commercial" job that he could do in a couple of weeks, but as he became more involved, what had started out in his mind as a sort of "booklet" was transformed into a collection of essays to accompany the photos, essays based in large part on his impressions from his recent tour of the country. Many of his thoughts were of things that he had wanted to write about in *Charley*, but because of the form had been unable to. He brought to the task his accumulated frustrations from the *Arthur*, which pushed him to do a more careful and thoughtful job and a more extensive one than he had planned. The result of this effort was *America and Americans*.

The second event was a call from President Johnson to help him with his acceptance speech for the nomination by the Democratic Convention. Since their dinner with the Johnsons before Christmas, the Steinbecks had been overnight guests twice at the White House, a correspondence between Steinbeck and Johnson (he wrote to the President through Jack Valenti) had begun, and they had talked on the phone. In mid-July John had been informed that the President would confer upon him the highest award presented to a civilian in peacetime, the Medal of Freedom. (John was pleased but complained that all these honors were making him feel as if he were already dead.) In a relatively short period the President had forged a bond between himself and the writer.

The friendship of these two men which grew over the next few years is an interesting juncture. Among the most prominent men of their time, they had succeeded in very different fields of endeavor, had different personalities and different interests, yet they were in many ways very much alike, and in the remaining course of their public careers they shared, to some extent, a common ironic fate.

Rough-hewn, big men, there was something about both that was larger than life. Both had been heavily influenced by F.D.R. and New Deal policy and ideals and shared a vision of an America of opportunity for all, without prejudice and without poverty. Yet in each there were strong elements of conservative values mixed into their overall liberalism. Both were intensely patriotic, suspicious of Russia, and very antagonistic to communism.

Both were Westerners who felt uneasy with the Eastern Establishment, were somewhat intimidated by Ivy League types, and tended to be defensive about their "provincial" origins. Both were very intelligent and knowledgeable, complex men, but they had an image in the media of lacking intellectual depth. Rather than simple men, or men of the soil as they were sometimes pictured, they were very sophisticated. Johnson assumed an air of modesty and Steinbeck was in fact modest, but they really enjoyed recognition enormously. And both men seemed to have an intense desire for approval, particularly by groups that tended to be antagonistic to them—the *Times* literary crowd for Steinbeck, and the old-line liberal establishment for Johnson.

The relationship between the two, as it evolved, was rather complicated, especially on John's side, for he seemed to carry certain doubts and reservations about Johnson with him to the end. Nevertheless, he gave the President his loyalty because he was the President, and his support, as the President won it through his strong domestic program. As their relationship continued and Johnson's popular support declined, Steinbeck's loyalty became firmer, almost fierce, and he developed, as Elaine noted, something like a protective stance toward the President in his difficulties.

Steinbeck never adopted a political position because it was fashionable, nor did he ever modify a stand because it had become unpopular.

Indeed, his instincts tended to drive him in the opposite direction—the more criticism the President received, the more positive and outspoken in his support John became. In the end, support for the war in Vietnam tragically affected the reputations of both men and unfairly tarnished their other accomplishments.

Johnson had enormous personal charm and was very skillful in getting what he wanted from people, and while he genuinely liked and admired Steinbeck, he also saw in John some political advantage. As a Stevenson supporter, John had ties with a wing of the Democratic Party that had been hostile to Johnson; as a Nobel Prize winner and author whose books were beloved by many readers, he would be a useful figure to have associated with his presidency; and as an accomplished writer with some speechwriting experience who shared many of the same values, he could become a valuable resource for a President, who must, perforce, try to communicate effectively with the general public.

Over the months before and after the 1964 convention, John felt himself being pulled into the President's magnetic field with mixed emotions. On the one hand, he had an inordinate respect for the office of the presidency and was vulnerable to the excitement and flattery that came from being around a president, feeling the history and majesty of the White House on an intimate basis.

When the Steinbecks were with the Johnsons, they were treated almost like members of the family. They stayed near the Johnsons on the second floor in the Queen's Bedroom or the Lincoln Room, and were able to have breakfast in the little office where Lincoln often breakfasted. When Steinbeck was asked to work on Johnson's acceptance speech, the materials came to him on Long Island by military airplane, and when they went to the White House to be with the Johnsons during the first few days of the convention, so that John could further polish the speech, a plane came to pick them up. Every once in a while in Washington, Elaine would turn to John and say, "You'd better get me out of here, back to New York. I'm getting to like this too much."

On the other hand, John had a certain amount of skepticism about Johnson and his politics. He viewed him with the same suspicion common to most liberals—as a too-conservative Democrat who in the Senate was a wheeler-dealer with too much willingness to compromise.

Johnson, a man who seemed to need constant reassurance from those around him, was apparently conscious of Steinbeck's reservations. Sometimes he would ask, "You really wanted Adlai Stevenson in this office, didn't you, John?" John would say, "Yes." "Well," the President would continue, "are you sorry?" John would answer, "Mr. President, that's water under the bridge. I can't tell whether he would have made a good President or not. I think he might have." In this the President seemed to sense correctly that no one would ever in John's mind quite measure up to Stevenson and that anyone else would always be subject to some criticism by comparison.

John also had, and frequently voiced to friends, a suspicion of what happened to the writer, scholar, or journalist in our society who became too entangled in the web of power and privilege and its pressures for conformity of opinion and approval. When John Kenneth Galbraith was appointed ambassador to India by Kennedy, John wrote a letter warning him, as Galbraith recalls, "that no writer, teacher, nor man of required independence of mind had any business becoming an ambassador, and that definitely included me. It wasn't necessarily that I would louse up the job or dislike it. Rather, I would like it too much." According to this standard, John himself probably became too involved with the Johnson White House and lost some independence of mind as it conflicted with stronger impulses of duty to country and loyalty to friends.

Real-estate photo of two houses purchased by Steinbecks on East 78 Street. The Steinbecks lived in one and rented the other to the Benchleys. *(Steinbeck Research Center, courtesy San Jose State University Library, San Jose, California.)*

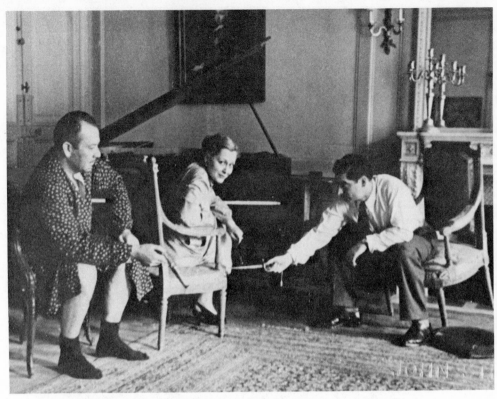

John, Gwyn, and Robert Capa in Paris hotel suite, 1947. *(Steinbeck Research Center, courtesy San Jose State University Library, San Jose, California.)*

John with sons Thom and John at Nantucket, summer 1951. *(John Steinbeck Library, Salinas, Steinbeck Archives.)*

John's initial meeting with Elaine Scott (right) at lunch with Ann Sothern (left) at the Pine Inn in Carmel. (Monterey Peninsula Herald *photo from The John Steinbeck Collection, Stanford University Libraries.*)

Elaine and John at their wedding reception, December 28, 1950. *(Courtesy Valley Guild, John Steinbeck Library, Salinas, Steinbeck Archives.)*

John with Elia Kazan, Ritz Hotel, Boston, during *Burning Bright*, October 1950. (*The John Steinbeck Collection, Stanford University Libraries.*)

Siasconset house where John wrote most of *East of Eden*. (*Jackson J. Benson.*)

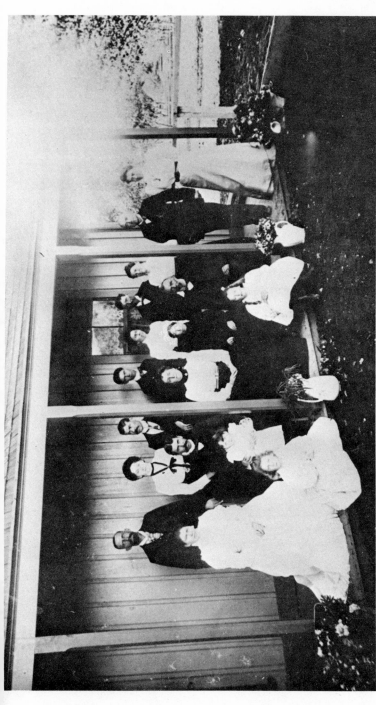

Steinbeck's maternal family, the Hamiltons, posing on the golden wedding anniversary of Elizabeth and Samuel Hamilton. Taken at the home of John and Olive Steinbeck, Paso Robles, California, circa 1899. Standing, left to right: J. E. Steinbeck; Mamie Hamilton (wife of George); Will Hamilton (husband of Adela); Joe Hamilton; Aunt "Lizzie"; Thomas Hamilton; Dessie Hamilton; Will Martin; Mollie Hamilton Martin. Seated (adults), left to right: Olive Hamilton Steinbeck; George Hamilton; Adela Winkler Hamilton (Dade, Will's wife); Elizabeth Hamilton; Samuel Hamilton. Seated (children), left to right: Elizabeth Steinbeck; Marian Hamilton (daughter of Mamie and George); Esther Steinbeck. (*Steinbeck Research Center, courtesy San Jose State University Library, San Jose, California.*)

Old Hamilton Ranch as it is today, looking north across Hamilton Canyon. Marks on hills are cow trails. (© 1983 Richard L. Allman.)

John and Elaine in Rome. *(Wide World Photos, courtesy Department of Special Collections, Stanford University.)*

hn, Elaine, Thom, and
ung John in Paris, 1954.
Courtesy Mrs. E. G. Ainsworth,
hn Steinbeck Library,
linas, Steinbeck Archives.)

Mary Steinbeck Dekker, John, and Elaine aboard ship, celebrating Mary's birthday, 1957. *(Courtesy Mrs. E. G. Ainsworth, John Steinbeck Library, Salinas, Steinbeck Archives.)*

Elizabeth Otis and Elaine. *(Special Collections, Bracken Library, courtesy Ball State University, Muncie, Indiana.)*

In July 1964 Pat Covici called Sag Harbor and asked for John; Elaine buzzed him in his workroom, and John came into the house in a bad humor, as he always was when he was interrupted by the telephone. The day before he had found out that Pat had "blown" an ulcer and had kept it a secret from him. He was worried about Pat, suspecting that his health might even be worse than he let on, but he was also angry with him for not telling him about the ulcer and for having to worry about him. And here was Pat on the phone, and John hated phones.

Pat had been feeling neglected for some time, and he complained to John of his treatment of him. He never sent him any of his writing any more, never even let him know what he was working on. He used to write long letters telling him of his thoughts, ideas, problems, and plans, but now he was lucky to get a short note commenting on the weather. About three years ago everything seemed to change between them, and John had been distant ever since. What did I do, Pat asked, to offend you so?

John's anger turned to irritation. His reaction was, essentially, "I don't want to talk about it now. I'm writing you a letter, and you should get it Tuesday." He went back to Joyous Garde and wrote to Pat:

> As for your suggestion of my inconstancy with mea culpa overtones, it seems to me that this was your late ulcer talking and I refuse to argue with an ulcer.
>
> Let's suppose I have an ulcer too and our ulcers get to arguing. Yours says—"You don't love me as you used to what have I done to deserve this?" And my ulcer says "Not so. It is you who have changed. I have remained constant."
>
> God damn it, Pat, that's school-girl talk and school girl thinking—fine for my kids at 16 but not good enough for two men

whose years should give them better counsel. Of course we have changed. If we hadn't it would be either a lie or an abnormality. I know I get tired when I used to be tireless. I am short tempered where I used to be calm and calm where I used to blow my top. That's simply age—to be accepted, not mourned over. I consider the body of my work and I do not find it good. That doesn't mean a thing except that the impulses have changed. If I have any more work in me, which I sometimes doubt, it will have to be of a kind to match my present age. I'm not the young writer of promise any more. I'm a worked-over claim. . . .

You say that about three years ago something happened and you are trying to find some blame in yourself, perhaps. Well, you know damn well what happened three years ago. I collapsed and got taken to the hospital. I don't know what it was and neither do you but I do know that something happened and that I never returned as I went in. Whatever it was made a change. Maybe maturity hit me and required an explosion to make me aware of it. [7/14/64]

He went on to say that he was not singling out Pat for neglect—he was neglecting everybody—and it was true that he had not been writing very many letters, nor had he been seeing very many people. The problem in terms of sending some of his writing to Pat was that he didn't have any writing to send. He had sent a copy of his most recent piece, the little essay that he had done on the origins of *The Moon Is Down*; he had even sent a copy of one of his letters to Mrs. Kennedy. Pat had his greatest joy in sharing in the work process of his authors, particularly John. John's creativity was almost his life's blood, and he could not believe that it was nearly played out.

In one of his last letters to John, sent in mid-August, Pat's plea was pathetic in its urgency: "It would be good if some time soon you sent me a chapter or two of your new writing. I need that badly for my morale" [8/13/64]. At the end of August, John sent him a tape of President Johnson's acceptance speech—it was all he had to send—and Pat responded with characteristic enthusiasm:

I know you are capable of tremendous work, but this was colossal. I listened to his acceptance speech, and I recognized the cadence and rhythm and phrases that were yours. He is no orator and he muffed many a fine line, nevertheless, it was a telling speech and his main points came over with downright conviction. [9/2/64]

At John's invitation, Pat and Dorothy Covici went to Washington on September 14 for the White House ceremony at which John and twenty-nine others received the Medal of Freedom. Just a month later, on October 14, Pascal Covici was dead.

For John the death was unexpected and a heavy blow, one that hit him harder than any other loss in recent years, except perhaps for Capa. For all the irritation that John felt in response to Pat's various stratagems, John had come to love very deeply the man who for thirty years had always been there, had always on his side. Pat's spirit had been indomitable, and his spirit had helped to carry John through the many bad times, through the self-doubt and despair, to an extraordinary career. Pat always believed, and there is absolutely nothing more important in this world to an artist than to have at least one person in his life who believes.

On the occasion of John's fifty-sixth birthday, Pat had written,

> That you were born and in some small way I have been of use to you in bringing your books to light means a great deal to me, possibly infinitely more than you may ever realize.
>
> When I look back at the long list of your books I am truly astounded. And if you don't write another book, you have written your name in American literature for as long as the human race can read. For you, too, have the poetry, the compassion, the laughter and tears we find in Cervantes, and Dickens and Mark Twain. A reading of your work will always add something new to one's imagination and will always have something to say. [2/12/58]

The service for Pat was in a small private room in a funeral chapel. John, Saul Bellow, and Arthur Miller spoke in tribute to the editor they shared. Elaine remembers that when it was John's turn to speak, "Never was a man so nervous," and when he was through, he told Elaine, "I'll never, ever do this again." In a voice that caught and croaked, he said:

> Pat Covici was much more than my friend. He was my editor. Only a writer can understand how a great editor is father, mother, teacher, personal devil and personal god. For thirty years Pat was my collaborator and my conscience. He demanded of me more than I had and thereby caused me to be more than I should have been without him.

To relieve his grief John and Elaine flew to California for a family reunion in Watsonville. (John wrote to Dook inviting him to join them at his sister's house, but Dook replied "that was too damned many Steinbecks" for him to handle all in one place. John borrowed Mary's Cadillac, and he and Elaine drove up to see him instead.) Back from California, John gave up work on *America and Americans* temporarily to work on President Johnson's inaugural address. Almost all his work ended up "on the cutting room floor." This made him angry, despite expressions of gratitude for his efforts, and he decided he could function better as the "loyal opposition," communicating occasionally with the President from a position of independent observation.

The Steinbecks were in New York that fall only a few weeks before they were off once again to Europe. John Huston invited them to come to his home in Ireland for Christmas, and they decided to go on from Ireland after New Year's to London and Paris for a several-week winter holiday.

John Huston liked good food, good drink and lots of it, good company and lots of it, and beautiful surroundings, which usually included one or more beautiful women. He had purchased a half-ruined house, St. Claren's, in County Galway, and spent a fortune restoring it, rebuilding it so well that it was written about and photographed as one of the most beautiful Georgian houses to be found anywhere. During the time that the Steinbecks were there, people came and went, some flying in from London, Paris, or Rome for just a day or two.

John and Elaine went to dinner parties hosted by Huston and to parties at other houses in the neighborhood. Huston was Master of the Hounds of the Galway Hunt, and the Steinbecks on a couple of occasions followed the hunt. But there was time, too, to soak up the atmosphere, to walk and to talk. John, in recalling the trip later for Dook, wrote, "The west country isn't left behind—it's rather as though it ran concurrently but in a nonparallel time. I feel that I would like to go back there. It has a haunting kind of recognition quotient" [2/2/65].

In the basement of his home, Huston had built a Japanese bath, and he and Steinbeck did much of their talking while relaxing in the hot water. Just as with Frank Loesser, Steinbeck sometimes discussed with Huston projects they might do together, although their plans, as with his speculations with Loesser, never came to anything—it was almost a kind of creative game. During this visit Steinbeck became interested in a story that came out of the history of Huston's house. He thought he might make a short novel of it, which, in turn, might be used as the basis for a movie script for Huston.

St. Claren's had been owned by an English family, the Burkes. One spring evening in 1820, when James Hardiman Burke was riding home from his land holdings, he was shot at from the bushes beside the road, and a young Irish rebel named Anthony Daly was arrested on trumped-up evidence. The story concerns his heroic behavior and martyrdom at the hands of English justice—a very colorful tale, but a bit too romantic, one would suspect, for Steinbeck at this stage of his career.

However, he did seriously consider writing it, since the story contained what he called "truth" and the "real," that is, it dealt with the heroic possibilities in man—what we might call the "Arthurian dimension." In a thank-you note to Huston, John wrote from London:

> I think often of Daly. And please believe me, I don't want to make a motion picture. But I do have still the hunger to make something beautiful and true. And I have the feeling that in this story are all the beauties and all the truths including the aching lustful ones. And so I'll write the little tale as well as I can and we will see whether the sound and color of it will translate to the visual. It does seem to me that in the late scramble for reality, writers have somehow overlooked the real. [1/5/65]

From London the Steinbecks went to Paris. During their trip they had been dogged by a certain amount of dread: Elaine's favorite aunt, who was quite old, seemed to be dying, and John's sister Mary had had three cancer operations and was getting weaker. The Steinbecks were staying in Paris with Leslie and Mary Brady (he had been the cultural attaché in Moscow during their visit there), and early one morning, she knocked on the door and handed Elaine a telegram edged in black. She opened it, as John looked up from the bed and asked hopefully, "Aunt Sally?" "Mary," she replied.

Elaine recalls, "I thought he was a goner then. He took it very, very hard, harder I guess than any . . . the loved sister, the one he really loved the most, the one he was closest to." Each death seemed to take a little more out of him, and the feeling that everyone he loved was leaving him began to overtake him.

It was typical that they had gone to Europe in part out of his restlessness in response to his inability to get any writing done, and once he was in Europe, it wasn't long before he was restless again, this time anxious to get home and back to work. He wrote to Elizabeth before leaving Paris:

> The mail [McIntosh and Otis was handling his mail while they were gone] must have been dreadful. I wonder whether it is neces-

sary to answer. Hemingway and Faulkner never answered anyone.

One thing might be suggested—that I am not home when I get home. I simply must try to get to work. The whole year and more has gone to politics and I am very tired of politics. I don't even think I have learned anything I didn't know from having read Machiavelli. [1/20/65]

His plan was to attack *America and Americans* with vigor, get it out of the way by summer, and then working at Sag Harbor through the summer into the fall, write a large chunk of the *Arthur*. He was, he wrote Huston and his assistant, Gladys Hill, in February, "taking 'the American' apart like a watch to see what makes him tick and some very curious things are emerging."

Elaine was called to Texas because the death of her aunt seemed imminent, and John was left alone in the apartment without even a dog for company, since Charley had died. The rain poured down, and it was so dark inside, he had to turn on the lights. In his misery he invented a new way to make enchiladas and named them *"Enchiladas a'l Cielo, hecho por la mano de Dios"* (enchiladas from heaven, made by the hand of God). John and Elaine did not write each other, thinking that any moment her aunt would be gone and she could come home, but after several days, he decided to write anyway, and he reported his lack of activity in great detail:

Life Magazine called today. They're doing a piece about Günter Grass. Asked me for two paragraphs. I said no.

June Havoc called. Has a radio show. Guess what she wanted! I said no.

Gina Lolla what you call it, phoned. Asked me to run off with her. I said no. [2/65]

He had put out the word that he wasn't going to go out while Elaine was gone, but urgent invitations finally pulled him to dinner at the Loessers', the Benchleys', and at Elizabeth's.

By mid-April of 1965, he was coming to the end of the first draft of his essays on America. He wrote his agent:

I know there is lots of work to be done on it, but I think it is good. I know I have been fascinated with it as it went down and I shall be sorry to finish it. . . .

Once it is down [I] will inspect it and add and subtract but the meat will be there. I should have it ready well before we move out here for the summer and then I can get to the Arthur which finally begins to grow and grow in my mind in the manner we spoke of but going much further. For the first time I have some confidence in it. And I can have the whole of the summer and fall to work on it. I am pretty excited about that too. The rains seem to be coming back after the long drought. And I never think they will. It always seems permanent.

His new beginning on the *Arthur* was delayed that summer until after the Whalers Festival. He was scheduled to judge the debate between New Bedford, Nantucket, and Sag Harbor, the whaleboat races, and a local beauty contest. When he was asked to do this last task, he told the committee he would be happy to do it providing the customary *droit du seigneur* was given him. They said sure, that would be fine.

For two years he had tried to get the President to make an appearance at the Festival, but had been unsuccessful. This second refusal was apparently somewhat embarrassing, because they sent a coast guard cutter instead. Jack Valenti wrote, "Sending a ship won't substitute for the President, but at least it helps your batting average, my friend."

John's letters that summer indicate that his new attempt at the *Arthur* was not a revision or continuation of his translation, but just what form his manuscript did take is not made clear, since no one saw the material or heard him read from it. Some clues to the nature of the manuscript he had planned do come out in a long, thoughtful letter to Eugène Vinaver in July.

He had occasion to write Vinaver after a lapse of some months in their correspondence, when the idea came to him that it might be possible to discover neglected or unrecognized Arthurian manuscript material in one of the private libraries of England's old aristocratic families. In late June he had written to Douglas Fairbanks, Jr., who was well acquainted with many titled families, to ask his help in locating these libraries and gaining access to them. Fairbanks shared John's enthusiasm for the Arthurian legends and had already reported some progress by the time John wrote Vinaver two weeks later:

I am moving along very slowly in my ms which I am calling as a working title The Matter of Arthur. It is such an outrageous approach that I want to have a lot of it done before anyone sees any of it. The reason for this is that there must be enough of it to bring its force to bear—or not—as the case may be. . . .

In all the years of fruitless exploring (not unlike a bumble bee in a bell jar) I come back again and again to one thought, planted perhaps when I was nine years old and never far away from me. And that thought is that the matter of Arthur is essentially a subjective matter. Geoffrey knew Arthur as belonging to his time or shortly before. Malory writes and thinks of a 15th century Arthur—Cretien speaks of his time and I, heaven help me, can only think of the Round Table as having existed in Salinas, California, around the turn of the 20th century. Caesar thought of his ancestress, Venus, as having been not so long before.

In all cases the manners, attitudes, techniques, weaponry and practices are contemporary, but the ethics, virtues, and codes of conduct belong to a recent past which has been violated and abandoned. Thus Arthur by his nature is a critic of the shortcoming of the present and his very existence criticizes our failures. . . .

This thesis has haunted me for a long time, first as a pestering thing but now I have accepted it and in the workings of my new work—the Matter of Arthur is the Matter of Me. In all of it I find myself. And I incline to the thought that it has always been so. The Wasteland was surely in the brilliantly dry and despairing mind of Eliot. Malory would have found it incomprehensible. Very well then—the humanity of Arthur ties us to him and our engagement with our times tie him to us. No 20th century man can write anything but a 20th or at least a 19th century Arthur. Once that is accepted, a large part of the barrier goes down. As long as my squyre is my sickker sistyr Sir Marye, I am on known and faithful ground. When I leave it, I have left the Matter of Arthur behind. . . .

The summer is quite beautiful here. Our garden is better than it has ever been. I don't go fishing as often as I could wish. I find myself bound to these yellow pads. I shall work here through the summer and into the autumn, and then in the winter I shall go to Ireland and of course to England. By that time I shall be ready for a break. But if I can be of any help in turning over the collections of the poor inheritors of a richer time, I would find it possible to come to you at any time. If only we could come on even a fragment of a pre-Caxton Malory, it would be a joy. [7/6/65]

The topic of the war in Vietnam began to surface in Steinbeck's letters to presidential assistant Jack Valenti during the spring of 1965. In part because of his relationship to the President, in part because of his sons' involvement in the war, and in part because he saw the controversy over the war as a demonstration of his ideas concerning the decay of our culture, Vietnam would become the topic that would dominate his writing during the last years of his life. His reactions to the war, however, would follow a curve, from great doubt about our involvement, to very strong support of our policy—particularly in defense of the integrity of our troops in Vietnam—and finally to doubt once again about the wisdom of our participation.

As much doubt as he had, at the beginning and the end, he never felt that what we were doing in Vietnam was immoral, except insofar as war itself was immoral. He saw our actions as inspired by idealism (at the end he thought of it as a misguided idealism), an attempt to help men who wanted to remain free do so. And our behavior was certainly in no way less moral than that of the North Vietnamese, the Chinese, or the Russians. If the war was wrong, it was wrong for both sides.

The roots of his attitude toward the war can be found in his experiences in Russia, which led him to think of that kind of totalitarianism as the worst fate that any society might have to endure—the complete lack of freedom, the thought control, and the gray conformity enforced by ever-present fear was a complete hell on earth. Attempts by Russia and China to extend this state was to him the ultimate immorality to be resisted by free men everywhere at whatever cost necessary.

He saw little connection between the totalitarianism of Communist Russia and the social programs of the New Deal in this country or the democratic socialism of countries in Europe. The Soviet Union, with its purges and political imprisonments, was far closer in his mind to Nazi Germany than to socialist Sweden. This was not a new attitude for him, but one that grew more intense as he grew older, not because he became more conservative, but because more information about Russia under Stalin became available and he saw Russia's excuses for repression to have less and less validity. But the politics of these matters, which concerned doctrines and justifications, were of little ultimate importance to him—what he cared about was actual human behavior, that is, what people do to help or hurt other people.

It is important in this regard to remember that he never lost his biological perspective, although in some of his later work little explicit reference to that perspective is made. Nevertheless, in the last serious essay he wrote, in *America and Americans*, he warns, "Perhaps we will have to inspect mankind as a species, not with our usual awe at how wonderful we are but with the cool and neutral attitude we reserve for all things save ourselves." It is this perspective that tended to reduce political considerations to matters which in the long view were ephemeral and superficial.

His attitude toward the war was also shaped by the "Arthurian thrust" of his thought during the last decade of his life which led him through what might be called his "moral trilogy"—*The Winter of Our Discontent, Travels with Charley,* and *America and Americans.* "Arthur" came to mean for him that quality in the human organism, a quality only man possessed, that emerges in adversity to show—as he said of President Kennedy—the best that is in us. All organisms thrive best in responding to the challenge of some adversity, but humans are able to face adversity through resources of the spirit; man's proven capacity, as he stated in his Nobel Prize speech, "for greatness of heart . . . for gallantry in defeat—for courage, compassion, and love."

Those who would understand not only Steinbeck's perception of the Vietnam war, but his canon from beginning to end, would do well to read *America and Americans,* particularly the essay on morality, "Americans and the Future," written during the months of July through October 1965. At the center of that essay he writes:

John Kennedy said his famous lines, "Do not ask what your country can do for you but what you can do for your country," and the listening nation nodded and smiled in agreement. But he did not say it because it might happen but because it is happening and in increasing volume. And it is historically true that a nation whose people take out more than they put in will collapse and disappear.

Why are we on this verge of moral and hence nervous collapse? One can only have an opinion based on observation plus a reading of history. I believe it is because we have reached the end of a road and have no new path to take, no duty to carry out and no purpose to fulfill. The primary purpose of mankind has always been to survive in a natural world which has not invariably been friendly to us. In our written, remembered and sensed history, there has always been more work to do than we could do. Our needs were greater than their possible fulfillment. Our dreams were so improbable that we moved their reality into heaven. Our ailments, our agonies, and our sorrows were so many and so grievous that we accepted them either as inevitable or as punishments for our manufactured sins.

What happened to us came quickly and quietly, came from many directions and was the more dangerous because it wore the face of good. Almost unlimited new power took the place of straining muscles and bent backs. Machinery took the heavy burden from our shoulders. Medicine and hygiene cut down infant mortality almost to the vanishing point, and at the same time extended our life span. Automation began to replace our workers. Where once the majority of our people worked the land, machines, chemistry and a precious few produced more food than we needed or could possibly use. Leisure which again had been the property of heaven, came to us before we knew what to do with it and all of these good things falling on us unprepared constitute calamity. We have the things and we have not had time to develop a way of thinking about them. We struggle with our lives in the present and our practices in the long and well-learned past.

Those Americans fighting the war in Vietnam seemed to Steinbeck to be the best among us. They displayed for him the same kind of nobility born of adversity as his characters faced in dealing with the Dust Bowl, the banks, and the jeers of native Californians. Our soldiers were fighting for the survival of others and for human dignity against those who would take it away, and they were doing so within a hostile environment, against a brutal and totally ruthless enemy, and with many restrictions on how they could fight and with less than total support and appreciation at home. Like the characters in his novels of the thirties, our soldiers were similarly victims and heroes—victims because they were plain folk caught in a mess beyond their control and because, like the Okies, they were reviled, and heroes because in the face of terrible discouragement, they were capable of great courage and sacrifice beyond the mere letter of duty.

Steinbeck saw the President in the same light. Despised equally by conservatives, intellectuals, and liberals, and vilified by the anti-war protestors, he moved to do what he thought was right, guided by principle and sustained by little more than his own courage. Steinbeck wrote to him at the time that his younger son, John, was going overseas in 1966:

I know that you must be disturbed by the demonstrations against policy in Vietnam. But please remember that there have always been people who insisted on their right to choose the war in which they would fight to defend their country. There were many who would have no part of Mr. Adams' and George Washington's war. We call them Tories. There were many also who called General Jackson a butcher. Some of these showed their disapproval by selling beef to the British. Then there were the very many who denounced and even impeded Mr. Lincoln's war. We call them Copperheads. I remind you of these things, Mr. President, because sometimes, the shrill squeaking of people who simply do not wish to be disturbed must be saddening to you. I assure you that only mediocrity escapes criticism. [5/28/66]

As for the war protestors, he saw them as a mixed group and had varying reactions to them. He had contempt for the Marxists, who praised and admired the enemy, who saw everything done by the North Vietnamese and the Viet Cong as pure, and who accused our troops of being deliberate murderers of babies. He admired and agreed in theory with those few who genuinely opposed all war and deplored the actions of both sides. He disagreed with friends who thought our presence in Vietnam was wrong and our role there immoral. In some cases, they agreed to disagree; in other cases, they simply avoided the topic; and in still other cases, he lost friends and was shunned by acquaintances.

On a less personal level, he strongly disapproved of the young people who vilified our soldiers, attacked the integrity of the President, and cheered the burning of draft cards. This to him was the product of an overly affluent America—spoiled and self-centered children who affected to be acting by principle, but whose only principles in fact were self-indulgence and self-preservation at the expense of others. They were the equivalent of those who close their windows to the screams of a victim being assaulted on the street outside their door. He was reinforced in these perceptions by the sight of the sons of the upper middle class and wealthy going to college and burning their draft cards, while the sons of the lower middle class and the poor went to war. Worst of all was the intense self-righteousness of these sudden converts to religion, morality, and conscientiousness.

When John got word that Adlai Stevenson had died on July 14, it was yet another blow, but there seemed to be always in his grief an element of anger. To Jack Valenti he wrote, "My first reaction to his death was one of rage that Americans had been too stupid to avail themselves of his complete ability" [7/16/65]. He put the case even more strongly to Eugène Vinaver when he wrote, "Many people loved him and many more are only now discovering his worth. It is one of the sad things about our nation that it has a number of times turned down our best men and elected the second rate" [7/65].

During the campaigns, John recalled, Stevenson had told him that he was "in charge of keeping him off balance, and he insisted that all public servants should be kept off balance all the time." Following the campaigns, the two saw each other several times each year, sometimes in Paris or London, but usually in New York. The Governor would come into town quietly and go to the Steinbecks for a long evening of talk and speculation. He was, John wrote Dook, "the kind of man who could sit in the gutter with a glass of wine and discuss things and he often did." When he became ambassador to the United Nations, the Steinbecks saw him more often. He would invite them to dinner on the servants' night out—Elaine and Marietta Tree would cook dinner—so that they could relax, even in the embassy suite of the Waldorf Towers.

In addition to being his friend, Stevenson became the representation for him of American politics brought to its highest level. Just as Dag Hammarskjöld had embodied for him the spirit of peace and world cooperation that might be achieved through patience and determination, so Stevenson came to stand for the possibility of a national policy that was rational and compassionate. With the death of each, some measure of hope within his spirit dimmed.

At first John did not intend to go to any of the memorial services, but then he realized that Stevenson would have paid him the honor if the situation were reversed. At this point the President called to ask him to Camp David for the weekend, and John declined, explaining that he was going to attend the service at the United Nations. Then the President said he wanted John and Elaine to accompany him on his trip to Bloomington for the funeral. John tried to decline again, but the President added, "I want to talk to you." John realized that the President was using him, but he was also sure that the President would know that he knew—with Steinbeck, Johnson would feel more comfortable attending the funeral of a man whom he had not treated well.

Johnson wanted to ask him at Camp David to serve as his special emissary, to go to Vietnam, observe and ask questions, and then report back to him. John didn't know what to say—the last thing in the world he wanted to do was to go to Vietnam, especially as an emissary of the President. Although he would defend the President and his policies if he thought they were right, he was determined he would do so as an independent, not as an appendage.

In Sag Harbor John worked on revisions of his essays, on the concluding essay, "Americans and the Future," and on "The Matter of Arthur." Progress on the latter, as he reported to Elizabeth several times during these months, was slow. He also still had in the back of his mind the idea that he might write a novelette about the death of Anthony Daly, and during the summer another publication idea came to him.

Several years earlier he and Pat, at Pat's suggestion, had talked of the possibility of publishing the journal he had kept while writing *East of Eden*. Nothing had come of it, but now, he told Elizabeth, it occurs to me that someone is going to publish it some time. It is one hell of a lot better than Henry Miller's letters. I wonder if we should not think of doing it now so that we could take advantage of it if there is any and I do think it would have some currency. Elaine has read it and she agrees. It is a fascinating account of the making of a book. So I am going to give it to Shirley this weekend both to read herself and to take to you to read.

Although everyone agreed that it should be done, it was felt that John should do some work on it first, and he never got back to it, resulting in its posthumous publication as *Journal of a Novel*.

On the domestic front, John had acquired a new dog, a bull terrior he named Angel (after Angier Biddle Duke), who turned out to be, perhaps, the best dog of all. That summer he wrote his doctor, Denton Cox:

> I never had such an agreeable beast. He is thoughtful, kind, faithful, and very funny. Furthermore, he enjoys his own jokes. He laughs all the time. . . . He is a most loving dog. Sometimes asleep, flat on his back, he dreams of love, wakes up, and flings himself in my lap. . . . I never had a dog like him—he listens and he can enjoy people and things without taking center. What human can make this claim? His manners are so good that when we are asked to dinner he is included. . . . I don't like trick dogs but by himself he learned when we say, "Let's go Mets!" he leaps into the air and runs in circles. I wish the Mets could learn this trick.

For Elaine's birthday John had a swimming pool built for her in the middle of the lawn between the house and Joyous Garde, and to go with it, he made a stepping stone on which he inscribed Lancelot's last words to Guinevere: "Ladye, I take reccorde of God, in thee I have myn erthly joye." But he soon encountered a problem he hadn't anticipated: local and migrating birds, particularly ducks, seemed pleased to use the pool as a travel stop and rest room. It became a sanitation problem that no amount of yelling and arm waving could solve, so it became a not uncommon sight to neighbors or visitors to see John rushing out wildly from the house, his robe flapping behind him, to fire his brass cannon. On the other hand, he was delighted when birds saw fit to use his property for nesting, and one afternoon Joe Bryan witnessed the unlikely sight of a duck leading her ducklings straight through the Sag Harbor house.

In the late summer he received a job offer from Harry F. Guggenheim, the publisher of *Newsday* on Long Island, to write a column that would involve documentation so that he could write off his trip to Europe that winter plus earn several hundred dollars for each piece, depending on the number of outlets signed up for syndication. Steinbeck would write letters, running usually from eight hundred to a thousand words whenever he found a subject and was moved to write about it. There would be no deadlines, no rigid schedule.

As it turned out, the job lasted far longer than he had anticipated. The articles ran from November of 1965 through May 1966 and from December 1966 through May 1967, averaging about four a month, although in one month, January 1967, he sent in nine. The series was titled "Letters to Alicia"—Alicia was Guggenheim's late wife, Alicia Patterson Guggenheim, who was publisher of *Newsday* from its founding in 1940 until her death in 1963. He wrote to Guggenheim: "When I tell you I intended to write these letters to Alicia, I meant just that. It is not mawkish or sentimental. The letters would not be to someone who is dead, but rather to a living mind and a huge curiosity. That is why she was such a great newspaper woman. She wanted to know—everything."

Although he would not have consciously admitted it to himself, since he always had plans for the future, the column came at just the right time. "The Matter of Arthur" was going nowhere, although he had not yet given up on it, and beyond it he had nothing of book length that he cared about doing. Indeed, even what he had intended to say in "The Matter of Arthur" may have already been said, in a different form, in *America and Americans.* But he badly needed some writing project in order to continue to function, and in many ways the column met his situation and needs perfectly.

He still had his curiosity and interest in—as he said about Alicia Guggenheim—everything, and his ability to observe and to present his observations from his own unique perspective with style, modest grace, and humor. And perhaps most important at this stage, he had a number of bits and pieces of things that he had stored up and had never had occasion to use. As he noted in one of his early columns, in answer to Max Lerner's question as to why he had "succumbed to the fatal itch and joined the gaggle of columnists":

Maybe it's like this, Max—you know how, when you are working on a long and ordered piece, all sorts of bright and lovely ideas and images intrude. They have no place in what you are writing, and so if you are young, you write them in a notebook for future use. And you never use them because they are sparkling and alive like colored pebbles on a wave-washed shore. It's impossible not to fill your pockets with them. But when you get home, they are dry and colorless. I'd like to pin down a few while they are still wet.

Although the column started on November 20, he began writing it several weeks before so that by the time they arrived in London on December 1, he would be three or four columns ahead. After ten days in London, they would drive north to Manchester where they would pick up the Vinavers and then go further north for their tour of private libraries. He wrote to Eugène in November, "I can't tell you how excited I am about this trip or quest. If we turn up nothing at all, it will still be wonderful. Aren't you looking forward to it?" [11/2/65].

Although Douglas Fairbanks had arranged for the Steinbecks and Vinavers to make their search for undiscovered or neglected Arthurian manuscripts through several private libraries, John and Eugène agreed that their most likely candidate was the library at Alnwick Castle near the Scottish border, the principal residence of the Percy family, who had been there since shortly after the Norman Conquest. It was evening by the time they arrived in their Rover sedan, the huge Norman keep before them barely visible in the fading light.

They drove through two sets of gates, opened for them by a gatekeeper, and on into the bailey. In the house they were welcomed by the Duke of Northumberland, who had just come back from a hunt. The library, the size of a very large drawing room, had a great stone fireplace and was impressively furnished with antique furniture. Books lined the walls on the ground level, and there was another story and a half of them above an encircling gallery with movable library steps. At the very least it contained twenty thousand books, and as for the visitors' hopes of finding something overlooked, they were, unfortunately, well cared for and meticulously catalogued.

After a night, a day, and part of another evening searching, Eugène found a curious catalogue entry for a bound manuscript that indicated that there might be something different in kind bound with the historical material listed. But the volume couldn't be found—the Duke even got on his hands and knees to search around at the bottom of the cases. Since it was late, they all went to bed, but the next morning, John was awakened by a soft knock on his door. In the half-light of the winter morning, Eugène stood there, smiling and a little pale, and said, "Come down. I've found something."

Restless, Eugène had come down early to the library and had gone to the same case they had searched the night before. He had reached up in the near-darkness, withdrawn a volume, and carried it to the light on the catalogue rest. He showed it to John: it was the volume they had been looking for. Vinaver leafed through the manuscript, page by page, and then suddenly that material was cut off and a new manuscript began. Forty-eight pages long, it started with a list of legendary kings and ended with the death of Arthur, his transport to Avalon, and the prophecy of his return: "There it is—a completely unknown manuscript, our pot of gold. We showed it to the Duke, who came in dressed in hunting pinks, ready to ride to hounds, and he went to the door of my wife's room and called to her, 'They've caught the fox!' "

The manner of the discovery was remarkable, but so was the appearance of the manuscript: the script appeared to be exactly like that of the Winchester Malory. And the sequence of wonders continued. Leaving Alnwick, the Steinbecks and Vinavers drove on across the Scottish border to visit the library at Sir Walter Scott's house at Abbotsford, where they came across a little book printed in 1582 which was an attempt to prove that King Arthur really existed. In it was quoted, word for word, a passage from the manuscript they had discovered the day before.

All of this was extremely exciting to John, who thought of these interlocking events as something close to magical. He very rapidly wrote two columns about his adventures for *Newsday* so as to have time to show them to Eugène before they parted, the Steinbecks to go to Ireland and the Vinavers to France. In his second article, John concluded:

> This [the scene at Abbotsford] and the dark Norman keep at Alnwick will be with us while we dig out meanings and suggestions from the ancient words set down by the scriverner, so it will be no dread and dusty record we stir, but something robust and young and as related to us as the seed is to the plant. For, if these wonderings do nothing else, they do stretch out for us the breakless line of continuity. What was, is and will be. Dragons and sorcerers— bombs and dark and devious plots. We read in the old records that it has never been easy, but we exist, which seems to mean that it is not hopeless.

After spending Christmas at St. Claren's with Huston, the Steinbecks began a tour of Ireland. Driving south they stopped at Ennis in County Clare, and the next day went out to Hag's Head, a point that sticks out into the Atlantic below Galway Bay, for a picnic. It was the anniversary of Mary's death, and John went out walking by himself along the cliffs overlooking the ocean. As he looked out across the edge of the water, the curve of the valley, and from head to sea head, he could see no living thing except the gulls that sailed along the cliffs. Perhaps it was the magical discovery of the Arthur, perhaps Ireland, or perhaps it was just Steinbeck, but when he returned he told Elaine that he had had an experience with Mary, that he had been with her and talked with her.

When they had finished their tour and returned to Dublin, John found that a great deal had happened in regard to the Alnwick manuscript while he was out of touch. Word of the discovery, perhaps from the duke, had leaked to the London *Sunday Times,* and the *Daily Mail,* which had contracted for John's column, feeling that it was being beaten on a story, took John's material and expanding on it somewhat, pushed it into the news columns. Somehow—perhaps because John had mentioned the Malory manuscripts and of the similarity in script between the Alnwick and Winchester manuscripts—the idea was spread in the London papers and from there into the wire services, that a third Malory manuscript had been discovered. It had nothing to do with Malory, of course, but was apparently a pre-Malory prose account of the Arthur legend.

When Eugène returned from France, he found himself in the middle of a terrible hullabaloo, which surprised and shocked him. He had the impression that John's articles would only be published in America and that nothing would appear in the British press until he had had a chance to study the manuscript at some length. In mid-January he wrote the Duke:

> [Steinbeck's] literary agent was clearly more interested in selling the story to the *Daily Mail* than in safeguarding the interests of scholarship. I only hope that as a result of this you have not been hounded by the reporters as much as I have. They have made my life hardly worth living and have in the end distorted the whole thing beyond recognition. Even my publishers, the Clarendon Press, have fallen into the trap to the extent of offering to re-set my new edition of Malory on the basis of the Alnwick manuscript! [1/11/66]

Apparently Vinaver was reluctant to blame Steinbeck, so instead he blamed Graham Watson, thinking that as an "agent" he would be interested only in the money and publicity for his client. In fact, Watson had acted in complete honor, thinking that Vinaver was leaving John out on a limb. No one is sure how the *Times* got the story, but the *Daily Mail* had already been contracted for, and neither John nor Graham had been responsible for the erroneous announcement. Graham went to Vinaver, after Vinaver had refused to comment to the press, to get him to back up John's story as John had written it, but Vinaver refused, feeling that he had been double-crossed and that his reputation was being abused.

So there was nearly complete misunderstanding all the way around, as well as hard feelings. To make things somewhat worse, it turned out that John's initial claim of "a completely unknown manuscript" was not entirely accurate. It had been microfilmed shortly after the war along with the other manuscripts at Alnwick, and copies went to the British Museum and Library of Congress, although apparently no one had as yet paid any attention to it.

John was upset that the *Sunday Times*, having made a low bid for the columns, would have jumped in and taken the meat for nothing; that he should have been misunderstood; that there was enmity between Vinaver and Watson, and that, by implication, Vinaver was distressed by his behavior. This last was particularly painful, since he was very fond of Vinaver and had great admiration for him. He wrote him, "I would do anything in my power to antidote the 'poison.' I will get out of the whole field if you think I am an interloper. . . . I am miserable if I have been a cause of unease or unhappiness to you" [1/15/66].

It had been an unlikely conjunction from the beginning, the cautious, meticulous, unworldly scholar and the impulsive, enthusiastic, worldly author-journalist. Without harsh words on either side, a breach developed between them that was never healed during John's lifetime, but when *The Acts of Arthur* was published after John's death, Vinaver went on the BBC to praise it.

In London John asked Elaine to call Harry Guggenheim and tell him that they were coming home. Elaine made the call, and Guggenheim said, "Ask John if he'd like to go on to Israel." John replied, "No, I'm tired, and I want to go home." (He wrote Elizabeth that he wanted to get home in time to plant his seedlings too early, just as he usually did.) Later, Elaine said to him that "after nearly six weeks in Ireland, in this dying civilization of lovely people with their lovely sentimentality, there is nothing in the world I'd like to see as a whole bunch of smart, energetic Jews." That made him laugh, and he said, "Let's go."

They had to wait for nearly a week before the next nonstop plane, so John settled down to write his column. He told Elizabeth:

> I want to try to get off some writing today if I can, some kind of a transition thing. Wakened with a funny idea but I don't know if it will work. I'll probably give it a try and throw it out if it doesn't.
>
> It's 9:30 and Elaine is still sleeping. I couldn't find my bathrobe in the dark so I am writing in a raincoat. Just as good.

The transition piece he wrote was a "colored pebble" that he had kept in his pocket a long time—the story of his great-grandfather Dickson's sojourn to the Holy Land to convert the Jews to Christianity.

They arrived just after February 1, 1966, and John found himself nearly overwhelmed: "The impact of the country is stunning. The energy of the people is incredible. . . . We are seeing too much to report. It will take time to iron it out. . . . This experience is like being trampled by the past while trying to catch up with the future" [2/5/66]. This last rings of Lincoln Steffens's statement when he returned from Russia, "I have been over into the future, and it works." But as John wrote to Elizabeth near the end of their visit, "These people are really doing the things the Russians are lying about" [2/19/66].

It is also significant that while Russia was intent on erasing any consciousness of the past from the minds of its people, here the past and the future were intimately joined—as they had always been in the mind of Steinbeck, biologist and historian. Israel was the animal that had survived, adapted, and became stronger through adversity; the U.S.S.R. had evolved into an overarmored dinosaur that would perish in the mire of its own self-deceit.

During their stay, the Steinbecks had a car and a driver, Sol Katz, who was also a history teacher. Elaine knew the Bible very well, better than John, and she carried one with her during their tour. Every once in a while, when the driver would say something had happened at a certain place, Elaine would disagree, finally getting out her Bible to read from it. John would laugh and say, "Sol, Sol, you haven't got a prayer." He reported to his agent, "You . . . will be glad to know that E. is in her element. In traveling, she and [Sol Katz], our driver and historian, engage in a sweet and friendly battle the whole time over the Old Testament. . . . Apparently Elaine knew all along that the Old Testament happened here. I think I always thought it was written by King James and by my grandmother" [2/12/66].

They saw everything and talked to people everywhere. John was relaxed, wore his old clothes all the time, and seemed to thrive in the informal atmosphere. They met officials—Teddy Kollek, the Mayor of
Jerusalem, for example—and John did his usual stint for the U.S.I.A.,
meeting with writers, students, and embassy people. (At one of the receptions, he got talking about his great-grandfather's journey to the
Holy Land and found out from one of the embassy staff that in a book
called *Journal of a Visit to Europe and the Levant,* Herman Melville
talks about meeting and talking to "Deacon Dickson" on his Holy Land
farm.) But they also made friends at various *kibbutzim* and even just
walking down the street.

One day they came out of their hotel in Tel Aviv and had to walk by
a boarded-up construction site nearby. On the boards was written in
chalk, "JOHN STEINBECK! If you want some good home cooking,
go to the corner, turn left, and go on until you come to number ——.
My wife will cook you a good dinner." John said, "Let's go." So they
found the house, knocked on the door, and announced, "Here we are."
John explained that he had an appointment right then, but asked when
they wanted them to come back. They did so the next evening and had
dinner with the family.

Who else but John Steinbeck would evoke such an invitation nearly
anywhere in the world? Or "John Steinberg," as his Israeli friends
began to call him after a humorous column by Ephraim Kishon described John's supposed encounter with a pushy Jerusalem waiter who
insisted on talking to John Steinberg about his novel *Zorba the Greek,*
rather than getting him breakfast.

Of all the many things they saw, the one that seemed to make the
greatest impression on John was Masada, a rock butte near the Dead
Sea where, in 70 A.D., 960 Jews fought off more than twenty thousand
Roman troops, the X Legion and its auxiliaries, for three years. The
Steinbecks drove to Beersheba, where they were met and then given a
tour by Yigael Yadin, the chief archeologist, formerly chief of staff of
the Israeli army.

An account of the siege is given by Flavius Josephus, an account that
sounds like legend, but which was verified in many of its details by the
excavation of the fortress by several thousand volunteer workers from
all over the world, as directed by Yadin. After months of effective Jewish resistance, the Romans had conceived of building a long earthen
ramp up the side of the cliff with the labor of thousands of slaves made
captive upon the fall of Jerusalem. Month after month the ramp crept

closer, as the slaves in an endless line carried their baskets of earth and stone to its forward edge. At last a battering ram was brought up to crush and topple the stone parapet, and then, after the breach had been repaired during the night with timbers and earth, the Romans fired flaming missiles at the new barrier and destroyed it.

The heat was too great for an assault, so the Romans retired to their camp, confident that the next day they would easily overwhelm the few hundred defenders. The defenders, as Steinbeck retells the story (quoting from Josephus), watched their last defense crumble under the flames. Then their leader,

> Elazar Ben Yair, made a long and moving speech. Their wives would be dishonored, he said, their children enslaved. "Let every man give the noble gift of swift death to his family. Then let us burn everything that can be looted. Finally let us die nobly by our own hands, leaving no victims for the Roman rage." His last words ring clearly over the nearly 2000 years. "In company with our wives and children, let us die unenslaved and leave this world as free men." . . . Then, as now—No Alternatives.

Josephus tells that ten men were chosen by lot. Each defender went home, embraced, and mercifully killed his family and then waited to be dispatched by one of the chosen ten. Afterward, the ten came together and chose one by lot, who killed the other nine, set fire to the fortress, and went to his family and killed himself. In the morning when the Roman legion stormed the fort, even the battle-hardened veterans were stunned to find nothing but ashes, silence, and death.

Steinbeck was extremely moved by the story, by the sight of the excavated fortress, and by ten shards of pottery shown to him by Yadin. They had been found together in a corner of a house, under a pile of ashes and rubble. On each, in Hebrew letters, was a male name.

Israel seemed to John to put the cap on what he had written for *America and Americans*, in that it demonstrated exactly what he had said about the survival of nations. Also, as the symbol of Masada clearly indicated, Israel was a country that had learned and taken strength from its own history, while the United States no longer seemed able to do so. Just before leaving for home, he summed up his thoughts about what this country meant to him:

> It seems to me that the Matter of Israel is a reservoir that stores material far more universal than the Fact of Israel. Here, it seems to

me, in this little area of the world is concentrated and almost graphed not only the limits of human experience, the incredible texture of human endurance and the tough inflexibility of human will power, but most important of all, the unlimited horizons of human possibility. All of these facts of our species are here, recorded and happening. And most important, all of these symptoms of survival and success have been fixed and honed and kept sharp by pressure, constant and unremitting pressure from nature, from geography, from accidents and enemies. It is a subject to study when we observe the trials, errors, successes and disappearance of other seemingly more fortunate groups and societies and nations.

The present-day Israeli nation, as apart from historical Jewry, is up to a point an exact replica of America up to the immigration laws of 1924. Here have come and been welcomed the hungry, the hurt, the driven peoples from nations, not the best but the worst, at least from the viewpoint of their places of origin. What we in America found early and have apparently forgotten is that the hungry are ambitious to eat, the hurt and hunted carry the dream of justice, the driven are most likely to make a stand, while only to the ignorant is knowledge an enterable heaven, available as well as desirable. This was our strength and our foundation. It is the core, or most of the core, of the Israeli nation.

CHAPTER XLIX

Like the radio and television detective of years ago, Boston Blackie, who was "a friend to those who made him a friend, enemy to those who made him an enemy," John Steinbeck's friendships and enmities were intense, and seldom was he neutral toward anyone who touched his life or his work in any significant way. His greatest personal virtue and greatest fault were thus tied together; once he loved you, he tended to love you regardless of your faults and offenses, and once he hated you, he would do so with unremitting intensity.

The pattern has its exceptions, but when he loved people, he seemed to take a kind of biological objectivity in regard to what they, as human beings, might do that would hurt or anger him or that he might disapprove of. This was an attitude that prevailed in the long run; for a time he might be angry, quarrel, or cut off relations with them. Such close friends that he associated with under varying circumstances as Toby Street, Bob Capa, Elia Kazan, and Pat Covici had all done things at one time or another that made him angry, irritated him greatly, or caused him severe disappointment.

He stayed with them not just because he believed in loyalty, but because he had a strong feeling of knowing what people were at bottom. When his anger was over, he came to see the occasion for his anger as an accidental, rather than essential quality of the person involved. He would say, "Oh, that's just Pat," or "You know how Capa is."

On the other hand, although he did on several occasions forgive those who had done him great personal wrongs, almost everyone who knew him well recognized that he could be very unforgiving and vengeful. Most people tend, in time, to forget if not forgive, but Steinbeck never forgot, although he might occasionally forgive, and he could take some pleasure in nursing over a lifetime his hatred of someone who had hurt him deeply.

His deepest personal hatred, as one might expect, was held for

Gwyn, and it was so deep that it spilled over from her to nearly anyone who was connected with her, except the boys. He struggled with himself when he saw anyone express traits that he associated with Gwyn, for in his mind such exhibits reflected qualities that represented the inherent nature of the individual, and he had come to believe that Gwyn's was not good. Yet this theory of biological determinism almost allowed him to forgive her, for he felt that because her behavior was so consistent it must be attributable to something so deeply seated that it was beyond her control.

By contrast, for all the grief that Carol had caused him and for all the dislike that he had for her during a certain period of time, he never really hated her and thought at bottom she was a good person. This was a frequent judgment that he made—"good man," "good woman," or "good person"—which had little to do with good or bad in a conventionally moral sense, although it might refer to the person's capacities for those qualities, such as kindness and courage, that he admired. Instead, it was almost a metaphysical judgment of basic character quality.

His greatest hatreds, beyond Gwyn, seemed to be those he felt for people he didn't know personally. It was as if he hated the idea or the essence of the person as he perceived him. For example, he hated Nixon, not, as one might expect, for his political position (he could get along with and even like conservative Republicans—most of his family and many of his friends in Sag Harbor were political conservatives), but because he saw him as basically an evil man.

The archvillain in his gallery of abstract hates was the critic Edmund Wilson. Wilson had been the first major critic to cut deeply into his work, but more than that he felt Wilson was snide, sneering, and personal. Unlike Mary McCarthy (who probably was second on Steinbeck's list and who by some bit of magical poetic justice, in his opinion, became Wilson's wife), who used descriptions like "childish" and "infantile," Wilson was more indirect.

At the end of a 1948 revision of an earlier essay on historical criticism, after proposing that it is after all an emotional reaction to literature that is the critic's "divining rod" in leading him to determining what is good or bad literature, Wilson concludes:

Crude and limited people do certainly feel some such emotion in connection with work that is limited and crude. The man who is more highly organized and has a wider intellectual range will feel it in connection with work that is finer and more complex. The difference between the emotion of the more highly organized man and the emotion of the less highly organized one is merely a matter of gradation. You sometimes discover books—the novels of John Steinbeck, for example—that seem to mark precisely the borderline between work that is definitely superior and work that is definitely bad. When I was speaking a little while back of the genuine connoisseurs who establish the standards of taste, I meant, of course, the people who can distinguish Grade A and who prefer it to the other grades.

This kind of incredible snobbery had great appeal for other critics, especially for those who by temperament were eager to demonstrate their own superior taste. As Wilson's influence spread and reputation grew, Steinbeck's hatred for what he stood for grew.

The novelist not only totally opposed nearly everything philosophically that Wilson seemed to him to represent, but he also felt, as he did about Gwyn and Nixon, that the quality of the man himself at bottom was totally corrupt. On the one hand, John tended to personalize his hatred in petty ways. He attacked Wilson briefly, but without naming him, in several places in his writing. He watched for unflattering references to Wilson in the press and gloried in them. He picked up gossip about the unsavory aspects of Wilson's private life and saw them as confirmations of his opinion. When the critic's novel *Memoirs of Hecate County* came out in 1946, he crowed over its awfulness and for months laughed in great satisfaction in reference to it.

On the other hand, his opposition to Wilson was also principled. The critic represented, or perhaps more accurately led, a movement in criticism that was extremely narrow in its sympathies and that placed emphasis not on the author's intentions or accomplishments but on the intellect and wit of the reviewer or critic in response to selected occasions for the exercise of his wit. But worst of all was the essentially elitist position occupied by Wilson and his followers and imitators.

This position was, Steinbeck was convinced, totally antithetical to what literature was and what it was for. It was destructive and insidiously so, since it was so seductive to the critic's ego. Literature, for Steinbeck, was a bold thing, as natural to humanity as speech, that came out of the people and was written for the people. The Wilson position was not only antidemocratic, but fascistic—for literature not only had the power to entertain, but the power to inspire, to provoke people to thought, and to get them to examine themselves, their lives, and their society. In doing so, *all* people have the power to enliven their existence, to extend their senses and widen their experience, and they have the tools of thought and experience to bring greater vitality, beauty, and justice to their environment.

Good literature in his view had never been what a select few decided in their wisdom was good for the people, nor had it been in our society something that only a few with self-proclaimed special sensibilities could apprehend. It was that which the people in their hearts and minds found meaningful and memorable and carried with them from year to year and passed down from generation to generation. Literature for Steinbeck was the stimulus to caring, the signpost to thought, and the passport to freedom. When he was asked on several occasions, what can we do for the oppressed peoples of Hungary, Poland, Czechoslovakia, East Germany, and Russia, he invariably replied, "Send them books!"

Although it is true in part that the most memorable passages in his Nobel Prize acceptance speech were inspired by personal hurt, it is also true that they constituted a personal declaration of independence and a declaration that literature belongs to humanity. He was proud, not apologetic, to be a writer:

> I am impelled, not to squeak like a grateful and apologetic mouse, but to roar like a lion out of pride in my profession and in the great and good men who have practiced it through the ages.
>
> Literature was not promulgated by a pale and emasculated critical priesthood singing their litanies in empty churches—nor is it a game for the cloistered elect, the tinhorn mendicants of low calorie despair.
>
> Literature is as old as speech. It grew out of human need for it, and it has not changed except to become more needed.

II

Among the good men of the world for Steinbeck was Budd Schulberg, who had had a difficult life in many ways and had emerged part shell-shocked victim, part street fighter, and part genius. The quality of the man, his toughness and caringness, is well illustrated by his founding of the Watts Writers' Workshop.

A month after Watts burned in the summer of 1965, Schulberg went in, the only white man in the middle of intense hostility, determined to do something to help. The only thing he knew how to do was write, but he thought if he could help some of the young blacks to do so, they might be able to get their message out to the world without having to burn down their own houses.

He posted a notice on the bulletin board of a community center, "Creative Writing Class—All Interested Sign Below." Nobody showed up. For weeks he stuck it out, sitting and reading newspapers in a small cluttered room, and as he walked on the streets, he was glared at and taunted. But gradually as he began to apprehend more fully what it meant to live in Watts, the people of Watts came to him, one at a time and slowly at first, and then they outgrew the room, moved to another location, and ended up at what they called Douglass House.

It was a nine-room house in ruins, but they got it for ninety-five dollars a month. Schulberg could handle the rent himself, but he would have to figure out some way to raise the money to rebuild it—plus money for furnishings, typewriters, a small reference library, and the salaries of a resident manager and secretarial help. In the meantime, the workshop found itself being solicited for literary contributions, individual members were being interviewed by the press and invited to conferences and seminars, and feature articles in periodicals described the group, its problems and progress. By the summer of 1966, the workshop had become "a kind of group celebrity," as poems from members were printed in *Los Angeles* magazine and *Time*, and NBC-TV presented an hour-long, prime-time special "The Angry Voices of Watts."

The workshop and Schulberg began to get mail, and he wrote back, asking for twenty-five dollars a month or three hundred a year to help support Douglass House. He also wrote all the writers he knew who he thought might have money enough to help. Among these was Steinbeck, who along with his check sent a letter:

> I saw the product of your project on television. I was astonished at the quality of the material. Some of it was superb. For one thing I was impressed with the growth of these people. I am so tired of one-note writing; sad homosexuality is not enough as a working tool for a writer. Your writers have learned early that one is not aware enough to scream with pain if one has not had glimpses of ecstasy. And both belong in our craft—else there would be neither.

Along with his praise he had, of course, an idea. Writing appeals to fifty or sixty writer friends must be time-consuming—what about Schulberg trying for a grant from the National Endowment for the Arts? Since he was a member of the Council, he would recommend the group to Roger L. Stevens, head of the endowment. After all, the Watts

Writers' Workshop was precisely the kind of thing, he thought, the endowment was for.

Today the idea seems obvious, but at that time it had not occurred to Schulberg or to anyone else with whom he had talked or corresponded about his project. Not only did they receive the grant, but they went on to get funds from the Ford and Rockefeller foundations, and the State Council as well. Schulberg gives credit to Steinbeck for turning the situation around: "It was damned good advice. I would really say that John was a drilling point in the workshop becoming really what it was, an institution." The workshop evolved into a school for about two hundred fifty students, which is now called the Frederick Douglass Center.

Steinbeck had been appointed to the Council of the National Endowment for the Arts by President Johnson in April, and it might not be too much of an exaggeration to say that by this time for Johnson Steinbeck was about the only real artist around. Johnson had been told by a poet that the poet would not come to dinner unless the President changed his ways; he had been lectured to at his own dinner table by a novelist. Johnson was, so to speak, fed up with the arts; he did not have much interest in awarding the National Medal for Literature.

Besides being on the Arts Council, John was also involved with P.E.N., with the State Department in trying to get Iron Curtain writers to visit the United States, with the Old Whalers Festival in Sag Harbor as its chairman, and even with the board of directors of his apartment building in New York. These activities all required meetings and letters and the expenditure of time that he hated to give up. He would complain about the time, yet he liked to be involved, especially if he had ideas he could contribute, and, as in his service on the apartment building board, he was curious—he liked to know what was going on.

He was as inept in organizing his time as he was sloppy in his personal habits and disorganized in his work environments, yet he spent a lot of time thinking and worrying about getting organized and saving time. His efforts were shot through with contradictions. He hated little tasks that weighed on his mind, yet when he was overseas, he was always promising to send books or other items to people or to report on something to them.

The mail was often a "horror" to him, especially following the publication of a book. Yet Elaine has testified that the mail was his "lifeline," so important to him that in the morning he wouldn't even look out the window until he had read it. Nevertheless, he saw the mail as a primary cause of wasted time, and in the spring of 1966 he once again was working on a form postcard, this time with a printed simulated signature, to ward off unwanted correspondence.

After he returned from the Near East at the end of March, his material on Israel was still being printed, and he went on to write five more columns from Sag Harbor, which ran the series out through May. In the first few of his "Letters to Alicia" the previous fall, he had made public his views on Vietnam, protesters, and the President.

In writing about these things during this period, he seemed to take on a new persona, to use a different tone than he had ever used in print. His historical sense, his biological objectivity, and his acceptance or willingness to reach out and understand "the whole picture," in the Ed Ricketts sense, seemed to wither away under the heat of his certainties and his scorn. Often he tried to use humor, but the humor was lame, and there was a snappy kind of sarcasm that surfaced in his writing that, along with the use of catch-words, was reminiscent of Walter Winchell or Westbrook Pegler, two journalists he did not admire.

That April, John, Jr., finished his basic training in the Army, requested Vietnam as his assignment, and asked his father if he would try through his connection with the President to make sure that he was able to go. (I will refer to him here as "junior" in order to make the distinction, although he had taken the name John Steinbeck IV.) Later, John, Sr., wrote to his son, "I was horrified when you asked me to get you orders to go out, but I couldn't have failed you there. Do you know, that is the only request I have ever made of the President? The only one. And I was not happy about making it. But if I had had to request that you *not* be sent, I think I would have been far more unhappy" [7/16/66].

John, Jr., spent part of his leave with his parents in Sag Harbor, and his father arranged for them to go to the White House in mid-May so that he could introduce his son to the President before he went overseas. Following the interview, Steinbeck wrote to thank the President for giving his boy "a pediment of pride," something that every good soldier must have, and added his reassurances concerning the antiwar demonstrations: "Remember that there have always been people who insisted on their right to choose the war in which they would fight to defend their country" [5/28/66].

Johnson wrote back:

Your visits and your letters never fail to refresh me. I was delighted to meet your son, and share your pride in him. He is a

Steinbeck through and through, perhaps the greatest of the many gifts you have given to this grateful nation. I shall pray for his safe and swift return to you.

Your own wise words of encouragement are a great source of comfort to me.

John's *Newsday* series concluded at the end of May, and in addition to Vietnam, war protesters, and the Berkeley "Free Speech" movement ("I hope when they get it themselves, they will allow it to others"), he had also written about a miscellany of subjects, some having to do with his travels (the ostensible occasion for the column) and some not. Along with the articles about England and the finding of the manuscript, Ireland and Irish Christmas, and Israel and the story of Masada, he had dealt with such problems as book piracy, juvenile delinquency, the accumulation of junk and trash in America, and prejudice against Jews.

That spring Ernest V. Heyn, editor of *Popular Science*, asked him to do an article as an introduction to a condensation in the magazine of Gardner Soule's *The Ocean Adventure*. It was something that John enjoyed—he still, of course, maintained his interest in oceanography (he hoped—against the reality of his physical condition—to accompany the next Mohole expedition and go down into deep water in the bathyscaphe), and he had, he wrote Heyn, been a *Popular Science* fan for years.

The sea, he wrote in the article, offered us immense opportunities, not only to feed the hungry and to provide scarce minerals, but also to learn about our as-yet-unexplored planet and ourselves. Twenty-one billion dollars, or many times that, may not be too high a price to get to the moon, "but it does seem unrealistic, unreasonable, romantic, and very human that we indulge in these passionate pyrotechnics when, under the seas, three-fifths of our own world and over three-fifths of our world's treasure is unknown, undiscovered, and unclaimed."

After finishing this piece, John sat down at his desk in Joyous Garde to write a novel. This time there was no formal announcement that he was abandoning the *Arthur*; he just let it go. Even with a novel, however, the old problems came back to haunt him. What was a novel? What is fiction? What is its relationship to reality?

He had given his proposed novel the title "A Piece of It Fell on My Tail," from the first line of the children's story about Henny Penny and Chicken Little, and, indeed, as he conceived the book, it would be based on the story itself. This may sound a bit like early senility, but it had always been his joy to take the obvious and turn it around or pick up the commonplace and take another look at it.

References to the story in his letters go back over many years, and it is referred to in *The Winter of Our Discontent*. The story had become a fable for him that dealt with several of his favorite themes: the nature of reality, the relationship of man to his environment, perspective as it produces our sense of reality, and intolerance and conflict produced by differences in perception. In early June he wrote down some of his thoughts about the story in a letter to Elizabeth:

> I came across it first in the second grade and so did you. . . . This may well be the most widely read story in the English language. . . . In the second grade we, who identified ourselves with clear-eyed Chicken Little, chuckled with pleased recognition. H.P. was obviously that nervous and wrong-headed adult we knew so well who screamed at us that if we got our feet wet we'd catch our death or that stealing and lying would get us in trouble or that if we climbed on the Tracys' barn we would fall and break our legs. . . . In the whole second grade there wasn't one kid who felt anything but contempt for H.P. We were all Chicken Littlers. . . .
>
> In the second grade and in the whole world, I guess, no one has ever come to the defense of Henny Penny. And that should give us some idea of the nature of human observation. What is cannot compete with what we want it to be. When what is turns out to be incontrovertibly opposed to what we wish or hope—we black the whole thing out and ignore it. . . .
>
> Now it may be that Henny Penny was indeed a foolish scatterbrain, an alarmist, and Chicken Little a cold and gimlet-eyed realist. But no one has inspected this story or these people. And also it is well to remember that no one was in the cabbage patch with H.P. when it happened. H.P. did not say, "The cabbage patch is falling." She said, "The *sky* is falling." Just because there was, or was said to be, a shred of cabbage leaf on her tail does not necessarily contradict her statement, at least to the extent that smart Alec Chicken Little indicated. He wanted H-P to be wrong and as we read, so did the writer of the story.
>
> We are told that Henny Penny came ranting and squawking out of the cabbage patch. But let us consider for the sake of contention that she said, "The sky is falling," in a quiet philosophic tone. . . . This would change the whole direction, intention and impact of the story. Far from establishing Henny Penny as a fool, it would make her an exact and penetrating observer of external reality. . . .
>
> For it does not require either a botanist nor a meteorologist to be aware of the proposition that, unless the sky is constantly falling

there could be no cabbage nor any Chicken Little for that matter. Without the falling nitrogens the plant could not raise its leaves to catch the falling sun's rays which create the chlorophil [*sic*] necessary to its and our existence. . . .

It is hard to give up a position one established in the second grade, but it is my conviction that all positions should be inspected. For generations Henny Penny has been held up to ridicule on the advocacy of Chicken Little. And actually what do we know about Chicken Little except that he jumped to a conclusion without proper preparation. [6/9/66]

He was playing here, but he was also serious. He saw in this story a metaphor for his own condition.

A major problem for him in attempting to write fiction during this period, as I have already said, was a strong feeling of intimidation— from receiving the Nobel Prize and from the severe criticism of recent years. The attacks by Mizener and by others at the time of the prize hurt him far worse than anyone could imagine. As disparaging of him as of his work, their condescension would have cut deeply into any man, no matter how confident or egotistical. But for Steinbeck, who was so terrified of exposing himself personally, who had a breakdown every time he was forced to give a one-line speech, they cut his heart out. He couldn't take any more risks.

It was his pride to exercise courage and not to reveal his wounds, but he longed to fight back. His eagerness to do the column for *Newsday* suggests he took it up almost as a weapon, which accounts for the belligerence of his tone on certain topics. In explaining to Max Lerner why he became a columnist, he wrote:

I can, if I wish, throw a punch or two at the critical semaphores who direct the traffic of literature and who sit in their warm blinds and blast me regularly like a sitting duck, which I am.

Now this is going to be one duck with brass knuckles. I never forget an injury nor forgive a compliment.

He had in recent decades "written out" his problems and deepest feelings, and now he was planning a novel to try to exorcise his artistic paralysis. Thus, his concern at the moment with the nature of fiction and its relationship with reality was in part the distillate from the bile he had accumulated in responding to his wounds.

Taking the scorned Henny Penny part himself in his metaphor, he can cast Mizener as the unemotional, hard-eyed realist, Chicken Little, a judge of truth and falsity without any doubts. What Mizener thinks is real turns out, in the story, to be a defect in Mizener's perception as well as a matter of prejudice. After all, the sky is falling—it's just that for Chicken Little-Mizener, it isn't real unless it meets his criterion. Since it was a particular point in Mizener's (and Wilson's and Kazin's) criticism scornfully to discount Steinbeck's scientific perspective as meaning very little, the parallel of the second-grade story is a remarkably close one.

However, two weeks later he wrote Elizabeth that he was planning on doing a piece on Sag Harbor before going on with "My Tail":

> Going on is an ambitious word. I haven't yet anything to go on from. It may well turn out that I not only do not know what a novel is but couldn't write one if I did. It's a real teetery position, complete with built-in doubts. I wonder indeed whether I am still capable of sustained effort.... But I'll go on twirling the pencil anyway. [6/22/66]

Early in July the Russian poet Yevtushenko published a poem in the Moscow newspaper *Literaturnaya Gazeta* that chided Steinbeck for not joining other American literary figures in coming out against the war. The poem was translated and printed in *The New York Times*, and John had not even seen it when newsmen were after him for a reply. He wrote a letter over the weekend, which he gave to Harry Guggenheim to release to all the news media at the same time.

In his poem Yevtushenko, who addressed his plea to "one of my most beloved writers and friends," took an approach that John had heard a hundred times on his recent trip to the U.S.S.R.: how could the compassionate writer of *The Grapes of Wrath*, defender of the people against capitalist exploitation, side now with the forces of oppression? He recalled Steinbeck's visit to Moscow in 1963 and his remark at a meeting of young writers who were under the shadow of discipline for criticizing the shortcomings of Soviet society, "Well, young wolves, show me your teeth."

> Understand
> These lines are not a provocative trick,
> But I cannot remain silent and isolated.
> Yes, we are little wolves.

> But John, you're an old wolf.
> So show your teeth,
> The teeth of John.

In his poem the poet speaks of Americans deliberately killing civilians—but Steinbeck had heard this all before, too. When he had been chided on the same basis in Rome, a decade before, for not opposing the American effort in Korea, he had taken the same position as he took now—we are in South Korea to help protect the South Koreans and you can't seriously suggest that our sons are baby murderers. In his open letter, he wrote in part:

> In your poem, you ask me to speak out against the war in Vietnam. You know well how I detest all war, but for this one I have a particular hatred. I am against this Chinese-inspired war. I don't know a single American who is for it. But, my beloved friend, you asked me to denounce half a war, our half. I appeal to you to join me in denouncing the whole war.
>
> Surely you don't believe that our "pilots fly to bomb children," that we send bombs and heavy equipment against innocent civilians? This is not East Berlin in 1953, Budapest in 1955, nor Tibet in 1959.
>
> You know as well as I do, Genya, that we are bombing oil storage, transport and the heavy and sophisticated weapons they carry to kill our sons. And where that oil and those weapons come from, you probably know better than I. They are marked in pictograph and in Cyrillic characters.
>
> I hope you also know that if those weapons were not being sent, we would not be in Vietnam at all. If this were a disagreement between Vietnamese people, we surely would not be there, but it is not, and I have never found you to be naive you must be aware that it is not.

He goes on to ask Yevtushenko to use his influence to have his government stop sending weapons, and he will devote every resource he has to persuade his government to withdraw its troops and weapons. But, he adds, even that is not necessary: "If you could persuade North Vietnam to agree in good faith to negotiate, the bombing would stop instantly. The guns would fall silent and our dear sons could come home. It is as simple as that, my friend, as simple as that, I promise you."

For a time Moscow delayed the publication of Steinbeck's letter. It put the editors of *Literaturnaya Gazeta* in a difficult position, since if they published it, this would be the first that Soviet readers had heard of American charges that Moscow, Peking, and Hanoi also bore responsibility for the war. They ended up deciding to "summarize" the letter, telling their readers that Steinbeck "repeated the hackneyed official American propaganda, distorting the truth about the war in Vietnam and its perpetrators." Alongside the summary was a picture from *Life* magazine showing a grief-stricken Vietnamese mother carrying the blood-splattered body of her infant child, a victim of a United States air attack on a South Vietnamese village.

The President, having read John's letter from a clipping sent to him by his staff, wrote to him:

> Your words say what I have been trying to say, and you say it eloquently and warmly—why our cause is right and why we must fight, and how peace can come to that little country if the aggressor will simply go home.
>
> As usual, John, you go the heart of the matter and that is what truly counts.

Steinbeck may have been right in his perception of communist propaganda, in his perception of the general character of our soldiers, but like most Americans who had not been in Vietnam, he had only a vague notion of the complexity and confusion of a war in which nothing was "simple." His certainties began to break down a bit after receiving letters from his son overseas. Young John, although not yet a "dove," quickly perceived that this was a far messier war than we had ever fought before, and that it didn't fit the neat terms applied to it and so heartily endorsed by the World War II generation of his father.

Our soldiers in the field were often surrounded by the enemy, although sometimes they couldn't be sure, and to cut down on the incidence of mistake, whole populations were being pulled from their homes and relocated. And the South Vietnamese government was so rotten, it was difficult sometimes not to feel as if one were protecting the bad guys from the good guys. What had come home to young John after only a couple of weeks in the country was that it was very often the civilians, caught in between, who suffered the most. His strongest feeling, perhaps, was neither for or against the war, but for the Vietnamese themselves, many of whom became his close friends. Like a considerable number of other Americans in Vietnam, he spent some of his off-duty time trying to relieve that suffering.

In August, John wrote to his son:

Your orphanage and hospital are very exciting. Let me know if there is anything I can do to help. I agree that the less government, the better. There is no reason why the Vietnamese should trust any government with their history. Hell, we don't really trust ours. But, would it make any sense if I tried to tap private sources for money for your orphanage? Would it make sense if the Authors' League or the Dramatists Guild or Actors Studio, for that matter, Actors Union—Stage Hands, etc.—couldn't they, as private organizations, endow beds, or adopt a wing and support it? If you, and your friends, think well of this and could give me some plans and programs, I could turn it loose among people who really care. [8/16/66]

In the meantime, he tried over and over again to start "My Tail," but like so many things that he had tried to do before, from *Burning Bright* through "Don Keehan," starting with an idea, he found it extremely difficult to translate that idea into fiction. How could he dramatize his idea to make it real, with flesh and blood people in a lifelike situation? Elaine recalls that "he talked about it a lot, talked about it to everybody. He talked it to death, you know—one of those ideas." Working on it from May through October, he never was able to make any progress. It was the last literary project he planned.

At the same time, however, a new idea was working on him, an idea that gained force in part from the frustration of his inability to write. As always when he was frustrated in such a way, he became restless, and when he became restless, his next move usually was to take a trip. He had resisted for some time the idea of going to Vietnam, but now that changed. "All he wanted to do was to go to Vietnam," Elaine recalls. "The minute John [Jr.] left for Vietnam, he was determined to go . . . the minute one member of the family went, he had to follow. . . . He always wanted to be where the action was, you know? He finally had to get into it and see what it was all about."

In November Yevtushenko came to the United States for a poetry reading tour, and in an ironic twist of his dispute with Steinbeck, he was accused by the Progressive Labor Party in New York of failing to speak out strongly enough against the war. After going to the Steinbecks' for dinner, he and John sat down and talked out their positions on the war at great length. Yevtushenko apologized and told John that he would never have addressed his poem to him if he had known that his son was in Vietnam. To the press afterward, the poet announced, "We explained our position to each other; now let history have the last word."

Later they did agree to try to go to Vietnam together—the Russian to accompany the American in the South and vice versa in the North— but then the Russian begged off. His reasons were vague enough to suggest that the Soviets had prevented him from going. It was too bad—the trip might have contributed to the education of both of them.

III

John went on his trip to South Vietnam and other Asian countries as a correspondent for *Newsday*. He avoided telling the President that he was going until he was gone, and he insisted on taking Elaine; he was too old, he explained, to want to go off by himself for any length of time. She too was accredited so that she could help him with his work.

On the way they stopped in California to see the family and Thom, who was in basic training at Fort Ord, and from there they flew to Hawaii, where John was briefed intensively by all three combat branches of the armed services. They also witnessed, and were deeply moved by, ceremonies aboard the U.S.S. *Arizona* marking the twenty-fifth anniversary of Pearl Harbor.

They took off again and flew through what seemed an eternity of darkness, until dawn caught up with them at Guam. As the rays of the sun streamed out across the expanse of blue-green water, from horizon to horizon, they began to look for land. When they spotted it, green and warm in the full sun, they knew that it was Vietnam, the place, not the word or the idea. Their introduction to what that meant came almost immediately as the plane continued at the same altitude and then suddenly dived nearly straight down to make its landing at Tan Son Nhut Airport. They realized, as their pulse rates returned to normal, that their pilot had taken this unusual approach to avoid being shot at.

At the airport their son stood waiting for them, looking, Elaine thought, "like a wise old owl" in "his fatigues and cap and specs." He went with them to the Caravelle Hotel, headquarters for the visiting press, and to their tiny room. For three days they talked and met their son's buddies, officers, and Vietnamese friends, while John attended further briefings and made arrangements to go into the field and Elaine unpacked and prepared for the campaign ahead.

Assigned to John by the Military Office of Information, to help him find his way around, get where he wanted to go, and accomplish what he had come to do, was Marine Major Sam M. Gipson, Jr. Sam was a tall, sandy-haired, freckle-faced Texan who looked too young to be a major. But he knew Vietnam, and he knew his correspondents, from the Caravelle cowboys who sat and drank on the roof of the hotel at night and watched the fireworks and filed from briefings and rumors, to the tough young men, out to make a name for themselves, who picked up their leads and charged out into the field.

There were big names, like Alsop; correspondents from foreign countries, even Yugoslavia; camera crews, like the fifteen-man Japanese television group; and there were reporters from the States who came out of small towns that no one ever heard of. Sam knew of Steinbeck, having read some of his books, but was surprised to find that a lot of the men they came across in Vietnam didn't know him—especially the young ones, who looked up in amazement to see this old geezer clamber from a helicopter and take off into the jungle swinging a blackthorn walking stick.

At three o'clock on the morning of the fourth day they were in Vietnam, Steinbeck got up and equipped himself for war: he had his glasses, his field glasses, his biologist's glass, his camping knife, special pills, ballpoint pens, pads, an extra bootlace, his toilet kit, change of underwear and socks, kaopectate . . . he knew exactly all the things that would happen. At four-thirty he left for the field.

He would spend most of his six weeks in the field, traveling for two, three, or four days and then returning for part of a day and a night to write his story and clean up, and then go right back out again, leaving early the following morning. He wanted to see and participate in every kind of operation, talk to as many different people, civilian and military as possible, and go to every part of the country. Sam was in very good shape, but John wore him out. After a long day of activity, he'd stay up late talking to the troops and then get up at the crack of dawn.

Elaine felt that to a certain extent he was trying to relive his experiences of World War II, although he was not so captured by that desire that he wasn't able to see, as time went by, that circumstances were quite different. Still, one of the first things he asked for was a weapon. Sam wouldn't let him have one, but he did arrange for him to take a short course in the firing of and familiarity with the M16 automatic rifle and the M79 grenade launcher. He also went through the booby-trap awareness course near Da Nang: "The course is about 400 yards long, winds through thick cover, and on the path and in the houses is every kind of booby trap that has been found. When you trip one a loud blank cap goes off. I set off three and it makes you feel foolish because you are looking for the trip wires and traps."

In the meantime, John, Jr., had gone back to his unit, and Elaine was left to learn to cope with Saigon on her own. Elaine got a lot of advice from the people she ran into and heard a lot of Saigon war stories from blasé American civilian workers. She found the advice and the casually recounted hairbreadth escapes equally frightening. One evening a Vietnamese couple took her to dinner on the outskirts of the city, explaining, "It's safer than being in the city tonight." It seemed to her it might be a tie, since she heard the reports of small-arms fire throughout the meal.

There was always the chance that while riding in a car, walking down the street, or sitting in a bar or restaurant you could get, as the soldiers put it, "a grenade in your ear." And among the thousands of bicycles there might be one parked with a pie-shaped explosive in its pouch, aimed to send projectiles into anyone standing at a bus stop or coming out the entrance to a shop. Once while the Steinbecks were in the city, a restaurant across the street from where they were was blown to smithereens.

Nevertheless Elaine was determined that she wasn't going to sit alone in her room or be overly cautious. She set out to learn the city and observe as much as she could, even though everywhere she went GIs stopped her to ask, "Ma'am! What's an American lady like you doing here?" She covered the daily press briefings, those that became known as the "Five O'clock Follies," for her husband, and she learned how to file his dispatches for him. All the time John was gone, she was worried sick about him, but she was determined not to say anything or let it show. Occasionally John went out with Vietnamese units, and Sam wouldn't know where he was and couldn't be sure he'd be protected. "Oh God," he'd say to her, "what if he doesn't come back in three days? We won't even know where to go looking for him." Then she and Sam would both worry.

John covered a lot of ground. He was able to get quickly from one place to another because of the helicopters, and for longer jumps, he was able to get space on C-130 aircraft. He went in with the lead ship (helicopter) of an assault team of the First Cavalry, joined a ground assault with the Marines, observed an artillery unit in action protecting the approaches to Saigon, and in the north sat in a spotter helicopter and watched B-52 strikes. He didn't write about a third of what he did during these first few weeks because the operations were still in progress.

He was fascinated with the various kinds of helicopters and managed to ride at least once in all of them except the single-place bubble, and to go along on nearly every kind of mission. One tactic involved using the little one-man helicopter to run over areas of suspected V.C. activity until it was fired upon, and then the pilot would call in the larger helicopters. A gunship would spray the area with fire while nearby a combat patrol might be dropped into the jungle to make its way to the target to engage the enemy and investigate.

Steinbeck was in the highlands with Sam Gipson when news came that a target had been discovered. They climbed aboard a Huey, and John took the door seat, which he liked because if you tightened the harness straps, you could look straight down: "I nod to the door gunner on my side," he recounted later, "and pat the twin handles of his weapon. . . . It is a joy to have him there. His potential burst of tracered fire may well be a deterrent to the casual part-time sniper who can take it or let it alone."

From the joy of weaponry he moves to the thrill of flight and the skill of the pilots:

I wish I could tell you about these pilots. They make me sick with envy. They ride their vehicles the way a man controls a fine, well-trained quarter horse. They weave along stream beds, rise like swallows to clear trees, they turn and twist and dip like swifts in the evening. . . .

We are now in V.C. country, where every tree may open fire and often does. Maj. [James Patrick] Thomas dips into a stream bed cascading down a twisting canyon and you realize that the low green cover you saw from high up is towering screaming jungle so dense that noonday light fails to reach the ground. The stream bed twists like a snake and we snake over it, now and then lofting like a tipped fly ball to miss an obstruction or cutting around a tree the way a good cow horse cuts out a single calf from a loose herd.

Low as we are flying, we are gaining altitude rapidly because these mountains are steep and high and our stream is cascade and waterfall. I wonder how the pilots find their way. On the hillsides are little fields chopped out of the jungle by Montagnards farmed for a season or two and left to overgrow. And these cleared places are not close together but separated and random with dense growth between.

Suddenly, up and ahead there is a burst of purple smoke, our landing signal, and we loop over to a chopped out clearing so small that our rotor blades barely clear the giant bamboo.

For those at home cheering for the other side, such pleasure in guns, tactics, and military maneuvering was enough to set their teeth on edge, and for those who were simply in doubt, there were some for whom such writing seemed overly bellicose. Several photographs of him in Vietnam published in United States periodicals further accentuated the warlike, superhawk image that his generally enthusiastic "Letters to Alicia" were projecting, particularly one with wide distribution showing him in fatigues and helmet, staring belligerently over the barrel of an M79.

Of course, many American reporters in Vietnam in 1966 tended to be hawkish, or at the very least sympathetic to the plight of the American soldier, but Steinbeck aroused the special ire of the antiwar Left as a "traitor." It was Steinbeck that they focused on and who became for them a symbol, a *cause célèbre* to prosecute.

He might have drawn special hatred also for his position in American culture. John, Jr., in his book, *In Touch*, speaks of his thinking of his father as "a kind of American-conscience figure," and it may be that he became so, and may even remain so, for many of the rest of us. If this is true, then it also explains the special antagonism that his judgment of the war as morally justified aroused in those who were convinced otherwise.

And, of course, he returned the antagonism, something that his column allowed him to do publicly—and quickly, without reflection. We see this in the continuation of the column cited above:

> Out of the undergrowth, thicker than any I have ever seen, faces, or really only eyes, appear. Mottled helmets and fatigues disappear against the background. Faces black or white from sweat and dirt have become a kind of universal reddish gray. Only the eyes are alive and lively. And when we settle and the rotor stops, the mouths open and they are men, and what men. Can you understand the quick glow of pride one feels in just belonging to the same species as these men?
>
> I suppose it is the opposite of the shiver of shame I sometimes feel at home when I see the Vietnicks, dirty clothes, dirty minds, sour smelling wastelings and their ill-favored and barren pad mates. Their shuffling, drag-ass protests that they are conscience-bound not to kill people are a little silly. They're not in danger of that. Hell, they couldn't hit anybody.

He learns that the V.C. have scattered from the target area and that on reconnaissance the GIs have discovered a large rice cache:

> D troop . . . smelled of sweat, hard-working sweat. On the back of every helmet, under the strap, was a plastic spray bottle of insect

repellent. I went into a V.C. trail so deep and covered with jungle that you are in perpetual steaming dusk. It was one of the V.C. transport trails over which they force the local people to carry their supplies. The rice cache was fairly large, a stilted structure deeply screened and disguised. The weary men were sacking unhulled rice to be air-lifted to the refugee centers, a good haul, 300 or 400 bags. . . . I started down the dark cave of a trail and a sergeant quite a bit bigger than a breadbox called "Don't go far. It's booby trapped." . . . I didn't go far.

His column tended to deal less and less with policy and the direction of the war as a whole, and more and more with the men he observed and talked to. Most did not want to be there, hated the danger and the ambiguity of the situation, but clearly felt an obligation to their country. They were in his mind a gallant crew, and when he left Vietnam, it was his respect for these men that he carried with him.

CHAPTER L

I f our troops were gallant, it was clear to Steinbeck that the Viet Cong was just the opposite. He saw a parallel between the movement of the civilian population here and in Eastern Europe and across the Berlin Wall: if the V.C. was of the people and for the people, why were the refugees coming always to us? "These people did not run from us," he wrote, "they ran to us. Doesn't it make any impression that there are no reverse refugees? Nobody runs north to escape the brutality of the South Vietnamese and the brutal Americans."

He perceived the V.C. as extortionists and terrorists who had not won the hearts and minds of the people and who had success primarily because of their extraordinary viciousness—they displayed no scruples, would balk at no horror in order to gain their ends. He saw the remains of villages that had been burned down because the people would not pay the V.C. "tax," and the bloody remains of Vietnamese who were tortured by cutting off little pieces of their bodies at a time, starting, apparently, with the tips of the fingers and toes, so that what was left was "a ghastly mound of butcher's meat." He would send pictures, he wrote back, but no American newspaper would print them.

It infuriated him that the two big lies of communist propaganda—that it was the Americans who were brutal and that the V.C. had the vast support of the population—were being believed by an increasing number of Americans at home. He saw no evidence to support either assertion. On the contrary, in Can Tho in the Delta Region in early January

at about 10 o'clock in the evening two strolling young men paused in front of a crowded restaurant and suddenly threw two grenades in at the wide open door. One was a dud. The other exploded and tore up the people and their children. There were no soldiers in the restaurant either American or Vietnamese. There was no possible military advantage to be gained. An American captain ran in and carried out a little girl of 7. He was weeping when he got her to the hospital and she was dead. Ambulances carried the broken bodies to the long building, once a French hospital and now ours.

Then the amputations, and the probing for pieces of jagged metal began and the smell of ether filled the building. Some of the tattered people were dead on arrival and some died soon after but those who survived were treated and splinted and bandaged. They lay on the wooden beds with a glazed questioning in their eyes. Plasma needles were taped to the backs of their hands, if they had hands, to their ankles if they had none. The children who had been playing about on the floor of the restaurant were the worst hit by the low-exploding grenade. The doctors and nurses of the brutal, aggressive, imperialist American force worked most of the night on the products of this noble defense of the homeland.

Meanwhile the grenade throwers had been caught and they proudly admitted the act, in fact boasted of it.

I find I have no access to the thinking of the wanton terrorist. Why do they destroy their own people, their own poor people whose freedom is their verbal concern? That hospital with all its useless pain is like a cloud of sorrow. Can anyone believe that the V.C., who can do this kind of thing to their own people, would be concerned for their welfare if they had complete control? I find I can't.

He observed here, as elsewhere, that the V.C. seemed to take pride and get genuine satisfaction from killing innocents, and he could not think of them as soldiers. In writing about the German soldier in *The Moon Is Down*, he had made him a human being—perhaps because he had not witnessed German atrocities. But such biological distancing failed him now, and he was unable to perceive the V.C. except as some kind of monster created by conditioning and indoctrination.

He was one of the few newsmen to report such atrocities at this stage of the war, and this, too, contributed to his hawklike image. Perhaps some of the others felt that to do so would echo too closely the American government's position on the war and cast doubt on their independence, or perhaps this kind of incident had become so common that for most correspondents it was no longer news. Sam Gipson recalls that when something happened, inadvertently or intentionally, that reflected poorly on the American forces, there were always a number of newsmen who clamored to get to the scene. On the other hand, when a large explosive went off in the middle of a crowd of women and children in a marketplace in the Delta area, killing and wounding dozens, not a single correspondent would go to see it.

John believed what he saw and heard, he was free to come and go and talk to whomever he wanted, and yet he was uncomfortable about the conclusions he had drawn as being too simplistic. He made an effort to talk to refugees in the camps, to Vietnamese on various levels of society—Buddhist monks, ARVN officers and enlisted men, musicians, poets, and students—to nearly every type of person he could find, except to high South Vietnamese government officials. The situation appeared to him more and more complex, and Elaine could see that his original doubts about American participation were returning. But he never changed his mind about the character and motives of the American soldier.

In viewing both combat and various efforts at pacification and resettlement, he came up with ideas, as one might expect—for weapons, tactics, propaganda techniques, and sanitation. He thought that twelve-gauge shotguns might be more effective in the brush than automatic rifles, and that a grenade the size and approximate weight of a baseball should be developed to take advantage of American experience. He talked to Sam about dropping cheap transistor radios fixed to one channel into enemy-held areas.

He wrote a column about using the Saigon Cowboys, ten- to fourteen-year-old street kids, as an intelligence unit, putting this reservoir of talent to work. "These boys," he wrote, "are more expert at concealment than the V.C. themselves. If they are thieves and lawbreakers, it is because nobody needs nor wants them for anything else." In another column he wrote about the water and sanitation problems in Vietnam. This was about the wettest country he'd ever seen, but none of the water, except from springs high in the mountains or from deep wells, was drinkable. This problem in turn was connected to the sewage disposal problem.

Cesspools or sewers were impossible, since anywhere you dug you hit ground water. Waste that went into the waterways and rivers was never purged, because the tidal range in the lowlands was so far that nothing was swept out to sea, but just moved back and forth with the tide. John suggested that a Taiwanese invention he'd heard of might be the solution. It was made of two fifty-gallon drums, copper tubing, and a sealing lid, and it not only fermented the waste until it was sterile, it also produced an odorless gas that could be used for cooking or heat.

Standing in waist-high water in the rice paddies and the necessity for American patrols to search for weapons caches underwater led to another suggestion. At home he had used a five-pound magnet to bring up as much as a hundred pounds: "If anything metallic falls off the dock I tie a line to the magnet and drop it to the bottom. I've brought up everything from a pair of pliers to an outboard motor with it." He promised an American officer in the area, who was interested in the idea, that he would try to have a magnet sent to him directly, since he would probably never get it through channels.

John made one trip to the Delta country with Elaine to see the pacification program near Tan An in Long An Province. The town itself was relatively secure, but to get there by helicopter, they had to fly over a "free fire zone," which was a bit worrisome to Elaine. One of the American officials gave up his room to the Steinbecks—luxury: twin beds, reading lights, and an indoor bathroom. All night long there was heavy firing, and Elaine kept asking, "Is that ours or theirs?" and John would say, "I think we can presume that's ours."

In the morning before dawn, Elaine recalls:

> John and I went down to the wharf to see the unloading of the sampans, watched the market stalls being set up—strange fruits and vegetables we were beginning to recognize and like, as well as baby ducks, fish, shellfish, baby pigs, plain rice, sticky rice and all the sweets of the Orient. We had breakfast at a stall with the farmers—Chinese soup and glasses of thick black sweet coffee.

They took a low-altitude survey flight in a Huey, and for two hours looked over the province. John wrote:

> The towns and villages forward of Tan An were very different. The bridges were invariably down, the roads broken and a kind of dilapidation, like a skin disease, spread over the land. The fields looked untended and many of the houses were unoccupied. The river, teeming with traffic in the secured area, was empty.

On the ground, John went a few miles deeper into the Delta from Tan An to a village, Rach Kien, that had just been recaptured a few days earlier. It looked as if it had been through a long sickness: the once neat paths overgrown, roofs collapsed, the public buildings gutted and made into barracks, and the canals filled with accumulated filth. He watched a squad of GIs cleaning out and rebuilding the schoolhouse and repairing and repainting the desks, and he talked to the hamlet chief, who told him of the things the Viet Cong had done while they held the village.

John was late getting back from Rach Kien, and he and Elaine were rushed to the outskirts of town, where the Huey was sitting on a concrete pad, rotors turning. They had barely time to get their belts hooked and Elaine was trying to tie on a scarf when the chopper thrust forward, hugged the tops of the trees for a moment, and then shot upward like a fast elevator out of control:

> My dear wife shouted in the ear of the door gunner sitting beside her. "What's the hurry? We're only five minutes late." The gunner swiveled down the mouth piece of his intercom.
> "Hell, lady," he complained. "They was shooting at us."
> "Where?" she asked.
> "Right back there on the pad, lady."

Until the third week of January 1967, John also continued to go on various combat missions, among them an afternoon and a night on a river patrol boat, a thirty-one-foot craft made of wood and fiberglass, while it covered a ten-mile stretch of the Bassac River. He went on a morning and afternoon flight with a Forward Air Controller in a single-engine fixed-wing Cessna which can fly about ninety to one-hundred knots per hour. There wasn't room for parachutes, and since the duty was somewhat hazardous—visual reconnaissance over V.C. territory—the pilots were volunteers. And he went on a night mission in Puff, the Magic Dragon, a twenty-four-year-old C-47, a two-engine, prop-driven plane that had been stripped and fitted with three six-barreled Gatling guns at two side windows and an open door. He was cold and he was scared, and since this was his last mission, on the way back he kept thinking of Ernie Pyle and Bob Capa.

One of the most memorable of times had been the night he spent on Pussi Mountain. He had been in nearby Pleiku and was able to arrange to visit his son's unit, Armed Forces TV Detachment No. 3, which was in the process of setting up a TV station on the mountain. They had pitched tents and had been waiting for two and a half months for the self-contained combat television van to come. John promised them that it would arrive soon—it would have to, since everywhere he went, action of some kind seemed to follow. The commanding officer, Captain Mike Luckey, agreed, and furthermore, if the van got up the hill by the end of the next day, he would burn his draft card by way of celebration.

At two o'clock the next day, the van arrived. That evening,

while the detachment stood as near to attention as possible, the captain whipped out his draft card and handed me his lighter.

I said, "You know, sir, this could get you five years at hard labor, by act of Congress."

"I know," he said happily. "Light her up." So I did and do you know—a draft card is nearly fireproof, but it finally caught flame.

The arrival of the van brought a great release of tension. The boredom of inactivity had been maddening, and so there was quite a celebration that night at the Pussi Mountain Culture and Rest Center.

But with property came responsibility. The next afternoon reports came over the radio of widespread V.C. activity and then the news that the road between the mountain and Pleiku had been cut with the explosion of a land mine. And then, as Steinbeck reported later, "The radio got that cold and detached tone of voice that comes when it is very serious. The situation was hairy, it indicated, and if we knew which side our bread was buttered on, we would look to our defenses." It seemed clear to them that with that huge brown van sitting on the mountain silhouetted against the sky, the V.C. was getting ready to overrun them and put their station out of business before it ever got set up.

The dry red earth was too loose to dig bunkers without sandbags, and without sandbags they had no means to screen the van. They did have weapons enough, and the captain and his NCOs set out a perimeter, assigning weapons and positions, one station to cover for another. Steinbeck joined his son (nicknamed by the outfit "Hemingway") and the others on the defensive line, and they settled down to wait.

While the previous night had been alive with the fire of gun ships and artillery, this night "was dark, a velvety crumbling dark, no firing, no earth-lighting flares swinging from their parachutes."

The [captain] had been very specific about posts. Mine was high and unprotected but I had a helmet and a vest and I can get down real flat if I have to. I knew where my son's station was below me, but I heard him say softly as someone walked by, "Who in the world could imagine that on a night like this, my dad would be up above me with an M-79 covering me?"

No one came, and when the dawn arrived they were glad. When John went to get up, he was so stiff and sore he could hardly move.

"I have often wished," he wrote later, "that if a war is necessary, it might be fought by men of my age rather than by boys with their whole lives ahead of them. The difficulty is that we wouldn't do it very well."

He liked these men, here and throughout Vietnam. He liked their comradeship against the misunderstanding of the world, their ironic humor, their sense of duty, their competence, and the fact that by and large, like his son, they really did care about the Vietnamese. For them, politics was nothing; it was people who really counted. And that, of course, was the politics that Steinbeck believed in, not doctrine.

Before he left Vietnam for Thailand and Laos, he wrote to Lyndon Johnson:

Dear Mr. President:
I have been in Vietnam about six weeks now, and most of that time I have spent in the field with our troops of all branches as well as with some of the Allied forces. From north to south I have been on every outpost, have flown with Air Cavalry, with Forward Air Control, with 1st Cavalry units. In fact I went in with the first strike of Operation Thayer II although I have not written about that since the operation is not completed.

I think I know our men very well now for I have lived with them and have been shot at with them.

I know, Mr. President, that you get many reports through your official channels of information. But I want to tell you by this completely unofficial means, that we have here the finest, the best trained, the most intelligent and the most dedicated soldiers I have ever seen in any army and I have seen soldiers in my time. These men are the best we have ever had.

In addition to fighting, they have taken on the duty of pacification and repair simultaneously and that is a new thing in the world. . . . The restrictions placed on them in carrying the war to the enemy must be and are galling to our soldiers. But they obey. I hope, sir, that in the near future you may find occasion to celebrate these men, to give verbal evidence of our love for them and our pride in them. They deserve it and I well know that you feel it. . . .

Yours with all respect,
John Steinbeck [1/18/67]

It may seem here that his admiration is more than a bit too uncritical, especially to anyone who has been in the Army and knows that sprinkled among the mass of ordinary people with decent impulses and a sense of duty there are also bigots, perverts, psychopaths, and con men. He was not blind to that, but it was not the essence of what these men as a whole were.

By the time Steinbeck left Vietnam, there had already been a number of sharply critical reactions to his reports. Not only did his support of our policy and of our men provoke cries of outrage, but his lifelong interest in weapons and tactics, and his enthusiasm for them, came to the fore and was interpreted as a superbelligerence. Furthermore, the sense that on occasion he was enjoying what he was doing and enjoying the company of our soldiers was interpreted as an enthusiasm for war.

Nevertheless, except for *The New Masses* and *Ramparts*, almost all the published attacks on him were delivered by communist papers in communist countries. Soviet publications accused him in a series of attacks of "betraying his principles" and having been "an accomplice in murder" by riding along on a helicopter mission. *Izvestia* called his reporting "disgusting." These were followed by denunciations in the Bulgarian weekly *Po Sveta*, which devoted twenty-one of its forty pages to criticizing him, concluding "your disgrace is appalling," and by an open letter by a Czech writer to P.E.N. President Arthur Miller asking that the organization as a whole vote to condemn Steinbeck for his Vietnam dispatches.

Except to report the communist attacks abroad, there was in this country very little reaction in print, at this time or even later. Later reactions were for the most part passing references to his "pro-Vietnam war" stand or to his "hawkish" views on the war (appearing in his obituary, for example), and his friendship with Johnson was the object of some ridicule or regret, but again, largely in passing. The real bitterness that his war reporting evoked at home seemed most often to be expressed personally, sometimes by a person who had been a friend, but more often by acquaintances.

Budd Schulberg recalls that during this period he had successive fist-fights with Joe Flaherty and Pete Hamill when they had some unpleasant things to say about Steinbeck. Schulberg didn't agree with Steinbeck's position on the war, but he felt "if you were going to criticize someone for some specific political act, Vietnam or something, you had to take in the whole picture of what he was about." Similar glib judgments had been made about him at times during his career, and he couldn't put up with a good man being called something on the order of a "fascist son of a bitch."

From the Caravelle Hotel in Saigon, with its dim lights, balky air conditioner, and "1947 Tijuana motel" furniture, the Steinbecks moved to the Oriental Hotel in Bangkok, into a suite of rooms once inhabited by Somerset Maugham. They went into a kind of culture shock, moving from constant suspicion to invariable kindness, from hell to something close to heaven. But after they had been there a few days, he wrote to Elizabeth, expressing the feeling that he might have come out of Vietnam too soon and that he had a sense of unfinished business. He also reported to her that he had come over the border with so much left to write that he had been desk-bound ever since they had arrived.

It was not long, however, before they were on the move again, this time to the northeastern provinces of Thailand, where in the very poorest area of the country, remote and backward, with hardly the soil or resources for the people to scratch out a living, communist cadres had begun their infiltration. As he reported in his column, it was suspected that many had come in under the cover of the thousands of refugees that had fled North Vietnam, but there were also night attacks across the river from Laos. It was the beginning of the same pattern that had been used in South Vietnam.

The Thai central government had belatedly begun to take an interest in the region and had enlisted the help of American technical experts to improve the agriculture, drill wells, build roads and bridges, and set up communication lines. For a week the Steinbecks toured the area with agronomists and engineers to examine to work that was being done and meet and talk with its people:

> In most of the villages we were accepted with pleasure and curiosity, and then one day we passed through three villages where the communists had been at work. No one has to tell you. You know. The children run away to hide. Only a few young men stand about sullenly, staring at the ground. They will not reply to a greeting. The women and old people peer from the semidarkness of the stilted houses.

Suddenly they were back in hell again, where fear governs life and someone watches everyone every moment to make sure that no one strays from political purity.

From Thailand they flew to Laos, a "neutral" country that was being cut to ribbons by the North Vietnamese, the Viet Cong, the Pathet Lao, and, much to the Steinbecks' dismay when they discovered it, by American bombing. The American public was not yet aware of this, nor was it aware of the extent of our involvement in Thailand and Laos, the dozens of agencies involved and the variety of projects and operations, both open and clandestine, that were under way. It was in Laos, in particular, that it came home to John just how widespread the war was and how intensive and complex was our involvement. At this point he came to see the war as a kind of quicksand of deceit and confusion.

We would be here for at least a generation, he thought, and there would be no victory.

But he did find one figure in Laos to admire greatly—Pop Ewell, a middle-aged, Midwestern American farmer who was devoting his life to the Meo tribesmen. He had founded the village of Sam Thong and brought in a hospital and school. "I think," Steinbeck wrote, "Pop is an example of how the ancient gods were born and preserved in the minds and the graven images of people all over the world." He continued:

> Remember . . . how the story invariably goes—in olden times the people did not live well as they do now and they practiced abominations. Then a stranger appeared and he taught us to use the plow and how to sow and how to harvest. He brought in writing so we could keep records. And he gave us healing medicines to make us healthy, and he gave us pride so we would not be afraid and when we had learned these things, he went away. He was translated. That is his figure there, carved in limestone. Well, I don't think Pop is likely to be taken up in a sweet chariot even if he had the time or the inclination, but that ancient story is Pop Ewell's story. Whether you believe it or not . . . there are still giants on the earth.

John and Elaine were taken back and forth from one part of Laos to another. From Vientiane they went to the Chinese border and then to Luang Probang, where they stayed with a C.I.A. man. One day shortly after they left their former host disappeared, presumed dead. They went to Ban Nam But, to Sam Thong, and to Tranninh on the edge of the Plain of Jars, which was a very active battle zone. They went on a rice drop, and John alone accompanied some Baptist missionaries on a trek to the top of a mountain to deliver medicine to a small Christian village.

The Steinbecks also visited an agricultural experimental and demonstration station on the Bolovens Plateau run by three American agronomists. The people in a cluster of forty-four villages nearby were being taught how to plant new crops, improve their husbandry of chickens and pigs, and manage and store water. While the Steinbecks were there, two battalions of V.C., crossing over from haven in Cambodia, overran Attopeu and, with artillery support, started to attack up the steep edge of the plateau below the station. Shells were coming in near the station when a helicopter touched down to deliver supplies. The chopper pilot looked at them with some disbelief and yelled, "What the hell are you two doing here?" He took them aboard and carried them to safety.

Without Elaine, John went on several combat missions in Laos, but he did not write about them, nor did he write about the bombing. Before leaving Vientiane, he went to the embassies of North Vietnam, Cambodia, and China to try, as he had before, to get visas to those countries. North Vietnam told him they would put his name on a waiting list, but nothing came of it.

From Vientiane they went back to Bangkok briefly for an audience that had been arranged with the King and Queen, and then took the train down the Malay Peninsula (on recommendation of a friend of theirs who hated to fly and who remembered it as a picturesque journey) to the point where they could depart for the island of Penang, where they could rest and John could catch up on his writing. It was now late February, and they celebrated his sixty-fifth birthday there. They had been away three months, most of which had been spent in the war zone, and John had sent fifty-two pieces to *Newsday* since the first of December. He was unhappy with himself that he was so tired, but he found after doing two articles on Laos, he couldn't force himself to go on and do more. He got up the next morning and sat and stared at his pad of paper. He wrote a letter. He took a long bath. He came back, sat down, and stared at his pad again. Then he thought, The hell with it. What in the devil am I running for?

They hired a car to go to Singapore, and from there flew to Jakarta, visited Bali, and returned to Jakarta. He wrote two meditative pieces about the war, one in which he tried to see it in the perspective of the history of the region and the other in which he examined the phenomenon of those having never seen the war being most certain about it. In the latter article he worries about not having looked long enough or hard enough, but decides that perhaps duration, of itself, is not the key:

> Some years ago, when Ed Ricketts and I were collecting marine animals for fun and very little profit, we would come to a beach or a tide pool near which people had lived all of their lives and they would never have seen many species that were constantly under their eyes. They had to be shown what was there before they could see it. This little example has often frightened me with the question, how many things are there under my eyes that I cannot see? I am sure there are very many.

But certainly during this trip, he goes on to say, he has tried to see, to set aside preconceptions. At a party he attended

> the Swedish ambassador to an East Asian country said to me, "You have been to South Vietnam. We only go to North Vietnam."

"Why?" I asked.
"Because we do not approve of your policy."
"But what has approval to do with seeing?"

In Jakarta they attended the ceremony, held in the Sports Palace on the outskirts of the city, at which "permanent" President Sukarno of Indonesia was removed from office by decree of the National Assembly and a new President, General Suharto, was installed. This led Steinbeck to investigate the history of the matter and do two columns in which he traced the life and times of Sukarno, a man who thought he was a giant but who was an incompetent with delusions of grandeur.

From Jakarta they went to Hong Kong, where John wrote a letter to Sam Gipson:

If this writing is bad, it is because "No good deed goes unpunished." Three days ago here in Hong Kong, I helped a poor heathen Chinee to pull a heavy hand truck of beer up a set of steps and slipped a spinal disk. So I am writing this flat on my back on a fracture board. What the V.C. couldn't do to me has been done to me by a decent impulse. However, I hope to be able to walk in a few days. I must—because Johnny is joining us in Tokyo for some leave. And I must get about. I know you haven't seen my pieces. When I get home I'll have my paper bind tear sheets for my friends. Some of them might amuse you. In R.V.N. where my impulses were not dove-like, I was safe. And now I have to be wounded by a beer truck.

After a time in Japan, we will go home, and about time. We have been all over Thailand, all over Laos, the H.C.M. trail included—the length of Malaysia and lots of Indonesia. Now in this pleasure dome of Hong Kong I am immobilized.

Sam, I don't know whether I properly told you how much you did for me. But you did. Apart from your guidance, it is such a pleasure to have a brave and a good man as company. And we did have a good time, didn't we. [4/67]

Not only was it ironic that he be hurt in Hong Kong, after having spent time in the war zone, but it was also somehow emblematic of him that the event that ended his career, in a sense, should be such a gesture of kindness toward a stranger. The injury turned out to be far more serious than it appeared to be at the time.

John did get on his feet, although it was very painful and difficult, in time to meet young John in Japan for five days of R & R, and they all went to Kyoto in the prime of the cherry blossom season. Back in

Tokyo, after his son returned to duty, carrying back a load of presents for Viet kids (as John made sure to point out in one of his columns), he wrote his last two columns for *Newsday*. Among the last words he would write for publication were:

> I'm moving in on an ending now. I know what I want to say but not quite how to say it. I have been accused by the interested but uninvolved of being a war-monger, of favoring war and even of celebrating it. I hope you will believe that if I could shorten this war by one hour by going back to Vietnam, I would be on to-night's plane with a one-way ticket.
>
> What I have been celebrating is not war but brave men. I have in a long life known good and brave men but none better, braver nor more committed than our servicemen in the Far East. They are our dearest and our best and more than that—they are our hope.

John and Elaine returned to New York the end of the third week in April. His back pain had eased somewhat but an attack of bursitis nearly immobilized his right arm. Nevertheless, he got off a typed letter to Sam in which he expressed greater fear for his safety in the jungles of Park Avenue than he had in those overseas: "The long haired boys and short haired women who prowl the streets make the hardcore V.C. look like friendlies. If you have any regard for your personal safety (you in your Marine uniform) you will stay where you are" [4/25/67]. In early May he retired to the protection of his friends in Sag Harbor who had been in the 101st Airborne in World War II.

The Steinbecks were invited to stay the weekend at the White House in mid-May, and John had an early and very long breakfast with the President, during which he told him what he thought we were doing wrong and made some suggestions. Johnson asked some questions and then asked him to stay over and repeat what he said to Secretaries McNamara and Rusk and Vice-President Humphrey; McNamara asked him if he would write it all down for him.

John's shoulder had gotten worse, so bad that he could neither use a pencil nor type, and he had a meeting of the National Arts Council in Tarrytown, New York, immediately after returning from Washington, but in between sessions, he put his comments on tape. McNamara had this transcribed—five single-spaced typed pages, classified "Eyes Only"—and took it with him on his next trip to Vietnam to show to General Westmoreland and his staff.

John's main suggestions were, first, that there be a sudden unannounced and unexplained cessation of the bombing north of the 17th parallel. Then after a week or two, an uninhabited area near Hanoi should be chosen, preferably something like the top of a mountain, and we should throw every B-52 we have against it with the heaviest possible explosives targeted on the smallest possible area. Following this strike, we should again stop, and after a cessation of three weeks, there should be another strike on an uninhabited area, this time closer to the city, if possible.

In the meantime, the only response to questions by the press should be "no comment," but with the implicit attitude that something was going on, that negotiations might be getting started. Speculation by the world press, the uncertainty of what we were going to do with our bombing, and increased pressure on Hanoi's troops in the south might combine in such a way as to put pressure on Hanoi actually to negotiate.

Second, since the V.C. is constantly using our ammunition when captured—our 81 mm mortar shells in their 82 mm tubes—we should reload some of our own shells and any captured Chinese shells with high explosive altered to detonate immediately on use. Since our troops have been trained not to use ammunition discarded or left behind in the field, such a procedure would be of no danger to us but cut off a significant source of ammunition to the enemy.

Third, since the incidence of infection and illness is very high among the enemy and they are short of medicines, we should package drugs such as Atabrine, quinine, and penicillin in foil and drop them from planes over enemy areas. On the foil there should be the message, "You'll be told this is poison. If you believe that, try it on the cat, and then give it to your friends." Since the foil would shine and flash as it is dropped and on the ground, the medicine would be easily discovered, and a propaganda message on the package would be read.

Fourth, instead of using Chu Hoi or V.C. that come over to us or are captured to work on rock piles, quarries, or road work, we should screen them and let them go back to work as soldiers. "They are damned good soldiers [contradicting his previous statements about them], and I'm quite sure they would do as good a job for us as they do for the other side if we made it worth their while. . . . What breaks their hearts is to make them do something they are not equipped to do and have no pride in." Loyalty to ideas may grow thin, but loyalty to family and country will never be touched and should not be undermined but encouraged.

On Memorial Day of 1967 the Steinbecks were in Sag Harbor when John's back gave out. He was subjected to that severe pain that simply leaves you without the ability to move enough to breathe. A young doctor of their acquaintance, Nancy Kester, was on a boat docked in the area, and she came immediately. She and Elaine took John into the city to a hospital, where he was thoroughly examined by a team of doctors and where he stayed, under observation, for several days.

The doctors accurately diagnosed his condition, but were understandably reluctant to operate on a man his age with his history of heart and circulatory problems, so they gave him medication and put him in traction. After about two weeks of treatment his pain eased and he seemed to be improved enough to warrant returning to Sag Harbor. However, his condition gradually worsened, and he spent the summer in a fog of pain and medication. Only occasionally was he able to do any of the things he wanted to do, and although while he was overseas, he had spoken several times of wanting to return to Sag Harbor—

> to go out to my little house on the point, to sharpen fifty pencils and put out a yellow pad. Early in the morning to hear what the birds are saying and to pass the time of day with Angel and then to hunch up my chair to my writing board and to set down with words—"Once upon a time . . ." [3/18/67]

—such an effort for him, although he tried, was impossible.

He did not write letters; he could not do much in the garden but walk about slowly and think of what should be done. Elaine tried to carry on what John called a "business as usual campaign," but it was no good. There was nothing usual about his situation, he thought, and his spirits sank very low. They did see friends, people like Ernest and Nancy Martin, Bob and Cynthia Wallsten, John and Shirley Fisher, but, as he put it to Elizabeth later, "I seem to be becoming a vegetable . . . thinking little thoughts or no thoughts or no thoughts at all."

He watched some television, but more as a curiosity than with much enjoyment. It was simply another window that looked out on a culture that had somehow passed him by. He felt as if his values were now suddenly old-fashioned, that even his ideas about writing seemed now old-fashioned. He spent some of his time reading new novels and decided that "the forms I am accustomed to are no longer admired—are, in fact, period pieces, only interesting if they were written a long time ago." And the pain was nearly omnipresent, driving him to a kind of detachment—for one of the few times in his life, he was not filled with plans for the future. Instead, he felt he was probably dying—"There is something sly about the whole thing," he concluded "as though I were the butt of an ancient practical joke."

At the end of August he wrote his first substantial letter in many months:

Dear Eliz.:

I know I have been greatly remiss about writing or even communicating, but this has been so in all directions. It starts with the stupid or wise feeling that I have nothing I can or want to communicate—a dry as dust, worked-out feeling. . . .

I do not mean to imply to you that I have been sitting out here pitying myself. But I am conditioned as a writer and I have been finding it impossible to write. The words will not form or if they do, there is no flavor nor any joy in them. The pain from spine and legs has been quite sharp but I halfway believe that the pain and the verbal impotence are a part of one thing in spite of what the x-rays say. . . .

I understand your feeling about this war. We seem to be sinking deeper and deeper into the mire. And it is true that we are. I am pretty sure by now that the people running the war have neither conception nor control of it. And I think that I do have some conception but I can't write it.

I know we cannot win this war, nor any war for that matter. And it seems to me that the design is for us to sink deeper and deeper into it, more and more of us. When we have put down a firm foundation of our dead and when we have by a slow, losing process been sucked into the texture of Southeast Asia, we will never be able nor will we want to get out. In the little I have seen, we, and I mean the Americans, are absorbing attitudes and thinking and some of the techniques of the East, but in equal measure the East is absorbing ours good and bad, except that it seems to me that any absorption is good.

If we should win this war, in the old sense of defeating and deadening the so-called enemy, then we would become just another occupying army, and such an army loses contact with the place occupied. But we are *not* winning in that sense and we will not. In many directions we are being defeated by more successful techniques and attitudes than our own. We have no choice in the matter. If we won we could reject but by partially losing or at best just holding our own, *we* are learning and absorbing.

Maybe it is the unformulated sense of this that causes so many men to extend their tour. Something new is happening to them.

The French could not change and so they were kicked out, but thousands of our men are changing very rapidly—giving a little but taking a lot. And unless something I cannot conceive should happen—we are there permanently, not as conquerors but as migrants. And when migrants move in they take what they can get but they deposit what they have. [8/31/67]

His reaction to the war had come almost full circle. Two years earlier, in July 1965, he had written Jack Valenti: "I'm afraid bad days are coming. There is no way to make the Vietnamese war decent. There is no way of justifying sending troops to another man's country. And there is no way to do anything but praise the man who defends his own land.... Unless the President makes some overt move toward peace, more and more Americans as well as Europeans are going to blame him for the mess, particularly since the government we are supporting with our men and treasure is about as smelly as you can get."

It was apparently the war that he thought to write about that summer, a long essay or short nonfiction book based on his articles, perhaps, but aside from the physical impossibility of it, there were too many moral restrictions on him to allow him to reveal his thoughts about the war frankly in public. Although because of his illness, his ties to the White House had slackened and would lapse almost entirely in the months ahead, he could not have publicly contradicted his President in a matter such as this nor, as he thought of it, turn against his country.

A month after he had written to Elizabeth the pain became so severe that he entered University Hospital of the New York University Medical Center on October 8, underwent a long series of tests, and was put back into traction. The doctors decided that they must operate, but on October 17, six days before the scheduled operation, his son John was arrested in Washington, D.C., on charges related to the discovery of twenty pounds of marijuana in his apartment.

Elaine had been at the hospital until very late—John was scheduled to have a very strenuous spinal test the next day and he was very nervous about it—and soon after she got back to the apartment, *Newsday* called and asked, "Mrs. Steinbeck, can you tell us a little more about your son's arrest?" That was the first she had heard about it. She tried to get hold of young John that night but was unsuccessful. Her main concern, however, was to get to the hospital as soon as they would let her in the next morning so that she could prepare her husband before the news broke in New York.

The next morning the doorman called to warn her that the press was waiting for her at the front door. She managed to sneak out the back:

All I wanted to do was to get to John, and I couldn't get a taxi, and so I got on the bus. Everybody on the bus was holding up the morning paper which said, "Steinbeck's Son Busted for Dope," which is a very unpleasant experience. I got to the hospital, and John had already turned on the early morning news and had heard about it and was very upset. We pulled ourselves together, and he said, "Just phone him. Get him in Washington and tell him he has two friends here. You and me. And ask him what we can do to help him."

The twenty pounds of marijuana discovered in John, Jr.'s apartment was not his, and so he had not been arrested for possession or dealing, but on the somewhat contrived charge of "maintaining a common nuisance." The situation was complicated by the fact that he was still in the Army, working for the Information Office at the Pentagon, and it was even more complicated by his having been working on his own time as a journalist on a story that was inimical to the Army's interest.

While in Vietnam he had observed the widespread use of marijuana by the troops, and he went on to investigate the drug use situation there. He had written an article that would break the story to the American public, in which he estimated that as many as seventy-five percent of the ground-based troops were regular users. Since anything he wrote for publication while in the Army would have to have Army clearance, which was highly unlikely for this story, he had made arrangements to have it published in the *Washingtonian* after his release from the Army, which was due in a couple of months.

However, his story broke earlier. When the narcotics agents had raided his apartment, they had taken a copy of the manuscript, and since the story also contained a rationale for the use of marijuana and a condemnation of the American public's attitude toward it, the agents quoted the article to the press in an apparent effort to justify the arrest. This in turn led the press to ask young John further about the article, and he obliged, citing among other things his statistics, which made worldwide news via the wire services.

Already feeling besieged and naturally sensitive about such allegations, the Army revoked its permission to John, Jr., to talk to the press about his arrest and connected matters, even ordering him not to discuss the fact that he had been ordered not to talk. A statement by General Westmoreland that called the entire story ridiculous was released to the press and a tape of the General denying the story was played on radio.

Actually, everyone else would seem to have come into more of a bind than the man arrested. The Army was embarrassed and had one more major problem along with all its others; the civilian drug authorities looked bad because they seemed to be persecuting the son of a famous man on the basis of a very weak case; and John Sr. seemed hurt for the article appeared to call into question his own articles about the behavior of the troops in Vietnam and his views about the war. Indeed, John's very arrest on dope charges seemed to act as a perfect refutation for all that his father stood for.

Throughout their lives both sons had repeatedly experienced situations in which they seemed to bring the house down on themselves, yet emerge unscathed. They seemed to have a kind of curious invulnerability, as if the hard shell of youthful callousness had been hardened further by the circumstances of their growing up.

This would seem to be another case of the same thing, particularly in regard to the relationship of son to father. In *In Touch,* his own account of his visit to his father in the period just following his arrest, there appears little consciousness of his father's very serious condition. On the contrary, young John's concern seems to have been devoted not to his father nor to himself, but to proving that the statements in his article were correct, and exposing the situation as he interpreted it.

His article was written "to dramatize the vast numbers of Americans who were smoking marijuana in Vietnam, and if they were smoking it as respected and lauded soldiers over there how could it be they were criminals in America. What I wanted to do most of all was paint this ridiculous contradiction. . . ." The article was written to champion the decriminalization of marijuana, and he had armed himself for an attack on the American public's hypocrisy.

Thus, young John came to his confrontation with old John, who, far from armed, was lying flat on his back in traction, trying to think of ways to help his son out of the mess he was in and warn him of certain pitfalls, such as retaliation by the Army, that he might not have foreseen. His head propped up on pillows, he was wearing a W. C. Fields T-shirt, and had a stuffed canary perched on the bridge of his glasses that seemed to be peering down into the book he had been reading. He told his son, by way of greeting, that the bird had stopped by on its way south to sample some of the tasty hospital food. On the wall, as a sort of topic sentence for the discussion to follow, was a poster that announced, SMOKE PEANUT BUTTER, NOT POT.

He listened as his son explained his situation and his plans. Young John was going to try to postpone the trial until after he was due to be discharged in December. That way, the Army would have to let him out on time, or keep him in for military trial. A court-martial was unlikely, he felt, since it would make the Army look as if it were trying to punish him for speaking out.

He had sent a copy of the manuscript of his article "The Importance of Being Stoned in Vietnam" to his father earlier, and now the conversation turned to that. John, Sr., had a continuing interest in the Vietnamese culture and the two of them talked of it for some time. The novelist complimented his son on some of the descriptive passages in the article and corrected him on a couple of points in regard to the use of drugs by the ancient Greeks. Then the major point of contention between the two finally came to the surface—what about this seventy-five percent figure that had caused such a sensation?

The older Steinbeck was concerned his son might be made to look foolish if that figure was proven to be exaggerated. Young John insisted that his motive was not sensationalism, but rather an attempt to make a point about our soldiers, who, in our ignorance of their marijuana use, are respected overseas, but who at home, if that use were discovered, would be subject to jail terms. He felt that if the juxtaposition were dramatized, it might stimulate people to rethink their positions on the subject. But, the father asked, was he using statistics that he knew might not be accurate? It was his son's "dramatization" that bothered him. If his son was trying to make a beginning as a writer, did he think it was a good idea to make exaggerated claims if he hoped his readers would take him seriously, now and in the future?

While the younger Steinbeck may have known that the figures he quoted could not be verified, he felt their use was justifiable. No exact statistics for use in Vietnam were available, and it was highly unlikely that any ever would be. In the meantime, although he might be mistaken in his estimate, if current trends in Vietnam continued, it would only be a matter of time before the facts caught up with the figures.

Young John felt at the end of their conversation that his father came to realize that in addition to exposing our hypocrisy regarding marijuana in the article, he was also making a deeply personal statement about the war and "the release from the confusion of being aware that you may die soon."

He left his parents two days before his father's operation, assuring them that he did not need their help. Although they had offered their lawyer, he had secured one of his own, and he would prefer that they were not "technically involved" in his trial. When they expressed concern that his lawyer might not be good enough, he reassured them that he was a highly respected Georgetown attorney. When young John departed, they wished him luck and asked that he keep in touch with them.

Sag Harbor house, pool in lawn to the right. *(Jackson J. Benson.)*

Receiving the Nobel Prize.
(Courtesy Mrs. E. G. Ainswort
John Steinbeck Library,
Salinas, Steinbeck Archives.)

Delivering the Nobel Prize speech. *(Courtesy Mrs. E. G. Ainsworth,*
John Steinbeck Library, Salinas, Steinbeck Archives.)

John with
Edward Albee (right)
in Prague, 1963.
*(The John Steinbeck
Collection, Stanford
University Libraries.)*

Budapest, 1963.
*(Courtesy Steinbeck House,
John Steinbeck Library,
Salinas, Steinbeck Archives.)*

At the Berlin Wall,
December 11, 1963,
with Hunton Downs (left),
Director of America House.
*(Courtesy Elaine Steinbeck,
John Steinbeck Library,
Salinas, Steinbeck Archives.)*

John with Carl Sandburg, June 6, 1963.
(*U.P.I., The John Steinbeck Collection,
Stanford University Libraries.*)

John (listening to music), Elaine, Thom, and Shirley Fisher, circa 1961.
(*Courtesy Elaine Steinbeck.*)

Elaine, Terrence McNally, John, John IV, and Thom begin "around the world" tour with passage on S.S. *Rotterdam* to Europe, 1961. *(Courtesy Elaine Steinbeck.)*

Mr. and Mrs. James Roosevelt, John, Elaine, with President Lyndon Johnson en route to Stevenson funeral in Air Force One. *(The John Steinbeck Collection, Stanford University Libraries.)*

John in door seat of Huey,
combat patrol, December 1966.
(Courtesy, © 1983,
Lt. Col. Sam M. Gipson, Jr.,
U.S.M.C., Ret.)

John with combat patrol,
Vietnam, 1966.
(Courtesy Elaine Steinbeck.)

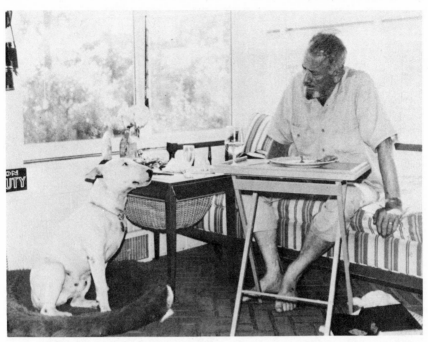

John with Angel, during the last summer, July 14, 1968.
(Courtesy Elaine Steinbeck.)

John's desk (adjustable drafting board) in Joyous Garde, looking out
over cove from Bluff Point. *(Jackson J. Benson.)*

John on Bluff Point, August 1966. *(Courtesy Elaine Steinbeck.)*

CHAPTER LI

The day before the operation, Budd Schulberg came into town and saw in the paper that his friend was in the hospital and had troubles. He called Elaine, who reported that with the pain, the worry about Johnny, and the newsmen trying to get a statement, her husband had had a very bad day. She wasn't sure that he would want to see anyone in the condition he was in—they had already started to prep him for the next morning—but he might like to hear from Budd. Schulberg phoned him at the hospital, and John asked him to come on over.

Schulberg entered a small, white room, antiseptic and depressing. It was evening, and Steinbeck was framed by the reading light, large head with rough-hewn features and jutting jaw, and a body with massive shoulders and chest that seemed far too large for the hospital bed. As they talked, John "grunted, closed his eyes in pain, cussed a little bit and snapped open and shut the blade of a large pocket knife." He pointed to a medicine cabinet on the wall and told Schulberg to make himself a drink. Budd did and went back to sit alongside the bed. He had brought with him a gift, a copy of *From the Ashes*, a book produced from the writings of the Watts Workshop, which James Thomas Jackson and the others had autographed for Steinbeck.

The two writers talked for a time about the workshop. Then John said, "I'll tell you something, I know they're angry and feel on the bottom that they've got nothing because we took it all—but I envy those young writers." They didn't have to search for material—they were living it. Having something to say burning inside you was a great luxury. John took a deep breath and sighed:

> That's my trouble. I don't think I have anything to say any more. And yet, I'm like an old tailor. Put a needle and thread in my hand and a piece of cloth and I begin to sew. My hands have to keep busy. I have to hold a pencil in my fingers. I need to write some

pages every day. When you do something for over thirty years, when you hardly think about anything else but how to put your experiences into the right words, you can't just turn it off and go play in the garden. I want to write every day, even if I don't have anything to say.

"How do you teach 'em?" he asked. "What can you tell 'em about writing except putting things down honestly, precisely?"

They talked about writing, the writers they admired, and the ones they didn't. Then they exchanged views on the times, disagreeing about the war and partially disagreeing about the hippies. John was troubled by their indolence and self-indulgence, and he compared the wandering hippies to the wandering knights of yesteryear, pointing out, as he had many times before, that our age was not so very different from theirs: "Something new was in the air but no one knew exactly what lay ahead."

The individual knights often roamed the land, searching for their own private grail. Maybe, John mused, we have our own Galahads and Mordreds on the street corners and along the highways of our day. But just as the knights in Malory's time needed direction, purpose . . . this movement today needed an Arthur and a Round Table to hold it together. Schulberg was fascinated, and sensing his friend's despair, he sought to rekindle his confidence and thoughts for the future. He told him he thought the idea marvelous and that he had never thought of the period in those terms before—sort of a *Grapes of Wrath* of the Middle Ages, he added enthusiastically.

The pills were taking their effect on John, and he ground his teeth, trying to resist their effect, and thrust out his jaw: "I don't know . . . nothing to say . . . did you see what the *Times* wrote about me?" He reached over to the top of a white porcelain table near the bed and indicated a clipping that lay near two others.

Schulberg reached over, picked it up, and read the editorial from *The New York Times* that questioned whether Steinbeck deserved the Nobel Prize and wondered if "a poet or critic or historian" might not have been a more appropriate choice as having made "a more profound impression on the literature of our age." Of the two other clippings, one was an editorial from the *New York Post*, which in an unforgiving tone scolded the author for having forsaken his old liberalism in his support of South Vietnam, and the other was headlined FAMOUS AUTHOR'S SON NABBED ON DOPE CHARGE!

Schulberg said, "Shove *The New York Times.* Why do you cut that out when you think of the presentation in Stockholm. God damn it, John, throw those lousy clippings away."

John flipped open the blade of his knife, made a kind of growling sound in his throat, and pointed the tip of the blade toward his stomach. "I don't want to come out of this thing in the morning a goddam invalid. When I'm not working on a book I've got to be outdoors, working on my boat, growing something, *making* something."

On October 23, Steinbeck underwent almost five hours of surgery for a ruptured spinal disk. The operation was successful, and the hospital reported his condition as "satisfactory." When his personal doctor, Denton Cox, came to visit him, he noticed that Steinbeck had persuaded someone to put a sign on his door: OFF LIMITS TO MEDICAL PERSONNEL.

A few days later, Elaine wrote to Dook Sheffield in California:

> You are very much on John's mind. Three times over the weekend he asked if I'd written you.
>
> It's a joy to me to tell you that he is doing marvelously. The doctors shake their heads in disbelief. Their diagnosis: a tough old bird. The main thing is that he *wanted* the fusion; in his condition anything short of that would have been patch-work. The doctors would promise him nothing. Who knew how well he would take the anaesthesia in a long operation or what the condition of the bone would be? Three times during the operation the two orthopedic surgeons told the anaesthetist: we can stop now and he'll have a pretty good back, and three times that blessed man said: John is fine—carry on.
>
> So we feel triumphant and optimistic for the future. I've always considered John's behavior with a common cold to be grounds for *divorce*—now, you've never seen such a great patient. He's been of good heart all along. Just before surgery when his special nurses came in to introduce themselves as "your day nurse, your night nurse," he said thoughtfully, "Well, I'm not quite sure whether I'm more fun in the day-time or at night." . . .
>
> I expect John will be home by Thanksgiving. At this point he can turn himself in bed, and by the weekend he will be on his feet for a few minutes. The doctors swear that after a few months his back will be stronger than it has been in years. Thank God he doesn't, at this point, have to try to come to terms with a restricted life.
>
> I'll keep you posted. Take care of yourself, dear one.

By mid-November he was learning to walk again, and he worked hard at it, but complained of himself that he was inclined to buckle at the knees and tended to panic. At the same time, he began swimming-pool therapy, which led him to invite certain selected nurses to join him in their bikinis. He had many visitors now, and Elaine set up a bar in the room so that he could receive his guests in style.

He received a little pamphlet from John Kenneth Galbraith on *How to Get Out of Vietnam*. The plan was to recognize our error, pull back, and negotiate our withdrawal from Vietnam, with provision only for the safety of those we left behind. Galbraith had sent it with some misgivings, but to his relief, he had not lost a friend. John wrote back:

> I like your book on how to get out of Vietnam. It is telling and effective, particularly in what it leaves out. Reminds me of a time during the last war. Meeting of services in Washington. Subject— what can we do to stop the rapid rise of V.D. No one could think of a solution except Gene Tunney. He had a beauty and it would work—Continence. [11/15/67]

Day after day he took his therapy, and by the first part of December he could get around well enough to be released from the hospital. He could lie down or stand up but he had been warned not to sit up for any length of time. On December 23 they flew to Grenada in the Virgin Islands, where they joined friends from London, and the two couples took cottages on the beach. It was a restful place with few other visitors, warm, but with a steady breeze off the bay.

John would put on his swimming trunks and lie with Elaine on the beach and every now and then go into the water. When they had drinks before dinner, he would lie on the couch on the terrace overlooking the sea, sit up during dinner, and then retire back to the couch. In what may have been his last completed letter to Elizabeth, he reported:

> There is absolutely nothing to do here which is fine for me. I haven't even written postcards. The days go by as the clouds do. We read, bathe, sun, drink, eat, nap, read, drink, eat and sleep. I have read old romantic novels, naval history, slavery history, mysteries and now am reading the long history of the love affair of Napoleon and Josephine. It is a small place on a small bay. Our cottage is right near the beach and available for every breeze....
>
> The only news, apart from local, is in the London papers three days late, so we know nothing that has gone on and for that we are pretty glad. My sister Esther writes, "I see that Johnny is imitating

your beard." I don't even much want to know what he is up to. King of the Hippies perhaps. I'm afraid he took his trial as a triumph rather than a lesson. [On December 18 John Steinbeck IV went to trial in the criminal division of the District of Columbia court of general sessions. After deliberating forty-five minutes, a jury aquitted him of the charge against him.] [1/9/68]

They stayed at Grenada for a month, and his condition seemed to improve daily as the pain subsided and his movement became freer. Of course he was still taking sedatives, and those plus the nervous shock had moved him into "another and rather fuzzy reality," as he reported to Dook at the end of January. Through all of this, it was Elaine's courage and her refusal to let him wallow in the trough of discouragement that kept him moving forward.

"He was less sick," Tom Guinzburg recalls, "because of her. I mean it's almost impossible to describe. The doctors who were involved with John were all marvelous people who cared very much about John, because Elaine had found them. They might have loved him had they known him, but they never would have got to know him unless Elaine had kind of ferreted them out." Nearly all their friends have made a point of remarking that without Elaine, or with a wife less spirited and capable, he would not have been able to find the peace to live with himself during what turned out to be a process of constant deterioration.

Near the end of March, John wrote to Dook from his room in their New York apartment:

Here in New York, we live 34 floors up with the whole city below our windows. It is a slender tower and there is an updraft around the building like a chimney. Right now it is snowing up because of this updraft. A startling thing to see. . . .

Here in my workroom, I have a sill garden. Four cucumber plants growing in pill bottles and one flourishing English oak I grew from an acorn I picked up in Somerset. I seem to require something growing. The cucumbers are just silly but I'll plant the oak at Sag Harbor. I have two English oaks out there I raised from acorns. They are about four feet high now. They are named Gog and Magog. Of course there are seventy or more American oaks on our point but I try to keep young ones coming. I don't know why. . . .

If my back recovers by next winter, we are going to Tanganyika to see the animals—not to shoot them or even to photograph them but just to look at them. I've never been in central Africa or south for that matter and I would love to see it. So much I haven't seen. [3/23/68]

Shortly after this, they did go to Sag Harbor, but as he wrote Toby Street, "They don't let me garden, go in a boat, fish, lift anything, bend over—all such things and it is a bloody bore."

II

Almost as if his life were on some kind of timetable of destruction, John was hit again by illness on Memorial Day Weekend, this time a small stroke while eating in a restaurant in Sag Harbor. He did not lose consciousness, nor was he incapacitated in any way, but Elaine took him to Southampton Hospital, where he was given tests and kept a week under observation. Then, in early July he suffered an episode of heart failure that was manifested as the sudden inability to breathe, as if one were drowning, and he was rushed to the hospital once more and put in an oxygen tent.

Long Island was having a heat wave, and there was no air conditioning in the hospital, so John's breathing problems were made even more acute. Over his objections—he wanted to stay and then return to Sag Harbor—Elaine and the doctors decided he should be moved to the city. Dr. Cox would come out in an ambulance to fetch him, and he and Dr. Kester would ride back, just in case there was another episode on the way.

A half hour before the ambulance was due to arrive, Elaine, who had been with her husband almost constantly during the past few days, drove back to the house to get what clothing and other things they might need in New York. Shirley Fisher came in to take over from Elaine, but because of the noise of the equipment and his restricted view, he didn't know that she was there.

He had some newspapers with him, and after Elaine left, he put them down, put his arm over his eyes, and wept. Shirley didn't move. After a few minutes, he picked up the newspaper again and was glancing vaguely at the tabloid's society page when he looked up and saw Shirley sitting there, apparently assuming that she had just come into the room. He said something that she didn't catch because of the whirring of the fans, so she went over and crouched against him, bending forward to hear what he was saying. Nodding toward the paper, he said, "I do thrill so to the exploits of Colonel Serge Obolenski."

Shortly after he arrived at New York Hospital on July 17, the nurses who had taken care of him before at University Hospital paid him the tremendous compliment of asking if they could come and care for him again at the other hospital. He had another very severe episode while he was there, but over a period of three weeks, surrounded by an extraordinary amount of love and care on all sides, he gradually grew stronger. Yet, after further tests and consultations with experts, it was clear to everyone that nothing could be done and that this was the road to the end.

John's relationship with his personal doctor, Denton Cox, was somewhat complex and perhaps unique in that not only was his doctor his friend, but there was a philosophical basis to both the personal and professional relationships. Cox had met John at a dinner party in 1956, not long after having passed his residency, and after dinner the doctor found himself in deep discussion with the writer. They talked about cellular biology, about tidepools and marine animals and ecology, and any number of related topics until four in the morning when everyone else had gone, and the fire before them had died.

Near the end they had been talking about John's Cannery Row days, and John asked him if he had read *The Log from the "Sea of Cortez."* Dr. Cox said he had not, and John offered to send a copy to him. When he received the book a few days later, he opened it and found the inscription, "For Denny Cox, who also proliferates in all directions. John Steinbeck, 1956, New York"—the quotation was from John's description of Ed Ricketts.

After seeing each other socially off and on during these years, John asked Cox to become his doctor in 1964, after his previous physician retired.

It was a very special thing to me, knowing me socially chiefly and in that way, and I am sure he had asked and found out other reasons to come to me, but it began a very special relationship.

The most important thing about his coming to me as a patient initially, apart from the choice of me, was that he made a gesture which is something he alone has done in that fashion, of writing a several page letter and document to me about the reasons for coming to a physician. This was not at a time of ill health, but for a checkup, and he was making a commitment he felt, to himself and me, and it involved communication—a new communication—in which he wanted to let me know everything that was important to him about his health and about life, and about future illness, if it came, and about pain, and certainly about his relationship with Elaine and how I should be aware, should the need arise.

Cox had given John a medical history form to fill out, thirteen pages of specific questions, which concluded with the questions, "Do you have anything to add of any importance?" It was in response to this that he had written his four-and-a-half-page letter, which read in part:

What do I want in a doctor? Perhaps more than anything else—a friend with special knowledge. If you had never dived and I were with you, it would be my purpose to instruct you in the depths and dangers, of the pleasant and the malign. I guess I mean the same thing somewhat. We are so made that rascally, unsubtle flares may cause a meaningless panic whereas a secret treason may be nibbling away, unannounced or even pleasant as in the rapture of the deep. Two kinds of pain there are—or rather a number of kinds. I think especially of the teaching pain which counsels us not to hurt ourselves as opposed to the blast that signals slow or fast disintegration. Unskilled, we do not know the difference and, I am told, even the skilled lose their knowledge when the thing is in themselves. It seems to me that one would prepare oneself differently to meet these two approaches, if one knew.

Then there is the signal for the curtain. I think, since the end is the same, that the chief protagonist should have the right to judge his exit, if he can, taking into consideration his survivors who are after all, the only ones who matter. . . .

I dislike helplessness in other people and in myself, and this is by far my greatest fear of illness.

Believe me, I would not go on in this vein, and never do, were it not for the nature of this communication.

I shall probably not change my habits very much unless incapacity forces it. I don't think I am unique in this.

Now finally, I am not religious so that I have no apprehension of a hereafter, either a hope of reward or a fear of punishment. It is not a matter of belief. It is what I feel to be true from my experience, observation and simple tissue feeling.

Secondly—I have had a good span of life so that from now on in I should not feel short-changed.

Thirdly—I have lived very fully and vividly and there is no possibility of cosmic pique.

Fourthly—I have had far more than my share of the things men strive for—material things and honors and love.

Fifthly, my life has been singularly free of illness or accident. At any rate the wellness has far overbalanced the sickness.

Sixthly—I do not come to you as a sick man. . . .

And now the last thing you should know. I love Elaine more than myself. Her well being and comfort and happiness are more important than my own. And I would go to any length to withhold from her any pain or sorrow that is not needful for her own enrichment. [3/5/64]

Dr. Cox read this letter two or three times, and reread it when John became seriously ill and was hospitalized, so that he would be aware of the things that his patient felt were important to him.

John had some emphysema, but his major problem was that his coronary arteries were clogged (the autopsy showed that you could not get a sewing needle through them), which led to shortness of breath. He was subject to periods of acute distress during his last months, when he had to have oxygen to survive. As time went by, these episodes became more and more frequent, especially at night, when he would suddenly choke and gasp for air. There was in early development an operation, a revascularization procedure of grafting to bypass the clogged arteries, but after consulting two eminent cardiologists, Cox concluded that the operation would not significantly affect John's chances for survival.

Still, he felt he should discuss the operation with John, who dismissed it very quickly. He said, "Denny, that's just a patch job, isn't it?" Cox replied, "Well, it might be better than a patch job." And John said, "Well, I don't want it."

When things were going very badly during the first part of his stay at New York Hospital, John asked Cox one afternoon, "Denny, have you read Ecclesiastes?" and Cox replied, "Yes, but a long time ago." "Which chapter or verse?" Cox asked, and John said, "The whole thing. It's not very long." And so the doctor wrote on the patient's chart, "The patient has sent me to Ecclesiastes," and went home and read it that night. Among the verses he noted, "One generation passeth away, and another generation cometh: but the earth abideth for ever" and the beginning of Chapter 3:

To every thing there is a season, and a time to every purpose under the heaven:

A time to be born, and a time to die; a time to plant and a time to pluck up that which is planted;

A time to kill, and a time to heal; a time to break down, and a time to build up.

The next morning Cox went into John's room and told him, "I read it, John, and I see what you mean, but how do you know that this is your time?"

Cox felt that when John was gloomy, he liked to toy with cynicism, but that in his heart of hearts he was a realist, that his basic quality was an affirmation in life. John was really concerned about two things: that Elaine should not be made to suffer through an extended period while his life was extended without hope, and that he not lose control of his own destiny. Behind both of these was the fear that he would either lose consciousness or become physically helpless and unable to move, and that in either case there might be some kind of elaborate, but hopeless operation performed or there be an extensive effort to keep him alive with tubes, wires, and apparatus.

In response to this fear, it became very important to him to get out of the hospital. If he were going to die, he wanted to die at home in his own environment, where he had more control over the circumstances. As he put it in his letter, "The chief protagonist should have the right to judge his exit," and there were times when he would tease Elaine and his doctor, now and later, about the possibility of his ending his own life. It would seem highly unlikely that he would do so, since he had also written that the chief protagonist should have the right to judge, but "taking into consideration his survivors, who are after all, the only ones who matter." Nevertheless, he was serious enough to squirrel away pills, which he collected into a little pill box shaped like a pig.

Every day Elaine was with him in the hospital, as long as the rules and the onset of crises would permit. One day she came in, and John asked her, "Are you for me or are you against me?" and she answered. "I'm for you—why?" He said, "I want to go to Sag Harbor." She said, "All right—do you want to go with or without a nurse?" "Without a nurse." She said, "Fine. Will you agree to come home to the apartment first and have nurses around the clock and let them teach me the routine? Of giving you any shots you need? And taking your blood pressure and doing all the things that you need—would you let them train me for a week and then we'll go?"

"Sure," he said, "that's fair enough."

They went back to the apartment for a week, and then moved to Sag Harbor on August 21. As soon as they got back to Bluff Point, John wanted to know where Angel was. Angel had been boarded at a kennel while John was in the hospital, and one day another dog jumped from behind a barrier, taking Angel unawares, and took off his eye. Elaine was frantic with John dying—what could she tell him about Angel? He kept asking, "Why isn't Angel here?" Finally, when she thought he felt strong enough, she told him, "Angel has had an accident." And John said, "Not his vital organs?" "No, his eye has been bitten." "Oh, well, that's all right."

Elaine told him that the kennel man had written and offered to let Angel "have a go" at the other dog—he felt so bad that he had been hurt while in his care—and since Angel was a pit bull, it would have taken him about a minute to kill the other dog. John said no, don't do that—that wouldn't do any good. When Angel came home, with his eye sewn closed, John put an eye patch on him, then changed his mind and painted a wink, with lashes, on the eyelid.

As difficult as the circumstances were, these were generally happy months. John could walk around and go outside, and he brought out a chair and watched the crew build a new dock. He could have visitors, and nearly everyone they knew stopped by, including Toby Street from California. There were times, during the day, when it seemed as if he were not sick at all, but Elaine had to be prepared for the sudden crisis, and always during the night, she would have to get up to help him. They had oxygen in the bedroom and in the sitting room.

Twice a week she would take him to Southampton to have a blood test, and they'd stop off at a diner and have breakfast. She would phone her grocery order into Schavioni's and then race down to pick it up and get the mail, afraid to leave him for fear he would have a crisis and not be able to get to the oxygen.

And there were times when his health seemed very poor, when he couldn't move, and it seemed as if he would never pull out again. During one of those periods, John had been in bed when he mentioned to Jean Boone, Elaine's sister, that he was going to get up and watch the news. She came in to tell Elaine, who was cooking, that John wanted to watch Walter Cronkite, and suddenly with a burst of energy that was startling, he stormed into the sitting room in his nightshirt and boomed, "Six o'clock!" and almost bounced into his chair.

He stayed to watch *The Wild, Wild West*. His technique for watching this program was to turn off the sound and make up his own dialogue. He did this also when he was waiting for one program to finish so that he could watch the next. Television, Elaine recalls, was always much better when John made up the dialogue.

John and Elaine wanted the late summer and the fall not to end. Somehow, as in Ecclesiastes, John's life had become attached to the seasons. They stretched their time as far as they could, but in early November he had a crisis so severe that Denton Cox was called from the city to attend him. By November 11 they were forced to return to town to the apartment.

They knew now that death was close, but the difficulty in facing it was that they didn't know how close. A friend told Elaine, "I hope you have a doctor who makes house calls," and Elaine was able to answer, "We've got one who makes one every day." Dr. Cox did come daily to check him out and take a blood sample, and they talked about literature, the opera, travel, or politics—they didn't talk much about John. Again, as in Sag Harbor, he had his good days and his bad. The Benchleys came for Thanksgiving, and they had a real party, almost like the old days, and friends dropped by in the late afternoon for cocktails or in the early evening to talk and visit.

Frank Loesser, who had always been a special friend, was a frequent visitor. He talked while he walked, and he walked all the time, with his hands stuffed into his back pockets, and told his stories all over the room. For John, to be with Frank was like a tonic, a sudden injection of life and laughter, and on one occasion, John was in his dressing gown sitting in the living room, when Frank went in to see him. At once they were in a world of their own, and it was as if nothing had changed. After a time, Frank came out to the kitchen where Elaine was cooking. "Elaine," he said, "we've all been wrong. He's not dying. Look at him. Why he's absolutely normal." Elaine could only say, "Maybe he's not—isn't that wonderful. Maybe he's going to be all right." And Frank said, "I wish that they would stop scaring us like this, the doctors. What do they know?"

At one point when the situation seemed to be getting very grim, John shocked Elaine by suddenly starting to chuckle to himself. She asked, "What's so funny?"

He said, "Honey, you're going to laugh like hell after I'm dead."

"What do you mean? I wouldn't laugh. I'd have nothing to laugh about."

"Sometime, suddenly, it will come to you that Gwyn won't be getting any more alimony, and you're going to laugh your head off."

The nights now were filled with crises, and Elaine lay by John's side and waited for the onset of the hoarse, guttural gasping. Then she would jump up, come around to where he would be sitting on the edge of the bed, and help him with the oxygen. She waited for the time that because of the sedation he would be unable to get to the mask by himself. Thursday nights they had a nurse come in so that Elaine could get a full night's sleep and regain her alertness. The nurse was a French-Canadian, Elaine LaTulipe, and John would say, "Let's have Tulips spend the night so that you can get a good night's sleep."

The Thursday night before the day John died, Elaine moved into the guest room for the night, and a few minutes after the nurse took over she came to Elaine and said, "I think he's better. He looks much better tonight. Why don't you get the car out and take him for a drive in the next two or three days?" Elaine replied, "Tulipe, you don't know what you are talking about. He couldn't possibly do that now." The next morning she woke Elaine at six and said, "Oh, I'm sorry for what I said. We had the most terrible night in the world. Not that the man is in pain, but he can't breathe. I don't think he has very much longer to live." And Elaine said, "I know he doesn't."

Elaine stayed very close by him that morning. She read to him, but after a time, he said, "No—let's talk."

"Okay."

"It's been a wonderful life," he said.

"It has, super."

"You've made my life bright."

"I'm glad."

"What's the best time we ever had together?"

"I think I've got it—but you have to say it first."

"I think I know."

"I'm not going to say it until after you've said. But I'll be honest with you and tell you."

"I've got it. The time at Discove."

"That's what I had, too."

Then he said, "Let's talk about champagne."

"All right. Where do you want to start?"

"You know what I mean."

"Oh, you mean when we went to the champagne festival."

Years ago when they had been staying at the Lancaster in Paris, Elaine had been reading a newspaper aloud to him in French in order to improve her vocabulary. As she read she said, "I think—I'm not sure—but I think that this says that in Rouen next Sunday they are going to celebrate the building of the cathedral, the invention of champagne, and Mother's Day." John roared and said, "The three great things in life, booze, the church, and mothers—let's go!" So they hired a car and had a very good time.

About twelve-thirty he said, "I would like Denny to come early, I surely hope Denny comes early today." "Would you like to see Denny right now?" "Yes, please." Elaine called Denton Cox, and he came at once, examined John, and then told Elaine that he was certain that it would only be a matter of a few hours. Elaine already knew this, but to hear it was still a shock, and she collapsed. After she had been revived and she managed to pull herself together, she called Elizabeth and Shirley to tell them that they could come over to the apartment at any time, if they wished.

At four Dr. Cox received an emergency call—one of his best friends had been seriously hurt in an automobile accident—but by this time, Dr. Nancy Kester had come to help, and, promising to return as soon as he could, he left John in her hands. He told her that he didn't know how many more hours it would be before John succumbed.

John began slowly to go into a coma, and Nancy said, "Elaine I'm not a rehabilitation doctor . . . I don't know." And Elaine said, "That's all right. It doesn't matter now. Just stay with us until the end." Elizabeth and Shirley had come into the living room, and in the bedroom, Elaine was lying next to John. He tried to say something, and Elaine leaned over him and asked, "What is it?" "I seemed to hear the sound of distant drums." Then he appeared to realize that that was a little corny, and so he looked up at Elaine and said, "Maybe it's just Shirley playing the bagpipes."

One of the nurses who had come from University Hospital to help John entered the room, as Elaine continued to lie beside him. Then, at the same moment, they realized he was gone. At five-thirty p.m., December 20, 1968, a few hours before the onset of winter, John Steinbeck was dead.

III

He had gone very easily and quietly. His eyes were closed and his heart just stopped. Elizabeth and Shirley, weeping, came down the hall, stood near the doorway, and blew a kiss to him. Denny Cox returned. "I cried," he recalls. "I don't cry easily or often, but the loss was a great one. I am a bad loser, and I couldn't get over the feeling that there was more I should have or could have done."

Elaine, with Elizabeth's help, had already made most of the arrangements, so that once the death certificate had been signed and the body taken away, there was very little more to be done, although everyone close to the Steinbecks rallied around Elaine to give her their support.

Dorothy Covici helped Elaine organize John's things, and they picked out "Burying Black" for the funeral. Thom had come home on special leave from Vietnam (John had gone back to Vietnam as a civilian and could not be reached in time to get back), and he went with his stepmother to pick out the casket.

At the showroom the salesman was outraged when they picked out the simplest wooden box available. "You can't do this, you can't do this to Steinbeck," he insisted in a shrill voice. "Don't you even want to look at this one? It is very comfortable." Elaine and Thom laughed, knowing how much John would have laughed at such sentiments. Elaine also refused to get a decorated urn for the ashes. John Fisher suggested that she use a little Georgian silver box that John had been fond of, and when Elaine agreed, he drove to Sag Harbor to get it.

Everything was done according to John's wishes. A few days before he died, he was sitting with Elaine and her sister, Jean, when out of the blue he said, "No man should be buried in alien soil." And Elaine said, "I know what you are telling me. You won't be." Then she paused for a moment as a thought came to her and said, "Oh, I will be." "No you won't," he said. "I'll be there." On another occasion he said to Elaine, "I want the Church of England funeral service—I want the 'I am the resurrection and the life, saith the Lord.' I don't want a bunch of people getting together for a memorial telling yarns about me."

Elaine asked Nat Benchley to get in touch with Henry Fonda, thinking that he was in New York, to read a few of John's favorite poems at the service. Fonda was making a film in California, but flew in for the funeral. Benchley also arranged for the honorary pallbearers—Tom Guinzburg, Denton Cox, Ernest Martin, John Fisher, Chase Horton, John Fearnley, and Edward Albee. Nat reported that Frank Loesser had taken John's death very hard and was in bad shape. He wanted to go to the funeral, but he hoped Elaine would understand that he didn't think he could; a day later he called to say that he had to do it, he just had to.

Although there had been an announcement in the papers that no flowers should be sent, they came anyway, and Nancy Martin and Marge Benchley went to the church to arrange them around the altar. An hour before the service a man came into the church, sat down, and prayed. The two women never spoke to him, but recognized John O'Hara.

The funeral, which lasted twenty minutes, was held at St. James Episcopal Church on Madison Avenue. Fonda read from Synge's "Petrarch's Sonnets to Laura," Tennyson's "Ulysses," and these lines from Robert Louis Stevenson's "Songs of Travel and Other Verses":

> Bright is the ring of words
>   When the right man rings them
> Fair the fall of songs
>   When the singer sings them
> Still they are carolled and said
>   On wings they are carried
> After the singer is dead
>   And the maker buried.

The rector read the beginning of The Order for the Burial of the Dead from the Book of Common Prayer and Psalms 46 and 121.

As the coffin was carried from the church, the professional pallbearers lifted it high in the air, at arm's length over their heads, and down the steps and out to the hearse. In the family room, Elaine was surrounded with a score of close friends, and as she embraced each, she said, "All I ask is—remember him. Remember him!"

Elaine and Thom took John's ashes to California the afternoon before Christmas. For two nights the silver box rested in the garden of the Eleventh Street house in Pacific Grove. John's sisters had arranged a small service for the family on Point Lobos, on a cliff overlooking Whalers Bay, a spot that John and Mary had loved and where they had played as children. A young priest with red hair and white robe said the burial service, took a handful of dust and let it drift with the wind. ". . . ashes to ashes, dust to dust . . ." An otter played in the sea below, and above, a gull circled and cried out against the sky.

Acknowledgments

Because John Steinbeck ranged widely in his activities and in the number and diversity of the people he met, this book could not have been written without the help of hundreds of people and many institutions, and it would be impossible to thank them all properly here. Those who talked or wrote to me about Steinbeck, or about topics related to him, have been listed as sources at the head of the notes for each chapter to which they contributed, and to all of them I express my profound gratitude for their kindness and generosity. Often they gave not only of their own time, but introduced me to other sources and provided letters, manuscripts, or photographs for my use.

As I have already indicated in my dedication, I owe a very great debt to Mrs. John Steinbeck, who not only gave me her authorization to proceed with the biography, but provided constant help in directing me to sources and materials. She gave me far more time and encouragement than any biographer has a right to expect.

I also owe a special debt to the generosity of John Steinbeck's sister, Mrs. E. G. Ainsworth, and to several close friends of Steinbeck who adopted me out of their love for John—Carlton Sheffield, Webster Street, Elizabeth Otis, and Shirley Fisher. I am most grateful to John's first wife, the late Mrs. William Brown, for breaking her silence on the subject to talk to me of her first marriage, and I wish also to acknowledge the help provided by John's second wife, Gwyndolyn Steinbeck, before she passed away several years ago.

Special thanks must be extended to others in Steinbeck's life who corresponded with me and gave particular help: Richard Albee, Nathaniel Benchley, Mrs. Lynn Loesser, Mrs. Virginia Scardigli, Jack Watson, Mrs. Polly Teas, and Mrs. Jerome Brody. Joseph Bryan III, a distinguished writer, shared his notes on his friendship with Steinbeck with me—no greater kindness could one writer show to another. And I would like to mention those who, although not connected with Steinbeck, gave me extended assistance with special topics: Mrs. Mary Alice Johns about her father, Tom Collins; Leo Shepovalov and Delbert H. West about the Tahoe area and the hatchery; Ross Riley about the Spreckels farms and factories; and Paul S. Taylor and Anne Loftis about farm labor in California during the 1930s. I appreciate the assistance of Edward F.

Ricketts, Jr., who was kind enough to review my biographical sketch of his father.

At the beginning of my research, I had the assistance of James Foxworthy, and at the completion of the manuscript, help with the verification of documentation by Alfred Bauer. I was also assisted by Mrs. Barbara Hopfinger, who for several years, out of her love for the material and her regard for Steinbeck, worked long and hard, reading, digesting, and abstracting from my notes and initial research to produce the basic chronology which I would build on in the years that followed. During the writing of the manuscript, I found occasion over and over again to thank her in my mind for the work she did so well.

From the beginning of composition, Mrs. Uni Poppert worked on my manuscript, typing draft after draft, making changes and following my revisions, proofreading and catching errors. Without her constant help, the production of a manuscript would have been a far more difficult task.

For financial assistance, I am indebted to the National Endowment for the Humanities for a summer grant and a research fellowship; to the American Philosophical Society whose financial aid enabled me to start this project; and to the San Diego State University Foundation. San Diego State University also provided a semester's research leave, two sabbatical leaves, clerical assistance, library assistance, and, for several years, a lightened teaching load.

I am grateful for the essential help and materials provided by the Stanford University Libraries, the John Steinbeck Library in Salinas, the Bancroft Library at the University of California at Berkeley, the Humanities Research Center at the University of Texas, and the Steinbeck Research Center at San Jose State University. Florian J. Shasky, Susan F. Riggs, and Carol A. Rudisell at Stanford; John Gross and Linda Plummer at Salinas; Maureen Pastine and Bernadine L. Beutler at San Jose; and James D. Hart at the Bancroft were of great help to me in my research, and I am thankful for their many kindnesses.

I owe debts also to the Pierpont Morgan Library, the New York Public Library, the Library of Congress, the Federal Archives in Washington, D.C., and San Bruno, the University of Virginia Library, the Harvard University Libraries, the Ball State University Library, and the Malcolm A. Love Library at San Diego State.

Friends and colleagues have come to my aid. Richard Astro and Joel Hedgpeth answered my questions and graciously allowed me to rely extensively on their scholarly work on Edward F. Ricketts. Robert DeMott gave me several leads and ideas coming out of his own work on a book on Steinbeck's reading. Peter Lisca, Philip Young, Richard Astro, Fred S. Moramarco, and Kermit Vanderbilt supplied references for my grant applications. Richard D. Davis helped me with my research in Los Gatos, and Richard L. Allman contributed the fine photography which has added so much to the total meaning of the book. Robert Wallsten read the manuscript and made valuable suggestions, and Susan F. Riggs was kind enough to read the galleys and, out of her extensive knowledge of Steinbeck materials, make a final check of my accuracy. My agent, Patricia S. Myrer of McIntosh and Otis, Inc., was instrumental in helping me acquire several important documents.

I should also like to give credit to those Steinbeck scholars whose work preceded mine, providing the foundation on which I was able to build. Among the many whose writings gave me an education in Steinbeck and influenced directly and indirectly the contents of this book, I would make special mention of Peter Lisca, Warren French, Joseph Fontenrose, and Richard Astro. Also, I am exceedingly grateful for the bibliographical work of Tetsumaro Hayashi, Adrian H. Goldstone, and John R. Payne.

Finally, I would like to express my gratitude to the many friends, neighbors, and students who provided research leads over the years, and to the many colleagues around the country who wrote periodically to encourage me in my work. The greatest debt of all is due my wife, Sue Ellen, and my two daughters, Katrina and Belinda, who put up with the pressure and my absences—physical and mental—over a period of many years and who in good spirits and with much love supported me and had faith in me.

Notes and Sources

EXPLANATORY NOTE

For each chapter I have listed (1) *interviews,* (2) *unpublished material by Steinbeck* (not including letters—for documentation of letters, see Prefatory Note), (3) *published material by Steinbeck,* (4) *published or unpublished material by others* (about Steinbeck or in some way related to him), and (5) *notes* (listed by page number and key phrase from text). Sections (2) through (4) can be considered a running bibliography of sources, primary and secondary.

The names listed under (1) for each chapter are for the most part people interviewed in person by me, but there are a few individuals with whom I only corresponded or talked to by phone. In several cases I have drawn on interviews conducted by others: by Anne Loftis of farm labor leaders, and by George Robinson and Pauline Pearson, acting for the John Steinbeck Library. I have noted the origin of these latter interviews by appending the label "Salinas tape" in each case. In two instances I was asked to omit any reference to the name of the informant, and I have done so, since the information was not controversial. In one other case I was asked to provide a pseudonym for the interviewee and have so noted in reference to him.

In order to simplify repeated references to Steinbeck's unpublished and published writings, I have listed these with full title and, in the case of published works, full publication information once in sections (2) and (3) for each chapter, and in the notes (5) I have referred to them only in abbreviation. I have used the same technique for multiple references to material about or related to Steinbeck written by others (4), except that once an item has been listed once for a chapter in full, it will not be listed under (4) for other chapters unless extensive use of it is made in that chapter.

When a work by Steinbeck is still in manuscript form, I have put quotation marks around the title; after a book has been published, I have put the title in italics. (Occasionally, I have referred to the published book, rather than the manuscript, prior to its publication and have indicated that by using italics.) Although there are a few instances when I have referred to a book long before either composition or publication, sections (2) and (3) provide a rough chronology of composition and publication. Nearly every work—book, story, and article or series of articles—by Steinbeck is mentioned in the text; those items omitted are largely prefaces written for books by other writers and a few short pieces of limited circulation, privately printed as gifts or tributes. References to Steinbeck books, unless otherwise indicated, are to the first edition, except where those first editions are so rare as to be nearly unobtainable.

Notes (5) have been kept to a minimum, with very few explanatory or expository items. In most cases, through identification in the text or context of use, sources can be located on the listings (1) through (4), and letters, as I explain in my Prefatory Note, are usually documented in the text itself. Where the source is not clear from its use in the text, I refer to the informant's last name. For quotations from published material by or about Steinbeck, I refer to the author's last name, or, in the case of Steinbeck, an abbreviation of the title, and cite the page number. Brief references or quotations from works about or related to Steinbeck are documented only in the notes section (5).

EPIGRAPH

Interview with JS, "Conversation with Bo Beskow and Bo Holmström," Swedish Broadcasting Corporation, 8/12/62.

PROLOGUE

(5) *Notes*
    Pages
    1. *Cannery Row* (New York: The Viking Press, 1945), p. 8.
    3–4. JS/Peter Benchley, 1956 (courtesy of Nathaniel Benchley).

CHAPTER I

(1) *Interviews*
    Max Wagner, Mrs. Mildred Hargis, Mrs. E. G. Ainsworth (Elizabeth Steinbeck), Mrs. C. J. Rodgers (Esther Steinbeck), Paul Pioda, Carlton A. Sheffield, Mrs. Lucille Hughes, Glenn Graves, Henry Renaud.
(4) *Published or Unpublished Material by Others*
    Peter Lisca, *The Wide World of John Steinbeck* (New Brunswick, New Jersey: Rutgers University Press, 1958).
    Joseph Fontenrose, *John Steinbeck: An Introduction and Interpretation* (New York: Holt, Rinehart and Winston, Inc., 1963).
(5) *Notes*
    Pages
    7. *East of Eden* (New York: The Viking Press, 1952), p. 5.
    7. "I can remember": *Eden*, p. 1.

8. *Travels with Charley in Search of America* (New York: The Viking Press, 1962), p. 161.

9. *The Red Pony* (New York: The Viking Press, 1945), pp. 91–92.

11–12. The Grosssteinbecks and Dicksons: "Letters to Alicia," *Newsday*, 12 February 1966, p. 3W.

13. "Neighbors": *Eden*, p. 151.

15. *Journal of a Novel: The "East of Eden" Letters* (New York: The Viking Press, 1969), p. 103.

15–16. Bally Kelly: *East of Eden*, pp. 8–12, and "I Go Back to Ireland," *Collier's*, 31 January 1953, pp. 48–50.

16. *Eden*, pp. 148–150.

16. "Olive had not": *Eden*, p. 149.

17. "External realities": *Eden*, p. 150.

CHAPTER II

(1) *Interviews*

Mrs. E. G. Ainsworth (Elizabeth Steinbeck), Mrs. C. J. Rodgers (Esther Steinbeck), Paul L. Pioda, Henry Renaud, Glenn Graves, John Murphy, William Welt, Max Wagner, William Black, Dorothy Vera, Mrs. Irene Church, Helen E. Ward, L. E. Johnson, Don Hitchcock, Ralph Storm, Dorothy Donohue, Mrs. Harry Ober, Mrs. William Brown (Carol Steinbeck).

(2) *Unpublished Material by Steinbeck*

Poem to his mother on her birthday (courtesy of Mrs. C. J. Rodgers).

(3) *Published Material by Steinbeck*

Various articles, signed and unsigned, *El Gabilan*, 1919 (Salinas High School yearbook).

(4) *Published or Unpublished Material by Others*

Alton Pryor, "Ignatious Cooper: He Knew Steinbeck When . . . ," *Salinas Californian*, 20 October 1962, p. 4A.

(5) *Notes*

Pages

19. "Loving and firm": *East of Eden*, p. 150.

20–21. "One day": from the manuscript at the Humanities Research Center, University of Texas (since published as part of the preface to *The Acts of Arthur and His Noble Knights* (New York: Farrar, Straus and Giroux, 1976, xi).

22. "Learn to walk": *Eden*, p. 150.

23. "Realer than experience": JS/BA, 2/36.

25. "The English room": "How, Where, and When of the High School," *El Gabilan*, 1919, p. 19.

25–26. "I remember": manuscript, "*The Grapes of Wrath* journal" (courtesy of the Humanities Research Center, University of Texas).

27. Birthday poem: manuscript (courtesy of Mrs. C. J. Rodgers).

27. "I used to sit": JS/Dorothy Vera, *Salinas Californian,* 11 January 1969, p. 14A.

31. "It must be": *Cup of Gold* (New York: Penguin Books, 1976), pp. 10–11.

32. "The Wizard": manuscript (courtesy of San Jose State University Library).

CHAPTER III

(1) *Interviews*

George Mors, William Black, Byron Madison Taylor, Mrs. E. G. Ainsworth (Elizabeth Steinbeck), Ross Riley, Paul L. Pioda.

(3) *Published Material by Steinbeck*

"Fingers of Cloud: A Satire on College Protervity," *The Stanford Spectator,* February 1924, pp. 149, 161–164.

(4) *Published or Unpublished Material by Others*

Robert Bennett, *The Wrath of John Steinbeck: or St. John Goes to Church* (Los Angeles: The Albertson Press, 1939).

(5) *Notes*

Pages

33. Academic record: transcript of grades (courtesy of Registrar's Office, Stanford University).

36. "Slipping behind": manuscript, *"The Grapes of Wrath* journal" (courtesy of Humanities Research Center, University of Texas).

37. "I was going": John Steinbeck, "The Golden Handcuff," *San Francisco Examiner,* 23 November 1958, p. 7.

39–40. "A coal fire": "Fingers," p. 144.

42. "Once in college": *Journal of a Novel,* p. 102.

44. "I have been working": *Wrath,* pp. 3–4.

44. "A lot of crap" to end: *Wrath,* pp. 7–8, *passim.*

CHAPTER IV

(1) *Interviews*

Budd J. Peaslee (Salinas tape), Frank Kilkenny, Frank Fenton, Dean Storey, Donald Stevens (pseudonym), Webster F. Street, Carlton A. Sheffield, Vernon Givan, Robert Cathcart, Glenn Graves, Nick Simon, Charles McNichols, William R. Gage, Katherine Carruth Grover.

(2) *Unpublished Material by Steinbeck*

"Ballad of Quid Pro Quo" (courtesy of Carlton A. Sheffield).

"Ode to the Virgin" (courtesy of Dean Storey).

(3) *Published Material by Steinbeck*

"Fingers of Cloud: A Satire on College Protervity," *The Stanford Spectator,* February 1924, pp. 149, 161–164.

"Adventures in Arcademy: A Journey into the Ridiculous," *The Stanford Spectator*, June 1924, pp. 279, 291.

(4) *Published or Unpublished Material by Others*

Edith Ronald Merrielees, *The Story Writer* (Boston: Little, Brown & Company, 1939).

Edith Ronald Merrielees, *Story Writing* (Boston: The Writer, Inc., Publishers, 1947).

(5) *Notes*

Pages

56. JS/Professor Carruth, n.d. (courtesy of Nick Simon).

57. "Ode to the Virgin": manuscript (courtesy of Dean Storey).

57. Academic record: transcript of grades (courtesy of Registrar's Office, Stanford University).

59. "Writing can never": Merrielees, *Story Writing*, p. 4.

59. "The 'lean, terse style' ": Merrielees, *Story Writer*, p. 246.

60. "Gasoline and alcohol": "Arcademy," p. 279.

60. "Gray goose": "Arcademy," p. 291.

61. "The sky was splitting": "Fingers," p. 149.

61–62. "The street," "a little hill": "Fingers," p. 149.

CHAPTER V

(1) *Interviews*

Carlton A. Sheffield, L. E. Johnson, Byron Madison Taylor, Frank Fenton, Dean Storey, Charles McNichols, Polly (Smith) Teas, Webster F. Street, Amasa (Ted) Miller, William R. Gage.

(2) *Unpublished material by Steinbeck*

"A Lady in Infra-Red" (courtesy of the Stanford University Libraries).

"The Nymph and Isobel" (courtesy of the Houghton Library, Harvard University).

"The Nail" (courtesy of the Houghton Library, Harvard University).

(4) *Published or Unpublished Material by Others*

Richard Astro, *John Steinbeck and Edward F. Ricketts: The Shaping of a Novelist* (Minneapolis: University of Minnesota Press, 1973).

(5) *Notes*

Pages

63. "The particular advantage": as quoted by Joel W. Hedgpeth, "Philosophy on Cannery Row," in *Steinbeck: The Man and His Work*, ed. Richard Astro and Tetsumaro Hayashi (Corvallis, Oregon: Oregon State University Press, 1971), p. 97n.

63. "In all parts of nature": as quoted by Astro, pp. 44–45.

63. "One's ability": Astro, p. 45.

64. "Mr. Steinbeck": Edmund Wilson, "The Californians: Storm and Steinbeck," *The New Republic*, 9 December 1940, pp. 785–787.

CHAPTER VI

(1) *Interviews*

Mrs. Margaret Judah, Frank Fenton, Webster F. Street, Robert R. Sears, Carlton A. Sheffield, Mrs. E. G. Ainsworth (Elizabeth Steinbeck), Amasa (Ted) Miller, William Black.

(2) *Unpublished Material by Steinbeck*

Untitled manuscript of a story about an Irish husband and wife (lost).

Untitled manuscript of a story about a woman and a cockroach (lost).

Untitled manuscript of a story of Christmas in New York (in private hands).

"East Third Street" (courtesy of the Houghton Library, Harvard University).

"The White Sister of Fourteenth Street" (courtesy of the Stanford University Libraries).

(4) *Published or Unpublished Material by Others*

E. B. Scott, *The Saga of Lake Tahoe* (Crystal Bay, Lake Tahoe, Nevada: Sierra–Tahoe Publishing Company, 1957).

(5) *Notes*

Pages

87. History of Fallen Leaf Lake Resort: Scott, p. 145.

90. "From a porthole": "Autobiography: The Making of a New Yorker," *The New York Times Magazine*, 1 February 1953, p. 26.

91. "My knowledge": "Autobiography," p. 26.

91. "Was red when he hit": "Autobiography," p. 26.

92. "Isn't this a nice address?": JS/MG, 2/26 (courtesy of Mrs. Margaret Judah).

92–93. "I remember Blaine's words": JS/KB, 6/28 (courtesy of Stanford University Libraries).

94. "They have been": JS/MG, 3/26.

94. "Margaret Gemmell": JS/MG, 11/25.

95. "They gave me stories": "Autobiography," p. 26.

95. "They pretended": "Autobiography," p. 26.

97. "Sixth Avenue cobbler": manuscript, "A Lady in Infra-Red" (courtesy of Stanford University Libraries).

97. "One of those trif": manuscript, "The White Sister of Fourteenth Street" (courtesy of Stanford University Libraries).

99. "But by that time": "Autobiography," p. 27.

CHAPTER VII

(1) *Interviews*

Mrs. Catherine Hill, Mr. and Mrs. Harold Ebright, Delbert H. West, Lloyd Shebley, Robert Cathcart, Webster F. Street.

(2) *Unpublished Material by Steinbeck*
"The Green Lady," novel manuscript, by J. S. and Webster F. Street (courtesy of Stanford University Libraries).
(3) *Published Material by Steinbeck*
"The Gifts of Iban" (by "John Stein"), *The Smokers Companion*, March 1927, pp. 18–19, 70–72 (courtesy of the New York Public Library).
(4) *Published or Unpublished Material by Others*
E. B. Scott, *The Saga of Lake Tahoe* (Crystal Bay, Lake Tahoe, Nevada: Sierra–Tahoe Publishing Company, 1957).
Webster F. Street, "Somethin' o' Susie's," story manuscript (courtesy of Stanford University Libraries).
Webster F. Street, "The Green Lady," play manuscript (courtesy of Stanford University Libraries).
Peter Lisca, *The Wide World of John Steinbeck* (New Brunswick, New Jersey: Rutgers University Press, 1958).
Joseph Fontenrose, *John Steinbeck: An Introduction and Interpretation* (New York: Holt, Rinehart and Winston, Inc., 1963).
(5) *Notes*
Pages
109. "Priceless secrets": "Somethin'," p. 11.
109. "When he don't": "Green Lady," p. 4.
111. "Remember": *Journal of a Novel* (New York: The Viking Press, 1969), p. 53.
112. *Sea of Cortez: A Leisurely Journal of Travel and Research* (New York: The Viking Press, 1941), p. 68.
115. Lisca, p. 34.
116. Fontenrose, pp. 8–13.
116. "Biological determinism": Lisca, p. 36.
116. "Healthy sexuality": Lisca, pp. 37–38.
117. "Despite the superficial": Warren French, *John Steinbeck* (New Haven, Connecticut: College and University Press, 1961), p. 38.

CHAPTER VIII
(1) *Interviews*
Mrs. Carl Wilhelmson, Amasa (Ted) Miller, Delbert H. West, Lloyd Shebley, Mrs. William Brown (Carol Steinbeck), Robert Cathcart, Mrs. Polly (Smith) Teas, Leo Shapovalov, Carlton A. Sheffield, Webster F. Street.
(2) *Unpublished Material by Steinbeck*
"The Green Lady," novel manuscript (courtesy of Stanford University Libraries).
(3) *Published Material by Steinbeck*
Cup of Gold: A Life of Sir Henry Morgan, Buccaneer, with Occasional Reference to History (New York: Robert M. McBride, 1929).

(5) *Notes*

Pages

118. "I have been eight months": JS/KB.

119. *Midsummernight* (New York: Farrar and Rinehart, 1930) and *Speed of the Reindeer: A Story of Lapland* (New York: The Viking Press, 1954).

136. Allan Pollitt: as quoted by Leo Shapovalov in a letter to me, 1/12/71.

CHAPTER IX

(1) *Interviews*

Lloyd Shebley, Delbert H. West, Jack Balbo (Salinas tape), Mrs. Josephine Van Deren, Bemis Bag Company, Mrs. William Brown (Carol Steinbeck), Polly (Smith) Teas, Webster F. Street, Robert Cathcart, Ned Brundage, Carlton A. Sheffield, Amasa (Ted) Miller.

(5) *Notes*

Pages

144–145. "A dark little attic": "The Golden Handcuff: John Steinbeck Writes About San Francisco," *The San Francisco Examiner: Pictorial Living*, 23 November 1958, p. 7.

145. "Saturday night": "Golden Handcuff," p. 7.

146. "We of that period": "Golden Handcuff," p. 7.

150. "What he intended us to have": after Steinbeck's death in 1968, material that he would have burned has come from two sources to be sold to manuscript brokers: from the estate of his second wife (Gwyndolyn Steinbeck appropriated all his papers at the time of their divorce) and from the private files of his agent, Elizabeth Otis, which were left as part of her estate.

153. "Edith Brunoni": from an interview with Mrs. Brunoni by Ned Brundage (courtesy of Ned Brundage).

157. "The fatal leap": JS/TM, 1/23/29.

CHAPTER X

(1) *Interviews*

Mrs. William Brown (Carol Steinbeck), Jack Calvin, Carlton A. Sheffield, Xenia (Kashevaroff) Cage, Marcia Hilton (Salinas tape), Mrs. Idell (Henning) Budd.

(2) *Unpublished Material by Steinbeck*

"Dissonant Symphony," novelette manuscript (lost).

(5) *Notes*

Pages

167. My thanks to Joel W. Hedgpeth for untangling the Kashevaroff family for me.

177–178. "The Depression": "A Primer on the 30's," *Esquire*, June 1960, p. 86.

179. "Large group of us poor kids": "A Primer," pp. 86–87.

179. "One great meat loaf": "A Primer," p. 87.

180. "She could infect": *Cannery Row* (New York: The Viking Press, 1945), pp. 160–161.

CHAPTER XI

(1) *Interviews*

Mr. and Mrs. Fred Strong (Frances Ricketts), Joel W. Hedgpeth, Rolf Bolin, Toni Jackson, Richard Albee, Mrs. William Brown (Carol Steinbeck).

(4) *Published or Unpublished Material by Others*

Richard Astro, *John Steinbeck and Edward F. Ricketts: The Shaping of a Novelist* (Minneapolis: University of Minnesota Press, 1973).

Joel W. Hedgpeth, "Philosophy on Cannery Row," in *Steinbeck: The Man and His Work*, ed. Richard Astro and Tetsumaro Hayashi (Corvallis, Oregon: Oregon State University Press, 1971), pp. 89–129.

Edwards F. Ricketts, "Non-Teleological Thinking" and "Philosophy of Breaking Through," manuscripts (courtesy of Edward F. Ricketts, Jr.). These have since been published in *The Outer Shores, II: From the Papers of Edward F. Ricketts*, ed. Joel W. Hedgpeth (Eureka, California: Mad River Press, 1978), pp. 69–79, 161–170.

(5) *Notes*

Pages

185–186. "Adults in their thinking": "About Ed Ricketts," prefatory essay by John Steinbeck to *The Log from the "Sea of Cortez"* (New York: The Viking Press, 1962), xlvii.

186. "It must have been wonderful": as quoted by Hedgpeth, "Philosophy," p. 90.

186. "At the age of 6": Hedgpeth, p. 90.

187. "This is a true book": "About Ed," lviii.

188. "Our early life": Hedgpeth, pp. 89–90.

189. College record: transcripts of grades, Illinois State University and University of Chicago (courtesy of Edward F. Ricketts, Jr.). Additional information courtesy of Gardner C. Van Dyke, Registrar, Illinois State University.

189. "I don't know when": "About Ed," xlviii.

190. "Walked among the farmers": *Cannery Row* (New York: The Viking Press, 1945), p. 108. Although in a novel, the truth of the story is confirmed by Ricketts's sister, Mrs. Fred Strong.

191. "For several years": Hedgpeth, p. 91.

192. "Got a holy look": Astro, p. 5.
196. "Very many conclusions": "About Ed," xlv–xlvii.
199. "I was dull": "About Ed," xliii–xliv.

CHAPTER XII

(1) *Interviews*

Carlton A. Sheffield, Amasa (Ted) Miller, Mrs. William Brown (Carol Steinbeck), Jack Calvin, Elizabeth Otis, Mavis McIntosh, Polly (Smith) Teas, Mrs. Carl Wilhelmson.

(2) *Unpublished Material by Steinbeck*

"Dissonant Symphony," novelette manuscript (lost).

"Murder at Full Noon," novelette manuscript (courtesy of Humanities Research Center, University of Texas).

Untitled novel manuscript (lost).

Untitled short story collection manuscript (lost—possibly a revision of "Dissonant Symphony" or a preliminary manuscript for *The Pastures of Heaven*).

(3) *Published Material by Steinbeck*

The Pastures of Heaven (New York: Brewer, Warren and Putnam, 1932).

(4) *Published or Unpublished Material by Others*

Nelson Valjean, *John Steinbeck: The Errant Knight* (San Francisco: Chronicle Books, 1975).

Clifford Lewis, "Jungian Psychology and the Artistic Design of John Steinbeck," *Steinbeck Quarterly*, Summer–Fall 1977, pp. 89–97.

(5) *Notes*

Pages

201. Valjean, p. 130.
215. Jack Calvin's "circle": although Steinbeck refers to such a circle several times in his letters, Calvin denies there was a literary clique that met regularly at his home.

CHAPTER XIII

(1) *Interviews*

Elizabeth Otis, Mrs. William Brown (Carol Steinbeck), Joseph Campbell, Francis Whitaker, Virginia Scardigli, Rolf Bolin, Richard Albee, Webster F. Street.

(2) *Unpublished Material by Steinbeck*

"To a God Unknown" (original title, "To an Unknown God"), manuscript and journal (courtesy of Stanford University Libraries).

(3) *Published Material by Steinbeck*

To a God Unknown (New York: Robert O. Ballou, 1933).

(5) *Notes*
Pages
226. "There are good": "Foreword" to *Between Pacific Tides* by Edward
F. Ricketts and Jack Calvin (Stanford, California: Stanford University
Press, 1948), vi.
226. "In conversation": "About Ed," lxvi.
227–228. "Great parties": "About Ed," xli.

CHAPTER XIV
(1) *Interviews*
Richard Allbee, Mrs. Margaret Judah.
(2) *Unpublished Material by Steinbeck*
"To a God Unknown," novel manuscript and journal (courtesy of Stan-
ford University Libraries).
"The Long Valley," story collection manuscripts and journal (courtesy of
San Jose State University Library).
(3) *Published Material by Steinbeck*
To a God Unknown (New York: Robert O. Ballou, 1933; New York:
Penguin Books, 1976).
(4) *Published or Unpublished Material by Others*
B.A.G. Fuller, *A History of Philosophy* (New York: Henry Holt and
Company, 1949).
Harold Chapman Brown, "The Problem of Philosophy," *The Journal
of Philosophy, Psychology, and Scientific Methods,* 17 (1920), pp. 281–
300.
Harold Chapman Brown, "This Material World," in *Animal Drive and
the Learning Process,* ed. Edwin B. Holt (New York: Henry Holt and
Company, 1931), pp. 265–287 (originally published in *Journal of Phi-
losophy,* 22 [1925], pp. 197–214).
Edward F. Ricketts, "Thesis and Materials for a Script on Mexico," man-
uscript (courtesy of Richard Astro). This has since been published in
The Outer Shores II: From the Papers of Edward F. Ricketts, ed. Joel
Hedgpeth (Eureka, California: Mad River Press, 1978), pp. 172–182.
Edward F. Ricketts, "Breaking Through," manuscript (courtesy of
Edward F. Ricketts, Jr.). Since published in *Outer Shores, II,* pp.
69–79.
William Emerson Ritter and Edna W. Bailey, "The Organismal Concep-
tion: Its Place in Science and Its Bearing on Philosophy," *University of
California Publications in Zoology,* XXXI (1931), pp. 307–358.
Lester Jay Marks, *Thematic Design in the Novels of John Steinbeck* (The
Hague: Mouton, 1969).
Richard Astro, *John Steinbeck and Edward F. Ricketts: The Shaping of a
Novelist* (Minneapolis: University of Minnesota Press, 1973).

(5) *Notes*
Pages
234. Fuller, p. 19
235. Brown, "Material," pp. 268, 278.
236. Brown, "Philosophy," pp. 281–282.
236. "The best situation": "Philosophy," p. 283.
238. Astro, p. 57.
239–240. *To a God Unknown* (Penguin), p. 133.
240. *To a God Unknown* (Penguin), pp. 179, 134.
241. Ritter and Bailey, pp. 341, 355.
243. Brown, "Philosophy," p. 297.
243. Ritter and Bailey, pp. 341, 355.
244. W. A. Swanberg, *Dreiser* (New York: Charles Scribner's Sons, 1965), pp. 60–61.
245. Marks, p. 44.
245. "The same kind": Marks, p. 45.
245. *The Grapes of Wrath* (New York: The Viking Press, 1939), p. 32.
245. "This man": *To a God Unknown* (Penguin), p. 147.
245. "You didn't know": *God*, p. 134.
247. "About Ed Ricketts," liii.
247–248. Ricketts, "Breaking," manuscript, pp. 7, 10, 4 (Hedgpeth, II, pp. 73, 74, 71).
249. *God*, p. 6.
249. Astro, pp. 55, 57.
250. "Proven capacity" and "Endless war": "Acceptance Speech," *Nobel Prize Library: William Faulkner, Eugene O'Neill, John Steinbeck* (New York: Alexis Gregory, 1971), p. 206.

CHAPTER XV
(1) *Interviews*
Carlton A. Sheffield, Francis Whitaker, Mrs. William Brown (Carol Steinbeck), Polly (Smith) Teas, Mrs. E. G. Ainsworth (Elizabeth Steinbeck), Richard Albee.
(2) *Unpublished Material by Steinbeck*
"The Wizard," play manuscript and journal (courtesy of San Jose State University Library).
"To a God Unknown," novel manuscript and journal (courtesy of Stanford University Libraries).
"The Long Valley," story collection manuscript and journal (courtesy of San Jose State University Library).
(3) *Published Material by Steinbeck*
Saint Katy the Virgin, separate publication of the short story, for Covici-Friede by The Golden Eagle Press, Mount Vernon, New York,

1936. (Reprinted in *The Long Valley* [New York: The Viking Press, 1938], pp. 189–200.)

(5) *Notes*

Pages

253. *Katy* (*The Long Valley*), p. 198.

259. *Life in Letters*, p. 64.

261. *Journal of a Novel* (New York: The Viking Press, 1969), p. 43.

268–269. "Argument of Phalanx," manuscript (courtesy of Richard Albee).

CHAPTER XVI

(1) *Interviews*

Max Wagner, Webster F. Street, Mrs. William Brown (Carol Steinbeck), Julia Breinig, Mrs. Alice (Cohee) Jackson, Mrs. George Mors, James Rodrigues, Mrs. Mildred Hargis.

(2) *Unpublished Material by Steinbeck*

"The Long Valley," story collection manuscript and journal (courtesy of San Jose State University Library).

(3) *Published Material by Steinbeck*

"The Red Pony," *North American Review*, November 1933, pp. 422–438.

"The Great Mountains," *North American Review*, December 1933, pp. 493–500.

"The Murder," *North American Review*, April 1934, pp. 306–312.

"The Raid," *North American Review*, October 1934, pp. 300–305.

"The White Quail," *North American Review*, March 1935, pp. 205–211.

"The Snake," *Monterey Beacon*, 22 June 1935, pp. 10–11, 14–15.

"The Leader of the People," *Argosy*, August 1936, pp. 99–106.

"The Lonesome Vigilante," *Esquire*, October 1936, pp. 35, 186A–186B.

"Breakfast," *Pacific Weekly*, 9 November 1936, p. 300.

"The Promise," *Harper's Magazine*, August 1937, pp. 244–252.

"The Ears of Johnny Bear," *Esquire*, September 1937, pp. 35, 195–200.

"The Chrysanthemums," *Harper's Magazine*, October 1937, pp. 514–519.

"The Harness," *The Atlantic Monthly*, June 1938, pp. 741–749.

The Long Valley (New York: The Viking Press, 1938).

"How Edith McGillcuddy Met R. L. Stevenson," *Harper's Magazine*, August 1941, pp. 253–258.

(4) *Published or Unpublished Material by Others*

Martin Bidwell, "John Steinbeck: An Impression," *Prairie Schooner*, Spring 1938, pp. 10–15.

(5) *Notes*

Pages

274. "Documentary evidence": for example, in the ledger containing *The Long Valley* stories and a journal, Steinbeck put down a list which he

headed "Record of Stories Completed Summer of 1934." But the list includes several stories which were certainly written before the summer of 1934, and several written during the summer are not included. It would seem, therefore, that the heading means "Stories Completed by the Beginning of Summer, 1934."

275. "The Chrysanthemums," *The Long Valley*, p. 10.

281. "A brave editor": "A Primer on the 30's," *Esquire*, June 1960, p. 93.

281. "Captain Billy": JS/EO–ALW, 3/19/37.

282–283. Bidwell, pp. 10–12.

283–284. Bidwell, pp. 12–14.

284. "Wrenching scene": *Journal of a Novel* (New York: The Viking Press, 1969), pp. 141–142.

289. "Lynching": see the account given in *Sacramento Bee*, 27 November 1933, pp. 1–2 (lead to source provided by Joel Hedgpeth).

CHAPTER XVII

(1) *Interviews*

Mrs. William Brown (Carol Steinbeck), Francis Whitaker, Mrs. Alice (Cohee) Jackson, Mavis McIntosh, James E. Harkins, Pat Chambers, Caroline Decker (by Anne Loftis), Ella Winter (by Elaine Berman).

(3) *Published Material by Steinbeck*

In Dubious Battle (New York: Covici–Friede, 1936).

(4) *Published or Unpublished Material by Others*

Stuart Jamieson, *Labor Unionism in American Agriculture*, Bulletin No. 836 of the Bureau of Labor Statistics (Washington, D.C., 1945), pp. 80–115.

Carey McWilliams, *Factories in the Field: The Story of Migratory Farm Labor in California* (Boston: Little, Brown & Company, Inc.,1939).

Ella Winter, *And Not to Yield: An Autobiography* (New York: Harcourt, Brace and World, Inc., 1968).

Justin Kaplan, *Lincoln Steffens: A Biography* (New York: Simon and Schuster, 1974).

Lincoln Steffens, *The Autobiography of Lincoln Steffens* (New York: Harcourt, Brace and Company, 1931).

(5) *Notes*

Pages

293. "Forty-four": T. H. Watkins, *California: An Illustrated History* (Palo Alto: American West Publishing Company, 1973), p. 411.

293. Jamieson; McWilliams; see also Porter Chaffee, an unpublished history of the C.&A.W.I.U., volume II of the manuscript, Bancroft Library, University of California at Berkeley.

295. "Steffens was stricken": Winter, pp. 153–154.

295. "Little gray beard": Kaplan, p. 326.

295. "Excessively shy": Winter, p. 212.

297. "I went": Winter, pp. 193–194.

298. "I have usually": Harry Thornton Moore, *The Novels of John Steinbeck: A First Critical Study* (Chicago: Normandie House, 1939), p. 102.

298. *In Dubious Battle:* for a full account of the novel's origins and sources see Jackson J. Benson and Anne Loftis, "John Steinbeck and Farm Labor Unionization: The Background of *In Dubious Battle*," *American Literature*, 52 (May 1980), pp. 194–223.

299. "When the apples": *Battle*, p. 37.

299–300. "The Tagus ranch": Jamieson, p. 94.

301. Strike settlement: Jamieson, p. 94; "Labor in California's Peach Crop," notes edited by Raymond P. Berry, from *A Documentary History of Migratory Farm Labor*, Federal Writers Project, Bancroft Library, University of California at Berkeley.

302. Cotton strike: Paul S. Taylor and Clark Kerr, "Documentary History of the Strike of the Cotton Pickers in California, 1933," *Violations of Free Speech and Rights of Labor: Hearings Before a Subcommittee of the Committee on Education and Labor*, U.S. Senate, Seventy-Sixth Congress, Third Session; Part 54, "Agriculture Labor in California" (Washington, D.C.: U.S. Government Printing Office, 1940), pp. 19947–19948; Jamieson, p. 101.

302. "Entire industry": Jamieson, p. 100.

304. "Whites, Mexicans": statement given in testimony at Visalia, California, 16 January 1934, quoted in Paul S. Taylor and Clark Kerr, *Notes for a Documentary History of the Strike of Cotton Pickers in California*, 1933, Taylor Papers, Bancroft Library, University of California at Berkeley.

305. Jamieson, p. 102.

306. "We protect": Taylor and Kerr, "Documentary History," p. 19992.

306. Leroy Gordon: Taylor and Kerr, "Documentary History," p. 19978.

307. Caravans: Taylor and Kerr, p. 19959.

307. "Leaving the Corcoran": *Visalia Times Delta* of 23 October 1933, as quoted in Taylor and Kerr, p. 19961.

308. "Power company truck": Taylor and Kerr, p. 19968.

308. "Arvin and Pixley": Taylor and Kerr, pp. 19990–19991, 19988–19990.

308. "Assembling": Tulare *Times*, 14 October 1933, as quoted in Taylor and Kerr, p. 19956.

CHAPTER XVIII

(1) *Interviews*

Mrs. Pascal Covici, Mavis McIntosh, Mrs. Idell Budd, Mrs. Joseph Henry Jackson, Mrs. William Brown (Carol Steinbeck), Carlton A. Sheffield,

Frank Lloyd, Richard Albee, Nathaniel Benchley, Ella Winter (by Elaine Berman).

(2) *Unpublished Material by Steinbeck*

"The Long Valley," story collection manuscript and journal (courtesy of San Jose State University Library).

(3) *Published Material by Steinbeck*

Tortilla Flat (New York: Covici–Friede, 1935).

"The Snake," *The Monterey Beacon*, 22 June 1935, pp. 10–11, 14–15.

In Dubious Battle (New York: Covici–Friede, 1936).

Of Mice and Men (New York: Covici–Friede, 1937).

Their Blood Is Strong (San Francisco: Simon J. Lubin Society of California, Inc., 1938). First appeared (without final section) as series, *The Harvest Gypsies, San Francisco News*, 5–12 October 1936. *Their Blood Is Strong* reprinted in *A Companion to "The Grapes of Wrath,"* ed. Warren French (New York: The Viking Press, 1963), pp. 58–92. (My references are to this reprinting.)

(4) *Published or Unpublished Material by Others*

"Authors and Others," *Publishers Weekly*, 27 July 1935, p. 273.

Mary McCarthy, "Minority Report," *Nation*, 142 (March 1936), pp. 326–327.

(5) *Notes*

Pages

315–317. This account of the rejection of *In Dubious Battle* differs from the account given by Donald Friede (in his memoir, *The Mechanical Angel* [New York: Alfred Knopf, Inc., 1948], pp. 127–128). The most important discrepancy concerns the telegram Friede claims was sent to Steinbeck to ignore Black's letter. Neither the correspondence of Steinbeck to his agents nor the recollections of Mavis McIntosh include reference to such a telegram—only a letter, sent much later, by Covici offering to publish the manuscript after all. (Friede's account called to my attention by Thomas Frensch, *Steinbeck Quarterly*, 14 [Summer–Fall 1981], pp. 114–115).

321. "Covici": *Journal of a Novel* (New York: The Viking Press, 1969), p. 15.

324. McCarthy, p. 327.

326. "Usual tract": JS/EO, 2/4/36.

327. Harry Thornton Moore, *The Novels of John Steinbeck: A First Critical Study*, second edition (Port Washington, New York: Kennikat Press, 1968), p. 41.

327. "I'm working": JS/EO, 4/15/36.

333. "He will die": *Their Blood*, pp. 59–63.

CHAPTER XIX

(1) *Interviews*

Lawrence I. Hewes, Jr. (F.S.A.), Professor Paul S. Taylor, Jonathan Garst (F.S.A.), Mary Alice (Collins) Johns, Patricia Collins Olsen, Milan Dempster (F.S.A.), John Berthelson (*Sacramento Bee*), Dewey Russell (F.S.A., courtesy of John Berthelson), Reginald Loftis, Webster F. Street, Robert Hardie (F.S.A.), Carey McWilliams, Helen Hosmer (Simon J. Lubin Society), C. B. Baldwin (F.S.A.), Mrs. William Brown (Carol Steinbeck), Mrs. Gwyndolyn Steinbeck.

(2) *Unpublished Material by Steinbeck*

"The Great Pig Sticking," story manuscript (lost).

"L'Affaire Lettuceberg," novel manuscript preliminary to *The Grapes of Wrath* (lost).

(3) *Published Material by Steinbeck*

Their Blood Is Strong, as reprinted in *A Companion to "The Grapes of Wrath,"* ed. Warren French (New York: The Viking Press, 1963), pp. 58–92.

"Dubious Battle in California," *Nation*, 143 (September 1936), pp. 302–304.

(4) *Published or Unpublished Material by Others*

Carey McWilliams, *Factories in the Field* (Boston: Little, Brown & Company, Inc., 1959).

Lloyd H. Fisher, *The Harvest Labor Market in California* (Cambridge: Harvard University Press, 1953).

Walter J. Stein, *California and the Dust Bowl Migration* (Westport, Connecticut: Greenwood Press, Inc., 1973).

Dick Meister and Anne Loftis, *A Long Time Coming: The Struggle to Unionize America's Farm Workers* (New York: Macmillan Publishing Company, Inc., 1977).

Donald Worster, *Dust Bowl: The Southern Plains in the 1930s* (New York: Oxford University Press, 1979).

Farm Security Administration papers at the Bancroft Library; the Federal Archives and Record Center, San Bruno; and National Archives, Washington, D.C. (including the Arvin Camp Reports at both the Bancroft and San Bruno).

Windsor Drake (Thomas A. Collins), unpublished novel manuscript, "Bringing in the Sheaves," with "Foreword" by John Steinbeck (courtesy of Mary Alice Johns).

Warren French, "The First Theatrical Production of Steinbeck's *Of Mice and Men,*" *American Literature*, 36 (January 1965), pp. 525–527.

(5) *Notes*

Pages

334. "National magazine": "I Wonder Where We Can Go Now," *For-*

tune, April 1939, pp. 90–94, 112–120; and "Along the Road," pp. 96–100.

335. "Exodus": McWilliams, p. 308; Stein, p. 16.

335. "Wages": McWilliams, p. 188–189, 314–315.

335. "Conditions": *Their Blood*, pp. 64–67.

336. McWilliams, pp. 314–315.

337. "Series of Camps": Stein, pp. 150–153 (as qualified by information provided by Lawrence I. Hewes).

339. "Foreword" to the unpublished novel manuscript by Thomas A. Collins, "Bringing in the Sheaves," since published in *Journal of Modern Literature* 2 (April 1976), pp. 211–213.

341. McKiddy and the Communist Party: Anne Loftis interview of Roy and Wilson Hammett, 9/12/82.

342. *The Grapes of Wrath* (New York: The Viking Press, 1939), p. 572.

342. "Uncle Bill": Loftis interview.

351. Joseph Henry Jackson, "Introduction" to *Of Mice and Men*, Modern Library Edition (New York: Random House, 1937), xix.

351. "Beatrice Kaufman": "Mice, Men, and Mr. Steinbeck," *The New York Times*, 5 December 1937, p.. 7.

351–352. "Theatre Union": French, "Theatrical," p. 525.

352. "By that I mean": "Mice, Men," p. 7.

CHAPTER XX

(1) *Interviews*

Annie Laurie Williams, Elizabeth Otis, Carlton A. Sheffield, Mrs. C. J. Rodgers, Mrs. William Brown (Carol Steinbeck), Reginald Loftis, Roger Condon, Webster F. Street, Helen Hosmer, Mrs. Joseph Henry Jackson, Lewis Milestone.

(3) *Published Material by Steinbeck*

The Red Pony, limited edition, containing the first three stories only (New York: Covici–Friede Publishers, 1937).

"Starvation Under the Orange Trees," *Monterey Trader*, 15 April 1938, pp. 1, 4 (courtesy of Webster F. Street).

Their Blood Is Strong (San Francisco: Simon J. Lubin Society of California, 1938).

(4) *Published or Unpublished Material by Others*

Nelson Valjean, *John Steinbeck: The Errant Knight* (San Francisco: Chronicle Books, 1975).

Harry Thornton Moore, *The Novels of John Steinbeck: A First Critical Study*, second edition (Port Washington, New York: Kennikat Press, Inc., 1968).

Carey McWilliams, *Factories in the Field* (Boston: Little, Brown & Company, Inc., 1939).

Farm Security Administration papers, Federal Archives, Washington D.C.

Windsor Drake (Thomas A. Collins), unpublished novel manuscript, "Bringing in the Sheaves," with "Foreword" by John Steinbeck (courtesy of Mary Alice Johns). "Foreword" and segment of the novel since published in *Journal of Modern Literature*, 5 (April 1976), pp. 211–232.

(5) *Notes*

Pages

353. Valjean, p. 158.

353. "Recognized": 3/19/37.

354–355. Moore, p. 87.

355–356. "Autobiography: The Making of a New Yorker," *The New York Times Magazine*, Part II, 1 February 1953, pp. 26–27, 66–67.

357. "Poker": JS/BB, n.d.

364. "Mice, Men, and Mr. Steinbeck," *The New York Times*, 5 December 1937, p. 7.

367. McWilliams, p. 315.

369–370. Collins, pp. 221–224, *passim.*

CHAPTER XXI

(1) *Interviews*

Mrs. William Brown (Carol Steinbeck), Elizabeth Otis, Annie Laurie Williams, Reginald Loftis, John S. Beggerly (Los Gatos *Times Observer*), Roger Condon, Horace Jones, M.D.

(2) *Unpublished Material by Steinbeck*

"L'Affaire Lettuceberg," novel manuscript preliminary to *The Grapes of Wrath* (lost).

"*The Grapes of Wrath* journal," journal kept during the composition of the novel (courtesy of Humanities Research Center, University of Texas).

Untitled manuscript of radio interview prepared for Joseph Henry Jackson (courtesy of the Bancroft Library, University of California at Berkeley).

(3) *Published Material by Steinbeck*

Of Mice and Men: A Play in Two Parts (New York: Covici–Friede, 1937).

The Long Valley (New York: The Viking Press, 1938).

The Grapes of Wrath (New York: The Viking Press, 1939).

(4) *Published or Unpublished Material by Others*

Pare Lorentz, "Ecce Homo!," a radio play.

Charles Chaplin, Jr., *My Father, Charlie Chaplin* (New York: Random House, 1960).

Alistair Cooke, *Six Men* (New York: Berkley Publishing Corporation, 1978).

Robert L. Snyder, *Pare Lorentz and the Documentary Film* (Norman, Oklahoma: University of Oklahoma Press, 1968).
(5) *Notes*
Pages
376. *"Of Mice and Men* Wins Critics Prize," *The New York Times,* 19 April 1938, p. 23.
384. Cooke, p. 28
384. Chaplin, p. 28.
386. Script: enclosed with a letter to Joseph Henry Jackson, n.d.
387. "John Steinbeck as Colorful as the Men He Wrote About," *San Jose Mercury,* 2 March 1969, p. 9 (quote from 1938 interview).
391. "Metabolic rate": JS/PC, 1/1/39.

CHAPTER XXII
(1) *Interviews*
Lewis Milestone, Max Wagner, Mrs. Gwyndolyn Steinbeck, Mrs. Stanley Heuit (Gwyndolyn Steinbeck's mother), Mrs. Lynn Loesser, Mrs. William Brown (Carol Steinbeck), Mrs. Nunnally Johnson, Annie Laurie Williams.
(2) *Unpublished Material by Steinbeck*
Untitled manuscript of radio interview prepared for Joseph Henry Jackson (courtesy of the Bancroft Library, University of California at Berkeley).
(3) *Published Material by Steinbeck*
The Grapes of Wrath (New York: The Viking Press, 1939).
(4) *Published or Unpublished Material by Others*
Richard Astro, *John Steinbeck and Edward F. Ricketts: The Shaping of a Novelist* (Minneapolis: University of Minnesota Press, 1973).
Robert L. Snyder, *Pare Lorentz and the Documentary Film* (Norman, Oklahoma: University of Oklahoma Press, 1968).
Edward F. Ricketts and Jack Calvin, *Between Pacific Tides* (Stanford, California: Stanford University Press, 1939).
Pare Lorentz, "Ecce Homo!," a radio play.
(5) *Notes*
Pages
395. "Wally Ford": JS/EO, 4/13/39.
396. Astro, p. 7.
399. Snyder, p. 98.
399. Joseph Henry Jackson, "Why Steinbeck Wrote *The Grapes of Wrath," Booklets for Bookmen,* No. 1 (New York: Limited Editions Club, 1940), p. 8.
401–402. "Boileau": radio script prepared for Joseph Henry Jackson.
403. Gwyndolyn Conger: when Steinbeck first met his second wife, she

spelled her name "Gwendolyn," later changing it to "Gwyndolyn." I have stayed with the second spelling (usually referring to her as "Gwyn") throughout.

403. "The people": manuscript, *The Grapes of Wrath* journal," Courtesy of Humanities Research Center, University of Texas).

409. Zanuck: *New York Post*, clipping, n.d.

CHAPTER XXXIII

(1) *Interviews*

Mrs. Gwyndolyn Steinbeck, Mrs. Xenia Cage, Mrs. William Brown (Carol Steinbeck), Robert Cathcart, John S. Beggerly (Los Gatos *Times Observer*), Richard Albee, Mrs. Joseph Henry Jackson, Ellwood Graham, Webster F. Street, Helen Hosmer (Simon J. Lubin Society).

(2) *Unpublished Material by Steinbeck*

"*The Grapes of Wrath* journal," journal kept during the composition of the novel (courtesy of Humanities Research Center, University of Texas).

"Second Try of Opening Preface," for proposed book on collecting tide-pool life in San Francisco Bay to be written with Edward F. Ricketts (courtesy of Bancroft Library, University of California at Berkeley).

(4) *Published or Unpublished Material by Others*

Joseph Henry Jackson, "Why Steinbeck Wrote *The Grapes of Wrath*," *Booklets for Bookmen*, No. 1 (New York: Limited Editions Club, 1940).

Martin Staples Shockley, "The Reception of *The Grapes of Wrath* in Oklahoma," *American Literature*, 15 (May 1944), pp. 351–361, as reprinted in *A Companion to "The Grapes of Wrath,"* ed. Warren French (New York: The Viking Press, 1963), pp. 117–131.

Frank J. Taylor, "California's *Grapes of Wrath*," *Forum*, 102 (November 1939), pp. 232–238, as reprinted in *"The Grapes of Wrath": Text and Criticism*, ed. Peter Lisca (New York: The Viking Press, 1972), pp. 643–656.

Carey McWilliams, *Factories in the Field* (Boston: Little, Brown & Company, Inc., 1939).

Dick Meister and Anne Loftis, *A Long Time Coming: The Struggle to Unionize America's Farm Workers* (New York: Macmillan Publishing Company, 1977).

Edward F. Ricketts, "Suggested Outline for Handbook of Marine Invertebrates of the San Francisco Bay," manuscript (courtesy of Richard Astro and Edward F. Ricketts, Jr.).

The Outer Shores: Part I, Ed Ricketts and John Steinbeck Explore the Pacific Coast and *Part II, Breaking Through—From the Papers of Edward F. Ricketts*, ed. Joel W. Hedgpeth (Eureka, California: Mad River Press, 1978).

(5) *Notes*

Pages

418. Jackson, p. 12.

418–419. Representative Lyle Boren: Shockley, p. 126.

422. "Speaking of Pictures: These by *Life* Prove Facts in *Grapes of Wrath*," *Life*, 19 February 1940, pp. 10–11 (see also 5 June 1939, pp. 66–67).

422. Eleanor Roosevelt: *The New York Times*, 3 April 1940, p. 25.

422–423. Meister and Loftis, p. 46.

423. "Bracero": Meister and Loftis, pp. 71–91.

423–424. "*The Grapes of Wrath* journal" (courtesy of the Humanities Research Center, University of Texas).

428. "Marine invertebrates": "Opening Preface," library page 462 (courtesy Bancroft Library, University of California at Berkeley).

429. "Jon": Hedgpeth, p. 31.

429. "All observers": "Preface," library page 463.

429. "With the coming": "Preface," library page 464.

430. "Realize": "Preface," library page 465.

430. "This handbook": "Preface," library page 467.

430. Joel W. Hedgpeth, "Philosophy on Cannery Row," *Steinbeck: The Man and His Work*, ed. Richard Astro and Tetsumaro Hayashi (Corvallis, Oregon: Oregon State University Press, 1971), p. 109.

432. Edward F. Ricketts, "Zoological Preface to San Francisco Bay Guidebook" in Hedgpeth, Part I, p. 35.

CHAPTER XXIV

(1) *Interviews*

"Flora's Girl" (Salinas tape), Captain James Rodriguez (Monterey Sheriff's Department), Horace "Sparky" Enea, Virginia Scardigli, Ellwood Graham, Ella Winter (by Elaine Berman), Webster F. Street, Hall "Tex" Travis, Anthony Berry, Mrs. William Brown (Carol Steinbeck), Max Wagner.

(3) *Published Material by Steinbeck*

John Steinbeck and Edward F. Ricketts, *Sea of Cortez: A Leisurely Journal of Travel and Research with a Scientific Appendix* (New York: The Viking Press, 1941), the journal reprinted as *The Log from the "Sea of Cortez"* (New York: The Viking Press, 1951).

(5) *Notes*

Pages

435. "Winchellii": *Log* (Viking Compass Edition, 1962), p. 215.

437. "Compactness": *Log*, p. 11.

438–439. *Log*, pp. 14–15.

441. *Log*, p. 41.

442. *Log*, pp. 216–217.

CHAPTER XXV

(1) *Interviews*

Carlton A. Sheffield, Horace "Sparky" Enea, Mrs. Gwyndolyn Steinbeck, Max Wagner, Lewis Milestone, Mrs. William Brown (Carol Steinbeck), Mrs. John Steinbeck.

(2) *Unpublished Material by Steinbeck*

"*The Grapes of Wrath* journal," journal kept during the composition of the novel (courtesy of Humanities Research Center, University of Texas).

(3) *Published Material by Steinbeck*

The Forgotten Village (New York: The Viking Press, 1941).

(4) *Published or Unpublished Material by Others*

Richard Astro, *John Steinbeck and Edward F. Ricketts: The Shaping of a Novelist* (Minneapolis: University of Minnesota Press, 1973).

(5) *Notes*

Pages

455. "Poor cousin": as quoted by Astro, p. 137.

455. "An emphasis": Astro, p. 57.

458. Roosevelt: JS/FDR, 6/24/40.

458. Herb Kline, "On John Steinbeck," *Steinbeck Quarterly*, 4 (Summer 1971), p. 84.

462. Herb Caen: *One Man's San Francisco* (Garden City, New York: Doubleday and Company, Inc., 1976), p. 104.

CHAPTER XXVI

(1) *Interviews*

Mrs. Gwyndolyn Steinbeck, Sandy Oliver, Mrs. William Brown (Carol Steinbeck), Ellwood Graham, Mavis McIntosh, Lewis Milestone, Webster F. Street, Mrs. Stanley Heuit (Gwyndolyn's mother), Burgess Meredith, J. B. Gilmer.

(2) *Unpublished Material by Steinbeck*

"Foreword" to novel manuscript by Thomas A. Collins, "They Die to Live," later rewritten under the title "Bringing in the Sheaves" (courtesy of Mary Alice Johns).

Tortilla Flat description written for *Life* (lost).

"God in the Pipes," novelette manuscript (lost).

(3) *Published Material by Steinbeck*

John Steinbeck and Edward F. Ricketts, *Sea of Cortez: A Leisurely Journal of Travel and Research with a Scientific Appendix* (New York: The Viking Press, 1941).

(4) *Published or Unpublished Material by Others*

Corey Ford, *Donovan of OSS* (Boston: Little, Brown & Company, Inc., 1970).

(5) *Notes*
Pages
471. "A field": JS/CS, 8/15/40.
471. "Knowing": JS/MW, 11/23/40.
474–475. "When I wrote": JS/BB, 1947.
487–488. "Reflections on a Lunar Eclipse," *San Francisco Examiner*, 6 October 1963, p. 3.
490. "Many people": "Lunar," p. 3.
490. "When the Grapes": JS/EO, 8/28/41.
490. "The Board": "Steinbeck Raps Censors," *Daily Worker*, 1 September 1941.
491. "Lunar," p. 3.

CHAPTER XXVII
(1) *Interviews*
Mrs. Gwyndolyn Steinbeck, Webster F. Street, Sandy Oliver, Mrs. Lynn Loesser, Max Wagner, Burgess Meredith.
(3) *Published Material by Steinbeck*
The Moon Is Down (New York: The Viking Press, 1942).
The Moon Is Down: Play in Two Parts (New York: Dramatists Play Service, Inc., 1942).
Bombs Away: The Story of a Bomber Team (New York: The Viking Press, 1942).
(5) *Notes*
Pages
497. Hyman: 10 December 1962, p. 10.
498. Review of *Moon*: 16 March 1942, p. 370; exchange between Thurber and Best, 20 March 1942, p. 431.
498. *Moon* (novel), p. 186.
499. "Reflections on a Lunar Eclipse," *San Francisco Examiner*, 6 October 1963, p. 3.
509. "Is running this thing": 9/23/42.

CHAPTER XXVIII
(1) *Interviews*
Mrs. Stanley Heuit (Gwyndolyn's mother), Mrs. Gwyndolyn Steinbeck, William L. Shirer, Burgess Meredith, John O'Reilly, Jack Watson, Douglas Fairbanks, Jr., Elizabeth Otis.
(3) *Published Material by Steinbeck*
Dispatches to the New York *Herald Tribune*, running irregularly from June 21, 1943, to December 15, 1943.
Selected dispatches reprinted as *Once There Was a War* (New York: The Viking Press, 1958).

(4) *Published or Unpublished Material by Others*
"Grapes of War," *Newsweek*, 5 July 1943, pp. 94–96.
(5) *Notes*
Pages
519. *War*, (Bantam Book edition, 1960), p. 7.
520. As quoted in "Ernie Pyle's War," *Time*, 17 July 1944, pp. 65–66.
521. *Newsweek*, p. 94.
530. *War*, p. 111.
531. *War*, p. 116.
532. "In the Wardroom": *War*, p. 161.
533. "One of the American": *War*, p. 163.
533. "The Five Americans": *War*, pp. 163–164.
534. "Action report": courtesy of Douglas Fairbanks, Jr.

CHAPTER XXIX
(1) *Interviews*
Mrs. Gwyndolyn Steinbeck, Mrs. Lynn Loesser, Burl Ives, Lloyd Shebley, John Hersey, Toni Jackson.
(2) *Unpublished Material by Steinbeck*
"The Wizard of Maine," manuscript of story for musical comedy (two versions in private hands).
(3) *Published Material by Steinbeck*
Cannery Row (New York: The Viking Press, 1945).
The Pearl (New York: The Viking Press, 1947).
(4) *Published or Unpublished Material by Others*
George Frazier, "John Steinbeck! John Steinbeck! How Still We See Thee Lie," *Esquire*, November 1969, pp. 150, 269, 273–275.
(5) *Notes*
Pages
541. La Paz: *The Log from the "Sea of Cortez"* (New York: The Viking Press, 1962), p. 103.
547–548. Hemingway meeting: Carlos Baker, *Ernest Hemingway: A Life Story* (New York: Charles Scribner's Sons, 1969), p. 387. The contradictory stories of this incident are discussed in Baker's notes, p. 636. My version comes primarily from Gwyn, who was on the scene, with dialogue recalled by John in a letter to Baker, p. 636.
548–549. Frazier, p. 150.
550. Bookstore: Frazier, p. 273. Frazier claims to have known Steinbeck very well indeed, when, in fact, he did not. He bases his report of Steinbeck's "lying" on the claim that he was "with him almost daily over a two-and-half year stretch." Since Frazier knew Steinbeck while the latter was living on Fifty-first Street—a period which lasted only a few months after the author returned from the war—the *Life* enter-

tainment editor must have followed him to Mexico and California, presumably in each location moving in next door.

550–551. "Wizard of Maine": at this writing, two versions of the manuscript are in the hands of manuscript brokers and unavailable for study. My description of the story comes from Mrs. Lynn Loesser, who recalled it as originally discussed by John and her husband.

555. "The word": *Cannery Row*, p. 14.

555. "Mack": *Cannery Row*, p. 15.

555. "Doc": *Cannery Row*, p. 28.

556. "Four doleful walls": JS/PC, 11/44.

557. "Millions": JS/PC, 11/44.

560. Ed and typescript: "About Ed," *The Log*, lvii.

561–562. Gabe: JS/PC, 1/45.

CHAPTER XXX

(1) *Interviews*

Mrs. Gwyndolyn Steinbeck, Nathaniel Benchley, Margery Benchley, Ned Brundage, Mrs. Lynn Loesser.

(2) *Unpublished Material by Steinbeck*

"The Pearl," film script.

"The Good Neighbors," novelette manuscript (lost).

(3) *Published Material by Steinbeck*

The Pearl (New York: The Viking Press, 1947).

(4) *Published or Unpublished Material by Others*

Eddie Condon, *Eddie Condon's Scrapbook of Jazz*, Foreword by John Steinbeck (New York: St. Martin's Press, 1973).

(5) *Notes*

Pages

574. "One man claimed": JS/GS, 10/24/45.

574. "Got tumbled": JS/GS, 10/45.

579–580. Condon.

580. Carey: letter to Ned Brundage, n.d.

580. Kaminsky: letter to Ned Brundage, 8/11/75.

580. Condon.

CHAPTER XXXI

(1) *Interviews*

Mrs. Gwyndolyn Steinbeck, Mrs. Lynn Loesser, Mrs. Portland Rynes (Mrs. Fred Allen), Nathaniel Benchley, Abe Burrows, Burgess Meredith, Mrs. Stanley Heuit (Gwyn's mother), Douglas Fairbanks, Jr., Lewis Milestone, Mavis McIntosh, George Robinson (Salinas tape), Cornell Capa.

(2) *Unpublished Material by Steinbeck*

"The Last Joan," a play manuscript (lost).

(3) *Published Material by Steinbeck*

A Russian Journal (New York: The Viking Press, 1948). (The articles which compose this book were published in and syndicated by the New York *Herald Tribune* from 14 January 1948 to 31 January 1948.)

(4) *Published or Unpublished Material by Others*

Robert Capa: 1913–1954, ed. Cornell Capa and Bhupendra Karia (New York: Grossman Publishers, 1974).

(5) *Notes*

Pages

586. "Reporters": "Literary Life," *Time*, 11 November 1946, p. 49.

589. "It is the art": *Cosmopolitan*, April 1947, pp. 18, 123.

593. De Voto: New York *Herald Tribune Books*, 16 February 1947, p. 2.

593. Redman: *The American Mercury*, May 1947, p. 631.

593. Broadcast: *The New York Times*, 19 February 1947, p. 24.

595. "Cellar": 2/16/47.

598–599. Capa: John Hersey, "The Man Who Invented Himself," *Capa*, pp. 14–15, 18.

599. "*Tribune*": *Time*, 26 January 1948, p. 58.

599. Hersey: *Capa*, p. 14.

602. "A critic": JS/GS, 7/47.

602. "Your own": *Russian Journal*, p. 27.

603. "Two little boys": JS/GS, 8/10/47.

604. "Dear Homefront": permission to quote from Robert Capa's letter to Gwyndolyn Steinbeck from Cornell Capa.

604–605. "Georgia": JS/GS.

CHAPTER XXXII

(1) *Interviews*

Mrs. Gwyndolyn Steinbeck, Mrs. Lynn Loesser, Virginia Scardigli, Richard Albee, Joel W. Hedgpeth, George Robinson (Salinas tape), Nathaniel Benchley, Elizabeth Otis, Elia Kazan, Alice Jackson, Max Wagner.

(2) *Unpublished Material by Steinbeck*

"Viva Zapata!" film script, posthumously published (New York: The Viking Press, 1975).

(4) *Published or Unpublished Material by Others*

Larry Schneider, "Cannery Row Revisited," *San Francisco Examiner*, 3 February 1963, Section IV, p. 1.

(5) *Notes*

Pages

610. "Literate": "Video v. Housework," *Time*, 19 July 1948, p. 66.

611. "Trees and bushes": JS/ALW, 2/10/48.

614. "Motorman": "Row Revisited," p. 1.

622. "A rain": "Le Rime of Petrarch: XVII," *Sonnets and Songs*, trans. Anna Maria Armi (New York: Pantheon, 1946).
623. "Simple life": 9/28/48.
623. "Won't be looking": 10/18/48.
628. "A man": JS/BB, 11/19/48.
630. "New snapshots": JS/PC.

CHAPTER XXXIII

(1) *Interviews*
   Mrs. John Steinbeck, Max Wagner, Mrs. Nunnally Johnson, Mrs. Gwyn Steinbeck.
(3) *Published Material by Steinbeck*
   "His Father," *Reader's Digest*, September 1949, pp. 19–21.
   Burning Bright, play (New York: Dramatists Play Service, 1951).
   Burning Bright, novelette (New York: The Viking Press, 1950).
(5) *Notes*
   Pages
   644. Peter Lisca, *The Wide World of John Steinbeck* (New Brunswick, New Jersey: Rutgers University Press, 1958), p. 256.
   646. Frederick Bracher: *Steinbeck and His Critics: A Record of Twenty-five Years*, ed. E. W. Tedlock, Jr., and C. V. Wicker (Albuquerque: University of New Mexico Press, 1957), pp. 195–196.
   646. "I'm not interested": JS/GA, 1/15/35.
   648. Peter Collier, "The Winter of John Steinbeck," *Ramparts*, July 1967, p. 61.
   648. "Allegorizing": see Arthur Mizener, "Does a Moral Vision of the Thirties Deserve a Nobel Prize?," *The New York Times Book Review*, 9 December 1962, pp. 4, 45.
   648. Edmund Wilson, "The Boys in the Back Room: John Steinbeck," *Classics and Commercials* (New York: Farrar, Straus and Young, 1950), p. 44.
   649. Nevius: Tedlock and Wicker, pp. 197–205.

CHAPTER XXXIV

(1) *Interviews*
   Mr. and Mrs. Jules Buck, Mrs. John Steinbeck, Burgess Meredith, Kent Smith, Elizabeth Otis, Mrs. E. G. Ainsworth (Elizabeth Steinbeck), Mrs. Harold Guinzburg, John Fearnley.
(2) *Unpublished Material by Steinbeck*
   "Viva Zapata!," film script posthumously published (New York: The Viking Press, 1975).
   A journal of letters addressed to Pascal Covici (posthumously published as *Journal of a Novel: The East of Eden Letters* [New York: The Viking Press, 1969]).

(3) *Published Material by Steinbeck*
Burning Bright, novelette (New York: The Viking Press, 1950).
"About Ed Ricketts," *The Log from the "Sea of Cortez"* (New York: The Viking Press, 1951).
"Critics, Critics Burning Bright," *Saturday Review,* 11 November 1950, pp. 20–21.

(5) *Notes*
Pages
656. "Universal language": "Critics, Critics" as reprinted in *Steinbeck and His Critics,* ed. E. W. Tedlock, Jr., and C. V. Wicker (Albuquerque: University of New Mexico Press, 1957), pp. 43–44.
658. "Range ponies": JS/GS, 8/22/50.
661. *Burning Bright* (New York: Penguin Books, 1979), p. 106.
663. "We found": "Critics, Critics," Tedlock and Wicker, p. 46.
663. "Negatives": "Critics, Critics," p. 46.
668. *Journal of a Novel,* p. 3.
669. "Most": "Critics, Critics," p. 46.
669. "I have had fun": "Critics, Critics," p. 47.
672. *Journal of a Novel,* p. 4.

CHAPTER XXXV
(1) *Interviews*
Mrs. John Steinbeck, Elizabeth Otis, Kent Smith, Mrs. Gwyndolyn Steinbeck.

(2) *Unpublished Material by Steinbeck*
A journal of letters addressed to Pascal Covici (posthumously published as *Journal of a Novel: The East of Eden Letters* [New York: The Viking Press, 1969]).

(3) *Published Material by Steinbeck*
East of Eden (New York: The Viking Press, 1952).

(5) *Notes*
Pages
674. "So much violence": *Journal of a Novel,* p. 47.
675. "I love him": *Journal of a Novel,* p. 50.
678. "I don't want": *Journal of a Novel,* p. 18.
681. "What he seeks": Carlos Baker, *Hemingway: The Writer as Artist* (Princeton, New Jersey: Princeton University Press, 1963), p. 186.
682. "Exact fact": JS/EO, 6/51.
685. "What a strange story": *Journal of a Novel,* p. 104.
686. *Eden,* p. 266.
686. "Here is": *Journal of a Novel,* p. 108.
687. "Tinshel," "Timshel," and "Timshol": see Joseph Fontenrose, *John Steinbeck: An Introduction and Interpretation* (New York: Holt, Rinehart and Winston, Inc., 1963), p. 123.

688. *Eden*, p. 294.

689. "Birthday symbol": 8/5/51.

691. The citations from *Journal of a Novel* which follow are documented in the text by date of entry rather than by page number and included in these notes.

CHAPTER XXXVI

(1) *Interviews*

Mrs. John Steinbeck, Elizabeth Otis, Arthur Miller, Gordon Manning, Jules Buck.

(2) *Unpublished Material by Steinbeck*

Screenplay for Henrik Ibsen's *The Warriors at Helgoland.*

(3) *Published Material by Steinbeck*

"The Soul and Guts of France," *Collier's*, 30 August 1952, pp. 26–28, 30.

(5) *Notes*

Pages

703. "Nostalgic": JS/PC, 2/56.

704. "Technique": JS/PC, 2/56.

711. "Continental trip": PC/JS, 5/23/52.

712. "No plumbing": JS/EO, 6/2/52.

712. "But the shoes": "Soul and Guts," p. 26.

713. "Dusty bottle": "Soul and Guts," p. 26.

713. Faye Emerson: JS/EO, 6/2/52.

714. "Duke . . . Duchess": JS/PC, 6/12/52.

717. "High mass": JS/EO, 6/17/52.

CHAPTER XXXVII

(1) *Interviews*

Mrs. John Steinbeck, Elia Kazan, Alan Ludden, Tom Guinzburg, Barnaby Conrad.

(3) *Published Material by Steinbeck*

"Duel Without Pistols," *Collier's*, 23 August 1952, pp. 13–15.

"I Go Back to Ireland," *Collier's*, 31 January 1953, pp. 48–50.

Adlai Stevenson, *Speeches of Adlai Stevenson*, Foreword by John Steinbeck (New York: Random House, 1953).

(4) *Published or Unpublished Material by Others*

Graham Watson, *Book Society* (New York: Atheneum, 1980).

(5) *Notes*

Pages

719. "Proletarian novelist": "Double Beating," *Time*, 7 July 1952, p. 48.

723. "Columnist once": "Duel," p. 14.

723. "Bacteriological": "Duel," p. 14.

723. "Refugees": "Duel," p. 14.

723. "Information was deleted": "Duel," p. 15.

724. "Underwater glass": JS/PC.
726. Watson, pp. 108–109.
727. Watson, p. 109.
728. "Sneering gentility": "Ireland," p. 49.
728. "Bleak hotel": "Ireland," p. 49.
728. "I guess": "Ireland," p. 49.
729. "Great Man": "Ireland," p. 49.
731. "Too blundering": "It Started in a Garden," *Time*, 22 September 1952, p. 110.
731. Anthony West, "California Moonshine," *The New Yorker*, 20 September 1952, pp. 121–122, 125.
731. "I wonder": JS/CS, 10/16/52.
731–732. "This, he says": Lewis Nichols, *The New York Times Book Review*, 28 September 1952, p. 30.
732. "I am getting": JS/CS, 10/16/52.
734. "I think Stevenson": "Foreword," *Speeches*, pp. 7–8.
736. "I liked Matador": JS/Barnaby Conrad, 12/29/52.

CHAPTER XXXVIII

(1) *Interviews*
Mrs. John Steinbeck, Mr. and Mrs. Ernest Martin, Elizabeth Otis, John Kenneth Galbraith, Arthur Miller, Joseph Bryan III, Mrs. Pascal Covici, Mrs. Jerome Brody.

(2) *Unpublished Material by Steinbeck*
"Bear Flag," a libretto for a musical.
"If This Be Treason," manuscript for article.
"Tailgunner Josephine," poem manuscript.

(3) *Published Material by Steinbeck*
Sweet Thursday (New York: The Viking Press, 1954).
"Autobiography: Making of a New Yorker," *The New York Times Magazine*, February 1953, pp. 26–27, 66–67.
"A Model T Named 'It,'" *Ford Times*, July 1953, pp. 34–38.
Articles (15) in *Le Figaro Littéraire* running from 12 June 1954 through 15 September 1954. My use of the first item, "An American in Paris" (*Figaro*, 12 June 1954, p. 1), and sixth item, "Kermesse aux Étoiles" (*Figaro*, 17 July 1954, p. 1), comes from the manuscripts in English (courtesy of Mrs. Jerome Brody and McIntosh and Otis, Inc.) used for the French translation. "An American in Paris" was also used as a title for the series as a whole. Several of the articles were later reprinted in English in *Punch* and *Holiday*.
"How to Tell Good Guys from Bad Guys," *The Reporter*, 10 March 1955, pp. 42–44. (Also as "Good Guy—Bad Guy," *Punch*, 227 [22 September 1954], pp. 375–378.)

(4) *Published or Unpublished Material by Others*
John Kenneth Galbraith, "John Steinbeck: Footnote for a Memoir," *The Atlantic Monthly,* November 1969, pp. 65–67.

(5) *Notes*
Pages
744. Galbraith, p. 65.
744–745. "To exercise power": Galbraith, p. 66.
745. "A list": 9/14/53.
751. "At first intemperate": "An American in Paris," ms., pp. 1, 3.
755. "The natural balance": "Kermesse aux Étoiles," ms., p. 2.
755–756. "My daughter": "Kermesse aux Étoiles," ms., p. 3.

CHAPTER XXXIX

(1) *Interviews*
Mr. and Mrs. Jules Buck, Mrs. John Steinbeck, Burl Ives, Joseph Bryan III, Norman Cousins, Bob Barry, John Fisher, John Harrington.

(2) *Unpublished Material by Steinbeck*
Statement to Satellite Countries for Radio Free Europe (courtesy of McIntosh and Otis, Inc.).

(3) *Published Material by Steinbeck*
"Always Something to Do in Salinas," *Holiday,* June 1955, pp. 58–59, 152–153, 156.
"The Affair at 7, Rue de M——," *Harper's Bazaar,* April 1955, pp. 112, 202, 213.
"The Death of a Racket," *The Saturday Review,* 2 April 1955, p. 26.
"Some Thoughts on Juvenile Delinquency," *The Saturday Review,* 28 May 1955, p. 22.
"A Plea to Teachers," *The Saturday Review,* 30 April 1955, p. 24.

(5) *Notes*
Pages
762. "There was a time": Statement to Satellite Countries, ms.
765. "Collaboration": "The Affair at 7, Rue de M——."
768. "About 70 volumes": 10/29/54.
769. Exchange between JS and Clare Boothe Luce from Mrs. John Steinbeck.
769. "Mycenae": JS/EO, 11/10/54.
769. "I am so full": JS/EO, 11/10/54.
776. "People need": "Juvenile Delinquency," p. 22.
778. "I am starting": JS/WS, 7/55.

CHAPTER XL

(1) *Interviews*
Ernest Martin, John Fearnley, Elizabeth Otis, Mrs. John Steinbeck, Shirley Fisher, Bob Barry, John Kenneth Galbraith, Joseph Bryan III.

(2) *Unpublished Material by Steinbeck*

Unfinished novel manuscript, untitled but referred to by JS as "Pi Root." (This is in private hands and has been given the title "Peter Root Legally Dead" by a manuscript broker.)

"Old Style and New Style Elaine," Calypso verses (posthumously published in *Steinbeck: A Life in Letters*, ed. Elaine Steinbeck and Robert Wallsten [New York: The Viking Press, 1975], pp. 519–520).

(3) *Published Material by Steinbeck*

The Short Reign of Pippin IV (New York: The Viking Press, 1957).

"How Mr. Hogan Robbed a Bank," *The Atlantic Monthly*, March 1956, pp. 58–61.

Articles (11) for the Louisville *Courier-Journal* (also syndicated), running from 12 August 1956 through 25 August 1956 (coverage of the Democratic and Republican conventions).

(4) *Published or Unpublished Material by Others*

Manuscript of a talk given by Shirley Fisher (a memoir of JS, untitled) given at Southampton College of Long Island University, Southampton, New York, 11 November 1978.

Joseph Blotner, *Faulkner: A Biography*, II (New York: Random House, 1974).

(5) *Notes*

Pages

779. "A good show": JS/WS, 9/23/55.

781. "What really is": JS/EK, 12/3/55.

785. "The young man": *Sweet Thursday*, p. 122.

790. "Nobody to interrupt": JS/WS, 6/4/56.

790. "Move out": Fisher memoir, ms., p. 2.

792–793. "To the Syndicated Newspaper Editors," 4/56, as quoted in Steinbeck and Wallsten, pp. 525–526.

793. "I want a combination": "Assisting John Steinbeck," *Newsweek*, 25 June 1956, p. 56.

794. "Five years": JS/EO, 9/1/56.

795. "Alan Lerner": JS/EO.

795. "I get daily": JS/EO.

796. "It is their failure": JS/EO.

796. "It kind of retires": 4/23/56.

799. "Your president": Blotner, p. 1629.

799–801. Blotner, pp. 1617–1629.

801. "Steinbeck was as little": Blotner, pp. 1625–1626.

801–802. JS/Arthur Larson, 1/12/57.

CHAPTER XLI

(1) *Interviews*

Marshall Best, Abe Burrows, Chase Horton, Elizabeth Otis, Mrs. John

Steinbeck, Ernest Martin, Robert Wallsten, Thom Steinbeck, Arthur Miller, John Fisher, Shirley Fisher, Burl Ives.

(3) *Published Material by Steinbeck*

"The Trail of Arthur Miller," *Esquire*, June 1957, p. 86.

"A Game of Hospitality," *The Saturday Review*, 20 April 1957, p. 24.

"My War with the Ospreys," *Holiday*, March 1957, pp. 72, 163–165.

Articles (23) for the Louisville *Courier-Journal* (also syndicated), running from 17 April 1957 through 17 July 1957.

(5) *Notes*

Pages

804–805. "All the vices": from the ms. (since published as "Introduction" to *The Acts of King Arthur and His Noble Knights*, ed. Chase Horton [New York: Farrar, Straus and Giroux, 1976], xii).

806. "Lovely nuances": JS/EO, 12/3/56.

806. "I called the curator": JS/ Stanford Steinbeck, 9/62.

806. "Since the economics": JS/EO, 2/57.

807. "Inspired convention": form letter, 3/6/57, sent to James S. Pope to be forwarded to subscribing newspapers.

807. "Pretty amusing": JS/EO, 4/16/57.

812–813. "Arthur Miller," p. 86.

814. "A great majority": "Hospitality," p. 24.

816–817. "Steinbeck in Sweden," *Courier*, 17 July 1957, Section I, p. 7.

819. "Garbage dump": JS/EO, 9/7/57.

CHAPTER XLII

(1) *Interviews*

Burgess Meredith, Elizabeth Otis, Mrs. John Steinbeck, John Fisher, John Kenneth Galbraith, Arthur Miller, Alice Jackson.

(2) *Unpublished Material by Steinbeck*

"Don Keehan," a novel manuscript (lost).

(3) *Published Material by Steinbeck*

"Conversation at Sag Harbor," *Holiday*, March 1961, pp. 60–61, 129–131, 133.

"The Easiest Way to Die," *The Saturday Review*, 23 August 1958, pp. 12, 37.

"Dedication," *Journal of the American Medical Association*, 167 (12 July 1958), pp. 1388–1389; reprinted and condensed as "The Spivaks Beat the Odds," *The Reader's Digest*, October 1958, pp. 153–154.

(4) *Published or Unpublished Material by Others*

Alfred Kazin, "The Unhappy Man from Unhappy Valley," *The New York Times Book Review*, 4 May 1958, pp. 1, 29.

(5) *Notes*

Pages

829. "Practicing": JS/WS, 3/14/58.

829. "Peaceful": JS/WS, 3/14/58.

831–832. "Your freedom": "Sag Harbor," p. 129.

835. "I have never": JS/EO, 6/15/58.

835. "I rather hope": 6/15/58.

835. "Vague essay": "Opinion: The Affluent Society," *Time*, 2 June 1958, p. 79.

837. "Heavily insured": "Easiest Way," p. 37.

844. "Man will disappear": from Alice Jackson interview.

CHAPTER XLIII

(1) *Interviews*

Mrs. John Steinbeck, Robert Wallsten, Elizabeth Otis, Chase Horton.

(2) *Unpublished Material by Steinbeck*

"The Acts of King Arthur and His Noble Knights," published posthumously, ed. Chase Horton (New York: Farrar, Straus and Giroux, 1976).

(3) *Published Material by Steinbeck*

"Atque Vale," *The Saturday Review*, 23 July 1960, p. 13.

"A Primer on the 30's," *Esquire*, June 1960, pp. 85–93.

"Conversation at Sag Harbor," *Holiday*, March 1961, pp. 60–61, 129–131, 133.

(5) *Notes*

Pages

852. *Travels with Charley in Search of America* (New York: The Viking Press, 1962), p. 177.

860. *The Acts of Arthur*, pp. 292–293.

863. "Left him resting": Steinbeck and Wallsten, p. 655.

CHAPTER XLIV

(1) *Interviews*

Ernest Martin, Shirley Fisher, Elizabeth Otis, Robert Wallsten, Mrs. John Steinbeck, Jimmy Costello, Allen Ludden, Barnaby Conrad, Webster F. Street.

(3) *Published Material by Steinbeck*

The Winter of Our Discontent (New York: The Viking Press, 1961).

Travels with Charley in Search of America (New York: The Viking Press, 1962).

"The Mail I've Seen," *The Saturday Review*, 4 August 1956, pp. 16, 34.

"Writer Catches Lion by Tale," originally in *London Daily Mail*, reprinted in *Monterey Peninsula Herald*, 7 October 1959, p. 1.

"Adlai Stevenson and John Steinbeck Discuss the Past and the Present," *Newsday*, 22 December 1959, pp. 34–35; reprinted as "Our 'Rigged' Morality," *Coronet*, March 1960, pp. 146–147.

(5) *Notes*

Pages

867. "Look . . .": "Writer Catches."

867–868. Jimmy Costello: "Prof. Toro" in "Peninsular Parade," *Monterey Peninsula Herald*, 3 August 1959, p. 13.

868. "Have live female": "Writer Catches."

868. City and county officials: Jimmy Costello, "County's Gift to British Warship," *Monterey Peninsula Herald*, 23 September 1959, p. 25.

870. "I was pretty far out": JS/Howard Hunter, 3/8/60.

876. Stevenson: "Adlai Stevenson and John Steinbeck," pp. 34–35.

877. Carl Sandburg: as quoted in "John Steinbeck Writes Column for Daily Californian," *Salinas Californian*, 17 December 1965, p. 1.

878. "An odd book": JS/EO, 6/60.

878. "Part Kafka": JS/Frank and Lynn Loesser, 5/25/60.

881. *Charley*, pp. 23–25; the trip had been in Steinbeck's mind for many years and had been originally inspired, according to his wife, by Ed Ricketts's walking trip through the South as a young man.

884. "Instant recognition": JS/EO, 6/60.

884. "Maine": JS/EO, 9/30/60.

884. "Presents piled": "Adlai Stevenson and John Steinbeck," p. 35.

885. "Columbus": JS/EO, 10/14/60.

886. "A woman journalist": Curt Gentry, "John Steinbeck: 'America's King Arthur Is Coming,'" *This World, San Francisco Chronicle*, 6 November 1960, p. 33.

887. Producer of "Flight": JS/Michael Neyman, as quoted in "Bay Youth Challenges Hollywood," *San Francisco Chronicle*, 22 September 1957, p. 22.

889. "I knew": *Charley*, p. 219.

889. "These blowzy": *Charley*, p. 228.

889. "The crowd": *Charley*, p. 227.

890. "Then the girl": *Charley*, p. 227.

CHAPTER XLV

(1) *Interviews*

John Kenneth Galbraith, Mrs. John Steinbeck, Mr. and Mrs. Willard Bascom, Terrence McNally, Mrs. Jerome Brody, Allen Ludden, Thomas Guinzburg.

(2) Unpublished Material by Steinbeck

Material excised from "Travels with Charley" manuscript (courtesy of the Pierpont Morgan Library).

"Travels with Charley" journal (courtesy of the Pierpont Morgan Library).

(3) *Published Material by Steinbeck*
  The Winter of Our Discontent (New York: The Viking Press, 1961).
  Travels with Charley in Search of America (New York: The Viking Press, 1962).
  "High Drama of Bold Thrust Through Ocean Floor," *Life*, 14 April 1961, pp, 111, 118, 120, 122.
  "Preface" to Edith Ronald Mirrielees, *Story Writing* (New York: The Viking Press, 1962).

(4) *Published or Unpublished Material by Others*
  John Kenneth Galbraith, "John Steinbeck: Footnote for a Memoir," *The Atlantic Monthly*, November 1969, pp. 65–67.

(5) *Notes*
  Pages
  891. "Toynbee": Galbraith, p. 66.
  891–892. "I got us": from the conclusion of the "Charley" ms. (courtesy of the Pierpont Morgan Library).
  892. "Political status": Galbraith, p. 66.
  892. "Syntax": Galbraith, p. 66.
  893–894. "Yesterday came": from journal written with "Charley" ms. (courtesy of the Pierpont Morgan Library).
  896. "Great core": "High Drama," p. 122.
  896. "Asked for a piece": "High Drama," p. 122.
  898. *The Atlantic Monthly*, July 1961, p. 122.
  905. "I hold no grief": from Thomas Guinzburg interview.
  909. "If Kazan": from Mrs. John Steinbeck interview.

CHAPTER XLVI

(1) *Interviews*
  Shirley Fisher, Mrs. John Steinbeck, Terrence McNally, Allen Ludden, Mrs. Harold Guinzburg, Nathaniel Benchley, Edward Albee, and others.

(2) *Unpublished Material by Steinbeck*
  Nobel Prize acceptance speech, published posthumously in *Nobel Prize Library: William Faulkner, Eugene O'Neill, John Steinbeck* (New York: Alexis Gregory, 1971), pp. 205–207.
  Papers and memoranda based on State Department-sponsored trip to the U.S.S.R. and East European countries, 1963.

(3) *Published Material by Steinbeck*
  Travels with Charley in Search of America (New York: The Viking Press, 1962).
  "Reflections on a Lunar Eclipse," *San Francisco Examiner Book Week*, 6 October 1963, p. 3.

(4) *Published or Unpublished Material by Others*
  Anders Österling, "Presentation Address" (of the Nobel Prize for Litera-

ture to John Steinbeck), *Nobel Prize Library: William Faulkner, Eugene O'Neill, John Steinbeck* (New York: Alexis Gregory, 1971), pp. 201–204.

(5) *Notes*

Pages

911. "This book . . . ": JS/EO, 6/25/62.

913. Princeton professor: Eric F. Goldman, "Steinbeck's America, Twenty Years After," *The New York Times Book Review*, 29 July 1962, p. 5.

913. "A book to be read": "Seeing Our Country Close," *The Atlantic Monthly*, August 1962, p. 138.

913. "The novelist's eye": William Rivers, "The Peripatetic Poodle," *The Saturday Review*, 1 September 1962, p. 31.

915. Press conference: "Novelist Learns of His Award Through Announcement on TV," *The New York Times*, 26 October 1962, p. 12.

915–916. Editorial: *The New York Times*, 26 October 1962, p. 30.

916. *Newsweek:* "The Old Steinbeck," 26 June 1961, p. 96.

918. "A costume": JS/BB, 11/14/62.

919. Osterling: *Prize Library*, pp. 203–204.

919–920. Steinbeck speech: *Prize Library*, p. 205.

921. *Publishers Weekly:* Alice Payne Hackett, "U.S. Bookstore Bestsellers of 1962," 21 January 1963, pp. 58–61.

922–923. Mizener: *The New York Times Book Review*, 9 December 1962, pp. 4, 45.

924. Sandburg dinner: Ralph McGill, "A Poet Is Not Without Honor" (newspaper clipping—no name), 14 January 1963.

925. "My days": JS/EO, 6/63.

925. "Pat wrote": PC/JS, 6/19/63.

926. To O'Hara: 7/63.

926. "Cobwebs": JS/EO, 8/63.

927. *The New Yorker:* "Our Man in Helsinki," 9 November 1963, pp. 43, 45.

930. "If it's royalties": Papers and memoranda, 1963.

931–932. Luncheon at *Izvestia:* Papers and memoranda, 1963.

CHAPTER XLVII

(1) *Interviews*

Mrs. John Steinbeck, Anatoly Gladilin, Edward Albee, Vladimir Maximov, Bob Barry, Dick Olmsted, Thomas Guinzburg, Mrs. Lyndon Johnson, and others.

(2) *Unpublished Material by Steinbeck*

Papers and memoranda based on State Department-sponsored trip to the U.S.S.R. and East European countries, 1963.

Draft for a platform for the Democratic Party, 1964.

Draft for acceptance speech for the nomination for President, delivered by Lyndon B. Johnson at the Democratic Convention, August 1964.

(5) *Notes*

Pages

940–942. Gladilin's account: letter to me, 1/81.

944–945. Professor Barghoorn: Henry Tanner, "Steinbeck and Albee Speak Out in Soviet for U.S. Professor," *The New York Times*, 15 November 1963, pp. 1, 5.

945–946. *Polityka:* as quoted in Papers and memoranda, 1963.

946. Polish press: as quoted in Papers and memoranda, 1963.

947–948. "I'm amazed": "Steinbeck at the Berlin Wall," *San Francisco Examiner*, 12 December 1963, p. 14.

948. Amerika Haus: as quoted in Papers and memoranda, 1963.

951. "I'm worrying": JS/PC, n.d.

958. "That no writer": "John Steinbeck: Footnote for a Memoir," *The Atlantic Monthly*, November 1969, pp. 66–67.

CHAPTER XLVIII

(1) *Interviews*

Mrs. John Steinbeck, Carlton A. Sheffield, Douglas Fairbanks, Jr., Joseph Bryan III.

(3) *Published Material by Steinbeck*

America and Americans (New York: The Viking Press, 1966).

Articles (27), first series, "Letters to Alicia," *Newsday*, running from 20 November 1965 through 28 May 1966 (courtesy of *Newsday*).

(5) *Notes*

Pages

961. Pat Covici: Charles A. Madison, "The Friendship of Covici and Steinbeck," *Chicago Jewish Forum*, Summer 1966, p. 296. (The statement made to the press was also the statement he made at the funeral.)

962. "Cutting room": JS/EO, 1/20/65.

962–963. Story of Anthony Daly: "Letters to Alicia," *Newsday*, 5 February 1966, p. 3W.

964. "Taking 'the American'": JS/John Huston and Gladys Hill, 2/17/65.

965. Jack Valenti: 3/26/65 (courtesy of Lyndon B. Johnson Library).

967. "Inspect mankind": *Americans*, p. 137.

968–969. *Americans*, pp. 140–141.

970. "In charge": JS/CS, 8/5/65.

970–971. "The kind of man": JS/CS, 8/5/65.

973. To Guggenheim: as quoted in "Steinbeck Will Travel, Report for Newsday," *Newsday*, 15 November 1965, p. 4.

973–974. Max Lerner: "Alicia," 4 December 1965, p. 3W.

974–975. Alnwick Castle: "Alicia," 31 December 1965, p. 3W.

975. Second article: "Alicia," 8 January 1966, p. 3W.

978. Dickson's sojourn: "Alicia," 12 February 1966, p. 3W.

979. Ephraim Kishon: as reported in *Newsday*, 26 February 1966, p. 3W.

979–980. Masada: "Alicia," 16 and 23 April 1966, p. 3W.

980. Elazar Ben Yair: "Alicia," 23 April 1966, p. 3W.

980–981. "It seems to me": "Alicia," 9 April 1966, 3W.

CHAPTER XLIX

(1) *Interviews*

Mrs. John Steinbeck, Budd Schulberg, Mrs. Gwyn Steinbeck, Phil Strong, Sam M. Gipson, Jr.

(2) *Unpublished Material by Steinbeck*

"A Piece of It Fell on My Tail," novel manuscript (lost).

(3) *Published Material by Steinbeck*

Articles (36), second series, "Letters to Alicia," *Newsday*, running from 3 December 1966 through 20 May 1967 (courtesy of *Newsday*).

"Let's Go After the Neglected Treasures Beneath the Seas," *Popular Science*, September 1966, pp. 84–87.

(4) *Published or Unpublished Material by Others*

From the Ashes: Voices of Watts, ed. and intro. by Budd Schulberg (New York: New American Library, 1967).

Elaine Steinbeck, "Half a World from Home," *McCall's*, June 1967, pp. 42, 137.

(5) *Notes*

Pages

983–984. Edmund Wilson, "Historical Criticism," *An Introduction to Literary Criticism*, ed. Marlies K. Danziger and W. Stacy Johnson (Boston: D.C. Heath and Company, 1961), p. 287.

985. Acceptance speech: *Nobel Prize Library: William Faulkner, Eugene O'Neill, John Steinbeck* (New York: Alexis Gregory, 1971), p. 205.

985–986. Workshop: *Ashes*, "Introduction."

986. "I saw the product": *Ashes*, p. 21.

988–989. Johnson letter: 6/21/66 (courtesy of Lyndon B. Johnson Library).

989. "But it does seem unrealistic": "Let's Go," p. 84.

991. Max Lerner: "Alicia," 4 December 1965, p. 3W.

992–993. Yevtushenko: "The Yevtushenko–Steinbeck Exchange," *Los Angeles Times*, 17 July 1966, Section G, p. 3.

993–994. Moscow delayed: Raymond H. Anderson, "Moscow Reports Steinbeck Reply," *The New York Times*, 17 July 1966, p. 5.

994. Johnson letter: 7/12/66 (courtesy of Lyndon B. Johnson Library).

995–996. Yevtushenko in U.S.: Henry Raymont, "Yevtushenko Irritated by Criticism, Answers Leftists," *The New York Times*, 11 November 1966, p. 8.

996. Tan Son Nhut Airport: Elaine Steinbeck, "Half a World from Home," p. 42.

997. Booby-trap awareness: "Alicia," 7 January 1967, p. 31.

999. Door gunner: "Alicia," 7 January 1967, p. 2W.

999–1001. "I wish I could tell you": "Alicia," 7 January 1967, p. 2W.

CHAPTER L

(1) *Interviews*

Sam Gipson, Jr., Mrs. John Steinbeck, Budd Schulberg, Elizabeth Otis, John Steinbeck IV.

(3) *Published Material by Steinbeck*

Articles (36), second series, "Letters to Alicia," *Newsday*, running from 3 December 1966 through 20 May 1967 (courtesy of *Newsday*).

(4) *Published or Unpublished Material by Others*

Elaine Steinbeck, "Half a World from Home," *McCall's*, June 1967, pp. 42, 137.

John Steinbeck IV, *In Touch* (New York: Alfred A. Knopf, 1969).

(5) *Notes*

Pages

1002. "These people": "Alicia," 7 January 1967, p. 31.

1002. "Tortured": "Alicia," 7 January 1967, p. 17.

1002–1003. Can Tho: "Alicia," 21 January 1967, p. 17.

1004. Saigon Cowboys: "Alicia," 18 February 1967, p. 1A.

1004. Waste problem: "Alicia," 18 February 1967, p. 16.

1005. "If anything metallic": JS/Harry F. Guggenheim, 1/4/67.

1005. "John and I": Elaine Steinbeck, "Half a World," p. 137.

1005. "The towns": "Alicia," 11 February 1967, p. 14.

1006. "My dear wife": "Alicia," 11 February 1967, p. 16W.

1006–1007. On Pussi Mountain: "Alicia," 28 January 1967, pp. 2, 16.

1007–1008. "I have often wished": "Alicia," 25 February 1967.

1009. Published attacks: see reports of, in "Steinbeck Up Front," *Newsweek*, 30 January 1967, p. 71; "Steinbeck Loses Bet," *The New York Times*, 12 January 1967, p. 2; "Soviet and Bulgaria Criticize Steinbeck," *The New York Times*, 23 January 1967, p. 18; "Condemnation of Steinbeck Is Urged on P.E.N. by Czech," *The New York Times*, 29 January 1967, p. 22.

1010. "Wrote to Elizabeth": JS/EO, 1/23/67.

1010. "Reported in his column": "Alicia," 4 March 1967, p. 16; 11 March 1967, p. 2W.

1010. "In most of the villages": "Alicia," 11 March 1967, p. 2W.

1011. Pop Ewell: "Alicia," 8 April 1967, p. 18.

1012. "Some years ago": "Alicia," 22 April 1967, p. 27.

1012–1013. Swedish ambassador: "Alicia," 22 April 1967, p. 27.

1014. "An ending now": "Alicia," 20 May 1967, p. 30.

1014–1015. Suggestions: transcription of tape by Steinbeck, memoranda on Vietnam to Secretary McNamara (courtesy Department of Defense).

1016. "A vegetable": JS/EO, 8/31/67.

1016. "The forms I'm accustomed to": JS/EO, 8/31/67.

1017. "Something sly": JS/EO, 8/31/67.

1020. "To dramatize": *In Touch*, p. 116.

1020–1022. John IV at hospital: *In Touch*, pp. 112–118.

CHAPTER LI

(1) *Interviews*

Mrs. John Steinbeck, Budd Schulberg, Shirley Fisher, Denton Cox, M.D., Jean Boone, John Kenneth Galbraith, Tom Guinzburg, Elizabeth Otis.

(4) *Published or Unpublished Material by Others*

Budd Schulberg, "John Steinbeck: Discontented Lion in Winter," *West, Los Angeles Times*, 23 February 1969, pp. 12–15.

(5) *Notes*

Pages

1023. "John 'grunted' ": "Lion," p. 13.

1023. "I'll tell you something": "Lion," p. 13.

1023–1024. "That's my trouble": "Lion," p. 14.

1024. "How do you teach 'em": "Lion," p. 14.

1024. "Something new": "Lion," p. 14.

1024. "I don't know": "Lion," p. 14.

1025. "I don't want": "Lion," p. 15.

1028. "They don't let me": JS/WS, 4/18/68.

1038. Stevenson: as quoted in "Steinbeck Rites Attended by 300," *The New York Times*, 24 December 1968, p. 20.

Index